THE ANNUNCIATION

François Lemoyne, *The Annunciation*, 1727
On display at The National Gallery, London
On loan from Winchester College
(Copyright: The Warden and Scholars of Winchester College)

THE ANNUNCIATION

A Pilgrim's Quest

Mark Byford

WINCHESTER
UNIVERSITY PRESS

Published by Winchester University Press 2018

Copyright © Mark Byford 2018

Mark Byford hereby asserts his moral right always to be identified as the author of this work in accordance with the provisions of the Copyright, Designs and Patents Act 1988.

First Published in Great Britain in 2018 by
Winchester University Press
University of Winchester
Winchester SO22 4N

British Library Cataloguing–in–Publication Data
A CIP catalogue record for this book is available
from the British Library.

ISBN: 978–1–906113–25–4

Printed and Bound in Great Britain

CONTENTS

THE GOSPEL ACCORDING TO LUKE

CHAPTER 1: VERSES 26-38

In the sixth month, the angel Gabriel was sent by God to a town in Galilee called Nazareth, to a virgin betrothed to a man named Joseph, of the House of David; and the virgin's name was Mary. He went in and said to her, 'Rejoice, so highly favoured! The Lord is with you.'

She was deeply disturbed by these words and asked herself what this greeting could mean, but the angel said to her, 'Mary, do not be afraid; you have won God's favour. Listen! You are to conceive and bear a son, and you must name him Jesus. He will be great and will be called Son of the Most High. The Lord God will give him the throne of his ancestor David; he will rule over the House of Jacob for ever and his reign will have no end.'

Mary said to the angel, 'But how can this come about, since I am a virgin?'

'The Holy Spirit will come upon you,' the angel answered, 'and the power of the Most High will cover you with its shadow. And so the child will be holy and will be called Son of God. Know this too: your kinswoman Elizabeth has, in her old age, herself conceived a son, and she whom people called barren is now in her sixth month, for nothing is impossible to God.'

'I am the handmaid of the Lord,' said Mary, 'let what you have said be done to me.'

And the angel left her.

FOREWORD

A few weeks ago, the British Social Attitudes Survey revealed that the proportion of those identifying themselves as non-religious is now in the majority. The National Centre for Social Research asked: 'Do you regard yourself as belonging to any particular religion?' For the first time since these statistics have been collated, 53% in Britain claimed no religious affiliation whatsoever. A victory for the irresistible march of science and secularism?

Yet, while formal religious affiliation may be in decline, other surveys suggest that people in Britain retain an appetite for spirituality expressed through a variety of devotional practices.

Or consider the American experience, analysed by the philosopher Charles Taylor in his masterful work *A Secular Age*. 'One of the earliest societies to separate Church and State,' writes Taylor, 'it is also the Western society with the highest statistics for religious belief and practice.'

One hundred years ago, the Moscow Theological Academy was shuttered. An institution, formed by a couple of Greek monks in the seventeenth-century, was rendered null and void by the Bolsheviks. Religion in Russia, seemingly buried by the Revolution.

Yet today the Academy thrives supplying ordinands, scholars and clergy to Moscow and beyond.

How to explain the conundrum? Why, despite our best efforts, does religious faith continue?

There are plenty of learned explanations available, from the social sciences to psychiatry, that may shed light on why we still seek out a place, a sphere, that C. S. Lewis refers to as 'something not yourself'.

One could also begin by reading Mark Byford's extraordinary devotional journey through *The Annunciation: A Pilgrim's Quest*.

Described in the New Testament, the Annunciation is celebrated annually in March – nine months precisely before Christians mark the birth of Jesus Christ on Christmas Day. It is the moment when the angel Gabriel visits Mary and announces to her that the child she is to carry, 'will be great and will be called the Son of the Most High... His Kingdom shall never end'. Elsewhere in the Bible, we are to understand that she is carrying 'the Word made flesh', the incarnation of the eternal God in human form.

In this unique and thought-provoking book, you will read of how such a mysterious visitation has inspired the work of artists and theologians alike for the past two thousand years. You will hear the voices of leading academics and clergy whose lives and work today bear testimony to this baffling event. You may also see how the Annunciation could be the most abiding explanation for why, to paraphrase the words of Mark Twain, reports of the death of religion have been greatly exaggerated.

If historians affirm, as most do, that Jesus Christ was born, lived and died – then this meeting between an angelic being and a soon-to-be pregnant woman offers an insight into how the spiritual became the physical; how mystery became material; when what was believed in the heart, was seen with the eyes.

Martin Bashir
BBC Religion Editor
September, 2017

PREFACE

The Annunciation is the gospel story of the encounter between the angel Gabriel and the Virgin Mary, informing her that she will conceive a son and must name him Jesus. A brief passage of fewer than three hundred words that takes less than ninety seconds to read. A story only mentioned by Luke within the four canonical Gospels and yet hailed by some as the most important event in human history. Certainly, it is a pivotal point in Christianity. Moreover, it is a story that has inspired some of the greatest artistic works over the past 2,000 years.

It is a chance encounter with a little-known French painting of the Annunciation hanging in the National Gallery that inspires the author to set off on a three-year pilgrimage, firstly, to discover the story of the picture and, most importantly, to learn about the subject matter and its meaning. It leads to an epic journey involving more than a hundred intimate, in-depth conversations with leading clerics, world-renowned theologians, academics, acclaimed art historians, artists, dramatists, musicians and poets. A long search that also leads the author to travel tens of thousands of miles around the world to stand before more than a hundred artistic compositions rooted in the annunciation story.

It is a monumental project of scale, ambition and innovation that is highly distinctive in its originality of approach. No book before has devoted itself to such a singular pilgrimage, setting out to understand the meaning of the Annunciation through a series of one-to-one encounters involving such a diverse and authoritative cast list. It is the intimacy, honesty and insightfulness of the revelations that give this book a real edge. The author wins the trust of his interviewees to speak as never before about the personal and profound impact the annunciation story has had on their lives, as the conversations explore the meanings of 'acceptance', 'calling', 'belief', 'certainty' and 'doubt'.

François Lemoyne's *The Annunciation* was painted in Paris in 1727 and arrived in Winchester two years later to be hung in Winchester College's stunning Gothic Chapel as the main altarpiece. For almost three hundred years, leading French art historians presumed its whereabouts was unknown although it had been in Winchester for all that time. Now, after recently being 're-discovered', it is on loan to the National Gallery in London – the only eighteenth-century French religious painting to be displayed on its walls.

As the author stands before the painting, it has an immediate and profound impact. Gazing at the angel Gabriel hovering above a meek and accepting Virgin Mary, the author recalls how, as a young boy attending his First Holy Communion classes, he heard the annunciation story for the first time and how, at his primary school, he would stand up in class regularly at midday to recite the Angelus prayer. Fifty years later, he starts to reflect on the Annunciation and its meaning. A long-term resident of the city of Winchester, his interest is piqued further when he sees a card next to the painting stating it is on loan from Winchester College, one of England's oldest and most prestigious public schools. The chance encounter that morning drives him, in the first instance, to research the origins of the picture and the life of the artist. Why was a contemporary French painting, created by a leading Parisian artist, chosen to hang behind the altar in Chapel in 1729? Why did the artist commit suicide less than a decade later, after creating one of the most ambitious works of eighteenth-century art at the Palace of Versailles? Why, for almost three centuries, did leading French art historians know the painting as Lemoyne's 'lost Annunciation'? Why is it now being displayed so prominently in one of the greatest art galleries in the world?

Walking the streets of Winchester, London, Paris and Versailles in search of the answers, the author examines the treasured archives at Winchester College before talking to world-renowned art historians including Pierre Rosenberg, the former Director of the Louvre; Xavier Salmon, the current Director of the Département des Arts Graphiques at the Louvre; Jean-Luc Bordeaux, the author of Lemoyne's *catalogue raisonné*; Sir Nicholas Penny, the Director of the National Gallery; Humphrey Wine, the Curator of Seventeenth- and Eighteenth-Century French Painting at the National Gallery; and Christoph Vogtherr, the Director of the Wallace Collection.

In the same way that Lemoyne's picture was 'lost' and then 're-discovered', the author questions whether the significance and theological meaning of the annunciation gospel passage has been lost in today's world. If so, then how can it be re-discovered? What is the story about? Is it fact, metaphor or what? How might its message resonate today? Is one bishop right to describe it as 'the most important event in human history'? Do the vastly different views on the painting's aesthetic qualities parallel the different perspectives held by Christians about the annunciation story and its meaning?

The author traces the historical impact of the annunciation story in Christianity, from the early Church through to the medieval cult of Mary, the Reformation, the age of the Enlightenment and on to the present post-modern world. He discovers how the role of the Virgin Mary at the Annunciation creates extreme responses – from deep adoration to condemnation – and asks why? He learns why the feast day on 25 March, so prominent and significant in previous centuries, has lost its importance today and asks if it can be revived.

The author sets out on a three-year voyage of discovery to understand more about the story's spiritual resonance and impact. Along the way, he documents a series of meetings, which provide him with fresh insight into the meaning of the encounter between the angel Gabriel and Mary. Effectively, Lemoyne's painting provides a focal point for searching discussions on the Annunciation in which each interviewee is given the opportunity to open their hearts and minds in a profound manner, often with surprising results. The revelations prove to be highly personal and edifying.

The series of encounters all happen between January 2014 and December 2016 (although they do not necessarily appear in the book in their original order for reasons of editorial coherence). One of the first is on the feast of the Annunciation when the author hears Rowan Williams, the former Archbishop of Canterbury, deliver a deep, meditative reflection. Later, they meet in front of the Lemoyne painting in the National Gallery, where they discuss the story's message. There follow more revealing one-to-one encounters. Both Cardinal Vincent Nichols and Cardinal Cormac Murphy-O'Connor, leaders from the Roman Catholic Church, proffer highly personal insights.

There are searching conversations with another former Archbishop of Canterbury, George Carey; Church of England Bishops Richard Chartres, Tim Dakin, Nick Holtam and Martin Warner; and leading authorities on the history of Christianity in Art, Dr John

Drury, Lord Richard Harries and Professor Ben Quash. Prominent women clerics include Libby Lane, the Church of England's first woman bishop, June Osborne, Vivienne Faull, Jane Hedges, Sarah Mullally, Judith Maltby, Rose Hudson-Wilkin and Lucy Winkett, who each offer intimate reflections on how the annunciation message has impacted fundamentally in shaping their own lives. Leaders from other denominations, including Methodist, Baptist, United Reformed, Pentecostal, Evangelical and Free Churches, also meet with the author on his journey. So, too, do leaders of the Eastern Orthodox and Coptic Churches.

In an extremely rare opportunity, and with complete access, the author stays with an enclosed order of nuns at the Carmel of the Annunciation at Thicket Priory near York. There, he has intimate conversations with the Carmelite nuns about their own 'annunciation moment' when they felt called to say yes to a contemplative monastic life.

He engages with two of the leading Christian historians of our time, Professors Diarmaid MacCulloch in Oxford and Owen Chadwick in Cambridge. He attends the International Congress of the Ecumenical Society of the Blessed Virgin Mary. He listens to Rabbi Julia Neuberger and the Muslim scholars, Mona Siddiqui and Tim Winter, offer their thoughts on the annunciation story from outside of the Christian faith. He also takes the opportunity, during his journey, to talk to his own family about their own beliefs or lack of them, and their own views on the Annunciation.

A range of contemporary artists, from painters to poets and musicians to sculptors, from across England and around the world, explain how a specific work of their own was influenced or inspired by the annunciation story. Some of the encounters are religious in character whilst others are secular. From the late Sir John Tavener to Grayson Perry, the revelations are heart rending, highly personal and profound.

He travels to Italy to track down what is claimed to be the first known depiction of the Annunciation in a catacomb in Rome and sees at first hand how the Annunciation inspired some of the greatest works of Renaissance art in Rome, Florence and Venice. He also views Annunciation masterpieces in Chartres, Paris, Amsterdam, Antwerp, Madrid and Barcelona, as well as the most acclaimed depictions from across England, created over more than a thousand years.

He heads to Nazareth and to the supposed location of the encounter between the angel Gabriel and the Virgin Mary. Today, it is a town with a Muslim majority population, situated in the northern part of the state of Israel and best known as a focal point for worldwide Christian pilgrimage. What does he discover new in contemporary Nazareth about the story of the Annunciation, and about inter-denominational understanding and interfaith dialogue?

Throughout his journey, the author, a practising Christian, does not impose his own views about the Annunciation. Instead, he lets the subjects describe and explain their thoughts and feelings, leaving the reader to come to her/his own conclusion. However, at the end of the book, the author assesses all that he has heard and seen over his three-year pilgrimage and reveals what he believes about the story and its meaning, and what has changed in his own faith over the course of his quest.

ACKNOWLEDGEMENTS

A big thank you to all the people I met and spoke with during my journey. I much appreciate the time, support, interest and input each of them gave to me.

A special debt of gratitude to the following:

Suzanne Foster, Archivist Winchester College, for her responsiveness and patience.

Dr Humphrey Wine, Curator of Seventeenth- and Eighteenth-Century French Painting, National Gallery.

Dr Jean-Luc Bordeaux, Art Historian with a special interest in the life and works of François Lemoyne.

Also thanks to:

Harry Byford for designing the book cover.

Daisy Hamblin and Peter Chittick for help with French translations. Merci beaucoup.

Dr John Crook, Andrew Honey, Fr Lawrence Lew OP, Joe Low, Ronald Neil, Andy Sollars and John Wallace for supplying specific photographic images.

Mark Stokes and Tom Marcinkowski at Winchester Photographic for their skill and diligence.

Professor Elizabeth Stuart for her warm encouragement from the start to the end.

Professor Inga Bryden, Chair of Winchester University Press Editorial Board.

Professor Neil McCaw, Commissioning Editor, Winchester University Press, for his passionate support for the book.

Professor Christopher Mulvey - a wonderfully encouraging Editor.

And especially Stephen Greenhalgh, for the excellence of his copy-editing, meticulous attention to detail in proof-reading, and constructive and wise suggestions. As a former Head of Theology and Religion at the University of Winchester he also offered me invaluable and insightful guidance.

Finally, a huge debt of appreciation to my wonderful wife and life partner, Hilary, for her endless creativity and ideas throughout this project. Although a non-believer, she provided extraordinary support and input, especially in relation to the writing of the manuscript. She also accompanied me to more cathedrals, churches, museums and galleries than she would care to mention.

LIST OF ILLUSTRATIONS

Cover and Frontispiece: François Lemoyne, *The Annunciation*, 1727. © The Warden and Scholars of Winchester College.

Spine: Statue of angel Gabriel, 1390s, Winchester City Museum. On loan from Winchester College. Photo by kind permission of Hampshire Cultural Trust and the Warden and Scholars of Winchester College.

1. Room 33, National Gallery. © The National Gallery, London.

2. Detail from François Lemoyne, *The Annunciation*, 1727. © The Warden and Scholars of Winchester College.

3. Detail from François Lemoyne, *The Annunciation*, 1727. © The Warden and Scholars of Winchester College.

4. Illustration by Elsie Walker in *My Lord and My God* by John Heenan, published by Burns and Oates, 1957.

5. Mike Chapman's *Christ Child*, 1999, St Martin-in-the-Fields, London. Photo: Ronald Neil.

6. Victorian mosaics at St Martin-in-the-Fields, London. Photos: Ronald Neil.

7. Shirazeh Houshiary and Pip Horne, East Window, 2008, at St Martin-in-the-Fields, London. Photo: Ronald Neil.

8. Statues on Middle Gate at Winchester College, 1390s. © The Warden and Scholars of Winchester College.

9. James Cave, *Interior of Winchester College Chapel looking east*, 1802. © The Warden and Scholars of Winchester College.

10. Lemoyne's painting on display in Room 33, National Gallery, London. By kind permission of The Warden and Scholars of Winchester College.

11. Left: The author in the Drawing Reference Room at the Courtauld Institute of Art. Right: François Lemoyne's drawing, *Annunciation*, 1727, chalk (black and white) on blue paper. © The Samuel Courtauld Trust, The Courtauld Gallery, London.

12. Laurent Cars' engraving after François Lemoyne's *The Annunciation*, 1727-28. © The Trustees of the British Museum.

13. Left: Church of Saint-Sulpice, Paris. Right: The painting after François Lemoyne's *The Annunciation*, in the Chapel of the Assumption. Photo: Eric Daviron.

14. Inside the Art History Library, École du Louvre, Paris.

15. The Salon d'Hercule, Palace of Versailles, featuring François Lemoyne's *The Apotheosis of Hercules*, 1736, Palace of Versailles. Photo: Ryan Hadley.

40. Dante Gabriel Rossetti, *Ecce Ancilla Domini* (The Annunciation), 1850, Tate Britain, London © Tate Images.

41. Henry Ossawa Tanner, *The Annunciation*, 1898, Philadelphia Museum of Art. © Philadelphia Museum of Art.

42. The author's personal copy of *Abraxas* by Santana, 1970. Cover art: MATI.

43. Mati Klarwein, *Annunciation*, 1961. © matiklarweinart.com By kind permission of Balthazar Klarwein.

44. John Collier, *The Annunciation*, 2000. © John Collier and Hillstream LLC.

45. Video image of Steven Sotloff and 'Jihadi John' (Mohammed Emwazi) 2014.

46. The peasants of Solentiname, *The Annunciation*, 1984 © Peter Hammer Publishing House on behalf of Fr Ernest Cardenal, Managua, Nicaragua.

47. Icon depicting an Annunciation scene.

48. WA 1850.7 attributed to Uccello *The Annunciation*, early 1420s, Ashmolean Museum, Oxford. © Ashmolean Museum, Oxford.

49. A.W.N. Pugin, Annunciation panels, 1843, University Church of St Mary the Virgin, Oxford.

50. Statues of the Annunciation, late fourteenth century, New College, Oxford. Photo: Baz Richardson.

51. Stained glass panels of angel Gabriel and the Virgin Mary, fourteenth century, Christ Church Cathedral, Oxford.

52. The author stands in front of Lemoyne's *The Annunciation*, National Gallery, London.

53. Duccio, *The Annunciation*, 1307/8-11, The National Gallery, London. © The National Gallery, London.

54. Fra Filippo Lippi, *The Annunciation*, 1450-3, The National Gallery, London. © The National Gallery, London

55. Cosimo Tura, *The Virgin Annunciate*, 1475-80, The National Gallery, London. © The National Gallery, London.

56. Carlo Crivelli, *The Annunciation, with Saint Emidius*, 1486, The National Gallery, London. © The National Gallery, London.

57. Nicolas Poussin, *The Annunciation*, 1657, The National Gallery, London. © The National Gallery, London.

58. Chris Ofili, *The Holy Virgin Mary*, 1996. Acrylic, oil, polyester resin, paper collage, glitter, map pins and elephant dung on linen. 243.8 x 182.8 cm. © Chris Ofili. Courtesy Victoria Miro, London.

59. Chris Ofili, *Annunciation*, 2006. Bronze. 200.7 x 213.4 cm. Edition of 3. © Chris Ofili. Courtesy David Zwirner, New York/London

60. Carmel of the Annunciation, Thicket Priory near York.

61. Lauds at Carmel of the Annunciation, Thicket Priory near York.

62. Sister Thérèse.

88. Peter Eugene Ball's initial sketches of an Annunciation sculpture. © and by kind permission of Peter Eugene Ball.

89. Left: David Wynne, *The Virgin Mary*, 2000 © John Morley. Centre: Close-up of the statue. Right: Dusk falls at The Lady Chapel, Ely Cathedral © Leslie Monk.

90. Marcel Barbeau, *Our Lady of Walsingham*, 1954, RC Slipper Chapel near Walsingham, Norfolk.

91. The 'Holy House' at the Anglican shrine, Walsingham, Norfolk. © Fr. Lawrence Lew O.P.

92. Roof boss of the Annunciation above the nave in Norwich Cathedral. © Paul Hurst ARPS.

93. Roof boss of the Annunciation above the North Transept in Norwich Cathedral. © Paul Hurst ARPS.

94. Domenico Veneziano, *The Annunciation*, 1442-48, The Fitzwilliam Museum, Cambridge. © The Fitzwilliam Museum, Cambridge.

95. Stained glass window of the Annunciation, 1530, in King's College Chapel, Cambridge. By kind permission of the Fellows and Scholars of King's College, Cambridge.

96. Alan Storkey, *Annunciation*. By kind permission of Alan and Elaine Storkey.

97. Medieval mural of the Annunciation in the Cathedral and Abbey Church of St Alban, St Albans, Hertfordshire.

98. *Benedictional of St Æthelwold*, tenth century, British Library, London. © The British Library Board MS 49598.

99. *The Winchester Psalter*, 1150, British Library. © The British Library Board F.10r.

100. Albrecht Dürer, *The Annunciation*, from the *Life of the Virgin* series, 1503, British Museum, London. © The Trustees of the British Museum.

101. Albrecht Dürer *The Annunciation*, from the *Small Passion* series, 1510, British Museum, London. © The Trustees of the British Museum.

102. Left: Henry Moore, *Mother and Child: Hood*, 1983, St Paul's Cathedral, London. © and reproduced by kind permission of The Henry Moore Foundation. Right: Henry Moore visits St Paul's Cathedral to view his newly installed sculpture, 1984. © PA Images.

103. Richard Hamilton, *The annunciation*, 2005. © R.Hamilton. All Rights Reserved DACS 2017.

104. Left: The author plays his personal copy of the Beatles single 'Let It Be'. Right: Paul McCartney soon after recording 'Let It Be' in early 1969. © Daily Mail/Solo Syndication.

105. The Mary and angel Gabriel encounter in Tony Jordan's BBC One drama, *The Nativity*, 2010. By kind permission of Tony Jordan and Red Planet Pictures.

106. John Lynch, Tatiana Maslany and Andrew Buchan star in *The Nativity*, 2010. © Red Planet Pictures.

107. Grayson Perry, *The Annunciation of the Virgin Deal*, 2012. By kind permission of Grayson Perry and the Victoria Miro Gallery.

138. Sandro Botticelli, *Cestello Annunciation,* 1489, Uffizi Gallery, Florence. © Gallerie degli Uffizi.

139. Tiled altar screen of the Annunciation, Lady Chapel, St Mary's Church, Ottery St Mary, Devon.

140. John Tavener, *Annunciation,* 1992. By kind permission of Chester Music Ltd.

141. Angela Conner, *Sir John Tavener Memorial,* 2016, Winchester Cathedral. © Joe Low.

142. Advent calendar window for 1ˢᵗ December.

143. Lectio divina.

144. Rembrandt, *The Annunciation,* 1635. © Besançon, musée des Beaux-Arts et d'Archéologie. Photo: Pierre Guenat.

145. Jill Coughman, *Mary Receiving the Call,* 1999. © Jill Coughman.

146. The Annunciation encounter at the Nativity service, St Paul's Church, Winchester.

147. Christmastime and the Byford family comes together.

148. The author's parents, Lawry and Muriel Byford.

149. Annunciation illustration from *Baby Jesus,* Ladybird book, 1961. © Ladybird Books Ltd 1961.

150. The central lancet window on the west façade at Chartres Cathedral features a stunning Annunciation panel, 1150s. © Fr Lawrence Lew O.P.

151. Statue of the Annunciation at the North Porch, Chartres Cathedral. © Jill K H Geoffrion, www.jillgeoffrion.com

152. Jean Soulas, stone carving of the Annunciation, sixteenth century, Chartres Cathedral.

153. *Sancta Camisa,* Chartres Cathedral. © Fr. Lawrence Lew O.P.

154. Jean-François Millet, *The Angelus,* 1859, Musée d'Orsay, Paris. © Musée d'Orsay. Dist, RMN-Grand Palais/Patrice Schmidt.

155. Rogier van de Weyden, *The Annunciation,* 1435-40, The Louvre, Paris. © Musée du Louvre. Dist, RMN-Grand Palais/Angèle Dequier.

156. Peter Paul Rubens, *The Annunciation,* 1628, Rubenhuis, Antwerp. © Rubens House, Antwerp. Photo: Michel Wuyts and Louis De Peuter.

157. Maerten de Vos, *St Luke painting the Virgin Mary,* 1602, Cathedral of Our Lady, Antwerp. © KMSKA – Lukas-Art in Flanders vzw. Photo: Hugo Maertens.

158. Tilman Riemenschneider, *The Annunciation,* 1486, The Rijksmuseum, Amsterdam. © The Rijksmuseum, Amsterdam.

159.: Francesco di Valdanbrino, *The Annunciation,* 1423, The Rijksmuseum, Amsterdam. © The Rijksmuseum, Amsterdam.

160. El Greco, *La Anunciación,* 1596-1600, The Prado, Madrid. © Museo Nacional del Prado.

161. Joan Flotats designed roof boss in the Crypt, 1882, La Sagrada Familia, Barcelona.

185. 'The site of the Annunciation', Roman Catholic Basilica of the Annunciation, Nazareth.

186. The grotto inside the Basilica, Nazareth. © Dennis Jarvis.

187. Guglielmo Schiavina, *The Annunciation*, 1990, Nazareth.

188. Cardinal Vincent Nichols prays inside the grotto, Basilica of the Annunciation, Nazareth.

189. Amy Bright Unfried, *Annunciation*, 2008. © Amy Bright Unfried.

190. Andy Warhol, *Leonardo da Vinci The Annunciation 1472*, 1984. © 2017 The Andy Warhol Foundation for the Visual Arts, Inc/Artist Rights Society (ARS) New York and DACS London.

191. Alfonse Borysewicz, *Beginning Comes Last*, 2016. © Alfonse Borysewicz.

192. Paulo Medina, *Annunciation*, 2006. © Paulo Medina.

193. George Bandele, *The Virgin Mary*, 1950, SMA African Art Museum, Tenafly, New Jersey © SMA African Art Museum.

194. Lamidi Olonade Fakeye, *The Annunciation*, 2007, © Dr Nicholas Bridger.

195. Vie de Jesus Mafa Project, *The Annunciation*, 1970s, Cameroon.

196. Evans Yegon (Yegonizer), *The Annunciation* © Evans Yegon.

197. Wood carving of 'an annunciation scene', 2002, Jakarta, Indonesia.

198. Junko Watanabe and Fujie Mase hold up Sadao Watanabe's *The Annunciation*, 1966. By kind permission of Mrs Fujie Mase (art dealer), Tokyo.

199. Tom Thompson, *Annunciation*, late 1960s-1970. © Manly Art Gallery & Museum.

200. Tom Thompson, *Annunciation, with distant town*, 1980s. © Sydney Grammar School.

201. Jill Coughman, *Overshadowed*, 2016. © Jill Coughman.

202. Annette Esser, *The Annunciation*, 2016. © Annette Esser.

203. Jana-Faye Jakumeit, *The Annunciation – bondage*, 2016. © Jana-Faye Jakumeit.

204. C.E. Kempe, *The Annunciation*, 1905, Winchester Cathedral. © Dr John Crook, Winchester

205. The Bishop of Winchester and the Dean of Winchester with the author at his licensing and installation as a Lay Canon and member of Chapter, July 2017, Winchester Cathedral.

PERMISSIONS

Over a three-year period, from January 2014 through to December 2016, more than 150 people agreed to speak with me for this project. They included a wide range of leading clerics, theologians, historians and artists, as well as members of my family. Each of them kindly agreed for their name to appear in the book.

In alphabetical order, they are:

Stephen Adam; Reverend Sally Allen; Reverend Canon Dr Keith Anderson: Dr Andreas Andreopoulos; His Grace Bishop Angaelos; The Very Reverend James Atwell; Peter Eugene Ball; Giulia Bartrum; Professor Tina Beattie; Dr Elizabeth Benjamin; Tim Bissett; Reverend Philippa Boardman; The Very Reverend Mark Bonney; Dr Jean-Luc Bordeaux; Alfonse Borysewicz; Sister Beatrice Bourrat; Professor Andrew Bradstock; Dr Nicholas Bridger; Reverend Canon Rosalind Brown; Reverend William Burke; Flora Byford; Harry Byford; Hilary Byford; Sir Lawrence Byford; Lily Byford; Molly Byford; Lady Muriel Byford; Sam Byford; Lord Carey of Clifton; Stephen Chalke; Michael Chapman; The Right Reverend and Rt Hon Richard Chartres; Steve Clifford; John Collier; Jonathan Cook; Theolyn Cortens; Jill Coughman; Professor Kenneth Cracknell; The Right Reverend Bishop Tim Dakin; Reverend Jeremy Davies; Professor Gavin D'Costa; Bishop John Dennis; Dr Kathleen Doyle; The Very Reverend Dr John Drury; Bishop Philip Egan; Annette Esser; Dr Caroline Farey; The Very Reverend Vivienne Faull; David Fawcett; Professor David Ford; Reverend Monsignor Canon David Forde; Suzanne Foster; Ann Furedi; Míla Fürstová; Fr Guy de Gaynesford; Reverend Dr Jill Geoffrion; Chris Gollon; Dr Paula Gooder; Reverend Sally Goodson; Professor Tim Gorringe; Professor Mary Grey; Reverend Malcolm Guite; Reverend Nicky Gumbel; Sophie Hacker; Caroline Hall; The Very Reverend Dr John Hall; Susie Hamilton; Stephen Hanvey; Lord Harries of Pentregarth; Reverend Canon Jeremy Haselock; Dr Colin Haydon; Dr Clare Haynes; Margaret Hebblethwaite; The Very Reverend Jane Hedges; Reverend Vanessa Herrick; The Right Reverend Bishop Nicholas Holtam; Reverend Rose Hudson-Wilkin; Professor Lisa Isherwood; Jana-Faye Jakumeit; Professor Steve Jones; Tony Jordan; Sir Nicholas Kenyon; Alice Kettle; Anne Keyte; Balthazar Klarwein; The Right Reverend Bishop Libby Lane; Professor Ora Limor; Professor Bill Lucas; Andrew Lumsden; Professor Diarmaid MacCulloch; Fr Bill O.S.M.; Milli McGregor; Dr Judith Maltby; Paulo Medina; Barry Miles; Arthur Morgan; Kate Morgan; Reverend Canon Philip Morgan; Reverend Canon Dame Sarah Mullally; His Eminence Cardinal Cormac Murphy-O'Connor; Nicholas Mynheer; Martin Neary; Rabbi Julia Neuberger; His Eminence Cardinal Vincent Nichols; Reverend Canon Mark Oakley; The Very Reverend June Osborne; Sir Nicholas Penny; Grayson Perry; Professor Ben Quash; Dr Chloë Reddaway; Reverend Canon Dr Brian Rees; Reverend Canon Dr Roland Riem; Archbishop Arthur Roche; Pierre Rosenberg; Christopher Rowell; Professor Miri Rubin; Jyoti Sahi; Gill Sakakini; Xavier Salmon; Anne Scanlan; Reverend Peter Seal; Dr Philip Seal; Professor Mona Siddiqui; Dr Fanny Singer;

Sister Ann; Sister Helena; Sister Mary of Carmel; Sister Thérèse; Fr Peter Smith; Bishop John Shelby Spong; Gloria Ssali; Elaine Storkey; Professor Elizabeth Stuart; David Suchet; Lady Maryanna Tavener; Lynne Tembey; Professor Elaine Thomas; Tom Thompson; Reverend Angela Tilby; Reverend Dr Bert Tosh; Dr Ralph Townsend; Sir Mark Tully; Amy Bright Unfried; Nicholas Vaughan; Dr Christoph Vogtherr; Reverend Dr Mark Wakelin; Reverend Canon Susan Wallace; Reverend Canon Dr Robin Ward; The Most Reverend Metropolitan Kallistos Ware; The Right Reverend Bishop Martin Warner; Reverend Dr Sam Wells; David Westin; Reverend Canon Andrew White; Dr Hannah Williams; Dr Rowan Williams; Dr Paul Williamson; Bishop Wilfred Willins; Dr Humphrey Wine; Reverend Lucy Winkett; Dr Timothy Winter; Patrick Wise; Professor Linda Woodhead; Professor Dennis Wright; Roger Wright; Evans Yegon

————————

Thank you to these poets and publishers for kindly allowing the following poems to be featured:

Mary C. Grey, 'The Annunciation', 2010. © Mary C. Grey.

James Atwell, 'Annunciation', © James Atwell.

Rosalind Brown, 'The Annunciation', 1997. © Rosalind Brown.

R. S. Thomas, 'The Annunciation by Veneziano', 1975, from the collection: *Laboratories of the Spirit*, published by Macmillan. By kind permission of the Publishers Licensing Society.

R. S. Thomas, 'Annunciation', from the collection: *Collected Later Poems 1988-2000*, published by Bloodaxe Books.

Charles Causley, 'Ballad of the Bread Man', 1968, from the collection: *Collected Poems 1951-2000*, published by Macmillan. By kind permission of David Higham Associates.

Elizabeth Jennings, 'The Annunciation', 1986, from the collection: *The Collected Poems*, published by Carcanet Press. By kind permission of David Higham Associates.

Denise Levertov, 'Annunciation', from the collection: *A Door in the Hive*, © 1989 Denise Levertov. Reprinted by permission of New Directions Publishing Corp.

Madeleine L'Engle, 'After Annunciation', from the collection: *The Ordering of Love, The New and Collected Poems of Madeleine L'Engle*, 2008, published by WaterBrook Press.

Jean Valentine, 'Annunciation', 2004, from the collection: *Little Boat*, 2007, published by Wesleyan University Press.

Luci Shaw, 'Virgin', 2006, from the collection: *Accompanied by Angels, Poems of the Incarnation*, published by Wm. B. Eerdmans Publishing Company, Grand Rapids, MI. Reprinted by kind permission of the publisher; all rights reserved.

David Scott, 'A David Jones Annunciation', 2005, from the collection: *Piecing Together 2005* and *Beyond the Drift, New & Selected Poems*, 2014, published by Bloodaxe Books. © David Scott.

Philip Seal, 'Annunciations', 2016. © Philip Seal.

Thomas Merton, 'The Annunciation', 1957, from the collection: *The Collected Poems of Thomas Merton*, © The Abbey of Gethsemani. Reprinted by kind permission of New Directions Publishing Corp.

Malcolm Guite, 'Annunciation', 2012. © Malcolm Guite. By kind permission of Malcolm Guite.

CHAPTER 1

A GROWING SENSE OF CURIOSITY

With an hour to kill before meeting a friend for lunch near Trafalgar Square, I decide to call in on the National Gallery. I amble through the East Wing, enter Room 33 and find myself facing a collection of eighteenth-century French paintings I have never seen before. There is only one other person in the room: a gallery assistant who sits with his arms folded and a resigned look on his face. We acknowledge each other with a smile and then he looks to the floor. A reverential silence hangs in the air.

I cast my eyes about the room then scan the wall facing me. Almost immediately, a large painting depicting the encounter between the Virgin Mary and the angel Gabriel catches my eye. There is something distinctive about it that demands my attention. I stand still and keep staring intently for a few seconds, then approach it slowly.

'Everyone tends to walk straight past that one,' says the gallery assistant, inclining his head towards the painting. 'I was brought up a Catholic so I often think about it when I'm sitting here. You know, the Annunciation and all that, the Hail Mary, the Rosary.' Seemingly happy to have a receptive audience, he shuffles his body sideways on the low, wooden chair and continues, 'By the time they have got to this room, they've probably had enough religion, to be honest. It's everywhere in the gallery.'

'Do you like it?' I ask.

'I don't like them cherubs up there. Ok, there's that commanding angel and the softly-lit Mary, but them cherubs aren't needed are they? It's all a bit over the top, to be honest. That's what I think. I like Caravaggio the best and the way he brings people to life. But that one, no, I don't particularly like it if I'm honest.' His crumpled black suit and dishevelled tie match his bored expression and dismissive tone. 'We're not supposed to give our view, but as you asked.'

1. Room 33, National Gallery. © The National Gallery, London.

Our conversation draws to a natural close. I move towards the painting, putting a little more distance between us. The lack of visitors allows me to spend more time contemplating the canvas in peace. I stand in front of it for several minutes, alone, undisturbed. My eyes dart around, absorbing every detail. I take several steps back, pause, and move forward again. Then I walk to the seating area in the middle of the room, sit down and study the image from a distance.

2. Details from François Lemoyne The Annunciation, 1727. © The Warden and Scholars of Winchester College.

First, my eyes settle upon Mary who fills the bottom left of the painting. She is kneeling in a subservient pose, her eyes cast down, her hands clasped together on her chest. The soft light on her face reveals a dream-like expression. She looks reflective, serene. A second glance reveals that she is gazing towards a manuscript that stands on a prie-dieu. A single sheet of plain paper appears to have fallen on the floor. The bottom half of the painting features a range of dark colours. Her long, voluminous robe is a deep shade of terracotta and the shawl draped over her shoulders is royal blue. I feel slightly confused: Mary's elfin-like features and peaceful demeanour are not at all the way I had envisaged her. If anything, this depiction of her seems rather cloying.

My eyes move upwards to focus on the agile angel Gabriel, who dominates the right-hand side of the picture. He shares Mary's soft, yet pointed features and has distinctive, arched eyebrows, the whole effect making him look androgynous. This rounded, unusually feminine depiction of Gabriel also takes me by surprise. But despite this look, he manages to appear authoritative and imperious. He hovers just above ground level, his large wings fanned out in motion, contributing a dynamic sense of movement to the scene. His right arm is raised in the air and his index finger points upwards in a dramatic gesture.

In contrast to the strong tones of Mary's garments, Gabriel is wearing much paler colours and is suffused by light. He is clad in a pale blue-grey tunic and has a flowing ochre shawl wrapped loosely around his body. His legs, including his upper thighs, are exposed. The blue and golden theme is continued in the clouds through which strong beams of light descend, providing a wonderful luminosity. In the top left hand corner of the painting float the disembodied heads of three cherubim: two looking down on Mary, the other appearing to look up to heaven. They seem out of place to me, imparting a saccharine tone to the scene.

I have spent so long looking at this painting. Extraordinarily for me, I have even written down some notes about it. But why am I so transfixed? It's not as if I find it particularly beautiful. In fact, I find the overall composition a little too florid. Is it because its style is so different to other more iconic depictions of the Annunciation I have seen in the past? That must have something to do with it, but it doesn't explain everything.

After a while, it dawns on me: it is the actual subject matter of the painting – the angel Gabriel's encounter with Mary – that is intriguing me. I have not thought about this story in any depth for years. It seems that my dormant emotional response to it has just been reawakened. I remember that as a child, I loved the story's sense of drama and found the consequences of Mary's quiet acceptance inspiring. I recall how it had a huge impact on my burgeoning childhood faith all those years ago. So the painting has triggered a myriad of thoughts and memories. But I wonder how I feel about the story now. Does it carry the same resonance as before or has its significance changed when viewed through my adult eyes?

I approach the canvas again. This time I notice the variety of delicate brush strokes, some individual hairs still stuck to the varnish, the uneven texture of the surface caused by the layering of the oils and a few small hairline cracks. However, this picture, almost three centuries old, is in remarkable condition. I crouch down and notice a faint signature hidden in the bottom right hand corner of the painting. Squinting, moving my head to the side to avoid the reflections, I can just make out the dark-brown lettering:

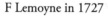

F Lemoyne in 1727

3. François Lemoyne's signature on the painting. © The Warden and Scholars of Winchester College.

A steady flow of visitors passes through the room but nearly all completely ignore the painting. One couple glances at it for two or three seconds but then moves on swiftly. A school party arrives and sits cross-legged on the wooden floor on the other side of the room. There are twenty boys and girls, aged around nine or ten, wearing smart blue blazers with matching ties. The group is placed in front of another eighteenth-century French painting opposite Lemoyne's, entitled *Psyche showing her Sisters her Gifts from Cupid* by Jean-Honoré Fragonard. A National Gallery education guide begins to address them and I eavesdrop shamelessly. As she speaks about Fragonard's work, I look towards Lemoyne's painting. Interestingly, what she says seems equally applicable to both.

'A lot of the pictures in this gallery tell stories,' she begins. 'We usually find stories through words, don't we? So an artist has to tell a complex story without words. They have to use body language. They speak with their hands. They use shades of light and dark. They use colour to create a mood. That's important. Think about the use of the colours here.'

She waves a hand across the painting as she commands the attention of every child through her simple eloquence and overt passion for her subject.

'This is a French artist who painted in the 1700s. He's telling us a story from a time much earlier than that. He's trying to capture a moment. Can you see how the light focuses in such a way that we look at that woman? She seems to be the key character in this painting.'

My eyes remain fixed on Lemoyne's depiction of the Annunciation, and my mind casts me back fifty years. I was six years old in early 1965 and living near the village of Hartley Wintney in Hampshire. I had just started to attend Holy Communion classes at the local Catholic church, along with several other children of the same age. The local priest, Fr Terry Walsh, gave each child a book that we read aloud together during the lessons. Entitled *My Lord and My God*, it was written by John Heenan, Archbishop of Westminster at that time. I still have my old, stained copy at home.

4. Illustration by Elsie Walker in *My Lord and My God* by John Heenan, published by Burns and Oates, 1957.

I recall the lesson where the class learned about Mary's encounter with Gabriel. First, we looked at a striking image in the book. I can remember it so clearly. Mary was pictured with her back pressed against a wall, her arms raised as if to protect herself. She was dressed in blue and white robes. Her head was covered in a simple headscarf and she wore a fearful expression as she looked in the direction of the angel, who was represented by several strong rays of light.

The class looked at the picture whilst Fr Walsh spontaneously acted out the story with great enthusiasm. 'The angel suddenly arrived from nowhere and...aagh!' he cried out loudly. 'Mary stepped back, anxious and frightened. What on earth was happening?' he asked us. The priest was getting into role, trying to convey some of the intense emotions the young Mary must have felt at the time. His body was shaking and his eyes looked wild. I recall how I felt shocked, scared and more than a little uneasy.

That lesson, and the image of Mary's encounter with the angel, was a strong influence throughout my early childhood and created a powerful, lasting memory. Now I understand why I have been surprised, perhaps even a little disturbed by Lemoyne's depiction of

Mary and Gabriel. The sweet subservience of Lemoyne's Mary contrasts strongly with the shocked expression on the face of the Mary in *My Lord and My God*. Likewise, the physical representation of Gabriel in the Lemoyne painting is totally different to the simple rays of sunlight I was familiar with as a child. This mismatch of images prompts a growing sense of curiosity and is starting to raise questions. Of course, I realize there are many ways to interpret this extraordinary event. But what is the essence of the annunciation story?

A couple of young adults stand in front of Lemoyne's painting and giggle as they attempt to copy the scene in front of them. The young man tries to hover in mid-air whilst pointing his index finger upwards. Meanwhile, the woman pretends to cower, holding her hands to her chest as if in awe.

'Didn't she break into a song after this when she visited Elizabeth?' the girlfriend asks. He looks confused and shrugs his shoulders. They both move on.

My attention switches again from the style of the painting to the subject matter of the Annunciation. I begin to wonder what the story is really all about and the questions start to tumble over each other. Did it really happen? Are we to believe that Mary was actually visited by an angel? Should we think of the story more as metaphor or as myth? What is it supposed to mean? What is its key message?

Suddenly, another childhood memory comes flooding back with great force. I attended a Catholic primary school in the 1960s where pupils were taught to recite 'The Angelus' prayer. A bell would ring at 12 noon and we would stand and begin immediately. Hands joined together. Eyes closed. 'The Angel of the Lord declared unto Mary and she conceived of the Holy Spirit…Hail Mary, Full of Grace, The Lord is with Thee…' I remember how we would chant those words automatically, scarcely considering their meaning or wondering why it was important to say them. But their familiarity and regular rhythm, coupled with the fact that this was a group activity, was rather engaging at the time. As I close my eyes, I can hear those young voices again.

More familiar words, this time from the Nicene Creed, float through my mind: 'By the power of the Holy Spirit, he became incarnate from the Virgin Mary, and was made man.' When reciting these words each week in church over a period of fifty years, have I been making an open declaration of my true beliefs or have I been merely following a ritual?

Feeling unsettled, I walk towards the picture again, perhaps hoping to find the answer to some of my questions hidden within. This time, I notice for the first time a card set to the left-hand side of the painting that reads:

François Lemoyne (1688 –1737)
The Annunciation 1727

According to St Luke's Gospel, the archangel Gabriel
announces to the Virgin that she will give birth to Jesus.
This depiction of the subject is signed and dated 1727,
the year the artist was awarded a prize for history painting
by Louis XV.

It may have been commissioned by the then headmaster of
Winchester College where it was installed in 1729.
Its painted arched top suggests an arched frame was
originally intended.

Oil on canvas.

L111 On loan from Winchester College.

The city of Winchester has been my home for thirty-one years so that last line, 'On loan from Winchester College', piques my interest in the painting even further. Why was this picture lent by one of England's leading public schools to one of the world's greatest art collections? And that line, 'It may have been commissioned by the then headmaster of Winchester College' intrigues me. Why did such a flamboyantly Catholic, early eighteenth-century painting of Mary, by a leading French artist, come to Winchester at that time? What is the story behind its commission and its journey across the Channel? I gaze at the top of the painting, noting its shape. I wonder if the artist originally intended it to be placed as an altarpiece in a site that had an arched niche.

I have been so absorbed in my thoughts, I have lost track of time. With a start, I check my watch. My hour is up. It is time to leave.

———

All through the lunch with my friend I feel distracted. I cannot stop thinking about the Annunciation and that painting. Afterwards, I decide to walk back down The Strand and return to Trafalgar Square. On the way, I notice a huge billboard outside the Savoy Theatre promoting a new Beatles musical. It features the Fab Four – John, Paul, George and Ringo – jumping out of a huge Union flag, across which are emblazoned the words 'LET IT BE'. Hang on a second. Wasn't 'Let it be done to me according to your word', Mary's response to Gabriel?

Opposite the National Gallery stands the church of St Martin-in-the-Fields. For some reason, I feel drawn to go inside. On my approach, I notice a line of tourists taking it in turns to stand on a small step. A closer examination reveals that they are all waiting to take photos of a stone sculpture of a male baby with his umbilical cord still attached. Around the base are carved the words:

IN THE BEGINNING WAS THE WORD
AND THE WORD BECAME FLESH AND LIVED AMONG US

The life-like, startling sculpture is highly unusual and inspires many fascinating comments from the people who queue patiently to see it close up. I usually carry a small digital voice recorder, a small camera and a notebook in my bag wherever I go – always the ever-ready journalist. Today is no exception. I ask a group of tourists if I can record their comments. Each is happy to oblige.

'So natural. It should be easy for people to understand. All the people around us are afraid of things in their lives but they should come up on this step, look at the baby not yet born and get peace from it,' says a German tourist, moving her finger slowly down the length of the umbilical cord.

'Is the baby about to be born or has it just arrived? Is it still in the sack?' a Brazilian woman asks me as she takes a photograph. 'So beautiful. It's so unusual to see Jesus Christ inside. I've never seen that before.'

5. Mike Chapman *Christ Child*, 1999, St Martin-in-the-Fields, London. Photo: Ronald Neil.

Three Polish sisters visiting London are transfixed. I ask them what they see.

'Hey, it's a sleeping baby with the, how do you say, the string still attached there. How unusual. Still inside the body,' declares one of them.

'No, no. He's just been born. Look, he's stretching out. There wouldn't be enough room for him in such a small place. I think he's outside,' her sibling responds.

'What do you think?' I ask the third.

'How do I know? I don't go any more to a Catholic Church…I'm not sure to be honest with you.' She shakes her head mournfully.

6. Victorian mosaics at St Martin-in-the-Fields, London. Photo: Ronald Neil.

Inside the beautifully restored church, I walk down the central aisle and sit in a front pew. In the sanctuary ahead, two Victorian mosaics on either side of the altar depict the Annunciation scene. To the left, Gabriel, dressed in red and gold and kneeling reverentially, holds a lily stem. To the right, Mary, composed and seated, receives his message with a hand placed on her chest. Rays of light break through a cloud to radiate her face, and her head glows under her halo. The words '*Benedicta Inter Mulieres*' – Blessed Among Women – are written below.

7. Shirazeh Houshiary and Pip Horne's East Window, 2008, at St Martin-in-the-Fields, London. Photo: Ronald Neil.

I gaze up at the recently installed large East window, which features a breathtakingly ambitious design by the Iranian artist Shirazeh Houshiary and her architect husband Pip Horne. The longer I look, the more I can see. From the abstract, etched glass and stainless steel latticed framework emerges the silhouette of a white egg set in the middle of a warped cross. Light floods in through the glass to the altar area. Annunciation. Incarnation. Crucifixion. Resurrection. Or is that simply my own interpretation? Abstract art inspiring my own reflection? It seems that today, wherever I go, wherever I look, I keep seeing references to Mary, the angel Gabriel, the Annunciation and the miraculous moment of the conception of Jesus.

I return to the National Gallery and to Room 33. The picture that is luring me back is not a Titian, a Da Vinci, a Rembrandt or a Van Gogh. It is a relatively unknown work by an artist I have never heard of. It isn't featured on the gallery's guided tour, nor is it mentioned in any leaflet or audio guide. There are many other much more acclaimed Annunciations on display as part of the National Gallery's permanent collection: Duccio, Fra Lippi, Crivelli, Poussin; a curatorial tour de force. And yet it is this François Lemoyne work that has captivated me, drawn me in, sparked my curiosity and raised a myriad of questions.

A group of art history students from Houston, Texas, stand in front of the painting. They have been in Rome, Florence, Venice and Paris and are now on the final leg of their 'grand tour'. I ask them to comment on the painting and its artistry. With their agreement, I record their thoughts.

'It's not like most Annunciations I've seen,' one of them tells me. 'Gabriel's on the right and Mary is on the left. It's building up a vertical rather than the traditional horizontal. And there's more movement here.'

'There's an S curve from the angel to Mary so you follow it down,' another explains. 'The first thing you see is the finger, then the spiral. I like the dramatic light…the fine, subdued tone of the colouring… azurite…Gabriel's ochre.'

'I'm not sure,' a third interve an extraordinary depiction. Humbling… demure…with wonderful movement. d wings and those masterly folds in the fabric…the free, sensuous brushwork. dle of something and whoosh! There's a big explosion. Amazing clouds. And that str l.'

'I love the light,' says another student.

'It draws me to the angel and to the finger. But I don't like the faces,' another comments. '1727 – you can see it's at the end of the baroque with its spectacular style. Spirituality and materiality mixed together.'

'It's not the best Annunciation I've ever seen,' says a fifth. 'Do you know that the Annunciation is the most painted religious subject in western art?' she declares. 'The earliest known image is a third-century fresco painting in the catacomb of Priscilla in Rome. We went there but, unfortunately, we couldn't go down to see it. We always have to remember most people who went to church in the Middle Ages were illiterate, so paintings were their main guide to the Bible and the iconography was the way the gospel stories came alive for them.'

They move on and a new group of four tourists replace them. I listen in on their conversation, standing a few inches to one side, and then ask them what they think of the painting.

'Gabriel is telling Mary she's going to have Jesus, right?' one enquires.

'She's been told what?' responds her friend. 'I don't know that story. And what are they?' She points to the cherubim.

'Are they just hanging around or communicating something? And why is that woman flying in?'

'That's not a woman, that's the angel Gabriel,' a third chuckles.

'Well, it looks like a woman to me,' she replies. 'I like her face but there doesn't seem to be much emotion here. She looks passive and demure. I'm still trying to work it out. What's going on? I'm not sure about the story. I think I've heard about it before…vaguely somewhere.'

'The moment is called The Annunciation,' I tell the group.

'What's that?' a handsome, bearded young man asks, headphones clasped round his neck.

'It's when the angel tells Mary she's going to have Jesus,' the first intervenes…'I'm more drawn to the colours than the story. To that angel space. Yeah, I quite like the colours. I wouldn't put it up at home though.'

'It's like a fairytale, don't you think?' the young man responds as he looks towards me. 'I don't like it and I don't believe the story. Do you?'

CHAPTER 2

MY OWN LONG SEARCH

I arrive home, head straight to my study and locate *My Lord and My God*, the book that played such an important part in shaping my childhood beliefs. I have not looked at it for fifty years but have always kept a place for it on my bookshelf. Turning the well-worn pages, I find the relevant chapter, 'The Infant Jesus', with its memorable picture of a startled Mary, and start to read its simple text:

> When a baby is born in your house your mother and father make up their minds what the baby's name is going to be. But Mary and Joseph did not have to choose a name for this Baby for an angel had told them before He was born that His name had to be Jesus. This is how he came to be called Jesus.
>
> One day Mary was saying her prayers at home. She was very kind and holy and everybody loved her. While she was saying her prayers she suddenly heard a voice speaking to her. This gave her rather a shock because she did not know that anyone was in the room except herself. She could tell that this was not the voice of an ordinary person. It was the voice of an angel and the angel's name was Gabriel. This is what Gabriel said to Mary: 'Hail full of grace, the Lord is with thee, blessed art thou among women.'
>
> Mary was very much surprised at what the angel said. She did not know what the angel meant by saying that she was 'full of grace and blessed among women'. Although she was the holiest woman God ever made, she did not think that she was better than anybody else. But God had chosen her to be the Mother of His Son because she was so holy and loved God so much. The angel Gabriel then said to Mary: 'God is very pleased with you and He wants you to be the Mother of His Son. When His Son is born you must call Him Jesus.'
>
> 'If I am going to be His Mother', Mary answered, 'who will be His father?'
>
> 'Oh!' said the angel, 'God will be His Father. That is why this Baby, when he is born, will be called the Son of God.'
>
> Mary smiled at the angel and said: 'I am God's little servant and I am glad to do what He asks me.'
>
> When the angel had gone away, Mary went on with her prayers. Now she had a great deal to talk to God about. From the moment when she said she would do what God wanted and become the Mother of Jesus, God came to her. God stayed with her until it was time for the Baby to be born. When you receive Holy Communion you are like Mary: you have God within you.

Reading these words casts me back to the time when I first heard the story. It was so dramatic and a little scary. To think that this simple girl called Mary was approached by an angel and told that her baby would be the Son of God. Of course, I was at an age when the difficulties facing Mary regarding the parentage of the baby went way above my head. To me, the story was wonderful, and coupling it with the picture in the book made the events seem so real. Those primary school years were a time of uncomplicated innocence, a time of acceptance. It never occurred to me to question whether the story was true. Why would it? I never knew then that the story is known as 'The Annunciation'. Indeed, it wasn't until early adulthood that I understood that the word 'annunciation' is derived from the Latin word *annuntiatio* and means 'announcement'.

While replacing *My Lord and My God* on the shelf, I notice a book next to it entitled *Ronald Eyre on The Long Search*. The book is based on Ronald Eyre's thought-provoking and ambitious BBC television series that I remember watching in the late 1970s. Over the course of thirteen hour-long programmes, Eyre explored the different beliefs and practices of the major religions around the world. 'The Long Search,' he said, 'was open to anybody. It doesn't have a tidy beginning, middle and end. You're on it the moment you start wondering where you were before you were born, where you go when you'll die, and what you're on earth for in the meantime. If you knew the answers, you wouldn't ask the questions. But other people's answers should be worth collecting. And so should other people's questions.'

You may be unlikely to get the definitive answer, he surmised, but the important matter was to search – to ask questions and be open to hearing new insights. Eyre's journey was primarily about listening intently to what priests, gurus, preachers, academics and lay people said to him about belief and meaning as he observed a variety of contemporary religious practices around the world. It was exploratory and open ended. During his search, as one reviewer highlighted, he discovered that beliefs were less important than he had expected. Indeed, he found that the power of symbol, ritual and community emerged as the living centre of religious experience.

But are Eyre's findings and interpretations enough for me? He was interested in the grand sweep of religious experience. A thought comes to me: why don't I try and approach the subject from a completely different angle? I could put one specific story – the Annunciation, told by Luke in the Bible in just 248 words – under a microscope and examine people's reactions to it and their experiences surrounding it. Could this possibly enable a deeper understanding for me of Christian belief, certainty and doubt?

Peter Taylor, the great investigative reporter, once memorably described his television documentary work thus: 'It's about listening to what they tell me, finding the revelations and putting them into context. The heart of current affairs is what people don't tell you, and what they do – those things that make your jaw drop.' In May 1990, Peter Taylor presented a BBC current affairs programme in the *Public Eye* series, entitled *The Church in the 90s*. As the Church of England awaited the appointment of a new Archbishop of Canterbury to succeed Robert Runcie, the programme investigated claims from critics that the Church of England had failed to be the nation's spiritual guide and asked whether a Church made up of liberals, catholics and evangelicals, can revive the faith.

In one memorable exchange between Taylor and the then Archbishop of York, Dr John Habgood, interviewed at his home at Bishopthorpe Palace, Taylor asked, 'Do you believe that Christ was born of a virgin, and was crucified, died and was literally resurrected?'

The Archbishop of York replied: 'I am very happy to take what the creeds say and also to read the Scriptures as they have always been read, namely as witnesses to the God-givenness of Christ and to the power of God in raising him from the dead. Now, the Virgin Birth has always been a difficult one because it forms a very minor part of the tradition. It's there in the Creed. I'm happy it's there in the Creed. If you asked me precisely what happened, I have to say, I don't know.'

'Do you believe it intellectually?' Taylor asked.

'It depends what you mean by *it*,' Habgood retorted.

'Do you believe it happened?' Taylor enquired again.

'This is…' Habgood hesitated. 'I have to answer as a symbol of the way in which God deals with humanity, as a symbol of a new beginning in Christ, yes I do believe it. If you ask me what it means biologically, I don't know and I don't believe anybody else knows or can know.'

Taylor followed up again: 'Are you saying it's symbolic rather than physical?'

'I am saying that a great deal of religious truth operates on a level which we can't easily translate into scientific, physical descriptions,' the Archbishop replied.

I feel gripped by a strong sense of purpose. I want to learn more about the Annunciation and the message it is trying to convey. This biblical story played a pivotal part in the formation of my own faith. Now, fifty years on, I want to discover what it means today for a wide range of people, each with different perspectives, beliefs and experiences, in the hope that a pattern may emerge. I intend to be receptive and open-minded in the hope that I will glean a new depth of interpretation and understanding.

Thirty years ago, David Jenkins, the recently appointed Bishop of Durham, created a national furore when he dared to question some of the fundamental beliefs of Christianity concerning the Annunciation and the Virgin Birth. He was Professor of Theology at the University of Leeds when the Prime Minister, Margaret Thatcher, recommended his appointment as Bishop of Durham. Soon after, in April 1984, David Jenkins said on the ITV religious programme, *Credo*, that the story of the virgin birth had been added later by early Christians to express their faith in Jesus as the Messiah. 'I wouldn't put it past God to arrange a virgin birth if he wanted, but I very much doubt he would,' he commented.

The words caused a storm of protest and considerable opposition to his appointment. Critics cited that he was an academic theologian with no experience as a parish priest and his views were inappropriate and wrong. For them, he became a symbol of the dangerous modernisation of the established Church as the split between its traditional and liberal wings intensified.

But was David Jenkins right? His beliefs caused distress and concern to many in the Church at the time but, surely, it was right that he was able to express such an honestly held position. Here was a cleric who believed with sincerity and passion that the Church had to break free of dogma if it was to retain a central place in the modern world. Thirty years on, I hope people will not be reluctant to discuss such a subject matter and that participants, particularly senior clergy from all denominations, will feel they can be open and honest in expressing what they truly believe about the Annunciation, the veracity of the story and its message today.

The well-known art critic and nun, Sister Wendy Beckett, once wrote: 'No one saw the Annunciation and yet perhaps no incident has been so repeatedly painted by artists and cherished by believers. The Annunciation is essentially about trusting God and letting him do as he pleases, secure in his fatherhood.' That's her interpretation, but is she correct?

My thoughts race ahead and my plan gains pace. Hopefully, I could conduct my own 'long search' through a series of intimate conversations with leading members of the clergy, world-renowned scholars, theologians, art historians, artists and musicians, all who have some connection to the annunciation story. I could engage with a range of people from different denominations of Christianity – Catholic, Anglican, Pentecostal, Evangelical, Orthodox, Coptic – maybe from other religions too. Hopefully, each encounter would provide me with fresh insight and perhaps make me re-think the Annunciation.

But before that journey can get underway, I want to set off on another expedition. I have to learn more about François Lemoyne and his 1727 painting, *The Annunciation*, and discover why the picture came to Winchester.

No painting has made such an extraordinary impact on me in recent years and yet I cannot describe why. I am not especially enchanted by its imagery or by its aesthetic value. My first acquaintance with it was pure serendipity. But there's something about it that has sparked an intense curiosity. The picture is a shining star, leading me down an unknown road to an unidentifiable destination.

The search for the story of the painting, François Lemoyne's *The Annunciation*, is about to begin.

CHAPTER 3

INSIDE WINCHESTER COLLEGE

Although I have lived in Winchester for thirty-one years, I am about to go inside Winchester College for the first time. One of England's oldest and most prestigious public schools, its presence is integral to the character of this ancient city. It is steeped in history, bound by tradition. Over the years, my walks around its boundaries have revealed snapshots of its medieval stone and flint buildings, impressive in their beauty and architectural grace. Add to the mix occasional glimpses of besuited young Wykehamists hurrying to lessons and you get a sense of a rarified community that is privileged, highly academic and enclosed.

Even before I set foot across the threshold, I am reminded why I have come here. Standing on the pavement opposite the medieval gatehouse, I notice a statue above the vaulted archway, of a crowned Virgin Mary holding her child. I pass the Porter's Lodge and see directly ahead of me, on the north side of Middle Gate, three more stone statues in separate niches, standing thirty feet above the ground. A recently replaced angel Gabriel on the left, a weathered Virgin Mary centre stage, and, intriguingly, on the right, the figure of a kneeling bishop.

I walk through Middle Gate and spot almost immediately three similar medieval statues on the gate's south side looking out on to the inner quadrangle of Chamber Court and to the Chapel beyond. Placed there in the early 1390s, all are battered and worn down after facing six centuries of prevailing winds. They are prominent depictions of the annunciation encounter and are carefully positioned on the school's main thoroughfare where pupils pass all day long.

I have come to meet Suzanne Foster, the College's full time archivist, with the hope of discovering why François Lemoyne's painting, *The Annunciation*, arrived here nearly three hundred years ago. We begin to talk in the darkly lit Warden Harmar room, an Elizabethan study filled with shelves of leather-bound books. Behind me is an original first edition of the King James Bible, displayed in a glass case. It was here at Winchester College that John Harmar, whilst Warden, helped to translate much of the New Testament in preparation for the publication of the King James Bible in 1611. Indeed, it was in this very study that Harmar, a Greek and Latin specialist and key member of the Second Oxford Company, worked on Luke's Gospel passage of the annunciation encounter (Luke 1:26-38), as part of his translation of the four Gospels, the Acts of the Apostles and the Book of Revelation:

> 26. And in the sixt moneth, the Angel Gabriel was sent from God, unto a citie of Galilee, named Nazareth.
> 27. To a virgine espoused to a man whose name was Joseph, of the house of David, and the virgins name was Marie

14

The room houses Harmar's precious collection of Bibles, which he bequeathed to Winchester College. As I sit on an old leather chair, almost immediately I notice there is a book cover placed in the centre of the main table showing a painting of a bishop. Something about him looks familiar.

Suzanne Foster tells me that the portrait is of William of Wykeham, the founder of Winchester College. It is his statue that is positioned alongside those of Mary and the angel Gabriel in the grounds of the school, and was placed there to remind generations of pupils – past, present and future – of both his pivotal influence and his special love of the annunciation story.

William of Wykeham was born in 1324, ten miles south-east of Winchester, to parents of modest means. At an early age, his intelligence was noticed by a local member of the gentry who financed his place at the grammar school in Winchester, then sited close to the west end of the Cathedral. A pious and diligent boy, William attended daily services in the Cathedral and was especially devoted to the Virgin Mary. He rose at dawn each day to attend Mass, and afterwards he would pray alone in front of a statue of Mary, which stood on one of the columns on the south side of the nave. His deep reverence for the Blessed Virgin Mary, nurtured at such an early age, was to stay with William throughout his long and extraordinary life. At that time, with Edward III on the throne, England was a singularly Catholic culture; there was little diversity of religious belief. The Protestant Reformation was still more than two hundred years away.

When he passed through Winchester on his way to prepare for another war against France, Edward III was alerted to young William's potential by a local grandee. After leaving school, William quickly developed an outstanding reputation for efficiency so that, in early adulthood, he was appointed the Clerk of the King's Works at Windsor and Chief Surveyor of Royal Castles. Then, in 1362, aged thirty-eight, he was ordained a priest and within four years, he was appointed Bishop of Winchester. Whilst Bishop, he served as Chancellor of England – the highest public office in the land – to King Edward III and then to King Richard II. It was a spectacular career and he built up a considerable fortune.

Powerful and wealthy, he lived in the Bishop's Palace at Wolvesey Castle in Winchester. By the late 1370s he'd begun to draw up a vision for his legacy, to be rooted in education. William recognized the urgent need to establish a regular flow of well-educated priests following the catastrophic losses caused by the plague or 'Black Death' – almost half the Winchester diocesan clergy had died – and also to address shortcomings in monastic life locally in his diocese. His plan was to build a new religious educational foundation in Winchester that was to focus on the teaching of Latin and Greek and that would produce a regular supply of pupils to his other new venture, New College in Oxford. Both educational establishments were to be dedicated to the Blessed Virgin Mary.

On 6 October 1382, King Richard II granted a Royal Licence giving permission, 'that the said Bishop may be able to found a College to the glory of God and the glorious Virgin Mary, His Mother.' A fortnight later, its Foundation Charter was written.

Suzanne Foster leads me to Muniment Tower where the school's most treasured documents, stretching back more than six centuries, are stored. The original Foundation Charter, a large manuscript on parchment, is laid out on a heavy, iron-bound oak chest. I scan the small, neat lines of Latin, written in black ink: '*Collegium Sanctae Mariae prope Wintoniam…*' – 'St Mary's College near Winchester will comprise a Warden, two Masters and ten Fellows providing education for seventy scholars together with three Chaplains, sixteen quiristers (choristers) and three Lay Chapel clerks to provide religious services and music in Chapel.' Revealingly, the wax seal, still attached by green silk cords to the document, depicts the Virgin Mary at the top and the kneeling figure of William at the base.

8. Statues on Middle Gate at Winchester College, 1390s.
© The Warden and Scholars of Winchester College.

Four and a half years later, on 26 March 1387, the day after Bishop William celebrated services throughout the day to mark the feast of the Annunciation, the foundation stone was laid and building work began. He had purchased a five-acre plot of land from the Benedictine Priory of St Swithun in an area near the Soke, just outside the city walls, next to the water meadows south-east of the Cathedral. On 28 March 1394, St Mary's College near Winchester opened its doors. Today, more than six hundred years later, the beautifully preserved original medieval buildings around Chamber Court, including Chapel, remain the focal point of Winchester College, which has the longest unbroken history of any school in England.

Returning to the Warden Harmar room, Suzanne Foster pulls out a large, heavy, leather-bound book, *Blackstone's Book of Benefactions*, drawn up in 1784 by a former scholar and Fellow, Charles Blackstone, which records all the gifts given to the College up to that date. One entry is central to explaining how Lemoyne's painting of the Annunciation came to Winchester. It relates to a Dr John Burton, the headmaster in post at the time of the acquisition of the painting. I look at the year 1729 where I see a reference: 'Dr John Burton's various valuable gifts from the year 1727 to 1774, the year in which he died.' A carefully handwritten entry in spidery shaped black ink states that he, 'gave a beautiful Salutation-Piece painted by Le Moine, placed over the Altar in the Chapel, which cost 80 guineas.'

There are no more references to the painting in the book. It leaves many questions hanging in the air: did Burton commission it directly from Lemoyne or did he contact a patron or agent? Did he travel to France, purchase the painting, and bring it back himself? If so, where did he find it? What happened between the painting being completed in 1727 and its installation in Chapel in 1729?

There is just one other historical clue, a possible reference to the painting's transportation cost. A brief entry in the Bursar's accounts, *Custus Necessariorum cum Donis*, for the fourth period of 1729 refers to a '*Monsieur Pugin*' who was paid £1.10s for his services.

I enquire about John Burton. The longest serving headmaster in the history of the school, his tenure lasted forty-two years from 1724 to 1766. Born in the Midlands in 1690, he claimed 'Founder's Kinship' which qualified him for a direct scholarship to the school. He went on to New College, Oxford, and returned to Winchester as a Doctor of Divinity. A Fellow from 1722, two years later he took up the post of headmaster at the age of thirty-four. I am eager to know how and why Burton came to acquire the painting for Winchester College.

'I don't think he commissioned it. I suspect he bought it,' James Sabben-Clare, former scholar, headmaster and now writer on the school's history, tells me. 'He was a generous man. He probably saw the painting as part of his legacy.'

Little is known about Dr Burton despite his long term in office. There is no portrait, no detailed biography. Suzanne Foster explains, 'The school was going through a quiet period. He wasn't controversial.' Indeed, there is no mention of the Lemoyne painting in any of the key books written on the history of the school – by Leach, Firth, Moberly or Sabben-Clare. As I trawl through each of them in the Warden Harmar room, I am left none the wiser.

However, a general guide to Winchester by Thomas Warton, published in 1770, describes the altar in Chapel 'being adorned with a beautiful Salutation Piece, painted by Le Moine and given by the Reverend Dr Burton, the late public spirited and learned headmaster.'

I track down a further reference in *The London Magazine* edition of April 1733, printed in the first year of the famous literary journal's publication. There, in a section marked as 'Poetical Essays', written four years after the painting's arrival, is an unattributed poem entitled 'The Annunciation in Winchester-College-Chappel, by Le Moine'. I scan the twelve verses:

> But oh Le Moine! what powerful skill
> Thy pencil's lively strokes can trace?
> Who can the hardy task fulfil,
> And imitate each nameless grace?
> Who so expressly, with so rich design,
> As though dost nature's works, can copy thine?

The poem ends:

> Oh may the piece unhurt by age
> To latest years preserve its grace!
> Never may time's devouring rage
> Thy noblest work, Le Moine, deface!
> But let it ever a memorial stand
> Of Burton's generous mind, and of thy skilful hand!

As I enter Winchester College's fourteenth-century Chapel, I am struck immediately by the magnificence of the red and white painted, original oak roof and the stunning beauty of its fan tracery vaulting. I look down the central aisle, taking in the classic Gothic architecture, the graceful windows either side, and focus my eyes on the place below the East window where Lemoyne's altarpiece originally was placed. I sit in the front pew and imagine how, at that time, almost three hundred years ago, the Quiristers would have risen at dawn for the early morning service and then begun their lessons before returning for the early evening service some twelve hours later. In those darkening hours, the boys would view the dimmed image of *The Annunciation* painting through flickering candlelight.

When it arrived in 1729, the painting was placed behind the altar and was set within exquisitely carved, oak panelling that had been installed four decades earlier. Either side of the picture's rectangular, gilt wood frame were ionic columns, and above the central panel was a broken pediment, the gap filled with a semicircular-shaped piece of wood and the Winchester College crest on top. That may be a clue as to why the painting itself has an arched top. The picture was positioned a few feet above head height and became a centrepiece of Chapel – a prominent reference point marking the Founder's deep devotion to the Virgin Mary.

However, at the time of its arrival in Winchester, such a Marian painting was a sensitive and somewhat controversial acquisition. Two centuries earlier, the College had faced the possibility of closure at the height of the Reformation. Later, it survived the Civil War. Protestants saw religious paintings as misguided distractions that were not required when the primary focus should be on the Bible and the word of God. By 1729, the display of a painting of Mary in a public school in Protestant England still had the potential to inflame the anti-popery sentiments of the age. Indeed, the school could be in danger of being seen to be promoting Catholic idolatry.

Burton was known for his High Tory, High Church stance and for Jacobite Catholic leanings. Therefore, the placing of such a flamboyant, late baroque style annunciation painting in Chapel may have been a subtle way of him expressing sympathy for the Catholic restoration of the Crown and the Stuart royal line as well as the promotion of his own religious conservatism.

Dr Colin Haydon is Reader in Early Modern History at the University of Winchester and an expert on eighteenth-century anti-Catholicism in the country: 'England was an anti-Catholic state at that time,' he tells me. 'Jacobitism was a tremendous problem – there was a rebellion in 1715, which misfired, but it crystallized the dangers of Catholicism. Winchester College had a reputation for Jacobitism. This painting must be tied in with that mindset and Burton's outlook on the world.'

Later, when I meet Diarmaid MacCulloch, Professor of History of the Church at the University of Oxford and author of *A History of Christianity: The First Three Thousand Years*, he explains to me the risk of displaying such a painting at that time: 'It's definitely odd that it got there but given the dedication of the College and the enormous pride that the College felt in that dedication, you can see how it could sneak past Protestant prejudice, particularly with High Church Tories in charge. They'd see an edifying and well-mannered piece of devotion. But, at that time, it would be very strange indeed. You could get away with most saints except Mary because she was the neuralgic one.

'Catholics had Mary everywhere and Catholicism was still an appalling threat to the country: Louis XV could invade. The anti-Catholic feeling was still extremely strong. Very carefully presented imagery was allowed – anything that wasn't Popish. And particularly not Mary – she was so prominent in Counter-Reformation Catholicism. It's a piece of local school patriotism – therefore, it can be excused. It's the totem of the College, the fetish of the College, and can be excused on those grounds. You could get away with much more at Oxbridge and its closely associated schools. People there are clever enough not to be seduced by Popery. I can't imagine this painting in a parish church at that time. Absolutely never. It's inconceivable. I think there would have been a riot. It was low risk only because of the dedication of the school.'

Clare Haynes is a historian whose book, *Pictures and Popery. Art and Religion in England 1660–1760*, was published in 2006. She tells me she thinks it could be the first instance of a foreign painter being commissioned to produce such an altarpiece in

England at that time, which would make the picture really rare. She agrees that it was only the strong connection with the Founder's devotion to Mary that allowed Winchester College to display such an annunciation scene at that time alongside the fact that it was such a well-educated community.

'Inside an elite semi-private setting, you can believe that such a painting will not be the subject of idolatry because you expect the people there to be so well educated as to not fall into that trap,' she tells me. 'At that time, it was thought "common people" were those most likely to fall into the trap of idolatry which was either to mistake an object for God or for it to be a sinful misrepresentation that wasn't true or wasn't strictly biblical. But Winchester College was a controlled, well-educated environment.'

Then, she reveals to me an important new piece of information. In the 1690s, she explains, an annunciation painting by Henry Cook was put up as an altarpiece in William of Wykeham's New College in Oxford. It was displayed similarly behind the altar at the east end of the College Chapel. Burton was a former student there between 1709 and 1710 and he would have seen the new painting each day when he visited the Chapel. (It was later removed in 1773, deemed to be old fashioned, and was apparently destroyed in a fire). *The Pocket Companion to Oxford,* published in 1761, in its entry on New College, states: 'As we enter the Chantry, the most striking object is the Altar-Piece; the painting whereof was done by our ingenious countryman, Mr Henry Cook…In the upper part of the Altar-Piece, which is painted in such a manner as to seem the finishing of the woodwork that supports it, between two columns rising in just proportion to the Corinthian below, is a Frame and Pannel, wherein is represented the Salutation of the Virgin Mary.'

9. James Cave *Interior of Winchester College Chapel looking east*, 1802. © The Warden and Scholars of Winchester College.

'Burton is pairing these two institutions again through their iconography in an act of emulation,' Clare Haynes tells me, suggesting why the headmaster bought the Lemoyne painting for the Chapel at Winchester College. She also speculates on how the lack of lily flowers and a dove in the Lemoyne picture may have been deliberate in order to reduce the level of its Catholic imagery.

Despite the potential sensitivity in 1729 of displaying the Lemoyne painting, it was to stay above the altar in Chapel for the next 135 years. A watercolour and gouache picture by James Cave from 1802, now hanging in the Warden's Lodgings, shows the painting in situ in Chapel at that time. The only other visual record of it in its original setting behind the altar is a black and white photograph taken in 1862.

In 1864, when the distinctive oak panelling in Chapel was removed to enable extra seating to be installed for an ever-expanding number of pupils, the Lemoyne painting went out with it. From then until 1998 it was displayed half way up the main staircase in the Warden's Lodgings, to be seen only by the Warden, his Fellows and his private dinner guests.

In 1996, it returned to Chapel temporarily, at the side of the altar, as part of an art exhibition featuring some of the College's historical art treasures. That move convinced Arthur Morgan, the Head of Art at Winchester College at the time, that it should return to its original home. The removal of the wood panelling more than a century before meant that it could not be returned to its original place but in late 1998, a space was found on a wall in Thurbern's Chantry in the south-west corner of Chapel. However, it was placed at such a high position that its detail was difficult to see.

In 2010, when a local benefactor offered to the College a gift of two new pieces by the contemporary sculptor, Peter Eugene Ball, the painting was removed again in order to accommodate them and was sent to a picture conserver, Simon Boback, in London for light restoration work before being put in storage.

It was at this point that an Old Wykehamist, Christopher Rowell, the Director of Furniture at the National Trust, suggested that the painting could be put on show in a major gallery. Rowell was about to reveal an intriguing and extraordinary story relating to Burton's acquisition of *The Annunciation*. Reading the *catalogue raisonné* of François Lemoyne, drawn up in 1984 by the French art expert Jean-Luc Bordeaux, Rowell noticed that the painting was listed as 'lost'. All that contemporary French art historians were aware of was that it had gone to England.

Indeed, in his 1752 biography of Lemoyne, the Comte de Caylus wrote: '*Une Annonciation, je crois pour l'Angleterre.*' Later, Pierre-Jean Mariette noted: '*L'Ange annonçant à la Sainte Vierge le mistère de l'incarnation…ce tableau a été fait pour l'Angleterre.*' So in France, for more than two hundred and fifty years, it was presumed that the painting had left France for England although its exact location was unknown. Indeed, among art historians in Paris, the picture became known as Lemoyne's 'lost Annunciation'. Upon this discovery, Rowell decided immediately to write an article for *The Burlington Magazine* entitled, 'François Lemoyne's "Annunciation" (1727) rediscovered at Winchester College'.

Following discussions with Rowell, the headmaster, Ralph Townsend, decided to contact the National Gallery and, after meeting with its Director, Nicholas Penny, an agreement was struck to lend the painting initially for five years from September 2011. It would be the National Gallery's only picture by Lemoyne and the only French eighteenth-century religious painting to be put on show in Britain's leading gallery. 'It's a misnomer to say it was lost. We knew about it,' Arthur Morgan, the former Head of Art at Winchester College tells me later over a drink in the nearby Wykeham Arms. 'I first saw it in 1980 in the Warden's Lodgings. There was no secret about it being there but nobody could see it. I knew it as *The Salutation of the Virgin*. I didn't know then that in France its whereabouts were unknown. I wasn't interested in that. I was most interested in the painting returning to its home in Chapel. It's a lovely painting, rich in grace and beauty. It should come back in 2016.'

———

Later, I meet the current headmaster, Dr Ralph Townsend, in the Headmaster's Office. He is the fifty-eighth headmaster of the school and has been in post for nine years. He is immaculately dressed in a beautiful worsted suit with a checked shirt and flamboyant tie, together with brightly coloured socks. His hair is neatly coiffured and he wears dark, round, tortoiseshell glasses with red arms. Confident and relaxed, he apologizes for having been slightly delayed and explains that the culprits who twice set off the fire alarms this morning have been preoccupying him.

Born in Australia, he was previously headmaster of Sydney Grammar School and Oundle School in England. Earlier, he had taught Theology at Oxford and English at Eton. We sit close together on two seats facing each other and, with a cup of tea close by, open our conversation.

'When I look at Outer Gate and Middle Gate and see those medieval statues of the Virgin Mary with Child and then the Annunciation, to me this embodies what a good school is about,' he begins. 'It's about children and parents being in a creative, responsive relationship. Parents, as the Virgin Mary does, saying yes to a creative opportunity. A child being grateful to his parent for having been given a life and the opportunity of a good education.

'This is not so much an academic school as an intellectual school,' he continues. 'There's a scholarly serenity here…a quietness of atmosphere. Everything stems from those sculptures of the Annunciation. They are recorded in the subconscious of a sixteen-year-old boy. I always say in my opening address to new parents, this is a school in which the presence of the Founder and his intentions are always referred to.'

Does he feel a particular bond with Luke's story? I ask.

'I've always felt that connection with the Annunciation,' he replies. 'It's what appealed to me about Winchester College. When familiarizing myself with the origins of this Foundation and the character of the school, there's an intimacy with its design, in its size, consistent with that image of mother and child and their mutual interdependence and adoration. I am very sensitive to the deepest roots of this institution.'

We move on to discuss Dr Burton and his alleged Jacobite leanings. 'So little is really known about him,' he says. 'The school, I think, was in the doldrums in the late seventeenth and early eighteenth centuries. There were periods when the school very nearly failed and that was one of them. The school was not confident so it wasn't writing much about its history then. The fact that he would have thought it important to acquire a painting of the Annunciation does suggest something about his churchmanship, his sensitivity to the history of the school. At the Reformation, Winchester College was a great resister. It had five martyrs at the Reformation. It always had a sense of being the crucible of the blood of the martyrs, which inclined it to religious conservatism and ceremonial. A strong sense that the Founder's intentions really mattered. Winchester was out of the way. It wasn't a Royal foundation and enjoyed both obscurity and independence to a greater degree. I think it is a credible suggestion, if you accept there is an in-built conservatism in the way this place looks at the world.'

Earlier in the day, a long-serving member of staff, who admires his leadership qualities, had described Ralph Townsend to me as 'a radical traditionalist and a curious mixture: deeply cerebral with a mischievous sense of humour; a dandy with a firm moral compass that guides all that he does.' I ask why he instigated the removal of the Lemoyne painting from the Chapel in 2011?

'It's a particularly dynamic presentation,' he responds. 'It's muscular, it's extrovert, it's confident. I don't see submission in the Virgin. Physically she's generous. Generosity is the word. I like it. I love it because it's so confident and dynamic, but I didn't think it was the appropriate place for it to be hung. It was too high and the space was too small to see it properly. It was too big for that area. It needed the full length of the Chapel to speak in the way it was designed to speak. We tried very hard to find another place in Chapel where it could be hung, be more visible and better appreciated but there was nowhere appropriate. Then there was the practical issue of a donor wanting to give us a Virgin and Child and a Christ in Majesty figure. We had to look at re-ordering Thurbern's Chantry. I took the decision to take it down.'

He continues, 'I wrote to Nicholas Penny [Director of the National Gallery] about it. His immediate, enthusiastic response made me realize just what a special picture it is. My view was that if this picture is as special as that, it should have a much wider public than it would ever have here. It would be properly lit there. It would look so much better in the National Gallery seeing it with the right perspective. From a purely commercial point of view, it's very good for Winchester College because a lot of people are seeing the name of this place there. My view will be that the loan should be extended for another five years. It's better that it's shown there. Its size, its provenance.'

I am intrigued to hear what the annunciation story means to him. He pauses for a while before responding, 'It means the importance in life of reflecting, pondering – the desirability of a boy to sit and stare, a spiritual grace which is an essential aspect of the human person who is fully alive. And, out of that pondering, to make a positive and confident response to the opportunities in life.'

Does he see the story as factual or metaphorical? I wonder.

'I take a rather literal view of it,' he answers. 'Yes, this is the way God works most creatively in human history, in the creation of children, of new life. And the most intimate relationship possible is that between a mother and a child. If you're going to believe in God, I don't have any problem with a virgin birth. That's the whole point; that this was unique, and, by definition, God is capable of being supernatural. I'm prepared to accept the reality of a creator God. I have never particularly intellectualized Christian faith. I've never felt I've somehow to make a concession to modern rationalism – it's all a metaphor – I don't think it is. I know that Luke tells the story. I know that the life of the Church has to be based upon some authority. And I know inwardly the power of the creative relationship between mother and child. That seems to me to express "Godness". I'm prepared to accept Luke's account because it's consistent with the things I can know in my own experience.

'The essence of the Annunciation for me is the creative response,' he continues. 'It's about the nature of creativity, which is why I've spent my professional life working with young people. That's the great theme and the thrill of it all. But it's not always going to be smooth. There is going to be suffering, a requirement for obedience, an act of faith when the going gets tough. I've never been through a period of doubt about the fundamental trueness of the Christian story – it's just true to human experience, human psychology. The Annunciation is the beginning of human history in that sense. We are always trying to express what is the great mystery of our experience. All of it is consistent with the mystery of the Incarnation. Rationally speaking, what's the point of believing in a God if you can't see that there has been God's activity in human history?'

Ralph Townsend is the first Catholic headmaster of Winchester College in almost five hundred years, indeed, since the Reformation. At the time his appointment was announced in 2004, a report in *The Tablet* mistakenly claimed that the statutes of the College would have to be amended because he'd earlier converted from Anglicanism to Roman Catholicism. The report claimed the statutes demanded that he be a 'communicant member of the Church of England'. Had leaving his position as an Anglican priest to go into full-time education and his switch to Roman Catholicism been a kind of calling, a message to him, like that for Mary in the annunciation story?

'I was an Anglican priest, the Chaplain at Lincoln College, Oxford and the Curate of the University Church,' he says. 'I'd married a Roman Catholic many years before that. I didn't really like professional religion. I just didn't like the job much in terms of the day to day and what it was about. I wouldn't call it conversion but a coming into full communion. It's about being true to yourself at the deepest level.'

He shuffles in his chair and leans forward, staring me in the eye.

'I remember the moment it happened,' he continues. 'I was walking down Parks Road having said Evensong in Lincoln College Chapel in November 1984 and saying to myself "I can't go on with this." It wasn't negative. It was "It's ok. I have to make this change." From the tentativeness of the Anglican expression of faith to the fullness of the Catholic expression of faith – I leave out the word "Roman" deliberately – to the universal expression of the faith which was a river flowing down from the Annunciation – the river of history, of faith, of life – from the Annunciation to the present day, I wanted to join the big river.'

CHAPTER 4

A PAINTING OF ENORMOUS CONTRASTS

I have returned to Room 33 in the National Gallery. I cannot resist the magnetic pull of the Lemoyne painting. This time, I want to hear more about its artistic merit. I want to learn how to read it as a picture and to appreciate at close hand the skill and artistry of François Lemoyne. A card on the wall informs me:

> Nowhere in eighteenth-century Europe was painting more sophisticated, technically accomplished and innovative than Paris. Knowledgeable patrons, thorough artistic training and, from the 1730s, the opportunities of regular public exhibitions all contributed to this.

Dr Humphrey Wine is the Curator of Seventeenth- and Eighteenth-century French paintings at the National Gallery. A former lawyer who switched to study art history, his doctorate thesis, published some twenty years earlier, focused on *Painting as a Career in 18th Century Paris.*

We sit on two small fold-up chairs directly in front of the picture and stare at the canvas in silence. Two long metal chains hold its large, gilt wooden frame in place. The painting rests on a wall covered in subtle, grey-blue patterned wallpaper and overhead spotlights help to bring out the richness of its radiant colours. It is a large oil painting – 208 cm by 127 cm – and is positioned slightly above normal head height. Earlier, I'd been advised that the artist intended it to be set higher when he painted it and that a good way to view is to lie down on the floor and absorb the way in which the angel appears to come out of the canvas.

Before meeting Humphrey Wine, I had read on the National Gallery's website a short feature he had written about Lemoyne's *The Annunciation.* The article states that François Lemoyne was among the leading French artists of his generation and that such an eighteenth-century French altarpiece in Britain is a

10. Lemoyne's painting on display in Room 33, National Gallery, London. By kind permission of The Warden and Scholars of Winchester College.

rarity. He describes the depiction of Mary: 'At the centre of the picture, heavenly light strikes Mary's forehead. Mary's features – slightly slanted eyes, pointed nose and a firm triangular jaw – are traits of Le Moyne's figures, but here their delicacy well suits Gabriel's appellation to her: "Hail full of grace".'

I start by asking him about his main impressions of the picture.

'It's a painting of enormous contrasts,' he begins. 'A moment of complete silence. A stillness when the Virgin Mary is saying, "Be it done unto me." A moment of realization, the gravity of which must have slowly, slowly sunk in. On the other hand, there's the constant movement in the picture. The upraised arm of the angel. You trace that curve through the angel's body, down the legs, to the body of the Virgin. You've got these two interlocking bracket shaped figures. There's the axis. At the top, the angel's finger. At the bottom that beautiful still life basket.' He follows the line of his description with his forefinger and speaks quietly and carefully, while he contemplates the picture before him.

'The dynamic of the painting is like a spinning top. At the moment a spinning top is placed on the floor, it's in constant movement but it stays in the same place.' He looks at me quizzically, checking I am following his train of thought.

'My second impression is about the year 1727. It's at the cusp of moving away from the rich colours of the Roman baroque to the much softer pastel colours of the French rococo. The deep blue and red of the Virgin's clothing and the grey-blue pastel colour of the angel Gabriel, carried forward into the tiles on the floor. It's a key year for Lemoyne. The year he jointly wins the first prize in a competition to encourage history painting. It underlines an already established reputation. And he shortly thereafter wins the biggest royal commission of the first third of the eighteenth century, namely the decoration of the Salon d'Hercule at Versailles.' His eyes squint above his half-rimmed glasses as he leans forward.

'See how he expresses the story,' he continues. 'There's a quiet acceptance. There's an element of pleasure in what she's hearing. It's a brilliant composition. One of his very best. The constant interplay of the hard and soft, the curve and the straight line. And the beautiful drapery.'

He rises from his chair and walks up to the canvas to inspect the fine detail. I ask him about his initial reaction when he first saw the painting.

'It was for me one of the most upsetting pictures I've ever seen…because it upset my pre-conceptions. One is normally taught…French eighteenth century – very good on portraiture – but when it comes to religious art…it's a bit so, so. Plus the fact is, of course, not much of it survived. A lot of it was destroyed. What does survive is certainly not in this country. And then up pops this painting and totally shatters my pre-conceptions. And it's been in this country since 1729 and was probably commissioned by the then Winchester College headmaster, John Burton. That's quite extraordinary. I didn't realize such a beautiful painting of a religious subject might exist here and be in such good condition.' His voice picks up a pace.

'We were alerted by the headmaster at Winchester. I went to Battersea when it was in store, with Nicholas Penny. I knew we had to have it. It's transformational because there's no other religious painting in this room…and, of course, because of its beauty. It's a stunning picture. This is already a beautiful room and this painting enhances it further. Part of the appeal is that it's a familiar subject. People are familiar with its story. And the artist has created something so beautiful out of it.'

I ask about its financial value. He shakes his head, apparently reluctant to engage on this matter. 'What shapes the value is determined by the market,' he says. 'The artist's reputation. The subject matter. Religious paintings are generally less popular. The condition is key. It's terribly difficult. Auction results are a constant surprise both ways.'

After Dr Wine leaves, I stay gazing at the painting and watching the movements in the room. The public looking at the paintings. The paintings looking back at them. There's an overwhelming stillness in the air. A nun wearing a brown habit pauses in front of the picture for a few seconds, then wanders away.

––––––––––

Christopher Rowell, the Director of Furniture at the National Trust, entitled his *Burlington Magazine* article, published in March 2012, 'François Lemoyne's *Annunciation* (1727) rediscovered at Winchester College' after, in his words, 'the penny dropped and I realized it was the lost original. The "lost Annunciation".' His eyes dart around the canvas before taking in a deep breath. He moves his head from side to side as he inspects the painting, then darts forward to get a closer look. He is keen to praise the quality of the artistry – 'the brushwork is astonishingly free – the beauty of the drawing and colouring, and the harmony and grace of the composition. It's rather magnetic. A great masterpiece. And in perfect condition.'

His careful enunciation and the deep, rich tone of his voice betray his Old Wykehamist past. Then he says something that strikes a chord: 'The provenance of this picture is crucial. To understand this picture, you cannot disengage the history of it from your appreciation of it as a painting. The more you know about its story, its commission, the more you will get out of it.'

So what does he think about the circumstances of Burton's purchase?

'I think it was most likely Burton commissioned it as the subject is so directly relevant to the foundation of Winchester College,' he says. 'Burton was a civilized man. He was well off, well connected, cosmopolitan. He was the sort of person who could have easily visited Paris. It's quite unlikely it was knocking about on the market in London. I think he was saying that Winchester College can be, in some way, at the summit of current taste. Part of the ethos of this picture is a statement by Burton that "my period at Winchester is going to raise the tone".'

I wonder what he thinks should happen to it.

'The ideal thing would be, if it were found to be environmentally safe and secure, and you can make it more visible, I would love it to go back in Chapel at Winchester,' he responds. 'On the other hand, it could have a double life, go back to Winchester in Chapel for a period of time and then come back here. It's a great picture. It fills a gap here. It's more than worthy of being in the National Gallery.'

––––––––––

'I see a finger first. It's clearly pointing to heaven. This is where the baby comes from. It's also saying, "One". The only begotten Son. This isn't a repeated event. This is the only event of this kind there's ever been.' Having stood by the painting for some time, the Reverend Dr Sam Wells, Vicar of St Martin-in-the-Fields, gives me his reaction. 'I can't help but see a sexual element to it too. To a virgin who's never been touched, a finger might be what one might say is a beginning. Gabriel is so fleshy. His wings are so luscious. He's really enjoyed the journey from heaven. He's the decision maker. He's dressed for action. His robe is about to come off. "Let's get on with it".'

He offers a gentle smile before continuing. 'Mary is in the foreground so we go through the emotions in the story with her. She's a mature Mary, well into her twenties. It's almost as if she's swallowing. Mary has not yet fully assumed her answer. It's not clear what shape "this photograph" has taken. She's not pretty – she has a huge nose, podgy cheeks, jutting chin. She doesn't fulfil conventional notions of beauty. She doesn't look as though she's having a good time. She's putting up with something. She's undergoing it. It begs the question, did she enjoy the moment of the Annunciation?'

Later, Sam Wells joins me for a bite to eat in the National Gallery Cafe. As well as serving as a Church of England parish priest for fifteen years, he spent seven years in the United States as Dean of Duke University Chapel in North Carolina. In addition, today he is Visiting Professor of Christian Ethics at King's College, London. His hair is light grey but he has a youthful air about him. His brisk delivery suggests an air of confidence and a sense of certainty. What does the annunciation story mean to him?

'It's the full revelation of earth to heaven and heaven to earth. The extraordinary thing about this painting is the subject isn't in the picture. The subject is the Incarnate Jesus and you can't see that. You have to infer it.' He continues, 'What we have here is Gabriel looking like he's really enjoying it and Mary looking as though she doesn't really know what to do about it. And I guess that's been the history of God's human relationship from the word "go". God has entered into it wholeheartedly and humanity hasn't quite known what to do with it. If you follow the logic of Christ being fully human, fully divine, this picture gets the fully divine part. What the Church has struggled with is what does the fully human part mean? Does it involve sex, the flesh? It clearly involved the messiness of childbirth. The Church came to terms with that. But did it involve the will of man?

'In many ways it is the most important moment in the history of the human world. This is clearly the re-affirmation of creation. This is creation again. This picture shows it is a new creation – the genesis of Jesus – with the billowing clouds. If Jesus was the reason for creation – in other words, God's utter being with us, inseparability from us was the raison d'être of creation in the first place – then this is the re-affirmation of that. To me, Incarnation, Resurrection, you can't choose between them.'

He grabs my arm and ends our conversation with what he describes as a 'provocative thought'. 'The Church doesn't know what to do with sex. To come to see sexual desire as a sublimative desire for God, that would be a fully challenging way of understanding desire. We have the slight fear that all desire for God is a sublimate sexual desire and it seems to me for Christians the challenge is the reverse. What this picture tells me is that God profoundly desires us. That's what I see in Gabriel. A profound desire. But we are so suspicious of desire that maybe we are missing the most exciting form of desire which is God's desire for us.'

———————

11. Left: The author in the Drawing Reference Room at the Courtauld Institute of Art. Right: François Lemoyne *Annunciation*, 1727, chalk (black and white) on blue paper. © The Samuel Courtauld Trust, The Courtauld Gallery, London.

In the Drawing Reference Room of the Courtauld Institute of Art at Somerset House, Stephanie Buck, the Curator of Drawings, brings out a small sketch of an annunciation scene and carefully places it on an easel. The atmosphere of the room is highly studious. You could hear a pin drop. I take notes with a pencil. Ink pens are banned here. Together, we examine the sketch with a magnifying glass. The drawing is black chalk on light blue paper and is by François Lemoyne.

It's a slightly different composition to his Annunciation painting although the style is instantly recognisable. Mary is still on the left but her body is positioned so that it turns away from the angel Gabriel. Her head looks down to the ground as he raises his right hand. The drawing is said to have originated in Paris sometime in the 1720s. Surely, then, this must be the original preparatory study for his 1727 painting of the Annunciation?

From the Courtauld, I move on to the British Museum's Prints and Drawings Room to inspect one of the three million prints and drawings that make up its vast collection. There I hold a striking black and white engraving, dated 1727–8, created by Laurent Cars after 'F. le Moine'. Wearing white gloves to examine the print, I notice that the composition is in reverse to the original Lemoyne painting but that all the features within the inverted image remain the same. I read that Cars was a former pupil of Lemoyne; that the engraving was presented to the Academie in April 1728, just months after the painting was finished, and was dedicated to Lemoyne's patron, the Duke d'Antin. I notice there are two rounded curves in the two corners at the top of the engraving, similar to those at the top of the original painting.

I know that next I have to head to France. To discover more about the 'lost Annunciation' in the place where the painting was created.

12. Laurent Cars engraving after François Lemoyne's
The Annunciation, 1727-28. © The Trustees of the British
Museum.

As I travel home from London on the train later that day, I open the *Evening Standard* newspaper, and immediately am taken aback by a large headline:

OUR SON GABRIEL WAS NAMED AFTER
MESSENGER ANGEL...
HE ALWAYS BROUGHT US GOOD NEWS

Parents of tower-plunge bank executive
vow to 'get to the truth' of his death

I read the article:

The devastated family of a JP Morgan executive who plunged to his death from the roof of the bank's European headquarters in Canary Wharf today said they were determined to get to the truth about what happened. Gabriel Magee, 39, fell 500ft from the top of the skyscraper shortly after 8am yesterday. Speaking from her home in Albuquerque, New Mexico, Mrs Nell Magee, 74, sobbed uncontrollably as she said: 'I've lost my baby. We are shattered beyond words. He was named after the angel Gabriel, the messenger who always had good news. He always brought us good news.'

CHAPTER 5

ONE OF THE GREAT INNOVATORS

I cup my hands around a small sixteenth-century font and feel the cold of the rough-hewn granite penetrate my skin. All is still and quiet. It is quite possible that I am standing in the place where François Lemoyne was baptized more than three hundred years ago. I am in a small church in rural Normandy. The building is simple and unadorned, the plaster on the walls is bare and there is very little ornament here apart from three statues, including one of the Virgin Mary holding her child. After a while, I head outside.

St Martin's lies at the centre of a sleepy hamlet called Belval, a community of around a hundred people located in the wonderful rolling, verdant pastureland of Basse-Normandie, six miles east of Coutances. The small sixteenth-century church has a pleasing demeanour, its low lozenge shape enhanced by a distinctive tower with a steep pitched saddleback roof. These days, only one service a year is held here.

It is a beautiful setting. As far as the eye can see lie emerald fields, some dotted with clover, others with cattle. A slow walk through the graveyard reveals that this has always been a small community. There are relatively few surnames here and those that are represented go back several generations. Typically, a family plot is populated with one or two large stones upon which are placed smaller plaques, some of the more recent additions displaying photographs of the deceased. These comprise moving tributes to loved ones as well as small, engraved tablets for other family members who have died.

I become very excited when I realize that the graveyard is scattered with 'Le Moyne' and 'Le Moine' family tombstones stretching back several centuries. But to my disappointment, there is no specific reference to either François Lemoyne or his parents.

I discover later that there is no formal record of Lemoyne's birth. Most of the biographical profiles state that he was born in Paris in 1688. But Jean-Luc Bordeaux, the author of Lemoyne's *catalogue raisonné* published in 1984, has his doubts. 'I think he was born in Normandy somewhere. The Lemoyne family were poor, of peasant origin,' he tells me.

Certainly, his parents, Michel Lemoyne and Françoise Dauvin, were married in this church on 8 October 1687. His father was a royal coachman, and his mother came from Paris. Their son was born sometime during the following year of 1688. The date and location of Lemoyne's birth are not the only details that lack precision. The spellings of his surname in art history books range from 'Lemoyne' or 'Le Moyne' to 'Le Moine' (The Monk). On the canvas of his Annunciation painting in the National Gallery, he signs himself as 'f. lemoyne' so that, I decide, is how I will record it throughout my journey.

I stand quietly, soaking up the stillness. I am reading a particularly large gravestone inscribed with the words 'Famille Lemoyne-Grandin', when I notice a woman wandering around the garden of the house next door to the church. She introduces herself as Catherine Labbe and enquires about my visit. Then she explains with enthusiasm how her parents told her many years ago that she 'is a distant relative of a famous artist through the maternal line.'

'I've heard the name François Lemoyne but I've never seen any of his paintings,' she tells me in French.

Lemoyne's father died when the boy was five years old. Just three months afterwards, his mother married a Parisian portrait painter named Robert Le Vrac de Tournieres. The couple stayed in Paris. Lemoyne's stepfather turned out to be violent, but he gave his stepson a grounding in art before sending him to the studio of Louis Galloche as an apprentice when he was thirteen years old.

From the beginning, Lemoyne showed promise. He focused on the 'grand genre' of history painting, religious and mythological scenes, and, at twenty-three years old, he won the Académie Royale de Peinture et de Sculpture's Prix de Rome. In 1718, his work *Hercules killing Cacus* was received by the Académie and seven years later, having spent nine months touring Italy, he exhibited eight paintings at the Salon. In 1727, the same year he painted *The Annunciation*, Lemoyne was controversially awarded joint first prize alongside Jean-François de Troy in the prestigious *Concours* competition for history painting, organized by his patron Duc d'Antin. He received a prize of 2,500 livres and five days later was promoted to the rank of adjoint-à-professeur at the Académie. The moves created a bitter, open rivalry between Lemoyne and de Troy and serious tensions were evident amongst members of the Royal Academy about the decision.

Jean-Luc Bordeaux has devoted the past fifty years researching the life and works of François Lemoyne. Now, aged seventy-seven, he spends most of his time in California as a Professor in Art History. I meet him at his magnificent, modernist summer home, designed by the radical French architect, Claude Parent, in Bois le Roy near Evreux, fifty miles west of Paris.

'From 1725, Lemoyne is using brilliant, brighter colours in his palette,' Bordeaux explains to me. 'Different brush styles, a spontaneity of the brush strokes. He applies pigment in a highly textured manner. His position is one of the great innovators of the early rococo. Without Lemoyne, Boucher would not have developed. Fragonard copied his female nudes. It all comes from Lemoyne.'

I ask him about the impact of Lemoyne in France at the time the painting was acquired by Winchester College.

'There's no question, between 1725 and 1730, in those five years, Lemoyne dominates among French painters. His reputation is very high. He's very prolific. He paints large historical paintings as well as easel paintings for private commissions.'

I wonder about the circumstances surrounding Burton's purchase of the painting.

'I have a feeling Dr Burton would have come to Paris with a recommendation from someone – we don't know who – he may, possibly, have contacted the Duc d'Antin (the chief arbiter of taste in Louis XV's France) or Lemoyne's patron, François Berger, and heard that Lemoyne was to be the big artist of the future. He was already established as a religious painter although that wasn't his vocation. But it's pure speculation because we have no record. In his estate papers there's nothing. We only know that it was commissioned for abroad. But the headmaster must have commissioned it. I think Lemoyne knew while the painting was still wet that it would be on its way to England.'

Bordeaux explains to me how it would have taken four to five months to complete the picture. Lemoyne's workload for that year suggests he is likely to have painted it in the second half of 1727. Once finished, it would have stayed in his Parisian studio to dry before being rolled up and dispatched by carriage and sea, to arrive in Winchester around five days later. Then, the canvas needed to be framed before being displayed in the College Chapel, possibly in early 1729.

Sitting on a large, comfortable white sofa surrounded by an impressive collection of richly coloured abstract paintings, he continues to reflect on Lemoyne's depiction of the encounter.

'The iconography often shows Mary in a stiff position but here there's that curvature, the humbleness, the downcast eyelids influenced by Correggio. The position of her hands. The angel hovering in mid-air – very Pellegrini – notice how he doesn't bother about securing the position of the angel. Wonderful.'

I ask him what precisely makes the painting so great. Speaking English in a strong French accent with a soft hint of Californian, he enthuses, 'Lemoyne would deal with the way textiles fall, how drapery folds, better than anyone else at that time. The three-dimensional form in the use of shadows, light and dark...it's superb. He knows the anatomy so well. He moves the brush to get the soft and hard texture of the body. The beauty of it is in its understanding of the humanity of Mary. He tried to be much more modern in his depiction. He's eliminated many of the traditional iconographic symbols. He tried to create something of his time. It's one of the most memorable interpretations of the Annunciation, especially of the eighteenth century. The way the Virgin receives the word. Of all the annunciations, it represents a very important moment in the history of religious art.'

Why had he not been aware that the painting had gone to Winchester?

'When the catalogue raisonné was published in 1984, I didn't know where it was,' he responds. 'For me it was the "lost Annunciation". I knew about so many of the copies in reverse. Then in 2004, Arabella Chandos, a senior specialist in Old Masters paintings at Sotheby's visited Winchester College. She was working on a private inventory there. She climbed a ladder to see it. She called me to tell me, 'I have seen an Annunciation with François Lemoyne's signature.'

'That's the original,' I said. It was the positioning of Mary on the left and Gabriel on the right that convinced him that the original had been found. At the earliest opportunity, Bordeaux went to Winchester. What was his reaction when he saw the painting?

'Wow, this is absolutely fantastic. Thrilling. I decided to wait in silence. To keep it to myself ready for my next book. Then Christopher Rowell contacted me while he was writing his Burlington magazine article. But I'd discovered it much earlier.'

He tells me he's just finished a comprehensive update of his work *François Le Moyne and his generation,* which, he hopes, will be published the following year with a detailed revision of the entry on *The Annunciation*. So what more does he want to find out about Lemoyne?

'That's it,' he says. 'When it's published in 2015, I've finished. It's for another generation now. I've exhausted the subject as far as I'm concerned. Lemoyne is a major figure of eighteenth-century French painting and I've served his memory.'

As well as being an academic, he describes himself on his business card as 'Expert/Old Master European Paintings and Drawings. Art Market Analyst/Research and Estimates.' What does he think is its financial value?

'It's worth five to eight million [US dollars]. A painting with so much history...so influential.'

Before I leave, I want to know what Luke's story of the Annunciation means to him. He takes a sip of fresh orange juice before answering, 'The Annunciation is a metaphor. I think it's a wonderful metaphor to celebrate the humanity of Christ. That's a beautiful way of showing the dual nature – the divine and the human. They had to find a way.

Son of God is fine but you need a woman,' he smiles. 'A mother, Mary, Christ and the emphasis on the nucleus of the family. It's a beautiful metaphor.'

———————

I arrive in Paris to try and locate the places where Lemoyne created his masterpieces and to view as much of his original work as I can. Firstly, I head to St Eustache Church near Les Halles to see his portrait, *St John the Baptist*, which was painted in 1726 just before *The Annunciation*. I notice the finger pointing upwards, similar to his angel Gabriel. From there, it is a forty minute walk to the Church of St Thomas d'Aquin on the Left Bank where I view his impressive ceiling painting of *The Transfiguration*, completed in 1724.

Next, I head half a mile to the towering St Sulpice in the Luxembourg district, the second largest church in Paris after Notre Dame. Inside, high above the chapel of the Blessed Virgin Mary, is an extraordinarily beautiful fresco painted on the cupola. Lemoyne started work on it in 1731, four years after *The Annunciation*, and it was completed fifteen months later in November 1732. Originally, Lemoyne had been selected to decorate the cupola in 1725, two years before he painted *The Annunciation* but for some unknown reason, the commission did not materialize at the time and was delayed six years. The magnificent fresco depicts the Assumption of Mary – the bodily elevation of the Mother of Jesus to heaven.

13. Left: Church of Saint-Sulpice, Paris.
Right: The painting, after François Lemoyne's *The Annunciation*, in the Chapel of the Assumption. Photo: Eric Daviron.

At seven o'clock the following morning, as Paris awakes for another day, I return to St Sulpice to attend Mass in the small Assumption Chapel alongside thirty other people. To the side of the altar, in semi-darkness, hangs a large painting of the Annunciation. It's a copy of Lemoyne's original but in reverse: Mary is on the right and Gabriel hovers in mid-air to the left.

There are other differences. It is a larger-sized rectangular picture in a plain, wooden frame. Gabriel wears a red undergarment with a green shawl. Above his pointed finger, a white dove emerges from the clouds, radiating beams of light. In the linen basket below Mary, there is a lily stem resting on a white sheet. It lacks the radiance of the original. The colours are more subdued and the detail in the drapery is less pronounced. Until the discovery of the original picture, *The Annunciation* in Winchester, this painting was a main reference point for Bordeaux when producing his *catalogue raisonné*. It is not clear who painted this copy and when, but it is likely to have been created by an assistant in Lemoyne's studio just before the original left for England. I notice there is no arch at the top of this copy.

The voice of the priest on the nearby altar fades into the background and my mind becomes crowded with questions. I wonder if the original intention was to hang Lemoyne's *The Annunciation* here in St Sulpice in the Chapel of the Blessed Virgin. Was it supposed to be displayed below the Assumption fresco that was created by him here at a later date? Had headmaster Burton thwarted this plan by persuading Lemoyne or St Sulpice to sell it to Winchester College? Or did Lemoyne's patron, François Berger, offer it to Burton just before it was due to be installed in St Sulpice? Was Lemoyne angry at the ongoing postponement of his cupola commission and thwarted *The Annunciation* going to St Sulpice in a fit of pique? Perhaps it is more likely that it was commissioned by Burton before Lemoyne had even begun work on it.

As the congregation leaves the chapel, I approach the painting. The two central figures shimmer in the flickering candlelight and I feel an overwhelming sense of curiosity. There are so many questions…but, as yet, no definitive answers.

Consulting the annual publications of the Royal Almanac at that time, I note there are three different locations listed for Lemoyne's studios. In 1725, he worked on Rue de Richelieu 'prés les bains de Bourbon, vers la fontaine de Richelieu'. In 1727, he lived and worked on Rue St Honoré, 'devant la rue de la Sourdière, chez Mr de Faverolles' and later, he moved to a residence on Rue des Bons Enfants. All three locations are a stone's throw from the Royal Palace on the Right Bank of the Seine.

I walk down these roads looking for possible signs of Lemoyne's residency. The original buildings have long gone and have been replaced by elegant five-storey sandstone houses with intricate wrought-iron Juliet balconies. To my disappointment, there are no plaques or signposts to mark his memory. I decide to focus on Rue des Bons Enfants, his last home, and try to envisage the likeliest of locations for his studio. The Royal Almanac reference states it was near the chapel of St Clair but that was torn down in 1792. I look around. It is early evening and the narrow road is empty. Did he paint *The Annunciation* over there, above what is now the 'Galerie Patrick Fourtin' or was the location in the same place as that current apartment above the 'Club Masculin Universe Gym'? I know it is somewhere around here but I feel frustrated that I cannot be more exact.

Early the following morning, using a copy of the famous Turgot map of eighteenth-century Paris, I track the route Lemoyne must have walked from his studio to the Académie Royale de Peinture et de Sculpture. Starting at Rue des Bons Enfants, he would have passed the Palais Royale, crossed the road at the junction with Rue St Honoré, strolled down the Rue du Chantre, then arrived in the magnificent courtyard of the Cour Carrée at the Vieux Louvre, before entering the Académie. Looking at the rooftops of the Lescot and Sully wings, decorated with caryatids in the classic sixteenth-century Parisian Renaissance style, these glorious grand buildings will have symbolized to Lemoyne that he had not only arrived at the Académie but also at the epicentre of French cultural life.

'He arrived at a very good moment. French art wasn't in very good shape. Everyone was expecting something to happen – for a reaction to the Venetian artists' occupancy of Paris. He helped create a new generation of great French artists,' Pierre Rosenberg, the Director of the Louvre from 1994 to 2001 tells me when I call his Parisian home. 'Lemoyne is a great artist. He is of crucial importance. There's a gracefulness, an elegance, great charm. All great French museums have to have a Lemoyne but his career was so brief.'

Seventy-seven-year-old Pierre Rosenberg is one of France's greatest art historians. I ask him for his assessment of Lemoyne's *The Annunciation*.

'He appreciated the idea of movement. French artists had been afraid of movement. *The Annunciation* is a very good example. It's a very elegant picture and yet the movement of the angel is well developed. It's a great meditative picture – you can dream in front of it.' He continues, 'It is one of the great Lemoynes. *The Apotheosis of Hercules* at Versailles is his masterpiece but *The Annunciation* is an important picture. I'm very pleased it's at the National Gallery in London – it's the kind of French picture that was missing from their collection.'

Inside the Louvre, I stand before *Hercules and Omphale* painted by Lemoyne in 1724 while he was in Italy. It is described on an accompanying information card as a wonderfully sensual work 'of chromatic luminosity and skilful elegance'. I read about the artist's love of colour, his admiration for the great Venetian artists of the sixteenth century, and his reinvention of the mythological nude.

In the nearby École du Louvre, on a shelf in the museum's vast art history library, I find six large box files of handwritten notes and papers devoted to Lemoyne. I rifle through them, searching for clues. One article written by Jacques Wilhelm for the Art Quarterly in 1951 immediately catches my eye. It soon becomes clear that Wilhelm's take on the artist is completely at odds with what I would expect. I had understood that Lemoyne's art was highly valued within his lifetime and was equally appreciated by art experts today. So how could it be that Wilhelm describes the name of François Lemoyne as 'falling into oblivion' and mentions that Lemoyne is held today 'in disdain'?

14. Inside the Art History Library, École du Louvre, Paris

I am intrigued and baffled as I sit there pondering in the quiet, studious atmosphere of the library. Certainly, in all the general guidebooks on Paris I have with me, there is no mention whatsoever of Lemoyne. A significant number of seventeenth- and eighteenth-century French painters like Poussin, Le Brun, Watteau, Nattier, Boucher and Fragonard crop up repeatedly and are described in glowing tones. But Lemoyne does not seem to be worthy of even a mention. This is at odds with the praise heaped on Lemoyne by the academics and art historians I have spoken to thus far. They all regard him as a hugely significant figure that greatly influenced the style of painting in France at the time.

There is a large folder in the Nouveau Testament box marked *L'Annonciation*. Inside, I find a photograph of an ivory carving created by Benetier in 1779 that copies Lemoyne's composition of Mary and the angel Gabriel and which is on display in a museum in Dieppe. There are notes on the locations of three different copies, all painted after the original, each of which show an inverted image. There is also a reference to a stipple engraving, made around 1747 by Johann Andreas Pfeffel Jr, with an accompanying illustration, entitled *Salutatio Angelica*.

I am struck by how many of the papers focus on the prints of Laurent Cars's reverse engraving which can be found in Le Havre, Algiers and Toulouse as well as the British Museum. The papers are tied together with various illustrations of the copy painting displayed in St Sulpice. I am surprised to see there is only one brief mention in all of these documents about the original painting having been rediscovered recently at Winchester College and indicating that it is now on display at the National Gallery in London.

In a box marked *Bibliographie*, I find details of two portraits of Lemoyne. One is a copy of a possible self-portrait from the mid 1720s, now in Kiel in Germany. The second is an engraving by La Live de Jully from around 1736. Both show Lemoyne as a man of medium build with large eyes and a long nose, wearing a long flowing wig.

Xavier Salmon is the Directeur du Département des Art Graphiques at the Louvre and a world-renowned expert on Lemoyne and eighteenth-century French painting. We sit together in his office above the library at the Louvre. He is highly cultured, softly spoken and immaculately dressed.

'He's part of the transition between the seventeenth century and eighteenth century – more softness, his use of colour, the way to paint quickly with the brushes. A new way to paint in France,' he tells me. 'In *The Annunciation* you can see the elegance, the beauty of Mary. What's really striking is the way in which the work is constructed because, very often, it's a confrontation between the Virgin and the angel. Very often the Virgin has an expression of panic, of concern. Here the image is one of a woman who accepts almost with a smile. There's a gentleness in the Virgin. But it's not very original. It's not innovative. It's done for a church so it's very classical, not very inventive.'

I wonder what is it in the picture that marks it out as a Lemoyne. He answers in English but, at times, has to revert to his native language, 'The way he paints faces. The face of Gabriel is almost feminine. The abundance of hair all treated in half shades. It is dealt with through colour and touch – a touch which dissolves. There are very, very gentle transitions, which is entirely emblematic of his style. The meticulous care in the colours of the angel. The way he stretches out his bodies – the contortions. Yes, that's it. The manner in which the body turns on itself.'

With some hesitancy, I ask about its likely value.

'Maybe hundreds of thousands of pounds,' he says. 'It's not very commercial. It's a religious painting. Only museums are interested in that.' Then Xavier Salmon makes a profound observation about the subject matter of the painting.

'When children come to the Louvre today and see our own Annunciation paintings, they don't know what it is about,' he says despondently. 'There's no religious education in French public schools. It has been a secular country since 1905. When you live in France today, and with no religious family background, you do not know the story. We have to explain it to our visitors.'

Does he believe the story?

'Not at all,' he replies. 'I had a religious education. But as an adult, I'm now an atheist. I see it as a painting. It has no religious impact at all. The emotion is in the beauty of the work.'

From 1998 to 2001, Xavier Salmon was Curator of Eighteenth-Century Paintings at Versailles and was heavily involved in the restoration of Lemoyne's greatest work, the enormous ceiling painting *The Apotheosis of Hercules* in the Salon d'Hercule. Located between the State Apartments and the Royal Chapel, the mythological subject matter depicts the hero raised to the rank of god by his father, Jupiter. I realize I have to see it.

15. The Salon d'Hercule, Palace of Versailles, featuring François Lemoyne's *The Apotheosis of Hercules*, 1736, Palace of Versailles. Photo: Ryan Hadley

Standing beneath this vast work at Versailles, I am humbled by its scale, ambition and sumptuousness. On completion, this was the largest ceiling fresco painted on canvas in Europe and is Lemoyne's masterpiece. The decoration demonstrates his desire to emulate the great Renaissance Italian painters in terms of skill, ambition and execution. The task took from 1733 to 1736 and demanded that Lemoyne should lie on his back each day for three years painting individually suspended canvas pieces before they were glued onto the ceiling to form the whole. The huge work features 140 life-size figures.

Hundreds of people are coming into the room as part of their tour of the Palace of Versailles. Nearly all stand in awe, holding up their mobile phones and cameras to take pictures. A few even lie down on the floor to soak up the whole splendid vista. I hear a tour guide nearby describe it to her group as 'the most grandiose of decorations, a pinnacle of eighteenth-century French art, never to be repeated.'

But there was a heavy price to pay. The immense scale and toil of the Hercules project took its toll on Lemoyne. The stress and physical strain of painting on his back for almost four years left him physically and mentally exhausted. In addition, his emotions were in tatters. His young wife had died shortly after he started work on 'Hercules' and by the end of the project his compulsive perfectionism was taking its toll. He was highly self-critical, obsessively industrious and short tempered. After working on the painting for three years it was nearly finished. But Lemoyne decided to make last minute changes that necessitated the repainting of an entire section.

At first, it seemed that the enormous effort had been worth it. Lemoyne's magnificent achievement was rewarded almost immediately when he was appointed Premier Peinture du Roi – First Painter to the King. But this was not enough for him. He became obsessed with being honoured and feted by the academic world and was desperate to become the Director of the Académie. However, his bid was unsuccessful and he had to make do with a token title that was created to appease him. Lemoyne took this badly as a personal snub.

Racked by self-doubt, he became deeply suspicious of his colleagues who, he imagined, were plotting against him. In addition, he faced serious financial issues. Although he had earned 30,000 livres for the decoration at Versailles, he found himself in debt because of his lavish use of expensive lapis lazuli from Afghanistan. This was a man under huge emotional strain who was rapidly descending into an unstable mental state, becoming increasingly depressed and paranoid.

During this time, Lemoyne worked on a commission for Berger, his long-term friend and patron. The painting was entitled *Time Saving Truth from Falsehood and Envy*. On 4 June 1737, Berger visited Lemoyne at his place on Rue des Bons Enfants, ostensibly to check on its completion and to discuss the framing of the picture. He knocked on the door of his room and after waiting for a few minutes he heard moans of pain coming from inside. Thinking that Lemoyne was ill and needed help, Berger called out for him to unlock the door. He heard Lemoyne stagger across the room to open it. Then, to his horror, Berger saw a terrible sight: his friend was seriously wounded, his face and clothes covered in blood. Nearby, on the floor lay his wig and a sword. Lemoyne staggered back and then fell on the floor in a pool of blood. Berger fetched help but later Lemoyne was pronounced dead at the scene.

It appears that, aged forty-nine and at the height of his career, Lemoyne had committed suicide in the most gruesome manner. The autopsy report, written by Elie Col de Vilars, a prestigious doctor of medicine at the nearby university, revealed that Lemoyne had pulled out his sword, stabbed himself and then repeated the process eight more times, on five occasions with enough force to go right through his body. The determination and strength of his ferocity is hard to digest. Lemoyne had inflicted three wounds to his throat and six penetrating wounds to the chest. De Vilars also noted five exit wounds on his back.

In eighteenth-century France, suicide was considered a serious crime. Many who ended their own life were dragged through the streets in disgrace and were denied a burial in consecrated ground. Their relatives were disinherited and maybe even punished. So, in 1737, there was neither a funeral service held for Lemoyne nor a memorial service. Today, the King's painter remains buried in an unmarked grave in an unknown location somewhere in Paris.

It appears that the manner of Lemoyne's death and the sudden curtailment of his career at its height may have affected his legacy. Perhaps the level of his talent and the extent of his achievements have been downgraded in the consciousness of the French art world. I wonder if the subject matter of the painting Lemoyne had so recently completed revealed anything of his state of mind at the time.

'I think it's autobiographical,' Bordeaux tells me. 'I think he meant with time they will find my worth. The allegory is self-serving: in time, they will realize how important I've been. There was a lot going on in his mind.'

––––––––––

Back in England, I head to central London. This time, my destination is Hertford House, home to the Wallace Collection. Comprising twenty-nine galleries, this rich and exotic display of beautiful paintings, furniture and porcelain is considered to be unsurpassed in quality as a private collection of French eighteenth-century art.

I am standing alongside Christoph Vogtherr, the Director of the Wallace Collection, in the large, imposing Great Gallery. In front of us hangs Lemoyne's final work *Time Saving Truth From Falsehood and Envy*. As the German-born art historian looks admiringly at the painting, he tells me Lemoyne was 'one of the greatest eighteenth-century painters of any country, one of the great geniuses of his generation.'

Could the subject of this painting refer to Lemoyne's imagined situation in his final days: the bearded figure of Time with a scythe holding up Truth, the nude female figure, whilst Falsehood and Envy have been pushed to the ground?

'At the time of the painting it would not have had a title,' he responds. 'It's only in the nineteenth and twentieth centuries that titles come in. Any title is ours not theirs. It's about what *we* see in it and how *we* call it. There's always this temptation to believe artists express their inner life and throw it onto the canvas, but this is a very un-eighteenth-century way of thinking. So how much this directly reflects what's happening inside Lemoyne is really difficult to prove but it just fits perfectly. One can only make the link if Lemoyne was in deep psychological trouble. If not, it doesn't make the slightest bit of sense. It's either coincidence or it's an indication he was already seriously ill. We can't prove anything. There will never be a way to know.'

When I press him further and ask him what his gut feeling is about the connection, he replies, 'I don't know but I tend to say yes.'

Later, I meet up with Dr Hannah Williams, an Australian art historian based at St John's College, Oxford, who specializes in eighteenth-century French art. Petite and arty-looking with a cropped spiky hairstyle beneath a flat cloth cap, she is preparing a paper to be published in the *Oxford Art Journal* entitled 'The Mysterious Suicide of François Lemoyne' describing it as 'a death as strange as it was violent'.

'I was looking for a conspiracy but all the evidence points to a suicide,' she explains. 'Looking at this final painting, you can't but think about the connection. It's correlation not causation. It's a poignant coincidence that it should be so evocative of what seemed to be going on in his mind. Maybe he was aware of that and how appropriate it was. He finished the painting that very morning or the day before, just in time. Maybe, he'd intended to finish it just before his death but it's all conjecture.'

CHAPTER 6

THE MOTHER OF GOD

I feel I have discovered as much as I'll ever know about François Lemoyne, his painting of *The Annunciation* and the reason it came to Winchester almost three centuries ago. For now, that particular journey has come to an end.

However, my curiosity and hunger for a deeper understanding of the painting's subject matter grows with every day that passes. The time has come for me to begin a second journey: to explore Luke's story of the Annunciation and to try to discover its key message. The plan: to have a series of intimate one-to-one conversations with a range of leading clerics, theologians, academics and artists. Hopefully these sessions will provide me with a unique opportunity to tap into their knowledge, and to hear about their perspectives, beliefs and doubts. I hope to gain a whole new level of understanding into what Dr Sam Wells described to me as 'the most important event in the history of the human world'.

My ambition grows by the hour. I start to make a list of possible participants. I hope there will be at least one hundred, each one sharing his or her views and personal experiences openly, intimately and sincerely. Moreover, I look forward to hearing their reactions specifically to Lemoyne's depiction of the Annunciation.

Whilst on my journey, I also want to see in situ as many of the world's greatest Annunciation works as I can. What can these acclaimed artistic interpretations teach me about the meaning of Luke's story?

Of course, in Britain today, the Christmas and Easter stories form the cornerstones of Christian belief. We have national holidays to celebrate them and have established rituals and traditions that mark them out as the most special of Christian festivals. However, neither could have occurred without Mary accepting Gabriel's request at the Annunciation. Logically, should this event not be afforded a similar status?

Catholic congregations, in particular, are asked to bow their heads at the moment in the Nicene Creed when they recite the words: 'By the power of the Holy Spirit he became incarnate from the Virgin Mary, and was made man.' Such an action emphasizes the profound level of religious meaning attached to the Annunciation. So why isn't the feast of the Annunciation celebrated in a more high profile way in Britain's Christian churches? Has it always been thus? I realize that before I go further, I need to find out more about the status of Mary and the Annunciation.

The scale and ambition of my plan seems crazy, ridiculous, but there's something on fire here that I cannot seem to extinguish.

———

As the nascent Christian Church established itself in the early centuries after Jesus's birth, the Incarnation and Mary's role in it became the subject of turbulent, heated and often bitter debate as the leaders attempted to agree on a doctrinal definition of the Church's teaching with regard to Christ's conception and birth. At the turn of the first century, Ignatius of Antioch wrote of Jesus being 'truly born of a virgin' and in AD 125, Aristides spoke of 'the Son of God taking flesh of a virgin'. Justin and Irenaeus of Lyon also wrote about Mary's virginal status. Justin Martyr stated Mary's response was a pivotal part of salvation. Irenaeus talked of her as the new Eve, whose obedience cancelled out the disobedience of the first Eve. Prayers described the faithful being 'under her protection'.

The doctrine of the Virgin Birth was first confirmed at the Council of Nicaea in 325. Later, at the first Council of Constantinople in 381, the Nicene Creed was amended to include the words: 'Jesus Christ was incarnate by the Holy Spirit and of the Virgin Mary and was made man.' Athanasius, patriarch of Alexandria, pronounced the Virgin Mary's ascetic life and female compliance to be a role model for women to follow. She was said to be perfectly obedient, more submissive than even a slave. In 401, Augustine of Hippo hailed Mary and Joseph as the perfect example of married life even though, apparently, it was a sexless union. When Jovinian denied the proposition that Mary's virginity continued with an unbroken hymen after Jesus's birth, he was pronounced a heretic and excommunicated. Ambrose, the Bishop of Milan, praised the virtue of Mary's virginity as a sealed gate that was wholly focused on a devotion to God. Jerome argued that 'We believe that God was born of a virgin because we read it' and insisted she was forever virginal. The rewards of a virgin in heaven were said to be sixty times greater than those of an ordinary Christian.

In his acclaimed 1995 book, *A History of Christianity*, Owen Chadwick, historian and priest, wrote:

> During the fifth century, the bishops came to a verbal war over Mary, the mother of Jesus. Was it right or wrong to speak of 'Mary the Mother of God'? This was really a war about how we should look on Jesus rather than how we should look on Mary. Some said that God cannot be born, so the right words are, 'Mary the mother of Jesus in whom God dwelt'; and if you call her the Mother of God you talk as though Jesus was not truly a man, and strike at one of the most important parts of the Gospel. Others said that by speaking of Mary as the mother of Jesus in whom God dwelt, you make Jesus in two, God with a man, rather than God-in-man who is one. The people wanted the phrase 'Mother of God', which fitted their love of her as a saint. The bishops cared more about how we should look on Jesus, the lay people more about how we should look on Mary. In 431 at the Council of Ephesus, the bishops approved the words 'Mother of God'.

The Council of Ephesus held a pivotal gathering, when the doctrine that Mary as 'Theotokos' – the God-bearer and the Mother of God – was finally agreed. This formal confirmation dramatically heightened Mary's status and increasingly made her an object of worship. In a sermon the following year, Peter Chrysologus, Bishop of Ravenna, described Mary as 'a virgin conceived, a virgin bore, a virgin she remains'. By 553, the bishops meeting at the second Council of Constantinople agreed that Mary was *aeiparthenos* – perpetually virgin – and 'Mother of God to Him alone'. By the end of the sixth century the devotion to Mary in Christianity was fully established. The Eastern Church gave her a title - *panaghia* - meaning all-holy or holy through and through. Proclus of Constantinople talked of a *conceptio per aurem*, the notion that the Virgin Mary conceived through the ear. Theodotus of Ancyra also proclaimed it was through her sense of hearing that Mary conceived the Lord.

At the Council of the Lateran in 649, it was pronounced that Jesus was conceived by the Holy Spirit, 'without human seed' and Pope Martin confirmed there that Mary's perpetual virginity was now a dogma of the Church. At the Council of Friuli in 796, Jesus was proclaimed as 'naturally Son of the Father as to his divinity and Son of his Mother as to his humanity but properly Son of the Father in both natures.' In the early eighth century, John of Damascus described Mary as 'more fragrant than the lily, redder than the rose, more florid than spring's verdure.'

Scholars began to promote a link between creation and the Annunciation, between the book of Genesis in the Old Testament and the Lucan narrative of the Incarnation. In the opening chapter of Genesis the earth was void and empty and God said, 'Let there be light.' This is echoed in Luke's Gospel narrative where Mary said, 'Let it be done unto me,' and the Light of the world was created.

Throughout the Middle Ages, the cult of the Blessed Virgin Mary spread throughout Europe. In the eighth century in England, Alcuin of York promoted Mary's bodily purity and majesty. In 1098, Anselm, explaining why God became Man to uphold the truth of the Incarnation, said it was 'as God had wished it'. People began to describe Mary as the 'Queen of Heaven' and some paintings depicted her sitting at Christ's right hand. In the twelfth century, the German nun and mystic, Hildegard of Bingen composed her acclaimed hymn 'Ave generosa' with the words:

> For your womb held joy, when all the celestial harmony resounded from you,
> for, virgin, you bore the Son of God when your chastity grew radiant in God.

A century later, the French writer Rutebeuf, in his play *Le Miracle de Théophile*, about a priest selling his soul to the devil and being saved by the Virgin, wrote: 'Just as the sun enters and passes back through a windowpane without piercing it, so were you *virgo intacta* when God, who came down from the heavens, made you his mother and lady.'

At the height of the High Middle Ages – the 'age of the Virgin' – Mary was hailed as 'the Window of Heaven', 'the Gate of Paradise' and 'the Mother of all Living'. The 'Ave Maria' prayer and 'The Angelus' were being recited across Europe. Thomas Aquinas wrote that she was so full of grace that it overflowed on to all mankind. John Duns Scotus, the medieval philosopher-theologian, and the Italian Franciscan scholar, Bonaventure, both described homage to Mary as neither *latria* (worship paid only to God) nor *doulia* (veneration paid to the saints) but *hyperdoulia* (veneration greater than that to the saints but not worship).

However, the Reformation dramatically diminished the veneration and status of Mary amongst Protestants. The reforming movements of the sixteenth century in Europe created not only a split with Roman Catholicism but also a new perspective on Mary and her role in Christianity. Many Protestant reformers emphasized *sola scriptura* (Scripture alone) and *solus Christus* (Christ alone) and stressed that the honouring of Mary should be kept to a minimum in line with the few mentions of her in the New Testament and the creeds.

Although Martin Luther believed in the Virgin Birth and supported the notion of Mary's perpetual virginity and her role as Theotokos, he stressed the need to be cautious in giving her a level of honour that was fitting: 'I worry that we give her all too high an honour for she is accorded much more esteem than she should be given or that she accounted to herself.' He considered members of the public making intercessionary pleas addressed specifically to Mary to be idolatrous. However, Luther supported celebrating the feast of the Annunciation because of its biblical foundation, saying it promoted Mary's humility, her strong beliefs and her willingness to say yes to God's word.

Later, John Calvin went further. He stressed that Mary could not be 'the advocate of the faithful' because she needed God's grace as much as any human being. To describe her as the Queen of Heaven, he said, was nothing less than blasphemous. The medieval historian, Miri Rubin, writes in her book *Mother of God. A History of the Virgin Mary*: 'While Lutherans diminished and Calvinists later banished Mary altogether from their world of affect and thought, this was neither a simple process, nor one whose contours were at all clear at the time.'

The Reformation led Protestants to view Catholic-based Mariolatry as distracting, unacceptable, and at times, obscene. They believed there were too many Marian feasts, too many images of Mary, too many Marian pilgrimages and too many so-called Marian relics. The Reformation called for the cult of Mary to be abandoned and for the sole focus to be on Christ and God's word.

A hundred years later, the Roman Catholic Counter-Reformation resurgence began with the Council of Trent from 1545 to 1564. Diarmaid MacCulloch, the Oxford-based Christian historian, describes Mary as the chief symbol of the Counter-Reformation renewal. The Council of Trent reaffirmed that Jesus 'was born of His Mother without any diminution of her material virginity...by the work of the Holy Spirit, who at the conception and birth of the Son so favoured the Virgin Mother as to impart her fecundity while preserving inviolate her perpetual virginity.'

At the beginning of the seventeenth century, Catholicism's obsessive focus on Mary's virginity and purity continued. The Spanish Jesuit, Francisco Suarez, wrote in his famous work *The Divinity and Virginity of the Mother of God* that the Blessed Virgin Mary 'in conceiving a son neither lost her virginity nor experienced any venereal pleasure' and that she suffered no birth pains as 'the troublesome weariness with which all pregnant women are burdened, she alone did not experience.'

Francis de Sales, the French born Roman Catholic Bishop of Geneva, in a sermon preached on 25 March 1621, described Mary as 'not only virgin par excellence above all others, angels as well as men, she was also more humble than all others. This was manifest excellently on the day of the Annunciation. She then made the greatest act of humility that was ever made or ever will be made by a pure creature.'

———

When the calendar system of Anno Domini was first introduced in 525 by Dionysius Exiguus, 25 March marked not only the feast day of the Annunciation but also the official start of the New Year. As well as being New Year's Day, it was also one of the quarter days of the year, close to the vernal equinox, symbolizing the arrival of spring and the beginning of new life.

For hundreds of years, the date, exactly nine months before Christmas Day, was steeped in religious significance. Accordingly, in England it became known as 'Lady Day', the special day to celebrate the Virgin Mary's acceptance of a new beginning. The move of New Year's Day to 1 January only occurred in 1752, when the switch from the Julian to the Gregorian calendar took place.

The earliest recorded date of a Mass being held to mark the birthday of Jesus Christ on 25 December was in 336 in Rome during the time of Constantine, the first Roman Emperor to legalize Christianity. A few years later, Pope Julius I declared officially that Christmas would be celebrated on that day, although the feast then had much less prominence than it does today. It followed that the day set to remember his conception should be nine months earlier on 25 March.

However, recently, Professor William Tighe, an American academic historian, has argued that the original decision was the other way around and that the date of Christmas

Day followed on from the day of both Christ's conception and his death on the cross being fixed on 25 March. It is certainly the case that some early Christian scholars thought 25 March was also the day of Christ's death, so that the day of Christ's conception and the day of his act of redemption were as one.

Records mentioning a specific annual feast day of the Annunciation on 25 March go back to the fifth century. In 430 it began to be celebrated in Constantinople and was called 'Conceptio Domini'. In 533 Abraham of Ephesus mentioned 'the Annunciation' in a sermon and in 656 the Tenth Synod of Toledo also spoke of 'the feast of the Annunciation'. By the eighth century, the feast day was almost universal across the Christian Church and the Patriarch, Germanos of Constantinople, described the Annunciation as the 'springtime feast of feasts'.

By the medieval period, the feast day, along with the Ave Maria and the Angelus prayers, was fully established in England. Thereafter, right through to the Reformation, 25 March was one of the most important days in the Church's liturgical year. As part of the medieval surge in devotion to the Virgin Mary, the feast of the Annunciation became the day when communities flocked to their local church to mark the moment God entered the human world in order to save humanity. This was the day to remember Mary's crucial acceptance in taking on the role of Mother of God. The day to celebrate when divine and human became as one.

But the sixteenth-century Reformation dramatically changed such a universal approach to Mary and the feast of the Annunciation. Although the Annunciation was retained as a feast day in Cranmer's Prayer Books of 1549 and 1552, the Reformed Churches saw it more as a feast of Christ's conception than as an annunciation to Mary. Reformers rooted Mary's position in the perspicuity of Scripture. She was the humble and obedient mother of Jesus Christ, as described in the Gospels, rather than an idol, an intercessor and Queen of Heaven. She was to be revered and respected rather than worshipped. She was still seen by Protestants as the bearer of the Son of God and a virgin at the time of the conception but she was no longer to be the subject of public devotion. Even in the twentieth century, the leading theologian Karl Barth was writing that the heresy of the Catholic Church remained its Mariology.

Today, the multiple Churches of the Anglican Communion have widely different views on the Marian doctrines with no universal authority. When the Oxford Movement was established in the late nineteenth century, high Anglo-Catholics once again began to celebrate the Annunciation on 25 March as an important Marian feast day.

Although Martin Luther always believed Mary to be '*semper virgo*' – a perpetual virgin – and Mother of God, the impact of the Reformation has meant that most Protestants today do not celebrate any Marian feasts and do not venerate Mary. They stress that she did not have any pre-existent divine or blessed nature but was completely normal in her origin like all other human beings and remained so until her natural death. Similarly, Methodists support Luke's scriptural account that the virgin Mary, through the Holy Spirit, conceived God in Jesus but, like Pentecostal Churches too, they pay Mary little attention.

In contrast today in Britain, Roman Catholicism continues to have well-established Marian traditions. Statues of 'Our Lady' are given a prominent position in all its churches and the reciting of the Rosary and the celebration of Marian feasts are also important parts of the veneration to her. Orthodox Church communities also have a particularly intense devotion to Mary, acclaiming her as Theotokos – the God-bearer – and icons of her are widespread in Orthodox churches. However, neither denomination, Roman Catholic or Orthodox, sees Mary as divine.

Two important doctrinal decisions about Mary, taken by the Roman Catholic Church since the Reformation, widened further the divide with the Anglican Communion and Protestantism in general. In 1854, an Encyclical of Pope Pius IX gave doctrinal authority to the concept of Mary's Immaculate Conception – that at her birth she was free from original sin. Orthodox and Reformed Churches do not support the doctrine. A hundred years later in 1950, an Encyclical of Pope Pius XII confirmed the doctrinal authority of the Assumption of Mary – that on Mary's death, her body and soul were 'assumed to heavenly glory'. Neither of these propositions is referenced in any of the four canonical Gospels.

Recently, I heard a sermon on Mary at St Paul's in Winchester, given by Dr Keith Anderson, a former Canon at Winchester Cathedral. He talked about the 'recent healing of relationships across denominations and the need now to talk about the place of Mary in our faith as friends.' He went on to describe 'the two poles of belief about Mary in the Church' and, using simple, bold language, highlighted how the 'Catholic' and 'Protestant' approaches are indicators of where 'the centre of the different beliefs lie.'

'From a Protestant perspective,' he explained, 'the centre of its theology of Mary is descriptive – she is the mother of Jesus. It is purely about what she did. From a Catholic perspective, the focus of its theology of Mary is the Mother of God and that is a title. It is not only about what she has done but essentially it is about who she is and her status before God. The first has human implications, the latter transcendent. In the first, the significance of Mary to Christ's ministry of salvation is minimized. In the second it is maximized. The Protestant would argue that any faith in Mary is, therefore, unnecessary for salvation and the place of Mary is not an essential belief of the Christian faith.'

For the Catholic understanding, he went on, Luke's account of the Annunciation is a focal point of biblical text: 'The announcement by the angel Gabriel of Mary's pregnancy and her unconditional acceptance of it is seen as the archetypal model of Christian life…The Catholic interpretation is that for salvation through Christ to happen, God called upon Mary to be a necessary and active participant in that process. Mary being Jesus's mother was not just an accident of sacred history but an integral part of God's saving grace in the Incarnation of the Son of God. She is the Mother of God. She is the spiritual mother of all Christians and, as such, continues to pray for us all.'

Dr Anderson was at pains to emphasize to his congregation that his words were a major simplification in order to offer a clear outline of the two poles of belief. He ended with this final reflection: 'The division in the understanding of the place of Mary is important in itself but also because it relates to our understanding of the Church, its authority, the working of the Holy Spirit in the Church after the New Testament period, the role of women and the nature of sexual relations. But behind all of this is a woman who became the mother of Jesus and, however you understand it, the Mother of God.'

Recognising such an uneven historical path and a wide diversity of views, I am intrigued to discover how contemporary Christian denominations mark the feast of the Annunciation, a day that has seen its status and religious significance change dramatically through the centuries. I decide that my new journey will begin on 25 March – the feast day of the Annunciation. I will carry out my own, admittedly unscientific survey on that date – visiting as wide a range of Christian churches in Winchester and London as I can in one day – to find out whether today the status of the feast is still alive or has disappeared altogether.

An obvious place to start my survey is Winchester Cathedral. On the previous Sunday, two days before the feast day, Canon Brian Rees preaches on the Annunciation at Evensong. Speaking from the finely carved pulpit in the Quire, he opens with what he describes as 'a gentle quiz'.

'To what am I referring?' he begins, 'It is related to the vernal equinox…one of the traditional quarter days for ancient tax purposes…it is one of the most frequent subjects of Christian art…musically, the texts that relate to the event are arguably the most set of any.' He goes on to describe Luke's story of the Annunciation as 'the most glorious text to match a stupendous event.' He remarks how, 'originally, it was a feast day of Our Lord; now it is generally seen as a Marian feast, but I would argue that this is a serious mistake and a misrepresentation of its true meaning.'

Then he highlights different reactions to Luke's story:

> Not surprisingly, I suppose, the profound concepts of the Annunciation – even though they appear straightforward – have caused problems. For some like the Donatists, Jesus was never really fully human. For others, like the feminist Simone de Beauvoir, writing in the early 1950s, this story is largely responsible for the subjugation of women through the past two thousand years. In her book, *The Second Sex*, she wrote: 'For the first time in human history the mother kneels before her son: she freely accepts her inferiority. This is the supreme masculine victory, consummated in the cult of the Virgin.' Others have noted that man has no part in the Incarnation whatsoever, and here in this unique event is emphasized the status of women. Still others find this young Mary – her selection and response – a herald of a new age, a spokesperson for the young, the vulnerable, the marginalised, who ultimately became the focus of Jesus, and ultimately of the Church and Christians.

When I look up the time of the Festal Eucharist service to be held on the actual feast day, I am surprised to see there is nothing planned. A notice states that the Cathedral's famous choir will be away on that day, recording music for BBC Radio 2. Instead, a 'First Evensong of the Annunciation' is scheduled for tomorrow, 24 March.

Twenty-six people attend the service. There is no sermon. During prayers, Canon Rees describes the Annunciation as 'the moment in time that changed time.' He asks us 'to think of Mary. We thank God she said yes. We thank God she was graced to fulfill that task. The grace of her life. Her obedience. Her loving care, humility and patience in fulfilling her task.'

Later, Brian Rees and I meet at William of Wykeham's Chantry on the south side of the nave at the very place where, as a boy, William prayed daily before a statue of the Virgin Mary. I ask about Luke's inclusion of the annunciation story in his Gospel.

'Luke is the great artist and he creates these wonderful word images – a wonderful ability to convey what's beyond conveying,' he tells me. 'A subtle nuance of taste. You can almost taste it in your mouth. It continues to inspire. If the event is as it was recorded, God emptying himself so he can fully understand us and bring us back into part of himself, it has to be set in that emotive language.'

He is smart, lean and athletic looking, a man who clearly cares about his appearance. He talks slowly and carefully in a distinct Canadian lilt. I ask him why he had said, in his Sunday sermon, that it was a serious mistake and a misrepresentation of its true meaning, to see the Annunciation as a Marian feast.

'The Church of England, when it went through the Reformation and then the nineteenth-century Anglo-Catholic revival, wanted to pick up the Marian feasts from medieval times,' he says. 'But it shouldn't focus on Mary. This is a Jesus feast when he freely becomes the Word made flesh. To see it as a Marian feast is a profound theological error. We must see it as the Incarnation, the very beginning of Christ. Mary is the instrument but it's a Jesus feast.'

I note his emphasis on the full title of the feast day as 'The Annunciation of Our Lord, Jesus Christ to the Blessed Virgin Mary.' A tour guide brings a group of foreign visitors to stand by the Chantry door. Canon Rees greets them warmly before continuing with his train of thought.

'A perfect seed is planted and continues to grow and is so lovingly nurtured both by God and by Mary. Whenever you are called to do something for God, you receive strength to see it through. We are called to sow seeds, to be faithful.'

As we move out of the Chantry and sit in the nave, I ask him if the status of the Annunciation is lost today?

'It is lost but that has more to do with the Reformation and medieval Marian worship,' he responds. 'If only somehow we could divorce it from all that and get it back. It's profoundly theological. It's one of those difficult ones that the faithful mainly don't consider. Maybe it's too hard to consider. Many people feel they cannot grasp it. But that misses the point that it's so simple really. This is the beginning. God wanting to be with us in a unique and profound way.'

16. Alan Durst *The Annunciation*, 1944, Winchester Cathedral

He takes me to the north transept, the oldest part of the Cathedral. There, tucked away in a sorry looking corner amid a pile of broken stones and rolled up, discarded carpet, he shows me a large wooden sculpture of the Annunciation by Alan Durst. Carved in 1944 to mark the death of Bertram Keir Cunningham, an honorary Cathedral Canon, it stood for many years at the side of the main altar in the nave before being taken away to this secluded place below the stunning Norman arches of this eleventh-century structure.

For many years, Dr Brian Rees was the headmaster of the independent Pilgrims School in the nearby Cathedral Close. Teaching has dominated his professional life and I am struck by his passionate engagement with the subject matter of the Annunciation. Has the story had a profound impact on his faith? I wonder.

'I think so because as a priest who doesn't serve parishes, I've always been in education so I've always had the luxury of being able to question,' he says. 'I don't have to wear some kind of concrete faith on my arm. So I've been able to be probing and questioning. If you try to unravel church history, it's like wandering through a field of wheat. When you take off the trappings of the Church, at what point do you come to that little wheat flower that is at the very centre of faith? It's so easy to miss it entirely. You have many people who have no faith who've got used to us saying, "this is mystery, this is theology, this is tradition." But what you end up with is the basic faith. And, in the end, to something profound like the annunciation story and John's Prologue. Both give you equal pause for thought.'

Does he see Luke's account as factual or metaphorical?

'It's very difficult. The joy of teaching teenagers especially is that they shoot straight through everything. They are not above questioning everything you say: "It's a pile of rubbish. You are believing it because you want to but there are no facts." That's fair as far as it goes but here we are dealing with faith, love, and life and death issues. So, often facts are irrelevant when you are dealing with these areas. For me, it must remain part of faith – to be fundamental to one's faith. If you have been touched by it, arrested by it so that it continues to be burnt in your heart, then although we don't have to believe things that are unbelievable, I think there are times when facts themselves can become incredible. And how can you explain the Annunciation except in artistic terms? We talk about falling head over heels in love but then we have to go back to poetry, to colours in art, to music, in order to communicate what it feels like. Visitations, at best, are about feelings – when you know you must do something. They're more profound, more spiritual, and more personal.'

As our conversation draws to a close, he leaves me with a final thought, 'The fullness of God's grace comes to Mary in her poverty and humility. In choosing a poor daughter of Israel, a young virgin, in an obscure little country town, God makes his grace and power shine forth in a most dramatic way – in the very midst of human weakness and helplessness. When she says yes, God gives his grace equal to the task she is given and accepts. For me, the story of the Annunciation remains awesome in its wonder and power to transform us.'

On the morning of 25 March, I rise early. I listen to 'Prayer for the Day' and 'Thought for the Day' on BBC Radio 4 but hear no reference whatsoever to the Annunciation. I note that the theme for the 'Daily Service' later in the morning will be 'Inside Anger'. The date of 25 March, nine months precisely before Christmas Day, sits in the heart of the Lenten season. Minds appear to be focused on other matters.

I head to St Peter's Roman Catholic Church on Jewry Street for eight o'clock Mass. There are twenty people in the congregation. Fourteen are women including three nuns. It is no longer a holy day of obligation and the vast majority of the seats are empty. One woman approaches me just before the service is about to start. 'What would have happened if she'd said no?' she asks, staring at me intently. Feeling slightly awkward, I shrug my shoulders and smile warmly.

The priest, Fr John Chandler, wears a shiny gold vestment with a richly embroidered image of Mary and her child on the front. Later, he tells me proudly how he bought the chasuble while visiting Poland. He opens the proceedings: 'It's hard to believe that it's only nine months away from Christmas. Today our Blessed Lady said yes to God. We celebrate that great day of decision.' With an innocent smile, he describes Mary as 'the ideal woman'.

During the Old Testament reading from Isaiah, (7:13-15) as the reader speaks the prophetic words, 'The Lord himself, therefore, will give you a sign,' a baby screams loudly from the back of the church. The reader pauses before going on, 'It is this: the maiden is with child and will soon give birth to a son whom she shall call Emmanuel, a name which means "God-is-with-us". A little later, when the priest reads Luke's story of the Annunciation and comes to Mary's words, 'I am the handmaid of the Lord,' the baby cries out again. People in the congregation turn around, look at each other and smile.

In a brief sermon from the pulpit that lasts less than three minutes, the priest reflects on the Gospel story: 'If we're ever going to understand something of the Incarnation, we need to know about the Old Testament foretelling the New. Mary said yes to God freely. God always knew that she would say yes but it was a free decision. Just as he can see you now on your chair freely choosing to be here.'

After the sermon, we are asked to pray 'for the courage to say yes to God. To freely do his will each and every day.' A young distraught woman arrives late as Holy Communion is being distributed. Standing next to me and about to receive the host, she falls prostrate to the floor and starts to cry, whispering that she is sorry about her poor punctuality but that she 'got the time of Mass wrong'.

At the end of the service, six members of the congregation walk across to the Lady Chapel, light votive candles and kneel in prayer in front of a fifteenth-century oak statue of 'Our Lady of Winton'. Standing high on a golden plinth, a crowned Mary, with long golden hair and red and blue drapery, holds aloft the Christ child. A nearby plaque reads:

> Following the lead of the great Bishop of Winchester, William of Wykeham, in dedicating his two colleges at Oxford and Winchester to St Mary of Winchester, this statue has been erected under the title of Our Lady of Winton.

After leaving St Peter's, I head to the United Church only a few yards away on Jewry Street. It is a joint Methodist and United Reformed Church and I am interested to see if there is any annunciation event scheduled for today. 'Sorry, there are no services at all today. But we're open for fair trade coffee and biscuits,' a kindly old gentleman responds.

Further along the road, the City Pentecostal Church is locked up and there is nobody there to answer the door. At the First Church of Jesus Christ in nearby Tower Street, it's the same story. A sign states that the Christian Science Reading Room will be open at noon. Similarly, the Winchester Family Church in Middle Brook Street is empty. Although the evangelical church in a converted cinema building has a congregation of many hundreds on Sundays, nothing is happening here this morning. The doors are firmly bolted.

At the Winchester Baptist Church on City Road, the main door is open. As I enter the building, a woman stops me in my tracks. 'I'm sorry, you can't come in. External music exams are being held here all day. There are no services,' she tells me brusquely. I see a young violinist playing in the body of the church with an adjudicator sitting nearby. I leave quietly.

Walking to Holy Trinity Church on North Walls, I wonder if it is necessary for a church to hold a service marking the Annunciation. What are feast days anyway? Are they simply a Roman Catholic and Anglo-Catholic tradition ranking specific days in the liturgical year by religious significance? Francis of Assisi guided us on this matter: 'Religious practices must never become more important than the end to which they lead: the love of God and the love of neighbor.'

But I keep hearing that the Annunciation is the pivotal moment in the Christian faith: 'the beginning', 'the moment in time that changed time'. In that context, should all

Christian denominations – high and low, traditional and evangelical – not mark the event in some way today? Or does a lack of recognition of the feast day demonstrate that the Annunciation's religious significance has been lost?

As I approach a large flint and stone early-Victorian church on North Walls, something feels different. A bell rings loudly from the belfry at the base of a thin copper-clad steeple at Holy Trinity Church. I am here to attend the ten o'clock service at a church that has been Tractarian in character ever since it was built in 1854. This high Anglo-Catholic establishment within the Church of England describes itself as a 'Forward in Faith' church, 'committed to the Catholic faith as the Church of England received it and to proclaiming it afresh in this generation.' In that context it states boldly, 'we are unable in conscience to accept the ordination of women priests.'

The Rector, Fr Malcolm Jones, wears a sky-blue vestment that, he tells me later, he always enjoys wearing on Marian feasts. After reading Luke's account of the Annunciation, he offers neither a sermon nor any comment. He calls on us to pray for Pope Francis and the Patriarch as well as for the local Anglican Bishop, before asking us to remember in particular Our Lady of Walsingham.

Three women attend the service, as well as a man called Clive, who assists the priest. 'We're higher than Rome here,' one of the women tells me later over coffee. When leaving, I notice a sign by the main door declaring: 'Take Mary to your home'.

Next, I call in at St Paul's, the Anglican church where I attend the Parish Communion service each Sunday. The main door is open but there is nobody inside, nor is there any service today to mark the Annunciation. On the church's wooden notice-board, set into a steep bank next to the busy St Paul's Hill road, there is a poster from the Taizé community in France showing a modern stained glass of the angel Gabriel and Mary encounter. Next to it, another large billboard proclaims the words:

WE ARE PILGRIMS ON A JOURNEY

I walk to the railway station, marvelling at the profusion of primroses, lilies of the valley and daffodils on the bankside, trumpeting the arrival of spring.

———

On my way to London, I read two starkly contrasting views on the Annunciation, written towards the end of the last century by two prominent but controversial Roman Catholic women.

Mother Teresa was born as Anjezë Gonxhe Bojaxhiu in what is now Macedonia. She became a nun at eighteen and, at thirty-eight, felt 'a call within a call' to found the Missionaries of Charity in 1948. For nearly fifty years, she was hailed for her compassionate work amongst the destitute in the Indian city of Calcutta. She died in 1997 and was canonized as a saint in 2016. She wrote: 'Mary showed complete trust in God by agreeing to be used as an instrument in his plan of salvation. She trusted in him in spite of her nothingness because she knew he who is mighty could do great things in her and through her. Once she said yes to him, she never doubted. She was just a young woman but she belonged to God and nothing nor anyone could separate her from him.'

The American radical feminist, Mary Daly, taught theology, feminist ethics and patriarchy at the Jesuit-run Boston College for more than thirty years before leaving in controversial circumstances in 1999 when she demanded that males be banned from her advanced study classes to encourage greater free thinking amongst her female students. She died in 2010. In her 1978 book *Gyn/Ecology: The Metaethics of Radical Feminism*, she wrote: 'the angel Gabriel appears to the terrified young girl, announcing that she has been chosen to become the mother of god. Her response to this sudden proposal from the godfather is total non-resistance: "Let it be done unto me according to thy word." Physical rape is not necessary when the mind/will/spirit has already been invaded.'

Six years later, in her book, *Pure Lust: Elemental Feminist Philosophy*, Mary Daly stated: 'The male-angel Gabriel brings poor Mary the news that she is to be impregnated by and with god. Like all rape victims in male myth, she submits joyously to this unspeakable degradation.'

As soon as I arrive in London, I make my way to Kennington Road near Waterloo station where I find the Oasis Church, a sprawling evangelical centre known throughout London for its vibrant outreach programmes. Once more I find that there are no services or special prayer groups to mark the feast of the Annunciation. A woman encourages me to visit their coffee shop. 'Is Steve Chalke, the Minister about?' I ask. 'He's away on business all day. Maybe you can call back tomorrow,' she replies.

Crossing the river to Westminster, I enter Methodist Central Hall, historically a major focal point for Methodism in England throughout the last century. I ask a doorman if there will be an Annunciation service today, and discover that I need to explain the meaning of the word to him. An official comes across and tells me the rooms are full, hosting external conferences and seminars. There are no services today, I am informed politely, but the regular midweek gathering will be held tomorrow lunchtime.

The next stop is Westminster Cathedral, the largest and most important Roman Catholic Church in England. The colossal early Byzantine style building offers Mass every half hour over the lunchtime period. I wander into the Chapel of the Blessed Virgin Mary where I find eight women and a man all kneeling. The place is rich with marble and mosaics. There is an air of deep reverence. Five of the women hold rosary beads and, as their lips move in silent prayer, all of them look towards an image of the Virgin and Child, set behind the altar.

Above the marble surrounding the Chapel, there is a colourful mosaic of the Annunciation that forms part of a frieze depicting the life of Mary. Designed by Gilbert Pownall in the 1930s, it shows a

17. Gilbert Pownall mosaic of the Annunciation, 1935, Lady Chapel, Westminster Cathedral, London. © Fr. Lawrence Lew O.P.

white-robed angel Gabriel kneeling before her. His wings appear to be long, curving tongues of fire. Mary, dressed in royal blue, sits below an archway clasping her hands. Gabriel is outside in a garden while Mary sits on a pink throne inside a building. A tall column separates them. A dove flies in from above Gabriel's face, heading directly for the Virgin. Inside the archway is a gold pot with three lily stems. The background is filled with shimmering pieces of gold that glitter in the light.

About two hundred people from a wide range of nationalities attend the one o'clock Mass that begins just four minutes after the previous one has ended. Fr Michael Quaicoe, from Ghana, delivers the briefest of sermons lasting only a minute. The office workers have to get back to their desks, I surmise. Standing next to the High Altar in the

Sanctuary, he talks about Mary receiving disturbing news, about her being afraid, and how the angel 'tells her not to be scared'. He guides the congregation: 'We all have fears about wealth, education, housing, our families, but we are told "do not be afraid". Fears can take us away from God. It's only when we make ourselves aware of God's presence and his companionship that we are able to see that we are free. That God is calling us. That God is with you.'

It is pretty simple stuff. The Mass moves on. He asks everyone to genuflect at the time in the Creed when the following words will be recited: 'By the Holy Spirit was incarnate of the Virgin Mary and became man.' Most of the congregation gets down on both knees. Even a frail woman next to me, who appears to be well into her nineties, is determined to kneel down, and gingerly uses my arm to steady herself.

As the faithful leave, I stay behind briefly to scan the weekly newsletter left on a pew seat. On the front page, Fr Alexander Master, one of the Cathedral Chaplains, describes the Annunciation as, 'the free choice of Our Lady which paves the way for Christ-less emptiness to end. A pivotal moment for humanity. Our Lady's *yes* made the whole story of our redemption possible.'

———

I am inside the magnificent Chapter House at Westminster Abbey, half a mile down Victoria Street, admiring two of England's finest Gothic stone sculptures. They stand above the inner entrance to the thirteenth-century structure, which was completed in 1253 as a daily meeting place for the monks of the Abbey and the assembly place for King Henry III's Great Court. Rightly, the Chapter House was described near its completion as 'beyond compare'.

Each of the stone statues, thought to have been designed by William of Ixworth, is just under two metres in height and stands in a trefoil-shaped niche either side of the twin doorway. The angel Gabriel on the left leans back slightly, stretching out his arms. The metal wing, originally slotted into his back, has been lost. On the right, the Virgin Mary raises her right hand accepting God's message while holding a book in her left. Originally, the two figures were painted in rich colours but today both are bare, light grey stone.

A guide tells me that for hundreds of years, the statue of the Virgin Mary was 'lost', hidden behind large wooden presses that stored vast numbers of public records

18. Statues of angel Gabriel and Virgin Mary in the Chapter House, Westminster Abbey. © Dean and Chapter of Westminster

in the Chapter House. It was only when the great architect, George Gilbert Scott, became Surveyor of the Fabric at Westminster Abbey in 1849 that he reopened the Chapter House and discovered the medieval statue, out of sight behind piles of documents. Similarly, the angel Gabriel had been moved from his original niche to a nearby vestibule. 'Now they are back together again in their rightful place,' the guide says.

I have come to Westminster Abbey to attend a special early evening Eucharist service to mark the Annunciation. I take my place in a top row seat in the stunning Victorian

Gothic Quire designed by Edward Blore. Tonight, the twenty-four boys and ten Lay Vicars of the Choir lead the congregation in singing the hymn, 'Sing we of the blessed Mother, who receives the angel's word, and obedient to his summons, bore in love the infant Lord.' The sound is triumphant.

The Dean of Westminster, The Very Reverend John Hall, delivers the sermon. His theme is uncertainty. I listen intently. He speaks slowly, in a precise, learned manner:

> Many of us have been disturbed by the recent disappearance of an aeroplane supposed to have been flying from Malaysia to China. What is most disturbing is the absence of any real news, the absence of any clear picture of what might have happened. For the time being, the families of the missing, just like the owners of the plane and airline, those undertaking the search, the governments of Malaysia and China and the watching media, must live with uncertainty.
>
> Today the Church calls to mind a decisive moment in the history of our salvation: the moment when the archangel Gabriel visited the maiden Mary with a momentous message from God. She had been chosen to be the Mother of the Son of God, to be the bearer of God to the world. From her flesh would the flesh of Jesus be made; he would be both Son of God and Son of Mary, fully human through Mary his Mother and fully divine through God his Father. Without her, God would not be able to be born into human flesh, would not be able to walk on this earth, would not be able to preach, to teach and to heal, would not be able to share in our human suffering. Without her, God would not be able to die for our salvation and rise to offer us new life.
>
> Everything hung on Mary's readiness to accept her calling, to respond positively, to say 'Yes'. But for Mary, what a moment that must have been. We see her hesitation. Mary said to the angel, 'How can this be, since I am a virgin?' And we hear her make up her mind. 'Here am I, the servant of the Lord; let it be with me according to your word.' But she must have remained uncertain what it would mean in practice. She could not surely then have foretold the missions of the adult Jesus, or her own role alongside him in his ministry, as one of many disciples. She could not have predicted her nearness to him in his suffering, his agony and his death. She could not have seen then that she would be given by her Son as the Mother of the beloved Disciple, the Mother of the Church. She could certainly not have predicted her presence with the early Church in Jerusalem at the time of the gift of the Holy Spirit at Pentecost. Mary too lived with uncertainty.
>
> For some of us, the thought that we live with uncertainty is rather alien. We who have a decent job and comfortable homes, a strong family life and plenty of friends, reasonably good health and a sensible life style – what could go wrong for us? We who have the good fortune to live in a temperate climate and in a democratic country enjoying generally incorrupt and reasonably efficient government – what could go wrong for us? In fact we know that there are many things that can go wrong and do go wrong. And for many for whom things do go wrong, the gap between comfort and disaster turns out to be surprisingly small. We do live with uncertainty and need to be conscious of uncertainty as a constant fact of life…Mary's 'Yes', her journey, took her through the shadow of death to the glory of new life in her Son, our Lord, Jesus Christ. We live with uncertainty until we learn to rely wholly on God and find our life in him.

At the Communion, the Choir sings Mendelssohn's *Ave Maria* with spine-tingling beauty, and at the end of the service, the bells ring out from the northwest tower.

Later, I visit John Hall at his large, book-filled office in the Deanery. As well as being Dean of Westminster, the sixty-five-year-old is also Chaplain to Her Majesty the Queen. Educated at Durham and Cuddesdon Theological College, Oxford, he served as a priest in south London for many years after his ordination. His great interest is education. We sit close together and I start by asking him about the meaning of the annunciation story.

'It's a beautiful and extraordinary moment,' he responds. 'From the point of view of our salvation, it is the moment when God takes to himself human flesh. The moment God breaks through to our human life and adopts to himself humanity. So divinity and humanity, from that moment are not like oil and water, two utterly separate, distinct things. He's stooped down to share our life in this most intimate and messy way and he's uplifted our humanity to share in his life in the most glorious and beautiful way. That's the big picture story.

'There's a secondary, important element and that is Mary responding. I see this as the cosmic yes. She takes an extraordinary risk. She gives us the example as insignificant, ordinary human beings, going about our everyday lives whatever that might be, as called upon by God to do things. They may be little things – do this at this moment, please – but the stance is that when God approaches in an unmistakable way, then we must say yes.'

I remind him how he had described the Annunciation in his sermon as a decisive moment but, for him, is it *the* decisive moment?

'It is the decisive moment,' he replies. 'I have no question about that. I have speculated what would have happened if Mary had said, "On your bike, this isn't for me." Obviously, the Church of England sees her as prepared, set apart for this moment. That is a very important concept. But also, the New Testament seems to me to be absolutely clear that God has been preparing for this moment throughout history.'

There's a pregnant pause as he looks through the window out onto Dean's Yard before his mellifluous voice breaks the silence: 'I'd say it's the most important moment in the history of the creation.' If it is so important, I ask him, why has the significance of the Annunciation been lost over the centuries?

'Where it was is very, very fascinating,' he says. 'I once tried to work out how many paintings there were of the Annunciation during the great Renaissance era. There are vastly more than of the Cross and, indeed, more than of Christmas itself. So why have we lost the centrality of that? Why have we lost that moment? I think it's because there are so many other ways of expressing the same truth. If I'm saying that God's entry into humanity is the decisive moment, then clearly that is what the Annunciation is. But it only becomes apparent at Christmas. You can see it then, which is much more immediately attractive and obvious rather than the invisible way in which it happens at the Incarnation. So it's no wonder that Christmas has become the focus. It's very difficult to express the Annunciation. The great painters find it difficult to express precisely what's happening and the significance of it, and they don't all do it brilliantly.'

He continues: 'At Christmas, there's a physical, human baby. I'm afraid the world has moved on from thinking that the moment of conception is the moment at which a human being begins. We've come to think these are expendable moments. We've come to accept this extraordinary idea of accepting a foetus can be terminated throughout pregnancy almost to the point of viability. The point is that the world has moved on from understanding that the moment of conception is the moment of the start of a human being. So I agree we've completely lost something. Why could we be tolerant of the extraordinary number of babies aborted if we hadn't somehow lost that importance of the moment of conception? That's all part of a much bigger picture about sex generally.'

I share with him that my wife told me she would be horrified if I did not know the birth dates of our five children yet she acknowledges that neither of us knows the dates of their conceptions. I move on and raise the central theme of his sermon: living with uncertainty. Why uncertainty?

'The way in which that *yes* is exemplary for us is that she has no idea of how it's going to pan out, what there is to come,' he responds. 'What would Our Lady have said if she had known at a later moment she'd be standing by the Cross? We have to be prepared to follow in a way that is risky, that is uncertain. Who knows exactly what the angelic appearance was like? For most of us the voice is not particularly clear and we are not very good at listening to it.'

He takes a sip of tea and shuffles in his chair. 'I have no doubt myself that Mary...' He hesitates and pauses for a while. 'Well, I have no doubt about the paternity of God, that Joseph was not the natural father of Jesus Christ. Beyond that, I would be confident that the angelic appearance was a genuine engagement with Our Lady. The voice of God heard in a very clear and definite way. Obviously with regard to the particular iconography, I wouldn't be confident about the detail attached to it. I'm not fussed about that. I do love the imagery of angels, the idea of angels worshipping God. All that means an enormous amount to me personally. I think God speaks to us but I think it happens in various ways.'

Does he believe the notion of a virgin birth to be critical?

'I absolutely believe that,' he says firmly. 'It is crucial to me. I believe in miracles and in God's direct intervention. I, personally, am quite comfortable with the belief that Our Lady was a virgin and remained a virgin. I think we see her wholly devoted to her vocation. I accept there's a vocation also to the married life and to Christian commitment in the married life. I don't think the vocation to celibacy or to the religious life is higher than the other but I think it is particular.'

But why should Mary remain virginal throughout her life?

'It's not vitally important to me,' he replies. 'I wouldn't want to hang a whole series of beliefs, ethical instructions or moral instructions upon it. I wouldn't want to elevate virginity over the married state at all.'

Does the positioning of Mary as someone who remained a virgin for the rest of her life make her seem unattainable and difficult to relate to?

'I don't see her as unattainable at all,' he says. 'But one of my former colleagues, a woman priest, never used to refer to her as the Blessed Virgin Mary but as "the Blessed Mary". One of my other colleagues said, "the most blessed and ever glorious Virgin Mary" rather than "ever virgin" which is a nice way of getting round it. Yes, virgin at the birth of Our Lord, but let's leave open the question of what happened afterwards.'

We discuss whether the feast of the Annunciation has got lost because it sits in Lent. He pauses again and reflects for a while before responding.

'There has been a great divide in the Christian community between those who've pinned all their trust on Christmas and those who've pinned all their trust on Easter,' he says. 'To see them as separate. We have to hold Christmas and Easter together. Incarnation and Redemption as both sides of the same coin is one way of looking at it. They depend entirely on each other.'

I tell him that I had first thought the Annunciation was about Gabriel telling Mary she was going to have Jesus. But I am now hearing that her ability to say yes or no is fundamental to the story.

'I think it's much more exemplary, much more exciting to see it as her opportunity to say yes,' he comments. 'Therefore, you must conceive what might have happened if she'd said no. I'm not going to speculate in that territory but I will say our ability to say no to God is incontrovertible.'

He continues: 'God reaches out to us. The most astonishing thing is that at the heart of the annunciation story is God's forbearance, God's humility. This is not just a detachment of God, somehow a sub-God rather than the great God himself. This is Our Lord Jesus Christ showing us what God is like. The wonderful Michael Ramsey said, "God is like Christ and in God there is no un-Christ likeness at all." There is in our loving God the most extraordinary humility.'

We discuss his proposition that Mary had the right to say no and yet, at the same time, was chosen by God to be the Mother of his Son. When I ask him how can she be chosen and still be free to choose, he tells me God can see the whole of time and knows absolutely what free choices we all shall make. 'God does not control us but he does know how in our freedom we shall respond to him,' he answers.

I move the conversation on. Does he feel there has been an annunciation moment in his own life; when, at a time of uncertainty, he heard a voice of calling?

'Well, there have been two moments really,' he responds. 'One was when I was twelve. We'd been very involved in the church as a family. I was in the choir. I was brought up in Eltham in south-east London. We had a vicar who then went on to Sheffield. We drove up to see him around 1961-2. I was twelve to thirteen. At some point after lunch, he said to me, "What are you going to do with your life? You should think about being ordained as a priest." It struck me forcefully. It played on my mind for four to five years. It kept coming back. There was then one particular moment when I was seventeen when our vicar had chosen to preach on the call of Isaiah. I was walking home from the church. I was on my own. I remember exactly the moment when I said, "If that's what you want Lord, well yes." It was very coherent. I was very captivated by it all.'

At the end of our conversation, he takes me to his private chapel that overlooks the nave in Westminster Abbey and faces directly towards the Tomb of the Unknown Warrior. It offers a magnificent open view of the inside of the Abbey. 'I come here at night when it is all silent and there's dimmed lighting. It's wonderful,' he says.

He has one final personal message before I leave him.

'The opportunity to say yes to God comes every moment, every day. This is the hardest thing I think to achieve – I'm way, way, way off achieving it but I long to achieve it – where I might be, as it were, able to hear the voice of God all the time and be able to respond all the time to what he wants me to do. He's always there and we have to open our ears.'

———

From Westminster Abbey, I head to Marble Arch for the final event of my day. One hundred and twenty people gather in the Anglican Church of the Annunciation close to the bustle of Oxford Street in the heart of the capital. It is an extraordinarily high Eucharist service. At times, it is difficult to see through the clouds of incense hanging over the sanctuary. At one point, a replica statue of Our Lady of Walsingham is processed through the Edwardian Gothic church with a long parade of priests and the whole congregation following behind.

Tonight's preacher has the appearance of a studious monk. Thinning on top with bushy white hair at the sides and a flowing white beard, he takes up his position in the pulpit. I sit directly below him.

19. Statue of Blessed Virgin Mary, Church of the Annunciation, London

The presiding priest, Fr Gerald Beauchamp, introduces him as, 'a man of many parts – priest, author, poet, Privy Councillor, noted linguist (apparently he speaks eleven languages including his native Welsh), preacher, prophet and Britain's foremost theologian.' Born in Swansea, Rowan Williams studied Theology at both Oxford and Cambridge Universities and was Professor of Divinity at Oxford before becoming Bishop of Monmouth. After ten years as Archbishop of Canterbury, he became Master of Magdalene College, Cambridge. I am eager to hear him share his insight on the meaning of the Annunciation. He speaks for eighteen minutes without referring once to any notes:

It is difficult to believe that the action of the Incarnate Son of God began today with the Annunciation – not with action as we understand it, but with receiving. The act that redeems the world, the act that turns the human universe on its axis, is an action of opening and receiving. Not only Mary's opening and receiving the Word of God through the angel and the Holy Spirit, but also the opening and receiving that God himself undertakes as part of being human.

What do babies do in the womb? They feed. They absorb. They are nourished by what they take in. The Saviour of the world begins with that action. The second person of the everlasting Trinity decides to be fed, to be made human, to be there in his mother's womb, absorbing life, absorbing the nourishment of her body. And when he's born into the world in Bethlehem, he continues to absorb that nourishment from his mother's body, and the nourishment of his mother's love. Humanly speaking, he becomes who he is because he is fed. Because he is not afraid to be human. And being human means being fed, being nourished.

It's quite a helpful corrective to our deeply held human tendency to want to go for heroics. We rather like to be doing things and to be seen to be doing things whether we are or we are not. And we get a little nervous about those patches of our lives when we're not seen to be doing things and making a difference. And yet, here we are told, the beginning of that greatest of all acts, the salvation of the human world, is in the apparent passivity or receptivity of the incarnate Son of God.

At the beginning of his earthly life, he is as active as he will ever be, taking humanity to himself, absorbing us into his life and we, in turn, absorb him into ours. A reminder that neither he nor we, as human beings, can do anything unless we are prepared to face the fact that to be human is to be hungry, to need nourishment and love. The incarnate Word does not come self-sufficient. He comes into the world as we do. This is for the eternal Son of God a supreme action and embrace – a willing embrace of what it is to be human.

We need to recognize that we need to be fed. To admit our need. To confess to God that we are not self-sufficient. That requires our energies in mind and body.

Where am I going to put myself to be fully human? Who is going to feed me? Where do I look for human nourishment? The short answer should be the Church of God. We come to church to be fed. We come with openness, saying help me to become human because I can't do it alone. We do it in our family lives, in our friends. But the Body of Christ is where we supremely come in order to be human. We are saying to our maker, to our redeemer, I can't be human without you. I can't be human unless I sit silent, empty, hungry. At the very heart of our faith is an act of feeding. We are here to be fed. To receive the nourishment to make us human.

There are some things that can't be hurried. Today is the beginning of a nine month wait. It's not Christmas yet. It comes after nine months of natural maturing. We would quite like things not to take the time they take. But pregnancy takes the time it takes and human growth takes the time it takes. We have to learn that we have to grow. That is as much a part of being human as being fed. We start a long journey of growth. We don't grow overnight. We need patience, putting one foot in front of the other. To look around and say, 'help me to grow'. To look within and say humbly and realistically, 'I'm not there yet'.

So, very simply, this feast celebrates the beginning of the mighty works of the incarnate Son of God. It reminds us that to imitate Christ is to imitate his humanity, His being human. We are called on this feast day to give thanks for an incarnate Lord who truly embraces our humanity, who tells us what we need to be human, which is each other and God. Who tells us that the time of growing is the time it will take, given who or what we are. It can't be rushed.

After the service, I approach Rowan Williams, and explain to him my interest in the Annunciation. We make an arrangement to meet several days later in the National Gallery. At the agreed time, Lord Williams walks into Room 33, wearing a black shirt with a clerical collar, black trousers and black shoes. He looks at the two central characters dominating Lemoyne's canvas. I ask him for his first impressions.

'I see a woman, hands pressed to her breast, looking relaxed...oddly,' he says in a quiet voice. 'Her body sagging. Mm, she's accepting, not resisting. She looks satisfied, at peace. The angel arriving in mid-air with the clouds behind.'

He looks at me intently then casts his eyes sidewards. He does this throughout our conversation, giving him a surprisingly shy demeanour.

'My main impression is an extraordinary, balanced and serene composition – very skilful and alive in the use of light and, oddly, a whole mixture of sources of light which is interesting,' he continues. 'It's a compression of the story and that's interesting too. A lot of the classical representations emphasize the alarm and distress that Mary has at the beginning of the story. But this shows the beginning and the end.'

What does he think is the spiritual meaning of the story?

'I've always been very struck that for many people the Annunciation is the real beginning of the Christian story,' he responds. 'We talk about God entering the human condition and that starts when Mary conceives. The Annunciation is very much a beginning time. Hence why Lady Day was the beginning of the New Year.' He pauses a while. 'I take Mary's yes as showing God never forces himself on the world but waits for consent. It shows God's patience, his respect, his humility.'

Does he see the story as fact or as metaphor?

'I see the virginal conception as fact,' he replies assuredly. 'I have no problem in believing that. What actually happened in Nazareth on 25 March I really don't know and

I'm not much bothered. It doesn't greatly matter what precisely happened. The conception of Jesus in the womb of Mary by God is what matters.

'I think it's a story that's very skilfully told. Luke is very deliberately telling it in an Old Testament style – the vocabulary, the sentence structure, everything about it is Hebrew Scripture. So it's as if Luke has picked up the stories of miraculous births – the Book of Judges, Genesis, the stories of angelic visitations and what people say, the promises to Sarah – Luke is writing a very deliberately measured Hebraic-styled Greek, quite unlike the rest of his Gospel. As if he's saying, "This is where the whole of Hebraic Scripture is summed up, this is where all the patterns of fulfilment are coming home, to focus on this moment".'

Does it trouble him that the encounter between Mary and the angel Gabriel only appears in one gospel?

'No,' he replies. 'There are many details, many stories in only one gospel. The fact that we have four gospels is a great providential reminder that no one gospel is going to tell you the whole thing. What you have to do is to read each one with a keen eye on what it is trying to say. Luke is saying, "You've read all the Old Testament stories. Let me give you the story to end all Old Testament stories".'

We move on to talk about the status of the feast today and he responds with surprising candour: 'It does trouble me that it is now one feast among others,' he says. 'It's a great pity because if you do believe that it is where the new creation begins, it's important. I'm sorry that it's not paid enough attention. It's a marker of how we've moved from pre-modern to modern. People move from one concept of time to another. In a pre-modern world, time is marked by a celebration of the acts of God. It's not mechanical. It is feasts at regular intervals re-enacting the stories that really matter. Take away the stories and all you're left with is numbers.'

We sit close together on the mahogany seating in the middle of the room, facing the Lemoyne painting, I ask about his sermon's central theme of 'nourishment, being fed, being human'.

'Our temptation is to think we can do it for ourselves. We can love ourselves into life,' he comments. 'We can consume our own fat as it were to keep ourselves going. But we all start with that dependence to be fed, to be nourished. Jesus is no exception.'

When I ask is there a single word that sums up the story for him, he pauses, then ponders on the word 'obedience'. 'Mm, obedience sounds a bit harsh,' he whispers. 'Someone imposing something from outside. The Annunciation is not a story about rape. It's about a promise and an acceptance. Receiving the Word.'

What does Mary mean to him?

'I see Mary as an elder sister rather than a mother. She's the first to believe the promise, to say yes to the promise. To trust, to receive Jesus in trust. So I see her as a sister as well as a mother – as a fellow believer touched uniquely by the grace of God. I think the idea of the "Mother of the Church" has been used sentimentally. Snuggling up to Mary when God seems to have been too strict – be careful with that also. I would like the Church to be a bit bolder. To say Mary does matter. She's the vehicle by which the Incarnation gets to happen. Therefore, there must be something about her faith, her love, her mothering that makes her crucially important. I'd like to put in a plea to take her very, very seriously.'

But, I observe, Mary's status today across the Christian faith varies hugely.

'It's a reaction to what people thought was an exaggerated devotion to her,' he responds. 'It also has to do with this sense of mediation. There is only one mediator between God and humanity and that is Jesus who rebuilds the bridge. Excessive devotion to Mary weakens that – that's the Reformation protest and I think it's an intelligible one.

'If you think the face of God is hidden by the jamming in of saints or that Mary is the one to go to when God seems difficult, then you are doing less than justice to the Christian message. That overreaction at the Reformation is still around. It shouldn't be an either-or. The Eastern Orthodox say you pray *with* Mary. There isn't an in-between. I don't think Mary is a barrier. Mary has often been a meeting point.'

We look ahead for a while in silence at Lemoyne's depiction of Mary. I note that she does not have anything like the appearance of a young Jewish girl. As I gaze at her wistful eyes and serene expression, I reflect on that profound description of Mary: 'the created who bore the creation'. I remember how Rowan Williams had once written that if we ignore Mary, shrug our shoulders, and say it doesn't really matter what kind of person she was, 'we deny the real humanity of Our Lord.' And if one believes the annunciation story then yes, Jesus must have looked like her and had some of her mannerisms.

He tells me he recites the Angelus twice a day, in the morning and evening. As a High Anglican and renowned intellectual, I wonder what would he say to those devout Christian believers who may think that the Annunciation did not really happen but, rather, is a story Luke crafted later than the rest of his Gospel to try to explain Jesus's beginning.

'To me the important question is this: Is the life of Jesus the action of God? If you can say yes to that, I'm not going to ask too many difficult questions,' he says. 'To me it has involved a particular action in Mary that took place nine months before Christmas. It's in the Scripture. I'm quite prepared to take that on trust. I've always been struck by the theologian, John Neville Figgis, who went from being a bit sceptical about it to then stating, "why not?" I'd like people to move into a world that is still open to receiving the act of God in this dramatic and specific way. Where the utter newness of God breaks in. And if you don't like the biology of that, I say, "Ok – give it time".'

CHAPTER 7

'THE MOST IMPORTANT EVENT IN HUMAN HISTORY'

Two days after the feast of the Annunciation, I am back in St Martin-in-the-Fields for a lunchtime gathering as part of the church's weekly *Great Sacred Music* series. This week's session is entitled 'Behold the Handmaid of the Lord – The Annunciation of the Blessed Virgin Mary' and is a thirty-minute sequence of music and readings led by Reverend David Jackson with the St Martin's Voices.

The grand neo-Classical building, designed by James Gibbs and completed in 1726, one year before Lemoyne's painting, recently underwent a £38 million restoration programme. The literature on display in the entrance describes St Martin's as, 'a church reflecting the world in which it operates. This makes for an honest but complex Christian Church. We don't restrict our understanding of the Gospels to simple, literal terms.'

The white interior looks spectacular as the light shines through the East Window on a fine spring day. Around a hundred and fifty people are in attendance. There are no candles, vestments or prayers. Rachmaninov's Vesper of the 'Hail Mary' is performed alongside Goldschmidt's 'A Tender Shoot' and a beautiful rendition of Henryk Gorecki's 'Totus Tuus Mater Mundi' [Wholly Yours Mother of the World], with the words 'I am yours completely, Mary; Mother of our Redeemer.' The main reading is Luke's Gospel account of the Annunciation.

After the gathering, I meet with David Jackson upstairs in the sacristy, where he explains the idea behind the *Great Sacred Music* sessions: 'We hope it draws people to the word of God. It gives them an entrée. Hopefully, the music draws you in and transports you to a place where you feel closer to God. A bit unself…you're taken out of the things we all carry and taken to a place where you are loved and valued and often challenged. So many people feel unloved and unworthy and so this is a starting place – a place to be nourished – it's a pretty good place to start.'

What does the Annunciation mean to him?

'This poor woman – how did it all happen?' he asks himself. 'The word "handmaid" suggests almost slave-like but I prefer "servant", in a dignified rather than a humiliating way. She became Theotokos – the God-bearer – through a physical birth. What a mystery it is.'

On the table in front of him lies a card of a twelfth-century fresco of the angel Gabriel that he saw on a visit to a small hillside church outside Sofia in Bulgaria. So great was its impact that he chose the image for his own Christmas card. 'Seeing such beauty was an unexpected gift,' he says, 'rather like that of the Christ child which Gabriel announced.'

On my journey home, I think of the number of sermons that must have been offered around the country on the feast of the Annunciation two days earlier. I head to my study and search the Internet to find all those that have been published and, after an intense and laborious exercise, three strike me as being of particular interest. One was given in

61

St Paul's Cathedral. Another was offered as a homily in Portsmouth. And a third was delivered at Evensong in Salisbury Cathedral. The next challenge is to track down the preachers for my next three encounters.

———————

I view St Paul's Cathedral in London as one of the most magnificent architectural glories in the world. Every time I visit this building, designed by Sir Christopher Wren, I stand in awe, inspired by the scale of its structure and the extraordinary beauty of its adornments. But, until today, I have never entered into the 'secret Cathedral' – the warren of rooms and passageways, inaccessible to the general public, which hold many of the Cathedral's great treasures.

Canon Philippa Boardman, the Cathedral Treasurer, was one of the first women to be ordained in the Church of England Diocese of London in 1994, and she recently presided over the national service to mark the twentieth anniversary of the ordination of women priests. She leads the way as we pass through a long room in the South Triforium. A tall pastel and chalk image of the Virgin Mary stands against a wall. Mary's right arm presses against her chin as she leans back, looking calm but pensive. 'You'll see that image again very soon,' Canon Philippa declares. She bounces along, warmly greeting everyone she sees.

We meet Jo Wisdom, the Librarian at St Paul's, who escorts me into the Cathedral Library. The pungent smell of old leather hits me as soon as the door is opened. Inside, surrounded by rows of antiquated books stacked on shelves thirty feet high, he guides me to a table to view one of the Cathedral's rarest treasures, laid on a stand. It is a small book, the size of a hand and, appropriately, is open on the page featuring Luke's narrative of the Annunciation.

On first sight, the words appear to be part of a hand-written manuscript but, on closer inspection, I realize the text is actually in movable type-faced print. I lean over to examine the book more intently. It is one of only three surviving copies in the world of William Tyndale's New Testament printed in English in Worms, Germany, in 1526 for export to England. Described at the time as 'the most dangerous book in Tudor England', its covert arrival in the country was critical in bringing continental Reformation ideas to the people of England. Until then, the Church and State had assumed hierarchical authority over the masses through their use of Latin and Greek and feared a loss of control if the general population was able to read the Bible in English.

Jo Wisdom explains how its unbound, loose-leaf pages were sent to England wrapped in wool in order to avoid discovery and that contraband copies were imported by the Bishop of London to be ceremoniously burnt at public gatherings at the nearby St Paul's Cross. Tyndale was betrayed by the clergy, condemned for heresy, and executed in 1536. His translation of the New Testament was the first version to be mass-produced in English. This enabled ordinary people to access the gospel stories, including the Annunciation, for the first time. Henceforth, the country's religious, literary and political landscape was changed forever.

We move on to the Cathedral's conservation offices where Philippa Boardman opens a small door and ducks through the entrance. I follow. We find ourselves in a precipitous position, high above the South Quire Aisle. The standing area is extremely narrow but the view is extraordinary. Directly opposite is a striking mosaic, designed by William Blake Richmond in 1899, which covers one of the choir spandrels over a central arch on the north side of the Quire. Shimmering in the light, it is a stunning illustration of the Annunciation.

20. William Blake Richmond mosaic of the Annunciation, 1896-1904, St Paul's Cathedral, London. © The Chapter of St Paul's Cathedral

A wide-winged angel Gabriel on the left hand side gestures towards the Holy Spirit in the form of a dove. A shy, retiring Virgin Mary stands on the right, wearing a long blue robe. Behind her is a green pot with three white flowers in full bloom. This is the very same image of Mary as the one I have seen just a few minutes ago leaning against the wall. Rays of light shine over orchard groves that lie between the angel and Mary. A central inscription reads *Ecce Ancilla Domini, Fiat Mihi Secundum Verbum Tuum* – 'Behold the Handmaid of the Lord, Be it unto me according to your word.' It is a beautiful, richly-coloured Byzantine style work, created by Richmond after visiting Italy, where the great mosaics from the ancient past had impacted on him deeply.

We look down on the wonderful woodcarvings of the choir stalls and gaze beyond to the area below the vast dome. When Philippa Boardman delivered her sermon here on 25 March, her theme was in marked contrast to the serene image of the Annunciation in front of us now. For this is what she said:

> Yesterday in London, the Centre for Social Justice launched their new report *Girls and Gangs*, revealing that girls in gangs are leading 'desperate lives' in which 'rape is used as a weapon and carrying drugs and guns is seen as normal'. Female gang members in their teens are being pressured to have sex with boys as young as ten to initiate males into gang life. As one of the report authors says: 'We see increasing numbers of girls dragged into this appalling world of exploitation, criminality and hopelessness.'
>
> A report from the British Board of Film Classification in January this year also makes sobering reading. Mothers of girls were found to be 'particularly sensitive to the increasing sexual and sexualised culture that their daughters are growing up in.' One mother of children aged between ten and fifteen said: 'I'm concerned about what they watch on music videos and young girls thinking that this is the norm.'
>
> Were we to travel back five hundred-odd years ago, however, the image of young women presented by popular culture would have been radically different. The popular culture of five hundred years ago would have been driven not by music videos on TV but by the Church whose cult of devotion to the Virgin Mary touched the lives of many, many ordinary people according to historians of that time. Seven great feasts of the Virgin were celebrated in pre-Reformation Europe: in February – the Purification; in March – the Annunciation, which we remember here today; in July – the Visitation; in August – the Assumption; in September – the Birth of the Virgin Mary; in November – the Presentation in the Temple; and in December – the Birth of Jesus. All these were full day Obligatory feasts, starting on the night before with

church services and the singing of the rousing chorus the 'Salve Maria', followed the next day with several masses with sermons, numerous processions bearing monstrances and relics, and ending with another evening service, with rousing singing, and the very last service at midnight! A great time would have been had in village after village after village – not once but seven times a year.

Those days have clearly gone but I believe that Mary's story can still speak to us and begin to give young people life-giving and liberating alternatives to the overtly sexualised models of womanhood thrust in their faces today. For we see in Mary's story a teenage courage.

In the first century, it was the custom for children to be betrothed in marriage at twelve or thirteen. Mary was young. But she would have been steeped from an early age in what was expected of her – modesty, propriety, no sex outside marriage, which would bring dishonour on her family and, if the law was fully applied, meant being stoned to death.

But when God spoke to her in the angelic vision, Mary set all cultural pressures aside: 'Here I am, the servant of the Lord, let it be with me according to your word.' Incredible courage especially from one so young. Incredible courage in the face of cultural pressure.

We see in Mary's story that, against the odds, she and Joseph create a stable, faithful, permanent relationship. It was against the odds, as the expected response to such a pregnancy was that the fiancé would call off the engagement, leaving the young woman with her reputation in tatters. It was against the odds because if Joseph had inflamed the situation, Mary could have been stoned to death. But visited by God in his own angelic vision, Joseph too, had the courage to go against cultural pressures and be faithful to God's call. And, according to the gospels, their marriage developed into one that was fulfilling, intimate and lasting. After the birth of Jesus, the gospels record that Mary and Joseph had at least six children together: the four brothers of Jesus: James, Joses, Simon and Judas and also Jesus's unnamed sisters – the plural implying at least two but it could have been many more!

A few years ago, Lily Allen wrote a song called '22'. For me, it sums up the rather bleak and desperate picture facing young women today. It includes these lyrics:

When she was 22 the future looked bright
But she's nearly 30 now and she's out every night
I see that look in her face she's got that look in her eye
She's thinking how did I get here and wondering why
It's sad but it's true how society says her life is already over

There is nothing to do and there is nothing to say
'Til the man of her dreams comes along
Picks her up and puts her over his shoulder
It seems so unlikely in this day and age

She's got an alright job but it's not a career
Whenever she thinks about it, it brings her to tears
'Cause all she wants is a boyfriend, she gets one-night stands
She's thinking how did I get here, I'm doing all that I can

I pray that on this day that we remember the Annunciation to the Virgin Mary, we may not collude with this counsel of despair but be emboldened to take the story of Mary back into popular culture and especially among young people. This story of teenage courage. This story that shows God's desire for young people to be in loving, stable, permanent relationships, not one night stands. This story that says that you do not have to wait for a man of your dreams to come and put you over his shoulder. For a young man, Jesus of Nazareth, has already taken our lives on his shoulders, loving us and bearing our sorrows and brokenness on the Cross. And by rising from death that we might be delivered from despair to live in relationships that nurture the best of what we can be. Let us pray that it is on Christ's shoulders of love that young people's lives can be founded and built and rebuilt.

Philippa Boardman and I head downstairs and sit together in the sacristy. I begin by asking what motivated her to write such a sermon for the feast of the Annunciation.

'Those relationships with teenage girls are still very much part of my lifeblood,' she tells me. 'Their stories are quite foundational to me. Issues around women's identity, their sense of self-esteem, their sense of self-worth, their relationship with a quite patriarchal culture and across different boundaries.'

Born in Harrow, she was a grammar school girl who went on to spend more than twenty years in Hackney and Tower Hamlets working in ministry with scores of different nationalities, cultures and languages. She came to St Paul's Cathedral ten months ago and says she is still in 'a transition phase'. She says it was her experiences in these inner-city districts that were the inspiration for her sermon.

'The starting point, focusing on Mary as a living, breathing teenager, made it relevant. I was trying to allude to the fact that her culture was very different. Then, there was a huge pressure for teenagers NOT to have sex before marriage whereas in our culture now, it is pretty much gone.'

She is clothed smartly in a black dress and grey jacket and wears a large, beaded necklace below her clerical collar. A warm, friendly smile radiates her face.

'Mary's culture was so different,' she says. 'In our church youth group, the girls just liked to hang out. But out on the streets, they had to be so tough. We tried to open up the possibility of building an alternative culture, where they didn't have to lose their virginity by twelve, thirteen, fourteen. They could be safe, playful and experience relations in a different kind of way. Being counter-cultural takes courage in the current sexual ethics of our society.'

She talks about Mary's own courage and describes how it can be a symbol of hope.

'Looking back to my past ministry, where the girls haven't lost their virginity at sixteen, seventeen, eighteen, you want to be able to affirm that…but not too loudly. One of the lovely stories from my youth ministry involved a seventeen-year-old. She went to a Tower Hamlets secondary school and set up a Christian group to talk about these issues. She had thirty to forty secondary school girls come along. That's saying a yes to God in quite a hostile atmosphere. Of course, it doesn't always work out but you pray it can work. I also have a friend who's based in north London. She spoke about how certain gang rituals are now all videoed. The pressure on the girls who have to do those acts and then they're always available to view. For those teenage girls, think what emotional and spiritual damage that does. And what damage in the past has there been to make such teenage girls have to be involved in such degrading, humiliating behaviour?'

I tell her that I found her sermon – delivered in St Paul's Cathedral to mark the Annunciation and set in urban gang culture – totally unexpected.

'I just want to give them so much self-esteem, so much affirmation that they are able to walk tall and feel good about themselves,' she responds. 'There may have to be leaps for them to get there but I want to say to teenagers, every one has a calling from God in life. Part of my work as a priest is to help people find their sense of purpose. As you can hear, my heart is still in the East End.'

To be a Christian, I wonder, do you have to believe Luke's account that an angel came to Mary and that there was a virgin birth?

'We say the Creed every day: "who was conceived by the Holy Ghost, born of the Virgin Mary".' she responds. 'What those words actually mean, I'd always want to give people a generous space as to what they believe by them. Personally, I do believe in miracles so for me it could have happened that way. But I wouldn't want to make it a stumbling block, something that has to be ticked off the list that you have to believe. For so many stories in the Bible, there are many different ways of explaining them. I wouldn't want to be prescriptive.

'One of the ways of experiencing the annunciation story is to focus on the way Mary made room,' she continues. 'How she made room for Christ in her womb, inside her. In the same way, women and men today are called to make room for Christ. For Christ to dwell in us. Faith isn't something you inherit. It is a "virgin experience" that you have to make for yourself to accept and receive Christ. An endeavour, with all our failings, to follow him. So the receiving of Christ, the dwelling of Christ in us is, for me, a good way to look at the story."

I bid her farewell. After walking down the steps before the West Front of St Paul's, I notice on Ave Maria Lane a newsstand emblazoned with *The Sun*'s latest front-page headline. Described as 'the story that shocked Britain', it reads:

> Dad of mum, 12,
> only knew of her pregnancy
> a MONTH ago.
> TEARS OF GRANDAD, 29

Later, I pick up the *Evening Standard* and notice immediately a headline on an inside page:

> Minister: we'll do more to stop
> gang violence against women.

I do not know how I am going to get on with Philip Egan. The Roman Catholic Bishop of Portsmouth has a reputation as a hard-liner, an ultra-conservative traditionalist. I am a little nervous. He has been in the news recently for reportedly declaring that a Roman Catholic MP in his diocese should not take Holy Communion because he voted in support of the Same-Sex Marriage Bill in the House of Commons.

Born in Accrington in 1955, he first felt a calling to the priesthood when he was eleven. It remained dormant in his teenage years but returned just before university. After studying Classics at King's College, London, he trained at the Allen Hall seminary in Westminster and then the Venerable English College in Rome. He was ordained in 1984.

---

* In January 2017, it was announced that Philippa Boardman would be leaving St Paul's Cathedral after four years there to take up a new post as Priest in Charge of St Mary Magdalene Church in Wandsworth, south London.

At one point he was Professor of Fundamental Theology and Dean of Studies at Oscott seminary in Birmingham. He was appointed Bishop of the Portsmouth diocese in 2012.

In his sermon on the feast of the Annunciation, he opened with the strikingly memorable line: 'Today, we celebrate the most important event in human history.'

When I first read his text, that opening sentence stopped me in my tracks. I paused to take in the enormity of the statement before moving on to read the rest of his homily:

> It's the moment when the Word of God took flesh in the womb of the Blessed Virgin Mary and initiated the redemption of the world. The angel Gabriel was sent by God to invite Mary's response. The model Christian, she welcomed the Word of God. She believed it in her heart and she gave her total consent.
>
> The Annunciation has changed the course of human history. In choosing to be born of a virgin, God has interrupted evolution. The Spirit who once hovered over the waters in Genesis now hovers over the Virgin to bring about a recreation, a new beginning, a step-change. Mary is thus the new Eve, and Christ the new Adam, the first-born of many, including you and me, who through baptism share this salvation history.
>
> We live today in an exciting world with advances in many fields. Yet our culture is highly secularized, and secularism has become the fertile breeding ground for a new conception of man, of what it means to be human. Abortion, euthanasia, eugenics, and now assisted suicide, all degrade the dignity and value of human life, while the breakdown and redefinition of marriage and the family, based on a misunderstanding of sexuality that sunders the unitive from the procreative, is creating a society of isolated individuals, fleeting relationships and unhappiness.
>
> Today's feast is a corrective. It sounds a note of joy and proclaims an alternative anthropology. It shows us Christ, the new Adam – the true Type of human being. It assures us that you and I are of infinite value and that the natural way of life in Christ leads to true happiness. That's what the Annunciation celebrates. It says there is another way. There's another way of being human. The way of hope. The way of Christ.
>
> Let us love saying the Angelus. Let us ask for Mary's prayers that we will become ever more like her, and so one day joyfully enter heaven, our true home.

Philip Egan greets me warmly in the main reception room of Bishop's House close to the Naval dockyard. He is dressed in a full-length black cassock and I am surprised to see that he has chosen not to wear his amaranth skullcap. The room is spotlessly tidy but he seems determined to create an atmosphere of warmth and informality. He encourages me to take a biscuit. We begin our conversation with his thoughts on the spiritual meaning of the Annunciation.

'Firstly, I'm human. I'm a creature. I belong to someone who made me,' he says. 'Secondly, because our humanity is fallen – I notice that in my own life there are sinful thoughts – there's need for redemption and salvation. The Annunciation means not only a celebration of creation but the beginning of redemption, the sending of our Saviour.'

I presume he sees the story as rooted in fact?

'There are certain elements of our Christian understanding that have to have the historical link with them,' he replies. 'Some are less important. Some are more important. There has to be a historicity to Jesus Christ. Therefore, the Annunciation, as the moment of the conception of the Saviour, has to be rooted in fact. Otherwise there cannot have been a human being.'

But, I observe, the encounter between the angel and Mary is only written down in one gospel.

'In God's providence, there are four people who recorded their impressions,' he responds. 'This corpus of writings is what God wanted as a secure, written record. Being candid, it does sometimes bother me that it's only in one. But then it doesn't really bother me. I trust in God's providence.'

What turns the story into belief?

'As long as you have the conviction of the theological, christological and ecclesiological – the existence of God, that Jesus Christ is the Son of God, and that his Church, despite its faults, at least in its teaching is guaranteed to be the truth that Christ willed – that gives me the underlying conviction that these texts are written by the early Church and are re-proposed to me today by the Church again, enabling me to believe in the truths that Christ wishes me to believe for the sake of salvation. But it's not naïve. There's truth and reason. It's unlike Islam where it's belief that counts. In Catholicism, we believe in the relationship of faith and reason. Reason has a history, a philosophy, a science. All that has a critical role to play in a dialogue with faith.'

So, does he think the Annunciation is factual rather than metaphorical?

'Why do you put it as an "either-or"?' he asks. 'Surely it's a "both-and". It can also be metaphor. It's symbol, it's scripture, it's sacrament, it's poetry, and it's the prophetic message of Luke as part of the proclamation of who Jesus Christ is. That doesn't take away necessarily the historical tether that somehow anchors it in the space-time continuum.'

He moves forward to be closer to me. I notice his thinning grey hair, his deep red complexion and his rimless spectacles. He appears to be relishing the conversation.

Does he believe a person can be a faithful Christian if he or she does not believe in the factual basis of the annunciation story?

'It's a central doctrine of faith but it doesn't mean they are stopped being a Christian,' he comments. 'Technically, they are in an impaired communion with the Catholic tradition. It would be a mistake, they could deny it, but they can still be part of the Christian Church and believe other elements. But the truths of faith form a connection of mysteries amongst themselves. If you take one bar out of a scaffolding, something has gone. Think of a horse. I don't agree with it but if you cut its tail off, it loses its balance. Other things are affected. All these mysteries are fragile, multi-faceted diamonds that, if you take one bit off, you've implicitly done something to somewhere else.'

What about the suggestion that Luke wrote the birth narrative later, after the rest of his Gospel, in order to try to explain how Jesus – divine and human – miraculously came on earth?

'I would say that's a bit like a scotoma, a blockage on a particular aspect of the great canon of faith. What we've got is what we've got. If this canon of Scripture is what God wanted the Church to have, and I believe that, surely I have to believe the elements that it is teaching me about. That's the difference between Catholicism and some of the other Christian traditions. In Catholic tradition, there's a nuance relationship between doctrine, what the Church teaches, and theological and personal opinion. I liken that to the flow of a river. The doctrines are the riverbanks, which are guiding the flow of the theology. Sometimes it's deep. Sometimes it's wide. Sometimes there's rocky bits and so on. But if you don't have a proper understanding of the relationship between doctrines and systematic theology, you end up with a flood plain.

'That I think is the weak thing in Anglicanism which doesn't have the same sense of magisterium, the same sense of doctrine and the teaching authority to sustain that, as Catholicism has. You have a theology as wide as the eye can see. You have some who don't believe in God. Some who are higher than Rome. Everybody has a view. It's a personal opinion.'

He smiles. I observe that Catholicism is criticized for its rigidity and Anglicanism is accused of too much diversity.

'Vatican II gives us that triadic relationship of Scripture, Tradition and Magisterium,' he says. 'The Catholic theological mindset is always directed by the bank of the river – the reference to Scripture, to the rooting in Tradition, and by the constant teaching of the Church. That's what gives us our strength. But Catholicism is also a massive place of debate, discussion and complaint. That's what gives it its vitality. The dialectical tension between the tradition and the teaching, and the fertile, vital imaginations of its members.'

He takes a sip of tea before returning to the main subject matter of our discussion.

'For me, the Annunciation is about beauty – the splendour of God, of being human. At the centre is call and response, so it's also about vocation. The freedom that Mary had to say yes or no. I've often thought about that in terms of vocation.'

He talks of his seven years in seminary being about vocation and discernment.

'I got to the point where I realized God is calling me and I'm totally free. Even if I said no, Our Lord will still love me. So I freely and one hundred and fifty per cent said yes. It was an act of freedom not restriction because with God there's something even greater than if I'd taken a different route.'

What about the lost status of the feast of the Annunciation?

'There's a hierarchy of truths,' he responds. 'The central truth is the Incarnation. The Annunciation relates to that. But we don't live in a Catholic culture here. You have to take into account the Reformation effect here. Luther, I think not logically, rejected the intercession of the saints. It's like cutting a finger off. Let's not go with Mariology – that's all Catholic stuff.'

I raise the issue, highlighted in his sermon, of a growing secularisation in Britain.

'I love living in the twentieth century – for example, the apps on my phone,' he comments. 'But I am alarmed about secularism. The hardcore secularism is to drive religion out of the public domain into a private, domestic ritual. In the public morality, its grounding, its mooring is eroded or corroded. Public morals become determined by the law, by precedent, by pressure groups. We've artificially separated the spiritual or religious from morality. They are distinct but they have to be together. My fear with secularism is it brings about moral relativism in our culture. It allows wriggle room and the alternative visions of the human person. And yet we know the real way to happiness is given in the life of Jesus Christ. Rightly, human beings are free. We can only propose, not impose on somebody else a different moral system, a different way of doing things. What the Annunciation, linked to the death and Resurrection of Christ, offers is a different route. It does include self-denial and suffering but it is the way that will have lasting happiness because it's a noble humanity, an authentic humanism.'

I wonder if for him the annunciation story carries an important message about the sanctity of life.

'Very much,' he replies. 'The purpose of religion is grace. Human life is a gift from God. We are co-authors, co-creators, but not the primary or principal.'

I note how he once described Mary as the 'true Christian disciple, brave and determined, passionate about truth and justice, a model of womanhood even for today's radically different world. No wonder she is the best loved member of the Church.' More recently, he called on the flock in his diocese to consider installing a Marian statue in their home, or to hang a rosary from the rear-view mirror in their car. I mention to him his reputation for hard line Catholic conservatism rooted in tradition but also observe that he seems to be very much up for discussing openly any of my questions.

'What damages a lot of Catholic thought is the glib football match politics of people who see something as left wing or right wing,' he responds. 'What they're showing is their own lack of philosophy. The critical thing is to have a worked-out philosophy underneath. Orthodoxy is a broad river. It's not about being conservative. I've always emphasized the importance of looking ahead. We have to be sound. We have to be grounded in the tradition and the truth we've received. But we have to be creative. We need to learn how to be Christ's disciples in the twenty-first century. Without that, we have nothing to offer.'

———

Ten years ago, Dame Sarah Mullally was the Chief Nursing Officer for England, responsible for 420,000 nurses and midwives working in the NHS. Then, forty-two years old and married with two children, she was an outstanding success story in health service management and was being tipped as a possible future contender for the top post of Chief Executive of the NHS. However, that same year she left her job to become a full-time priest in the Church of England, having been ordained two years earlier. After serving as a parish rector in south London for six years, she is now Canon Treasurer at Salisbury Cathedral.

Her roots as a child were in the evangelical Church. She felt a calling to faith at sixteen; a calling to nursing at eighteen; and a further calling at forty-two to give up her highly successful nursing career for full-time ministry. So the theme of the Annunciation – a calling and saying yes to God – she acknowledges, has been central to her life.

On the feast of the Annunciation, when she preached in Salisbury Cathedral, she used a painting by an Indian artist as her main theme. Jyoti Sahi's *Dalit Madonna* had been displayed in Salisbury a few weeks before as part of the travelling Methodist Art Collection. 'The picture uses the colour of harvest and the artist has sought to illuminate the Christian faith through the cultural traditions of India'; she began her sermon.

21. Jyoti Sahi *The Dalit Madonna*, 2000. © Jyoti Sahi

The figure of Mary and her son are seen in relation to the symbol of the grinding stone. A grinding stone is found in the heart of every traditional Indian home and is often secured in the ground. The grinding stone consists of a mother stone, which generally has a hollow centre into which fits a smaller seed or egg shaped stone that is called the baby stone.

In Jyoti Sahi's picture, this creates an image of the Madonna who is predominant as the mother stone and she is embracing the Christ child at her heart as the baby stone, within her womb.

Dalit is the current name for the caste previously called 'the untouchables'. Dalit women are oppressed and marginalised because they are women. And because they are Dalit, they live in poverty and so are marginalised again. They often find themselves open to exploitation including sexual exploitation.

Today in India, even in Christian churches, people often refuse to drink out of cups used by Dalits. When the picture was painted in 2000, it met with a great deal of shock. How could he paint Mary like this? How could God choose such a woman? But he did – although Mary was not a Dalit, she was from the lower parts of society, a refugee and unmarried, marginalised and in poverty.

Today we celebrate the moment when God announces his intention to enter our lives and world, and he does this not in a palace or through a princess but through the powerless and marginalised. What does that tell us about the nature of God?

The word Dalit means broken. The grain and other items of food are broken in the grinding stone for eating. As Ignatius of Antioch said, 'There is no bread without the process of breaking and transforming.' Today, as we celebrate the moment when God announces his intention to enter our lives and world, knowing that his son would be broken for the possibility of life and hope, what does that tell us about the nature of God?

The image of the Madonna and Child in the Dalit Madonna demonstrates an intimacy in their bond. Today, we celebrate that for God's intention to enter our world and lives, this was made possible because of Mary's faith and faithfulness. Mary's faith seen in her obedience, her faithfulness seen in her endurance of social scorn and grief that would pierce her heart which bore fruit. We know the fruit of her faith and faithfulness as Christ who is the fruit of God's deep love for us.

Let us hear God's intention to still enter our lives and the lives of the world, and open ourselves up to the possibility of knowing his deep love. Then, by showing the same faith and faithfulness demonstrated by Mary, we hold the possibility of bringing hope and life to others.

A few weeks after delivering that sermon, Sarah Mullally has agreed to meet in her immaculate home that looks onto the soaring spire of Salisbury Cathedral. Immediately, I am struck by her focus and efficiency. 'We only have thirty minutes precisely,' is her opening greeting. She seems cautious and asks me to explain exactly what I am up to. 'I will see what you use from me before publication – yes?' she asks.

She is warm and pleasant but at the same time no-nonsense and directional. I can see how she became a successful executive and senior civil servant. We begin our conversation by talking about the Jyoti Sahi painting and why she chose to focus on it for her annunciation sermon. The oil painting features a rich palette of yellows, greens and blues and its mother and child image, according to the Methodist Collection of Art, depicts the relationship of Mary and Jesus as being 'symbolic of the transformed earth which becomes like a full vessel of life.'

'It spoke to me strongly about the nature of God – his choice of Mary – unwealthy, a migrant, an outcast,' she says. 'In the painting, you can debate whether Christ is sitting in the womb or is she hugging him? There's the whole sense of the grinding stone – bread being broken, Christ being broken and the sense that he was being broken against Mary. That sense of the link to Mary's heart being pierced was very powerful too. The painting said more to me than just the Incarnation – that there's also the pain to come later.'

So, what does the annunciation story mean for her?

'It's about the announcement of God choosing to come and dwell with us in all our pain and suffering as well as our joy,' she responds. 'For me, it's about learning from Mary about that sense of obedience and recognizing that obedience isn't straightforward. Obedience is still a choice. To be obedient is sometimes easy and sometimes it isn't.'

Does she see it as fact or metaphor or something else? She pauses for a long time and shuffles in her chair before responding.

'I think for me,' she begins, before pausing again, 'I'd say I don't know the truth about that one way or the other. So I hedge my bets. I certainly think there are facts within it. The fact of Mary and of her hearing God. We hear God and we can describe that as angels talking to us. How much of it is fact or metaphor I don't know but I do believe that God chose to announce to Mary that he was to dwell with us. I would say there are roots of metaphor in it and roots of fact. Who am I to say? It's one of those mysteries. The bigger issue for me is what do I choose to do with it? What difference does it make to me about my understanding of who God is and about what he has called us to be and to do? What's the response from me to that gift?'

We move on to discuss her evangelical background. In that context, I wonder what Mary means to her and has that view changed during her life?

'There's concern in the evangelical community that people perceive the false worship of Mary,' she responds. 'The evangelical Church is always cautious of her because of that. Her status is low. As my faith has developed and grown, I have a greater knowledge of how God chose to work through her and what she means to other people. I'm very respectful of that.'

I wonder if she venerates Mary.

'No,' she replies firmly. 'I certainly wouldn't pray to her although I venerate her as part of liturgical worship when it helps other people. In my previous parish in Sutton, there was a statue of Mary and she stood there by the side of the chapel looking into the nave and I didn't move her because it would offend other people if I did.'

Is Mary an inspiration in her own life journey?

'Yes, in the sense of how we learn to be obedient,' she replies. 'I would see that as an inspiration. Also, as a mother, you learn deeply about the pain she must have borne. I've understood through her about the vulnerability of being a mother.'

If the Annunciation is about a call and response, was there such a moment for her?

'I became a Christian at sixteen. It was a personal decision. My parents didn't attend church when we were children. We went to Sunday school and our grandparents took us. Out of the four of us, one sister is now a non-stipendiary minister and another is a youth worker in a church. There was definitely a call to faith – to bring the kingdom of heaven to earth. There were no women priests then, of course, so I went into a vocation of nursing – to care. I had a strong calling from God to do that. But I still had moments of feeling called to ministry.

'The church that I was at were conservative evangelicals and they didn't agree with the ordination of women. So it was a difficult place to work out how you respond to that calling. I did part-time training for full-time ministry. But a year into the training, I had a clear calling from God to apply to be the Chief Nursing Officer for England but I knew I would be ordained. It was a tussle trying to discern the calling. So I did a part-time curacy while I was in the Department of Health. But then I thought, if I believe in God, if I believe in the Church, and I am hearing the call of God to use my gifts, then I shall follow it. People didn't understand why I'd give up such a big job and big salary for something of lower status and non-existent pay.'

I ask if she sees in her calling a parallel with the annunciation story.

'Yes, there may well be a parallel in the sense of how do you discern, how are you obedient and how do you listen to God? I'd describe the step for me as "canyoning". That's where you climb up some wonderful mountain, say in the Alps. You have all the safety equipment on, the wet suit, the hard helmet. You go up to the top of the mountain and come down the waterfall, like on a water chute in a swimming pool, and you fall into a huge pool of water. At some point, you have to take that big step over the waterfall and you do that step in faith. You feel when you hit that pool of water that you are drowning. And that's how my decision felt in 2004.

'I could have carried on at the Department of Health but, at some point, you take that leap of faith. You make the step and then God does for you the best he can. If God calls you to do something, then there's this developing process. There's a conversation. You listen. Then you take the step. You're doing the best you can but it's not always easy – as demonstrated by leaping off a canyon. You think you're drowning and that you've made the wrong decision. So there's probably a parallel. In all that struggle, it says, Mary was perplexed. That's a good description of the struggle.'

My time is running out but I feel we have only just begun. Where will she go from here?

'I do my best for God in this moment, where I am,' she says. 'I'm called to this place at this time. My longing is to keep my ear close to God with my feet in the world, to do what I believe he wants me to do.'

My time is up. Twenty-eight minutes have flown past. She bids a warm goodbye. I walk across the tranquil, green lawns of the Cathedral Close, towards Salisbury's fine Early English Gothic Cathedral and stand before the West Front. It is the most beautiful of settings.

The central doorway has three gabled roofs each with a shallow niche holding a comparatively modern stone statue made by James Redfern in 1870. A youthful angel Gabriel stands on the left, wings outspread, carrying a lily stem. St Mary of the Annunciation is seated on the right, eyes closed in contemplation as she holds her prayer book. Unusually, in the middle, there's another statue of the Virgin Mary, standing directly over the great west door, as if to emphasize to all would-be visitors that they are about to enter the Cathedral of the Blessed Virgin Mary. The same gospel story. The same central characters. Yet another fresh, creative expression.*

22. Statues of the Annunciation on the West Front, Salisbury Cathedral

---

* A year after my interview with Rev Dame Sarah Mullally, she was appointed Bishop of Crediton in the Diocese of Exeter. Two years later, in December 2017, she became the new Bishop of London, the third most senior position in the Church of England.

CHAPTER 8

EMPOWERMENT, EMANCIPATION, INDEPENDENCE

I am fascinated by Sarah Mullally's reference to Mary being depicted as a member of the poorest caste in India. I want to learn more. So shortly after our meeting, I visit a touring Methodist Art Collection in St Mary's parish church in Banbury, Oxfordshire. There I find what I am looking for: the original *Dalit Madonna* oil painting by Jyoti Sahi.

My eye is drawn immediately to the Madonna's tender, loving expression as she cradles baby Jesus. I love the rich earthy colours and the thick brushstrokes that flow across the canvas in a fluid, swirling composition. I stand there in admiration for a long time.

On my return home, I decide to try and contact Jyoti Sahi. Using the wonder of search engines and email, I discover that he lives at an art ashram in a small village called Silvepura, fifteen miles north of Bangalore in southern India. I email him, outlining the bones of my project and suggesting that we arrange a telephone or perhaps a video-linked interview.

To my surprise, he responds immediately, informing me that, by chance, he is in the United Kingdom for a few days. He suggests we could meet at his next destination: Hartley Wintney in Hampshire. His reply amazes me. Hartley Wintney is the very village where I attended Holy Communion classes fifty years ago and received the *My Lord and My God* book. The same place where Fr Walsh first showed us that iconic illustration of a perturbed Mary as she heard the voice of the angel.

There are more surprises in store: Jyoti Sahi indicates in his email that he knows Laurence Wolff, the Head of Art History at Winchester College. Moreover, he visited the school and even saw Lemoyne's Annunciation painting there a few years ago when it was hanging in Thurbern's Chantry.

A few days later, I head to Hartley Wintney. I have not seen St Thomas's Roman Catholic Church since I was seven years old. The memories flood back as I unlatch the gate, pass under an arched hedge and approach the small, plain yellow brick building. Unfortunately, it is locked up and I can't go inside. However, I recall standing here fifty years ago on 20 June 1965 – my first Holy Communion Day. The weather was gloriously sunny. I was wearing a new white shirt, red tie, grey shorts and polished black shoes. The girls were wearing white dresses with white veils, white tights and white shoes. Each of us on that day was given a rosary, a crucifix and a certificate. And we could keep our class book.

From the church, I walk across the picturesque village cricket green to meet Jyoti Sahi at his friend's terraced house. He greets me warmly and I feel immediately at ease; like I am meeting a dear old friend. He has white shoulder length hair, a long flowing white beard and kind eyes. Dressed in a white knee-length linen shirt and a cream cotton jacket with a long red scarf, he walks in bare feet and wears round glasses. The overall effect is that of a wise spiritual guru. He brings tea and biscuits and we sit together in the back garden filled with trees, flowers and shrubs.

Jyoti Sahi is seventy years old. He describes himself as an artist-theologian and was a founder member of the Asian Christian Art Association almost fifty years ago. His British mother, who was brought up in the Unitarian Church, went to India in 1936 where she met and married his father, who was a Hindu from Punjab. As a boy, he was raised in north India as a Protestant in 'the Church of Scotland tradition'. When he was a teenager, his mother converted to Catholicism and he was baptized with her. However, he says he has always felt his spiritual roots in the non-conformist tradition and describes himself as 'a non-conformist Catholic'.

His mother was a teacher whom he loved dearly. She was very interested in Carl Jung and especially liked Jung's thesis on archetype ideas: found all over the world, these are universal truths that are expressed through stories and myths that are adapted to different cultures.

Jyoti's mixed background, coupled with ideas like this, has instilled in him a life-long fascination with the subject of identity. 'There's a universal wisdom,' he tells me. 'God didn't just talk to one set of people and save them. There is wisdom to be found in all cultures. The cultures have come out of this wisdom, which relates to their own place, their geography, their landscape, their traditions.'

He places his paintings of Christian stories in the classical tradition of Indian cultural myths and symbols because this makes them more relevant for Indian audiences and 'creates more understanding'. So, in his annunciation works, he always depicts Mary as Indian and the landscapes are always Indian in style. He describes this unusual mix of Christian stories, Indian cultures and the South Asian folk tradition of story telling as reflecting his Indian identity as a Hindu Christian.

Jyoti Sahi came to England aged fifteen and trained in the early nineteen sixties at the Camberwell School of Arts and Crafts. After he returned to India, he met his English wife who was a Quaker. Thirty years ago, he set up his own art ashram, the Indian School of Art for Peace, north of Bangalore.

We begin our conversation by discussing the *Dalit Madonna* that he painted in 2000. He tells me that probably the majority of Indian Christians come from a Dalit or Adivasi tribal tradition. As 'untouchables', he explains, they've felt alienated, broken, marginalized and rejected.

'In the UK, Christmas is a time when there's no life in the land but in contrast in India it's harvest time. So the *Dalit Madonna* is a harvest picture. Dalit means earth – people of the earth. She is the richness of the harvest and Christ is part of that harvest,' he tells me in a soothing, gentle voice.

He says it is important to capture 'the spirit of the place' and not to relate the Incarnation and the birth at Christmas to a cold mid-winter scene like that so often done in the West, which would be seen as 'very foreign and colonial' in India. He tells me many Indian people are interested in Christian stories but they don't like the idea of the Christian Church as an institution. 'I am a Catholic. I still go to church,' he says. 'But I've been involved in all types of churches. In India, all these Christian denominations are a headache because they are all about emphasizing what has happened in the West.'

He sits next to me looking at my laptop. We find his paintings of the Annunciation. He clicks open and describes various depictions that he has created over the years. One, in particular, fascinates me.

'I went to a temple in Mangalore and painted it as part of a series on the life of Christ,' he says. 'She is playing the veena here like the goddess of wisdom. The angel is coming down from above. There's a well in the background. There are parallels between the angel descending and the bucket going down to winch up the water.'

His slow, mellifluous voice enhances his aura of spirituality and wisdom. I move on the conversation to ask him what the annunciation story means for him personally.

'I see it as the Word coming,' he says. 'The angel is a messenger and announces the Word. He is the Word but in an image.'

So, for him, is the story fact or metaphor?

'Oh dear,' he responds. 'It all depends on what you mean by fact. I don't hear the story in the literal sense. Of course, it's a metaphor but I also see

23. Jyoti Sahi *Annunciation*, 2007. © Jyoti Sahi

it as real, as a Christian myth. St Thomas Aquinas, of course, thought the Incarnation was fact. As a result of the period of the Enlightenment in Europe, there was then the distinction made between fact and myth – the rational approach. When the missionaries came to India, they said, "Our religion is fact and yours is myth." That's how they attacked Hinduism – they said, "Krishna didn't exist but our Jesus did. All the stories you tell are myths."

'The western argument has been how can such intelligent quantum physicists and information technologists in India believe such a dreadful thing? That has deeply hurt Indians who say how can we fight this degradation of us believing in myths? How can we counter-act this? There is a Jungian centre in Bangalore where one psychoanalyst argued that these myths are true but they function at a more unconscious level – at a deeper meaning which doesn't mean they are untrue. And the people who were listening were all highly intelligent IT specialists in Bangalore.

'So for me it's Christian myth. I don't like the distinction between fact and metaphor. For me, it's true. Empirical truth is all mixed up with myth. A lot of what we call fact is myth. Like the understanding of the dark holes in quantum physics. All that comes back to myth. Myths are cosmological. We think we can verify it empirically but the more we look at it, we're not quite sure.'

He leaves his seat, takes hold of a leaf from a nearby tree and holds it in the palm of his hand. I join him by the tree.

'We touch this leaf. We know what it is,' he says. 'But it's got a whole universe inside it. There's the cosmos, the planets, the earth, this bush, then this leaf, and then the atoms inside it. It gets deeper and deeper and we find what's inside here is the same as up there. It's a myth. If you look up "myth" in the dictionary, one of the meanings is that it's not true. But I'm saying the exact opposite. Myths are often more true than empirical facts. They affect us more than empirical facts – our feelings, our integration. So, for me, the Incarnation is a myth. There was a man called Jesus. He was born. He suffered. Whatever happened in the early Church was they discovered that inside this person whom they interacted with was a whole mythic world. So the right question to ask me is "how does this myth affect our lives?" '

As we sit down again and he pours out some tea, I ask him to consider that specific question in relation to the story of the Annunciation and his own life.

'Personally, I'm interested in the yoga philosophy – how the spiritual world enters into the physical world and transforms it,' he replies. 'A transformation takes place. So the Annunciation is about the spiritual coming into and meeting the physical, tangible, sensual world. It's not unique. All religions have virgin births. All the gods were born by virgin births. Every religion believes in virgin births. But the virginity of Mary is not just a physical thing. It's more about her integrity. Her power. She is a full woman. She doesn't have to depend on a man for the child. But the problem with fundamentalism is that it says she had no sexual relations. I don't know why we have to drag that in. The literalist position doesn't understand that a faith, a spirituality is not literal in that sort of way. It's a myth – it's the spiritual Word coming to earth.'

I wonder what he makes of Bishop Egan's phrase, that it is 'the most important event in human history'.

'I would say the Annunciation is one of the most important concepts in all faiths, not just Christianity. Christianity doesn't have a copyright over it. The concept of the coming together of the spiritual, the tangible and the material. All religious systems, all faiths are concerned with that but they articulate it in different ways. The annunciation story is archetypal.'

As I get up to leave, I ask him what he thinks of Lemoyne's painting of the Annunciation that he viewed some years ago while visiting Winchester College.

'I don't like it', he responds firmly as he grasps my hand. 'It's too literal. I call myself a symbolist. Bad art is bad theology when taking it too literally. Good art is more abstract. I don't mean non-figurative. But it doesn't try to represent things like a photograph. Mary is too flesh and blood. Modern art, rightly, has gone back to the metaphor.'

My return to Hartley Wintney has sparked a desire to see Fr Terry Walsh once more. I want to ask the priest – the first person to teach me about the story of the Annunciation – what he makes of it now.

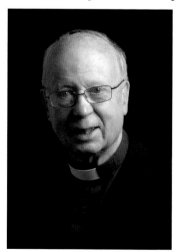

Sadly, I discover that he has died recently, aged ninety-one, having been a priest for almost seventy years. To my surprise, I learn that he had been living in a care home in Romsey, only eleven miles from my own home in Winchester. I feel sad and frustrated that until only a few weeks ago, I could have visited him.

His funeral was held at St Boniface Church in Southampton, where his friend Fr David Sillince delivered the eulogy. He reminded the congregation that Terry Walsh had studied Theology at the English College in Rome and, after many years serving as a parish priest, he had spent fourteen happy years as Head of Theology at La Sainte Union College in Southampton. Apparently, Terry had hoped that one day there would be both married clergy and female priests in the Roman Catholic Church. One particular section of his eulogy struck a chord:

24. Canon Terry Walsh. By kind permission of St Boniface RC Church, Southampton

One of Terry's abiding passions in Scripture was that you shouldn't take something in one mode (image, myth, parable) and transfer it to another (literal truth). In fact, he had an abhorrence of arguments, which began 'But it says in the Bible…'. Not that Terry wanted to wreck faith. But in all his encounters with people 'as far as they were capable of understanding' he wanted to lead them on gently to see a deeper truth. He wanted to pass on a mature faith without recourse to the tooth fairy while respecting people's intelligence and leading them on. In short, possibly without knowing it, he was a real 'new evangelist'. Terry was very clever but he was sensitive to those whose faith could easily be shaken. He wanted to help them over the reefs, not leave them to sink.

Terry Walsh's death has shaken me up. I realize that I need to see some of the people I want to meet, sooner rather than later.

Fr David Forde was the local Catholic parish priest in Lincoln throughout my teenage years. Although I listened to his sermons every Sunday for almost a decade, I have never had a conversation with him about his faith. The last time I saw him more than thirty years ago, he was standing next to Mark Fitzwilliam, an Anglican vicar, at my marriage to Hilary in her local Anglican church in Beaconsfield.

Now he is eighty-three and has the early signs of Parkinson's disease. He is retired as a Monsignor and lives on his own in a small, detached house in a residential suburb of Nottingham. His home is plain and spartan except for a large screen television in a corner of his front room where he indulges in his favourite past time – watching live football. His 1956 ordination certificate from All Hallows College, Dublin, hangs on one wall next to a framed faded photograph of him cutting the cake at his silver jubilee celebration at Our Lady of Lincoln church back in 1981. Now, he tells me, he spends each day praying, reading and reflecting, 'getting ready for the next life,' as he describes it.

Brought up in County Cork in Ireland, the son of a farmer and one of seven children, he recounts how as a young boy every evening he'd kneel down with his family in front of the fireplace to say the Rosary. He remembers with fervour how they would recite the First Joyful Mystery of the Rosary with its focus on the Annunciation and, as he puts it, the important theme of humility.

I remember how back in the 1970s, it seemed to me that David Forde's faith was characterized by humility and certainty. He never struck me as being a great intellectual but he was extraordinarily hard working, humble and kind. Forty years on, I am keen to hear his take on the annunciation story.

'It's pivotal to the whole of our belief,' he tells me. 'It's the beginning of our journey back to God. It's a story about acceptance.'

If it is so pivotal, I ask him, why is it no longer a holy day of obligation?

'All the feast days have become less prominent. It was big at one stage but it's been diluted. We live in a different society. There isn't the same commitment. We've changed so much. There's been a bit of back-pedalling but you're in this business for saving souls and you must do the best you can. There's a lack of faith now in the general public and a lack of commitment. There's only a handful of us go to church now compared to the population and it's getting less and less.'

I wonder if he sees Luke's account as fact.

'It's fact – no question about it,' he answers. 'It's written in black and white. There's no doubt about it at all. I wasn't at the Leicester City football match last night but I know for a fact it was a draw. I rely on the evidence of others. But more than that, Luke's Gospel is the inspired word of God. It is God's word.'

So, for him, the Virgin Birth definitely happened.

'It may be very hard to accept it all as fact but this is God's hand working at things. It was written down and has stood the test of time.'

And there were no other children? I ask.

'Mary had one child and that was it,' he responds firmly.

A thought crosses my mind. Should Catholic priests be able to marry?

'We should stay as we are,' he replies immediately. 'That's not the problem. Commitment is the real issue.'

When I ask him whether he feels a sense of disappointment at the reduced status of the feast of the Annunciation, he recalls with a real sadness in his voice how many people

whom he remembers were devout twenty years ago, no longer go to church. 'There's less guilt,' he tells me.

Is guilt a good thing? I ask. There is a very long pause. 'There's the commandments in front of you,' he responds before his voice tails off.

As I pack my bag and prepare to leave, he shakes my hand and then envelops me in a bear hug before making a final comment: 'I have no doubts about the Annunciation. No doubts at all.'

25. Mgr David Forde meets Pope Francis 2016, Rome. By kind permission of Mgr David Forde

---

I am inside York Minster gazing up at the magnificent Great West Window that dominates the entrance to the nave. Glazed in 1339 by Master Robert Ketelbarn, it is one of the largest and most spectacular medieval stained-glass windows in the world and is known as 'the heart of Yorkshire' because of its central tracery. Using binoculars, I focus on two specific panels high up on the left side that show the annunciation encounter, one of a series of themes in the window which, taken together, depict the 'Joys of the Virgin'. Sarah Brown, the Director of York Glazier Trust and an internationally renowned expert on stained glass, describes the scene to me.

'I see the Virgin holding a book, engaging in private devotion. The angel is kneeling, which shows a familiarisation at the time with Italian iconography. The heads of Gabriel and Mary are not the originals but the rest of the figures are well

26. Stained glass of the Annunciation, Great West Window, York Minster. © Chapter of York: Reproduced by kind permission

preserved. It's a slightly swaying elegant posture of the Virgin and the lily nearby signifies her purity. It's a beautiful piece.'

I move on to the North Choir Aisle to view another window, this time from the early fifteenth century. Both Mary and the angel Gabriel are robed in blue. To the right of Gabriel's peacock wings is a dove and, most interestingly, below is a pot containing a lily with a depiction of the crucifixion set within the flower itself.

27. Stained glass of the Annunciation, North Choir Aisle, York Minster. © Chapter of York: Reproduced by kind permission

'This is a very interesting iconographic development. The window is there for devotion in the more liturgical area of the Minster,' Sarah Brown explains. 'Mary is looking over her shoulder and has just been disturbed. We are witnessing a very private moment. Anyone looking at the Annunciation also knows that lying ahead are moments of tribulation and sorrow. It's a way of bringing together the Incarnation and the Crucifixion.'

I have come to York to meet one of the most renowned and respected Anglican priests in England. Fifty-nine-year-old Vivienne Faull is the Dean of York. In 1994, she was a member of the first wave of women priests appointed by the Church of England. Brought up in what she describes as 'a middle of the road Anglican household', at nineteen she was a student at St Hilda's College, Oxford, and attended an evangelical church in the city. 'I'm not sure we would have mentioned Mary then. She was dangerous,' she tells me in her office a few yards away from the Minster. Today, however, she says she is inspired by 'her emancipation and freedom to choose'. When I ask her if she venerates Mary she smiles before responding, 'I'm not sure I have but I might.'

We sit close together at a plain table. The room is functional and sparse. She is well mannered with a lovely, soft face but she admits she is worn out due to diary pressures. Even so, I get the clear impression she wants to engage with me about the Annunciation, however tired she may be feeling. I wonder what the story means for her spiritually.

'It's a story of vocation,' she says. 'A response to a messenger. A "yes" that took her way beyond her wildest imaginings. I think of it as an event. Clearly something happened that enabled that young woman to respond to what was clearly going to be a difficult set of consequences. The risk of death as well as the effect on her relationship with Joseph. I see little reason to doubt the veracity of the bones of that story. It's so simple and yet so powerful. Whoever St Luke was, he was interested in fact as well as interpretation. By and large, he sticks with fact and puts weight on that.'

She says she is agnostic as to whether an angel actually appeared. It does not matter. What matters is the message.

'The fact that the Church interprets it as Mary becoming the God-bearer is huge – historically, theologically – and particularly for women. It's not important that Mary is a virgin or not, but it is that she is to carry God. It's the most extraordinary thing. I find it almost incomprehensible but there's something about the mystery of that which is hugely powerful. The idea of Mary as Theotokos – God-bearer – is the primary metaphor.'

We move on to discuss the declining status of the feast day within the Church of England.

'There are all sorts of cultural reasons,' she suggests. 'We've been very frightened until very recently about talking much about Mary because of the inheritance of the Reformation and we're only just beginning to recover from that shadow. The whole story probably does need more prominence but there's this whole question of how Mary's power is constructed. Because so many people have lived through Mary being used as a weapon against them, particularly women, we have backed off from finding another way of interpreting her.'

I wonder if Mary is an inspiration for her.

'Sometimes,' she replies. 'More as I get older, which is slightly contrary, partly because I've stopped feeling the force of this impossible role model of a virgin mother which doesn't work for women and for Christians generally. I've started to re-think what that might mean. A young woman prepared to defy convention, to say yes to God, an older woman who saw her son die and stuck with it – that model of resilience is very powerful.'

Does the concept of the Virgin Birth present difficulties for her? She sighs before responding.

'Yes, partly because I think it is a biological impossibility and I think God doesn't routinely so defy the biological.' She sighs again. 'It feels manipulative. If you look at the antecedents, this is about Isaiah saying, "Behold a young girl shall conceive" and for me that's what's important. This is a sign that a young woman, who would have been marginal, not empowered in her society, was placed in the centre. So to focus on certain bits of the body, which I don't think the Christian faith does when it is healthy, to focus on mechanisms for reproduction, I just don't think that was the point. It's a distraction alongside the impossible role model of the virgin mother. On top of that, if she was a virgin, I don't think she could have had the baby. That's the most down to earth response. So it's a mystery that I haven't yet resolved.

'When the Gospels say there were brothers and sisters, for me there were brothers and sisters. Why not? Why is she claimed to be perpetually virgin?' She runs her fingers through her short dark hair, ruffling its neatly trimmed shape, before rubbing her forehead. 'The Annunciation signals that there was something profoundly special happening at this point,' she continues. 'The Church has marked it out by talking about virginity. I don't think the Virgin Mary label is helpful but I haven't come up with another label. The Church doesn't allow it.

'Certainly, I think when I was younger, I didn't find the Anglo-Catholic and Roman Catholic interpretation helpful. I was also alienated by this concept of virginity; not least by the way the Church used that as a weapon for control of women much more generally. I remember at my fairly conservative theological college, we discussed the virginity of

Mary. It was quite clear the majority of people in that room were as uncomfortable with it as I was. At that point, I realized it was acceptable to ask open questions about that. I began to see there were other ways of looking at Mary that allowed me to dodge that. Only recently have I come back full circle to say "Ok, I don't know what the Virgin Mary label means but it does signify that there's something profound here".'

I am interested in her use of the word 'control'. She breathes in heavily.

'If you tie up virginity with the significance of someone like the mother of Jesus, virginity becomes something that is prized. If a woman is deflowered, she becomes impure. The whole link between non-virginity and impurity has been so dangerous for women and continues to be in many countries.'

She mentions a favourite sculpture of Mary, sited in the Lady Chapel at Ely Cathedral and designed by David Wynne. She says she loves the freedom and independence that it symbolizes.

'She's claiming the space there. In many depictions, the angel seems to be the most important figure. Mary is either resigned or serene or fearful whereas in that one she can claim the whole space of the Cathedral and that's wonderful. I say, "Wow! I can take that with me for the rest of the day".'

Again, she runs her fingers through her hair and offers me a gentle smile before declaring, 'The Annunciation is about empowerment in so many ways. Empowerment. Emancipation. Independence.'

I enquire whether these themes of emancipation and empowerment have parallels in her calling?

'My journey with the Church has been one of saying yes to God but finding in that *yes* new possibilities that have been created that haven't necessarily been easy or straight-forward or painless. Obviously, I haven't had to suffer the grief that Mary had to suffer but there is something about a whole life's journey that has seen profound change all around me in the Church's relationship with women.'

She has an air of serenity about her and speaks movingly yet wearily.

'I have observed very significant changes in attitude in those who are now leading and guiding the Church. The voice of women is now heard, tested, responded to, and acted upon. They're now treated as fully human. We're not quite there but almost. It's getting to the point where normalisation happens very quickly.'

As our conversation draws to an end, I show her a print of Lemoyne's *The Annunciation*. Immediately, she bursts out laughing.

'The finger!' she proclaims.

'Some see it as phallic,' I tell her.

'That's what I noticed,' she responds. 'I think it is. It looks absurd rather than abusive.'

She looks at the composition in silence for some considerable time. 'It doesn't fit with the reality of the encounter. It doesn't do it for me. Mary kneeling, looking down. There's a submissiveness there. It doesn't impinge positively. It's disempowering.'

Today, of course, modern, contemporary Britain is a country marked by a diversity of faith and, indeed, no faith at all. As the number of self-proclaimed churchgoers slips below 15 per cent, Rowan Williams, the former Archbishop of Canterbury, has described it as a 'post-Christian country'.

'Britain is post-Christian in the sense that habitual practice for most of the population is not taken for granted. A Christian nation can sound like a nation of committed believers and we are not that,' he told *The Daily Telegraph* in 2014. 'It's a matter of defining terms. A Christian country as a nation of believers? No. A Christian country in the sense of it being very much saturated by this vision of the world and shaped by it? Yes.'

An accompanying ICM poll in the newspaper article reveals that just 14 per cent of the population see themselves today as practising Christians. But the number identifying themselves as Christian rises to 52 per cent while 41 per cent say they are non-religious. Fifty-six per cent say Britain is Christian compared with 30 per cent who say they think the country is non-religious. Five per cent say they are a member of another faith including Islam or Judaism. *The Daily Telegraph* reports that the same poll also reveals that two thirds of practising Christians in Britain appear to be wary of speaking about their beliefs with 62 per cent saying religious fundamentalism has made Christians afraid to express their faith.

Soon after the release of the poll in April 2014 and Rowan Williams's accompanying comments, the incumbent Prime Minister, David Cameron, wrote an article in the *Church Times* calling on Britain to be unashamedly evangelical about Christianity and its Christian tradition:

> I believe we should be more confident about our status as a Christian country, more ambitious about expanding the role of faith-based organisations, and, frankly, more evangelical about a faith that compels us to get out there and make a difference to people's lives.
>
> First, being more confident about our status as a Christian country does not somehow involve doing down other faiths or passing judgement on those with no faith at all. Many people tell me it is easier to be Jewish or Muslim in Britain than in a secular country precisely because the tolerance that Christianity demands of our society provides greater space for other religious faiths, too.
>
> People who advocate some sort of secular neutrality fail to grasp the consequences of that neutrality, or the role that faith can play in helping people to have a moral code. Of course, faith is neither necessary nor sufficient for morality.
>
> Many atheists and agnostics live by a moral code – and there are Christians who don't. But for people who do have a faith, that faith can be a guide or a helpful prod in the right direction – and, whether inspired by faith or not, that direction or moral code matters.
>
> I am a member of the Church of England, and, I suspect, a rather classic one: not that regular in attendance, and a bit vague on some of the more difficult parts of the faith.
>
> But that doesn't mean the Church of England doesn't matter to me or people like me: it really does. I like its openness, I deeply respect its national role, and I appreciate its liturgy, and the architecture and cultural heritage of its churches.
>
> I have felt at first hand the healing power of the Church's pastoral care, and my children benefit from the work of a superb team in an excellent Church of England school.
>
> Some fault the Church of England for perceived woolliness when it comes to belief. I am not one for doctrinal purity, and I don't believe it is essential for evangelism about the Church's role in our society or its importance.

Follow up letters in the national press criticized the Prime Minister's stance. One letter signed by thirty-four leading public figures stated: 'We are a plural society with citizens with a large range of perspectives, and we are largely a non-religious society. Constantly to claim otherwise fosters alienation and division in our society.'

Soon after, a worldwide survey reveals that two thirds of the global population have a faith. Countries such as Thailand, Bangladesh, Georgia and Morocco report that 90 per cent of their population is religious. The UK is six places from the bottom of the list with only 30 per cent of the population giving themselves that status. Below that lie Japan, Sweden, the Czech Republic and the Netherlands. Last is China where 6 per cent say they are religious and 61 per cent say they are convinced atheists. Interestingly, in this Win/Gallup International poll, those under thirty-four are more likely to be religious than other age groups.

––––––––––

My wife and I sit with three other couples at Stuart's birthday lunch. Six of us met whilst at university and have known each other for over thirty-five years. Whilst catching up on each other's news, I explain that I am working on a book about the Annunciation. This leads to a discussion about the role of Church and the relationship that each individual has with it.

Pete tells me he goes to church once a year on Christmas Day because it is a way of getting away from 'all the commercial stuff and focusing on why we have the day.' He says the best thing about Christianity is the teaching to love your neighbour. He concludes: 'It provides a good system of values.'

Steve, a non-believer, says he may call in a church a few times a year, especially in France where he has a second home. 'It's a place to reflect, have some quiet time and to think. I don't believe in God but it takes me to a world apart – the darkness, the austere atmosphere, the history, the peace, the trinkets, even the lingering smell of the incense. But I don't go to a service.'

Hilary states, 'I don't go to church because I don't believe the biblical story. I think that religion serves a purpose for those who need it; it attempts to explain why we are here and offers guidelines for morality. Also, it offers comfort to those who are fearful of death, of not existing any more, by promising eternal life.'

Helen reveals, 'We go to a Catholic church regularly but don't take communion. We're not Catholics. But the priest gives a good sermon that's short and makes you think.' Her husband, Stuart, intervenes, 'Of course, the Virgin Birth is a metaphor. The whole thing is a metaphor. If more priests had the courage to say that, more people would feel Christianity was relevant and would go...the meaning lies in its metaphysical interpretation,' he states resolutely. He goes on to mention Anselm of Canterbury who proclaimed in the eleventh century something along the lines of 'One should not seek to understand in order to believe, but one must believe in order to understand.' He continues, 'If Darwin and Grayling are right, this is all evil, twisted fairy tale nonsense but the best and most compelling stories and lasting truths emerge not from cold facts but from the human imagination.'

Hilary retorts that the real problem is the 'institutions of religion'. 'They're simply not relevant anymore,' she exclaims.

Bridget comes in at the end of the conversation and reveals how she goes to her local Anglican church once every so often. 'I used to go religiously as a child with my mother and I know I don't go enough. I feel guilty about it. I say to myself on the Friday or Saturday I'm going to go but then by Sunday morning, I decide to stay in bed. Also, it is becoming more "happy clappy" and I don't care for that. I like the more traditional approach.'

Linda Woodhead, Professor in Sociology of Religion at Lancaster University, is considered to be one of Britain's leading thinkers on the role of religion and faith in society. Her special interest lies in the relationship between religious and social change worldwide, particularly over the past twenty-five years. She is especially interested to explore the ways in which older, established forms of religion are being increasingly challenged by issues such as gender relations, global consumer capitalism and social media.

She gained a double first in Theology and Religious Studies at Emmanuel College, Cambridge. Now aged fifty, she has written a number of books including *An Introduction to Christianity, The Spiritual Revolution* and *Religion and Change in Modern Britain.*

Today, the Church of England still has twelve thousand parishes, sixteen thousand buildings and a presence in every community. But Linda Woodhead believes it to be in crisis, facing collapse, and being on 'its last chance'. She has highlighted how, in living memory, it has gone from being a Church of the majority to a shrinking minority. 'We are living through the biggest religious transition since the Reformation of the sixteenth century. The Church has lost touch with our everyday life and has become inward looking rather than being a broad Church for the whole of society,' she told the BBC recently.

As Director of the 'Religion and Society' research programme, she supervised the most comprehensive survey ever of religious attitudes in Britain, involving the in-depth questioning of more than nine thousand people. In the 2001 survey, 71 per cent said they were Christian but ten years later the figure had fallen to 59 per cent. She tells me that people dying off and not being replaced by a new generation has caused the drop. The fall is accelerating as more and more younger people say they have 'no religion'.

'It's about the failure of parents to transmit religion to their children and the failure by religious institutions to connect with the new generation,' she tells me. 'People are leaving the Church of England but they're not necessarily not believing in God. They are open to being spiritual beings but not in an institutional religion. Spiritual vitality has come adrift from the institutions that used to contain it and nurture it.'

I have arranged to meet her in front of Lemoyne's painting in the National Gallery. When she arrives, she leaves me sitting in the centre of the room and walks up to the picture, gazing alone at the canvas for several minutes in silence. Then she calls me across. 'It's not really human and I think the divine comes through the human,' she says. 'It lacks realism. I'd walk past it. It seems a bit stereotypical of female piety rather than being arresting and new. It's conventionally pious. There's nothing strong about Mary – pure, meek femininity. Supplicatory even. But I want her to have the same force of character as the muscular angel – the pretty boy.'

She takes out her mobile phone and shows me some of her own recent photographs. One is of the red carpet of more than 880,000 ceramic poppies placed around the moat at the Tower of London, each one commemorating a British fatality during the First World War.

'Look at it – that's amazing,' she says. 'It's spectacular. It's ritual. It's a memorial. It's not religion but it's extraordinarily meaningful. I'd say that's spiritual vitality today.' She scrolls down to a photograph she took recently of a statue of an angel at a cemetery near her home. 'I love walking in graveyards,' she says. 'They're much more personal now. Angels are back in a big way in society. Here's a grave in Lancaster I saw recently with the words "In memory of a little angel". It's nothing to do with institutionalized religion but it's providing meaning to someone who's lost a child. The angels are looking after the child and the child herself has become an angel. Angels are becoming really important now. People are becoming much more creative at using Christian symbols to make greater meaning within their own lives. And the Church has got nothing to do with it anymore.'

So, what do religious institutions have to do to make the annunciation story more relevant to today's generation?

'Go and listen to people and make a church that treats people as spiritual people rather than saying, "we've got the only truth and we're going to tell you". Respect people's spiritual wisdom.'

Does she think the Church of England is a listening Church?

'No, exactly the opposite,' she says. 'It's not even interested in what the people inside it think. It's a tragedy. It's obvious that the Jesus story is not engaging people. You just have to look at the numbers. Whereas for 1,900 years, it was a story where people could make sense of their lives, it isn't anymore. The Church hasn't faced up to that. It just thinks if you keep turning it over and over again, they'll get it. But that's not true.

'There are parallels with the annunciation story that would make it very meaningful to people, especially working-class women who would be much more interested in the angel than in Mary. Angels are increasingly relevant as guardians – they help people interpret their lives but Mary is very difficult.'

Linda Woodhead has shoulder length blonde hair, striking, wide eyes and a distinctive gap between her two front teeth. Her upright posture imparts an elegant poise. She listens carefully to each of my questions, offers a smile and then pauses before answering.

What does the annunciation story mean for her?

'I don't see it as clearly historical or factual as other parts of the Gospels,' she replies. 'I see it as an incredibly powerful story into which you can read lots of different meanings. Even though it's one of the latest parts that were written, it is one of the weightiest.'

So, does she think it actually happened?

'It's irrelevant whether it actually happened or not. It's much more important to get the messages from the story. For any great religion, why do some stick around and others die? It's because their stories and symbols can be read in so many different ways. That's the power of them. We all read the story through our own times and lenses. It's impossible for me to read that story outside of feminism and the issue of women's equality. Jane Schaberg [former Professor of Religious Studies and Women's Studies at the University of Detroit Mercy] claimed it was an illegitimate birth and could be a way of covering up a rape. Once I'd heard that, I can't get it out of my head. I don't find it particularly plausible but it makes you concentrate on the power dimensions. Here's a woman being told by a male you are going to have a son and you are going to do what you've been told. Is it just re-enforcing what women should have done unto them, whatever one tells them? If so, that's a dangerous message.

'As a child, I had Anglican parents but I went to a strict Catholic convent school and it had similar images [of the Annunciation], and that message that you don't have the power to say no is a really dangerous message. I'm sure those images have been destructive to people who've been abused and didn't feel able to resist because passivity is being commended here as divine. But there's a weird contradiction because I also think it's a beautiful image. Even out of something awful whether rape or whatever, something good can come out of it. It's a positive story. In the cases of abuse, some people can transform it into a positive and become some of the most compassionate people there are. That's what transformation can be about.'

Is there one word that sums up the annunciation story for her?

'For me, it's about subversion.' She pauses again for quite a while before reframing her answer. 'Taking things that happen to you, however badly they are meant, and making the best of them. It's a story of hope.'

I tell her that Bishop Philip Egan believes the Annunciation to be 'the most important event in human history'. She shakes her head.

'It isn't the most important event in human history. That's very Christo-centric. What's that saying about other religions, "My religion is the one that counts"? I don't believe that's the case. I'm not that kind of person. God comes in human form in all kinds of times and in all kinds of places. I think God has revealed other religions on other planets. You could say that about any part of the Bible stories but they all need to hang together. And I believe God is powerful and mysterious enough to appear in any religion in many forms and in many places.'

What part does Mary play in her life?

'She's become more important to me as my faith has gone on. She wasn't a real character to me. "Mary – so meek and mild – behave child!" She was about obedience and I've never been very obedient so she never really appealed to me. As a teenager, I was much too obedient and I wish I hadn't been. At the time I didn't like it. It was a deeply powerful formation. There was anger, not particularly focused on Mary but on having to behave in that way. You could never be fully yourself – "be good, be quiet, be perfect".

'But I've come increasingly to realize the importance of the goddess – the female way of thinking about God. As I've done that, Mary has become much more important. I don't think she is saying you have to chop off these bits of yourself. She is inspirational to some extent – seeing her in the context of the female goddess, the female divine. Mary is the closest thing we have to thinking about God in female terms. I want a much bigger God, less narrow, as God really is. A much more powerful representation of what it is to be a woman and not just in relation to a man. A more realistic depiction of womanhood like in Hinduism.'

Does she venerate Mary?

'I don't know if I venerate God even. I don't pray often. I try to open myself to God, clearing my mind. I don't think of God anymore as a person that I might have a conversation with.'

I am becoming increasingly aware that many women associate the annunciation story with the Church's view of sex and desire, together with negative concepts of power, subjugation, lack of freedom and possession. She talks about the concept of an 'empty space' and how she's moved by that idea.

'One woman once said to me about Christianity, "You've taken something away from me and I don't know what it is." That resonates with me. It's not allowed me to be as fully as I should be but I don't know exactly what it is that's been taken away. But I know my life could have been fuller, richer in another context.'

We return to talking about the present state of the Church.

'You're not represented,' she says. 'You're on the outside. You're never really part of it. You're there by sufferance. The stories. The images. The hierarchies. It sounds like an abusive relationship – so why don't you leave then? – but there's always been enough in it and I was brought up in it. You can't start again. I may have liked to have been brought up a Hindu but it's not going to happen. You make do. Like Mary, you make do with what you've got.

'I wish there was something that was richer that could encompass people in their variety and wholeness that was on much more equal terms – something much bigger in terms of the whole planet, even other planets, and not be just focused on our little human race and men within it. Our faith is rather small now and more and more people feel that. They want more variety these days.'

CHAPTER 9

BELIEVING IN THE MEANING

After hearing Linda Woodhead talk about the rapid growth of interest in angels, particularly amongst women, Theolyn Cortens seems like the ideal person to meet. She describes herself as a mystical teacher who combines ancient wisdom with 'inspiring, practical suggestions for personal spiritual development'. Her mission, she says, is to help people open their inner shutters. She has written several books about angels: *Living with Angels: Bringing angels into your everyday life* (2004); *Working with your Guardian Angel: An inspirational 12 week programme for finding your life's purpose* (2006); *Working with Archangels: A Path to transformation and power* (2007); *Your Guardian Angel Needs You! How to step into a remarkable future* (2011).

Sitting in the busy cafe in the Herbert Jarman Building on the University of Winchester campus, she tells me, 'It all started from an experience of my own forty years ago. It was like an annunciation. I certainly thought at the time, what are these bright lights that have appeared suddenly? And then thinking, oh, angel Gabriel has arrived. I hadn't any background then to suggest I'd think like that. I wasn't brought up in a religious way.'

Theolyn Cortens has been teaching about angels and taking angelic meditation classes for the past twenty years. She studied the history of human interaction with angels for a Master's degree at the University of Wales and is currently studying for a Ph.D. at Winchester. Her subject focuses on the emergence and development of 'Angel Spirituality among British Women 1985–2015'.

'I was always on the lookout for the perfect religion,' she says. 'I joined a Buddhist society when I was fourteen. In my twenties, I went for a while to a Roman Catholic Church. I then went to Quaker meetings. Later, I settled into transcendental meditation. Around 1972, I started to get a profound spiritual awareness and, after a while, it culminated in a very specific experience. It was in June 1974. I was thirty. I'd been quite ill with mumps and having a stressful year as a probationary school teacher. I was at home upstairs in bed, meditating. Then I had this experience. I'd known something was coming my way a couple of days before. I was off the planet in a slightly altered state. Then just before lunchtime that day – even talking about it today is still a very intense experience – I heard some words in my inner mind, which felt as though they were being spoken by another. All it said was, "Be prepared to meet your god".

'I took that as meaning I was about to die. I was in a complete state of surrender. I had no resistance to it at all. Then I found myself in a state of light, like when you lie on a beach directly facing the sun. I can't say if it came from inside or outside but it was such an intense light. It started to move within me and expand. I thought, what is this? I said in my mind, are you Gabriel? The light moved right through me like a light bulb being switched on inside and that was inherent in my whole body. When I heard the voice, my whole being vibrated with an awe-inspiring energy.'

She wears a brilliant-white loose shirt underneath a beautiful, multi-coloured embroidered jacket. It is no surprise to me to discover that she was once a dressmaker to the Pop music world. With her long blond hair, intense eyes and high cheekbones, she bears a striking resemblance to the singer/songwriter, Joni Mitchell.

'I wasn't really a biblical person until I started researching angels,' she tells me. 'I came across this biblical expression in Matthew [6:22] where Jesus says: "The light of the body is the eye, if therefore thine eye be single , the whole body shall be full of light." I thought of what the Orientals may call "the opening of the third eye". It wasn't a vision. It was a physiological happening. Was it an encounter with God, through an angelic interface, that allowed such a communication to take place? I remember the light was rushing through me with a pulsating sensation. I can't remember how long it lasted. It had a flow through it, which came right up.'

She moves her right hand slowly upwards from her stomach to her head to help describe the feeling.

'Then it rushed off. I sat up in my bed and part of me wondered if it was some kind of seizure, a fit. The only place I thought I could understand what had happened was through the religious texts. I read intensely about Mary's encounter with the angel and Teresa of Avila's encounter with an angel "piercing her side" and thought it was a profound mystical experience. It was the event of my lifetime. In that sense, it was an annunciation. It was a spiritual awakening that has provoked me to continue asking questions for all these years.'

She continues to talk passionately about being surrounded by this intense light and hearing an angelic voice. I have so many questions I want to ask but decide it is best not to interrupt her flow.

'I still felt very other-worldly, in a very mystical state,' she says. 'The boundaries of my everyday self felt dissolved and very beautiful but it wasn't very good for running a busy household. I had two young children. I felt I had to return to my ordinary self in the everyday world. But I also thought, how do you carry that experience, the oneness with creation, with the everyday and still think about paying the rent? In my teachings now, I ask that question regularly, "how do you keep the heaven with your feet on the earth?" The intensity of that message was isolated to that one event – it was like an invasion – but I kept getting more messages. I felt a communication with celestial beings. I started looking at the Tree of Life and the Jewish mystical tradition and saw that you can meet angels as you climb it. In my own inner meditations, I started to experiment and go on an inner journey – a path working – where you ask to meet different beings. I visualized it like a block of flats with a lift and I was going up. I'd go on the inner journey and first see traditional images of Gabriel, like on the Christmas cards, but I was looking for the archetype image. I kept meditating and, eventually, a real, genuine image came up. It was like a sudden opening of the cinema curtains and it had a lot of its own power. I didn't see a face but swirling colours with some sense of sound like a drum beat.'

She fiddles with her hair, adjusts her necklace and then takes a sip of water.

'I was doing that through the 1980s – working with these energy fields – out of my own personal curiosity,' she continues. 'I then thought, we've characterized them. We've put names on that kind of experience like Gabriel to allow us to have a conversation, but I think they're deeper than that. They're embedded in creation and human consciousness. In religious texts and art, we've put faces and images to them in order to have some dialogue.'

She describes angels as powerful meta-beings, whom we can meet when we are in need of spiritual support and guidance.

'They can transform our lives,' she says, 'enabling us to recognize our own creative power. They allow us to open our heart to a higher direction.'

She looks me straight in the eye as she emphasizes how angels can give us all inspiring messages that can reassure and encourage us as we cope with the ups and downs of life. She explains how the past three decades for her have been devoted to learning more and more about angels and mystics who understood how to live in both Kingdoms – the heavenly life and the everyday, earthly life.

'I was brought up in a very rational household so I was continually questioning, what does this mean?' she says. 'Where does it fit with the great mystics? I wanted to keep a foot in both camps – to hold on to the mystical but also have a rational conversation about it. I started to talk about it and realized how, over the past forty years, there's been a huge burgeoning interest in angels, particularly across Europe. So I did the MA with a dissertation on angels and the spiritual experience, using traditionalist Jewish mysticism as source material.'

In the early 1990s, she developed 'The Angels' Script', a set of thirty-six cards, featuring twenty-three sacred symbols, twelve Archangels of the Tree of Life, a card for the divine space of the Holy Spirit, and an accompanying guidebook. As she takes them out of a box, she says she understands that people may think they are like Tarot cards but these cards do not predict the future. They offer a gateway to angelic wisdom, she says, which allows users to access the channelled messages that she originally received.

As she lays out some of the cards from the deck on a nearby table, she insists she is not a psychic, nor a medium, nor a clairvoyant or kabbalist. She says she began channelling the messages after discovering 'The Writing of the Angels', a set of powerful symbols that date back to King Solomon. 'The Angels' Script' is a tool to enable access to the transformational energy of angels, she tells me, and acts as the gateway to angelic realms.

'I'm a mystic, engaging with mystical traditions to explore levels of consciousness. Teresa of Avila's "interior castle" is something I'm really interested in. It's to do with maps of consciousness – a metaphor for a journey to meet God. If people come with a question about their life, I channel the energies of the words in my book that come from a source of wisdom that's more than my everyday self.'

She acknowledges that most people who come to her probably have some belief in angels already. If someone says they are feeling unstable or unsure, she will ask them to pick a card to engage with an angel. If they draw the Gabriel card, it will be 'serendipity and synchronicity' working together. However, if the clients indicate they need to find their Archangel Gabriel, then she will go straight to that card.

For our conversation, I ask if I can take the Gabriel and Holy Spirit cards from the deck. She shows me a chart of the Tree of Life with Gabriel below the Holy Spirit. She says energy sits in each

28. Theolyn Cortens *The Angels' Script*, 2004

sephira or container on the Tree of Life and each sephira has a guardian angel. 'You're going on a journey through Sandalphon to go through to Gabriel,' she says. She shows me Sandalphon's card. He is a steward who rules the Kingdom, which I take to be earth. Sandalphon, apparently 'binds each blade of grass, each creature, each movement of the elements, into a coherent world. Thus, we are able to trust in the Kingdom for our support.'

I look at the Gabriel card. How would I know I've got to him? I ask.

'It's an interior experience of an expansive kind,' she responds. 'It's very subjective. You cannot share it directly with anyone else. Each archangel is a messenger and Gabriel is a messenger par excellence.'

I hold the Gabriel card close up. The illustrated figure is dressed in a white shawl with a blue collar. He holds a scroll in his right hand symbolizing the gift of language and the words of wisdom. His left hand contains an orb, representing the possibility of 'communion with each other and the Divine'. A halo of golden rays shines around his head and symbols that are letters from the Writing of Malachim fall from his mouth. As I hold the card in my left hand, I read the passage about Gabriel in the accompanying book:

> Gabriel brings messages from the Divine and heralds Change. Sometimes Change comes as a shock, sometimes it shifts us lightly. When Gabriel invades our lives, he demands our wholehearted attention; we are not permitted to ignore the requests of the Divine. Our lives may be overturned and we may feel chaos has entered; in order to move forward, the old and the outworn must be stripped away.
>
> Gabriel may startle you but his guidance is true. He may arrive with a request, or a gift; be assured if Gabriel presents himself to you, your life will be enriched, not threatened. Such a visitation means no more or less than a reminder of your purpose. Gabriel does not always speak directly but may drop hints and use tricks to call you to attention; watch out for small pointers and signs along the kerbside since you will not necessarily see a sign lit up with bright lights.

It sounds a bit like astrology to me, I say. Surely everyone goes through changes in their life. What would she say to those who claim this is just platitudes?

'It's always part of a bigger conversation of how a person is feeling, using my own intuitive skills,' she replies. 'This isn't like astrology like in newspapers although the very best, most detailed astrology is incredibly accurate. I'm allowing them to access something that's been given to me all those years ago. When it's read, it's almost like spiritual guidance. It's quite poetic in its delivery. Each time I do an angel reading, there's the opportunity for them to access the same wisdom I accessed all those years ago and it will enrich the way they then go on.'

I start to read the accompanying Angel Wisdom passage for Gabriel: 'It is a time of change in your life. Gabriel guides you out of your old world into your new one. He is the Messenger who reminds you of the commitments you made before you were born. He works with your Guardian Angel to create new situations that encourage your spiritual growth. Sometimes change is frightening, because we are stuck in our old ways, but we need to welcome changes that bring us back to our true purposes.

The illustration of the Holy Spirit shows a circular shape of brilliant white rays of light set against a purple-blue background that resembles Space. The guidebook states the Holy Spirit 'is an Empty Room where all is silent, perfect and complete. It is an Abyss into which we step in faith, knowing that the Divine seeks only what is good for us. This Room is veiled with a Cloud of Unknowing, but when we surrender to its oblivion we shall know, even as we are known.'

On the Tree of Life map, the Holy Spirit resides at 'Da'at' meaning knowledge. She says the Hebrew for the Holy Spirit is Ruah ha Kodesh – the breath of the Divine. She describes it as an invisible space or an 'empty room'. So, is this different to the Holy Spirit of Christian tradition, which is part of the Holy Trinity? I ask.

'In Jewish mysticism,' she replies, 'we have the Tree of Life, and the energy of the Divine flows through the template out of which everything is created. These signs are like pathways. It's like a plumbing system.'

When she was a teenager, Theolyn read a book about the Perennial Philosophy, which is the perspective that all religions have the same universal, single truth embedded in them as the foundation for the growth of their different dogmas. The book had a profound impact on her.

Would she describe herself today as religious?

She tells me she's not religious in the conventional sense but rooted in a mystic spirituality, with an empathy with the Liberal Jewish tradition although she doesn't practise in a synagogue.

'I would describe myself basically as a mystic with a very wide perspective,' she replies. 'Any mystical tradition appeals to me – Sufi, Christian mysticism, any language and writings of mystics.'

I ask her to imagine that I have come tonight for an angelic session and, at the start, I mention the angel Gabriel and Luke's annunciation story. What would she do?

'If we take the Annunciation as a moment of conception for a new idea to be born,' she says, 'an incarnation of something, then from a Jewish mystic perspective, it comes down from the Crown of the Tree of Life and the energy of it flows and is grounded in the Kingdom. It's where heaven comes down and touches earth. So if I was looking at the annunciation story, I'd say the Godhead wants to deliver something that's coming to be grounded in the Kingdom in the form of Jesus Christ.'

She shuffles through her pack of cards and finds Sandalphon.

'The character of Sandalphon is often described as Messiah because he bridges heaven and earth,' she continues, 'and the energy is channelled through the Holy Spirit – the breath of the spirit of God. Through the Spirit, it allows the action to happen and something is born. Gabriel announces this as a bridge between the visible and invisible – the psychopomp – and is informing. He's putting it into form. So, in the story of the Annunciation, Gabriel is informing, not telling Mary, of the planting of that conception.'

When I reflect that there seem to be obvious parallels with Luke's story, she refers to Margaret Barker's book *The Great Angel* which states that, at the time Jesus was born, there was a tradition in Judaism of perceiving that God had sent a great angel as a prophet. Some of Jesus's followers would later suggest he was Elijah returned.

What does Luke's story mean for her spiritually?

'I would say that my whole approach to who Jesus is, is that he has been sent, incarnated, as a very specific person with a very high state of consciousness embedded in who he is, to encourage humanity to get its act together.'

Does she see Jesus as both God and human?

'He is divine in human form,' she replies. 'He expresses the Divine in the human form rooted in the Jewish mystic tradition. I believe in divine intervention.'

I tell her I am a little confused.

'The Divine can come into the human form,' she says. 'I'm not technically a Christian because I don't believe that was the only person ever. That idea, intellectually, doesn't work for me.'

So, does she consider Luke's story of the Annunciation to be factual, metaphorical or something else?

'It's mystery,' she responds immediately. 'I can certainly imagine a woman having that kind of experience and coming out of it and feeling that something had been predicted for her specifically. I think the conception of Jesus was physiological. That's fine by me. A natural conception. But that doesn't make it any less. She's pure. She's been given a message. She's receptive. She's had an angelic experience about the child she is going to have. I'm very open to unusual things happening. I think the Divine energy can do double back flips on the material world. I'm very open to the business of how spiritual beings can be conceived. I don't want to dismiss it all entirely with rational, scientific materialism. I admit I wrestle with it like any practical, modern person does.'

What does she think about the claim that it is the most important event in human history?

'I think it might be the most important event in Western cultural history,' she says. 'I'm not sure about the whole of humanity. There are large swathes of humanity not touched at all by the concept of Jesus. But there's something there. The story was passed down. The woman said she had a very special experience of either an angel appearing to her or an intense dream. I'm quite happy for it to have been an event. I've had my own event back in 1974 that was an awakening for me. I may not have had a baby but...'

Her voice tails off. She looks around the room at all the students in the cafe, nearly all of them fifty years younger than herself. As a mother and a grandmother, she says she feels youthful and vibrant being surrounded by all these students on campus.

I show her the Lemoyne picture of the annunciation encounter.

'I'm intrigued by that pointed finger,' she tells me. 'That's a classic pointed reference summoning the energy from the light up above down to the ground below and she's accepting and surrendering to what she's been told to do.'

Does she see a clear parallel to the Tree of Life framework used in The Angels' Script?

'Absolutely,' she says. 'It's all to do with states of consciousness.'

I feel the need to call in on John Dennis, a retired Anglican bishop who lives a few hundred yards from my home. Both of us attend the Communion service at St Paul's in Winchester every Sunday morning. He always strikes me as a wise, tolerant and open-minded cleric who has seen it all.

Educated at St Catharine's College, Cambridge and Cuddesdon College, Oxford, he was ordained in the late 1950s and served in the tough urban parishes of Armley in Leeds and the Isle of Dogs in London before going on to become the Bishop of Knaresborough in 1979 and then Bishop of St Edmundsbury and Ipswich in 1986, where he stayed for a decade. In recent years, he has become something of a mentor to me about faith, certainty and doubt. I want to update him on the initial progress of my journey and to ask what the annunciation story means for him spiritually?

'It's not meant a lot to me, to be honest,' he replies. 'Obviously, the Incarnation means much more. And for me, Easter is the climax of it all.'

How does he view Mary?

'I see her as a real human being,' he replies. 'That's why I don't like the horror face idea when she's told she's going to be the mother of God. It wasn't like that. I think she showed quiet, peaceful devotion. A real woman doing a real job as a mother. She went through the agony of the growth of the baby in her womb and of childbirth and all the mess that was involved in that. That's the Mary I see. She was willing, shocked maybe, but not aghast.'

Does he see Luke's story as fact, metaphor or something else?

'I don't know,' he admits. 'Was it a virgin birth or not? I don't know. Where I am on that is, I don't think it matters. The reality for me is, it was the coming of the Son of God into the world. I can see geneticists saying that it couldn't possibly happen. I'm inclined to agree. Certainly, in human experience, it couldn't have happened. Some of the answer why the Church picked on this story so importantly is that it didn't know a lot about genetics. You can have virgin births but they're always of females not of males. Ok, this is God's world. It could have been the way that Scripture describes it, but I don't care. It's like many other things in Scripture. They're either true or they're not. We'll find out. If Mary realizes she's going to have a baby in the normal way of her periods going haywire or what, a physical indication of a baby on the way, I don't find any difficulty in thinking that God, whether the coming of the angel at the Annunciation or through dreams or whether through' – he pauses, realizing he's lost his train of thought before continuing – 'whether the Annunciation happened as it says or she found she was pregnant and began to wonder how that could be, and the idea developed in her mind that she knew she was in for a really rough road ahead and this was no ordinary child, well ok. In that sense, it's mythology but mythology describing reality. Is there a tidying up? It's not impossible that Joseph and Mary had sex before. Unusual yes – they would have had to be very quiet about it, so a story goes she didn't know anything about it. Ok, ok. What matters is that God came into the world through Christ.'

The eighty-three-year-old retired Bishop, who still conducts services regularly at St Paul's as well as taking confirmation classes, is now classed as an honorary assistant bishop. Married with two adult children, one a successful diplomat, the other a leading comedian, John Dennis has a kind, jovial manner. We sit in his modest study. He is dressed in a crumpled jersey and baggy trousers. As he presses the basket down on the coffee percolator, I ask whether he sees the Annunciation as the most important event in human history.

'Yes, because without it, nothing else could have happened,' he says. 'The central message of the story is the willingness of a young Jewish girl to be a mother and all that followed from that. A loyal mother and with all his joy and pain being born in her. The message is the way she bore that and remained faithful.'

I wonder what he thinks about the notion of Mary's perpetual virginity. I quote Matthew 13:55-6: 'This is the carpenter's son, surely? Is not his mother the woman called Mary, and his brothers James and Joseph and Simon and Jude? His sisters, too, are they not all here with us?'

Does he think Mary had other children? Or were those referred to the offspring of Joseph and his widow? Did Mary marry Joseph then take the vow of chastity for life after Jesus was born?

'I think that's cock,' he replies. 'It's rubbish and it all comes out of a false concept of sex really, I think. There are Roman Catholic bishops being summoned by Pope Francis to make decisions about marriage. What the hell do they know about marriage? Why must Mary act as a single-birth mother? That's not the pattern we're supposed to be brought up in. We're supposed to be brought up with parents, who have happy sex together, and that's a strength of their relationship – what they do in bed together – and that results in brothers and sisters and that strengthens the family relationship. Why on earth should she have been deprived of that? Only because somehow this holy Mary having sex was somehow abhorrent and sex itself is rather disgusting.' He sighs heavily. 'Perpetual virginity is totally unnecessary. And the Immaculate Conception is even worse. It just doesn't make any sense at all. I not only feel entirely comfortable with the notion she had other sons and daughters, I feel very uncomfortable about any other view really. You talk of an act of sex. I think she needed lots of acts of sex. She needed to have a happy married life and the result of that, as contraception was not available, was she had lots of children.'

'Why doesn't the Church talk like that publicly?' I ask him.

'I don't know the answer to that question.'

'Is it that it may confuse a congregation?'

'I think that's right,' he responds 'You can say it in a house group or a Bible study group and people can feel free to disagree. That's alright.'

Does he pray to Mary?

'No I don't but I don't pray to any of the saints either. I don't have anything against that but I haven't been brought up in that tradition. I haven't ever felt the need to. The nearest I ever get to it really is to call on my local angel to look after something for me or to say thank you for something.'

He has an angel he talks to?

'My guardian angel,' he responds. 'I haven't met him personally but he's around. He's sort of there.'

I love his honesty and openness. I pass him the Lemoyne picture.

'Crikey!' he responds. 'It's a bit of a surprise. It's saying more about the attitude to the reality of this coming child than all of that "aagh".' He acts out an expression of shock using his face and hands. 'She was more serene, more prepared to face it. Look at that chief of the angels, the captain of the army,' he says as he points to the angel Gabriel. 'I can't quite buy that one. But who knows? That's maybe what she saw. It's all she could absorb.' He then looks at the cherubs. 'They look like play school to me. It's so full of symbolism.' He keeps studying the picture. 'Actually, I think it would grow on me. I like the light up there. Yes, I think I could use it for prayer but I'd have to transfer the symbolism of there to the symbolism of today.'

Seventy-eight-year-old Philip Morgan is another retired Church of England clergyman who lives in Winchester. Brought up in South Wales, he graduated with a Law degree from Gonville and Caius College, Cambridge, and then trained at Wells Theological College. He was ordained in 1961, served as a parish priest for many years, and retired as a Canon at Winchester Cathedral in 2001.

'Where I start from is the fact all the Gospels were written after the resurrection,' he tells me. 'Everybody who had anything to do with the production of the Gospels was convinced that the resurrection had taken place and that this had made all the difference to everybody's life. They then had the oral tradition of Jesus, a couple of generations old, by the time of the Gospel of Mark. They were working backwards from the resurrection with the oral tradition and their imagination about what must have happened. They were convinced that Jesus was undeniably and uniquely the Son of God and, therefore, to go right back to the beginning, must have been born in a special way. So it leaves us with a great deal of interpretation to do if we take that seriously. That's why I feel the Annunciation was a metaphorical way of describing how the Son of God began to come into the world as a foetus.

'I feel it's better not to concentrate on whether it's fact or not. I think as I have gone on, my phrase is: "Believe more and more in less and less." Believe more and more in the resurrection and less and less in the rest of the gospel story as accurate, historical information. The crucifixion can be historically attested. The resurrection is a matter of faith. It will never be proved. But I don't think the Church would have got to where it is today if it had just been flannel.'

So, if a Christian says, 'I believe in the Resurrection but I'm not sure if the Annunciation happened,' does he think that is a reasonable view?

'In my view, yes,' he responds. 'If I was in a discussion group with friends at St Paul's, like the Pilgrims group, I'd say that. But it wouldn't be something I'd preach about. It would have to come in a discussion group. You don't bowl a fast leg-cutter to the congregation saying, "I don't believe in the Annunciation," when you're preaching. It's just not on. It produces a sense of shock and confusion. It's all too complicated a story to say in a ten-minute sermon.'

He has a beautifully rich voice, and sounds like a Shakespearian actor or a Radio 4 continuity announcer. He speaks slowly and with regular pauses, clearly thinking carefully about what he wants to say and how to phrase his responses. As he sits in a comfy armchair in his first floor living room, I wonder what the story means to him spiritually.

'I think a great deal was lost at the Reformation,' he replies. 'The Roman Catholic emphasis on Mary is a very important element in believing in God without gender. She, as Mother of God, holds a very important place in the balancing of the Church between genders. The consequences of the Reformation have been to help lead to the loss of Mary. I think that's a blind spot that means we're losing something. Anglicanism has begun to recover some of that in putting Mary in a more prominent place. She was Jesus's mother. It's the conception that's really the challenge. Was it Joseph or some miraculous event?'

Does it matter? I ask.

'If we look back at the four Gospels,' he responds, 'Mark and John don't pay any attention to the Annunciation at all. Not a word. Yet it's in John where Mary is at the front of the Cross. So you can't say John was trying to minimize the role of Mary. Luke is the storyteller par excellence. It was crucial that Jesus was born into the world as a human being. That was the great new start of God coming into the world afresh. Not just through the words of the Prophets. So God must have determined in some way that this was going to happen and brought it off in some way we can't explain. But that Jesus was the Son of God is a vital part of the jigsaw for me. I always end my prayers "through Jesus Christ Our Lord".'

What place does Mary hold in his spirituality?

'A figure central in the Scriptures but not somebody I think a great deal about in my own spiritual life, I think it's true to say. I pray to God through Jesus Christ. I think that the Crucifixion and the Resurrection are the indication that that is the right channel. Deeply saintly though Mary was, she is not part of the Godhead.'

Does he think the Annunciation is the most important event in human history?

'No,' he replies. 'I'd put the Crucifixion above it but Jesus had to begin. The process had to begin.'

I show him the Lemoyne painting.

'I see a very dominant angel and a wishy-washy Mary. It looks typical of the baroque period. It's not my favourite. I have a collection of Annunciations that probably stop around 1530. I love the early Renaissance. The simplicity, the innocent faces. But if she did have a vision with that message, then it's an entirely appropriate posture.'

He gets up and brings over a series of scrapbooks he's compiled of his travels. He takes out a whole series of Annunciation postcards from various European galleries and museums.

29. Philip Morgan's collection of postcards of the Annunciation

'The thing is we've all had nudges. What we need is the grace to recognize them whenever they come. For whatever reason, a change of course or whatever. This is not religious – it's not a nudge into religious life. It's a nudge about a fuller life. We've all had those. And if we have the grace to spot them and act, then it's a blessing. If you can achieve that, it's pretty good,' he laughs. He collected the cards on his travels with his wife Kate, a singing teacher. Five years ago, she suffered a severe stroke on an aircraft as they

30. Kate Morgan's drawing of angel Gabriel 2015

travelled on holiday to the south of France. Ever since, she's been in a nearby care home and he visits her every afternoon. He shows her the scrapbooks as part of her recall therapy. He passes a drawing of the angel Gabriel, which she's copied from one of the postcards with her left hand. He says she wanted me to have it. I thank him profusely and say I will visit her.

As I begin to leave, he says something rather profound.

'There's a lot of unlearning to do as we grow up, isn't there? I often think the great number of the stories that are told to children are part of the unlearning in another ten years for them. I hope they will ditch it without washing out the Crucifixion and the Resurrection.'

I wonder aloud if I am going through that process.

'If so, it's a blessing,' he replies. 'It's sometimes a hassle as well. But it all comes out as a blessing. Don't worry.'

The following day I visit Kate Morgan in the Brendon care home in north Winchester. She is sitting in a chair by her bed in her small room and it is clear she has no movement on her right side. I notice immediately a postcard of Lippi's *Annunciation* pinned onto the wall and a Renaissance painting of the Annunciation stands on the little desk directly in front of her. There is a tumbler full of pencils and crayons next to it. I thank her for the drawing of Gabriel. Her speech is difficult to decipher and delivered very slowly. She tells me she likes to look at the annunciation scene every day. 'So lovely. Beautiful,' she says. 'A lovely angel.'

I talk with her about my annunciation journey. Philip had advised me earlier that she will be able to understand all that I say. I wonder if, for her, the story is fact or metaphor.

'Somewhere in between,' she replies slowly. There's then a long pause. 'But believe in the meaning.'

———

Seventy-two-year-old Mary Grey lives with her husband, Nicholas, in a lovely thatched cottage called 'West Mill' on the banks of the River Test at Wherwell in Hampshire. She takes me to the bottom of her garden to view the crystal clear, flowing waters of one of the world's finest chalk streams, abundant with trout and grayling. I comment that it is like being in heaven. 'You'll have to wait for that moment,' she chuckles in a voice still marked by a childhood raised in County Durham.

A Roman Catholic theologian and social activist, Mary Grey is Professorial Research Fellow at St Mary's University College, Twickenham, and has held professorial chairs at the Universities of Wales, Southampton and Nijmegen in the Netherlands. Her work has focused on feminist liberation theology and spiritualities, and most recently on social justice and reconciliation. For more than twenty years, she has been heavily involved in a charity she helped to found with her husband. It is called Wells for India, and its aim is to secure water supplies in the desert areas of Rajasthan in India. She's written more than ten books and, in 2010, SPCK published *The Advent of Peace: A gospel journey to Christmas*. A chapter entitled 'The Annunciation' begins with her own poem:

O radiance, radiance of morning's new dawn,
O speak not a word, lest you miss what is born
From the womb of the Godhead creating with pain,
The nourishing gifts of the earth's fruit and grain.

'Is there one here who is hearing?' God's heartbeat is pleading,
She is listening, listening, the bread she is kneading,
The silence enfolds her, deep-hidden in her power,
O daughter, beloved, know this is the hour!

O deep is the yearning, for healing she longs
For a people's deliverance from oppression and wrongs.
While moulding the loaf – wheaten flour which earth yields,
She connects with her sisters still toiling the fields.

O daughter, beloved, I heard Rachel's cries,
For the vulnerable children who forever will die
Through the violence of culture, my compassion will stream,
in your waiting, responding, lies my hope and my dream.

O strong is the spirit, instant and wild,
Evoking response – 'I am Wisdom's child!
Let my body, my life, as love's gift remain
For God and my people, for all children in pain.'

The silence is broken, there is rushing of wings,
The cry of the wild goose, exultant it sings —
'O rise up, daughter, love's power will unfold,
Revealing the healing of stories untold.'

We make our way up the gentle slope of her back garden and return to the glass-fronted living room where we sit down and start to chat. I begin by telling her about the image from *My Lord and My God*, which has stayed with me these past fifty years.

'For me, it's exactly the absolute opposite image,' she replies. 'For me, the Annunciation is a moment of mutuality – a paradigm of mutuality of the Spirit working between people. It's a metaphor for encounters. My work is all about a theology of connectedness and the Annunciation is the inspiration that started me on that journey.'

What does she mean by 'mutuality'?

'In normal secular terms, you could say a spark develops between people,' she replies. 'They know they're on the same wavelength and spark each other off. People are led to a deeper sense of inspiration that's lasting. The sense of an encounter that ends but goes on. The encounter between Mary and Gabriel may have lasted only a few seconds but the meaning of it carries on and inspires later actions. You know when the spark is re-animated. It takes you on more deeply than the moment you are living.'

I ask what the annunciation story means for her.

'The word 'annunciation' epistemologically means announcing from one person to another but I feel it's more about an epiphany of connectedness,' she says. 'To move from the world of separation to the world of connectedness. And it's not just Gabriel and Mary. It's being led by the power of the Spirit – a powerful encounter that leads Mary beyond. It's about attentiveness and so much of life is about blotting that out. In George Elliott's *Middlemarch*, she says: "If we only learn to listen, we could hear the grass grow, the squirrel's heartbeat and the roar that lies on the other side of silence." Isn't that amazing? It's the power of listening but not listening alone. It's the power of action. She has to move. She can't just be passive.'

Does she see the Lucan passage as factual or metaphorical?

'We'll never know,' she replies. 'I want to believe it. I do believe it. But there's a strong argument that Luke's account is in order to get Jesus to Bethlehem. He has to have a reason to get us from Nazareth to Bethlehem But I want to believe it. I won't go further down that road. I've made it the anchor point of my own theology – that connectedness of the Annunciation – so I'll hang on to that. I don't think there's anyone authoritatively who can disprove it.'

I ask what she means by the 'anchor point of my own theology'.

'Because of its metaphoric significance,' she responds. 'Also, because I'm nourished by it. It's a moment of such deep significance. It takes you out of time.'

What does the Annunciation mean for her as a feminist liberation theologian?

'We have to use theology in the plural here,' she says. 'There are lots of feminist liberation theologies. The first lot would be rather crude and I don't go along with it. They'd go for justice for women right through society. Mary Daly wouldn't talk to men. It was extreme. But I would use mutuality. I deliberately don't go with anti-patriarchy but I don't go with matriarchy either. We're not trying to replace patriarchy with matriarchy. We're in for mutuality and justice, which means just relationships between women and men and also beyond the West to the context of India and Africa, for example. It's an ongoing journey of mutuality.'

So how does she view Mary in that context?

'She's an image for the power of the Spirit,' she replies. 'She said yes. Her receptivity is so positive. The Catholic Church has tamed and domesticated her in a hidden life in Nazareth. "Behold the handmaid of the Lord" used to be seen as submissive but it wasn't like that in my view. She was a model of full attentiveness and action on behalf of the Spirit.'

Would she agree that it is the most important event in human history?

'Without Mary's assent, we wouldn't have Jesus is what that means. I think it's right if you go down the historical, factual line. He had to be born. He had to have a mother. If we have that attentiveness and belief in the spiritual encounter, we can make a lot of what comes our way.'

She looks at the Lemoyne painting and pulls her spectacles half way down her nose. I watch her eyes scanning the picture.

'The angel is very powerful with a wonderful sense of movement,' she observes. 'Look, he hasn't touched the ground. Amazing! He could be a woman. He [Lemoyne] has left it open, hasn't he? Mary has a sense of life. She's not canonized. She's a real woman here. I see receptivity in Mary, attentiveness and humility. She's open to the sense of glory of the heavens. Mary is looking down but the angel could be saying to her, "Look up," at that very moment. Yes, for me, that would increase the sense of the power of mutuality of it all.'

I leave Wherwell and head down the Test valley to Romsey Abbey, a stunning example of twelfth-century architecture and the largest parish church in Hampshire. Dedicated to Mary and St Ethelflaeda, who was the Abbess of the Benedictine nunnery here at the beginning of the tenth century, all the Abbey's original stained glass was badly damaged during the English Civil War when Parliamentarian troops entered the building in March 1643. The Abbey was filled with replacement plain glass until richly coloured Victorian windows were installed in the late nineteenth century.

Inside, on the south side of the nave, directly opposite the main entrance, there is a distinctive twentieth-century Annunciation window designed by Hugh Easton. The coloured figures of Gabriel and Mary stand out against a background of clear glass. Rays of light from heaven above and the descending dove flying over Mary's head, create an intricate lattice design. Below Gabriel and Mary, attached to three lily stems, there is a mandorla showing the crucified Christ on the cross. As Gabriel points towards Mary and she accepts his extraordinary message,

31. Hugh Easton *The Annunciation*, Romsey Abbey. Photo by kind permission of Amanda's Arcadia

she appears to be looking down to see the pain and suffering that she will face in later motherhood. In a small glass panel in the bottom right hand corner of the window, there is a weather vane pointing east.

'Presumably,' I say to an Abbey guide, 'it's a sign recognizing the ancient tradition of the first Christians, who faced east when praying towards the rising sun.'

She opens her bag, takes out a pamphlet, and starts to read from it: 'It's a symbol not just of the Resurrection and the rising of the sun, but of the notion that when the Messiah returns, he will come from the east,' she says. 'Indeed, even before the Christian Church came into being, pagans prayed to the rising sun in the east, and then, of course, there's the whole idea that Christ will return through the Golden Gate of the eastern wall of Jerusalem. So Easton is encouraging us to look east towards Jerusalem. Images of the Annunciation are crammed full with signs and meanings – lilies, doves, gardens – and here, Hugh Easton has just added even more.'

––––––––

Dressed in a black cassock with a flowing black beard, Andreas Andreopolous is a striking figure. Greek by birth, he is married to a Romanian and is now a priest in the Romanian Orthodox Church. Andreas is a Reader in Orthodox Christianity at the University of Winchester. He studied in Greece, Canada and the United Kingdom and has a Ph.D. in Theology and Art. His area of expertise is Orthodox Theology, Iconography and Sacred Art.

I have returned to the university campus to seek a one-to-one tutorial with him about an Eastern Orthodox view of the Annunciation. It is a rambling session that lasts nearly two hours. Andreas is certainly loquacious and I spend much of our time trying to keep him focused on the subject matter in hand. He is extraordinarily passionate and needs little encouragement to digress at length on all matters connected with the Orthodox Church.

'There's always the question about the Annunciation, did it happen?' he says. 'It's an important question. A shocking question. But I want to start at the other end, what does it mean? What's its significance? It's a scandal for God to become involved in the world, for God to be human. Even if the events were not precisely as Luke recorded, there was a moment when the divine and human came together and worked together to give substance to that divine-human person. A secret moment. A synergy. A co-operation. A free will, when divinity and humanity came together. For all we know, things like that may have been requested before. Someone may have said, "No Lord, I don't want to do that." Many pious people I know say they would have answered, "I'm not worthy Lord. I'm not prepared to do that." So the free will element is absolutely vital.

'Although God is God,' he continues, 'he's not omnipotent. We have a choice to say yes or no. God asks and we respond by giving ourselves or not. Mary represents the whole of humanity here. She is one of us. If she can say yes, it means we can also say yes.

'The Annunciation of the Theotokos, the Mother of God, is more important theologically than Christmas, and the word "Incarnation" used by the early Fathers was focused on the Annunciation rather than on the Nativity. It was celebrated before Christmas. It's a more ancient feast. The celebration is a little bit subdued today because it falls in Lent but there's a trade-off. In the Eastern Orthodox tradition, it's given a pre-eminence almost as high as Easter.

'In the entire life of Christ, there's one date that we can be precise on – his death and the beginning of his resurrection, which is 25 March. The early Christian Fathers then made connections. The spring equinox and various other things. The early Fathers thought it was also the first day of creation. So on this day, the world is re-created. We know that it's the date Christ died before emerging from the tomb. The early Fathers made the connection between the womb and the tomb. They saw it as the same date, 25 March, that Christ entered the darkness of the womb of Mary and then dead, entered the tomb before coming out. He gave his life by uniting with Mary in her womb and then brought life again after he left the tomb.'

I say the standard interpretation is that the Annunciation was fixed on 25 March because it is precisely nine months before Christmas Day, which had already been allocated as 25 December. Does he see it the other way around?

'Yes, that's right,' he responds. 'We find the connection between the tomb and the womb earlier than we see the connection with the birth of the sun in the pagan context and with Christmas being fixed on 25 December.'

Yet today, Christmas is celebrated much more than the Annunciation, I observe.

'It is and it isn't,' he says before correcting himself, 'no, you're right. For many centuries, in both East and West, when you were asked what is the greatest feast, people would say Easter and then the Annunciation. That only changed in Victorian times with Christmas.'

He shows me the *Apolytikia* for the Great Feasts and opens it on the page for 25 March, 'The Annunciation of the Mother of God'. It reads:

> Today is the crowning moment of our salvation, and the unfolding of the eternal mystery. The Son of God becomes the Son of the Virgin, and Gabriel brings good tidings of grace. Therefore, with him, let us also cry aloud to the Mother of God. Hail, full of grace! The Lord is with you. Awed by the beauty of your virginity and by the splendour of your purity, Gabriel cried aloud to you, Mother of God. How can I praise you as I should? By what means shall I invoke you? I am troubled and amazed. Therefore, as I was commanded, I cry to you, Hail, full of grace!

We place the Lemoyne painting next to an icon of the Annunciation known as the *Icon of the Holy Mother of the Annunciation of Ohrid*.

'It's an icon of the evangelisation of Mary, made near Skopje' Andreas explains. 'It expresses the theme of the Annunciation: Mary as Theotokos. For the Orthodox Church, an icon is like the word of God. We don't change it unless there's a real need for a fresh expression. The bright colours here emphasize the joy of the event. Gabriel is on the left with his feet apart and one of his wings is raised and the other is down, showing he's just arrived. He's been running to share the great news. In his left hand is a staff, the symbol of a messenger, and his right hand points to Mary. She is on the right holding a spindle of scarlet yarn, referencing the apocryphal story of her weaving the veil of the Temple. Her right hand is raised, accepting Gabriel's request, and her head is lowered, also symbolizing her agreement. Mary is on an elevated throne. She's clothed in deep red and the three stars on her garment symbolize her

32. Icon of the Annunciation, fourteenth century, Ohrid, Macedonia

being a virgin before the conception, then at this very moment, and then, after the birth of Christ, throughout her life. This is a courtship between divine and human that results in Jesus Christ, wholly divine and wholly human.'

He describes how the icon speaks to us in a theologically correct way and conveys deep meaning about the spiritual realities that are beyond our comprehension. Importantly, he emphasizes, icons are not religious pictures but 'windows into eternity'. An icon is not naturalistic but reveals, in line and colour, the nature of the spiritual world. Icons are also sacramental, canonical and liturgical art forms of ancient origin whereby the figures are stylized and dematerialized as they live above and beyond this world in the eternity of heaven.

Andreas asks me to direct all my attention on the icon and to try and resist any distraction. Purity, he says, must include a singleness of attention. We look at the Lemoyne painting side by side with the icon.

'The basic grammar is the same,' he says. 'The angel, Mary, the spiritual light. There's no disagreement, just a slight difference of emphasis. I can accept this Lemoyne painting as a theological statement but it's not conducive to me either personally or liturgically, although it can facilitate my reflection and prayers in the here and now about what the Annunciation means.'

Does he like it? I wonder.

'Could I have it in my house?' he responds. 'Yes, I could but not to be identified as an icon but only as a religious painting. I wouldn't be comfortable to see it in my church.'

We move on. How important is it to him that Mary was a virgin at the time of Jesus's conception?

'Yes, it's important in Orthodoxy that she is a virgin,' he replies, 'but it's not something we need to prove in order to make a theological point. If it was shown somehow that this wasn't the case, it is not going to destroy anything in the way we accept and understand Jesus Christ. But we believe it happened and we still believe it today, even with a more critical eye, not just in blind faith. Yes, rather than a blind faith, I'd prefer to call it a deep spiritual presence. One way to understand it is to say Mary gave herself to such an intimate contact with God that she could not then enter into a similar relationship with a man. It's a very erotic, intimate relationship with God.'

Why does the Orthodox Church also support the notion of Mary's perpetual virginity?

'There's nothing that could be destroyed in Christian theology if we assume that after the virgin conception of Jesus, Mary had a full human life and other children,' he says. 'It could have happened but we believe it didn't happen. The full life of Mary was immersed in the Holy Spirit. The brothers and sisters could have been Joseph's children through a previous marriage, when he was then a widower. I believe what we see through the path of the Holy Spirit is that even if she had given birth to other children, she would have remained a virgin. Yes, I do think she would have remained a virgin and the Holy Spirit would have preserved her virginity. But I believe she had no sexual contact throughout her life.'

So, I suggest, when Mary says, 'Let it be done,' she's not just saying yes to Jesus but she's also saying yes to remaining a virgin for the rest of her life?

'Yes, very much so,' he replies. 'She had a deep mystical relationship with God. She surrendered her own natural needs.'

'Some would say that's an unnatural suppression,' I say.

'She's entering into a wedding with God,' he says.

'But there's no scriptural evidence to back up a doctrine of her perpetual virginity, is there? There's no certainty on that.'

'Well, it brings us back to the historicity. Did it happen?' he replies. 'It's much easier to accept the Cross and the Resurrection if we accept that. It's about a trust. A commitment. A belief. A paradox.'

What would he say to his students? I ask, if they said, 'I don't believe the annunciation happened. It's all a metaphor.'

'I would say we have a different understanding of what symbolism is. I appreciate there's a wide range of beliefs in the Anglican Church. The most difficult thing to accept in this story is not whether an angel came down with wings and spoke to a young girl from Nazareth in an angelic apparition. I'd say that's just detail. Very few people would have a problem with that. The main issue is the central event itself in any dispute about the historicity. Is it possible there was union between the Holy Spirit and this young girl from Nazareth? Is it easier to accept that it was a natural birth and that the baby later became enlightened? The early Christian tradition debated all that intensely. We have no historical evidence or source but that's not important. This is the moment.'

Does he think the feast of the Annunciation should have a higher status in the Western Church?

'Yes definitely, because, as I say, this is the moment. It is the active moment when God and humanity come together.'

I observe how there is a certainty here in his responses that reminds me of Roman Catholic teaching.

'I think that's absolutely right,' he replies. 'There's very little difference between Orthodox and Roman Catholics about the Annunciation. Just some small emphases. For me, what defines the Christian tradition is that in Jesus Christ, we recognize the only union between God and creation, which allows us to share in the life of God. It won't go very far if we start to dilute that and say, "No, it's only a metaphor".'

CHAPTER 10

QUESTIONS THAT PIERCE THROUGH THE COURSE OF EXISTENCE

I am ensconced in my study with my Bible, which has been a daily companion for more than twenty years. The cover of the spine fell off some time ago and many of its thin pages are marked and worn through constant use. The red ribbon page marker has been in the same place for weeks – at the story of the Annunciation. I read the same passage – the Gospel according to Luke, chapter one, verses 26-38 – over and over again. The story is only 248 words long and takes just over a minute to read.

Most biblical scholars believe that Luke's Gospel was written sometime around AD 80–85, but the precise date is unclear. It is thought to be a second or third generation account of the life of Jesus but the original sources that helped to shape its content remain uncertain. In the early second century, authorship was ascribed to a person named Luke, who is described variously as a physician, a painter and a travelling companion of St Paul. In addition, he is often said to be a master storyteller, a historian who recounts Jesus's life in a logical, biographical and factual manner. Dante memorably described him as 'a scribe of the kindness of Christ'.

An apocryphal story claims that Luke made an icon of the Virgin Mary while she posed for him, thereby suggesting he knew her personally, but there is no hard evidence to support this. Moreover, tradition in the eleventh century claimed the Hodegetria icon at the Hodegon monastery in Constantinople was a Lucan painting of Mary but it was lost or destroyed in the fifteenth century.

Luke's Gospel is one of the four canonical Gospels decreed by the early Christian Church to be imbued with 'truth'. Its authentic status means that Luke's work, alongside those of Matthew, Mark and John, is central to Christian belief, can be read out in all churches and is decreed by the Christian faith to be not only authoritative but a work inspired by God.

It is thought to have been written about fifteen years after Mark's Gospel and probably soon after Matthew completed his own account. The earliest reference in the New Testament to Jesus's conception was made briefly by Paul in his Letter to the Galatians around thirty years earlier: 'But when the fullness of time had come, God sent forth his son, born of a woman.' It is thought that Paul's letter was written around AD 57, just twenty years after Jesus's death, but, interestingly, he makes no mention of a virgin conception. The primary source material for Luke's Gospel as a whole is understood to be Mark's earlier work, as well as another written source often called 'Q' or Quelle, the German word for 'source'. This is a collection of Jesus's sayings, together with other oral accounts that may have been handed down by eye witnesses, possibly Jesus's disciples, during the five decades or so after his death.

Luke's annunciation story forms part of what is called his 'Infancy Narrative' in which he recounts Jesus's birth and early life. It is placed at the start of his Gospel but many scholars think it was actually written later, after the bulk of his work was completed, and was inserted afterwards in order to explain to his audience how Jesus, as Son of God, came into the world. By doing so, the reader could understand right from the start of Luke's narrative how Jesus was truly God and truly human from the beginning of his life and how his birth was the result of a divine conception involving the Holy Spirit and the Virgin Mary.

Throughout his Gospel, Luke is at pains to emphasize that the Incarnation and the Resurrection are the critical foundations of faith: from the womb to the tomb. Luke's work spreads the message that God entered human history, thereby opening the way for forgiveness, and rescued humanity from sin through Jesus's actions of redemption. The Annunciation is the pivotal start of that message.

At the heart of Luke's account of the Annunciation are three great interwoven paradoxes: a virgin becoming a mother; a human being becoming the mother of God; and a natural birth despite a conception that did not involve a human father.

Although none of the details in his account of the Annunciation are verifiable by hard evidence, Luke is keen to make the reader aware that he has given an accurate account of Jesus's life. Indeed, at the very beginning, he takes the time to mention his careful research. He claims that he has 'investigated everything accurately from the start'; that he has drawn up 'an orderly account of the events that have been fulfilled among us, just as they were handed on to us by those who, from the beginning, were eye witnesses and servants of the word.' He is keen for the reader to know, 'the truth concerning the things about which you have been instructed.'

It is believed that Luke was a Gentile who was familiar with the Hebrew Scriptures. He wrote his account in grammatically perfect Greek, using minimal description and offering only the barest of detail. For instance, at the moment of the Annunciation, Mary's physical appearance, her age and her home environment are all left to the imagination of the reader.

Luke addresses his Gospel to 'Theophilus' meaning 'lover of God'. It is possible that this may be a reference to a literary patron who tasked him to write an account of the life of Jesus or perhaps it is more likely to relate to Luke's target audience – those eager to know about Jesus, his life and work. These people are thought to have been Greek-speaking Gentile Christians but, importantly, the content is positioned in such a way that it could be read and understood by both Jews and Gentiles. Whatever, Theophilus seeks to know 'the truth concerning the things about which you have been instructed.'

For centuries, biblical scholars have studied the original Greek words used in Luke's account and debated their precise meaning. When the angel greets Mary, for example, he calls her, 'kecharitōmenē'. This could mean either fully graced or highly favoured. The word, 'dietarachthē' is used to describe Mary's reaction to Gabriel's voice. This can be translated as greatly troubled, much perplexed or disturbed. Although the angel appears to announce to Mary that she will conceive a son and commands her to name him Jesus – 'kaleseis to onoma autou Iēsoun' – most biblical scholars are at pains to emphasize that it is a commission story inviting Mary to become the Mother of God. The Incarnation, they say, depends on Mary's assent, a deliberate, affirmative answer, freely given. The humility of Mary is demonstrated in her response – 'hē doulē kyriou' – but does the word doulē best translate as I am the 'servant' or I am the 'handmaid' of the Lord? Indeed, some radical feminist theologians have claimed that a more accurate translation of the original Greek word would be 'slave'. Such apparently subtle differences in translation can make a significant impact on the overall interpretation of the story.

Although Luke uses formal Greek word construction in his Gospel, the content shows that he is fully aware of the Hebraic books of the Jewish faith as it is full of Old Testament references, both direct and implied. It becomes clear from Luke's text how much of the story of Jesus's birth, life and resurrection were pre-figured in the Hebrew Scriptures, emphasizing a notion of prophecy and fulfilment.

For example, Luke highlights that Mary's son will receive the throne of his ancestor, David, thereby revealing himself as the awaited Messiah from David's royal line. This fulfils God's earlier promise to David that his family would have an everlasting dynasty as prophesied by Nathan. Also in the annunciation passage, Luke writes that Jesus will reign over the house of Jacob, thereby leading the tribes of Israel and of all nations forever.

Crucially, as part of a potential prefiguration, it is claimed that Luke's annunciation account recalls the prophecy made in Isaiah 7:14 of a promise made to King Ahaz that a son, Emmanuel, meaning 'God with us', will be born to a maiden as a sign:

> The Lord himself, therefore,
> will give you a sign.
> It is this: the maiden is with child
> and will soon give birth to a son
> whom she will call Emmanuel.

Interestingly, the Hebrew word used in Isaiah's original Old Testament passage is *'almāh* – young girl or maiden – and not *b'tulāh*, the Hebrew word for virgin. But the word found in the Greek translation of Isaiah and used later by Luke in his New Testament account of the Annunciation to describe Mary's status is *parthenos*, which means 'virgin'.

Although some theologians highlight how this Isaian text prefigures the Annunciation – 'a maiden with child will soon give birth to a son' – the time lapse between King Ahaz's reign and the birth of Jesus was more than seven hundred years and, therefore, many other biblical scholars cast doubt on any serious historical connection.

Another link between the Old and New Testaments (the Hebrew Scriptures and the Christian Scriptures) is the appearance of the angel Gabriel, whose name means 'strength of God'. The Old Testament Book of Daniel recounts how the angel Gabriel appears as one of God's messengers to the prophet Daniel to help him interpret his visions (Daniel 8:15-26). Then, directly before his New Testament account of the Annunciation, Luke describes how the angel Gabriel visits Zechariah to inform him that his elderly, barren wife Elizabeth is to give birth to a son. That encounter heralds the coming of John the Baptist who, at both the start and the end of Luke's annunciation passage, is described as having been in Elizabeth's womb for six months: 'In the sixth month…' and, later, 'And she whom people call barren is now in her sixth month.'

Luke links the conceptions of John the Baptist and Jesus by placing them close together in the opening part of his narrative. Both events are extraordinary but there is a crucial difference. Elizabeth's experience references other barren women in the Old Testament who, miraculously, found themselves able to conceive naturally in old age. For example, Sarah unexpectedly was able to conceive a son Isaac with her husband Abraham after she had gone through the menopause, and Hannah suddenly became pregnant late in life with a son, Samuel, through her husband, Elkanah.

However, by contrast, Mary's experience is unique. There is no natural father and life enters Mary's body without sexual intercourse taking place. Instead, it is the work of the Holy Spirit 'overshadowing' the Virgin Mary that leads to her pregnancy and the birth of Jesus. The overshadowing power of the Holy Spirit at the Annunciation echoes previous mentions in the Hebrew Scriptures of God's presence covering the Ark and the Tabernacle (Exodus 25:20 and 40:35). The story is so extraordinary that the reader is left in no doubt that Jesus will be much more than a prophet; that Mary's virginal, supernatural conception, a one-off event that has never happened before or since, is the unique moment when she becomes the mother of the Son of God.

At the time of Gabriel's announcement, Mary was betrothed to Joseph. The betrothal would have lasted a year, during which time the couple were legally married but not yet living together. By Jewish tradition, Mary, probably, would have been twelve to thirteen years old, just starting to menstruate, still a virgin and living with her parents at home. Most Christian art mistakenly depicts her to be much older at the time of the Annunciation, often showing her to be a woman in her early twenties and, therefore, a fully-grown adult. However, the likelihood that she was an adolescent makes both the angel's message and her acceptance of it even more startling. It is unclear from Luke's story whether the conception happens immediately following the verbal exchange but most biblical scholars believe that is what Luke intends to convey.

The author provides no detailed visual descriptions within his text: where, precisely, the angel appears; what the angel looks like; how Mary is dressed; at what hour it happens; what Mary is doing at the moment he arrives. Luke only writes that Mary lives in Nazareth – a small, obscure Galilean village located on the northern edge of the Plain of Esdraelon, twenty miles from Tiberius and fifteen miles west of the southern bank of the Sea of Galilee. A nondescript, unknown village of no religious significance, the location of Nazareth for the angelic encounter highlights the ordinariness of Mary and her background.

Luke's encounter between the angel Gabriel and Mary has a narrative structure that takes the form of a series of stages: an introduction; the angel's arrival and greeting; Mary's pondering; the angel's response of reassurance; Mary's questioning; the commission of her conception; Mary's response and acceptance – her 'fiat'; and, finally, the angel's departure.

In the fifteenth century, Fra Roberto Caracciolo described the Annunciation as taking the form of an angelic mission, an angelic salutation and an angelic colloquy. Within the colloquy, the conversational exchange between the angel Gabriel and Mary, he observed that there are five stages: the *Conturbatio* (Mary's disquiet at Gabriel's arrival); the *Cogitatio* (her reflection); the *Interrogatio* (her inquiry or questioning); the *Humiliatio* (her submission or acceptance); and the *Meritatio* (her merit and meditation on what has happened). These stages are the component parts of Mary becoming the 'Virgin Annunciate'. A more recent commentary describes the sequences as, 'Comfort – do not be afraid'; 'Assurance – you have found favour'; 'Annunciation – you are to conceive'; 'Questioning – how can this be?'; and 'Agreement – let it be done.'

British art historian Michael Baxendall, has explained how these different stages are reflected in artistic depictions of the Annunciation through the various expressions of Mary. For example, he highlights how the positioning of Mary's hands is key to demonstrating the different stages of the encounter. Her raised hand shows her disquiet; a hand on her heart indicates her reflectiveness; both hands extending upwards demonstrates her sense of inquiry; and her hands crossed in front of her heart symbolize her submission.

Interestingly, in Lemoyne's picture, the artist seems to combine two different stages within the one scene. The painting appears to depict the angel Gabriel at the opening stage of the story, at the time of the Salutation, his first greeting to Mary. But at the same time, it shows Mary at a later stage – at her fiat – when she says, 'Let it be done to me.'

The annunciation encounter between the angel Gabriel and Mary is found in Luke's Gospel alone. However, the opening chapter of Matthew's Gospel (1:18-25), believed to have been written a little earlier than Luke's, recounts a meeting between an unnamed angel and Joseph:

> This is how Jesus Christ came to be born. His mother Mary was betrothed to Joseph; but before they came to live together she was found to be with child through the Holy Spirit. Her husband Joseph, being a man of honour and wanting to spare her publicity, decided to divorce her informally. He had made up his mind to do this when the angel of the Lord appeared to him in a dream and said, 'Joseph, son of David, do not be afraid to take Mary home as your wife, because she has conceived what is in her by the Holy Spirit. She will give birth to a son and you must name him Jesus, because he is the one who is to save his people from their sins.' Now all this took place to fulfil the words spoken by the Lord through the prophet:
>
>> The Virgin will conceive and give birth to a son
>> and they will call him Emmanuel,
>> a name which means 'God-is-with-us'.
>
> When Joseph woke up he did what the angel of the Lord told him to do: he took his wife to his home and, though he had not had intercourse with her, she gave birth to a son; and he named him Jesus.

According to Matthew's account, Joseph realized he could not be the natural father of Mary's child as they were not yet living together and had not consummated their marriage. He was not present when Mary was told her news. Joseph would have suspected gross infidelity on her part and would have recognized she could be stoned to death for her behaviour. Indeed, as the prospective husband, he could have been called upon to throw the first stone. However, as written in Matthew's story, he had decided to divorce her quietly to spare her the adverse publicity. Mary would likely have had to be confined to her parents' home, vilified and shunned by the rest of the village. According to Matthew, the appearance of the angel in the dream changed everything for Joseph, and the carpenter accepted the angel's instruction in a huge leap of trust. In Matthew's story, which in effect is the telling of another annunciation encounter, Joseph is the central character. Mary is in the background without a voice. In contrast, Joseph is the missing person in Luke's account. Luke makes no reference to the dream of Joseph, which may suggest that he was unaware of Matthew's version at the time he wrote his own work.

There are other differences between the two gospel accounts. Matthew's indicates that Joseph and Mary lived in Bethlehem, the place where King David was born; after the birth they fled to Egypt for safety and then set up home in Nazareth. Luke, on the other hand, writes that they lived in Nazareth from the start of their relationship, headed to Bethlehem because Joseph had to register for the Roman census, and then returned to Nazareth.

Matthew makes a direct reference to the Old Testament prophecy of Isaiah in his text. But in using a later, Greek translation of the original Hebrew wording, Matthew states: 'the virgin will conceive and give birth to a son'. The original Hebrew text of Isaiah used עלמה or *'almāh*, meaning young maiden but the later Greek translation used by Matthew has παρθένος or *parthenos* meaning virgin. It is *parthenos* that is also used by Luke in his account of the Annunciation. Its use underpins the notion of Mary's virginal state when she conceives.

As well as recounting Joseph's dream, Matthew explains in a detailed genealogy at the start of his Gospel that, through the paternal lineage of Joseph, Jesus is directly linked to

King David and beyond to Abraham, the father of Judaism. And yet, in the next passage, Matthew then tells us that before Joseph and Mary came to live together, 'she was found to be with child through the Holy Spirit' and that Joseph is not Jesus's natural father.

Luke does not mention a genealogy until much later, after the annunciation passage and the birth of Jesus, when he places it between his baptism and the start of his ministry. He traces Jesus back to Adam and to God. Lineage and the family tree of Jesus play a key part in both Luke and Matthew's Gospels. As the theologian, Jane Williams, explains in her book *Faces of Christ*:

> The Gospels are very precise in saying that Jesus is born at a particular place and time, when a unique confluence of circumstances and people make his existence possible, and that it is this set of influences that make Jesus who he is.
>
> Luke's Gospel traces Jesus' ancestry all the way back to Adam, the first human being made by God. Through Adam's line, all human beings come into existence, but they also come into an existence that is flawed, because it no longer knows its connection to God. Luke is telling us that it is this real humanity that Jesus has in common with us. He is born into this inheritance, as we all are. The story that will unfold in the life and death of Jesus is a story about all of us. It will leave none of us unchanged.
>
> Matthew's Gospel does not go back through Jesus' genealogy quite as far back as Luke does, but Matthew adds another dimension. He traces Jesus' family tree back to Abraham, the great founding father of the Jewish people. God calls Abraham to be the source of a new nation of people who will live by God's Law and so show the rest of the world the character of the God whom they have begun to forget because of Adam's sinfulness. Matthew is reminding his readers that Jesus is born into the people whom God is using to fulfil his purposes for the world. That is part of Jesus' inheritance, and part of what shapes him.

The late American theologian and Roman Catholic priest, Raymond E. Brown explains how the Infancy Narratives of both Luke and Matthew contain the basic revelation of the first identity of Jesus and act as a transition from the Jewish Scriptures to the story of Jesus's ministry:

> The liturgical preparation relives in a microcosmic way the long historical preparation for the coming of Christ in the history of Israel (seen through the eyes of the Christian faith)...The Messiah did not come without the preparatory period of Israel's history or without the preparatory responses of fidelity by Joseph and Mary.

Neither Mark's nor John's Gospel makes any reference to the angelic encounter between Gabriel and Mary. Indeed, Mark makes no mention at all about Jesus's conception and birth. His first mention of Jesus is as an adult at his baptism. However, John, in his later Gospel at the start of chapter one, famously writes of Jesus's pre-existence as God:

> In the beginning was the Word:
> the Word was with God
> and the Word was God...

> The Word was made flesh,
> he lived among us,
> and we saw his glory,
> the glory that is his as the only Son of the Father,
> full of grace and truth.

So, after all this research, I am left asking the question: did the Annunciation actually happen? If so, did it happen in the way that Luke describes? It seems there is no definitive answer so I wonder if I am on a misguided search for hard evidence, rooted in a rationalist approach that abandons both the Church's authority and teaching, and lacks any theological imagination. Rather than a search for historicity, should I be focusing more on identifying the theological meaning of the story? I recall the American writer and historian, Garry Wills, stating in his book, *What the Gospels Meant*: 'the virginal conception of Jesus is not a gynecological or obstetric teaching, but a theological one.'

I decide to broaden my enquiry outside the contents of the Holy Bible and the four canonical Gospels. I turn next to the Protoevangelium of James, an apocryphal gospel, written around AD 145, approximately sixty years after Luke. Early Church leaders rejected the work, believing it lacked sufficient authority and authenticity, so it has never been given the same status as the canonical Gospels. However, its content became hugely popular with early Christians who had an insatiable hunger for information about the early life of Jesus and the back-story of Mary.

In his apocryphal infancy gospel, James describes the story of Mary's early life and makes the assertion that she was perpetually virginal. He recounts first how Mary's mother Anna, an elderly barren woman, and her wealthy husband, Joachim, yearn to become parents but remain childless. While the grieving Joachim leaves home to spend forty days in the desert, Anna prays to God that in the same way he had blessed the barren Sarah's womb and enabled her to have a son, he would do the same for her.

Later, an angel visits Anna to tell her that they are to have a child: 'The Lord has heard your prayer and you shall conceive, and shall bring forth,' the angel says, 'and your seed shall be spoken of in all the world.' The thrilled Anna and Joachim meet at the Golden Gate in Jerusalem and embrace. She proclaims: 'Now I know the Lord God has blessed me exceedingly for behold, the widow is no longer a widow and I, the childless, will conceive.' Nine months later, Mary is born in Jerusalem.

Anna makes a sanctuary in Mary's room and allows nothing common or unclean to pass through her on account of the special holiness of her daughter. James then describes how at three years of age, Mary is presented in the Temple in Jerusalem and Mary's parents, along with the Temple priests, decide she will be offered to God as a consecrated virgin for the rest of her life and enter a chaste marriage. According to James, her betrothal to Joseph happens when she is twelve. It is through the direction of an angel that Joseph, an elderly widower with children of his own, is selected by lot to be her husband and 'to look after the virgin of the Lord'.

James recounts how Mary is specially chosen to spin scarlet and purple thread for the veil in the Temple. Later, he writes how Mary first hears the voice of an angel when she goes to a well to draw water near her home. The angel appears a second time in her home and it is there that he announces to Mary that she is to conceive a child through the Holy Spirit – as was recounted similarly by Luke in his own earlier Gospel.

Although James's legendary account has never gained authoritative status in the Church, it has influenced depictions of the Annunciation in religious art and religious teaching. In the early fifth century, Augustine of Hippo described Mary's mother Anna as, 'the flower of the field from whom bloomed the precious lily of the valley. Through her birth the nature inherited from our first parents is changed.' At the turn of the seventh century, the celebrated Syrian monk and priest, John of Damascus, wrote of Anna and Joachim: 'O blessed couple. All creation is in your debt. For through you is presented the noblest gifts to the creator, namely a spotless mother who alone was worthy for the creator.'

After studying these religious texts, together with a rich variety of bible commentaries, I yearn to leave my study and to engage with experts – leading theologians, biblical scholars and historians – and to hear each of them offer their perspective specifically on Luke's account of the Annunciation. There are so many questions I want to ask

What is the spiritual meaning of the story? What is its key message? Is it, as Bishop Egan described in his annunciation homily, 'the most important event in human history'? Did it really happen or is it a mystery rooted in metaphor? Was Mary a virgin at the time of Jesus's conception? Was she perpetually virgin throughout her life? Of course, only Mary knows the answers to these latter questions. There were no other witnesses at the Annunciation.

I like the way Professor Elizabeth Stuart described the challenge in a recent sermon in Winchester Cathedral. A former Professor of Christian Theology and Director of the Centre for the Study of Theology and Religion at the University of Winchester, she said:

> Questions are at the heart of the Christian faith because those of us who are Christian are plunged into a mystery as deep as an empty tomb. Such mysteries invite questions from us and pose questions to us. To question is emphatically not to show a lack of faith, rather it demonstrates a willingness to dive deeper into faith. Questions lure us deeper into the mystery without allowing us to think that we can ever capture and own it, nor ever reach its end.

In addition, she talked of Jesus as a great asker of questions. Apparently across the four Gospels, Jesus is recorded as asking 307 questions. He was a questioner, she said, because he was a question. 'Indeed, he is *the* question. His very being poses questions that pierce through the core of existence, and blow through the gossamer of our human constructions and send us sliding into the mystery of the heart of God.'

Dietrich Bonhoeffer, the German theologian who was jailed in 1943 for his anti-Nazi sentiments, wrote from his prison cell how, 'all Christian theology has its origin in the wonder of all wonders: that God became human.' Without the conception and birth of Jesus, Bonhoeffer argued in a daily reflection entitled, *The Mysteries of God*:

> 'there is no theology. "God is revealed in the flesh," the God-human Jesus Christ – that is the holy mystery that theology came into being to protect and preserve. How we fail to understand when we think that the task of theology is to solve the mystery of God, to drag it down to the flat, ordinary wisdom of human experience and reason! Its sole office is to preserve the miracle as miracle, to comprehend, defend and glorify God's mystery precisely as mystery.'

The American theologian, Raymond E. Brown commented in his 1973 book, *The Virginal Conception and Bodily Resurrection of Jesus*: 'From AD 200 to 1800, the virginal conception was attacked almost exclusively by those who denied Christianity in general or the divinity of Christ in particular. For the mass of Christians, it was an unexplained doctrine taken for granted.'

My journey is about to recommence.

CHAPTER 11

THE HINGE

Dr Paula Gooder is a widely respected writer and lecturer in biblical studies. Educated at Oxford University, today she occupies the position of Theologian in Residence for the Bible Society. When we meet, she is working on a book exploring the birth of Jesus (published in 2015 entitled *Journey to the Manger*). We begin by talking about Luke's Gospel as a whole before focusing specifically on the annunciation passage.

'It's clear Luke has a text in front of him, a story of Jesus – a lot of scholars would say it's Mark's Gospel or the hypothetical gospel called Q – and he's then got his own unique sources especially, for example, for his birth narrative,' she tells me. 'It's classic Luke in the way it's written. He likes order. He very carefully puts things next to each other. He describes something that happens, then they speak.'

She is a bubbly conversationalist, and talks in an easy, accessible manner. She tells me she is troubled by Luke's rendition of Mary's encounter with the angel Gabriel.

'I really struggle with the annunciation story because of how it's been used. The way it portrays Mary as absolutely obedient, gentle and mild without any particular character behind her. So often, Mary is portrayed in the Annunciation as an obedient, good girl and nothing more than that. Reflecting on Mary more recently, I think she is a remarkable, feisty, vibrant and interesting woman.' Her comment makes me recall the description of Mary's response to the angel Gabriel's message in my First Holy Communion book: 'I am God's little servant and I am glad to do what He asks me.'

'The Lemoyne painting epitomizes what I really dislike about the way the annunciation story is traditionally portrayed,' she continues. 'It shows her passive, meek, not engaging – just doing what she's told. I don't like it at all. Where do I start? Her eyes are downcast. Gabriel is androgynous but domineering. I deeply object to the cherubs too. The finger is striking, suggesting the only thing that Mary can do is to be subservient. Mary has no choice. It characterizes the tradition I don't like. It's saccharine and non-effective.'

She focuses on Mary's character and behaviour.

'Mary has been held up as what a woman's meant to be like – obedient. When things are announced to us, we are supposed to say yes with no engagement. To be the gentle woman. But since I've been engaged in a lot of ecumenical work, I've had to engage more with Mary and, for me, she's now become the epitome of what a disciple should be. She comprehends and then responds.'

Does she see the story as factual, metaphorical or something else? She pauses before responding.

'That's interesting. I like not to ask the question about history because it's got us in such a lot of mess over the years. If you pressed me, I do think it's fact but just asking the historical question sends you off in the wrong direction.'

I wonder what she thinks is the key message of the story.

'I think it's about the joy that comes when you're able to accept the gift that God wants to give you, however unexpected that is,' she responds.

How important is it that Mary could have said no?

'That's one interpretation,' she says. 'Some would say that's not what the text says. Is it a genuine question or a rhetorical question – it's not clear. Personally, I think it's a statement of what's going to happen rather than a question from Gabriel. What would have happened if she'd said no? I think God would have asked again and to someone else.'

Does she see it as 'the most important event in human history'?

'I would say it is part of a chain. Personally, I'd say the Resurrection at the other end of the chain is more important.'

She tells me how Mary has become increasingly important to her since she discovered that she is quite a mysterious character. She describes her as 'not passive but actually a remarkable leader'. In that context, can Mary be a bridge in inter-denominational dialogue?

'I do think she's still a big barrier,' she replies. 'It's still a real problem. That's why, originally, I reacted in the way I did to her. I was brought up in a Protestant, evangelical, Anglican environment so it was an instinctive reaction to ignore her. The way in which devotion to her developed in the Roman Catholic Church – the shrines to Mary – it's hard to get that extreme out of your mind when you think of Mary; it just presses that Protestant button – even today it does. Interestingly, though, feminist Roman Catholic scholars are very opposed to Mary but Protestant feminist scholars are much more welcoming. That's interesting, eh? It's because within Roman Catholicism, Mary is often used to put women in their place. In Protestant circles, she isn't positioned like that.'

It sounds as though she thinks the way Mary is depicted in the annunciation story has caused lasting damage.

'Personally, I think it's done enormous damage and, particularly, it's difficult for those of us who are, ourselves, mothers,' she says. 'Mary is held up as the ideal but it's an ideal none of us can achieve – to be a virgin mother. To be an acceptable woman in the Church you have to be a virgin mother. Either you manage the virgin bit or the mother bit but not both. So what is held up is impossible to attain. The text stresses it because of the importance of being able to explain that Jesus is divine – that's why it's there in the text. It's making a theological point. But what tradition has done is expanded that position so that virginity becomes an ideal.'

As we draw to a close, I ask if she believes in the Virgin Birth.

'I believe in the virginal conception, not in the virginal birth,' she explains, 'the difference being that she conceived as a virgin but the doctrine of the Virgin Birth is that she remained a virgin after the birth and I don't go with that. The biblical references to brothers and sisters, I think, are genuine.'

I follow Diarmaid MacCulloch as he pedals along Oxford's Woodstock Road at slow speed. Today, he has replaced his signature Panama hat with a cycle helmet. Making his way from lunch at St Cross College to his office half a mile away, he looks the archetypal Oxford don. Professor of the History of the Church at the University of Oxford and one of the world's leading Christian historians, Diarmaid's book *A History of Christianity*, published in 2009, sparked an acclaimed six-part television series on BBC Television. When we meet, he is working on a new series, this time examining the historical link between sex and the Church. Before meeting him, I had read how he describes the Gospels as 'down market biography' so that is how we open our conversation, focusing, in particular, on Luke's account of the Annunciation.

'It's generally thought of as a bit posher than the other Gospels,' he says. 'The beginning material is interesting because it doesn't seem to have much connection with the rest of the Gospel. It's patently unhistorical except perhaps the vague date of the birth of Jesus before Herod's death. Otherwise, it's not history. It's a theological meditation in story form and a lot of its stories are ridiculous – for example, the idea of there being a census. But it's trying to do a job of explaining the puzzle of a human who is in some sense a God. You have to think of ways of making that sound sensible in first-century terms.'

He peers at me over the top of his spectacles before offering a gentle smile.

'The Annunciation is one of those bits of it which, after all, couldn't be historical,' he continues. 'Early Christians were desperate for stuff about Jesus's life and they hadn't got much. The Gospels are descriptions of three years or one and nothing else apart from the odd anecdote. And once Mary gets off the ground in the second century, they're desperate for anything about her too.'

When I ask if he regards Luke's account of the Annunciation as metaphorical he responds decisively.

'It can't be anything else because of its context. It's a set of events that are manifestly fairy tales. It's the sort of event you expect in a fairy tale but it's trying to square a circle and describe the impossible – that a human being can bear God. It's not a bad story to do it. The trouble about conception and birth is that they are pretty indecorous. They touch the physicality of the Incarnation in a way the Church has never been happy to do.'

So, is he suggesting that the opening to Luke's Gospel is primarily a device to explain how Jesus arrived on earth, recount how he carried out his ministry, and describe how he was crucified and rose again?

'That's exactly it,' he says. 'It's intellectually dishonest to treat it as history and those who try, eminent though they may be, are indulging in woolly thinking.'

I ask for clarification. Am I right to think that he sees the Annunciation as a pure metaphor?

'I do,' he replies, 'and, of course, you judiciously use "pure" as the adjective rather than "mere" because metaphor is often more real than fact. It does jobs that facts cannot reach. The great thing that Christianity has that gives it an edge is the audacious statement that reality can be divinized. That the everyday can be charged with the grandeur of God. That's what the Annunciation does. It makes the Incarnation work metaphorically when opposites – divinity and humanity – shouldn't work together, can't be together. The Annunciation is the hinge on which they work.'

He stares at me intently, seeking affirmation, then continues.

'If you can't have a physical conception, the Annunciation is rather neat. It provides a means of contact between God and Mary without it being messily physical. It's through the ear that she hears the message – that nicely sidesteps a lot of the indecorous questions that might arise as to what happened. If it's going to enter any orifice, the ear is the most decorous of them all. It links up with us being cognitive and relational beings. Our discourse is one of the things that makes us human. For speech to be the agent is pretty neat and solves a lot of the problems.'

He urges me to seek out a rare, fourteenth-century font in Suffolk that displays the Annunciation scene.

'It's a sculptured stone panel on a medieval font in St Matthew's church in the centre of Ipswich,' he explains. 'Given that she is depicted prior to the birth of Christ, she is not crowned, but the dove of the Spirit, flying from the end of a scroll held by Gabriel, is whispering his message in her right ear. The common medieval belief was that the conception of Jesus occurred through Mary's ear since this was how she had heard the news. Mm, yes, I like that one,' he smiles.

33. Stone carving of the Annunciation on the Font, St Matthew's Church, Ipswich. By kind permission of St Matthew's Church, Ipswich

I move on the conversation. What about the description of the Annunciation as 'the most important event in human history'?

'In mythological terms, if you are working within Christian terms of reference, then I think it is,' he replies. 'Myths are frequently more important than facts. It is fact that I had breakfast this morning but I think the plot of Hamlet is more important than my breakfast, though it never happened, because it tells us things about being human. The Annunciation is like Hamlet although Hamlet is lower grade than the Annunciation on the mythological scale, but both are the same sort of truths, which are totally different to historical truths.

'The problem with religion in the West, thanks to Protestantism, is we've got stuck with the idea there's one sort of truth – an historical one – and that the Bible is a text book of history. Well, it's not like that and it wasn't generally taken like that before the Reformation. So get off whether it's fact or metaphor and interrogate the message as part of myth. Of course, bishops are frightened of saying that, aren't they? Church leaders think the faithful will be cross but often they are liberated by such thought. If only they trusted the faithful with a bit more nous. They should man up. It infuriates me. They're afraid of the *Daily Mail* and what they don't seem to realize is that the faithful have deserted the Church because they can't believe any of the stuff. Because they've been given the wrong clues about it by the Church hierarchy. But that's the sort of leadership the Church now needs.'

In *A History of Christianity* Diarmaid MacCulloch writes about the existence of 'a tangle of preoccupations' about Mary's virginity. What does he mean by that?

'Not just Christianity but the general presumption in ancient religion and philosophy is that virginity is better than the married state,' he answers. 'Therefore, if you've got a super-heroine, she's got to be a virgin. When the monastic movement became really big in the third and fourth centuries, virginity was prioritized. It was already there with the Protoevangelium of St James. Even Mary's mother becomes a virgin. It's absolutely crazy and it's a syndrome the Church has not got over yet.'

As we draw to a close and together look at the print of Lemoyne's painting, he tells me it is not for him. 'A soppy looking angel, a simpering Mary. There's no danger in it, no awe or terror about it,' he sighs.

———

Gavin D'Costa arrives in Room 33 at the National Gallery, dressed casually in a yellow shirt and crumpled jeans. He walks over to the painting and stares at it intently for over five minutes, looking closely at the canvas through the glasses perched on the bridge of his nose. Then he breaks the silence by exclaiming about the 'wonderful light' coming from the top of the picture; how the broken plaster on the wall possibly emphasizes how Mary was rooted in her earthly home at the time and how the brickwork contrasts with the heavenly sky above. Bending down to focus for a while on Mary, he describes her as his 'heavenly mother' and says that he admires the tenderness that exudes from her.

'I feel a closeness in vocational calling when I look at it and realize that my life is identified with this figure,' he tells me. 'Every other day, there's a moment of call and a challenge when the angel of the Lord comes to me and calls me and I potentially say no. It's not quite as dramatic as in this image but it's a dramatic call to vocation. I feel the Annunciation is a constant Christian moment of demand – quite terrifying at times, quite tender at others. And there has to be a moment of decision.'

Gavin D'Costa was born in Nairobi, Kenya, fifty-six years ago and came to Britain in 1968. After gaining his doctorate at Cambridge University, he began a career in teaching and today is Professor of Catholic Theology at the University of Bristol. He takes a special interest in the theology of religions and has acted as an advisor to both the Roman Catholic Church and the Anglican Communion on inter-religious dialogue and theology.

He continues to stare at the image through his metal-rimmed spectacles. He walks back a few paces then moves closer to the canvas, his arms folded and his head bobbing from side to side.

Does he think the Annunciation really happened? I wonder.

'What is portrayed in the text actually addresses reality – what happened,' he responds. 'We'd have to talk about each particular detail. Do I really believe angel Gabriel came into a room? The text is clear, there was an interruption in ordinary life by something extraordinary. My feeling is we do see angels today but we don't recognize them. The angel is the mediation between God and the human and I meet angels wherever I see the beauty and act of God.'

I tell him some leading theologians, who are practising Christians, have told me that they believe the story is simply a metaphor.

'It's a legitimate type of view to hold,' he replies in a quiet voice. 'Ultimately the whole notion of divine action challenges us about how we conceive the world. So when we say it's a metaphor, immediately it suggests we know how the world operates – this is the meaning of this action – and this is being used as a front to get this message out. But I think there's a great danger with that kind of attitude, privileging our own prejudices and our own sense of decorum of how God acts. Why couldn't an angel have appeared for example? I think angels do exist. Modern angels can appear in different guises. The stunning beauty and shining radiance of truth is what the angel is a form of.'

Does he think it is crucial to believe in a virgin birth?

'I'm aware that some Christians do not. I'd be loath to exclude a whole group who are sincere – who give their answer in good conscience – but I would say yes. Firstly, in belonging to a tradition of continuity. In Roman Catholicism and Orthodoxy, it's not a negotiable bit of furniture. It's given implicitly and explicitly in Scripture. The whole concept of Christianity is based on the concept of miracle.'

But does it worry him in any way that the encounter between Mary and the angel is only mentioned in one of the four canonical Gospels?

'I think what would undermine it is if in the other Gospels, or somewhere else in Luke, we found evidence that went against what is pointed out there. Veracity is not dependent on multi-tellings.'

Does its veracity stand or fall by a virgin birth? I ask.

'I'd say it should stand by that but if someone was having difficulties but could accept the Incarnation, I would say that's a more primary belief.'

I am particularly interested, given his background, on whether Professor D'Costa sees the Annunciation as a bridge or a barrier to interfaith dialogue.

'It's a really interesting question. It tends only to come up with Muslims. It can be both a door that opens onto a common heritage and sharing, or it's a door that brings into focus the profound differences between us. So the answer is both yes and no.'

But Christianity, I suggest, is the only monotheistic religion that proposes God has come to earth in human form. Surely that makes the Incarnation a block?

'Christians believe this story is about God becoming flesh which is problematic for nearly every other religion,' he replies. 'It is a scandal for a Jew, a Muslim, a Buddhist, but the notion of it being a scandal doesn't mean it has to have a violence in it which makes it problematic for interfaith dialogue. For interfaith dialogue is characterized by people who have a strong conviction that they have the truth but that if they were all right, it couldn't be possible in making sense intellectually of what's going on. You can recognize these incredible tensions that can't be reduced but the real issue is how do we live with these fundamental differences?'

So how does such an inclusive approach relate to the annunciation story?

'I no longer call myself an "inclusivist",' he says. 'I've now moved to what I call "open access exclusivism". I have a worry about inclusivism which is the notion of including other people's truths in our own vision because it means we don't take them seriously in what we say – we just take the bits we like and agree with. I've become uncomfortable with that. For example, with Muslims we can say that we both affirm that we believe in one God who is creator and judge. That commonality stands even though we believe in the Trinity. But when the Roman Catholic Church comes to the Incarnation and the Virgin Birth, it bares a disconnection that can't be minimized. We just have to live with things we disagree with and profoundly think are wrong but still keep open the conversation. Open access means there will be many people who aren't Christian but who by virtue of that are not lost.'

Does he believe the Annunciation is 'the most important event in human history'?

'Yes, that's right in one way,' he says. 'What if Mary had decided to go and have an abortion or decided to rush off the scene and say, "No way, it's too embarrassing"? There is a crucial sense in which the turning around of history depended on the obedience of this woman. The Incarnation is the turning point in history and Luke shows how human cooperation was a vital part of it.'

Seventy-nine-year-old Kenneth Cracknell shuffles into Room 33, clutching a small Bible. He stands in front of the Lemoyne painting and stares, mesmerized, at the canvas.

'I see the clouds. The figures get in the way,' he tells me. 'The clouds represent the invisible, the transcendence. We can't get there from here but God does get to us from there. God eternal speaking to us, creatures of dust. I'm looking at the light – not the figures at all. It's a painting of a metaphor.'

He has just flown into London from his home in Vermont, USA, to celebrate his daughter's birthday. He retreats from the painting and makes his way slowly to the centre of the room where he sits on the mahogany circular bench.

Kenneth Cracknell has had a long career that started in West Africa where he served as a Methodist minister. In the late 1970s he became Director for Inter-Faith Relations at the British Council of Churches and held that role for ten years. He also taught at Cambridge and was Professor of Theology and Global Studies at Brite Divinity School in Fort Worth, Texas. His specialism is the Christian theology of religions and interfaith dialogue. He describes the Methodist Church as 'a Protestant Church with a Catholic theology'.

'I expect the word "midrash" is familiar to you?' he asks me. 'The great rabbinic way of interpreting Scripture by telling another story – a story which deepens it and enlarges the original story. What I see Luke doing is offering us a midrash on something that doesn't actually happen but ought to have happened and deepens our understanding of what did happen and which begets enormously powerful Hebrew poetry when he speaks. That is the transformation of the whole world in pure psalm metre and style.

'Mary couldn't have composed it herself – I don't suppose she did for a moment but I don't care – because what Luke and his friends have done is give us an enormous sense of what it was actually all about. The great theological moment when that which is bright, the divine, breaks out into very earthly circumstances. Here's all the transcendence of heaven and here's a little Jewish girl. That's the breaking moment when heaven cracks open and you hear a new time is about to happen. From the beginning, nothing has happened like this before – the breaking in from ultimate transcendence to this world.'

I listen intently, trying to follow his every word. So, is it too simple to say that the annunciation story is just a symbol – an imaginary explanation of how God became human, rather than recalling precisely how it happened?

'That's right,' he says. 'Nobody is an eyewitness of this. It's a mystical experience, a transcendent experience. All the first Christians are ministers of the word. That's the key phrase. Luke wants to make it speak. He uses words to describe something ineffable – something very strange, very ultimate, and very unusual indeed. He thinks he is a minister of the word. The word is not the events. It sounds as though he wants to put things in order but he's not doing that. He wants to say this is the inner meaning and the inner meaning is much more certain than the history.

'Theophilus is a symbolic figure too. It simply means the lover of God. So Luke states, "I'm writing to you, the lover of God, that you may hear the intensity of what actually happened. I wasn't there. I didn't see these things but here's the ultimate meaning of what happened. And boy has it reversed the universe".'

He pauses for a while. He is looking at his tiny Bible and some notes he has written.

'This picture in front of me represents the certainty not the history,' he says. 'The certainty that is an inward expression of faith and, by faith, there is a certainty.'

There is much to take in here and I want to make sure I understand his position. Am I right in thinking that he does not see the story of the Annunciation as a historically accurate event?

'It's a way of explaining what is to go on now. There is no historicity going on here. There is an expression of faith,' he replies.

So, what about other Christians who believe it actually happened?

'It's like trying to square a circle,' he responds. 'There are people who are bound by history. The world is divided into those who think religion is metaphor and those who think it is part metaphor but is really an explanation of history. If they found out it didn't happen – southern Baptists, many Roman Catholics, some Methodists – they'd be profoundly disturbed because they have been instructed, informed by everything they've had in their catechisms, in Sunday schools and in other teachings that these are historical events and, if they're not true historically, then their faith is at an end. It's profoundly meaningful to them. But for me and for many others, what we are dealing with is human beings trying to find words to express the inexpressible and you can't do that. No journalist, no theologian, no historian can express the inexpressible. It's not possible. Therefore, some people – the God deniers – say, "There's nothing here, it's all stupidity." No, it isn't. It's human beings trying to express that which cannot really be expressed. So in that, I see it as a metaphor.'

Where does Mary fit in? I wonder. Does he see her as a metaphor for acceptance, for submission to God? And if so, does he find this liberating rather than suppressive?

'Yes, yes,' he responds. 'After all, we know nothing about her as a person.'

Do most Methodists think like him? He pauses for a long time before answering.

'Mary doesn't normally appear in Methodist churches but she's around a great deal in the four Sundays of Advent,' he responds.

How does he see the position of Mary in the context of interfaith dialogue?

'She's an absolute unifier between Christians and Muslims but I've never had a discussion with a rabbi about Mary. The notion of the Incarnation is impossible to Jewish people. For Hindus too, she also can be a great unifier as a mother of God. For Buddhists, she also resonates.'

How can the annunciation story inspire interfaith dialogue?

'The world's religious traditions, as a whole, represent to human kind that we are not alone in the universe. There is transcendence,' he explains. 'The idea that God has spoken, has broken through what is invisible to us and has burst through and spoken, that's what all religions are pointing to.'

Soon after he departs, a couple walks into Room 33 and stands in front of the Lemoyne painting. I listen in on their conversation.

'This is all about the heavenly sphere crashing into the human sphere,' the woman tells her partner. 'The angel from heaven meets the woman from earth. It's an allegory, of course. It never happened.'

Professor Lisa Isherwood is the Director of Theological Partnerships at the University of Winchester and is regarded as one of Britain's most radical feminist liberation theologians. Her work explores 'the nature of incarnation within a contemporary context including areas such as the body, gender and sexuality.' She has written a number of books including *The Power of Erotic Celibacy* (2006).

The walls of her small, cramped office are filled with pictures and memorabilia. I notice a painting entitled *The First Supper* by an Australian artist, Susan White, in which Christ and all the apostles are depicted as women. Nearby is a caption by the American black feminist poet Ntozake Shange stating: 'i found god in myself and i loved her, i loved her fiercely.' There's an icon of Mary described as *Mother of God: Mother of the Streets*; and another Byzantine icon of *Christ Sophia* in which God as Wisdom is depicted as feminine. Intriguingly, opposite her desk, there's also a tall statue of Mary as Our Lady, robed in traditional blue.

Lisa Isherwood opens our conversation by telling me how feminist theology has, at its heart, 'the radical idea that women are equal in religion' and how it asks why women's contribution in Christianity has been silenced. 'We ask the questions male theologians don't ask,' she declares. 'For example, the violence, abuse and unacceptable stances in the Bible such as rape and the place of women.'

As a liberation theologian, she explains, her focus is also on poverty, inequality and social justice. I ask what the Annunciation means for her.

'If you look at how feminist theologians have approached the Annunciation,' she responds, 'there's on the one hand Mary Daly [the late American radical feminist theologian] saying this is just a rape scene – "you will do this", "be it done unto me", "I can either get battered or accept it" – it's not a happy situation at all. And if it was a rape by a Roman soldier or whoever while living under occupation, well that's no different to the situation for many women today. But then say for some Latin American feminist theologians, the annunciation story is a very positive thing because they'd say: "Here's a man who is going to give me a baby and then just disappear…and that happens to us all the time…a young single woman who, alone, raises a son who then fights for social justice…we can relate to that." I'm more with the Latin American approach.'

Once an international golfer who represented Wales, her voice has a distinct lilt that indicates her Celtic roots.

'I wouldn't say it was some kind of supernatural birth,' she continues. 'I don't know if it was an act of love or an act of abuse but there's definitely been an act. But this was not a virgin birth – a virgin Mary. The important thing for me as a feminist liberation theologian is that she brought up her son to fight for justice. And incarnation isn't a once and for all event about the birth of Jesus and the mythology around it. It is telling us about our own divinity.

'Yes, there was this man Jesus. He must have had a mother. That must be fact. But the Incarnation is really about all of us. It's much more important to get that sense of the story. If we reflect on that and what it means, reality comes bigger, a lot bigger. In the past though, we've got it horribly wrong and that's because we're not told in Church that that's who we are. We're told we're sorrowful sinners so we act like sorrowful sinners. We're told we need forgiveness so we act like we need forgiveness. We're not told, "you are the original blessing, the beautiful outpouring of the divine – live it!" Psychologically, it's awful. This man died for you because you are so sinful rather than this man died for you because he was so committed to a better world that he didn't run from death. It's like at the heart of Christianity is an image of divine child abuse. God saying, "I need a sacrifice and I'm going to watch my son's horrible death in some way that then I might forgive the people." That's shocking. But Jesus, for me, is a big example of what divine incarnation in the flesh might look like but it's our flesh as well as his. It's every birth.

'If Mary is just the kind of "be it done to me" then I think she becomes just wallpaper. But if she becomes the person who helps shape this baby, this adolescent, this man – then she becomes a much stronger message for women. But she's been an appalling message for women – "you can be a virgin or a whore" – and most women are neither. You can't win. If you're not passive and meek, then you're going to run into trouble.'

I am trying to take all this in. There are lots of messages here and I don't want to conflate or misread them. Intrigued, I am keen to know what she believes is the key message of the annunciation story?

'Panic,' she replies. "How do I do this? I'm twelve to thirteen years of age. What do I do?" That is such a real message for so many women in the world today. It's not all about "Oh, isn't this lovely, this is a divine calling." It's much more about, "How do I do this?" There's backbone there. "I will do it. But I will then raise this child to realize that the wild injustices are so wrong that he will stand up against them and try to change it." She must have been one hell of a woman to cope with all she had to and to show such love, compassion and fight.

'If we're saying that the Incarnation is everybody's incarnation, then it is about our body, gender, sexuality. We have to explore all these from an incarnational point of view. For me the Incarnation is the most inspiring part of Christianity if we see it enfleshed...a flesh and blood youngster taking a gritty decision...and not "oh, what an honour this is". A woman who took it by the scruff of the neck and said, "I will raise a justice-seeking son." That's the message.'

She looks at an image of the Lemoyne painting and sighs.

'It's a pretty picture but it doesn't feel right. It doesn't feel right at all. It wouldn't spiritually empower me. Not at all.'

———

Hearing this feminist perspective on the Annunciation, as well as a Latin American liberation theology dimension, inspires me to make contact with Margaret Hebblethwaite via a video link. For the past fourteen years she has lived and worked in the small community of Santa Maria de Fe (St Mary of Faith), four hours south of Paraguay's capital city, Asunción. In the seventeenth and eighteenth centuries, the village, set deep in the Paraguayan countryside, was a thriving Jesuit-Guarani 'Reduction' or mission settlement for indigenous people before being ransacked.

A feminist and liberation theologian, Margaret Hebblethwaite has established a pioneering charity – the Santa Maria Education Fund – that is rooted in basic education and mission work. She teaches English and Bible studies as part of a group of volunteers devoted to improving the lives of the 4,000 poverty-stricken *campesinos* who live in the local area. 'I was drawn here. I wanted to be with the poor,' she tells me as she extols the achievements of some of her students who went on to study at university.

A writer, journalist and activist, Margaret Hebblethwaite graduated in Theology and Philosophy at Oxford in the early 1970s and then studied at the Gregorian University in Rome. She came to Paraguay after the death of her husband, the journalist and Vaticanologist, Peter Hebblethwaite, a former Jesuit who left the priesthood to marry her. She has written many books including one entitled *Motherhood and God*, and she is a former Assistant Editor of *The Tablet*. Today she calls herself 'a teacher and freelance missionary'.

She links up with me from her home in Santa Maria de Fe, as the temperature there rises to 33 ºC. She is sitting under a bamboo and thatch verandah, surrounded by a cacophonous soundscape provided by the numerous birds and monkeys in the nearby trees.

She opens our conversation by recalling her convent school education in England fifty years ago when pupils would 'leap to their feet as regular as clockwork at noon each day' to recite the Angelus prayer. This, she remembers, told how 'Mary received news that shattered all her plans and symbolized how we are all interrupted to have a new plan, to set out on a new footing, and to be ready.'

Now aged sixty-four, with striking, long red hair and a warm, caring smile, she speaks passionately about what the annunciation story means for her.

'It's a complete attitude of receptivity to God. Here I am. A self opening. Mary accepting the will of God. The message of the Incarnation is on another plane but, to some extent, we should put ourselves in the position of Mary, opening up and accepting the will of God.

'There's also a sexual overtone to the Annunciation. I remember one painting in Florence has a depiction of the angel Gabriel holding the lily in an incredibly phallic position – most embarrassingly. You have the purity of the lily but you also have the echo of female sexual receptivity. Like St Teresa says, "Fill me." Religion is a very sexual affair. The Song of Songs shows that.

'I do think something happened. I don't think it's a complete make-up. There's a source for Luke. Mary told her story. The idea of an angel flying in with wings into a room is nonsense but that she had an intense spiritual experience I assume happened and she recounted it to Luke or to some intermediary who then recounted it to him. I would doubt that a man or angel walked into the room and said those words…well it could be, I suppose…but it doesn't matter. The most important thing is that she felt quite certain that this was a message from God.'

She makes reference to the late American feminist theologian, Jane Schaberg's work, *The Illegitimacy of Jesus.*

'I thought hers was quite an interesting line – that Mary was raped and that she wasn't defiled by this but that the will of God was done through it. And all this talk of the virginity of Mary – I think that the point that is most clear is that Jesus was not Joseph's child. But whether he was someone else's child is not quite so clear. The language of the Holy Spirit overshadowing means for me that she received the protection of God. There's a strong feeling, obviously, in the Catholic Church about her virginity. Schaberg suggested virgin meant she was a woman never subdued, undefeated, one not destroyed by her relationship with men. I think that's quite important.

'But over the centuries, that's not what "virginity" has meant – all these nuns, all these religious orders – but for me, this was a woman saying, "I am not going to be reduced to being a machine for producing babies." This was a way in which women could retain their independence and freedom. The adoption of virginity for Mary is not necessarily a physical one. The idea that her hymen didn't get broken – that's just silly.'

So, to clarify, does she think it is possible that Mary may have been raped?

'Exactly, that's what I would say,' she replies. 'Many Catholic women would see it as completely destroying the spirituality and doctrine of Mary but that's not the point. We get hung up on physical details.'

But surely the idea of an incarnation generated through rape would seem utterly abhorrent and, indeed, deeply blasphemous to so many Christians?

'That's the flaw in the rapist theory,' she responds, 'but I don't completely dismiss it. It makes you think. It draws your attention to what is important – not the physical details but to who he was. Go to the message.'

I wonder if she feels that the feast of the Annunciation has become lost.

'Well, we have Christmas, don't we? That's the moment when we see a child. The birthday. We pay more attention to that than the conception, which is a hidden moment we don't know about. It's all the same mystery – the Incarnation, the Nativity – it doesn't matter.'

She laughs loudly. Then, with a twinkle in her eyes, she tells me that the reason she was called Margaret was because her parents knew she was conceived while on a trip to Edinburgh.

What does Mary mean to her today?

'I've had a lot of difficulties with her in my life because she is so emphasized in the Catholic Church,' she says. 'I found that off-putting. Her virginity was so stressed. It went far beyond the biblical evidence. It was so exaggerated.

'I went to a convent school. As an adolescent girl, I didn't like this virgin as a role model. It went along with this goody-goody kind of thing. And you're discovering your sexuality at that time. I now understand the virginity reference differently. It's really about female independence and emancipation, and that gives it a completely different read. In so many areas of the world, you can't own property if you're a woman. You can't travel independently. That independence of Mary – that she didn't depend on a man to conceive a child – that is a liberated, independent Mary. That part of the message of the Annunciation appeals to me.'

Has Mary has been a source of inspiration for her?

'I'm not sure she's been that much of an inspiration to me other than in that prayer of the fiat,' she replies. 'It would shock people around me here in a deeply Catholic country of Paraguay to hear that. But also there's the idea of Mary as priest – she offers her son who dies. That would inspire me. I don't think it matters whether she had other children. In the Bible it appears to say she did. Then you have tradition saying she didn't. That's a counter-weight. I just don't think it matters.'

She emails me a photograph of a statue of Mary that is in the town's museum. I see Mary sitting in a chair with her right hand placed on her heart and her left holding a book. She looks down at her newborn baby who lies on a white cloth. Her long brown hair falls over her shoulders onto her yellow dress that is emblazoned with flowers. An anonymous Jesuit-Guarani artist created the statue as a

34. Statue of Blessed Virgin Mary, Santa Maria de Fe, Paraguay. © Margaret Hebblethwaite

seated Mary at the Annunciation but today it is an integral component of a nativity scene in the museum.

'I now live here in this little town called Santa Maria,' she continues, 'and being in Latin America changes one's impression. Mary is so important to people here because she was so poor, gave birth in a stable, she was a refugee in Egypt. "She's one of us," they feel. And the hymns here – so many are of Mary as the Mother of the Poor. You don't hear that line in the developed world. Everyone reverences her here. She has a good influence on people. And the virginity thing is a good model for the men. The men here are very sexually unfaithful and yet here is a woman whom everyone reveres, who is not a woman to be used for sexual exploitation. It's good they have that respect for her. It's only one woman but it's good that the Latin American male has one woman he looks up to.'

Hang on a second, I say to her. There's a dichotomy here about Mary's virginity. She's a good symbol for men and yet a difficult symbol for women?

'You're right. The virginity in a physical sense is a good message for the men but not for the women,' she chuckles. 'For women, it's the independence that should be the message. Some people need one kind of message. Others need another message. I don't think these messages are in opposition at all. Men treat women as sex objects because they do not accord them a dignity and independence. The message for women is, "Don't let them exploit you!" Nearly all the men here are unfaithful. Women's liberation in

Paraguay is so far behind. The man is still the boss. I think both the messages from the Annunciation are relevant.'

————————

The idea that Mary may have been raped or seduced haunts me. I admit that I had never considered this to be a possibility until I set out on this journey. I track down the book *The Illegitimacy of Jesus* by Professor Jane Schaberg, published in 1985. In it she argues that Luke and Matthew were aware that Jesus was conceived illegitimately, probably as a result of a rape, and had hinted as such in their Gospels: 'By having the Messiah born out of the exploitation of a woman of the poor,' she writes, 'God demonstrates the vindication of the oppressed in a truly miraculous manner.'

The book proved to be highly controversial. Schaberg was vilified, received thousands of letters of abuse including death threats, and her car was fire bombed. Unfortunately, I can't make contact with her as she died a year ago. However, I read her book from cover to cover.

Going against the general scholarly consensus, Schaberg claims the Infancy Narratives were about an illegitimate conception, rather than a miraculous virginal conception. Before the gospels were written, she states, the illegitimate conception had already been understood theologically as due in some unexplained way to the powers of the Holy Spirit. 'In their telling,' she writes, 'they presupposed the illegitimacy tradition, of which Christians soon became aware.'

According to Schaberg, Luke inherited and passed down this tradition of the illegitimate conception of Jesus. Instead of referencing Isaiah from the Old Testament, Luke was really alluding to the law indicated in the book of Deuteronomy (22:23-27) that concerns the seduction or rape of a betrothed virgin. That law, Schaberg indicates, has to do 'with sexual relations without the woman's consent or without her full consent.' Mary was consenting to a future pregnancy and motherhood but she was not depicted in the annunciation story as consenting to the act that will cause the pregnancy. The act is never mentioned or discussed. God, through Gabriel, does not specify how Mary will become pregnant but promises the presence of the Holy Spirit, especially in terms of divine empowerment and the protection of Mary.

Schaberg agrees that Luke purposely wrote about the conceptions of Jesus and John the Baptist to demonstrate that Jesus had greater status due to his virginal conception. But she writes: 'What is "greater" in the case of Jesus is not the miraculous manner of his conception but God's overcoming of the deeper humiliation of his mother…Elizabeth's humiliation was that she was barren…but the humiliation of a betrothed virgin who was seduced or raped, and who became pregnant by someone other than her husband was far worse.' The Lucan narrative, she writes, against all expectations, challenges the reader to believe that the Holy Spirit was involved in a pregnancy resulting from such humiliation.

Schaberg concludes that the question whether the pregnancy was the result of a seduction or rape of Mary or the result of her free choice to have sex with someone other than Joseph must remain an open one historically.

Supporters of Schaberg's illegitimacy proposition point to the verses in Luke that immediately follow the annunciation story. Mary has to leave Nazareth in haste immediately after conceiving. She sets out on a journey of hundreds of miles to see Elizabeth in the far away Judean hill country. Humiliated, Mary describes herself to Elizabeth as the 'lowly handmaid' but Shaberg suggests the appropriate translation of the Greek word *doulē* should not be 'handmaid' of the Lord but 'slave'.

Schaberg resigns herself to the fact that that by the end of the second century, the virginal conception 'had become the dominant Christian understanding of Jesus' origin, the dominant Christian reading and meaning of the New Testament narratives. The tradition of his illegitimate conception was lost to Christians but it was passed on and developed in Jewish circles.'

Of course, the proposition of Jesus's illegitimacy has been around as long as the history of Christianity. After Jesus's death, and especially from the second century, Jewish rabbis condemned him as illegitimate and cited how the Talmud made cryptic references to bolster that view. Jesus was nicknamed 'the manzer' – the bastard son of a menstruating woman. Celsus, a second-century, anti-Christian Greek philosopher, also proclaimed the legendary story that a Roman soldier called Panthera impregnated Mary. But I find it somewhat unsettling that there are Christians today who believe serious consideration should be given to the idea that Mary was raped or seduced. I want to explore further and try to understand why many believe the virgin conception should be rejected outright.

———

John Shelby Spong is a retired American bishop of the Episcopal Church. He served as Bishop of Newark in New Jersey for more than twenty years from 1979 to 2001. He doesn't promote the idea of Mary being a rape victim but he doesn't dismiss it either. The doctrine of a virgin conception is, in his words, 'nonsense'.

He calls himself a committed Christian and 'an authoritative voice for believers in exile'. A liberal theologian and part of the Progressive Christian movement in the United States, the eighty-three-year-old promotes a faith that is willing to challenge assumptions, is not afraid to ask hard questions nor to admit doubt. For decades, he's been calling for a fundamental re-thinking of Christian belief away from theism and traditional doctrines. He emphasizes that popular and literal interpretations of Christian Scripture are not sustainable, nor do they speak to modern Christian communities. He believes that to regard the Virgin birth as historical would turn it into 'nonsense' and 'fantasy'. He believes it to be an allegory, a proclamation of a living faith.

When his book *Born of a Woman* was published in 1992, the subtitle on the front cover stated: 'A Bishop Rethinks the Virgin Birth and the Treatment of Women by a Male-Dominated Church'. In it he wrote:

> No one in scholarly circles that I know of is willing to defend the historicity or the likeness of the virgin birth story. Continued belief in a literal, biological virgin birth for Jesus is based only on a faith or a dogmatic commitment. It cannot rest on the evidence. Such a belief is no longer defended on the basis of Scripture, not even by Roman Catholic scholars, who have much more invested theologically in the possibility than Protestant Christians do.
>
> The fact that these ideas are commonplace among the biblical scholars of our world and yet are all but unknown among the average worshippers in either church or synagogue is, in my opinion, scandalous. It cannot help but be a reflection of the ecclesiastical hierarchy's fear that such knowledge, if broadly shared, would render the faithful faithless. Conservative bishops and priests content themselves by asserting that biblical scholarship is an ever-changing, inexact science that cannot be counted on for final answers. They argue that we must, therefore, trust the church's historic teaching authority. It is a weak and almost pathetic argument.

Bishop Spong argues that you cannot understand the birth narratives of Matthew and Luke unless you see their connections with the Hebrew Scriptures and recognize the Jewish antecedents. It is a rich narrative but it is not history, he claims. Rescuing the Bible from the fundamentalism of literalism, he states, is now one of the necessary steps Christianity must adopt on its pathway to survival in the twenty-first century: 'Literalism is not only an expression of biblical ignorance, it is a distortion of the Gospels so dangerous as to be destructive to Christianity itself.'

John Shelby Spong's critics vehemently oppose his views. Rowan Williams describes them as embodying 'confusion and misinterpretation'. Others say he mistakenly sees the world through the eyes of eighteenth-century rationalism, as promoted in the Enlightenment. However, his supporters praise his courage to challenge and to speak out, his promotion of inclusivity, and his ability to offer fresh, relevant interpretations of the Gospels for the people of today. His books have sold more than a million copies and, even though he is now in his eighties, he still gives more than a hundred public lectures a year. As he stresses on his website, religion in general, and Christianity in particular, must continually evolve:

> Jesus was a first-century experience in which people perceived that what they called divine and what they understood as the human had somehow come together. The New Testament is a first-century attempt to explain that experience. The creeds of the Church are a fourth-century attempt to codify that experience. No explanation can ever become identical with the truth it seeks to explain.
>
> Historically, Christianity then proceeded to make excessive claims for the authority of its explanations, freezing them in their first and fourth-century frames of reference. Literalised words are always doomed words since the perception of truth is always expanding and changing.
>
> The explanation of knowledge over the last five hundred years in the West has rendered most of the biblical and credal presuppositions to be unbelievable. They rise out of a world that no longer exists. Yet churches continue to operate as if eternal faith can be placed in these earthen vessels, proclaiming that in both the Bible and the creeds ultimate truth has been captured forever. The result is that Christianity seems less and less believable to more and more people. Can we separate the Christ experience from the dying explanations of the past? If we cannot, then surely Christianity will continue its relentless journey into a declining irrelevance. If we can achieve this separation, however, the result will necessitate a reformulate of Christianity that is so radical that Christianity as we know it may well die in the process. Death or radical revisions, however, appear to be the only realistic alternatives. I cast my vote for the latter. I would rather die in controversy than die in boredom.

Bishop Spong calls for a 'new reformation' and among his twelve theses, he focuses on God, Jesus – the Christ, and the Virgin Birth. In his manifesto, he states that understanding God in theistic categories 'as a being supernatural in power, dwelling somewhere external to the world and capable of invading the world with miraculous power' is no longer believable. Most God-talk in liturgy and conversation has thus become meaningless. On 'Jesus – the Christ', he says if God can no longer be thought of in theistic terms, then the conceiving of Jesus as 'the incarnation of the theistic deity' has also become a bankrupt concept. He describes original sin as the 'Myth of the Fall' stating that the biblical story of the perfect and finished creation from which human beings have fallen into 'Original Sin' is pre-Darwinian mythology and post-Darwinian nonsense. He emphasizes once again that the Virgin Birth is biologically impossible and far from being a bulwark in defence of the divinity of Christ, the concept actually destroys that divinity.

I ring Jack Spong at his home in Morris County, New Jersey. I ask why he entertains the possibility that Mary may have been raped and why he believes we should take seriously the notion of an illegitimate birth.

'It's awful hard to do an investigation on something that happened two thousand years ago in which you can present evidence to a court,' he tells me. 'The tradition is that there's something about the birth of Jesus that caused scandal like there was in the crucifixion causing scandal. The idea the Messiah could be executed as a common criminal is a scandalous idea. Jesus being born illegitimately is also a scandalous idea. But the fact is that the experience of the Christian community, beginning with the disciples, was that through some means, somehow through the life of this Jesus of Nazareth, the God presence was made known to human life. That's a pretty powerful statement in itself.'

Does he think that the Church's teaching today on the Virgin Birth is scandalous?

'The Church is in the position of trying to defend its power and if people began to get the idea it is not based on a lot of history, they may well decide to say, "I'm not that interested anymore" and take their money away and then the Church would be in bad trouble.'

Is he saying that if it is to survive, the Church should stop promoting the annunciation story and the Virgin Birth as literal truths?

'Let me say it a different way,' he responds. 'There are two movements in the Christian Church that are growing today: the growth of fundamentalism and the growth of total secularisation. And secularisation is winning that battle. The two groups that are growing are the people that are giving up on all religion and those that want to literalize everything. And they're growing because literalizing offers people some kind of security and that's very appealing. But the fact is that America is becoming more secular every day. The Christian Church is not challenged enough on literalism. There's an enormous religious hunger for something that the Church is not giving people. And there's not an enormous hunger for the doctrine of the Annunciation.'

He says that if you look at the Bible literally, Paul and Mark appear to have never heard of the Virgin Birth. Writing first after Jesus's death, Paul states in his letter to the Galatians (4:8), written in the late 50s, that Jesus was 'born of a woman' with absolutely no connotation whatsoever of a virgin conception. It is clear, he says, Paul had never heard of a miraculous birth. It's the same with Mark's Gospel, probably written in the early 70s. For Mark, Jesus is a completely normal human being until his baptism in adulthood. Then God enters him as the Holy Spirit descends from heaven like a dove and a voice proclaims him as the divine Son. John in his later Gospel appears to have purposely rejected a virgin conception. Christians have taken it out of the Matthew and Luke tradition, he says, literalized it, and put it into the Creed so that people then think it is the essence of Christian faith when, really, it is a tangential issue.

I wonder if he recites the Creed.

'Yes, absolutely,' he replies. 'I think all of that is mythical language. It points to truth but it never captures truth. You can't capture truth in human words. I think creeds are a love song written by fourth-century Christians to their understanding of God. I have no difficulty joining in with such a love song. But I don't think any love language is literal. I tell my wife every day she's the most beautiful woman in the world. That's true but then she knows I haven't examined everyone else to make that statement objective history. It's the language of love. That's what we are talking about. It's not literal language. It's love song language.'

He reiterates that neither Luke nor Matthew's Infancy Narratives are literally true. They are interpretive narratives intended to convey the message that Jesus was the designated Messiah from the moment of his conception. What the virgin birth story says is that human life alone could not have produced the God presence that was found in Jesus of Nazareth, that the writers are stating it mythologically, and in that, it's a profound truth. It forces us to see truth in dimensions larger than literal truth. It seems that we know how to say non-literal things except in religion. "I feel like a million dollars" of course, shouldn't be taken literally', he says. 'Nor should the description of himself as "a big-hearted man". It doesn't mean I've got an enlarged heart.' He says it is 'a sad way to treat a pretty wonderful faith tradition.'

So, what does the annunciation story mean for him?

'Not much,' he replies. 'The Annunciation is all pre-Jesus mythology. It doesn't mean a thing. The Church in its wisdom puts the Annunciation on 25 March, nine months before December 25. The Church understands a little about biology but we have no idea when Jesus was born. We have no idea.'

Bishop Spong comments how, in the age of the first century, the writers had no sense women had anything to do with genetic reproduction. The whole life of an infant was assumed then to be genetically present only in the sperm of the male and the female was merely a vessel.

'They assumed a woman was like a farmer's field. A man plants the seed and the farmer's field nurtures it but doesn't add anything to the man's seed. So the woman has no role in reproduction,' he says.

I tell him how Bishop Philip Egan described the Annunciation as 'the most important event in human history'.

'I would disagree with that,' he responds. 'Incarnation language like that doesn't make sense. To me that's like saying Jesus is Clark Kent. He's God in disguise like Clark Kent is Superman in disguise. That kind of thinking is fourth-century nonsense to today's world. What happens in the Christian story is that in the fullness of the life of Jesus, we begin to see the meaning of the reality of God. It's not about God becoming flesh. The Annunciation is a meaningless symbol to me. An affirmation that Christians must make that God was in Christ. The real experience, however, was that in the life of Jesus you met the presence of God.'

CHAPTER 12

SAYING YES

I am in London again, this time in Millbank Tower, on the banks of the River Thames. Swarms of workers go about their business, some talking earnestly on mobile phones, others tripping over themselves to meet their guests. The energy is electric. I receive a warm enthusiastic welcome and am led to a small meeting room where I discover an oasis of calm. There, sitting behind a desk, is the man I have come to see.

Fifty-eight-year-old Steve Chalke is a Baptist minister, a prominent and outspoken Christian evangelical leader and a well-known social activist. Born in Croydon, he was brought up in south-east London in humble surroundings. His Indian father arrived from Madras in the 1950s, struggled to find work, then became a railway ticket collector. Steve left school with no O levels but later qualified and served as a Baptist minister in Tonbridge, Kent, in the early 1980s before founding the Oasis Trust in 1985. The charity has since become a huge, multi-million-pound venture employing more than five thousand people. It focuses on housing, healthcare and education projects across the capital and around the world, and is hailed for its successful outreach and impact.

'I've been a Christian from the age of fourteen. That's when I decided I was going to follow Christ,' he tells me. 'Walking home near Crystal Palace football ground from a youth club run by the local Baptist church, I said I'm going to be a Christian. I got the idea there and then of setting up Oasis – to start a school, start a hospital, start a hostel for homeless kids. It's true every single day of my life since then, over the past forty-four years, has been a pursuit of who Christ is. I felt God speak to me that night. It was internalized. I was given a gift of purpose and direction quite outside myself. That event that night changed everything. I was rescued. Salvation. I was saved.'

Steve Chalke is married and has four children. He has written more than forty books and remains the Senior Minister at the vibrant, independently run Oasis Church situated across the river in Waterloo. His watchwords are 'drive', 'enthusiasm' and 'delivery'. But in recent months, he has courted great controversy within the evangelical Church over his support for monogamous same sex relationships. Chalke believes that such relationships are part of the central tenet of faith – 'God is love'. So shocked and offended were much of the evangelical community across the country that Oasis was removed from the Evangelical Alliance.

However, it is not gays and lesbians that I want to talk about today. I am interested to find out why his Oasis church did not mark the feast of the Annunciation on 25 March. 'In my tradition of Baptist churches, we did Christmas, Easter and Pentecost,' he says. 'Advent and Lent were not part of the rhythm. Nothing else was celebrated. We would never read Luke's Gospel account specifically on 25 March. We didn't mark that day.'

When I ask what he thinks is the spiritual meaning of the Annunciation, at first he is reluctant to respond.

'The thing is…I've learnt I can read something in the Bible, be inspired by it, teach it and then, three years later, I read it again and I think why have I never seen that – the deepest thought I've been blinded to – and then, three years after that, the same thing happens again. Everything in me is reticent to say, "this is the meaning" because I may have precluded other meanings. But in the story there's a vulnerable teenager who, in some ways, this terrible thing happened to her, in a society that doesn't just frown upon sex outside marriage, pregnancy outside marriage, but will stone you for it, would have killed you if the Romans hadn't stopped that. It makes Mary an outcast, casts a huge shadow over her and her morality as a person. But it is good news that God brings to her. Really good news,' he smiles.

He takes a sip of water and continues. He is in full flow now.

'She hears then responds. It brings her great happiness and terrible pain and yet through her struggle, God is at work and because of her willingness to embrace the plan, the world is changed. So a central message is about that calling but everything in me, the way I'm wired, is not to say, "The central message is…". I've learnt the more you look at these things, the deeper they are. The Annunciation is like a gold mine that I can never finish mining. Even if I was still a hundred and fifty, I'd still be finding truths about it I'd never seen before.'

Does he consider the story to be factual, metaphorical or something else?

'I think…I'm sure it's fact,' he replies. 'However, the whole thing about the glowing angel…mm, do I believe that? I don't know. But the thing I would say *is* literal is that she heard a voice and she knew something about the destiny of her life and God calling her. How do we know about it? She must have told someone and said, "that night God spoke to me".'

Does he believe in the Virgin Birth?

'I would say there's lots of discussion about that precise word and what it meant,' he says. 'I am not a Hebrew scholar. I know some Christians think that. I've also read that the word could mean "young girl". I can't say who's right or wrong. If it was a natural act outside marriage, there's an extraordinary power in that. If you look through the Bible, the kind of people God uses constantly are messed up, screwed up, have made giant moral errors. A catalogue of ordinary people with messed up lives whom God gets hold of and that's my experience in my own life and in my own church which I lead. The number of people with broken pasts – they've done all sorts of things and if they could turn the clock back and do it differently, they would, but they can't. But the great thing is, God does great things to pick you up to do extraordinary things. That is the most powerful thing for me out of the story. So when I say I think the story is literally true, what I mean is that this girl called Mary senses that God has chosen her and gives over her life to God.

'The important question for us all is to ask and answer the question, "What am I here for?" "What am I called to do?" and then to be obedient to that calling. It's the only question you have to answer in life. What's my calling and how do I live in obedience to that? Whether she's a virgin or not is a completely secondary thing to me. Some may say that's apostasy but for me the centrality of the story is about God's interaction with ordinary people to bring about extraordinary outcomes.'

As we close and bid each other farewell, he offers a final comment:

'My appreciation of 25 March as an important day has grown by about a thousand per cent,' he chuckles. 'In the Baptist calendar we don't mark it, but perhaps we should.'

George Carey, the Archbishop of Canterbury between 1991 and 2002, has asked me to meet him in the tearoom at the House of Lords. We sit in the corner of the wood-panelled room looking out onto the River Thames and across to Lambeth Palace, which he inhabited during his eleven year tenure.

During his period of office, women priests were ordained in the Church of England for the first time. When he took up the archbishopric, George Carey declared that he wanted his time in office to be a 'decade of evangelism'. However, as an evangelical who sought greater ties with the Roman Catholic Church, he faced strong criticism from all sides of the Anglican Communion, especially on the issue of homosexuality. Now, aged seventy-nine and a member of the House of Lords, the grandiose surroundings of the Palace of Westminster are far away from his humble childhood in the East End of London.

The son of a hospital porter, he failed his eleven plus and left school in Barking to join the Central Electricity Board as an office boy. At seventeen, he became a Christian and during National Service he felt a calling to be ordained. He studied intensely, gaining O levels, A Levels, a Bachelor of Divinity degree at King's College and then a Master's and Doctorate in Theology. He has been married for fifty-four years, has four children and thirteen grandchildren, and remains an active lecturer and commentator. Recently, he made the headlines claiming that society is becoming increasingly illiterate about religion and that Christians are being forced to hide their beliefs in the workplace.

'I'd like to start with a positive and a negative,' he begins. 'I've always been slightly dubious of the cult of Mary and all that. It came later in the Patristic period – fourth and fifth centuries – when it came out of a positive reaction to the negative approach to women. In the early Church, women were regarded as inferior to males. They didn't know then what we know now – that nothing could be further from the truth. There was a negative reaction from the Fathers of the Church but then the theology of Mary came, saying women can't be all that bad if God used a woman as the vehicle for salvation.

'So, as an evangelical, actually I have a very positive response to Mary. I think evangelicals have lost something in their reaction. At the Reformation, in order to get to the importance of the Bible, we forgot that the Bible says a lot about Mary. I'm positive about the portrayal of her but I find most of the paintings of her too saccharine, too sweet – they do not speak to my spirituality.'

White haired and balding, with a distinctive gap between his two front teeth, he speaks with a drawl.

'The interesting thing about the Annunciation,' he continues, 'is the way Simone de Beauvoir describes it as the total capitulation of women to men – the submissive Mary saying yes to the maleness of God. But on the other side, which I take, the Annunciation is all about the surrendering to the will of God, the submissiveness is all about the freedom to choose. She could have said no but she said yes. That becomes a model in the Christian Church to do the will of God.

'From a Low Church end, you could react against the Catholicism, the focus on Mary by being negative, but a more balanced view is that it's part and parcel of the story of redemption, which starts with the acceptance of birth on the part of Mary. Therefore, it becomes a really positive thing. It's part of the story of our salvation, which Mary participates in. I think it's a very positive thing – the acceptance, the willingness to go the extra mile.'

I ask if he thinks the story is rooted in history.

'It's clearly more than a metaphor,' he replies. 'Jesus is born. Mary is the mother. Is it a theologizing of the birth – a romantic version of something then that was probably dirty?

The birth is real. Was it a virgin birth? That's a theological question. I accept as a Christian what the Church teaches. There were times I doubted a virgin birth. I worked my way through it. I accepted it because all the other versions seemed implausible to me.'

I wonder if the Annunciation's theme of 'calling' and 'doing the will of God' chimes with his own experience.

'I wasn't born into a church-going family,' he says. 'I lived in a secure, loving working-class family. I'd been evacuated three times. I discovered faith as a teenager, going to an Anglican evangelical church. The evangelical teaching of the Rector, I found both very attractive and very disturbing because he was so anti-Catholic. I thought it can't be as bad as that. I did cross the line in May 1953. I was seventeen. I knew something spiritually was happening – "I have found Christ." But it's a process. It's not a once in a lifetime event. You struggle, you doubt. You doubt the arrogance, the ecumenical disunity. But I'm still with it. At times, I'm at deep peace. At times, I question. I think the Annunciation becomes a reflection of that journey: to see the story as freedom, discovery, acceptance and choosing. The Christian way is one of acceptance and following the will of God before oneself. Being true to oneself like Mary was.'

Is it right to describe it as 'the most important event in human history'?

'It was probably a Catholic Bishop who said that,' he responds. 'I would say the Crucifixion and Resurrection – the other side. It shows how the Church looks at different incidents and puts their money there. What would Mary say to that? She was there at the beginning of the story. She was there at the foot of the cross. I would be quite unrepentant to say, for me it's still the Crucifixion. But the two belong together. The beginning is important but not as important as the end.'

What is his view on the Virgin Birth?

'There are many, many Christians who would reject the Virgin Birth. When you look at it, it's pretty slight in the New Testament. In terms of one's journey, we start at different places and we accept and reject different parts of the story. For example, William Temple, to his dying day, wasn't too sure about the Virgin Birth. Personally, I can say with certainty, I accept the Resurrection. With the Virgin Birth, I'm not so sure but I accept it because it's the most satisfying version to make sense of the story. But I do actually think Mary had other children. That is the clearest, most worthwhile conclusion and Joseph was the father of the other children. It doesn't diminish Mary. It makes her more of a woman.'

I ask whether Mary remains a barrier to the pursuit of greater unity of the Christian Churches.

'What we have in common exceeds by far all that separates us,' he says. 'Pope Francis could do it. The character of the man. If he said, "I'm going to call an ecumenical conference next year of Catholics, Protestants, Methodists, Church of England, the Anglican Communion; let's try to unite with our differences." Rather like some of the Churches in the Middle East – retain their identity but they're still Catholic. Why can't we do that? This Pope could do it. I see no reason why we can't live together as one family with our differences. In our family of twenty-three, when we get together, children and grandchildren and all, we disagree over many different things but we're still together because we love one another.'

But the status and role of Mary varies so greatly within the Christian Churches, I suggest.

'The essence of leadership in the Church is the breadth, the ability to hold disparate groups together,' he replies. 'You don't lose your own identity and beliefs. But wrong leadership is to narrow the views of others. To say, "it's only orthodox if you believe what

I believe." The breadth to understand there are different approaches, I think, gives an Archbishop or a Pope the ability to sympathize with an extraordinary range of evangelical or catholic interpretations. Your authority, given your understanding of all sides, gives you the ability to gently correct where you think the distortions are. The word "catholic" means you embrace everything. Surely, evangelicalism can settle in the breadth of that. There's an extraordinary incoherence in our Churches today. But the Annunciation is all about inclusion. It's about a woman being included in the central story of redemption. The early Churches rubbished the position of women so, theologically, it's absolutely amazing.'

Does he venerate Mary?

'I don't pray to Mary. I can't say I have ever done so. But I don't criticize those who do so.'

As we draw to a close, he holds up to the light a large print of Lemoyne's painting and stares at it intensely.

'She's not terror struck. It's actually a look of wonder and a willingness to go on the next journey. Isn't it lovely? It re-enforces what I've said. There's no weakness there but acceptance. Look there's a smile there. Excitement. He's brought that out so well. It's very, very powerful.'

———————

A few hundred yards from the House of Lords, on the corner of Tufton Street and Great Peter Street, stands Mary Sumner House, the international headquarters of the Mothers' Union. With four million members worldwide, seventy thousand of them in Britain, and with branches in seventy-eight countries from Nigeria to Mauritius, I am interested to hear what the story of the Annunciation means for its Worldwide President.

Mary Sumner founded the Mothers' Union in 1876 when she was living in Old Alresford Place, ten miles east of Winchester. Her husband George was the local rector of St Mary the Virgin church in the village and his father was the Bishop of Winchester. When her eldest daughter gave birth, Mary Sumner was reminded of her own experience of first-time motherhood and how difficult she had found it. She was moved to call a regular meeting of mothers in the parish so that they could offer each other mutual support.

Mary Sumner promoted her parish group as a model that recognized motherhood as a vocation and emphasized the importance to society of upholding Christian family values. She established an annual day of prayer on the feast of the Annunciation and, in the founding of the institution, the Virgin Mary and her role as a mother was placed centre stage in Anglicanism for the first time since the Reformation.

More than a hundred and thirty years later, the Mothers' Union still proclaims its mission to raise children in the love of God with their lives firmly rooted in prayer, and recognizes the importance of loving, respectful and flourishing relationships.

'We're about the protection of children, caring for women with problems in life, supporting marriage but looking out for all families and nurturing the Christian faith in children,' the Worldwide President, Lynne Tembey tells me. 'I hold dear that on 25 March every year, our members are called together all over the world to celebrate the life of Mary and their membership of the Mothers' Union. The feast of the Annunciation is vitally important as part of what it means to be a member.

'We are called to be united,' she continues. 'As a wife and mother, I have tried to be caring, gentle but firm in the mother role and have looked at Mary as an inspiration.

She was an incredible lady. Very young, very vulnerable and yet there's that total and utter acceptance – let it be according to your will. I wonder if today women would act as gracefully as she did.'

Lynne Tembey is from the small coastal town of Whitehaven in Cumbria and calls herself 'an ordinary mother'. Warm, bubbly and friendly, she says she doesn't pray to Mary and describes herself coming from a 'middle to high Anglicanism'. Becoming the Worldwide President of the Mothers' Union, she tells me, has been a gift, a blessing, a privilege and a calling.

'Spiritually, for me, personally, the annunciation story is about a response to God's call. Total acceptance. Mary could have said no. History would have been changed. But wow, she didn't. Through her vulnerability, she never thought of herself. She immediately said yes.

'The annunciation story is both fact and metaphor for me. I believe passionately in the word of God and what it says, but there will be some things that aren't quite fact in there. But she accepted totally. I don't think for one second she thought, Oh my goodness, I'm going to be an unmarried mother.

'As a teenager, I always felt God was inviting me to do something. I was always excited by the worldwide Church. I felt he may be calling me to be a nun or a missionary. I then met a young lad and the rest is history. I became a mother and, through the love of Scripture, the door was opened for my membership of the Mothers' Union thirty-five years ago. I believe that God's golden thread has been with me from day one and intertwined and inter-knitted the pattern that has been my life. I was taught that ordinary people can achieve extraordinary things for God and his Church. That's the message of the annunciation story.'

———

One national newspaper's Religious Affairs Correspondent has described Lucy Winkett as 'one of the most loved and admired women priests in the Church of England.' Lucy tells me she has no regrets about her ordination in 1995 but admits that it's been, 'very, very hard at times'. She first served as a priest in Manor Park, Newham, in the East End of London before arriving at St Paul's Cathedral where she rose to be Canon Precentor. It was a tough assignment. Soon after going there, she was spat upon by a member of the congregation who objected to the concept of women priests. She stayed at St Paul's for twelve years.

In 2010 she became the Rector at St James's Church in Piccadilly. It is here that I have come to meet her. She says its mission is to be 'an inclusive, adventurous and welcoming Christian community, honouring God and one another.' There is a busy market outside the church and inside, many of the pews are filled with the homeless. Many are sleeping; some are just escaping from the bustle. In the latest edition of her parish magazine, Lucy Winkett writes: 'A guiding principle of St James's is that rigid or defensive orthodoxy has no place here, most especially when we ourselves think we're right.'

She was brought up in Buckinghamshire and her original goal in life was to be a professional singer. She won a choral scholarship to Cambridge. While she was a student, her boyfriend Andrew died after a climbing accident in the Alps, an event that, understandably, had a profound impact on her.

Whilst adored by her community at St James's and by fellow priests, she has a reputation for guarding her privacy. However, when I meet her in her office next to the church, she could not be more open. Sitting in her chair with her legs tucked under her, she looks relaxed and much younger than her forty-six years.

She begins by explaining what the annunciation story means for her.

'The best way to describe it is, *yes*. It means *yes*. Sometimes it's hard won, or reluctant, or obvious. Sometimes it's the most automatic thing to say and sometimes it's the most impossible thing to say. There's something about the encounter. She mysteriously assents to a path unknown. The "yes" is a sustaining energy and trajectory. Women priests put themselves in the place of Mary. It's a vocation you can refuse. No one compels you to do this stuff. So all of us have said yes to what we believe is a vocation.'

I ask her about her own calling.

'I said it quite quietly but irreversibly. It was like a door closing behind me and I knew I couldn't come back. You believe you've been called. You're answering some kind of invitation and the answer is yes. But the danger is if you try to discern what the "actually happened" is, you're going to judge that. You're going to place a value on it. A quick "yes" is good because you're faithful and joyful. But what of a hard "yes", the reluctant "yes"? It's not a case of putting a value on each of them.

'Saying yes for me was sudden. I was aged twenty-four or twenty-five. The actual experience was I thought, I am going to be a priest even though at the time women couldn't be priests. I wasn't going to church at the time. I was having a bit of an off period, thinking it was a load of nonsense. I was visiting my parents. It was a Sunday and I decided to potter down to the church in Buckinghamshire where I'd sang. I went to Evensong. I was the youngest woman sat there. It was like *Dibley*.

'The vicar talked about "the appearance of success". At the time, I wanted to be a professional singer. I realized then that what I wanted was the recognition and that's wrong. Truthfully, it was one moment when I sat in the pew in a quite boring service, and I just knew, and I was so excited: I'm going to be a priest. It was like an uncovering – that God had placed something in one that wasn't there before. It was astonishing and it's never gone away.

'I was working for a market research company at the time demonstrating photocopiers to get some money to finance my singing. It was the most tedious job in the world. The next day, I was in a hotel just down the road in Piccadilly. I said to the MD, "I'm going to be a priest." It was very funny – there was no recognition whatsoever.'

When I ask her how tough it has been as a woman priest, she visibly flinches.

'There's the woman-priest bit and the priest bit. The woman-priest bit has taken me to the edge of what I can bear as a person at times. There was a particular time when I went to St Paul's. I had stalkers, nasty sexual letters. I believed I was doing good but it was met with fury. "You're spoiling our church." "You're the reason why the Church of England is in decline." People described me as feisty, ambitious, wanting power, wanting to take the men's jobs.

'So here's a story, like the Annunciation, that happened there. I was celebrating the Eucharist at the main altar in St Paul's. It was huge. There was a chap who worked there and he got all the serving team to refuse Communion from me. I'd been there a couple of weeks. Six years later, he opened his hands to receive Communion from me and said to me, "There's no fool like an old fool." There's an annunciation there. He eventually said, "Yes".

'Most of the congregations at St Paul's are international tourists and Catholics. They've never heard of Anglicanism. In they pour. They see a woman priest. So, few said how terrible. Most thought the Pope had said that in England they can have women priests. Once, all the women on the front row were crying. They were Mexican. They asked if I was real. And then they said, yes. Instead of saying how outrageous, they said, yes. That was an annunciation moment. A new future. I'm not translating it in denominational terms but all denominational barriers were blown apart there and then, and they said yes to the unimagined future. A paradigm-shifting thing. They saw it and said yes.'

I note that her eyes are filling with tears. It is clear that she finds it very emotional to recount those times.

'I do find a lot of inspiration in the Annunciation because I do think it's about that new, unimagined future. What do you do when that is presented to you? You either run away or say yes and how extraordinary it is when you say yes.'

Does she see the gospel account as factual, metaphorical or something else?

'I think it could have happened,' she says. 'But a metaphor is more true for me than a fact. It's beyond a fact. I get to the truth behind it. So I think it's profoundly true. It could have happened – in real time with two bodies – but I don't know. And "I don't know" is a very inspiring place to be. If you spend time questioning it as fact or not, it's displacement activity from what faith is about – which is accepting the "I don't know". From beyond the question "Did it really happen?" where I land is "I don't know but I believe." Knowledge here is unobtainable. I believe it could have happened but it doesn't matter to me. I believe its message. What I'm challenging in myself is the supposition that facts are better than truths. My experience is that's simply not true.'

I share with her Bishop Egan's statement that the Annunciation is the most important event in human history.

'I don't agree with him,' she responds. 'Rather than important, I'd use the word "vital". God finds a way to redeem humanity. The truth of that is greater than the events themselves. I get where he's coming from but it's too linear for me. God is much more creative than that.'

Does she think that the status of the feast of the Annunciation has got lost and, if so, why?

'One of the reasons why is because in a modern Church people are a bit embarrassed by a virgin birth,' she says. 'We can sing all the stuff and circle around it a little bit. But the slightly prosaic fact that it's the 25 March and then precisely nine months later, it's the 25 December – life doesn't work like that. It feels a bit clinical. Then they feel they have to address this problematic doctrine, which feminists see as their moral duty to oppose and Catholics see as absolutely axiomatic to their faith. It becomes a bit embarrassing. This nine-month thing. People are a bit squeamish about it – about the woman's stuff. It's all clinical. No pain. Not earthy. But in a modern church, if we can say it's about those beautiful icons, Mary and Gabriel and their eyes in parallel – there's a mutuality – and then with all the gold, rich red, and lapis lazuli – that's how to talk about the Annunciation and get people in. The reason I find the Incarnation so compelling is God is there in the mess, the ambiguity, the unfinishedness of what it is to be human.'

She talks movingly about an icon of the Annunciation displayed upstairs in her private quarters before we move on to discuss the status of Mary.

'Mary is an impossible ideal – a virgin and a mother,' she tells me. 'Women have been beaten over the head with that paradigm for over two thousand years. Women have quite a high degree of ambivalence to Mary if she's sold to them as this obedient, submissive, "let it be", head-bowed image. Is that how women should be like? For many women, that would be very problematic. For me, her encounter with the divine presence is the irresistible invitation, which, itself, is a paradox. You are free to say no but you can't resist it.'

Does she believe in the Virgin Birth?

'Some feminists would say it's a duty not to believe in the Virgin Birth. It distances women and keeps Mary apart as an unreachable goal. An image of perfection to beat women up with. I feel very ambivalent to it as a doctrine but, truly for myself, I have no difficulty with it. It could have been. But it doesn't take away from the truth of the Incarnation if Mary wasn't a virgin. But I would be absolutely with the proposition that Jesus had brothers and sisters. Her immaculate conception, the Virgin Birth, her dormition, her assumption removes her from humanity and is the root of very problematic attitudes to women, and to sex and relationships in the Christian tradition. They're all unhelpful. That's making her a fantasy figure and I want to resist anything that reduces, atomizes, distances, makes fantasies about real people.'

I ask if she venerates Mary.

'I think I do,' she replies. 'I don't pray to her. I've said the Hail Mary. I'd happily say it.'

She ponders more on Mary and her impact. 'The Annunciation is vital to her but I'd put it with her by the cross. That's very important too. I'd also make a link with Cana. She knows it's time for his first miracle. I love her for that.'

I show her a print of the Lemoyne painting and ask what she sees.

'I interpret it as Mary being too meek and submissive and that's not on,' she responds firmly. 'I feel sorry for her being portrayed in that way because the *yes* was such a courageous thing to do. However, I do see a kind Gabriel and that's lovely. What I would love Gabriel to be saying is: "Get up. Stand up. Stop being so reverential. We're off now. There's a great adventure ahead of us and I'm not leaving you".'

As I leave her office, I notice directly opposite her door a large, original abstract painting of the Annunciation in striking shades of greens, blues and greys, created and bequeathed by a parishioner. I look at the wording on the frame: 'Annunciation by Eve Moore aged 91 who loved this progressive church'.

35. Eve Moore *The Annunciation*, St James's Church, Piccadilly, London. By kind permission of Rev Lucy Winkett

I am in Bloomsbury, at the heart of academic learning in the capital city. The Housman Room, the Senior Common Room at UCL (University College London) is full of professors, fellows and lecturers drinking coffee, reading papers and books, debating and arguing. In walks Steve Jones, wearing an open-necked shirt, casual trousers, an old jacket and sandals.

One of the world's leading geneticists, Professor Steve Jones led the Department of Genetics, Evolution and Environment at the University and is now Principal Research Associate. At the Galton Laboratory, he has carried out internationally acclaimed, groundbreaking research into evolution and variation, sex, inherited disease and genetic manipulation. He has developed a lifetime special interest in snails and how their anatomy sheds light on biodiversity and genetics. He broadcasts and lectures widely. In 1991, he delivered the Reith Lectures on 'The Language of the Genes'.

Immediately, and with great enthusiasm, he shows me two slides from one of his academic lectures entitled, 'Snails in Art and the Art of Snails'. One is described as 'The Resurrection of Theba Pisana'. Better known as the white garden snail, the theba pisana, he tells me, is capable of 'explosive reproduction rates'. In the photograph, hundreds of them are shown clinging to a tree. In the next slide is the Italian Renaissance painter, Francesco del Cossa's depiction of the Annunciation. Between the angel Gabriel and the Virgin Mary, a snail slithers across the marble floor. Above the painting, Steve Jones has included the following quotation from Francis of Retz in 1400: 'If the dew of the clear air can make the snail pregnant, then God in virtue can make His mother pregnant.'

He tells me the symbolism of the snail in the painting turns on the belief that a snail is insulated from sex by its shell and, therefore, gives birth by miraculous means. He laughs out loud as he explains that it is completely wrong and snails have sex in very complicated and highly imaginative ways.

The world-renowned malacologist takes delight in telling me that many snails are hermaphrodites and that, during courtship, the boy-girl and girl-boy fire love darts to try to penetrate the other's body wall. 'The idea of a virgin birth is simply nonsense,' he proclaims.

Steve Jones is also a prominent member of the British Humanist Society and, as a vocal non-believer, twice has been awarded prizes as 'Secularist of the Year'. Just before I met him, *The Times* published a major feature written by him, entitled 'God and science don't mix, right? Wrong.' with the sub-heading, 'Yes, miracles stand outside physics. But scientific inquiry can explain biblical events and why we turn to religion.' In the article, he wrote: 'What makes us human is that urge to explain. In biblical times, the explanation was obvious: God did it. Since then, scientists have begun to use logic rather than assertion in the search for truth.'

In this context, I am interested to hear his point of view on the story.

'The Annunciation, like many themes in many religions, comes from a fear of death and a longing for re-birth,' he tells me. 'I'm a geneticist and my job is to make sex boring. But if you look at the biology of sex – sex, age and death are three sides of the same coin. Sexual organisms die. Asexual organisms tend not to die. The trouble is, asexual organisms then build up errors and go extinct. So you have this constant tension between death and life. Obviously, people, even in the most primitive formats, were aware of death. It is said Neanderthals may have buried their dead with bouquets and horns – they were obviously expecting some kind of resurrection. The idea of resurrection goes back to the beginning of language. Once you could say, "Here he is; here he isn't; is he going to come back?" then you have a powerful narrative that appears again and again.'

He continues: 'The Annunciation is the inevitable equivocation that comes out of sex. Most religions are very interested in sex – the Catholic Church more than most. Sex is obviously a central part of human life and the notion you can generate life without sex is very attractive to people who are concerned with cleanliness. And it's noticeable many priesthood sects are enjoined not to have sex, for example, in the Catholic Church. If you can separate reproduction then you've done a kind of ritual purification.

'It is noticeable that virgin births are everywhere. In Greek legends. It's ancient. It's tied up with this guilt about sex. If you look at the Genesis story about Adam and Eve, they committed the first and least original of all sins to eat the fruit from the Tree of

Knowledge. Then they had sex. That gives us original sin. Cleanliness and uncleanliness. I think the notion that Jesus can be originated without original sin, without sex, is a very entrancing one. But there are plenty of reasons why it's not possible in mammals. There's plenty of reasons why it's possible in other creatures.'

We talk about the fact that some see the annunciation story as factual and others as mythical. But what about Christians who see it as metaphorical? Those people may believe that the event did not actually happen but choose to interpret the story as a message of calling and acceptance.

'The difficulty for me,' he says, 'is an awful lot of religions have at their centre the desire of a rational being to believe something that is irrational. I think everyone knows in the real world a virgin birth is impossible but in the form of Christianity, you have to persuade yourself that it is possible. Once you've made that dishonest decision, there's no limit to where you can go. That's the crux. Believing something that you're not willing to disprove. That is the exact opposite to scientific method. You don't believe anything. The claim is that your only interest is to destroy your own theory. In practice, that is not true. But you can see it to be at the base of all science that it is true. People are reluctant to give up their ideas but when they have been proved wrong, they profoundly swear they've been proved wrong.

'But you never find with the Virgin Birth and Resurrection a true believing Christian saying, "I don't believe in it." They will say "I don't believe in Noah's Ark and all the animals on it." But the sticking point is virginity, sex and re-birth. It is basically impossible to have a virgin birth in humans. Quite surprisingly, in the last five to ten years, we've come up with the fact you cannot feminize a male to make an egg and a female to make a sperm. You need both male and female to get together, not just X and Y chromosomes, you need the actual maleness and femaleness to put marks on the DNA that they pass on to the next generation. Without those male plus female marks, you cannot do it. Fish do it. Lizards can do virgin births. But they don't have the systems mammals have. You cannot have virgin births in mammals.'

What does he say to those who respond, 'But that's the point. It can't normally happen. But this was a unique one-off occurrence. A miracle.'

'I can see that,' he responds. 'But it's like death and resurrection. You can't come back to life. It trivializes the whole story. If you're willing to swallow this, you can swallow all the rest. As someone who doesn't have that mindset, I can't understand it. It's like being colour blind. I just don't see it. I don't have a receptor.'

Can he understand those who say the Annunciation was an action by a power that can defy science?

'Science is very bad at dealing with the unique,' he says. 'The Big Bang was said to be a unique singularity but now the only way to get round it, some are now saying, is that there were millions of Big Bangs – like an annunciation happening every month,' he chuckles. 'And that shows the difficulty of science dealing with unique events. It's foolish for a Christian person to say the Annunciation was a unique event because the same stories of virgin births are in many religions. They seem to me to point to human curiosity rather than they do with any real event. The joy of science is you ask the methods of science to ask would the Annunciation be possible biologically and the answer is no. That's my take on it.'

So, can a scientist be a Christian? I wonder.

'Absolutely. Sure. I have no problem with that as long as you don't let your Christianity interfere with your science. Then, it doesn't matter.'

But if a scientist thinks a virgin birth is impossible, how can he/she also believe in the Christian teaching?

'Science is science. Anyone can do it. It's arts for the mediocre. Any fool can do it. It's just a method. A tool,' he responds somewhat sarcastically. 'Whatever else you believe is irrelevant so long as you use that tool. I don't see that as being an issue.'

Some may say that science is rooted in certainty whereas faith and belief are based on trust and commitment.

'Oh, God no!' he exclaims. 'I would never say science is based in certainty. I have a strong suspicion that the theory of evolution is correct. But you've always got to be willing to accept things may or will change. It's happening with genetics now. This constant tearing down of the idols that makes science what it is. That's the difficulty for me with religion. There are certain idols you are not allowed to tear down.'

I persist with my questioning on this. What about those who believe in God, Jesus Christ, the Resurrection, but say the Virgin Birth did not happen? That it's a metaphor.

'If you decide to wilfully believe in something you know is not factually true,' he says, 'then you open the door to believing anything you like. That's my problem with religion. One of my problems I never understand with Christians is, why do they need an excuse to be good people? It's what puts me off it.'

So, are those who describe the Annunciation as purely metaphorical still being sucked in to something that is plain wrong?

'The factual thing is they are being sucked in to something that is plain wrong – but they would not explore it in factual terms. But when you've opened up the metaphoric door, where do you stop? That's why I don't open up that door. If you take somebody like Martin Rees [Lord Rees, cosmologist and former President of the Royal Society] who's a very nice guy. He talks about being a non-believing Christian. But that's a contradiction in terms. I say to him, "What the hell are you on about?" There's a confusion in it.'

Steve Jones comes from a Welsh Presbyterian background, having been brought up near Aberystwyth. As a child, he attended Chapel three times a week. On his maternal Morgan side, there's a line of preachers. He tells me when he went to grammar school on the Wirral, he attended religious instruction classes, 'but it was clear to me at the age of eleven, the people in charge didn't believe it.'

I ask him if he's ever prayed.

'Never. God, no. I was a field biologist for many years and I took a lot of risks. But I've never said, "Please God, get me out of this".'

He ends the conversation with a last thought. 'I don't challenge the ideas of faith anything like as much as religions challenge science. I say the battle between religion and science is like a fight between a shark and a tiger. So long as they stay on their own territory, they're bound to win. But it's much more likely for the shark of religion to challenge the tiger of science than the other way round. And then it always loses.'

After I leave, my head is full of questions. Would Mary be any less holy if she had had sexual intercourse with Joseph resulting in the conception of Jesus? If Joseph was his true father, would that stop Jesus being the Son of God? If the pregnancy was natural and Jesus was illegitimate, would that really matter? Is the concept of the virgin conception critical to the theological understanding of Jesus, his status and role? If Jesus as Son of God pre-existed his birth, what is the benefit of a virgin conception?

CHAPTER 13

THE MODEL OF FAITH

Eighty-one-year-old Cormac Murphy-O'Connor greets me warmly at his home in leafy Chiswick in West London. He ushers me into a comfortable sitting room that leads into a bright conservatory, and invites me to take a seat. I look around. The first thing I notice are sheaves of clearly annotated papers and piles of books stacked neatly on a nearby table. He tells me that these are reference points for the autobiography he is working on. He seems to be enjoying retirement, relishing the process of looking back on his extraordinary life.

He speaks emotionally of his admiration for his father, describing him as 'a deeply pious man' who went to Mass every morning. This had a strong impact on his family: three of his sons opted to join the priesthood. Cormac remembers clearly the moment when he told his father of his plans. He was fifteen years old and he made his announcement in the family car. Three years later he was attending the English College in Rome where he gained a degree in Theology.

Between 1982 and 2000, as Bishop of Arundel and Brighton, Cormac Murphy-O'Connor was the Co-Chair of the Anglican Roman Catholic International Commission (ARCIC) and was described then as a 'pioneer in ecumenicalism'. In 2000, he was appointed Archbishop of Westminster, the head of the Roman Catholic Church in England and Wales, and the following year became a Cardinal. On his seventy-fifth birthday in 2007 he submitted his resignation but Pope Benedict did not accept this until 2009. He remains a close confidant of the current Holy Father, Pope Francis.

In a recent speech, he condemned the country's growing secularism:

> Our danger in Britain today is that so-called Western reason claims that it alone has recognized what is right and thus claims a totality that is inimical to freedom. No one is forced to be a Christian. But no one should be forced to live according to the new secular religion as if it alone were definitive and obligatory for all humankind. The propaganda of secularism and its high priests want us to believe that religion is dangerous for our health. It suits them to have no opposition to their vision of a brave new world, the world which they see as somehow governed only by people like themselves.

His assistant, Sister Damian, brings us cups of tea on a tray. There is a natural pause in the conversation so I look more intently at the man in front of me. Cormac Murphy-O'Connor has a ready smile, a smooth, ruddy complexion, and he exudes an amiable, avuncular air. However, I am very aware that ascending the ranks of the Roman Catholic Church, culminating in the role of Cardinal, requires a great deal more than being merely avuncular. We resume our discussion. He listens intently to my questions and is careful how he phrases his responses.

'The main thing, the central part of the Annunciation, is Mary's "Be it done to me",' he tells me. 'The intervention of God in a mysterious way. The most dramatic intervention of God in human history. Where we have the Old Testament and God's chosen people, here we have an intervention which brought about the greatest mystery. One of the three great mysteries: the Incarnation; the Trinity; the Redemption. How does it come about? She says "If that's what you want, I'm ready." It's that openness. And I think one needs to understand the sanctity of Mary not just as his mother but as the first disciple.'

He speaks slowly. There are long pauses. At times, he stumbles over his words, and occasionally his sentences trail off into the distance.

'When we say in the Creed, "Born of the Virgin Mary", that's part of the self-understanding of the Church – it meditates on the deposited faith,' he says. 'There are some things that can't change and some things that can change. What you can't change is what's in the Bible and what has been handed down through the ages – the Tradition. The people have a role to play in upholding the deposited faith…the three great mysteries including the Incarnation. I would go along with the idea of faith and belief being about trust and commitment. We have faith, hope and charity. How did it happen? We know through faith that it was through Mary. That he was born in such a special way. That his mother was by divine decree.'

What does 'faith' mean for him?

'For me it is trust in God, trust in Jesus Christ, and trust in the Church. It would never have lasted unless somehow the reality of Christ was contained there in the word, the Sacrament, in the Holy Spirit. I once told Henry Chadwick, a very intelligent historian, in our ARCIC discussions, "I would want a certain submission of mind and heart to the mind of the Church." "I bow my head to that", he replied. It doesn't mean I believe totally in relics or something but it does mean I believe totally in the mind of the Church when it is talking about Jesus Christ. Is he Son of God? Is he truly human? The details of the cows and sheep at Bethlehem – that doesn't matter. But what Luke is trying to say here is that this is an extraordinary, phenomenal event. I believe the intervention of God in history. The way he puts it is true but not all the detail. In a way, I don't think about all the details but I do think about the Incarnation and on the meaning of Mary.'

So, an angel appearing is not really relevant.

'I don't have faith in Gabriel in that sense,' he says. 'I don't know…What does matter is the Incarnation. That's the moment it began. And how Mary accepted the question – there's a bit of a mystery there too. All the great artists have imagined the event. But you could depict the Annunciation without the angel, without her saying her prayers. The pivotal moment is the Incarnation.'

Referencing the ARCIC report from 2005 entitled *Mary: Grace and Hope in Christ*, I ask whether he believes that the status and role of Mary is a barrier to greater ecumenical progress. The Cardinal explains that it has been another issue that has been the key stumbling block.

'In ARCIC, the chief talking point after total agreement on the Eucharist, on Ministry – accepted by the Anglicans and by Rome – was Authority,' he says. 'We couldn't agree. The key difference is the Catholic Church believes in the Scripture, Tradition – handed down over the years – and in teaching Authority. That means the Apostles through the ages. Anglicans believe in Scripture, Tradition and Reason. It's very English. Ever since they lost the authority of the Catholic Church – the Pope with the Bishops – the Anglicans have come to decisions through a body of bishops, clergy and lay people. That's not a Catholic view. Ours is the Pope with the Bishops. The Bishops with the Pope. But we have things to learn from the Anglicans. The consultation of laity on doctrine is important.'

I tell him that many people I have spoken to in relation to their understanding of the Annunciation have used words such as: 'calling', 'acceptance', 'surrender', and 'emancipation'.

'It's nearing the surrender for me,' he responds swiftly. 'In other words, there's something in me that says "I give myself to the will of God and the mystery of Christ and the mystery of the Church. That's how I believe it. I'm here to do the will of God. We're here involved in the mystery of salvation and we somehow have to surrender to it".'

Does it really matter that Mary was a virgin?

'I'd never say it doesn't matter because it's part of my spirituality, to be like Mary, the first disciple. If she's the first disciple, what she said, how she surrendered to the will of God, is crucial to my spirituality. I would never say it wasn't important.'

What about Jesus having brothers and sisters?

'I don't really know. I just don't know,' he replies. 'It could have been Mary's sister. There are so many theories. I'm not going to worry about any of them. It could have been cousins, children of Joseph, the extended family or whatever.'

I ask whether the feast of the Annunciation has lost its previous status. He talks at length about the importance of Mary to him before returning to my question. He tells me how, in the past, Holy Days were holidays but all that has changed. 'If I was Pope, I would say the Assumption is just a minor holy day and the Annunciation is *the* Holy Day. Maybe we have diminished it.'

He holds up a print of the Lemoyne painting.

'It's an extraordinary painting. It's so unusual. I like it. The angel is so strong. Mary is bending over – she's bowing. "I'm here. I'm willing. I accept it." It's a lovely depiction.'

––––––––––

The Victoria and Albert Museum collection of European Medieval and Renaissance art and design is among the finest and most comprehensive in existence. I have come here to meet Paul Williamson, one of the world's leading medievalists and curators, whose job title is rather a mouthful: Keeper, Department of Sculpture, Metalwork, Ceramics and Glass at the V&A. I feel honoured and excited to accompany him on a special personal tour of ten great Annunciation treasures.

As we peer inside a glass cabinet at a tiny ivory carving made in Liege or Cologne in the eleventh century, he talks with an infectious mixture of passion, enthusiasm and deep-seated knowledge.

'The angel approaches from the right,' he enthuses. 'Mary is looking rather Queen-like, a frontal pose, rather different from the vast majority of Annunciations, particularly the later ones when there's the concentration on the human aspects. She's almost caught by surprise here, she's shocked, lifting her hand up.'

We walk slowly through the magnificent Medieval and Renaissance rooms that have been recently refurbished as part of a £35 million restoration programme.

'So much of our collection was acquired in the nineteenth century when Cathedral treasuries had been broken up after the French Revolution, the end of the Napoleonic Wars, the unification of Italy,' he explains as we walk through the rooms. 'Objects were beginning to percolate onto the market by the middle of the nineteenth century and we were in the right place at the right time. The great museums like the V&A, the South Kensington Museum as it was then, were in the very lucky position of being very well funded at that time and the materials were available.'

––––––––––

* This conversation turned out to be one of Cormac Murphy-O'Connor's last ever interviews. He died on 1 September 2017.

36. *Master of the Louis XII Tryptych*, 1498-1514, Limoges. Victoria and Albert
Museum, London. © Victoria and Albert Museum, London

We stop to examine a beautiful portable altarpiece called the *Master of the Louis XII Triptych*, part of a collection of painted enamels on copper, made in Limoges in France by an unknown artist between 1498 and 1514. The Annunciation forms the image of the central scene and the rich variety of blues, both vibrant and subtle, together with a patchwork of reds and purples, make it one of his favourite pieces.

'It resonates on all sorts of levels,' he tells me. 'This is an extraordinary object made for Louis XII and the Royal Court, possibly for his wedding. It's a work of the highest quality, so beautiful. The King and Queen are either side of the main plaque. It's rather like a great stained glass. They're almost taking part. Look, there's God the Father above,' he points out enthusiastically. 'This would have been a travelling altar packed in its own leather case. It would have been opened out in the tent or wherever they were staying. Put out to pray to. As the figures can't speak, the angel points to the words on the scroll. Mary's at a lectern, turning.'

We move on. He guides me towards more Annunciations. A fourteenth-century stained glass from a pilgrimage church dedicated to the Virgin Mary at Strassenegel in Austria; a lovely thirteenth-century crosier in enamel and gilt from Limoges with the spiral of the crook extending into an elongated curl with the figures of the angel Gabriel and Mary set within; and a fourteenth-century miniature Byzantine mosaic used for private prayer by a wealthy household in Constantinople.

Next, we stand before the *Troyes Altarpiece*, an elaborate French work from 1525, crafted in limestone before being painted and gilded. The Annunciation forms the scene directly above the Crucifixion in the central section. The piece depicts Gabriel rushing in from the left. A dove flies down on the right-hand side of God the Father who wears a crown. Further on the right is Mary, robed in blue and gold, kneeling at a prie-dieu with her right hand raised. There is a four-poster bed behind her and a large pot of lilies sit between her and Gabriel. The setting is exquisite and lush.

37. Detail from *Troyes Altarpiece*, ca. 1525, Victoria and Albert Museum, London.
© Victoria and Albert Museum, London

38. Arnolfo di Cambio, *The Annunciation*, 1295-1302, Victoria and Albert
Museum, London. © Victoria and Albert Museum, London

'These pieces tell us a lot about private devotion, the things people owned from the upper and middle tiers of society,' Paul Williamson explains. 'Travelling items of devotion brought out to aid people in prayer. They would often think, engage, empathize with the suffering the Virgin went through. They're visual anchors.'

He moves on to stand in front of a white marble relief, carved by Arnolfo di Cambio in Florence between 1295 and 1302, and describes it as 'one of the greatest Italian Gothic pieces; the best Tuscan Gothic sculpture on offer by one of the great, great sculptors. It's a peculiar construct. It's unusual in giving so much prominence to the building in the centre. Mary with her lovely head down and Gabriel's parted lips…the understanding… masterly! Her hand on her heart…It anticipates the great sculptures of the fifteenth century like Donatello.'

We go on to admire an early fifteenth-century French statue of the angel Gabriel. It is carved in oak then painted and gilded. Originally it formed part of a large altarpiece. Gabriel's right hand is raised and his forefinger points upwards, referencing heaven and the Holy Spirit. The statue of Mary that was intended to accompany the angel has been lost.

A few feet away, we are confronted by a tall willow statue of Gabriel by Nino Pisano, made in 1350–1368 in Tuscany, probably for the cathedral in Pisa. He has lost his wings, his halo and much of the original paintwork has faded away. Next, we admire a fantastic altarpiece, created by Giovanni della Robbia in Florence between 1510 and 1520. It is composed of white and porphyry enamelled terracotta, and illustrates God the Father, who is placed above Gabriel's head, releasing the Holy Spirit in the form of a dove towards Mary.

It is not only statues and sculptures of the Annunciation that are on display. He shows me a sixteenth-century Spanish

39. Giovanni della Robbia *The Annunciation*, ca. 1510-1520, Victoria and Albert Museum, London. © Victoria and Albert Museum, London

wall hanging with a large monochrome painting of the Virgin Mary, hands wide open as she reads a book, with the dove hovering by her head. It was used to cover an altar during Lent, recognizing that the feast of the Annunciation fell in March. Next to it is a fifteenth-century Italian chasuble, made of silk velvet, with intricate embroidery depicting the life of the Virgin. One exquisitely designed scene, using silk and metal thread, shows the Annunciation with Mary sitting on a throne as the angel Gabriel kneels in homage. Above, God the Father looks on as his messenger delivers his words.

We retire to Paul Williamson's office where he unpacks a small box with great care. When he is ready, he hands me tentatively a tiny object made from ivory. It is a wing of a Tabernacle Polyptych made in thirteenth-century England. I notice immediately that the first of three scenes shows the Annunciation. It is so small that both Mary and the angel Gabriel appear wedged close to one another. I learn that this beautiful piece, made in 1240, is one of the earliest examples of the depiction of a lily in an Annunciation scene.

As I hold the precious carving carefully in my hand, I ask Paul Williamson what the annunciation story means for him.

'I have my own baggage,' he responds. 'I was brought up by the Jesuits. They cast a long shadow. I'm not a practising Catholic now so it doesn't have religious resonance. For me, these objects speak rather than as a doctrine. They give me a window into how people thought in the medieval period, the way they believed, the way they used the objects. They often take you right to the heart of religious belief in the Middle Ages. You can understand how people perceived the Annunciation. There's no doubt they believed it absolutely…a comforting certainty about the Gospels. Everywhere you look with medieval objects, there's an obsession with the shortage of life and the need to prepare for a good death. The sublime, stunning beauty, the level of craftsmanship, almost tempts you to think…they believed their work was for the greater glory of God…it almost makes you want to believe it yourself.'

What stops him crossing that line?

'Just not knowing. Agnosticism really. It's a big leap. My mother and father were extremely pious and believed it all. My father was extremely well educated, he had a tough mind, he wasn't a romantic at all, but he accepted every word of Catholic dogma, he took it all on.' He smiles as he wraps up the Annunciation ivory carving and carefully places it back in its box.*

––––––––

A stone's throw from the V&A stands one of Britain's most successful and vibrant churches. The Holy Trinity Brompton (HTB) stands behind the Brompton Oratory, which has a lavishly ornate neo-Classical Roman Catholic edifice. The two churches could not be more different.

As well as the main site of Holy Trinity Brompton on Brompton Road, there are three satellite churches nearby. HTB proclaims itself to be a church 'that loves and accepts everyone' and is focused on the 'evangelisation of the nations and the revitalisation of the Church'. Eleven services are held each Sunday and each week the churches are packed full to the brim.

HTB is also the engine room of the Alpha course, the most successful recruitment initiative devised in recent years to engage potential Christians. This is significant because attendance at Church of England services has gone into free-fall in recent years. The framework of this introductory course for 'outsiders' to Christianity is a structured programme of eleven weekly interactive group sessions. Using a group leader, DVDs and written course materials, each session focuses on a question such as 'Is there more to life

––––––––

*   In January 2016, Dr Paul Williamson retired as Keeper, Department of Sculpture, Metalwork, Ceramics and Glass, after thirty-seven years distinguished service at the V&A.

than this?' 'Who is Jesus?' 'How do I pray?' More than a million people in Britain have attended an Alpha course. It has also been a success internationally, reaching more than thirteen million people in over one hundred and sixty countries.

The pioneer behind this huge expansion in the Alpha course is fifty-nine-year-old Nicky Gumbel, the evangelical Anglican vicar at HTB. His book *Questions of Life* has sold more than a million copies and has been published in nearly fifty countries. But its severest critics have described the Alpha course as the work of a cult-like organisation that, it is claimed, tries to brainwash people using manipulation techniques and encourages participants to believe they can talk in tongues.

As I walk up to the vicarage, I notice that Alpha is not the only session on offer at HTB. There are Connect groups, Prayer groups, a variety of courses in Relationships, Post-Abortion Healing, Recovery and Wellness, the latter specifically aimed at those who've suffered sexual abuse and rape. Everywhere I look, there's a poster for a different group or activity.

A tall, lean figure with neat, grey-flecked hair rushes towards me and opens the front door of the vicarage where I have been standing for more than half an hour. Out of breath, Nicky Gumbel is deeply apologetic, saying he has 'mucked up his timetable'. We walk through his comfortable yet modest home to the garden.

Quickly, I discover that we are not to be alone. It appears that his Communications Director, Mark Elsdon-Dew, will sit in on our session. This is to be the only encounter I experience on my entire journey during which an official is present to take notes. Is that a precautionary measure? I wonder. Has he been hurt or damaged by journalists in the past? Or is it a surprising sign of insecurity on his part? I don't know the answer but I am intrigued that such an apparently successful and dynamic church leader doesn't feel he can talk with me alone.

The son of a German Jew who fled to Britain, Nicky Gumbel was educated at Eton and read Law at Trinity College, Cambridge. He practised as a barrister and was a member of the Holy Trinity Brompton church community before giving up the law in the early nineteen eighties to read Theology at Oxford and then train for ordination as an Anglican priest. He returned to HTB as Curate in 1986 and was appointed Vicar in 2005. He is married to Pippa who plays an integral part in HTB and they have three adult children. The Archbishop of Canterbury, Justin Welby, was a fellow member of the HTB community when Nicky Gumbel first attended the church.

He uses social media to promote his evangelical messages. Earlier, I had connected to his Facebook page, and read his latest posts that will be read by thousands of his followers:

> Children laugh on average a hundred and fifty times a day. Adults laugh an average of six times a day. Jesus tells us to be more like children.

> Stop looking for a perfect church. It does not exist. Join an imperfect church and serve in every way you can to make it nearer perfection.

> Be selective in your battles, sometimes peace is better than being right.

We sit on wooden garden chairs around a table with the noise from the bustle of busy central London ever present in the background. Nicky Gumbel sits beside me and places his Communications Director strategically opposite him so that he is directly in his eye line.

What does the annunciation story mean for him?

'I guess it's the start of the Incarnation so it's a pretty important moment in Christian history.' He laughs nervously and then continues, choosing to focus specifically on Mary. 'She's the model of faith. The most influential person in human history after Jesus. A role model for us all. The second most influential leader of all time. Bearing God in her womb – what a challenge. Her response is taken for granted by us all today but at the time she wasn't married, it was such a major challenge within her culture. I do see it as fact, as what happened. That's what I believe. That's how I take it.'

He talks in clipped, Received Pronunciation and keeps looking across at his Communications Director. It feels like he is looking for approval. He is well mannered and warm yet at the same time surprisingly nervous and lacking in confidence, very different from the charismatic man I had watched on the Alpha course DVD.

'Some see Mary as a model for women but I see her as a model for everyone,' he tells me. 'She has an amazing, simple faith. Obedience, calling, surrender, all rolled into one. She's a very attractive role model of women's leadership. If leadership is about influence, that's why she's the greatest leader after Jesus. She's there at all the key moments...the Incarnation, the Atonement, the Resurrection, Pentecost. No one else is there at all those moments.'

I ask whether she is a bridge or a barrier to greater inter-denominational dialogue. He hesitates before responding and once more looks across at his colleague.

'She should be a bridge but unfortunately we need to get back to...' suddenly, he stops talking, gets up and rushes off back into his house.

A few minutes later he returns with a wad of papers – the notes he used for a recent talk he gave on 'The Call of Mary'. He shuffles through the papers and keeps reciting key headlines and paragraphs. 'What can we learn? That Jesus's DNA came from a combination of her and the Holy Spirit. He had her genetics. He must have looked like her. Had her features. He was trained by her for thirty years.'

He searches through the loose sheets of paper and continues.

'The leading woman of women's liberation. She began the women's liberation movement. At the time when women were regarded as inferior, the fact is that God was born through her.'

He is racing through his notes, scanning them quickly then seizing on ideas and quotes he wants me to hear. I try several times to ask him a question but he appears oblivious and keeps firing new headlines at me. He looks down intently and describes Mary as being involved in a three-stage time bomb. That's interesting, I think, and I try to pause him but he continues talking. Eventually, I manage to interrupt, observing that often Mary divides opinion within the Christian community.

'Really?' he exclaims. 'Some people don't like her?' he asks somewhat innocently.

I squeeze in another question: 'If I came to an Alpha course and explain that I can accept the Crucifixion and the Resurrection but find the Annunciation and a virgin birth really hard to believe, does that matter?'

'Alpha doesn't work like that. We're not telling people what they should or should not believe,' he responds.

But what would he say if I came to the session curious but doubtful about the Annunciation?

'The way Alpha works is everyone makes up their own mind,' he replies. 'In the first half of the session, we say what we believe – it's about presenting Jesus – and in the second half, everyone says what they think. There's not a categorisation of people. If someone declares they're a Christian, then they are a Christian. If they say they're not, I accept that. It's up to God to judge us. Our church is made up of Christians and non-Christians.

We embrace everyone. We're a community. Faith is a belief in Jesus. It's as simple as that. You're not going to be judged on doctrine.'

If Alpha is about teaching, guiding, explaining, I say to him, then surely what Christianity says – he interrupts me.

'Yes, I teach about the Incarnation but I would never ever say if you don't believe this, you're not a proper Christian. I don't like the idea of proper Christians and others. It's heresy,' he responds. 'Galatians says it's just faith. If you believe in Jesus, you're justified by your faith. It's not that I don't care where they are. I don't know where they are. So don't add to it by saying to me you're not a proper Christian. It's not an exam.'

He pauses for a short while before continuing.

'I wouldn't say it doesn't matter. What we encourage is to explore for yourself. You are on a journey. We're all growing. I think what we're confusing in our discussion is what I believe passionately and strongly and, pastorally, how you handle someone who has a different belief. HTB operates as a very hands-off approach to everybody's life. For me, it's the Incarnation, the Atonement and the Resurrection – three in one. You can't separate them. And Mary, as I say, is the model of faith. Facing possible stoning and yet says, "I'm going to do it." Her act is the greatest and most decisive act of faith in history.'

We move on to discuss the declining status of the feast of the Annunciation and he agrees that it's an important issue.

'It's a very good point. I am as guilty as anyone. I do think it's a mistake. It probably has huge implications on how we treat unborn children. We should celebrate the Annunciation because what we're playing into is the modern culture that says you're only a person when you're born and you're not a person beforehand. The Incarnation gets to what personhood is. Right, so in future, it's 25 March,' he proclaims with a chuckle.

I ask if there was a single moment in his life when he realized that he was being called.

'I did have that moment,' he says, 'while studying Economics in my first year at Trinity in Cambridge. (He switched later to Law.) It was 16 February 1974. The day I said yes. I was such a vociferous atheist. I hadn't been brought up a Christian. I was reading the New Testament and was convinced it was true but my initial response was, "Oh no, this is the worst thing that could possibly happen. If it's true, life is going to be terrible from now on." I wanted to say no because life would be so boring. Everything I associated with Christianity was boring. So I thought I'd have a deathbed conversion. I'll enjoy my life now. Then I thought that's intellectually dishonest. So it was a resigned 'life is going to be very different now.' I hope for others it isn't like that – that it isn't a single moment. I hope for others, like my children and my grandchildren, they can have belief from the start, that they're brought up in the faith. But if you're not, then I hope there is a moment. So, as you can see, the Alpha message is "everything is fine". He then looks at me and smiles.'

I show him a print of the Lemoyne painting. What does he see?

'I'm sure it's a great painting but it's quite religious for me. I see Mary more as an ordinary person. It's not how I imagine you getting the message of God. This painting takes it away. When I think of faith, I think of the ordinariness of people and this, to me, is not what life is about. What we're trying to do on Alpha is to stress that faith is not just for religious types who live in a religious world, it's there for the ordinary world of the workplace and the family.'

I have come to the London borough of Hackney to meet the local Anglican vicar who has served at All Saints Church for the past sixteen years. I walk across Stonebridge Gardens, a green open space surrounded by high-rise flats, and enter the mid-nineteenth-century building. The church is dark, unadorned and basic. A drum kit stands by the altar. The vicar and I sit on two oak chairs nearby.

Each Sunday around a hundred people attend the morning service here but today the church is empty and silent. 'We're Anglican in the Catholic tradition – we have vestments, the Eucharist, a band but we're not happy-clappy. It's not entertainment. We're not here to put on a show. It's important to remember why we come together,' the vicar tells me.

As well as being the parish priest at All Saints, fifty-three-year-old Rose Hudson-Wilkin is Chaplain to the Speaker of the House of Commons and a chaplain to the Queen. She is the first black woman in the country to hold such offices.

Born in Montego Bay, Jamaica, in 1961, her mother left home to come to England when Rose was two so she was brought up by her Aunt Pet. She didn't see her mother again until she was ten. She grew up in a tenement yard with no electricity in the house. A standpipe supplied the water. When her mother returned to Jamaica, Rose went to live with her for two years but things did not work out and she spent all her teenage years back with her father (who never married her mother) and his sister, Aunt Pet. She endured a disruptive childhood that she describes as being 'a scar that I didn't allow to become an open wound. That was the dice that life had thrown me and I got on with it. It's a part of my life I still don't fully understand.'

She tells me that at fourteen years old, she had her own annunciation moment.

'I had an overwhelming sense of being called by God. I was dreaming one night and I suddenly woke up. There was somebody in the dream and I was calling out, "Hallelujah, Hallelujah, Hallelujah." It woke me up and the rest of the house. I was disturbed. Someone was calling me. I went to the verandah but I couldn't see who it was. The voice said, "Invite me up." I went to find a light and it was as though the voice vanished. And I heard something say, "Don't invite, that's evil."

'I lay back down in bed and picked up my Bible. It fell open at Luke Chapter 4: "The Spirit of the Lord is upon me because he has anointed me to preach." I then fell asleep. The next morning I woke up and read the Isaiah passage: "The Spirit of the Lord is upon me." It was the same wording. At that moment I felt there was a yes moment. A call to serve – a priestly calling. Of course, in the mid-1970s, there were no women priests then. But I said to God, "I really believe you have called me. Although there are no models for women in this role, you will have to work it out".'

Her local Anglican church in Montego Bay provided her with some much needed stability in her teenage years. She came to England at eighteen and trained as an evangelical Church Army Officer, passionate to share the gospel with others. There she met her future husband Ken and together they had three children. She became a deacon in 1991 and was ordained a woman priest in the first wave of Church of England appointments in 1994. Does she feel there was a direct link between her ordination and her teenage dream?

'Absolutely, absolutely,' she proclaims in her strong Jamaican lilt.

When she appeared on *Desert Island Discs* she proclaimed, 'I'm a Caribbean woman at heart. I'm a world woman. But I bring my Jamaican with me in all I do. It's who I am.' Her head is completely shaved; she smiles widely and has a large, wonderfully engaging laugh that erupts loudly and frequently. She is warm, open and friendly but as soon as I engage with her, I detect a vein of steel and determination.

What does Luke's story of the Annunciation mean for her?

'It draws me to a God who uses the powerless,' she says. 'A God who comes to his people, not waiting for his person to come to him. A God who identifies the poor, the underclass, the people who society says are irrelevant. And he looks at them and says, "You are my people and I'm going to do something really special with you." It invites me, draws me closer, to a God who I believe, as he came to Mary, also comes to me – of humble beginnings in a society that is known as the Third World. And yet this God touches and makes something special. There is something of the personal. He seeks a relationship with Mary and he seeks a relationship with me.'

She stares at me intently, then smiles and moves her chair even closer.

'It begins with Mary. I see her as an underclass woman. She somehow, even though it was very costly, decided to say yes at huge cost to herself. With me, there is a sense that I can identify with her background and life. I have great admiration for Mary and that she had the gall, the courage to say yes. I see her as earthy. In the Anglo-Catholic tradition, they put her on a pedestal but she's not meant to be there, to be idolized in that way. She is gritty and she is real. She's like me and because of that, there's a connection with her journey. If I go in a building and I see her, I may give her a wink and say, "You go girl!" instead of "Holy Mother of God" and all that stuff. That doesn't do anything for me.' She leans back on her chair and shrieks with laughter.

'Is the story rooted in fact or metaphor?' I ask.

'Coming from my background, a little girl from Montego Bay, when I first came to this country to theological college, I came with the very basic knowledge that if the Bible says it, then it is so,' she replies. 'Then at theological college, I learnt that it may not necessarily be so. I don't think my lecturers and fellow students were aware of this but I would go back to my room in floods of tears, shattered because everything that I held dearly was being taken away from me and was being thrown out of the window. That it wasn't all literal. I went into a dark place where I had to wrestle really strongly with my faith. If all I had believed was being thrown away from me, what did I have left in faith to stand firm with? And so, in that wrestling, I remember saying to myself, "Ok Rose, it's clear there's some historical factual things here." So I had to ask myself, "What is going to be the core that you're not going to let go of?" And the core was I believe in God. I believe in a God that became incarnate. Whose Son died for me. Whose Son rose again that I may have life. That much I will not part with. But how he did it is irrelevant as far as I'm concerned.

'For instance, I don't know why I'm breathing in oxygen now. Why oxygen is there. But I am jolly well alive and I'm jolly well grateful it's there. I don't understand it but just because I don't understand it doesn't mean it's not real and that it's not happening. So my way of going forward is that it really doesn't matter if it's proven that she really wasn't real and that it's only a metaphor. That metaphor is so important to me because it's telling me something profound about my own journey and my own connection with God.

'That's why I won't ever get into endless conversation with those atheists who say that it didn't happen and try to disprove it. It's a fool's game. For me, that's faith because faith is about things that are unseen. You go forward accepting it, living it in a way that makes it real. The story leads me. Whether it's real or unreal, it leads me to this great God who decided that this poor girl is going to be the one. The meaning of the story is more important than the actual story if that makes sense.'

So, what does she think is the precise meaning of the story?

'God turns upside down society's way of looking at things. Society goes for the wealthy but...' her voice falls off temporarily. 'But here is the God who could have had anybody – the wealthy, the leaders, the famous. He bypasses Herod, he bypasses the wealthy and choses this poor girl and makes her the mother of his Son. Yes, that's it. It's God turning upside down society's way of looking at things.'

I tell her that Bishop Philip Egan called the Annunciation 'the most important event in human history'.

'Yes, it is – the Incarnation,' she says. 'It's as though God is saying, "I'm giving, I'm giving, I'm giving" and then decides, "Yes, I'll give myself." It's about this endless giving of oneself. The parent who would say take me instead of my child. The partner who would give up their life for the other. The bodyguard who would take the bullet. For me, it's about a God emptying himself.'

How important is it that Mary had the right to say no?

'That is what has always drawn me to the Christian faith. I'm part of a religion that actually allows me to say no. That has been so important to me. If God has given me a mind, he has given me a mind to challenge, to do my own thing. Look at the parable of the Prodigal Son as well as the Annunciation. He decides to go off but the Father does not give up on him. There is a free will. We choose whether we say yes to God and follow in his footsteps.

'I remember my daughter, an actor, coming home from university and saying she doesn't believe any longer. She said "Mummy, what if I don't believe?" I said, "Darling, I don't care whether you believe or not but while you live in this house and partake of the things that the God whom I serve provides us with, you will worship".'

She emits a chest-rattling burst of laughter.

Hang on Rose, I say. That did not give her the right to choose!

'But she still had a choice to come back to the house within the framework of this home,' she responds. 'While you live in this household, this is what we do. You cannot participate in what God has provided here and then say, "I don't believe in God nor worship him." What is interesting, whenever she is home, she plays the organ here and helps with the children. She's found faith in her own way. If I'd said, "Ok, it's fine, if you don't want to, you don't have to", I think the nurturing would not be there. There has to be a framework especially when they're younger.' There is another explosion of laughter.

So, for her, there are limits to free will, I suggest

'I don't know if it's "limits". You have to provide a framework so they can see what it looks like and they can say this is for me or not for me. If you haven't provided that framework, that experience, that nurturing of faith, then they have nothing to choose from.'

I wonder if she venerates Mary.

'I don't pray to her,' she says. 'I pray in thanksgiving for her, that she said yes and that I am able to say yes. I see her as a comrade, a companion on the journey. I also relate to her in the fact that she allowed Jesus to wander off. She's not possessive but there's an overarching care.'

Does it matter to her that it was a virgin birth?

'It doesn't matter. For me, the Virgin Birth is there to show she wasn't sleeping around and that it wasn't someone else's baby.' She giggles. 'It doesn't mean virgin as in virgin. It's God's child and she wasn't sleeping around. And yes, she probably had other children. Scripture says so. I'm sure Joseph had a very fulfilling sex life and they didn't have birth control in those days.'

She shrieks loudly.

'I don't relate to the idea of perpetual virginity. That's about men having problems with their own sexuality.' Her laughter bubbles over effusively. 'I'll be persecuted for that,' she proclaims. 'It's about men not knowing what to do with women. They think, we can't ignore this one because she's Mother of Our Lord so let's put her up there.'

She said earlier that Mary was there for the underdog. Does she feel like an underdog herself?

'I know I'm sometimes treated like an underdog. I don't feel it. I know it. For instance, when I first came to this church, they didn't want me because of being a woman and my colour. One of them who was at the church said, "We are not accustomed to black people leading the church." He left soon after.'

The time has flown by. We have been chatting for seventy-five minutes. It's time to say farewell. I show her the print of Lemoyne's painting.

'Oh, my God, oh, my God, oh, my God. I don't believe it,' she shouts out as she focuses her eyes on the depiction of Mary. 'I can identify with that. I'm looking at her whole demeanour. For me, this is a real OMG moment.'

I leave with her laughter ringing in my ears.

Tina Beattie was born in Lusaka, Zambia, in 1955 and lived much of her early life in Africa. Today, she is Professor of Catholic Studies and the Director of the Digby Stuart Research Centre for Religion, Society and Human Flourishing at the University of Roehampton. She is one of Britain's best-known theologians, and much of her work focuses on the relationship between the Catholic tradition and contemporary culture, especially in areas of gender, sexuality and reproductive ethics.

She has a keen interest in Marian theology, art and devotion. Her doctorate from the University of Bristol, completed in 1998, focused on the theology and symbolism of the Virgin Mary. She has written many books including *Rediscovering Mary: Insights from the Gospels* in 1995 and *God's Mother, Eve's Advocate* published in 2002. Married with four grown-up children, she has a reputation as a liberal modernist and is a regular commentator on religious affairs in the media.

She converted to Roman Catholicism from Presbyterianism in 1987, after the birth of her fourth child, and was attracted to Catholic spirituality while living in Zimbabwe in the early 1980s. As an evangelical Protestant Christian, she tells me how previously she had been deeply suspicious of 'Marian worship' and that Mariolatry had been a great obstacle in the way of her becoming a Catholic.

Before meeting Tina, I read a selection of her work and noted down some of her most interesting phraseology. For example, she wrote that, unlike many Catholic women of her generation, she did not grow up in a Church that 'used the Virgin Mary as a weapon against my own developing sexuality.' She points out that whereas Catholics are taught in childhood to come to Jesus through Mary, she had to find a way to come to Mary through Jesus. It may be easier, she explains, 'for a woman who has had a non-Catholic upbringing to enjoy and celebrate Mary than for a woman who has always been taught to see Mary as a rebuke to her own sexual desires.'

The Annunciation, she claims, 'was not an act of seduction but a free invitation to a woman to participate in God's salvic action. But if this encounter was an occasion of profound joy for Mary, it was also one of risk.'

At the Annunciation, which she calls the 'secret ecstasy', Mary is 'neither subordinate nor subjugated but stands as an autonomous agent in the presence of God, without any need of man to make her complete. The Annunciation means more than the restoration of woman to spiritual wholeness. It also means the end of the God of patriarchy.'

She has also written how priestly homilies on Marian feast days are more likely to alienate and frustrate women in the congregation than to inspire them. It is essential to salvage Mary and the values associated with her, she claims, in a way that is relevant and liberating for all modern Christians, men and women. 'Mary offers men the opportunity to reclaim the motherly aspects of their own natures,' she writes, 'just as she offers women the opportunity to reclaim their sense of autonomy and self-worth before God.'

We meet in her small office on the upper floor of a drab administrative block on the university campus. I learn that when she comes to Roehampton she lives on a houseboat nearby. Right from the start, she demonstrates her extraordinary passion for the annunciation story.

'It's the shock of the new. It's when you think you know what your life is about and there's an interruption, a calling,' she says. 'Perhaps it's catastrophic, sometimes it's an unexpected joy. But it's about our capacity to take the unexpected and make it of God. So something breaks into your life and how do you interpret it and give it meaning? How do you orientate this event towards God in the future? How do you understand what's happening towards your vocation to God? Our word 'crisis' comes from the Greek word *krisis* and it means a time of radical opportunity and decision. It always needs a response from a place you haven't been before. A new thinking. A new reaction to life. The Annunciation is an interruption whereby life can never ever be the same again and how do you make meaning from it?'

This tiny woman speaks slowly, with great precision and intensity. Each syllable is stretched to its limit, and the space left to hang between each utterance draws the conversation to an unexpected length.

When I ask her if she sees the Annunciation as factual, metaphorical or something else, she pauses.

'I believe it happened but that doesn't rule out it being metaphorical,' she says before pausing again. 'I think there's a difference between fact and truth. I do believe in the Virgin Birth. I do believe there was a miracle and no sexual act was involved in the conception. That's a doctrine of the Church. I can't explain it but I believe it. Believing it makes sense to me. Facts are important but facts are facts, they're not truths. Truths are what we make of the facts. We can string along a load of facts but we won't have meaning. Meaning is the truth we use to interpret the facts. There are truths that don't have real scientific facts. I believe it to be true that my husband loves me but if you ask me for scientific proof of that, I can't give it. I can talk about his behaviour, but I can't prove it. I trust it, so I trust that the Virgin Birth is true. A great many profound truths flow from that. If we believe in the Incarnation, we have to believe in a God that doesn't just do symbols and metaphors. We have to believe in a God who is active in the fleshy fabric of being and I do believe that. The Virgin Birth is part of that activity. From the moment Mary conceived Jesus Christ, there was no going back – that was the re-creation of the world.'

Her reply takes more than three minutes to deliver. We move on. Does she see the Annunciation as 'the most important event in human history'?

'Yes, that is the moment – the conception – but I would go further,' she says. 'It created the world because I think it brought creation to its fulfilment. The early Christian Fathers used to call Mary the rational paradise because her body was the creation and what was conceived in her was the new Adam. Just as the earth brought forth the original Adam, so Mary was the paradise that brought forward the new Adam. And she was rational. She was a human who could have said no. She brought forward the new. Eve is a metaphor for the possibility of Mary's no. The first Eve is a metaphor for the human condition. We're alienated, conflicted, divided, tempted. But that is transformed from an animal condition of hopelessness to becoming redeemed because of Mary. The Incarnation, the conception, is the moment creation comes into the fullness of its being. The moment creation finds its meaning.'

She laughs as though to ask, 'are you keeping up with me?' If it is *the* moment, why is the feast of the Annunciation barely acknowledged today?

'Well yes, except the moment of conception is unknown. There's a lovely saying by St Augustine: "Mary, Mary, why are you waiting? The angel is waiting at the gate. All of creation is holding its breath. And you keep the messenger of God waiting while you think about it." She laughs loudly.

'How long was it between Mary's intuition that it was angelic and her knowing that she was pregnant?' she asks rhetorically. 'Mary deciding in her heart this could be. Was it a moment, a year, ten years? I think there was a time Mary knew there was something being asked of her. Then there was a time she was able to say, "let it be". And then there was a time she knew she was pregnant. There wasn't a single moment. I have no idea but I think of it as a long period. It's such a dense mystery. That sense of something happening and us looking back and saying when was the moment? There's something about interpreting it all that's a mystery. The unfolding of a mystery that is a process. So maybe there's wisdom in the Church in marking the actual birth so clearly. A birth happens on a specific day and time. But a conception slowly dawns on us. We can witness birth and death but we can't witness conception and resurrection.

'For me, there are certain things we take on faith because we will never get there logically. We start with the given. Like in mathematics, we start with some given rules to get there. We start with the revealed mysteries from faith and we think from them, not behind them. There's a difference say between the Church teaching that artificial contraception is wrong and the Annunciation. Now I've tried very hard to think with the Church on the former but actually I really do think one must use one's reason in situations like that and there's a mismatch. Whereas when the Church offers me a mystery – the Virgin Birth – I have taken that as non-negotiable. A part of being a Christian is to accept it. But what happens when I accept it and then think what comes from it? It becomes very deep and very rich theologically and personally as a feminist. The Virgin Birth "is" and a great deal flows from that.'

So, is it essential for a faithful Christian to believe in the Virgin Birth?

'You've been with liberal Anglican clerics haven't you,' she laughs. 'You don't have to believe it but, if you do, it becomes very coherent in the wide unfolding spectrum of Christ.' She pauses again for a while and closes her eyes in contemplation.

'You don't have to but you'll never have a theological acceptance of what the Incarnation is if you don't believe in a virgin birth,' she says. 'The virgin mother, until the advent of modern genetics and test-tube babies, was a paradox. Just as something being Word as Flesh is a paradox. It's the reconciling of impossible opposites – one couldn't be a virgin and a mother. The motherhood inserts the Christ into the human story horizontally – he's one of us, he's part of our history. But the virginity makes it vertical. And it's very important that it's a woman who does this because this overturns the order of the fallen world. From the man's dominance of the woman in Eden, it's now a woman who has the voice of authority on behalf of creation. The Catholic Church has yet to discover this.'

She chuckles to herself, takes a sip of her hot drink, smiles again and then continues.

'Therefore, through the Annunciation and the virgin conception, I see the whole story turned inside out. The woman conceives free from an all-male domination. And this is an anticipation of the fulfilment of our restoration by God. In Mary, we see its beginnings.

In Eve we see the story of life as it is for a woman and in Mary we see the promise fulfilled. The two have to be held together.'

What about those who see the Annunciation as a symbol of surrender?

'But she's surrendering to God, isn't she?' she responds firmly.

And what if she'd said no?

'That's the story of Eve. It's a paradox,' she says. 'Eve belongs to the story of the human condition as it is. If it was an unredeemed condition, that would have been the story, but it never has been unredeemed.'

Does she believe that Mary had no more children after giving birth to Jesus?

'I wouldn't put as much weight on that as on the Virgin Birth,' she says. 'I think it is important but not in the terms of the mystery of faith. She was the first woman of a new creation. To be that woman and then for her to return to traditional married life would take away her eschatological significance. Yes, she's a person, a woman. But she is powerfully symbolic as well. A woman who symbolizes the renewal of everything and, therefore, she doesn't get inserted back into the old order. She is a powerful symbol of that which is God's alone. I think of nothing degrading in that…the problem is we immediately think of virginity in the biological terms of sexual intercourse. Mary married Joseph. She had all the love and companionship of a good marriage but she also retained that virginal wildness that is the nature of God. A mother who then has sexual intercourse and children, well there's then a world of justice. If she'd been an ordinary wife and mother, it would have been very difficult for her to be part of Christ's ministry.

'So I think he had cousins. I grew up in Africa. The idea of talking about "brothers and sisters" in tribal groups and kinship groups like that is the norm. So why is that a problem? I grew up a Presbyterian so I'm sometimes very literal about the Bible. Jesus on the cross said to a disciple "Here is your mother." That's an odd thing to do if she had other children. Why would he do that? No, he gave her to the Church, as the symbol of discipleship.'

Of course, if you take a literal meaning in the Bible, I suggest to her, then he did have brothers and sisters. I reference Matthew's Gospel 13:54-58: 'This is the carpenter's son surely? Is not his mother the woman called Mary, and his brothers James and Joseph and Simon and Jude? His sisters, too, are they not all here with us?'

She shakes her head slowly and smiles. Does her view – that Mary was a mother who never had sex throughout her life – make Mary unapproachable and unnatural?

'Incarnational talk means we have to talk in human and divine terms so we're always talking in paradoxes,' she says. 'In human terms, it's not just about Mary as a woman. It's about Mary as a creature in whom we see what total intimacy with God means. If a woman said to me, "I don't understand all of that, other than in the context of sex with my husband", I'd say you've got a real problem with your psyche if you don't have that inner core of your own being which should not be projected onto any sexual or parental relationship. It's the God-shaped space within us and it's an insatiable desire that nothing of this creation should quench. That's who Mary is for me. She's that desire for God that is so focused, so attentive, that it materializes itself. She is that space of virginal attentiveness – an empty, formless self to a life we don't know. She is also God's assurance to women in a world in which women are so defined by their sexuality. Hers was a unique vocation and she was given the grace to fulfil it. She is creation.'

I hand her the print of Lemoyne's Annunciation painting.

'It doesn't grab me,' she says. 'It's quite romanticized. It's not earthed. There's nothing of the natural world apart from the beautiful clouds. The Annunciation is the marriage of heaven and earth and earth has to be there. It's too ethereal. It's too resolved. She looks too docile and he looks too commanding, too muscular. There's too many associations…of almost…I don't want to say a rapist God. That sounds like cheap feminist rhetoric. But yes, some masculine power swooping down from the heavens on this very feminine girl. It's beautiful in a sweetish kind of way but mm, yes, there's no hint of trauma. There's no shock of the new.'

Suddenly, she walks across to her desk and fires up her laptop. She clicks on an icon but it takes an age to load. 'You have to see this,' she insists. Eventually, a PowerPoint presentation appears on the screen that shows the images of many famous paintings of the Annunciation. The presentation is entitled 'Virgins, Lechers and Angelic Encounters: the visual representation of theological ideas'. Many great Renaissance works are featured – Botticelli, Fra Angelico, Lorenzo Monaco, Martini, Baldovinetti, van Cleve, Lotto, del Sarto – as well as later pictures by El Greco, Rubens and Tissot. There are even Annunciation images from China, Sri Lanka and South Korea. She includes forty-three images in all.

We talk at length about Dante Gabriel Rossetti's *Ecce Ancilla Domini*, Henry Ossawa Tanner's *Annunciation* and two controversial twentieth-century depictions by the surrealist painter Mati Klarwein and the American artist John Collier.

Much to my surprise, as I bid Tina Beattie farewell, I feel compelled to tell her that I am going to discover more about those four works as part of the next stage of my journey. I want to consider the different approaches of Rossetti, Tanner, Klarwein and Collier – artists who paint the same story at different points in history. Perhaps they may reveal new depths to the annunciation story?

CHAPTER 14

WHAT YOU SEE IS WHAT YOU GET

I head to Tate Britain in London, eagerly anticipating the moment when I can cast my eyes on *Ecce Ancilla Domini* (Behold the Handmaid of the Lord) by Dante Gabriel Rossetti.

I arrive at the gallery and search everywhere but it is nowhere to be seen. Eventually, I discover that it is being held in storage in south-east London.

So several days later, I find myself passing through a set of high security gates leading into a bleak industrial estate off the Old Kent Road. My destination is Tate Stores, an enormous warehouse. Here, thousands of works by eminent artists hide away, stacked on shelves and in racks, as there is not enough space at Tate Britain and Tate Modern to display them all.

Leaning against a wall on the floor, near to an Andy Warhol screen print of Marilyn Monroe, I catch sight of Rossetti's famous painting wrapped in protective plastic sheeting. Next to it stands a vacuum cleaner.

I cannot quite believe that possibly the most famous nineteenth-century painting of the Annunciation lies on the floor in a warehouse where no one can view it. The member of staff accompanying me says she is unsure whether it has just returned from being on show at another gallery, has been undergoing restoration or, more likely, has been removed temporarily from Tate Britain to be replaced by another painting. 'I don't think it's been shown there for ages. There isn't space for everything,' she says.

I crouch down on the floor directly in front of it. The artist completed the work in 1850 when he was twenty-two years old. When it was first exhibited at the National Institution, its style and iconography were met with stinging criticism, and initially it failed to sell. Today, however, the painting is widely acclaimed for its originality and radicalism. Traditionally, Annunciation scenes show Mary in her study or garden,

40. Dante Gabriel Rossetti *Ecce Ancilla Domini* (The Annunciation), 1850, Tate Britain, London
© Tate Images

dressed formally in blue and red, often in quiet contemplation. This painting is very different. Mary is pictured sitting on her single bed dressed in a nightgown, having been woken by the angel. Her body leans against the wall in an awkward pose. She looks like she is in a trance.

The room has the appearance of a nun's cell. Mary's nightgown, the bed sheet, the angel's cloak and the walls and tiles are all painted in brilliant white, as if to emphasize her innocence and purity. A wingless angel Gabriel holds what art commentators often describe as a 'phallic-shaped' lily stem diagonally placed in the direction of her womb. A long slit in the side of his white garment reveals the angel to be naked. The psychosexual dimension to the encounter is clear. The perturbed eyes of Mary are transfixed on the lily stem that has three buds, only two of which have opened. Above the lily flutters a white dove, synonymous with the biblical description of the Holy Spirit at Christ's baptism in the River Jordan.

In contrast to the dominant white of the picture, a screen behind her displays the traditional blue usually associated with Mary and heaven. Around the angel's feet are golden flames as he hovers just above the tiled floor. A piece of red embroidery hangs on a pedestal next to her bed, displaying a lily stem, its crimson colour referencing the blood of Christ and the suffering to come. An open view at the back of the bedroom shows a tree outside – the Tree of Life in the Garden of Eden. By placing the event in an ordinary bedroom and implying that the meeting between Mary and the angel Gabriel was of a sexual nature, Rossetti made a radical and innovative departure from past Annunciations.

To fully appreciate the iconography in the picture, it is important to have viewed Rossetti's earlier painting, also owned by the Tate and currently displayed in Tate Britain's 1840 room. It is called *The Girlhood of the Virgin Mary* and was completed the year before his Annunciation in 1849. The picture shows the story of Mary as a young girl at home working on embroidery with her mother, Anna. The red material is the same as that hanging in Rossetti's Annunciation painting. Mary looks similar too, with pale skin and long golden hair flowing down the full length of her back. There are other symbols. A red shroud hanging over an aperture is the one that Jesus will wear later in his life. Mary's father, Joachim, is outside the house pruning a vine, which traditionally symbolizes truth. Nearby, a dove sits on a perch and there is a trellis nearby shaped like a cross.

This first painting emphasizes that Mary was chosen well before she knew she was to bring the Saviour into the world. *Ecce Ancilla Domini*, completed a year later, focuses on the fulfillment of the prophecy. It occurs to me that surely they should be displayed side by side?

―――――――

In 1996, I attended an eight-week advanced management course at the Wharton Business School in Philadelphia. Whilst there, I had the opportunity to visit the Philadelphia Museum of Art, where I viewed Henry Ossawa Tanner's oil painting *The Annunciation*.

I remember loving the realism of this painting, although, at that time, it did not spark any profound questions in the same way that Lemoyne's painting has done. In those days I had other things on my mind. However, since my interest in the Annunciation has been wakened, I have revisited Tanner's painting and have realized that it is possibly my favourite depiction of the encounter.

As a child, Henry Ossawa Tanner was brought up in a religious home – his father was a bishop in the African Methodist Episcopal Church. Born in Pittsburgh in 1859, he lived his early life in Philadelphia and trained at the Pennsylvania

41. Henry Ossawa Tanner *The Annunciation*, 1898, Philadelphia Museum of Art.
© Philadelphia Museum of Art

Academy of Fine Arts as its only black student, before moving to Paris where he studied at the Académie Julian. He made the French capital his home and exhibited regularly at the annual Salon. Tanner became the first African-American artist to gain international acclaim.

He painted this Annunciation work in Paris in 1898 soon after returning from his travels to the Middle East including Jerusalem and Cairo. One reference suggests that the model for Mary was the opera singer Jessie Macauley Olssen, who became his wife the following year. Another entry suggests that while he was in the Holy Land, a young Jewish woman agreed to pose for him. Certainly, Tanner made many sketches of the clothing styles and architecture of Palestine, as well as recording its intense colours and light. All would inform his depiction of Mary and her home. On his return to Paris, apparently, he was so taken by a groundbreaking demonstration of electric light that it became the inspiration for his characterisation of the angelic voice.

The warm glow in Mary's face, her rumpled peasant clothing, the crumpled Middle Eastern rug laid on the stone floor and the overall simplicity of her bedroom are all important features of this painting. So too is her modest pose as she leans forward calmly to listen to the voice, her hands clasped together. Tanner reveals part of her bare foot below her nightgown to add to its humanity. And there's no winged angel present – just a shaft of light.

Of course, at the time of the Annunciation in Nazareth, Mary probably would have been a member of a local peasant family and slept on a basic mattress on a raised platform just above a stone or dirt floor. She would have worn a simple cotton robe down to her ankles. She may have had a candle or an oil lamp to provide a basic, dimmed light.

The sense of realism, the serenity of Mary and the dazzling radiance of the vertical beam of light make this painting so compelling. It also has a spiritual quality that captures brilliantly the intensity of the moment. I love it.

In 1972, I was thrilled to be able to buy one of my very first long-playing records, using money given to me for my fourteenth birthday. The album was *Abraxas* by the American group Santana.

Two years previously, it had topped the Billboard album chart in America. As much as its unique blend of high-energy Latin rhythms, rock guitar solos and jazz-fusion beats, it was the album's cover that intrigued me. I would stare for hours at its psychedelic style, extraordinary detail, fantastic range of colours and symbols, and the strange characters that it featured. My eyes would fix upon a white dove, placed strategically between the legs of a beautiful, naked black woman's body, his beak resting by the mass of her pubic hair. Then they would stray to the figure hovering above her: a svelte, bald headed, heavily tattooed, red painted female angel pointing to the sky. I found the images beautiful, erotic and yet disturbing.

42. The author's personal copy of *Abraxas* by Santana, 1970. Cover art: MATI

Eight years after its completion, the legendary guitarist Carlos Santana saw a reproduction of this painting and knew immediately that he had to feature it as the cover of his next record. Many years later, Rolling Stone magazine named *Abraxas* the thirteenth greatest album cover of all time.

I remember studying the back cover to find out the names of those who had worked on the album. The only mention of the artwork was expressed in three words: Cover art: MATI.

Wind the clock forward forty-two years. When Tina Beattie showed me her presentation: *Virgins, Lechers and Angelic Encounters* on her laptop, I discovered that the album cover is from a painting called *Annunciation* and was created by the artist Mati Klarwein in 1961 when he was twenty-nine.

Subsequently, I learn that, as well as being heavily influenced by the Christian story of the Annunciation and the great Renaissance works on the subject, Klarwein's painting also references the birth of the Buddha by showing an elephant impregnating the side of the black woman's body. The naked black woman symbolizing Mary is surrounded by images of fertility, and the angel is pointing upwards to the first letter of the Hebrew alphabet, the symbol aleph, to signify the beginning.

Matias Klarwein was born in 1932 in Germany and, having fled the country with his Jewish parents as Nazism tightened its grip, he spent his childhood in Palestine. When the State of Israel was established in 1948, he left for Paris where he trained as an artist. He always liked to emphasize that he had grown up in three different cultures: Jewish, Islamic and Christian. He declared that 'these circumstances and my family's stern resistance against being part of any orthodoxy made me the outsider I am today and always have been.'

He has been described as an illustrator, an easel painter and even an extra-terrestrial. 'What you see is what you get. Nothing less, nothing more' he once said of his work. 'Anyone can interpret their own message in my painting. That is the message.' Andy Warhol said Klarwein was probably his favourite artist. His artistic style is heavily

43. Mati Klarwein *Annunciation*, 1961. © matiklarweinart.com By kind permission of Balthazar Klarwein

shaped by surrealism, pop culture, psychedelia and religious symbolism. An important influence was the Viennese painter, Ernst Fuchs. Klarwein once described himself as 'the most famous unknown painter in the world'. He died of cancer at his home in Majorca in 2002.

Mati Klarwein started painting *Annunciation* in New York City soon after moving there at the beginning of the 1960s and he completed it in Deia in northern Majorca two years later. He said it was the first picture he painted 'after my initial New York awakening' and was completed while at 'the peak of [my] molecular bio-energy'. It was part of a series of paintings for a major project he called the *Aleph Sanctuary*, which was to be a chapel featuring a wide range of biblical interpretations. The woman depicted as the Virgin Mary was Jill, his Guadeloupean girlfriend at the time, and there is also a self-portrait in the painting of himself as Joseph. The rich variety of background images references many of the views he saw from his home in Majorca. Today, a private collector, living in Barcelona, owns the original painting.

I contact Mati's twenty-nine-year-old son, film director Balthazar Klarwein, who helps to conserve his father's artistic estate. I want to discuss what motivated Mati Klarwein to paint such an extraordinary depiction of the Annunciation.

'In his private writings, he says he was influenced by the energy of moving to New York,' he tells me. 'He'd also been travelling in Africa, India and Central America and all these travels and experiences influence it. When he was a child at school in Jerusalem, he first heard the biblical stories and then when he was living in Paris he saw some of the great Renaissance works on the Annunciation. But he was always looking forward.

'He was an amazing father. He had a very open mind in the way he saw the world. He was so on top of culture and art. He had a clear view of how he wanted to see a globalized world. He wasn't making fun of the Annunciation at all. He was making a point of mixing races and cultures to show the true globalisation of the world. Everyone knows the image but no one knows the artist. It's his most acclaimed work.'

We discuss a highly relevant quote from his father: 'I choose to believe in free will. We have to believe that we have a choice. Not to choose is the worst choice of all...unless your choice is not to choose.'

'He wasn't religious himself but he was highly spiritualized,' Balthazar Klarwein tells me. He often said he was 'part of the undefined religion of everything'.

––––––––––

The American painter and sculptor, John Collier's depiction of the Annunciation, completed in 2000, is set in present day American suburbia. It shows a young teenage girl, having arrived back from school to start her homework, being confronted on her doorstep by a young pious-looking angel, his praying hands clasped together and his heavy wings dropping down behind him. The soft colours of the plumage match those of his full-length cloak. He leans forward, inclining his head towards the girl. Although the painting acknowledges the great Renaissance artists of the past in its use of iconography and symbolism, what makes this depiction so interesting and so controversial is the way in which Collier places the encounter in a contemporary setting.

44. John Collier *The Annunciation*, 2000. © John Collier and Hillstream LLC

Commissioned by St Gabriel's church in McKinney, Texas, the image is widely available to view on the Internet. Indeed, when using a search engine to produce a list of the best-known paintings of the Annunciation, the Collier picture is frequently featured. But it is one of those paintings that deeply divides opinion. Those who like it speak admiringly of its realism, simplicity and relevance. Critics damn it as sickly, childlike and 'mind boggling'.

Aged sixty-five and living in Texas, John Collier is a former award-winning book illustrator who turned in later life to sculpture and oil painting. He was chosen as the chief sculptor for the Catholic memorial at Ground Zero in New York City. I am keen to hear about the inspiration behind this Annunciation work and what he wanted to communicate.

'I thought it would be interesting to see an ancient story set in contemporary times,' he tells me. 'Just like the way the great paintings were done in Renaissance times. It hasn't been done too often in so long. Also, I had the desire to show just how young Mary was – aged thirteen to fourteen.

'It's traditional in some ways. She's wearing blue and reading a book, probably Isaiah. There are lilies in the foreground. There's the sealed window behind the angel's head, symbolizing her virginity. The Holy Spirit as a dove is on a roof nearby waiting for Mary's answer. But I put some untraditional things in too. The welcome mat, the doorbell, her untied shoes. It's the extraordinary and the commonplace together and the Bible is full of that. The house she comes out of is palatial but the neighbourhood area around her is poor. That's symbolizing the condition of her soul. She's been doing her homework, absorbed in a book, and suddenly she's looking at the most extraordinary thing she's ever seen. But she's not recoiling. I wanted to portray her as if she was your own sister or daughter. The contrast of what an angel looks like and the girl from down the block.'

I ask him about the church's reaction when it was unveiled.

'They liked it but they were afraid of it,' he says. 'They didn't know what to do with it. So they put it in the narthex rather than in the main body of the church. The women in particular liked it because it looked like an everyday daughter instead of what so often Mary is portrayed as – not like us.'

I wonder what the reaction has been outside of St Gabriel's church.

'Quite extraordinary,' he responds. 'I feel gratified so many people have noticed it. Priests from everywhere write to me saying how they use it when they recite the Rosary. Kids write to me about how much they love it. I'm very happy and touched that so many people are looking at it all around the world. It's now so well known online. I see reactions using Russian Cyrillic lettering and Chinese fonts and I love the fact that people from so far away have found it interesting. The Internet has democratized everything and here is a powerful example. I'm so happy.

'They could have thrown rocks at it so to speak although that's difficult to do online,' he chuckles. 'There are so few religious painters in the twenty-first century. My work is narrative and objective in its approach and that makes it suspect in the mind of a modern art critic. But I decided why don't I just paint what I want to paint. I don't care what they think. I could paint the Annunciation for the rest of my life and be happy. There's so many ways of showing its meaning.'

CHAPTER 15

THE CUSP OF SALVATION

The waiting room of Archbishop's House in Westminster displays a large print of Fra Angelico's *The Annunciation*. When summoned, I make my way up the grand staircase to find Cardinal Vincent Nichols waiting for me at the top. He proceeds to tell me about each of the Cardinals who are depicted in a series of oil paintings lining the length of the landing. Vincent Nichols is the leader of the Roman Catholic Church in England and Wales. He is sixty-eight and immediately appears relaxed and friendly. There is no visible sign of high office reflected in his clothing; he is wearing a plain black cassock and clerical collar. There is no media advisor or assistant anywhere to be seen.

The scouse lilt in his voice is easily detectable; something he would be pleased to acknowledge. He is proud of his Liverpool roots and extols them from the very start of our conversation. The fortunes of Liverpool Football Club seem to be as important to him as the major issues of the day. He was born in Crosby and was educated at the nearby Christian Brothers establishment, St Mary's College, with its motto *fidem vita fateri* – 'show your faith by the way you live.' He went on to the Venerable English College in Rome, studied Philosophy and Theology at the Gregorian University before being ordained in his home Archdiocese of Liverpool in 1969. He spent fourteen years as a priest during which time he also gained a Master's degree in Theology.

At one time, he served as the General Secretary of the Catholic Bishops' Conference of England and Wales where he gained a reputation as a dynamic administrator before becoming Archbishop of Birmingham. In 2009, he was appointed by Pope Benedict to succeed Cormac Murphy-O'Connor as Archbishop of Westminster and in 2014, Pope Francis admitted him to the Sacred College of Cardinals. Those close to him describe him as: wily, a master politician, a shrewd tactician, ambitious, a champion of the suppressed, a strong and confident media performer, kind yet tough, humane yet determined. All of them agree on one thing – that he was destined to become a Cardinal.

We sit on two comfy chairs in the middle of his large office and I begin by asking if he can pinpoint a single moment when he felt a calling to be a priest.

'I would say to begin with, from the age of twelve and thirteen, there was a gnaw, a profound, uncomfortable sense of something I have to do,' he recalls. 'I couldn't speak about it. I hated it. I can remember being on the Anfield Road end [at Liverpool's football ground] where I would stand, and saying, "God, will you just leave me alone? Will you just let me disappear into this crowd?" Eventually, around sixteen, I remember vividly going to see the local priest, Michael O'Callaghan. He took me upstairs. It was very unusual. I said, "I feel God wants me to be a priest." Astonishingly, he responded by saying, "I want you to understand it's not a sin to refuse a vocation." He didn't want me to do it out of obligation. There had to be a free will. You have the right to say no. So there was a whole vortex of things going round. It was more gradual, organic.'

Does he see a parallel between his story and Mary's in the sense that both heard a call and both had the right to say no?

'You're quite right. That's true,' he responds.

Was it the power of the calling that made him say yes?

'Some years on, literally the night before I was to be ordained a priest, my elder brother said, "What on earth are you becoming a priest for?" I said, "Peter, because I know it makes sense of who I am".'

He crouches forward as though he is going to let me in on a secret.

'I'll tell you another story. It's not publicly known. I was in the seminary in Rome, five years in and with two to go. I'd more or less made my mind up that it was too much and I was going to leave. I was writing the letter. Then, an airmail arrived from a priest from India saying once you've set your hand on the plough, you keep on going, so be encouraged. To this day, I have no idea who he was but I thought, good Lord, maybe I should stay.'

I wonder what he thinks is the spiritual meaning of the Annunciation.

'The Annunciation is an invitation to remember transcendence,' he begins. 'That each of us is addressed by God, each of us is esteemed by God and is, at least in potential, full of grace. It's a reminder of the dignity of every person no matter how lowly or simple or confused or angry or bitter that person might be.

'It's also from the other point of view a place to remember how we radically comport ourselves in life. Life makes best sense when we can echo Mary's words. The recognition that the providence of God is the strongest reality in our lives. It's even more fundamental than a calling. It's like the platform on which I stand, the starting point, the foundation. It is that strange contradictory truth of how we think of ourselves – that we get closer to our fulfilment with a degree of passivity.'

Does he see the story primarily as factual, metaphorical, mythical or something else?

'Oh, I would very simply take it as the narrative of an event that happened,' he replies assertively. 'We don't know by evidence but we take as true many things on less evidence than we have here. There's nothing to suggest the gospel writers are not reliable witnesses. There's no sense of deliberate ploys to deceive. Yes, there's a greater emphasis on infancy in Luke and I wonder, was Luke close to Mary personally? I don't have any trouble with it. I must admit I don't spend much time pondering the substantive literal truth of it. Regarding the question, it's not an either/or answer. I see it as both. If what we are given in the Gospels is an incarnation of the truth of God, then clearly that's going to work on all sorts of different levels.'

He makes reference to having looked earlier at the Lemoyne painting, which he describes as 'a bit fussy'. He comments that the usual eye contact between Mary and the angel is lacking and mentions that the angel Gabriel is summoning Mary to something that is almost beyond her understanding.

'I love the fact that in France, it may be known as the "lost Annunciation" because you could say in our society today, it is now a "lost Annunciation". It is an annunciation of our transcendence and of both our capacity and our calling to understand and share in the life of God, and that is being lost. And we need to recover that annunciation.'

I remind him that in a recent sermon at Walsingham, he described the Annunciation as 'the most important word of consent ever uttered in human history.' He responds, 'There's a lovely commentary or meditation by Bernard, I think, [the thirteenth-century French Cistercian abbot, Bernard of Clairvaux] in which he says something along the lines of "the whole world, prostrate at your feet, is waiting Mary on your word of consent. What will you say? Do you know what hangs on your answer?"

'Of course, the real importance of the Annunciation is the person who is not portrayed – the Word that is taking flesh. And if this annunciation of who we are, of our calling, and our depth of being, and our transcendent nature, if that is to be understood and followed, then it is the hidden person of Jesus, hidden in the picture, who is going to emerge and teach us how to enter and live and share. It's only because of Jesus that it is a unique event in human history.'

We discuss the idea that God asks and never imposes, as well as the importance of Mary's freely given consent to the Annunciation.

'That's part of our transcendent nature. You cannot force God,' he tells me.

I wonder if he accepts that the importance of the feast of the Annunciation is played down somewhat today.

'I think that's fair,' he replies immediately.

I tell him that my wife says we all mark birthdays but not conception days.

'Yes but no conception day is quite like this one. A natural conception is of its nature intensely private and mysterious. But this is known, this is asked for, this is announced, this is the start. I agree we've lost the importance of the feast but, more importantly, we've lost its core meaning – of what it is to be human and how it announces the true depth of our humanity.'

Is the Virgin Birth fundamentally important to him?

'It's not something about which I'd ponder. But I do think the positive affirmation of the fatherhood of God is essential. I would say I quite understand and accept the insistence in the Church's teaching on the Virgin Birth for that purpose. To be unequivocal, that what took flesh in the womb of the Virgin Mary was the eternal Son of the Father and not a borrowed being.'

Has he ever contemplated that the conception was virginal but that Mary went on to have other children naturally or does he believe that she gave birth to Jesus and remained a virgin throughout her life?

'I would take the second option,' he says. 'It may be that Joseph accepted her as someone who had made this promise of virginal life but he already had children and hence the description of "brothers and sisters". He was very much the protector husband rather than a teenage bridegroom. I'd take it as it is and move on and try and understand the meaning of it.'

Thirty minutes into our conversation, the tone shifts dramatically. Cardinal Vincent Nichols asks me to come over to his desk. I see an image of the Lemoyne painting on his computer screen and notice nearby on his desk a copy of today's edition of a national newspaper. The stark headline reads:

45. Video image of Steven Sotloff and 'Jihadi John' (Mohammed Emwazi) 2014

A Briton will be next warns 'Jihadi John' as he beheads second captive

Underneath these words is a chilling picture of the kidnapped American journalist Steven Sotloff, kneeling down with his eyes open, taken moments before his execution. To the side of him, the masked Isis terrorist 'Jihadi John' stands holding up a knife.

The composition of both images – the Lemoyne painting and the image taken from the recently released Isis video – is strikingly similar.

'When I was thinking about the Annunciation this morning and then looked at the morning papers, I said I know what I will say to you,' he explains. 'The absolute inverse annunciation, the absolute antithesis of the annunciation story is the photo on the front of this newspaper. The man there kneeling down and the man standing over him with a knife. That's an annunciation too. An annunciation of terror, an annunciation of the irrational, destructive side of human nature. The two images can be stood next to each other. The Lemoyne painting image here and that one there. And the terrifying things that the Jihadist is trying to say is: "This is God's work" and it isn't. That is the ultimate horrific thing for me. That it is a total corruption of anything we understand about God and thereby ourselves. It's a corrupt, blasphemous human nature announcing itself whereas that there [he points to Lemoyne's painting], in its light and beauty, is the transcendent human nature being announced to us.'

He peers at the computer screen and looks closely at the depiction of Mary.

'If you look at the Lemoyne painting, she shows her neck. There's a whole biblical thing about being a stiff-necked race and the race has to learn to bend its neck before God. And of course the executioner requires the exposure of the neck too.'

He continues to stare at the Lemoyne painting.

'I think what you see here is love in the face of the angel. This raised arm of Gabriel is not a forthright, abrupt summons but a call of love with great gentleness and tenderness. Mary is utterly not presumptive but open to be raised, to be lifted up to fulfil God's plan for her.'

He picks up the newspaper, looks at the shocking image of Steven Sotloff then puts it down, shaking his head.

'It's a message of defiance, of hatred, of revenge, of destruction. The angel comes to seek Mary's consent. The hooded Jihadist John comes to impose his. The angel brings a message of life. Jihadist John announces death. They're both annunciations,' he declares solemnly.

For the last nineteen years, The Right Reverend Dr Richard Chartres has been the Bishop of London. Appointed in 1995, he is third in line in the Church of England hierarchy, after Canterbury and York. Married with four grown-up children, he is an imposing figure with a formidable intellect. A graduate in History at Cambridge, he abandoned his theological studies at Cuddesdon, taking a job in Sainsbury's, before returning to complete them at Lincoln Theological College. He was ordained in 1973. 'For you, I am a bishop but with you I am a Christian', he says of his role.

We meet at his residence in the Old Deanery, a few yards away from St Paul's Cathedral, shortly after he has bid farewell to a group of touring American theologians. He is a big man in every sense. With his white beard, red cassock and booming voice, he is hard to miss. The press has reported regularly that he did not put his name forward to succeed Rowan Williams as Archbishop of Canterbury because he thought he would be too old to take on such a gruelling task. However, at sixty-four years old, his energy levels appear to be unbounded. He says he tries to follow the example of St Augustine – 'unity through diversity' – and does not ordain either males or females to the priesthood in his London diocese so that he does not cause offence.

We ensconce ourselves in a small meeting room on the first floor before he explains what the Annunciation story means for him.

'Much religion is spurious – a business of the bruised and humiliated ego surreptitiously re-ascending to worship some projection of itself,' he says in a powerful, almost thunderous voice. 'So much of religion is confected. It's a God we make in our own image. In the Holy Scriptures is the communication of the authentic God, the God who created us, not the confection of our imagination. He had never been seen at anytime, says St John, and we would never know anything about him unless he had, as we believe he had, communicated himself. Right the way through Scripture, there are these extraordinary annunciations: "Adam, where are you?"; "Samuel, Samuel"; "Abraham, leave your household goods and set out on a journey"; and, of course, the supreme annunciation to Mary. That is how it all begins.

'So, spiritually, it alerts you to the presence of the divine messages in everyday life and that you don't hear them or see them unless you're looking for them, unless you're expectant. There is a receptivity that is in our gift. Being there to be found which, of course, most of us aren't most of the time because we live in the mental ego level and we are anywhere but where we appear to be. We are all over the place.'

He sounds like a Shakespearian actor in full flow.

'So it's being there to be found and having the conviction that flows from something… it's rather like Solzhenitsyn and his experience in the camp. He went as a very perturbed intellectual and it was in the camp that he recovered a communication through some other prisoners in the depth of his own being. Working in the cold and discomfort beyond the camp walls, he received communication of the kind a person can never forget, which is a taste that means you find nothing else remotely comparable and which you can't argue with. And, therefore, you are given a gift of faith and conviction, which is not susceptible to being destroyed by argument. It was an overwhelming annunciation. It unnerved him for a lifetime. And, so in the same way for the Blessed Virgin Mary, there's a being alert to the movement of God. So, in a nutshell, I start from a very awry, biblically-formed view of the spuriousness of much religion.'

Within minutes of meeting him, I find his self-confidence, the sheer force of his personality and his highmindedness almost overwhelming. Apparently, he adored drama at school and he seems to have lost none of his love for taking centre stage. He speaks with forceful authority and deep conviction and, at times, seems to be talking to himself or into the distance. Throughout the conversation, he never seems to pause and he hardly ever looks at me.

I ask warily, if he regards the Annunciation as fact or pure metaphor? He closes his eyes before answering.

'I don't know what you mean by pure metaphor,' he replies. 'I regard it as poetic language, which is the most extraordinary accurate way of describing what is an overwhelming reception of the communication of God. I suppose if you're asking me "fact or fairytale?" then I'd say fact. But I don't think fact in the way we understand it really does justice to it. Was it a locution? Was it a vision? I think I'm agnostic about that – the methodology, the mechanics.'

His eyes remain closed as he continues to elucidate.

'To me, and this is utterly fundamental, what rescues you from the spurious, confected religion is communication from the side of the Other and which happens in all sorts of ways. Words come to life and reverberate in the depths in a way in which it is not the case if you had them in your field of vision and you dominate them within your framework. If there's a genuine communication of the word and it enters into a dialogue with you, as from the Other, practically speaking, the voice of God, through the messenger, through the angel, then I would say if you're using the word "fact" then it is definitely on the fact side.'

Phew! I am trying to keep up here. I am listening as carefully as I can to his pronouncements but I am already feeling somewhat intellectually inadequate.

I tell him that some theologians and clerics have told me the annunciation story did not actually happen, but that the story is a metaphor with a profound message.

'No, no, that's deeply, deeply distressing and awry,' he says emphatically. 'This is not the case. The weakness of much western religion is that God has become so many ideas in the mind. God himself has become an object. Scripture has become objectified. The whole meaning of the Annunciation is that a channel of communication, heart to heart, subject to subject, is opened up. If you are still in the realm of the Cartesian eye of a world of objects then I would say, with the greatest love and respect, you haven't even got to the starting point.'

Is his phrase 'ready to be found' the key message he receives from Luke's story?

'Yes, "ready to be found". Most of us aren't ready to be found because for some reason in your life a Copernican shift has occurred and you recognize that you are not a solitary, dominant eye around which everything constellates. That you are in the presence of life. You are part of the constellation of life and life is living through you in a way that abolishes the subject/object distinction and division. And the way this starts is with a word associated with the Blessed Virgin Mary – humility – an extraordinary difficult word to use in contemporary English. If it means "close to the humus", close to the body of a young woman full of perturbation, full of the seeds of life but vulnerable, then I think that what we're talking about is beginning, without too much by way of a carapace of interpretation, to be about being part of the earth, part of one's body and in that state of real humility, not beating yourself up, not an elaborate self-abrogation or an attempt to pretend to other people that you're worse than you really are. This immense humility is what I see. And it begins with not too much ideological coverings but with an experience of the life that is being lived through you, through your body, your individual circumstances.'

I nod as he speaks. However, his eyes remain closed as he continues talking. I listen attentively.

'That's why I'm so disturbed by the idea "It's simply a metaphor." What is a metaphor for? Some kind of preaching to oneself. Some kind of communication that comes from one's own unconscious?' he asks rhetorically. 'I'm really rather distressed at that interpretation of the Annunciation.

'I put an enormous emphasis on it in the economy of Christian faith because we would know nothing about God if he had not communicated with us. The constant danger of religion is to confect gods in our own image. And the breakthrough is being ready to be found, being humble, close to the humus, an annunciation.'

His voice is really booming now. He sounds quite perturbed.

I wonder if he believes the annunciation to be 'the most important event in human history'.

'It's all part of the most important event in human history which is that God has communicated with us,' he replies. 'It's an aspect of that. He's communicated with us in his word. Supremely, in the birth, life, death and resurrection of Our Lord Jesus Christ who is God's plan for the whole spiritual evolution of the whole human race.

'Yes, the Incarnation changed the world but that statement suggests that the Annunciation was the time of impregnation, doesn't it? It's all part of one mystery. That statement is a typically Latin analytical way of thinking, not at all a Greek and mystical way. Of course it is part of, a vital aspect of, the great event in human history. But the Greeks never asked such a question because they're synthetic, not analytical.'

The Great Tom Bell in St Paul's Cathedral rings out to mark the hour. It reminds me that my time with The Right Reverend Dr Richard Chartres is coming to an end. Before I leave, I show him a print of Lemoyne's Annunciation.

'I don't like it very much. Mm…a soppy virgin. Anaemic. That for me is not humus. It's a spiritualized version and the blood and guts of the woman has been taken out of her.' *

———

The Reverend Dr Mark Wakelin was born in Africa to missionary parents. He studied Theology at the University of Nottingham, and then trained for the Methodist ministry. He's served for over thirty years in the Methodist Church and has a Master's degree and a Ph.D. in Education. Married with three grown up children, he served as President of the Methodist Conference in 2012–2013.

John Wesley, the Founder of Methodism, was the first President of the Methodist Conference. After his death, it was agreed that in future, the President would be elected to sit in Wesley's chair for one year only. During that twelve month period, the President's role is to represent Methodism to the wider world as he travels the length and breadth of Great Britain preaching widely on the Bible.

Mark Wakelin, now Minister at Epsom Methodist Church, has been described as a 'quietly inspirational, thoughtful, down to earth speaker who talks directly to people in ways they can apply to their own lives.' I am keen to hear what the Annunciation means for this nonconformist who has devoted his life to the 'methodical pursuit of biblical holiness'. We arrange to meet at the National Gallery in front of the Lemoyne painting.

On arrival at the Gallery, I discover that the contents of Room 33, including the Lemoyne painting, have been moved downstairs temporarily for a year, whilst the room undergoes extensive refurbishment including the installation of LED lighting and the introduction of more natural light. The chains that held the picture frame in place hang loosely against the empty wall in what is now a desolate space. The new location – Room E on the ground floor – is quieter and more private. The Lemoyne painting has been positioned lower down the wall so it hangs at eye level. This gives a closer perspective than before.

After exchanging niceties, I ask Mark Wakelin what he sees.

'The strongest image is Mary,' he notes as he casts his eyes over the canvas, squinting at times as he examines the detail of the brush strokes. He then takes ten steps back and gazes ahead. 'The colours strike me strongly. A very muscular and dominant angel. Some quite cute cherubim. And a brooding cloud behind it all. The focus is on the face of Mary, which is intriguing. It feels like the moment of "Let this be done to me according to thy will". She's gone through the point of lots of thinking and has got to the point when she submits.'

He walks closer to the canvas and casts his eyes all around the painting before returning to his original spot.

'It's a big picture. It's best to stand back or it's too overwhelming. I see the presence and watching of heaven in the cherubim and that's always intrigued me about the Annunciation – the watching of heaven. I've often thought about the stillness and

———

* Subsequent to this interview, Richard Chartres retired as Bishop of London in February 2017 after twenty years in the post.

quietness of heaven in the narrative in which the promises of God to the human race, to creation, are resting on the thin thread of a human being's obedience. Her acceptance is of huge interest to creation rather than just to her alone.

'I don't like the angel but that's not important because it's somebody else's attempt to reproduce something that is not representable – an almighty, all powerful God wanting to communicate to a very fragile part of creation. The dominance holds an ambiguity. It's quite an oppressive presence and that has all sorts of connotations of male dominance and oppression of women over the centuries. It's possibly why I feel uncomfortable with the painting. The experience of women in our world today, and almost certainly then too, is one of pretty regular abuse and hurt, and men being oppressive.'

His face grimaces and he shakes his head sidewards.

'The angel's face is incredibly feminine but the finger and the posture present an ambiguity,' he says. 'Mary doesn't seem a weak person here. She's allowing, she's giving permission and doing so with sincerity.'

I suggest that a Methodist minister would not normally experience a Marian painting like this one.

'No. I think if I came to it as a young man from that background, I'd find it quite problematic. But I've been a Methodist minister for thirty years and my ecumenical experience with people means that some of the things in the Roman Catholic Church that I would have been profoundly suspicious of, I've now had the privilege of seeing them from the perspective of friends and fellow human beings which has helped me.

'The Methodist spirit is in the Enlightenment and the puritan end of Enlightenment – an austere, rationalistic approach, a word approach not an image approach and especially in church. We are warned about idolatry. But it's a long time ago that I had the arrogance to assume that is what's going on for other people. My family background is Calvinist where no image, not even a cross, is admitted. My Nana once walked out of a church when they put a cross on the communion table. My parents were far less austere than that.

'I've become more interested in the Annunciation and Mary over the years. It goes back to when I was studying Theology at Nottingham. In the heart of Methodism, there is a very strong emphasis on what Luther called the *capax infiniti* – the capacity of the human being to bear the infinite. Luther and Calvin divided on this. Calvin's very strong sense of the brokenness of the human race made him argue that human beings did not have that capacity. The Methodists tend to follow the more Lutheran side, a gentler view of creation. And in the Annunciation, you have a statement about the degree to which God trusts humanity. In which the mighty weight of his promises hang on the thin thread of human obedience.

'This picture in front of us is that cusp moment in salvation. This moment must be conceived because as God creates the best, human beings being able to say no is a much better world than human beings unable to say no. In which case, it's bound to come to a point when the mess has to be fixed and has to rest upon the point where it almost could go wrong on whether the human being says yes. That debate we have with God is not on whether we believe in God but whether God believes in us and whether we believe God trusts us. Mary stands for humanity, which is ultimately trusted by God.'

I ask whether he sees the story as fact or is it just a metaphor.

'It depends whether you put the word "just" before metaphor,' he replies. 'I see the story as a story and you can't unpick a story that expresses theology. It's kind of the wrong question. It's probably the most truthful thing we can say about God and humanity – that he trusts us and requires individual people to say yes and his promises rest upon that fulcrum. I'm agnostic on whether it's fact or metaphor. How do you know? It's an unfair question because it assumes that a literal truth is somehow superior to a narrative and ancient story. Certainly, an ancient story cannot do things that a literal truth can do but it can do things that a literal truth can't do.

'So in Shakespeare you may say, "look how the floor of heaven is thick inlaid with patinas of bright gold," and you'd say, is that truthful? Well, no it isn't because they are made up of a huge nuclear fission reaction burning tons and tons of hydrogen to make helium. But if you're out with your partner looking into the night sky and feeling romance upon you, you're more likely to say, "Look, heaven is thick inlaid with patinas of bright gold," rather than "Look, there's hydrogen burning into helium".

'There're different kinds of knowledge and theology is a different kind of knowledge again. It isn't literal truth. It doesn't mean it's fact free and that facts don't matter. You are talking about something that is incomprehensible, which you reach out to. So Luke writes the annunciation story but is it true? On this, it doesn't matter because that's not the point. The point is I don't know.'

I share with him Philip Egan's description of the Annunciation as 'the most important event in human history'.

'That's interesting,' he says. 'I think I'd agree with that. Mm…the Cross is the most important event in God's history. Mm…yes, in Mary you see a human being saying, yes and she's one of us. The Annunciation is what it is to be human.'

Is Mary a bridge or a barrier to inter-denominational relations?

'A bridge to ecumenism which we need to grasp,' he replies.

Does he pray to her?

'The tradition I came from would wonder why you are doing that and they would wonder is Christ not all in all? But I wouldn't find it offensive for someone to pray to Mary.'

Does he think she had other children? That Jesus had brothers and sisters?

'I've never questioned it that she had other children,' he responds. 'I'd never realized it was an issue. I was quite surprised it was an issue. One of the things I find offensive is this "keeping yourself pure for your marriage". The idea sex is impure and once you've had sex, you're no longer pure. I think that's blasphemous against a God who's created human beings to be sexual and to be sexy creatures. It's a male perspective on female sexuality and it's about possession. It really upsets me.

'Did Mary conceive without the help of a man?' he asks rhetorically. 'Again, it's not an issue for me. I don't think Mary, if she had a natural child, was impure. She might have been unfortunate. She might have regretted it. But sin is not a sexually transmitted disease.'

For three years, Professor Andrew Bradstock led the Centre for Theology and Public Issues at the University of Otago in Dunedin, New Zealand. He is also a former Co-Director of the Centre for Faith and Society at the Von Hügel Institute in Cambridge. In the 1980s, he took a big interest in Liberation Theology, focusing on the political situation in Nicaragua. He returned recently to England to be Secretary for Church and Society in the United Reformed Church.

The URC brings together English and Welsh Presbyterians with Scottish Congregationalists. It has 68,000 members across more than a thousand congregations in Britain. It has a commitment to the Reformed tradition with 'a belief that all God's people should be one.' Central to the URC is a respect for individual belief and a conviction that majorities are not always right. It is not a dogmatic Church and embraces a wide range of opinions. Andrew Bradstock's work is 'to facilitate the public witness of the URC on issues impacting Church and society and to enable the voice of the URC to be heard in the public space.'

We meet in the United Church in Winchester. Although he works for the URC, he is not a member of it and, therefore, talks to me in a personal capacity.

'My background was firmly Calvinistic, brought up strictly in the Baptist Church, so Mary was a bit off limits to me,' he begins. 'Of course, she was part of the gospel narrative but I wasn't encouraged to worship her or see her as an object of devotion. She's important but certainly not a co-redemptrix, which I would see as Roman Catholic overlaying.'

I ask how he'd describe himself today and he responds, 'Low evangelical Anglican but not abandoning my Baptist roots.'

'What I see in the annunciation story,' he tells me 'is the meeting of the divine and the human and I agree that it is the most important event in human history in the sense that it is the ultimate expression of God's identification with human kind. That's pivotal to my personal faith – that God is not detached from humanity. In Scripture, we encounter a God who is deeply concerned about an involvement in human affairs. How societies operate is important to God and that they are based on foundations of social justice.

'The Incarnation is the ultimate expression that what goes on here in our supposedly mundane flesh and blood existence matters deeply to God because how could God more profoundly demonstrate a concern for humanity than to become human himself and become incarnate in human form?

'It is significant that Mary is a woman who is probably not that important socially, possibly poor, possibly a peasant woman because there's a sense in which the whole orientation of her son's life is at the lower level. He identifies with the ordinary people of society and there's an explicit rejection of earthly power and earthly riches.'

Does he see Luke's account of the Annunciation as factual, metaphorical or something else?

'I certainly see the Gospels as founded on real historical narrative,' he replies. 'Jesus lived and walked in Galilee. As Francis Shaeffer once said, "If you walked up to the cross and ran your finger down it, you'd get a real splinter." I've wrestled with it for years but I do think the resurrection had to have happened. I'm not sure that believing the Annunciation literally – an angel appearing – is essential to understanding what's going on. Most biblical scholars would accept that Luke and the other gospel writers are struggling for ways to express something that they, themselves, have felt very deeply and they want to find the language to say there is something mega here that's hugely significant. We wouldn't use angels now but that was the tradition they inherited.

'I think the dressing around the Incarnation of an angel, maybe they're not the right words, is one thing Luke may be using to say to us you need to sit up and listen because it's so important, rather than it being literal. I'm not ruling it out either. I don't know what it would mean to have an angel in front of you. I believe there are angels around today who can help you, advise you and bring you out of difficult situations, but whether it happened like that shown in Lemoyne's painting, I just don't know.'

What, for him, is the key message of the annunciation story?

'I think it's about acceptance. If you take the story literally, here's a woman completely overwhelmed by what's going on but there's also a sense of her understanding she's in a privileged position and saying, "who am I to refuse God?" It's not a surrender to some kind of male domination. I think it's an active acceptance of the enormous task that's been given to her. God is with us and the kingdom of God which Jesus comes to announce is so very much about this world – turning upside down the values of our society and privileging people whom society likes to marginalize. The Annunciation and the Incarnation are all of this.'

He brings out of his shoulder bag an example of a Nicaraguan depiction of the Annunciation, showing a scene involving the peasants of Solentiname who lived on an archipelago in Lake Nicaragua.

46. The peasants of Solentiname *The Annunciation* © Peter Hammer Publishing House on behalf of Fr Ernest Cardenal, Managua, Nicaragua

'Look, there's the angel,' he tells me as he opens a book. 'An ordinary Nicaraguan guy dressed in white shirt and white trousers appearing in front of an ordinary Nicaraguan woman. You haven't got all that heavenly stuff here.'

The painting is set in an everyday Solentiname home with a woman sitting on a chair by her sewing machine. She is dressed in red. There are four empty rocking chairs in the room. The angel looks like a waiter approaching her. The doors of the room open out onto a lush garden, full of fecund vegetation and brightly coloured flowers. Behind her is a bedroom.

The painting was created when the people of Solentiname were backing the Sandinistas in their attempt to overthrow President Somoza in the 1970s. They were interpreting the gospel teachings in relation to their own lives, he says. The accompanying text next to the painting reveals how they saw the angel as 'a subversive' and that Mary was about to join as a subversive too by saying yes. Her obedience is 'revolutionary because it is an obedience to love.'

I ask whether he feels that we've lost something about the significance of the annunciation story?

'I think it would be an interesting idea to revive the Annunciation and take some of the focus off Christmas,' he replies. 'It has become so secular – the presents, the spending, the gorging. Christmas is all about consumption and all about us. There's so much over-layered at Christmas. The Annunciation would strip all that away and get us back to the bare bones of what's going on.'

Does he see Mary as 'Mother of God'?

'Well no, that idea of absorbing her into the Trinity is awfully problematic.'

So he sees her as the mother of Jesus, chosen and special, but finds it problematical to describe her as the Mother of God?

'There's a logical incoherence to my position because if Jesus is the promised Messiah and is God coming to earth, then she is the Mother of God in that sense but not in a role where she's been elevated and new stuff has been added over the centuries which I do find problematic. So, as a Calvinist, I would strip it back to what we have in Scripture which is fairly basic.'

So we should subtract the concept of the Immaculate Conception and the Assumption, and concentrate on Mary being the mother of Jesus?

'Yes, that's not to undervalue what's going on, but keep to the Scripture and don't add things on,' he says.

I ask him if he feels Mary is a bridge or barrier to inter-denominational unity?

'She can become a barrier,' he says. 'It depends how she's interpreted. When I was looking at liberation theology in the 80s and 90s, I saw that so many women found her an impossible figure to emulate. The Church held her up as a perfect virgin and a perfect mother and, apart from her, you can't be both. She's a one off. In that sense, she made women feel very vulnerable. But I think you can see her as a one off, specially chosen but don't overlay too much extra kind of doctrine. She can become a bridge because she is at that point when the divine meets the human. She is that vessel.'

Does he believe in the Virgin Birth?

'I don't necessarily and I don't think Luke did either actually,' he replies. 'I think you can look at the Luke account and the Matthew account without actually seeing that that's the only way to read it. There's a wonderful ambiguity about the whole thing.

'In the early Church, there was one tradition that held that Jesus was illegitimate and that seems to me to be quite profound. I don't think the Virgin Birth adds anything to the special nature of Jesus. He could still be the promised Messiah, the Redeemer, without that extra dimension. I don't rule it out. With God anything is possible. But I just wonder if that provides an unnecessary barrier. Tom Wright [New Testament scholar and Bishop] says what's absolutely fundamental to the faith is that you could take away Christmas altogether and you'd still have a faith but take away Easter and…the secular world doesn't celebrate it anything like Christmas…but it's absolutely crucial.

'What does intrigue me is how much influence Mary had in the gospel narratives and the traditions on which the gospel writers drew. The whole thing is problematic. I don't say it's not worth wrestling with but not to the point of missing the kernel of what lies right at the heart of it, which is the meeting of the divine and the human in human form.'

I show him the print of Lemoyne's painting.

'It's the antithesis of what I'm trying to say.' He breathes in deeply and sighs. 'Because it doesn't lead you to think…it's not earthed…maybe I'm waffling here…but the real worldliness of the story has gone here. I certainly wouldn't put it up over the fireplace."

––––––––

Sixty-year old Steve Clifford stands before the Lemoyne painting in deep concentration. He is the General Director of the Evangelical Alliance that represents two million

_____

*   In 2015, soon after this interview, Professor Andrew Bradstock was appointed Convener, Centre for Theology and Religion in Public Life at the University of Winchester.

evangelical Christians across the United Kingdom. Seventy-nine different denominations are affiliated to the coordinating body.

Born in Bradford, he is a former teacher who switched to being a Christian worker, then studied Theology at the London Bible College, and since then has been in a number of high profile roles in the 'Pioneer' network of churches. He has been the driving force behind some of the UK's most dynamic and successful Christian projects, including 'March for Jesus'; 'Soul in the City'; 'Soul Survivor' and 'HOPE Together'.

He lives in west London, is married and has two children. He is tall, slim and fit, and although he has a full head of white hair, he looks youthful. He speaks with warmth and positivity, and smiles constantly.

I begin by asking him to define an evangelical.

'They're passionate followers of Jesus. There is the centrality of an experience of a personal relationship with Jesus – a new birth, a conversion, a transformation,' he says. 'They're activists, actively involved in society. They see the Cross, the Resurrection as pivotal to understanding what God is doing, and they have a high view of Scripture. The Bible is not just another book. It's a unique book.'

In that context, what does the annunciation story mean for him?

'There has been a danger in evangelicalism of almost forgetting the importance of Mary in the story,' he says. 'Partly out of a reaction, we've ignored the role and place of Mary. Personally, I find the story profoundly moving. I wonder if there's ever been a more significant conversation that's taken place. It's a profoundly honest conversation. This isn't a chance encounter taking place. Gabriel makes it clear she's been chosen. He's been sent with a message for her. She has a choice. That's important. She asks the questions.'

Is the Annunciation fact, metaphor or myth?

'I see it as fact. It happened,' he responds firmly. 'In two thousand years of Church history, the Church community have always, until recently, regarded this as a true narrative of what took place.'

Does he see it as a revelation of 'truth'?

'Yes. You're using words I probably wouldn't use. But yes, I don't have a problem with what you say but it's not how I would express it. I read the Gospels and they ring true for me.

'I go back to my own watershed moment in my own life. I was seventeen years old. I'd got a job over the summer working in this conference centre in Lancashire and it was full of Christians. My dad was an Anglican vicar but he died when I was five years old, killed by a drunk driver. By the time I was a teenager, I believed there was a God but there wasn't a lot of faith in my life.

'I was working on a farm associated with the conference centre. They dragged me along to some of the events. I remember vividly one evening in the chapel a guy recount the events of the cross and their significance. I knew the events but as he told the story, at that moment, at the core of my being, I just knew it was true. I had a choice. Should I decide to embrace it? I just knew it was true. I received it. It was a watershed, profoundly important event for me.

'And Mary's response at the end of her encounter, "I'm your servant", is truly amazing. That submission to the will of God in her life, I think, is what happened to me in that little chapel in Lancashire that night. There wasn't an angel there but the word of God came to me. As that preacher spoke, it was as though I heard God speak.'

Is Mary of low status to evangelicals?

'There's a danger of that,' he responds. 'I'm trying to remember how many sermons I've heard from evangelical leaders on Mary and there aren't that many. There is a concern to make sure we don't add another person to the Trinity. Yes, there's her amazing act of obedience but Mary was a flawed human being like the rest of us.'

I note that a couple of minutes ago, Steve Clifford had referred to the Annunciation as 'the most important conversation in human history.' I tell him that Bishop Philip Egan had described it as 'the most important event in human history'.

'I'd find it difficult to use his phrase,' he says. 'If I had to talk about the watershed moment in human history, it would have to be the events at Easter. However, the Incarnation is absolutely central to our understanding of God working through our humanity and how God can be amazingly surprising. But the Incarnation was always leading somewhere. There have been hundreds of deaths on a cross. The empty cave is the watershed moment. God shouting to all humanity that the rescue plan for salvation has been achieved.'

He sees Mary as the mother of Jesus. Does he see her as the Mother of God?

'No,' he replies immediately but then pauses for a while. 'Again, that's not the language I'd choose to use. We are in the realms of mystery. We struggle to find the right language to explain all this.'

I ask whether the phrase 'Mother of God' is too close to the Trinity for him.

'It's open to misinterpretation. That would be my fear if I used that label.'

Does he venerate her?

'We don't use the word "venerate". Again, we'd speak of worship. We couldn't worship Mary. We worship the Trinity.'

Would he celebrate the feast of the Annunciation on 25 March?

'The majority of evangelical churches wouldn't celebrate it,' he says. 'We're not strong on using the liturgical calendar of the Church.'

Is Mary a bridge or a barrier?

'I wouldn't use either of those words,' he says. 'I do think there are important conversations to be had. The evangelical wing is the fastest growing part of the Church. There are areas where we need to have more conversations to understand those of other traditions and how they understand Mary. The thought of her as part of the Godhead, someone to pray to, would be problematic for evangelicals. Mary as a significant part of God's intervention in humanity, who made such a wonderful response to the angel – yes, evangelicals can embrace that. It's how you interpret the story that can create issues and misunderstandings.'

He gazes at the Lemoyne painting. I ask him what he sees.

'I'm drawn to Mary. "I'm your servant. Let it be according to your word".'

I ask him to close his eyes and to imagine the encounter between Mary and the angel. What does he see? He stays silent for about a minute.

'I see a teenage girl, living on a social housing estate in the East End of London and she's in twenty first-century dress. She goes to the local Academy. She's not religious by way of persuasion but she's not closed to spiritual things. There's a humility and honesty to her. She's your average teenager. She's not stupid. She's not super bright. She doesn't have much ambition. She's on a stairwell and she's met there. Her first words might well involve a swear word.'

He chuckles and smiles but continues closing his eyes. He goes on. 'Hang on a second, "I've had my sex education lessons",' she says. 'But the encounter is so profound for her. She's touched. She's humbled by it. The angel touches her humanity. The words speak of significance in a world around her of insignificance. There's something both earthy and heavenly in the angelic voice she hears on the stairwell. Is it possible for angels to be missed in the crowd? I think the stranger could be missed but the words cause Mary to stop and to ask questions, to hear the response back and then to say yes. A bit like me as that seventeen year old.'

He is standing a couple of feet in front of Lemoyne's painting. His eyes remain firmly closed. He is still smiling.

———

Eighty-year-old Archbishop Kallistos Ware, titular metropolitan Bishop of Diokleia under the Ecumenical Patriarchate of Constantinople and monk of Patmos, is probably the best-known Eastern Orthodox theologian in Britain.

Born as Timothy Ware in 1934, he was brought up as an Anglican before embracing the Orthodox faith when he was twenty-four. After gaining a double first in Classics at Oxford and studying Theology, he was ordained an Orthodox priest in 1966 and took the name Kallistos when he became a monk. He lectured in Orthodox Studies at Oxford for more than thirty-five years and has written numerous books including the acclaimed work, *The Orthodox Church*. Bespectacled, with a long white beard and white hair, he wears a black cassock that covers fully his diminutive figure.

I have come to visit him at his flat in north Oxford. We are in his study that is littered with piles of books. On his desk sit three cameras that, I learn, are there to record his regular video talk to audiences in the United States.

The Orthodox and Latin Churches broke apart in 1054 in the Great East-West Schism over a series of ecclesiastical differences and theological disputes. They included the source of the Holy Spirit within the Trinity and the Pope's claim of universal jurisdiction.

I am eager to hear the Orthodox interpretation of the annunciation story and how it differs from other denominations.

'In the event of the Annunciation, I see two decisive aspects,' he begins. 'The first is the divine initiative. The second is the human response. Clearly, without the divine initiative, there would be no event at all. But God does not simply announce the divine initiative to Mary. He also waits for her response. Initially, she is bewildered. It's only when the angel has explained further and sought to persuade her that she responds.

'So at the Annunciation, we are to see not only the angel announcing the divine initiative to Mary but we are to see Mary in full freedom accepting the divine plan. I think of the words of the Second Letter to Diognetus, "God persuades. He does not compel, for violence is foreign to the divine nature." This is exactly what we see at the Annunciation. She could have said no. It was an invitation, not a compulsory order. God waited for her in full freedom.'

What would have happened if she had said no?

'We don't know,' he replies. 'We cannot answer hypothetical questions. But no doubt God would have sought to realize the divine plan, the salvation of the world, in some other way.'

He sits completely still in his chair, talking very slowly and precisely in a deep, mellifluous voice. I remind him that he once described the Annunciation as a 'model of listening with obedience'.

'Mary listens to the annunciation and then responds,' he says. 'We have to listen to God but God will wait for our response. She is not just a passive instrument. She is an active participant in the mystery. There's a creative and active receptivity. She's not just a passive woman. She makes a courageous and decisive choice.'

I remind him how he also said that Mary serves 'as a mirror, a living icon of the biblical Christian'.

'She is in some ways unique,' he responds. 'God did only become incarnate once. It's a unique event. So there could only be one woman who is the mother of Christ. But looked at from another point of view, she is an example to us showing us the common path that we are called to follow, that God has a vocation for each of us. We are all different. Each of us has a unique true vocation. Each one of us is called to make something beautiful in our own distinctive way.'

What does he mean by 'true vocation'?

'Some people might interpret vocation as something overwhelming and imposed upon us but in its true meaning it means an invitation,' he replies. 'We have to make the decision and the true meaning of vocation allows for personal freedom to say yes or no. I like the words "engagement" and "partnership". Mary cooperates with the economy of the divine plan. She actively consents. Mary is the supreme example of what it means for us humans to cooperate with God. Grace is always a convergence between God's plan and our consent.'

I wonder if all Christian denominations should see Mary as Theotokos – the God-bearer – or to be exact in its translation, the one who gave birth to the one who is God.

'For us Orthodox, the title sums up the whole of the mystery of salvation and in that way is fundamental,' he explains. 'All Christians can accept this title although some may have reservations. The title is not simply an honour to Mary but safeguards the unity of Christ's person. Mary is birth-giver of God. She did not bear a person loosely united with God. She did not bear a prophet or saint but God himself incarnate. She is mother not only of the human nature of Christ as a person, but also as the Logos of the Trinity, who has existed for eternity in the Trinity but now undergoes a human birth.'

She gives birth to God in human form?

'God as God cannot be born. But God incarnate, made human, can and is born from Mary and he does die on the Cross. What Mary bore is a single, undivided person who is God and Man at once. She herself is fully human as we are.

'Roman Catholic teaching is that Mary was conceived immaculately, without stain of original sin. The Orthodox approach is she was subject to original sin like all the other righteous men and women of the Bible including John the Baptist, but she bore God. Christ is the Saviour for her just as much as he is for each one of us.'

I understand that Orthodoxy says Mary was next to a well when she first heard the angel's voice but Luke makes no mention of that in his Gospel. So, what is that Orthodox belief based upon?

'It is true we embellish the gospel account and much of Orthodox worship represents a meditation on the Gospels. But these embellishments are not matters of dogma. They enable us to enter more fully with the mystery being described. All the additional details are part of tradition and treated with reverence but we do not insist upon them. I find my faith being enriched by me being able to think of her by the well but it would not matter if it had happened somewhere else.'

Is her virginity crucial to him?

'Absolutely,' he says. 'This is affirmed both in Scripture in both the Gospels of Luke and Matthew and has been believed since the early years of the Church. I'm quite clear from the narrative, she's not just a young woman but a young woman who hasn't had sexual intercourse with a man. I accept it as part of evangelical gospel tradition. Why is it important? I would answer I do not impose a necessity on God but it seems to be fully appropriate, it fits together that God did not have a human father. There is a difference between the birth of Christ and the birth of humans normally. In a normal birth, through the union of man and woman, a new person comes into existence. But in the case of

Christ, no new person comes into existence. Christ has existed as a divine person from all eternity and what happens at his human birth is simply that he who has existed from all eternity as God now exists in addition in a new way as human as well as God. A new beginning but no new person. It points to the uniqueness of Christ.'

Does he think it is important that she is perpetually virgin?

'That's another question. It isn't stated in Scripture. It came to be believed gradually in the Church and isn't clearly affirmed until the end of the second century. One thing it does not mean for me is that somehow we are to think that sexual union is sinful in itself and somehow defiling, and, therefore, God couldn't be born from sexual union. Many people think of it as somehow impure. If she was ever virgin, it doesn't mean she would have become impure if she had sexual union later. That would be a false inference. I do not put the perpetual virginity on the same level as the virgin birth of Christ. I think the reason the Church came to believe in her perpetual virginity was from a position of extreme reverence.'

I show him an Orthodox icon of the Annunciation. Its jewel-like colours and gilded background invite a closer inspection. The angel is running to share the good news with Mary. In his left hand he carries a staff and his right hand reaches out to Mary. She has

47. Icon depicting an Annunciation scene

been sitting on an elevated seat and now stands upright. In her left hand, she holds a spindle of scarlet yarn that she is using to make the veil in the Temple in Jerusalem. Her right hand is raised in a gesture of acceptance. Her posture expresses her willing cooperation with God's plan of salvation. At the top of the icon is the segment of a circle representing the divine realm and from it, the Holy Spirit, in the form of a dove, descends on rays of light shaped like the blade of a sword.

Kallistos Ware stares at it intently and starts to move gently backwards and forwards in his chair. After a while, I ask him what is going through his mind.

'The angel is in movement, which expresses him being sent to deliver a message revealing the divine initiative to her...In the literal form, it's a statement but we should interpret it as an invitation. I notice in the icon she's not standing by a well but in a house. The idea of her at the well is tradition with a small "t".'

In the Orthodox Church, one talks about 'going inside the icon'. What does that mean?

'The icon is a point of meeting,' he explains. 'The theology of the icon is presence and encounter. Through the icon, we meet the person depicted. When it shows an event like the Annunciation, again the icon acts as the point of encounter and meeting. It brings us into the mystery. We enter the Annunciation as it happened. When it took place, it was just the angel and Mary but, through the icon, we too become part of the event. It's not just something that happened two thousand years ago. It's something that's happening to you and me, here and now.'

Is one meant to feel joy?

'When the angel says to her "Hail", the original Greek word, *chairē*, means literally "Rejoice",' he replies. 'The angel brings tidings of joy to Mary that she will bear a child but joy to the world that this child will be the Saviour of all humankind. But joy goes with sorrow and that is shown in a special icon when the feast of the Annunciation falls on Good Friday.'

The full title of the feast in the Orthodox Church is 'the Feast of the Annunciation of Our Most Holy Lady, the Theotokos and Ever Virgin Mary.' I ask if the feast has much greater status in the Orthodox Church than in the Western Church and, if so, why? He responds somewhat diplomatically.

'I'm not sure about that. It's not for me to pass judgement. It has a primary status in Orthodoxy and it is of very great importance. You must ask those in the Western Church to answer that one. I am sad to hear if it has been reduced in status there and I pray that it never may happen to us in the Orthodox Church. It is a great feast and our churches will be full on that day. It's a high point in the Christian year and we would not wish to see it being downgraded. We would lose the full value of the Incarnation of Christ and it would rebound on all the other feasts of Christ. The Annunciation, the birth of Christ, his death and his resurrection are all part of a single drama of an undivided event but if we are to make distinctions, without the Annunciation there could not have been a divine birth.'

I tell him about how Bishop Philip Egan described the Annunciation as 'the most important event in human history'.

'I can see why he says that,' he says. 'We could also say that the death and the resurrection are the most important events in human history. We say in our special hymn, "The Annunciation is the inauguration of our salvation." The first act and without that first act the other acts could not have followed, so it is a fair comment.'

Is Mary a bridge or a barrier in inter-denominational relations?

'Historically, she's been a barrier but she can be a bridge to bring us together. I do believe she is praying for Christian unity at this very moment.

'One feature of Anglicanism is its comprehensiveness. A wide variety of different opinions. Very many High Church Anglicans hold, in effect, a faith undistinguishable from that of Orthodox. Then there are many Anglicans of the evangelical tradition who would feel unhappy to honour the Virgin Mary and the saints. There's a clear difference between them and us. Then there's the liberal Anglicans who, in my view, are even further from Orthodoxy. They may question the Godhead of Christ, the Virgin Birth and his resurrection.'

I wonder whether there was single moment that made him switch from Anglicanism to Orthodoxy.

'When I was still at Westminster School aged seventeen, in my last year, 1952, I went to the Russian Church in London by chance,' he tells me. 'As you might say, by divine providence. I was walking past it and in I went. They were having the Saturday evening vigil service and I was deeply moved. I had an experience of heaven on earth. When I first entered, I thought it was empty. Then I saw the icons with lamps in front of them. Then I saw a few people. Then I realized the church was full of invisible presences – the saints are here, the angels are here, the Mother of God is here, Christ is here. There was a fullness. It was an overwhelming experience. I decided this is where I belong. I waited another six years. The more I learnt in Orthodoxy, the more I realized this is what I believe. I didn't think I'd changed my faith. It was renewed in a new way.'

Was it in a sense his own annunciation moment?

'I suppose I could say that. I certainly felt that call in 1952 but I didn't respond immediately and say, "yes, I'm going to become Orthodox" until 14 April 1958. I'm glad I waited. It was the most important single event in my own history. True.'

I show him a print of the Lemoyne painting. He studies it for some considerable time.

'I see it as a painting of beauty,' he says. 'The angel is in dynamic movement, pointing up to heaven. A different symbolism to the icon but probably the same truth. I find the Orthodox icon conveys to me a greater sense of transcendence. This painting is shown as a more human, more naturalistic event. The Orthodox icon shows the divine rays coming down from heaven with the dove. The angel points up to heaven but we don't see the movement down from heaven. The Orthodox icon is more theologically exact. In the Annunciation, the angel doesn't say look up to heaven. He says God is coming down from heaven. There is a different movement. The angel and Mary are at the same level in the icon. I prefer the Orthodox icon which is a little less naturalistic.'

He tells me about his favourite icon of the Annunciation. In his words, the one that 'most impresses and moves me,' is an early fourteenth-century icon from the Peribleptos church (St Clement), now in the National Museum in Ohrid in Macedonia. He starts searching his many bookshelves looking for the image when suddenly a friend arrives ready to record his latest talk for America. We have to bring our conversation to an abrupt close. I tell him I'll look it up when I get home.

It's six-thirty in the evening. The eighty-year-old Bishop has been on the go all day and there are still more appointments to keep. 'I keep going,' he says. 'I haven't seen my obituary yet in *The Times* so I keep busy.'

CHAPTER 16

ARTISTIC SYMBOLISM IN ANNUNCIATION PICTURES

———————

Since starting this project, I have carried a pocket-sized book with me everywhere I go. It is called *Annunciation*, and is a collection of 120 artistic depictions of the biblical encounter, brought together in a single book by the creative arts publisher, Phaidon. From a fifth-century mosaic in the Santa Maria Maggiore church in Rome through to late twentieth-century abstract pieces by Brice Marden and Andy Warhol, the images show how the dramatic meeting between angel Gabriel and Mary has inspired artists throughout the ages.

The Annunciation has been one of the most popular subjects in religious art, dating back almost two thousand years. The Lucan text provides hardly any descriptive detail so the visualisation of the encounter is all in the imagination of the artist. Each great period in art history brings its own style and conventions: Roman, Byzantine, Celtic, Carolingian, Renaissance, Venetian, Mannerism, Baroque, Rococo, Neo-classical, Romanticism, Cubism, Surrealism, Pop Art, Postmodernism. Take your pick, whatever the school or styles, there will be a plethora of Annunciation paintings to view. At the heart of so many of these pictures is symbolism, which has developed through the ages.

The majority of the images in the Phaidon collection come from the fifteenth to seventeenth centuries, at the height of the Renaissance and baroque periods. At that time, Catholic churches across the European continent and many private homes were filled with pictures of the Annunciation. After the 1550s, the impact of the Reformation saw a dramatic collapse in the commissioning of such Marian work, especially in predominantly non-Catholic countries such as Germany, Holland and England.

Initially, I was disappointed to see that the Lemoyne painting is not included in the Phaidon collection but, of course, no one knew of its whereabouts when the book was first published in 2000.

The first known image of the Annunciation, a fresco in the Catacomb of Priscilla in Rome, dating back to the early part of the third century, is a simple, naive rendition. On the left side, an unveiled Mary sits on a chair facing forward as a wingless angel arrives from the right. It isn't until the following century that Christian art begins to depict angels with wings. Then, from the early sixth century through to the Renaissance period it became the tradition in western art for the angel Gabriel to approach from the left side of an Annunciation picture. In contrast, Eastern Byzantine icons continued to show him entering from the right.

From the early Middle Ages, Mary would most often be seen kneeling on a prayer stool or sitting reading a book, probably the Book of Hours or the Bible. Frequently, the book is opened on a page containing the words: '*Ecce virgo concipiet, et pariet filium*'.

The space that lies between the angel Gabriel and Mary is used regularly by artists to highlight important symbols of the angelic message. The hand of God, representing God the Father, often emerges from the top of a picture. The white dove, symbolizing the Holy Spirit, may be seen gliding down rays of light towards Mary's ear or her womb. From the early fourteenth century, the rays of light were sometimes depicted carrying a tiny figure of Christ holding a cross. However, that image soon became highly controversial as it went against the very idea of the conception having taken place in Mary's womb and was soon dropped.

From the early fifteenth century, an enclosed garden started to feature regularly in the central background of an annunciation picture. This symbolizes the Virgin's womb and references the Song of Solomon (4:12): 'You are a garden locked up my sister, a spring enclosed, a sealed fountain.' A tightly shut gate adds to the symbolism. This '*hortus conclusus*', representing Mary's perpetual virginity, is also often rich in vegetation to represent the coming of spring and the fact that the feast day of the Annunciation is held on 25 March.

By the late fifteenth century, Mary is more often placed in a formal, enclosed room that leads on to an adjacent bedroom. The room is her private, protected inner sanctum and the angel Gabriel usually stands or kneels outside. The door or archway to the room symbolizes Mary's role as '*porta coeli* ' – the doorway to heaven. The virgin's bedroom – '*thalamus virginis*' – is the nuptial room where traditionally a conception would take place. A neatly made-up bed signifies Mary's conception without sexual intercourse. An opened curtain shows she has conceived and the Incarnation has happened. A luminous yellow or golden background with billowing clouds represents divinity and the unseen God, whilst cherubim, the first hierarchy of angels, represent divine wisdom.

If the angel's wings are in motion, it signals he is supposed to have travelled fast to deliver God's message and has just arrived. One of the wings is often portrayed overshadowing Mary to symbolize the power of the Most High overshadowing the God-bearer. Often, the angel's wings are made of peacock-eye feathers, designed to attract a female mate. As well as the obvious sexual connotation, they are also a symbol of holiness, of eternal life between heaven and earth, and of guardianship to royalty. They can even be a symbol of resurrection as the male peacock loses his feathers in the autumn before new ones grow again in the spring.

From the twelfth century, the lily has been a regular and significant symbol in so many annunciation works. Originally, it was used to represent the flower of paradise, before becoming the prime symbol of virginity and purity. For that reason, it became a classic feature in nearly all annunciation paintings throughout the Renaissance period. A palm branch held by Gabriel represents Christ's peace and a sceptre symbolizes God's authority and sovereignty.

Knowledge of all these historic, artistic signs may be interesting and insightful, but does such an understanding of Christian symbolism in art bring me any closer to a better understanding of the spiritual meaning of the annunciation story and its key message?

CHAPTER 17

GOD'S ABSOLUTE COMMITMENT TO THE HUMAN RACE

I have arrived in Oxford and I am entering the magnificent Ashmolean Museum, founded in 1683 as the first public museum to be established in the country. Climbing the grand stone staircase to the right of the main entrance, I walk into Room 42, focused on Early Italian Art, and spot it immediately.

The Annunciation is a small, fifteenth-century panel created with tempera and gilding. It is attributed to the Italian, Paolo di Dono, better known as Uccello and is thought to have been painted in the late 1420s. One of his earliest known works, Uccello was a mathematician as well as a painter and a pioneer in visual perspective.

Here, there is a lavish use of gold and ultramarine blue made from lapis lazuli and, at the time, this devotional image would have been expensive to produce.

What makes this particular picture distinctive for me is the way God the Father is depicted at the top, dressed in blue robes with the angel Gabriel kneeling at his feet. Behind him are three blue-dressed angels trumpeting as though to announce the angel's forthcoming journey. Behind them are three more red-dressed angels banging drums and behind them are three more in pink, playing more musical instruments. You can almost hear the cacophony of sound and you get the powerful sense of an introduction heralding a major announcement.

48. WA 1850.7 attributed to Uccello *The Annunciation*, early 1420s, Ashmolean Museum, Oxford. © Ashmolean Museum, Oxford

Further down the painting, you see angel Gabriel again, this time hovering above Mary's abode. At the bottom of the picture, in the third stage of Uccello's depiction of the annunciation story, angel Gabriel kneels on the step of a twin-arched porch, where Mary sits inside reading her prayer book. Behind her, a white curtain is rolled back slightly to create an opening that reveals her bedroom. In contrast to the dark blue building rooted in earth, the picture's backcloth of gold represents heavenly glory. As I lean forward and examine the canvas close-up, I notice a tiny white dove with red feet standing on a ledge of the blue pillar, directly in front of Mary's ear. His wings are opened out and he is ready to fly. The Incarnation is about to happen.

———

In 1999, Dr John Drury wrote a book in association with the National Gallery entitled *Painting the Word: Christian Pictures and their Meanings.* A former Dean of Christ Church Oxford from 1991 to 2003, and Dean of Chapel at King's College Cambridge, from 1981 to 1991, he is now Official Fellow and Chaplain at the graduate-only All Souls College, Oxford.

As I arrive, the morning sun pours over the fifteenth-century honey-coloured sandstone buildings, drenching them in golden light. The lawn spreads out in front of them like a crisp emerald green linen tablecloth, all straight lines and clean edges.

Sitting at his desk, the seventy-eight-year-old Anglican priest, author and theologian gingerly puts down his cup of coffee. John Drury is wearing a collar and tie, a pullover and a well-worn suit. Piles of papers surround him and columns of stacked books and handwritten notes are scattered all over his desk. He presents me with a gift – a copy of his newly published book, *Music at Midnight. The Life and Poetry of George Herbert,* which has been well received in recent reviews.

He looks quizzically at a large print of Lemoyne's *The Annunciation,* commenting on the diagonal entry, the brick wall, the plentifulness of the sky, describing it as a Baroque affair. Then he makes an observation that nobody else has mentioned to date. He gestures to the area directly behind Mary in the background, on the left hand side of the picture. I squint my eyes to focus, and then notice a grey-blue cloth merging into the clouds. 'That's a curtain being blown aside,' he proclaims. 'That's important.'

'Lemoyne is a very good painter but not great,' he continues. 'Perhaps I'm being a bit snooty. He's a good colourist, he can deploy well the conventional things of the Annunciation including Mary's attitude. It's a proper job but it's not quite Rubens and that sort of brilliance.'

So, I ask him, what makes a truly great annunciation painter?

'Originality,' he answers immediately. 'You have to take it further. From the reader's point of view, rather more is required of them.'

He moves his metal-rimmed spectacles down the bridge of his nose to take a closer look and runs his hands slowly through his white hair as he peers at the picture.

'It's all there, he's done his stuff, but there's more to notice say with Duccio, Fra Lippi and Poussin (three of the other annunciation works hanging in the National Gallery, which he highlights in his book). You hit the buffers earlier after five or ten minutes with Lemoyne's. It doesn't puzzle at you. You can admire it greatly but you're there pretty quickly.'

In *Painting the Word,* he wrote that in the annunciation story, 'St Luke's imagination twisted eternity together with our historical world of time, people and place.' What did he mean exactly?

'It is for him a historical matter,' he replies. 'Luke's imagination is quite horizontal. He sees Christianity in the succession of history from the Old Testament. He starts quite gently – "I'm going to write this cathexis in sequence." His annunciation is very much like the birth of Samuel. Hannah can't conceive and then there's her surprising and divine conception. It's an Old Testament topos to have this kind of miraculous birth. He wanted to show that the birth of Jesus was like the births of Isaac and Samuel. It's part of the long story in which God constantly does the same thing. There are prohpecies and then they are fulfilled.'

I remind him that in his book he also wrote that Luke 'was a historian who delighted in circumstantial details and a fabulist who enjoyed making the impossible actual and palpable. In the fabric of his work, the two are woven together.' I tell him I particularly liked the way that he described the Incarnation as a 'charter for the painter's task of transforming the words of Scripture into figures.'

'There's a magic realism, treating it realistically, but it's weird and improbable,' he comments.

He says a painting is powerful because it 'infuses and metamorphosizes the visible with the invisible. It has to transubstantiate the talk between Gabriel and Mary into silence and frozen action.' Does he think that Lemoyne has achieved that?

'I think he does. It's effective, it's exciting, it's splendidly thought out in terms of movement,' he replies as he continues to examine closely the composition. 'It's very deliberate on light. The different postures. Mary's attitude is rather courtly. She looks a very well brought up girl – she's been doing her sewing. There's the expensive piece of furniture and the marble floor. She's certainly not a peasant.'

He continues to examine Lemoyne's composition.

'Mm, yes,' he goes on, 'her downcast eyes and her gesture of submission and humility. She's moving backwards, recoiling. A nice interaction of humility and grandeur. The poses are very dramatic with a lot of movement. I like the confidence of the airborne figure bringing in the light, with his floating legs, very much in flight. The angel is good – quite an ambivalent, meditating angel with a lot of light and force.'

A studious silence hangs in the air. You get the feeling John Drury has entered into a world of his own as he takes another sip of his coffee.

'You sense it's come from an aristocratic society with exquisite manners. The elaborate, social world of the Court of Louis XV,' he continues. 'Yes, it's good. It has got some force. The colours are well contrasted. Mary, appropriately, has more solid colours as someone in the world and Gabriel's are more ethereal. Mm, an expensive marble floor and a flaky brick wall with its breaking plaster, which suggests Gabriel has come through a barrier. It's a very vertical picture, Gabriel coming down and Mary coming up but there is a diagonal, horizontal element coming across the wall.'

I ask him whether he thinks the annunciation story is a metaphor. It's not rooted in fact.

'Yes, yes. Well it had better be because a metaphor, as it were, will have some religious value. But what's the religious value of...' his voice tails away. 'This moment doesn't happen usually and the metaphor takes it into the usual. If it's a metaphor, it's an image, it's part of you already.'

I ask again, wanting to interpret his comments correctly. Is he saying that the Annunciation did not actually happen but is a metaphor for something much bigger about God coming into the human world?

'Yes, and you can see that in the painting. It appeals to me visually. The illuminating light and the clouds would catch my eye. Being a human being, you respond to that lovely light.'

So, in his view, is it possible to be a Christian without believing that the Annunciation actually happened'?

'Yes, the trouble is,' he replies, 'is religion an orthodoxy or a tradition? I believe it is a tradition. It's not like Soviet Marxism that is an orthodoxy – what it says is, ipso facto. But this is a tradition like the tradition of a regiment or a country. It's a very foggy situation. If you got a lot of clergy together, lots would think like me. It's a question of whether you want to run your religion on authority, doing as you are told, or on imagination, entering into the spirit of it, as you might say.'

How does that square with his belief in Jesus as Christ; that he was God in human form on earth?

'Yes, a revelation of whatever we mean by God,' he responds. 'I'm a bit like Luke. I'm quite content with him being a prophet. The value of him is in the truth of his utterances, the conduct of his life and his morals. Of course, by the time Christ is available to us with St Paul in the New Testament, he's a composite figure. He's attracted other people and you can't pull them away. It's quite important he was an oral teacher. And then the central symbol to go with that is the Eucharist, which is consumed. Christ is consumed. So there's that religiously important consideration.'

So, in the context of the annunciation story, the key would be to see it as the coming of Jesus as a prophet, and his teachings, and not necessarily that he is God in human form. It is what he teaches that is the crucial thing.?

'Yes, just to get hold of something you can understand,' he replies.

So you can quite comfortably be a believer, have faith, and yet not believe the Annunciation actually happened?

'Oh yes. That's the least of my problems. Absolutely,' he responds.

So, what does he want people to take from the annunciation story?

'What is its religious value?' he asks rhetorically. 'I would say a lot is to do with Mary's passivity. To conceive something intellectually, you have to be rather like that in order to let it penetrate you, to use a pseudo-sexual metaphor. You need to be relaxed but alert, a receptive attentiveness, an appetency.'

He ponders further. 'Leave the doctrine, I feel. It's not the thing that counts. Not with ordinary people. The doctrine mostly consists of metaphors misunderstood as facts and that's not a good idea. No, it's not a good idea to mistake a metaphor for a fact and then to make it authoritative fact.'

So what should I take from the annunciation story? I wonder.

'I think that's very easy,' he replies. 'The various attitudes that Mary can have are very, very human and you'll be deploying them as you consider the Annunciation. You're in this attitude of expectancy, enquiry, that it's worth a go. You're going to take what comes. That's it really. It's a journey but it includes navigation. You looking at the map carefully.'

———————

I leave All Souls and walk just a few yards west along the High Street to the University Church of St Mary the Virgin. There has been a place of worship on this site for a thousand years and it is steeped in ecclesiastical history. I stand in front of the flamboyant baroque-style Virgin Porch, built in 1637. Above the door is a stone statue of the Virgin Mary and Child, which the Puritans attacked for being papist. It is easy to spot the bullet holes in the stonework, made by Cromwellian troops.

This is the church where the trial of Thomas Cranmer took place in 1556. Author of the English Prayer Book and architect of the English Reformation, he was tried here for heresy along with Latimer and Ridley during the reign of the Catholic Queen Mary, and all three were burnt at the stake. It is the place where John Wesley argued from the pulpit for moral and spiritual reform in three sermons between 1738 and 1744 as he launched his non-conformist vision that would later become Methodism. It is where John Henry Newman and John Keble gave sermons in the nineteenth century calling on the Church of England to re-discover its Catholic traditions and spirituality, as the Oxford Movement was about to be established.

I sit in front of a magnificent stained-glass window, designed by Augustus Pugin in 1843. Two panels at the bottom show a golden winged angel Gabriel on the left, holding out his hand to Mary as he stands on a black and white triangular shaped marble floor. In the panel to the right, Mary hears the message and begins to look around as she kneels in prayer, her hands joined firmly

49. A.W.N. Pugin Annunciation panels, 1843, University Church of St Mary the Virgin, Oxford

together. A halo of golden stars surrounds her head as a dove flies towards her ear. Two ornate pillars separate the angel and Mary. I keep my eyes focused on Mary's image, and reflect. An ordinary young girl wholly rooted in humanity; Theotokos – the God-bearer and Mother of God; her virginal conception; her perpetual virginity; the Queen of Heaven; her Immaculate Conception. No person from the Holy Bible has divided the Christian Church and its teachings as much as Mary and, in so many ways, I have come to realize that everything hinges on the way the moment of the Annunciation is interpreted.

I move on and head down a narrow, winding road called New College Lane, walking under the Bridge of Sighs, before facing a tall medieval gatehouse. This is the original main entrance to New College, Oxford, founded by William of Wykeham in 1379 and

dedicated to the Virgin Mary as the 'College of St Mary of Winchester in Oxford'. There on the west face, above the porter's lodge and the Warden's Lodgings, is a group of three stone statues. Similarly, on the east side of the gatehouse, looking onto the picturesque Front Quadrangle, there are three more statues in the same positions. Angel Gabriel is on the left, the Virgin Mary takes pride of place in the middle, set in a higher niche, and to the right Bishop William kneels in reverence. On the other side of the quadrangle, on the west

50. Statues of the Annunciation, late fourteenth century, New College, Oxford. Photo: Baz Richardson

face of Muniment Tower, there's the same configuration of three statues. The figures are positioned in exactly the same way to those that stand above Middle Gate at Winchester College. A New College guide stands below, addressing a group of Spanish tourists: 'William of Wykeham wants you to remember him wherever you look; to remember his great love of St Mary, whom he exalted; and to show his deep spiritual connection to the story of the Annunciation.'

I head south through the city of dreaming spires. Walking through the magnificent Tom Quad at Christ Church, I see a woman waving vigorously at me from the south-east corner of the large quadrangle near to the entrance to Christ Church Cathedral. As I get closer, I can see it is the person I have come to see, Angela Tilby, a regular presenter of 'Thought for the Day' on Radio 4.

Having read Theology at Cambridge, Angela Tilby embarked on a career at the BBC lasting more than twenty years as a radio and television producer in the Religious Programmes department. In 1997, she was ordained as an Anglican priest and was formerly Vice-Principal at Westcott House Theological College in Cambridge where she specialized in Early Church History. Now aged sixty-four, she has been based at Christ Church as Diocesan Canon since 2011.

She tells me how she first felt a calling to be a religious broadcasting producer and then later experienced a second calling to be a priest.

'It was a moment at a retreat where you let your fantasy lead you,' she explains. 'The fantasy was a statue that was supposed to be me and it was wearing a white stole. I felt it was saying there was a priestly potential that needed to be tested. Then, over time, I could see it wasn't a one-off moment but part of a continuity of moments.'

Having climbed up a narrow flight of stairs, we settle down in her small study. It is rather dark but extraordinarily neat and ordered. Her voice has a lovely rich tone and she talks in a slow, warm manner. She has a winning smile that often breaks into a big toothy grin. I ask what the annunciation story means for her?

'It has a strong sense of childhood, of mystery and of angels,' she responds. 'It reaches back into those parts of childhood that found the mystery of Christmas enchanting and enticing. Much later, as an adult, what strikes me about the Annunciation is the directness of a woman's encounter with God and the sort of critique that authority and identity was always with the male at that time, so for a woman to be free to obey the will of God just like that is still a shattering thing for me. Even though I've been ordained for more than fifteen years now, it's still so shattering in a positive sense. It's a massive hurdle. The extraordinary story of God making contact with an Israelite woman of no great social standing is still amazing. But it then gets taken over by the Church in benign and not so benign ways.

'The pictures that show Mary in terror and fear are trying to re-emphasize the submissive, the obedient – "You jolly well say yes" – but other paintings, like Fra Angelico's, are very different. There's humility there. She's completely self-possessed. There's an acceptance. She is empowered by his visitation, not disempowered, and I think that is what Luke is trying to say. He's always interested in women and the disadvantaged. The natural order is reversed and the Annunciation is where it begins. In Christian terms, she stands on the cusp of the old era and the new. She's both the entirely authentic daughter of Israel and the mother of the Church. A hinge point of history summing up the old and pointing to the new.'

Does she see the story as factual or metaphorical?

'That's really difficult,' she replies. 'I'll put on my academic side. I was taught to think very critically about the sources and to be aware that this story only happens in Luke's Gospel. Does it have historical weight? I suppose that scepticism thinking is deeply engraved in me. But I also say there's a long tradition of Luke having a personal contact with Mary and I don't think you can discount that. It doesn't terribly matter because the creative imagination is always where God has spoken to the people and I can take that. I don't have to resolve that issue.

'The problem is the way fact has been separated out from meaning,' she continues. 'Facts are bare facts. They don't come with any emotional colouring. They mustn't. To say it didn't happen is very prejudicial to it having any meaning at all because you can't ascribe meaning to something you don't know how to. Metaphors aren't given their context in contemporary culture. So on one level, I'm pretty agnostic as to whether it occurred in the way Luke described it. But to say it didn't happen is loaded with such useless and reductionist implications that I don't want to go down that route either. So, if that puts me on the fence, well, that's where I am.'

So, for her, what is the key message of the annunciation story?

'God's absolute commitment to the human race,' she replies immediately. 'It's an extraordinary promise. Nothing shows more clearly God's investment in and willingness to be part of humanity. It's the portal into the Incarnation. It's startling. From the Jewish oneness of God to a God where there is a relationship. Both being outside the whole system and within it.'

So, is it, in her view, the pivotal moment that separates Judaism from Christianity?

'I think that's true. It takes the story in a radical new direction,' she replies. 'What's more complicated is mapping out exactly when the separation happened. What we get left with is a picture of what that separation means. There are things in first-century Judaism that allow that jump in understanding. The fact there are hints and echoes in Jewish Scripture and Jewish practice of what might come shouldn't surprise us.'

I tell her about Philip Egan's description of it being, 'the most important event in human history'.

'I could go quite a long way with that,' she responds. 'Some would say the resurrection but hey, why not both? I can see the logic of that statement and I'm sympathetic with it. There are some whose faith pivots around an Incarnation axis and others who pivot around the Cross and the Resurrection. Your particular draw is to one or the other. Most of the time, I'm an Incarnation person: that means the mystery is the humility of God in coming to be one of us and everything clusters around that. The more Catholic minded see the Incarnation as what makes everything happen. Then there's a certain sort of Protestant, nervous about Mary, who sees the Cross as the ultimate moment in human history.'

Why does she think the feast day has lost so much status?

'I don't think it's ever carried the weight of Christmas, the actual event of when the birth happens,' she says. 'That's in at least two of the Gospels. I agree it has lost its status. Even English Catholicism has played down Marian feasts. It's sad in a way because the Marian cycle is both important and enriching. I'm very pro-Mary and her prophetic role. It was such a great mistake at the Reformation to downplay her role. It left the Protestant communities somewhat impoverished.'

Angela Tilby was christened a Catholic but was brought up in the Church of England. Does she venerate Mary?

'Yes, I do. I say the Hail Mary when I can't get to sleep. Then I drift off,' she chuckles. 'In an Anglican culture, she's played down but I've come to see more and more that Mary as Theotokos is critical to a fully-fledged incarnational faith. There's something in the Protestant mentality that is very afraid of anything standing between the naked human soul and God. It's rather silly and it's incredibly diminishing to think Jesus's mother is not important. Jesus would have had Mary's face. Doesn't that matter? She taught him his faith. Surely that matters.'

Does she think Jesus had brothers and sisters?

'There's a scriptural warrant for believing she had other children and led a normal married life,' she answers. 'We are not as embarrassed about sex as in the ancient world.'

So, what does she want to believe in the story?

'I like the Virgin Birth because of what it says about the autonomy of a female before God. Something very important is being said. That God can intervene directly without a male intermediary either protecting or acting for God in sex. I want to hold on to the theological truth of the Virgin Birth while being agnostic about whether or not it happened. The important word in the story is birth not virgin. That he was to be born. That he really did undergo birth. That's where the scandal lay for the early Christians. It was a normal human birth. A virgin birth was of secondary importance.'

So, if a practising Christian said to her, 'I don't believe in the Virgin Birth,' how would she respond?

'I would say what the Creed says is important,' she responds. 'The Christian mystery is contained within the Creed but as soon as you take it apart, line by line, you misunderstand what a creed is. "I believe this part but not this bit." It's the whole package really. You've done a post-Enlightenment reductionism and missed the point. This is a profound mystery of God's relationship with all humanity and once you start hair splitting over particular clauses, you've lost it. I think the creeds should be sung like hymns because they're saying this is the truth of the Church through all generations. What I am doing is I'm just hoisting my little flag and saying I go along with this lot. I don't think you are being asked to say: "Do you believe on the dotted line that this happened?" '

As I bid her farewell, I show her the large print of Lemoyne's painting.

'Gosh!' she exclaims. 'I'm looking at the angel's figure and seeing how muscled he is. He's certainly been to the gym,' she chuckles. 'Mm, she looks transported. I don't warm to it. Partly it's the era and the extravagant style. But the angel is unsympathetic. I don't like the hand. That finger. No!'

I head downstairs and enter Christ Church Cathedral next to her office and make my way to the Latin chapel. A three-panelled stained-glass window, installed sometime between 1333 and 1366, shows the angel Gabriel and the Virgin Mary either side of an unknown bishop. It is described as 'a jewel of Christ Church'. The angel is dressed in a flowing long white robe that falls to the ground yet reveals the toes of his bare foot.

He has curly blonde hair and holds a scroll as he stands looking at Mary. A tall, elaborate church building stands behind him. Mary looks downcast, perturbed, with her left hand raised. The angel has just arrived and she appears to be in shock. Her long golden hair tumbles around her. Behind her is a lush, richly coloured garden, set within the archway of another tall, ornate church building. A guide describes it as a 'sinuous, elegant depiction of a young maid, compliant and humble'. Angela Tilby would not like that!

51. Stained glass panels of angel Gabriel and the Virgin Mary, fourteenth century, Christ Church Cathedral, Oxford

Anglican priest and theologian, Dr Judith Maltby, was born in the United States and educated at the University of Illinois before going to Cambridge. A specialist scholar in the history of the English Church in the century following the Reformation, she was ordained as part of the first cohort of women priests in the Church of England in 1994 and is now Chaplain and Fellow at Corpus Christi College, Oxford. She is also a member of the General Synod.

When I meet her, she has just returned from Baltimore where she presented a keynote address on the Virgin Mary as part of a major international conference held at the Johns Hopkins University.

As we sit in her elegant study, she smiles as she looks at the print of the Lemoyne painting.

'She's inclining her head to the angel. "Alright, I'll do it," she's saying to herself. Mm, that fine gown – more a member of the Royal Household than a peasant girl.'

I ask what the annunciation story means for her?

'The key is God becoming a human being like us. The Annunciation is about human participation and contribution in the work of salvation. Mary's yes is entirely a freely given consent to participate in God's redemption. Her freewill is very important.

'Are human beings totally depraved and awful?' she asks rhetorically. 'A so-called low anthropology? To be a good human being, is that eradicated by the myth of the Fall? I guess I'm more of an Erasmian rather than a Lutheran on this – that is the goodness of human beings, although impaired and damaged, has not been completely extinguished. The idea that a human person, Mary, can contribute to God's work of salvation is to me fundamental about what it is to be a human being.'

Does she think the Annunciation actually happened?

'Yes, I think it did,' she replies. 'I've never had a problem with the Virgin Birth, theologically or historically. The how I'm quite agnostic about. I'm not saying the narrative in Luke is historically how it happened. I'm happy to think of Gabriel as a fictional character in that story. Luke is saying something about transformative grace here. I just feel in my guts, it's more than a metaphor. For me, Mary's consent is freely given. She's not coerced.

'Some people see the Annunciation almost as a rape but to me what is so key is that she consents. There is a sense that any human being is subordinate to God. You can read it as not about subordination to patriarchy because God isn't a man and doesn't have a gender.

'Mary is the model disciple for all Christians. I become really cross when she's seen as the role model just for women. She's the role model for all Christians, male and female, because it's about saying yes to God and that's not a gender thing. To me, she's a great saint. I'm a High Church Anglican but I've never prayed to her. I pray to Christ and to the Trinity.'

I wonder why the feast of the Annunciation has lost its status.

'The Annunciation is the prologue and Christmas is the main delivery,' she says. 'The Annunciation is about leading up to the Incarnation. The birth is about God coming into the world.

'There are some very interesting points around Mary's virginity. Why does she have to be perpetually virgin? Why can't Mary and Joseph have had normal spousal relations after the birth of Jesus in the way you'd expect any healthy marriage to have? I find that bordering on the offensive and completely unnecessary. The biblical evidence is against that and I think the attempts to airbrush that out are deeply unconvincing. I do think around Mary and her virginity are lots of unhelpful things – the Immaculate Conception and her perpetual virginity which are based on an unease about female sexuality.

Does she think it is possible to be a Christian and yet not believe in the Annunciation?

'Yes,' she replies before pausing. 'Well, I wouldn't make the Annunciation a deal breaker. It is important because the Incarnation is central to Christianity. Heck, I'm in the Church of England. We don't throw anybody out,' she laughs. 'I know Anglicans who have trouble even with the idea of the Incarnation but to me it's so central to the understanding of Christianity and why it matters. We are the world religion that says God became fully invested in human history, not as a visitor. It's not God in a human zipper suit on a divine gap year. It's God's total immersion into human history. Without the Incarnation, I can't see the point of Christianity.'

I say it strikes me that the Roman Catholic view on the Annunciation is characterized by rigidity and certainty and the Church of England's stance is rooted in diversity and, possibly, a lack of coherence.

'I'll push back on that,' she responds, 'and say one of the big differences between Roman Catholicism and the Anglican Communion is that our differences are out in the open. Talk to any Roman Catholics privately and there's a huge diversity of views there too. What we lack in the Church of England is the social control of the Church of Rome,' she chuckles. 'Look at what John Paul did to the liberation theologians. It isn't that Roman Catholicism is this monolith. It's just that it has this monolith presentation. But you peel it away and it's a quarter of an inch thick and you see all the diversity and differences you see in any denomination. It's presentational. It's not reality.'

Is it possible that the Roman Catholic Church and the Church of England will ever agree about Mary?

'There was an attempt with the ARCIC report on Mary a decade ago but I think it was a pretty poor report. I thought the Anglicans capitulated on the Immaculate Conception and her perpetual virginity. It was an almost entirely male body talking about female virginity. I'd quite like that to stop. I'd like an embargo on male theologians discoursing on female sexuality. For a hundred years, just knock it off guys. The idea of a room full of men discussing female sexuality is something a bit grotesque.'

As I stand up to leave, she offers me a final message.

'You're an actor, not a passive participant in God's work. That's the key thing about the Annunciation. God seeks our partnership in his work. We're good enough to be partnered with God's activity in the world – the work of love. And remember the ordinariness of it all. The breaking in of God to the ordinary.'

––––––––––

Forty-eight-year-old Robin Ward is the Principal of St Stephen's House, Oxford, an Anglican theological college rooted in the Catholic tradition of the Church of England. An external inspectorate report on St Stephen's House recently describes it as 'a community at ease and comfortable with embracing a variety of perspectives and traditions on numerous issues whilst situated clearly within a distinct theological and spiritual tradition.' Educated at Magdalen College, Oxford and St Stephen's, Robin Ward studied for his Ph.D. at Kings College, London, in the field of Patristics. Married with two sons, he was ordained in 1991 and is a representative of the traditional Catholic Group on the General Synod.

He is an elegant-looking man with short salt and pepper hair, and is dressed immaculately. He sits in his office, his Bible placed on the desk in front of him, opened at the page of Luke's Annunciation.

'It is the hinge of human history because it is the moment in which the Word becomes flesh,' he tells me. 'Yes, it is the most important moment in human history. Consequently, hanging on that is everything – the entire sanctification of matter, the sanctification of creation, the redemption of humanity, the promise of glory given in the image of God. This fallen race is given not simply a chance to go back to the place where it was before but a dignity that is in fact much higher because the Word takes on a human nature. The promise that we have is to be partakers in the divine nature, which comes through our incorporation through to Christ, the God/Man. The Word made flesh.'

So, if it is such a 'hinge' moment, why has the feast of the Annunciation been so marginalized? I wonder.

'Yes, I think that's true as a liturgical feast. Yes, Lady Day and the importance of it as the start of the New Year, has been lost,' he concedes. 'Liturgical observance is an odd thing, I think. Sometimes there are fashions in the way holy days and feast days are observed. It certainly doesn't have the profile it had. But it falls in Lent and there's a psychological issue switching suddenly from fast to feast. And it also gets moved around. Again, psychologically, that impedes its impact. But it's a ubiquitous mystery. It's there in everything. The whole action of the Mass when it is celebrated is testimony to the mystery of the Incarnation and when we recite the Creed too.'

I ask if he sees the annunciation story as factual?

'Oh yes,' he responds immediately but then stutters. 'Oh well, well yes, the Incarnation is fact. I don't have any reservations about that. The Lucan infancy narratives are very particularly associated with drawing out Old Testament themes and connections. The Annunciation falls into that pattern. Mary is seen as the culmination of Israel. This is absolutely something that hinges on consent, which is why the Church in a very curious way has sometimes seen it as both marriage and motherhood. The sense of the spousal bride and bridegroom as well as motherhood because the Incarnation happens through the language of consent.'

I note his precise, scholarly use of language and the quiet confidence and certainty in his voice. I am reminded of an article in the *New Yorker* magazine in 2010 which refers to his 'chilling intelligence'.

'The tendency of modern Biblical criticism is to discount portions of the narrative,' he continues. 'Obviously, the infancy narratives are a different sort of thing to other parts of the Gospels but, theologically, they are tremendously rich in emphasizing that Mary is the one in whom the old covenant culminates. Mary, in her consent and giving of herself, is fulfilling her role as mother, daughter of Israel, exemplar of the human race, and as the new Eve reversing the conversation that took place in the Genesis narrative.'

So, what does the annunciation story mean for him?

'It teaches me that the Word became flesh,' he says. 'It encourages me to see both in the angel and in Mary a sense of obedience. The fulfilment of the teleology of each thesis – the angel "angeling" and Mary "Marying" – anticipates the most perfect divine communication in human history which is the Incarnation. It doesn't come out of the blue. It's the culmination of the whole of the revelation of the Old Testament.'

In his role as educator, does he root the annunciation story in certainty or does he welcome a diversity of views about it?

'There are two issues here. If one is teaching about it, first there is that body of creedal belief in the Church of a belief in the Incarnation, and the Annunciation is an important part of that story. The testimony of the Church is reflecting Scripture and, therefore, authoritatively one will teach that. But if they [the students] are doing a critical study of the Bible, they will want to absorb techniques of thinking about the scriptural text that include what really comes from Bultmann [the twentieth-century German theologian] – the demythologizing thing – that mythic presentations can be just as important; there can be such a thing as a true myth that you can describe. Luke was not present at the Annunciation so how did he know what happened? Did he make it up? Yes, for them to ask these questions. It's a narrative context to a mystery, to a truth that the Church understands.

'That's a tide that's beginning to go out a bit now. It was certainly the case in the 1960s and 70s in Anglican seminaries, there would have been a Bultmannian attitude to the scriptural narratives that would have said what we need here is demythologizing. This complex mythical junk can still speak to us so long as we are intellectually rigorous in saying this didn't actually happen. It's a myth and it's not designed as an historical narrative. And you come out of that German idealist position seeking to extract religious truths from mythical material but being rigorous about making the distinction. I mean, you could actually see the Annunciation as a mythical narrative but that doesn't disqualify you from believing either in the Virgin Birth or the Incarnation. And as far as that narrative is concerned, you can't prove it one way or the other because Luke is the only evidence for it.'

With regard to the virgin conception, I am intrigued to know his view.

'The Virgin Birth is very, very important,' he says. 'It's extremely important because it emphasizes the divine fatherhood of God. It emphasizes the absolute integrity of the Incarnation. That the Son is the Father's Son. There is one subject in the Incarnate Christ. He is not a mixture or a combination of individuals, a hybrid, but is True God and True Man. The Virgin Birth is testimony to that. And the traditional doctrine of the Church is that Mary was a virgin before, during and after the birth and I'm happy with that too. It was a true marriage with Joseph but one that was not consummated sexually. What's the importance of her virginity? It's not simply because of its physical integrity but also it's a form of consecration.'

I suggest that many people think those views portray sex as something sinful, something associated with guilt.

'I'm quite sympathetic about Catholic guilt about sex in some ways. It's better than what's proposed now,' he laughs. 'Because the sexual instinct in human beings is so strong and human beings are fallen, a certain scepticism about the capacity of human sexuality is important.'

Does he believe in the Immaculate Conception?

'Absolutely!' he replies.

What role does Mary play in his life?

'I venerate Mary. I pray to her. I recite the Rosary regularly.'

Does he struggle, with the wide diversity of views about her within the Anglican Church?

'Yes, I do,' he replies emphatically.

Twenty years on, does he see the ordination of women priests as a regressive step or a progressive one?

'I don't accept the ordination of women priests myself. As a Catholic Christian, I'm very anxious about sacramental assurance. I want to make sure that when I receive the Blessed Sacrament, it is the Blessed Sacrament. I want to know that when I'm in hospital and dying, I will be anointed by someone who can hear my confession, who I can be sure is a priest. The anxiety is that it is excluded by the vast majority of Christians of a Catholic character, of both Roman and Orthodox. That makes me anxious. I couldn't propose to you a good reason in itself from Scripture and Tradition, other than it has never happened, to say why it is wrong. But no, I wouldn't take Communion from a woman priest.'

If I came here as a theological student and admitted to him that I did not believe in the Virgin Birth, would he ask me to leave or would he try to convert me?

'I would say this is a place of intellectual formation. The important thing is for people to say not why do you believe this or not believe this. You have got to be public exponents of the gospel. Once ordained, you have to understand your public responsibility. You cease to be people whose private theological speculations can be presented as the message of the Church. But the Church has nothing to fear from frank intellectual investigation of her teaching. If a person is going to be a Christian apologist, that person has to know whether their doubts are well founded as well as their beliefs. So that person who has an anxiety about the Virgin Birth would need to come and study it.'

But isn't it a good thing for people to question what they really believe and sometimes to admit doubt?

'Yes, that's right but one of the vulnerabilities of Christianity in our present culture has come through national compulsory education to the level we now give it. In the past, people were carried along by the structures. You will know yourself the Roman Catholicism in northern England before the Second Vatican Council in the 1960s and that communal emphasis which carried people forward. Now people are educated in a way that they have enough education not to take things on trust but not quite enough to be able to work things out rigorously on first principles.

'If I had to say if there is one really significant issue for evangelism and apologetic in the Church now for all Christians, it is dealing with that particular problem. You can't say to people any more "This is how we do it, just get on with it. You've got to obey orders and that will see you alright. Come to Mass on a Sunday until the undertaker comes for you and you won't go badly wrong and all of that. People won't take that now but the education they have is not enough to be philosophers – to work it out from first principles. It places a strong burden on the training of the clergy.

'At the Counter-Reformation, what did the Catholics decide to do? The Jesuits and nine years of training. We're not committed in that sort of way. Indeed, to keep the show on the road, the Church of England has made the choice to ordain people with very little training – part-time training even to keep the churches open. The fundamental issue is how you expound the Christian faith to an educated population but one that is vulnerable to impressionistic and emotional responses to truth propositions.'

Before I leave the Principal's study, I ask him to take a look at the large print of the Lemoyne painting. He studies it in silence for what seems like ages…at least three to four minutes. The stillness in the room feels tangible. Then, he begins to speak.

'The first thing that strikes me is how unusual it is for a French, early eighteenth-century painting to see a Virgin Mary kneeling to a standing angel. Normally, the convention would be the other way around. Has it been commissioned by somebody who clearly doesn't want to make a Catholic point? It's for a Protestant chapel. Would it be too risky at that time to have her standing and the angel kneeling? It makes me think it has been designed for a very specific English setting and has been toned down.

'It has a tremendously lively sense of movement,' he continues. 'Mary hasn't noticed the angel is there yet. She's engrossed in devotion. Mm, I like it. It's growing on me. When I first saw it, I thought it was a slightly bland academic exercise in early eighteenth-century piety. But the issue of Mary kneeling, reading, and that paper on the floor. Is there a sense the angel has dropped the message?

'There's a very particular French devotional strain here. The Sulpicians from St Sulpice who ran the French seminaries had a very strong emphasis on the interior life of Jesus and Mary. That strong sense of interiority is very important in the strand of French piety at that time. And the way her fingers point inwards. Yes, the interiority of her life is being highlighted here.'

I tell him that a copy of the painting hangs in St Sulpice church in Paris and that Lemoyne was very familiar with the place and the priests who were based there because he worked inside the building for three years after painting his *Annunciation.*

'For me, that's very, very important,' he responds. 'It's a very Sulpician take on the Annunciation. A profound sense of interiority and the interior life of the Blessed Virgin Mary. Look how she's unveiled as well. That's quite curious. You can see her ear. It shows it's good art. It's a powerful hook for meditation and to contemplate the mystery. Yes, that strikes me now. The more I look at it, the more comes out of it for me.'

The room returns to silence as he continues to study the picture. I look at him closely. He is staring transfixed at the detail. Then he closes his eyes in contemplation. It's as though he has entered the painting itself.

———

I head to the Houses of Parliament to meet Lord Richard Harries, the former Bishop of Oxford who served from 1987 to 2006. Educated at Wellington College and the Royal Military Academy at Sandhurst, he left the Army in 1958 to study Theology at Cambridge. He was ordained in 1964 and is a former Dean of King's College, London.

From 2008, Lord Harries has been the Gresham Professor of Divinity and has delivered a wide range of highly acclaimed public lectures, many of them on religion and art. He is the author of more than twenty books that focus on the interface of Christian faith and wider culture especially the visual arts. In his book, *Art and The Beauty of God*, published in 1993, he writes eloquently about the way in which the beauty in a painting is shaped by its symmetry, balance, harmony and proportion. 'Art is related to the "meaning" and the "truth" of things not just as they can be copied but as they can be envisaged in the mind of the creative artist,' he writes. 'And this mind will reflect, in however cloudy a manner, the way God sees things.'

Sitting on the outside terrace, overlooking the Thames, he tells me the Lemoyne painting 'is very good of its kind but it's not my favourite period to say the least. I think art stopped being properly Christian in the fourteenth century. There, they're still imbued with a Byzantine sense of holy.' He says he prefers icons for 'self-effacing' devotional purposes, and because they 'inspire the most effective direct manifestation of God and Christ.' In contrast, he sees Lemoyne's painting as 'trying to impress'.

He describes how in the Lemoyne picture, there is 'the humility of Mary in a very beautiful gesture; a very refined Mary. She's obviously very well bred and comes from a fine house. She knows how to do the rituals in that docile way. There's a much more dynamic, dominating angel, very authoritative, very powerful, and very androgynous. He's arrived with such a wind that the pages have been blown off the lectern. Obviously, a keep-fit angel,' he laughs. 'It's a beautiful composition. This is clearly a statement about divine light and divine power. It's very powerful but not overdone. There's no getting away for Mary. She hasn't got much choice.'

He tells me he prefers Fra Angelico's and Duccio's depictions. 'It's the sheer grace and beauty of the annunciation story that is not to be underestimated and they're not trying to show off.'

Does he believe the encounter actually happened?

'My view is, in the end, it doesn't matter all that amount,' he replies. 'We simply don't know the historical truth. I prefer to take it as it is – a very beautiful story. I'm concerned with fundamental issues about the existence of God, suffering and who Christ is. I regard the Virgin Birth as a secondary issue. For me, there are certain things that would collapse the whole edifice: the Resurrection; life after death, the divinity of Christ.

'I'd like to believe the Virgin Birth and I'm happy to accept it at the level of that the story is. There's a wonderful dialogue in *Brideshead Revisited* where Sebastian is challenged about believing in the Christmas story. He answers that it's because it's so beautiful. "You can't believe something just because it's beautiful," he's told. "But that's why I believe it," he responds. Well, that's the annunciation story for me. I'm not concerned to bother myself. I don't want to worry myself. There are much bigger things that are absolutely fundamental. So, if someone says it's simply a metaphor, that wouldn't worry me.'

I ask him if it is possible to be a Christian yet not believe in the detail of the annunciation story.

'It depends if one came to the conclusion that in some unique way God was in Christ reconciling the world to himself. That's the fundamental plank,' he responds. 'There has to be Jesus Christ. There has to be a unique manifestation of God in him. It wouldn't stop those three pivotal things. It would destroy the romance and the beauty of the story but it wouldn't destroy my faith.'

I wonder what he thinks of the claim that 'it's the most important event in human history'.

'Yes, I quite agree if it's the Incarnation, but the Incarnation is not necessarily totally identifiable with the appearance of Gabriel. But the Incarnation is totally fundamental.'

He says he understands why people put together the story of Mary and Gabriel and the events in the stable and bind them all together as the Incarnation.

'For them, those stories are about the Incarnation and they can't think of the Incarnation without all that. But some people, not because they're cleverer, are capable of thinking about the Incarnation without all of that. I'm happy to accept the story and receive it as it is.'

So, what does he believe is the key message of the Annunciation?

'The divine initiative,' he responds immediately. 'Taking the first step. And for Mary, the recognition and response.'

We walk a few steps to the edge of the terrace wall. Below, the pleasure boats and barges make their way slowly down the Thames. A striking, crepuscular sky hangs over the water. In the distance, through the arches of Waterloo Bridge, the river merges into the horizon.

CHAPTER 18

TRANSFORMATION

52. The author stands in front of Lemoyne's *The Annunciation*, National Gallery, London

Every time I am in central London, I go to Room 33, say hello to Mary and the angel Gabriel, and watch the ways in which people respond to the picture that has come to dominate my life. Most walk straight past it, without acknowledgement; some look at it for a long while. One day, I conduct a mini-survey and discover that the average time spent in front of it is sixteen seconds. I approach each individual and explain that I am writing a book about the painting. I ask what he/she is thinking whilst looking at it and make a record of each response. Here is a small selection:

'It has a very Western feel…look at those silky, porcelain skin tones. It isn't Jewish hair…where's her swarthy skin? And all the heavy drapery. I don't relate to it. And that sexually ambiguous angel…that's rather odd. As for those cherub heads, they are utterly repellent.'

'I see a profound humility. Our Lady saying, "Who, me?" The light coming into the darkened place captures so well the story of our own human lives.'

'I'm not a believer but you don't have to be to like it. It's striking. But she's too…what should I say…she's not…what's the word…she looks too obedient. Not weak…just acquiescing…and that flirtatious angel with its fabulous, spread out wings…saying get up and get on with it…it's not a good message for women, is it?'

'The artistry moves me even if the subject matter doesn't.'

'There's lots of all that Greek mythology in here. It's too remote for me.'

'It represents a miraculous moment beyond our comprehension. It's so vibrant. It forces you to move in and out. You have to go inside the painting to get it. To be actually there present with them both in their meeting.'

'It said it's called 'The Annut' (*sic*) or something. I can't remember the right word. What is that? And how can she give birth if she's a virgin? I didn't understand it to be honest.'

'It's exquisitely tender. The folds in the drapery are outstanding. You can almost feel the weight of the cloth. I like being able to get close up and see the layers of oil paint and the varnish. I love the picture, particularly as a woman.'

'It's not for me. It means nothing. I gave it a cursory glance and thought those faces are so weird.'

'In the first century, all men believed their sperm made up a hundred per cent of the foetus and the woman was there simply as a vessel to carry the baby. What a load of old cobblers. That's at the heart of the Virgin Birth and all that male dominance. I was thinking what a very damaging story it is, both for women and men.'

'I was looking at it and, funnily enough, thought of The Beatles. *Let It Be* and all that. I hadn't really thought about it before. I hadn't realized it was a religious song until a minute ago. "Mother Mary"; "words of wisdom"; you know what I'm saying, and then, "Let it be." You remember those words? Now I know what it's about. That's cool.'

'I'm not into religious paintings but I like the light. The way the picture is bathed in that spectacular light. That's why I stopped.'

'Art is a two-way experience, yeah? What's the artist trying to express? What does the viewer see? Has the painter been able to absorb the viewer's fascination? The most important thing about any painting is whether it draws a reaction. This one didn't move me at first when I glanced at it. But I came back and had another look. Even though I'm not religious, it made me mull over about what an amazing story.'

'What was I thinking when I was looking at it? Virgin births. How Paganism is also all about divine intervention in the cycle of life. Classical mythology is full of supernatural births. The Greeks thought Plato was conceived by Perictione through the god Apollo. I remember in Luxor once hearing how one of the Pharaohs was born miraculously to an Egyptian Queen. And Buddha, he was a miracle birth too. All religions and beliefs are full of them. Virgin births are used to pump up the divine character of someone. They're not fairy tales…they're a kind of metaphor…well no, they're more like myths. It's the same with this one.'

'I kept looking at that tear drop on the floor tile below her. By those two exposed toes on her right foot. Is Mary crying a tear of joy or a tear of sadness at what she is now giving up and what she is about to face as a mother? I've never seen a tear before in an Annunciation painting.'

'That's not a tear drop, you daft thing. It's just a chip on the floor tile. You're always seeing things no one else sees.'

'You have to understand nobody could read or write then. Well, very, very few. So I suppose it was bringing alive the story for the vast majority of the people looking at the painting, who were all illiterate. But it's like that other one we saw upstairs. The woman looking down and the angel pointing. They're always the same.'

'There's a growing agnotology about the Annunciation. No one talks about it today. No one teaches it. No one even acknowledges it anymore. Most people today are completely ignorant about it. That's secular Britain for you.'

'I'm Jewish so it means nothing to me. It's quite good though isn't it?'

'All of these, apparently, [he points around the room] are some of the best paintings in the world but you wouldn't put many of them up in your own home, would you? Certainly not that one.'

'I'm transfixed by Mary. She knew the joys and pains of motherhood. She was open to God's call and she trusted, she accepted. He captures that brilliantly.'

'I noticed you were looking at it for a long time so I thought I would too. The subject matter is not for me. I'm quite taken by the painting though, especially that light. That's good.'

'You can sum it up in one word: "Yes".'

'I couldn't take my eyes off it. It's a picture about us.'

———

It is one o'clock. Twenty-eight people gather in front of the painting, waiting to hear today's free lunchtime talk. The seats are positioned in eight rows of five. The guest speaker walks towards her place just in front of the picture and composes herself.

Dr Chloë Reddaway is the Howard and Roberta Ahmanson Curator in Art and Religion at the National Gallery. She read Philosophy and Theology at Trinity College, Oxford, before completing her doctorate on the theology of Florentine fresco cycles. Her current work focuses on visual theology and 'how images can facilitate a relationship between the viewer and God.'

She begins her talk on François Lemoyne's painting by stressing to her audience that she is not an expert on French eighteenth-century art but that she is 'very interested in Annunciations'.

Her slender figure, upright posture and elegant poise are striking, almost balletic. Her brown hair is tied back; she has bright red lipstick and she wears a brilliant white shirt. Her precise, clipped enunciation showcases a highly articulate erudition. In some ways, she appears and sounds like she is from a bygone age. Later, she tells me that she has no television in her home and 'has no need for one'.

Speaking from her script, she explains how the painting would have been hung much higher in Winchester College Chapel. Apparently, the best way to get the true perspective is to lie flat on the floor, looking up at it. Then you will see the angel's flexed knee appearing to project out of the painting.

Some people take notes. Others listen intently. One person, irritatingly, keeps shuffling a map of the gallery, planning where to go next.

Dr Reddaway observes that Mary's eyes are cast down, averted from Gabriel's gaze, so there is no direct interaction between them. However, she emphasizes that there is a strong connection 'in the way his wing is sheltering her, and in the way the spiral of his drapery seems to exercise a kind of compositional pull on her as she leans forward.' She moves on to describe the iconography as showing 'a certain kind of interiority. The Virgin's experience is a very interior one. She's not talking and not, obviously, reacting to something. It's a miraculous conception and, of course, that is a very interior event.'

She says there's an ambiguity about which precise moment of the annunciation story is being depicted in the painting but she believes it is right at the end of the encounter, as the angel is about to leave and Mary is absorbing the enormity of it all.

Most interestingly, she concentrates a latter part of her talk on the chipped, 'shabby' plaster and brickwork in the centre of the painting.

'We might read that chipped plaster as the first stage of peeling back the top layers,' she says, 'to let us see something underneath – a kind of material metaphor for the first stage of a revelation which begins at the Annunciation and which will continue through the Nativity, the life of Christ, and on through to the Crucifixion and the Resurrection. In other words, what we can only begin to understand at the Annunciation will ultimately be fully revealed at the other end of this story, when the veil in the Temple, which separated the Holy of the Holies – the place of God's presence – from the people, was torn in two and the barrier between God and man removed.

'We might also want,' she continues, 'to read the chipped plaster and brick more literally as a reference to true materiality. The Incarnation is the taking of flesh – the becoming material. The Virgin's own flesh in the painting is mainly covered and what we can see of it is glowing and beautiful, rosy and smooth. The rough plaster and brick behind her speaks of a different kind of materiality, something much grittier. And that aspect of the Incarnation is one which can easily be lost in the beauty of such images. The Incarnation is about the Virgin's beautiful flesh but it's also about the rough, gritty materiality of human life on earth and it's that human life and that earth for which Christians believe that Christ became incarnate.'

She says we might read the paper as blank because it is ready to receive the Word – the Logos – the Christ. We might read the empty basket as the future cradle for the anticipated child who will come from the empty womb of the Virgin. And we might remember that the Virgin is, herself, the unsullied, pure matter on which God's word is to be written when her empty womb is filled. She ends: 'There's a wholly appropriate sense of anticipation here; of matter waiting to be marked; of emptiness waiting to be filled. It is, literally, a very pregnant moment.'

As soon as she has finished, most people leave the room immediately. Three people stay on to continue looking at the painting.

'It's the lighting that has the most striking effect on me. That's the best part of the painting but, surprisingly, she didn't talk about that,' one of them says. 'I don't like the vagueness of the wall and how it disappears into the cloud,' another tells me. 'It looks half finished to me. The picture is too frilly and unnatural. Where's the authentic, long black-haired, olive-skinned Mary as a fellaheen, wearing a simple tunic and mantle?'

A third person approaches me coyly and describes the painting in a whisper: 'It's so very beautiful. I would have walked straight past it if I hadn't stopped to listen to her talk. I've gone from merely looking at the picture to now seeing it…I understand it.'

A few minutes later, the room is empty and I sit with Chloë Reddaway in front of the painting. I wonder how effective it is in facilitating an understanding of Luke's story and the relationship between viewer and God. There is a long pause before she responds.

'It's not just about understanding the story. It's about understanding the significance of the story – the meaning of the meaning,' she says. 'You can read the text and you can know exactly what it says and you can read it backwards but if you don't know why it matters, that's no help to you. Paintings are particularly good at the "why it matters" bit, and particularly with something which is about the Incarnation and the human experience of God.

'If I just walked past this painting,' she continues, 'I wouldn't find anything new about the Incarnation and about Luke, but if I spend a few hours looking at it, I realize this is happening and that is happening and I start to make connections and, in that process, I'm having an experience rather than just noting a fact or writing down a chapter and verse. I'm feeling it in some way. There are almost no paintings worth looking at that you can get a huge amount out of in the first thirty seconds. What you need is a long period of attentive viewing in which you really look. The longer you spend with it, the more there will be and the greater the richness.'

As she gazes at the painting, she praises the sculptural quality of Lemoyne's two main figures as 'very three-dimensionally modelled. You can really sense the weight and the volume of them. They're proper life-like figures.'

I ask what the annunciation story means for her.

'The Incarnation is the hinge on which everything else works or fails,' she replies. 'If not the Incarnation, then none of the rest of the story makes sense. The Annunciation is what makes that possible. The true volition of human beings says something enormous about the capacity for transformation that human beings have, and the Virgin Mary's acceptance is a model for everyone else to transform and change.'

Did the event actually take place? I wonder.

'It might be historical fact, it might not be,' she says. 'I'm never going to be in a position to know. I would never rule it out. On balance, given my experience of the world and the way it seems to work, I'd say it's probably quite unlikely. But then again loads of things are quite unlikely and we experience unlikely things every day and don't think about it. I would not die in a ditch for the Virgin Birth being historical fact but I really don't mind if it isn't. It really doesn't make any difference to me to the power of the story and what it means.

'In the same way, I said the point of the painting is the meaning of the meaning. If the painting can't tell you why this matters, then it isn't working as a painting and I don't see painting a story as particularly different. To me, they're both an attempt to put into some kind of form an essential element of human experience. And if humans are God-experiencing creatures, then those are two ways in which they have tried to shape that kind of experience to make some kind of coherent sense. We live in a largely linear narrative fashion, so one of the ways in which we make sense of things and by which we shape meaning is in a linear narrative way with all the possibilities that that then has for doubling back, for pointing forwards, for layering things.'

So, what does she think is the key message?

'I think the key message for me about Christianity, full stop, is transformation. The possibility of something becoming unlike what it is now. I would see that in the crucifixion and resurrection narrative, that death can be not death but death can be life or re-life re-lived; to me, that's what's happening in all of the miracle stories, that something is being transformed into something else, somebody who is ill is no longer ill, someone who has no wine suddenly has wine. It's about a complete change of events in a way you do not anticipate is possible. I think that's one of the primary reasons for continuing to talk about the Virgin Birth. It emphasizes the extreme transformation involved in that. A woman who is a virgin and yet she is pregnant is a complete transformation both of her and of everyone's expectation of what can happen. If you look at it in a symbolic, narrative sense, it's so powerful.'

Does she see the Annunciation as 'the most important event in human history'?

'Fair enough,' she replies immediately. 'If you say none of the rest of the Christian story is going to happen without that, then that's where it really starts. It's the pivotal moment where Mary could have said no.'

––––––––

Ben Quash is the Professor of Christianity and the Arts at King's College, London. After studying English and then Theology at Cambridge, he was Chaplain of Fitzwilliam

College and Dean at Peterhouse. Now, he runs the only Master of Arts degree course in the world in which there is collaboration between a Theology and Religious Studies department in an academic institution (King's College), and an international art gallery (The National Gallery).

Twelve students, from a variety of backgrounds, are currently taking the inter-disciplinary course. Ben Quash specializes in art as a theological medium and focuses on the idea of beauty in western theology and the devotional use of art in Christianity.

He arrives at the National Gallery dressed in an open-necked shirt, smart jacket, well-pressed jeans and brogues. He is tall and slim with a matinée-idol face. I am interested in what he sees. He scans his eyes across the Lemoyne canvas, before taking a place to the right of the picture and looking upwards.

'The first thing that strikes out at me is the angel and its similarity to Leonardo da Vinci's image of John the Baptist,' he tells me. 'He's often described as a messenger – *angelos* in Greek – and Eastern Orthodox often depict him as a winged figure. In some of the earliest English Anglo-Saxon sermon texts, the Blickling Homilies from the end of the tenth century, John the Baptist is described as an angel. So, whether from a theologically intelligent decision or just because he liked Leonardo's John the Baptist, it looks as though something special and mesmerizing has been done here. Mm, yes, an elfin-like, androgynous angel representing the other worldliness. He, she, it is mesmerizing and Lemoyne has good instincts.

'Mary's posture though looks very awkward. It's really very odd. I'm trying to work out how her body is working. The state of humility is beautifully evoked by the positioning of her hands and the angle of her head. There's this sense, almost literally, of putting her head below a yoke. She's bending her head to the task facing her like a yoke. But I can't see her other leg and where's her knee?' he asks. 'It's far too long. Anatomical accuracy is not the be all and end all but, in this case, it creates a sense of disquiet in me because I can't work out how she's supported. Maybe as well as her quiet resignation, disquiet is part of what's going on here – a huge step into the unknown. A burden that could bring her down.'

He takes a couple of steps sideways to the left so he is standing in front of the middle of the picture, then crouches down, his arms still folded, and moves his head forward to within six inches of the canvas.

'I'm very struck by the tattiness of the interior. The plaster falling off the wall to reveal the brickwork. You don't see that often in annunciation images. The marble is chipped too. And there's this odd material, sackcloth almost, to the left of the Virgin. She's in fine robes. And then there's the glory of heaven in the upper reaches of the picture.'

'Across this diagonal,' he continues as he stands up and sweeps his right hand across the picture, 'it's driving a powerful contrast between the heavenly realm which is luminous and radiant, and this broken worldly space. It's a fascinatingly evocative image but a little bit derivative and it's too saccharine for me. My favourite part of the painting is this brickwork. It's very centrally placed. The space between the Virgin and the angel is the most charged space. What an artist decides to do in that space matters greatly. It's never accidental or an off-the-cuff decision. So the exposed brickwork is extraordinary. It's like a metaphor for revelation. For stripping back the linear. An apocalypse. Literally the unveiling. It's wittily subversive.

'It's just bricks and another barrier, of course. But you've got a moment of insight that's almost minute. All you've gained is this half inch of depth and then there's another barrier. But barriers matter a lot in the Annunciation – the meeting of heaven and earth is a significant threshold. It's not one you can cross from this side but you can be brought across it if you're worthy. I love the brickwork. It's so earthy. It's about the real stuff human beings make. A lot of things in this picture I don't want to touch because they look too unsubstantial or I don't have faith in them as real. But those bricks, I want to touch them.'

As he continues to peer closely at the brickwork, he sees some individual brush hairs stuck to the canvas. 'That's a lovely trace of its materiality,' he proclaims.

We move a few yards back from the picture and sit together in the central seating area of the room. I ask what the annunciation story means for him.

'This is where redemption begins,' he replies. 'It begins at that moment of conception. It's an incredibly important moment – the point when the threshold is crossed and from then on, redemption is unstoppable.'

I wonder if he sees the story as factual or metaphorical.

'It depends what you mean by fact,' he responds. 'I don't see any reason to suppose an angel didn't come to see Mary. I have no problem with an angelic visitation. It's quite possible it didn't happen just as Luke's Gospel constructs it because Luke wants to make every detail theologically meaningful. A lot of complex literary things are going on in terms of parallels between Elizabeth and Mary, and John and Jesus, which are building the layers of meaning. I don't think the Gospels are written as the sort of historical document we now expect. They didn't observe the same rules.'

I reflect that the encounter between Mary and the angel only appears in one of the four canonical Gospels. Does that give him pause for thought?

'No. I'm happy with that,' he says. 'It's a loaded word but Luke's Gospel is pregnant with meaning in those first chapters. They're a gift that are specifically his to the traditions of the Church and are very, very eloquent about the meaning of Christ's Incarnation.'

I tell him how Bishop Egan described the Annunciation as 'the most important event in human history'.

'I'm with him on that,' he replies. 'My way of capturing it is that the Cross and Resurrection are already implicit in this but you can't say that the other way around. You can have a gospel that doesn't tell this story. You can't read the Passion Narratives in Matthew and find implicitly in them this but, my goodness, it works the other way around. Cross and Resurrection are what this is all about and is leading to. So, in that sense, it trumps them.'

He walks back up to the painting and looks at the basket at the bottom of the picture.

'The white cloth in the basket here is evocative of death – the shroud with which Jesus's body will be wrapped,' he says. 'I'm also intrigued by that scroll on the floor. My instinct is that it is connected with both Gabriel and the artist. See how there's a very strong horizontal axis moving from the Virgin's head and shoulders across to the text she's been reading. And there's a strong vertical axis from Gabriel's finger right down through the exposed leg and on to the scroll. To me, the scroll symbolizes "message". It's a visible rendering of what Lemoyne can't make the painting be – to be audible – and he shows how something so special is being delivered from heaven to earth.'

He tells me his favourite depiction of the Annunciation is Domenico Veneziano's fifteenth-century painting displayed in the Fitzwilliam Museum in Cambridge. He describes it as 'eloquently simple and unadulterated. It invites you to peddle back from all the accretions and preconceptions that gather around an annunciation image and, having seen so many of them, to just go back to the purest form. It wipes the slate clean and gives you the space to think about the story. It's the same with the Fra Angelico in Florence.'

So, what does he think of Lemoyne's painting as a source of contemplation and revelation?

'The more I look at it, the more I find in it,' he responds. 'It doesn't have everything you'd expect in an Annunciation – no dove, no lily. But it's that centrality of the brickwork and the basket of linen. I didn't clock them at first. It's standing in the presence of it for a while that elicits those insights and possibilities. Good paintings keep on giving. They're temporal events because the human mind and the human eye have to take time with them. What I've started to discover is just the beginning. There's a lot more here still to discover. It's a very theologically intelligent painting. It does have an emotional impact but it isn't only going for emotional effect. It's carefully constructed to encode meaning. I'd love to bring my Master's students here to stand in front of this painting.'

I take him up on that wish and a few days later ten of his Master of Arts students gather around the painting in Room 33. As they view the picture, I listen keenly to their observations:

'For me, this is very much a moment of the spiritual and the material. It's expressed in the way the wall blends into the clouds and the sky.'

'I can't help but be completely distracted by the three absurd angel-like children that are so bored by what's going on between Gabriel and Mary that they're dive bombing each other in the corner.'

'I see something most unexpected. I see a John the Baptist like angel with wings because of his distinctive finger gesture.'

'I see Mary looking very unusual. She could be stoned to death and yet she doesn't look shocked. She almost looks pleased.'

'I'm a fashion designer so I'm immediately drawn to the fabric. I love the colour palette and the fluidity of the fabric. So much synergy and movement and yet so static as well.'

'First of all, I didn't like it. It was too heavenly and, for me, that doesn't help get into the Annunciation. I thought, how extraordinarily mundane it was. But then I noticed she isn't aware of any of all this around her. She's centred in her mundanity. I then saw the washing basket and the plaster coming away from the wall. You have to see God in the ordinariness and dirtiness of life and, as I look at it now, I see it as a better way in. It's a very clever painting.'

'I first look at Mary and her devotional love. She hasn't realized Gabriel has come down.'

'When I think of the Annunciation, I think of Mary not having a choice and her complete submission and I see that here. But the way the light has been painted, hitting the hand and face of the angel and the face and hands of Mary is just a complete romanticism of the scene.'

'It looks like my kitchen floor – dirty – and the plaster coming off the wall. I also see a face at the top of the blanket hanging over the prayer stall and Mary is looking at the face.'

'Whenever I see an Annunciation picture, there are two types: the shocked face – "Oh my God", or the more sedate version. And I always ask myself, what is the artist's view of the story? Who's it being painted for? Where's it going to be placed? Who will be the audience?'

'It's the painting of a myth.'

'I would say it is truth, not fact. Fact is not the highest form of truth. Fact is the most easily definable truth. I wasn't there, only Mary was. Yes, there was an event but it's very difficult to be factual in the way we think of facts today. But I'm very happy to call this event I'm looking at truth and not fact. It doesn't lessen its reality.'

'From an Islamic perspective, the story was re-revealed 400 years later to the prophet Muhammad. I'm a Muslim. I don't see why we have to question whether it's factual or not unless we are dependent on something, which makes that problematic. If someone believes it could not happen, they either reject it or try to reinterpret it. For me, I don't have a problem in accepting it as fact. I wasn't there but I'm depending on revelations that confirm it.'

'I'm a massive Irigaray fan [Luce Irigaray, the Belgian born French feminist and philosopher]. She talks about how the Annunciation is a type of crucifixion and she has this wonderful quote, that as soon as Mary says yes, she has nailed her lips to the Cross. That's what I see here.'

––––––––––

I have come to the Sainsbury Wing of the National Gallery to join a guided tour led by Dr Caroline Campbell, the National Gallery's Curator of pre-1500 Italian Paintings. The tour is called 'The Immaculate Conception' but this turns out to be a misnomer: what it actually focuses on are paintings of the Annunciation. The ones I am particularly interested to see are by Duccio di Buoninsegna, Fra Filippo Lippi, Cosima Tura, The Master of Liesborn, Carlo Crivelli and Nicolas Poussin.

Duccio's *The Annunciation*, using egg tempera on poplar wood, was painted in 1311. It forms the first of seven scenes from the infancy of Christ that made up the predella of a magnificent double-sided altarpiece for the high altar in Siena Cathedral. At the time of its creation, the Virgin Mary was the protectoress of Siena, and Duccio was the city's leading painter. The overall piece, known as the Maesta, was huge – at least sixteen feet square – and was one of the largest and most complex altarpieces ever produced. Its main image, facing out to the nave, showed the Virgin Mary and Christ enthroned in majesty. The Maesta was broken into several pieces in 1771 and the National Gallery acquired the Annunciation panel in 1883.

53. Duccio *The Annunciation*, 1307/8-11, The National Gallery, London. © The National Gallery, London

Although it is small, it is a stunningly beautiful work. Dr Caroline Campbell tells the group, 'The architecture here plays a deep role in making the message of this sacred picture more obvious.' The two central figures stand in their own architectural frames. The Virgin stands inside a covered grey porch, underneath an arch, symbolizing the *porta coeli* or doorway to heaven. The porch encloses Mary to emphasize her isolation and to highlight her holiness, purity and separation from the world. Dr Campbell points out, 'There's a door partly open that refers to the entry of the Holy Spirit and also to the believer once they follow her way.'

I stand close to the Duccio picture, my nose almost touching the frame, noting more of its detail, including a tiny heraldic-shaped white dove descending towards Mary on golden rays of light. Mary's unusually long, right hand index finger points to her left, indicating that the next scene on the predella is the Visitation. The British sculptor, Sir Anthony Caro, greatly admired the stillness of the picture and the way Duccio understood the use of architecture to organize the internal space and to shape the narrative. He acclaimed Duccio's 'tenderness,' calling it 'a painting with feelings of love…a delicate, almost feminine picture.' The painting inspired Caro to design *Duccio Variations* in 1999–2000, a series of seven sculptural pieces using bronze, cast iron, steel and walnut.

We move to Room 54 to view Fra Lippi's fifteenth-century Florentine masterpiece, *The Annunciation*, hanging high in a corner of the room. Lippi painted this beautifully refined work, using egg tempera on wood, between 1448 and 1450. It is one of a pair of panels originally displayed in a Medici palace in Florence and may have been used as a bed head or placed above a door. The famous Medici logo, three feathers within a diamond ring, can be seen on the end of a wall in the centre of the picture.

54 .Fra Filippo Lippi *The Annunciation*, 1450-3, The National Gallery, London. ©
The National Gallery, London

'So many of the paintings from this period are closely related to their devotional function but this Annunciation is represented on secular furniture,' Dr Campbell explains. 'What's very extraordinary here in fifteenth-century Tuscany is that the domestic accoutrements of the Virgin are very important to the tale. Lippi shows a really accurate Florentine domestic interior. And she's open to our gaze. The artist plays with the question of access.'

On the left of the painting is an enclosed garden, the *hortus conclusus*, symbolizing Mary's purity and virginity. The angel approaches her from the garden, taking care not to squash any of the delicate yellow flowers below his feet. The curve of his opened peacock wings skilfully matches the curve of the painting. He leans towards Mary and looks at her face. Between them is an urn full of lilies and he carries a lily stem in his hand.

55. Cosimo Tura *The Virgin Annunciate*, 1475-80, The National Gallery, London. © The National Gallery, London

'Gabriel is not touching her with the lily,' Dr Campbell observes. 'Mary is *"virgo intacta"* and a virgin is not meant to be touched. It plays with the pure lily getting very close to the pure virgin. She's meant to be penetrated by the Holy Spirit so the lily stem, although not penetrating her, is making that connection.'

Moving on to Room 55, we stand before Cosimo Tura's *The Virgin Annunciate*. Originally, this was one of a pair of panels forming part of an altarpiece with a companion picture of the angel Gabriel. Tura painted this small Annunciation between 1475 and 1480 when he was employed as a court artist in Ferrara.

'Tura was a very strange, unusual artist who doesn't follow iconographic traditions, with his elongated fingers, his sclerotic limbs and forms, and his strange architectural structures, says Dr Campbell. 'He likes to play with shape. His figures look like they're jumping out of the pictures.'

One woman in the group tells a friend, 'How horrible. That's not how Mary looked at the Annunciation!' As if she would know!

We head to Room 64 to view the Master of Liesborn's *The Annunciation*, one of four panels that made up the shutters of a fifteenth-century high altarpiece in the Benedictine Abbey of Liesborn, Westphalia, Germany. The painter's real name remains unknown but it is believed that the work was completed between 1470 and 1480. The large imposing altarpiece was divided into parts in 1807 and sold off. The National Gallery acquired this particular piece in 1854.

Crivelli's masterpiece, *The Annunciation, with Saint Emidius* is displayed in Room 59. The altarpiece was painted in 1486 and is one of the most extraordinary annunciation pictures created during the Renaissance era. The town of Ascoli in the Italian Marshes was under papal rule when in 1482 Pope Sixtus IV granted it partial self-governance. The altarpiece was commissioned for the Church of SS Annunziata in Ascoli to celebrate that event. News of the town's new status reached its people on the feast of the

56. Carlo Crivelli *The Annunciation, with Saint Emidius*, 1486, The National Gallery, London. © The National Gallery, London

Annunciation and, from then on, 25 March became a special annual feast day for the townsfolk to celebrate both the Annunciation and Ascoli's new status.

Crivelli's painting conflates the annunciation story and that political event. St Emidius, the patron saint of Ascoli, stands next to the angel Gabriel outside Mary's home as the angel delivers his message to the Virgin. St Emidius, dressed as a bishop, carries a model of the town and appears to be telling Gabriel the news about Ascoli's new status. It is rare to see a third major figure feature in an annunciation encounter although the painting reminds me of the statue of William of Wykeham standing alongside the angel Gabriel and Mary in the three niches above Middle Gate at Winchester College.

On a later visit to the National Gallery, I head to Room 18 on my own and stand in front of Nicolas Poussin's beautiful but austere picture, *The Annunciation*, painted in 1657 during the final part of his career. Born in Normandy and frequently hailed as the greatest French painter of the seventeenth century, Poussin travelled to Rome when he was thirty years of age and stayed there for most of his life. Greatly influenced by classical sculpture, he painted mainly for private patrons. It is thought this picture may have been destined to hang above the tomb of Poussin's patron, Cessiano dal Pozzo, in the church of Santa Maria sopra Minerva in Rome.

57. Nicolas Poussin *The Annunciation*, 1657, The National Gallery,
London. © The National Gallery, London

Poussin was known as the embodiment of the painter-philosopher tradition and was not fervently religious. However, *The Annunciation*, is an outstanding work revealing the artist's personal meditation on God. It speaks of interiority, solemnity and acceptance. Red-haired Mary, dressed unusually in a yellow garment, opens her arms as she hears a voice reveal her destiny. The dove hovers above her head, its wings similarly outstretched. The pages of Mary's book are also opened out as she closes her eyes and absorbs the message.

Next to the Poussin in Room 18, the Yves Saint Laurent Room, are two paintings side by side by Philippe de Champaigne. The first is called *The Dream of Joseph* from 1643 and shows a sleeping Joseph being visited by an angel, as told in Matthew's Gospel. Mary looks on in the background with her arms crossed. A year later, the French baroque painter created *The Annunciation*, which is on loan from the Ferens Art Gallery in Hull. Angels encircle the Holy Spirit in the form of the dove. Rays of heavenly light shine through a gap in the sky, as Mary and the angel Gabriel stand on plain floorboards, representing Earth, with the nails clearly visible. Two depictions from Matthew and Luke's stories of the Annunciation displayed together.

I return to the ground floor of the National Gallery. To my surprise, I notice that the doors of Room A are open. During previous visits, this room has been closed to the public, but a Gallery assistant informs me that it is open for a limited number of hours each Wednesday. The room houses extra works from the National Gallery's collection, focusing on the latter part of the Middle Ages up to the High Renaissance from 1250 to 1600.

The walls are covered with paintings of Mary. I count twenty-four pictures featuring the Virgin and Child; one depicts the marriage of the Virgin; another shows her death. There's yet another 'Annunciation' picture, this time a fifteenth-century altarpiece by the Florentine artist, Zanobi Strozzi. The room is a clear indication, if ever I needed one, of the strength of the cult of Mary during the Middle Ages through to the Renaissance, demonstrated by the preponderance of churches and homes, particularly across southern Europe, that were adorned with devotional images of her.

I reflect that no woman in history has inspired such an extreme range of reactions, from devotion to rejection, from admiration to contempt, from inspiration to abnegation.

———

I head to Room E where a striking woman with frizzy black hair and distinctive large black-rimmed glasses stands waiting for me in front of the Lemoyne canvas. Miri Rubin is Professor of Medieval and Early Modern History at Queen Mary, University of London. She is the author of the book *Mother of God: A History of the Virgin Mary*, which traces Mary's journey 'from virtual unknown to virginal icon and ultimately God-like figure.' It was ten years in the making, and when it was published in 2009, academics and theologians hailed it as 'masterly' and 'breathtaking…the finest account of Mary's impact on world culture.'

Fifty-eight-year-old Miri Rubin was brought up in Israel and is a mother herself. I want to hear her views about the most famous Jewish girl in the history of the world. But first, I ask for her assessment of the Lemoyne painting.

'I see a very strange Annunciation,' she says. 'I'm a medieval historian. I deal with medieval materials where there's usually far more parity between the angel and Mary. But in this early eighteenth-century picture, there's an androgynous angel descending on Mary and telling her what's what and dominating the composition. She's not prominent. It's an arrangement that would be very unusual in earlier centuries. It's made in France, it's still a Catholic culture, but it's very, very different.

'In the Middle Ages, what's emphasized is Mary's domesticity,' she continues. 'Artists suggest Mary is a well brought up Jewish girl, she's indoors, modest, pure, worthy of this mission. So, for me, it's really strange looking at this early eighteenth-century picture, where she's in an undetermined, unspecified space. The emphasis is not on domesticity. The centuries long tradition of Mary being visited where she feels safe, all her routines are predictable and then this extraordinary surprise lands on her – that's lost here by the lack of a very secure domestic setting. Gabriel usually faces her but here he descends upon her while Mary sits meekly. Of course, I do understand in the baroque there's a real transformation in the emphasis – the loftiness, the other worldliness, the clouds. But for me, schooled in hundreds and hundreds of works of medieval art in many media, it strikes me as very, very different – the exalting, the putti, the sense of over the top. Usually I see an encounter, a parity but here he's telling her what's what. It's a sensual object for the Court. I find it less interesting. It doesn't move me in terms of human insight.'

She speaks in a fluent, forthright manner and waves her arms enthusiastically when making a point. I ask how the positioning of Mary changed during the period from the early Church through to 1600?

'Really dramatically, I think,' she responds. 'Within the Byzantine empire, within the Christian Eastern Mediterranean empire where Christianity became established and was allowed to flourish intellectually, within the Eastern ports that became Christian, Mary was imagined as a very good lady indeed. She was enthroned, looked serious, solemn, dressed with jewelled garments, majestic. Christianity was an imperial enterprise.

'In Western Europe, on the whole, artists and theologians up to 1100 were quite beholden to that Eastern tradition. But Europe then developed its own way. A different language of Mary, emphasizing alongside her regality a deep humanity, a motherliness. An emphasis on feelings, on a human familiarity. The vision of Mary that wins and that appeals to most people in the rural parishes is to experiment how far you can go with Mary's humanity. The draw was for a Mary that could be embedded in people's everyday lives.

'The really big intervention then, of course, is the Lutheran one, the Protestant one,' she says as she gazes at the Lemoyne painting. 'But the scene of the Annunciation never goes away. That's why the Anglican Winchester College in the 1720s can interpret Mary through a scene of the Annunciation but they cannot interpret her through a scene of Mary's birth or the Assumption because they're not biblical. The Annunciation is kosher. And the eighteenth century is not the seventeenth century. All the killing is over. It's a little more sensible. But religious art is still dead in this country in the early eighteenth century. It's still so controversial. There's been so much removal and iconoclasm. So people paint dogs and horses as they do. Then the headmaster says "we really need a good picture (for the Chapel) and the French still do it and an Annunciation would be less controversial".

'This painting is also a mark of trade and commercial society developing,' she explains. 'You know who the great artists of France are; you are able to go to Paris and commission them; and there are ways of paying. I'm really intrigued by the nitty-gritty of how this headmaster, Burton, actually acquired it. Was he on a Grand Tour? Did he visit Paris specifically for this picture? That would be extraordinary. Did he see a collection or what? It's all absolutely fascinating.'

What does she think is the key message of the annunciation story?

'I think the Annunciation must surely bolster the idea of the dual nature of Christ,' she replies. 'It's an assurance. He had to have a proper mother, flesh and blood, and no ambiguity. That's why the Immaculate Conception is a real problem. I can see why it's necessary – in the nineteenth century it became an article of faith – but I find it an unhappy compromise. You want Mary to be as ordinary as can be because you want Christ to be as human as can be. On the other hand, you want to show she's part of a bigger pattern, a big, big providential story that's unfolding. And she's told, "you're part of it" and she takes a leap of faith. She's in her home, she's domesticated but she could also see history unfolding. That's such an interesting idea, that faith is all about accepting and identifying with something you can't see. It doesn't seem reasonable but it's important. She's afraid but she accepts.'

I tell her that I have asked a range of people whether they think the story is factual, metaphorical or something else. What does she think?

'I don't know how we can know what happened,' she responds, 'except to say Mary may have reported it to someone within the circle of Jesus who ultimately became one of the evangelists. But this is not important to me. What's important to me is that this is one of the early binding ideas of Christianity and it's absolutely necessary if you are going to say that Jesus is the Messiah and that he is also the Saviour. Jews never imagined the Messiah would be Man and God but rather would be an elevated figure. But to not be Jewish, to be Christian, to build on Judaism and go beyond, you then create this Good News of God and Man. And that's so challenging and so powerful that the immediate issue of maternity becomes absolutely crucial.'

Does she view the Incarnation, rather than the Annunciation as the lynchpin of Christianity?

'Absolutely,' she replies. 'The Annunciation only becomes an important scene in art much later. Christianity got on very well for hundreds of years thank you very much without constantly dramatizing the event. It shows that the Annunciation is not that formative but it's much beloved because of all the incongruities that are resolved within it. She's afraid but she accepts.'

What did she learn about Mary when writing her book?

'I wouldn't say I learned about her but definitely I learnt about us,' she says. 'The most important thing about Mary is that just like in any cultural system, of course, you're going to find a wide array of interpretations. That's the nature of symbols and narratives. They strike us in different ways. What I also learnt is that the thing that is most dear and most beloved can be a tremendous inspiration for people but also can be a thing of which they will be most intolerant and be willing to kill for, willing to judge, willing to interrogate, etc. So Mary is a symbol of conversion of faith but also a touchstone that separates groups, religious faiths and even Christians amongst themselves.'

Does she see Mary as a bridge or a barrier to greater interfaith dialogue?

'She's now more a bridge. There's been a decline in literalism and Christians are now less literal about her. Although in 1999 you saw in the British artist Chris Ofili's wonderful work, *The Holy Virgin Mary* and his use of the very holy substance of elephant dung, how a massively organized Catholic activism can still really put the pressure on. Even New York's Mayor Giuliani had to take a position on the painting not being displayed in the city.'

As we draw our conversation to a close, Professor Rubin offers a final thought: 'In my experience, on the whole, everybody wants to love through Mary. Feminists want to have Mary. Mary is interfaith. She was Jewish. She was Christian. She's held in great esteem in Islam. She's about maternity and nurturing. She's a bridge and it's dangerous to be too ahistorical. There are lots of cases in Judaism where an angel informed, inspired, struck fear in figures. The whole issue of how do you receive a divine mission, how do you confront a destiny, and that moment when the penny drops and you have to be a part of something that's very scary but very worthwhile. So we can discuss Mary and the annunciation story through issues that are humanly universal. It has cultural resonance. It has something to work with everywhere.'

———

Chris Ofili's *The Holy Virgin Mary* is a prime example of the way in which a serious, aesthetically inspiring work of religious art can become the subject of huge controversy when it is hijacked by an outraged, hysterical section of the community who fail to understand the serious motivation of the artist.

Forty-six-year-old Ofili was twenty-seven when he created his best-known work in 1996. Born to Nigerian parents, in a working-class Catholic household in Manchester, he once described himself as 'believing in God but not dominated by it.' His initial ambition was to become a furniture designer but he ended up studying Art at the Chelsea School of Art and Design and the Royal College of Art. Today he lives and works in Trinidad.

In the book *Chris Ofili* published by Rizzoli in 2009, which examined his artistic career to date, Ofili's intricately constructed works are described as creating 'a unique iconography that marries African artistic and ritual practices with Western art historical traditions and contemporary hip-hop culture.'

He once said he recognised that religion can be a springboard for spiritual enlightenment: 'I don't think it necessarily takes you to a greater place but it can put you in the mood.'

The Holy Virgin Mary is a work that became part of the 'Sensation' touring exhibition, featuring works from Charles Saatchi's collection of Young British Artists (YBAs). First, it appeared at the Royal Academy of Arts in 1997, then moved to Berlin and finally to the Brooklyn Museum of Art in New York City in 1999. By the time the exhibition arrived in Brooklyn, Ofili had become the first black artist to be awarded the Turner Prize, in recognition in part of his deeply moving work, *No Woman, No Cry*, featuring Doreen Lawrence, the mother of the murdered black teenager, Stephen Lawrence, that he had created the previous year.

The Holy Virgin Mary created a storm of protest in the Big Apple. The *New York Daily News* described it as the 'Brooklyn Gallery of Horror', claiming the Virgin Mary was 'splattered with elephant dung'. Cardinal John O'Connor, Archbishop of New York, called it an attack on religion itself whilst the Republican City Mayor, Rudolph Giuliani, described it as 'sick stuff'. Indeed, so offended was the Mayor at the prospect of Ofili's work being displayed in his city that he took out a legal action in a doomed attempt to prevent the exhibition going ahead. Neither the Cardinal nor the Mayor had even seen the piece.

'Religion should be used in the appropriate way,' Ofili told *The New York Times* at the time

58. Chris Ofili *The Holy Virgin Mary*, 1996. © Chris Ofili, Courtesy Victoria Miro, London

of the exhibition. 'The Church is not made up of one person but a whole congregation and they should be able to interact with art without being told what to think. This is all about control. We've seen it before in history. Sadly, I thought we'd moved on.'

The eight-foot-tall *The Holy Virgin Mary* is a sensual, lustrous, and provocative mixed-media work that features a voluptuous black Madonna nursing her newly born baby. Ofili uses paint, glitter, resin, pointillist dots, map pins and, most controversially, elephant dung and magazine collages, to shape its exuberant content. The Madonna's blue robe is parted to reveal an exposed breast, made from lacquered elephant dung adorned with glitter. Around her, on a bright yellow-orange background, appear to be an array of fluttering putti or small butterflies, which, close up, reveal themselves to be a collage of genitalia, cut out from pornographic magazines. Two balls of elephant dung provide the two feet that prop up the picture, one displaying the word 'Virgin' and the other 'Mary'.

Before creating the work, Ofili had visited Zimbabwe as part of a British Council sponsored travelling scholarship. He immersed himself in his African heritage and spent time studying the ancient art in the paleolithic caves. He discovered that elephants and their dung are sacred in many African countries. When discussing his painting with Paul Miller in 2000, he explained, 'It's about the way the black woman is talked about in hip-hop music. It's about my religious upbringing and confusion about that situation. The contradiction of a virgin mother and the stereotyping of the black female. And it's about just being confused.'

Three months into the exhibition, the painting was vandalized by Dennis Heiner, a seventy-two-year-old Catholic and retired school teacher from Manhattan, who daubed it with white paint, claiming it was blasphemous.

'I don't feel as though I have to defend it. The people who are attacking the painting are attacking their own interpretation, not mine,' the artist told *The New York Times*. 'It all seems very distant and confusing to me.'

Eleven years later, this metaphorical and ambiguous work, imagining Mary as a black African, formed the centre-piece of Chris Ofili's retrospective exhibition at Tate Britain in 2010. Speaking to the Ghanaian British writer Ekow Eshun, Ofili commented, 'I was an altar boy and heard the Bible being read out repeatedly. The stories have stayed with me, although they're completely re-mixed in my head. And often, when I do further reading, I'm quite surprised by the difference between the real story and my memory of the story. I'm interested in that difference and how it's affected the way I think about making images…Stories within the Bible still have a relevance to my life and contemporary life in general. I'm still interested in morality. The stories are so well put together that they evoke very powerful images.'

The Holy Virgin Mary was feted with praise rather than criticism when it returned to New York in 2014 as part of Ofili's first US solo exhibition, 'Night and Day', at the New Museum on the Bowery. By then, it was more than a decade since he'd represented Britain at the fiftieth Venice Biennale. 'Perhaps the actual elephant in the room back then was that the Virgin Mary was depicted as a black woman,' commented Massimiliano Gioni, the curator of 'Night and Day'. 'Art that was striking at one point becomes normal after a while.'

In June 2015, *The Holy Virgin Mary* sold for a record $4.5 million at a Christie's auction in London, easily surpassing the expected price.

The story makes me reflect on the myriad of perspectives on the Annunciation I have heard so far. Everyone I have spoken to has offered her/his own view honestly held. Each has given a personal interpretation shaped by her/his life, belief and experiences. To one reader, some of these thoughts may seem questionable, provocative, irrelevant, controversial or shocking. To another they may offer fresh insight, stimulation and revelation. But for me each encounter has opened a new door. And each depiction of the Annunciation has offered a new view. Ofili's experience demonstrates how ignorance, closed minds and bigotry are the worst enemies of the search for the message and the meaning.

In 2006, Chris Ofili created an edition of three startling, provocative sculptures entitled *Annunciation*, one of which shows a black angel on its knees as a golden woman figure wraps her legs around his thighs. The coarse, dark matte finish of the angel, with its large, swan-like wings, contrasts starkly with the polished, gleaming sheen of Mary.

59. Chris Ofili *Annunciation*, 2006. © Chris Ofili.
Courtesy David Zwirner, New York/London

In a conversation with Thelma Golden, the Director and Chief Curator of the Studio Museum in Harlem, New York City, he described the inspiration behind the work.

'*Annunciation* came from an interest in that subject and wanting to do something with it, and the beauty of the idea of one person coming to another bearing news – the idea of a meeting, but the news being very dramatic. It was dealt with fantastically by Fra Angelico,' he says. 'The challenge of *Annunciation* was to make two figures come together but in one form.'

Later in the conversation, she observes how he expresses that describing beauty can also cause trouble.

'Because at times, I'll try and take it quite far,' he responds. 'I'll push it in a way that is very, very close to the imagination and I'll try to close the gap between reason and fantasy. It definitely exists with The *Holy Virgin Mary*.'

'And obviously with *Annunciation*,' Thelma Golden comments.

'Yes, I describe it as pushing it but it's an attempt to look at things from a new perspective, to confront contradictions between ideas of purity and impurity and different forms of representation in terms of your private point of view in relation to a general public point of view. In doing that, I'm aware that a line is being crossed, and crossing it can be seen as taboo.'

The journey goes on.

CHAPTER 19

AN ACT OF FAITH

I head down a long straight driveway, flanked by lush green fields. After half a mile, I see a building nestled within a cluster of trees. The gentle rustling of branches breaks the silence of this remote place. I have arrived at Carmel of the Annunciation at Thicket Priory, set in the Derwent valley eight miles south of York. This is the home of nine Carmelite nuns who are part of an enclosed religious order devoted to prayer 'under the spiritual protection of the Blessed Virgin Mary'.

I approach the building and notice a woman emerging from the main door. She is dressed in a brown scapular, her head covered by a white wimple and black veil. She gives me a welcoming smile and beckons for me to follow her. We pass through the main entrance, lined with religious books, to the room where I will be staying. Sister Ann tells me in whispers that the nuns here see Mary as an inspirational role model because, in her simplicity, she was totally open and receptive to God's action.

The nuns aim to live a life that is poor, chaste, obedient and wholly dedicated to prayer 'as true daughters of the Blessed Virgin'. Total silence is maintained throughout their twenty-four-hour day, other than the seven occasions when they attend Chapel to recite the Divine Office, and in the two half-hour periods of recreation when conversation is allowed. If the message of the annunciation story is about a 'calling', saying yes to God, and seeking to give over oneself totally to the divine, these nuns have interpreted it in the most extreme way. That is why I am here: to learn more about their calling and submission and to witness their unique lifestyle.

I never expected them to allow me in. The nuns, aged between thirty-six and eighty-three, are willing to let me – a fifty-seven-year-old male stranger – stay in their closed community and experience life as they know it. They tell me they have never done this before.

Teresa of Avila, a Spanish mystic, and John of the Cross founded the reformed Carmelite Order in the sixteenth century. Their teachings, based on simplicity, silence and the interior life, remain the framework of today's contemplative practice at the monastery: '*No pensar nada es pensarlo todo*': to think without thinking. The aim is for *nada* – a state of nothingness. 'When we are nothing, we are in the best place to receive all from God,' one of the nuns later tells me. A Carmelite aims to empty her mind of all thoughts to enable her soul to journey towards its union with God – a process named by John of the Cross as 'the dark night of the soul'.

The Carmel of the Annunciation was founded in 1926 in Exmouth. It moved to a large Victorian mansion house on the Thicket estate in 1955 and five years ago moved to a brand new, purposely-built monastery located on the old vegetable garden, just a few hundred yards south of the house. There were nuns at Thicket Priory more than eight hundred years ago, when the site was originally home to a convent of Cistercian nuns attached to Fountains Abbey. Indeed, today's monastery is sited on the medieval nuns' burial ground.

On first impression, the new monastery looks like a modern single-storey block of sheltered housing. It is one of seventy Carmelite monasteries around the world, eighteen of which are in the United Kingdom. In total, they house approximately two hundred nuns across the country.

Each nun here has her own 'cell' that contains a single bed, a desk, a chair and a table. A crucifix hangs on the wall. No food is allowed in the room. No other person is allowed to enter. In this simple, spartan, sacred place, the nun spends much of her day in solitude and total silence, focused on prayer and reading.

A nun rarely leaves the monastery except to visit the doctor, the dentist or the optician. When I arrive, Sister Elizabeth, who suffers from Parkinson's disease, is due to return from a weeklong stay in hospital.

The Mother Prioress, Sister Mary of Carmel, sets the rules and culture within the monastery. Discipline is strict, but not as severe as in some other Carmelite establishments. The metal grille that used to separate the nuns from occasional visitors to the Chapel has been removed. A small meeting room by the main door enables the Mother to meet members of the public as and when appropriate. The rest of the monastery is out of bounds. There are no radios, televisions or daily newspapers readily available. However, the Mother allows the nuns to watch television on special occasions such as Remembrance Sunday, a royal wedding or a papal visit.

Sister Ann, who deals with much of the general administration of the monastery and is connected to the internet 'in a limited and appropriate way', pins up a printout of the home page of the BBC News website on a corridor wall each morning, but most of the nuns do not look at it. A print copy of the weekly edition of *The Guardian* is delivered, but not all choose to read it. Apparently, the weekly edition of *The Tablet* is the most popular publication.

After settling myself down in my room, I make my way to the Chapel for Vespers. Just before 5 p.m. a bell rings. Seconds later, each nun enters in silence and walks towards the altar before taking her place on one of the red chairs facing the tabernacle. There is no eye contact, no acknowledgement of my presence. I sit behind them. They use the *Liturgy of the Hours*. One of the nuns asks us to pray for all those being lost in wars and for those suffering in the ebola crisis in West Africa.

This is followed by another hour of silence. Three nuns remain in Chapel with me; the others go back to their cells. I am struck by the remarkable stillness of this place. No one shuffles or moves at any point.

60. Carmel of the Annunciation,
Thicket Priory near York

At 6 p.m. we head to the dining room. Two nuns have prepared the evening meal for the rest of the community. Tonight it is cheese and leek flan with potatoes and carrots followed by carrot cake and fruit. There is water to drink. All look down as they eat. Not a word is spoken.

When I have finished, I go to the kitchen and gesture that I will help to wash up. One of the nuns smiles approvingly so I get straight to work. I go to my room for half an hour only to return to the dining room at 7 p.m. for the recreational half hour. I find one nun knitting, another drawing. One tells me she is learning to play the electric guitar 'like Eric Clapton'. Another, I am told, has gone back to her cell to practise her saxophone. I introduce myself and tell them briefly about my project.

Along the main corridor near to the cells, I notice a 'Reminder Board' fixed to the wall. In bright red lettering, there is a stark command: 'Remember It!' In black marker pen below, the following words have been written on the whiteboard giving details of yesterday's timetable:

MONDAY
      7.00 Lauds
      9.15 Terce
    11.50 Sext
    12.00 Dinner
      2.00 None
      5.15 Vespers
      5.30 MASS
      Supper
      7.15 Recreation
      8.00 Office of Readings
      9.00 Compline

At 9 p.m. I return to Chapel to attend Compline. I find the nuns standing in front of their allotted chairs. They sit quietly; stand to sing psalms, then pray. They close by singing in Latin:

> *Flos Carmeli,*
> *vitis florigera;*
> *Splendour caeli,*
> *Virgo puerpera, singularis.*
> *Mater mitis, sed viri nescia;*
> *Carmelitis da privilegia;*
> *Stella maris.*

> Flower of Carmel,
> Tall vine blossom laden;
> Splendour of heaven,
> Childbearing yet maiden, none equals thee.
> Mother so tender, who no man didst know;
> On Carmel's children, thy favour bestow;
> Star of the Sea.

At the end of the service, they remain in their seats, reflecting and meditating for at least ten minutes. Then each of them leaves in her own time to return to her cell. I wait for the last to depart, by which time it is 9.45 p.m.

At 5.30 a.m. dawn breaks. I decide to take a short walk to the nearby lake. The murky air is filled with birdsong. Ducks quack in anticipation of food when they see me. I stand there for a while, thinking about the life that the nuns lead and the extraordinary sacrifice they have all made. They are so sheltered from the outside world that I find it hard to imagine what spending an entire lifetime here would be like. I am fascinated about the circumstances that led each one to commit herself to a life of silence, prayer and contemplation as part of the Carmel of the Annunciation community. As I return, I see the shadowy silhouette of a nun through the blinds of her cell. She is kneeling, her head bowed.

I return to my room. From 6 a.m. there is an hour to pray then it is time for Lauds in the Chapel. The nuns return just before the service begins. They sing Psalm 89 and the reading is from the Book of Judith, 8:21b-28: 'Remember that our fathers were put

to the test to prove their love of God. Remember how our father, Abraham, was tested and became the friend of God after many trials and tribulations. The same was true of Isaac, Jacob, Moses and all who met with God's favour. They remained steadfast in the face of tribulations of every kind.'

Breakfast is at 8 a.m.: bread and margarine with a cup of tea. Marmalade is served only on special feast days. I sit in silence at a table next to the oldest nun who is eighty-three. I learn later that she is from Accrington and used to be a school teacher.

61. Lauds at Carmel of the Annunciation, Thicket Priory near York

After breakfast, I go for another walk in the grounds before heading to a room where Sister Helena is packing communion wafers into boxes for delivery to churches up and down the country. I offer to help and she whispers instructions to put 500 into each plastic bag. I fill ten bags before sealing the contents in a cardboard box ready for dispatch.

I can hardly believe my luck, but The Mother Prioress and three other nuns have agreed to meet me to discuss their lives in a series of one-to-one recorded conversations throughout the course of the day. I wait anxiously, as I am not sure if any of them will turn up.

However, on the hour, Sister Thérèse walks in to the room by the main entrance and takes a seat. She is tall, slim and wears metal-rimmed spectacles. She has a mild complexion and the hairline below her black veil shows flecks of grey. She tells me that she is thirty-six years old. She flashes a warm smile at me and I begin by asking her what the Annunciation story means for her.

'It is about an act of faith on the part of Mary,' she responds. 'She's faced with this call – an enormous thing she has to accept, agreeing to be the mother of God – and she doesn't know where it's going to take her. Her whole life is changed by it. When she says yes at the Annunciation, it carries her through to the crucifixion. It's a whole life.'

I ask whether she thinks the story is factual or metaphorical?

'Oh, I believe it happened,' she answers. 'I suppose with a lot of Scripture, some is symbolic, some is historic and some is a mixture of both. Luke presents the Annunciation in this way but we don't know whether it happened like that. Each person interprets it slightly differently. I don't know what it means to say the angel Gabriel came to Mary. Luke doesn't say what the angel looked like. But I believe she had this encounter with God.'

What key word or phrase sums up the story for her?

'An act of faith,' she says. 'We often put Mary on a pedestal. It's right that we venerate and honour her. But she was human. She was an ordinary girl and she had faith. She was graced by God as we all are but it wasn't something supernatural. It was an act of faith. It's not just a story. We are all in there somewhere.'

She seems surprisingly at ease and happy to converse. I ask if she models herself on Mary.

'Mary is a role model for all Carmelites. We profess our vows as an echo of Mary's *yes* at the Annunciation,' she replies.

She tells me she venerates Mary every single day. I wonder if she prays to her as much as to Jesus Christ.

'No, definitely not,' she replies. 'She's not on the same level as Christ. She's his disciple. She's a model of faith.'

I ask her what 'being under her special protection' means.

'She's someone we can turn to,' she responds succinctly.

Is the Annunciation the 'most important event in human history'?

'Yes. I agree. The Incarnation is the starting point.' Then she quotes the German twentieth-century Jesuit priest and theologian, Karl Rahner: 'For one split second in the history of humanity, God's *yes* and humanity's *yes* were fused in one single moment.'

And yet, I suggest, the feast of the Annunciation doesn't mean much at all today in the outside world.

'Yes, I understand,' she acknowledges in a North West, Lancastrian accent. 'People think the Immaculate Conception is the same as the Incarnation which is the same as the Annunciation. It seems to be lost now in the liturgical year.'

62. Sister Thérèse

Sister Thérèse tells me that she grew up in Warrington in Lancashire. Then, she was known as Clare. She went to Catholic schools and studied mathematics, economics and psychology at A Level. Then she followed a Business Operations and Control degree at the University of Salford that, she hoped, would be the springboard for various choices of career.

'When I went to Salford, I got involved in the Catholic Chaplaincy and then moved into the Chaplaincy house,' she tells me. 'It was like a quasi-religious community with daily prayer and I was going to daily Mass on campus. I discovered my faith as my own. Towards the end of the second year, I kept hearing a call to be a nun – to enter religious life. At first, it frightened me. I kept pushing it away and ignoring it. I prayed for it to go away but it was still there. I came to the realization that Jesus had become the most important person in my life.'

We look at each other intently as she continues to talk slowly.

'One particular day, I was reading some Carmelite materials and I just said to myself, yes. It was like an annunciation moment.' She laughs to herself quietly. 'I found this little booklet about Carmelite life. It had a quote from the Book of Kings from Elijah: "Why are you halting between two ways? If the Lord is God, follow him." I then read about Teresa of Avila when she says, "The things of God please me but I'm following the things of the world." That was my situation at the time and I had to make a decision. I felt a powerful calling to religious life.'

'The next day I spoke to the University Chaplain and he said, "Oh yes, I was wondering when you'd realize that." Everyone else could see it,' she says. 'I felt an inner peace. I was twenty. My parents were shocked and surprised. My dad accepted it well. They said, "We just want you to be happy".'

She finished her degree, and then did office jobs in Manchester and clerical work for the diocese of Manchester. It was a year later before she made contact with Carmel of the Annunciation at Thickett Priory.

'In one sense my heart was drawn to Carmel and the whole lifestyle,' she says. 'The balance between solitude and community and the centrality of prayer.'

She entered the monastery at twenty-four. Did she know what she was letting herself in for?

'No, and I still don't know now. There were aspects of the life I didn't see coming. The way the Sisters work so hard.'

'What makes a good Carmelite nun?' I ask.

'You have to be a good Christian,' she replies. 'There are qualities that lend themselves to this way of life. A sense of perseverance and determination. It's both demanding and liberating. For example, the sense of enclosure. For an outsider looking in, it's very demanding. You only go out of the monastery if absolutely necessary – maybe once a year. Your family come to you. You don't visit them. That's the demanding part. The liberating part is that it frees us to experience that atmosphere of silence and solitude. It widens your horizons.'

I wonder whether she can cope with that level of solitude.

'Yes. Even though I had siblings, they'd left home by the time I was thirteen. So I spent a lot of time alone as a teenager. After I decided to follow the calling, I tried to cultivate that silence and solitude. I was an ordinary teenager. I loved football. I went to see Liverpool football matches at Anfield. I went to Take That concerts. Obviously, it was a challenge. The most challenging time wasn't when I was alone in the cell for that's where I most encountered God. The thing I found most challenging at first was working with another person and not talking. It was difficult to grow into that.'

Has she experienced entering the 'dark night of the soul'?

'I think I've had aspects of it,' she says. 'Sometimes you can describe it as periods of doubt and uncertainty. It's a test of faith. It's a very human thing.'

'Like a crisis of confidence?' I ask.

'That's a good way of putting it,' she responds.

Did she ever wish to be a wife and a mother? Has she ever regretted not having children?

'Personally no. There are times, of course, when you think, did I do the right thing? But I've never had a great crisis about it. I have a different kind of motherhood in which I use the maternal instinct in prayer.'

Is she praying for herself, the local community, or the whole world?

'It's all inclusive. It reaches out,' she says.

So, she is praying for me?

'Yes,' she replies firmly.

How does she know her prayers have been answered?

'You don't know,' she responds. 'We must trust that God answers prayer. We might think it hasn't been answered but it has, but in a different way. We get a lot of people asking us to pray for them. That can be a great comfort. Some people ring us and say there's been a miraculous response.'

She tells me how each nun has a different style and pattern of praying. I ask her what she does in that first hour of silent prayer in her cell at 6.00 a.m.

'I offer the hour to God. I try to be aware of the presence of Jesus. It's a silence to allow God to speak.'

She explains how it is important to be disciplined and responsible. With no television, radio and regular daily newspaper, is she truly removed from the outside world? I ask.

'In one sense, yes, but we do have an acute awareness of what's happening in the outside world. It's hard to explain. In the outside world, you have constant, continuous news. But when I got here, I realized so much of it is speculation and gossip and details you don't need to know. By having a weekly newspaper, you get the basic facts on the main things that are happening. And if you have a major disaster, people will soon ring the monastery and ask us to pray.'

She tells me when her parents had a car, they would come to Thicket Priory once a month and would see her for part of an afternoon. Now they come less frequently on public transport. They never come into the private parts of the monastery. They stay in the special visitors flat, away from the cells and the working area, and meet up with their daughter in this very meeting room.

'When I was accepted to make my final vows and was received, I was able to phone my mum and dad. My mum has said since that she'd always hoped I'd ring and say to her "I want to come home" but now she says she'd be disappointed if I said that. They've made a journey of acceptance themselves.'

How have her two brothers reacted? I wonder.

'One practises and the other doesn't. Funnily enough, the one who doesn't has found it much easier,' she says.

Some people, I suggest, would say that the nuns are escaping and wasting their lives away.

'I'd love to say to them, "Come and see us." God gave us free will as he gave Mary free will. The commitment is not just for one moment. It's for life and every day when you wake up, you re-affirm that commitment.'

63. Ceramic of the Annunciation at Aylesford Priory, Kent

I show her a print of the Lemoyne painting. She flinches.

'I don't like it. Something in me reacts against it immediately. I think it's the angel. There's something quite nice about Mary going on interiorly. But it's that finger pointing that I don't like, not at all. My favourite Annunciation is a ceramic work at Aylesford Priory in Kent made for the Rosary Way wall there.'

Later, I track it down. The work is a three-dimensional figurative piece rooted in folk art with Romanesque styling. The designer is Adam Kossowski who was 'deep in calamity' as a Polish prisoner of war during his captivity in a Soviet labour camp in Ukraine during the Second World War. He made a promise to himself that if he came out of 'this sub-human land' he would tender his thanks to God. When he arrived in Britain, he spent more than twenty years creating religious art based among the Carmelite friars at Aylesford Priory.

'Mary has a very contemplative stance in the ceramic but her eyes are bulging. She's saying, "What me?",' Sister Thérèse proclaims.

'Just like herself sixteen years ago,' I suggest. She smiles affirmatively.

We say our farewells and I tell her I hope to see her again later. Whether I will speak with her again, of course, is a different matter.

Soon after she leaves the meeting room, the Mother Prioress, Sister Mary of Carmel arrives. A petite, elegant woman in her seventies with beautiful teeth and rimless glasses, she talks fluently and appears to be completely relaxed. 'I've never done this sort of thing before,' she tells me, but you would never know. She turns out to be a consummate interviewee.

'For me, the Annunciation is all about one's fiat,' she begins. 'Everybody makes a fiat and you don't just do it once. You do it all the time. Giving yourself to God in whatever you are doing – in every moment, in every day. A yes to God.'

Does she see the annunciation story as a fact or a metaphor?

'Something happened but it may not be as depicted,' she replies. 'Human beings have got to put it into words to make people understand it. Whatever it was, Mary realized then she was being asked to be the mother of God. She didn't say yes straight away but then she said yes.'

If she closes her eyes and tries to picture the moment, what does she see?

'Nothing in particular. I think of words not pictures. We've seen depictions so often but I don't want to think of a particular picture.'

How important is it that Mary could have said no?

'Very, very important. We all have free will to say no. The fundamental part of the story is asking her *if* she would say yes. We all say no quite often. She didn't know then what it would entail. You took marriage on, Mark, and I took on a religious order. We didn't know then when we said yes what even the next minute would envisage. So it's a choice. We make choices all the time. Trusting in God. We are all aiming for wholeness. Yes, you have to make a choice and they're all fiats.

'I have a thing about wholeness and humanness,' she continues. 'Mary was a proper, whole human being. She had a normal baby with everything that we've got – a complete human being. I was told years ago he couldn't suffer like we could because that's the result of sin. But I felt that was rubbish. Jesus was wholly human.'

Does she see the Annunciation as 'the most important event in human history'?

'Yes it is, because of redemption,' she says. 'The metaphor is heaven's gate opened for everyone.'

We discuss the feast of the Annunciation and she agrees that its significance has been greatly reduced if not lost in the outside world.

'I don't have an answer to that,' she comments. 'It's a big feast for us here obviously. And those of us who were brought up in convent schools learned all these things but now, today, they've hardly heard of the Annunciation.'

How central to her life is the Virgin Mary?

'She's special to us all in Carmelite life,' she says. 'She's the Mother of Carmel, the Queen of Carmel. We look to her for inspiration.'

Sister Mary was named Bridget and was brought up in rural Somerset. She attended a convent boarding school. Her elder sister became a Carmelite nun and joined the Carmel of the Annunciation community. When Bridget was a teenager, she would go and visit her.

'I'd always had ideas coming to me now and again about joining a religious order from a young age,' she tells me. 'I didn't want to be a nun. I lived life pretty well. I had boyfriends. But the older I got – well, there comes a time in life when God calls you for a life of prayer. But I was telling him, "Please, not for me." I remember I was at college in

64. Sister Mary of Carmel

Manchester and I visited my sister two or three times. I realized this is what I wanted but I still fought it. I said to myself I'll write to my parents and tell them I'm going. My older sister had entered without telling them. She said she was going for a fortnight and never came back. I sent them a letter from Manchester saying, I'm going to give up college. I then went home at Easter. We kept quiet. I knew they were very upset but they didn't stop me.

'The other Sisters knew we were sisters but didn't say anything,' she continues. 'The Prioress would let us share family news at Christmas and Easter. My mother came up to see us once. My father never came. They felt very bitter. It was a very long journey. They didn't have a car. He only had one arm because of the war. It was pretty awful.'

Was there conflict within herself? I wonder.

'Yes, of course. But you're headstrong at that age,' she says. 'You think about what *you're* doing in life. You feel you are giving to God.'

Did they ever recover? I ask.

'Yes. After seven years here, my mother became a diabetic. I went back home now and again when she got ill. They got to love me coming back. I still wore the habit all the time I was there.'

So, what makes a good Carmelite nun?

'For each Sister to develop their own relationship with God and to be whole – a whole human being,' she responds before emphasizing that the calling is both a joy and responsibility.

How does the Order guard against people using it as escapism?

'You have to watch out for that,' she replies.

Many people, I suggest, say that the way the nuns live *is* just escapism.

'There are times when people could try to come here to escape but they'd never get past the process of formation. They'd soon see there's lots of hard work and coming here you are not escaping anything.'

How did she feel about giving up the chance to be a mother?

'That's part of the giving up,' she responds. 'But you feel yourself being more open to nurture. You do it because that's what you want to give to God.'

Does she ever feel doubt or regret?

'Everyone feels doubt. There are moments when you've felt, is it worth it? But everyone has coping strategies.'

To have any understanding of what you have done and why, does one have to believe in the power of prayer?

'Even priests don't understand that,' she replies. 'It's surprising how the Anglican churches often understand us more as a powerhouse of prayer. Many Catholic priests like nuns to work for them.'

Is responding to the call demanding or liberating?

'Both,' she says. 'It's liberating in that your heart and mind are free to be with God.'

I show her the Lemoyne picture.

'It's too glitzy. Too flowery. Mm, it's too gaudy. She looks simpery. I like her as a sensible girl. This doesn't give a sense of normality. I want a straightforward picture and this isn't one.'

I tell her I noticed she had prominently displayed a large postcard of the Fra Angelico fresco of the Annunciation on the cluttered desk in her office.

'It just says to me the Annunciation. The calling. But this one, oh dear, it's horrible.'

After a short walk in the grounds to reflect on her comments, I head to midday prayer in the Chapel. The sun shines brilliantly through the glass doors and the colours of the stained-glass window shimmer on the parquet floor. The nine nuns dressed in habits, some wearing crocs, others sandals or black leather shoes, sit in line again. Each has arrived with her Bible and her personal copy of the Divine Office. Lunch follows in the dining room and is taken in silence. A leek and sardine bake is on offer with mash potato and sprouts. Rhubarb pie is the pudding of the day.

At 1.30 p.m. I go for a recreational walk down the long drive with three of the nuns. We talk about the weather, my family and the health of Sister Elizabeth who has returned from her hospital stay in York. When we reach the gate by the main road, we turn round immediately and head back. It is clear that no one must leave the grounds. Although this is one of only two times each day when they can converse together, surprisingly much of it is spent in silence. By the lake, we go our separate ways and each nun returns to her cell.

Soon after I return to the meeting room, Sister Helena walks in and sits down. She is a delicate, quietly-spoken woman with a quirky smile. I estimate that she is in her fifties. We start our conversation by focusing on the annunciation story.

'It's a mystery,' she tells me. 'You live it. It always deepens. Although we've got the gospel narrative, there's always deeper and deeper depths to it. What's my part connected to the Annunciation? You're dealing with something vast here.'

Did it actually happen or is it a metaphor?

'She must have received a communication whatever that was,' she answers. 'She understood what was being asked of her very clearly. It says she intellectually asked questions but somehow you have to let go to the huge dimensions of what it means. I do believe in angels. They're way beyond our human understanding. You have your own guardian angel, your friend, whom you can ask for help.'

She agrees that it is 'the most important event in human history' and says the story hinges on Mary's ability to say no.

'That's essential. It's *our* human free will, which is essential to us all. It's what makes us human. There's that beautiful reading from Bernard: "What's going to be your reply, O Lady? The whole of creation is waiting on you." He brings out that free will. It overturns the disobedience of the fall of the human race. It's pivotal. I know in my own life I can say no to God's will at any time. That's part of the challenge.'

What does being under Mary's special protection mean?

'In our medieval hymn, *Flos Carmeli*, there's the line: "Under thy mantle, hard pressed in the fight, we call to thee." The Christian life is a battle. And she's there to protect us from evil.'

Does she believe in evil?

'Oh yes. My God, yes,' she proclaims. 'We are weak and fallen. Elements come in that whip up fear. I'd attribute that to evil. We constantly need God's grace to uphold us.'

65. Sister Helena

Sister Helena was born as Helena Guzman and brought up in a Catholic family in Reading. Her father was Polish and her mother was Irish. She was the second of four children with an elder sister seven years older, and a younger sister and brother.

'Even then, I was marked out for solitude. My sister was too old to be my companion and the two younger ones did everything together. My path was being sort of prepared,' she tells me. 'I came to university in York to study Economic and Social History. I really enjoyed it at the time. When you leave home, you have that freedom. Do I keep up my faith? Because I didn't know anyone, I got in touch with the Catholic chaplaincy. I started a prayer life at that age. Once you ask up to God, he just comes in for a complete takeover. I was very naturally being drawn to prayer.

'One vacation, when I went back home,' she continues, 'I asked my parish if I could go somewhere alone to pray. I was guided to Quidenham [a Carmelite community in Norfolk]. I wasn't seeking monastic life. I just wanted to be alone to pray. I remember I saw the Sisters over by the altar and I saw one of them praying. I thought, my God – like a thunderbolt – this is what I must do. I was nineteen.

'I was terrified at the prospect. I came back to the university at York. I had lots of friends including a boyfriend. But something was going on underneath at a deeper level. I remember there was a notice on a board from the Prioress here asking if people wanted to come here for a weekend of prayer. I discovered there was a bus service so it was all very simple. It felt laid on.

'After graduating, I came to do a live-in here, to be sure. I didn't like the experience at all. It was a very ascetic life. It was a lot harder then. No heating. Living with women together. I was repulsed. I thought I'd just forget it. I applied to do nursing.

'Then one Christmas, I went to Ampleforth and called in to see the Sisters again on my way back. There was a heavy snowstorm and I was stuck here for a week. It was as though God had laid that on as well. I really felt God brought the country to a standstill in order to get the *yes* out of me. So, I said to myself, I'll give it three years and see.

'My mother's reaction was, "What have you done?" My dad was all about education and he thought it was a prison. He couldn't comprehend it. They were both bewildered. My mother came to see me once and, after then, she said she hoped I'd stay. They have both died but my siblings still come to see me once or twice a year. They don't practice and I accept that.'

What do they feel about her and her decision? I wonder.

'I've never asked them,' she says.

I am struck by how open she is being, considering she has only just met me. I ask if she has ever pined for a child and reflected on not being a mother.

'Of course, of course,' she acknowledges. 'It's a renunciation and a sacrifice every day because you're a woman. But you get something much bigger in return. The mystery of God present within me. You experience that as a presence and it's very real. The whole purpose and design of this set up is that you can enter and connect with it. If I'm connected with God, it's such a strength. I feel I'm sending out peace. It's palpable. The mind has to let go.'

Has she ever had doubts about what she has done?

'Yes, I've had struggles. There comes a point when you reach a certain age. Once you reach forty. You know that's it [regarding motherhood]. So it's quite a crisis time. You have to get deep, deep, deep, to get to the meaning of the sacrifice. Your faith deepens when you go through that. Redemption is too important, and this is what I'm being asked to do, and it's such a worthwhile thing to do with my life.'

What makes a good Carmelite?

'Basically feeling God's grace. You can have any kind of temperament – gregarious or reserved. But you have to have that call to God. It's God's choice for you to do a certain job.'

'But hang on,' I exclaim, 'you said earlier that human free will was essential.'

'We're always free,' she replies. 'But then if I knew God was asking something and I said no, I'd be turning my back on him. You have this abiding presence of God – the cell of the heart. He's made his love in your heart. It's a life of love.'

She tells me how much she values silence. 'Here, you can get in touch with it. As human beings we've lost it. The animals all have it. But we're out of touch with it now.'

When I hand her a copy of Lemoyne's picture, immediately she starts to laugh.

'I find it really difficult to get into it,' she says. 'It's so simple.' She keeps staring at the picture and laughing at the cherubim. 'It's so over the top,' she declares as she leaves the room.

A few minutes later and I am joined by Sister Ann of the Holy Spirit who describes the Annunciation as 'the most influential thing in my life and in creation. It's the pivotal point.' She emphasizes that Mary's ability to say no is extremely important. It could have meant stoning. According to her, Mary saying yes was a complete break with her own tradition.

She tells me how she sees Mary more as a sister than a mother. She agrees that the Annunciation is the most important event in human history because 'this being we call God somehow was so caught up in love with the human that God became human at that moment and with it gave humanity the ability to become divine.'

Why, if it is so pivotal, has the feast of the Annunciation lost its status? I ask.

'I think Christmas is seen as the culmination of the Annunciation and the Incarnation. The spectacular moment of the birth. But the real moment, of course, is the Annunciation. I've missed out on the feminist advancement. I haven't joined forces with it. But let me say it's suited history to highlight Christmas. You are engaging with an insignificant Jewess. She redeems herself by giving birth to the Messiah. What happened before that has been brushed aside.'

Sister Ann is the *Infirmatur* within the Thickett Priory community with a special interest in caring for anyone who is weak or ill. She is small and wears large metal-rimmed glasses. I have noticed that she always seems to be one step behind the Mother Prioress wherever she goes.

Does she see the story as fact or metaphor?

'I don't see it as a photograph of what happened,' she replies. 'For me, the message is what's important. A journey into the unknown. It's a very, very simple story and a very barren text. It's about listening, which leads on to obedience.'

Ann Dodd was brought up in Bromley, Kent. Her parents were practising Catholics but were not particularly devout. She was the eldest of four children. She attended the same Catholic primary school as her mother and both of them had the same head teacher, who was a nun. She remembers in her childhood how the Sisters at St Joseph's in Downham fostered a sense of grace in the pupils. 'Without God, we don't exist,' she was told at a very early age. She recalls hearing the annunciation story for the first time.

66. Sister Ann

'It was like a fairy tale. The fantastic is very real at that time.'

There are long pauses between her sentences. But then, suddenly, she warms up and the words start to flow.

'When I was seven, we had student teachers from the local Catholic training college regularly come to our school. One was a nun who wore blue. She was a missionary. She told us about her own calling. I realized then that nuns were real people. The headmistress was keen for us to realize the Church was full of very different people. A White Father came to talk to us about China. I was fired up about becoming both a nun and a nurse serving in China but I didn't tell anyone. Then, at fourteen, I heard about Carmel. It sounded dreadful but there was something in that moment of a glimpse of a praying presence for the world. Even though the closeness sounded frightful, in some ways I felt this was something I had to do. It was just a sort of imperative. Like when you fall in love with someone. You can't define it. I made up my mind. I didn't tell my parents. It was madness really when I look back at it. I got the Catholic Directory and wrote to the nearest Carmel community at Notting Hill. I can resonate that action with Our Lady's own calling. How can this young girl of fourteen say yes to such a life changing invitation? But I knew then, that's what God wanted of me.

'While on a day trip to London with friends,' she continues, 'I persuaded them to come with me to see the Carmel at Notting Hill. I then joined them at eighteen, straight after leaving school. I told my parents just before. My mother was horror struck. She said, "What do you want to join a group of back-biting women for?" My father was very, very quiet. My siblings thought it was a joke. I stayed at Notting Hill for four years. The family came to see me once a month for half an hour. My mother changed tremendously and became very, very supportive. I left Notting Hill after four years because I started to faint. I seemed as happy as Larry. I was advised to leave and was very, very disappointed. I had seizures. However, I think it was a wonderful grace. I then trained as a nurse. But the calling didn't go away. I began to seriously discern whether it was a call again. I knew one of the Sisters here. I decided to come and visit. And the Prioress invited me in – she was very compassionate. I'm now the *Infirmarium* here, both nun and nurse. It's a wonderful twinning.'

I ask her what makes a good Carmelite nun?

'A determined determination,' she replies immediately. 'St Teresa said don't go for the pious ones because you have to knock the piety out of them. It's very demanding yet it becomes very liberating. But it takes a lifetime. There's a critical joy in it all. "I'm doing great things for God and the world." There's so much that's being offered here. It's a story of mercy. And mercy becomes not just things to help other people but receiving.'

Is she regretful that she couldn't be a mother?

'Yes, I felt it very poignantly at eighteen when I was about to enter Notting Hill,' she tells me. 'I remember being out shopping and seeing women with prams. It made a tremendous impression on me then but I felt another calling. I've never regretted it. There were times I felt I wished I was as far away as possible from it but I've never regretted it. I'd do it all again.'

I ask if she has ever felt serious doubt.

'No, not doubt about the importance of the life. I've had doubt about whether I could do it. It's all caught up in that *yes*.'

She looks at the Lemoyne picture and, like her colleagues, frowns at the depiction.

'It's very dramatic. The figures don't touch me at all, aesthetically or emotionally.'

As we close our conversation, I ask her how does she know that her prayers have been answered?

'Just look up at the sky,' she responds. 'And see what's going on up there. There's so much beyond this planet that we just don't know. A Carmelite has a connection with all of that. It's so sad – I don't mean to be patronizing – that so many people can't see any more than within their own four walls. Life has become so insular for so many.'

———

An hour later and I am back in the Chapel where a Mass is underway. A local priest from York leads this regular weekly service that the public is allowed to attend. Today, I count five people, all elderly. The nine nuns sit in line on the front row and look straight ahead. At the end of the service, slowly they all march out in line and return to the private, closed-off area of the monastery.

At dinner time, the Mother Prioress, Sister Mary, announces that she is relaxing the vow of silence for fifteen minutes so that the nuns can converse with 'their special guest'. She bids me well on my journey and tells me to 'continue listening'.

'You're writing the book and, therefore, at the end, you've got to take from all the things you'll hear what you feel resonates with you. And you've got to be honest in the way you're writing it. Not that you don't have to take anybody's ideas. I don't really know the reason you're writing it. Do you want to portray it in a religious sense or just as a travelogue? But be yourself. You've got to always be yourself. That's what wholeness is. But it's good to hear what all these people say to you and to take their advice. Then you've to take it all in, drink it all in, and be honest and, at the end, write about what you believe. We've all got to be whole. Whatever you do, you've got to be genuine, it's no good trying to please everyone or be someone else. We've got to be the person who God made us and be whole.'

A few weeks after leaving the Carmel of the Annunciation, I receive a photograph from them via my email account. It shows the setting sun shining through frothy clouds above a silhouetted line of distant trees. The day is drawing to a close at Thicket Priory.

Accompanying the image is a message from Sister Ann: 'The Annunciation Sky! – I hope you can see it.'

67. 'Annunciation sky' over Thicket Priory

CHAPTER 20

MAKING THE IMPOSSIBLE POSSIBLE

I am back in Winchester, a Hampshire city steeped in history and an important centre of Christianity since the seventh century when King Cenwalh, following the conversion of his kingdom to Christianity, founded a monastery here known as Old Minster in 648. I am about to embark on a new part of the journey much closer to home, this time around the precincts and surroundings of the world famous Winchester Cathedral.

As I walk along College Street, south of the Cathedral Close, once again I catch sight of the medieval stone statue of the crowned Virgin Mary and Child, standing in a niche on Outer Gate at the main entrance to Winchester College. I pause and reflect on how much the project is enveloping me before I continue to nearby Wolvesey, the home of the Bishop of Winchester for at least 900 years.

The chalk and flint ruins of the Old Bishop's Palace, built by Henry of Blois between 1130 and 1140, stand hidden behind the city walls in the shadow of Winchester Cathedral. In medieval times, this castle was the luxurious main residence of one of the most powerful and wealthy men in the land, whose diocesan estates stretched from Somerset to London. As well as being his administrative centre, Wolvesey was the showpiece of the Bishop of Winchester's wealth and power. Ransacked and destroyed by Roundheads in 1646 during the English Civil War, much of the palace was demolished and a new residence, commissioned by Bishop Morley, was built in 1684 next to the ruins.

In 1729, when Lemoyne's painting arrived across the street at Winchester College, Richard Willis was ensconced in Wolvesey as the seventy-seventh Bishop of Winchester. Today, the ninety-seventh bishop, Tim Dakin, lives in a wing of the large baroque style mansion, less than a hundred metres from the main entrance to the school. He was appointed in 2012 to the fifth most important bishopric in the Church of England and says 're-discovering Jesus and his mission' is his top priority in the post.

The son of missionary parents, fifty-six-year-old Bishop Tim, as he likes to be known, was born in Tanzania and grew up partly in Kenya and partly in England. He says he 'felt hit by a call to ordained ministry' aged fifteen while attending a Christian festival. 'I knew then the Lord had his hand on me.' Ordained in 1993, he returned to Kenya to work as a principal at a Church Army training college in Nairobi before serving as General Secretary of the Church Mission Society for more than a decade. Evangelism, Mission and Africa have shaped his life and faith. 'I'm African by background and African by foreground,' he says. He is a member of the evangelical group on the General Synod and has described himself as an 'out of the ordinary priest, not run of the mill'.

When I walk into his office, there are stacks of cardboard boxes full to the brim with copies of Esther de Waal's spiritual book, *Searching for God: The Way of St Benedict*. He tells me he wants to distribute hundreds of them to churches throughout his diocese. 'Have you read it?' he asks me directly, 'It's an extraordinarily powerful book.' When I tell him that I used it as a Lenten study a few years ago, his eyes light up and he shakes my hand vigorously as though he has met a kindred spirit. With short, neatly parted black hair, he has a youthful air about him.

There is a striking sense of the ascetic as well as the evangelist about him. He asks if I would like a glass of water. I notice on the nearby table that his Bible is opened at Luke's Gospel account of the Annunciation. This gives me the cue to ask what the story means to him.

'You've come at this from the angle of the Lemoyne painting and, therefore, the meeting of Mary with the angel,' he says. 'But that's always been accompanied for me by the other side of the story and that's the angel with Joseph. That there was another meeting of an angel with the man betrothed to Mary. In the genealogy in Matthew's Gospel, Mary is one of a number of women mentioned, all of whom are dubious in their social background. None of them are respectable. Mary is the last of the women mentioned and the implication is she's one of them. And yet, all the ones mentioned are very significant to the story of Israel. They include Ruth – she's not Jewish. So the origins of Jesus include a non-Jewish mother somewhere – that's a bit dodgy. Rahab, a prostitute – what on earth is she doing in there? The mother of Solomon (Bathsheba) who had been Uriah the Hittite's wife before David – that's dodgy too. Jesus has a somewhat dodgy ancestry. Matthew is trying to tell us, "I know that it looks a bit odd and even odd enough that Joseph needed a visit by an angel so he could be reassured." But in an African context, dreams are normal and a natural way in which you are led. In a Middle East world view, as in Africa, dreams and encounters with God and spiritual realities in dreams are normal.'

He remembers the name of another 'dodgy woman' mentioned in Matthew's genealogy – Tamar, a seductress who disguised herself as a prostitute to lure her father-in-law, Judah. Prostitution, adultery, seduction, Matthew's genealogy line certainly emphasizes a sense of female earthiness and 'dodginess', as the Bishop points out.

So, is it crucial for him to see Luke's and Matthew's gospel accounts side by side? I ask.

'Yes. There's another annunciation there and that's essential for you to get the whole picture of the history of Israel,' he replies. 'The genealogy in Luke goes back to Adam and the genealogy in Matthew goes back to Abraham. There is the integration of some of the dodgy bits of the history of Israel included in Jesus and his story, and in the way, therefore, he understands his identity. The history of the people of Israel is an essential part of understanding the mission of Jesus. It gives you a reference point. God is committed to history. The mission is historical.

'The Annunciation is not just a personal encounter,' he goes on. 'This is God re-engaging with the history of this people, that he might, in his mercy, engage with the wider history of the world. That's the extraordinary thing here. This particular people are going to be used again to bless the world, which is the calling that Abraham had.'

I ask him whether he thinks the encounter between Mary and the angel is fact or perhaps metaphor.

'Those categories themselves presume you have to answer the question in a particular way,' he says, 'and I think one of the things that happens with our engagement with the revelation of Christ is that he changes what the facts are. So there's an adjustment about what your world looks like when you look at the world with Jesus. So one of the things that is happening to Mary, I suspect, is that her world is changing. She has this encounter. Is that fact? Well, the facts have been changed. This is the re-birth of history around this extraordinary event. The facts are being re-worked. It's not entirely clear in the way that we now understand what facts are any longer. We look at things and that adjusts what we're looking at. If an angel speaks to you, it adjusts the way you see things and the way you see the world.'

His diction is precise and his delivery slow. He talks in a quiet manner and looks at me with an eagle stare as he makes his points.

'From the African perspective, the world is bigger,' he says. 'It isn't reduced to boxes. There isn't the historical and the scientific or nothing else. There is so much more. C. S. Lewis talks about angels as moving too fast for us to see them. We occupy so much space but what if there is more? That's part of the way God engages with us particularly at moments of great significance where he's wanting to change the direction of how things are happening. That implies that God is both personal and engaging with us in his story. I know there are big scientific discussions about that. How God can do that at a cosmological and micro level? My sense is that there is also the question, where's the world going? Not just in the way God intervenes but in the trajectory of the way the world is going to end up.

'And so there is something about the angel's engagement that isn't just reduced to that encounter but it's also about where does the future now go?' he says. 'What new future might there now be because of this new encounter, this new development? The fact that Jesus is going to be the Messiah is a statement about the future of the world. An extraordinary adjustment to reality at that moment.'

I ask what the meaning of Luke's annunciation story is for him personally.

'We are tempted to reduce it down to the personal. We tend to operate in those categories in religious belief, which has been reduced to the personal because our social-liberal societies in the West understand religion in those terms. That's the safe place to put religion. But you could hardly say that was the case for Mary. Getting pregnant isn't a personal event. It's a community event. If Mary is pregnant, and for the wrong reasons, the community will have to deal with it. And that will depend on the community relying on its wider culture and the covenant they have with God as to what to do in those circumstances.

'This is more than a personal encounter,' he emphasizes before again asking another rhetorical question. 'How will God adjust the life of his people? How will the worldview get re-adjusted now this new individual who is going to be the light to the Gentiles is to happen? And it begins with this woman who's been accused of getting pregnant before she's married. This is more than a personal vocation. This is the vocation of this people and God's commitment to bring his kingdom into reality within history, dealing with people as they are. It's a community event. It's a cultural event.'

We move on to discuss whether among Christian communities in East Africa, the teaching of the annunciation story would be different. He tells me it is impossible to generalize.

'There are forty languages in Kenya alone. What can I say? The dream element would not be a problem. Dreams remain really important there. They wouldn't necessarily think of angels with wings. The spirit world there is very closely associated with the physical world.'

I mention a book by John Taylor, a previous Bishop of Winchester, entitled *The Go-Between God* that emphasizes the centrality of the Holy Spirit in the annunciation story. Does that heavy focus on the spiritual dimension chime with him?

'Very much so,' he replies immediately. 'John was one of the first to articulate what would be recognized as the African world view. What John picks up, which is very African, is the inter-connectedness of all things. The nature of all things being part of life. Vitality is central. One of the key things, therefore, is fecundity. Mary being pregnant before she is married is not a major problem in some African cultures. It's proof she's ready for marriage. So, whereas in the western culture, we struggle with that, "gosh, they had sex before marriage", in some African cultures you have sex before marriage to make sure you are ready for marriage because you show you can have a child. Vitality and the ongoing life of the tribe is so important and people need to know you can have children.'

I remark that in Nazareth at the time of Mary's conception, the culture was very different and she could have been stoned to death.

'Yes,' he responds, 'hence how does God intervene without causing the death of Mary? He has to talk to the husband to be. An African would fully understand the challenge of that. Being fertile is so important. Getting pregnant before marriage in some African communities is a good thing and, therefore, for the man to know this child was an acceptable child to God and was not someone else's child is a very powerful thing. I understand within some African values, pregnancy can mean something else. But Matthew writes of a way forward that plays back the story and challenges African culture in that you don't have to get someone pregnant before marriage. It works the other way. You need to trust God with the fecundity you want.'

He takes hold of his Bible and reads through the Luke's Annunciation passage in silence before speaking again.

'God's grace is just written all the way through this. He can use you as you are to bring the Messiah and his purposes into fruition. It's back to the history. Do I know where I fit in? Does my calling correlate with the way the world is working? Do I have a sense of "fit"? What's wonderful is when you have that sense of calling to be and it fits. How does Mary discern where she fits? She has this encounter where she's suddenly given a sense of "you fit into history like this". Personally, it's going to mean this with Joseph. In the community, it's going to mean that. Culturally, it will mean this. But in terms of God's great history, this is where you are called to be. Can you say yes? Most of us say no or most of us can't quite hear the call and misunderstand what we're called to be. But Mary is, in some extraordinary way, able to say yes and follow through and, therefore, be who she's meant to be so that we might be who we are meant to be in a similar way. She is the disciple of Jesus in a way we are all called to be.'

When I ask him whether the Annunciation is 'the most important event in human history', he shuffles in his chair and looks uneasy.

'Jesus grew in wisdom and in stature and in favour with God and Man,' he responds. 'So the one event of the announcement of Jesus's coming has to imply that he is also growing. The atomisation of truth into these key events...this is the point...that's why I struggle when people say, "I have an incarnation theology"...as human beings, we don't have a choice. We are bodily...God chose to become man, to be human in Mary. But that was then a growing and expanding engagement with what it meant to be human.

'So, for me, it's the announcement of his ongoing engagement. He's coming. The Messiah is coming and he will grow into all that we are, and glorify all that we are, and turn it into something that can be with God forever. He will redeem, heal, glorify humanity and creation. It is the fulfilment of God's original intention to make creation a companion with God. The only way that change will happen for all of us is that we follow that journey that Jesus took. Hence the mission of Jesus. A journey from being announced to the fulfilment of all hope and longing through the historical life.

'You have no idea what that moment means without the later moments,' he continues. 'We read Jesus through his history. We can't jump back and say, "Ah, it was that event", because that event has no significance without an understanding of the history of Jesus's engagement with us as a way of interpreting what that event was. If he hadn't died and risen again, we would not be what we are as Christians. I'm not a philosopher. I'm a Christian. I don't believe in the Incarnation as a philosophical process. I understand there was an Incarnation. He was announced and born as a human being. But I only understand the significance of that event afterwards.'

We move on to talk about the status of Mary, the concept of the Virgin Birth and the Roman Catholic doctrine of the Immaculate Conception.

'I would want to say she was a virgin,' he says. 'I can definitely understand that to be an essential part of how God worked with her. But whether she was immaculate...for me she needs to be *not* immaculate in order for her discipleship to be the model that I want to follow. The fact that she said yes despite all the challenges she faced as an ordinary human really helps me.'

He tells me he doesn't pray to Mary – 'I'm not so sure I have access to her,' he comments.

Before I leave, I show him the print of Lemoyne's painting.

'What's interesting is how often the finger is pointing upwards in Annunciation paintings and particularly in this one because of the light. It's very striking. "You will receive power from on high." And then Mary's acceptance, "Wow, it's God – I'll accept it." I don't see a lot of fear. I see gracious acceptance of the calling she has. But it's very stylized. It's too chocolate box for me. It doesn't really grab me. For me, the Annunciation image in my head is of a young African girl on her way to get some water somewhere and she has a strange, extraordinary encounter as she walks past a sacred tree. That's how I imagine it can happen.'

———

I sit within the ruins of Wolvesey Castle under a brilliant blue sky and read the opening chapter of John Taylor's book *The Go-Between God*, published in 1972, two years before he became the ninety-fourth Bishop of Winchester. The title of the opening chapter is 'Annunciation' and in it, John Taylor argues how, 'the chief actor in the historic mission of the Christian Church is the Holy Spirit. He is the director of the whole enterprise.' He describes the Spirit, as in the old Hebrew word *rūach* as the 'breath of God' and as 'that which lies between making both separateness and conjunction real'. He references the impact of several Renaissance paintings of the Annunciation which emphasize, 'the mutually enraptured gaze of the angel and the Virgin, and the dove symbol of the Holy Spirit spinning, as it were, the thread of attention between them.' The 'truth of the Annunciation' consists simply of *yes*. The encounter is about 'mutual giving' and 'Annunciations last only as long as truth faces truth.'

In one particular thought-provoking passage he writes: 'In every such encounter, there has been an anonymous third party who makes the introduction, acts as a go-between, makes two beings aware of each other, sets up a current of communication between them. What is more, this invisible go-between does not simply stand between us but is activating each of us from inside.'

Christians find it quite natural, he writes, 'to give a personal name to this current of communication, this invisible go-between. They call him the Holy Spirit. The Spirit of God. The first essential activity of the Spirit is annunciation. It is always he who gives one to the other and makes each really see each other...The Holy Spirit is the invisible third party who stands between me and the other, making us mutually aware. Supremely and primarily, he opens my eyes to Christ.'

———

I leave Wolvesey and head for Winchester Cathedral. On the way, I notice in the bay window of the Kingsgate Books and Prints shop, an engraving of the city viewed from St Giles Hill in the early eighteenth century. The tag attached to the gold framed picture reads: 'East Aspect of the City of Winchester: after S&N Buck 1736.' It is clear how seven years after Lemoyne's painting arrived in the city, the Cathedral and the College dominated the Winchester landscape.

At that time, Winchester was flourishing after recovering from the aftermath of the Civil War. Its size and prosperity were growing and parts of the city walls were being demolished as the expanding population moved outwards. The professional classes of doctors, lawyers and teachers serving the local gentry, as well as the growing sector of tradesmen, were the heartbeat of an increasing economic vibrancy in the city. But it was the Cathedral that was then, as now, the iconic symbol of Winchester. Indeed, the magnificent building and the ecclesiastical activities taking place daily within its surroundings have shaped the city's character since medieval times.

Above the tiny Kingsgate bookshop is a thirteenth-century church called St Swithun-upon-Kingsgate. In the Middle Ages, churches located above a city's main gates were not uncommon but very few survive today. Kingsgate was a southern exit point from the city out to Winchester College and the water meadows.

Climbing a steep flight of stone stairs, I enter the small first floor room above the arch of Kingsgate that constitutes this simple, early English church. The walls are whitewashed and the striking wooden beams above form a lovely steep-pitched open collar ceiling. Straight ahead, set within the plain east window, are fragments of medieval glass that originally were part of a depiction of the Annunciation.

Sitting alone on the front pew, praying quietly, is fifty-year-old Reverend Sally Goodson, the Assistant Curate. A former speech therapist, she was ordained as a priest less than one week ago. I sit alongside and ask about the meaning of the annunciation story for her.

'The predominant thing for me is about obedience,' she tells me. 'Mary must have been absolutely flabbergasted by the encounter and yet was obedient. That's what comes through for me. Despite her bewilderment and angst, she's obedient. She does what she is asked to do. Yes, she questions it. We don't hear a lot about that but she must have questioned it but then doesn't waiver. Did she really have the right to say no? I'm not convinced that she did. I suspect there was a bit inside her head that said no or "that can't be right" but actually not "No, I won't do that".'

I ask her what she would have done in the same situation.

'Much like Mary,' she responds. 'I would have thought, what will people think? She's a young girl, unmarried, it would have been seriously frowned upon, her life put at risk through her accepting.'

Does she see the story as fact, metaphor or something else?

'I see it as fact,' she replies firmly. 'Why isn't it fact? is good enough for me. Nobody has convinced me it isn't fact and, therefore, like many things in my faith, it's fact and I'm happy to accept that. Nobody has come up with a good alternative why it isn't fact. Angels coming to tell people things are going to happen occurs loads of times in the Bible – in the Old and New Testaments – so why wouldn't it be fact? It's the divine becoming human so why not a human girl hearing such an announcement?'

Does she see the Annunciation as 'the most important event in human history'?

'I can see why. It's the boundary between divine and human. The turning point,' she says. 'In order to get to the rest of the story – for Jesus to walk on the earth and do the things he did, to give us the teaching – he had to arrive on earth as a human being. How does he arrive as a human being? He doesn't arrive as an adult. We have this concept of how he came to be and how that was announced. It was through Mary – a nobody. And that's how it came to be.'

When I ask her if Mary is an inspiration for her, she hesitates slightly before responding.

'I don't know. I've never thought about her in that way. She's not centrality. But her acceptance and obedience certainly chime with me. As a mother, there's a relevance for me too.'

We talk about her calling to ordination, which took place in the Cathedral less than a week ago.

'When I felt I was being called, my reaction was how on earth do I get from being a wife and mother to also being a priest? That went on for a while. I suppose lots of people who are called will say there's that niggling nagging feeling that just won't go away. That's absolutely right, there is. I didn't recognize it as a call to ordination for a long time. I thought it was a call to do something different with my life.

'As a child, I grew up in Sunday school. We went to church. Then I went to university. I didn't really find a church in Birmingham in which I felt I belonged. After university, I met Kelvin and we knew we would start a family. I found a church in Winchester and settled in there. I led the children's work team for the next ten years. I then became Church Warden.

'Then, ten years ago, I can clearly remember walking up to church thinking, what are you doing? It was about, this is significant for you. It rumbled on. It wasn't an angelic presence. It was something in my head nudging at me. I can remember clearly thinking something is going on here. I'm paying more attention to this than my day job [as a speech therapist]. Then my fellow Church Warden asked me, "Could you ever see yourself wearing a dog collar?" I was absolutely flabbergasted. And that was it. Nothing else was said. As I walked home, there were roses in the hedgerow and they were shining. I thought, wow!' The effect of all this was, "You need to listen".'

Hearing her story, I suggest there is a parallel for her with the story of the Annunciation.

'There is,' she replies. 'My big concern was that this was really arrogant. Who am I to say I'm being called to ordination? But it was other people around me and supporting me who convinced me. I was relatively calm and it was one step at a time to get there but it was certainly an upheaval.'

Indeed, during this preparation time, her husband Kelvin was diagnosed with a grade three brain tumour and lost part of his vision so she had to put the process on hold for a few months.

'It was really challenging but the calling didn't go away,' she says.

I show her the print of Lemoyne's Annunciation.

'I look at Mary's hands and see, "What me?" She's not saying, "no". She's saying, "What me?" And the wing and the arm [of the angel] is very much about "I'm here. It's going to be ok."

"I can't do this."

"Yes you can. I'll look after you."

That's what this is all about.'

I enter the Cathedral Close from Kingsgate, and meet with the Cathedral's new Canon Precentor and Sacrist, Reverend Sue Wallace. She has degrees in both Music and Theology, and is also a composer and an artist. A recent Cathedral newsletter welcoming her to Winchester comments on the 'red flecks in her hair and a diamond stud in her nose' and how she is 'a thoroughly modern addition to the Chapter'.

'The Annunciation is an amazing moment in history,' she tells me. 'What strikes me is Mary flagging up the sheer impossibility of it all. There's this kind of double play here. How can this be as I'm a virgin? I've never had sex. I'm unmarried. But also, how can this be because I'm a woman? Women have been neglected. Women couldn't get anywhere near the Holy of Holies and yet suddenly this woman is becoming the Ark of the new Covenant. That's incredible. I love that amazing juxtaposition of the impossibility of it all with the possibility of God making the impossible possible. Suddenly, everything changes. God wants to dwell in a woman and a woman becomes the God-bearer. That's incredibly important for ordained women and, indeed, all women. It's all about new life. Impossible and wonderful new life and the potential, therefore, for all of us.'

It is true she has strikingly coloured hair. It is more a warm shade of purple than red. Her diamond nose stud is tiny and rather subtle. We sit together at her plain office table, and she starts to reminisce about her childhood.

'My father was Roman Catholic and my mother was Anglican and I was baptized and brought up a Catholic. It was impossible then for women to become priests in either denomination. I remember once being allowed into the sanctuary area of a Catholic church because I was helping my dad fit the microphones under the altar and him saying, "This is a spot you are never normally allowed in." And now being free to enter that spot is very striking for me.'

She tells me how, as a child, she went to both Mass and Evensong.

'Mum's vein of Anglicanism was very much middle of the road. We don't go too far up the candle. We don't talk about Mary – that's too High Church really. That's still the case for Mum. For my dad's side of the family, it was OTT with Mary.'

I ask her if she sees the annunciation story as fact?

'Absolutely,' she replies straight away. 'It's vitally important for me that it's fact because of the blending of divinity and humanity, the joining of heaven and earth. It's so important for humanity's salvation. It gives hope for flesh. Without that, it's all fluffy and spiritual. We desperately need hope for our own flesh and this announcement of the marriage of the physical and the spiritual is so important.'

Does she agree it is 'the most important event in human history'?

'Absolutely,' she responds firmly again. 'I totally agree that everything changes at that point. Actually, God is outside time anyway and that moment permeates throughout history and permeates into my life.'

She talks about her own experiences of 'being called'.

'I remember some time ago a sense of God calling me to be a Precentor and it was impossible because I hadn't been ordained for six years. And yet I felt a really strong calling then to what appeared to be impossible. My only reply was like that of the Virgin, "How can this be but let it be done to me." And, then, suddenly, a job comes up that's a Precentor job but not a Cathedral Canon's job, that I could apply for because it didn't matter that I hadn't been ordained six years. So God constantly makes the impossible possible if we're willing to say yes to the potential of a new plan that God may have.'

She recalls another moment from her childhood: 'When I was four, I remember a Vocation Sunday service and the priest talked about God needing more workers for the harvest. And I said, yes, if you need people, I'm here. And I announced to my dad I was going to become a nun. He laughed. As I got older, I unpacked it to realize it was some kind of calling to be a Christian. And then it developed further to an initial seed to be called to the priesthood, even though at that time it was impossible for a woman to become a priest.'

We talk about the feast of the Annunciation effectively being lost today and she tells me it would be better to celebrate it in Advent. Even though the day would no longer be nine months before the celebration of the birth on Christmas Day, contextually, she explains, it would sit much better there than in the middle of Lent.

We move on to Mary and I ask what she means for her?

'In many ways she's the perfect model of how to be a priest,' she says. 'She brings Christ to the people. There's something inspiring about her being the Ark of the Covenant.'

Does she venerate Mary?

'I'm probably in that Anglican thing where we do not pray to saints,' she says. 'I honour her position but I don't pray to her. It's a very close line between veneration and worship and it's very easy to cross that line. Liturgically, occasionally, it's sometimes appropriate to walk that line but not to go too far across it.'

Does she believe in the virginal conception?

'Absolutely. The DNA or whatever of both God and Mary is crucial for salvation. It's important it's a marriage of divinity and humanity.'

Did Mary have other children after Jesus?

'I think the most likely explanation is that Joseph is an elderly widower and already had children. But I'm wary of anything that does not make Mary properly human. So I'm very uncomfortable with the Immaculate Conception. I'm uncomfortable also with the idea of her perpetual virginity. The jury is out for me. It doesn't really matter. What is vitally important to me is that she was a virgin when the angel came to her.'

I show her the print of Lemoyne's Annunciation. She laughs out loud.

'Ha ha, writhing bodies. It isn't my favourite period of art. I like Orthodox icons and Modern Art. That bit in the middle is not my favourite bit. I walk faster in the National Gallery when I walk through those particular rooms. Mm, Mary's white. I suppose it speaks of God in our culture. She's too serene. It's not a realistic treatment…although the holes in the walls are interesting.' She squints as she looks closer. 'It all looks very lovely until you notice the holes in the plaster. All this grand thing is a veneer and underneath it all are people who are in just as much a mess as everyone else.'

―――――――

I enter Winchester Cathedral via the West Front to be confronted by the sight of multi-coloured banners hanging on each of the sixteen piers of the long nave. Created by Thetis Blacker to celebrate the nine-hundredth anniversary of the foundation of the Cathedral back in 1979, the batik-styled paintings focus on the theme of creation.

The first, hanging directly above me, is called 'The Incarnation'. It portrays a crowned Virgin Mary holding the Christ Child close to her womb above a blooming garden of flowers that appears to form the rest of her body. A glowing sun and crested moon appear either side of her golden face. A nearby card reads: 'After the Fall of Man, primordial darkness is upon the earth in the hearts of men. Through the Incarnation of Jesus Christ, the darkness is dispelled. The Virgin Mary reigns as the Queen of Heaven, for the darkened universe is transformed as she brings the Light of Lights into the world.'

68. Left: Banners by Thetis Blacker on display in Winchester Cathedral, which has the longest nave of any Gothic cathedral in Europe © Joe Low. Right: Thetis Blacker's *The Incarnation*. © Dr John Crook, Winchester

I make my way up the long, soaring nave, transformed into its present two storey Perpendicular Gothic style by William of Wykeham when he was Bishop in the late fourteenth century. I pass his chantry chapel, completed just before his death in 1404. There, daily masses were said for him after he died in the hope of speeding his soul through purgatory and on to heaven. I enter the south transept and climb the stairs up to the Williams Room where the Cathedral's Curator and Librarian, Jo Bartholomew, awaits my arrival.

There, with great care, she takes out of a locked glass case one of the four huge volumes of the twelfth-century Winchester Bible and lays it on a large marble-slab table. The Winchester Bible, a masterpiece of medieval art, is hailed as one of the finest Bibles in the world and is the largest of the great English Bibles of the late 1100s. It is the only Bible to remain in the place for which it was created. It is the Cathedral's greatest treasure.

Jo Bartholomew opens it on the page featuring Luke's story of the Annunciation. There are no lavish illuminations on that particular page, just the beautifully inscribed text in black ink that uses Jerome's fourth-century Latin translation of the original Greek text as its source, commonly known as the Vulgate. I lean over and start to follow the relevant words from the Gospel '*secundum Lucam*' – according to Luke:

> *in mense autem sexto missus est angelus gabrihel a deo in civitatem galilee cui nomen nazareth. ad virginem desponsata viro cui nomen erat Ioseph de domo david. Et nomen virginis MARIA.*

The Winchester Bible was created sometime between 1160 and 1175 in the scriptorium, directly below us on the ground floor of the south transept. It is thought that Henry of Blois, grandson of William the Conqueror and brother of King Stephen, commissioned it when he was Bishop of Winchester. The Bible was intended for everyday use by the seventy or so Benedictine monks and also would have been displayed in public on important feast days. Indeed, in medieval times, it would probably have been carried at the head of a procession on the feast day of the Annunciation.

A single scribe, thought to have been a monk from the Priory of St Swithun, wrote it over a five year period. I had read earlier how he used quill pens made from goose feathers, and ink made from oak apples that had been crushed and soaked in rainwater. The parchment required more than two hundred and fifty calfskins. The calligraphy is exquisite. The tiny Carolingian script is written with great precision and uses fifty-four lines per page as it follows the scored rulings on the vellum.

Extraordinarily, the Curator allows me to hold the huge book for a few seconds with the page open on Luke's Annunciation passage. I experience a rush of excitement as well as trepidation. For here in my hands is one of England's oldest surviving accounts of the annunciation story in a book that is more than eight hundred and fifty years old.

69. Extract of Luke's Gospel passage of the Annunciation in the Winchester Bible, twelfth century. © and by kind permission of the Dean and Chapter Winchester Cathedral

Roly Riem arrives in the Epiphany Chapel at our arranged meeting place directly below an Edward Burne-Jones stained-glass window of the Annunciation. Unexpectedly, he is armed with two prints, one of Botticelli's 1489 painting of the Annunciation which is in the Uffizi gallery in Florence and the other, Titian's dramatic 1535 work displayed in Venice. Immediately, he asks me what I see in the two pictures and how Gabriel's message is being delivered.

I tell him that I notice Mary stands at a higher level than the angel in Botticelli's picture.

'Exactly. It's a beseeching Gabriel, almost grovelling,' he declares. 'Will she give her assent? It is that moment of absolute tension. There's a dance. Gabriel's eyes are absolutely fixed on her hand. It's like the X-Factor. Will she say yes?' In contrast, in Titian's painting the angel hovers above Mary. 'She's serene, in prayer, meekly accepting,' he tells me. 'Gabriel is like a ballet dancer arriving from heaven. He comes in a great flourish. The divine light heads to Mary like a laser beam. It's not a "maybe", it's a definite "yes".'

We then look up to the Burne-Jones stained-glass window. I see that the two central characters in his Annunciation design are standing side by side on the same level. He enthuses on how this exercise demonstrates how each Annunciation depiction has a very different take of the encounter.

Reverend Canon Dr Roland Riem is the Vice-Dean and Canon Chancellor at Winchester Cathedral and, among his many duties here, he leads the education and visual arts programmes and has a special interest in spirituality, pastoral care and ecumenical relations. He comments on the exquisite detail of the window's Pre-Raphaelite design.

'The drama here is more subtle. There's no big emotional bang of a Titian angel hurling himself down from heaven. It's rather demure, gracious, measured. If you took away his wings, it would be just a conversation between two people. She's approachable. She's an ordinary person who has an extraordinary gift of grace. She's not fazed by the decision facing her. She's turning back. Her attention has been caught. This is the moment of calling.'

The striking window was made

70. Edward Burne-Jones *The Annunciation*, 1910, Epiphany Chapel, Winchester Cathedral. © Dr John Crook, Winchester

in the William Morris workshop and was based on an earlier cartoon from the 1870s that Burne-Jones had created for Castle Howard in Yorkshire. It was installed in 1910 as one of four Nativity windows in the newly created Epiphany Chapel that today is the quietest part of the Cathedral, reserved for private prayer and silent reflection. Surrounding the rich colours of the Annunciation scene is green foliage characteristic of the William Morris studio and at the base of the window are the words: 'When Thy Word Goeth Forth It Giveth Light And Understanding Unto The Simple.'

'To me, one of the key words about this design is simplicity,' Roly Riem tells me. 'He is willing. She is responding. They are encountering each other at the same level. There's a lovely rhythm. His right hand is raised up in a blessing and her right hand goes up too. See the encounter of their eyes. She's prepared to hear what Gabriel says from his soft, gentle lips. She's listening modestly. There's a hugely strong threshold line that his hand crosses, created by the great bar of the stained-glass structure in the middle. And there's the tree of life from the Garden of Eden between them with a serpent wrapping itself around it. It's slithering down the trunk. It's losing the battle. It was complicit in the first Fall but that's being undone by Mary's *yes*. Mary is going to re-make the whole story of God being with his people. The dove is resting in the tree and light is emerging. It's a new age. The Spirit is just about to do his overshadowing crossing over the line. There's a lot of attention to the materials of their clothes. The tones match beautifully.'

He tells me how the window speaks to him and how it is a key feature of the spirituality of the Cathedral building.

'The sentiment here is a modest one and on a human scale – the ordinary and simple business of listening and responding. A pedestrian way of thinking about obedience. I might be able to manage that. It's approachable. She's approachable.'

Edward Burne-Jones once wrote about the aims of his work: 'I mean by a picture a beautiful romantic dream of something that never was, never will be – in a light better than any light that ever shone in a land no one can define or remember, only desire – and the forms divinely beautiful.'

A few rows further up in the Epiphany Chapel, we notice a man, lying prostrate across four chairs, fast asleep. As we move to the north transept where we can view the window at a distance through the round Norman arches, I ask Canon Roly what the annunciation story means for him.

'It's about the possibility that the reality we think of as earthly can be shot through with the glory of heaven, but only with God working in and through the human condition and circumstance, and for there to be something of a dance. God isn't just going to dictate terms to the world about how it's going to be glorified. He waits for us to be so caught up in that drama. We are taken into it so long as we allow it to be – "Let it be according to your will" – if we can just do some of that, the dance can begin.'

I note that he talks as though the annunciation story is a metaphor.

'Even if it were fact, and I believe Jesus must have come into the world in a way that was unique and extraordinary, I don't put it beyond God to have done that,' he says. 'Even if it happened, I wasn't there. It comes to me as a story that I listen to and learn from. So, inevitably, it carries the air of a metaphor or a parable. That's what it was like for Mary. What can it be like for us now? It's not that history doesn't interest me. Obviously, I believe Jesus came in the flesh. But I don't spend too much time worrying about the facticity of it. I worry about the details of the narrative and the little chinks and twists that Luke describes. The Holy Spirit is guiding that in my imagination. That's ok. That's the creative process.'

He pauses and looks up in admiration towards the Annunciation window before continuing.

'That's the balance of my approach. I want the metaphor to be grounded in the actualities of the events but I leave that to God really. I feel that it's important that it should always be a fresh message as we listen. The story is God-given. The more you listen to the story and the way it's constructed, the more you take in, like you see in pictures. Luke might have put in all his artistic turns the way he fancied to on that particular day but somehow it's all in the act of God and God's imagination and God's creative capacity to communicate with us.'

Does it concern him that the encounter between Mary and the angel Gabriel only appears in Luke's Gospel?

'No, I don't think so,' he responds. 'Every Gospel gives you a different window on the divine truth. It would make a difference if Jesus had never been born and there was no sense of the marvellousness and uniqueness of his birth.'

When I tell him that the Annunciation has been referred to as 'the most important event in human history' he laughs and puts his left hand up to his face to stroke his beard.

'I remember going on the buses in Malta and they had signs on them: "The Word was made Flesh". That's the Catholic emphasis on Incarnation. Other Churches like the Orthodox would say the Resurrection, the Evangelicals the Cross, and the Anglicans would hedge their bets,' he chuckles. 'For me, it's the whole sweep. So, to talk about a point in history…what is a moment? For me, it's God's hand painting the story of grace. He gives us so humble a message and we just have to listen carefully and find a way into the story. We get too hung up on which is the most important part. The most important thing is that we jolly well hear and act.'

What single word sums up the Annunciation for him? I ask.

'Let's take the word "glory". Mary found this portal into the glory of God,' he responds. 'She found a way of being whipped up into the story of God's grace among us and taking her part in it. She is the tree of life who joins earth and heaven to her womb. She is the pivotal point. It's the glory in the yielding.'

We move on to talk further about Mary.

'I'm not particularly Marian. My history is Protestant evangelical. I resist all the sentimentality and the easy worship around Mary. "Let's not go to Jesus. He's too stern. Let's go to Mary, our compassionate mother." All that I shy away from. I eschew the sentimentality and the adoration that spills over into a worship of Mary. But I come to Mary as a real woman.'

Does he venerate her?

He chuckles again. 'On a good day, I can say the Hail Mary and put myself into that story.'

Should the feast of the Annunciation be more prominent in the liturgical calendar? I wonder.

'I think we need soft ways into hearing the gospel and this lovely, gracious story,' he says. 'That's the key. All the festivals are there to help us approach God through the different windows of the truth. And yes, Mary is an important treasure of the gospel story.'

———

'As a child, 25 March was always hugely significant for me as a Wiltshire dairy farmer's son. It was a Quarter Day. It was the day the rent was due.' James Atwell is ensconced in his chair in his office in the Cathedral Close, overlooking the south transept of the magnificent medieval structure.

'There was a real sense of fear and dread as 25 March came because you had to somehow or other scrape together the rent for the tenant farm,' he tells me. 'I remember that very well. Therefore, it's an especially significant milestone in the calendar for me – almost like Christmas Day – and I'm staggered that people don't know about it. I chose to be installed here at Winchester on the feast of the Annunciation and every time 25 March comes around, I think of it as my *yes* to coming here. I'd been in Bury St Edmunds for eleven years, built a tower, became a bit of a hero, and then I came to Winchester, had no "street cred" at all and had to learn it all over again.'

The Very Reverend James Atwell was appointed Dean of Winchester in 2006, with overall responsibility for coordinating and developing the life of the Cathedral, after eleven years as Dean of St Edmundsbury Cathedral in Suffolk. There, he'd led a successful campaign to fund and build a new Millennium Tower.

He studied Theology at Oxford and then gained a Master's at Harvard. His country roots still run deep – he keeps hens in the Deanery garden and drives a Land Rover. He waxes lyrically about the Annunciation as we continue our conversation.

'Ah yes, is it poetic?' he asks himself. 'Is it historical? Is it actual? What was going on?'

The sixty-nine-year-old cleric is an affable and whimsical man with a lovely kind face, white hair and red cherubic cheeks. I ask if he thinks the Annunciation is the most important event in human history.

'I'm not sure I would say it's an event. You're on the edge of poetry, imagination, instinct. It's a big question,' he responds. 'I would rather say myself it's Good Friday and Easter Day. It was only because of what happened there that people were interested in the birth of Jesus. In a strange sort of way the interest in the birth came after what happened then. The traditions of Jesus's conception and birth are the most poetic, mythological and wondrous.'

I ask him whether we should see the story as fact or metaphor.

'I'm on the frontier between fact and metaphor,' he replies. 'Jesus has to have been born. The Magnificat – where did that come from? Was it a spontaneous piece of poetry by Mary? We don't know. That's why we're on the fringe. I try not to think too much about what's history and what's not because it's such a lovely story to enter into and in many ways the birth pre-configures the Crucifixion and the Resurrection. I suppose for me what is fact is that, somehow or other, Mary must have had to say yes. God never overrules a human being's free will. If he was going to use a human being, he must have won her assent. The Annunciation is Mary's *yes*. In what way she said yes…well, I don't know…but I'm sure it was freely given.'

I wonder whether it matters how it came about. Was there an angel present? Was Jesus an only child?

'Look, it's all very intriguing,' he responds. 'I don't think…' He pauses for a moment to frame his thoughts. 'For my own self, I think Jesus was her first born but it's pretty difficult to say he didn't have brothers and sisters because they occur in the New Testament. We know his father and his brothers. The only way you get round that is by saying that Joseph was older and had previous children but…' His voice tails off. 'Did Mary have some kind of spiritual encounter?' he continues. 'The whole business of angels? It seems to me…well, I don't believe they had names and there was a squadron of them and you can identify them. If you look at the Old Testament and the story of Abraham and so on, the angel is the angel of God's presence – it's a veiled presence of God. Angels in the way we think of them came out of the change from polytheism to monotheism and what happened to all these gods around the place is they became angels.'

So, is it better to think of it as some kind of spiritual force coming to Mary rather than an angel with a name and all that entails?

'Yes,' he replies, 'and with some sense of vocation and calling.'

When I ask what he believes to be the key message of the annunciation story, at first he digresses a little.

'Very often, when you get people like Richard Dawkins who have this rather primitive notion of God – if something goes wrong, why hasn't God put it right – what sort of world would we be living in if every time something went wrong, God picked it up and put it right?' He chuckles to himself, 'The idea in some way God must suffer in the world and call it to himself.'

Then, he focuses on the question. 'What you got in Mary and the Annunciation is a sense of God being powerless to make the world come to him. What he's got to do is to draw it to him of its own free will and Mary is the world saying yes to God. The Church is prefigured in Mary and maybe the consummation of creation is prefigured in Mary. It shows us transparently the way God works.'

He believes that the scene of the Annunciation, captured by so many artists through the ages, is all about Mary's assent. And it is that yes to God that will form the basis for his sermon on the Fourth Sunday of Advent: 'The events of our redemption need the *yes* of Mary,' he writes. 'God cannot use her as a channel of his grace without her own complicity in the plan. It would deny all that God is as the author of love, justice and reconciliation if even he did not respect the integrity, the dignity, the will of the creature coming to be in his image. God needs a door of opening into the world he has made. He is here limited by the independence of a teenage girl. His love has to win a free assent.

'The Annunciation undermines many of the concepts of God we craft in our own image. It redefines the notion of "God is king". We often have an impatience with the way the world is. Just as earthly rulers have a temptation to want to control everything in their charge, so we feel God ought to be continually interfering to put things right. However, if the nature of God is to gift the creation with his own identity, then he has to withdraw sufficiently to allow creatures true independence, true initiative and to become true centres of generosity. There is a tension, something of an enigma, that if God is love then it requires of him a generous silence. He has to wait for the response of love in his creatures. There has to be space for his creatures to respond: Let it be with me according to your word.'

He writes of 'a generosity, a humility, a patient love in waiting, which is the nature of God. The Annunciation and the *yes* of Mary encapsulates Mary as of significant stature in the story of our redemption. However, it also throws into high relief the way God works. There has to be a waiting between the angel's message laden with the love of God and the willing response of Mary, that answers love with love. It represents a pattern of God's activity. God cannot wish upon Mary the sacrifice to which she is called, he can only invite her to the task and wait.

'In Mary's *yes* is hidden the *yes* of the Church to God's love. The life of Christ is an invitation to discipleship. He trail-blazes the path of divine humility. We see something of the divine waiting of thirteen billion years that has brought us here today; the divine humility which has never overwhelmed creation, but gives it space for a free response.

'It is in that context that we should understand prayer. It is part of our *yes* to God, our holding people and affairs in his love and inviting him into his world. God needs our *yes* as well. Mary is not simply a one-off; she is a prototype. We are all invited to respond to the invitation of Christ's life with our own assent: "Here am I, the servant of the Lord; let it be according to your word".'

I show him the print of Lemoyne's Annunciation.

'I see an innocence of Mary here,' he says. 'Her hands are almost laying her life before God. "If that's what you want me to do." She's almost resigning herself to that. I see a slightly effeminate angel and I see a finger that's very sexual, very phallic. It reminds you that this is the moment of conception. He's very cleverly woven a moment of innocence in Mary with a moment of conception. There's not a lot of pain in the picture is there? But in the "Let it be" there is a huge pain, a huge sacrifice.'

He studies the picture in silence for quite some time. I ask him whether he likes it.

'Funnily enough, it's growing on me,' he says. 'I'd have probably passed it by but you're making me look at it and I'm realising there's more and more to this picture. You're lifting a veil for me in many ways. I'm now seeing the picture as a piece of poetry almost. It's no longer a snapshot of the moment. It draws you into it, it works its magic and gets under your skin.'

As I prepare to depart, James Atwell gives me a poetry-prayer for 25 March that he wrote some years back, when he was Dean at Bury St Edmunds:

ANNUNCIATION

O God, before all things is your selfless love.
An act of renunciation enables the word that calls creation into
being: your goodness involves restraint that the creature may have
dignity. In your waiting is nurtured the free response of creation's
very being: the hard fact of rock, the delicate complexity of life,
the harmony of nature all return their Creator's praise.

O God, before all things is your selfless love. An act of
annunciation seeks redemption's invitation. The permission of
the creature must precede a Sabbath of healing. You wait upon
the word of Mary, the maiden daughter of the house of David.

Your love coaxes Mary's 'yes' and in that affirmation is creation's
will to win its destiny and final consummation.

Alleluia! Alleluia! Your Kingdom comes, your will be done, Alleluia!
Amen.

————

Sometime later, I return to the Cathedral Close and head to the Deanery. I am here to
meet a man who has come to be interviewed for the *Winchester Dialogues* – a series of
interviews about the changing relationship between Church and State and the challenge
of faith in the twenty first century.

Sir Mark Tully was born in Calcutta, and came to Hampshire as a child immediately
after the Second World War to board at Twyford School, three miles south of Winchester.
Then he went on to Marlborough and Cambridge where he read History before switching
to Theology.

He intended to become a priest in the Church of England but says he was too wild and
did not have the 'moral stability' required. Instead he joined the BBC in 1964, reported
from India for over forty years and was knighted for his outstanding contribution to
journalism. Not only did he broadcast brilliantly and incisively on South Asian affairs
but he also presented a highly acclaimed BBC television series in 1996 called *The Lives
of Jesus* and he still regularly presents the early Sunday morning Radio 4 religious and
ethics programme *Something Understood* that 'examines larger questions of life through a
spiritual theme.'

I've heard him speak eloquently about India's multi-religious culture and how he is
able to feel the presence of God in cathedrals, temples and mosques.

'No religion has a monopoly of truth,' he once declared. 'Truth is many sided and there
are many ways to God. I do not feel any difficulty in believing that not only Christianity
but also Hinduism is a way to God. I had thought Christianity was the one and only true
way to God. But I then realized that was nonsense. In a way it was an enormous sense
of relief. The most important thing I've learnt from living in India is there are so many
different ways to God. We're all searching for the same thing. There's no single way.'

Although he regularly attends services in the Anglican cathedral in Delhi, he says he
finds the idea of karma and re-incarnation helpful. It's in this context that I am fascinated
to hear Sir Mark Tully's take on the Annunciation. Now aged seventy-nine, he is a large
framed man with a wonderfully rich, mellow voice.

'In many ways, the Annunciation means the start of Christmas for me,' he says. 'It's
about the way human beings can communicate with God and how God can communicate
with human beings. I don't see it as fact. But that doesn't mean I see it as a lie. I also don't
say it could not have happened. If one is being cynical, it's Luke trying to explain how a
virgin can conceive a child. But for me, the story's meaning is about obedience to God
and how we as human beings can be called to do something. That's the message of it. For
Mary, it must have been very frightening for her.'

I mention that the phraseology of his last comment suggests he believes the event
actually happened.

'Let's go back to the many sides of truths,' he responds. 'In many ways, whether it's
fact or not doesn't really matter to me. That question isn't relevant to the way I feel about
it. The whole story is important to me.

'The strongest proof of the divinity of Christ is the Church. I don't believe an
institution like that could have been founded on a lie or even an illusion. So something
remarkable must have happened particularly at the resurrection. Of that, I feel a hundred

per cent certain. Of course, Jesus lived and I'm certain he was crucified. The most likely explanation for me was that, like in Hinduism, he was filled with God, had realized God in such a deep way that he became something quite different to ordinary human beings. Son of God is too anthropomorphic.'

He continues: 'My partner once said, "The trouble with you, Mark, is you love the Church more than you love Jesus." I absolutely have to agree with that. "Jesus, my friend" and all that and talking directly to Jesus is not very meaningful to me. But the Church, and the history of it and the liturgy is hugely meaningful. I can't describe my love and loyalty to that. It means a hell of a lot to me.'

He acknowledges that when he attends the Eucharist service in the Anglican cathedral in Delhi most Sundays, he will recite or sing the Creed including the words, "For us and for our salvation he came down from heaven, was incarnate from the Holy Spirit and the Virgin Mary and was made man." But he re-iterates that whether the Annunciation happened or not doesn't matter.

'One of the things I'm very keen on is balance. Of course it's not rubbish. People have been inspired by this vision of the Son of God and the Crucifixion and I still share some of the hope of the Resurrection. I'm not saying it's all rubbish. What I am saying is, don't worry too much about exactly what happened or exactly what it means. That's the way I'll put it.'

He goes on to tell me how he sees Mary as the mother of Jesus rather than the Mother of God.

'But I can't even explain it myself. It's not a case of this is what I believe or not believe. Rather, this is what I find helpful to me to remain a Christian. It's a personal framework. An experience of being infinitely small, part of something infinitely bigger than myself, but still mattering. And for me, nature is the symbol, the embodiment, almost the idol of all that.'

I wonder if he ever prays to Mary.

'I was taught as a young man that that was dangerous Catholicism,' he replies. 'She's never been a really important part of my life.'

I show him the print of Lemoyne's Annunciation.

'I see a very surprisingly young, human Gabriel. The only angelic thing is his wings. And there's a totally obedient Mary. She seems to be rejoicing in her calling which, considering the momentous nature of that calling, would be rather surprising.' He takes in a deep breath. 'I find it a bit sentimental, a bit too sweet,' he continues. 'I'd like to see the struggle going on in Mary, the alarm, the concern. This looks to be a totally happy experience. It can't be like that.'

I then show him Jyoti Sahi's Annunciation and immediately he smiles.

'Look, Gabriel here is a frightening, alarming figure,' he exclaims. 'The colours are quite frightening as well. Mary is subservient but you can see the fear. This is a much, much stronger picture. It's absolutely wonderful. This would not be a comforting picture to have. The "Indian-ness" is there with much more colour. There's the confusion of the situation and the tremendous motion. Yes, it's very Indian – that lack of linearity. The wiggles. The lack of straight lines. To me, the lack of straight lines symbolizes this whole business about religion and faith not being a linear thing, not being a rational thing. There's no straight way through it, no absolute certainty about anything.'

CHAPTER 21

A GIFT

A couple of miles off the M6 motorway in Cheshire lies the small town of Sandbach. I head to the picturesque, cobbled market square and spot immediately what I have come to see: two tall sandstone crosses that display one of the earliest known images of the Annunciation in England and are amongst the finest examples of Anglo-Saxon sculpture in Britain. They are positioned side by side and stand five metres and three and a half metres high respectively. Sunlight hits the shafts, imparting a rich red-brown glow to the lavishly carved stone. The crosses were crafted in the early ninth century when Sandbach, then known as Sanbec (sand valley), lay at the centre of a large early Saxon parish, possibly the site of a minster church linked to the powerful Bishop of Lichfield.

Originally, they were brightly painted, adorned with jewels and metalwork, and stood as symbols of Christian authority. A plaque nearby explains that the stone carvings draw heavily on the motifs and techniques of metalworking, reflecting the prestige of the jeweller in Anglo-Saxon society. The biblical scenes which adorn the eight faces of the shafts contain references to both Scottish and Continental figurative art.

For many years it was believed that the crosses were created in the early part of the ninth century to commemorate the coming of Christianity to the kingdom of Mercia two centuries earlier, in the reign of the Saxon king Penda. However, it is now thought more likely that they were placed originally at an unknown site in the area, between AD 800 and 850, and used either as boundary markers for a religious establishment or as the site for religious services. They were moved to the market square in the late sixteenth century but torn down by Puritans opposed to religious imagery in the early seventeenth century, when the stone blocks forming the crosses were dispersed. The shafts were reassembled in 1816 and both the crosses were restored.

71. Carving of the Annunciation on the Sandbach Crosses, ninth century, Sandbach, Cheshire

Half way up the west face of the taller cross, a well-worn angel Gabriel stands looking straight at me. His wings are outstretched and he holds a scroll. To his right sits Mary in profile on a high-back chair that emphasizes her nobility as the future mother of God. She appears to be listening to Gabriel. Much of the bottom half of the carving has been badly eroded by more than a thousand years of English weather but experts think that, originally, she may have been carrying a spindle. The panel above Gabriel and Mary features Jesus being led to his crucifixion. Next to him, Simon of Cyrene carries the cross as Jesus makes his way to Calvary. At the top, I see the cross-head is badly damaged.

Remarkably, 1200 years after their creation, these extraordinary stone carvings remain open to the elements. Equally surprising, a small metal railing is the only protection from vandals.

What did the people of Sanbec make of the annunciation story back in the early ninth century when they first saw this image? The vast majority would have been illiterate and would have relied on the local priest to tell them the story of Mary and the angel Gabriel. He would use the carving on the stone cross to guide his narrative. Presumably then, nobody questioned the story's authenticity or meaning. Today, the citizens of Sandbach walk past the crosses, not giving the images so much as a glance.

I have come to The John Rylands Library in the centre of Manchester for the first time. The building is unlike any library I have been in; its late Victorian neo-Gothic splendour resembles a cathedral both inside and out. It houses one of the world's finest collections of rare books and manuscripts, including one of the most important collections of Egyptian papyri.

I make my way to the high security Elsevier Reading Room, identify myself, and an assistant from the Special Collections team goes off to collect something that I am very excited to see. After a while, he returns with a silver metal case from which he carefully removes a glass frame containing a small, badly damaged piece of Egyptian papyrus. This tiny fragment, measuring 18 cm by 10 cm, was acquired in Egypt for the Library in 1917 by the biblical scholar and palaeographer, Rendel Harris, but was not catalogued and published until 1938.

What makes it so special is that the words, written in Greek, form the oldest evidence anywhere in the world of a prayer specially dedicated to the Virgin Mary and seeking her intercessionary power as Theotokos, the God-bearer. The word *theotokos* is used clearly in the text, as is the partially visible Greek word [*lut*]*rōsai*, meaning 'deliver'. The papyrus dates back possibly as early as the middle of the third century.

I place the frame at an angle and with a magnifying glass examine the brown lettering, which, reconstructed, uses Koine Greek to state:

> *Mother of God [theotokos]*
> *hear my supplications*
> *suffer us not to be in adversity*
> *but deliver us from danger*
> *Thou alone*

It is the earliest known version of the Marian prayer, 'Sub Tuum Praesidium', which was recited in Latin throughout the Middle Ages and is still said today by some Catholics:

> *Beneath your compassion*
> *We take refuge, O Mother of God [theotokos]*
> *do not despise our petitions in times of trouble*
> *but rescue us from dangers,*
> *only pure, only blessed one*

72. Greek papyrus 470, Rylands Collection, third-fourth century, The John Rylands Library, Manchester

In Volume 3 of the *Catalogue of Greek and Latin Papyri*, published by the Library in 1938, the compiler, Colin (C. H.) Roberts, a lecturer in Papyrology at the University of Oxford, described the tall, upright lettering to be 'of a peculiar type to which I know no exact parallel.' He dated the fragment to the fourth century because he did not think Egyptian Christians would have known Mary as *theotokos* until then. Indeed, it was not until 431 that the doctrine that she was the Mother of God was formally declared at the Council of Ephesus. However, it is known that Peter of Alexandria, Athanasius and other theologians were already using the word *theotokos* in their writings at the beginning of the fourth century and some palaeography experts now think the style of the lettering on the papyrus indicates it is more likely to have been created in the third century, possibly around AD 250 to 280. I look in wonder at this small scrap of papyrus. It looks so bland and insignificant, yet I appreciate its immense importance historically.

Critically, what this papyrus fragment shows is that Marian veneration existed well before the Council of Ephesus and that Mary's pivotal role in the annunciation story, as laid out in Luke's Gospel, made her the subject of veneration amongst Egyptian Christians 250 years after the death of her son, Jesus.

I leave Manchester and continue up the M6, past Carlisle, and arrive in Ruthwell near Dumfries, close to the northern edge of the Solway Firth. In the eighth century, this part of south-west Scotland lay within the recently Christianized Anglian kingdom of Northumbria.

I am here to see the Ruthwell Cross, the most famous Anglo-Saxon sculpture in Britain and one of the greatest monuments of the early Middle Ages anywhere in Europe. Its stone carvings, part of the Insular Art tradition, are the largest reliefs on any surviving Anglo-Saxon cross. Originally, it was used as a preaching tool and stood on the site of a small monastery near to the Solway Firth. Today, it is housed inside the tiny, whitewashed Ruthwell church in a specially designed apse.

Records show that the imposing seventeen-foot-tall structure was placed in the church in 1600. However, in 1642 the Church of Scotland deemed the monument 'idolatrous' and ordered its destruction. Two years later, it was smashed to pieces, its remains scattered in the churchyard. In 1802 various pieces were moved to the nearby manse garden and by 1823 they were re-assembled. Finally, the Ruthwell Cross was re-erected inside the church in 1887.

73. The Ruthwell Cross and stone carving of the Annunciation, eighth century,
Ruthwell, Dumfries and Galloway

I stand in the apse looking at the south-facing side of the cross. So tall is the structure that the base has been sunk five feet into the ground in order for the church to accommodate it. Various reliefs depict Martha and Mary, Mary Magdalene anointing Jesus's feet, and Jesus healing the blind man. Below them is a relief of the Annunciation. Mary leans away from the angel Gabriel in apparent surprise or fear. A Latin inscription reads: '*Et ingressus angelus ad eam dixit ave gratia plena dominus tecum benedicta tu in mulieribus*' (And an angel came to her saying, 'Hail, full of grace, the Lord is with you, blessed are you among women'). The bottom part of this south-facing column is severely worn away but below the annunciation relief one can just about make out a panel showing the Crucifixion.

I have to pinch myself. I am standing in front of the earliest known image of the Annunciation in Britain, created in the first half of the eighth century. It is an extraordinarily powerful moment. I think of the priest who would have stood here on the bleak, flat Northumbrian landscape on the north side of the Solway Firth, dwarfed by this tall cross, preaching to a gathering of local people about Luke's story, using the carved relief as his aid. Thirteen hundred years later, the story still fascinates, still inspires, still connects.

Below four arcades of arches in the centre of the narthex, she stands passively on her own, her eyes closed in contemplation. She is about five feet tall, looks calm and serene, and is stunningly beautiful. Her back is straight but her smooth head bows down slightly. There is a tension in her neck and she stands motionless. Her stomach forms a gentle curve. Indeed, seen front on, the shape of her slender body, from shoulder to hip, suggests her invisible arms are wrapped under her outer garment and are covering her womb. Presumably the angel Gabriel has fulfilled his task and departed some time ago.

I am alone in the Galilee Chapel in Durham Cathedral, the first Romanesque church in England, built between 1175 and 1189. Originally, this was a place of arrival – the one area of the Cathedral where women could worship in what was home to an all-male Benedictine community. Nearby, at the door to the lower nave, a black line on the marble floor indicates the boundary beyond which females were forbidden to cross.

74. Josef Pyrz *Annunciation 2*, 1992, Galilee Chapel, Durham Cathedral

The figure is *Annunciation 2*, an evocative sculpture in ash, made by Josef Pyrz and gifted to the Cathedral by the Jerusalem Trust and an anonymous donor in 1992. Born in Poland in 1946, Pyrz left his homeland in 1979, aged thirty-three, 'to secure his artistic freedom', and settled in Paris. A plaque describes how the sculptor 'uses the accidental fissures and gnarls of his medium but also imposes his own pattern on it so that there is a perceived struggle between the natural state of the wood and the spiritual yearning which makes the work of art.'

Josef Pyrz called his Mary, 'everywoman'. Certainly her appearance is far removed from that of a young Jewish peasant girl. With closely shaven hair and African features, she looks more like a Masai woman standing alone on the Kenyan plains. I imagine Tim Dakin, the Bishop of Winchester, would love this sculpture. At the bottom of the plaque is a poem, written as an accompaniment to the sculpture, by an unnamed author:

> Annunciation to virginity, yes
> Inscribed on life's blank page
> Virginity is not a relic of the past
> for nothing passes,
> but it is the very condition of our existence.
> Virginity is our present time.
> As much as we are virginal
> as much as we see our very selves
> opened on the world till we can holy be seen through
> as Mary is 'yes' comes from her purity

> but purity is not ourselves
> it is the symptom of our being alive
> it is the door through which we pass
> with closed eyes
> the door of the Annunciation.

I approach the statue slowly and move my hands across its smooth, undulating surface. Light streams through the windows, illuminating the top of her head. I take a seat, look around me, and then shuffle through some notes I have with me. I come across a sermon on the Annunciation given in December 2005 by Reverend Rosalind Brown, the Canon Librarian here at Durham Cathedral. She began with a series of questions that she had posed in a poem she wrote eight years earlier:

> Did Gabriel come half-hurtling in –
> wings waving, stirring up the dust
> of Galilean tracks you trod (until this day)
> with familiar oblivion?
> glory trailing in his wake,
> did he shine that luminous, incandescent aura
> we ascribe to holiness?
>
> Or did he approach with reticent reserve,
> gingerly; softening the shock
> of the abrupt invasion
> of worldly space by heaven's word?
> Did he knock, or just unfold
> before your startled eyes?
>
> And was he a loud, majestic
> messenger of God
> more used to fanfares in the heavenly court
> than twittering of bird song
> in the Galilean hills?
> Or was he your first ally in the fear that gripped your heart,
> calling you by name, serene with words of calm
> and favour found with God?
>
> Well might you wonder what kind of greeting this might be!
> Had anything prepared you for this day
> when glimpses of God's way of seeing
> were unlocked to you,
> simple Galilean girl
> and favoured one of God?
>
> In Nazareth, whence nothing good can come,
> suddenly your home becomes the place where
> heaven touches earth
> and neither are the same again.
>
> Was it a request or statement that you heard?
> and was there fear or faith within your heart
> when you said 'let it be'?

The rising tide of hope and co-creating energy,
welcomed and embraced the 'yes, let it be
with me – with me – according to your word.'
And did you laugh, or cry or pray
when you were left
to wonder at the wonder
of God's grace?'

Rosalind Brown goes on in her sermon to describe how Luke left the question hanging, 'tantalisingly unanswered', and observes how in so many Annunciation paintings, 'there's something of the ballerina about both of them as they dance around each other.' She suggests that Saint Benedict echoed Mary's response when he formulated his three monastic vows of stability, obedience and conversion of life. I am intrigued by this proposition and want to learn more.

I arrange to meet her at her tied residence in the Cathedral precinct in an area called The College. This was once the outer court of the original Durham monastery and her home is medieval in origin with a Georgian frontage. For many years, she was a town planner but left for the United States in the early 1990s to join an open Benedictine religious community in a steel town in the Rust Belt. She went on to study at Yale Divinity School on her road to becoming a priest. Before arriving in Durham, she trained candidates for ordination at Sarum College in Salisbury.

A single woman with wavy, greying hair, she is dressed in a purple, fluffy jumper and an elegant scarf together with a clerical collar, black skirt and black tights. She looks scholarly and talks clearly and precisely.

We move to her study where she takes great delight in showing me over five hundred images of the Annunciation that she has collected over the past twenty-five years. Postcards, prints, newspaper cuttings are all neatly filed in large ring-binder folders in chronological order, many of them marked with handwritten notes. She giggles as she shows me a tiny angel Gabriel 'trying to climb up Mary's tree-trunk of a neck to whisper in her ear.'

She finds Braccesco's painting from the Louvre and observes how 'Gabriel zooms in from the top right on a fifteenth-century skateboard and how Mary has to duck as he heads straight for her head.' She tells me she is especially intrigued by a rather understated Andy Warhol screen print, created in 1984, three years before his death. It focuses on Gabriel's raised right hand and Mary's tense fingers and was inspired by Leonardo da Vinci's famous painting of the Annunciation from 1472. 'Extraordinary,' she declares. She even has a picture of *The Annunciation of the Virgin's Death* by the seventeenth-century Dutch painter, Paulus Bor. 'Look at her expression,' she proclaims. 'I only found it this year.'

As she wades through a fraction of the hundreds of Annunciation images, I tell her I think I have met my match!

She puts the files aside and explains how the three Benedictine vows echo Mary's response to the Annunciation. She tells me that 'Stability' is about the fidelity to stay put when God has called us; the refusal to run away when things get too hard; and the vow is reflected in Mary's statement, 'Here am I.' She says 'Obedience' is about more than just doing what we are told; it is the recognition that we are not on our own; we are not totally autonomous individuals and, ultimately, we are God's people as reflected in Mary's statement that she is the servant or handmaid of the Lord. 'Conversion of life' is about an openness to grow in holiness as God leads us, exemplified in Mary's prayer, 'Let it be with me, according to your word.' As she emphasized in her sermon a decade ago, she says she believes the three vows are the tried and tested parameters for our lives as we follow Mary's example.

'Stability and Conversion of life are two sides of the same coin,' she says. 'Stability is not being in a rut and if you have Conversion of life without Stability, you're all over the place.'

We move on and I ask her what Luke's story of the Annunciation means to her today.

'It means, in the biblical context, the Incarnation. It says something about God's creation of humanity in his image; God's honouring of humanity and the importance of humanity. For today, it means God still comes to us, in unexpected ways and in the midst of ordinary tasks.'

When I ask whether she believes the story to be factual, she sighs heavily.

'I have no trouble in believing there was a virgin conception,' she says, 'I see no reason not to, but I don't go down the Catholic line of Mary being forever virgin. Whether that means literally or theologically, I'm prepared to say God was born in human form of a woman and so why not the way that it happened as it's described? Maybe if I get to heaven that will be one of the questions I'll ask and then say, "Oh yes, I should have understood that." It doesn't bother me. You end up always with the theological question, just who is Jesus? How is he human and divine? I think for theological reasons this is an explanation of how it happened. In that sense, I don't go down the metaphor-only line. It's more to me than just an encounter. It's God taking human form and that had to happen in some form.'

Does she believe Mary had more children after Jesus?

'It's the conception that seems to be the miraculous part,' she replies. 'She gives a natural birth. I don't go with the Roman Catholics that somehow she was left intact and didn't go on to have any more children. Once she was pregnant, it was normal family life.'

What are her thoughts about the Annunciation being the most important event in human history?

'I would say the Incarnation, the death and the Resurrection of Jesus Christ together are the most important events in human history. You can't have one without the other. So I would say that lot together. Many Christians would say it's the Cross but you can't have the Cross without the Incarnation – God entering the world in human form in order to save it.'

What does Mary mean for her?

'Mary is a very strong woman who knows her own mind and is totally given to God,' she responds. 'She's a fully human, down to earth, confident, self-determining woman, which is remarkable in first-century Nazareth. All this notion of perpetual virginity and her assumption – that puts her as no longer a woman like me and, therefore, if she's no longer a woman like me, then I can't relate to her. I want to say that Mary is the model. She's liberating. But if she's not like me, what hope is there then for me? I'm surprised at all that concern about the brothers and sisters. It says it in the Bible. What Galilean family would stop at one child?' She sighs heavily again. 'She's got to be real. She's got to be a first-century Jewish peasant woman.'

Does she venerate her? I ask.

'I honour her,' she replies. 'We keep the Marian feasts here at Durham. The Cathedral is dedicated to her. But I don't pray to her. I don't venerate her.'

Does she feel that the feast day of the Annunciation has become lost?

'I think it has in the Church at large but we keep it alive here in Durham.'

I wonder if Mary is still a barrier to inter-denominational dialogue.

'She certainly has been in the past but not as much now. History has moved on,' she says as she points to an icon she bought recently in a United Reformed church.

I show her the print of Lemoyne's painting. Interestingly, she doesn't have a copy of it in her collection.

'There are hardly any eighteenth-century paintings in here,' she says as she points to her files before examining the picture. 'I see a very pious Mary, unduly passive. I'm not sure what that expression says. If I was having that vision, I think I'd be doing more than that. To me it doesn't seem real.'

Does she like it? I enquire.

'No,' she says firmly. 'I can't be doing with those cherubs up there and angels like that. It smacks to me too much of pious Catholic art. If I was living in early eighteenth-century Paris, I may be able to relate to it, but it takes away her humanity. She looks human but there's something wrong with her expression. She's not reacting like a human.'

She starts to open up her files again, trawling for depictions that she particularly admires. 'I like that one,' she says, pointing to a print of the Tanner painting in Philadelphia. 'And I like the Rossetti in the Tate.'

She holds the print of Lemoyne's Annunciation in her hands.

'I'll now have to add this one to my collection…even though I don't like it,' she laughs.

Thirty-five miles south of Durham, on the bank of the River Swale, lie the ruins of Easby Abbey. Nearby stands St Agatha's church, built in early Norman times when Breton Lords came to nearby Richmond and established a castle in the town. Roald, Constable at Richmond Castle, founded Easby Abbey next to St Agatha's church for a Premonstratensian order of White Canons. This religious community, recognized by its simple yet distinctive undyed robes, comprised a small number of ordained priests who served local parishes. The Abbey was suppressed in 1536-7 after the community took the fateful decision to support the 'Pilgrimage of Grace', a popular rebellion in the north of England against King Henry VIII's break with the Roman Catholic Church. In February 1537, Henry ordered 'St Agatha and such places as have made resistance…shall without pity or circumstance cause the monks to be tied up [hanged] without delay.'

The magnificent Abbey buildings were stripped, demolished and fell into ruin. Today, the towering remains of the refectory, dormitory and gatehouse offer a powerful reminder of that time of ecclesiastical conflict and destruction. However, St Agatha's church survived intact and still functions. Inside, I discover a superb set of thirteenth-century wall paintings, one of which depicts the Annunciation.

75. Fresco of the Annunciation, 1250, St Agatha's Church, Easby Abbey, North Yorkshire

The series of New Testament frescos starts on the upper tier of the south wall. Angel Gabriel holds a scroll on which are written the words '*Ave Maria*'. In the centre of the wall painting stands a large vase containing a bunch of lilies. Mary is on the right holding her hands aloft in prayerful acceptance. Along with the rest of the collection, the Annunciation fresco was whitewashed during the Reformation before being re-discovered in Victorian times and restored by the specialist conservation firm, Perry Lithgow, in 1994.

A two-hour car journey from Easby through the North York Moors and along the east coast leads me to the seaside town of Scarborough. I have come to see St Martin-on-the-Hill, an Anglican Victorian church set a hundred yards back from the Esplanade, overlooking the South Bay. At first, I am disappointed and wonder if I have come to the right place. The church does not look very promising – its shape is non-prepossessing and its stone exterior is blackened, austere and nondescript.

However, to my relief I discover that first appearances can be deceptive, for inside I find what I am looking for: a unique artistic treasure trove; one of Britain's most comprehensive collections of nineteenth-century Pre-Raphaelite religious art, with outstanding works by William Morris, Dante Gabriel Rossetti, Ford Madox Brown and Edward Burne-Jones. I have come specifically to view two particular works, both depicting the Annunciation: a rose window on the west wall by Burne-Jones and an oil-painted double panel on the pulpit by Rossetti.

At first, the church interior seems empty and dark, in stark contrast to the azure sky outside. But as my eyes adjust to the gloom, I see rays of brilliant sunshine filtering through the stained glass, bathing the nave and aisles in shimmering, luminous colours.

So, what is the story behind this great artistic collection? In the late 1840s, Scarborough's South Cliff area began to flourish. Large hotels and impressive crescents and terraces were built and the town became England's pre-eminent seaside resort. Mary Craven, a wealthy local resident, agreed to finance the building of St Martin's – a new High Victorian Gothic Revival church on the South Cliff – and commissioned George Frederick Bodley, a young architect, to design it. Bodley was a member of the newly founded Hogarth Club, which put him in close contact with the Pre-Raphaelite Brotherhood, a group of controversial new artists whose works had recently emerged on the London art scene, harking back to the simple, medieval style before Raphael. In 1862, Bodley commissioned William Morris and members of the artistic group to decorate the interior of the church in readiness for its consecration the following year.

High on the church's western wall I find Burne-Jones's stunning rose window with a central roundel of the Annunciation. A wide beam of intense light projects diagonally onto the western wall, showcasing the jewel-like colours of the window. Nine cusped panels surround the main image. Eight of them display an angel playing a musical instrument and a ninth has an angel holding an Alleluia banner of praise. Jane Morris, the wife of William Morris but also Rossetti's muse, was the model for both Mary and the angel.

Gabriel, wearing a robe of yellow and gold, holds a willow twig in his left hand symbolizing the renewal of spring and rebirth. The thumb, index and middle fingers of his right hand are raised to symbolize the Holy Trinity. A pot of lilies separates the angel from a perturbed looking Mary, who turns towards him from her kneeling position at her prie-dieu. Also between them is a scroll with the words '*Ave Maria Gratia*', a fitting

Catholic sentiment for what was to be a brand new Tractarian church established to support the revival of controversial Catholic rituals.

Apparently, the introduction of candles on the altar, the wearing of embroidered robes by the priest and the celebration of Marian doctrines was an unwelcome Anglo-Catholic intrusion into evangelical Scarborough at that time and was resisted by local residents who bombarded the Archbishop of York with complaints. However, the church remains Tractarian to this very day.

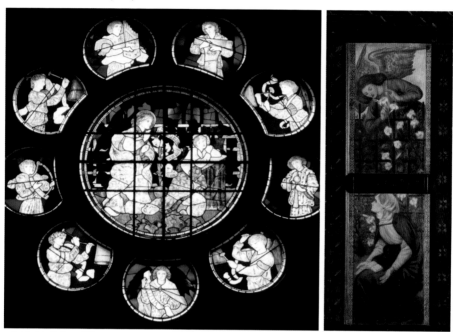

Left: 76. Edward Burne-Jones stained glass window of the Annunciation, 1862. St Martin-on-the-Hill, Scarborough. Right: 77. Dante Gabriel Rossetti's panels of the Annunciation on the pulpit, 1862. St Martin-on-the-Hill, Scarborough

I walk down the main aisle towards the sanctuary, to see Rossetti's highly decorative pulpit. The pulpit's two left side panels, one above the other, are painted in oil and depict a distinctive Annunciation scene. The top panel shows the angel Gabriel arriving from above, his right hand holding a lily stem whilst his left hand offers a blessing. His long auburn hair rests on his shoulders and he looks down at Mary as he proudly displays his peacock-feathered wings. Behind him is a luminous background of gold. Between him and Mary is a wall of flowers set within a metal trellis, a medieval rose garden symbolizing the enclosed garden as referenced in the Song of Songs. The second panel below the angel shows a calm, confident looking Mary dressed in a white top and blue cloak. Her hands are open wide and rest on her lap, as if she's willingly receiving Gabriel's message at that very moment. A prayer book lies on her lap and a flimsy veil covers her light brown locks. A haloed dove beside her proclaims the coming of the Holy Spirit. Behind her, a rich garden of flowers blossom within the lower trellis. Jane Morris was the model for Rossetti's Virgin and one of Burne-Jones's young girls is understood to have posed for the angel.

The two panels separate the angel and Mary. The sensual modelling and intricate detail of Rossetti's design, with its intense colours, so characteristic of the Pre-Raphaelite movement, is a very different take on the Annunciation to *Ecce Ancilla Domini* that he had painted twelve years earlier. When I had seen that picture in storage at the Tate warehouse, I had been struck by its sheer simplicity, its pale colours and its naturalistic depiction of Mary as a vulnerable and frightened young girl, sitting on her bed as the angel arrives. The two pictures could not be more different. I am fascinated how the same artist can interpret the annunciation encounter in such different ways.

Rossetti painted the Annunciation many times throughout his life. As well as being a great artist, he was also a poet and the encounter between the angel and Mary inspired his literary prowess as well as his artistic skill, as demonstrated by this sonnet written in 1847:

> The lilies stand before her like a screen
> Through which, upon this warm and solemn day,
> God surely hears. For there she kneels to pray
> Who wafts our prayers to God—Mary the Queen
> She was Faith's Present, parting what had been
> From what began with her, and is for aye.
> On either hand, God's twofold system lay:
> With meek bowed face a Virgin prayed between.
> So prays she, and the Dove flies in to her,
> And she has turned. At the low porch is one
> Who looks as though deep awe made him to smile.
> Heavy with heat, the plants yield shadow there;
> The loud flies cross each other in the sun;
> And the aisled pillars meet the poplar-aisle.

———————

I leave Scarborough and travel twenty miles south to Bridlington. I have come to meet Patrick Wise who creates paintings influenced, he says, by Christian religious iconography, cubism, art deco, Mexican muralist art, folklore, spirituality and even psychedelia. The end result is certainly individualistic and distinctive.

'I think I have a unique style, my very own,' he tells me. 'I picked up a pencil before I could walk, according to my mum. My dad was an artist as well. He was a bus conductor, then a gas fitter, but he always painted. It was through my dad that I developed a love of art and drawing. It was through him that I saw a lot of paintings as a child – Botticelli, Russian icon paintings. The images were often quite Catholic I suppose, the colours, the stylized figures. The feel I got from those paintings had a mystic quality. They evoked mystery, almost a magical quality. I've always been fascinated by stories and that's what I try to capture in my work. I hint at stories but I don't want to tell people what's going on. People should take whatever they want from them.'

We sit in two comfortable red armchairs in the small front room of his Victorian terraced house. I take in my surroundings and realize that this is a man who clearly loves Victoriana. The room is filled with art and trinkets. There is a large glass display cabinet filled with tiny ornaments and the walls are festooned with pictures, mirrors and small sculptures. It feels homely. His cat sits on the windowsill looking out to the street.

The forty-nine-year-old artist and illustrator was raised in Hull and studied Fine Art at Bretton College in West Yorkshire. Today, he is dressed casually in T-shirt and jeans. First impressions suggest a kind, warm hearted, thoughtful man, somewhat lacking in self-confidence. He is clearly very shy and often struggles to find the right turn of phrase. He

78. Patrick Wise *Encounters with Light*, 2015, © Patrick Wise

smiles regularly, is passionate about his art but does not earn enough to wholly devote himself to the cause.

He unzips a large, black portfolio case and inside, on top of a pile of other art works, is the painting I have come to talk to him about. It is much smaller that I had envisaged – around 12 inches by 8 inches – but the size does not diminish its impact. Made with acrylic, watercolour and pen, it is called *Encounters with Light* and the composition is clearly influenced by the annunciation story.

'I have to admit, I know I shouldn't, but sometimes I paint almost for the sake of painting,' he says. 'I'm passionate about it. It's about who I am. With this painting I tried to evoke and capture something that is slightly otherworldly or magical. I'm not really into realism. That's all too literal and you might as well just take a photograph. I've always tried to create something "other" that you wouldn't see anywhere else. I wanted to capture an essence of light. I've always been fascinated by images of angels, I don't know why, and especially by the Annunciation. The idea of this visitation by an angel. I think it's all about somebody presenting a gift.' He laughs nervously. 'I always think I sound crazy when I talk about my work but that's how I see it.'

I tell him that, although the painting is semi-abstract, I can see the angel Gabriel and a woman who looks very much like Mary. Am I right to see that?

'I think you are,' he acknowledges, 'although there could be an ambiguity there as well. But yes, there's definitely the influence of the annunciation story. You're not way off the mark at all. Yeah, that's what's behind it.'

I hold the painting in my hands and admire the multitude of colours and exotic imagery. In some ways it looks Indian in style. It also has a touch of the psychedelic. An angel figure appears to be passing a heart to a woman dressed in green. She looks away. An enormous sun shines over the whole composition. When I ask him what he would like people to see in it, he hesitates for a while before responding.

'It's difficult to say. I want people to take away what they want from the work but I'd kind of like people to think about more than the everyday, not necessarily about religion but about spirituality. People have forgotten how to be contemplative, if that makes sense, and that maybe there's more to life than what we see.'

What does he make of Luke's biblical narrative on the Annunciation?

'Well I know the story and all the Annunciation paintings I've seen over the years that have influenced me.'

Does he believe in angels?

'I'm not sure,' he says, laughing nervously again. 'I'd like to believe in them. I like the idea of there being more than what we see around us. Even the idea of angels is quite comforting. Sometimes, I think I believe in everything. Other times, I think I believe in nothing. I go from one to the other.'

The painting now forms the album cover for Yorkshire musician, Heath Common's *Encounters with Light*. I ask him how the painting came about.

'I was approached to work on an album cover featuring another painting I'd already done,' he says. 'At the time, I was working on this piece and when Heath Common told me what the title of the album was going to be, I instantly thought this work suited it ideally. I sent it and he got back to me immediately and said, "That's the one!" '

I ask again what he makes of Luke's story.

'As a story, I've always loved it. I'm fascinated by what Mary must have been thinking and going through. I don't really understand why I have such a fascination with it but I see it as quite a beautiful, human story, particularly that point when Gabriel arrives. Visually, that's very beautiful.'

Does he see it as fact or metaphor?

'I don't see it as a load of old nonsense but I don't necessarily see it as fact,' he replies. 'I'm not a church-goer, I'm not necessarily religious. I see it more as a beautiful story. I believe in it and I don't believe in it. As I say, sometimes I believe in everything and sometimes I believe in nothing. You don't have to take it literally to get something from it. I find it strange that I paint the things I paint. I don't follow any one religion or belief system but when you look at lots of religions, you see their values are not a million miles away from each other. And you find virgin birth stories repeated in folklore all around the world. I love tales of transformation. I see the annunciation story really as about a gift.'

Is that what the heart that the angel holds symbolizes?

'Yes,' he says, 'it was the idea of a gift.'

What is going to happen to the painting? I wonder.

'It's never been on show yet, that one,' he tells me. 'Sometimes when I sell my work, it feels like you're selling your children. It's like a body of work and then it's gone. But I quite like this one. I'm quite happy with it. It has nice memories. I would sell it. It would be nice to know it would be hung in someone's house and that they like your work enough to show it. I do think it needs to be seen so I will exhibit it sometime in the future.'

He looks at Lemoyne's Annunciation picture on his iPad.

'In comparison to some of the other Annunciation paintings I've seen, it wouldn't grab me as much,' he tells me. 'The colours are subdued and the way Mary is looking down is quite odd. It's different to what I usually see in Annunciations. Usually there's a dialogue but I don't see that here. I don't think I would walk past it. I'd stop and study it.'

As I bid him farewell and walk down the street, I keep thinking about that response, 'Sometimes I believe in everything. Sometimes I believe in nothing. You don't have to take it literally to get something from it.'

CHAPTER 22

INTERSECTION

On the banks of the gently meandering River Wharfe in the Yorkshire Dales National Park, stands one of my favourite sights in the world: the ruins of Bolton Abbey. Beauty reigns as far as the eye can see: lush green fields; steadily flowing water that babbles over stepping stones before cascading down a lively weir; a backdrop of heather clad moorland and, most importantly, the ruined edifice of the old Augustinian priory. This is a truly idyllic place that had a huge impact on the likes of Turner, Ruskin and Wordsworth and cannot fail to inspire all who see it today.

The black-robed Augustinian canons arrived here in 1154 and dedicated their priory to the Blessed Virgin Mary. However, by 1540, the lead roof had been stripped away, the interior decoration had been destroyed and the east end was in ruins as the dissolution of the monasteries took hold across the country. However, the nave in the western end of the building was left intact and continues to function as a parish church to this day.

In 1851, with the Gothic revival underway, the sixth Duke of Devonshire commissioned Augustus Pugin, the celebrated Victorian artist and architect, to design

a set of stained-glass windows to replace six plain panes of glass on the church's south side. Pugin's mission was to reproduce the beauty and magnificence of the original glasswork of the thirteenth century in six early Gothic style twinned lancets. His ornate designs display thirty-six scenes of the life of Christ, starting with the Annunciation and ending with Pentecost. The windows were installed in 1853, a year after Pugin's death at the age of forty.

I use binoculars to view the detail of the Annunciation medallion on the top left hand corner of the south wall. On the left, Gabriel wears a white undergarment and golden shawl. His wings are green and red and a red halo surrounds his head. The index finger of his right hand points upwards to heaven whilst

79. A.W.N. Pugin *The Annunciation*, 1851-53, Bolton Priory, North Yorkshire. © Father Lawrence Lew O.P.

his left hand holds up a scroll on which are written the words '*Ave Maria Gratia Plena*'. He stands opposite Mary and they look into each other's eyes. A flask of water and a lily stem are positioned between them. Mary, dressed in red and blue and wearing a head scarf, holds up her right hand as the white dove of the Holy Spirit flies down from above, heading towards her left ear. The overall impact is glorious.

I sit in a front pew in the church and look directly ahead to a distinctive wall painting on the east wall. Five Madonna lilies, referencing the Priory's dedication to St Mary the Madonna, stand between single stems of barley, olive, vine, passionflower, wild rose and palm. For many years, the wall painting, created by Thomas Bottomless in 1880, was considered too secular to be displayed behind the altar and was covered over by a tapestry. Now, the lilies have been unveiled and take centre stage in this beautiful church, proclaiming the purity of the Virgin Mary.

After travelling along the A59 through the south-eastern corner of the Yorkshire Dales National Park towards Harrogate, I divert northwards for a few miles and arrive at one of Yorkshire's greatest sights, the magnificent ruins of Fountains Abbey, nestling in the Skell valley.

The long history of the Abbey began in 1132 when a group of disaffected Benedictine monks from St Mary's Abbey in York came to an isolated, heavily wooded area in search of a simpler and more devout life. They switched to the Cistercian order and endured particularly austere lives focused on prayer and meditation. They were known as the 'white monks' because of the coarse, undyed sheep's wool they wore as a *cuccula* or choir robe, the white celebrating Mary's purity. The community's new Abbey was dedicated to the Blessed Virgin at a time when the cult of Mary was expanding rapidly across Britain and Europe. They received instruction from one of the monks of Bernard of Clairvaux's Cistercian community in France such that the daily Divine Office at Fountains Abbey commemorated Mary's unique devotion and ended with the singing of the *Salve Regina* at night. Like all Cistercians, the monks at Fountains Abbey praised Mary's humility and virginity.

As I sit alone in the roofless nave of the Abbey church ruins, I read one of Bernard's twelfth-century homilies on the Annunciation: 'You have heard, O Virgin, that you will conceive and bear a son; you have heard that it will not be by man but by the Holy Spirit. The angel awaits an answer; it is time for him to return to God who sent him. We too are waiting, O Lady, for your word of compassion; the sentence of condemnation weighs heavily upon us.'

Within a hundred years, Fountains Abbey became one of the largest and wealthiest religious houses in the country as a leading producer and exporter of wool. Scores of laybrothers joined the monks as shepherds, farm workers, tanners and stonemasons. But in 1539, the Abbey was closed as part of the dissolution of the monasteries and its great wealth seized.

The dank weather, and a heavy mist that hovers over the ground, adds to the mysterious, eerie atmosphere as I walk through the extensive ruins. Pigeons, jackdaws and sparrowhawks fly around Huby's Tower as the Skell river burbles past the ancient sandstones. 'You've got the place to yourself today, it seems,' says David, a jovial National Trust volunteer guide.

But I have not only come to see the ruins. I meander past the mirrored ponds and follies of the nearby Studley Royal Estate water garden and head up the main avenue towards an elegant, steepled, grey church, perched on a hill. A herd of more than forty deer including four stags stand watch in front of the building.

St Mary the Virgin church is one of the finest High Victorian Gothic Revival churches in England. The opulent edifice was designed by William Burges and commissioned by the Marquess and Marchioness of Ripon in 1870, when they were the owners of the estate. Inside are intricately patterned floor tiles and mosaics, together with stunning carvings, richly coloured stained glass and splendid columns.

80. Stone carving of the Annunciation on the entrance porch, St Mary the Virgin Church, 1870, Studley Royal, North Yorkshire

But it is the outside gable end of the South Porch that, for me, holds the special attraction. The welcoming sight for visitors as they enter the church is a wonderful stone carving of the Annunciation with the angel Gabriel kneeling and pointing to heaven on the left as he looks towards Mary, standing in a separate niche on the right. She raises her hand in alarm, having been disturbed whilst reading. The dove of the Holy Spirit hovers above them.

Today, the Fountains Abbey-Studley Royal Estate is a UNESCO world heritage site. Whether it is the magnificently preserved ruins of the nine-hundred-year-old Abbey or the stunning Victorian structure of the church of St Mary's, it is clear that the cult of Mary imbues this special place.

————

Nearly fifty years ago in 1968, my family moved from the West Riding of Yorkshire to Lincoln. I was ten years old and attended Our Lady of Lincoln Roman Catholic primary school for a year before moving on to the local boy's state grammar school, Lincoln School. I lived in Lincoln for eight years before heading off to university.

Whilst undertaking this annunciation journey, I have had a bit of a niggle that will not go away. I remember vaguely that somewhere in Lincoln during those childhood years, I regularly used to see a depiction of the Annunciation. I cannot remember what it looked like or where it was sited but I know it played a significant part in my life somehow. I decide to head to Lincoln to try to discover the whereabouts of the mystery image.

The magnificent, imposing edifice of Lincoln Cathedral stands in a commanding position on the northern edge of a gap in Lincolnshire's long limestone escarpment. High on the steep hill, its distinctive three towers can be seen from twenty-five miles away across the flat Lincolnshire countryside. A thousand years after the Romans had developed a legionary fortress called Lindum Colonia, the Cathedral was established on the orders of William the Conqueror in the late eleventh century and dedicated to the Blessed Virgin Mary of Lincoln, celebrating her pivotal role as the mother of Christ, first revealed at the Annunciation.

In the Middle Ages, Lincoln became a major centre of Christian pilgrimage and was regarded as the most Marian city in England. Thousands of people came to the Cathedral each year to pray before a statue of the Virgin and Child that was later destroyed during the Reformation. By the twelfth century, Mary had become the patroness of the city. To this day, Lincoln still has strong Marian connections, hence the name of my former primary school – Our Lady of Lincoln – and the clear memory I have of the Lincoln School sixth-form badge, comprising a fleur-de-lis alongside a figure of the Virgin and Child.

I enter Lincoln Cathedral via the stunning West Front and walk along the spacious nave looking for clues. Accompanying me is a former headmaster and now volunteer guide, Bill Stead. We come to a Victorian stained-glass window half way down the north side of the nave, which contains a panel showing a classic Annunciation scene.

At the Reformation, iconoclasts destroyed all the original stained glass in the nave and the present windows were installed during the 1860s and 1870s as the Oxford Movement became established within Anglicanism. This richly coloured window was designed by the Victorian stained-glass design firm, Ward & Hughes, and, according to the bottom of the panel, was presented to the Cathedral 'by George Tomline Esq of Bilby Grove in this county' in 1869. It is a lovely depiction but it is not that Annunciation image I remember as a child. We find three more Annunciations in windows in the south transept and south-east transept but none of them, unfortunately, spark any recognition.

81. Ward and Hughes stained glass window, nineteenth century, North Aisle of the nave, Lincoln Cathedral

I walk towards the great East Window – the largest thirteenth-century window in the world –and notice a striking statue in a side chapel at the far south-east end of the building. It is called 'Our Lady of Lincoln' and is a seven foot high, three-dimensional sculpture of the Virgin Mary. It is one of the largest works to be commissioned by the Dean and Chapter at Lincoln since the Reformation.

82. Aidan Hart *Our Lady of Lincoln*, 2014, Lincoln Cathedral

Created by the liturgical artist and sculptor, Aidan Hart, an ordained Reader of the Greek Orthodox Church in Britain, it depicts Mary as the Mother of God with Christ as a baby in front of her, surrounded by a *vesica* representing heaven and his divinity. The *vesica* also represents her womb, which, uniquely, held God, divine and human. The sculptor aimed to create a striking artistic work that 'manifests the world transfigured in Christ in accordance with the Byzantine icon tradition.'

Hart carved it by hand from a three-tonne block of Lincolnshire limestone, quarried near Grantham. The final product weighs one and a half tonnes. The statue was polychromed using egg tempera and azurite and ochre pigments, together with gold leaf. Mary wears a red dress to represent Earth and her humanity. Her blue mantle symbolizes heaven and the Lord's divinity. Jesus's robe is orange to represent the sun 'because he is the giver of light and life.' He holds an orb, a blue sphere of the world, in his left hand, symbolizing God as creator of the universe and sustainer of the cosmos. He raises two fingers on his right hand to represent his divine and human nature. Mary sits on a throne as the Queen of Heaven and below her, at the base of the statue, are the words: 'The Word was made flesh.'

Aidan Hart hopes his statue can give fresh insight into the mystery of the Incarnation as well as providing a place of contemplation that can inspire people to pray for reconciliation for the whole Christian community.

'The Incarnation is the greatest paradox of them all,' he said in a recent lecture about this sculpture. 'The Pantocrator dwells in the womb, the Creator becomes created. He who is boundless becomes bounded by flesh and yet is still sustaining the universe by the word of his power.'

The Dean of Lincoln, the Very Reverend Philip Buckler, states: 'This sculpture will draw many to reflect upon the obedience and trust that Mary displayed when called to be part of God's redeeming works.' For me, the statue is striking because it can be seen along the full length of the Cathedral. Mary's piercing gaze has an extraordinary impact, her expression a mixture of sadness, joy and sorrow.

I leave the Cathedral no wiser as to the whereabouts of that lost Annunciation image but enriched at seeing this memorable sculpture, a fine example of old and new conjoining. It was an exciting and risky commission, and I feel that Aidan Hart's courage and sensitivity has paid off.

A mile and a half from the Cathedral, I come to Our Lady of Lincoln Roman Catholic church on the Ermine estate. I served as an altar boy here in the late 1960s, soon after it was built. Next door is the primary school that I attended. I have not been back in almost forty years. Is there anything here that can offer a clue to that childhood image that is parked in my distant memory? I walk into the Lady Chapel, lit by a number of blue votive candles. A small stone statue of the Virgin and Child stands on a white altar cloth embroidered with the words: 'Our Lady of Lincoln Pray for Us.' I find nothing relating specifically to the Annunciation here.

I leave the church disappointed and head down Steep Hill to the bustling shops and arcades of the city's main retail area, resigned to the fact I will not be able to resolve the mystery. I walk over the twelfth-century High Bridge – the oldest bridge in Britain still to have buildings on it – feeling frustrated and a little despondent. But then something stops me in my tracks. I turn round and look back and there, straight ahead, is The Stonebow, an early sixteenth-century Tudor building. It forms an archway over the High Street and houses the Guildhall where the city council has held meetings in session over the past 500 years.

I retrace my steps and walk towards The Stonebow, situated on the original site of the historic south gate to the Roman settlement and which derives its name from the Norse word *stennibogi* meaning stone arch. It was built of limestone in 1520 by William Spencer, eleven years before Henry VIII stood up in Parliament and demanded that all members of the Church in England recognize him as Supreme Head and Sole Protector of the Church in England. Today, it is a Grade One listed building and is a regular meeting place for Lincolnians who use the catchphrase, 'I'll see you at the Bow.' When I lived here, cars and buses passed under the archway and I can remember double-decker buses moving gingerly through the tight space, before this area of the High Street became pedestrianized in 1972.

It suddenly hits me like a stone to the head. This is the place I have been looking for. I remember now…each time I passed by, I would see Mary and Gabriel. I rush forward and stand in front of the south façade. There, in niches on either side of the central arch, stand the two familiar figures of the Annunciation.

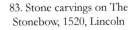

83. Stone carvings on The Stonebow, 1520, Lincoln

On the west side, stands the long, narrow statue of the Virgin Mary, with flowing hair and hands crossed over her chest. On the east side is the angel Gabriel, holding a bunch of lilies in his right hand and a scroll in his left, with his feet firmly on the ground and his wings dropping behind him. I remember now why these statues were so important to me. I know it sounds crazy but nearly every time I would meet a friend here or pass through the archway on the bus on the way home, I would whisper the opening lines to the Angelus when I saw the statues. Looking back, it became a teenage ritual. I would look at Gabriel and quote: 'The Angel of the Lord declared unto Mary' and then at Mary when saying: 'and she conceived of the Holy Spirit.' It was more a sense of habit and superstition than a moment of deep reverence. But now, nearly fifty years later, I wonder. Did this ritual indicate a strong early identification with the story that became sublimated for many years until I saw Lemoyne's painting at The National Gallery? Did exposure to that picture reawaken ideas, beliefs and memories that I had forgotten were there? Perhaps a psychiatrist could answer that, but as I look up at those two familiar figures and recite those words once again, I feel relieved that I have resolved my niggle, yet intrigued by my teenage ritual.

Southwell is the smallest cathedral town in England. There's been a place of Christian worship on this site for almost fourteen hundred years. Its Minster is dedicated to the Blessed Virgin Mary, and is the Anglican cathedral for the Southwell and Nottingham-shire Diocese as well as being the local parish church for the town.

Set amongst the rounded Norman arches and intimate chapels, is an exhibition entitled *The Art of Mary*, in which twenty-two nationally acclaimed artists consider 'Mary, one of the most significant but neglected figures in our shared cultural story.' In the accompanying guide, an essay by the Reverend Canon Dr Julie Gittoes from Guildford Cathedral entitled 'The Art of Mary: her Maker's Maker', describes Mary as, 'an exemplar of faithfulness, trust, obedience and humility. She has become for us a pattern of grace, endurance and hope. She is receptive to the outpouring of the Holy Spirit from the moment of annunciation to the day of Pentecost. She ponders and praises, she protests and prays…Mary's story is a tapestry of joys and sorrows; depictions of her are drenched in symbolism. Her story is overlaid with our hopes and fears; we interpret her words, celebrate her character and fill her silences.'

Three works in particular grab my attention as soon as I set eyes on them. All depict the Annunciation in some form. Susie Hamilton's *and the angel departed from her* is a small oil painting that depicts Mary pondering the news soon after Gabriel has departed. She sits alone on a stool looking ahead towards a rather bleak, dark area made up of thick black and green brush strokes. In contrast, the departing angel leaves behind an intense radiance. Susie Hamilton focuses on 'figures in emptiness' and likes to use light as a spiritual metaphor.

84. Susie Hamilton *and the angel departed from her*, 2015. © Susie Hamilton

As the artist describes it, 'Mary is on her own, abandoned by the divine messenger, but she is illuminated by the orangey glow of his message.' I decide to contact her at her studio in Stepney, east London. I ask what she is trying to express in the painting?

'Silence. A meditative stillness,' she replies. 'Balance. A sense of the uncanny. A lot of my work is on a hinge of pain and pleasure, ecstasy and something rather more melancholy. I wanted to express a period of fear and doubt with the black sky and the absent divine, as well as inspiration about the promise and the idea of a shower of gold from the angel's presence. I thought the idea of the angel Gabriel there felt a bit phony. I have an interest in negative theology and so I wanted to have her with a suggestive, pulsating light around her but no other figure in the picture. That sense of abandonment rings true for me. I think if I'd been in that situation I'd think, What on earth was that all about? Where's he gone? I'd be very alarmed and mystified.'

What does the annunciation story mean for her?

'Intersection,' she responds. 'The crossover between what we know, what we think of as real and actual, and what we think of as "Other". I do see it as fact in some odd way. If Christ was born from Mary, there must have been some kind of communication to her to say she would give birth to him. I can't see how it could have happened without some sort of communication between the human and the non-human, the divine.'

And what does Mary mean to her?

'She's a great mother figure and I could do with a mother figure,' she says. 'I'd like her to mean more to me. She means obedience, humility in the best sense of the word, openness and emptiness to what may come along. I wish she could be for me the Mother Mary that people pray to.'

The second picture I view is entitled *Eclat* by the mixed-media artist Gill Sakakini. Again the painting captures a post-Annunciation moment but this time shows Mary, alone in her room, responding to Gabriel's news 'through a bursting, embodied "YES!".' Working in acrylic and crayon, Gill Sakakini depicts a contemporary scene: a teenage girl jumping for joy in her bedroom.

Gill Sakakini used her daughter as the live model in the painting. A bold, botanic wallpaper design forms the backcloth behind Mary. This intimates an enclosed garden (*hortus conclusus*) and is a vehicle for 'emphasizing Mary's emotional interior space'. The artist states in the guide that 'the "garden", like creation itself, shares the immediacy of her joy through the shape of wide open, fully ripe petals which reinforce the openness of her limbs in this accepting gesture.'

85. Gill Sakakini *Eclat*, 2015. © Gill Sakakini

Later, Gill Sakakini tells me how the moment she captures is one that would have been entirely private.

'I was interested in what Mary would have been thinking in her own mind when all the shenanigans had finished and the angel had left. What really would Mary have been thinking when she was left in her own interior space? I've been a mother of three teenagers and a secondary school teacher and so I'm familiar with how so many teenagers today regularly take pictures of themselves jumping. Sometimes Annunciations can be a bit stuffy and a bit adult. I wanted something that didn't necessarily resonate with a middle-aged, art-interested person. I wanted a more contemporary scene of a teenager taking a photo of herself jumping as they all do now. Every part of her body, her whole physical being, is involved in that gesture from fingers to toes and it's a very human, highly energetic response. I thought when everything had settled and she'd said yes, how would she feel? For me, that was my interpretation of her *yes*.'

I am intrigued that she feels an unmarried teenager who found herself unexpectedly pregnant in such extraordinary circumstances would feel so elated that she jumps for joy.

'I'm not denying there were other stages,' she replies, 'but this is the fruit of all those other interior conversations. How can this be? What will become of me? I'm not saying none of that didn't happen but she works through all that and this is when she's finally arrived. I've spent so many days in the Sainsbury's Wing at the National Gallery looking at medieval paintings of the Annunciation. The symbolism of the medieval and Renaissance art is profound but now we don't think that way. The symbols don't mean the same anymore. We're the opposite. So the only symbolism for me here is in the wallpaper with its fecundity of open, ripe petals.'

What does the annunciation story mean for her?

'It means being noticed, being singled out, being chosen. Someone through whom God can fulfil his purposes. As a believer, I read the story with faith. I do think Mary existed and that she was the mother of God. A real, true story rather than myth. We certainly can't explain it but yes, I do believe it.'

86. Nicholas Mynheer *Annunciation*, 2015. ©
Nicholas Mynheer

I leave the north aisle of the nave and head to the north transept. There, a whole range of pictures of Mary are on display but one small painting, by the Oxfordshire artist and sculptor, Nicholas Mynheer, stops me in my tracks. It's part of a series of eleven small oil paintings depicting *Scenes from the Life of Mary*.

Annunciation, the one I am particularly interested in, shows Mary and Joseph asleep in bed together as the angel Gabriel arrives as in a dream, presenting a bunch of lilies and holding his hand above them, seemingly in an act of blessing. I've never seen such a rendition of the Annunciation before and I am unsure of my own response to it. Is the subject matter scandalous or is it simply realistic?

I contact Nicholas Mynheer and he begins by telling me that he could quite easily work on the Annunciation for the rest of his life. 'Each time I look at it, I end up saying something or being told something quite different. It's so open.'

So, what was he trying to convey in this particular painting?

'I wanted to portray that moment that Mary feels the angel speaking to her in a dream and, because I'm not a biblical illustrator, things just appear. As I sketched it out with paint, Joseph appeared in the bed and I thought that was a really powerful message. The Annunciation was speaking to Joseph as it was just to the Virgin, even though there's no scriptural reference to that happening together. It refers to him being told in a dream not to be afraid to take Mary, but it's an annunciation that's to both of them. Mary is hearing her own message too.'

Is he suggesting that Mary and Joseph were in bed together before they were married?

'That comes out of my own confusion about exactly what betrothed meant in their times,' he says. 'At what point was one married? It was understood that when you were betrothed that you were with that person so, yeah...I just felt they were in a partnership and it would have been perfectly natural for them to be in bed together. It didn't cross my mind whether it was a marriage in the old or modern sense but they were clearly together in a relationship. It wasn't intentional that I wanted to do something different. It just appeared. And as soon as I drew it, I knew it was right. What comes out for me is that the angel was speaking to them both and not just to Mary. Biblically, I know it seems that the angel was speaking slightly later to Joseph but for me here he was speaking to them both together. In that sense it was a new beginning for them both. They were both giving themselves to God. Ok, it might not have happened at that precise moment in time but it was only when I was painting it that I realized yes, it was an annunciation to them both.'

I wondered if Southwell Minster staff had expressed any concern about this controversial depiction.

'No,' he replies. 'I don't think people really look. They look at the whole scheme of things and don't really look at the detail. However, there's a good chance someone will have mentioned it by the end of the exhibition. I'll be glad if it creates a response.'

What does Luke's story mean to him?

'The draw for me, what fascinates me, is the relationship between the angel and Mary and how she responds. She wasn't horrified, she accepted it, whether in a reality or in a dream. Maybe there's no difference. The fact is she accepted it. She was more bothered about how she was going to deal with it rather than whether to accept it. That's so intriguing. Presumably such was her faith that she wasn't horrified. I've always felt that she was an incredibly strong, powerful, single-minded person who I see not as meek and mild but almost ripping the lilies out of the angel's hand. I'm a very simple person really, brought up as an Anglican in the Anglo-Catholic tradition, so I see the story literally. I've never questioned that it's just a metaphor. I assume it happened but whether she dreamt it and this is the right expression of it or whether the angel appeared in bodily form doesn't interest me. I don't care. It happened in some form. It wasn't apocryphal.'

On a leafy suburban road in Newark, Nottinghamshire, I find the house I have been looking for. I am invited into the large semi-detached Edwardian red brick home, then led through the well-nurtured garden to the artist's workshop that is situated in the grounds. I enter and find myself confronted by an extraordinary range of wooden sculptures of all shapes and sizes. There are crucifixes, Christos figures, various saints, a Pieta, Madonnas and angels. Some are completed. Others are works in progress. Pieces of driftwood and yarra wood, ready to be carved and shaped, lie piled up on a table and on the floor. Medieval sacred music plays in the background.

Peter Eugene Ball is Britain's most prolific and best-known contemporary religious sculptor. His work adorns more than eighty cathedrals and churches around the country. In 1993, Winchester Cathedral hosted a solo exhibition of his work to mark the nine hundredth anniversary of the building. Twenty years later, Winchester College mounted a major exhibition and it is Ball's large Christos figure on the wall of Thurbern's Chantry in Chapel that replaced Lemoyne's *The Annunciation* painting when it was taken down in 2011.

Seventy years old, with gleaming white hair, he looks fit, lean and healthy. Dressed in a denim shirt, white T-shirt and tight blue jeans, he looks more like a rock star than a sculptor of religious art. He is extraordinarily open, warm and friendly from the moment I shake hands with him. He has an infectious enthusiasm and a loud, bellowing laugh that erupts at regular intervals.

Born in Coventry, he attended Coventry College of Art and by twenty-four he had his first solo exhibition in the Marjorie Parr Gallery on the King's Road, Chelsea. His work then was described as diverse and eclectic and, certainly, there was little hint of the transcendent religious figures that would come to dominate his highly successful work in later life. During his early career, he travelled widely with a friend studying Romanesque, Celtic and pre-historical works and says he realized then how art can be both innocent and sophisticated simultaneously.

He made his first religious piece fifty years ago – a simple crucifix that was bought by a priest at Westminster Cathedral – but it wasn't until 1986 that regular church commissions became an integral part of his life and art. Although devotional pieces now dominate his work, he still creates witty and idiosyncratic secular figures that reflect his wry sense of humour.

As we start to talk about his creativity and inspiration, he tells me, 'It's completely mine. I'm not swayed by modern trends of art. Yes, I produce contemporary art but it's not pastiche. The religious objects have to be devotional and yet theatrical at the same time.'

He was baptized, although the household in which he grew up was not religious. His father was an ardent communist and he describes his mother as 'superstitious'.

'When I was fourteen, I was sort of religious in an adolescent sort of way but no longer,' he says. 'But I don't want people to think I'm doing it all for reasons of income. There's a paradox in all this. I tend to be quite a simple person really. As far as religion is concerned, when I open a church door I need all the help I can get. There is a sense of theatre in being in a church…in the liturgy and the art. When I make the pieces, I'm very touched by them. You don't have to believe in Christ to know there is suffering. And as a sculptor, I'm not only dealing with a philosophical subject, I'm also dealing with form. When I'm dealing with these highly emotive subjects, when you think about it, they are the most important subjects confronting us as human beings. They are questions of life and death. Not many modern artists today deal in these subjects.'

He says his work has 'to give out something'. I ask what he means by that.

'People have to take something from it personally,' he responds. 'They have to go away with something. When I see a lot of modern art, semi-abstract art in churches, I find them non-decorative. When people pray in front of an object, it's a one-to-one relationship and they need something out of that and it's awfully difficult to give something out of an abstract image. People need a recognition.'

He pauses and checks I am content with the way the conversation is proceeding, before continuing.

'You're absolutely right that I don't go there myself but there is something.' His voice tails off for a short while before he picks up the thread again. 'I had a big conversation once with David Stancliffe, the former Bishop of Salisbury, about the relationship between the objects I'm making, what other people get from them, and what I can give to them. I don't know the answer to it. The Master of St Cross in Winchester once said to me, "You're a sacrament." I can't understand this. I think he meant I can't help it. I'm literally an instrument.'

I suggest that, being able to produce work that enables people to feel such deep emotion and acts as an aid to prayer, is an extraordinary gift.

'I feel slightly embarrassed about it if I'm honest. I've got pieces in more than eighty cathedrals and churches. It's not my intention to be religious. The work that comes out when I make religious art is accidental in many ways. I'm not conscious of making a religious object even though some of the qualities like the serenity of Mary may come out. I'm an artist who works. I'm in a studio working. I'm seeing them in an aesthetic way. I think the worst artists are Christian artists because they're too literal and too intense.'

He has created many different images of Mary – devotional pieces with titles such as the *Madonna and Child*, the *Pieta*, *Our Lady Seat of Wisdom*, *Black Virgin* – but also humorous pieces such as *Virgin Adrift* and *Contraption for Elevating the Virgin*.

'The humorous pieces I make for myself,' he tells me. 'It's looking at the way the Virgin has been elevated over the centuries. But also, without being irreligious, the Church can make mistakes with canonisations. But they wouldn't go into a religious setting. They're too critical.'

I comment that Mary seems central to his work and that many of his commissions feature her holding a maturing Christ-child rather than a baby.

'It's a matter of taste. A hundred and fifty years ago, you'd have produced a Madonna with a baby. I don't produce babies. My Christ figures sitting on their mother's lap are eleven to twelve years old. You can't express the inevitability of the crucifixion through a very young child. If it's an eleven-year-old, he sees his eventual doom. Babies tend to be too sentimental.'

I ask for his thoughts on Mary.

'It's a mixture,' he says. 'She comes in all forms and guises from the wise to, these days, the ordinary mother. It hasn't got to be too hieratic. Not "Mary above us". Women want to relate to her being part of their own experience – an ordinary woman giving birth to a child. But some times you do want to make her a Queen of Heaven and that's part of the theatre. It just depends on the commission.'

On a worktable nearby stands a beautifully crafted angel entitled *Gabriel*. He is made of driftwood and is just over two foot high. His face is covered in gold leaf, his chest is inflated as though he is announcing 'I'm here', and he stretches his wings out like a proud peacock displaying his feathers.

87. Left: Peter Eugene Ball *Madonna and Child*, 2011. Right: *Angel Gabriel*, 2014. © Peter Eugene Ball

'Because of my interest in classical art and ancient art, angels on the surface are a Christian concept but, of course, well beforehand, the minor gods brought messengers,' he explains. 'I think of my angels basically as messengers.'

I am intrigued that, over the years, he has created so many versions of Mary and many single pieces of the angel Gabriel but has never brought the two of them together in an annunciation work. He tells me he once almost had a commission for an annunciation piece from a church in Brighton but, in the end, they couldn't afford it.

'Perhaps it's not relevant to the way people think. You're dealing with a subject that even those who are religious may have grave doubts about. The advancement in medicine and childbirth in the last hundred years or so cuts out the idea of falling pregnant without sexual intercourse. I think it's very difficult, even for people who on the surface are religious, to accept it.'

Although the Annunciation was hugely popular in inspiring so many great works of art in medieval times, for Peter Ball, commissions for an annunciation are non-existent.

'I think it's difficult for the reason I said. People can relate to Mary herself – an ordinary woman or Queen of Hearts or even Stella Maris – but the idea of the Annunciation seems ridiculous to most people now.'

We look at the detailed sketches he made some years ago for the potential annunciation commission for the Church of the Annunciation in Brighton. The sculpture would have been made from wood, copper and gold leaf and the design is highly unusual. A winged angel Gabriel, around six foot tall, stands directly behind a seated Mary, and they are both positioned facing straight ahead. Her left hand is outside of her garment and resting on her right breast. Gabriel has placed both his arms round the front of her body in a comforting gesture. Their eyes are closed.

88. Peter Eugene Ball's initial sketches of an Annunciation sculpture. © and by kind permission of Peter Eugene Ball

What was he trying to show in this piece?

'First of all, I don't believe in the Annunciation,' he says. 'I think it's a metaphor as most religious precepts are metaphors. I believe in metaphors but not in actualities. I was thinking of the angel Gabriel being very protective – much more personal than just appearing and you know, "I've come from heaven and you're pregnant". I wanted something more intimate.'

I mention that it is unusual for Gabriel to be depicted standing directly behind Mary.

'It's the same protector idea as the Virgin having her hand around the child,' he replies.

I ask what he considers to be the message of the annunciation story. There's a long pause before he responds, 'I don't really know. Protection…Calling?'

Was there a sense of disappointment that the commission did not go ahead?

'Yes, I thought it was a good design.' He pauses and looks at his sketches before moving on. 'Unless you're a religious person who actually dispenses with any rationality…' He pauses again. 'You see as an artist, I have to be conscious of making rational decisions in art and, although I believe in metaphors, I don't believe in literal things. When you're talking about the Annunciation, you're asking people to believe that Joseph didn't go to bed with her, which is very difficult in these days when everyone is sexually conscious. It's such a difficult subject to most people. You've got to have a rational sense about you. They can accept suffering and the crucifixion. Suffering is a common thing – it touches us all. But a phantom pregnancy does not.'

Why does he think he receives regular commissions for angels but not for the Annunciation?

'I think angels, because they're messengers of the gods, have always been attractive to people. They're accessible. Angels can be a metaphor for all sorts of things in life – good luck, bad luck.'

Does he feel that he has had a calling?

'It's such a paradox, isn't it?' he replies. 'Yes, but not a religious calling, rather an artistic calling. And I've only found that because the subject matter is such a big one – life and death, suffering, which is ever present and relevant all the time all through the ages. It's the biggest question of them all. That's one of the motivations for doing it. I don't know why I do it reasonably well. The idea of making art is communication.'

But has he had any sense of a religious calling?

'No,' he replies firmly. 'I feel a calling to be an artist. I'm very conscious I'm trying to say something about an ongoing important subject which I have an input into as an individual. The great thing about it is that people relate to it and that's the only reason for doing it.'

When he is working on a religious sculpture, does he ever pause and wonder?

'I do, of course, particularly after I've made the object.'

What happens then? I wonder.

'I dismiss it because I don't have a faith,' he replies. 'The other paradox is when I see a Romanesque crucifix in Spain or the south of France, I'm very, very moved by them because they're exquisitely beautiful. But how can they be exquisitely beautiful when they are about suffering? But, of course, they can be. It's the aesthetics. When I see those objects, I believe. I believe in Christ on the Cross. But when I'm away from the image, I don't. It's the actual image and, just for that moment, that makes me feel, well…'

So, just for a split second, I suggest, he may believe, but then he goes back to where he was.

'It has to be,' he responds. 'Whether that's got anything to do with believing in God or Jesus or is a reaction to our aesthetic, theatrical experience…I think now it's a bit of both. I don't believe in God but in that moment I could have.'

He takes hold of a Madonna sculpture that he has recently completed. He then grabs another angel Gabriel he has made from driftwood, covered with pewter, copper and gold leaf. His large wings look as though they're flapping furiously behind him, billowing in the wind.

'The gravity of the message is in the face,' he declares.

He stares intently at the two figures. It is as though he has unintentionally created a makeshift Annunciation piece here and now.

'I believe when I look at my work, I believe in hope,' he says. 'That's what makes me go on. The objects are about hope. Even though I don't believe in the actual nitty-gritty things of whether Christ was a man or whether he was God or part of the Trinity – these things don't interest me – but the images are all about hope. The great untold subject, which nobody has got anywhere near to.'

What does he hope will be the legacy of his work?

'Hope is the subject I want to convey. The idea will always be going on. Trying to solve our problems. Hoping to be happy.'

Would he like to have a faith?

'Yes, I would like to,' he replies. 'It would give me the chance of thinking all this work I've done is not in vain. But I can't go that far. I don't believe in Christ's Incarnation and his resurrection but I do believe in the metaphor. I believe in the hope it gives us.'

I take out of my bag the print of Lemoyne's Annunciation.

'I've already seen it at Winchester College,' he declares. 'The first thing is when I look at it, it doesn't move me. The aesthetic elements do not give me that intense idea of its subject matter. That's my personal opinion. I find it superficial. It doesn't tell me anything. It gives me an illusionistic idea like God being a white bearded guy sitting on the clouds. It's very simple. There's no intensity. It's fitting for the early eighteenth century but it's far too literal and sentimental. It doesn't say anything. It's gesture. And that's what's wrong with Christian art generally.'

As our conversation draws to a close, I ask him if he thinks he'll ever create an annunciation piece.

'Yes, if someone asks. But you've got to have a reason.'

Three hours later, and the splendid sight of Ely Cathedral, standing prominently on the east Cambridgeshire fens, comes into view. Inside, I make my way along the recently constructed Processional Way that stands on the foundations of the original Lady Chapel passage used by medieval pilgrims. I pass under a newly installed ceiling boss of the angel Gabriel. Designed by Peter Ball, the angel's golden face and open palms glisten in the light above me. Just a few seconds earlier, I would have been admiring a striking *Christ in Glory* statue by the same prolific sculptor that hangs above the Cathedral's main pulpit and was installed in 2000 to mark the new millennium.

I head towards the largest Lady Chapel in Britain. It was built between 1321 and 1349 to honour the Blessed Virgin, when the cult of Mary was at its most intense. Upon its completion, the huge chapel was elaborately decorated with stained-glass windows and elegantly carved stone statues, all marking the story of Mary's life. However, during the Reformation two centuries later, much of that decoration was destroyed. Statues of saints were removed, paint stripped off the walls, and windows broken. Today, a number of stone statues whose heads have been smashed act as a stark reminder of the damage caused by the iconoclasts.

A cathedral guide describes the chapel as 'a place of brokenness and an eloquent reminder of the power of religious ideas and the way they can be used destructively.' We are asked to pause for a moment in silence and consider praying about the brokenness, loss or grief that we, too, may have experienced in our lives.

Above the altar, at the far eastern end of the chapel, stands an extraordinary statue of Mary, commissioned in 2000 to mark the millennium. Designed by the British sculptor, David Wynne, it is a life-size effigy of Mary, who stands fifteen feet above the ground on a stone window ledge, with her arms stretched high above her head. Carved from Portland stone and weighing half a ton, it captures the moment when Mary exults at the news of her conception and says yes to her new vocation. On the base of the statue are the words: *Behold the handmaid of the Lord.*

Mary wears an electric-blue dress with a gilt belt around her waist and leans back in delight. Her long golden hair hangs loosely down her back and her eyes are closed. Part of her bare left foot is visible below the hem of her dress. When viewed from the side, her tummy appears to protrude slightly.

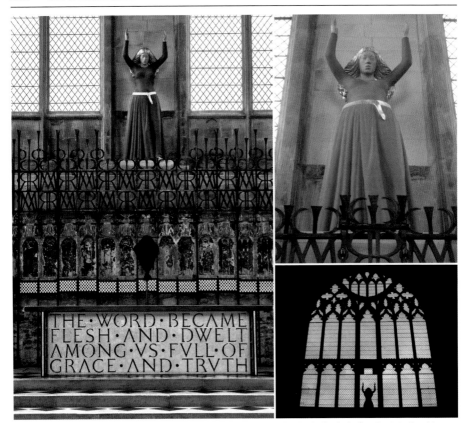

89. Left: David Wynne *The Virgin Mary*, 2000, Lady Chapel, Ely Cathedral. © John Morley. Top Right: Close up of the statue. Bottom Right: Dusk in the Lady Chapel, Ely Cathedral. © Leslie Monk

The Prince of Wales unveiled it fifteen years ago, and immediately the statue proved to be highly controversial. The striking clash of the modern sculpture set against the medieval Lady Chapel was too much for many of its critics. 'Unspeakably hideous'; 'blasphemous'; 'a bra-less Charlie Dimmock' (referring to the TV gardening presenter); 'a cheap looking, shabby, sub-standard travesty'; 'bad art and feeble fakery' were just some of the more printable descriptions.

But other reactions following its installation could not have been more different, praising 'such a positive image'; 'a wonderful, uplifting vibrancy'; 'at last, a statue of Mary that promotes the importance of women, not their subjugation.' Indeed, Vivienne Faull, the Dean of York, had described it earlier on my journey as one of her favourite annunciation pieces. She loves the freedom and independence in Mary and the way in which she is 'claiming the space'.

The label next to the statue acknowledges this apparent polarisation of views: 'since its unveiling, it has been a source of controversy, bearing little resemblance to a first-century girl from Palestine. Yet, unlike many images, which show Mary as a rather meek, passive figure, this one portrays her as strong, determined and attractive. She is a "real" woman, stepping forth into God's costly call upon her life.'

A cathedral guide tells me, 'She's like marmite. You either love it or you hate it with very little in between. I'd say the majority dislikes it. Many intensely. Some say it should be moved to another less prominent place in the Cathedral. Others want it taken out altogether. Then again, yesterday, one visitor told me it was the best and most moving Mary she's ever seen. "Yes!" she exclaimed to me. Actually, she became very emotional.'

Sitting directly below the statue in the twilight of the late afternoon, I am joined by Mark Bonney, the Dean of Ely. After studying Music at Cambridge and then Theology at Oxford, he was ordained in 1985. He served as Precentor at St Albans Cathedral, then Canon Treasurer at Salisbury Cathedral, before arriving here less than two years ago to lead the Cathedral Chapter. Aged fifty-seven, he is married with two daughters and my first impression is of a studious, reserved, rather shy intellectual with short, neatly cut grey hair and metal-rimmed glasses perched on his nose. However, the Dean soon turns out to be surprisingly open and loquacious.

He begins our conversation by recalling a particular moment when he 'felt challenged' and then 'being turned around'. He says he was brought up in a Christian family and always went to church. He never seriously doubted the existence of God but 'in my mid-teens, I was quite happy for God and me to go our separate ways.'

Then at Cambridge, as a choral exhibitioner, the chaplain invited him for sherry and suddenly asked, 'Do you have a faith?' and he replied 'No.'

'It was a very important moment for me, recognizing where I was, because it was the moment I began my own journey,' he tells me. 'I didn't like my answer although it was honest. So my attendance at Chapel increased very dramatically from that moment. Seven or eight months later, that same chaplain said, "Oh Bonney, you'd make a good priest." That niggling idea then never went away.'

What does he make of the annunciation story?

'It's a critical moment. A focal moment of a "yes to God" that is the beginning of God incarnate,' he replies.

Does he see it as a fact or a metaphor? I ask.

'I see it as metaphor. One of the reasons for that is it only appears as an account in Luke's Gospel. There's the angel and Joseph in Matthew. There's nothing in Mark and John. And St Paul can quite happily preach without any reference to the birth of Christ whatsoever. I veer to the metaphorical understanding of what that story is about.'

So, he doesn't think the encounter between Mary and the angel actually happened?

'I'm agnostic about it,' he responds. 'That's a good Anglican answer,' he chuckles to himself before continuing. 'When I say in the Creed "incarnate of the Virgin Mary", I think I am heading to the metaphoric rather than the literal virginal conception, probably on biblical grounds.'

I ask him if there's a single word that sums up the story?

'It's certainly about calling, obedience…and also about recognition, an entering into a deeper relationship with God. The ability to hear and to listen.' He continues: 'We think of angels with wings but the word *angelos* means messenger. God's message comes to us in all sorts of hidden ways. So it's about our receptiveness and our being open, getting to hear those messages and clearing away the things that stop us from hearing and being obedient.'

What does he think of the Annunciation being described as 'the most important event in human history'?

'It is,' he replies, 'because without it, there couldn't have been the Incarnation. Although we don't know if he would have asked someone else…indeed, we don't know if he asked ten women before that who said no, do we?' he chuckles again. He pauses again for a while in thought before continuing. 'Paul preaches without any reference to it at all. If we didn't have Luke's Gospel account, we'd be seriously deprived at many levels but I still think we could preach the gospel because the Resurrection for me is at the heart.'

Does he feel that the feast of the Annunciation has become a bit lost?

'Yes, with Lady Day, yes,' he says. 'Here at Ely, we have an extra Eucharist on the feast day. We don't have a sung Eucharist. There's a rather solemn Evensong on the day. We mark the Annunciation but not many come. It has been lost since the Reformation. Within the Anglican tradition, devotion to Our Lady is still tainted with Popery, even today. I'm a funny old mixture. I'm a priest associated with the Shrine of Our Lady of Walsingham and when I'm here in this chapel on a Friday morning, I always use the "Hail Mary" as part of the intercessions.'

Does he venerate Mary? I wonder.

'Yes, I ask for her prayers. I use the Angelus. She is the mother of Jesus.' he responds.

And yet he describes the annunciation story as a metaphor.

'I think it's a theological statement,' he says. 'It's theology. What it's saying about Jesus is what's important. And Mary as somebody pointing to Jesus is what's important to me and her obedience.'

We look towards the David Wynne statue. The light is starting to fade in the Lady Chapel and the sculpture forms an extraordinary silhouette against the large plain-glass window behind the altar.

'I know what I think the artist wants me to see,' he tells me. 'An exuberant, rejoicing Mary. Personally, I don't find it a satisfactory image. I don't think it's very subtle. As I understand it, the maquette wasn't painted. I find the colours rather brash. She looks more like Maid Marian. I don't have a problem with Our Lady not being meek and mild but rejoicing. But it is very unusual to have an image of Our Lady without Our Lord, certainly in an Anglican Lady Chapel.'

We walk towards the statue and look more closely at the silhouetted figure, her arms raised in the air.

'Some people say she's already pregnant but if it's the moment of the Annunciation she wasn't pregnant,' he comments. 'Some people say David Wynne modelled her on a woman four months pregnant and shaped her on that. I'm disappointed by it really. Yes, it brings colour to this place that was missing but the reason the reredos and screen were put in later was to try to ameliorate the sharp distinction between her and the building.'

I ask him to compare Wynne's depiction with the Lemoyne painting.

'Artistically, there's a sense of movement in the whole of Lemoyne's picture that's interesting. Gabriel pointing upwards and Mary looking down. The folds in her clothes are more delicately done. She still looks like a woman of her period.'

Which does he prefer? I ask.

'I wouldn't want either of them in here in some ways,' he responds. 'The Lemoyne painting is too baroque for me…a lot of icons work more powerfully for me.'

I ask him if the Wynne statue still remains controversial here.

'Yes. I don't find it devotional. I've just set up an Exhibitions Advisory Committee. It may not stay. We have another David Wynne piece, *Noli Me Tangere*, in the south transept (where Jesus greets Mary Magdalene after the resurrection). I think that's fantastic. You'd never guess they were by the same person – it's quite extraordinary.'

So, would he prefer it if the sculpture of Mary wasn't here?

'Yes. I'd like a statue of Our Lady here of some description,' he says. 'It may be interesting to treat it like the fourth plinth in Trafalgar Square and try out a number of different representations to see what works. But a Canon colleague here likes it because of the way people can react to it one way or the other. That can be a good thing about a piece of art. I just feel…I don't know…I want it to be…I don't know…I'm not sure I want it to be challenging like that…If that challenge leads people to pray, that's fine but I'm not so sure it does…I'd prefer a Mary figure with a child. Our Lady pointing to Our Lord. That becomes her role.'

CHAPTER 23

PROFOUNDLY TRUE

Walsingham, a picturesque village in north Norfolk, holds a special place in Church history as the most important pilgrimage site in medieval England, a status revived in the early twentieth century and still thriving today. It is known as 'England's Nazareth', and the reason millions of people have come to the village for over almost a thousand years is rooted in the story of the Annunciation.

The Shrine of Our Lady of Walsingham was established in 1061 as a memorial of the Annunciation when, according to tradition, Richeldis de Faverches, a wealthy local noblewoman and devout Christian, prayed that she might undertake some special work in honour of the Blessed Virgin Mary. In answer to her prayer, Richeldis had a vision in which Mary took her to her house in Nazareth where the Annunciation occurred. She asked Richeldis to build a replica of her simple dwelling back in Walsingham 'as a house built in honour of my Salutation'. Mary is said to have declared, 'All who seek me here will find succour.'

Richeldis instructed work to begin straightaway and, guided by Mary, built the replica, which became known as the 'Holy House'. At the time, England was under the Anglo-Saxon King, Edward the Confessor, and the Norman Conquest was still five years away. Marian devotion was growing intensely across the country. It was also the time immediately prior to the first of the medieval Crusades, when it was almost impossible to visit the Holy Land. Pilgrims could feel that, by going to Walsingham, they were visiting Nazareth in their own land. Although the legend claimed that the 'Holy House' was Mary's home transported by angels, the small Saxon structure belied any Galilean character. Rather, it is thought to have been a simple, single-storey construction made from wood, wattle and daub, with a pitched roof.

Around 1130, a community of Augustinian Canons took charge of the structure and built a vast priory church on the site. Inside the 'Holy House', they placed a statue of Mary, Our Lady of Walsingham, with the infant Jesus seated on her lap. By the middle of the twelfth century, Walsingham had become one of the most famous shrines in Europe. Indeed, the four great shrines of medieval Christendom were Jerusalem, Rome, Compostella and Walsingham, the latter being the only one dedicated to Mary, the Mother of God. Thousands of pilgrims flocked to the 'Holy House' each year and the taking of the water from the nearby wells drew the sick and infirm in search of healing.

Much of the information about Richeldis and her vision comes from a medieval ballad printed in 1495 by Richard Pynson, which became known as the 'Pynson Ballad'. It describes how many of the sick were cured at Walsingham by 'Our Ladyes Myghte' and concludes that England has great reason to be glad that it has 'a new Nazareth'. For 400 years, it was said to be the hope of every good Christian in England to visit Walsingham.

As was the custom then, those that sought blessings, healing or forgiveness, brought with them gifts and money, and so the Priory accumulated great wealth. All the kings of England from Henry III in 1226 to Henry VIII in 1511 travelled to Walsingham on pilgrimage. However, when Henry VIII pronounced himself Head of the Church in 1534 and then began the destruction of the monasteries, he ordered the wealth of the Priory to be seized and handed over to the King's Commissioners. In 1538, the Shrine was destroyed and the statue of Our Lady of Walsingham was taken to London and burnt. Nothing remains of the Anglo-Saxon Shrine today but the site of the original 'Holy House' is marked by a small plaque on a lawn in the grounds of the ruins of Walsingham Abbey in the centre of the village.

After the destruction of the Shrine, Walsingham ceased to be a place of pilgrimage for four centuries. But in 1896, Charlotte Pearson Boyd, a recent convert to Roman Catholicism, purchased the Slipper Chapel situated in Houghton St Giles, just outside Walsingham. In medieval times pilgrims would stop there to pray and confess their sins before removing their shoes or slippers to walk the last mile to the 'Holy House' barefoot. When the Shrine was destroyed, the Slipper Chapel passed into disuse, becoming a barn and then a cow byre. Following Ms Boyd's purchase, the chapel was restored but, initially, was little used. Then, Roman Catholics gradually began to return to Walsingham. In 1934, the Slipper Chapel was designated as the Roman Catholic National Shrine of Walsingham and the first public Mass in 400 years was held there. Two days later, Cardinal Bourne led a national pilgrimage of more than ten thousand Roman Catholics and a Pilgrims Mass has been held in the Slipper Chapel at noon every day ever since.

Meanwhile, Arthur Hope Patten, an Anglo-Catholic Church of England priest, became Vicar of Walsingham in 1921. He, too, was determined that Walsingham would become a place of pilgrimage once more. In 1931, he oversaw the building of a new 'Holy House', a replica of the medieval building, set within a new Anglican shrine church in the centre of the village, close to the original site. During the construction, an ancient well was discovered, a link to the pilgrims of the past. Soon, this place became the Anglican Shrine of Our Lady and grew in national importance.

Today, over two hundred and fifty thousand people visit the Shrines each year. I arrive in Walsingham in Christian Unity Week and it strikes me as somewhat sad and ironic that here there are two separate national shrines designated in the name of Christianity. As one guide puts it, the village 'is filled with the spirit of the evangelisation of England and the traumas of the Reformation.'

My first port of call is the Slipper Chapel. I am struck by its diminutive size and stark simplicity. A small prayer card for visiting pilgrims states: 'In 1061 Mary Our Mother promised: "All who are distressed or in any need, let them seek me here in that little house you have made me in Walsingham"... Now let us follow Mary's example by declaring our own Fiat before God by saying: "Let it be done according to your will." Let our thoughts turn to the Mother of Mercy.'

I sit quietly and, after a while, start to look through a small book published by the Catholic Truth Society called *Message of Walsingham* that

90. Marcel Barbeau *Our Lady of Walsingham*, 1954, RC Slipper Chapel near Walsingham, Norfolk

has been left on a table. In one section, entitled 'Understanding Our Lady', it reads:

> Mary is an enigma. On the one hand so close to God; on the other so ordinary and human. It is so easy to exaggerate her role until she seems to be indistinguishable from God himself; it is also easy to minimise her role so she appears to be an ordinary woman indistinguishable from the rest of the human race. To exaggerate or to minimise is not to do justice. The heart of the matter is Mary's relationship with God. As long as she is seen as the 'Christ-bearer', the Mother of God, then she will be seen in her true perspective.

I head into the village to enter the replica of the 'Holy House', a twentieth-century creation with roots firmly in the period of medieval Marian devotion. A sign outside invites people to reflect on life's purpose. I sit inside for half an hour, all alone. It is a tiny room that fewer than ten pilgrims can enter at any one time. Lamps hang on either side of the small altar. Above the altar table is a replica statue of Our Lady of Walsingham and just below is an icon of the Annunciation. Scores of candles flicker on both sides of the

room. Intercession cards are pinned to the walls: 'For Rupert's healing', 'For Ian, that he may come to faith', are just two of them. There are more than fifty Rest-in-Peace messages from relatives of loved ones recently deceased, and prayer cards from different parishes.

A nun enters the room with a mop and starts to clean the floor. I leave quietly and drink a small cup of the holy water that is

91. The 'Holy House' at the Anglican shrine, Walsingham, Norfolk. © Fr. Lawrence Lew O.P.

being offered, taken from the well below.

I walk through the village, passing various gift shops selling Marian wares. The Shrine's shop window is crammed full of statues and icons of Mary as well as various small presentation boxes with rosary beads inside. I notice in the main square, a sign to an Orthodox Chapel. Curious, I walk a few hundred yards up the hill to find St Seraphim's, a Russian Orthodox chapel housed in the former Gentlemen's Waiting Room of the old village railway station that was closed back in 1964. St Seraphim's has been a centre for Orthodox iconography for nearly fifty years. There is no heating inside and it is very cold.

Inside the small, dark room, I stand before the iconostasis, the screen that normally separates the sanctuary from the nave. Here, the screen divides the unseen altar from the rest of the tiny room. The iconostasis has three doorways. The double doors in the centre are called the Royal Doors because 'the King of Glory passes through in the Holy gifts of the Eucharist for the Communion of the faithful.' On the doors is a beautiful icon of the Annunciation. On the left of the Royal Doors is another icon of the Mother of God and beside it on the third door is an icon of the angel Gabriel.

I read how the icons express the heavenly dimension as 'windows into heaven' and how we must look at God and his saints through the icon in order to reveal the way to the Kingdom of Heaven and the nature of the spiritual world.

In this week of Christian Unity, I remember how the Eastern Orthodox Church was united in communion with the Roman Catholic or Latin Church until the East-West schism in the middle of the eleventh century. Indeed, just six years before the legendary vision of Mary by Richeldis de Faverches was alleged to have occurred in this village, the mutual excommunications by the Pope and the Patriarch in 1054 created the biggest watershed in Christian Church history.

What a fascinating place Walsingham is. Two national shrines – one Anglican, the other Roman Catholic – and a tiny Orthodox chapel, all focused on Mary, pilgrimage, and the 2,000 year old story of the Annunciation.

—————

I am lying prostrate on the floor, two-thirds of the way down the central aisle of Norwich Cathedral. I am aware that I may appear ridiculous, but there is method in my madness. The delicate fifteenth-century stone ribbed vaulting above me is studded with bosses that have been intricately carved and decorated to highlight stories from the Old and New Testaments. The reason I am lying on this cold stone floor is because I am trying to get the best possible view of these amazing bosses. There are 255 of them stretching along the nave to the choir, and nowhere in Britain has such a large and impressive collection.

92. Roof boss of the Annunciation above the nave in Norwich Cathedral. © Paul Hurst ARPS

I am interested to see one in particular, at the eastern end of the nave directly above the altar, but it is seventy-two feet up. Luckily, I have come prepared and have brought binoculars to help me make out the details. Eventually, I pull the lenses into focus and see the angel Gabriel running towards Mary, his golden wings flapping behind him. Mary is wearing a gold veil, gold dress and gold mantle, with her right hand placed on her breast. On her left side lies a prayer book, and two lily stems stand between the two figures.

To my embarrassment, an amused Cathedral guide indicates that the best way to see the roof is to use a nearby portable wooden trolley with a large mirrored surface. I thank him, move the wheeled mirror in place and soon I can see not only the magnified Annunciation roof boss but also one close by that shows the angel of the Lord appearing to Joseph in a dream. Joseph has a golden beard and golden cloak. The angel stands behind him and appears to be whispering in his ear. The natural light reveals wonderful, rich colours. Both bosses form part of a twenty-four-piece bay that displays different biblical scenes from the Nativity story.

It is thought that the scenes on the roof bosses were inspired by the travelling mystery plays that were performed regularly in the city during medieval times. The Gothic vault was built in the 1470s after lightning hit the Cathedral's timber spire and the subsequent fire destroyed the wooden roof. Designed by Reginald Ely and created by

master stonemason Robert Everard and his team, the bosses were covered in a wash after the Reformation to hide the biblical stories but this was removed in 1870 and they were all re-painted in the 1930s. It is such a pity that so many visitors seem to be totally unaware of their presence. As they make their way up the nave, nobody cranes their neck to admire the magnificent craftsmanship although, admittedly, it is impossible to see their intricate detail with the naked eye.

I move to the north transept, where the four bays of the vaulted ceiling house a series of bosses that focus on the births and early lives of John the Baptist and Jesus Christ. No fewer than nine of them relate specifically to the story of the Annunciation.

93. Roof boss of the Annunciation above the North Transept in Norwich Cathedral. © Paul Hurst ARPS

Reverend Canon Jeremy Haselock, the Precentor and Vice-Dean at Norwich Cathedral, arrives as planned and comes to sit next to me directly under the bosses. Although the light is starting to fade outside, he has kindly arranged for the spotlights to be switched on, illuminating the whole roof. A former art historian and medieval iconographer, he studied History and Medieval Studies at York before being ordained a priest in 1984 and he has been the Precentor at Norwich for the past seventeen years. A stocky, balding sixty-four-year-old, he is dressed in black with a clerical collar and carries a black Fedora hat.

I ask him about the bosses.

'They tell stories from the life of the Virgin,' he begins. 'It was a complicated but well known story in the Middle Ages, derived principally from distilling incidents and images from the Old Testament and setting them into a Christian context. To answer questions that are posed by the gospel narratives but not answered by the gospel narratives. The Virgin Mary comes into the story at the Annunciation and that begs a whole lot of other questions – who was she, where was she from, how did she get herself into that position? What happens in the apocryphal gospel of St James and other apocryphal gospels is a whole set of stories invented to answer those unanswerable questions.'

He talks about the legendary story of Joachim and Anna: how the barren Anna conceives Mary, how they embrace at the Golden Gate in Jerusalem and how Mary is pledged to the Temple at a young age.

'Of course I believe the Annunciation happened,' he says, 'because it is the central doctrine of the Christian faith – the Incarnation – that God meets man at the point of his greatest need, in human flesh, and the only way to do that is to be born. Perfect God and perfect Man linked in the one person. The Incarnation must have happened and the Bible tells us a story of how it happened. But you can't read that gospel narrative without looking back to the Old Testament. Every word of that gospel is profoundly and deeply true but it is not necessarily historical fact. That was understood in the Middle Ages by the Fathers and the theologians. They could see how these themes were taken from the Old Testament and developed in the New Testament, and they saw it all as a wonderful narrative to enshrine, frame, whatever word you like, the essential truth of the Incarnation. The Annunciation is a wonderful story but it's not new. There are annunciations all through the Old Testament. In order to root the narrative in the expectations of the Jewish people, you use images and language with which they are already familiar.'

So, what does he think is the meaning of the Annunciation?

'It means the most important thing in the world – that the Word was made flesh and dwelt among us. It is the most central fact of the whole Christian revelation. In order to save us from our sins, to meet us at our point of need, Man could be divinized – God became Man that Man might become God. It's this great exchange.'

Does he see it as the most important event in human history?

'Yes,' he responds. 'It is the event that all human history is pointing up to.'

But is he saying that it doesn't really matter if the story did not happen as Luke documented it?

'It can't be proven to be historical fact but it is profoundly true. You have to look at the ingredients of what you need. The theological need is for God to devise a method of redeeming us. There's no time in God. He exists in the eternal now. The moment of creation and the moment of ending is all one in God. When Adam is made, he's envisaging the possibility of the Incarnation then. The Incarnation is always in God's plan. When the time is right, Scripture says, the time to intervene in human history comes again and the Word is made flesh. The pre-existent second person of the Trinity is sent by God and is made flesh.

'The first centuries of Christianity were absolutely dominated, of course, by christological disputes,' he continues. 'How could it be that God could be both fully God and fully Man? Was he not really God or not really Man? This wasn't resolved until the Councils of the fourth century and the problems were there right from the beginning. So when you are devising a gospel story to proclaim the Good News and it's just seventy or eighty years after the birth of Christ, it's written to try and solve some of these problems. And the way to solve them is to say Jesus has no earthly father. There is a virginal conception. He has to be born physically from the womb through the vagina of a woman to be fully human but to be fully God he has no paternal human father.'

So, does he believe that the encounter between the angel Gabriel and Mary actually happened?

'If the story was history and the story was common currency,' he replies, 'then I think Paul would talk about it, the other Gospels would talk about it, rather than starting at the beginning of Jesus's ministry. There are hints there was something odd about Jesus's paternity but they're underneath the level of the Gospels. I believe the annunciation narrative to be profoundly true because it is a beautiful way of expressing a profound theological fact. It's the best possible way there could be to express it. It's not the least important whether the details of the story actually happened historically. It's the theological reality being enshrined, the profound use of Old Testament language – the images and the parallels. It's not a new story. It's a rejigged story. That's why I don't believe it has to be historically true. It has to be theologically true. Even if we didn't have Luke and Matthew's infancy narratives, we'd still have the Incarnation because John says it all in his opening few words – the Word being made flesh. It's the most important intervention there is in human history.'

Is the notion of a virgin conception important to him?

'Yes, but not as a point of history,' he replies. 'If someone said parthenogenetically, it was scientifically impossible here, the medieval mind would say yes, but then for God all things are possible. The really important point is not the gynaecology but the theology – a complete equal pairing between God and human kind – of the Holy Spirit and the Virgin Mary. The true translation of the Greek is that they were absolutely equal partners in that conception. Jesus Christ is totally and truly God and totally and truly human. If there had been a story that Jesus was born of a passing Roman soldier who took advantage of a pretty young girl and then went on his way, if that had been the case, the Incarnation could not be seen in the way it is theologically. The child would be wholly human and wholly human.'

So, what does he say to those who do not believe in the virginal conception?

'They put scientific rationalism above theological import,' he replies abruptly.

Is the concept of Mary's perpetual virginity important?

'Not in the slightest,' he responds firmly.

We move on. What does Mary mean to him personally?

'I have a very high doctrine of her,' he says, 'because of the story of the Annunciation. "Let it be done according to your word." That's what all Christians should do.'

Does he venerate her? I wonder.

'Most certainly. I use my rosary. I say my *Ave Maria* as part of my daily prayers. I venerate her as someone who I believe to have been taken near to the presence of God because she was so crucial. She benefitted from the redeeming behaviour of her Son.'

What does he feel about the current status of the feast of the Annunciation?

'The twenty-fifth of March was deliberately chosen because that previously was known as the date of Good Friday. The patristic mind and the need for it all to be neat and tidy meant that it was important Christ died on the same day as his Incarnation. That's why twenty-fifth of December became Christmas Day. The twenty-fifth of March was fixed as the day of the Annunciation and the Incarnation well before Christmas Day and Christmas is dependent on that. The Incarnation happens at the moment the embryo is, as it were, implanted in the Blessed Virgin's womb, by whatever means.'

So, what does it mean to him when he sees that the roof bosses tell the story of the Annunciation?

'It means so much,' he responds emotionally. 'It means that the story is so important that the medieval mind, and the patristic mind before, saw it as so important that they needed to give it a narrative framework – in order to communicate it and for people to inhabit that truth.'

Before Evensong, I walk round to the Deanery to talk to the Very Reverend Dr Jane Hedges. She came to Norwich from Westminster Abbey eighteen months ago and is the first female Dean in the history of the Cathedral. Married to a teacher and with two sons, she was ordained a deaconess in 1980, a deacon in 1987 and was one of the first women priests to be appointed in 1994. A first tranche pioneer.

We meet in her living room, a large space with three big settees, piles of books ranging from Ruth Rendell and Robert Harris novels to more weighty theological tomes as well as stacks of DVDs. It has a homely rather than studious feel, especially when her two cats start jumping all over the furniture and chasing each other round the room. She talks about her early life: living in Locks Heath in Hampshire and then leaving school to work as a bank clerk. Her mother went to church, but not her father. At seventeen, she first felt God calling her to be ordained a priest although she did not know at the time she could not be one. 'Girls were in the choir; girls were servers; it never occurred to me that we couldn't also be vicars,' she tells me.

Aged fifty-nine with short blonde hair and wearing a pink pullover and black trousers, she has a no-nonsense way about her and says she cannot imagine how we will use the allotted time of an hour to talk about the Annunciation.

I begin by asking what she thinks is the significance of the Lucan story.

'During the time the Church of England was thinking seriously about the ordination of women and all the arguments that were going on,' she says, 'for me, Mary, as a complete character, and not just in the story of the Annunciation, was a huge inspiration. I remember someone in a sermon then describing how Mary had been put on a pedestal in the past, not like a real woman, whereas the story of the Annunciation is very real and down to earth. If you think about it, it was shocking. If I try to relate to how that may have impacted on her, it's a complete disruption on her life, a scandal and the fact she wouldn't be believed – there's so much to it. At one level it's a beautiful story but, when you unpick it, it's really quite shocking. And yet at the same time the "let it be according to your will" offers a huge amount for us to meditate on. What do we want in our own lives? What does God want for us? And how do those things come together?

'Certainly for me, putting myself in the shoes of Mary, she may have had certain assumptions about her life and how it was going to be that, all of a sudden, were shot apart. We might have all sorts of assumptions about what our lives may be like. We live in a world where, to some extent, we take life for granted and then there are times in our lives when something happens suddenly that makes us sit up and makes us realize we can't just take our lives for granted. It's also interesting that Mary did have a choice. She could have said no. For me, that is fundamentally part of my spirituality. God has a will and purpose for us but, with that, we have free will – bringing our will into line with God's will, and that's what Mary did.'

I notice that she avoids direct eye contact with me when she speaks. I tell her some people have said to me that God knew she would say yes even though she had free will.

'That's fascinating,' she replies. 'I can get my head around that even though it does sound odd. Philosophically, God is outside time. Of course, we've all got free will but somehow God does hold it all in some kind of plan. I also believe God makes himself vulnerable and let's us say no. That's why the world goes wrong. God being so loving means letting us go free and that's the painful thing for the Godhead. God can watch us all mess up and make a pig's ear of the world and yet God is all powerful.'

When I enquire if she sees the story of the Annunciation as factual, she pauses for some time before answering.

'I do think it's fact actually,' she responds. 'Whether it happened just like that, I don't know, but, for me, the story is in some sense historical but also it's symbolic. God was in Christ and that could have happened as a normal conception rather than the other way around. I can see why the story was told as they struggled to explain how Jesus was Christ, fully God and fully human. But I can't get too excited about the Virgin Birth. If it wasn't one, it wouldn't bother me too much. But the idea of her perpetual virginity, for me, is nonsense.

'I definitely see Mary as an actual real person who brought up Jesus and had some big calling moments in her life,' she continues. 'For me, there's a lot of reality there. Whether there was an angel or not, I don't know. People have different pictures of angels, don't they? There's a very wide range of pictures of what angels might be. The fact that the story is only recorded in one Gospel doesn't trouble me. The gospels come from different traditions and different faith communities and those stories were around in some communities and not in others. That doesn't make them less true. Not everybody knows everything. With all of the birth narratives, they are all highly theological and once you try to take them apart a bit, they become even more symbolic, and yet, within them, there is such a lot of richness and things to pull out that have so much meaning for us.'

What does she feel about that statement that it is 'the most important event in human history'?

'It depends how you look at it,' she replies, 'but yes, the Incarnation is the foundation of it all. God coming into the world in person in the form of Jesus is a climax.'

What does Mary mean for her personally? Is she a bridge or a barrier to inter-denominational dialogue?

'Mary has become very, very important in a lot of people's spirituality and she's started to be taken more seriously. In the past, there was all this removing of Mary from being an ordinary human being. I think now people have got much more in touch with the reality of Mary and the incredibly important part she played in the ministry of Jesus.'

Does she venerate her? I ask.

'Yes, we do here,' she replies. 'Unusually there isn't a Lady Chapel here at Norwich Cathedral. It was lost at the Reformation. We don't even have a statue of her in the Cathedral. But for many people here, she'd play a very important part.'

I can tell she is a little anxious to draw our conversation to an end. There is time for one last question. Does she feel a parallel between the story of the Annunciation and her own calling?

'There's the phrase "Stepping out in Faith" and that's what we are all called to do,' she says. 'To step out to a place where we don't really know where we are going, where we don't know what's going to happen, but if you trust in God, there is a sense, in the words of Julian of Norwich [the fourteenth-century anchoress and mystic], that "it will be well".'

CHAPTER 24

THE ARCHETYPAL DISCIPLE

I have been invited to Cambridge to attend the Nineteenth International Congress of the Ecumenical Society of the Blessed Virgin Mary. Held over four days in Magdalene College, thirty-five of the six hundred worldwide membership have come together, 'to advance the study of the Blessed Virgin Mary in the Church and, in the light of such study, to promote ecumenical devotion.' The aim of the ESBVM is to show that Christians of many traditions may find a focus in their search for unity in the Blessed Virgin Mary. Delegates have come from the United Kingdom, Ireland, United States, Africa and Lebanon.

Inevitably, the Roman Catholic Church and the Anglo-Catholic wing of the Anglican Communion dominate the group of delegates although individuals such as Fr Jonathan Hemmings, an Orthodox priest from Lancaster, are also present. During the meeting, papers are tabled, lectures are delivered, a variety of Eucharistic services are celebrated, and Marian discussions take place over meals and coffee.

Fr Bill, a member of the mendicant Order of the Servants of Mary, is the Society's General Secretary. He tells me the Annunciation is 'the starting point of our own theological reflection. Without it, the work of salvation would have taken a different character. Everything hinges on it.'

He wears the uniform of a Servite priest: a black tunic, scapular and cowl with a hood attached. When I ask if he thinks it's the most important event in human history, he agrees, stating unequivocally, 'The Church says that very clearly.' He becomes a little prickly when I suggest that the status of the feast day may have been lost and that few people nowadays attend church on 25 March.

Surprisingly, he contends that it is still a central feast within the Church's liturgical year and has not been lost. 'That's headcount importance. I don't think that enters into it really in the terms of its significance and importance. The Annunciation is understood as the sine qua non. If you don't have the Annunciation, nothing else happens.'

We sit either side of a small table late in the evening, and he stresses: 'Good theology is not so much having the right answer; it's having the correct question. So if one asks the right question, things flow from that.'

Again I put forward the argument that the status of the feast day has been diminished.

'The liturgical year is a cycle,' he emphasizes. Then he asks me to name the three birthdays that are celebrated in the Church's year. I name Jesus Christ and Mary but fail to remember John the Baptist. 'They are all highly significant in the unfolding of the story of what salvation is telling us,' he proclaims.

I ask him about Mary's role in inter-denominational dialogue.

'Mary is a central catalyst for ecumenism,' he replies. 'In some ways, she was a factor of disunity during the Reformation. She was seen as a distraction from Christ. The hope now is to return to a continuity of unity and ecumenical devotion to the Virgin Mary.'

At 7 a.m. the next morning, delegates gather in the College Chapel for an Anglican Holy Communion service. Two hours later, I attend a special ecumenical service held in a large lecture theatre before joining a Roman Catholic Mass in an upstairs seminar room. By mid-morning, we've all gathered for the keynote lecture by Rowan Williams entitled 'Holiness and the Sovereignty of Grace: Mary's Discipleship'.

He opens by explaining how Mary embodies discipleship. A disciple is a learner, he says, who is in the process of being formed into a fullness of love.

'The disciple is formed by response…who with open hands and heart responds to an invitation to grow. A disciple is always responding to a calling and a gift, and is always a listener.'

He describes discipleship as a new life that is about to come to birth and that listening is a constant process of being re-born.

'Mary is the archetypal disciple,' he says. 'She heard and believed. Mary hears the word that quite literally creates new life in her. A life that will both feed on her as a child feeds itself from the body of a mother and will form her in that hearing of the word. She receives. She recognizes all that loss and risk involved in becoming a disciple. She says yes from the first moment. That loss of safety and security involved, that moment of the Annunciation is a moment of scandal. That of an unmarried woman, standing on the edge or threshold of her society. Her "yes" is a yes to the fact of scandal and insecurity.'

He emphasizes how we have to think of Mary undergoing a *kenosis* – a self-emptying. 'An emptying that does not add up to passivity. She says yes. She affirms. She welcomes. She opens. As the first of the disciples, she has to shape Jesus's humanity as he shapes hers. She has to bring up the child, form his imaginations, his perceptions, his sensibility.'

He then moves on to pose a question.

'Did Mary become the mother of God on 25 March or whenever precisely it was, at that moment of the Annunciation? In a sense no, because her yes to the angel doesn't come from nowhere. She's a daughter of Israel. She's framed very clearly in Luke's narrative in the context of very deliberately Old Testament style stories. Luke's literary style is Old Testament almost to the point of caricature. He's writing a Greek which is soaked through with the rhythms and idioms of the Old Testament as if to say the story doesn't begin in Nazareth. It begins with the entire record of Jewish Scripture.

'Mary becomes the mother of God,' he continues, 'in one obvious and physical sense at the moment of the Annunciation and yet the beginning of the story is not there. It is as someone rooted in the beginning of the history of Israel that she becomes the mother of God…The promise she affirms and welcomes is the promise built into the very identity of God's people from the first. Where do we begin to tell this story? Surely, at the very beginning of Mary's own existence and beyond and before that too. Grace is always there before us. That's the key.'

He says for Mary to become the human being that she becomes is a mystery that takes us well beyond a simple reflection on Mary's psychology.

'Mary is formed by Christ in order to form Christ in a unique way,' he emphasizes. 'Her openness to Christ is the barest act of faith, hope and trust. Christ's life in her is a grace of a unique kind.'

He ends by explaining that in that shocking moment, God knew what was going to happen but that Mary did not. His audience, although small in number, has been transfixed. Some have been taking notes furiously. Others smile in admiration and affirmation.

After the sermon, I ask Rowan Williams how important it was during the annunciation encounter for Mary to pause and to question.

'Our own questions, "just a moment" moments, are not betrayals or refusals,' he answers. 'For Mary to ask, for Isaiah to ask, for Moses to ask, is part of a narrative pattern of "Are you sure? I'm not worthy. Can't someone else do it?" What we are being told in the annunciation story is that that moment of sheer human shrinkage and uncertainty is not incompatible with a wholehearted and holy response. That is a very significant point in giving us permission to say, "What on earth is going on?" '

After our chat, I have some time to myself. I start to think about denominational affiliation and my own experience of going to church. I reflect on how ecumenism has become important to me and, as it lies at the heart of the ESBVM, I realize that I have a golden opportunity to bring together one Roman Catholic and one Anglican delegate to talk about the Annunciation.

Dr Mary Frances McKenna is an Irish Catholic theologian. She read History at University College, Dublin, and recently gained a Ph.D. in Theology from All Hallows College, Dublin City University. Aged forty, she is currently undertaking post-doctoral research on Mary in relation to the Trinity, Creation and Anthropology.

Reverend William Burke went to Sandhurst and was commissioned into the Royal Inniskilling Fusiliers. After commanding a battalion, he left the Army to train as an Anglican priest. Today, aged sixty-eight, he is Rector of a Church of England country benefice that takes in six parishes west of Peterborough. He is also an honorary Canon at Peterborough Cathedral.

On a sunny, pleasant afternoon, we sit outside in the garden of Cripps Court, the conference centre attached to Magdalene College. Mary Frances and William sit side by side on a wooden bench facing me. I read the relevant passage from Luke's Gospel, 1:21-38. They sit in silence, listening to the words. After a short period of reflection, I ask what the story means for them.

Mary Frances

'I thought how would I have reacted to having this powerful spiritual experience and could it have remained a constant response throughout my life? Life happens, there are disappointments, you can forget about God, you can be consumed by your own problems. But Mary had this powerful, unique encounter with God – a nobody from nowhere – who was chosen and responded and, importantly, continued that response throughout her life.'

William

'In the Greek New Testament, the loveliest phrase and the most satisfying piece of language used is *kecharitōmenē*, "Hail, thou that art highly favoured and full of grace". So Mary becomes like a royal residence full of grace and favour. The Queen's houses are grace and favour houses and God wants her to become a grace and favour house. It's such a beautiful phrase. I come from that tradition that says when the angel is speaking to someone in the Bible, they're speaking to us too. So we are also highly favoured and full of grace. We have that potential to be the acorn that can become the oak tree. And Mary had free will to say, "On your bike, mate!" She didn't have to accept. The Incarnation means nothing unless we have free will. Above all, Mary is the symbolic guarantor of the Incarnation… We don't know if she lived in poverty. No one knows. We presume she's young. Joseph was a *tektōn*. We translate that as a carpenter but he could have been an extraordinarily successful and wealthy builder or craftsman for all we know. We make assumptions.'

I ask them if they see the story as factual or metaphorical.

Mary Frances

'It's definitely a story that comes from Mary, either directly to a source of Luke's or from a family member. There's no reason why it can't be of a historical nature. Science describes the physical world. It explains the phenomena. But it can never explain where all the world comes from, where the intelligence comes from. Science can't be used as a mechanism to say this couldn't have happened. It's God breaking into the world. It's a unique event. God is the initiator.'

William

'I don't mind if it's a fact or not. It's irrelevant to me. It's the only story we've got and we have to try and make sense of it and work out what it means. For me, it's a sign that Mary, like us, is full of grace and favour and we have the free will to take that gift of life and do what we can with it. It's the guarantor that God knows what it's like to be one of us. The meaning is more important than the fact.'

Mary Frances

'The truth of the account is important to me. Joseph Ratzinger said the Incarnation is about whether God has power over matter. I would trust the gospel account that it is historical. Some people would be adamant about the virgin conception. Others would not be. I think the important message is that God is becoming human, breaking into humanity and I don't think Christianity has fully got to grips with what that actually means. That we talk about Jesus as fully man and fully divine. The whole phenomenon, the power of God taking flesh and walking on this earth like all of us is so huge that we might…we can't comprehend it.'

William

'I agree with this idea that God breaks into our lives, not just Mary's then but our lives now, and continually does that. The ordinary to become the extraordinary. We have to be open to possibility like Mary was. She reminds us all to be open to possibilities, to allow things to happen.'

I ask them if there is a word or phrase that sums up the story.

William

'It's just a beautiful story. I just love it. It's so important. I love the humanity of it all. I love the antecedents of those women in Jesus's genealogy. I love the fact that his great, great grandmother x 14 or 28 or something seduced her father in law to get a child. I love that his great, great grandmother x 70 seduced Boaz in the threshing shed when he'd been on the piss. I love the humanity of it all. The grit. The earthiness.'

Mary Frances

'The word for me is "response". God is continually reaching out to everyone and is hoping there's going to be a response. It gets lost that dialogue. But it's so important.'

William

'Yes, God needs us as much as we need him. He needs us to bring in his kingdom. It's mutual like any good relationship. Mary is the sign of that.'

Mary Frances

'I would say that the Annunciation and the Incarnation need to be more closely connected. The Annunciation can be more easily depicted in paintings. My favourites are the Tanner in the Philadelphia Museum of Art and the Fra Lippi in the National Gallery. Mary being so still because she was listening to something with real substance.'

William

'The Annunciation is the start of the Incarnation. It starts in her womb.'

Mary Frances

'The Annunciation needs a response. There's no Christianity if God just said, "I'm going to incarnate myself and off I go." God sends Gabriel to someone full of grace, asks them, there's a dialogue, and then she said, "Yes, be it done according to thy will." And that is so, so important and I think we miss that. People think God is out there doing this and that and is totally disconnected from us, whereas, in fact, the whole Christian story depends on God reaching out and then there being a whole human response.'

William

'Where did she learn these responses? Those phrases that resonate with Mary.'

I ask them for their thoughts on Bishop Egan's description of the Annunciation as 'the most important event in human history'.

William

'It changed history. Whatever you make of the story, it changed history and the direction of the way the world went. It changed human behaviour forever and how people judge the world.'

Mary Frances (who looks down to the ground and pauses)

'Today, history is a very secularized history. There's no place for God in any notion of history. God can be used. God is on our side or not. There's a desire for facts. So it depends on the individual's acceptance that faith and history, faith and reason, are compatible. I wouldn't have articulated it that way myself but God entering into history...we haven't fully grasped what the Incarnation in history really means. But yes, God entering history has to be the most important, the most decisive moment.'

If it is so pivotal, I ask, why has the status of the feast been so lost and the relative importance of the Annunciation in the Church become so low?

William

'England used to be known as Mary's Dowry. Post the Reformation, we were still having New Year's Day on 25 March. It had so much more significance when it was on New Year's Day. It was when we secularized the calendar and went along with that heathen Napoleonic calendar next door across the Channel. I'm being facetious now of course.'

Mary Frances (smiling affectionately)

'Part of the issue is that it falls in Lent, sometimes in Holy Week, and I would argue that the Annunciation is a relatively minor feast now. It's not like Corpus Christi. The Annunciation is not marked in relation to the power of the Incarnation. It's like "God appeared to Mary. Oh, that's lovely and great. Now Mary is a bit of an embarrassment to modern theology so we'll ignore all of that ugh." There's an awful lot of that in there. I think it's imperative the Annunciation is reconnected with the Incarnation because in many ways the meaning of each is so very different. It means reconnecting the Mother with the Son. There's no Mother without the Son and there's no Son without the Mother.'

William (anxious to intervene)

'Of course, the Annunciation is one of the most common Christmas cards. The angel talking to Mary. So people now think it's a Christmas story. A child will think that the angel came to Mary the day before Christmas. We've got confused about when it is. It's now part of the Nativity plays and all the rest of it. It's lost its distinctiveness about God breaking in.'

Mary Frances

'Yes, and the Incarnation is the other side of the Resurrection. No one can say they witnessed it. Nobody can say "I saw what happened." The parallels between the Annunciation and the Resurrection haven't been drawn out. You don't have many pictures of the Resurrection nor of the Incarnation. The sight of it is very important to human beings to understand what an Incarnation means, but it's so difficult to depict.'

As they sit together talking so freely, I wonder whether they think Mary today is a bridge or a barrier to greater inter-denominational understanding.

William

'I think reasonable non-Roman Catholics have come to understand the importance of Mary in the story of man's redemption. If I'm honest, I find something deeply moving and haunting about Mary. I can't put my finger on it. It's visceral. I can't quite explain it. It's about potential, love, being open to God, to new possibilities. I'm not an emotional person but there's something about Mary that gets under my skin. I was once told that those who love the Church love Mary and those who love Mary love the Church. Yes. I'd say yes.'

Mary Frances

'Mary is the crossroads of Christianity. So many aspects of her are reflective of wider Christian dialogue. If people call her a barrier, it's because she is the most clear manifestation in terms of differences. Mary can be used as an embarrassment – an immature spirituality. Yes, there are differences between denominations. There's no point in saying there aren't. But let's talk. Dialogue can mean we all learn.'

Do they wish for a single, unified Church, I ask them?

William

'Yes, I think it's a Christian command. We should be completely one. We say we believe in one, holy, catholic church. There's something seriously dysfunctional about the Church because it isn't one. It damages its role in the world. It should now be a very, very high priority.'

Mary Frances (nodding in agreement)

'We are all one in our creedal statement and expression of faith. It's the same Creed that's said every day. On the one hand there's unity through our expression of belief but, on the other hand, there's these manifestations of divisions. I sometimes wonder that these are very clearly institutional divisions whereas in the early Church there was a huge dialogue and diversity of view. The important thing is the unity in that creedal declaration of faith. Some of the attempts at bringing the Church together can be man's attempt to force us together because it makes us feel good. It's like these ludicrous photo opportunities bringing together world leaders at summit meetings and they claim they're all united. We just need to let God work through us.'

They look at the print of the Lemoyne painting, holding it jointly in their hands.

Mary Frances

'I see Mary in prayer, consumed by the event. Something internal is happening. She's not looking at the angel.'

William

'She's having some internal encounter. Her hands are almost pointing to inside herself.'

Mary Frances

'I wouldn't be drawn to it.'

As we draw the conversation to a close, I talk with Mary Frances about the current debate in Ireland where there are calls to change the broadcasting of *The Angelus* by the country's national broadcaster. Reciting the Angelus prayer at 6 a.m., noon and 6 p.m. has been a part of Roman Catholic devotion for centuries but RTE is the only broadcaster across Europe to reflect that ritual each day in its scheduling. At noon on radio and at 6 p.m. on the main television channel RTE One, 'a reflective minute' called *The Angelus* is broadcast that includes the sound of the eighteen peals of the Angelus bells. The main news bulletin is even delayed by a minute to incorporate this. Secular critics in Ireland argue that it no longer reflects a pluralist Republic of Ireland. Supporters say it is part of Ireland's cultural identity. For now, *The Angelus* on RTE remains in place.

I head back into the conference centre to hear the next keynote speaker. A small make-shift bookstall by the main door offers the latest ESBVM publications: *Mary For Time and Eternity*; *Mary For Earth and Heaven*; *Mary Is For Everyone*; *Mary A Bridge of Unity*.

Bishop Angaelos is a bishop of the Coptic Orthodox Church. He enters the lecture theatre wearing black robes and 'emmeh headwear. Born in Cairo, he spent his childhood in Sydney, Australia, and graduated in Political Science, Philosophy and Sociology. It was while he was a postgraduate law student in New South Wales that he felt a calling to join a monastery. He left Australia to return to Egypt and entered the monastery of Saint Bishoy in Wadi-El-Natroun, between Cairo and Alexandria, where he was consecrated a monk. 'It was just a realisation and I pursued it quite rationally,' he tells me. 'It wasn't dramatic.'

In 1999, he was made a General Bishop of the Coptic Orthodox Church in the United Kingdom, based in Stevenage. 'Coptic just means Egyptian,' he says. There are 20,000 Copts in Britain but it is the largest Christian denomination in the Middle East and was founded by St Mark in the first century AD. Bishop Angaelos is here to talk about 'The Holiness of Obedience' and he describes Mary's obedience as 'empowerment'.

'When the archangel visited the Blessed Virgin, he did not say to her, you need to do anything,' he tells the audience. 'He said, "It will be done through you. All you need to do is accept and to say yes. To be obedient." To Saint Mary, obedience meant being led. Obedience is that which brings us into power when we obey the right things. It is embodied in the Virgin. We don't like to call ourselves servants. But servants serve the people. Mary was that grain that willingly fell into the ground and into the dark unknown. What did she know about becoming pregnant? What prepares you for that? Nothing but the grace of God.'

After his talk, we go outside into the garden to discuss his interpretation of the annunciation story.

'It represents a huge element of trust to be a vessel, literally, for the will of God,' he observes.

When I ask him whether he sees it as fact or metaphor, I am not surprised by his answer. But his certainty shines through.

'It is absolute fact,' he replies. 'The Scriptures are divinely inspired. It then applies metaphorically in our own lives.'

What makes him so certain the details of the encounter are fact?

'All Scripture is inspired by God,' he replies. 'There is no need for it to be made into a metaphor or for it to be symbolic. Why would this be a metaphor?'

So, what is the message of the story?

'We are all called for something in God's will as His agents, His vessels and it is up to us to respond to that call. He is never going to force something on us. He is never going to force His will in our lives. But He wants us to be part of His story and His mission.'

I wonder if there is a word or phrase in the story that resonates for him.

'Trust and obedience,' he replies immediately. 'Obedience has become a derogatory term in this day and age. We think of it as a mindlessness or a lack of character. But in our monastic order, one of our three pillars is Obedience. And I'm not a mindless follower. Obedience is a good thing as long as we are doing the right thing. It should always be an informed obedience.'

We move on to further subject matters. Does he see the ability to say no as an important element of the story?

'God gives us the freedom to determine our lives,' he says. 'I can say no to anything that God calls me to do.'

Does he see the annunciation encounter as the most important event in human history?

'I do not think it was the pivotal moment. For God, salvation was a process. There is no one most important moment. They are all steps in a process along the journey. God could have found another vessel if Saint Mary had said no. But salvation was not going to stop because one person resisted his will. And she was a chosen vessel. There was no option for God because He already knew her answer. Knowledge is very different to determination. He knew she would accept.'

But how can that be free will? I say.

'If I know you really well and we go out for lunch, I know what you are going to order but I do not force it on you,' he responds.

Does he think God chose Mary because He knew she would say yes?

'No. He chose Mary because she is the one whom He wanted to do this,' he says.

There's a confidence in his voice and a swagger in his stance that I find quite surprising. He seems so certain about everything. Next, I ask him about the status of Mary.

'She is a saint,' he replies. 'We venerate her as a saint but we do not follow the idea she was immaculately conceived. We believe she was an ordinary human being but then became *theotokos,* the God-bearer. She remained virgin all her life. She was perpetually virgin, on the basis of Scripture and tradition.'

I comment that he seems to put great emphasis on her being an ordinary human being and yet, at the same time, says she must also have been perpetually virginal. Why?

'Surely the Virgin Birth is a much greater incomprehensible mystery than her perpetual virginity. Why do you find that so difficult?' he replies. 'I'm celibate as a monk. It does not mean I think married life is impure.'

But why is it so important that Mary remained a virgin all her life? I wonder.

'What is central to salvation is that she gave birth to the Incarnate Word. If she had not stayed a virgin, it would not effect salvation. It does matter though. We often say things do not matter. We must accept Scripture as a whole for what it says and we cannot have this supermarket approach of taking certain things and leaving behind the rest. The literal reading of the text would be Jesus's brothers and sisters but our reading is that, in the tradition of Jewish custom at that time, it would have been his cousins.'

He tells me how the feast of the Annunciation has always been a significant feast in the Coptic Church and remains so today although it is more focused on the coming of Christ and his Incarnation than about Mary. I ask him if Mary remains a barrier to interfaith dialogue.

'Muslims believe Mary is the mother of Jesus and they believe in the Virgin Birth,' he says. 'They venerate Saint Mary. They see Jesus as a prophet and her as the mother of the prophet. She is a connection between Christianity and Islam. She is not an obstacle. We believe we have received our Messiah, while Jewish believers maintain they are still waiting.'

What about her role in inter-denominational dialogue?

'I feel with my Anglican friends that they, too, believe she was human and a prepared vessel,' he replies. 'With Catholics, we have other things to discuss about Mary such as the Immaculate Conception. There is a difference between theological dialogue and ecumenical discussion. Theological dialogue is a much longer process.'

As we say our farewells, he says he wants to offer me some advice.

'Be open to listening. But you cannot just keep listening. You have to make a decision. There are always choices to make and the journey has to come to its destination at some point. You need to know what you believe – your anchor point – and then be exposed to other people's views and respect them. Do not ever expect it will make logical sense. It has to be a decision of the unknown, from the heart. We're talking about the super-human. It is not limited or confined to logic. But you will have to get to a point on your journey when you have to make a decision.'

CHAPTER 25

THE DNA OF OUR FAITH

I have been invited to stay overnight in Cripps Court at Magdalene College and in my room I find a meditation book, *Venite Adoremus!* by Fran Godfrey. The author declares that Mary had been 'groomed from before birth to be the perfect woman, the perfect, unstained carrier of the Son of God' and that her patience, her trust and her acceptance of her fate, made her 'a truly awe-inspiring role model'.

This adoration forms a stark contrast to the words of a woman I had met earlier on my journey – a Church of England woman priest who had asked to remain anonymous:

> I think the Roman Catholics have put her onto such a pedestal, interceding for us, her perpetual virginity, her assumption in heaven, that for them she's ceased to be human. My hunch is because they've got such a male dominance…they've suppressed womanhood in the Church to such a level that they have to elevate Mary as the perfect one. I think it's all to do with Roman Catholic priests being celibate. A lot of them were separated from their mothers when they were twelve or thirteen and there was this yearning by them for the idealized feminine.

After breakfast, I head to the Fitzwilliam Museum and stand before one of the smallest but most beautiful renditions of the Annunciation. Domenico Veneziano's painting, created in Florence some time between 1442 and 1448, originally formed the central section of the predella as part of an altarpiece in the small church of Santa Lucia dei Magnoli in the city.

94. Domenico Veneziano *The Annunciation*, 1442-48, The Fitzwilliam Museum, Cambridge. © The Fitzwilliam Museum, Cambridge

Gabriel, on the left side, kneels in reverence before Mary with a long lily stem in his left hand, phallically positioned at an angle. The index finger of his right hand points upwards. Mary, on the right, dressed in flowing scarlet and blue robes, stands inside a *loggia* with her arms crossed over her chest as her head tilts down. She is accepting the angel's message at that very moment. The four columns of the portico separate her from Gabriel.

What makes this work so special are the gentle, pastel colours and its wonderful luminosity. Although at some point the painting was trimmed by about two and a half inches on the left side, art historians acclaim its careful symmetry – its spatial construction, sense of balance and Veneziano's ground-breaking understanding of linear perspective. All points converge on the centre of the bolted door at the rear – a *porta clausa* – that encloses the garden to symbolize Mary's virginity.

I gaze at the serene figure of Mary. I can almost hear her speaking the words, 'Let it be done unto me.' I recall Rowan Williams' memorable comment that, at this very moment, she undergoes a *kenosis*, a self-emptying, as she accepts Gabriel's request.

I sit a few feet away and read R. S. Thomas's 1975 poem, 'Annunciation by Veneziano', that was inspired by the painting:

> The messenger is winged
>   and the girl
> haloed a distance
>   between them
> and between them and us
> down the long path the door
> through which he has not
>   come
> on his lips what all women
>   desire to hear
> in his hand the flowers that
>   he has taken from her.

In a film profile of R. S. Thomas, made in 1972, the Welsh poet and Anglican priest talked about poetry and religion:

> To me, any form of orthodoxy is just not part of faith's providence at all. Faith must be able to claim a certain amount of poetic licence, a freedom to follow the imaginative vision of poetry. After all, what is today's orthodoxy is tomorrow's antiquity. I don't bother much about that at all. In any case, poetry is religion and religion is poetry. The message of the New Testament is poetry. Christ was a poet and the New Testament is metaphor. I feel perfectly within my rights in approaching my whole vocation as a priest and my whole vocation as a preacher in presenting poetry. When I preach poetry, I'm preaching Christianity and when one discusses Christianity, one is discussing poetry in its imaginative aspect – the core of our imagination. I'm not worried about it.

'I consider the Resurrection is metaphorical use of language,' he continued, 'as is the Incarnation. The Incarnation and the Resurrection are metaphors. My work as a poet has to deal with the presentation of imaginative faith. Christianity, it seems to me, also is a presentation of imaginative faith. There is no conflict between them at all. As a priest, I am committed to the ministry of the word and the ministry of the sacraments. Word is metaphor. Language is sacrament. Sacrament is language. The combination is perfectly simple.'

R. S. Thomas died in 2000. As more visitors arrive in the room and admire the Veneziano painting, I read another evocative poem by him, entitled 'Annunciation', written towards the end of his life:

> 'She came like a saint
> to her bride-bed, hands
> clasped, mind clenched
> on a promise. 'Some
>
> fell by the wayside,'
> she whispered. 'Come, birds,
> winnow the seed lest
> standing beside a chaste
>
> cradle with a star
> over it, I see flesh
> as snow fallen and think
> myself mother of God.'

I leave the Fitzwilliam Museum and head down Trumpington Street to King's College Chapel, the best-known building in Cambridge. It is a magnificent edifice dedicated to the Virgin Mary and is a jewel of grand, late Perpendicular Gothic architecture. I tilt my head in awe at the largest fan vaulted stone ceiling in the world, designed by John

95. Stained glass window of the Annunciation, 1530, in King's College Chapel, Cambridge. By kind permission of the Fellows and Scholars of King's College, Cambridge

Wastell, and then gaze at the amazing radiant colours that seep through the early sixteenth-century stained-glass windows as sunlight filters in. There are twenty-six windows. All are tall and narrow and are sited around the Chapel. In part they depict the life of Mary, referencing the New Testament Gospels as well as the later legendary apocryphal stories. The illustrations begin with Mary's conception and end with her ascent into heaven to be crowned by the Holy Trinity, reminding us that Mary's story is also the story of the foundation of the Christian Church.

I focus on one window in particular, installed in 1530 just before Henry VIII's split from Rome. It's a type/anti-type pairing that shows the Virgin Mary as the new Eve and focuses on disobedience and obedience. In the top two panes on the left side, Eve stands in front of the Tree of Knowledge having just accepted the fruit from the serpent. The two panes directly below show Mary, dressed as usual in red and blue, turning round to hear the message from the angel Gabriel, who is dressed in a jewel-encrusted robe. The index finger of her left hand points towards the angel, indicating her agreement to become the mother of Christ. The window is an edification of the way in which Mary's acceptance of the will of God helps to save humanity from the sins perpetrated by Eve's earlier disobedience.

I head down King's Parade and Trinity Street to nearby Trinity College where I have arranged to meet one of the world's most eminent theologians. Professor David Ford has been the Regius Professor of Divinity at the University of Cambridge for more than twenty years and is also Director of the Cambridge Interfaith programme. Educated at Trinity College, Dublin, where he read Classics; St John's College, Cambridge, where he studied Theology; and Yale where he took a Master's before returning to Cambridge for his Ph.D., he has a worldwide reputation for outstanding scholarship and is renowned as a brilliant public theologian.

At lunch, Professor Ford is an engaging companion who speaks enthusiastically about being raised as an Anglican in the Church of Ireland, how unusual it is at Cambridge to be a Regius Professor of Divinity without being an ordained priest, and what hermeneutics of the Bible — a special focus of his research and scholarship — is all about. He has retained a lovely soft, gentle Irish lilt and laughs regularly. Although he is clearly a serious intellectual, he loves making witty jokes. I am eager to pick his brains about Luke's story but he says that can wait a while.

After lunch we take a circuitous route from Trinity to the Faculty of Divinity. He has to get back to his office for an upcoming tutorial and pushes his bicycle as he walks along at a fast pace. Becoming increasingly out of breath, I just about manage to throw a few questions in his direction. He says the Annunciation passage encapsulates 'all of the drama of Faith': Jesus, Mary and the Holy Spirit; the Old Testament and the New Testament; history and theology.

When I ask him if he sees it as the most important event in human history, he says we cannot take it down to a single event. They are all interlinked and mutually dependent. 'I see the whole of the word as one,' he says as he picks up speed.

Eventually, we settle down in his office. He tells me we have twenty minutes before he has to take his next class. When I ask what the annunciation story means for him spiritually, he pauses for a long time.

'My goodness,' he sighs. He breathes in heavily. He is deep in thought. 'It's the DNA of our faith. It has everything. Your DNA has all these sequences out of which everything else unfolds. It has the logic of your being, so to speak. It has the recipe for your life. It seems to me Luke has that extraordinary gift in those opening chapters of giving, in an intense, deeply inter-connected, resonant way, the key elements that unfold later in the Gospel...It's a story that has everything.'

He stands up and walks to the window, continuing to reflect. I ask whether he regards the story as fact or metaphor?

'I refuse the dichotomy,' he says. 'It seems to me that realistic narrative is one of the ways you can convey "truth" that is both historical and fictional. Because every history has a fictional dimension — you have to fashion it as well as find it — and because every good fiction has a deep reference to life — Luke, it seems to me, is writing extraordinary, dense, rich, resonant, realistic narrative using Old Testament resources and giving us the framework within which to understand the rest of his story.'

Does that mean he believes the essential ingredients of the story: the Incarnation, Mary's calling and the naming of Jesus, but thinks that the exact details of the story are not necessarily true?

'The most important thing is who God is; who Jesus is; and this is testimony to that,' he answers. 'Testimony can come in all sorts of shapes and forms. It can be imaginative as well as coldly factual. And if what you are giving testimony to is God-sized, extraordinarily rich and deep and comprehensive for the whole of history as this was, and is about a very particular person, then to think that facts get that is just inadequate.

'You know that there has to be sufficient truth to reference in it for it to ring true and I think the main areas of Luke's Gospel where that rings true are later on. But we just don't know. There is no claim anyone else was present at the Annunciation. We just don't know what sort of experience it was for Mary. There are all sorts of different ways you can experience these things. I feel that in Luke's Gospel, the pivot of reliable testimony is not in the opening chapters but later on when Jesus is carrying out his ministry.'

I suggest that the Birth Narrative in Luke may have been written later to try to explain the unexplainable.

'It's a God-sized event and Luke is stretching our categories, our imaginations, stretching our hearts and minds in order to be open to something amazing, unique, unprecedented and yet deeply resonant with especially the Old Testament.'

I remind him how I'd asked him earlier whether it was, as Bishop Egan has described, 'the most important event in human history'.

'My fundamental category would be person not event,' he responds. 'And so, person means you cannot identify one event. It's a whole drama. And it's a set of relationships. You can't divide Jesus from his mother, from his disciples and so forth.'

When I ask whether it troubles him that the feast day has lost some of its significance, he chuckles.

'I'm an Irish Anglican. The Church year was important in certain ways but one didn't rate importance by whether it was a feast. I do think it should be celebrated more. I would love that. I do think it is so worth celebrating, meditating on deeply, and not just doing that individually but communally.'

How does he rate the significance of Mary to himself?

'Mm,' he pauses, 'she's got more important over the years interestingly. In Irish Anglicanism there's a bit of a reaction against the prominence of Mary in the surrounding Catholicism so I was slow getting started but she certainly has become more important. Mary is just gently present more and more. More significant.'

Does he venerate her?

'What do you mean by "venerate her"?' he asks.

'Do you pray to her?'

'Mm, I don't in a direct way…but I do think that Mary and all the saints are part of the worship in that broad Anglo-Catholic tradition. I'm deeply at home with that. Just as I'm at home in an evangelical tradition. I don't see them as contradictory. It's not the same veneration as for Jesus or as for the Trinity.'

He looks at the print of the Lemoyne painting.

'How wonderful. Wow!' he says in a soft voice as he breathes in heavily. 'Wow,' he whispers again. 'Oh, I feel wonderful. The first thing I see is this wonderful face of Mary in the centre. This face and with those hands. It's the heart. It's the face and the heart together.'

He keeps looking at the picture and smiling.

'And then there's this dynamism of the relationship with the angel,' he observes. 'Also the relationship with this text on the right here which seems to get beautifully the relationship with the Old Testament. One sees there the way in which the word is given by the messenger, the word coming in person so to speak, and the glorious relationship between the word in the text, the word now and the Word becoming flesh. That's all there. Wow!'

He shakes his head slowly in wonderment. He is becoming rather emotional.

'I love it. It's beautiful,' he says. 'There's an interiority about Mary. She's taking it in, almost literally. There's that sense of her being both amazed and yet interiorizing what is to be so generative. It's the energy of the angel too that also gets you. He's extraordinarily active. The energy of the Holy Spirit with the Word there coming. And her receptiveness.'

I wonder if, in his view, Lemoyne's rendition captures the essence of the annunciation story.

'It gets a great deal of it.' he replies. 'Oh yes, it's lovely. It's really powerful. One of the distinctive things about it is the energy that's there and the receiving of energy through a word relating to the word of Scripture. The very body of Mary is being overshadowed by the Holy Spirit. Oh yes…oh yes.'

He breathes in heavily again.

It is time for the professor to go to his tutorial. He gathers his papers, presents me with a copy of his latest book, *The Drama of Living: Becoming Wise in the Spirit*, offers a warm handshake, and darts off.

———

For many years, the Archbishop of Canterbury has commissioned a book for Lent to be used by Christians up and down the land for the purpose of spiritual meditation and reflection. Twenty years ago, the focus of the Lenten book centred on Mary. Written by the philosopher, sociologist and theologian, Elaine Storkey, who lives in Cambridge, it is entitled *Mary's Story, Mary's Song*. The opening chapter, 'God's Initiative', focuses on Luke's account of the Annunciation. Here is how it begins:

> The modern tabloid newspapers could hardly dream up anything more sensational, more full of 'human interest', and more unlikely.
>
> The story is difficult for us today for many reasons. First, of course, we live in a world which would hardly know how to recognize an angel. Frankly, most of us do not believe in them. We can somehow believe in astrology, and take great interest in the signs of the zodiac. We may believe in the demonic, or even dabble with witchcraft or the occult. Yet few of us expect visits from angels.
>
> Perhaps it is that angels are too benign, too personal. They do not belong to a universe which accepts fatalism or chance. They do not remind us of evil and hatred. They are not part of the sinister, the pantheistic or the psychic. Compared with all of these, angels are fairly ordinary creatures who crop up unannounced in apparently everyday situations. They might be unlimited by the space-time boundaries which affect us mortals, but it would seem that they are otherwise quite average. In the Bible they busily flit between time and eternity as willing messengers sent from God. Today people find all of that hard to grasp hold of. For the modern mind is very perverse. Some people find it easier to believe that their next Tuesday morning will be affected by the relationship of Jupiter and Saturn on the day they were born, than to believe in a God who cares about us. So it seems doubly hard for some people to believe in angels. For if we accept that angels exist, we have to accept that there is a God who has been sending them to communicate with human beings for the last few thousand years. We might even have to accept the possibility that God could do that even today.

Elaine Storkey and I sit close together at the end of a large room in the Master's Lodge at Selwyn College that has been freed up for our meeting. She has a winning smile and a strong West Yorkshire accent. The seventy-year-old was brought up in Wakefield as an Anglican but tells me that she is now an 'open evangelical', comfortable with all parts of the Christian Church.

Twenty years on from writing those words in *Mary's Story, Mary's Song*, what are her reflections today on the annunciation story?

'God actually intervenes in human history,' she says. 'There is a blending and melding, a mix between humanity and divinity, between the temporal, the here and now, and the eternal. God chooses an insignificant human being for the most extraordinary human task in the history of the human world. Mary is a bridge between the Old Testament and the New Testament. She comes from the Old Covenant – a faithful Jewish woman – and takes us into the New Covenant, redemption times, and she does it through her own body. That's very exciting. A woman's body bridges the covenants and changes the direction of human history.'

Does she think the story is rooted in fact?

'I believe the Annunciation. I believe that it happened. For me it's not an interesting myth that's attached itself to a belief system. So it is crucial and it is interesting.'

In that context, what does belief mean?

'I think I believe it was a historical event. If I'd been there at the time, I would have seen something that took place in human space-time. What it was like, I haven't a clue. What the angel looked like, how Mary responded, I don't know. I just go on how it was written. I believe the Scriptures are many kinds of different literature and we get terribly confused because we take these things literally when they were never meant literally. They were meant metaphorically or they were meant in terms of poetry or song. But then there are things that are historical and, for me, this is.'

So she trusts rather than knows that it happened.

'Yes, I'd be one hundred per cent with that,' she says. 'Knowing is arrogant. We go by faith with mud on our boots and get bogged down every now and then and then we have to work out our faith. So knowledge is much more concrete. But knowledge is based on faith. The fact that I believe, that changes the way I see other things and changes my knowledge framework.'

What does she think is the key message of the story?

'Total trust. Obedience. Openness. A sense of adventure,' she replies. 'Heck, where is this taking me? Being open to possibilities you never dreamed of or that don't even come into your horizon.'

I ask if she believes it is the most important event in human history.

'Yes. Of course, it leads on to other very, very key events too. I think human history is not simply a beginning, a middle and an end. It's not a temporal system in which all events are of equal nature. It's peppered with completely significant moments. The Annunciation makes the Incarnation possible and opens up, because of Mary's acceptance, its meaning and its actuality and then the rest follows, and all the events that will change human life follow on from that.'

Does she think the status and significance of the feast of the Annunciation has been lost?

'It's completely erased from human history,' she replies in a sad tone. 'We are struggling in our culture to even get some proper understanding on the Resurrection. The Annunciation has gone way back into the ether. How we get it back, I'm not sure.'

Why has it been lost?

'People are very wary about angels,' she says, 'although angels have come back into fashion recently so we may be able to cash in on that.' She laughs gently.

'It was lost in the modernist period when angels were connected with human foreboding and were seen as weird. We're also unsure about the status of women. The way that Mary is terrified and on her knees. The more radical feminists have seen it as a cosmic rape scene – Mary Daly and others – the idea Mary was raped mystically and divinely in order to bring this child. That's actually soured the nature of the Annunciation for a lot of thinking, authentic women. There's a lot of work to do to recapture what it actually means.'

As our understanding of the modern world has become so science-based, does she think this impedes the acceptance of a virgin birth?

'Yes. The Christians who are scientists are not battling in these areas. They're focusing on whether God exists and the chance the world evolved out of nothing. But the scientists I know are quite happy with the Annunciation and a virgin birth. I know a young professor of Physics at Oxford who's happy about it. He said, "Science fits in where science fits in." It's about the nature of a miracle. The Annunciation was a miracle. The Incarnation was a miracle. This is the point. When God intervenes directly in human history and we believe there is a God who is the author of time, the author of history, then it's a God of miracles who will change things.

'We are struggling to mark anything now as the calendar more and more becomes secular,' she continues. 'We'll get it back sooner or later. If we are going to recapture the Annunciation, we have to recapture it for authentic women. The radical feminists have already demolished it, claiming it's a way of the Church keeping women down, making them subservient to the biddings of their male masters and this story re-enforces that. The frightened picture of Mary or the submissive, passive Mary plays in to all that. They say you need strong, strident women who say, "I'm not allowing my body to be used in this way. Let me go away and think about it." We've got to re-present the story to say that's not what it's about. It's the reverse. It's the choosing of a person of insignificance who is a woman and offering her the opportunity of significance and trust. It's the whole package of working with God and there's nothing demeaning about working with God. It's the highest asking possible.'

So what is her kind of feminism? I ask.

'It's Christian feminism,' she replies. 'There is a God who loves us and is calling women and men together in partnership – in complete equality – to realize these ends.'

Later in that opening chapter of her book *Mary's Story, Mary's Song*, Elaine Storkey focuses on the notion of Mary being the servant of the Lord:

> Mary could not have accepted the role of servant if she had not first abandoned her own autonomy: the 'right' to live her life independently of the call of God or the needs of others. And it is the demands of human independence, which lie behind so many of our problems of unbelief today. Not only do we reserve the right to have everything brought within our intellectual autonomy, we also insist on the right to our own personal and moral autonomy. We draw up our own agendas. We live with our own decisions. We write our own scripts. If a given morality doesn't suit us, we change it. If our friends are too demanding, we drop them. We try our hardest to construct a world that assures us that we can live the way we want, that we are what we have, and that truth is what we say it is. And then we wonder why we cannot believe in God.
>
> Mary shared none of these assumptions. Although she could presumably have rejected the angel's story and refused her assent to the proposal, she did not. With this

young, believing Jewish woman there was no question of living life according to her own rules or requirements. For even if this were possible (and few even today are any longer convinced by this myth) her life would be the poorer, not the richer as a result.

To be the 'servant of the Lord' has enormous implications for anyone. It means nothing less than death to self; giving up our own small ambitions, putting ourselves at God's disposal. It requires an abandonment of pride and the acceptance of a more humble assessment of ourselves. It also means embracing others as our equals. For the implications of servanthood are mutuality and acceptance.

In that context, how does she view the status of Mary?

'She's a really gutsy person. I can identify with her nervousness, her sense of protection, her motherliness, her anxiety of being a mother but also her authority. She's an inspirational figure. Tremendously so. Very human. Very normal. But, at the same time, she ponders things in her own body.'

Does she venerate her?

'No,' she responds straight away. 'I see her much more as a sister. I wouldn't pray to her. That's my tradition.'

Does she think Jesus had brother and sisters?

'I'm sure she went on and had other children. Well, I believe that she did.'

Is Mary a barrier or a bridge to greater ecumenism?

'More of a bridge now,' she responds. 'There's been an awful lot of interest in Mary in the last twenty years. People discover more about her humility and get away from the problem of statues.'

Has she ever experienced an annunciation moment and felt a calling?

'There was a moment in a field funnily enough at a Methodist gathering in Derbyshire,' she remembers. 'I'd gone with a friend. I was seventeen. I climbed to this place at Froggart. It was crystal clear. "This is it. This is it." And the choice was mine.'

Did she feel the choice was like Mary's?

'I hadn't thought about it like that but yes,' she replies.

She then tells me that, when she was studying Philosophy at university, she was 'knocked sideways, particularly by an atheist philosopher' and then had a second moment when she was 'on her own in a room and the light was on but there was no light in the room.'

96. Alan Storkey *Annunciation*. By kind permission of Alan and Elaine Storkey

I show her the print of Lemoyne's Annunciation. She comments immediately on the very muscular, sexless, androgynous Gabriel. She notes that although Mary isn't looking at the angel, she is fully aware of him.

'I think her face is incredibly beautiful. It's not passive, submissive in the negative sense. It's expectant. It's full of authority. A recognition that something very profound is happening. I love it. I don't like a lot of Catholic art but I really love it.'

She rifles through her bags until she finds a small oil painting by her husband, Alan, that she is keen for me to see. The picture is set in the countryside on a remote hillside on which sheep are grazing. Mary kneels in a penned area in front of a stone bothy with a thatched roof. She appears to be a very poor, simple girl looking after her sheep. She is wearing a long ragged, red dress. The angel, a young man dressed in rough brown cloth, stands just outside the stone walled area with his right hand raised in the air. The sheep continue to graze unaware of what's happening. This is the moment of the announcement.

'It's a very Protestant way of seeing the Annunciation,' she comments. 'It's so earthy.'

———————

There's one last person I want to meet before I leave Cambridge. Owen Chadwick was Professor of Ecclesiastical History and then Regius Professor of History at the University of Cambridge for fifteen years from 1968 until 1983. Academic, writer and clergyman, he is regarded as one of the greatest religious historians of the twentieth century. Twenty years ago, I much enjoyed reading his book, *A History of Christianity*, described then as an 'original, sweeping history of the Christian faith from the perspective of a people's religion and the effects of the faith on the lives of believers over two thousand years.'

Today he is ninety-eight, frail and living in a modest house in Newnham, with a care assistant at hand. His beloved wife, Ruth, is also alive but lives in a nursing home nearby. They have been married for sixty-five years and he still tries to visit her every day. He sits in his favourite chair in the front room with a blanket wrapped around his thin body. He has the manners of an English gentleman and exudes great charm. He offers me a cup of tea and a biscuit.

He talks in short sentences with long pauses in between, and chooses his words carefully. I know I should not press him too hard and realize that I must not tire him out. But I am keen to hear his thoughts on the annunciation story, however brief.

'She has a choice but there is no choice,' he tells me.

I ask him to clarify what he means by this. There's a long pause.

'Mary has free will but the question was so big, how could she say no? God knows the answer.'

I ask him what the annunciation story means for him.

'It's the most beautiful story in Scripture and the most important one. "Let it be done"; she's the first disciple. But it's not really about Mary. It's about Jesus. The coming of the Messiah.'

I show him the print of the Lemoyne painting.

'It's the most beautiful painting,' he tells me. 'A lovely sight.' He studies it in silence for more than a minute.

'It has a depth of grace and humility and it has legend in it. I don't mean legend doesn't have force. Mary is too serene though. She would have been so frightened when she was told, don't you think?'

He is fascinated by the painting's history so I tell him what I have learned so far. He describes its acquisition at that particular time in the eighteenth century as 'rare and quite remarkable'. He keeps studying it, his eyes darting back and forth and, as he does so, his impressions seem to change.

'I think it's altogether so beautiful and a lovely Mary. I like her demeanour. Do you think it's too cosy?' he asks. 'Some may say it's too sweet but for me it's a virtue. I think it's rather marvellous. I like Mary more than the angel but then humans in life are better for historians than angels,' he chuckles.

As I tell him it's time for me to leave and thank him for his hospitality, he offers a final observation.

'What an interesting project. Everyone will have a view. They will all be different. And yet it's the same story.'

He puts his thumbs up slowly.

'That's religion for you,' he says before a last smile and then he closes his eyes.'

*   Owen Chadwick died at his home on 17 July 2015, a few months after this interview. His wife, Ruth, passed away just before him.

CHAPTER 26

AWAKEN

St Albans is the oldest place of continuous Christian worship and pilgrimage in England. I am in the Cathedral and Abbey Church of St Alban walking up the longest nave in the country. It's built on the very spot where the first English martyr was executed around AD 245.

Alban was a citizen of the Roman city of Verulamium and worshipped the Roman gods. He became a Christian after sheltering a priest called Amphibalus who was fleeing from persecution. Alban refused to renounce his faith and was put to death, proclaiming, 'I worship and adore the true and living God who created all things.' He was beheaded and buried here on a hillside just outside the city.

Throughout the medieval period, his shrine was a focal point for Christian pilgrimage and the abbey became the leading Benedictine foundation in the country until it was disbanded at the Reformation. As pilgrims made their way slowly up the nave towards Alban's tomb, they would stop and pray in front of various altarpieces painted on each of the west-facing Norman pillars, between the nave and the north aisle. The brightly coloured thirteenth-century wall paintings were important aids for contemplation before the pilgrims arrived at the shrine.

Each mural is a secco and was made by craftsmen first covering the wall in plaster, allowing it to set, then dampening it and adding a coat of lime, before sketching the outline of the painting and finally adding the various colour pigments. With the coming of the Reformation in the sixteenth century and the destruction of what was seen to be decorative idolatry, the altarpieces were covered with whitewash and were not rediscovered

97. Medieval mural of the Annunciation in the Cathedral and Abbey Church of St Alban, St Albans, Hertfordshire

until 1862. The restorative attempts to remove the lime-based wash destroyed much of the detail and colour of the paintings and most of the upper layers of the artists' work flaked off or faded away. But together they remain the most extensive set of medieval wall paintings in existence in any English church.

I touch the medieval plaster, close my eyes and think of the thousands of pilgrims who have stopped at this very place over the past 800 years to reflect on the annunciation encounter; to pray to God, to Christ and the Virgin Mary; to ponder on the story of the Annunciation. Some may have seen the Annunciation wall painting whitewashed away in an act of iconoclasm. Others may have seen it return to reveal its mystery. A mystery focusing on a brief encounter that Bishop Philip Egan described to me some months ago as 'the most important event in human history'.

My focus on medieval depictions of the Annunciation continues. I am feeling very excited as I am escorted to a small, nondescript room in the British Library in central London.

A few minutes later, Kathleen Doyle, Lead Curator of Illuminated Manuscripts at the British Library, wheels in a trolley that holds two large boxes. Inside are two of the British Library's greatest treasures. They have been brought here from a nearby strong room.

'We want them to last for another thousand years,' she says in a soft American accent. 'They're stored in a controlled temperature area. With extreme humidity and temperature, the vellum would revert to the original shape of the animal.'

Kathleen Doyle spent her childhood in Seattle and has lived in Britain for twenty-five years. She gained her Ph.D. in Art History and wrote her Master's dissertation on the Winchester Bible. Indeed, Winchester will feature heavily throughout our encounter. For the objects inside the boxes are two of the greatest medieval devotional or liturgical books anywhere in the world: *The Benedictional of St Æthelwold* and *The Winchester Psalter*, were both made in Winchester and used throughout the late Middle Ages.

She opens the first box and takes out *The Benedictional of St Æthelwold* from its leather case, taking care to support its spine to alleviate any point of stress. 'It speaks for itself,' she says as, delicately, she turns over the parchment pages, eventually settling on a stunningly beautiful illumination of the Annunciation. 'It's such a fine example of the Winchester School of Illumination,' she declares, as she points to the lush acanthus sprays in the rectangular decorative borders and the lavish use of gold, which glows in the natural light.

St Æthelwold was born in Winchester around AD 909 and was Bishop of Winchester between 963 and 984. It is thought the book was commissioned and completed sometime between 971 and his death in 984. The texts of the book contain solemn benedictions for a bishop to speak at Mass on different days of the ecclesiastical year. It is likely Æthelwold commissioned it for his own personal use. The scribe who created it is thought to be a monk called Godeman who was based at the Old Minster in Winchester. There are twenty-eight full page illuminations. The page featuring the Annunciation miniature would have been used when the special blessing was given on the First Sunday of Advent.

I bend over this masterpiece of Anglo-Saxon art, one of the earliest illustrated Benediction books still in existence. It is in extraordinarily pristine condition. Close up, the magnificent beauty of the illumination is breathtaking. The intimacy of my encounter with the book is truly thrilling.

'At a time when everything today is mass produced rather than handmade, everything here is hand done. It's incredible,' Dr Doyle tells me.

Mary sits under a dome-like baldachin with a spindle in her left hand and a book by her right hand. What makes this depiction so special, as well as it being one of the earliest illuminations in the West, is its portrayal of Mary's interiority. It is said to have 'wielded a powerful effect on insular art with many of its iconographical features being copied in the

98. *Benedictional of St Æthelwold*, tenth century, British Library, London. © The British Library
Board MS 49598

last quarter of the tenth and the eleventh centuries.' A professor quoted on a British Library blog describes it thus: 'All manuscripts are unique but the Benedictional of St Æthelwold is more unique than most.'

Kathleen Doyle puts the book back in its leather pouch and closes the box firmly before placing it back in the trolley.

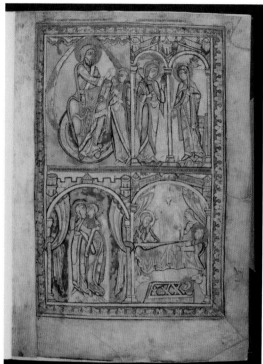

99. *The Winchester Psalter*, 1150, British Library. © The British Library Board F.10r

Next, she places the *Winchester Psalter*, also known as the *Psalter of Henry of Blois*, on the table. This twelfth-century book, another masterpiece of medieval manuscript illumination, is known for its cycle of miniatures, which precede the text of the Book of Psalms. Indeed, it has been described as the pinnacle of English Romanesque manuscript illumination.

It was designed for use as a prayer book in Winchester and is likely to have been commissioned by the wealthy Bishop of Winchester, Henry of Blois – brother of King Stephen – who served at the Cathedral from 1129 to 1171. Its creation is estimated to have been around 1150. There are thirty-eight full page miniatures grouped at the beginning of the manuscript featuring scenes from the Old Testament, the life of the Virgin Mary and the life of Jesus. The drawings are in black ink, with some of the coloured pigments having flaked off over time. Kathleen Doyle carefully turns over the pages before stopping at a full page with four compartments.

The top panel on the left shows God in heaven sending the angel Gabriel to convey the Salutation. The second scene, in the top right panel, is a depiction of the annunciation encounter between the angel and Mary. The Anglo-Norman French caption reads: 'ICI ENTRET LI SAINZ ESPIRS EN LI' (Here the Holy Spirit enters into her). The words emphasize to the faithful how this is the very moment of the supernatural conception.

'It's a visionary scene that places you in a mystical place,' Dr Doyle comments. 'The goal is to create a scene that is contemplative to show how extraordinary the moment is – life changing for her and for the redemption of the whole world.'

The third panel shows the Visitation, when Mary meets her cousin Elizabeth, and the final panel shows the Nativity.

I ask Dr Doyle whether she believes the Annunciation is the most important event in human history.

'For those people of Christian faith, presumably it is,' she answers. 'It's the act that leads to the redemptive act of the Crucifixion. But I'm an art historian. I leave that to the theologians.'

The last time I was inside the British Museum's Prints and Drawings Room was at the start of my journey, when I came to view Laurent Cars's 1728 engraving of the Annunciation that used Lemoyne's original painting as its reference point. Now I have returned to see two original early sixteenth-century woodcut prints by the great Albrecht Dürer.

The first is part of a *Life of the Virgin* series he produced in 1503 and the second is from his *Small Passion* series from 1510. I place the two prints onto two small easels in front of me.

Born in Nuremberg in 1471, Albrecht Dürer was a prolific draughtsman who built a reputation as one of the greatest artists of his day, north of the Alps. He was gifted and highly versatile, working as a painter, drawer and engraver but was most renowned as a printer of woodcut designs. Aged twenty-four, he set up his own workshop in Nuremberg specializing in the production of innovative, high quality prints. He travelled widely, especially to Italy where he engaged with the leading Renaissance artists of his day who greatly influenced the subject matters of his work.

The British Museum has a fine collection of Dürer's prints and some of the original blocks used to create his woodcuts. Giulia Bartrum, Curator of German Prints and Drawings from 1400 to 1900 and an expert on Dürer, joins me at the British Museum. She studied art history at the University of London, then worked at the Royal Collection before joining the British Museum thirty-six years ago. Her major work, *Albrecht Dürer and his Legacy*, was published in 2002.

Elegantly dressed in a sky-blue top and black trousers, with blond-brown hair and metal-rimmed glasses, she tells me, 'His main desire was to create a market for high class, good quality prints for wider sections of society, to broaden the market…primarily for the middle class but to target a lesser market than for engravings. He was creating an aesthetic for the medium of print – to admire and appreciate it. This was a time before the Reformation so we are into standard Catholic fare and we want narrative treatments of the most popular stories around Christ. But Dürer is on a grander scale. This Annunciation from 1503 fits into his *Life of the Virgin* series of seventeen images. The quality of this design, the elaborate architecture, the cross between the old and the new, enabled his audience to appreciate all the clues. Dürer used the obvious clues and symbols but he also introduced a more elaborate setting.'

The print is smaller than I had imagined: 295 mm x 210 mm. But it is the incredible detail that is most striking. The way the arches promote a strong linear perspective to the vanishing point of the garden beyond; the angel arriving down the stairs with both wings open, his two fingers and thumb pointing at Mary…you can almost hear him declaring, 'You're the one'…the covered canopy; the drawn back curtain; Mary's closed eyes and her arms crossing her chest in a gesture of acceptance; God the Father holding a cross as he looks down from the sky above.

'Northern artists like Dürer are very good at portraiture,' Giulia Bartrum says, 'but they also want to tell a story and make it clear what's going on and to make it realistic in a contemporary setting and with that hint of the landscape beyond. It's the wonderful texture that he is able to convey here in black and white.'

She comments further on Durer's determination to raise the aesthetic quality of northern art, and of printmaking in particular, such that it would be treated on equal terms with the great works produced by the fashionable artists of the Italian Renaissance.

100. Albrecht Dürer *The Annunciation*, from the *Life of the Virgin* series,
1503, British Museum, London. © The Trustees of the British Museum

'He works very hard on the architecture and the interior look,' she continues. 'These prints had a wide circulation across Europe and then were copied in other media too such as glass. He was interested in how many he could print of high quality from the blocks.'

We turn to his second Annunciation, designed seven years later for the *Small Passion* series. There's God the Father again in the clouds; the dove descending on the beams of light; Mary turning around having been disturbed whilst in prayer; and the familiar *AD* trademark sign of the artist. But it is the magnificence of the drapery and the splendid architecture of the bed chamber setting that catches my eye, as well as the stunning detail of Mary's wonderful long, curly hair flowing down her back.

'The woodcut was very robust and would yield thousands of impressions,' she says. 'That was Dürer's whole idea – to create as many high-quality prints that remained sharp.'

Dürer designed the woodcut by drawing in reverse directly onto the block. Professional cutters would then cut out the wood round each of the lines of his highly detailed and intricate design.

101. Albrecht Dürer *The Annunciation*, from the *Small Passion* series, 1510,
British Museum, London. © The Trustees of the British Museum

'I always look at the quality of the impression,' she says. 'This is a particularly fine one. The black lines almost stand up and that's what we really admire – the impression of the block on the surface. Here, you've got very fine lines indeed.'

We move on to talk about the impact of the prints at that time. Long before most people would be able to read a book, they could read an image. The effect of Dürer's woodcuts, and the thousands of prints issued, was to enable so many more people to engage in an intimate one-to-one dialogue between the viewer and the viewed.

'I'm not religious myself but I'm astonished how little the students of today know about the basic Bible stories,' she sighs. 'You've got to know these stories inside and out or you lose out on the clues and your appreciation of it. They knew the annunciation story and Dürer is trying to make it more realistic, to bring it home to you, that it could happen close to you or in a particularly beautiful setting that you admire or aspire to. It's the extra details and the extra dimensions he created so that it's not just a basic tale.'

Standing in the North Quire aisle of St Paul's Cathedral is a seven-foot-tall sculpture by Henry Moore. *Mother and Child : Hood* was created in 1983 and installed in 1984. It is one of his final works. The subject matter of mother and child was a common theme for Moore but this one is rather different.

In *Celebrating Moore – Works from the Collection of the Henry Moore Foundation*, published in 1998, Gail Gelburd recounts the following comment from one of the greatest sculptors of the twentieth century: 'There are two particular motives or subjects which I have constantly used in my sculpture. They're the "reclining figure" and the "mother and child" idea. Perhaps of the two, the "mother and child" has been the more fundamental obsession.'

Moore recognized the mother and child to be a universal theme from the beginning of time and realized how some of the very earliest sculptures from the Neolithic Age depicted the two figures together. The Dean of St Paul's Cathedral in the early 1980s was Dr Alan Webster and he was a great admirer of Moore's work. Following his suggestion, Moore agreed with the Dean that a madonna-like mother and child sculpture would be an appropriate installation to display inside one of Britain's greatest architectural glories.

Moore was not a religious man but as Roger Berthould revealed in his 1987 biography, *The Life of Henry Moore*, the sculptor always recognized the importance of ecclesiastical art through the ages: 'Religious art has been the inspiration for the greatest works of art in the world because the Church at one time was the greatest patron and gathered up all the artistic talent.'

Moore later made another relevant observation: 'I'm not sure what people mean by religious art. If you believe that life is something wonderful, that is worth living, that's religious. It's a belief in life.'

Henry Moore was recovering from a serious illness at the time of the commission from St Paul's and the project is said to have done much to reinvigorate him. He rang his friend Sir Denis Hamilton as he began work on it. 'I can't get this Madonna and Child out of my mind,' he said. 'It may be my last work and I want to give it the feel of having a religious connotation.' After creating the maquette and then a working model, the design was sent to the artisans of the Henraux studio in Querceta in the Carrara mountains of northern Italy, where the specially selected travertine marble was carved.

Interestingly, when he had previously worked on a madonna and child way back in 1943-4 for St Matthew's church in Northampton, the religious element of the commission appeared to trouble him: 'It was to strengthen religious beliefs. I tried to fit in with the accepted faith. It was a real worry and gave me many problems.'

In contrast, this time, as his career and life were starting to draw to a close, Moore realized that the location for the new piece in St Paul's would mean it would be viewed by millions of people. In addition, the fact that the subject matter would focus on birth and the sanctity of the mother-child relationship, could make this one of his most iconic works.

The result is a stunning abstract version of the mother and child theme and more specifically the Madonna and Child. To me, the figure immediately looks like a seated Virgin Mary holding her child. The smooth crescent shape at the top of the sculpture suggests her veil. The curved line of her back, apparently modelled on an animal bone Moore found in the garden of his home, implies that the figure is leaning forward, in act of protective love.

Simon Carter, the Collections Manager at St Paul's Cathedral had informed me before my visit, 'It's a generic mother and child group rather than specifically the Virgin and Child. But it's intended to show conception, gestation and post-birth toddlerhood.' One website indicates the recess in which the smaller figure rests suggests both a womb and a tender embrace – a theme of new life as well as mother and child.

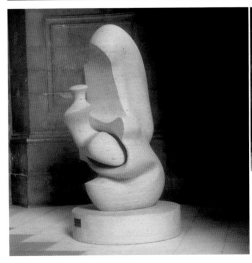

102. Left: Henry Moore *Mother and Child: Hood*, 1983, St Paul's Cathedral, London. © and reproduced by kind permission of The Henry Moore Foundation. Right: Henry Moore visits St Paul's Cathedral to view his newly installed sculpture, 1984. © PA

The sculpture was given to St Paul's as a gift, on long term loan from The Henry Moore Foundation. The minutes from the Chapter meetings at the time reveal that St Paul's saw it as devotional: 'the carving was not intended as an exhibit but rather an object of spiritual evocation.'

Moore himself insisted there would be no protection around the sculpture.

In 1986, two years after Moore came to St Paul's to see his new work in situ, he died aged eighty-eight. A plaque in the Artists' Corner of the Crypt commemorates his life and work. I contact The Henry Moore Foundation that promotes and protects his artistic legacy. Is there any indication from his personal papers that Moore was trying to infer in this sculpture a moment of conception – incarnation, birth and toddler all in one? Archivist Michael Phipps responds: 'It hasn't been possible to discover any reference or allusion to the Annunciation. Moore's statement, "It may be my last work and I want to give it the feel of having a religious connotation" is hardly enough. Although he periodically acknowledged the influence of religion on much great art, he wasn't a practising Christian as such and indeed preferred not to ascribe definitive sources of inspiration to his works.'

I touch the smooth marble stone, feeling its curves and indentations. I stand back and then move around the sculpture, viewing it from different angles. I can just about work out what Simon Carter has suggested. Many visitors stop and view the sculpture as they walk out of the High Altar area onto the North Choir Aisle.

A beautifully dressed middle-aged American couple stands in front of it, holding hands. I ask them what they see. The woman laughs gently.

'Oh, my God,' she replies. 'You don't wanna know.'

'Go on,' I say, 'tell me.'

'Well it's the Virgin Mary and Jesus, right? But when I first saw it, I thought it was the foetus in her uterus. I know that sounds crazy but that's what I saw first.'

She moves back a few yards to view the sculpture from a certain angle and points her finger towards the smaller figure.

'Hey, I see what you mean,' her partner responds. 'I didn't clock that at all but now I see it. Hey, the moment of conception. And then you move and the child appears as a young kid in her arms. That's really smart. That's amazing.'

Another young couple stand in front of it. She tells me she is called Ana and lives in Madrid. I ask them what they see. Her partner, Alvaro, seems reticent and walks a few steps away but she responds enthusiastically.

'It is La Virgen Maria of course,' she answers in a strong Madrileños accent. 'It is different. It is very sexual. How do you say?…the action and the child. Fantastic.'

Another couple tell me it's the Virgin Mary holding the Christ Child. Do they see anything more?

'It's Mary with her young son,' the woman responds.

Next, a young man from Nottingham says he doesn't know what it is. I tell him it is called *Mother and Child : Hood*. 'Ok,' he replies indifferently as he moves on.

Two women from Peru describe it as the Virgin Mary holding the baby in the stable immediately after the birth.

Five minutes later and a middle-aged English woman gazes alone at the *Mother and Child : Hood* for quite some time. I approach and tell her I am writing a piece about the sculpture. I ask her what she sees.

'Obviously it's suggesting Mary and baby Jesus. It's rather phallic,' she declares without an ounce of inhibition. 'The tip, the head,' she says, as she points to the top of the smaller figure, whilst she moves to its right. 'It points to the act of impregnation. Then there's the gash in her stomach. It looks like a cross-section of her womb. Very provocative and sensual.'

I am taken aback. I cannot believe her openness, nor, as I look at the sculpture, can I fathom out what she means. I tell her I cannot see what she's talking about. To me, it looks like a gracious and tender depiction of the Virgin Mary holding the baby Jesus lovingly in her arms.

'We see what we want to see,' she replies. 'For me, it's highly erotic.'

As I sit in front of the sculpture feeling rather stunned, I read two interesting comments made by Moore that I had noted down before the visit: 'Artists, in a way, are religious anyway. They have to be; if by religion one means believing that life has some significance, and some meaning, which is what I think it has. An artist could not work without believing that.' And in a conversation with John Hedgecoe, published in his 1986 book *Henry Moore My Ideas, Inspiration and Life as an Artist*: 'Just because throughout my sculpture I've been interested in the same subjects, mother and child, reclining figures and so on, doesn't mean I was obsessed with these themes. It just means I haven't exhausted them and, if I were to have another hundred years, I would still find satisfaction in these subjects. I can always discover new thoughts and ideas, it is inexhaustible.'

As I make my way out of the Cathedral, I recognize that I have the same type of fascination for my subject – the Annunciation – and I am starting to realize that the different thoughts, perspectives and ideas I have discovered seem inexhaustible too.

I walk round to Amen Corner Court to meet St Paul's Residential Canon Chancellor in his home. The courtyard is tranquil, only yards away from the noise and bustle of Ludgate Hill. Canon Mark Oakley has a particular responsibility for engagement with the arts in the Cathedral. I tell him I have just been in front of the Moore sculpture and he starts to pace around the room, gesticulating with great enthusiasm as he speaks.

'You go over here and look this way,' he proclaims. 'You have to be sexually alert. It's conception. It looks as though conception is going on. Then you move here and you have the womb and the nurtured foetus.' He then changes direction. 'Then you go here and you have the outline of a woman holding the child. You get the three stages all in one piece of stone. I think it's incredible, one of the best pieces in the Cathedral. I often show GCSE students that. They obviously love the sex bit but then they go, "this is really cool". But sometimes people miss all that.'

The forty-eight-year-old cleric sits down on a comfy chair and strokes the dog lying next to him. 'Poor Fritz,' he sighs. 'He's got a poorly paw and is rather lame. He's not himself today.'

I have come to see Mark Oakley primarily because he takes a special interest in poetry and I want to engage with him about some of the great poetic works that focus on the Annunciation. But I also want to take the opportunity to discuss its spiritual meaning.

'The word annunciate means "awaken",' he begins. 'It's about awakening us out of surface existence to a sense of numinous, the depth, whatever metaphors we want to fall into. Awakening us out of our daily lives to another voice. It's an important image. Today, we've never had so many voices in our lives aimed at us from advertisers to politicians. It's a key theme in the Gospels, particularly the beginnings of the Gospels, where people hear another voice. Awakening the soul to a resonance that is beyond the human – the mirror of God, the transcendent – and we all know when it happens.'

I am interested that he refers to metaphors straight away. Is this how he sees the Annunciation?

'Mm, my theology is done through narrative and poetry,' he responds. 'In the same way you wouldn't ask that of a poem, it's a false question for me. It is what it is. The Japanese have a lovely phrase for it – mu (無) – what you say when the question is wrong. It's the wrong framing of the question or the wrong question altogether.'

He pats Fritz, then continues to stroke his tummy while he talks. Clearly the two are very close.

'It's a wrong question,' he repeats. 'It's based on an understandable Enlightenment approach. Did it happen or didn't it happen? For me, religion is about living a poem. To rationalize it is missing the point. That's why we ritualize it. We make a drama of it.'

He speaks gently.

'The Annunciation is mythology. It's so important that it can't just be factual,' he explains. 'It's not about what happened. It's about what happens. It may be a story about the past. But the resonance for preaching is, does it happen now? People are awakened out of High Street muzak into awe and to a voice that matters. Most human beings discover it in some sort of trauma or happiness. Something awakens them to something that matters.'

I presume that voice is the voice of God, I say.

'Yes,' he replies. 'Being somebody immersed in the poetic view and the metaphor, I'm cautious in over-using the word but yes, I do believe that this is of ultimate reality. And for me, belief in God is to say, ultimately reality is trustworthy. You can trust.'

What does he make of the statement that the Annunciation is 'the most important event in human history'?

'Yes, because of that rupturing into history,' he replies. 'I think as a Christian you would say that this is the moment when God communicates in a body language called Jesus. So yes, I can see that. But whether or not it is the moment? Do I really want to get into a beauty contest of Christian doctrines?' he laughs.

Mark Oakley was an only child brought up in Shropshire by his grandparents. He describes himself as a solitary boy, a 'reflector', who made his own company. His grandparents did not attend church. However, one day he walked past his local church, saw the vicar wearing green vestments and thought, I want to do that! It was, in his own words, the beginning of his romance with God and the Church. He would pretend to be a vicar – draping himself with a sheet, lighting a couple of candles in his bedroom, and playing choral music and hymns he had recorded from the radio. He joked with an amused audience at a recent St Paul's Sunday Forum, 'Nothing's really changed thirty years later.'

He read Theology at King's College, London, where 'questions started to throw themselves up'. He says his time at university was about 'thinking critically, wondering how to live faithfully'. After a period of serious doubt about religion and bewilderment with God, having worked on an HIV-Aids ward at St Mary's Hospital in Paddington, he returned to his Christian faith and was ordained in St Paul's Cathedral twenty years ago. On first impressions, he appears to be soft and sensitive and there is an integrity and openness about him that is striking. He tells me that truth, honesty and resonance are the watchwords of his own faith.

Does he agree that the feast of the Annunciation has lost its resonance?

'Yes, yes,' he sighs, 'I think it has. Although if you started to preach, to spell out the themes I've just been talking about, they may say, "now that's a different take on it" instead of just hearing about a flapping angel walking into a room. That may not do it for people now. So, what if I said something like, "Is life about spending money you don't have, on things you don't need, to impress people you don't particularly like? Is that it? The moment you realize it isn't, there's been an annunciation." Of course, I believe this was an annunciation about God and about his communication. But today it is about an awakening, an awakening to the beyond, to things that matter.'

He gazes out of the window at the pink apple blossom from a nearby tree fluttering to the floor.

'The one thing I would say about the Christian faith for me is, my understanding is, that you can sum it up like this: God loves us just as we are but he loves us so much he doesn't want us to stay like that. It's about transformation. Annunciation. Resurrection.'

Twelve years ago in a lecture entitled, 'Spiritual Society, Secular Church?' which he delivered at both Westminster Abbey and Keble College, Oxford, Mark Oakley argued that the Church, in its search to be relevant, was ironically becoming too secular for the British public and that it should be the deeper human resonances that the Church must seek to identify, explore and have dialogue with.

'We're not always as imaginative about our feasts as we could be,' he says. 'We live down to people's expectations. But through preaching, events, creative liturgy you could frame this feast to be more relevant. Of course, the story ends with a pregnancy. But so many people today don't think that the Christian faith is pregnant. That it's clapped out with not much resonance. It doesn't push our contours like a pregnancy does. It deflates us. You could have a more imaginative, playful, allusive approach where things did become more pregnant with more meaning. An annunciation.'

Mark Oakley says that everything he does should be to relax people into the poetry of Christian living. He has been described in a national newspaper as 'one of the finest preachers in the Church of England of our age.' As he speaks, one can hear his love of words and his passion for the rhythm and feel of poetry. He tells me he is normally a script person. 'Every word is normally written there. But today it's just coming out spontaneously.' He asks me if he is expressing himself satisfactorily. I nod back appreciatively.

'There's something about the vulnerability of love in that story of the Annunciation,' he says. 'We get all that imagery in our prayers…Almighty God, All Powerful Father, a "Thor" like…it seems to me any God who is love is not going to be all-powerful because love isn't. You see it in how you annunciate your love. Everyone knows the first time you tell someone "I love you" there's huge risk in that because it may just come back in your face. The most precarious and intense thing you've ever said to somebody could be rejected. There's something hugely worrying and hugely exhilarating about it. Well, here is God doing the same to humanity. "I love you and I'm waiting to hear the reply".'

Mark Oakley will spend the rest of his day working on his forthcoming book, *The Splash of Words*, in which he explores the power of poetry and how it can, in his words, 'stir our settled ways of viewing the world and faith, shift our perception and even transform who we are.' In the book's introduction, he writes, 'the phrase 'Splash of Words' is a good description of poetry. When you read a poem there is an initial splash like a pebble thrown into a lake. The words disturb your surface and have their impact. Then, as the poem begins to do its work, the ripples of meaning head out towards your shore, often slowly, but relentlessly, and you realise that these words are shifting your perceptions and consequently even transforming who you are and how you understand.' He goes on to observe, 'poetry is not an easy running river. It is not a quick read. It is a fountain, a source from which meaning can be slowly, patiently drawn. We have all heard of "creative writing" but poetry demands of us a creative reading. Poetry is a language that listens. There is no quick clarity. No seductive easy answers. There is no one meaning to be had either, no conclusive evidence to give to the court. Get a group of people together talking about a poem and you'll discover this very quickly. As you read a poem you have to persevere for the meanings that begin to work their way out, resonating and demanding in equal measure.'

I take a short walk from Mark Oakley's home to a newly opened garden in the south-east precinct of St Paul's Cathedral. There, I sit quietly next to a recently unveiled bronze bust of John Donne, one of Britain's finest ever poets and a former Dean of St Paul's. In 1610, after a period of personal religious turmoil when he converted from Roman Catholicism to Anglicanism, John Donne wrote 'La Corona' in the form of a crown of sonnets – a single poem made up of seven linked sonnets. I study the second one which he entitled 'Annunciation':

> Salvation to all that will is nigh:
> That All, which always is all everywhere,
> Which cannot sin, and yet all sins must bear,
> Which cannot die, yet cannot choose but die,
> Lo, faithful virgin, yields Himself to lie
> In prison, in thy womb; and though He there
> Can take no sin, nor thou give, yet He will wear,
> Taken from thence, flesh, which death's force may try.
> Ere by the spheres time was created, thou
> Wast in His mind, who is thy Son and Brother;
> Whom thou conceivst, conceived; yea thou art now
> Thy maker's maker, and Thy Father's mother;
> Thou hast light in dark, and shuts in little room,
> Immensity cloistered in thy dear womb.

Over the past few months, I have created a personal compendium of poetry inspired by the annunciation story. Whilst sitting in the garden by St Paul's, I take this poetry notebook out of my bag and focus on three of the poems. The first was written by the sixteenth-century Spanish Carmelite friar and mystic, St John of the Cross. Born Juan de Yepes y Álvarez in 1542 at Fontiveros near Ávila, his poem is called 'The Incarnation' and was translated into English in the late 1940s by the acclaimed South African poet, Roy Campbell:

Then He summoned an archangel,
Saint Gabriel: and when he came,
Sent him forth to find a maiden,
    Mary was her name.

Only through her consenting love
Could the mystery be preferred
That the Trinity in human
    Flesh might clothe the Word.

Though the three Persons worked the wonder
It only happened in the One.
So was the Word made incarnation
    In Mary's womb, a son.

So He who only had a Father
Now had a woman undefiled,
Though not as ordinary maids
    Had she conceived the Child

By Mary, and with her own flesh
He was clothed in His own frame:
Both Son of God and Son of Man
    Together had one name.

The second poem I read is entitled 'Annunciation to Mary' and was written in 1912 by the Bohemian-Austrian mystical poet, Rainer Maria Rilke:

The angel's entrance (you must realize)
was not what made her frightened. The surprise
he gave her by his coming was no more
than sun or moon-beam stirring on the floor
would give another, – she had long since grown
used to the form that angels wear, descending;
    never imagining this coming-down
was hard for them. (O it's past comprehending,
how pure she was. Did not one day, a hind
that rested in a wood, watchfully staring,
    feel her deep influence, and did it not
conceive the unicorn, then, without pairing,
the pure beast, beast which light begot, –)
    No, not to see him enter, but to find
the youthful angel's countenance inclined
so near to her; that's when he looked, and she
looked up at him, their looks so merged in one
the world outside grew vacant, suddenly,
and all things being seen, endured and done
were crowded into them: just she and he
eye and its pasture, visions and its view,
here at the point and at this point alone: —
see, this arouses fear. Such fear both knew.

The Irish poet, William Butler Yeats was one of the twentieth-century's greatest literary figures. In 1923, he won the Nobel Prize for Literature and ten years later Yeats wrote this poem, titled 'The Mother of God':

> The threefold terror of love; a fallen flare
> Through the hollow of an ear;
> Wings beating about the room;
> The terror of all terrors that I bore
> The Heavens in my womb.
>
> Had I not found content among the shows
> Every common woman knows,
> Chimney corner, garden walk,
> Or rocky cistern where we tread the clothes
> And gather all the talk?
>
> What is this flesh I purchased with my pains,
> This fallen star my milk sustains,
> This love that makes my heart's blood stop
> Or strikes a Sudden chill into my bones
> And bids my hair stand up?

I cross the slender Millennium Bridge over the Thames, to the Tate Modern. I have come to see a relatively modern image entitled *an annunciation (b)*. The picture shows a naked woman sitting on a chair by a window in the corner of a sparsely furnished bedroom. She is speaking on a cordless telephone while playing with her blonde hair. Her legs are crossed and some of her pubic hair is just visible. Through the window is a leafy tree and it is clear that daylight is starting to take its leave. A lamp on a table next to her is switched on, illuminating her upper body and the corner of the room, casting shadows on the floor and walls. She appears alert and pensive.

The work forms part of the Tate's major retrospective on Richard Hamilton, often described as the godfather of pop art in Britain and one of the most significant British artists of the latter half of the twentieth century. Hamilton died in 2011 aged eighty-nine and worked right up to his death. He is known for his highly innovative paintings, collages, print designs, photographs and computer graphics.

Mark Godfrey, the curator of the exhibition, neatly sums up Hamilton's artistic impact on the exhibition's audio guide. In a career spanning seventy years from the late 1940s to 2011, in which he took a consistently original and experimental approach to art, Godfrey says Hamilton 'moved from one style to another approaching all the historic genres of art in distinctly modern ways.'

an annunciation (b) is a painting he created on canvas in 2005 as part of his final body of work. Godfrey explains: 'He produced several versions of a particular work rather than a single finished piece. He explored new printmaking methods and leading edge digital techniques, locating the boundary of abstraction and figuration in enlarged images.'

The image used in this painting is actually an iteration of a more famous, original work by Hamilton – a high resolution inkjet digital print called *The annunciation*, completed earlier in the same year. In that larger work, the image of the naked woman taking the call is depicted as a picture hanging in what looks like a modern art gallery, with white beams and walls jutting out at all angles. A spotlight illuminates the picture and an air-conditioning grille is pictured above it. It is a lustrous print that utilizes a series of digitally enhanced photographs taken over a ten-year period. One photo shows the corner of Hamilton's bedroom. Others show different angles of a room in an art gallery. Hamilton used advanced computer graphics to blend together different parts of the scanned images. The end result looks like an untouched photograph.

The annunciation was inspired by Fra Angelico's fifteenth-century Annunciation frescos in the San Marco monastery in Florence, which Hamilton first saw thirty years earlier. He kept a postcard of them in his studio in Northend, Oxfordshire, and at one time, was hoping to exhibit some of his own work at San Marco.

I head back north over the River Thames and make my way to Mayfair, the heart of London's contemporary art galleries. I enter the Alan Cristea Gallery in Cork Street where I am keen to view one of the original digital prints of Hamilton's *The annunciation*. I walk down the stairs into the private basement area with the Gallery's Director, Helen Waters, and immediately see the framed print on the floor. It is much smaller than I had expected and is nestled alongside various contemporary artworks including a self-portrait by Julian Opie. I pick up the picture and inspect it closely. I notice how, to the left of his signature, Richard Hamilton writes the title as *the annunciation*. Has he purposely omitted a capital 'A' to indicate that this is a secular work? On the back it is marked as the forty-fifth print of a limited edition of sixty.

103. Richard Hamilton *The annunciation*, 2005. © R.Hamilton. All Rights Reserved DACS 2017

The art historian, Fanny Singer, has written numerous articles for the Tate and *The Burlington Magazine* on Hamilton's artistry and innovation including a scholarly analysis of this particular annunciation work. In them, she observes how, 'Hamilton did not intend for his increasingly frequent use of recognisably Christian motifs to substantiate or defer to any given belief system to which he did not subscribe. His idiosyncratic aim was to achieve a kind of secular numinosity through technical fluency and layered narrative.'

She explains how Hamilton 'encouraged an analogy between the theme of the

Annunciation (that is the moment of Mary's super physical impregnation by God) and digital creation (an artwork created without physical touch). The medium and the message becoming one.'

Richard Hamilton wanted to create hundreds of digital prints of the Annunciation to echo the trends of the past. As Fanny Singer reflects: 'The Annunciation image appealed on an aesthetic level but equally for its wider cultural ubiquity as one of the most visualized stories in western history.'

I make contact with the thirty-year-old Californian writer who studied Art History at Yale and whose Ph.D. at Cambridge focused on Richard Hamilton's work. She starts our conversation by recounting how she sat with the artist in 2007 as he read the part of her dissertation focused on this annunciation work.

' "Ten out of ten" he very kindly proclaimed after reading it,' she tells me from her home in St Ives. 'For him, it was about developing some kind of conversation with Fra Angelico, an artist he admired as a genius, more than it was about the religious aspect of the subject. I've been to San Marco myself many times. I'm always amazed. I'm in no way religious but those images are incredibly moving. Hamilton was adamantly, vocally atheistic but he saw the magical aura of them which was impossible to ignore.'

So, is this a purely secular work?

'I think there was an increased tendency in his late work to remove the hand from the making. That chimed with the Annunciation theme more broadly. There was this touchless conception,' she responds. 'What's interesting for me with the print is that he doesn't intervene at any stage with paint or he only does so at the end stage. The brushwork was beside the point because the real interest in the work was the artistic aim to achieve *acheiropoieta*, but in the uncanny, sleek, twenty-first-century medium of digital technology. It's a perfect resolution to a problem. How do you re-engage this story that is appropriate for right now?'

Hamilton continued the Annunciation theme in 2007, two years after creating *an annunciation (b)*, with a new digital montage print called *The passage of the angel to the virgin*. There, he directly references Fra Angelico but depicts the angel and Mary as female nudes.

The sound of the seagulls drowns out Fanny Singer's voice so we pause a while. She explains how, in viewing the images, we are suspended between the illusory and the real in the same way that, in Christian theology, the Virgin has been suspended between God and humanity. Importantly, she says, they are images that come into being without an intervention from a human hand.

'It is interesting that someone so vigorously atheistic gets into these subjects. It's not simply a witty take on things. It's much more than that. It's entering into a colloquy with another master who he revered and studied. It's a meditation on how Fra Angelico's masterpiece can be re-visualized but with his own trademark. It's incredibly beautiful not to have any interruption of any brush stroke. For the plane to be completely resolved…a feeling of total integration. Like the Fra Angelico fresco on the wall, there's a seamlessness to it. He was never disparaging about the annunciation story. Yes, there were the witticisms, the cordless phone, the naked woman as the virgin. But he was very willing in his art to go into the complicated territory of what's real and what's fabricated, what's a religious miracle, what's myth, what the Annunciation is to people and however they want to define it.'

I leave Cork Street and walk just around the corner to Savile Row. Five decades ago this area was the epicentre for high-end male fashion and bespoke tailoring as a vibrant London was building its worldwide reputation as 'The Swinging City'. I have a song buzzing in my ears as I make my way to my next destination. The opening words rolling around my head focus on troubled times, a mother called Mary, hearing wise words and the phrase, 'let it be'. I find that the building I am looking for is undergoing a process of refurbishment and is due to re-open soon as an 'Abercrombie Kids' shop. However, it is not children's clothing that interests me today but the basement room at the bottom of the iron staircase. As I peer down at the cellar window of 3 Savile Row, my mind imagines the scene here forty-five years ago, on Friday, 31 January 1969.

Then, this basement was a small recording studio directly underneath the main entrance to the headquarters of Apple Records. The day before, The Beatles, the most famous group in the world, had given their last live performance on the roof of the building. Afterwards, the quieter songs that could not be recorded on the roof were performed in the studio. One of those new songs was called 'Let It Be'.

Nine takes of 'Let It Be' were recorded that Friday. One was released more than a year later and became a chart-topping single. Another was included in a feature film of the recording sessions, showing a bearded and straggly haired Paul McCartney at the piano looking directly at the camera as he sings his poignant lyrics. Although no one realized it at the time, that session would be the last ever filmed performance of The Beatles.

'Let it Be' is frequently voted one of the greatest popular songs ever written. As with many of The Beatles' lyrics, there have been many different interpretations of its meaning. Priests, scholars and Christian believers around the world have imbued it with spirituality, many of them believing it to be a beautiful rendition of the annunciation story. I remember seeing the words 'Let it Be' on a poster of a Beatles musical, the same day I first set eyes on Lemoyne's painting. That day, I saw images and reminders of the Annunciation everywhere I looked. Shortly after this, a woman told me that the song came into her mind when she was looking at the Lemoyne painting.

104. Left: The author plays his personal copy of the Beatles single 'Let It Be'. Right: Paul McCartney soon after recording 'Let It Be' in early 1969. © Daily Mail/Solo Syndication

The Beatles were at their lowest point at the time of the song's recording, riddled with angst, unhappiness, acrimony and tension. Two months before saw the release of the famous double LP, *The Beatles*, which quickly became known as the 'White Album' in recognition of its plain white cover, designed by Richard Hamilton. The follow-up record was supposed to be a return to their rock 'n' roll roots and was to be filmed throughout its gestation.

The initial filming of the rehearsals at Twickenham Studios proved to be fractious and problematic, just as the recording of the 'White Album' had been throughout the summer of 1968. The reality was that the four members were starting to go their separate ways. Paul McCartney was trying to hold the group together and to organize proceedings. That made him increasingly unpopular and the others saw him as too controlling and dictatorial. The band was disintegrating, slowly and inevitably. Paul McCartney set the scene and described how the song came to be written in a conversation with his friend and biographer, Barry Miles. (*Paul McCartney Many Years From Now*, published in 1997):

> This was a very difficult period. John was with Yoko full time, and our relationship was beginning to crumble: John and I were going through a very tense period. The breakup of the Beatles was looming and I was very nervy. Personally, it was a very difficult time for me, I think the drugs, the stress, tiredness and everything had really started to take its toll. I somehow managed to miss a lot of the bad effects of all that, but looking back on this period, I think I was having troubles.
>
> One night during this tense time I had a dream I saw my mum, who'd been dead ten years or so. And it was so great to see her because that's a wonderful thing about dreams: you actually are reunited with that person for a second; there they are and you appear to both be physically together again. It was so wonderful for me and she was very reassuring. In the dream she said, 'It'll be alright.' I'm not sure if she used the words 'Let it be' but that was the gist of her advice, it was 'Don't worry too much, it will turn out okay.' It was such a sweet dream I woke up thinking, Oh, it was really great to visit with her again. I felt very blessed to have that dream. So that got me writing the song 'Let It Be'. I literally started off 'Mother Mary', which was her name, 'When I find myself in times of trouble', which I certainly found myself in. The song was based on that dream.
>
> For many people 'Let It Be' was to become an inspirational song, one that got them through the bad times in their lives. Paul is proud of the number of fans who, over the years, have written to thank him for writing it. It is a song that still goes down well in concert and for which the audience shows its appreciation with candles, matches and disposable lighters.

Although the 'Let It Be' sessions were recorded many months before the Beatles final album *Abbey Road*, the recording tapes were shelved and 'Let It Be' wasn't released as a single until thirteen months later in March 1970, by which time the band had broken up and the song sounded like an epitaph.

When the *Let It Be* LP was released eventually three months later, John Lennon introduced the title track in a childlike voice, 'And now we'd like to do Hark the Angels Come' – a typical example of his caustic humour. On an earlier out-take, he had declared at the end, 'Country and Gospel. It's C&G.' Whether or not he liked the song, Lennon clearly identified a spiritual element within it.

Both Paul and his younger brother Michael were baptized Catholic, which was their mother's denomination, but it is fair to say that religion played little part in their childhood in Liverpool. Barry Miles writes that they were not sent to Catholic schools 'because their father Jim thought they concentrated too much on religion and not enough on education.'

Paul McCartney outlined his thoughts on a religious interpretation of 'Let It Be' to Barry Miles in his biography (*Paul McCartney Many Years From Now*):

> Mother Mary makes it a quasi-religious thing, so you can take it that way. I don't mind. I'm quite happy if people want to use it to shore up their faith. I have no problem with that. I think it is a great thing to have faith of any sort, particularly in the world we live in. My mother was Catholic and she had me and my brother christened but that was the only religious thing we went through other than school, and occasional visits to church, where I sang in a surpliced choir. The first time I ever heard about religion was when I was in hospital when I was eleven, and the sister on the ward lifted up my case sheet and said, 'What religion are you? It's not on here.' I said, 'I don't know.' She said, 'C of E?' I said, 'Probably.'

I have seen McCartney perform 'Let It Be' at Earls Court, Glastonbury, Hyde Park and at a more intimate gig at the Roundhouse in north London. Each time, his adoring fans closed their eyes and raised their hands in the air as if at a religious gathering. They showed their appreciation with lit candles and torchlight on mobile phones, holding them aloft so their lights flickered across the crowd. It was a very moving experience.

Hunter Davies, author of the Beatles official biography and aficionado of all things Beatle, describes the song particularly well in his more recent book *The Beatles' Lyrics*: 'Whilst it is almost a pastiche of a choral hymn, with lots of biblical overtones and allusions such as "hour of darkness", "a light that shines on me" and, of course, the image of Mother Mary, it is nonetheless sincere and moving.'

Mary McCartney died on 31 October 1956 when Paul was fourteen years old. Understandably, it was a shattering experience that has stayed with him for the rest of his life. Fifty-seven years later, when asked by a fan on his website in 2013 what he would do if he had a time machine, he replied, 'Go back and spend time with my mum.'

I meet with Barry Miles who has known Paul McCartney for more than fifty years. We begin by talking about the death of Paul's mother.

'It was an enormous shock to him. Jim had kept the boys ignorant of just how ill she was. He was a really good father. When it happened, it must have really undermined Paul's confidence. Despite being one of the most famous people on earth and having God knows how many number ones, he's still very much lacking in self-esteem, I think. He's always desperate to get people's approval. I would put it down to that. I know one of the things he regrets most of all is that his mother never saw his success. Imagine, you're a Beatle and she never knew.'

I ask about McCartney's creation of 'Let It Be', a song that has been described since as an elegy for the band's collapse.

'He did become very insecure. It was a very difficult period,' he tells me. 'I'd forgotten about that dream he had. It's very beautiful. I'm sure it's accurate. He wouldn't make up something like that. I think he believes there's a spiritual dimension to our lives but as far as I know he's not religious in any sense. Presumably being of Irish Catholic background, it's there, it's part of the culture so it might be unconscious. But it's very common up north to say, "let it be". It's a common thing to say. It doesn't have to relate to religion. It may be that on an unconscious level that information was there but whether it was a direct quote, I doubt it.'

So, what about those people who think it is connected to the Annunciation?

'I think that's fairly normal in rock 'n' roll quite honestly,' he replies. 'People are always interpreting things in their own way. Usually the more successful the rocker, the more they are like a *tabula rasa*. People project onto them and get back what they need. I'm sure it wasn't a religious song when he wrote it, certainly not. It just came out that way. The Beatles have been misinterpreted endlessly.'

Many of these misinterpretations are to be found in the acres of blogs and speculation posted on the Internet. For example, Charlotte Allen wrote an article on a website called *'beliefnet'* entitled 'Mother Mary Comes to Me: The Beatles and Catholicism':

> There is no lovelier hymn to Mary in modern English than 'Let It Be'. Those pellucid lyrics stand out as peerless against the backdrop of the saccharine Marian hymnody of today's Catholicism…It is difficult to listen to a Beatles song without hearing… Liverpool. Many of the songs are specifically infused with the Catholic culture of Liverpool which, as a port on the Irish Sea, has more Catholics than any other city in England because it has more Irish.

A daily Christian meditation website states boldly: 'The Beatles lyric concerns the Annunciation when Christ came to be Mary's son in the quietness of a spring evening.'

Another religious website calls on the faithful to listen to the song and hear its message: 'From the perspective of Advent, I invite you to hear the Beatles "Let It Be" as if for the first time. Listen with the words of Mary echoing in your ear. Listen with an openness to how God may be calling you to slow down, open your eyes in wonder, and expectantly wait, for he is already in the process of being born. How is God inviting you in the coming days and weeks to echo some form of Mary's words of humble openness and acceptance?'

On the website, *The Beatles Bible*, which features almost everything anyone may want to know about the group and their songs, a fan called Terry writes: 'What a coincidence that in Luke 1:38 Mary says "Let It Be". Or is it? Perhaps there is a more spiritual purpose and application here that is bigger than even The Beatles!'

Perhaps the most balanced observation I came across is this one: 'All of these interpretations (right or wrong, or stupid) are why the Beatles are so great…it's all about ambiguity, because no matter what the actual song meant, it means different things to different people.'

CHAPTER 27

A REFUGE OF CERTAINTY

I am watching a sixteen-year-old Jewish girl on a huge screen. She has long black wavy hair and an innocent looking face with rosy cheeks. We learn that she goes to synagogue every day and her loving father describes her as 'gentle and pure'. We see her meeting an older man for the first time and telling him about her faith: 'You feel safe, as though God is controlling you in his arms.' It becomes clear that they are about to become betrothed. He is a thirty-year-old manual worker, used to honest hard work. He tells her he plans to have lots of children and swears that he will be faithful forever. He appears to be kind and straightforward, always wanting to please. 'We'll be married for fifty years and have ten children,' he declares. The names of the characters are Mary and Joseph.

This is a scene from the BBC One television drama, *The Nativity*, first transmitted in December 2010 as a mini-series of four half-hour programmes in the run up to Christmas. It was broadcast at seven o'clock on consecutive nights, from 20 to 23 December, and was considered by the BBC to be one of its boldest commissions of recent years.

I am in a meeting room at Red Planet Pictures, just off Regent Street. Sitting next to me is fifty-six-year-old Tony Jordan, the creator of *The Nativity* and we are watching the plot unfold on the television screen on a wall. Tony wears a crisp, white shirt and a gold neck chain. He is tanned, has shiny white teeth, a long prominent nose and carries a small paunch. As he talks, he runs his fingers frequently through his curly greying hair. Born in the North West of England, he was expelled from school at fourteen years old and became a market-stall trader. Now, he is one of Britain's most successful dramatists. He is the man who brought us *Hustle, Life on Mars* and, as lead writer on *EastEnders*, introduced the nation to another couple, Kat Slater and Alfie Moon. When I see him, he is fully focused on writing a new twenty-part drama series with the working title, *Dickensian*, based on the interweaving of characters from different Charles Dickens's books.

As soon as we are introduced, I am aware of the force of his personality. He is so gregarious and loud his presence fills the room. We start to talk about Mary and I discover that he believes most people see her as 'a one-dimensional character with a halo round her head'. He describes how she fascinated him: 'She's not saccharine. Just a nice kid – real but fallible.'

He believes that the story remains hidden for so many people because they cannot get past the first bit – the Annunciation and the idea of a virgin conception. He felt that the key to making it compelling was to focus on the tension created between Mary and Joseph after the Annunciation. He spent four years working on the drama.

'This is it now, coming up,' he bawls in a cockney accent that could have come straight out of Walford. We're sitting behind a large table on which his original script lies. The Annunciation sequence is about to appear. It forms both the end of the first episode and the beginning of the second. Jordan constructed it as a cliffhanger, a device for which he is renowned.

It begins with Mary lying awake in bed at night at her home in Nazareth. She gets up to go outside and have a drink of water. All is quiet apart from the insect sounds that fill the night. She sits alone in a small garden, enthralled by the beauty of the velvet sky that is studded with bright stars. Suddenly, a bearded man with long hair and a full-length white robe appears and sits on a nearby rock. As well as watching the screen, I follow his original script:

GABRIEL: Hello Mary. Don't be afraid.

MARY: Who are you? My parents are just inside.

She stands up quickly.

GABRIEL: They're sleeping…and you mustn't worry, the Lord is with you…He holds you in much favour…Please…Sit.

Gabriel smiles kindly, Mary glances back at the house.

GABRIEL: You're safe, I promise.

MARY: (slowly sits down) What do you want with me?

GABRIEL: My name is Gabriel. I have stood in the presence of God and he has sent me to you.

MARY: I don't understand…

GABRIEL: You have been chosen.

CUT TO: NIGHT SKY.

On Jupiter, spinning through space, a booming mechanical sound of the universe being moved by unseen forces.

Spin off towards Saturn, then finally approach Regulus at speed, spinning all the way around it.

A sense of enormous scale as the three bodies edge ever nearer.
The noise increases to a crescendo… END OF EPISODE ONE

EPISODE TWO

Mary sits looking at Gabriel sitting on a rock a few feet from her.

MARY: I don't know what you mean…chosen for what?

GABRIEL: (smiling) The world is about to change forever…Mankind will be given a new testament, your sins will be forgiven and the path to eternal life will be revealed…the word will be made flesh.

MARY: You're talking in riddles

GABRIEL: You will bear a child. A son…you will call him Jesus.

MARY: Jesus?

GABRIEL: He will form a bridge between heaven and earth for all time. He will be called the Son of God and he will take up the throne of David. There will be no end to his reign.

MARY: But I'm not married.

GABRIEL: That's as it should be.

MARY: No!

GABRIEL: You have nothing to fear Mary. God is with you.

MARY: But I've never been with a man. How could I be with child?

GABRIEL: The Holy Spirit has found you.

MARY: (Stands) Why are you saying this? It isn't true. I don't know who you are but I don't believe you. Now leave me.

Gabriel stands as she walks back to the house.

GABRIEL: Do you love your God, Mary?

Mary continues

GABRIEL: Do you trust in him?

MARY: Yes.

Gabriel stands in front of her now.

GABRIEL: Then close your eyes…

Mary looks at Gabriel, he smiles and nods…

She closes her eyes.

GABRIEL: (CONTD) Look inside yourself, feel the Holy Spirit within you…Understand where your faith has brought you…It will be shown to you now.

A moment – Tears fall from her eyes and then she gasps, both hands move to her stomach and her eyes snap open wide… She looks at Gabriel and falls to her knees.

Gabriel kneels too – in front of her.

GABRIEL: (elated) You are blessed among women…You carry the Son of God!

MARY: It can't be.

He nods, smiling. Mary looks at him, tears in her eyes. A thought…

MARY: (CONTD) Joseph!

GABRIEL: He is a good man and he will care for you and the child.

He looks deep into Mary's eyes, he's elated.

GABRIEL: (CONTD) The light of the world is within you!

A moment and Mary knows it's true…

MARY: I am the Lord's servant.

Gabriel holds her hands gently.
Soon he has gone and she's left alone in the garden.

105. The Mary and angel Gabriel encounter in Tony Jordan's BBC One drama, *The Nativity*, 2010. By kind permission of Tony Jordan and Red Planet Pictures

'You can see the love in that relationship between Gabriel and Mary,' Tony Jordan proclaims as he points to the screen. 'It's key. Because of the way he arrives and the way he disappears, it gives you the opportunity to interpret it in any way you want to. But it's quite faithful to the original story. It's as faithful as I could make it because if I'd changed the text of the Annunciation so that it was completely different, it wouldn't have validated what was there. It had to be the same thing. It's what's in the Gospel but I've allowed for the oral sharing of it.'

Later, Mary tells Joseph that she thinks she has had a strange dream. He notices the slight swelling in her belly and immediately presumes she has been with another man or has been raped. He is so angry, incredulous and distraught that he calls off the marriage. As her pregnancy becomes steadily more obvious, the Nazareth community shuns her and calls her a whore.

Joseph hears that he has to head to his hometown of Bethlehem to register in a forthcoming census. Reluctantly, he agrees to take Mary with him only to save her from being stoned and assaulted. They hardly speak on the journey. She walks along behind him, heavily pregnant and increasingly tired. When she grows too weary, she sits on the donkey as they make their way through the sparse landscape. Joseph is depressed and shattered. Mary is sad and lonely. She tries to gain eye contact but he ignores her. The tension between them is palpable. One night, Joseph has a dream and tells Mary he is unsure what it means. Mary explains that the words he heard were similar to those delivered to her by Gabriel.

When they finally get to Bethlehem, no one wants to put them up because of the shame of her unmarried state. In the final scene of the serial, we see Mary giving birth to her baby in a stable.

Tony Jordan and I return to his nearby office. I ask him how *The Nativity* came about.

'Over half a bottle of rum with BBC drama colleagues in Cardiff,' he chuckles. 'I pitched off the top of my head a ninety-minute soap opera version of the Nativity. We don't see any of Mary and Joseph. We start in the inn, the Queen Vic of Bethlehem, with the landlord and we create a story about that time. It's full inside of Roman soldiers. Then at seventy-five minutes in, there's a knock on the door as a couple ask for a room. The landlord says, "Are you mad?" and sends the couple off into a barn at the back. The landlord then admits his own infidelity. Then at eighty-nine minutes he goes, "Shit – what about that couple in the barn?" He runs round to see them, opens the door and

106. John Lynch, Tatiana Maslany and Andrew Buchan star in *The Nativity*, 2010.
© Red Planet Pictures

there's the picture of the Nativity. It was half tongue-in-cheek – half me messing about. We had a laugh about it, telling the story of the Nativity without telling the story of the Nativity. That's certainly different.

'Four days later,' he recalls, 'I was told the idea was pitched to the BBC. They loved it and wanted to commission it. "Really?" I said. "The Queen Vic of Bethlehem?" "Yes, it's a really fresh idea," they said.

'I then went away to start writing the version. I was cock sure of myself. I thought, I don't need to do any research. I've got the image of the manger, the donkeys for the last five minutes and, before it, I'll sort of write my own thing. I got about twenty minutes in and I felt a bit dirty. I wasn't taking this seriously or whatever. It was like *'Allo 'Allo*. It's not my way. When I'm writing, I'm passionate about it. I'm fearless as a writer. If that's what I want to write, that's what I'll write. But I felt different. I thought it was silly. It had all come about because of that conversation in the pub. It had amused me but it was for all the wrong reasons.

'I put the script aside. I started to research the subject. I talked to bishops. I looked at lots of paintings. I read lots of stuff, trying to get my head round it all. What occurred to me then, in a kind of blinding light, was that all these biblical stories, and that story in particular, are denied to people like me. You know, northern working class, no education, expelled from school, no university education. Imagine if my wife came round to me and said, "I've got some good news and bad news. The bad news is I'm pregnant but the good news is I haven't been unfaithful. It's God's." Well, I'm not going to say, "Blessed am I. Let's go to Egypt," am I? I'm going to start throwing crockery around. Ask whose is it? Do I know him? So that story meant nothing to me. It never did. It was just part of the Christmas story. It had no resonance. It had no truth at the heart of it. It was closed to people like me. I couldn't get past that first bit so it didn't make any sense. If you don't believe there's truth in the DNA of a story, you're never going to buy into it. I knew that more than anyone. People have to believe, have to have empathy with the characters. Then you can take them on a journey. But if they look at it and say "What…really…come on," then you've lost them. So I suddenly realized the story wasn't accessible to people. It was on the shelf over there. Then I started looking at other films and television pieces about the Nativity. I realized they were doing the same f*****g thing. It was up there. It was beyond you. You'll never understand it. Angel Gabriel's always standing on rocks with a "Ready Brek" glow. Always looking down.

'I suddenly felt a do-you-want-a-real-test-of-your-craft? moment. Do you really want a challenge to your gift? Then make this story believable. Make it so that guys in the pub can watch it and not go, "F**k off, that never happened." That gave me an *in* to it. The relationship between Joseph and Mary became key. If I could make that believable, it would be ok. Make you believe her acceptance and his acceptance. That it would be ok for him not to have faith so long as he had faith in her.

'I started to feel a real air of responsibility when I started to write the second version. Once I'd got a handle on it, as a writer I could smell the truth in the DNA of it. I got halfway and I suddenly started to smell truth in it. With that, I felt, f**k, I've always discounted this. I've always thought it was a made-up story by religious institutions to keep the masses happy but, you know what, I don't think that's right. It's got truth to it; beauty to it. I thought, shit, I'm now going to deliver this to a mainstream audience for which this story has never been accessible before. This could well be their take on the Nativity story. That's quite a big thing to do that. It's five million people. Pre-watershed. Families. Believers and non-believers.

'So it had to be about her. I didn't know how you could have that kind of faith. I felt you could have the beginning of that kind of faith. There's an acceptance at that age, a trusting. A trust in your parents, your culture, your God. That acceptance worked for me. The beginnings of faith. Why wouldn't she accept? So I thought I can buy into that beginning of faith but I then had to find solutions to the things that bothered me.'

What particularly resonated with him?

'In the Annunciation, she accepts immediately. She doesn't say, "I'll wait and see if I am pregnant" or "I'll do a test in the morning Mr Angelman. If I am pregnant, I'll remember this conversation." No. She accepts immediately this huge chasm of faith. And that's what I also thought was so important. Angel Gabriel saying it will be shown to you now. She closes her eyes and feels the moment. People of faith often talk of a physical thing; a warmth; a light; a tangible thing. So that's what I focused on.'

I tell him that I loved his depiction of Mary, who changes from an innocent happy go lucky girl to a troubled, depressed outcast as the story develops.

'I placed her as a sixteen-year-old but I wish I'd made her a twelve-year-old,' he says. 'But then I thought, this is BBC One. Can you imagine the papers? It would have been a f*****g nightmare: "Joseph portrayed as a paedophile".'

Ah yes, Joseph.

'Joseph was the forgotten man of this story. For me, what I found fascinating was how it was just as big a leap of faith for him. So I had to take him on this journey of disbelief, not accepting it, and the idea of him being forced to take her to Bethlehem rather than her being stoned to death. A journey that felt real and truthful. Then the story came to life.'

It sounds as though he almost had his own annunciation moment when writing it.

'I can get my head round messengers,' he responds. 'I don't know what Gabriel was in reality and whether he came to her in some kind of dream state. I don't know if it was inside of her. But I knew I had to dramatize that, to physicalize it. I was adamant what my angel would be. He'd not be standing on a rock looking down on mankind represented by Mary. My angel would not have a "Ready Brek" glow or a halo or wings. He wouldn't have anything that distanced himself. My angel was delivering the best news ever. I wanted him to be excited and elated. I didn't want him to look down on her. I wanted him to kneel down with her and hold her hands and look in her eyes because they were sharing this amazing news together. It's not God from on high. That's what makes these stories inaccessible to people. Organized religion and all that says: "If you come through those big oak doors and walk down the aisle and sit in that little wooden seat, I've got God in a little bottle under the pulpit and if you're really good and quiet, I'll take the top off and let you have a little look. Now f**k off and come back next Sunday." That's what they do to us. Putting the angel on a rock above us. Better than us. Condescending to us. That's why in my Annunciation, Gabriel is just a man who kneels. He's a messenger. When my postman delivers my bill from Her Majesty's Inland Revenue, he just does it. He doesn't have to have a f*****g crown on his head. So I don't see why an angel would have to have wings or put on all the ermine.'

He says he'd never really thought about the Nativity story, other than watching his kids in their school plays, until he started writing about it.

'It was really weird but in the story writing process, I came to believe that the story is true. I believe there was a child called Mary. I believe she was betrothed to a man called Joseph. I believe that she had a child. I believe that child was Jesus Christ. I find it really, really difficult to say…look, if you believe Jesus Christ was the Son of God…which I have to because of his clear words of truth…if you accept his words as a true paradigm of the way for us to live our lives…the truth of the things he said…if you accept that is truth…then you can't cherry pick some bits and not others.'

His voice tails off and he pauses a little while.

'What you can't say is there is no God,' he continues. 'If you say there was no God, no virgin birth, then surely you have to understand everything in order to be able to say those things with such certainty. And if you think you know everything, you're a f*****g idiot. That's the rationale for the Nativity from my fevered brain. I can't say it was a virgin birth but I can't say it wasn't. I can only go by what I feel. And I feel it was because I feel there's no reason it couldn't be if he was the Son of God. If you accept he's the Son of God, it could not only have been a virgin birth, however weird it may sound, it could have been anything. He could turn this pebble into something else. Once I got there, the truth gradually showed itself to me. It was just hidden by the idiots with the big hats who say the angel must have wings, Mary must have been blessed, and all that other stuff.'

He is fidgety and cannot keep still. He fiddles with some paper clips on the desk. Then he picks up a pen and puts it down again. He rocks back and forth in his chair and his right leg taps on the floor continuously.

'I don't know what people will remember of my work in a hundred years,' he reflects. 'I suspect no one will be settling down to watch *Life on Mars* or *Hustle* or *Holby Blue*. But this one I hope is different. The story is timeless. In a hundred years or two hundred years time, I hope the BBC or whatever then will still show *The Nativity* and people will be moved in the same way as the first audience. I'm convinced of that and that makes me feel very proud. I'm so proud to have taken a story that everybody knew and make it accessible and allow you to believe in the story if you want to. If you want to believe it, I hope I've given you a way to believe it and not feel a right idiot.'

So, was the process of writing it a profound experience?

'I've not gone from Neanderthal to some kind of spiritual intellectualist in a single leap. I'm fifty-six. I'm on a continuous journey through my writing. I'm trying to find the truth of things. That can happen with *EastEnders* and with Dot Cotton and spiritual things.'

So, he is not religious in the sense of going to church but he feels he is on a journey of spirituality.

'Yes, that's well put,' he responds. 'I have a healthy mistrust of organized religion. Whenever I'm in a church, I like to go in and feel quiet. I think about my family, the kids, God. I feel almost child-like again. I'm just Anthony. I like that. I don't have a problem with the buildings and the pews. My problem has always been with the people who say to me, "If you don't do it this way…" and they don't understand the basic concept. Two thousand years ago the telling of stories was done orally, right? There was no *Sky News*. It was, "I've heard something. I've just come back from Bethlehem and heard this." And then I tell someone who then tells someone else.'

So there is an embellishment?

'Of course,' he replies. 'So, if you understand that, you can't then say, "It definitely happened like this…" What's it matter? It's those very details that get blurred in the telling of the story. What stays constant is the reason for telling the story in the first place. The heart of the story that never changes. The punch line.'

He sounds increasingly frustrated and angry. Timidly, I take out a print of Lemoyne's *The Annunciation* and pass it to him.

'I see everything I dislike about religion here,' he bawls. 'An angel raised higher. I see Mary as "Blessed am I. I'm so lucky. I'm the handmaid of the Lord. I'm a vessel." And then those cherubs. It's everything I dislike and everything I tried to avoid in the telling of the Nativity story. My angel knelt down in front of her with tears in his eyes and he felt love in him. A real genuine love and joy in the news he was bringing. He wasn't above her. There were no stars.'

I recall that his rendition of the Annunciation involved Gabriel taking Mary's hand.

'God said we are all equal,' he replies. 'We are love. Do not judge each other. Be inclusive. It was a message of love. Not this.' He looks disparagingly at the Lemoyne print. 'That's Man doing: that there has to be a hierarchy. You have the angel, then the sergeant angels by him and then, above it, all that.' He points to the light. 'If this is about Christianity, about the Virgin Birth, about the Annunciation, then you have to understand…it's the beginning of something…and you also have to understand the message of Jesus Christ. It's the same thing, isn't it? So, if you understand the message of Jesus Christ, he wasn't into hierarchy. He washed people's feet and said, "I am not worthy". God's not up there and looking down from that light. That's Man that's done all that. Bollocks. It's done to keep us in line. You've been doing it for two thousand years. Well no, f**k off.'

At its launch in December 2010, Tony Jordan said that if you've got faith, *The Nativity* could re-affirm it. If you haven't, it may make you think twice. Ten million people watched *The Nativity* over four episodes. It was was lauded by critics for its quality, ambition and distinctiveness. One wrote that the strength was its relevance today, its humanity and the lack of a preachy tone. Another described it as impressive and compassionate and 'a valiant attempt to infuse the story with some contemporary resonance.' It praised the central performances of Tatiana Maslany and Andrew Buchan 'who wear the haunted but determined looks of humble people suddenly endowed with terrifying responsibility.' As well as winning such huge viewing figures, the BBC's audience services department received more unsolicited contacts of appreciation for *The Nativity*, through email, text and phone calls, than for any other programme that year.

At the heart of my next encounter is another acclaimed television series that features the Annunciation. In this case, Grayson Perry fills the lead role.

For many years, Grayson Perry was almost as famous for cross-dressing as for his art. But that reputation has shifted and he has risen rapidly to become one of Britain's leading artists and the first potter to win the coveted Turner prize. The fifty-four-year-old uses different mediums to express his imagination and creativity – in particular, ceramic pots and tapestries. In addition, he writes and presents television and radio programmes. Last year he delivered a highly praised four-part Reith Lectures series entitled, *Playing to the Gallery* on BBC Radio 4.

This time, the television programme in which I am interested is the Channel 4 BAFTA award-winning documentary series *All in the Best Possible Taste* in which Grayson Perry explores his fascination with class. We see him visiting three different regions of England, discovering the likes and dislikes of the different social groups he encounters. He interacts with members of each class, and then creates a tapestry that reflects his insights and observations. The artist named his series of tapestries, *The Vanity of Small Differences*.

Grayson Perry is intrigued by the subject matter. 'Class is something bred into us like religious faith,' he writes in the book that accompanies the series. He goes on to observe:

> Making knowing reference to older artworks is itself a very middle-class thing to do, as it flatters the education and cultural capital of the audience. The paintings I borrowed from are mainly early Renaissance religious works as encapsulated by the collection shown in the Sainsbury Wing of the National Gallery. This is my favourite era of art and, as this television series is very much a public work, I wanted to use the audience's familiarity with the Christian mysteries depicted to lend weight to my more modern moral subject.

I learn that he took particular inspiration from William Hogarth's *A Rake's Progress*, which tells of the rise and fall in the fortunes of Tom Rakewell in the early 1700s. Grayson Perry adapts the character, calling him Tim Rakewell and putting him in a contemporary setting.

Each week, I watched the television series, transfixed by Grayson Perry's revelations and the tapestries he created. Now I want to see his work with my own eyes. To do this I have to travel to Temple Newsam, a beautiful Tudor-Jacobean mansion on the eastern edge of Leeds. The house is famous for its magnificent collections of old furniture, ceramics, silverware, paintings and wallpapers, as well as for its 1500 acres of beautiful parkland designed by Capability Brown. It is here that I find *The Vanity of Small Differences*.

The tapestry I am particularly keen to see is called *The Annunciation of the Virgin Deal*. This was inspired by the artist's encounters with a group of residents who live on the newly built Kings Hill estate in Tunbridge Wells, Kent. He declared that these upwardly mobile people are 'synonymous with conservative middle class values' and noted that their 'shared tastes help bind the tribe.' It's a large piece, 200 cm by 400 cm, and is made with wool, cotton, acrylic, polyester and silk. I feel it is no accident that it is displayed in the dressing room next to the State Bedroom; this references historical Annunciation works that depict Mary in a bedchamber.

107. Grayson Perry *The Annunciation of the Virgin Deal*, 2012. By kind permission of Grayson Perry and the Victoria Miro Gallery

As I stand there admiring the large, vibrantly coloured work, I listen to Grayson Perry guiding me on its rich detail via an app on my iPad:

> Tim (Rakewell) is relaxing with his family in the kitchen of his large, rural, second home. His business partner has just told him that he is now an extremely wealthy man, as they have sold their software business to Richard Branson. On the table is a still life demonstrating the cultural bounty of his affluent lifestyle. To the left, his parents-in-law read, and his elder child plays on the rug. To the right, Tim dandles his baby while his wife tweets. This image includes references to three different paintings of the Annunciation by Carlo Crivelli (the vegetables); Mattias Grunewald (his colleague's expression); and Robert Campin (the jug of lilies).

Three elderly women stand to the side of me, laughing. 'I didn't expect to see that here,' one of them says. 'It's not a Temple Newsam thing, is it?' The other says in a thick Yorkshire accent that she loves the bright colours. 'It lights up the room, don't it? It's smashing. I'd luv to take it home.' The third describes the tapestry as 'clever and respectful'.

I continue listening to Grayson Perry explaining the concept behind *The Vanity of Small Differences*:

> I usually choose a medium because of the resonances it has acquired. Tapestries are grand. They hang in the vast bedchambers of ancestral piles. They often depict classical myths or military victories. A lot of the status associated with tapestries historically was due to their huge cost and the enormous amount of skilled labour required to produce them. The British care about taste because it is inextricably woven into our system of social class. I think that more than any other factor – age, race, religion or sexuality – one's social class determines one's taste. Class is bred into us like a religious faith. We drink in our aesthetic heritage with our mother's milk, with our mates in the pub, or on the playing fields at Eton. We learn the texture of our place in the world from the curlicue of a neck tattoo to the clink of a Le Creuset casserole dish or the scent of a mouldering hunting print. A childhood spent marinating in the material culture of one's class means taste is soaked right through us. Cut me and beneath the thick crust of Islington, it says Essex all the way through. We often only become aware of these conscious choices when we move between social classes.

The artist always envisaged that the public would see these tapestries and they've already been on show in London, Sunderland, Manchester, Birmingham, Liverpool, Ankara and Istanbul before coming to Leeds. I have much fun spotting the teasing, symbolic references to the Annunciation: the angel wings, the pointed finger, the woman receiving the message on her mobile phone, the ceramic bird hanging above Tim's head while he holds the baby, the iPad with the Financial Times news headline declaring, 'Bakewell sells to Virgin for £270m.'

I understand that Grayson Perry is not a religious man but I am intrigued by this particular work. I wonder what he thinks about the annunciation story. He acknowledges that he likes to bring together the secular and the religious in his work. Recently, in a television interview with Professor Laurie Taylor, he said, 'The way we look at art comes from religion, the sacred object in the special place. That's how the idea of art came about. Most of the art that I love and my peak aesthetic experiences have been in churches and cathedrals. You don't need to believe in God to enjoy going into a church.'

A few weeks later, I enter his single-storey studio on a leafy well-to-do road in Islington. There is no sign of cross-dressing today. He is wearing work clothes and his dark blonde, asymmetrically cropped hair is slightly greasy and unkempt. He offers me a cup of tea and a broken teddy bear biscuit. He tells me he is fascinated by my annunciation project and wants to hear more.

He perches on a chair whilst I sit on a sofa facing him. Pots and other ceramics, many of which are works in progress, surround us. Behind him is a green pushbike – his primary form of transport. The light outside is fading fast as dusk takes its hold. He says it's the end of a long day but he seems to be jovial and engaged. It is not long before I hear his distinctive bellowing laugh. We begin by talking about *The Vanity of Small Differences* and, in particular, *The Annunciation of the Virgin Deal*.

'Each tapestry in the series has a biblical religious reference,' he begins. 'People would know the imagery. It gives them a hook. A slide in to the familiar. What they already think is beautiful is also actually familiar. I wanted the tapestries to have a monumental, religious frieze aspect. There's pathos there. Using a grand motif to tell a new story. I wanted it to be "pregnant" with middle class taste.'

He explodes with laughter at his deliberate pun.

'I had a series of religious scenes I wanted to portray to shape the whole story. They came organically. It's a delicate dance when you're putting them together. I took a real risk. When I finished them I was incredibly nervous that they were too kitsch, a bit garish. But now they've been validated not by the tasteful, intellectually pretentious section of the art world but by the public – a Middle England audience, which is the bedrock of the country's art audience. That one is an annunciation about a shit load of money, not a conception. Maybe the woman is the backer and that's why she's shown as an angel.'

Amusingly, he tells me, he once played the angel Gabriel in a modern version of the Nativity when he was ten years old at his Church of England primary school in Essex. The Annunciation scene, he recalls, was based in a supermarket.

Although most things that have shaped his life as an artist have come from religion, he is not religious himself mainly because he did not grow up with it. 'Religion evolves out of a human need,' he observes. Although he is not a believer in Christianity, he says he can understand those who are.

'It offers a refuge of certainty,' he tells me. 'I understand the fatalism of it. I've got a lot of time for religion. I just don't sign up to any formal religion for myself. I'm always suspicious. Whenever anyone says, "What do you believe in?" I always reply, "Gravity".'

He continues, 'The very nature of belief is that the only evidence you have is emotional. That's the nature of belief. That's why people become so angry and defensive around belief, because you're attacking their feelings, not facts. Feelings that are very dear to them, that are deeply ingrained in their emotional upbringing and character. There's a hell of a lot of emotional stuff that's added on to that belief and me, I've never had that. I've never felt emotionally connected to belief. Even though I love religious architecture and religious art and religious culture, all the different belief systems around the world, I don't believe in a fixed religion at all. I'm a Christian atheist.'

I show him a copy of the Lemoyne painting.

'It's not to my taste,' he tells me. 'I must say, the angel pointing up is odd. The basket down there – is that foretelling the swaddling clothes about to be filled? What's weird is that blending of the plaster on the wall. I'm not big on baroque paintings. Cherubs, clouds, mythical over-muscled figures, generic robes. I wouldn't be able to tell you where that style came from. What was the collective emotional impulse in society that got artists to develop that style? I prefer rococo to baroque. Rococo at least is in your face, sugary, over the top, quite camp whereas baroque is a bit over-ripe that I find distasteful. It's a little bit insincere, the language of earnestness. It's not a style of painting I'd ever go to reference.'

I tell him about Bishop Egan's description of the Annunciation as the most important event in human history. He leans back in his chair, seemingly shocked and baffled.

'I'm always fascinated by the way that religion seems to have incredibly bonkers ideas and religious officials often feel obliged to rationalize them. I think it's a mistake. The story is working at a subconscious level. Don't pull it apart. Don't dissect the frog because the frog dies and you never learn anything. The brilliant thing about religious narratives is that they're very specific. This happened now and this happened now. I love the way religions over time build up a set of traditions and symbols and rituals. They come from a need for those specifics. And the fact they're specific means all the airy-fairy stuff happens in the background. As Alan Bennett says, all his best ideas come from the corners of his eyes. So when you're listening to a specific story, then perhaps the more soulful, even spiritual ideas can float in through the window when you're not looking.'

So, he does not like the word 'spiritual'.

'I hate it because it's so woolly,' he says. 'It's often banded about by Notting Hill types who go on retreats and have a Buddha in the hallway. It's been taken over by too many people wanting to borrow some kind of mystical insight.'

But he likes the word 'religion'.

'I don't mind the word religion. What works about religion is that people do it. They go every week. They listen every week. They hear the same message every week. They go to the same building, meet with the same people. You can't say, "I'm spiritual" and then hope for something to happen. That's not how religion works. It's not about you read a book and then you've got it. It's something you do. You go to the building. You do the ritual with your fellow believers and it forms a community. That's how it works.'

I ask him whether Luke's story of the Annunciation has any resonance for him at all.

'I don't find any parallels to it in my life. I've never had a moment when I've felt a calling or anything like that.'

But he felt a calling to art, I suggest.

'That's the nearest I've got to a religious calling, yeah. It's a rational thing being an artist. You do it. I'm not interested in people wanting to be artists. I'm more interested in people doing art. In the same way, I'm more interested in the person who says they're religious and they do it – who go to church every week and say, "I'm not particularly spiritual".'

He starts to pack up and get his bike ready. By the door is a large etching entitled *The Map of Days*. This is a detailed map of a fortified town that portrays his inner self and changing identity. The city walls represent his skin and inside are named areas and buildings that are shaped by personal events, experiences and emotions. The map illustrates how the self is moulded by everything that it encounters. One area is called 'The Truth', another is 'Deeply Held Beliefs'. There's a road called 'Bullshit detector' and another place is named 'Reality Check'. A large church that looks like Southwark Cathedral is labelled 'An Imaginary Refuge'.

I bid him farewell and make my way home. On the long journey back, I read his book *Playing to the Gallery* based on his 2013 Reith Lectures. One paragraph focuses on the challenge facing somebody who walks into a contemporary art gallery. This resonates strongly with me because it strikes me as a particularly relevant description of my long search to understand the Annunciation: 'It can be tricky to get to the place where you can start to understand because, although you can intellectually engage with something quite quickly, to emotionally and spiritually engage takes quite a long time. You have to live with it.'

CHAPTER 28

ABANDONMENT

The General Synod – the Church of England's national assembly and leading legislative body – gathers twice a year, and I have come to watch it in action. Looking down from the public gallery on the members sitting in the Assembly Hall, I can see the Archbishop of Canterbury scrolling through the pages on his iPad, the Bishop of Winchester listening intently to the proceedings, and nearby, an elderly gentleman with snowy hair, who appears to be fast asleep. It is a predominantly white membership and to describe the age profile as 'mature' would be kind. Even the public gallery is filled with oldies.

This morning, the debate focuses on attendance figures. We learn that, according to internal projections, the Church of England faces at least thirty more years of decline in this area. Until recently, it had been predicted that the fall was likely to continue for a further five years before recovering. But even if there were to be an influx of young people, the sheer number of imminent deaths among the elderly congregations means that the Church is unlikely to see any overall growth in attendances until at least 2050. John Spence, the Church of England's finance chief, tells the Synod that at present, 18 people per 1,000 regularly attend church. However, it is expected that this will fall to 10 per 1,000. The debate comes a month after the Church of England revealed that the number of people attending services each week has fallen below a million for the first time, with Sunday attendances falling to 760,000. The rate of decline is now so severe that it could drop as low as 425,000.

In response to this crisis, we hear that the Church of England is about to inject £72 million into a 'renewal and reform' programme. The plan is to ordain six thousand more clergy comprising a younger priesthood that is less male dominated and less white. The previous day, the Bishop of Burnley informed Synod members that the Church of England is 'dying and dying very quickly' in many poorer areas of the country. He said not even one per cent of the population on many housing estates ever attend services. Too many resources, he warned, were focused on the middle class and the middle aged and many vicars preached to the converted rather than actively seeking out new recruits.

'The battle for the Christian soul of this nation,' he proclaimed, 'will not be won or lost in Kensington or Cobham or Harrogate but on the estates where life is hard and church life is fading fast.'

I look carefully around the auditorium. On the third row, I spot a woman wearing a green-blue woollen jacket and black trousers. She has short black hair with reading glasses perched on top and rather pale skin. She is wearing a clerical collar, a bishop's cross and has a red bag by her side. Although she blends in with the rest of the crowd, I recognize her for the true pioneer that she is: the first female bishop to be appointed in the Church of England.

Forty-nine-year-old Libby Lane hails from Glossop near Manchester. She studied Theology at St Peter's College, Oxford, and was one of the first women priests to be ordained in England in 1994. A year ago, and against all the British newspaper predictions, the relatively unknown Vicar of St Peter's Hale and St Elizabeth's Ashley made ecclesiastical history when she was appointed the Suffragan Bishop of Stockport in the Diocese of Chester.

After the Synod deliberations finish, I head to the Farmers Club off Whitehall to meet her. She tells me that she stays here, as a member, because her new role means she spends more time in London and part of her new diocese is rural in character. Tall, upright and slim, she has a warm, engaging personality. Married to a fellow priest, George, whom she met at Oxford, and with two children aged twenty and eighteen, she seems confident in her own skin, pleasingly relaxed and actively engages with the detail of my annunciation project.

We sit together in the reading room of the club overlooking the Thames, surrounded by comfy sofas and leather chairs, and she tells me what the annunciation story means for her.

'It's a story of hope and inclusion. It's a story of affirmation of humanity. On a very personal level, it affirms that my femaleness is part of God's story. Beyond that, it's about the fact God chose that person whom otherwise history would have ignored. She would never have been part of the grand narrative of history. But that's where God is. It says something to me about where God chooses to be. It's an encouragement about what we should be doing ourselves – being alert to God and in places we would not expect.'

She speaks slowly, in a Mancunian accent with long pauses between sentences.

'It's the most transformational moment in human history and transformation should exactly be the place we seek to be,' she continues.

She describes the annunciation story as one of hope. What does she mean? I ask.

'Because God's people have been yearning to be saved,' she replies. 'We yearn to be made whole. This is the moment of God's *yes*, his answer, his fulfilment.' She talks about Mary being 'a model of discipleship, she asked questions.'

Did Mary really have a choice?

'Yes. God gave her a choice,' she says. 'I simply can't conceive that God would have insisted. That's not my understanding of God. To have had that imposed on a person would be shocking and an act of abuse. The sexual abuse of women in warfare is quite rightly recognized as a terrible war crime and the idea God would impose that kind of experience on a young woman who didn't choose it feels to me like a terrible abuse of power and that's not my understanding of God. I would always want to rationalize it as Mary's choice but it wasn't easy.'

But did Gabriel not simply tell her that she would be having a child?

'I think inevitably we read these stories through our own lenses and I need this story to work,' she replies. 'This is a crucial part of the Gospel. If I could only read it in ways that offended me, that would be really difficult for me to hold together. So I recognize my own take on it is shaped by who I am and my culture and my particular history. I just have to be honest about that. It's part of the Good News and I want to speak of it as good news.'

What about the idea that comes from feminist theologians like Mary Daly and Jane Schaberg, that Mary may have been raped?

'If you don't hold to the theological conviction that Jesus is God made flesh, you have to come up with some rationale to explain the story,' she says. 'I have sympathy with what motivates that rationale – the idea that Mary's full humanity doesn't diminish Jesus's divinity – but for me personally, having made the choice about who I understand Jesus to be, that is the bigger choice. Accepting that his birth is inexplicable I can sit with. I don't need to have a more rational, straightforward understanding of how someone who was unmarried became pregnant. That's a relatively small part of a much bigger risk I have taken – believing Jesus to be fully God as well as fully human.'

She stresses Mary's ordinariness. To make Mary more than that makes her less rather than more.

'She's like the guy on the bench outside,' she says. 'She was unremarkable and that's more precious.'

Does she read the story as fact or as a metaphor?

'I read it as fact but I'm not disconcerted by those who don't,' she replies.

So, if a Christian simply cannot believe that the Annunciation happened, would she be relaxed about that?

'Yes, because I think the nature of faithful discipleship is continuous and we do it as part of a community rather than as individuals. One of my answers about the creedal statements is that that's why we say it together as a Church. You individually walk with us and you are part of a community and if you say there are some parts of the creedal statement you can't say together, that's ok. If you continue walking with us, you're in. To ask that question is a very kind of past nineteenth-century western grasp of what it is. I have a bigger perspective. Are you faithful to Jesus? Are you striving to follow Christ? Do you continue to live out your faith and are wrestling with those things that are hard? If the answer is yes, well join the club.'

She is in full flow now. 'All our language is limited. All our conception is limited. We simply don't know it all but there's a necessary recognition of being human,' she tells me. In her mind, belief is all about trust. 'For me, the conceptual, rational, intellectual rigour is important but I recognize where my exercise of that has made me land is that I can say every word of the Creed without any sense of dislocation. But I recognize it's not necessarily the place others may land when they exercise the same kind of rigour. It's not just logic and rational but emotional and relational, and it is alive. It's not a fixed thing in terms of belief. But I can say this is what I believe in Christ.'

I ask if the virginal conception is fundamental for her.

'Yes, in the sense it makes sense to me,' she replies. 'It is a way of understanding how Jesus is fully divine and fully human. How Jesus's coming is a collaboration between God and humanity. Mary's choice to participate in the salvation history of God is an extraordinary moment of human and divine collaboration, which says something to me about both the nature of God and how God chooses to engage with us and also says something extraordinary about the honour of our created bodilyness. It matters to me that Jesus was gestated and born of a woman and that that was painful. I can say the Creed but I can't sing those Christmas carols that suggest that it was all soft, fuzzy and lovely and that Jesus never cried. I really can't because it undercuts what's important.'

I tell her how I have been trying to understand the theology that Jesus as Son of God pre-existed before his human birth. I say it is an extraordinarily difficult thing to comprehend.

'The Second Person of the Trinity pre-existed the Incarnation,' she says.

So, does that mean Jesus existed before his conception?

'The Second Person of the Trinity, that we call Son I would contend pre-existed Jesus' she replies. 'The full nature of what was enfleshed in Jesus was pre-existent and post-existent. What changed was God chose to enflesh that. I don't understand that Jesus as a human person was pre-existent but I do think God has the eternal dynamic of mutuality and inter-dependence and that creative dynamic that is the relationship of the three persons of God. Regarding John's Gospel account, the Word was pre-existent but the flesh was not.'

Earlier in our discussion, she had described the Annunciation as 'the most transformational moment in human history'. I tell her that Bishop Philip Egan had told me it was 'the most important event in human history'. She agrees.

'Yes, because it is when God chose to be with us. That changed the whole...well, that's the moment of absolute shift. All that was then lived out by the Jesus that became...' She pauses before picking up her thought process again 'It's real in that moment of God choosing to become flesh. I don't think the Crucifixion or the Resurrection is subservient to that. It's all in there.'

If it is the most important event in human history, why does she think the status of the feast of the Annunciation has been lost today?

'I think it has been and as a Christian community we're diminished by that,' she replies.

I observe that it always falls in Lent, sometimes even on Good Friday and, therefore, is overshadowed by the Easter story.

'That's really interesting,' she says. 'It makes you re-think Good Friday. Mary was there as well and at Pentecost.'

We move on to discuss the status of Mary.

'She really matters to me because she's like me. Her participation, her choice, her wrestling, all in her ordinariness, I think marks Mary as someone through whom we can understand why these events are so important. It's through her human experience and that's a gift.'

Does Mary inspire her?

'That's a really difficult word,' she says. 'I find her story and her example and what I have learnt of myself through her, stimulating, challenging and formative. If that's what inspiration is, then yes.'

Does she ever pray to her?

'No,' she replies firmly.

But is she relevant to her?

'Absolutely,' she says.

Is Mary a bridge or a barrier?

'She can be both. It depends how we engage with her and how we talk about her. It's important to me that we talk about her as accessible and see the comparable things in ourselves. Mary has been intended to be viewed as a bridge between the divine and the human and in that she's a bridge builder. But the unintended consequence of Mary being the bearer of our prayers to the throne of God becomes a barrier to our relationship with God because it's interpreted that we can't do it ourselves and, therefore, that puts further distance between us and God. That's an unintended consequence of such Mariology. She was flawed like all of us and yet God chose to work with her in the most extraordinary way.'

Whilst at secondary school, Libby Lane's ambition was to become a civil engineer, like her father, and it was only when she was studying Theology at Oxford that she thought about the possibility of being ordained as a deacon. In that context, does she see any parallel regarding her own calling and that of Mary in the annunciation story?

'Not at the time,' she says. 'My sense of vocation was not specifically centred on Mary but retrospective reflection on my own experience and the account of her experience has and does help to think through my own story and challenges me to walk more closely with Christ.'

I tell her of a sermon I read recently given by a canon treasurer at Coventry Cathedral. He made a direct comparison between the unknown Mary being chosen by God in the annunciation story and Libby Lane, unknown to the vast majority of the population, being chosen for such a historic appointment. She smiles graciously.

'If my appointment as the first woman bishop inspires young women to recognize because they're women, they shouldn't be limited, and that God does extraordinary things, and their horizons can be lifted, then that's a good outcome of my appointment,' she responds. 'I can see it has the potential for people to see new possibilities.'

I show her the print of the Lemoyne painting. What does she see?

'I see a narrative of a theology that I have a lot of sympathy with. The direction of travel through Mary's laundry. I'm interested to see she seems to be reading as well as washing.'

What does Lemoyne's painting communicate to her?

'I wish her head was up not down, looking more outward and forward' she says. 'Accepting and participating in God's call in your life is not solely about submission or subservience. Faithfulness to God is about participation.'

So, does she think the painting stresses interiority too much?

'Yes, yes,' she replies. 'But it doesn't feel static. She doesn't feel static and I like that.'

She continues to study the picture quietly for a while before offering a final comment.

'If that's what the moment of the Annunciation says about Mary, the capacity to be calm in the centre of a storm, and that's what is said about me, then I'm content with that description.'

108. Arthur Hacker *The Annunciation,* 1892, Tate Britain. © Tate Images

I walk down the Victoria Embankment, pass the Houses of Parliament, and continue along the north side of the Thames, eventually arriving at Tate Britain. I have come back to the gallery specifically to view a beautiful, late nineteenth-century painting: Arthur Hacker's *The Annunciation.*

This large picture was created in 1892. It shows a bare-footed Mary in a garden, about to fill her flagon with water from a nearby pool. She is draped in an ivory-coloured dress that hangs from her shoulders down to her feet and her long veil flows around her. Her hands touch her chest and the angel Gabriel swoops down behind her, carrying a lily stem. In the distance is a house, possibly the family home in the hamlet of Nazareth.

What makes this painting so enigmatic is Mary's face. She stares directly at the viewer, as though she is asking, 'What shall I do?' Whilst the rest of the painting has a soft pastel style, her face is precisely defined, almost like a photograph. Her dark eyes are so piercing, innocent and yet fearful. She is about to come to terms with the most momentous of encounters and the scene is one of trepidation.

As I step back, it is that extraordinary face that keeps staring at me. Those eyes that are so transfixing. It is one of the most captivating depictions of the Annunciation I have seen so far.

'Can we go from "I cry to thee" and let's have just a little bit more air,' shouts a small man dressed in black. 'Let's all breathe in please. Tenors, you can afford to hold on a little longer on the E flat.' The conductor moves his hands and head to the rhythm of the voices. Clearly, he is feeling the music very deeply. David Fawcett turns around and looks at me with a proud smile. 'It's not always the case that a composer knows how to conduct the performance of his own piece,' he says.

It is 9.30 a.m. on a Saturday morning and I am inside St Mary's church in Balham in south-west London. It is a large Anglican edifice on a busy road, dedicated to the Blessed Virgin Mary. The church choir, numbering thirty members, is gathered at the end of the central aisle in front of the altar. Fifteen singers to the left: Bass, Tenor, Alto and Soprano. Fifteen singers to the right: Soprano, Alto, Tenor and Bass. All staring intently ahead at the Director of Music at St Mary's as he draws the final rehearsal to a close. There is a tangible air of tension and excitement. David Fawcett is about to make the first ever recording of the most important composition of his life. The piece is a new arrangement of the classic fourteenth-century English carol, *Hymn to the Virgin*.

I have the sheet music in my hand. Next to the title of the composition are two words: 'For Holly'.

The church falls into complete silence. Buttons are pressed on the bank of recording equipment in the middle of the central aisle and a row of red lights start to flicker. The conductor holds his hands in the air and signals the start of the inaugural recording. Written on the score above the opening notes is the guidance: 'Simply and with dignity'.

Thirty exquisite voices soar harmoniously into the rafters as the choir sings these early fourteenth-century words:

> 'Of one that is so fair and bright,
> Velut maris stella,
> Brighter than the day is light,
> Parens et puella,
> I cry to thee, thou see to me,
> Lady, pray thy Son for me
> Tam pia,
> That I may come to thee,
> Maria!
>
> All this world was forlorn,
> Eva peccatrice
> Till our Lord was y-born,
> De te genetrice.
> With 'Ave' it went away,
> Darkest night and comes the day,
> Salutis;
> The well springeth out of thee,
> Virtutis.

Lady, flow'r of ev'-ry thing,
Rosa sine spina,
Thou bare Jesu, Heaven's King,
Gratia divina;
Of all thou bear'st the prize,
Lady, Queen of Paradise,
Electa:
Maid mild, Mother
es effecta

The glorious, multi-layered vocals swell to fill every nook and cranny. I find the music and performance inspiring, haunting and emotional.

'Well done, well done!' the conductor exclaims proudly at the end of the recording. The choir members cheer in satisfaction and relief that a successful take has been achieved.

Fifty-one-year-old David Fawcett first dabbled in religious composition as a teenager in the Lincolnshire market town of Gainsborough and whilst attending university in Nottingham where he studied Music as an organ scholar. Nothing more came of it. Now, more than thirty years later, after a successful career working in the civil service and as a strategist in large public service organisations, he is started to compose again. This time he is taking it much more seriously.

Today's recording is the climax of a journey that began in August 2011 when he first started working on a new musical treatment for *Hymn to the Virgin*, originally a medieval anthem glorifying the Annunciation to the Virgin Mary. It took a life-changing event to start the process.

Over a fifty minute conversation he tells me the story behind his composition, speaking quietly and movingly, in an extraordinarily open and composed manner.

'My wife, Hatty, and I had been trying for a family for some time,' he begins, 'and we'd had unsuccessful IVF treatment. Eventually, after two or three years, we managed to conceive naturally. It had been a difficult road we'd been travelling on – one of raised hopes and plenty of disappointments. In the summer of 2011, my wife carried our baby for nineteen weeks and six days. We got past all the first danger moments. We'd been for all the check-ups. We'd started to tell family and friends after sixteen weeks. The congratulations were still coming in when, very suddenly, we lost Holly at nineteen weeks and six days.

'We went into hospital and it was a couple of days later that Holly was delivered – a natural delivery. We'd been told there was no chance of her surviving or being able to be helped in any way. So it was a case of spending that couple of days really getting our minds round it all. We were at St Thomas's [by the Thames opposite the Houses of Parliament]. We'd sometimes leave the room and sit by the river. It was a time of a lot of questions of each other, of digging deep into ourselves, and also a lot of silence. A lot of grieving. A lot of crying. Why is this happening? It can't be fair. Some were spoken out loud but a lot of time was spent in private thought. There was anger as well as sadness and grief. The child was still alive in her.

'While Holly was inside Hatty she was being kept alive through the umbilical cord but all her waters had gone so there was no chance of Holly being kept in the womb and continuing to grow. We were told that when Holly would be delivered, it would happen immediately and she wouldn't survive. It felt almost like we had to decide the time she was going to die. Holly would die the moment she would leave the womb and be separated from the cord and that was an added puzzle. She was going to be born and to be dead.

'I tried to find a quiet, reflective place even though I felt angry and grief stricken. It was in those quieter, reflective moments that the thought of music and Mary came to me. I'd just come back to being a church organist after fifteen years off, partly because I'd lost my faith. I'd come back into St Mary's, Balham, without having regained a faith in a Godhead but having seen the value of the community of faith. It just chimed there. The vicar, the very diverse community, its High Church nature. It felt like home. And the dedication of the church and the focus on Mary.'

I am reluctant to break into his thoughts but I ask him why it was Mary who he turned to in that darkest hour?

'It may have been an alternative to railing against God which is quite hard to do if you can't claim to have a faith in the existence of God,' he responds. 'In those situations, it is easier to look outside yourself for the answer, either for a reason or as an example. And for whatever reason, Mary came into my mind as an example of calm, quiet acceptance and a suffering mother. She had accepted what was given to her without knowing where it was going to take her.

'As I thought about her and the story of the Annunciation, Benjamin Britten's setting to *Hymn to the Virgin* kept coming into my mind – a piece of work he wrote in his teens – a really splendid setting that made me remember those specific words. I started to think in the hospital room and on the riverbank about my own setting. The first couple of lines of a melody came to me and throughout that night those lines kept coming back over and over again. I started to write something down on paper. It was the first time I'd ever used that technique of something being in my head, going over and over again in my head, and only when you feel a sense of rightness do you write something down. It gave me the confidence to start to apply the harmonies that I was beginning to feel as well.'

Was he thinking at that very moment about Mary's annunciation story and the theme of acceptance and incarnation?

'Yes, absolutely,' he replies. 'I was thinking of motherhood and what my wife was going through. The loving of motherhood and the pain of motherhood. I didn't know if I was calling out to Mary because I don't have that kind of faith but I was certainly calling out to her example, her acceptance. Mary's *yes*. In the absence of someone to blame, I just had to trust that it would all be alright in the end for Hatty, and for Holly as well, in the same way that Mary trusted. Her trust in accepting the conception and then her trust later in having to witness the death of her son. For us, it was all happening in the space of two to three days. It's quite a journey going from this idea of loving the fact that we were finally going to have a child to where we were. We didn't know her sex then until she was born. Because her due date was Boxing Day, we'd had a joke that if she was a girl, she'd be called Holly. When she was born and we were told she was a girl, there was no other name.

'The seventh of August 2011 was when we lost Holly. I was determined that day to write the piece and I wrote it very quickly, finishing it within a week. I remember writing the description at the top of it: 'Simply and with dignity'. We were troubled by how we could allow our daughter dignity, protection and love. We didn't want it to be a procedure or a problem that had to be solved. This was a child that was about to be dead that was now alive. Up to that point and after, we wanted our baby to be treated with dignity and the minimum of fuss. The main shape of the melodies was there by then in my head and were still coming together at the time she was being born. It was a very tender moment. It was a deeply personal moment for all three of us.

'She died on the way out of the womb. I cut the umbilical cord and sat with her in my hands. She was the size of my hand. The midwives took care of Hatty. I saw and felt two movements of electrical impulses. For me, it was like two breaths. It was quite alarming and disturbing. The time I spent with Holly in my hands then was one of amazement about life at the time of death and the amount of love that had gone into her creation. We had a naming process in the hospital. We lit a candle. We had a service in our own church and a burial in a cemetery in Lower Morden. It's a beautiful resting place for her. I completed the work in time for a copy of the work to be included in her casket. So she's buried with the score by her because, as it says at the top, it's "For Holly". There's also a photo of the three of us in the hospital and a palm cross from St Mary's.'

I ask how it feels to be conducting the piece and hearing the choir as it is being recorded.

'Musically, as a conductor, I can get through very emotional music,' he answers. 'But this is "simply and with dignity". I've always approached the piece that way. It's not a maudlin piece, a sad piece. It's soft and gentle rather than raw. I could have written a piece that could make a lot of people cry but I didn't need to make it emotional. The people at the church knew our story.'

Was there a line that particularly chimed with him?

'Yes, I think it was "I cry to thee, thou see to me, Lady pray thy Son for me." I just thought Mary was a symbol to be admired.'

So, what does the annunciation story mean for him?

'I think it still goes back to the symbolism of being able to trust,' he says. 'Whatever it is we choose to trust, however dark things are, the darkest of nights, then will come the day. All can be well. I still don't have a faith in a deity but I have a faith in a community of mutual support and healing.'

I presume he does not see the annunciation story as fact.

'I don't need to see it as fact,' he replies. 'I don't question whether it is fact. It's strong enough for me as fiction if that is what it is. The metaphor, the symbol is the important thing. The symbolism in religion is the most important thing to me. I've always been a religious person without necessarily being a faithful person. I like the practice of religion, the ceremony, the symbolism, the architecture, the music. Many, many people are also in that position if we're all completely honest about it. So it's that calm listening to a profound message and being able to accept that. For me, that's the meaning of the story.'

He tells me his *Hymn to the Virgin* piece will always be the most special one that he has created. However, although he is increasingly successful as a composer, it's unlikely to be commercially published. He explains, 'It's too personal a piece to want to assign the copyright to anyone else. I might self-publish if there's enough demand from people who want to perform it say on the feast of the Annunciation or during Advent.'

The conversation is drawing to a close. And then Lily came along, I observe.

'We knew we wanted to try for another child as soon as possible. Hatty managed to get pregnant naturally soon after. Holly made everything possible, maybe physically but certainly in terms of preparing us for parenthood. The love and the pain at the same time.'

Soon after attending the recording of *Hymn to the Virgin*, I look at David Fawcett's Facebook page where I see a photo of a small white gravestone on which are engraved the following words:

HOLLY FAWCETT

7TH AUGUST 2011

VISITED BRIEFLY STAYED FOREVER

Directly behind it stands a small holly bush with a red ribbon tied around its stem. In front of it is a row of six small shells. Below the photograph, David Fawcett has posted a message:

> Full of love for my daughter Holly who visited us three years ago today and changed our lives, teaching us the joy and heartache of parenthood all at once. We spent time together as a family. Delighted to see the holly bush is flourishing. We had a picnic at her graveside, lit the birthday candle we had used at her naming ceremony and Lily enjoyed leaving gifts of shells and pebbles we had picked up on holidays and days by the sea. Sleep softly my darling girl.

109. Holly's headstone, 2015.
© David Fawcett

Of course, not every painter is a critical and commercial success. For every artist whose work is commissioned by wealthy patrons, hung in trendy galleries or sold for thousands of pounds at auction, there are literally hundreds of thousands of others toiling away, trying to improve their craft, hoping and praying for any success. Some have given up everything to pursue their passion. They have felt a calling and have followed it, whatever the financial penalty and burden. One such case is the Ugandan born Gloria Ssali.

She was born forty-two years ago in Kampala and, after a brief stay in Kenya, left for Britain aged eleven. Her father was a doctor and professor. She gained two degrees in toxicology and pharmacology at the University of London, and pursued a career as a pharmacist. Six years ago she gave it up in order to pursue her art, primarily ceramics and painting, inspired by her cultural origins and the divine.

'I feel like I've found my soul,' she tells me. 'I'm not striving to sell but to create what's in my mind. I think about how much of my Catholic upbringing can I express in a particular liturgical season. I'm driven by expressing the Bible and feeling my faith.'

I first saw her work when trawling round the Internet. One of twenty-three depictions of the Annunciation she has posted online is a stunning watercolour she made in 2011. The two main characters stand side-on facing each other, bathed in vibrant shades of red and yellow. Gabriel's hand almost touches Mary. Both their mouths are open in conversation. The empty space between them is like a golden fire. The whole painting is a mixture of scarlet, rust and vermilion shades that contrast with brush strokes of gold, saffron, mustard and sunglow.

Gloria Ssali and I meet up over coffee in a large nondescript shopping centre in the heart of Harrow, near to her home in north-west London. I start by asking her the story behind the painting.

'Mary has just left the Temple. She's just been betrothed to Joseph. I wanted to express her poverty. For me, she wasn't a lady of wealth. That's why I only used one paint colour. Just to keep it minimal and to suggest that when the angel came to her, she had nothing. Just to keep it simple. The "Africanness" is something I wanted to emphasize. You don't

110. Gloria Ssali *The Annunciation*, 2011. ©
Gloria Ssali

often see Our Lady in an African setting. Here, she's wearing traditional Ugandan clothes.'

I observe how Mary appears to have a shaved head and looks pencil thin.

'I wanted to show her vulnerability,' she says. 'But it was also important for me for the angel to be humble and to be below her. The angel arrives with this brilliant message for her to absorb. In African societies, the male is usually more important and dominant. But I wanted him to be lower to show how special she was. She's a queen and I wanted to express that. Mary is very popular in Uganda but I wanted to give it my own African twist. People are passionate about Our Lady in Uganda. Everybody has a picture of her in their home but they're mainly very European in style. I don't like modern Marys. I like a humble one like I grew up seeing her. I stick to the Catholic viewpoint of Mary, what my upbringing taught me. I wanted the different shades to reflect the beauty of the words that were coming from the angel for her to absorb.'

Why did she use only one paint colour from which she created so many different shades?

'I wanted to show she is of the earth. She looks like she's from my tribe. The wings of the angel are matting, like that used by my tribe, and are protecting her.'

Gloria Ssali is a Mugandan from the Baganda ethnic group. She is single and a devout Catholic. Eighty-six per cent of Ugandans class themselves as Christian and the largest denomination in the country is Roman Catholic.

I ask her what happened to the painting.

'It only took two hours to make. The watercolours dry very quickly so I had to work very speedily. I painted it at home. It was on A3 size paper that I stuck onto the wall while I painted. It got more than three hundred views when I put it up on the website, which I was pleased at, but it didn't sell. I'm afraid it's lost. I don't know where it is now.'

Does she pray when she is making her art? I wonder.

'I close my eyes and pray about it and a vision comes into my mind,' she says. 'Sometimes it's quite quick. Other times it's more slowly…a few hours…and I try to interpret it. It finds its own way. It depends on the season of the year. Usually it's influenced by the Catholic calendar and I try and draw something in my mind that I then can bring out in a relevant image.'

What does the annunciation story mean for her?

'It means a lot to me. The absolute abandonment of Our Lady. The abandonment to the will of God. That's how I feel I am as well. I've left pharmacy. I've abandoned myself to the art. I'm doing Christian art. Not many people are successful at it, I have to agree. But it's working well for me.'

Abandonment is a very strong anti-feminist word, I suggest.

'It's a celebration of her womanhood,' she replies. 'She agreed to be a mother. That's a very noble thing to do. It's not a negative word at all. We are all servants of the Lord. It's not a subjugation. It's a celebration. It's liberating. In your humility, you're accepting. You're trusting God with the role he's planned for you. You don't know what it is but you follow it according to your faith. Once you receive the message, you say yes. Everything feels right about that abandonment.'

So, does she see a definite parallel between the annunciation story and her own?

'Certainly. Yes, definitely. The last job I did was at Boots at Waterloo. I left late after a long shift and got home. I realized this is my chance and said yes. I gave it all up there and then, six years ago. This is my chance to contribute to the world in this dimension. This is a higher calling. I thought there would be hard times but as I would be celebrating my faith in a higher calling, I felt free. Free to serve God.'

Does she believe that the annunciation story actually happened as Luke recounts it?

'Of course it's true,' she says. 'You have to have faith that the angel did visit Mary. We have constant signs from God today that he is supernatural. I have it in my heart that it did happen. I feel the message is true. I don't see it only as metaphor.'

I ask what success means for her.

'I don't paint to earn millions. I create my art to please God. The motivation is to bring honour to God. It would be nice to evangelize but mainly to draw people to God. I want to move people with my work.'

What does her family think?

'I've had all sorts of reactions but mainly supportive,' she responds. 'As the years go by, they see I'm not going back to pharmacy.'

In five years time what does she hope for?

'I don't expect to have huge success. I would love people to enjoy my art and to make the world happy. As the world becomes more secular and I can please a few people and bring them nearer to God then that's good.'

I show her a print of François Lemoyne's *The Annunciation*.

'It's lovely,' she says. 'What I see is the glory of God being reflected in Mary. It's very moving. It's the kind of painting I like to see. Her humility is the most important thing to me. Here, that's beautiful. I also see the strength of Mary even though she's almost faint as the message is entering her heart.' She tells me humility is the most important characteristic of Mary and she tries to replicate that virtue in herself.

What does she mean by humility? I ask.

'Although it troubled Mary, she was willing to take this message. To say yes. So listen to that voice. Don't compromise on the dream. Never dilute the message. I see a lot of people who say to me don't do Christian art – "Gloria, don't do Christian art." But I have to say yes. It's this African thing, we have to show humility. It's a beautiful cultural thing to see in my tribe. Humility is to listen and to be obedient. It's a very good thing. A good child is a humble child.'

CHAPTER 29

I LOVE THE GLORY

I am in unfamiliar surroundings, inside a church in Kent, which has no altar, no statues, no decoration and declares that its mission is about 'lives transformed by the generosity of Jesus'. Tonbridge Baptist Church, or TBC as it likes to call itself, states: 'We believe that everyone is on the edge of something greater. We are committed to awakening the God-given potential in lives.'

It's a vibrant community, located on a large housing estate in the north of the town, with a membership of more than five hundred. Two hundred and fifty normally attend the Sunday morning worship service and a hundred and fifty come on Sunday evening. On this particular Saturday afternoon it is packed to capacity.

I am come to witness the ordination of one of TBC's members as a Baptist Minister for Evangelism. Fifty-four-year-old Sally Allen is dressed elegantly in a pink cardigan, white top and an above the knee, dark blue skirt. She looks excited. That is not surprising. It is one of the biggest days of her life. I have been invited here because Sally Allen is my sister-in-law.

I look around the large space that forms the main room of the church. People are mulling around, greeting each other warmly. The atmosphere is convivial and noticeably full of positivity. It reminds me of a Billy Graham convention but on a much smaller scale. There are no images of Mary here. In fact there are no images at all save for a modern stained-glass window of the cross on a side wall. I ask one member of the congregation why this is the case.

'We don't need adornments. They're an unnecessary distraction. That's all far too Catholic. Here, we focus simply on the Word,' he responds.

In the Tonbridge Baptist Church's Statement of Faith, Article 5 declares a belief in, 'the incarnation of God's eternal Son, the Lord Jesus Christ, born of the virgin Mary, fully divine and fully human, yet without sin.'

The service gets underway. From the stage, Sally presents herself to the congregation to 'tell her story' although, for most of them, she needs no introduction. She stands at a lectern and talks of a time in the early 1980s at Sheffield University when she was studying Psychology and 'because of the radiant witness of a Christian friend, I had a radical encounter with Jesus Christ.'

111. Sally Allen at her ordination at Tonbridge Baptist Church, Tonbridge, Kent

She highlights how her father was 'incredibly hostile to my faith'. She describes how, later in life, she spent months in bed with a painful back problem and cried out to God, 'there must be more to the Christian life than this.' A friend who had been involved in the 'Toronto blessings' offered to pray for her. 'That was the beginning of a new walk with God,' she declares. 'Up until then, I knew I loved God with a passion but I didn't really know his passion for me.'

She began to lead various Alpha courses in the local community before hearing a call to Christian ministry. She enrolled at Spurgeon's College in south-east London to study theology and then extended her studies in order to become an accredited evangelist. 'It's been an amazing work of grace in my life,' she says. 'All glory to God. Amen.' Several members of the congregation raise their hands in the air as they respond, 'Amen'. I notice that the woman directly in front of me has tears streaming down her face. Revd Derek Hills, the former leader of TBC, who retired in 2010 after twenty-three years service here, tells the congregation, 'I've been a minister for forty five years. This lady is the most natural evangelist I've ever met.'

There's a Laying of Hands, then a Declaration and Blessing before the formal Induction. The service ends with the TBC Gospel Choir singing 'This Little Light of Mine'. Afterwards, everyone retires to an outer room for tea and a huge spread of sandwiches and cakes, made by the congregation.

Sally's husband, Gareth, is Chairman of the elected Elders at Tonbridge Baptist Church. Their four sons all played an active part in the TBC community throughout their childhoods and two of them met their future wives through the church.

Later, I meet up with Sally Allen to explore more about her calling and her own thoughts on the annunciation story.

'My childhood was incredibly active at weekends,' she begins, 'sailing, canoeing, climbing, walking and it meant church never featured because we were never at home. My father was quite antagonistic about going to church. My mother would go at Christmas, maybe Easter, and I think I went to Sunday school twice. I remember wanting to be confirmed at twelve but I hadn't a clue what they were talking about at the first lesson. I remember at my confirmation, the Bishop jumping up and down with his shepherd's crook and shouting, "Jesus is alive" and me thinking, what planet are you on? I had no understanding about it. I then went out with a guy at seventeen and recognized he had a faith and I didn't, and realized there was a difference.

'In my first year at Sheffield University, I was searching. I felt a deep loneliness in my gut but I didn't know what it was. I met Julie [Kitlowski], a medical student, and she blew me away. She had a quality about her that I didn't have. In the second year, we moved in together. The Holy Spirit is called the hand of heaven and I remember feeling pursued at that point because she and the rest of the household were praying for me at that time. I borrowed a book from her room by John White about the pearl of great price. As I read it, I started weeping. I was on my own. After a few weeks, I realized I had a decision to make. I had no doubt God was the Creator and I had this incredible longing to know the Creator. I realized it could change my life forever and that really scared me because I didn't want to become a "weird Christian". I realized I was sitting on the fence.

'I was nineteen when I was at a Bible study led by a barrister. At the end he said, "Do you want to pray?" I thought, what have I got to lose? If it's not true, I can walk away and if it is true, this is huge. As I prayed, this liquid love poured into my body. It was like cold water going into my body on a hot day. It was as tangible as that. Oh my goodness, this stuff is real, I thought, and I heard a voice, "I love you, I forgive you, you're mine." At that point, I knew that my life had changed forever. For me it was real and powerful and God radically transforming his glory. It was an incredibly active thing, not just a nice religious feeling.'

She tells me how later in her life in the 1990s she went to see someone who had witnessed at first hand the so-called 'Toronto blessing' at the Toronto Airport Vineyard church in Canada's largest city. The 'blessing' at the neo-charismatic evangelical church involved being 'slain by the Spirit', sometimes described as getting drunk in the Spirit, resulting in church members laughing uncontrollably, growling, shaking, dancing, 'crunching' and some being in a state of physical paralysis. It was claimed these extraordinary experiences were attributed to the Holy Spirit entering people's bodies. Sally recalls her own experience: she was in the Pilgrims' Hall in Herne Bay and fell to the floor, exploding in laughter for more than half an hour. She describes it as being like a champagne cork popping out of a bottle, 'a waterfall of joy. There's not an earthy thing that gets near it. God was just healing my heart.'

Twenty years on, what does her ordination ceremony mean to her,

'Incredible joy,' she replies. 'I was pinching myself, getting to do something I was born to do – to share faith.'

In that context, what does the annunciation story mean for her?

'It's good news, fantastic news, that God comes to live with us. Mary was a woman who loved God with all her mind and strength. I hold her in high regard for that but I think we are all called saints when we give our lives to Jesus. Hats off to her, it was so counter-cultural what she did, incredibly brave. She could have been stoned.'

Does she see the story as fact? I enquire.

'Totally,' she replies firmly. 'Yes, totally fact. I believe in angels and the heavenly realm. Mary was clearly a historical figure. Why wouldn't an angel have approached Mary?'

I explain to her that some Christians see it as metaphorical rather than factual.

'If that had been written in the Gospel and it wasn't right, someone would have said something – "you need to leave that bit out because it happened like this." People were still alive to refute these stories or validate them. It was too big a fact. If it hadn't been fact, it wouldn't have been there.'

What does she see as the key message of the story?

'I think God knew she would say yes. When we do surrender to God's will, the best will come. God wants to totally bless us so that we can be a blessing to others.'

We move on to discuss the status of Mary.

'In front of the cross, she was on the same level as everyone else,' she tells me. 'We are all sinners. Mary needed a saviour just as much as you and I do. She's no different in her calling.'

Does she venerate her?

'No, not at all,' she exclaims, almost in shock. 'No, I don't need to. I have Jesus. I can't find any evidence that I need to change my mind about Mary.'

Is she relevant to her?

'No, not really,' she says. 'What she went through, so many mothers go through. How many mother's sons are on heroin?'

But she was the bearer of God, I say.

'Ok, yes,' she says defensively.

Does she view Mary as the mother of God but regards her as not particularly relevant because she was a normal human being like us?

'Yes,' she responds. 'There are so many examples in the Gospels where Jesus has to rebuke her. She's on the same status as all the others are. Of course he deeply cared for her.'

I ask her to imagine she is inside Notre Dame Cathedral in Paris and sees people kneeling and praying in front of a statue of Mary in the Lady Chapel. What would she think?

'I'd be really offended,' she replies. 'I get really offended by all that. In some countries, the whole Mary worship is demonic. That's strong language but I mean it. It is Father, Son and Holy Spirit – the Trinity – not Father, Son, Holy Spirit and Mary. To bring Mary into that is demonic. I'm deeply, deeply offended by it.'

What does she think about the statement that the Annunciation is 'the most important event in human history'?

'I'd say yes to that and the Crucifixion which is where it's all leading.'

When I tell her that some people believe that it's possible to be a Christian whilst not believing in the Annunciation, she replies, 'I would say that when we get to heaven, what we will be asked is, "Have you put your faith in Jesus Christ?" God won't say, "Did you believe in the Annunciation?" There are some things that are central to the Gospels...the life, death and resurrection of Jesus Christ.'

But the life of Jesus Christ begins at that moment of conception, doesn't it?.

'Yes, but I don't think that's what we will be judged on,' she responds. 'I believe in the Annunciation totally but that's not the key question we will be asked when we go to heaven. "Have you put your trust in Jesus Christ to forgive your sins?" – that will be the key question.'

So, I wonder, if a Baptist minister came to her and said, 'I believe in God, I believe in Jesus Christ, I believe in the Resurrection, but I don't believe the Annunciation actually happened,' what would she say?

'I would say that's fine. There are all these other things around it that are true but some is doctrine and some is dogma.'

Is she saying that Jesus being fully God and fully human is the key, not how he came down on earth?

'Yes,' she responds. 'It says if you confess to Jesus Christ as Lord with your mouth, you'll be saved. I'd also say face the journey. When you come to Christ, you don't have all the answers. Faith isn't about ticking boxes. It's about a relationship.'

Is it important to her that it was a virgin conception?

'Yes,' she says. 'The reason there is a hymen, I think, is that when it is broken, blood is shed and blood is all about covenants. God doesn't want a marriage without a covenant agreement. So that's why sex outside marriage is not God's intention. He wants children to be born within a covenant. That's why blood is shed. That's why there's a hymen. For Mary that wasn't a part of her impregnation. I haven't worked out why yet but I think that's why it's important. There wasn't blood shed.'

I suggest that although some women find the emphasis on virginity to be offensive, she does not see it like that.

'No I don't,' she replies. 'And the fact she went on to have loads of children – the Gospels say that.'

Some have suggested they were cousins, I say.

'No, no. It doesn't say cousins. It says brothers. And it doesn't just say it once. It says it throughout the Gospels.'

So she believes it was a virgin birth, but what about the notion of Mary's perpetual virginity?

'It's ridiculous,' she intervenes, 'and it's not biblical.'

She is becoming increasingly restless. So, I ask, for her, were there brothers and sisters who came after Jesus?

'Yes,' she replies. 'But the hymen was intact when she slept with Joseph for the first time.'

We move on to talk about the feast of the Annunciation. She admits she did not know the date was 25 March.

'Partly it's because Baptists don't follow a liturgical calendar. Partly it's been a kickback to this veneration of Mary, which we really do find distasteful. It's a reaction to the whole Catholic/Mary thing,' she says. 'I personally love the Lectionary and the idea of a Church calendar and I do think us Baptists miss out a lot because we don't follow it like the Anglican churches do. Theologically, it widens your scope and allows you to meditate on different aspects of the Christian faith.'

I wonder if she has big hang-ups about Mary.

'No, only when she's venerated,' she replies. 'I don't think she's sitting up there with the Godhead. But I can't wait to meet her. She has my utmost respect and honour. I do honour her.'

I take out the print of the François Lemoyne picture of the Annunciation. She looks at it in silence for a while.

'I love it,' she exclaims. 'I love the finger pointing to God. It's all about him, not her.'

I observe that she is becoming rather emotional looking at it.

'I love the glory,' she says. 'Your eyes are immediately lifted up. I like her attitude. The listening servant. The humility. That maid servant. To follow him is all about love, grace, glory, forgiveness, but it's also about obedience. It's a beautiful picture of submission. I think it's wonderful. I love it.'

Would she put it up in her home?

'Yes, I would. Yes. Do you know what most people's spiritual journey is?' she asks me. 'It starts off being converted. Then a lot of us go completely charismatic like I did. But then you become contemplative. I've been to a nunnery and spent ten days in silence. I love the contemplative and spiritual side. That's a common journey for a lot of people. The pentecostal stuff happens and it's "whoosh" and then you land up eventually more contemplative and you go deeper and deeper. It's a revelatory faith and the whole time God reveals more and more who he is.'

My journey takes me to a tiny lime-washed, Saxon church in the hamlet of Hardham in West Sussex, one mile south of Pulborough. A large sign outside declares that the church contains 'probably the earliest nearly complete series of medieval wall paintings in England,' dating back to the beginning of the twelfth century. When I open the ancient wooden door and enter St Botolph's church, the sight inside is stunning. The walls are saturated in beautiful Anglo-Norman religious paintings. A complete set has survived virtually intact although, not surprisingly after 900 years, the colours are somewhat faded.

A single travelling workshop of artists created the paintings around 1100. They are known as the 'Lewes Group' because the Cluniac monks based at the priory in Lewes supervised these artists. When they arrived at Hardham, they applied a thick base of plaster to the church's rubble walls and painted the frescos whilst the plaster was still wet using cheap, locally available pigments such as red and yellow ochre, lime white and carbon black. There is still evidence on some of the haloes of the most expensive pigment used – a blue-green copper carbonate produced from malachite. It is thought the frescos were lime-washed over as early as the thirteenth century before being discovered in 1866 and then uncovered in the 1940s.

My eyes focus on one particular painting on the upper tier of the east wall, at the end of the nave, on the south side of the chancel arch. There, Gabriel stands on the left holding a sceptre while the dove descends towards Mary and hovers on her forehead as she raises her hands. Next to this fresco is one of the Visitation – Luke's story that directly follows the Annunciation, when Mary visits Elizabeth. Above the two paintings is a clearly visible inscription: 'VIRGO SALUTATUR STERILIS FECUNDA PROBATUR' (The Virgin is saluted. The barren is proved fruitful).

112. Lewes Group's wall painting of the Annunciation, early twelfth century, St Botolph's, Hardham, Sussex

It is a surprise to find Andrew White, the Vicar of Baghdad, living in a large bungalow in Liphook, east Hampshire. However, in the week I visit, he has been ordered by the Archbishop of Canterbury to stay in England because to return to St George's church in the Iraqi capital would put his life in extreme danger. He and the Archbishop worked together at Coventry Cathedral fifteen years ago and are old friends. Like White, Justin Welby has experience of working in hostile environments, particularly in West Africa, so his decision to forbid his former colleague to return to Baghdad will not have been taken lightly.

'He's very, very worried about ISIS and my own safety. If they get into Baghdad, no way would they let us go,' Andrew White tells me. 'But I want to be back with my people. I'm very, very concerned for them. I'd take any risk. I'm not worried but I know I should be. I know he's right and I'm wrong.'

St George's church, in the Red Zone of Baghdad, has been bombed five times in the past three years. One of Andrew White's assistants, a lay pastor, was kidnapped and then reportedly released when a ransom sum was handed over. Some of his staff and many of his faithful congregation have been murdered and now, most are fleeing for safety by heading north to Jordan. Previously, White has been kidnapped and then released and says that ISIS have warned him indirectly in recent weeks that they want to cut off his head as a prized target. If that was not enough to contend with, he has suffered from multiple sclerosis since the age of thirty-three and both his mobility and speech have become severely affected.

His study is large and crammed with theological books and memorabilia. Crucifixes and icons from different parts of the Middle East vie for space with personally signed photographs from President George W. Bush, Yasser Arafat, and Shimon Peres. There is a photo of him alongside Pope John Paul II and another from Justin Welby, signed 'To my dear friend'. It is clear that he likes his work to be recognized, thrives on praise and relishes the regard in which he is held. He comes across as an eccentric and flamboyant character. I soon discover how he loves to be the centre of attention, has a large ego and does not hesitate to blow his own trumpet. But there is a reason for this. He is a man of steel, passion and enormous courage. He has much to be proud of and has shown an extraordinary level of bravery in fulfilling his ministry.

He sits in an armchair in the corner of the room. I realize as soon as I meet him that his multiple sclerosis greatly restricts his mobility and forces him to speak in a slightly slurred drawl. He starts our conversation by reminiscing about the early influences on his life. He was brought up in a strict Baptist and Pentecostal household in Wanstead, London, before the family moved to Bexley in Kent. I ask about the place that Mary held during his childhood.

'Mary was non-existent to me as a child. You couldn't have any religious images and especially of Mary. That would mean you're a dodgy Roman Catholic,' he recalls. 'I was told we were the pre-destined people and they were heretics.'

He stares at me intently through owlish glasses. He tells me how he used to visit regularly a bed-ridden old lady whom he called Aunty Hilda. She was a staunch Anglo-Catholic and had a huge impact on him.

'I wanted to go to her church for her, even though she couldn't get there. So I started going. My parents weren't happy. I'd come back singing "Glory be to the Queen of Heaven". Right tune, wrong words. I'd go to Evensong almost every day. I was told, "You're going to get indigestion with all this church. You're really crazy".'

When the family moved to Bexley, he found that he did not like the local Anglican church.

'I could cope with the wacky charismatics and the high Anglo-Catholics but middle of the road was far too boring so I went back to the Baptists and then became a charismatic Anglican.'

He had ambitions to be an anaesthetist and became an operating department practitioner at St Thomas's Hospital. But then he heard a calling from God to become a priest in the Church of England, and trained for ordination at Ridley Hall, Cambridge. After various postings, he became a Canon at Coventry Cathedral and Director for the International Centre for Reconciliation. He spent a lot of time in the Middle East and built up a reputation as a trusted facilitator in reconciliation initiatives between Christians and Jews, Jews and Palestinians, Sunni and Shi'ite Muslims. 'You listen to all sides and you hear all perspectives,' he says.

Today, as well as being the exiled Vicar of St George's, he is the President and original founder of the charity, Foundation for Relief and Reconciliation in the Middle East. He says he was greatly inspired by Donald Coggan, the former Archbishop of Canterbury, who told him, 'Don't take care, take risks.' He started working in Baghdad in the late nineties, and after the fall of Saddam Hussein in 2003, he returned to re-open the Anglican church in the city where he became known as 'Aboona' or 'Father'.

In the room with him this afternoon is a staff of three. At regular intervals, he shouts out orders in a brusque manner that makes me feel slightly uncomfortable: 'What was his name?', 'I want to speak to him later', 'Let's have some tea and biscuits.'

I move the conversation on and ask what the annunciation story means for him. He calls it the 'Announciation [*sic*] of the Coming of the Lord to Mary' and says, 'It is about hope, that everything is changing, it causes us to look forward, always to look forward. Even in the dark, dark state of Iraq, it makes me realize I have to look forward.'

Does he see the story as factual?

'It's absolutely factual,' he responds. 'It is so much part of the Christian history and tradition. I can't see it as anything but fact. I believe in the oral tradition, passed down.'

Does he see it as 'the most important event in human history'?

'Absolutely. It's when the whole messianic hope becomes reality.'

He tells me at St George's the feast of the Annunciation is designated as a fasting day and, in past years, the church has been full for the festal service. 'No other Anglican church does that,' he says. 'Everyone comes to light a candle.'

I ask whether he venerates Mary.

'Never. I would never pray to her but I would always respect her and I love the story of her.'

What about the virgin conception?

'It's central to my understanding of who the Messiah is. Who Jesus is as the chosen, anointed one of God.'

I wonder if Mary is a bridge or a barrier to interfaith dialogue.

'She's a barrier,' he replies firmly. 'She's not someone or something you'd ever bring up.' However, he goes on to describe with much affection the Byzantine-styled icon of Mary that he has by the side of his bed in his private room in Baghdad. It is a metal image of the Virgin holding a scroll. He goes on to explain how Orthodox icons inspire him.

Did he feel a definite calling from God to go to Baghdad?

'Yes. I felt a need to go because no one else was there,' he says. He left his wife, Caroline, and two young children back in England to commit himself to serve in Baghdad. He would try to return home to see them every six weeks. At its peak, six to seven hundred people would come to Sunday services at St George's but now that number has reduced dramatically. Now fewer than fifty attend. There used to be more than a million Christians in Iraq; now there are fewer than a quarter of a million and most live in fear of reprisals and the spectre of ISIS. 'Christians can no longer live safely in any part of Iraq,' he says. He accepts, with great reluctance, that soon, centuries of Christianity in the country will come to an end.

He established a clinic at St George's where free medical and dental treatments were offered. It was funded through his charitable foundation and Christians and Sunni and Shia Muslims worked there together side by side. He claims that as many as 2,000 would access the service each month.

While in Baghdad he received stem cell therapy to try to stabilize his multiple sclerosis. He becomes agitated as he tells me it is the only place where he is able to have the controversial treatment other than in Abil in Jordan. He is worried that without it his physical condition will decline rapidly.

A phone rings. It is the Archdeacon at Lambeth Palace. Andrew White tells him he wants to return to Baghdad as soon as possible. However, he is told there are very serious worries about bombs being thrown into the church and his personal safety will be greatly at risk if he returns. He is informed that the Archbishop of Canterbury has a duty of care to him and it is in his best interests not to go back. He looks disconsolate but resigned to his fate. 'It doesn't look as though I will be returning soon,' he sighs.

I sense it is time to close our conversation but before I leave, I show him the print of Lemoyne's *The Annunciation*.

'Oh yes, oh yes, oh yes,' he says. 'I see her saying, "Me? What me? I'm wholly available. Here I am".'

He becomes highly emotional as he continues gazing at the composition.

'It's great. This is very profound. It speaks of servitude, calling, acceptance and one proud woman prepared to take risks.'

CHAPTER 30

AMBIGUITY

The Right Reverend Dr Martin Warner is the Bishop of Chichester and takes a special interest in Mariology and Christian art. A traditionalist, the fifty-five-year-old is a member of the Society of the Holy Cross, an international Anglo-Catholic society of male priests. He trained for ordination at St Stephen's House, Oxford, and in 2003 was awarded a Ph.D. at Durham for his thesis entitled, *Virginity Matters: power and ambiguity in the attraction of the Virgin Mary*.

At the 2012 General Synod he voted against the motion to allow the ordination of women as bishops in the Church of England. He will not ordain women as priests but is content to work alongside them as part of a team. The Diocese says he has worked 'resolutely to encourage provision in which people of all integrities can remain together.'

I meet him in his large sunny office at the Palace – his official residence that is situated close to the cathedral. Bishop Martin is a bald-headed, diminutive man with a wiry physique. He wears metal-framed round glasses and has a distinctive silky, rich voice. I find him to be cerebral, warm and friendly.

I begin by asking about the meaning of the annunciation story.

'This is the point at which we give to God the one thing God does not have, and Mary is the person who makes that gift, which is flesh and blood,' he says. 'A time-limited existence on earth. It is the turning point in history because it is the point of restoration. The English text that it connects with in my mind is from *Paradise Lost*. The moment Milton brilliantly describes the biting into the apple and "nature shudders". This is the next point that nature shudders again. That sense of shudder in the Fall is about something that introduces dislocation. I think metaphysically but also in terms of our human experience, this translates into something being amiss. We don't know how or why or what but we know its symptoms and experience them individually, socially, globally, but we also experience them within the very nature of the earth – for example, the tsunami and its destructive force – all of this is about dislocation. That's the context out of which we emerge in the light of the Annunciation. It's about the new creation and the healing of this dislocation.'

Does he have any concerns about the veracity of the story as it only appears in Luke's Gospel?

'John's Prologue gives us the whole spectrum in which the detail of Luke's Gospel is illuminated,' he replies. 'We have four people in a room and each of them speaks from a different experience, in different terms, about the same truth.'

Does he regard the encounter as fact or metaphor?

'Yes, it's as profoundly fact as the love and engagement between the two parents of any human person,' he responds confidently. 'No matter what questions people may want to raise from a point of scepticism about a particular woman who was Mary who lived in Nazareth, the truth of the Christian faith in the Word made flesh, God taking human experience to God's self, being born, means that somewhere there is a woman of whom God is born. Either you say I don't believe that, you don't buy into the Christian story, but, if you do, as soon as you do, then the fact Mary has existed becomes fundamental.'

I tell him about the wide range of views that I have heard on my journey.

'The difficulty for us now is that it has been so overdrawn, we've had so many representations and they're so specific, that perhaps there's a surfeit in our minds about the visual. It's very difficult to eradicate what is commentary and heavily freighted by a particular culture and age. Because there have been so many of these versions, we'd even be nervous about adding our own cultural layer to this by saying there was no angel, there was some other message. It would just add to all the rest. I'm not sure how helpful all that reductionism is. We are talking about an exchange between a human being, whom we call Mary, and God, at a point when something happens in her, which is about conception in which she is also an agent. Some sense of free will is profound in our conviction about God's dealings with us. There's a marvellous description in the imagination that St Bernard gives. He sees at this moment that history turns. The angel comes and says what he says and then everybody holds their breath, all creation, waiting for Mary's reply. Will she say yes or no? Just that sense she may say, "Sorry, I'm busy, ask someone else," but then says "Let it be done to me." Of course, it was possible for her to say no. It's as though the whole thing breathes a sigh of relief. This is humanity doing what humanity is capable of at its best.'

We move on to discuss how the status of the feast day has diminished in modern times and I ask if he feels that something important has been lost.

'Without doubt,' he answers assuredly. 'I go on and on about our patterns of prayer. We can enrich society at large by returning to the attention of the rhythm of nature and the idea of morning and evening prayer. If we were to recover some of the wonder of the rising and the setting of the sun, we would notice more than we do a different pattern to our year. The Annunciation was the day around which the year worked pivotally. I think it's something to do with the status of touching the rhythm of the nature of the earth's patterns, connecting them with the rhythm of the human person in terms of the nine-month gestation period. I don't think it would mean that it will suddenly become as important as Christmas Day but it might help us understand why the Annunciation day was so important in the past and help connect faith with the reality of the material world.'

I ask what Mary means to him.

'I think she represents ambiguity in a way that encapsulates both the human condition and our experience of God,' he says. 'The human condition is profoundly ambiguous at so many levels – in the tentative nature of our relating to each other and our capacity to know and understand ourselves. For the Christian, the journey into oneself simply expands that sense of the mystery of the human person.'

He tells me he venerates Mary 'profoundly'. In that context, is she a bridge or a barrier, I wonder, to greater inter-denominational dialogue?

'She's less of a barrier now,' he replies. 'Evangelical Christians have seen a pattern of discipleship in Mary and found their own ways of looking at her. In a scholarly way, they've recovered some of the insights of the Reformers who were uniform in believing in the perpetual virginity of Mary. Much of what we think of as a barrier is about iconography and excess in terms of devotion to Mary. The freedom for difference of approach, the respect for differences of approach, has probably grown.'

Does he hold to the view of her perpetual virginity?

'Yes I do,' he replies. 'It's an important statement.'

But does that not imply that virginity is an aspirational state and that sex is somehow sinful? I point out that many people I have spoken to believe that Mary had more children after Jesus and believe that a part of her strength is her ordinariness and her humanity.

'I think that's the thin edge of a very dangerous wedge to be honest,' he responds, 'because you can then say: "Of course then the stuff about Jesus, the point about Jesus is he is one like us." You're going down the line of emphasizing the humanity. And then, of course, it's necessary to say, of course, Jesus didn't walk on water, he didn't cure the sick. So the reductionist stuff goes further and further and at what point do you then say he was just a very special human being who communed with God in a remarkable way? The full force of the scandal of the gospel – Jesus of Nazareth, born of the Virgin, is the human and the divine – that's the scandal of it, and holding on to that is the real challenge for all of us.'

But doesn't the notion of her perpetual virginity make her unapproachable and distant?

'I completely see how the danger emerges. But it's worth remembering in the eleventh century, as the Decretalists get going and the Western Church wants to begin on a process of wanting answers and they want to start regulating stuff such as marriage and the ordering of celibacy in the Church, so the rules begin to emerge. For them the problem is Mary and Joseph have to exemplify everything that is proper in marriage so what are they going to do about sexual relations between the two of them and the issue of her perpetual virginity? It's a real problem. Their determination to say it's a real marriage and yet to validate men and women who enter into a real marriage and somehow to square that circle. Of course, for men and women like us, sex has a place like it doesn't have for Mary and Joseph. Nevertheless, how Mary and Joseph enfold those who are sexually active in their mantle of marriage seems to me to connect with what I love about the ambiguity of Mary. That's where the ambiguity of Mary falls.'

I tell him about Vivienne Faull's view of the annunciation story and how the Dean of York sees it as a story of emancipation.

'Yes,' he says firmly, 'this is not just the woman but a human person who says, "My body is the temple". She gets there before Paul does. She got there first. The emancipation is that Mary is saying that not just as a human person but as a female person. The consequence for women of that has been hugely varied by the culture in which they have lived. At its very best, it has said to women you model for us what it is to be human in terms of the body being the temple.'

I wonder how the annunciation story has shaped his life.

'Staying with the theme of ambiguity, I suppose something about both limitation and freedom; something about discipline,' he responds. 'Here I am, a single person living a life that's constrained in a number of ways, through ordination, and yet the fruitfulness and liberation of thinking my affections, desires, relationships, nonetheless find outlets and expressions that need not be limited and constrained by the disciplines that are placed on me. For a single person in ordination, the limitation would be sexual. That's clear. On the other hand, the expression of sexuality as an aspect of being human, to eradicate it, strikes me as being weird, de-humanizing it. But it finds expression in a wide and rich range of other ways, which expresses itself not only in physicality between two people. That comes back to perpetual virginity. All the time, virginity is registered as the negative, the fruitless statement that we have to undo. As soon as it becomes the positive, dynamic, fruitful sense of potentiality, it seems to me that it has something that offers human beings enrichment.'

I am listening very carefully. I feel the conversation is taking us to a very intimate area of his life. I ask if the concept of the perpetual virginity of Mary inspires him personally.

'Yes, absolutely, absolutely,' he replies. 'What do I do with this aspect of my life that is not expressed in a marital relationship and that has the fruitfulness in children. I need to find other ways of doing that or it shrivels and I diminish something about myself. Mary models how that can be. And actually much of the whole paraphernalia of the iconographic interpretation of the Annunciation is trying to work that through.'

I ask whether he would discuss his own perpetual virginity in the pulpit.

'I've always felt that touching on virginity and human sexuality is an important thing for us to articulate as clergy and to articulate it in a positive context. One of the things that is profoundly damaging for Christianity at large and especially for the Church of England, even more so than for the Roman Catholic Church, is the fact that our language, our talk about sex, particularly around same-sex relationships, is becoming toxic. It already is, I think. We need to stop talking in those terms and in that way and talk in other ways that are more positive. I remember a woman in a big church in London telling me how troubled she was talking about sex and Christianity with her children. "What do I say to them?" she asked. "They're late teenagers. They can't get enough of it. And I'm saying, don't do it." I said, "You say to them, 'It's sacred, darling. Use it carefully.'" I do want to talk about sex as something sacred.'

I show him the print of Lemoyne's *The Annunciation*.

'I see some of the familiar ingredients in the later development of Annunciation pictures and I also see some of the seeds of difficulty. There's a sort of verismo quality in an odd way that leads straight into the piety of the nineteenth century in ways that have not been helpful subsequently as we look back. We're beginning to look at the psychology of the woman here. That's the focus here. The real Mary. There's something that takes away any physical sight between Mary and the angel. She's really looking at the book. The angel is an auto-suggestion cue. So there's a whole dimension here of psychology beginning to break in. The beginnings of the modern world. A post-Enlightenment Mary stripped of a range of accoutrements that belonged to the medieval world. What does this experience feel like?'

Does he like it?

'Personally no,' he responds. 'It's a very interesting examination. She's on a pavement…through an arch.' He stares intensely at the image, almost talking to himself. 'We are looking outside. Are we coming out of Eden to a building environment? I'm not sure where I am here. It reverses the angel coming in from the left and being at Mary's eye level. That disturbs me, just in the way that canvases work. Why have you done that? You haven't said why. I'd be saying to the artist, "Where are your workings? You haven't given me the answers here." So it's rather irritating. It jolts.'

Inside Chichester Cathedral, I find a touring exhibition of paintings entitled *Incarnation, Mary and Women from the Bible* that features seventeen works by the British figurative artist, Chris Gollon. Eve, Hannah, Rachel, Salome, Delilah, Judith, Job's wife, Mary Magdalene and, of course, the Virgin Mary are all featured. Even Mary's mother, Anna, gets a look-in although there is no mention of her name in the Bible. There are also portraits of the early Christian martyr Lucy and the fourteenth-century mystic Julian of Norwich. But that is not what intrigues me. Yes, there is a Virgin and Child here, yes there is a Pieta, but in an exhibition entitled *Incarnation, Mary and Women from the Bible,* I am surprised at the absence of an Annunciation.

Chris Gollon is a self-taught painter with a provocative style. Although primarily a secular artist, he is described by art critic Tamsin Pickeral, as 'a chronicler of the soul'. His figures are stylized, dark and intense, often set against stark backgrounds. The fourteen Stations of the cross he painted for the church of St John on Bethnal Green – a mammoth project that took ten years to complete – has been widely acclaimed. This current exhibition is touring many of the great Cathedrals of England including Guildford, Durham, Norwich, Chichester and Hereford, and he creates a new painting for each one to add to the core exhibition. But I am intrigued: why is there no Annunciation here? I contact Chris Gollon's agent, David Tregunna, curator and collector at IAP Fine Art in London, hoping to find the answer. Within a few weeks, I am sitting inside the artist's studio in Surrey listening to the explanation from the horse's mouth, so to speak.

Chris Gollon's workplace is a small barn on the outskirts of the village of Worplesdon, four miles north west of Guildford. It is more like a large shed or converted garage than a trendy artist's studio. Branches of ivy invade the workspace through gaps between the walls and roof. The roof beams are exposed and two single glazed windows look out onto the nearby woods and pastureland. Electric heaters glow in the dusky light and rock music plays softly somewhere in the distance. A large table stands in the middle of the room. It is entirely covered with paints, sponges, spray cans and brushes, but the artist tells me he knows exactly where everything is placed. Nearby, scores of art books are piled high with a Robert Hughes publication on Goya on the top. Below it lie books on Bruegel, Picasso and another entitled, *The Art of the Renaissance.* There is a mannequin by the window, a large sombrero hat hanging from the ceiling, and two prominent signs on the wall written in thick black marker pen: 'DRAW PROPERLY!' and 'DREAM CATCHER'. Suffice to say, the nearby toilet reminds me of my student days at Leeds University in the 1970s.

Sixty-two-year-old Chris Gollon is a good-looking man with the air of a seventies rock star. He has spiky, silver hair, a goatee beard and a slim figure. He is tanned, dressed in brown chinos and a black V-neck pullover and blue collarless shirt.

Behind him stands a large canvas that he has just started working on. Already, I can see two figures emerging: on the left, painted in black and gold, an angel with disproportionally muscular arms and tiny head and, on the right, a woman dressed in yellow and grey with outstretched arms and a slightly protruding belly. Its title will be *The Annunciation.*

113. Chris Gollon begins work on his painting of the Annunciation

'When David mentioned your communication and asking why I hadn't done it,' he tells me in a slow drawl, 'I thought I was being a bit cowardly in not attempting it so, as is usual with me, I don't like being defeated. So I thought I will do one, I'll see what I can do with it. I'd thought it would take me a long time to work it out. Like with the Resurrection, all the ones I'd seen don't really work for today's society – not because it's an impossible thing to believe in but I couldn't quite work out how to do it.'

Was it too hard to imagine? I ask.

'Partly that and I hadn't seen a decent, contemporary interpretation of it. Lots of artists depict her recoiling. I don't know but…' He pauses for a while. 'It was partly because I hadn't done enough research. I thought at the time it was too much for me to look into and I wasn't entirely sure I'd be able to make a convincing image anyway. But I find if I do too much research, I end up turning out a picture that people know about already. I like to get a little bit of theology from the clergy and then I make something that may be slightly wrong in its factual content but there's no point in me making something people already know. It needs to be an image that makes you re-think the situation. With the Annunciation, traditionally, there's the archangel Gabriel, the Holy Spirit represented by the dove and Mary, of course. But for me, the whole thing is going to rest on her expression. It must be with her.'

He describes himself as deeply spiritual but not conventionally religious.

'I have some faith. I don't practise. There are aspects of the Bible I have some problems with.'

So will this be a secular painting about a religious story?

'I don't know. That's a good question. Quite possibly. It's a difficult one that.'

Does he believe the annunciation story?

'I don't know. It's hard to put into words,' he says. 'I do believe the story but I don't know how to represent it. The factual side is where the difficulty is. I believe in Jesus slightly more than God, which I know is nonsense. It's the wrong way round but because of the Incarnation, I kind of do.'

What has shaped his initial thoughts about the painting?

'I looked back at some imagery including the van Eyck in Washington. He almost did the first speech bowl quote and I thought I might do something like that here. I'm not quite sure yet. I was interested that he'd written Mary's words upside down so God could read them more easily. I thought that was interesting with a little bit of humour there. I thought I'd keep the three main elements of the archangel Gabriel, the dove and Mary. I wanted to do a volatile sky. I started to paint the canvas in yellow oxide and then painted it in black over the top, and with some sponges managed to create this sky – just taking paint off – so you actually end up with some lovely marks you couldn't make otherwise. Of course, it still needs tidying up. I've then painted the three figures in black and white over the yellow but Mary is hardly worked up at all at the moment.'

I tell him that to the untrained eye, it looks well on its way.

'I can see things emerging already,' he replies. 'It's too fussy there, [he points to the angelic figure] and if I paint this, [he points to a part of the background] it could be quite dramatic. This has got to be more 3D here, [he looks at the Mary figure]. I'm pleased with the sky. You've got to be brave when you're painting. I'm quite pleased with the composition as such. It's a very difficult story for people to relate to today somehow. To believe in. I don't think people like their imagery to be too corny today. If you've got shafts of light coming into Mary as though it was the moment, I don't think anybody could take it nowadays so I need to find a way of…' His voice tails off. He has been working on the picture for four days and says he expects it will be another three weeks before he finishes it. It is a large painting, 5 foot by 5 foot. I notice that Gabriel's eyes are closed firmly and I wonder why.

'Because it's such a severe moment, such a special moment. I know it's an angel but human beings often do that.'

I tell him I like that feature. I have never seen it before.

'Apparently, I have an ability to freeze a moment in time,' he says modestly. 'I like the idea of her acceptance. I'd like her to have no expression at all. Then everyone who looks at it can make up their own mind on what she's thinking because I don't know what she was thinking. I can't begin to understand how she felt. Was it a gift or a burden? I don't know how I would have felt. Maybe it's because I'm a man. So if she's expressionless, I feel it will be more profound and that's the clue to the whole painting as far as I'm concerned. I don't know how she felt. I never will know but if I can get her face to be somehow expressionless, then you [the viewer] will make the facial expression for me – I'm giving you a little bit of work to do yourself. I don't want to have an opinion, otherwise it's little me's interpretation of such a momentous moment. I'm just the receiver of the story.'

He looks at the painting in silence, moving his eyes around different areas of the canvas.

'With religious art, I spend more time thinking about it than actually painting. After a couple of glasses of wine, I had an idea of receding nails in the background but...' His voice tails off again. I tell him that some of my interviewees have described the Annunciation as the start of salvation which then leads on to the Crucifixion, so that may work well.

'Thanks,' he says. 'I've kind of got it but I haven't got a painting yet. It's a seed now. Parts of it I'm not happy with. Her face needs working up. It doesn't quite work yet. Once you've said all you want to say, that's when it will be finished.'

I leave him to get on with the task in hand and say I will return when he has completed the work.

Three weeks later, I return to his workshop. The painting is finished. Two fluorescent lights hanging between the exposed roof beams, light up the canvas. What has changed since we last met, I ask him?

114. Chris Gollon *The Annunciation*, 2015. By kind permission of Anne Gollon and IAP Fine Art

'I've been thinking about that very awkward but very important question you asked me,' he replies in his distinctive London accent. 'Is this a secular painting about religion or a religious painting? I hadn't really thought about it before and it has affected the way I've finished the painting. I've also been thinking about a couple of artists in the twentieth century, Max Beckmann and Marc Chagall, and about Bruegel's methods too.

'In my case, depending on whether my faith is high or non-existent, it does fluctuate and I don't think that makes me an agnostic or atheist,' he says before pausing. 'I've been remembering what Fr Alan Green at Bethnal Green said to me, "When in doubt Chris, just paint the characters as being human because, after all, they were human." There's one word they don't seem to like in the Church and that's if a painting is described as "spiritual" but I disagree with them. You can have a painting of faith in a still-life. It can be spiritual. That led me to think,' – he pauses for a while to gather his thoughts – 'I probably always start it as a secular painting about a religious subject and then it seems to become religious when it's installed in a religious place. If you were to take a Picasso of the *Mother and Child* and put it in a cathedral, it kind of takes on, you know, a religious feeling. And it can work the other way round. The El Grecos in the Prado don't have the same effect as when you see them in the sacred places in Toledo for where they were originally intended. So even though for me the procedure is secular, then, possibly, it can become a religious image. I seem to have an ability for religious people to relate to it.'

His answer rather reminds me of Peter Eugene Ball's comments earlier in the year. Chris Gollon goes on to tell me how, from a technical point of view, he's made various adjustments.

'I tidied up the angel, worked on the hands but left him pretty much as he was. I loved the sky but it was far too fussy and was taking away from the expression of Mary, but then I decided to leave that too. We'd discussed about the nails and I thought I'd go further and I'd spray in a cross and that's the two shadows here, (he points to a cross shaped shadow at the bottom of the canvas.) The picture then becomes stage-lit because, obviously, you can't have one shadow going one way and another going another. So I decided to make it like a stage in which the scene is enacted. I also used the nails for perspective. What we have there is the future. It could also be a comment on how she's feeling. Does she know or does she not know? I left Mary here (he points to her stomach). She's sort of pregnant but isn't – that's mucking about with time. I looked through loads of wallpaper designs to see if I could find one for her tunic but couldn't, so I bought a bunch of lilies and worked on it myself. (He points to her golden tunic, festooned with lily logos.) I've gone for the golden tunic because that's not normal for her. I like the seriousness and the severity of the moment so I started painting out bits of the sky. In the end, I didn't have to do too much to her face. I wanted to leave the under-paint coming through. Whether I've managed to get an expressionless expression, I don't know, but, hopefully, I've done that.'

Would he be pleased if viewers of the painting interpret the expression on Mary's face in their own way?

'Yes,' he responds. 'I thought if I worked it up too much I'd put my opinion into the matter and my opinion isn't worth anything. As the artist, I'm just a receiver to put something out. It's really important to me she doesn't have a specific expression. It could be acceptance but it could be a hundred other different emotions. That's for the viewer.'

So he still wants the viewer to focus on her, that is the centrality of the painting?

'Yes, definitely. The whole success of the painting rests on that. If that doesn't work, then the rest doesn't work.'

I notice he has kept the idea of representing speech. By Gabriel are the words '*Ave Maria*' and next to Mary is a speech bubble with upside down words reading '*Ecce Ancilla Domini*' (Behold the Handmaid of the Lord). He stares at his completed canvas, standing before it in silence for at least a minute before he opens up again.

'What I wanted really was just her without all these other attributes but that wouldn't work as an Annunciation without that label. Her face is just black and white paint over yellow with a little bit of sienna. I think it makes her look quite real.'

Has painting an Annunciation over the past month changed his view of the story? I wonder.

'A little but I still find it a remarkable story to believe in somehow,' he says. 'That's why I'd never attempted to paint it before. I wanted to make my own version, of this woman...of this situation...it's crazy what happened to her. I still don't know but I've got closer to thinking what she'd thought about it. But I'm a man trying to interpret a woman's point of view and that's impossible. But I am quite pleased with it. I'm glad I did it in the end. It's pretty traditional in the three elements but it's also very different.'

Now he has finished, does he regard it as a secular painting of a religious subject or a religious painting?

'If it's looked at by people with some faith, they may well see a religious painting. I don't think my paintings can convert anyone. It's always difficult to talk about your own work actually. If it works with you as a religious painting, that's fine by me.'

Has it changed him?

'Only in the sense that I've looked at Mary a bit more and tried to get into her skin. I'm not confirming it's a true story but I'm saying if it was a true story, this is perhaps how she'd think about it. It does make you think a lot. When I see my own paintings in a religious setting, it also lifts me to a place,' – his voice tails off before starting again – 'they're not like my images anymore. If I hear a choir in a cathedral and I'm looking at one of my pictures there, I feel it's taken away from me, it's not mine anymore and the painting takes on something else that I didn't do with it.'

He looks at me poignantly.

'It would be nice if it was to be enjoyed by someone or some place but it's gone for me now,' he says.

I show him a print of Lemoyne's *The Annunciation*. He looks first at Mary, then the angel and then the putti before asking about the meaning of the linen in the basket and the writing on the prie-dieu.

'It's a marvellous expression on her face,' he says and then pauses as he keeps looking at the image. 'She almost looks...you can't say pleased...not grateful...it's quite a remarkable expression. She's certainly thinking inwards, not outwards. It's not corny, you know, "I can't believe this is happening to me." Yes, it's quite remarkable. To us now, it looks very old fashioned but you can take works of art from any period and if an artist can manipulate expressions like that, it doesn't matter when it was painted. I don't like the top half – the angel and the putti – but that expression is really...mm, peculiar...it's not an expression one can describe. Quite remarkable.'

As I pack up to leave, he reveals that he used his thirty-one-year-old daughter Alice as the model for Mary's face in his own painting whereas the angel was all in his imagination.

'It wasn't a portrait,' he stresses. 'She just gave me the idea for Mary's expressionless face.'

He peers again at his painting on the easel.

'It's Mary's vulnerability,' he says quietly. 'Imagine the stress for her. I want to make her look as though she's asking for our help. That's my view. She's asking us all for our help in order for her to get through it. That's what I want to convey. That wasn't the feeling I had when I first started painting her, but I can feel it now, looking at it.'

In April 2017, Chris Gollon died after a short illness, aged sixty-four. This was the last interview he gave in which he discussed his biblically influenced work.

––––––––––

'You have to earn this audience from the very beginning. Think how are you going to feel the emotions of the character you are playing. And how are you going to change in the telling of this story?' The director, Ashley Herman, has gathered his cast together minutes before the play gets underway. 'When the angel appears, you're almost on top of her,' he proclaims to genial laughter. 'But it's not a comic event – remember that, and give it great punch audibly.'

It is his last piece of advice before proceedings get underway. The cast holds hands. 'This whole thing is a prayer,' he tells them. 'We pray that the Holy Spirit will be in our hearts throughout the day.'

I have come to the Wintershall Estate just outside Guildford to witness an open-air performance of the Passion play *The Life of Christ*. Over the next five and a half hours, more than a hundred actors will perform the three-act play. The audience, numbering around eight hundred, sits on the grass, eagerly awaiting the opening scene.

It is a dank, grey morning and light drizzle starts to fall as Phil Street, who plays St Luke, the Narrator, addresses the crowd.

'I was a doctor,' he tells the audience, 'and therefore I was able to make a careful study of everything I'm about to tell you so you can rely on what I say.'

He is wearing multi-coloured robes and a yellow and purple headdress.

'Our story begins with a lowly country girl, chosen amongst all women by God for the purity of her heart,' he tells us.

Mary appears in front of a small shack, sweeping the ground with a long brush.

I look around at the audience, the majority of which are school children aged between seven and eleven. All are transfixed. For the rest of the day, the actors move to different locations around the fields of the Wintershall Estate, followed by the crowd, recreating Jesus's life from his birth in Bethlehem to his ministry in Galilee and Jerusalem, ending with the crucifixion and resurrection.

Peter and Ann Hutley have lived on the Wintershall estate for more than fifty years. It was their idea to utilize the rich pasture, lakes, plantations and ancient woodland as an atmospheric backdrop for a play about Jesus. It was first produced in 1999 and has been enacted annually ever since. A charitable trust has been established 'for the purposes of ecumenical evangelisation and sharing the Christian faith.' Ten thousand people are expected to come to this year's performances that stretch over four days. More than a hundred and fifty thousand people have seen *The Life of Christ* since it began.

115. Mary is confronted by angel Gabriel during the Wintershall Estate production of *Life of Christ*.

Peter Hutley's simple but captivating script, matched by the beautiful scenery, the impressive acting and the clarity of the sound, make it a compelling production. The producer, the Hutley's daughter, Charlotte de Klee, explains the aims of the production on the Wintershall website: 'I'd love as many people to see it who might not know the story. It's not just for faith reasons but for educational reasons too.'

The director, Ashley Herman, states, 'You don't have to have faith to come to the play. It's not a religious play. It's a play that explores the phantom head of western civilisation. We try and portray this as real and not as a religious play.'

As I follow the production as it weaves around the estate, my mind still is fixed on the opening scene. Who would have thought that I would get to see the annunciation story coming alive in a field in Surrey?

All Saints church on the Isle of Wight is perched high above the picturesque village of Godshill. There's been a church on the site since Saxon times and the present building dates back to the fourteenth century. The churchyard gate is situated in front of an elegant stone tower, near a series of pretty thatched cottages. It is a classic chocolate box English village scene.

Inside the church's rather ramshackle interior, I make my way to the south transept to view a unique mural, popularly called the 'Lily Cross'. This fifteenth-century wall painting depicts Christ being crucified on a triple branched lily. The three branches of the lily symbolize the Trinity and the open golden stamens symbolize the pure and sinless Virgin Mary. Christ has long limbs, a painfully thin body, and is wearing a short loincloth and a cap of thorns. It is thought that an unknown travelling craftsman created the mural around 1450. Then it was lime-washed at the Reformation, and re-discovered in Victorian

116. Lily Cross, fifteenth century, All Saints Church, Godshill, Isle of Wight

times. There is no other wall painting like it in the British Isles and that's why I have come here to see it for myself.

Uniquely, it encapsulates the beginning and end of Jesus's life in one image: the moment of his conception and his crucifixion. Most interestingly, it references the notion that Christ's conception and death took place on 25 March. The idea that Jesus entered the world and died on the same day, forming a perfect circle, goes back to the third century and was a firmly held view in patristic and medieval tradition. Augustine wrote: 'He is believed to have been conceived on the 25 March; upon which day also he suffered. So the womb of the Virgin, in which he was conceived, where no one of mortals was begotten, corresponds to the new grave in which he was buried, wherein was never man laid, neither before him or since.'

The coincidence of the Annunciation and Good Friday falling on the same date only happens two or three times each century. It is a rare event because Christian Churches use different methods to schedule holy days. The feast of the Annunciation and Christmas Day are fixed feast days, always occurring on 25 March and 25 December respectively. Movable feasts like Easter fall on different days depending on the lunar calendar.

The overlap happened on three occasions in the twentieth century: 1910, 1921 and 1932. In the twenty-first century it has happened twice, in 2005 and 2016. The next time will be in 2157. The coincidence has been described as presenting a tension for Christians – the joy of the Annunciation and the darkness of Good Friday. In that context, the Western Christian Church holds the view that celebrating the feast of the Annunciation on the same date as the solemnity of Good Friday is inappropriate and in 2016, therefore, the feast of the Annunciation was postponed until the Monday after Low Sunday on 4 April. However, in churches of the Byzantine rite, the solemnity of the Annunciation and Good Friday will still be marked on the same day with the divine liturgy of the Annunciation being spoken in the morning and the Good Friday commemoration starting from noon.

In 1608, when the Annunciation and Good Friday fell simultaneously on 25 March, it inspired the metaphysical poet John Donne to write one of his most acclaimed Divine Poems: 'Upon the Annunciation and Passion falling upon one day':

> Tamely frail body' abstain today; today
> My soul eats twice, Christ hither and away.
> She sees him man, so like God made in this,
> That of them both a circle emblem is,
> Whose first and last concur; this doubtful day
> Of feast or fast, Christ came, and went away;
> She sees him nothing twice at once, who is all;
> She sees a cedar plant itself, and fall,
> Her maker put to making, and the head
> Of life, at once, not yet alive, and dead;
> She sees at once the virgin mother stay
> Reclused at home, public at Golgotha.
> Sad and rejoiced she's seen at once, and seen
> At almost fifty, and at scarce fifteen.
> At once a son is promised her, and gone,
> Gabriel gives Christ to her, he her to John;
> Not fully a mother, she's in orbity.
> At once receiver and the legacy;
> All this, and all between, this day hath shown,
> Th'abridgement of Christ's story, which makes one
> (As in plain maps, the furthest west is east)
> Of the angels' *Ave*, 'and *Consummatum est.*

Reverend Paul Kennedy, parish priest at St Faith's in Winchester, says the coincidence of the two events happening on the same date in 2016 would be 'as if the wood of the crib and the wood of the cross are hewn from the same tree. When Mary says yes to the Incarnation in her womb, she is also saying yes to the sacrifice of her son at his crucifixion at Calvary.' In that context, he says, the moving of the feast of the Annunciation to a later date in April in 2016 is an act that 'impoverishes the Annunciation/Good Friday Day. It's unfortunate that our Church calendar will not allow space for the conflicting emotions which afflict and enrich our lives.'

The most extraordinary story to arise from the Annunciation/Good Friday coincidence comes from southern Italy. A single thorn, which the local priesthood claim was taken from Jesus's crown of thorns, has been kept in a reliquary in Andria Cathedral since 1308. Tradition has it that the thorn bleeds each time that the Annunciation and Good Friday coincide. This occurrence has been recorded since 1633, and in 2005 the Cathedral claimed that independent scientific analysis backed the proposition.

As I look up at the beautiful mural of the *Lily Cross*, I wonder if this is the painting that most accurately encapsulates Bishop Egan's phrase, 'the most important event in human history'. Conception and death brought together. The whole lifespan of Jesus captured in a single image.

I have crossed the Solent by ferry and I am now searching for another Annunciation. This time I am in Southampton, meandering through darkly lit passages underneath the City Art Gallery, heading towards a locked-up storage area where thousands of paintings are stacked away. Thankfully, the gallery's curator, Tim Craven, is with me. Two floors above sits one of England's best civic art galleries that displays a superb collection of paintings spanning eight centuries. As well as wonderful sculptures by Epstein, Rodin and Degas, there are works from leading Post-Impressionist and Surrealist artists. One such Surrealist picture is by the celebrated Belgian painter Paul Delvaux and is entitled *Annunciation*.

To my surprise, I discover that Paul Delvaux's painting hasn't been displayed in Southampton City Art Gallery for years. Tim Craven tells me there simply is not enough space to show all of their great works.

'There are 4,000 pieces in the collection but only a fraction are on show,' he says.

But this is one of the most celebrated and original takes on the Annunciation created the last century, I respond, pleading with him to move it upstairs for more people to see.

117. Paul Delvaux's painting in the vaults of Southampton City Art Gallery

'I know, I know,' he replies.

I show him the Phaidon handbook of great Annunciation works that features Delvaux's *Annunciation* alongside Magritte, Dali, Richter, Marden and Warhol. He breathes in and sighs almost apologetically.

Paul Delvaux was born in Antheit in Belgium in 1897 and painted his *Annunciation* in 1949 soon after the end of the Second World War. After working in the art movements of neo-Impressionism and Expressionism, he focused on surrealism in the mid-1930s.

Tim Craven explains that Arthur Tilden Jeffress, the London art collector and gallery owner, who committed suicide in Paris in 1963, bequeathed the picture to Southampton. Jeffers had lived at Marwell House between Winchester and Southampton from 1934 with his lover, John Deakin. Craven's formidable knowledge about the history of the painting and his passionate enthusiasm for it makes it even more difficult to understand

118. Paul Delvaux Annunciation, 1949, Southampton City Art Gallery. © Foundation Paul Delvaux, Sint-Idesbala – SABAM Belgium/DACS 2017

why it is hidden from public view. He pulls a heavy rack towards him and gradually, Paul Delvaux's *Annunciation* reveals itself. Immediately I see it is a stunning picture.

The female angel is clothed in an off the shoulder dress made of thick green leaves that she has pulled apart to reveal her bosom. A chain of daisies flows through her long hair and she carries a small bunch of daisies in her left hand. She leans towards Mary, her eyes looking downwards. Each appears to be in a dream-like state, as if hypnotized. Mary does not look at the angel and yet she has heard the message; her right hand is raised. She sits on an open terrace in a beautiful garden near to her palatial home. She wears a silver tiara in her hair and her silky, blue mantle has fallen off her shoulders to reveal her white breasts. The sexual dimension to the encounter is clear, accentuated further by the finely trimmed topiary archway between them. The clipped yew tree, shaped around a metal arch, forms a long, shaded pathway that leads to the sea. Above the two figures is a brilliant clear blue sky.

I cannot take my eyes off the picture. Tears well up in my eyes. It is such a beautiful, clever and highly unusual depiction. I have learned recently that surrealism aims to unleash the sub-conscious imagination, revealing the unconscious mind, and reconciling it with rational life. So what does this painting tell me about the Annunciation? Is it rooted in the sub-conscious? Is the message in the dream?

I leave the Civic Centre and head to a large office building on the corner of Cumberland Place and London Road. It's the headquarters of Paris Smith, a large law firm, and I am coming to meet its Managing Partner, fifty-eight-year-old Nick Vaughan. Before I reach my destination, I spot his familiar figure walking towards me, dressed smartly in a black suit, collar and tie.

The sight triggers a fond memory. Thirty-eight years ago, I was walking across Woodhouse Moor in north Leeds having just attended my first lecture at the university. A young man, dressed in a smart, camel-coloured coat and brown brogues, caught up with me, and then asked the memorable question, 'Are you a Catholic?' That was the beginning of a life-long friendship. Nick Vaughan and I both studied Law and lived in the same hall of residence. We would talk endlessly about anything and everything (how to change the world, what is the meaning of life?) as young students do. And we'd have meandering conversations about politics, ambitions and belief.

After we left university, armed with our Law degrees, life changed and we went our separate ways but still kept in regular touch. Our conversations thereafter would focus on careers, music and family life. My wife and I went on to have five children and we asked Nick to be godfather to three of them. Sadly, he and his wife Karen were not able to have a family of their own but that has not stopped us talking about conception, fertility and parenthood. We are too close to make it a taboo subject.

Today I want to hear his views about the meaning of the annunciation story. We go to a dreary cafe nearby. He has to send his meal back twice, firstly because it is not what he ordered and then because it is under-cooked. It is hardly conducive to a deep discussion on religion and faith but, as ever, the conversation soon begins to flow. He recalls his first memory of the annunciation story:

'I remember it was the school Nativity play at St Mary's Catholic primary school here in Southampton. I was around five or six years old. It was an all boys school. I was Mary. Apparently I was given the role because I had fair hair and an angelic face. It started with the Annunciation and ended with the Three Wise Men. Instead of one Gabriel, we had about twenty in order to get everyone involved. There was a main person Gabriel and then all his followers. I remember saying, "I am with child." At the school, there were lots of Renaissance pictures all around of the Annunciation. They were like the Stations of the Cross.'

What did he think about the story then?

'At that stage, you simply soak up the information. You don't understand it,' he replies. 'There's lots of things coming at you. I remember staying at my grandmother's house and she used to have medallions hanging at the back of each bed. One was of the Sacred Heart. Another was of Mary at the Annunciation. Then, as a teenager, I suppose I thought about the Annunciation more artistically than religiously.'

When he was seventeen years old, did he know what 'The Annunciation' meant?

'Yes, definitely,' he replies. 'Partly because I was a regular churchgoer and also because lots of our Christmas cards had paintings called *The Annunciation*.'

What does the story mean to him today?

'It's the start of everything,' he responds. 'If you had no birth of God as Man, there'd be no New Testament. It starts there. It starts from something not normal, that's completely different: "You have been chosen." That message sets it aside as unique and very different from any child you or I would have.'

So, does he think it is factual or metaphorical?

'I suppose…' he starts to answer but then pauses hesitantly, 'it's difficult isn't it? Part of you sees the romantic view in those pictures. Two figures. Did those two people ever exist? Do we know Mary existed? We assume she did. We believe she did. And then part of you thinks, well, that's probably nonsense. I just want to see it in black and white. Why should I believe it? The humanist view. And somewhere in between is where I'd be. There is an element because of all your personal history…you know, I see God as a person with a white beard and all that, which has come from pictures. Part of me thinks, well I don't know that something happened and yet part of being a Catholic is that you believe in that.'

I think I understand where he is coming from. In this case, does 'in between' mean being on the fence?

'No,' he responds firmly. 'I can't prove it so I can't say that it definitely happened or that those people definitely existed. But if I believe, as I do, that God came down on earth and there was a reason for that, and that that belief has been there with us for more than two thousand years, and I believe that there is a resurrection, then I've got to believe it even though I can't prove it. That's what being a Catholic, being a Christian should be about. Believing it even though you can't possibly prove exactly what happened.'

When he says it is 'the start of everything', what does he mean precisely?

'I think it's about the start of a completely different chapter. Something amazing. You have to put it in some historical context. You have to think where it happened, how long ago it happened, and in what community it happened. It was a Jewish community not known for being very keen on women in those days. Yet here we are talking about a woman and about something slightly smutty. She's not married and yet she's going to have a child. Whoever wrote the account of that story came from that background and yet thought it was important enough to put down. That's very moving. It's human.'

Has he ever questioned the story and its veracity?

'I quite often think about the whole story,' he says. 'Can this be possibly true? And the answer is, I've no idea. And nor has anyone else. If someone knew, we wouldn't be having this conversation. You have to take things on trust and that's all about belief isn't it. It can't be about proof. It has to be about something that makes it worthwhile.'

Nick Vaughan's father was an Anglican and his mother a Roman Catholic. Consequently, he would go to two church services every Sunday. He attended Catholic schools throughout his childhood and his mother's relatives were deeply devout Catholics, some of whom would travel miles to attend a Latin Mass. He says the main thing he learnt from his parents was 'goodness'.

Does he think the way he views the annunciation story today is shaped by his upbringing or does he approach it now with a complete sense of free will?

'I think how my view started was very much influenced by how I was brought up, the household I lived in, by my grandmother who was a very staunch Catholic, and my Catholic schools,' he says. 'But after a period of time, you grow more independent of all of that and so you suddenly think, it's a nice story but what do I make of it? You can say I don't believe any of it or, instead, you can say I can't prove it but I have some belief in it because if not what's the point of being here?'

Is it a feeling of 'I want to believe it' or that 'I'd like to believe it' or 'I do believe it but I don't know'?

'I think it's probably "I believe it but I don't know",' he replies.

What about the statement by the Catholic Bishop, Philip Egan, that 'it's the most important event in human history'?

'I do believe that,' he replies. 'But I'm not sure about "in human history". There are billions of people who wouldn't hold to that view. But if you're a Christian then it is the most important event in their history. What comes after may have more impact, the Crucifixion and the Resurrection, but they couldn't have happened without that original event.'

I move on the conversation to talk about Mary. What does she mean to him?

'She's a sort of motherly support,' he says. 'I would pray to her probably more than to God. In all the workings of that story, she's the one who's human. Yes, there's Jesus but he's also God. She was always down here. She was fully human. So, she's more easy to talk to, she's more approachable, more understandable than somebody like God, Jesus, the Holy Spirit or whatever.'

Does he believe in the Immaculate Conception and Mary's perpetual virginity?

'I suppose you have to but that's much more difficult. I suppose they're just showing she's more special than any other person. I don't spend a lot of time thinking about that, to be honest.'

What about the notion of the virgin conception?

'Yes, I do believe that,' he replies. 'If you presume she's given birth to God, then yes it was a virgin birth or he'd be tainted with whatever. Yes, that's important. If you're accepting that she gave birth to a god, and you either do or you don't, then any of those other ways of conceiving would not be possible.'

Does he think she gave birth to other children who were Jesus's brothers and sisters or does he hold to the view they were cousins or friends?

'I've never really thought about it to be honest. I don't think it makes much difference. But if you are selected for that particular role, such an amazing role, you'd dedicate your whole life to that role wouldn't you? Someone who isn't married, who presumably wanted to have children in future, who's then told it's suddenly all going to happen now, that's fairly extraordinary isn't it?

'I was thinking when we went through IVF, for example, if somebody had come along to us and suddenly said, "Karen, you're going to be the mother of a child," how amazing would that be? That side of the story is very human. Your expectations, your hopes, and then suddenly somebody comes along and says, "Yes, it is going to happen." It would be an amazing experience. It's not a god you're talking about there of course but it's a similar amazing experience. For me, it emphasizes the human side of what she went through.'

Has experiencing the disappointment of unsuccessful IVF treatment re-shaped his view of the annunciation story?

'Not the general concept of what happened or what might have happened. But from her point of view, I know what Karen went through when it didn't work, having gone through it on three separate occasions. And then if suddenly she had been told she was going to have a child, I can't imagine what that would have been like. So for Mary not to be married, and with no prospect then of having a child, and then suddenly to be told she was going to have a child, to be a mother, she must have been...' his voice tails off. He looks out of the window wistfully. 'You've got the divine intervention, whatever that was, and then there's a human person. She's accepting something she has absolutely no concept of. Amazing.'

When I ask him if his faith is rooted in certainty or doubt he pauses for a long time before responding.

'It can't be rooted in certainty because I don't have the facts,' he says. 'But it's a strong belief in something that I can't prove.'

I wonder if he feels his faith is stronger today than it was thirty-eight years ago when I first met him.

'It's gone through phases,' he says. 'Up to my teenage years, like most people, it was very strong because I had no option. Then there was a period where, ok, it's in the background, maybe I believe or not, it was more challenging about the things you can't prove. I went along in that phase for quite a period I think. Now, in some ways, although I don't go to church anything like as much as I used to, I probably have a stronger general faith as opposed to being in a church community, than I did before. I do think there's an emphasis on too many things that shouldn't matter.'

What does he mean, I wonder?

'I played the organ in both an Anglican and a Catholic church for more than twenty years. I suppose I saw too much of the politics. Too much time being spent on the people who were there rather than on why they were there. I will still go to church but not as regularly now. I enjoy the experience but the church community isn't as important to me now.'

CHAPTER 31

DESTINY

I am back in my home city ready to meet six women artists, who have each created a work inspired by the Annunciation.

Sophie Hacker studied Fine Art at Oxford and graduated from the Slade School of Art in 1989. Her work comprises oil paintings, pastels, acrylics, sculpture and stained glass and can be found in public and private collections in the United Kingdom and abroad. She is currently Arts and Exhibitions Consultant at Winchester Cathedral and is married to the Vice-Dean, Roly Riem. In the 1990s, she created two works called *Annunciation* and *Annunciation II* and I have come to her home in the Cathedral Close to discover the stories behind both pictures.

She looks every inch the artist in residence. Trendy spectacles and a beautiful knee length jacket match a distinctive, spiky hairstyle that seems to have a mind of its own. She is ebullient and extrovert and yet, at the same time, appears sensitive. She tells me how she wanted to be an artist from the age of four. She lived in a house where her parents, both professional musicians, encouraged her to value the importance of the creative arts.

The two Annunciations, created in 1994 and 1997, are both pastels on handmade water colour paper.

'It was all very tactile,' she remembers. 'You roll the pastel, feel the colour, there's no intermediary between your thought process and the colour. It's very direct. It's about rubbing the surface, very fleshy, using colour and finger, and the image evolves.'

She was in her early thirties when she created the two works but has not worked in pastel for more than a decade.

'The first Annunciation work was about the ordination of women,' she tells me. 'I got married in 1992 and soon after, my sister Katy was training for ordination at Westcott just before the vote was to be taken on women priests by the General Synod. I wanted to give her a gift that was about the genuine calling of her life to God and to the priesthood, which she was honouring by training to be a deacon at that time. For me, the Annunciation was highly appropriate because it's about the calling of a woman to a unique ministry. It was a gesture of love to my sister.'

119. Sophie Hacker *Annunciation*, 1994. © Sophie Hacker

We sit at the breakfast table looking at a postcard of that first Annunciation work. It is semi-abstract, and shows a seated female figure moving her head round to face a bright light.

'Her body seems to be facing towards the dark but her torso is gradually turning and her features are diffused by the intense light,' she observes. 'She's gradually turning to respond to the call.'

Sophie Hacker says the figure is not her sister.

'It's about Mary and without her *yes* the redemption of creation could not happen. We are in darkness and have been called by a great light. The whole of creation, groaning and longing for Christ to enter the world, is dependent on Mary's *yes*. The intense light is from the angels dancing in heaven as she's about to say, "Go on then, let it be." So, it's at that moment of the call just before she says yes – the Salutation.'

I note that there is no Gabriel in her depiction.

'I absolutely feel the description of Gabriel as a messenger doesn't have to be embodied in any way at all,' she says. 'I don't need an angel. For me, it's the metaphor of light and dark. When light enters as the messenger. That's why for me I am always seeking to express the presence of light in a dark world. That's what grabs me.'

I also note that Mary is dressed neither in blue nor red.

'She's naked in fact,' she replies. 'She's only barely there. She's only defined by the same sorts of marks as the space around her. You only read her as an image because of the placement of those marks. Her nakedness is about being stripped bare in the face of God. That's what a calling is. If you clutter calling with layers that are obscuring, in what way are you responding? So her nakedness is there to make it as honest and articulated a response as possible – a genuine meeting of love.'

She tells me that her sister Katy has kept the original throughout her ministry.

'It's been relevant and important to her as an expression of her vocation.'

As she looks at the image on the postcard, she ponders. 'For me, the Church is extremely male. Everything about it…God the *Father*, God the *Son*,' she says, emphasizing each word. 'So many also call the *Holy Spirit* "he", but for me the Holy Spirit is always feminine…the original Hebrew word was *rūach*…breath, wind, spirit…it's a feminine word, a feminine form of language. God is God. It seems entirely authentic within the Trinity for the Holy Spirit to offer a model of parental, creative and communicative love that's based more in a feminine form. It's different to a masculine personhood. It feels utterly right for the Holy Spirit to be fundamentally feminine in the language form.'

She keeps staring at the image.

'I called it *Annunciation* because it was about my sister's calling to the priesthood. The Annunciation represents a calling to all Christians but there is a particularity about the calling to Mary that is about "what is my vocation?" and that is what my second Annunciation work is all about.'

Without warning, she stands abruptly from her chair and asks me to follow her to the first-floor landing where the pastel is hung outside her bedroom. 'I want to talk to you about this one in front of the picture,' she declares.

Annunciation II is more abstract. After looking at the image for a long time at the artist's request, I tell her I see two black figures standing together in the centre of the image. I also see a belly button to their right and possibly a woman's pubic area below. I am almost too embarrassed to reveal my observations.

'You can see how the finish on the pastel has this fleshy, velvety quality,' she says. 'Everything is very softened around it. This one is extremely personal to me. I made this in 1997. Today, my daughter is seventeen. There is a relevance there. Roly and I had been

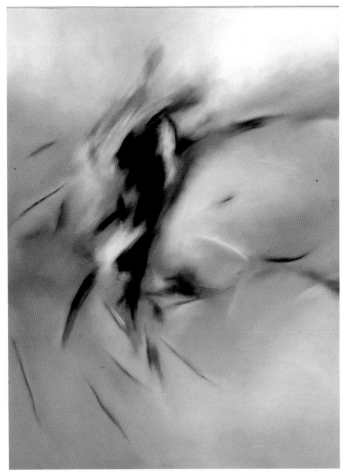

120. Sophie Hacker *Annunciation II*, 1997. © Sophie Hacker

married for five years and very much wanted to have a child. For various reasons, it took quite a while for me to get pregnant. This painting was created when I became pregnant with Abigail, having waited some years. What we've got in terms of narrative here are two figures.'

She points to what is, in fact, a dark blue figure with a bowing head, thin torso and two legs. Behind it is a softer second figure that she describes as, 'an echo alongside, slightly melting away.' The landscape across which the two figures appear to be travelling is shaped like a belly.

'Notice the head is looking down, and around the abdominal area is a strange scarlet mark. That's the heartbeat of my daughter,' she says, pointing to a red squiggle on the dark blue figure in the foreground. 'Before I became a mother, I was an artist. When a woman becomes pregnant, you go through such physical and emotional changes. The emotional and spiritual changes that happen – you almost have to relinquish who you are and who you know yourself to be – means the person you are going to be is not entirely known. Mary went through that too. She was the virgin who became a mother. The Annunciation is about becoming a mother and the calling is about bearing a child. Her body went through all the physical changes. But she also went through the emotional and spiritual changes with, of course, the nightmare of being unmarried and potentially being stoned to death by her community. When I became pregnant, I became extremely conscious of what must have happened to Mary as Jesus grew in her belly, whilst Abigail was growing in mine.'

Placing this picture outside her bedroom means she sees it every day, first thing in the morning and last thing at night.

'I made this work between conceiving and giving birth. It will never ever leave my side as it's the most personal piece of work I have. It's the most significant event that ever happened to me, having Abigail. The journey wasn't all that easy to get her – she's my only child – and she's been on my journey with me all the way. I've had offers for the picture but…no, never…never would I sell it.'

She is clearly emotional now after talking about it at such length. 'It's also about my journey as an artist,' she continues. 'I was genuinely scared what would happen to my career knowing that I was about to become a mother. I knew there would be changes and I didn't know how I would experience that. So, this work is saying that it's also another journey. My physical journey to motherhood and also my journey of creativity, side by side.'

I ask her to tell me a little more about what she was trying to express and she confirms that the figure and its echo represent her roles as mother and as creative artist.

'They're walking over a landscape,' she explains. 'Some people interpret that there as a belly button but, originally, I didn't make it to be that. Now, I see it all the time.'

She points to what looks like a small black smudge mark within a pink surround in the middle of the picture.

'The figure is me but it's also meant to be any woman who engages with that internal quandary.'

I tell her, somewhat nervously, that when I first saw the abstract picture and tried to interpret it, I thought I could see two figures looking down at a woman's pubic area. I am a little anxious how she is going to respond.

'That's lovely,' she replies. 'I can exactly read that area as a pubis as well. I don't have any problem with that at all. The body is the landscape and the landscape is the body. That's what the picture is all about. The growth of a new life and that the person who is bearing that new life is asking herself "Who am I? What will happen to me as a mother?" But also, "How will I now understand myself as a creative person?" So, *Annunciation II* is all about the acceptance of a calling and this *Annunciation II* is all about consequence.

Why did she call them both *Annunciation*? I ask.

'Because *Annunciation* II is about my own calling to make art to the glory of God. It's all about my own calling to God and the fact I'm doing that alongside the very special role of me being Abigail's mother.'

What do contemporary artists have to do in order to make the annunciation story relevant for today?

'You can't answer that question without engaging with what Christianity currently has to offer the art world,' she responds. 'An artist must be engaged with integrity and with where we are in the world now. How we communicate with God and how God communicates with us to steward our world and the people in it with fairness and integrity. I genuinely feel that the Annunciation is a profoundly symbolic moment in history that happened but continues to happen. For God to have come into this world, he has to continue coming into this world. The "Let it be" is important for Mary accepting being the mother of Jesus as it is for my sister's calling for ordination.'

Does she think the Annunciation is the most important event in human history?

'Yes, and the most important word there is "human". Mary was just human. What happened in her womb at that moment, I agree, was the most significant activity and action that ever happened to humankind because everything else happens from it. What the Annunciation offers us now, if we can be really honest about who we are, what we are called to be, how we lead our lives, is about a response to a call that never goes away. We're reminded every day to live our vocation and, for me, that is being an artist, a mother and a Christian.'

———————

Alice Kettle is one of Britain's most acclaimed textile artists. World renowned for her canon of distinctive and ambitious work, she was originally a painter who turned to embroidery to express her creativity with startling impact. Her machine-stitched, richly coloured works are displayed in public collections across the United Kingdom. 'Creation' and 'Identity' are important themes in her work.

Born in Winchester in 1961, the second of three sisters, she spent nearly all her childhood living in the confines of Winchester College where her father was a housemaster and teacher of modern languages. She found that living in the male-dominated community was intimidating, and sharing her family home – the boarding house – with fifty teenage boys, was stifling.

'We were always stuffed into the background,' she says. 'The female presence was secondary. There was a clash of the outside and the inside worlds, the male and the female worlds. My mother's way of dealing with it was to find soft, aesthetic places of decorative art where she could make her female presence known and that's what I took from it. So I also challenged that environment by adopting those female forms too – to express the alternative, the other – in colour, form, surface and texture.'

As a teenager, her bedroom became her 'magic domain' where she kept her treasures and created an imaginary space that was her own. Dominating her room was a poster of Fra Angelico's mural of the Annunciation from the San Marco convent in Florence.

'I think subconsciously it was something about the female. Something struck a chord and I fell in love with it. I took the colours from it to paint the walls in yellow ochres and the woodwork in pink. You could be subversive in a passive kind of way. No one would be able to know. I wonder now if I was creating my own cell. Most of my counterparts had pop groups on the wall but I had Fra Angelico,' she laughs. 'I just saw this beautiful woman and the pattern and the composition of her being held within this arch. The way they looked at each other. The calmness of the womb-like space. It felt very protective. Everything in that room revolved around it.'

After studying Fine Art at Reading University, she focused on Textile Art at Goldsmiths College, London. Her very first public showing in 1986, featured a figurative piece called the *Harlequin Madonna* and its inspiration was the story of the Annunciation. It is that particular work that I have come to talk about.

We sit in Alice Kettle's living room in the Hyde area of Winchester and she explains the techniques involved in her work. She talks slowly and precisely, describing the way in which she uses the sewing machine like a paintbrush, and the needle as a drawing tool. Alice tells me she finds that the tactility of textile art enables her to express her thoughts and emotions and that the physical action in creating these pieces is conducive to meditation and is a 'transformative process'. I find it fascinating and realize this is an art form that I know absolutely nothing about.

She is slightly built, softly spoken and self-effacing. She comes across as warm and highly intelligent, and there is an almost tangible sense of fragility about her. After talking for some time, she reveals that she was very vulnerable as a teenager. I ask whether the Fra Angelico *Annunciation* poster spoke of a quality in Mary that she could relate to at that time?

'It must have done but I wasn't aware of it then. I was a very mixed-up teenager, clinging onto something unconsciously. I think looking back, when I saw my mother in that male dominated environment, I saw her struggle, being trapped and I felt equally trapped. I wasn't terribly religious but I related to the symbolism of the work.

'I'd just left to go to Reading University,' she continues. 'I had fought to do Fine Art. Three weeks in, my mother dropped me off and died in a car crash on the way back home. She was the defining figure of my life. I really struggled for ten years after that rupture and I was very badly ill for some years after that. Yes, I did associate the Mary of the Fra Angelico with my mother. In fact, this conversation now is making me think very deeply of how all these things came together. I just submerged myself in my art. I was searching and restless. I knew I could use my work to recover. Textiles was very much my mother's thing. I knew it was something deeply resonant. It was about being myself. I knew the day I got to Goldsmiths and began to work in textiles that I'd found myself.'

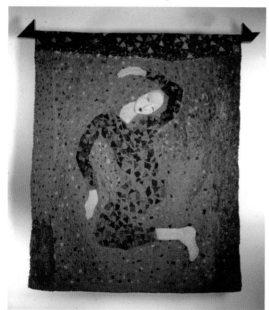

121. Alice Kettle *Harlequin Madonna*, 1986. © Alice Kettle

At Goldsmiths in 1986, she created the *Harlequin Madonna*. Influenced by Gustav Klimt's *The Woman in Gold*, it was exhibited in Chichester as her first publicly shown work.

'I started working figuratively at a period when abstract expressionism was pre-eminent,' she says. 'As part of my recovery, I first started painting small pictures that were about myself and my sanctuary. When I went to Goldsmiths, I started to think how I could present the female condition much more symbolically and the *Harlequin Madonna* emerged. When I was a child, there was a book called *Kitchen Madonna* and we used to make Madonnas with paper and fabrics and all that came together.'

She tells me how she now realizes the *Harlequin Madonna* was very much influenced by the annunciation story and, in particular, that poster of the Fra Angelico mural in her room.

'There is that sense of containment. There is a stillness but also a movement,' she says.

In that context, is the *Harlequin Madonna* both Mary and her own mother?

'Yes, very much so. It's all mixed together,' she replies. 'I was acutely in need of a mother figure. Even now, I feel a gooey warmth about it. I wasn't particularly religious then but, in a symbolic sense, Mary gives you a role model. She represents the entirety of womanhood in humanity. You don't imagine her speaking much – it's more her gaze, her benign presence of being woman.'

Did she find something inspiring in Mary and in Fra Angelico's depiction of her that led to her creating the *Harlequin Madonna*?

'Yes, I think so,' she concedes. 'There's something about the Madonna being submissive, but in her submission I see that as essentially powerful. She has something deeply resonant within the core of her being which exudes this powerful presence without her projecting or imposing it. She has it within her. That's how I felt. I knew there was something strong within but you don't have to articulate it because it has its own internal power.'

Why did she subtitle the work as 'A Circle Within a Square'?

'Because it's about purity – pure form. In that knowledge, there is something profound in its simplicity.'

She created both *Harlequin Madonna* and *Eve Falling from Grace* in 1986. One shows an upright woman dancing. The other depicts a woman who is upside down and falling. Was she conscious of the link between the two: the themes of obedience and disobedience and of Mary being called the 'Second Eve'?

'I never realized that then,' she says. 'That's very interesting. I did the Madonna first, icon-like, whereas the Eve actually falls from the wall onto the floor. It must have been in my sub-conscious.'

She moves on and reveals another bizarre connection with the annunciation story. She got married, became pregnant but lost the baby. A second pregnancy followed immediately but she cannot understand how it happened.

'To this day, I don't know how I got pregnant with my first daughter. I had a miscarriage and, apparently, conceived her at the time of the miscarriage, which, as I understand it, is impossible. The dates show I conceived on the day of the miscarriage. Everything had come out. I was not in a condition to have sex. Nothing happened. I have no idea at all how I conceived Poppy. It's weird, isn't it? Obviously, I wouldn't equate myself with Mary in any form but it has been one of those mysteries to this very day. I thought, this child wants to be here.'

She takes hold of her cup of coffee and gazes wistfully out of the front room window of her Victorian house.

'I've realized talking to you, and thinking again about that Fra Angelico poster, how the Annunciation has been a core theme throughout my work. Motherhood. Womanhood. A calling. It's an extraordinary thing but I think it is. Stitching gives me that inner light. It's a gift from my mother and from the universal mother.'

So, what does the annunciation story mean?

'There's something about destiny,' she replies. 'I have to do good. I have to have purpose and for a reason. I have to rise above, transcend above the difficulties of life. To realize that there is a calling. I don't know what it is but it's enormous.'

Does she see the story as fact or metaphor?

'I don't see it as fact. I see it as something deeply spiritual in a kind of celestial way. I'm not sure what it is. It's an archetypal myth that's humanizing. We need to lift ourselves from the everyday. A transcendence. It's a mix of the sub-conscious and the conscious. You're not absolutely aware of it. But it's about something that can transport me and give me the power and energy beyond the everyday experience. If I acknowledge and accept it, it will enable me to gift something back to life.'

I tell her how Bishop Philip Egan described the Annunciation as 'the most important event in human history'.

'I think it's about creation – the human capacity for creation. It's about imagination, potential, relationships with each other. It's similar but framed in a different language. It's never reached. It's a gift that makes us "Other". It makes us have infinite potential as beings. It's something unimaginable.'

I show her a print of Lemoyne's *The Annunciation*.

'It's very sentimental. The Fra Angelico evokes something transcendental but this is so funny. It's so comical. It's quite suggestive and quite phallic. It hoards you into the constraints of the portrait whereas the Fra Angelico allows you to open up your imagination. She looks so much more submissive, more downtrodden here. I wouldn't feel inspired by it at all. I don't have any sensations of wonder whereas with the Fra Angelico I can feel a gasping, a wanting to believe, an opening up of a space. With this, it closes it down. It's too allegorical. I really dislike it.'

I arrive at the Link Gallery on the University of Winchester campus for the opening of an exhibition entitled *Divine Antics*. The artist is Elaine Thomas, a former Vice-Chancellor at the University for the Creative Arts, who's recently returned full-time to painting. The exhibition features her latest figurative works in watercolour and acrylic, strongly influenced by Romanesque frescos, Indian carvings and Greek and Roman sculpture that she has seen on her travels. She describes the subject matter as, 'People and their behaviour; mannerisms and relationships; the many layers of meaning and understanding that exist between people.'

As luck would have it, the first picture I see is *The Annunciation*. The painting shows a multi-limbed angel on the left pointing at a female who is sitting on the floor with her hands wide open. Crouched behind her appears to be a second angel. However, I cannot work out if the image of the angel depicts one figure in motion, or several figures. The more I look at it, the more confused I become. Thankfully, Elaine Thomas joins me. First, she tells me about her craft.

122. Elaine Thomas *The Annunciation*, 2012. © Elaine Thomas

'The process of the painting is important,' she tells me. 'I start off by creating a ground with acrylics which is scrubbed and washed with my hands and run under the tap so I've got a surface like a fresco that has a semi-destroyed feel. I then work on top of that with a paintbrush and watercolour paint and discover images. The painting evolves. It comes out of my imagination combined with the surface I have in front of me. I have no sense whatsoever what the subject matter is at that time. It's like how the surrealists work in terms of automatic writing and automatic painting. Creating a surface and shapes which then suggest an image to you and then you find it. You work automatically and quickly and then go, "Ooh, ooh, I've found something".'

She tells me that her work is both autobiographical and autographic in its use of gestures and flourishes that represent a sense of personal identity and identification. Irony and hidden meaning pervade her work, and the stance she adopts can best be described as that of a satirist, caricaturist and cartoonist, seeking to communicate the many things that go unsaid.

'I'm always concerned with people and their behaviours,' she continues, 'the postures, poses and stances they adopt. I hold back on the details of the hands and faces until I've got the bodies. Limbs that may be wings. Is there one or two or three figures? Multi-limbs that may suggest an ambiguity. I like ambiguity. The figures start to emerge. I then put their hands and faces in. I hope people have to work to read my paintings. The actions are implied so, for the viewer, they can discover and find things for themselves. It may not necessarily be what I've committed to and what I see in the painting. I like that.'

She is a striking sixty-four-year-old with greying, tightly cropped hair. She is dressed smartly in black, and wears silver rings of various sizes and shapes on each of her fingers.

'I didn't know it was an angel Gabriel then,' she continues. 'I began to see a hand making a gesture and there was a point where it began to look like an angel. I gave it a halo. I allowed one head to take over and the halo became an echo. Then the wings appeared. At the same time, I was also working on the figures below, at least two figures then, maybe more.'

I intervene to ask whether Mary is the same figure in motion or two different figures.

'Either,' she replies. 'It could be that's a static Mary and that one is potentially a flying-away Mary. I can take responsibility for that afterwards but mostly at the time I'm an artist who doesn't plan. I follow my instinct and allow things to emerge.'

Her voice has a lovely Lancastrian lilt. I ask whether the great Medieval and Renaissance artists influenced her as she created this work.

'I think I must have been. First of all, I look at them all the time and go to places like Siena and Florence. I'm always in Italy and always looking at those powerful images everywhere. But I also have to say Indian dance is there too. I like hands and I'm always using hands to suggest things too. So, the influences will have been from both the annunciation story and other things too. All my figures are naked but they don't have rude bits. This is important. They're quite innocent, most of them. I very rarely draw naughty bits. It's all by suggestion and ambiguity. This painting was an early one I did in 2012, the first one of this collection. Very few of the others have such a literal title. When I saw them all together, I wondered what all these works were communicating to me and I eventually came up with something connecting the biblical divine with this cheeky dancing choreography and the two words 'divine' and 'antics' came together. Something high, something low and something cheeky. My relationship with religion is definitely cheeky. I like to poke at it and make it naughty.'

What motivated her to paint the annunciation encounter?

'Yes, what did I take responsibility for?' she asks herself before declaring, 'Power relationships. My work is to do with people and their behaviours, and relationships between figures. The Gabriel figure here, in a sense, is powerful while the figure on the right is more supplicant but not entirely. You can see a struggle going on there. A dominant figure meeting a more submissive figure or figures. The gender is ambiguous and the faces are quite feminine but not pretty. I've made the angel slightly androgynous and the figure on the right slightly female. The two figures there on the right are both Mary in a way and represent the idea of struggle, discomfort, agitation. Although I said the figure was, in a sense, supplicatory and submissive, what you actually see in fact in Mary is quite active, struggling with whatever's going on. It's not straightforward. There's more turbulence.'

I ask what the annunciation story means for her.

'I'm not sure,' she says. 'Iconographically, it's a very familiar image presented in lots of different ways. There's a familiarity there. But now I'm older I see it as the notion of the male God and the female human. I'm an atheist who was brought up a Methodist. I don't have any faith in any sense now but I'm a great believer in the Christian stories in what they can tell us. I'm somewhat intrigued by the image of it. The notion of the virgin conception I would disregard as a necessary story to help people believe in the character. But the image of it is powerful. It transcends time. An Annunciation image can vary enormously in tone and in message. In that respect, artists impose their own interests and own predilections. The Annunciation definitely has a message and for me it's holy osmosis. Something is happening between them. The angel Gabriel is the vertical one here. There's stature and there's gesture with the hand bestowing authority. Dominant but not necessarily achieving dominance. There's a fighting back and quite rightly,' she laughs. 'In those two figures, basically composed to represent Mary, you can find supplication, a figure looking submissive, but you see the sense of an inner struggle. There's no contact with the angel. But there are gestures with the hands that are expressing a struggle and a dialogue.'

So, is this picture of *The Annunciation* both secular and feminist in its stance?

'It's a secular piece. It has connotations for me to do with gender and power and the notion of male dominance. God has always been described as male. Angel Gabriel is always male. And Mary is just this vessel, this receptacle. The story now would anger me. To be fair, when I was brought up as a Methodist, this story didn't have much connection, much relevance. We didn't have images in our Methodist upbringing. I had an image free religious experience then. But it has become much more powerful now, looking at the images in Italy within the Catholic faith there. I adore so many of the Annunciation images there.' She then qualifies what she means. She loves the images as paintings rather than necessarily loving the story itself.

She tells me that in her late teens she felt that she was being indoctrinated and lost her faith. 'There was an almost "ding" moment when I realized that what I'd been taught at Sunday school and church was just a version of stories and events and wasn't real.' However, the more educated she became, the more she started to understand why many people seem to need a faith.

After graduating in painting from Manchester Polytechnic, she took up teaching posts in higher education in Northern Ireland. This had a pivotal impact on her.

'One of the many things I learnt from my students there was that the Catholics did work that was figurative and the Protestants did more that veered to abstraction. When I'd been a student, abstraction was everything and when I turned to figurative work, it was like a revelation. In a way, I think I'm making a statement about Catholicism here and the power of the human image in Catholicism, the importance of images and figures in telling stories.'

I wonder if male dominance, and women's anger about that dominance, is a key part of her work.

'I think it must be. As I gradually became more senior in university education, I really did come across prejudice and some terrible behaviour. I was in a world of the male in my early career and I observed their behaviours. Pomposity, for example, and how you couldn't get a word in. I had to suppress what I was thinking because I was on my own. It was painful feeling excluded. But as a woman, I grew more in confidence. All of that was going on in the background. In these paintings, made after I left, it's more ambiguous just as in life it's more ambiguous. There is an underlying sexuality in terms of relationships with men and the complexity of them – the tensions, the battles, the struggles. It's not simply male dominance. I'd say my art work is softer, strategic, but the things you suppress come out.'

Several people hover, wanting to talk to her, but she is in full flow now and doesn't notice them.

'When I was young, about seven or eight, and did still have faith, I saw an angel. I imagined an angel while I was away in the middle of Cumbria. I was visiting an aunt and I was missing my dad. I saw an angel at the end of the bed and for a long time after that it sustained my faith. I thought, crikey, I've seen an angel. Now, I can rationalize that and say what an amazing imagination I had. But thinking about it now, it was androgynous, something like this.' She points to the angel Gabriel figure in her painting. 'I'm only thinking about it now, talking to you. You connect all these things. I've never really thought about the angel and why they appear in my work but talking to you has made me think back and realize that I thought I saw one. I've never thought about that since it happened until now and the significance of that. I'm an atheist now but I'm not naive enough to think that these things don't matter. There's so much behind it all. Power relations in religion fascinate me and I don't have to have a faith to be interested in the role of religion in society.'

I tell her how one bishop described the Annunciation as 'the most important event in human history'.

'Mm, interesting,' she says, not committing herself to an answer.

I show her the print of the Lemoyne painting.

'I see a very feminine Gabriel. It looks like a woman. Look at those legs. My eyes are drawn there. Mary looks rather wimpish, a bit pathetic. It's the combination of her hands and her face. It goes to the heart of my preference for strong women. I want to resist the cliché of the dominant male and supplicant female but this painting presents that challenge. But it's interesting that Gabriel is so dominant and yet so feminine. It's beautiful. I like the painting.'

We draw to a close. I tell her I have much enjoyed the conversation.

'I've never thought about seeing the angel at the end of my bed and the significance of it, that is until now,' she reflects. She looks again at her Annunciation painting for a few seconds and smiles before being whisked off to meet other guests.

As soon as I enter Caroline Hall's Studio and Gallery in Little Minster Street, I see a dramatic oil painting named *Roller Coaster*. The title could easily be used to describe her life, which has undergone seismic changes in the last decade.

I first knew Caroline thirty years ago when she was a reporter on the BBC's regional television news programme *South Today*, and I was the programme producer. A journalist and mother of three children, she changed direction in 2004 when she decided to study Visual Art at Winchester School of Art. She graduated with a first class honours degree and then continued her studies, gaining an MA in Painting three years later. Today she is in her mid-fifties and is a professional artist whose style has moved from abstraction to figurative landscapes painted on aluminium. Without so much as referencing the painting I noticed earlier, she describes her new career as a 'roller coaster' experience. Furthermore, the change in her professional life has been more than matched by dramatic developments in her personal life.

Caroline Hall is steadily building a reputation for flair and originality. Three months ago, a mixed media installation called *Walking on Water* was exhibited in Winchester Cathedral and was well received. It comprised a video loop that gave the impression of the River Itchen flowing out of the medieval tiled floor of the South Aisle. When I arrive, she informs me that she has just heard that the Elena Shchukina contemporary art gallery in Mayfair plans to show her work. She hopes that will be her big break in London.

Her stunning oil paintings are displayed all around the gallery. One, of bluebells dancing in the wind, against a backdrop of dark green foliage, particularly catches my eye.

A delivery of aluminium panels arrives and Dexter, her lively chocolate-coloured dachshund puppy, darts out of his covered basket, barking loudly in a valiant attempt to declare himself the gallery's security guard as well as artist's pet. As the space is a gallery as well as a working studio, it seems curiously refined and quirkily chaotic at the same time. Caroline Hall perches on a tiny stool in a corner and stares intensely at a set of nine charcoal drawings pinned to the wall.

Two weeks ago, I bumped into Caroline in the High Street and told her about my Annunciation project. Subsequently, she has asked me to come and view something she created as a result of our conversation – a series of nine abstract drawings, inspired by the annunciation story and its message. She tells me that she went to the National Gallery immediately after our chat to view its medieval and Renaissance paintings of the Annunciation. The first picture she saw as she walked round the Sainsbury Wing was the Duccio.

'I love the colour palette, the simplicity and the fact they're both level with each other,' she says. 'There's an intimacy and a mutual respect.' That was enough. She did not want to study any more Annunciations, nor read Luke's Gospel passage again because she did not want her head to be filled with visual imagery. She explains the creative process of the

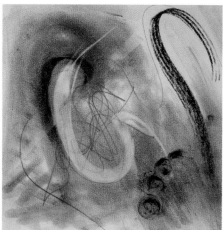

123. Caroline Hall Annunciation Study 2, 2016.
© Caroline Hall

past fortnight, claiming she approached the work without any preconceptions. The drawings were entirely intuitive, linked only by a pencil line at the start, which gave each study a story to follow.

'I bought a load of charcoal which I haven't done for ages and I bought these blocks that can create ridges and I started to carve. I'm playing with it, grating it and the charcoal dust falls onto the drawing. I decide that's interesting and decide to go with that. Then I start to rub it and the ridges start to make lines. The first effort I liked but then I ruined it by overworking it. I put too much in. Every one of them starts with a line – a beginning, middle and end – that's highly gestural and spontaneous. I see where it takes me and I don't take the pencil off. It's a very free way to start with a squiggle that's a moment. I like the idea of nurturing.'

I notice that under the first drawing, she has written: story, journey, narrative, spontaneous. In the second drawing, she tells me, she stripped right back and blurred the charcoal with her fingers and created 'splodges' through wetting the area. At the very end, she turned the image upside down.

'It didn't begin that way. I moved it round at the end every which way and thought it looked better that way up.'

I say I can now see Mary, the developing foetus, and an angel's wing. Over the course of the past two weeks, each of the nine drawings marked a progression.

'The last was the ninth. I knew I had to stop. I can't even tell you why but I knew that was it, straight away. I'd taken elements of every single drawing before. I'd got to the point where I thought, this one works, the balance, the harmony, the symmetry. It just had something for me and I called it *Annunciation*. As soon as I gave it a title, I knew that even though it was abstract, the viewer would find meaning in it. My partner saw a head, things being embraced, a wing.'

When she looks at it now, what does she see?

'I see visual things that I never set out to do. A head, an arm bending over, the chaos of the moment. The rectangles, which give it balance and stability. Are they windows, containers? Remember that you are looking at an abstract. The viewer does the work.'

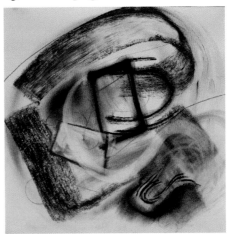

124. Caroline Hall *Annunciation Study 9*, 2016. © Caroline Hall

Does she view the annunciation story as a mixture of chaos and balance?

'Yes, there must have been turmoil and yet, at the same time, a calmness in it. A mixture that I was unconsciously looking for.'

I say that within the picture I can see a Mary figure looking downwards.

'For me, it's more an embracing,' she responds.

Is that a foetus in the bottom right of the drawing? I ask.

'For you, it is now,' she replies. 'I've had such a great response already on Twitter. I'm going to make them a series of nine to sell although I may not sell number nine. I may make that one a limited edition print and take possession of it. That one's become very special. Not for any religious reason. More, it's an example of what I can do with charcoal and I've learnt a lot while doing it. It's an experiment that's worked. It was only when I got to this point that I really decided I didn't want to paint it. Up to then, I was organizing how I'd transfer that image onto an aluminium panel. Then I stopped. I thought the essence of it would go if I try to transfer it. Why would I want to do that?'

Nine drawings, from concept to delivery. Nine different stages and then *Annunciation* is ready to be revealed. It is like the stages of a pregnancy, I observe.

'That's spooky,' she replies.

What does Luke's annunciation story mean for her now she has finished the project?

'I think of it from the point of view of Mary and did she have a choice or didn't she have a choice? That's fundamentally important. If she didn't have a choice that's a heck of a big ask. I think of it in the context of my own life, artists following their heart. Was she able to follow her heart or was she given an instruction? That's really important in how you see the story. I always see visually and I see a visual image of that story transferred as a moment of light and life. But there's a large question mark now in my mind. If you take it at its most simple level, someone being offered an opportunity – and in terms of my own life being thrown a curve ball and deciding to run with it – you either catch and run with it or you drop it; there's this definite parallel in the story with my own life in terms of opportunity, something coming out of the blue, that causes huge turmoil, hardship and angst, and everything else. It's very trite to say there are parallels because this is on a completely different level but in its simplest term it is the idea of being offered something and deciding whether to go with it.'

Caroline Hall loved art from the very moment she could pick up a pencil as a young child living in Dulwich in south London.

'Literally, I was always creative. I could lose myself in the process of drawing. It completely absorbed me. But it was then put on hold.'

So in her adult life, was there a sudden moment when she felt a calling to art?

'When everything failed in Germany as a family and my children were so unhappy, and we came back [her husband was working as a correspondent in Berlin at the time], Pete and I said we have to make it a positive and move our lives on in some way. He left journalism and I went to Art College. As soon as I got to Winchester School of Art, I felt, at last, I've arrived! Of course, I'm still learning to be an artist but I feel I've got a whole well waiting to come out, so much is waiting to be painted.'

Caroline Hall feels that another event in recent years can also be described as a calling. Four years ago, while on a skiing trip, she met and unexpectedly fell in love with a woman. She returned to England and almost immediately moved out of the family home, leaving behind her husband of thirty years and three children, to live with her new partner, Lucy.

'I feel both were callings,' she says. 'It was literally in a week, in fact on the very day. "Calling" gives it a religious connotation but it's more accurate to call it a blast, "Oh my God, this is how unhappy I've been. I've ignored this and I've ignored that." I knew with absolute certainty this is what I needed to do. I just knew. Effectively, I did the hardest thing I've ever done in my life in terms of pain, marriage, religion, the sanctity of marriage. People talk about all the people divorcing but you think it doesn't happen to you. It was like someone had turned on the engine of the train and it was rolling. I couldn't jump off. I absolutely had to go with it and say yes. The idea of a roller coaster is so apt.'

Did she see the announcement as one that would cause utter chaos but would also bring balance and harmony?

'Yes, yes,' she replies. 'I now know about all the soul things that I put on hold. I've found someone who wants to do these things with me. I'm not religious in the conventional sense but I've had the opportunity to go into Winchester Cathedral to find…It's very difficult to justify being happy when you've made someone else so unhappy and everyone else. Everything is fine now but I will have that legacy for the rest of my life. It's a momentous thing to break up a marriage. There is chaos. You can read too much into it, I know, but it's how I am as a person. I understand spirituality. A harmony and understanding of yourself which comes with age, experience and getting in the right place. I think it's that idea of spirit and person rather than an actual story in the Bible.'

Although she is talking about matters so profound and highly personal, she remains surprisingly calm and collected.

'When I go in the Cathedral, I'm not thinking about God and Jesus but I do think, this is an extraordinary place where I can stop and think. It's being at one with yourself and thinking beyond the selfish world we live in. As an artist, you spend so much time on your own. I love climbing a hill and looking at the whole landscape. I understand religion. I went to children's church. I brought my children up similarly. It saddens me people don't get going into the Cathedral, sitting there and feeling a sense of being, a sense of now, a sense of mindfulness.'

So, when she reads the story of the Annunciation now, what does she think?

'I see it as a metaphor,' she replies. 'Angels with wings, people will struggle with that today. We live in a world of science and technology. A virgin conception – it's a very difficult thing to grasp. But as a metaphor? Well yes, of course. Who couldn't relate to it as a metaphor? For me though, there's a downside to the story. This lack of choice. The way it's written: "You must do as you're told; you have this fantastic opportunity and it doesn't matter what you think about it, you're the one." That's very different. So, it depends how that story is – you're told you're having a baby or you have the free will to choose.

'Because I've been extraordinarily lucky and I've taken risks and I've used my free will a lot more than a lot of people in my personal circumstances, that to me would deny everything that I've done if I didn't have a free choice. I've chosen to go against convention and I don't know if Mary had the same choice. I've thought a lot about that in the past fortnight. I don't know if she did have free will. But then maybe…if you've ever been in love, you can be bewitched. There's that side of it about choice too. Maybe it was such an extraordinary moment, she said, "Wow, how could I say no?".'

———————

I climb the rickety, steep steps of an old dairy building that has been converted into artists' studios in the Fulflood district of Winchester. Thirty-nine-year-old Milli McGregor works in a large area on the first floor. As I enter the room, I notice a large oil painting of a heavily pregnant woman in a bathing costume propped up against a wall and next to it is a lovely drawing of the Virgin Mary.

Milli was born Amelia Du Plessis and was brought up in a strict Afrikaner household in Johannesburg, South Africa.

'The idea of wearing a T-shirt and jeans to church would have been unthinkable,' she tells me. 'You'd always wear your formal dress and be so neat and tidy.'

She spoke both Afrikaans and English at home and always wanted to be a creative artist. She lived her teenage years through the extraordinary period of South African history in the 1990s: when the National Party President F. W. de Klerk unbanned the ANC and repealed the remaining apartheid laws. Then, Nelson Mandela was released from prison after twenty-seven years and became President in the first non-racial elections.

Milli wanted to study Fine Art but her father told her that she needed a 'proper career' so she studied advertising, graphic design and marketing at the Red and Yellow School in Cape Town. Afterwards, she travelled to Europe, lived in London and the United States before settling down in Winchester with her partner and two children.

She describes herself as an Illustrator and Design Artist. Her website states she feels 'change is the only absolute'. The reason I have come to see her is because our local church, St Paul's, recently commissioned her to create the image for its Advent prayer booklet, and I was gripped by the result – a stunning image of Mary entitled *Lady in*

Waiting, rooted in Luke's annunciation story. As she begins to tell me about its gestation, it soon becomes clear why those two other images are leaning against the studio wall.

'She's waiting to give birth,' she says about *Lady in Waiting*. 'She looks like an angel herself with her halo. There's a feeling of knowing the message from the angel.'

She says she started with a charcoal drawing before adding colour on her computer.

'I love charcoal, the rawness, the messiness. She needed a rawness, I felt. I love the way her head is tilted, that peacefulness, and the way her hands are crossed in acceptance. I feel it really works.'

I comment that it looks more like an icon.

'It has a certain tackiness if you know what I mean. A good tackiness,' she replies.

125. Milli McGregor *Lady in Waiting*, 2016. © Milli McGregor

Lady in Waiting speaks to me in a powerful way. The wistful eyes, the calm pose of acceptance, the rich colouring. Milli tells me there is a clear South African flavour to parts of the image – her neckline, the pattern of the background, the emblem holding her cloak. I note that her facial features look neither European nor African but are more a hybrid.

She says that her Mary image was influenced by the works of Pisanello, together with Gustav Klimt and Marc Chagall, and especially by two of her previous works. She points to the painting of the heavily pregnant woman by the wall.

'That's a self-portrait of me in late pregnancy with my first child, fourteen years ago. He was unplanned. It just happened. And the other [she points to a black and white drawing of the Virgin Mary] speaks of motherhood. That's not usually my style. The very strong lines, incredibly strong, almost purposefully made.'

As a young Afrikaner brought up in the strict, Calvinist influenced Dutch Reformed Church, I am intrigued to find out what Mary means to her today.

'I feel I've always had a tug to faith. I have a strong belief. To me now, she means "freedom". As a woman who still feels there are certain restrictions, it's wonderful to resonate with her. Yes, she means "freedom".'

When I ask what the Annunciation means to her, she hesitates a while.

'I don't know it well enough. A lot of the time I think in my own language of Afrikaner and we use different words. When you say the word "annunciation", I'm not sure what it means. You're making me feel very…' She laughs out loud in supposed embarrassment. 'I'm in trouble here.'

She starts to speak in Afrikaans. 'Aankondiging, aankondiging, aankondiging. Die Bybel in die Afrikaans, aankondiging – die boodschap aan Maria. The announcement – the message to Mary. That's how I know the Annunciation,' she says.

As I prepare to depart, she reveals something she has never shared before.

'I always put some scripture words in a painting, underneath it at the start, before I get working on it.'

What is that about? I wonder.

'It's just a message that goes away with the work to somebody. A message of the day or something that's connected. I often give a quote in Afrikaans from St Paul to the Philippians: "I can do all this through Him who gives me strength".'

———

Every morning when I wake up, I open my Weekday Missal, and the first thing I see is a long, thin bookmark with a striking image of a bright golden cross on a multi-blue background. I cannot remember where I acquired it but the words 'Anne Keyte – contemporary handmade glass' are printed on the back with a mobile telephone number and an email address. I decide to find her.

Her website reveals that she is a 'contemporary glass designer' from Winchester whose studio and gallery offer 'the opportunity to view finished glass works including her signature blue dishes.' Her biography mentions that she trained as a Craft and Design and Technology teacher at Shoreditch College, graduating in 1980, before becoming a teacher. She gave up her job when she became pregnant with her first child in 1986. Two years later, she started going to the evangelical Winchester Family Church and in 1988 became a Christian. She had two more children before returning to supply teaching. Then she went on a stained-glass course and writes: 'I fell in love with the medium of glass and felt that was how God wanted me to express my creativity.' She returned to teaching to finance the building of a studio and kiln at her home.

For the past ten years, fifty-seven-year-old Anne Keyte has been experimenting with the art of fusing glass. She sells her pieces at the city's Christmas market, local craft fairs and open studio events.

I realize that she lives only a mile from my home and an idea occurs to me. I wonder if she would be willing to make a fused glass piece inspired by the annunciation story and let me follow its progress from conception through to gestation and then on to completion. We meet at her house and, after hearing my proposal, she agrees, saying she is excited and up for the challenge. Two weeks later, we are sitting in her studio looking at her initial designs.

'I always picture Mary in royal blue. There are lots of icons and pictures of her in blue and blue is my colour,' she tells me. 'I first thought about the angel Gabriel and how she was sent by God from the high heavens. She was pure and from God whereas Mary was a lowly human and low. Before that moment she was separate, then there was a coming together and her life and our lives changed forever. So here are my thoughts.'

Interestingly, she keeps identifying the angel Gabriel as 'she' throughout the conversation. She shows me three large pieces of card on which she has sketched her designs. Next to figurative drawings of Gabriel and Mary are lines of different shades of blue that form the shape of a square. By them are a series of highlighted words and phrases:

High/Heavenly/Pure/Above; Lowly/Human/Royal Blue/Below; Separate/Together/Union/Changed Forever;

Mother of God – Jesus!

'I want to do something three-dimensional, symbolic, representative rather than literal,' she explains. 'My thought is they're separate, Gabriel and Mary, but then they come together like in the kiln when the separate pieces of glass are fused together. So, there'll be a union. When the glass is fused it becomes completely different, just like Mary becoming the mother of God. Different things come to us at different times. They're all separate pieces of glass that will come together as one. The royal blue base is Mary at the bottom looking up. Surrounding the base are different shades of blue with the pure, clear glass at the very edge at the top. I am comparing the purity of God, the heavens and the angels at the top with the dark, sinful nature of the earth below. Mary was a sinner like all of us. Once those pieces of glass are fused as a flat piece, it will then go over a mould and become something else. It will go back in the kiln and slump and sink into the shape. The slumping is the symbol of the yielding, the submitting to God's will. She drops. She's on the bottom. And so when it's complete, you can say she's looking up at the pure glass or God, or the pure glass or God is looking down at her, the royal blue, and the darkness of the world. It's bigger at the top because God is so immense. The glass becomes something else once it's been in the kiln, like she becomes something else when she's submitted. There may be some air bubbles in the glass between the flat and the ripple but that's ok, they can represent the Holy Spirit giving life as the angel and Mary come together.'

When it comes out of the kiln, will she see it as a bowl representing the Annunciation or the Annunciation represented in a bowl?

'I see it as the Annunciation represented in the piece,' she says. 'I think about the art, the symbolism of the Annunciation and how I can represent that in my creation. For everyone else, they'll see it as a blue dish but for me, God has spoken to me. It's difficult to separate your own creative thoughts but I'm sure it's spirit led. God is leading me to do this work with passion and in the colours I love. I don't think it's by chance that you contacted me or that the design has turned out like this.'

Has she thought of a title for it?

'I was in church thinking about it yesterday and then when I went to bed, I thought about the word "Submit" but I'm not sure about a title yet.'

After having designed the piece, what are her thoughts on the Annunciation?

'It's about God being able to speak to each and everyone of us directly. Why he chose her I don't know. Does anyone know? Was she open to it?' She pauses for a while before continuing. 'Did I think subconsciously about the submitting, yielding and the dropping before I started to work on the design? It's difficult to know but that is what it symbolizes for me now. I can relate to that on a personal level. When God speaks to us, it's a union, it's relational.'

Does she see her work with glass as a calling from God?

'I've always been creative,' she says. 'I'm a teacher, a Christian counsellor, a pregnancy crisis counsellor, I spin a lot of plates. I found this quite late in life but as soon as I came to the medium of glass, I just knew that was it. Yes, it's an expression of my Christian faith. The gifts God has given me. God's beauty. It's my testimony. A witness to my faith.'

I leave her to put the pieces of glass in the kiln where they'll fuse together during the first firing that will last over thirty hours. Then they will cool down before being returned to the kiln for a further thirty hours to fuse to the mould and take on the shape of a three-dimensional bowl.

Ten days later I return to Anne Keyte's home. We are sitting in her Gallery – a large, converted garden shed. A range of her work, displayed on whitewashed shelves, surrounds us. There are about a hundred pieces, but there is one in particular I have come to see. On the table in front of us, a cloth covers the bowl. She whisks it away with a flourish to reveal the finished product. 'Here it is, all done and dusted,' she proclaims.

She is concerned there is a bubble in the royal blue coloured base, where a little bit of water may have been trapped. 'I wanted it to be perfect,' she says, 'but then I thought, actually, we're not perfect but God still uses us in our own imperfection. When I first saw it, I realized the whole piece is shaped like a star. I thought people may not like it but I do with all the symbols.'

When she looks at the finished piece what does she see and what has she learnt?

'I can't see it as a specific thing as I've been involved in such a different process here. This time, the title has led me into the design. I'm a perfectionist

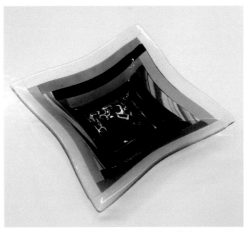

126. Anne Keyte *Annunciation*, 2014. © Anne Keyte

and I've learnt here that it doesn't have to be perfect. Beauty is in the eye of the beholder. It's what's inside the heart that matters. And that's what being a Christian is.'

Has she given it a title?

'I still haven't come up with one. I've never given any of my work a title. If it was a picture, it would be easier.'

Does she see the annunciation story as factual or metaphorical?

'Oh, I've always believed it to be factual,' she responds firmly.

And the notion of a virgin conception?

'Yes, I believe it did happen and that it's all possible. I believe the Bible is the word of God and if it said it happened, it happened.'

What does Mary mean to her?

'She has a part to play but to me…I don't put her…I don't hold her…I only hold Jesus and the Holy Spirit and God up there.'

Then, Anne Keyte says something I wasn't expecting to hear.

'I thought I'd lost the passion over the past two years for glass design, trying to sell my work, but this project has really brought it back to life,' she comments. 'It's given me the passion again and it's time to push fusing glass again. It's about God's timing, isn't it? It's re-ignited my calling.'

I ask her how much she will sell it for and she quotes seventy-five pounds. I tell her I will buy it and will call it *Annunciation*. She is thrilled.

Before leaving, I show her the print of the Lemoyne painting. Immediately she says she doesn't care for it.

'Mary is not looking up. It's not something I particularly like. Her looking down. The colours. I expected more brightness. There's too much else going on here. It's too busy.'

As our own encounter draws to a close, we talk about her work as a pregnancy crisis counsellor.

'It's about loving unconditionally as Jesus would and being non-judgmental,' she tells me. 'Before I did it, I thought I can't do this as a Christian. I can't promote abortion. But I've learnt it's about being non-judgmental and loving unconditionally as Jesus would. You may be the only person these people ever have to come to who listens. You go through the pros and cons of each of the options for them – pregnancy, adoption, abortion. You're not putting words into their mouths. You're just helping them to separate the head knowledge from the heart knowledge. What you believe in your heart rarely changes.'

She stresses that every case is unique: the people involved, their backgrounds, the context behind the pregnancy. I wonder whether the annunciation story may have relevance in the debate about the sanctity of life – when does a life begin in the womb – and about the fundamental human right of a woman to choose her own destiny.

'I think I can be pro-life and pro-choice at the same time,' she says. 'I'm free to have my choice about the sanctity of life, that's my personal belief, I have my own personal choice, and they are responsible for their choices. I'm never telling them what to do or enforcing any thoughts on them at all. I'm giving information and listening. Their freedom of choice is their accountability.'

Annunciation, the star-shaped glass bowl in varying shades of blue, now takes pride of place on a table in my home.

Reading my local paper, the *Hampshire Chronicle*, I come across details of an upcoming event to be held on the University of Winchester campus. It is entitled 'Big Questions: What to make of abortion?' The promotional material catches my eye: 'Is abortion good for women? When does a foetus become a person, and what are the implications of our answer? Is our abortion law the right one? We explore all these issues with Ann Furedi, pro-choice advocate and chief executive of the British Pregnancy Advisory Service and Anne Scanlan, Head of Education and Media at LIFE.'

I remember some months ago, the Roman Catholic Bishop of Portsmouth, Philip Egan, wrote in his sermon on the feast of the Annunciation that abortion 'degrades the dignity and value of human life' and that the Annunciation is a corrective, sounding a note of joy and proclaiming an alternative anthropology. 'That's what the Annunciation celebrates,' he wrote. 'It says there is another way.'

It is estimated that 26 per cent of all pregnancies worldwide are aborted. Most of those are unwanted conceptions, with fewer than 2 per cent thought to involve genetic issues. Forty-four million abortions are performed globally each year and half of them are claimed to be unsafe. The law of the land in Britain simply focuses on the point when a life is sustainable. Originally the gestation period was set by Parliament at twenty-eight weeks but this was reduced in 1990 to twenty-four weeks other than in exceptional cases. In England and Wales, of the 185,000 abortions that happen each year, 79 per cent are within the first ten weeks of pregnancy, 91 per cent within thirteen weeks and 98 per cent before the twentieth week. Since the Abortion Act was passed in 1967, abortions have been freely available on the NHS through registered practitioners in England, Scotland and Wales. There have been more than eight million legal abortions in Britain since the Act was passed, which equates to around 500 a day.

I have decided to attend the debate between Anne Scanlan and Ann Furedi to hear their opposing ideas. It occurs to me that it would be interesting to meet them beforehand to ask their views on the message of the annunciation story in relation to their beliefs about abortion and the right to choose. Luckily, they both agree.

127. Left: Life campaign poster. © Life charity. Centre: Anne Scanlan and Ann Furedi present the arguments in the abortion debate. Right: bpas information leaflet. ©BPAS charity

Anne Scanlan was born in Ireland and moved to England as a young adult. She gave up her directorship at an architectural firm to train as a pregnancy advice counsellor and is now Head of Education and Media at LIFE, the largest pro-life charity in the UK. She argues that from the moment of conception, a new human being with a fully human genetic make-up has been created and that abortion is the deliberate termination of that new human being, violating its right to life. She believes that abortion has caused devastation and damage to a society that's becoming increasingly less compassionate. A referendum in her Irish birthland in 1983 voted to introduce a constitutional ban on abortions, emphasizing the rights of the unborn child.

'One night when I was pregnant, I was lying on the sofa and my daughter-to-be kicked in the womb and I could see the imprint of her foot,' she tells me. 'I thought, there and then, this is an independent human being growing inside of me that has every right to be born. It was like a clarity moment. It struck me really strongly and solidified what I thought. Then, when I became pregnant again with my third child, I was working as an architect in London's West End and I was coming home on the Tube one night and saw an advert for LIFE, offering counselling. I contacted them and then trained as a counsellor for four and a half years.'

LIFE is not a religious organisation and claims that its arguments are grounded in the humanist principles of justice, equality, democracy and human rights.

'The organisation is not about condemning women for the choices they make,' she explains. 'It's about saying, "there is another way". I want to help women make better choices. I want to be an educator. I see it as a vocation. I made a big sacrifice but when I go into a school, I see how the penny drops and that makes it so worthwhile. I want to be telling kids 'this may not be the best choice.' Life begins at conception and, therefore, taking that life must be wrong regardless of the reason how it was conceived. Taking a life is morally wrong.'

We are sitting together in a corner of the student cafe on the University campus. It is full of young people laughing and joking and is very noisy. We continue our conversation above the din.

Does she believe that every abortion, at every stage of pregnancy, and in all circumstances, is wrong?

'Absolutely,' she replies in her soft Irish brogue. 'We have to be careful and sensitive how we answer the rape question. Obviously that's the best of all reasons but the reality is I don't think it's a natural thing for a woman to want to end the life of her child at any stage and in any circumstance.'

But doesn't she think there is a difference between a pregnancy resulting from rape and a woman having an abortion after a one-night stand?

'There's a difference in motivation but there isn't a difference in that you're ending the life of a child. In a rape, it's a truly, truly tragic case. The woman has done no harm but so hasn't the unborn child.'

What if a member of her own family was raped and subsequently discovered she was pregnant??

'I genuinely believe abortion is wrong,' she replies. 'If it was my own child, I don't think abortion would be the answer for her. When you decide some abortions are ok and others are not, whose job is it to decide they're ok? It is a bit totalitarian in some ways, I know, but it has to be. Ending a life is ending a life. Picking any other point during a pregnancy other than life begins at the moment of conception is extremely arbitrary. The law focuses on viability. Does that mean that children in this country have more or less rights than those in the developing world where viability is later? You can't base it on that. A foetus is fully formed at eight weeks. Where can you draw the line? Any moment after the moment of conception is completely arbitrary.'

Like all Pro-Life campaigners, she cites the endorsement of the world community through the 1959 United Nations Declaration of the Rights of the Child that the child, 'needs special safeguards and care, including appropriate legal protection, before as well as after birth.'

Does the annunciation story chime with her arguments?

'Big time!' she responds immediately. 'Mary was a single mother. She was far from being in an ideal situation. To have accepted that announcement must have been remarkable but she did accept it as something she had to do. The pro-choice argument is entirely about "my bodily autonomy. It's what I want and it has nothing to do with anyone else." But it does. We're talking about an independent, unique, living human being. It's not about you. It's about more than you. The moment of conception is when life begins.'

But does that not ignore a woman's right to choose her own destiny? Surely that is a fundamental part of the annunciation story, I suggest.

'I would fight for women's rights but I just don't see that a woman has the right to choose to take away somebody else's life,' she says. 'That's the beginning and the end for me. We've invented this right to choose. Yes, of course, women need authority and you have bodily autonomy but if they become pregnant, they have to consider the other person, the person growing inside of them. I'm a feminist. I'd fight for women's rights. I just don't see how anyone has the right to choose to take away someone else's life.'

Does she think that Mary had the right to say no to the conception but after conception had occurred she did not have the right to change her mind?

'Correct. Exactly,' she replies. 'She was in a magical situation but anyone who has sex knows there's a possibility they will get pregnant and we have to take responsibility. Bodily autonomy means we will use that body in an appropriate manner.'

But in some cases, such as a pregnancy resulting from rape, the right to say no was never an option for the woman. Surely there's a difference?

'I can see a difference in motivation but it comes down to have I the right to take away the rights of a defenceless child that hasn't harmed anyone?' she responds. 'Regardless of how much I feel for that woman, I cannot think differently about the child and, as the annunciation story shows, life begins at conception. It's a clutch of cells that divide and divide. Am I human when I am an embryo? Yes, I'm just a much earlier human. I must confess I never saw the Annunciation as a story about the right to choose but I can see it now. It's a very interesting angle. But she has the right to choose whether to carry the baby, to conceive it, but she never has the right to choose to take away a child's life.'

So, what does the annunciation story mean for her?

'It's about a poor, single woman who was humble enough to take all that on. Rather than the right to choose, Mary thought about what was the right thing to do. Not what was right for her but what was the right thing to do. There's a difference.'

Does she believe that the encounter between Mary and the angel Gabriel happened?

'My relationship with religion has shifted in recent years. I don't know if I believe anything. When my dad died when I was twenty-five I was thinking, I'll never see you again. It shook my certainty. It was the same with my own son's death. I'm not saying I've lost my faith but I don't know what I believe. I was ridiculously unquestioning. So I don't know whether it happened. I wish I could say yes it did, but I don't have the faith I used to have. I regret that. Faith is very comforting.'

I show her the print of the Lemoyne painting. She breathes in heavily.

'I see acceptance. Doing something for something higher than herself. "I will do my bit", she is saying, "It's going to be hard for me. People will criticize me but, yes." She was given a choice and she made the right choice. And that's at the heart of the abortion debate too.'

Half an hour later and I have switched to another cafe on the campus. I've also switched to the other side of the debate. I am with Ann Furedi, chief executive of the British Pregnancy Advisory Service. An English and Sociology graduate, she tells me how, previously, she worked in human rights organisations, was politically active for years in left wing causes and at one time in the early 1980s campaigned for the Republican hunger strikers in Northern Ireland.

At first she seems a little anxious.

'I can't claim to have any informed perspective to bring on the Annunciation,' she says. 'I'd describe myself as an atheist but I haven't got a lot of time for the Richard Dawkins trendy new atheism. It tends to verge on philistinism. I'm an atheist now but I was once a Sunday school teacher and served in church in my mid-teenage years. I was very drawn to the Church. Then I had an epiphany in the opposite direction. I realized quite suddenly I just didn't believe in God. I was more a rationalist, a humanist. But I'm quite respectful in considering the views of those who do believe. We have to appreciate the Catholic Church in the broadest sense has played a huge part in the development of ideas and philosophy.'

She explains that the British Pregnancy Advisory Service is a charity with a two-fold remit: providing services for women in distress, and education.

'We promote that women should be able to freely make a choice about the future of their pregnancy. I'm as opposed to the idea of women being compelled to have an abortion – those people who say a woman is not fit to be a mother – as I am being opposed to the idea of someone having to continue with a pregnancy. I think, as thinking individuals with a sense of ourselves, all of us have a destiny, an idea of what we'd like to do with our lives and it's one of the things that makes human beings special. To take away somebody's ability to make that decision – "you cannot do this" – when they are making a choice that morally they think is the right decision, to step in and overrule someone, is completely wrong.'

She is becoming visibly more relaxed. She can see that this is a discussion, not a confrontation, and now she is fully engaged.

'When I read Luke again, what struck me is how it didn't correspond with the feminist view of Catholicism. Oppressing women. I was struck very much by the angel's offer.'

So does she think that the right to choose our destiny lies at the heart of the abortion debate and the annunciation story?

'Yes, absolutely,' she replies. 'My ambition that I'm discussing with our trustees is possibly also starting doing assisted conception work as well as abortion advice. Women should have the right to decide if they want a child as well.'

Does she believe that a woman has the right to choose to terminate a pregnancy at any stage?

'I'm speaking for me here. BPAS believes a woman has a right to choose but doesn't actively campaign for the law to change. My own view, really strongly, is that the law doesn't have a place. When you look hard at the weeks, everything is arbitrary. By the time you get to twenty to twenty four weeks, very few are not conscious they're pregnant. Why does a woman request an abortion at this late stage? I know from our women, if the law reduced the time limit, which of them would be forced to have the baby. You have women who have concealed the pregnancy because they don't know how to talk to their parents about it. One woman already had a child with Down's Syndrome and then decided to terminate the other at twenty-three weeks. Another woman was quite happy to have the baby until she found her partner was abusing her other two daughters. All these cases show life is full of complications. Women very rarely request an abortion after twenty weeks. Very few doctors are prepared to do them. The later the request, the more there's a story behind it. In my heart of hearts, I genuinely trust people to make good decisions for themselves. If someone is an adult, you should trust them to make the decision. We at BPAS put forward the choices that they have. I think it would be much clearer and much more honest if we actually decriminalized abortion. Take it out of the criminal law. Trust the judgement of people to make intensely personal decisions.'

We return to Luke's description of the annunciation encounter. What did she think when she read it?

'It's interesting to look at the Bible as a text,' she says. 'I love the language of the King James version. It was really interesting. How we are so judgmental about assisted conception for older mothers and yet there was Elizabeth, barren and then being able to conceive. With Mary, I'm very interested in the permission she gives for this act to take place. What I found incredibly moving is that here is someone who is accepting the role being offered to her but she has the ability to say "No, I'm not having it". What it says to me, and I was surprised to read it because I'm much more accustomed to a feminist narrative around Christianity and the way women are treated, is that it emphasizes choice and decision making by women. It reminded me of the discussions I've had with an American organisation called "Catholics for Choice". It is about the importance of conscience and you deciding to do something because you think it is the right thing to do. The notion that you have the ability to make the decision.'

I tell her that some women have told me that the annunciation story is about surrender and suppression.

'I tell you what I think,' she responds. 'Whenever we look back at the Bible and at any old books, we read them in the context of how we are living today. It's very easy to imprint those twenty-first-century notions onto what was written then. I wouldn't say whoever wrote it was trying to convey a sense of choice and agency and women making sense of reproductive decisions because it was written at a time when women had hardly any choice in their lives. There was no contraception. Life was just what happened to people. But what I can say in reading it from a twenty-first-century perspective is I can pull a different story out of it that's completely opposite to supplication. It's wrong to look at it and say, "That just goes to show, men have been forcing their will on women all the way through history." It's what you see in it. Clearly those who look at it from a more traditional perspective in relation to Mary's situation would say Mary had no choice. That you can't possibly say she was in a position to say to the archangel, "Go away!" '

What about those who say the Annunciation emphasizes the sanctity of life from the moment of conception?

'That's exactly the point,' she replies. 'You can look at the Annunciation and interpret it and draw from it completely different stories. But for me, the fact we can take decisions is the most brilliant, fulfilling thing about humans.'

I show her the print of the Lemoyne painting. What does she see?

'There is something that is…I see Mary, this woman, looking serene and thoughtful. Those hands. She's thinking about *me*. She's smiling. A sense of "This is happening to me. Where is it taking me?" I don't see archangel Gabriel as a terrible, terrifying, oppressive figure but someone who is showing her the potential of what can happen and then she is choosing to take this on herself. That element of choice makes it, for me, a far more compelling and touching story. It's an absolutely beautiful painting, superbly structured. It has a sense of connection, drawing you into it and upwards and with a sense of uplift. In contrast, as I'm looking at it, I can't help but feel that she has, in that moment, what many women feel when they find they're having a baby, that sense of hopes and dreams and imaginings of what that future will be…and then what happens in the end is so terrible.'

An hour later and I am in the Chapel on the University campus ready for the start of the debate. Unfortunately, the size of the audience is very disappointing. I learn that the University website's promotional page for the event has had more than a thousand hits in recent days. However, only thirteen people have turned up. 'It's a shockingly bad turn-out,' says, the Reverend Dr Peter Waddell, the chair of the debate. Unsurprisingly, with so few people present, the discussion is rather stilted, flat and predictable. As the two women leave the Chapel, I express my sadness that such eminent leaders of their respective organisations have come all this way for nothing.

'Far from it,' says Ann Furedi. 'It was worth it to come and discuss the Annunciation. I've never done that before in relation to a debate on abortion,' she smiles.

'I agree, I agree,' says Anne Scanlan. 'I've thought a lot tonight about the right to life and the right to choice but in a whole new dimension.'

CHAPTER 32

THE WILLINGNESS TO GO WITH IT

I am full of intrigue about the encounters I have had on my journey so far. There is so much to absorb, so many opinions to digest and I feel that the time has come to reflect a while on everything I have heard up to now. The weather forecast is good and I decide to walk the Clarendon Way, a twenty-six mile route between Winchester and Salisbury. It'll give me an opportunity to be alone, to have the chance to think, and to read some more annunciation poems.

I get up early to make full use of the available light. A slash of red, orange and pink glows over St Giles Hill as I head westwards out of Winchester on this crisp, dry morning. Soon I am rambling along beautiful rolling Hampshire chalk downland, following the track of an old Roman road, then passing through tranquil Wiltshire forests and pastureland with buzzards, starlings, kestrels and roe deer for company along the way.

Just over an hour into my journey, I divert half a mile from the official path to visit the tiny church of St Mary's in the hamlet of Ashley. Nobody is sure when it was built but ecclesiastical historians think it was sometime in the late twelfth or very early thirteenth century. Originally, the simple construction stood next to Gains Castle, a medieval fortification that has long since disappeared. The church walls are made of flint rubble with chalk block dressings and quoins, all rendered with lime mortar. For the past thirty years it has been a redundant Anglican building but for eight centuries St Mary's faithfully served its local agricultural community as a place of worship and quiet contemplation. Now it is in the care of the Ashley Church Conservation Trust.

Inside, on the splay of a Norman window on the south side of the chancel, I notice a thirteenth-century wall painting of a haloed woman. The simple red lines depict her holding a book against her chest with her left hand. I think I can make out a lectern by her right side, but when I look further, I realize it may be a palm branch. It is difficult to work out. The woman's eyes look down as she stands underneath a canopy. The lower part of her figure, unfortunately, has been destroyed. One website devoted to the study of medieval wall paintings speculates that it may represent the martyr, St Catherine, but the more I look at it, the more I see Mary at the Annunciation. Interestingly, directly opposite the painting is

128. Wall painting at St Mary's Church, Ashley, near Winchester

409

evidence of secondary plasterwork. I wonder if originally below this later rendering there was once an image of the angel Gabriel. I sit on a green mound outside the church and open up my special compendium of annunciation poetry. The first poem I read is by the Victorian poet, Christina Georgina Rossetti, who wrote 'Annunciation' in 1866:

> Whereto shall we liken this Blessed Virgin Mary,
> Faithful shoot from Jesse's root graciously emerging?
> Lily we might call her, but Christ alone is white;
> Rose delicious, but that Jesus is the one Delight;
> Flower of women, but her Firstborn is mankind's one flower;
> He the Sun lights up all the moons thro' radiant hour.
> 'Blessed among women, highly favoured', thus
> Glorious Gabriel hailed her, teaching words to us:
> Whom devoutly copying we too cry 'All hail!'
> Echoing on the music of glorious Gabriel.

I turn the page and find this poem called 'Ave Maria Gratia', written by Oscar Wilde in 1881:

> Was this His coming! I had hoped to see
> A scene of wondrous glory, as was told
> Of some great God who in a rain of gold
> Broke open bars and fell on Danaë,
> Or a dread vision as when Semele,
> Sickening for love and unappeased desire,
> Prayed to see God's clear body, and under fire
> Caught her brown lis and slew her utterly.
> With such glad dreams I sought this holy place
> And now with wondering eyes and heart I stand
> Before this supreme mystery of Love:
> Some kneeling girl with passionless pale face,
> An angel with a lily in his hand
> And over both the white wings of a dove.

I need to return to the main route of the Clarendon Way if I am going to reach Salisbury in daylight. There is time to read one more poem, this time by the American Roman Catholic poet, Joyce Kilmer, who wrote 'The Annunciation' in 1917:

> "Hail Mary, full of grace," the Angel saith.
> Our Lady bows her head, and is ashamed;
> She has a Bridegroom Who may not be named,
> Her mortal flesh bears Him Who conquers death.
> Now in the dust her spirit grovelleth;
> Too bright a Sun before her eyes has flamed,
> Too fair a herald joy too high proclaimed,
> And human lips have trembled in God's breath.
> O Mother-Maid, thou art ashamed to cover
> With thy white self, whereon no stain can be,
> Thy God, Who came from Heaven to be thy Lover,
> Thy God, who came from Heaven to dwell in thee.
> About thy head celestial legions hover,
> Chanting the praise of thy humility.

Three hours later I reach the lovely village of Broughton, the halfway point of the Clarendon Way, and visit another church that is dedicated to the Virgin Mary. Inside, behind the organ on the north side of the Chancel is a stained-glass window, featuring the angel Gabriel and Mary, a gift from a parishioner in 1904.

It is time to move on. I enjoy taking in the magnificent, panoramic views; crossing the clear chalk stream waters of the River Test, occasionally catching sight of a brown trout or grayling; gazing up at the ash, beech and ancient oak trees that straddle the route; walking through picturesque villages and hamlets with their thatched cottages and flint-faced houses; and meandering through lovely, undulating farmland teeming with wildlife and autumn flowers.

By late afternoon, in the far distance, I catch sight of my destination – Salisbury Cathedral. Officially known as the Cathedral Church of the Blessed Virgin Mary, it was built in the thirteenth century and possesses the tallest spire in Britain. The first cathedral sited at Old Sarum, two miles north of Salisbury, was also dedicated to the Virgin Mary by Bishop Osmund, when it was consecrated in 1092. It is one of the two thousand or more churches across the country that are dedicated to her.

Wearily, I enter the beautiful, genteel Cathedral Close some nine hours after setting off from Winchester. My legs and back are aching beyond belief and it is difficult to focus on anything other than reaching the cathedral and sitting down to rest. However, thirty yards north of the West Front my attention is grabbed by a modern, life-size, figurative sculpture of a woman, sited on the lawn. From a distance, she appears to be walking away determinedly from the Cathedral and heading towards the city centre.

129. Elisabeth Frink *Walking Madonna*, 1981, The Close, Salisbury Cathedral

It is called *Walking Madonna* and was created in 1981 by Dame Elisabeth Frink. It is unusual because Dame Elisabeth hardly ever sculptured the female form. As I approach the figure of Mary, the dark brown and turquoise patina of the bronze casting reveals itself and the figure's sense of purpose, striding away from the Cathedral, becomes ever stronger. It is one of Frink's most famous and celebrated works, seen by hundreds of thousands of visitors each year. Many of them like to photograph themselves next to the Madonna, sometimes holding her left hand, other times walking behind her in the same strident pose.

Close up, she is more than six feet tall. She is a mature woman and wears an authentic, early first-century, Galilean-styled headscarf. The Elisabeth Frink Estate describes the work as such: 'For many, the figure is seen to reveal depths of emotion and spiritual truths and is seen as one of the very few genuinely religious works of our time.'

A woman passing the figure tells me it is her favourite ever image of the Virgin Mary: 'She's walking away from the Cathedral so purposefully. Perfect!' In a sermon at Salisbury Cathedral in 2010, the Precentor, Jeremy Davies, commented:

> For all her humanity, the *Walking Madonna* is a disconcerting figure. Not only does she speak of singleness of purpose, not only does her gaunt frame speak of a spare idealism, not only does she proclaim an integrity and a truthfulness as all great art must – but she

130. Elisabeth Frink's *Walking Madonna* leaves the Cathedral and heads for the city

is walking away. The *Walking Madonna* walks away from the Cathedral which bears her name and which was built to enshrine the gospel verities her life proclaimed. She walks away from shrine and altar and liturgies of infinite beauty, away from the shimmer of silver in candlelight and the platitudes of parsons and preachers. Away from the green sward of quintessential Englishness and the elitism and privilege and comfortable living that surround it. She turns her back on the well-polished route to God, as though determined to seek him and find him out there in the city of noise and clamour and in the struggle to survive, where relationships are made and broken; where laughter and love and human goodness are joyfully celebrated right on the edges of living, in the pain and the squalor and the meanness of life. The *Walking Madonna* walks away from the shrine as though she is searching still for some outhouse to bring forth God's Word and some hill outside the city wall where alone God's great work of redemption may be achieved.

> I rejoice that the icon of the Blessed Virgin Mary, which we daily encounter here in Salisbury, steps outside the gilded cage that we have built around her, steps outside the doctrines that have controversially accompanied her heavenward journey, steps outside the sentimentality of the simpering madonnas that have been the focus of so much mawkish adoration. The *Walking Madonna* brings us down to earth, to the place where the angel first encountered her, on the road to the market place, amidst the noise of the traffic, to those places where ordinary people live, where the hungry are still hungry and the poor still poor. She seems to say to us, as she strides away from her shrine, 'Follow me, and I will show you where heaven is.'

> With the *Walking Madonna* as our companion we are challenged to leave behind the narrowness of our polemic, the limitations of our dogma and the lack of imagination of our intellect. We are invited instead to think again about what God's grace and mercy and love may achieve in a human life. For beyond all the titles which the Church has bestowed on Mary over the Christian centuries – Queen of Heaven, Star of the Sea, Mother of God – she remains what she was before and after the

moment of Annunciation: an ordinary human being transformed by her extraordinary capacity to be open to God to say: 'Yes Amen, so be it: Be it unto me according to thy Word.'

Jeremy Davies graduated in English and Theology at Cambridge as a choral scholar at Corpus Christi College. In 1985, he became Canon Precentor at Salisbury Cathedral, a post he held for twenty-six years until his retirement in 2012. After stepping down, he wrote a book *In Season and Out of Season* in 2014 on the art of sermon creation.

I settle down on a park bench facing the West Front of the Cathedral as twilight descends and start to read a sermon, delivered by him here back in 1994. It is entitled 'Annunciation - what if she'd said, "No"?' It begins with a poem written by the Orkney poet Edwin Muir in 1925:

The Annunciation

The angel and the girl are met.
Earth was the only meeting place.
For the embodied never yet
Travelled beyond the shore of space.
The eternal spirits in freedom go.

See they have come together, see,
While the destroying minutes flow,
Each reflects the other's face
Till heaven in hers and earth in his
Shine steady there. He's come to her
From far beyond the farthest star,
Feathered through time. Immediacy
Of strangest strangeness is the bliss
That from their limbs all movement takes.
Yet the increasing rapture brings
So great a wonder that it makes
Each feather tremble on his wings.

Outside the window footsteps fall
Into the ordinary day
And with the sun along the wall
Pursue their unreturning way.
Sound's perpetual roundabout
Rolls its numbered octaves out
And hoarsely grinds its battered tune.

But through the endless afternoon
These neither speak nor movement make,
But stare into their deepening trance
As if their gaze would never break.

What if she'd said, 'no!'? What if she had been too busy, or too conventional, or too afraid? There were a hundred ways of getting out of it: 'It's market day', 'I'm not that sort of girl', 'It's the wrong time of the month.'

For a fleeting moment, the consequences of saying 'Yes' ran past her. The stranger saw the fear and panic in her eyes and hastened to reassure her. 'Do not be afraid, you have found favour with God.'

Well! God's favour was one thing, an important thing I'm sure, and thank you very much but I've got to go on living in *this* community, with these particular neighbours, and this particular tight-knit, traditional, hard-working peasant village. I'm not sure that saying 'Yes' to you will find favour with them.

And the shape that God's favour would take? To be the mother of God's son. The joy of every Jewish woman's heart, to be a mother: to put off the shame of virginity or sterility and join the matriarchal throng; responsible for the continuation and nurturing of the covenant people of God. But what a sour joy – to be an *unmarried* mother in a Jewish village; more degraded and ostracised than simply being an unmarried virgin.

What if she'd said, 'No'?

No one would have blamed her: in her position we would have done the same. Indeed, though Christian iconography has persuaded us that this particular woman was God's only choice, it is possible that the stranger had knocked on several doors before this one. Like some Dandini in the Christmas panto seeing if the slipper, as it were, would fit. After all, God's plans had been thwarted by women and men – even highly favoured ones – saying 'No' before. Maybe, in Mary, the barrel was being scraped and God was truly exalting the humble from their lowly estate.

What if she'd said, 'No'?

All heaven held its breath as God's almighty plan for the redemption of the world hung upon the 'Yes' or the 'No' of a slip of a girl from Nazareth. That perhaps is the most remarkable thing about the whole episode: that all the divine eggs were put into one highly vulnerable basket. I suppose there might have been a contingency plan. After all, you could read the Old Testament as God's great contingency plan. Not so much the story of God's constant initiative of love and judgement in human affairs: but God reacting, trying to find another way around human intransigence; coping with our God-given capacity to say 'No'. There might have been a contingency plan if yet again this maid, true to her humankind, had opted for convention, for safety, for obscurity. But nothing in any contingency plan could change the fact that the almighty God had tethered himself and his good purposes once and for all to the 'Yes' or the 'No' of the beautiful but wilful creatures he had made in his own image and likeness. Their co-operation, their participation, their freely given 'Yes' to him, was a crucial and indispensable ingredient in whatever redemptive plans the great God might have. There were no shortcuts; there are no shortcuts. God has put himself entirely in the hands of a Jewish girl; because only from this acceptance, this God-given capacity to say 'Yes', could God's original creative purpose come to fruition. Which is why Edwin Muir in his poem *The Annunciation* sees the encounter between Mary and the stranger (who is none other than God himself) as a meeting between lovers:

> See they have come together, see,
> While the destroying minutes flow,
> Each reflects the other's face
> Till heaven in hers and earth in his
> Shine steady there. He's come to her
> From far beyond the farthest star,
> Feathered through time. Immediacy

> Of strangest strangeness is the bliss
> That from their limbs all movement takes.
> Yet the increasing rapture brings
> So great a wonder that it makes
> Each feather tremble on his wings.

There's a suggestion of sexual encounter in the 'increasing rapture' and the 'trembling feather', but much more than that, this is a meeting of mutual self-giving in which both the maid and the stranger are reaching out to each other in mutual esteem: both saying 'Yes' to the other. As they look into each other's eyes, they see not only their own faces reflected in the other, they see heaven and earth joined together. Of course this is a love poem – pure and simple (if either love or poetry could ever be so simply and purely described), but it is a love poem that sees the gospel truth that God's disclosure of himself arises and can only arise within the relationship of mutuality, and self-offering to another, and saying 'Yes', that we call love.

What if she'd said, 'No'?

She had no choice. At one level she had all the choice in the world; she could have said 'No' or 'Wait' or 'Perhaps'. She saw the consequences – or some of the social consequences at least, of saying 'Yes'. But when the angel and the girl are met, when the moment comes, there is no possibility of saying 'No' for either of them.

Muir's poem continues: while this secret love-making is going on, life goes on outside the window; as though to remind us that the Annunciation did not take place in some rarefied atmosphere of sanctity – but on the main concourse, in the midst of the traffic.

> Outside the window footsteps fall
> Into the ordinary day
> And with the sun along the wall
> Pursue their unreturning way.
> Sound's perpetual roundabout
> Rolls its numbered octaves out
> And hoarsely grinds its battered tune.

Which moves us from sacred story to ordinary day: to the places we inhabit; where we buy our lottery tickets; where we worry about money, especially in the midst of a financial downturn; where we grieve and feel guilty over the relative who has had to go into a home; where we over-indulge; where we do our shameful things, as well as the things that surprise us by their generosity. I'm talking about Monday morning: with Sunday and its story a half-forgotten memory. As we hurry into town, the leisure of Mary's love tryst will be the very last thing on our list: turkeys, cards, wrapping paper, presents for forgotten friends who just happen to be passing on Christmas Eve; as we hear the hurdy-gurdy organ in the Market Square churning out comfort and joy, we may offer a hurried £1.50p for the latest edition of *The Big Issue*, or press a hurried 10p into the begging hand of a wayfarer, or a quid into the rattling boxes of a local charity. Over a quick cup of tea before getting the children from school, we may turn on the radio and hear the point-missing syncopation of a John Rutter carol. We may even be seduced by his saccharine view of Christmas with shepherd boys piping and angels manger-hovering like demented midwives. But if we are persuaded by that sentimental view, I fear that what we celebrate today and what we shall be celebrating on Christmas Day will be little more than a fairy story. The story of the Annunciation is not simply a two-thousand-year-old fable that it pleases us to embellish and gaze at like some Old Master we can wonder at and turn away from. The Annunciation is the most relevant New Testament story for us today. Just the other side of the window where our footsteps fall, just the other side of the ordinary day, just at the end of this road to the market square, an angel waits: God waits. The question is not, what if she had said, 'No'? (An idle speculation: we know she didn't). The question is: what if we say, 'No'?

Or more importantly, what if we say, 'Yes'? For the Annunciation, like the sacrifice of Calvary, is something that happened once for all, and can never be repeated; and yet, annunciations like crucifixions take place every ordinary day as God encounters us, addresses us, discloses his love to us and longs for us to answer 'Yes, Amen, Be it unto me according to your Word.' The consequences of saying 'Yes' may run before our eyes; the excuses – the understandable excuses – will form upon our lips; but if we can get past John Rutter, we may find in the business and busyness of this week that God, having put a wafer in our hands as a token of his presence today, is staring into our eyes tomorrow, yearning for us to say 'Yes' to him and to cradle his new life with all its terrible demands, and transforming joy.

> But through the endless afternoon
> These neither speak nor movement make,
> But stare into their deepening trance
> As if their gaze would never break.

It is a terrific sermon and I make no apologies for publishing it here in full with Jeremy Davies's agreement. Later, I meet up with the sixty-nine-year-old retired priest in Winchester. I ask what the annunciation story means for him.

'The great thing about the great stories in the New Testament is that they are told in story form that allow you to inhabit them,' he tells me. 'So, although a lot of the doctrine has been shaped around the Annunciation, I prefer to see it as some kind of metaphor – a story that allows us to get in. The Annunciation happened once but it also happens every day. It's about the way God comes to us. Waiting upon God for that surprising event for which we can never prepare, and that happens day after day after day, moment after moment.'

So does he see the story as fact or as a pure metaphor?

'It's a very interesting question,' he replies cautiously. 'Because I believe...', he pauses, hesitantly, before continuing, 'I want to think about the Annunciation as an event that happened, maybe as a vision, maybe as a reality, but most of all, it stands for something true. I would take the same view of the Resurrection. I do not want to dispute the historicity but the important thing is its truth. Does it have something important to say? How can we learn the truth beyond the evidence and the facts? Christianity has always wanted to claim the historicity of the facts – this actually happened – but the Gospels don't often describe what actually happened. It's more the impact of what happened, you might say.'

What does he think of the statement that 'it's the most important event in human history'?

'Right,' he laughs before pausing. 'I don't really like talking in that way, isolating it from everything else. You can't take Incarnation, Atonement and Redemption out of Creation. We're talking about the whole panoply of salvation history and it's part of it.'

What does he think would have happened if Mary had said no?

'As I tried to say in that sermon, Mary wasn't the first person God had asked to be the bearer of the divine word,' he replies. 'You can read the Old Testament as God coming where we are in order to respond and eventually he finds someone. That's why I describe it as like Dandini and Cinderella. He's almost scraping the barrel when he comes to Mary. There at the bottom of the barrel he finds someone who will say yes. God doesn't give up with humans saying "No".'

Does he agree that a fundamental part of the story is Mary's freedom to say no?

'Yes, yes,' he replies enthusiastically. 'She could have said no. She had every reason to say no.'

He is a small bespectacled man with silvery hair and a ruddy complexion. He is thoughtful and articulate, and tells me that as a child he used to give sermons to his sisters and regularly went to listen to preachers at three different Sunday schools. He says he knew then that he was destined to be a priest. I ask why he referenced that poem by Edwin Muir at the start of his annunciation sermon.

'It takes a fundamental story and recasts it. It places it in the ordinary concourse of the ordinary day. I love the idea of God coming where we are amid the pressure and pace of life. It says something to me about the contemplative poise. Taking a story we know well and recasting it. And I like the sexual frisson.'

He comments that 25 March, the date of Mary's conception of Jesus, has been identified as the moment of the Annunciation and that the early Church tried to pin Good Friday to the same day, thereby bringing the whole story together as one.

I show him a print of Lemoyne's painting. He studies it for quite a while before responding.

'It's very interesting in all sorts of ways. The way Gabriel is pointing upwards. It has an implication of the Assumption. This is Mary's direction of travel and that of all humanity. It has that air of triumphalism about it. Usually Gabriel is lower than Mary and more subservient. I wouldn't say it's my favourite Annunciation. It doesn't have the stillness that I like. This one is full of energy. It's a new take. He sees something else in the story. That's what I like about painters and poets. The way each of them re-casts the story.'

A few weeks after our meeting, Jeremy Davies hits the national headlines after being 'banned' by the Bishop of Winchester from officiating in any priestly duties in the neighbouring diocese of Winchester. Ten years ago, on his sixtieth birthday, Jeremy Davies entered into a civil partnership with his partner, Simon McEnery, a composer and opera singer eighteen years his junior. Recently, to celebrate their relationship that has lasted twenty-eight years, they decided to get married. The Bishop of Winchester responded by citing the current Church of England rule that permits its clergy to enter into a same-sex civil partnership so long as they give assurances that the relationship is celibate, but same-sex marriage is banned for all clergy.

Jeremy Davies says he hopes that, as a retired priest, he will be able to continue officiating at baptisms, weddings and funerals in his home diocese as well as taking services in his local church in Farley, eight miles east of Salisbury. He wants to carry on with occasional priestly duties in retirement, he says, alongside his new roles as a freelance liturgical consultant, lecturer and spiritual director.

'I don't need to feel angry because there are so many people feeling angry on our behalf. The theology of marriage is not about a man and a woman,' he is quoted as saying in one national newspaper. 'The marriage vows are about mutual society, human relationships.' The Bishop of Winchester's controversial decision may be clear and consistent with present rulings, but once again it has opened up the deep divisions on homosexuality within the Church of England.

Sixty-year-old Nick Holtam has been the Bishop of Salisbury since 2011. Previously he was the Vicar at St Martin-in-the-Fields in central London. He grew up in a church-going family in north London and knew from an early age that he was going to be a priest but tried to rebel against it. He read Geography at Durham where he spent nine months avoiding church. 'I thought I was allowed a little rebellion,' he tells me. During this time, he says his life became a muddle. He ended up going back to church, and re-discovered his faith. 'Life didn't add up without a Christian faith,' he says, and after Durham he began training for the priesthood at theological college in London and then Cambridge. Today, he is married and has four adult children. A year into his tenure at Salisbury he became the first Church of England bishop to publicly support same-sex marriage.

He takes a keen interest in Christian art. In his book *The Art of Worship* he describes the National Gallery as a reflective space and reminds his readers that a third of its paintings are of Christian subjects. Religious paintings (like Lemoyne's *The Annunciation*) must always be seen in context, he stresses – that originally they were devotional pieces created for a sacred space.

I visit him at his beautiful home in the south-west area of the Cathedral Close in Salisbury.

'One of the things about the Annunciation is why her?' he says as he opens our conversation. 'Some of the depictions of her are of a very young girl and you just think, my goodness! The Hebrew doesn't use the word "virgin". It's in the New Testament that she's called a virgin. There must have been a sense for her of "what is all this about?" One of my favourite depictions is Jacob Epstein's statue where this young girl with pigtails is wringing her hands. She's perplexed. There's a sense of "I really don't get it" and "why me?" Part of the connection (of the Annunciation) for me is that whatever I've been called to be, I know I'm not up to it.'

Is it important for him that Mary had an opportunity to say no?

'We all have the opportunity to say no,' he responds. 'An incredibly important part of the story is the acceptance – the willingness to go with it. She's an archetypal person there like each of us and has the chance to respond or not to God. Our acceptance is down to you and me.'

Does he see the story as fact or a metaphor? I wonder.

'This isn't just a Bishop hedging but I don't think it works to say either this is or isn't history or fact. It works well as metaphor, as archetype, as a universal story. I think Luke uses it in that way. Fact or metaphor wouldn't have been his thought forms but I think he could own it as both. The way it's structured in the Gospel bears that sort of weight. How does an angel appear to us? As a messenger of a divine being somewhere between the supernatural and this reality. I can't tell you what sort of angel it was. I can't be precise on that and I don't need to be. But it was experienced by Mary and that's the best answer I can do. What I'm saying is, it was experienced by Mary and that is the fact on which the story was constructed. Something has been given to her uniquely that was unchosen, unwelcome but accepted. That is fact.'

Does he believe that Jesus had brothers and sisters?

'The idea that Mary did not engage in sexual relations for the rest of her life is not scriptural,' he says. 'The Christian tradition is that there was a family and, indeed, in the Scriptures there is reference to his brothers. Her perpetual virginity makes no sense to me. Where I would want to stick is that Mary received an angel, a messenger of God, asking her to take on this role on behalf of the world. I'm really not that interested in the

Virgin Birth. I can see what in terms of Christian doctrine the notion of a virgin birth is intended to preserve. I do not know. There isn't enough weight to put certainty but that's not where I put the weight. What the story is conveying is that Mary received a message she believed to be from God that came from an angel, whatever form that angel took, and it's the message from God that is the key thing.'

What does he make of the statement that the Annunciation is 'the most important event in human history'?

'I respond emotionally to that very warmly,' he replies. 'I certainly warm to that,' He then pauses and seems a little troubled by what he has said. 'It doesn't help to separate out different parts of Christ's life,' he continues. 'This is more important than that. It works as a piece – the life of Christ is the most important thing. That's why I'd draw back a little from saying that it's the most important moment. It's the start of it but it only works as a whole piece – the life of Christ – and the Annunciation is the historic start of it.'

I wonder what he thinks about a person who may say, 'I can believe in the Crucifixion and the Resurrection but I don't necessarily believe in the Annunciation. That doesn't matter to me.'

'I'd have trouble with the answer, "It doesn't matter to me". The story of Jesus is a big story and for quite a period of the last two thousand years, at least in the West, it has functioned as the overarching meta-narrative of how the world has lived, the notion of Christendom. I have got some doubts whether Christendom really existed but it was the story through which life was interpreted. It was the "Big Story". With the Big Story, there will be different interpretations and we've got fixated on different parts of the Big Story at different times for different reasons. I don't think people always take the whole of the story but I think that the Church, corporately, represents the whole of the story. That's why we continue to say the creeds.

'If you took a straw poll of most congregations on a Sunday morning and really pressed them in the way you are pressing me now, they'd say "I've always had difficulty with that bit. It's not that I'm standing with my fingers crossed behind my back but, for example, I don't understand the philosophy of two natures." They may say I don't really understand all of that. Most people don't think very hard about it all and, if you pushed them, might begin to question some of the philosophical assumptions. But the Church is upholding all of that. At a particular point in the Church's early history, it became the normative way of expressing the Big Story and that's what we are operating out of. Bishops have a responsibility for holding that whole story for the Church but most Christians are going to focus on different parts – Jesus the moral teacher, for example – and probably not take all the doctrinal stuff.'

Does it concern him that the story of Gabriel's encounter with Mary is recorded in only one of the four canonical Gospels?

'We're having quite an intense conversation here. You'll write it up differently to how I might write it. They'll be different and it won't appear to be the same conversation. Do the different accounts diminish the reality of the conversation or are there different ways to see that conversation from different perspectives that adds to the reality of the conversation? They're four views of the life of Christ from different perspectives and contexts. That doesn't diminish the reality of who Jesus is but strengthens that sense of really giving us insight to what was happening there. Four different views but with some overlap.'

He then says he wants to go back again to an earlier part of our conversation. He wants to be clearer.

'That statement, "the most important event in human history". The more I've thought about it, I think my initial reaction was warm and to say it's fine but actually the moment only works as part of a whole person's story. You have to take the totality of Jesus's life. I'm resistant to the notion of one part being the most important moment. What I really believe is, now is the most important moment in the history of the world and Christ is the most important story in the history of the world. The significance of the story is not just as a piece of history. It has a significance now. This story has got a life to it now.'

We move on and discuss the status of Mary in his life. Does he pray to her?

'I see her as praying alongside and for us,' he replies. 'That's the language of the classic prayers that the Anglo-Catholic tradition of the Church of England use. Asking her to pray for us. Praying with her. It's not unreasonable to ask the saints to pray for us.'

Is there one word or phrase that sums up the annunciation story for him?

'The start of the journey,' he replies immediately.

He asks me whether I am familiar with a poem focusing on the Annunciation by the Cornish poet Charles Causley, written in 1968. I say no, and he then takes a piece of paper from the table and starts to recite the first six verses from 'Ballad of the Bread Man':

Mary stood in the kitchen
Baking a loaf of bread.
An angel flew in through the window.
'We've a job for you,' he said.

'God in his big gold heaven
Sitting in his big blue chair,
Wanted a mother for his little son.
Suddenly saw you there.'

Mary shook and trembled,
'It isn't true what you say.'
'Don't say that,' said the angel.
'The baby's on its way.'

Joseph was in the workshop
Planing a piece of wood.
'The old man's past it,' the neighbours said.
'That girl's been up to no good.'

'And who was that elegant fellow,'
They said. 'in the shiny gear?'
The things they said about Gabriel
Were hardly fit to hear.

Mary never answered,
Mary never replied.
She kept the information,
Like the baby, safe inside.

He chuckles with amusement. I show him the print of Lemoyne's *The Annunciation*. What does he see?

'There are various bits that bother me,' he says. 'She's not looking at the angel. Then there's that paper on the floor and that basket. Her face is quite serene, open and smiling. It's the exact opposite to the Epstein I like where there's a degree of anxiety. This is joyful, accepting, serene. I'm not sure about her eyes. I'd love to know what she sees of the future. At first, the angel troubled me quite a lot. "Come on, get on with it." But I think now the angel is saying something about the connection between heaven and earth. It's strong and directive. It is what it is...of its time and style. It's not my sort of theology but it's beautifully done. Here's an interpretation that I can get but I don't respond emotionally to it.'

He continues studying it in silence. He brings forward the picture and then moves it away from his face.

'It's a really great painting of the Annunciation. I've spent a lot of the last week thinking about this. How much did the artist know? How much research did he do or did he land it intuitively because he stood in a Christian tradition and really understood it? It offers us an interesting interpretation of the Annunciation but how much did the artist get it from the inside?'

We realize we've been chatting for well over an hour and he is now behind schedule. I pack up my things and ask him what advice he would give me as I continue my journey.

'You need to look in and you need to look out,' he replies.

131. Ernst Blensdorf
Annunciation, 1957, Salisbury
Cathedral

I enter Salisbury Cathedral and head to the south transept, to the Chapel of St Margaret of Scotland, a descendant of King Alfred of Wessex. For many years, the chapel has been a focus of prayers for the Mother's Union in the Salisbury Diocese. Standing to the side of the altar is a wonderful wooden sculpture by the late Ernst Blensdorf entitled *Annunciation*.

Blensdorf fled Nazi Germany in 1935 and eventually settled in Bruton, Somerset, where he was a teacher and sculptor for over forty years. His favoured material was elm, sourced from local woodland. His three-foot *Annunciation* was carved from a trunk in 1957 and, with his chisel and mallet, he created a single figure in semi-abstract form. For me, it captures Mary in a wonderful rhythmic movement as she is suddenly confronted by the appearance of the angel. A sculpture of great natural beauty and outstanding craftsmanship, its dynamic carving suggests a young, petite Mary turning away in trepidation as she hears the angel Gabriel's unexpected greeting.

I leave the Cathedral and head to the nearby Deanery where I meet with the Dean of Salisbury Cathedral, sixty-one-year-old The Very Reverend June Osborne. We begin the conversation talking about football. I learn that, although she and her husband are Tottenham Hotspur season ticket holders, she remains true to her roots and is really a die-hard Manchester City fan. Good humoured and clearly very sharp, she looks and sounds more like a confident secondary school headteacher than a member of the senior clergy. She has short silver hair and glasses, and wears a plain jacket, a sensible skirt and flat black shoes. Her big voice transmits authority and no-nonsense leadership.

She studied Social Sciences at Manchester University in the early 1970s and afterwards 'felt the hand of heaven' and decided to study for ministry. She has spent her professional life smashing through glass ceilings. Becoming a deaconess in 1980, a deacon in 1987 and a priest in the pioneering first wave of 1994, it is thought that her passionate speech at the General Synod in 1992 helped sway the historic vote in favour of women priests. She is the eightieth Dean at Salisbury and her historic appointment ten years ago marked her out as the first ever woman in the job and the first woman Dean to lead one of England's major medieval cathedrals.

'The Annunciation is about two things,' she begins. 'Firstly, an encounter with God. My own Christian story began with an encounter with God. So I don't find it implausible, it doesn't stretch my sense of rational belief, to think an individual can have a deep, profound sense of God putting his touch on their life. The other is about this whole dynamic of surrender, obedience, acceptance, calling. In many ways, the language of calling and vocation has become so very narrow but actually what this story is about for me, as someone who's had a vocation as a minister of the Church, is a calling in which over thirty-five years, the Church has struggled with validating at points the whole sense of me pursuing a vocation, a destiny, a purpose, a sense of fulfilment and it's been a road that's not been easy.

'These are the two big themes that come out of it for me. The fact that Mary is a woman, the calling is about a pregnancy, and that God is going to share human life through a woman's womb, is clearly very significant for me because gender has been a contentious issue, an issue of dramatic change in social history during my life. The story couldn't be more relevant. We're meeting in the week of action against gender violence. The big issue that is facing the global community that compares with slavery in the previous century has got to be the issue of gender violence. I've lived my whole professional life in an institution that has an ambivalent relationship with gender. The fact that this narrative is about a young woman, unformed, sensing where God is taking her, is extraordinarily powerful.'

So, does she see a direct connection between gender violence and the annunciation story?

'I think in the West, we've lost sight of what a unique and significant Christian contribution to civilisation the equality of humanity is. I listened to the Today programme this morning on Radio 4 for about an hour and a half. There wasn't a single subject that wasn't about diversity and respect in human relations. I've just come back from India. In such a pantheistic society, not only do they not hold to equality of all human life, they positively have a theology that builds in inequality. One of the great rallying calls of the Christian faith, without which the Enlightenment movement would not have happened, is that glorious belief that God made human life in his image, male and female, and the equality of each individual.'

Does she see the story as rooted in history or is it a metaphor?

'A bit of both really,' she replies. 'I don't have any difficulty with holding to a sense of God's revelation. We are a revelatory religion. Yes, we should always be sceptical. One of the gifts of the Holy Spirit is common sense. But I do believe that God is at work – the grace of God – in all mundane, material existence. So what I hear in the story is that God is capable of treating a peasant woman just as validly as a king. He wanted to reveal himself through a woman.

'When I was a child,' she continues, 'I grew up in a completely non-religious family. We never talked about religion. We never went anywhere near a church. I was baptized at six weeks and that was it as far as going to church. I had no expectation whatsoever of God activity. But at eight or nine years of age, I became spiritually curious. I can remember clearly having an "annunciation moment". I looked at the night sky. You couldn't see the stars that often above Manchester,' she chuckles. 'I came from a fairly brutal, working-class background. It did happen in a single moment. I remember I thought the sky goes on forever, for eternity and I felt small. Where am I in it all? I couldn't fathom why I thought everything was so significant when I was so inconsequential. It was a moment that I felt met by God. I needed to know what God looked like. For Mary, it was an encounter with a manifestation of a messenger from God. I don't think the angel Gabriel looked like how Botticelli saw him. We're looking at something that conveyed glory and personal revelatory significance to her. For me, the natural world above me that night was capable of doing that but I then became very clear that the manifestation of that revelation was Jesus Christ. It was kept private. I knew where my parents' comfort zones were. I said to myself rather than to them, "I'm seeking spiritual answers", and that went on through being a teenager to entering adult life. However, it never crossed my mind in my teenage years that the calling would be church related. So, looking back, is that the moment that changed my life? I suppose there are lots of moments. I don't believe that at that moment Mary knew exactly what God was up to. God's hold on your life and his calling is like a developing photograph. An image coming out very slowly is how I describe my own vocational calling.

'I took seriously the call to faith. I always knew there was going to be a cost. I remember as a teenager praying to have the resilience to be faithful. That element of sacrifice. Yes, I knew it would be costly and there have been the darkest of days. Most of the jobs I've done, I've been the first woman to do it. But that breaking new ground hasn't been the most difficult bit. That came relatively recently, around 2012, when it looked like the Church of England wanted to travel in the wrong direction so that women bishops would be treated differently. I've met prejudice and real abuse from people in leadership in the Church who've been shoddy in their treatment of women. Most of my energy now is to make it better for the generation behind me.'

I welcome her candid responses. It sounds as though her path towards being accepted as a leader in the Church has been extremely bumpy.

'You said to me earlier the story is all about love and acceptance,' she says. 'I don't see those two things primarily in the story. I think, yes, God does always add grace, he adds his love of us when he stretches us, when he asks us to do something, and of course it comes with the promise he will give us resilience, he will give us the strength, but Gabriel is not a loving presence. Gabriel is demanding something of Mary that's terrifying. Mary is bewildered, questioning, frightened, anxious. Which of us, when we meet a moment of destiny, can see all the consequences of it, but we have the emotional intelligence to know it's trouble ahead. If someone had told me when I was twenty-two and going to theological college what the next thirty-five years were going to hold, I would have thought a great deal harder about it all. I'd have still done it, just like Mary did it, but let's not pretend that Mary could see it all and say, "I'm in for all of that".'

I observe that the annunciation story obviously touches her very deeply.

'There's a very difficult nugget of issues in the Annunciation which is, there is suffering, God calling her to suffer. It's through her suffering that she will be fulfilled and further God's purposes. She will be the best she can be. She'll embrace it as best she can. That's really tough for the contemporary mind to grasp because we like to think that freedom and liberty is about rescuing ourselves from pain and grief and loss and unhappiness. If we were truly free, we'd be able to manage ourselves out of suffering. But what this story says, and there's an authenticity about it, is that sometimes what life asks of us and God asks of us is deeply painful and yes, somewhere in that experience we can say "I'm a better person" out of it. The journey is not just about material comforts and living a long life. It's about eternal values and building the virtues that make us proud to be who we are.'

What does she think of the statement that it is 'the most important event in human history'?

'I'd say it's rather a hierarchical statement in terms of its impact. It underperforms in terms of contemporary Christianity. We're very bad now at stimulating the biblical imagination to make people see it is very relevant today to their own life journey. We are very poor at conveying the potential of the Annunciation today.'

So how does she feel about the status of the feast of the Annunciation today? Has it been lost?

'Absolutely in terms of the Church's calendar,' she replies. 'But tomorrow, Saturday and Sunday, for the Advent weekend of services here at Salisbury, we'll have nearly six thousand people in the Cathedral but on the feast of the Annunciation in March, there are fewer than fifty. The Church's calendar has lost its power with regard to the Annunciation.'

With a twinkle in her eye, she suddenly diverts the conversation towards something highly personal.

'Do you know Mark, I conceived a child on the feast of the Annunciation?' She laughs out loud, a real full-on laugh. 'A bishop once told me it was the most stupid and incompetent thing he'd ever heard a clergyman ever tell him. Forty weeks from Christmas Day is 25 March and my daughter was due on Christmas Day. I told him if he didn't know what his clergy did at that time it was his problem not mine.' She laughs again. 'But then just this year, on the feast of the Annunciation, I had an experience of God. I was in Cornwall and I couldn't find a service anywhere. I had to take myself off to Truro Cathedral for a Eucharist service. You're right. The feast of the Annunciation has been seriously downgraded. But one of the jobs for me, and for you with this project, is to keep people's biblical imagination going when they no longer get stories of the Bible like this either at home or at school.'

I tell her of my wife's view that a feast around conception is difficult to celebrate because many people do not know the day that their baby was conceived. Instead, we tend to focus on the birthday, as it is more tangible.

'That's really interesting,' she responds. 'When I tell my daughter she was conceived on 25 March, the feast of the Annunciation, she says, "Oh no Mum! Too much information, ugh." It's because it's associated with the act of sexual intercourse. "I don't want to think of you and that",' she says. She shrieks with laughter again. 'But I do think women who are much closer to the rhythms of their cycle will understand its profound meaning. You only have to talk to women who are infertile or have lost a child in pregnancy to know conception is absolutely profound. May I say, I think one of the major problems of this story is that we come at it through too masculine a view of the world. I like Ursula Le Guin's distinction between "mother tongue" and "father tongue". "Father tongue" is the public language we use in the public world. "Mother tongue" is the language of stories and narratives and the power of daily life. I think we largely tell the Christian stories, especially the Annunciation, through the "father tongue". We tell it that way in church and schools. But if I talk to my daughter and her friends in a "female tongue", they'll get things under that narrative in a completely different way. In the annunciation story, it's not just that Mary has a personal journey and has got used to the fact she's got all that stuff to deal with. It's also that, as a woman, she's shifted to being a prime mover of God's purpose.'

Does Mary inspire her?

'Enormously, enormously,' she replies. 'It's quite difficult to clear the undergrowth with Mary. There's so much symbolism and projections on her. I grew up, when I started going to church, in a very simple, Protestant tradition and it was all about obedience.'

Does she venerate her? I wonder.

'Quietly,' she whispers. 'We do Morning Worship in the Trinity Chapel and, by and large, I sit opposite an exquisite wooden statue, a very simple image of her holding the child Jesus. I come as close to praying to Mary as ever I'm going to in my reformed and Protestant spirit. What she does for us is enable us to enter into the Trinity from the female experience. I do not think she was divine but our imagination needs a way into the divine. One of the things the Church has done in the way it has treated women is to have locked down so much potential for understanding how the creative feminine spirit could flow.'

I show her a print of Lemoyne's painting. After a while, I ask for her thoughts.

'I see something rather romantic. I also see questions I would ask myself about what's going on. I don't like it much. I wouldn't choose to live with it. I wouldn't let it inform my imagination. It's too cherubic. There is an awfulness about that moment when God enters a person's life. Yes, there's wonder but there is…terror is probably too great but…'

She studies the painting and then declares it to be rather mannered and pietistic.

'Her gesture is only there in order to convey a message. But it's too reflective of a calm inner attitude. Life is challenging. Life is really tough. I'm a great believer in decisions cultivating themselves but in that moment when you have to take one path and not another and have to foreclose, there has to be a much greater sense of the grittiness than this conveys.

'If people are going to experience this narrative in terms of their own life, I think…' She sighs before picking up her thread again. 'I don't want to be dark about people's lives but I think it takes real courage to live an ordinary human life. And this painting does not speak to me about courage. This is an afternoon tea party. Are you with me? Mary was going to experience social exclusion and be totally misunderstood by those closest to her. Anyone who has had the experience of being humiliated and vilified and being treated with contempt knows the cruelty of that. If this narrative is going to work for people, it has to articulate both the gruesome reality of suffering and the extraordinary virility and potency that you can find within it.' *

———

It is seven o'clock on a Friday evening in late November and Salisbury Cathedral is packed with more than seventeen hundred people. The congregation remains completely silent as it sits in total darkness. A few minutes later and a single Advent candle is lit half way down the nave. Over the next hour, in a service entitled 'From Darkness to Light', more than thirteen hundred candles are lit in this magnificent space. It is an extraordinarily moving occasion.

Advent music and readings form the backbone of tonight's 'Advent Procession' service. The choirs create a wonderful polyphony as two processions make their way from the

---

* In April 2017, it was announced that June Osborne will be the next Bishop of Llandaff, based in Cardiff.

west end of the building along the north and south aisles. Dean June Osborne, wearing a richly embroidered, festive cope, takes up the rear of the procession on my left, and Bishop Nick Holtam, wearing his mitre and holding a staff, walks at the end of the other line to my right. Some of the procession members are carrying banners. One states 'Jesus is God'. Another proclaims 'Jesus – God is with us'. This is a night to experience high Anglican pomp and ceremony and to witness the Salisbury Diocese declare its readiness for the Advent season.

Twenty minutes in, the taperers, in an impressive, well-drilled routine, have lit the scores of candelabra that are placed strategically along the nave and in various spaces around the Cathedral to create maximum impact. The processions come together around the altar under the spire crossing, and a small, bald-headed man walks towards the golden eagle lectern directly in front of me. He starts to read Luke's Gospel, 1: 26-38, the story of the Annunciation.

There's a magnificent richness to his voice. His slow, measured delivery, precise pronunciation and dramatic phrasing make it the most stunning oral rendition of the Annunciation passage I have ever heard. This man is communicating the story in a way I have never heard before. At the end of the reading, he returns to his seat directly in front of me. It is only as he approaches that I realize he is David Suchet, the actor known around the world for his work on stage and television. A former member of the Royal Shakespeare Company, he is most famous for playing Hercule Poirot, Agatha Christie's much loved detective, in more than seventy television episodes spanning the past quarter of a century. When the service ends, I go to congratulate him on his wonderful reading. He thanks me graciously and we arrange to talk later.

Sixty-nine-year-old David Suchet was born in London. His father was of Lithuanian Jewish descent and his mother was English and baptized as an Anglican. He was raised without religion but converted and became a practising Anglican aged forty. For years after that moment, he dreamt of reading the whole Bible for an audio recording and recently achieved his goal: 752,702 words, from Genesis to Revelation. 'The Bible says: "Hear the word of the Lord",' he tells me. 'It was written in order to be heard because no one could read then.'

He is speaking to me by phone from his London home. During our conversation, he has the image of Lemoyne's *The Annunciation* in front of him on his computer.

'I've struggled with the Annunciation and I've struggled with paintings like the one I'm looking at now for many years,' he begins. 'Because I'm a convert, I've found both Church and Art in contradiction to what I read in the Bible and that disturbs me. Most of all, much of the art about the Annunciation romanticizes something that is very fundamental regarding Mary. I think we all look at the Bible too much from a Western perspective and, certainly, this picture is from a Western, romantic perspective.

'When I read the Bible, which took me over two hundred and fifty hours and another three to four hundred hours in preparation, I approached each book, chapter and verse with the firm knowledge that this was written for Eastern people inspired by the Holy Spirit. The Bible is a Middle Eastern book. Most of the people were illiterate. The only way people could know about it was to have it read out to them on a high platform day after day after day and there were people in the crowd explaining what they were hearing. So, it's holy oral testimony. That's why I wanted to read the Bible out loud because it's by listening to the words that you actually take it in inside of you.'

What was he thinking when he read the annunciation passage in Salisbury Cathedral?

'When I first started looking at the Annunciation, I was reading it and thought, it's so pretty, but then I thought this is Middle Eastern. Let me go back to the books of Law and let me read what it meant for a young girl to be pregnant out of wedlock. What was going on here? We are given to understand in Luke's Gospel that a young girl was engaged and sworn to be married. What did it mean for her to be told she was going to bear a child out of wedlock? The angel says, "Do not be afraid". She was scared stiff at hearing the angel. She was terrified and wondered what it all meant. She hears, "You will be with child. You will give birth to a Son. You are to give him the name Jesus." There were three orders. That's extraordinary. Today, we still speculate on what the sex will be of an unborn child and to have known the sex of the baby before its birth was completely unheard of in her day. But she is told even before she's conceived that she is going to have a boy, what to call him, and that he is from God. Extraordinary.

'Then there are Mary's questions,' he continues. 'I like to think Luke got this from Mary herself. "How will this be because I'm a virgin?" What did this all mean in Middle Eastern terms for Mary? That's why this painting disturbs me so much. This meant that if she's discovered to be pregnant, she could be stood outside her father's house, rather like with Al Qaeda and ISIS, and be stoned to death. This is extraordinarily terrifying. What's more, we learn she goes to Joseph and tells him. Imagine Mark, if you or I learnt that our wife-to-be was pregnant? We'd say by whom? Is it anybody I know? And your fiancée answers "God". The whole annunciation story throws into relief what actually Mary faced when she said yes – a growing sign in her stomach that she was pregnant out of wedlock and, as such, faced a penalty of death and the first stone being thrown by her father. It's my conviction, my belief, that when Joseph had to go to Bethlehem for the census – men normally went on their own – he took Mary with him to protect her as she was about to give birth and would have been murdered.'

So when he delivered the passage so powerfully, so dramatically, was he trying to bring across the terror as well as the profundity of that moment?

'It's very important we look at the text of the Bible. We can only look at the different translations we are given, Greek, Hebrew, Aramaic. For Mary it was not a moment of pure joy. And the reason she goes to see Elizabeth straight away is for protection. So it's important to give it some form of due weight and to rescue it from romanticism.'

Does he see it as fact or metaphor?

'I see it as fact,' he replies firmly. 'It's very hard today with our intellectual, sceptical minds to doubt miracles. I believe there was a time when people did experience miracles. I think miracles are legitimate. They are real. I think Luke got his account from interviews and stories. He would not have been around so I would like to think a lot of the account came from Mary herself. One other thing that also convinces me is that Luke is purported to be a doctor. My dad was an obstetrician and gynaecologist. I would have found it very difficult not to have believed him if he'd said it.'

I tell him that many people have told me the central message of the Annunciation is about 'calling'. He felt a calling at forty after reading St Paul's Letter to the Romans. Does he see any parallel between his own conversion and the theme in the Annunciation of Mary saying yes to God?

'No,' he replies immediately. 'I call my conversion "dragged, kicking and screaming". I saw a way of being and of thinking at the end of reading that Letter. I was confronted with this question, where did he [St Paul] get this? The answer was that it was from somebody called Jesus. I went back through the whole of the New Testament, which I'd been thinking was a load of romantic twaddle. At the age of forty it's very difficult to be convinced, so I call my conversion the journey of kicking and screaming, after asking questions all the time, but somehow it never let go.'

What does Mary mean to him?

'Courage more than anything,' he replies. 'I think the visitation of the angel must have been absolutely terrifying and I don't think she recovered that quickly. That's why I think this picture is such a romanticized image of Mary. I think she said yes but, personally, I don't think she was given much choice. If an angel came to you in your house at 3 a.m., surrounded by light, and you were told what was going to happen and you said yes, after the angel had gone you'd think, do I need to see a doctor? I think we have to look at this in real terms, not romantic terms. It frustrates me because the message it gives – what the world, when it sees it, will take away – is one of serenity and calmness, and it moves us out of the East and to the West. We have to cling on to the Bible. There's no other source we have, and if we romanticize it through a Western view, we are losing all that real meaning it had for Mary, for Joseph, for the whole family and the reaction of all the people all around her. This to me proves it's true and not make-believe. Nobody could write like that and it be just make-believe.'

If there's a phrase that sums up the annunciation story for him, what is it?

'The change in the world,' he responds. 'It's the new promise of God. It is the beginning of the new covenant. From that moment, the world has changed.'

I tell him about the Roman Catholic Bishop's statement that it is 'the most important event in human history'.

'Yes, it certainly changed the world at that very moment,' he says. 'All God's covenants were leading up to that very moment. It's got nothing to do with Catholic belief or anything else. In a sense, the Reformation demoted Mary too much. They moved away from Catholic devotion to Mary and she got diminished, but I think in the Protestant world we need to restore her to a rightful place. She was the vehicle literally of God coming into the world and changing the course of time. Gabriel says to her that he will be called the Son of God. Theologically, it doesn't mean that God is Jesus's literal father. When she is told Jesus will be the Son of God it means more than the Messiah. It's God in person and that's such a mind-blowing event. So I concur that it is the most important event in human history. The two events I always focus on are the Annunciation and the Crucifixion/Resurrection. They are the greatest miracles for us – God coming in human form and then dying and resurrecting in human spiritual form. They are absolutely linked and it all begins with the Annunciation.'

CHAPTER 33

SURRENDER TO WIN

Wimborne Minster, built from New Forest stone and local Dorset limestone, has a distinctive grey and rust-brown patterned façade. Dedicated to St Cuthburga, who founded a Benedictine nunnery here in the eighth century, it has been, as the guidebook puts it, 'a living centre for pilgrimage, prayer, mission and worship for more than a thousand years.' In the Holy Trinity Chapel, a beautiful stained-glass rendition of the Annunciation forms

132. Stained glass of the Annunciation, Holy Trinity Chapel, Wimborne Minster

part of the first light of a five-lancet window. Gabriel, wearing a green tunic, confronts the Virgin Mary who sways backwards, holding onto her prie-dieu for support.

Vanessa Herrick has been the Rector of Wimborne Minster since 2012 and leads a ministry team comprising mainly women. Previously, she was the Director of Ministry and Ordination for the Diocese of Ely and before that taught Theology at Cambridge. She was the first woman to be appointed as the leader of a church within the Greater Churches Group of the Church of England and considers herself to be a pioneer with 'the responsibility of proving a woman can do it.' She talks movingly about a key moment in 1992 when she was going through the discernment process. She recalls watching a report on the BBC Six O'Clock News about the vote being taken at the General Synod to approve women priests. She tells me it felt as if a child had leapt in her womb.

'It was an extraordinary physical experience like my tummy being turned upside down. It was a tangible experience of connecting to the spiritual.'

We sit in her small, cosy study in the nearby Rectory where she describes the difficulties she has faced since becoming the first ever woman Rector at Wimborne, particularly at the beginning of her tenure. Her husband, also a priest, works in East Anglia and for much of the week they lead separate lives.

'The particular challenges I've had here have not just been about being female but whether a woman could deal with management, finance – competence issues in running a large organisation. That's been the main question in the background, which is different to should a woman be a priest. The woman priest stuff has been there all the way through since I was ordained back in 1996. The way some people then would walk out when they saw me, clearly that rejection was very painful, but I'm older and wiser now.'

Short haired, bespectacled and undeniably determined, she explains what the annunciation story means for her.

'It's only taken on meaning in recent years,' she begins. 'I grew up in a very evangelical wing of the Church and Mary was off-piste. You didn't do stuff about Mary. It's only in the last ten or twenty years that Mary things have become part of my awareness. The Annunciation has been different things at different times to me. That's the great strength of Scripture and art. You come to it in whatever culture or circumstance you are in at the time. For instance, I've gone on silent retreats every year in recent times and meditated on the Annunciation as part of that. But the outcome has been different every time that I've gone back to it.

'The fundamental theme is about God breaking into human existence,' she continues. 'I believe God has been part of existence since before the Big Bang but it epitomizes how God chooses to work with human beings. As a woman, the Annunciation has taken on particular meaning in terms of trying to explore what was going on for women in that culture at that time, and what it says today for the hundreds of thousands of women in a similar culture today. Also, what it says in my own particular journey as an ordained person and for women growing into the service of God in a different kind of way. My gut internal reaction to any artistic representations of the Annunciation is just how much of an underdog is this woman depicted as? How much is she seen as being suppressed by an angel male character or are they on a level? What sort of expression does she have – is she strong and courageous? I look at all the Annunciation paintings as a woman priest in terms of how are they seeing me? Am I seen as an underdog? Do I fit into their culture? Am I being told what to do?'

What would she like to see in an annunciation painting?

'I want to see genuine human response,' she replies. 'I want to see the worth and value of Mary as she is depicted. I want to see strength and courage in her. I don't want to see an overbearing figure. Of all the human beings who've lived, she has undertaken the most immense task that anybody could be asked to undertake. There's a clash between my own understanding of that and the way in which many cultures have depicted her over the centuries. So many cultures make the woman inferior. The Roman Catholic Church elevates her but, forgive me, in a pastiche sort of way that's rarely had an integrity in terms of her as a human being.'

During her childhood, was Mary considered irrelevant?

'I'd say it was much stronger than that. As I say, she was off-piste. We saw her as idolized in an inappropriate way. I didn't think it was bizarre. It was the way I was brought up. Then shortly before I went through the discernment process to become a priest, I was on a retreat at a Jesuit spirituality place in north Wales called St Beuno's. I first went there in 1992 and I was invited to take away the annunciation story and meditate on it. It was the first time I'd really thought about Mary. I remember the Director on that particular retreat writing to me saying that Mary would become more important to me on my Christian journey. That was permission-giving for me. I'd already crossed the abyss by going to a Jesuit retreat centre but actually it was the beginning of a pattern of annual retreats that has been really important to me.'

I ask her to explain her thoughts about the Annunciation whilst on those retreats.

'I can recall one, focused on the ordinariness of Mary. The fact she was an ordinary teenager, nobody special, but had faith. That's fundamental for God breaking into human living and taking it as it is. Another theme has been about risk, the choosing to say yes.

I often ask myself, what would have happened if Mary had said no, because she had the freedom to do that? It would not have been the Incarnation. It's crucial that it's a human being with free will. "Let it be" is an amen. It's an amen at the beginning of God breaking in that is balanced by the amen of both the Cross and the Resurrection, and the ultimate amen of heaven. We make a great deal of the Crucifixion and the Resurrection and about heaven but we forget the "Let it be" of the Annunciation.'

Does she see any parallel between Mary's calling and her own?

'I think it has been a sort of *cantus firmus* throughout my journey to being a priest. I think vocation is ongoing rather than "that's it" and you have it for the rest of your life. The themes that have come from my meditation on the Annunciation – the ordinariness of who I am, the risk of being ordained, the way that Mary had her own plans but actually God transformed those plans and made them his own – I can see how they have resonated in my own life. I've had to say yes to that, it hasn't just happened. The other theme that hits me about the Annunciation is what sort of yes it was. When God calls, like when Gabriel met Mary, you can have a yes that's kind of "yes alright then"; you can have a yes because there's no alternative; or you can have the yes that I believe Mary offered, which was "I haven't a clue what this means but I trust God." Those different sorts of yes have echoed in my own vocational journey. It means I have said yes to things that I don't know yet whether they'll happen. Saying yes to being the Rector here was the right yes, but boy was it hell for the first two years I was here. It was extraordinarily difficult but, two and a half years in, I can see that yes now bearing fruit.'

Does she see the story of the Annunciation as fact or metaphor?

'I see it as recorded fact in the life of a woman,' she replies. 'I don't necessarily see it as artists depict it. How do you depict an angel? I've never seen an angel in a vision or in reality, as depicted in art, but I have known people whom I've had conversations with, who have said things that have been hugely significant, that can equate to a revelation from God. In that respect, I see it as both fact and metaphor. I think an encounter with the divine happened. Just as it happens to all sorts of people in ordinary living. I do believe that God broke in not only to her life in particular but to human living at that particular moment. I'm agnostic about angels. I believe God sends messages. They can be ethereal beings. Equally, I believe, they can be you.'

We talk about the difference between West and East: in the West, much time is spent trying to find explanations – did it happen, could it happen? In the East, the emphasis is on the spiritual experience – what is the message, what does it mean? In that context, what does she think about the statement that the Annunciation is the most important event in human history?

'Yes, I think it is,' she responds. 'God breaking into human existence. It's because of the fundamental truth of Jesus becoming a human being as well as being God. If Mary had said no, God would have to have found another woman to give birth to the Son of God or the rest of it would not have made any sense.'

So why has the feast of the Annunciation been downgraded in recent times?

'I could be cynical and say because it's about a woman,' she replies. 'The Roman Catholic Church would mark it, wouldn't they?'

Yes, I respond, but even there, it has lost much of its status within the liturgical calendar and is not a holy day of obligation.

'If I can draw a parallel with the Transfiguration,' she says. 'I think it's a feast that has very little tangibly that people can connect with but it has a huge amount spiritually that people can connect with. Christmas is popular because people like the baby and the animals. Easter is popular in a different way because people can identify with people being beheaded and crucified and persecuted in the world today. They can make some sort of connections. The Christian Church, and I'm part of that responsibility, has lost our ability to communicate with people on a spiritual plain. We've certainly lost our ability to communicate theological truth in a way that connects and makes any relevance to people. Therefore, if you're trying to celebrate a festival that primarily has as its presented meaning a spiritual encounter, then you haven't got a great deal to go on in communicating it. As an aside, you could say the same about creation. I'd say the Annunciation is the most important event in the history of humanity. You could argue the most important event in the history of the world was its creation. The two are closely related because the Cross is the redemption of creation as well as the redemption of humanity. You can't separate them.'

Is there a phrase that sums up the Annunciation for her?

'God's yes to humanity and our yes to God,' she responds.

Is Mary central in her life now?

'I don't think I'd say she's central,' she replies. 'She's a significant resource in particular circumstances for particular people. Mary has been very helpful in pastoral work, particularly with those who have lost a child or who face a difficult decision.'

When I ask whether she venerates her, she replies no, rather firmly. I wonder if the doctrine of a virgin conception is of critical importance to her.

'I think it is critical theologically because of the idea of breaking in, of accepting the weakness of humanity, of severing the cord of sinfulness that allowed God to be both God and human. That's a very theological way of putting it. It's part of the creeds that I accept. If you were to ask me would it affect my faith if I was to be told the Virgin Birth didn't happen, the answer would be no.'

Does she believe that Mary had other children and that Jesus had brothers and sisters?

'Absolutely,' she says. 'Actually, part of me is sad she has been made into something else. I feel particularly in art she has been removed. The Roman Catholic Church will say, "Praise to Mary, she's so much like you." But, actually, the Church, particularly the Roman Catholic Church and artists coming from that, have separated her off, made her unattainable and alienated her from ordinary women. I get it that over the centuries ordinary women may have wanted to adulate and honour her in a cathartic sense to make their lives more bearable, but I'd far rather that Mary was like me.'

I tell her that many women I have spoken to believe that the Roman Catholic model of Mary has caused damage to women.

'I think that's been particularly poignant for me, and some of the other women priests you will have interviewed, in this parallel journey towards the priesthood of women and women now joining the episcopate' she replies. 'There's often been an undercurrent, or often an explicit current when women first became priests, of men sitting in the congregation and fancying them – a sexualisation of the priesthood that would not have happened with male priests. Should women wear earrings when presiding? To caricature, the image of women has been the wife at home looking after the family and not about leadership in the Church. That's the virgin woman image. Yet women who were called to ordination were feeling something very different. They were wanting to say yes in the same gritty way that Mary said it. But the Church was painting a different picture of who they should be.'

I show her the print of Lemoyne's painting.

'I don't like it as a painting at all,' she tells me. 'I don't like the baroque and all the cherubs stuff. I think Gabriel is being extremely rude. It is the first finger. I think unholy thoughts. I see it as phallic or "up yours". By contrast, the Sistine Chapel is very different and the use of the finger in that depiction is significant. Here I see the angel as saying, "God is over and above you." The posture of Mary is extraordinarily subservient. I hate the fact that she's not even looking at the angel in the eye. It's above her. The meekness is completely wrong. Fear would be a far more human response. And if I think about their conversation, it would be much more on the same level. I'm more comfortable with Renaissance paintings. This doesn't do it for me at all.'

I pack up my notepad and pen and prepare to leave.

'Pray with the story of the Annunciation,' she tells me. 'Read it, go into silence and allow God to connect in any way. Say to God, "what is this for me today?" and see what will happen. Different things will emerge.'

It is some months since I first saw Mike Chapman's life-size sculpture of a baby in the portico of St Martin-in-the-Fields. Nick Holtam, Bishop of Salisbury, commissioned the piece to mark the millennium when he was the Vicar. Recently, I was told that some women touch the baby's penis in the hope of getting pregnant. It is clear that the sculpture has an extraordinary impact on many people and I am very keen to meet its creator.

I pass a row of nondescript terraced houses in Monmouth Road, Dorchester, and make my way down a narrow back garden path towards a rickety garden shed. There, I find sculptor Mike Chapman displaying his wares in an open studio exhibition as part of 'Dorset Art Week'. Paintings, drawings and small sculptures adorn the walls of his modest workshop. A huge wooden crucifix placed in the centre of the shed dominates the small space. I've come here because I want to discover more about the *Christ Child* sculpture and the inspiration behind such a distinctive work.

Mike Chapman is a gregarious character with receding snowy hair and a white-grey beard. He reminds me of a sea captain. For the next thirty minutes, he opens up about his extraordinary life and the story behind that sculpture. He starts by talking about his childhood in Derby. He says he came from a troubled background and suffered abuse.

'I was very uneducated but quite bright. I passed no exams except the 11+. I went to Art School at fifteen. I wasted such a lot of educational opportunities but it's how my mind worked then. It didn't fit in with that system. It's only when I went into advertising that it all worked because they thought I was a manipulative, lying git,' he laughs out loudly. 'I was exactly what they needed. I could mind read, which is what they wanted. A positive out of a negative start and I took off like a rocket. I joined an ad agency called Dorland that was part of the Saatchi group. It was then the second largest in England and, eventually, I became its Creative Director. I really got in my stride in the 1970s and had a stratospheric rise.'

He says many would find it hard to believe that he found the awards, the flash cars and the posh restaurants lacking in appeal. Instead, he dreamed every day of something more rewarding.

'There was an instantaneous moment when I packed it all in,' he says. 'By my 40s, I was multiply divorced, an alcoholic, drug addict, a really-in-trouble human being due to the pressure of life and a really unhappy soul. The career had foundered. I walked into a shop where I got my newspaper each morning. I couldn't speak. Opposite there was a phone box and I rang an old girlfriend. I got into a treatment centre for three months. I didn't know what I was going to do but I knew I wasn't going to do that again. Everything fell into place. The badge in the treatment centre said, "Surrender to Win". That's exactly what happened.

'I decided I must do something that isn't bullshit. I'd stopped smoking and drinking. There was a postcard on the wall of the treatment centre of donkeys on the beach at Weymouth. A guy who was studying stone carving in Weymouth sent it. I thought that's for me and I took to it like a duck to water. Within months, I was at Weymouth College, in my late forties, learning about stone carving. I studied for two years with men from the Dorset limestone quarries. It was a massive change but I felt completely familiar with it. It changed my life. I love stone. I love the sound of it under a mallet; the smell of it when it's cut; the colour and the texture. The smell is amazing – like diesel – the smell of dead, organic material, of creatures released into the air after hundreds of millions of years. It's so evocative. I love the permanence. It moves me. It's so different to my previous life. You can't bullshit a stone carving. It's either good or it isn't.'

We sit close together on two small wooden chairs. Occasionally, we have to break from the conversation when visitors come inside to view his pieces. One woman writes in the visitors' book: 'What a joyous surprise. Magnificent.' When she leaves, we continue where we left off.

'I came out of Weymouth College in 1996 and soon after in 1999 I was commissioned to work on the *Christ Child*,' he says. 'There was no brief. I worked on it continuously for three months. I'm not a Christian, anything but, but I thought people were missing the point of the millennium…the Dome and all that. I was brought up in the Church for good or bad. I said I just want to carve a life size baby. It was to replace the crib in Trafalgar Square for that year. I've got to tell you, it did look amazing when the cranes placed it on its spot in Trafalgar Square in late November at 4.30 in the morning. It was a very emotional time for me.'

After the Christmas festive season and the millennium celebrations, the sculpture was moved to its present site in front of St Martin-in-the-Fields.

133. Mike Chapman *Christ Child*, 1999, St Martin-in-the-Fields, London. Photo: Ronald Neil

'I'm quite fond of the idea of Christ but I'm not fond of the Church,' he says. 'He brought me some comfort – a benevolent kind of hippy before hippies were even invented. Talking about being kind to people, redemption, forgiveness. As a kid, I saw God as this thundery, frightening, punishing thing. I don't know.' He laughs out loudly again and asks me if this is all irrelevant. 'The reaction to the *Christ Child* has been phenomenal. The art establishment are very stuffy about it. It's too representational, it's too obscure. It's not clever. But it doesn't half move people. I still get letters from all over the world.'

So, does the sculpture depict Jesus in the womb or has he just been born?

'I always intended it to be the newborn Christ arriving on earth. I wanted it to look like a time traveller who'd just arrived. For me, it was about vulnerability. That's what so moved me. If you are God and you want to have a presence on earth, I think it's extraordinary to choose to appear as a baby. They are utterly helpless. Naked. They've got no fur, half blind, the brain only a third developed. So the idea that that's the entry point into mankind is so trusting. That's what I loved.'

I tell him I'd spoken to some women who thought the baby is still in the womb, about to be born.

'That's great,' he responds. 'They're moved by it. I don't think it's mine anymore. I can be objective. I think it's a very spiritual piece. I went back three years ago to see it and observed the difference in our relationship. It was always mine up to then but it wasn't mine anymore. It was quite moving. I knew I could now trust the world with it. I sat in a corner and observed people's reaction to it. I saw one woman cry there. That's fabulous. If your take on it is that it's a baby in the womb, it's still Christ. That's fine. The whole point of Christ is that he was born naturally from a womb. And with the words around the sculpture, you're not going to mistake it for anybody else.'

When he says it's a spiritual piece, what does he mean?

'I'm spiritual. I'm a believer in God – in a higher power. Alcoholics Anonymous is passionately non-doctrinaire but encourages you to find a higher power. It's a spiritual programme but passionately not religious. My view, when I went into rehab, had been that God was a vengeful bastard who'd wrecked my life. God was responsible for that. I'm now a believer in a benevolent God but not in the Church. My own take on the Church was that it was about punishment and guilt and shame. I'd already got enough shame to sink a battleship. I didn't need Church.'

Does he see the annunciation story as a fact or a metaphor?

'I don't really believe it as a story,' he replies. 'It's a lovely idea. It's a beautiful metaphor – God on earth. For that, I'm prepared to believe it. My personal take is there's a massive presence of God on this planet. It's central to me in my life. I pray every morning. I celebrated the annunciation story for years as a child but now I completely reject it as fact. But as a metaphor, I find it profoundly moving. I love those words, "And the Word was made flesh and dwelt among us." And the idea of her acceptance, "Let it be". Acceptance is the key word in recovery.'

So, is there a kind of parallel between the annunciation story and his own story?

'That's why you hook onto that phrase "Surrender to win",' he replies. 'When I was commissioned to create the *Christ Child*, it was very early days for me in terms of my recovery and my own journey. I was living on my own. I was very poor. My dog had just died. I had no identity. My children were all in London. The idea of a baby was incredibly important to me. The idea of a new start. Acceptance, redemption, forgiveness, the end of shame.'

He tells me he is now married to a lovely woman and has a precious eight-year-old daughter. Unexpectedly, his life has completely turned around and he has never been happier. In addition, his sculpture is displayed in the centre of London and is viewed by thousands of people every week. Who would have thought?

'Surrender to win. I won by losing. Everyone in London I knew thinks I'm a loser. In their perception I lost everything. I lost my career, I was bankrupt, and I pissed it all up the wall. But I know I've won. It may never have been critically acclaimed but I'm very proud of the *Christ Child* because it's honest. So many people love it as inspirational and true. The critics may think my work is crap but I don't give a monkey's.'

Five years before meeting Mike Chapman, I attended the Christmas Midnight Service at my local church in Winchester. Peter Seal, the Rector at St Paul's, gave the sermon, in which he focused on the *Christ Child* sculpture:

> In the carved entrance porch to St Martin-in-the-Fields is a huge piece of stone in the shape of a cube. It stands some four feet high. Carved in relief on top of the stone is a naked baby boy. He's lying on his back, immediately vulnerable and beautiful in the same instance . . . Somehow that baby, whom we immediately conceive to be the Christ Child, represents all humanity – every man, woman and child of every race who has lived, lives today and will live tomorrow and beyond. It speaks of human vulnerability . . . To be vulnerable is to be open to being wounded or hurt, physically or emotionally... If God is to be real for us, we need to accept and embrace not only our vulnerability but also God's vulnerability. When we begin to do this, we discover a very great truth. The truth, that to be vulnerable and be open, is actually to be strong in the most real way. We find this hard but we need to respond because the fullness of our lives depends on us being as open and vulnerable to God, as he was to us when he came wearing nothing and trusting human hands to hold their maker.

At Sarum College in Salisbury, a day of spiritual reflection for Advent has been planned and will focus on Mike Chapman's *Christ Child* sculpture. An Anglican priest will lead the six-hour session. The programme states: 'It is a daily reminder to the thousands who see it each day of the coming of God incarnate, not as a powerful overlord but as a small vulnerable baby. We will allow the *Christ Child* to speak afresh to us as we look forward once again to his coming.'

It is clear that Mike Chapman, who surrendered to win and discovered a new calling, will, through his sculpture, continue to inspire thousands of people to think and reflect for years to come.

Glastonbury has been a religious centre since pre-Christian times and is a place filled with mysteries and legends. One early tradition claimed that Joseph of Arimathea visited in the early part of the first century, accompanied by Jesus before he began his ministry. Another legend from the twelfth century claimed that Joseph of Arimathea visited Glastonbury later in AD 65, thirty years after he had removed Jesus's body from the cross at Golgotha and placed it in a linen cloth in the nearby tomb. Both these stories are now dismissed as make-believe. However, for many centuries, tens of thousands of Christian pilgrims have flocked to Glastonbury, known as the 'cradle of Christianity in England' and as the oldest shrine to Our Lady north of the Alps. The small, Somerset town claims to be the only sacred site in Britain to have been continuously Christian since the first century.

The first church, St Mary's of Glastonbury, was established in the middle of the seventh century and dedicated to the Virgin Mary. By the eighth century, it was being recorded as 'the foremost church in Britain and the fount and source of all religion.' In the tenth century, a new Abbey was constructed around the wattle church and was then rebuilt nearby under the Normans. The Abbey developed to become the richest Benedictine monastery in England. Tragically, in 1184, a great fire burnt the 'old church' and almost completely destroyed the Abbey buildings. Only an ancient wooden statue of the Virgin Mary survived – the result of a miracle according to the monks. Immediately afterwards, as rebuilding began, a Lady Chapel was established on the site of the original church. Today, its surviving Norman doorway shows sculptural scenes from the life of the Virgin

Mary, including an Annunciation scene in the bottom left corner of the archway. Much of its detail has been weathered away. But as I place my fingers on the stone relief I can just about work out an angel dressed in long robes with his wings fully displayed whilst Mary kneels in apparent acceptance.

134. Stone carving of the Annunciation, twelfth century, Glastonbury Abbey

Throughout the Middle Ages, thousands of pilgrims would pass through this doorway in order to venerate the statue of Our Lady of Glastonbury. The feasts of the Annunciation on 25 March and the birthday of Mary on 8 September, were key dates for the pilgrims. However, the Abbey became a major casualty during the dissolution of the monasteries in 1539 and today all that is left to indicate its extraordinary scale are the extensive stone ruins that stand in the lovely Abbey grounds. Sadly, the original statue of Mary was lost when the Abbey was ransacked.

Today, across the road from the Abbey ruins, the mid-twentieth-century Roman Catholic church of St Mary's stands as Mary's restored shrine and as the present day focal point for Catholic pilgrimage. A new statue, medieval in appearance and bearing the ancient title of Our Lady, St Mary of Glastonbury, was blessed in 1955 in front of thousands of Catholics, and comprises Mary clutching her child with her left arm as she holds a flowering rose bush in her right hand, symbolizing her flourishing motherhood. Ten years later, the statue was taken to the Abbey's ruins and crowned in front of 20,000 people who had gathered there for a special service.

As I leave the church and walk up the town's main street, I notice how many shop windows are filled with angel statues and 'New Age' books about angelic powers. Advertisements for healing, transformation, natural energy and meditation services, proliferate. As well as being 'the cradle of Christianity in England' and a focal point for Marian veneration, Glastonbury is also a centre for Paganism at the heart of the sacred isle of Avalon. There are said to be more than seventy practising 'spiritual faiths and paths' here and many more individuals have developed their own ways for exploring the divine. One building is named the Glastonbury Goddess Temple and is the first official Pagan establishment in England to be granted a license to conduct heterosexual and same-sex marriages. The Temple, based in the loft of an old house, is described as 'a sacred space set aside for the exploration and celebration of the Divine Feminine in all Her forms.' It proclaims: 'Come and get married within the loving energies of Goddess, in the heart of Avalon, in the Glastonbury Goddess Temple, a Sacred Place dedicated to the Lady of Avalon.'

Our Lady, Mary of Glastonbury is named as one of the many goddesses. On a notice-board nearby in the High Street, I see a poster featuring a picture of the angel Gabriel along with the invitation: 'Discover what your angel has in store for you. If you feel a moment of change, I can help you connect to Gabriel, the archangel of love and compassion, the guardian of rain, the bringer of new life.'

I am in Wells Cathedral in the St Calixtus Chapel, crouching on the floor in front of the ornate fifteenth-century tomb of Thomas Boleyn, former Master of Gonville College, Cambridge. Below Boleyn's effigy, set in the bottom left hand corner of the tomb, is an alabaster relief of an annunciation scene. Unusually, the angel Gabriel is still in the process of descending and is heading towards Mary who stands by her prie-dieu, having been clearly disturbed whilst reading her psalm book.

A Cathedral guide calls the relief 'The Annunciation of the Virgin of the Lilies'. He refers to the depiction of Mary's shock but, to my eyes, her open hands raised to her chest signify her acceptance of Gabriel's request. The guide describes how the alabaster was transported to the West Country from Nottinghamshire in the 1470s and how, remarkably, the tomb survived intact from the Puritan raids. Then, he sums up the panel's aesthetic rather well as 'a rare, distinctive and most wonderful Annunciation, breathtaking in its beauty.'

135. Alabaster relief, fifteenth century, St Calixtus Chapel, Wells Cathedral

---

In the week I visit Míla Fürstová in the Regency spa town of Cheltenham, I calculate that her latest work must surely be the biggest-selling artistic image in the world at that time. The British band Coldplay has just released its latest album, *Ghost Stories*, and Míla designed its front cover. At present, the album is number one in the United States, Canada, the UK, France, Spain, Germany, Australia and New Zealand, and sold more than a million copies in the first few days of its release. It is also top of the charts in Míla Fürstová's native country, Czech Republic.

The artwork comprises a detailed etching of two wings. The plumage of each wing is filled with meticulously designed drawings and symbols that, when viewed close up, reveal an extraordinary level of intricacy and detail. The wings are placed in such a way that they form the shape of a broken heart. The image is clever, highly original and enigmatic.

Míla Fürstová was born in 1975 in Hradec Kralove in the former Communist, Eastern-bloc country of Czechoslovakia. She tells me how, in her childhood, religious services were not totally banned in the surrounding villages where she lived but were mostly attended by grandmothers.

'It was tolerated but not promoted,' she recalls. 'I remember a teacher walking between the desks at school and saying in a threatening voice, "I bet some of you here believe in God." I was terrified. I thought, I do believe.'

She was christened a Catholic and her grandmother took her to Mass on Sundays.

'I remember seeing so much art there,' she says. 'Catholicism is dependent on imagery and Protestantism on words. That really influenced me. When I went to church, it was like visiting a gallery. I'd be looking at all the art, the statues and the paintings. It was so amazing for a young child's mind. I was allowed to grow with an open mind.' Her parents were married in a Catholic church and the family said a prayer together once a year around the table on Christmas Day. They 'acknowledged God but didn't talk about it.'

At fourteen, she went to boarding school to pursue her love of art and then attended Charles University in Prague, where she studied English Literature, Psychology and Art.

'There are artists interested in form and artists interested in content. Studying Psychology helped me understand the fundamental importance of content, of being human and the depths of humanity,' she says.

She came to England and gained a Master's degree at the Royal College of Art. In 2003, she became the first artist in residence at Cheltenham Ladies College and today is internationally recognized for her outstanding etching, hailed for her 'exceptional technical skills and brilliant creative imagination'. The printmaker and Royal Academician, Eileen Cooper, has lauded her talent and body of work: 'She is a storyteller. Her stories are both contemporary and personal, yet they reference art and history, culture and mythology.'

I have come to Cheltenham to visit her on the outskirts of the town. Although the cover for *Ghost Stories* features a pair of wings that look like they belong to an angel, it is not this particular image that I have come to learn about today. Instead, I am keen to talk about a series of five etching and mixed-media works she created in 2007, entitled *Annunciation 1-5*.

In her small studio, sited above a car mechanic's workshop, she tells me about the technique of etching that is rooted in the fifteenth-century tradition.

'I work on a zinc plate. I heat it up and cover it with brown wax, which I roll on. Then when it cools down, I turn it round and smoke it with a candle to make the surface black. There's an alchemical feeling to it. I then draw with a needle into the wax, scratching away so the plate underneath gets exposed. When you work on the black surface, this silver thread appears. It's like lace.'

She talks eloquently about the female voice in her work, how she delves into the darkest corners of the female psyche and how the resultant image can appear out of the unconscious.

'I'm searching. I often don't know where I'm going with the needle. I love it. I'm curious and excited. That's the point of art and life, isn't it? I'm tracing a future image that will be there through chance and hope. You work with a needle like with embroidery. It's like a tapestry. It's very intimate. All your feelings, sensitivities and mind go into this silver point. It's a sensual, beautiful experience.' She describes how she likes to let the mystery of etching flow through her hand. 'It's a thing of love. You see it grow.'

I ask her to explain the term 'etching and mixed media' as she has used both techniques in her *Annunciation* pieces.

'Etching as a medium was originally created as a technique to make reproductions,' she explains. 'People soon realized you could make prints from etchings of very famous paintings. When I say mixed media, I take the etching further by chopping it up and collaging it together and printing it on different coloured papers or cutting into it, or printing it in different inks so it becomes an even more inventive process. Some have materials added to them and some etchings are printed on wallpaper. It's very tactile. There's a layering of materials and a layering of thoughts.'

We return to her apartment. Her newborn daughter sits in a baby chair on the floor in the living room. Her delightful cooing sounds and spontaneous chuckles break up our conversation regularly. We discuss the five *Annunciation* works, each a separate piece but all connected.

'I always like to talk about things that are universal but also have to extend from my own experience,' she says. 'The main inspiration for this body of work for me was the concept of an annunciation coming from heaven, the space above us, and the key for me was that Mary was absent. She wasn't there. She's supposed to be announced to but here she's lost. We wonder where she is.'

The angel and a chair feature in all five works but each piece builds a different part of her story. Although they were created sequentially, she did not know how each one would develop when she started.

'I played with accident and coincidence,' she says. 'I really didn't know how the second, third, fourth and fifth would turn out. The essential things in these works always are the angel and the chair and the absence of Mary. Everything around is kind of fluid. The chair with no one on it symbolizes the missing Mary with the enquiry, "where is she?"'

I am interested to know what was the inspiration behind such a depiction of the Annunciation. 'I just felt lost myself. I was in a long-term relationship and it had ended. It was all I had known,' she replies.

In 1994, aged nineteen, she had fallen in love with an Englishman whilst in Prague and followed him to England, but thirteen years later, the relationship ended. 'I felt lost but I also felt there was a higher purpose to my life. I was in a labyrinth. Sometimes, I knew there was a metaphorical Gabriel somewhere, an angel, but I couldn't find him. I also felt I may have missed an annunciation. In my sub-conscious I also knew I was brought up in a Catholic background but in a communist country. I wondered about that. I remembered the Annunciation a little as a child as a story floating around. Obviously, I also knew it through art. I've always been drawn to angels. My grandmother would tell me how an angel is looking after you. I'd say I can't see it but she would say it's there. As a young child, I accepted it. You learn about the world by what you see and partly by what people tell you. It seemed totally acceptable to me.'

So the works are rooted in her childhood, her relationship with her grandmother and her belief in angels.

'Yes,' she responds. 'The main association is with Mary. I am kind of her here. I know how she feels.'

Is she the missing Mary in the Annunciation sequence? I ask.

'I'm not trying to elevate myself to Mary. The story in mythology and Christianity is very human and very humble. They tell my personal story.'

When she began the work, did she have any idea of what it would involve?

'Not really, other than the angel and the chair, and the absence of Mary' she replies. 'What's really exciting is how I can wander in my own mind and create it as I go along. That's another element of accident. It's as if angels are speaking to you. I'm approaching it in faith that I'm going to be led to something that makes sense to me. It's not religious though. It's spiritual. With etching, you have options to print it so many times. It's like a thought that you can bend in different ways. Go on different journeys. I didn't know there'd be five. I knew I was going to make one. Then I thought, there is much more of a story in it here and I wanted the elements of accident and coincidence to play a role. I wanted to play with it. I wanted to see where Mary gets to. Like a bird. Like a presence. A metaphor for the soul. Something without gravity. She's there but then she flies away before he [the angel] gets there. She's almost a challenge for the angel. Of course, sometimes the story is being made at the same time the art is being made. I didn't really illustrate what I was thinking. The story just developed as I was making it.'

We look at all five Annunciation images. *Annunciation I*, the foundation of them all, features a medieval-styled angel Gabriel dominating the scene, kneeling before a red chair, with flowers and pine trees that she remembers from childhood and an airport sign.

136. Míla Fürstová *Annunciation I-V*, 2007. © Míla Fürstová

We move on to the second, *Annunciation II*, where the environment becomes more dramatic. 'It's a human story. A woman falling,' she says as she points to an image of Prague and a big Japanese style wave. There are naked female bodies swimming in a wave of emotion that she describes as a narrative of her own story. There are other personal stories from her life etched in extraordinary detail. She points to Rodin's *The Kiss*. Then there's a gate being broken by more water. 'They're all full of personal, intimate meanings,' she says.

She turns to *Annunciation III*.

'Look, there's a further development of the story. Now there's London. I was often there. Look, the Millennium Bridge and Tate Modern. That was the centre of London for me, not the Houses of Parliament. I loved the proximity of the river. There's St Paul's, which I've drawn many times. Then there's a map of Bristol. I was making journeys to the Royal Academy of the West. I was also going to New York.'

She fixes her gaze on the Chrysler Building. The detail in the etching is incredible. Then she points to the outline of an imaginary door, which obscures part of the angel, saying she likes the symbolism of it. I notice that a dove has appeared by the chair.

'Birds and angels come from the same...the lack of gravity, the sense of escape...the bird becomes the soul of Mary. She's becoming a bit more present but not in a physical sense. She can't remain still in the chair.'

Does it depict her spirit? I wonder.

'It's a human spirit. It's all of us,' she replies. 'I have a problem with people thinking because etching is a medieval art, it's not modern. It's timeless and I'm trying to capture a timeless story, a timeless theme.'

When we look at *Annunciation IV*, she says it becomes even more of a labyrinth.

'I'm representing a three-dimensional story on two dimensions. But I'm chopping it up to suggest a fourth dimension. This all sounds crazy, yes?'

What does the labyrinth represent?

'It's my own mind and the universe at the same time. How we orientate and understand ourselves and question our humanity.'

We move on to *Annunciation V*.

'It all becomes broken; and when I was making this piece, I wasn't thinking of illustrating a particular story. I was allowing the medium to take over. It's all fragmented. Even the angel is disappearing. I leave it to you to interpret. It's a good thing if the artist allows you to find your own story there. I love that. It's like landing a seed and it's fabulous that it can then grow into so many different things.'

I ask her whether the series was commissioned and why she has kept them.

'There is a strange story,' she replies. 'They were done for an exhibition. I was working with a guy called Dermot Chichester. They were shown once in an exhibition at a gallery in Piccadilly for a few days and they were going to be shown in his gallery but he died suddenly. So I brought them back. I then started on a new work so they became frozen in time. Now I'd be quite reluctant to sell them as single pieces. I'd like them to be kept together. Hopefully, there'll be a bigger exhibition where I can show them. But they represent such an intimate journey.'

I thank her for talking so openly about such personal works and their significance. I wonder if, like Mary, she ever got to hear the announcement that would change her life forever.

'I think my whole life has been a series of announcements,' she replies. 'It's probably too intimate for me to talk about any further but yes, the announcement has happened,' she says.

She is now in a loving long-term relationship with Quintin, her partner and the father of her three-year-old son and baby daughter. She says she has never been happier.

'I knew as soon as I saw Quintin, he was going to be such an important part of my life. The moment I saw him, I felt I'm no longer lost. I didn't start dating him straight away but I knew something was happening and I felt I had to follow it. It was this feeling...I looked at him and felt happy. I was waiting for something to happen. It's such a joyous thing when you find a true soul mate.'

As the conversation draws to a close, I ask what Mary means to her.

'A woman,' she says. 'A mother who managed to listen to the bigger things from above and understand their meaning.'

What does the annunciation story mean?

'It's about a calling. She knows she's meant to do that.'

Does she see the story as fact?

'Nothing is ever fact,' she replies. 'If you look at these flowers here, they're a fact from one angle and another fact from another angle. Everything is a myth but also a truth. It's like a divine truth that can mean many different things. It's universal. I don't have anything against religion but I think spirituality is the essence from which religion builds. Spirituality comes first. Then religion tries to order it into things. I'm interested in it before it's ordered, before it becomes a set of rules. The soul. The centre of each religion is a God figure. In spirituality, there's one God which is the same for all religions but looked at from different angles.'

I show her Lemoyne's painting of *The Annunciation*.

'I really like it,' she says. 'It reminds me of a piece of art in my grandmother's main living room. The dining table was in front of it and I'd always sit and have this view of it. The Mary here has a very similar face. It reminds me of that and I know the feeling of it. I love the drapery in that baroque style. It's what I experienced as a child. One day I'd see something in the painting and then, the next day, I wouldn't see it again. I love that. I love her hand gesture here and the way the light hits her face. The fact that she's in the middle of doing something and is ready to accept the calling. He [the angel] doesn't have to be there. The light is on her. She has the contact directly with God, if the God is light.'

As I prepare to leave, I comment that it must feel wonderful to have her artwork so prominently featured by Coldplay.

'The commission was an absolute dream for any artist,' she says. 'I listened and listened to the music and started seeing images. I drew and drew and drew in a whirlpool of activity. I was treated with such respect. It has been true art and true love for me.'

As I drive away from Cheltenham, I realize that this extraordinarily talented artist eventually received an annunciation that would change her life. But most importantly, she listened to it and accepted it.

CHAPTER 34

GRACE IS GIFT

Exeter's magnificent Gothic Cathedral is home to the largest single collection of medieval figure sculptures in England. In the south porch of the West Front I can see the figures of Gabriel and Mary. Both have been badly damaged, their heads destroyed by sixteenth-century iconoclasts.

137. Desecrated statues and door painting of the Annunciation, Exeter Cathedral

I move inside to St Gabriel's Chapel at the east end of the Cathedral, keen to find a particularly special painting of the Annunciation that was created in the 1290s. My research informed me that I would find it displayed on two panels on the bottom left hand side of the elaborate wooden entrance to the Chapel. Without any trouble, I locate it. Angel Gabriel is clearly delineated on the left panel, wearing a blue tunic and green wrap. His bare right foot is raised at an angle, showing he has just arrived. His red hair shines brightly and he holds his right hand aloft. A scroll reads: *'ave gratia plena dominus tecum'* (hail, full of grace, the Lord is with thee). Mary, on the right side, wears a red dress and blue overgarment and looks down in shock at the angel's sudden arrival. A small white dove heads for her ear and a lily in full bloom, with three stems representing the Holy Trinity, stands between the two figures.

I am amazed at the clarity of the images and the depth of colour. Unlike the statues, the painting has survived surprisingly intact. George Hood, a Cathedral guide, explains that it was covered over at the Reformation and later, at an unknown date, the secondary paint was scraped off to reveal the original medieval artwork. 'It's quite remarkable that the original paint is still here and that it's not been rubbed off. A miracle in itself, like the Annunciation.'

Sixty-eight-year-old Tim Gorringe is the Emeritus St Luke's Professor of Theological Studies at the University of Exeter. Ordained in 1973, he worked in India for seven years teaching Theology and was then Chaplain and Tutor in Theology at St John's College, Oxford. His academic interest is the interrelation between theology, art, social science and politics.

He is dressed casually in a multi-coloured woolly jumper and heavily creased trousers. Bald on top with grey hair and a grey beard, he has joked in the past that people should consult Judith Kerr's *Mog The Faithful Cat* to discover an uncannily accurate picture of him. He begins our conversation by explaining what the Annunciation means for him.

138. Sandro Botticelli *Cestello Annunciation*, 1489, Uffizi Gallery, Florence. © Gallerie degli Uffizi

'We were married on 25 March. In our bedroom, we have a copy of the Botticelli Annunciation from the Uffizi Gallery. For me, Botticelli gets closer to the Annunciation and what it's about than anyone else. The painting is framed around a courtyard and a dance between Gabriel and Mary. The angel has just arrived and he's on his knee before Mary. It's a gesture of respect but also of engagement, and Mary meets it with a reclining from the angel. There's a wonderful sense of dance and movement. I think what Botticelli thinks the Annunciation is all about is a kind of dance between the divine and the human in which the divine approaches but doesn't overwhelm; in which there's a kind of respectful distance between the divine and the human, and the human, represented by Mary, has the opportunity to say yes or no. For me, the Botticelli painting is at the heart of what it may be all about. Did it ever happen? Probably not.'

So he doesn't see the story as fact?

'No,' he replies. 'It probably didn't happen at all. It's a metaphor…a metaphor for the human condition…and it's a metaphor for the way in which, whatever God is, God encounters the human. There are all those other ghastly tyrannical metaphors for the way in which the divine encounters us, those kind of Calvinistic and Augustinian ideas where God is the supreme judge and is waiting for us to step out of line and then we'll be cast out to darkness. It's just ghastly. The Annunciation is something absolutely different. If there's one word to sum it up, it's "grace". It's gift and what you do in response to gift. Usually, if someone gives you something really precious, you'll say, "I couldn't possibly take that." But part of the idea of gift is, even though you say you couldn't possibly take it, you do have to accept. And then the acceptance brings with it responsibility and discipleship.'

How important is it that Mary had the ability to say no?

'If what Mary is, a representative human being, then all of us, all of the time, can say no,' he responds. 'A lot of the time we do say no. That ability to say, "I couldn't care less about the gift. I'm quite happy to trash it. I'm quite happy with dominative relationships. I'm happy with relationships of oppression." All of that, which theology has commonly called sin, is a way of refusing it, saying no to it.'

Does he think it is more important for Christians to understand the message rather than believing everything to be factual?

'I think so,' he says. 'Those early chapters of Luke are extraordinarily beautiful and, in the history of world literature, this is some of the most beautiful story telling ever. But this is not reportage. It's not John Humphrys at Aberfan. It's Luke with incredible artistry talking about what it might mean for God to engage with human affairs at its ultimate depth and where humans fit into the picture.'

Does he think that the prominence of the feast of the Annunciation has diminished?

'Yeah, ok. There's two things about that,' he says. 'So first, there is a problem for anyone brought up in a Protestant tradition as to what's happened to Marianism in the Church. Karl Barth says Marianism is an excrescence that must be excised. There's too much dotty stuff about Mary. The Marianism gets in the way of people really appreciating the Marian feasts. Secondly, it's a real shame that Protestants, by and large, have lost the articulation of time through feasts. The Catholic and Anglo-Catholic practice of marking the passage of time by thinking of these feasts is terribly precious, I think. With the Annunciation, they've just lost it and don't know what it's about any longer, and that's such a shame.'

How does he react to the statement that it is 'the most important event in human history'?

'I can understand that if you think the Incarnation is at the heart of your faith. Roman Catholics will want to say that Mary saying yes to God is what allows the Incarnation to happen. Without it, we wouldn't have the Incarnation. I myself wouldn't say that, precisely because I think Luke is writing a poem, if you like, between the divine/human relationship. For me, it's more about the truth of poetry than about historical reportage of when God decided to get involved in human affairs on 25 March, AD 4 or whenever.' However, he stresses he believes in the Crucifixion and the Resurrection. 'They're not metaphors. They did happen,' he emphasizes.

So, is the annunciation story trying to explain how Jesus Christ came to earth?

'No, I don't think it is,' he replies. 'Lots of people think that's how it is. In this country, we have a rather empiricist view and so we think in terms of fact and if it isn't fact, it isn't worthwhile. But if you're an artist, it's different and Luke is, by tradition, an artist and he tells these most beautiful stories. I mean the walk to Emmaus. Did that happen? No, no, probably not, but if you see the Caravaggio in the National Gallery, it's amazing. Now the truth of that is quite independent of whether it happened or not. So, of course it's true. But read it as poetry, sublime poetry. It's not the Gradgrind world, the world of the British empiricist. That's a world without imagination. That's hopeless really.'

I show him the print of the Lemoyne painting and place it next to Botticelli's depiction.

'It's pious kitsch really, isn't it?' he says about the Lemoyne picture. 'Look at Mary and her attitude of old Bourgeoise, and those ghastly cherubs hovering above. It comes out of a particular piety of that Versailles world at that time. If you ask, why do we have the art of the twentieth and twenty-first century, like Francis Bacon, part of the answer is because we had this world in the past. It's because of this bollocks really. Tied to a social order, which is impossible. Tied to a view of God, which is impossible. If you put the Lemoyne and Botticelli side by side, it seems to me there's a kind of depth of spirituality and integrity in the Botticelli that's not there in the Lemoyne. That's what I would say.'

As he gets up to leave, I pose one final question. How has the annunciation story impacted his life?

'I never use the word "grace" because grace is gift. When we say God is grace, what we are saying is the origin and end of all things is self-gift. That God is self-gift in God's self. The world is gift. We are gift. We are called to live in response to gift. To understand ourselves as gift. Gift ourselves to others. I screw that up just as much as anyone else does. My thinking about gift has shaped every aspect of my existence in every dimension. Gift in response to gift. That's the core of my spirituality. This whole panoply, this whole universe that we are part of, is in its essence self-gift. That's amazing, truly amazing.'

———————

A dawn chorus greets me as I awake inside a monastic guesthouse at Buckfast Abbey in south Devon. It is 5.45 a.m. and I get dressed quickly, then go to join the Benedictine community of ten monks as they start their day celebrating Matins in a small chapel within the cloisters of the monastery. An hour later, we are back in the chapel to attend Lauds, before breakfast is taken in silence at 7.15 a.m. in the Refectory. The Abbot, Rt Rev. Dom David Charlesworth, sits alone at a top table. I join three monks who are sitting at a long table, dressed in black habits. Nobody acknowledges my presence. It's only 8 a.m. as I attend the public Mass in the main body of the Abbey but it feels like half the day has gone already.

A religious house dedicated to the Blessed Virgin Mary was founded here in 1018, and by the twelfth century, the Abbey was absorbed into the Cistercian order. It was destroyed in 1539 as part of the dissolution of the monasteries. In 1882, a group of Benedictine monks, exiled from France, settled at Buckfast and set about rebuilding the Abbey. It is claimed that over a thirty-year period, six monks, using primitive building methods, built the impressive Abbey, which was completed in 1938. It is hard to believe that a small team of amateurs achieved such an extraordinary feat.

Today, the monks generate an annual income of nearly £9 million, mainly through the sale of its Buckfast Tonic Wine. The caffeinated wine, sometimes known as 'Bucky' has been made at the Abbey since the 1920s. However, recently, it has been linked to violent crime in Scotland. BBC News has reported recently how one Scottish sheriff claimed there was 'a very definite association between Buckfast and violence'. The Abbey said it was 'saddened by the sheriff's unfair comment'.

Over the next thirty-six hours, I plan to follow the daily routine of the monks. However, I am mainly here to learn about a new venture that has been founded in a medieval house close to the Abbey. It is called the School of the Annunciation and I want to hear more about its mission as it sets out on its task. Created as part of Pope Francis's 'New Evangelisation' initiative, the school plans to offer online distance learning courses, Master's programmes, retreats and summer schools. The publicity leaflet states that 'at the School of the Annunciation, you can find a place to study the Catholic faith, joyfully transmitted in all its beauty, depth and vigour' as part of the formation of Christian adulthood at all levels. Its logo is a stone statue of angel Gabriel holding a scroll declaring '*Ave Maria*'. Above is the phrase, 'Do not be afraid.'

The School's small, basic rooms, contrast with the Abbey's lavish, well-established modern Conference Centre and Educational Activities Centre. From these modest beginnings, the School hopes to establish a worldwide reputation for innovative Catholic teaching..

While the monks go about their work, cooking, cleaning, gardening and creating the famous Buckfast Abbey tonic wine and honey, I head to the School to meet a senior member of the new staff.

Dr Caroline Farey is the Director of Studies with overall responsibility for student learning. She says her background is 'too complicated to describe'. She is clearly a very private person. She says she has chosen to be single, and most of her adult life has been devoted to academic study and teaching. I manage to tease out that she was once a professional embroideress, restoring specialist ecclesiastical vestments.

We sit in her modestly furnished office on the first floor. A large computer screen dominates her desk and academic certificates and religious images hang on the walls. She takes a specialist interest in Thomism (the philosophy of Thomas Aquinas) and sacred art. Bespectacled and slim, with short, greying hair, she seems rather anxious at first but soon starts to relax. She makes noticeably strong eye contact when she speaks, occasionally delivering a piercing stare.

She tells me how, when she became more interested in faith, she saw 'the need for philosophy', and decided to study at University College, Dublin, in the Department of Metaphysics. She then took an M.Phil. at Cambridge before going on to teach religious education in various places. She says she became ever more interested in theology and ecclesiastical philosophy in order to understand her faith more. She describes passionately how her life over the past three decades has concentrated on learning and passing on the faith to other people. When she studied for a Doctorate in Philosophy, she focused on the meaning of a single phrase in one of the documents from the Second Vatican Council. The sentence had stated: 'The Son of God, by his incarnation, united himself in a certain way to every man.'

'What does "in a certain way" mean?' she asks herself rhetorically. 'Once you've got that, then there's something tremendous about Jesus's relevance to every human being that has ever existed or will ever exist. What happened at the Incarnation to the whole of humanity, when God took human nature? Most people concentrate on Jesus but very few people ask what happened to the human race? Our destiny changes, our kinship changes, because he becomes a human being.

'The account of the Annunciation is the greatest event in human history,' she continues. 'Divinity and humanity become united in the words of Our Lady at that point. Once she gives her fiat, let it be done unto me, you have this incredible shift in the dignity of the human person at the Incarnation that totally respects human freedom and yet changes the whole of humanity at the same time. That whole account of what happens at the Annunciation is how we here want to help everybody appreciate how God is trying to reunite himself with every human being. The word religion means "to link". In Christianity, God does the linking by becoming man. That's what the account of the Annunciation really brings out. One can help everyone appreciate what God is doing. We use the phrase, "the primacy of grace". It's a liberating thing; rather than "I have to be good"…there's a kind of "allow me to enter in". It's a different way of teaching the Christian faith. It's Christo-centric rather than anthropocentric. It all follows from the story of the Annunciation and Our Lady saying, "Be it done unto me." It's the passive tense. It brings people to tears when they realize God wants to do everything…we teach receptivity…of all the wonders and the glories and the beauty of God and his way and his truth and his life…to grow in receptivity. Our Lady gives us the most perfect response to God, which is a response of receptivity.' She speaks with such enthusiasm and passion that her evangelistic fervour shines through.

What inspires her about the story of the Annunciation?

She opens her marked up Bible and starts to read the Luke passage slowly, line by line.

'It's such an extraordinary account of how to be receptive to God and how God is so lovingly respectful of humanity,' she says. 'His way of treating Mary is so exquisite through the angel Gabriel. We teach people to pass on the faith by looking at the angel Gabriel and the way he relates to Mary and to learn how God exquisitely relates to man.

The angel Gabriel is lower than Mary and yet he is passing on the message from God. You have to realize the message is from God, not your own. You are passing on something utterly precious. That whole dialogue between the angel Gabriel and Our Lady is a fantastic model of passing on. When Our Lady says, "what does this mean?" and "how can this be?" it is so wonderful. Her response is so positive. All we must do through the account of the Annunciation as human beings is recognize the need to receive the truth of the message of Christ and hear it in such a way that we can respond like Our Lady.'

I ask why the phrase 'Do not be afraid' has been chosen as part of the logo for the School of the Annunciation.

'Do not be afraid of the Good News,' she replies. 'Don't be afraid to learn. It's all good. It's all from God. Be ready to receive. A lot of people are afraid of the Catholic teaching, especially the moral teaching. But you will hear it here as something beautiful and you don't have to be afraid. If you are receptive, the Holy Spirit will do the work in you. You become more free, the more you are receptive.'

Does she see herself playing a similar role to Gabriel in that she is passing on the message from God?

'Yes, we are messengers. Human messengers,' she replies. 'You've got it. It's such extraordinary stuff,' she responds.

Where does her calling come from?

'If it's a vocation or a charism, God has put it in me. It's not my own,' she says.

Extraordinarily intense now, I move the conversation on to discuss different paintings of the Annunciation. She shows me various pictures and icons that she uses in her teaching. Then we look at Lemoyne's depiction.

'I think different artists had different depths themselves for understanding the account of the Annunciation,' she observes. 'You can look at different images and some would have more depths in them than others. Fra Angelico, rooted in the love of the psalms and the liturgy, has heard year after year about Adam and Eve, the promise to Abraham, and all that. He understands through the liturgy of Our Lady that he will have been participating in purposefully and receptively, such that he was clearly able to put into a painting what other artists couldn't do. They put into a painting technical expertise but they couldn't necessarily put in the grace and the truth that could enable a picture to carry the depths of what's going on in the Annunciation.'

She holds the Lemoyne print closely and studies it methodically.

'What Lemoyne tries to do with all the clouds and the cherubs is show there is something of the divine uniting with the humility and purity of the woman. That's another way of doing it. The almightiness of God and the angel is not of this world – there's a message there. It's one way of doing it. There's that fabulous passage in one of the Prophets: "Pull back the curtain of your tent because your maker is to espouse you to himself forever".'

She points to the curtain behind Mary on the left of the picture. I tell her very few people notice that particular feature. I explain that some also see the breaking of the plaster on the wall as a breaking through of the message.

'Lots of nativity scenes,' she replies, 'have broken stones and broken plaster a) as part of the poverty and b) to show the old covenant is breaking down now and the new covenant is born. The heart of stone is being changed for the heart of flesh.'

As she keeps looking at the painting, she notes that Mary has been reading Isaiah and that the sheet of paper on the floor means the sign is now being fulfilled. She looks at the white linen in the basket.

'The white linen cloth means a lot of things,' she says. 'The swaddling clothes and the corporal clothes of burial. The white cloth wrapped around Christ at birth and death. I would say the whole sweeping arm of the angel is too dominant to what I read. I don't think that angel, theologically, is very good. There's something about the angel I don't consider sufficiently helpful to understand the angelic world at the moment here.'

When I ask whether she likes the painting, she hesitates before responding.

'I say to my students I don't mind them saying they don't like a painting. But sometimes, the more I investigate a picture, the more I see in it, the more I want it on my wall, and I then realize it's an amazing picture. So don't worry about whether you like it or not. More, stop and see what's being said here. Once you know the message, it might change your experience of the visual.'

I tell her that some people find it too saccharine or too flamboyant, or they don't like the angel's finger. She acknowledges these views and nods her head, 'Yes, yes, yes.' It's as though she needs permission to criticize it.

'I really try to help people to be receptive to the message,' she says almost apologetically. 'Many young people don't go with any of this. Their eyes are not attuned to beauty anymore. They've gone down a different path. I'm not saying...' She stops her train of thought.

What would appeal to them? I ask.

'That's a good question,' she replies. 'I try to re-form them. Let someone tell you what beauty is and let yourself be soaked in that.'

I tell her that I ask everyone I meet on my journey the same question: is the story fact, metaphor or something else?

'Yes, one has to understand how the Church sees Scripture as a) divinely inspired and b) truth. What the Church says is the Scriptures are the truth that we need for salvation. That's a very careful distinction of what is meant by faith. It's the truths we need for our sake. So I accept that story as truth that we all need for understanding who God is, how Christ has come into the world in order to bring us home to our Father's house.'

If it is truth rather than fact, I start to ask, but she intervenes before I finish the question.

'It's absolutely fascinating. Catholics say Genesis is so deeply true that it can only be given to us in a story form. It's containing such a truth of divine mystery. That somehow such a simple story, with just a few words, can carry the depths of truth more than explaining every tiny detail – this happened, that happened, I don't know what.'

I am listening to her really carefully. She has slowed right down now and is delivering her words with clear precision.

'The Incarnation is impossible to explain. It's almost beyond human understanding. But the story of the Annunciation, the moment of the Incarnation, is truth. Yes, and everything in this story is even more true than how we read it at a literal level. That's true as well. The spiritual depths of meaning depend always on the truth of the literal.'

So, does she believe the story is literally true?

'Yes, that's right,' she replies. 'It's both. God did create Mary as a human person. I do believe the Annunciation happened. That's how the Church understands the literal truth. But it's a much bigger truth about divinity and humanity coming together. Exactly...the whole of Scripture operates in the same way.'

What about those Christians who say that the encounter never happened and the story is only a metaphor?

'Metaphors are very interesting,' she responds. 'The problem with that is that you are removing Jesus and the Incarnation as a historical act. The most important event in human history. You're saying it all depends on how we see things in our heads. That it is all to do with my set of beliefs. So long as what's going on up here,' she points to her head, 'guiding my life, that's enough. The Catholic Church doesn't follow that at all. If something is not objectively so, then we shouldn't be telling it...the faith of the Church over two thousand years doesn't go along with that interpretation. That is somebody's way of working it out for themselves.'

Does it trouble her in any way that the story is only mentioned in Luke?

'No, because the four Gospels give us everything we need together for what we need to know about truth,' she replies.

But if the Annunciation is the most important event in human history, is it not remarkable, I suggest, that the Gabriel-Mary encounter is not even mentioned in the other three canonical Gospels?

'They've obviously come from different groups of disciples,' she responds. 'This wasn't an event that was widely known. It has to have come from Our Lady. There's no one else who could have said anything about it. Someone has heard this from her as a very precious, intimate encounter that has then been passed on to Luke. Then later, John may have thought, I have not been a witness to this, and left it out. But he's writing a very different account anyway.'

I observe how the feast of the Annunciation is hardly marked now, even by practising Catholics. She concedes that its status has been somewhat lost.

'It's because he's conceived. How many women know when they conceived? It's very, very hard. Yes, he becomes known at that point. I do wonder whether contraception has affected people's thoughts. We've crept into a conception being less relevant than the actual birth.'

We've been going for nearly two hours, much longer than either of us had envisaged. She says she has enjoyed the conversation.

'Mary had the freedom to say no,' she reflects as we draw to a close. 'And remember, she is also saying yes to the likelihood of being stoned to death. She's saying yes to the Incarnation and also to her own death, if that's what it's going to mean. That receptivity is such an extraordinary act.'

I leave her office and rush back to the Abbey to attend Midday Office with the monks and then walk with them to the refectory to have lunch. Once more, the meal is taken in total silence. A slice of meat pie and vegetables is offered with a glass of water. I spend much of the afternoon in the monks' private library reading the *Catholic Catechism* and passages from theological books about the Annunciation before retiring to my room to read a homily about Mary, posted on the Buckfast Abbey website:

> Belief in the Incarnation, with the Sacrifice of the Cross, together form the bedrock of faith in the Holy Eucharist. Because of Mary, we are all able to be one with Jesus, spiritually and physically. Is it little wonder that those who have little or no regard for Mary and shy away from her veneration also have a weakened understanding and respect for the Holy Eucharist and can even attack and belittle the doctrine...Through Mary we have, today, the possibility of a share in the life of God. By grace we may be united to Christ, and in Christ become the adopted sons and daughters of God.

I continue to search different posts about Buckfast Abbey and its monastic community on my iPad. Suddenly, by chance, I find a series of news reports from eight years ago that shock me to the core. The previous Abbot, Philip Manahan, resigned in 2006 and a year later was sent to prison for fifteen months for sexually abusing boys in the 1970s at the

Buckfast Abbey Preparatory School that has since closed. Two years previously, another monk, Paul Couch, was jailed for ten years for a string of sexual abuse offences.

I go for a walk by the River Dart. It is such a beautiful and tranquil place and the monastic community here seem completely devoted to God and to Benedictine values. But the revelations have made me feel uneasy and angry. Of course, those past incidents have nothing whatsoever to do with the new School of the Annunciation but the enjoyment of the day has been significantly tarnished and diminished.

Later in the afternoon, I return to the School of the Annunciation to meet Fr Guy de Gaynesford, Rector with responsibility for overall governance and the spiritual welfare of the students. The priest sits behind his desk with a Fra Angelico painting of the Annunciation on the wall. I ask him to explain the vision for the school.

'It's all about the phrase, "the new evangelization" and making that phrase realistic. It's vital for the Church, particularly in the West. It's about calling all nations to Christ. The purpose of the Church, as well as being a field hospital, is also to be the tool of evangelisation of proclaiming Our Lord, making it possible in order to bring salvation to the human race.'

But why has it been called the School of the Annunciation?

'The Annunciation has this extraordinary profound and prominent place,' he responds. 'It's the only place in the Creed where we make a physical act of reverence, to bow. It used to be to kneel. Think also of the devotion to the Angelus. That's focused on the Annunciation too. The Church keeps coming back to the Annunciation. It is the most beautiful description of what a catechist is. The School of the Annunciation will walk in the footsteps of the archangel Gabriel, the messenger who carries the invitation of God to a human being with absolute authenticity. He gives the message to Mary in such a way so she can understand. It's not over-technical. It's not dumbed down. You could say that every single Christian is called to echo the role of the archangel Gabriel in the Annunciation. Every Christian.'

What does he think is the spiritual meaning of the story of the Annunciation?

'Firstly, God wants to be heard and he wants me to hear him,' he says. 'He's not running away from me. He's there. So keep listening because he wants to be heard. It's a reassurance to me. Secondly, what happens within Our Lady biologically is what God is seeking to do in you and me supernaturally, spiritually. She's conceived the person of Our Lord within her. Grace conceives within us, through the sacraments, the person of Our Lord. The Annunciation describes that as an analogy for what God is doing within me, and that's very moving.'

After Vespers, I head to the dining room for supper. One of the monks passes me a pamphlet, with a marked-up page called 'The spirit of the true Oblate'.

'You may not want to be a Benedictine monk but you may want to live by the Benedictine values,' he whispers. 'If you feel the calling, remember, you can live life to the full outside but in the true spirit of the Rule of St Benedict.'

I smile politely, thank him for the information and take the pamphlet back to my room.

At 9 p.m. I return to the Abbey to join the monks for the last time, at Compline. At the end of the service, in semi-darkness, we stand in front of Our Lady of Buckfast in the Lady Chapel in the north transept. It's a flamboyant medieval statue. Mary is richly robed and wears a gold and jewelled crown whilst holding in her arms the young boy Jesus, who carries a sovereign orb. Desecrated in the sixteenth century, the statue was restored in 1903 after it was found hidden in a wall of the ruins of the original monastery building.

Before the Benedictine monks head to their cells for the night, they sing their communal prayer, '*Memorare, O piissima Virgo Maria,*' in front of the statue:

> Remember, O most loving Virgin Mary,
> that never was it known
> that anyone who fled to your protection,
> implored your help,
> or sought your intercession
> was left unaided.
> Inspired by this confidence,
> I fly to you.
> O Virgin of virgins, our Mother!
> To you I come,
> before you I stand,
> sinful and sorrowful.
> O Mother of the Word Incarnate,
> despise not my petitions,
> but in your mercy
> hear and answer me.
> Amen.

Between Exeter and Honiton, just off the main A30, is one of England's most beautiful medieval churches. The parish church at Ottery St Mary is dedicated to the Blessed Virgin and the list of its vicars can be traced back as far as the late twelfth century. The present edifice was the work of John de Grandisson, Bishop of Exeter, who built it in 1342 as a Collegiate church on the lines of Exeter Cathedral.

Above the Chancel, at the centre of the fan tracery, are a series of five fourteenth-century ceiling bosses, which include: a depiction of Mary with her mother, Anna; the Annunciation; the Virgin and Child; and the Coronation of the Virgin. In the Choir, on the magnificent west face of the St Mary's Altar Screen, is another carving of the Annunciation. The original screen was smashed during the Reformation and covered over with plaster. In 1935 this sculpture by Herbert Read of Exeter was inserted, together with a crucifixion and nativity scene.

139. Tiled altar screen of the Annunciation, Lady Chapel, St Mary's Church, Ottery St Mary, Devon

Further east in the Lady Chapel is perhaps the most interesting decoration: a striking altarpiece of the Annunciation made from painted tiles. The tiles tell the story behind its creation: 'To the Glory of God and in memory of Percy Duke Coleridge, Lieutenant and Adjutant, Plymouth Divisional Royal Marine Light Infantry, who was accidentally killed at Devonport in the execution of his duty on 29 March 1881, aged 30 years. This tablet is erected by his fellow officers in affectionate remembrance of one who, both in public and private life, was respected and beloved by them all.'

The most famous son of Ottery St Mary is another Coleridge – poet, philosopher and naturalist Samuel Taylor Coleridge, who was born in 1772. He grew up in the town and regularly attended services in the parish church. One legendary local story describes his ability to read a chapter of the Bible at the age of three.

Coleridge's life was dominated by 'a quest for the truth'. A preacher in Unitarian chapels throughout the country, his love of 'the Great and the Whole' dominated his life as he tried to reconcile the scientific and philosophic thought of the day with his Christian beliefs. As the story board in the church and an accompanying leaflet proclaim, he opposed purely rational explanations and emphasized that poetic imagination was as valid and valued as scientific evidence and rational thought. He was an apologist for the integration of Romanticism and Christianity, seeing imagination as the bridge between the two. He stressed the spiritual interpretation of life rather than one based on materialism and rationalism.

I wonder whether Samuel Taylor Coleridge's approach can help point the way to discovering the meaning and truth of Luke's story. Unfortunately, Coleridge did not write any poetry focused on the Annunciation. However, after leaving the stunning St Mary's, I sit in the tranquil churchyard and take out my poetry compendium. This time, I spend more than an hour reading five poems – all inspired by Luke's story and all created in the past thirty years by highly acclaimed female poets.

The first is titled 'The Annunciation' and was written in 1986 by the Oxford-based poet and devout Roman Catholic, Elizabeth Jennings, who died in 2001, aged 75:

> Nothing will ease the pain to come
> Though now she sits in ecstasy
> And lets it have its way with her.
> The angel's shadow in the room
> Is lightly lifted as if he
> Had never terrified her there.
>
> The furniture again returns
> To its old simple state. She can
> Take comfort from the things she knows
> Though in her heart new loving burns
> Something she never gave to man
> Or god before, and this god grows
>
> Most like a man. She wonders how
> To pray at all, what thanks to give
> And whom to give them to. "Alone
> To all men's eyes I must now go"
> She thinks, "And by myself must live
> With a strange child that is my own."
>
> So from her ecstasy she moves
> And turns to human things at last
> (Announcing angels set aside).
> It is a human child she loves
> Though a god stirs beneath her breast
> And great salvations grip her side.

Denise Levertov was born in the London suburb of Ilford in 1923 but lived most of her life in the United States. A prolific and highly respected poet, much of her work was grounded in religion. She died in 1997 in Seattle, aged 74. Her father was a Russian Jew who converted to Christianity, moved to England and became an Anglican minister. As a child, she was exposed to both Judaism and Christianity. Many of her poems, in her own words, 'trace my slow movement from agnosticism to Christian faith, a movement incorporating much doubt and questioning as well as affirmation.' Her poem, 'Annunciation', is often cited by priests and religious commentators when marking the feast day on 25th March.

Annunciation
'Hail, space for the unconfined God'
From the Agathistos Hymn,
Greece, VIc

We know the scene: the room, variously furnished,
almost always a lectern, a book; always
the tall lily.
      Arrived on solemn grandeur of great wings,
the angelic ambassador, standing or hovering,
whom she acknowledges, a guest.

But we are told of meek obedience. No one mentions
courage.
      The engendering Spirit
did not enter her without consent.
      God waited.

She was free
to accept or to refuse, choice
integral to humanness.

———

Aren't there annunciations
of one sort or another
in most lives?
      Some unwillingly
undertake great destinies,
enact them in sullen pride,
uncomprehending,
      More often
those moments
      when roads of light and storm
      open from darkness in a man or woman,
are turned away from

in dread, in a wave of weakness, in despair
and with relief.
Ordinary lives continue
      God does not smite them.
But the gates close, the pathway vanishes.

———

She had been a child who played, ate, slept
like any other child – but unlike others,
wept only for pity, laughed
in joy not triumph.
Compassion and intelligence
fused in her, indivisible.

Called to a destiny more momentous
than any in all of Time,
she did not quail,
        only asked
a simple, 'How can this be?'
and gravely, courteously, took to heart the angel's reply,
perceiving instantly
the astounding ministry she was offered:

to bear in her womb
Infinite weight and lightness; to carry
in hidden, finite inwardness,
nine months of Eternity; to contain
in slender vase of being,
the sum of the power -
in narrow flesh,
the sum of light.
               Then bring to birth,
push out into air, a Man-child
needing like any other,
milk and love

but who was God.

This was the moment no one speaks of,
when she could still refuse.

A breath unbreathed,
            Spirit,
                  suspended,
                         waiting.

————

She did not cry, 'I cannot. I am not worthy,'
Nor, 'I have not the strength.'
She did not submit with gritted teeth,
                  raging, coerced.
Bravest of all humans,
           consent illumined her.
The room filled with its light,
the lily glowed in it,
              and the iridescent wings.
Consent,
        courage unparalleled,
opened her utterly.

The American writer, Madeleine L'Engle was primarily a children's and young adult fiction author. An Episcopalian, she believed in universal salvation. Her religious meditations and spiritual writings often proved controversial. She died in 2007, aged 88. This poem, taken from *The Ordering of Love: The New and Collected Poems of Madeleine L'Engle*, was published a year after her death by Shaw Books and is titled 'After Annunciation':

> This is the irrational season
> When love blooms bright and wild
> Had Mary been filled with reason
> There'd have been no room for the child.

Another short poem comes from the American, Jean Valentine. Written in 2004, it is entitled simply 'Annunciation':

> I saw my soul become flesh   breaking open
> the linseed oil breaking over the paper
> running down   pouring
> no one to catch it   my life breaking open
> no one to contain it   my
> pelvis thinning out into God

The Christian poet, Luci Shaw, is Writer-in-Residence at Regent College, Vancouver, and a member of St Paul's Episcopal church across the US/Canada border in Bellingham, Washington. In her acclaimed 2006 collection, *Accompanied by Angels, Poems of the Incarnation*, there is this wonderful poem called 'Virgin':

> As if until that moment
> nothing real
> had happened since Creation
>
> As if outside the world were empty
> so that she and he were all
> there was – he mover, she moved upon
>
> As if her submission were the most
> dynamic of all works: as if
> no one had ever said Yes like that
>
> As if one day the sun had no place
> in all the universe to pour its gold
> but her small room

CHAPTER 35

HAIL!

Christmas is fast approaching and the Winchester Cathedral Choir is ready to perform at one of the biggest events of its year: the annual Advent Procession.

The Cathedral is plunged into darkness. Soon, we become aware of robed candle-bearers walking slowly up the nave and the side aisles, lighting the candles of the people who stand at the end of each row. They, in turn, light the candle of the person next to them and so on. At this point, candles are lit only at the west end of the Cathedral. Then, after a reading from Isaiah, people sitting in the lower part of the nave take part. The building gradually fills with golden light and half an hour later, it looks magical with more than fifteen hundred glowing candles held aloft. The slow movement from darkness to light, the Dean tells us, 'mirrors the journey from the darkness of sorrow and death into the light of Christ's dawning kingdom of justice and joy.'

Half way through the service, Sue Wallace, the Precentor and Sacrist, walks to the podium and reads Luke's story of the Annunciation. She may not have the same rich intonation as David Suchet in Salisbury Cathedral, but she more than makes up for it in her emotional delivery. When she has finished, the final candles are lit on the nave altar and at the west end of the Quire. The congregation is deadly quiet, its candles creating a sea of shimmering lights.

Then, the silence is broken. In the far distance, the sound of four pure voices can be heard. The soprano, alto, tenor and bass quartet sing in unison: 'How shall this be, seeing I know not a man?'

The full, unaccompanied Winchester Cathedral Choir, comprising boys, girls and men, stands behind the nave altar and faces the congregation. With perfect timing, it responds to the question with a thunderous barrage of sound: 'Hail! Hail! Hail! Hail! Hail! Thou art highly favoured. Hail! The Lord is with thee. Hail! Blessed art though among women.'

The quartet asks meekly again, in soft, pure harmony: 'How can this be, seeing I know not a man?'

They sound even further away. The Choir responds again with the same dramatic chant, this time delivered even louder. The slow, repetitive exchange continues for over six minutes. The sound is extraordinary – powerful, emotional, magisterial, transcendent. At the end, there is a stunned silence. The woman sitting next to me takes a deep breath. Other members of the congregation look at each other and smile, some shaking their heads almost in disbelief.

We have been listening to Sir John Tavener's anthem *Annunciation* in which words from Luke's story are used to create a stunning sound.

'I get shivers down my spine when we perform it,' the Director of Music, Andrew Lumsden, told me earlier. 'It's very difficult to control the emotions afterwards. It just sails away around the whole building and you think, wow! That was really very special.

Our job as musicians is to uplift people and make them feel drawn to the faith and to God. That's the crux of what we do. And that is always one of the very big moments.'

I first heard the piece eight months earlier, performed by the Romsey Choral Society in St Cross church, Winchester as part of an evening of choral music called 'There's Something about Mary.' The Musical Director, Jamie Hall, also a member of the BBC Singers, told me in the interval what it was like to conduct the piece.

'Everyone has the experience of having a mother. It makes the experience more real. The ideas here are so massive. She's in shock. She's numb. She's drawing a blank. I think it's where we truly comprehend how huge this idea is. It's been going on since and will go on forever. I'm dipping into something that exists whether I'm there or not somehow. It's so meditative and makes you go somewhere else. Art misses a trick by presenting the angel basically as a person in fancy dress. There's no real sense of the awe that Mary must have felt. That for me is the key point and Tavener captures that brilliantly – the interaction between essentially the voice of God and Mary. The music tells me that he absolutely believes. He clearly believes what he's writing about. There's such an honesty there.'

Sir John Tavener was born in London in 1942 and died in 2013. He made a very striking figure: he was 6′ 6″ tall, had long blond hair and often wore white suits. He studied at the Royal Academy of Music, was a highly accomplished pianist, and became one of the most significant composers in British music in the past fifty years. His oeuvres ranged from large-scale choral and orchestral works to song cycles and string quartets. He was a deeply spiritual man with a profound conviction. As Sir Nicholas Kenyon, former Director of the BBC Proms and Controller BBC Radio 3, and now Managing Director of the Barbican, told me, he dedicated his life to music and religion but he never recognized a division between the two.

'For him, music was absolutely not an expression of the man but of man's aspiration towards the divine,' Sir Nicholas observed. Indeed, Tavener said himself that all good music comes from God. 'If I have no music, I have no God. The two are together,' he once explained.

His Christian faith took a convoluted route. His parents were Presbyterians and, as a child, he played the organ in his local church. He moved to Catholicism in early adulthood but left after finding it too oppressive. In 1977, he converted to the Orthodox Church, which he described as 'a homecoming'. Orthodox theology and liturgical traditions became a major influence in his work but towards the end of his life, he came to believe that all religions and denominations are part of the same thing – man's relation to what lies beyond – and he identified himself as an ecumenical 'universalist'. His most famous work is *Song for Athene*, sung as the recessional music at the funeral of Princess Diana in 1997 as the coffin was carried slowly down the nave before leaving Westminster Abbey. The impact was memorably haunting.

Roger Wright, the Controller of Radio 3 and Director of the Proms, tells me John Tavener was, 'such a distinctive voice compositionally. He cut through as a composer to general audiences but he was always his own person. If you hear ten bars of Tavener, it couldn't be anyone else. There's an honesty about his work that connects, a spirituality that was in him but was always questioning. He was always on a search and that's what made him such a compelling figure. For those of us who feel most comfortable in our faith when we are on the edge of doubt, you can see him too as someone struggling and always asking questions. I've known him a long time and last saw him just before his death in the cafe at Broadcasting House. As ever, we talked about ideas. In so much of John's work, he always talked about the text that had inspired him. That's where he started from. The texts inspired him and focused him.'

What makes Tavener such a distinctive voice?

'Some hear the music as endlessly repetitive,' he responds, 'but I hear it as an opportunity to ground you and enable you to go deeper into the textual material. It might not come back to you as the same sequence that you've just heard. It's like a favourite statue or painting you know really well. It sits there but in our lives, because we change and develop, our relationship to it changes. It's the same with John's music. There are elements to John's music that are simple but you can never describe his approach as simplistic. There's a lot of complex thought there.'

Tavener suffered from ill health for much of his life. In 1990, he was diagnosed with Marfan syndrome, a genetic disorder that causes disproportionately long limbs and a weak heart. He survived a stroke, the removal of a tumour, two heart attacks and a long drawn out coma. After a long period of frailty, he died in November 2013, aged sixty-nine.

His funeral service at Winchester Cathedral was one of the most extraordinary services ever to be held there. Lasting more than two hours and led jointly by His Eminence Archbishop Gregorios of Thyateira and Great Britain and the Dean of Winchester, James Atwell, much of the service focused on Tavener's great love for Mary as Theotokos – the God-bearer. Tavener's own compositions *Mother of God, here I stand* and *A Hymn to the Mother of God* were performed alongside prayers dedicated to Mary with words such as 'Hail, honoured one, who bore God in the flesh for the salvation of all' and 'Pure Virgin, gate of the Word.'

Sadly, I will never get to meet Sir John Tavener and will not have the opportunity to ask him about his composition. However, I want to discover what lay behind the creation of *Annunciation*, and what makes it such an emotional, absorbing and highly original piece. So I set out to meet three people who can offer me the best possible insights: Martin Neary, the organist and choral conductor who first requested the piece and conducted its premiere at Westminster Abbey; Sir Nicholas Kenyon who gave the main address at Tavener's memorial service at Westminster Abbey; and Sir John's widow, Lady Maryanna Tavener, who vividly remembers it being composed at their home.

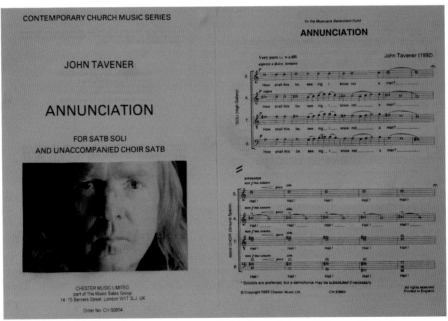

140. John Tavener *Annunciation*, 1992. By kind permission of Chester Music Ltd

I am in seventy-three-year-old Martin Neary's front room, listening to him playing the opening part of Tavener's *Annunciation* on the piano. He seems relaxed, and wears a light blue open-necked shirt and navy blue V-neck pullover. The room is filled with books, paintings, manuscripts and family photographs but the piano dominates. As Musical Director at Winchester Cathedral, and then Organist and Master of the Choristers at Westminster Abbey, Martin Neary knew Tavener well – indeed they were close friends – and he conducted more than twenty premieres of his works. In 1992 the Musicians Benevolent Fund approached Martin Neary, requesting a new commission. He recalls hearing from John's publisher, Chester Music, that the composer was working on a new work focusing on the Annunciation.

'I had no idea what he was going to produce at all,' he tells me. 'It wasn't a request specifically for an Annunciation piece. I explained to him there'd be a large choral group. That, of course, greatly appealed to him and also being able to use the vast open spaces of the Abbey, where there could be echo effects, spaces of intimacy and also huge grandeur.

'He was living in Sussex then and I went down to see him. The first time he showed it to me I was startled, even before he played a note. He showed me the text: "How shall this be, seeing I know not a man?" Throughout his creative life, he picked up on unusual texts. As soon as he started playing it, I heard that very questioning open chord.'

He starts to play, reading the manuscript in front of him.

'It's nearly pure harmony and then there's this extra note – the C sharp against the D – as if he's really trying to work out "how shall this be?"…and in great humility,' he says. 'He was greatly conscious of the humility of Mary.' He continues following Tavener's score.

'He could write just one simple phrase like that, and that's all it is, but somehow it registered immediately. One of his extraordinary gifts was to write in such a way that it touched people. A lot of people would have thought it was too simple but no, it went straight there.' He points to his heart. 'After that questioning, we then have this theophany, this huge sense of wonder, which was really the same chord, but with this extra ingredient.'

His hands strike the keys hard as he sings, 'Hail! Hail!'

'That's so incredibly passionate,' he says. 'I remember John would have to take a breath at every phrase. So you have a contrast between this meek question and then, bang! I mean it's so full of drama. It's the sweep of it all. He has a concept of a mood. You can feel that in the specific phrases. A question suspended and then answered by this extraordinary response. It's beyond just musical. It's using music to transport you into a deeper spirituality about it. That's how he actually felt about it. As ever, it was his personal interpretation of a Marian story. He felt so deeply about the humility of the woman but also this incredible sense of adoration. These are the two extraordinary elements you can hear. I remember he sang it to me in a pretty breathy manner but with such passion. You could tell, as he was playing, how it just came forth. It was a total addiction to him. I remember wondering if part of it sounded too grim, almost gruesome. But somehow, it was so extraordinary. He had such an ear and I thought it became increasingly beautiful. What he felt so much was a melody. He had a great gift for melody and this extraordinary musical invention – going upside down, then back to front.'

I am sitting right next to him as he plays. It is like being part of a masterclass. Martin Neary recalls how he and Tavener sat like this at the time.

'John got very excited when I suggested to him how he could take advantage of the vast spaces of the Abbey and put the distant quartet up at the Henry V Chantry, seventy yards away. John loved spacial elements. On the morning of the service, when the piece began, nobody knew where anything was.' He chuckles and continues playing. 'How shall this be?' he sings again. 'We're waiting for that response of total acceptance. The way he created that sense of drama was superb. He immediately hit the spot. I wonder how many pictures of the Annunciation can manage to bring that shock, that sense of astonishment.'

Twenty years on, Tavener's *Annunciation* has become part of the regular canon of Advent services all over the country.

Is there one single ingredient above all others that makes it so great? I ask.

'The originality,' he replies immediately. 'It suited John's vision of religion, which was to be so much in awe and majesty and yet be so incredibly intimate. Over time, whenever you go back to it, you find something new. The more times you hear it, the more you realize what's in it. I can feel his passion. We came from different religious traditions but there was a complete rapport between us. His music has made so much impact. Some critics couldn't take the repetitive religiosity of his work and they said it was too long. But I think he was a genius. He had this endless fascination with the eternal feminine. For him, it meant purity, something beyond him, acutely beautiful and touching, and he used these Marian pieces as a starting point for his own adoration.'

I ask him to play the whole piano version of *Annunciation*. Luckily, he agrees and for six minutes, I enter another world. At the end, I ask Martin Neary whether the piece, in any way, made him re-interpret his own thoughts on the annunciation story.

'Definitely, definitely,' he replies. 'First of all, that arresting opening, with those words: "How shall this be?" It's so easy for us to assume that everyone knows this is how the Virgin Birth happened. No! Let's take this on board. Did the Virgin Birth actually happen? How could this be? He brought it alive. The beauty and the shaping of it. How did Jesus enter into the world? You don't necessarily understand it any more but you are gripped by the concept. I think John's piece does something that words alone can't do. That's great music's power, isn't it? It goes beyond the expression of words.

'The comprehension of the Annunciation is beyond me,' he continues, 'but that doesn't mean I don't believe it. In a way, it doesn't matter that I can't comprehend it. I would not go so far as to say, just because it can't be proven, that I dispute it. When you hear John's piece, it makes you want to believe it and it makes me believe it and to love the concept, whatever it is. It's the exultation matched by the lowliness. John loved that.'

Before I leave, I place the print of the Lemoyne painting on the music desk next to the sheet music of Tavener's *Annunciation* and ask Martin Neary to comment.

'Oh, John would have loved it,' he responds as he sits on the piano stool looking at the picture. 'He would have loved the eroticism of it. Particularly the angel and that finger. How many Annunciation paintings are there with a finger like that? It's very striking. And the sense of enrapture. Those eyes of Mary. It's all pointing to those eyes and her joyful acceptance. It's a very, very, very powerful picture. Oh yes, John would have loved this one.'

————————

I am attending a service of thanksgiving for the life and work of Sir John Tavener. The congregation in Westminster Abbey is an eclectic mix. His Royal Highness, the Prince of Wales is here; it is well known that he is a huge admirer of Tavener. I can see the choral composer John Rutter and the former Rolling Stones bassist Bill Wyman. The acclaimed soprano, Patricia Rozario and the cellist Steven Isserlis both perform. The order of service is a unique mixture of Orthodox chants and prayers, High Anglican ceremonial and the performance of some of Tavener's most acclaimed works. The former Controller of Radio 3 and Director of the Proms, Sir Nicholas Kenyon, now Managing Director of the Barbican Centre, delivers the main address. 'He was never a remote or theoretical composer but passionately involved in performance,' he says. 'Music was his lifeblood. He always wanted to communicate. There was no one quite like him.'

Later, I head to Nick Kenyon's office at the Barbican. I want to learn more.

'He was a totally individual figure and one of the most significant voices in British music of the past hundred years,' he tells me. 'He leads you to another dimension.'

Was the music a reflection of his spirituality or of his search for spirituality?

'That's a very good distinction. A bit of both. He doesn't give you something instantly harmonious or instantly static. There's a process of getting towards it, which often involves dissonance, conflict, and then there's something that is arrival and consonance. It wouldn't be as effective if it didn't have that sense of struggle, that sense of search in it. He had this extraordinary spiritual quest. His whole life was a quest. He was still exploring different avenues of spirituality right to the end.'

We move on to focus specifically on *Annunciation*.

'You're seeing action and reaction and isn't that one of the things about the Annunciation that is key? She's going about her ordinary business, doing the washing or whatever, and something happens suddenly, out of the ordinary, that is going to completely change her life. You have here what is the reaction to this eruption, what we would now call a supernatural or spiritual force that has an incredibly practical impact on her. She's no longer just going to continue doing the washing. Her life will change forever. This is the moment. There's something symbolic in the separation of the forces here.'

He plays a CD track of the Westminster Abbey Choir's 1994 recording of *Annunciation* conducted by Martin Neary. The sound fills his office.

'I haven't heard this for ages,' he shouts above the music from across the other side of the room. 'Call and response. That's the idea of it. It's almost as though you have to say these things three times in order to get them through. It's not that she doesn't believe it. It's just that the import doesn't really strike home. Then she suddenly realizes, "this is going to change my life forever".'

Sixty-three-year-old Nick Kenyon, wears a light blue open-necked shirt and black suit, and walks around the room as he listens intently to the track. He stops often to close his eyes and stroke his chin in deep concentration.

'There's something about the way he designs these pieces. There's a beautiful plan with these five chords on the "Hail!" and then from the call, the response. You feel the puzzlement because the import doesn't get through. When someone says something to you important, you often don't get it right away. You have to let it soak through and absorb it. It's like saying, "Your father is dead." You can imagine receiving it but you have to take time to understand the full import and for it to strike home.' Another sequence of 'Hails!' plays out. 'Ah, the call to attention again,' he proclaims. "This is really important, don't turn away and keep doing the washing up. I've got something really important to say here." That's absolutely incredible. So typical of the way John stretches things out. That huge bass note there and the increasing elaboration to draw you in. It's wonderful, isn't it?'

When the track finishes, I show him the print of Lemoyne's *The Annunciation*.

'It's incredibly beautifully put together and proportioned. That's one thing I see,' he says. 'In contrast to the music we've just heard, I see her here as very accepting, very compliant, whereas before we heard Mary questioning and reflective. She looks very obedient here. She's very honoured. "How kind of you to come," he laughs, screwing up his face in mirth. 'Mm, that finger pointing up beyond, and I see the angel has a supporting chorus [the cherubim] to re-enforce the message,' he chuckles. 'It's not my style of painting. I find in this period, there's too much focus on the purely beautiful. I like the medieval period where you get the real sense of ritual, of confrontation, and what the angel will expect of her. They're a bit too complicit here. The interesting question is would Tavener have liked it as a picture? Would he feel it matched his spirituality? My instinct is "not quite" but I may be completely wrong. I don't know.'

Nick Kenyon was educated at St Bede's College, the independent Roman Catholic school in south Manchester. What does the former choirboy think is the meaning of the annunciation story?

'One always has to be open to the possibility of something coming along that can disrupt your life and expectations, and you need to be aware that that could happen at any moment,' he replies. 'Some of us who've had life too easy and do something we love as a job probably ought to be a bit more aware of the possibility of something that can disrupt all that, just like that.' He clicks his fingers.

Does he see the story as fact?

'Mm,' he says as he puts his right hand on his chin again. 'Like so many of the stories associated with biblical tradition, I see it as meaningful myth. It embodies a great truth so that the actual factual accuracy of it is not the main point about it. The central message is of accepting something from the outside over which you have no control. The possibility of shock. It could happen tomorrow. Who knows?'

———

In 1985, Maryanna Schaefer was studying Physics at Oxford University when she was invited to accompany her father to the dedication of a Cecil Collins stained-glass window. The venue was All Saints church, Basingstoke and John Tavener's *Angels* was being premiered there that same night. Later, she met the composer in the nearby vicarage and went to a talk he gave in Oxford the following week. He sent her a composition he wrote specially for her but they did not see each other again for four years. They came into contact again when *The Protecting Veil* was first performed at the Royal Albert Hall. They arranged to meet and he took her out a few times in his Bentley. Initially, she thought he was too tall, too longhaired and too old, but within two years they were married. He was forty-seven, she was in her mid-twenties. Tavener had been married seventeen years earlier but had never left his parents' home in Wembley Park and his first marriage collapsed after just eight months.

A few days ago, Lady Maryanna Tavener returned to the city to hear *Annunciation* being performed in Winchester College Chapel. I arrange to meet her in Winchester Cathedral and we sit in the same place she occupied during her husband's funeral service. She talks about hearing *Annunciation* again.

'It's so wonderful to be reminded of it,' she tells me. 'Every time I hear it, it's so stunning, so forceful and yet deeply accepting at the same time. It's so beautiful and spacious. It has such a huge sense of space. I always love hearing it now more than when he was alive, partly because I don't have his anxiety sitting next to my elbow, which took up quite a lot of space, and partly because I'm constantly amazed how brilliant the music is. I wasn't thinking in those terms at the time he was alive. All the performances we ever heard together, he was so nervous and I was anxious for him. You couldn't really entirely listen. But now it's like a gift. When he wrote that, he meant one hundred per cent what he was writing. You can hear the effort in him trying to communicate the text.'

They were married in September 1991 and he wrote the piece in the first year of their marriage. Does she remember him composing it?

'Yes, I remember him being quite excited,' she recalls. 'It was March 25, the feast of the Annunciation, and I remember getting a card from Mother Thekla on my "second birthday". He started working on it that day and finished it four days later on the twenty-ninth.'

Mother Thekla was a Russian Orthodox Prioress who lived in a small monastery on the North York Moors near Whitby. She became John Tavener's spiritual mother and muse after his mother's death in 1985 and was also, on occasions, his librettist.

Was the composition in any way connected with those first few weeks of marriage? I wonder.

'Yes, I do think it was connected,' she says. 'The Mother of God, as Mary is in the Orthodox Church, was always incredibly important to John, and her struggle and then acceptance as a young woman was something he loved. We'd got married and moved into our house in December 1991. He was forty-seven and still lived at home with his parents. So it was a huge change. We got married on the understanding he would at least consider having children. I wouldn't have done it if that hadn't been the case. He had to accept the possibility. Did we try straight away? The possibility was there but you need some breathing space in that first year of settling in, don't you? But let's say the idea of children was more than in the air.'

She lets out a cheeky chuckle and looks at me with a twinkle in her eyes.

'I'd never been baptized as a child but when I met John and Mother Thekla, his friend, I joined the Orthodox Church. I was baptized on the Annunciation Day and was known as Maryanna.'

So the story of the Annunciation, I suggest, has huge significance for her personally and for them as a couple.

'Yes, John found that wonderful,' she replies. 'That's why he wrote the piece two years later on the "second birthday" of my baptism, on Annunciation Day, and also at the beginning of a marriage where he was accepting that children would be in the air. It's terribly powerful and terribly sensitive. I hear it as John's vision of the Annunciation and the power he felt about it.'

Two years after their marriage, Maryanna gave birth to a daughter, Theodora. Three years later, they had Sofia and in 2006, they had a son, Orlando.

'I remember, [when *Annunciation* was finished] he and his composer manager, James, looked for a commission,' she says. 'That's important when you're newly married and have a mortgage. I think this commission came up quickly. Martin Neary came down to our house in Sussex and John played it to him with a view to it being premiered at that St Cecilia Day concert in Westminster Abbey. John was so happy because it was such an ideal event, in a beautiful building, with a beautiful choir. I also remember going with him to the premiere at that St Cecilia's Day event. We both instantly loved it when he first composed it. It was so powerful. But I remember the anxiety of him listening to it that day. He knew it would be performed well but he worried so much inside.'

I comment that it seems Mary – Theotokos – was very important to him.

'Yes, she was an inspiration and a refuge as well from difficult, other relationships,' she responds. 'A completely safe place at the root of the Church.'

Did he ever reach the destination on his long search before he died?

'No. He was completely happy with Mary and the Orthodox Church but he also recognized she was present in the Islamic world and in some Indian theology. He was always searching.'

What did the story of the Annunciation mean for him?

'You can hear it in the music. It was an aural embodiment of complete human acceptance of the power of God, and accepting that truth and taking it into your own body.'

Does she see the story as fact?

'The marvellous thing is we really don't know what happened,' she says. 'It could have been a physical reality. I'm happy to think that it was a physical possibility and that it might have happened.'

Before we go our separate ways, I show her the print of Lemoyne's painting.

'It's a really wonderful picture,' she says. 'I can see the "Hail!" through the finger and the sun. It's quite a musical painting. She's deeply accepting. It's terribly western. It's not like an icon. But I can hear John's music when I look at it.'

As I leave the Cathedral, I remind myself of some words Sir John Tavener spoke on the occasion of his sixtieth birthday: 'The one thing that exists is God. Everything else is an illusion. If you love someone, you don't really love that person, you love God. I can't see it any other way. There's only one being, one thing. There's only one God and only one thing that exists, and that is God. We are God and we have to find that in ourselves. It's you and I, there is no other. It's all one.'

––––––––––

A year later, a special Choral Evensong is held in Winchester Cathedral to celebrate Sir John Tavener and his close connections with the Cathedral. Canon Roly Riem describes how Tavener can 'drill further into our hearts' and Canon Brian Rees says, 'he leads us higher to the mystery that is God' through his music, which is 'like an icon in sound'. Church leaders from both the Anglican Communion and the Orthodox Church are present and the Cathedral is full.

Lady Maryanna Tavener looks proudly towards her son, Orlando, now a Cathedral chorister. I catch her eye before she unveils a specially commissioned sculpture in memory of her late husband. The sculpture, by Angela Conner, is a waterfall of molten glass, and is on permanent display in the south presbytery aisle. The sculptor comments: 'Water is such a classical symbol for cleansing and John's work will flow on into the future and be part of the history of spiritual music.'

141. Angela Conner *Sir John Tavener Memorial*, 2016, Winchester Cathedral. © Joe Low

CHAPTER 36

WOW!

142. Advent calendar window for 1st December

It is time to open the first window of this year's Advent Calendar. As chance would have it, the picture inside is of a feminine looking angel Gabriel, about to make an announcement to Mary, accompanied by words from Luke 1:26-33. Soon, Christmas will be upon us.

Large billboards and magazine advertisements proclaim Winchester as 'England's Christmas Capital'. In recent years, the city has marketed itself heavily as the perfect place for Christmas shoppers to visit as the festive season approaches. The Christmas market in the Cathedral Close attracts 350,000 visitors from mid-November through to 20 December. Scores of coaches arrive each day. One hundred German-styled wooden chalets, located within the picturesque setting of the Cathedral's south precinct, offer luxury gifts, decorations and festive foods. An open-air ice rink, surrounded by illuminated Christmas trees, is also sited in the Inner Close with the magnificent medieval Cathedral as its backdrop. It is a magical sight.

This is a big commercial success story, bringing in hundreds of thousands of pounds to the Cathedral to help run its operations and maintain the magnificent building for the future. However, it is somewhat ironic that few of those queuing to visit the market will enter the Cathedral to visit the crib and contemplate the religious meaning of Christmas. The Dean of Winchester is keen to emphasize that as well as supporting the Cathedral's finances – it gets no funding for its upkeep from central government or the Church of England – the market also serves a pastoral role: 'We've put the Cathedral back at the heart of the community at Christmas and managed to make it a friendlier and welcoming place, where people feel at ease,' he says.

I am aware that for some years now I have felt increasingly disillusioned about the commercialisation of Christmas in Britain. But perhaps I should gain heart at the knowledge that every year the Cathedral is full to capacity – more than 1,000 people – for each of its three evening Christmas carol services.

I leave the Christmas market and head towards The Square, walking through an attractive avenue of twenty-eight lime trees, all festooned with white fairy lights. I call in at St Lawrence's church, a haven of peace from all the hustle and bustle. St Lawrence's stands on the site of the chapel of William the Conqueror's Palace. It is the only church of Norman foundation within the old city walls that survives as a parish church.

Inside, stuck to the right wall, is a large poster of a statue of the Virgin Mary that is located outside the Church of Santa Sofia in Anacapri on the Italian island of Capri. Next to it is a handwritten Advent meditative prayer: 'God our Father, the angel Gabriel told the Virgin Mary that she was to be the mother of your son. Though Mary was afraid, she responded to your call with joy. Help us, whom you call to serve you, to share like her in your great work of bringing to our world your love and healing. We ask this through Jesus Christ, the Light who is coming into the world.'

I sit there all alone and reflect on those words: 'The angel Gabriel told the Virgin Mary that she was to be the mother of your son.' There's little sense in this prayer of Mary's free will.

———

I leave the city centre and walk northwards up St Peter's Street, a place of special resonance for Roman Catholics in Winchester. A plaque on the Winchester Royal Hotel indicates it was once known as the Bishop's House and was a secret centre for local Catholics in the 1580s. Later, towards the end of the eighteenth century, it became a convent of refugee English Benedictine nuns. Further along the street I peer through a wrought iron gate and down an archway to see a stone statue of the Virgin Mary in a well-tended garden, next to what looks like a small Gothic styled chapel.

For more than two hundred years after the split with Rome, Mass was held secretly on this site in an upper room at St Peter's House. Then in 1740, a garden shed was converted into a tiny, makeshift chapel. In 1792, after John Milner arrived as the priest and the Roman Catholic Relief Act permitted Catholics to exercise their religion, he built a new chapel here dedicated to the Blessed Virgin Mary and St Peter, which served the city's Catholic community for the next 130 years. Importantly, this was the first Catholic church in England to be consecrated since the Reformation. When a new church, St Peter's, was built in the 1920s, it was no longer needed as a place of worship and became a community hall named Milner Hall. It was restored in the 1980s.

I open the thick wooden entrance door of the nearby St Peter's church and enter the building. The interior is dark and silent. All the church pillars are decked with flower arrangements, comprising red carnations, poinsettias, red berries and greenery. The glowing light of the sanctuary lamp hangs in front of the tabernacle, indicating the presence of the Blessed Sacrament. An electric light bulb illuminates the crib, which is positioned by the altar. Statues of Joseph and Mary are in the stable but no baby yet has been placed in the manger.

I am the only person around. I sit in a pew and start to read some words from a homily about the Annunciation, written by the resident priest, Canon Paul Townsend: 'In these days of scientific evidence being of paramount importance, the conception of Jesus through Mary's faith and the action of the Holy Spirit is, for some, hard to appreciate. Nevertheless, Mary's experience and example offers us all a challenge to really believe in the presence and action of God in our lives.'

———

I stop off for a coffee in a cafe on Jewry Street and open my iPad. An email from America has popped up in my Inbox. It is from an old friend, David Westin, who was President of ABC News in the United States for thirteen years from 1997 to 2010, and was responsible for all ABC's broadcast output across news and current affairs in one of the most prestigious jobs in American journalism.

'What a wonderful idea for a book,' he writes. 'Part Dan Brown, part *The Goldfinch*, part *The Girl with the Pearl Earring*, but all true. Congratulations both on having the idea and for pursuing it so thoroughly and creatively. I'm excited for you.'

'I've heard various sermons on the Annunciation, but haven't really given it much thought – with one tiny exception,' he continues. 'Three years ago, our church in Bronxville asked those of us who served as Elders (please don't laugh too hard) to write up very brief reflections on specific passages of Scripture around Christmas to be printed in the bulletins used for the various services. I was assigned the Annunciation. I'm attaching my very brief reflection, not for its profundity, but just to show the connections we happen upon in the most unlikely of places.'

I click on the attachment:

> The angel Gabriel comes to a young, unsuspecting girl and tells her in no uncertain terms that she will bear a child and that God will be the father. How many times have we heard sermons on this passage, sermons that make us marvel at how accepting Mary was, how trusting, how obedient? But I confess to always having one slight reservation. Mary did have a difficult path in front of her, but she also had the advantage of being certain that it was the path God wanted her to take. She did, after all, have an angel come and lay it out for her. Most of the time, I don't have that clarity about what is the 'right' path in a complicated world with so many competing interests and so many unintended consequences. Obedience is hard, but sometimes discernment is even harder. And perhaps the trickiest question of all is whether the two may be connected – whether we sometimes lack conviction about the right path to take because, deep down, we're not willing to take it. Unlike Mary.

It is a bitterly cold afternoon in Winchester. The sky is brilliant blue and the air is crisp. I am standing next to the tall, floodlit Christmas tree on the pedestrianized High Street, next to the Buttercross. Dressed in a black woollen overcoat, a scarf and blue jeans, I am holding a small notepad and pen, together with a black ring-file binder containing a large print of Lemoyne's painting. Around me swarm throngs of Christmas shoppers.

Two young women, raising funds for charity, play 'The Holly and the Ivy' on a flute and ukulele. Nearby, a market stallholder is doing a roaring trade selling woollen hats and scarves. Another is selling handcrafted bread and pastries; next to her is a man promoting various beers from the local Mash Brewery; further along, there is a meat stall called 'Flavours of South Africa' selling biltong, stokkies and boerewors. Kevin, The Big Issue seller, wears a Santa Claus hat and a Christmas tree cape over his donkey jacket. Many people have been to the Christmas Market and are continuing to shop or are returning to their cars and homes.

So, what am I doing here? Lately, I have become aware of some recent research from the highly reputable US based Pew Research Center. Its findings suggest that in the UK, if current trends continue, the proportion of the population identifying themselves as Christians will fall from 64 per cent in 2010 to 45 per cent by 2050. The proportion of the population claiming no religion at all – the 'unaffiliated' – will also rise significantly from 28 per cent to 39 per cent. In response to the Pew Report, Linda Woodhead, Professor of Sociology of Religion at Lancaster University, told BBC News, 'We are living through the biggest religious transition since the Reformation of the sixteenth century.'

However, Justin Welby, the Archbishop of Canterbury, has a different view. At a New Wine leadership conference, he stated, 'The long years of winter in the Church, especially in the Church of England, are changing. The spring is coming. The ice is thawing. There is a new spring in the Church. There is no despair in the Church because we serve the God who raised Jesus Christ from the dead.'

I want to find who has judged the mood of the British public most accurately and the reason I am standing on Winchester High Street clutching my folder is because I have decided to conduct my own mini survey. I am just hoping people will not think I am odd, and scurry away before I have had a chance to chat with them. Conscious that most of the people I have encountered on this journey are Christians or have some Christian belief, I am hoping that this moment on the High Street will provide a more accurate flavour of the voice of the people. Of course it is far from being a scientifically robust sample size but I think it is worth a try.

During the afternoon I speak to a cross section of the population: men and women, teenagers, young adults, middle aged and the elderly. Only one person tells me to 'bugger off'. Two think I am a 'chugger' and say they haven't the time. Incredibly, thirty-two agree to stop and converse.

I want to know how many people have heard of the annunciation story, what they think it means and whether they believe it happened. I show each person the image of the painting as an introduction. Only five people recognize its subject matter, although eleven identify that Mary is standing next to an angel. Just three people say they know about the annunciation story and after I give them a quick explanation, more than twenty others tell me they definitely don't believe it, five say they do and the rest don't know.

'It's a religious painting and that means very little to me,' says Mary, a middle-aged woman. 'I'm not religious. I remember the story at primary school. It meant something then but not now. I like art but not religious art.'

Lee from South Africa says, 'It has no meaning.' She adds, 'I'm not religious.'

Dennis is retired, having served in the Army. 'It's the lady and the what do you call him? I don't believe it. Serving in the army taught me how bad religion is. People have been kicking the shit out of each other for six millennia and more often than not it's been about religion. It's a bad thing is religion. Not good. I quite like the painting but not the subject. No, not at all.'

Joao is a young man from Portugal. 'It's the Virgin Mary and an angel…yes? The meaning? It is nothing. I am agnostic.'

Jasmine is a Sikh married to a Christian. 'We go to church for the children,' she tells me. 'We tell them there's one God but different messengers – Jesus, Guru Nanak, Buddha, Mohammad. They're all friends up there with God. It's a nice painting but as a Sikh it means little to me.'

A man in his thirties gives me short shrift. 'It's religious is that,' he says looking at the painting. 'That's enough for me. No thank you. No religion. Never.'

Cambridge educated barrister Jonathan recognizes the painting as, 'Mary and something…Oh yes, an angel! I didn't see the wings.'

I tell him it is called *The Annunciation*.

'What's that?' he replies.

I say it means the announcement.

'Of what?' he asks.

'The conception of Jesus.'

'Isn't it awful that I didn't know,' he responds. 'It's symbolic. People needed meaning all those years ago. It was all symbolic.'

'I've never believed any of it,' another woman says. 'It's invention. We question much more nowadays and that's good. Of course, it never happened.'

The painting intrigues a middle-aged man.

'It looks French to me – rather baroque in style. Those cherubim. It's the Annunciation, of course. It's the moment. The big moment when the message is being delivered.'

'Do you believe it happened?' I ask.

'Of course not. It's a story. It's telling a fantastic story. It's trying to explain something that can't be explained.'

'The Annunciation? I've never heard of it,' a man says. 'I'm an atheist. All religions are the same. Forget it.'

At first, a young couple is reluctant to stop. 'Mm, that's Mary, ok?' says the male. 'I'm not a Christian so there's no point talking with me.'

His partner looks at him disdainfully.

'I don't believe either. It would be nice to. It's a striking picture but it doesn't move me. I never go to church. I haven't been since I was a child.'

Mick, aged sixty-three, wears a peak cap with a Manchester United logo.

'It's fantasy, is that, a fairy story. I mean it's not like other fairy stories. They're imagination. This one's – how do you say? – make believe too but there's a purpose, yeah. It's there to explain the coming of Jesus. Jesus as God. But I don't think any of it happened. Well, not like that.'

'You don't believe it?' I ask.

'Of course not. Why, do you?' he replies. 'People need hope and that's what all this stuff does. That Jesus is more than a man, more than a prophet. There's nothing wrong with that. I'd like to believe it but I don't.'

'Why not?' I ask.

'There's no proof, I suppose,' he replies. 'It's imaginary. Made up. Anyway, nice talking to you.' He holds out his hand.

A good looking, rather suave male, dressed in a suit and navy blue woollen coat, holds out his arm to indicate he cannot stop. I tell him I want to ask him a couple of brief questions about the Annunciation.

'That's when Jesus goes up to heaven,' he responds with some certainty.

'No, that's the Ascension,' I say.

'It's all the same for me,' he replies as he tries to move on. 'It all passes me by. Religion? It's not for me. But keep the faith, mate. Have a good Christmas.'

Two girls studying at Winchester University decide to stop.

'I believe it,' one of them tells me. 'I was taught it at Sunday school and it has never left me.'

I turn to the other.

'I used to believe it but no longer. I've moved on. I'm amazed Amy still does,' she giggles.

A woman called Katherine carries a large box containing a model train.

'It's all mystery. All religions. Christianity. Jews. Muslims. I may go to the carol service at the Cathedral. I usually go. It's so lovely, isn't it?'

'Do you believe the story of the angel appearing to Mary?' I ask.

'I simply don't know. Does anyone?' she replies. 'Probably not. It would be delightful if it were so. But no, if I'm honest.'

'No chance, absolutely no chance mate,' says a young man to all my questions.

'I've no interest in it. You won't want to hear what I think,' says a man who says he is from Southampton. 'Religion? No thank you. Respect for those who believe but no, not me.'

A woman called Stephanie, a general practitioner, holds up the Lemoyne print for some time, not saying a word.

'The Virgin Birth. Did it happen? Do I believe it?' she then asks rhetorically. 'It's a good question in a world of, what do you call it now, spin and all that. I don't know what to believe anymore. I suppose it's no less true than some of the rubbish that's out there – the fiction on the Internet purporting to be truth. Fake news. Conspiracy theories. It was Pontius Pilate, wasn't it, who asked, "What is truth?" It's certainly not factual but in a sense it's not untrue. Do you understand? I used to think it kind of holds truth within it even though it never happened. That sounds weird, doesn't it? I didn't believe it but in another way I did. Well, that's where I was with it. But I'm no longer religious. That's gone I'm afraid. I'm now what you'd call a non-believer.'

I am keen to continue talking with her but she says she has to leave or she'll get a parking ticket. She rushes off up the High Street.

It is getting dark and I need to go home. I stop one last person – a middle-aged man – in his tracks.

'We're now encouraged not to believe and that's a good thing,' he tells me. 'Some people think they're so superior because they say they're believers. But they're no better than me. It's got nothing to do with intelligence. Faith is all about conviction not proof. That's why I don't go with any of that and never will,' he says sternly as he points to the painting.

The results of my tiny survey suggest strongly that the Pew research may be overly optimistic and the Archbishop's comments more hope than reality.

Every Tuesday, a Christian Meditation group meets at my local St Paul's church for prayer and lectio divina.

Lectio divina is a traditional Benedictine practice that dates back before medieval times and describes a way of reading Scripture that encourages people 'to let go and open themselves to hearing what God wants to say through the "Living Word".' The first stage normally is *lectio* – reading and letting the words sink in; the second stage is *meditatio* – reflecting and ruminating on the text; the third stage is *oratio* – responding through prayer and letting the heart speak with God; and the fourth and final stage is *contemplatio* – digesting the word, listening at the deepest level possible to God and, hopefully, being transformed within in order to gain an increased knowledge of Christ. The point is not simply to analyse the texts but 'to enter' the words and absorb them. There are no fixed procedural rules.

Some weeks ago, I asked the group whether they would consider focusing on Luke's story of the Annunciation, and if so, would they permit me to witness the gathering. They have kindly agreed.

On a cold Tuesday evening in early December, I walk into a small room adjacent to the church, to find five women and five men sitting in a semi-circle on office chairs. One of them is the Rector, Peter Seal. Another is Kathleen Freeman, a psychodynamic counsellor. Most are middle aged. Two could be described as elderly. The fluorescent lights have been switched off and the curtains drawn. There is a small table on which six candles are lit, providing the only light in the room. A red rug and two cushions lie on the floor.

One woman opens the session with a preparatory thought-piece on meditation. A bell rings, followed by a twenty-minute silence, and then it rings again. Kathleen Freeman then reads the gospel passage. There is a further five minutes of silence before she reads the passage once more. Her delivery is measured and steeped in feeling.

After a while, the silence is broken. In the darkness, it is difficult to work out exactly where the voices are coming from but I hear a woman's voice, 'What stayed with me was that Mary was deeply disturbed, unsurprisingly perhaps.'

A man responds immediately, 'It was a virgin conception but a natural birth.'

There is another quiet period. Gradually more people start to comment. Everyone's eyes remain closed during the following discussion.

'I was struck by Mary asking for information. Her acceptance only came once she'd got clarification.'

'It can't be history, not in a sense of a post-1850 meaning of the word "history". It's something else.'

'I'm thinking about the unfolding of this encounter and how much is condensed in a few paragraphs. How long did it really take?'

'Yes, I'm puzzled by just the different times. How long was Mary troubled for before the conversations carried on?'

'There's a very set historical location back to the house of David and a reign that would last forever,' an older man observes. 'There's an extraordinary expansion and contraction of time all at once.'

'Another thing that struck me was that final line, "And the angel left her." It's a bit too soon to leave.'

'I'm really struggling with the density of the words as opposed to the image that keeps coming into my mind. It's all so much simpler in the paintings. Mary is there. She's present. I realize in the visual representations that the detail is stripped away. These words are so dense.'

'I find I almost want to tremble at what the angel says to her. I can't imagine how she could bear to listen to him. They're such beautiful words, so huge. This little woman in Nazareth. It's like it zooms in from a worldview to a continent, to a country, to a village, to a house, to a bare little room, and then there are these words. It's beauty beyond measure.'

'She was so ordinary, amongst ordinary people.'

'It sounds very irreverent but it feels like it's been written for a primary school play. You've got a stage. The angel enters stage left. When he's said his wonderful words, you almost expect a puff of smoke as he exits. The scene is set. I'm also struck by your words, "It's not history." I doubt if there was one of those things recording the words.' He points to my small digital recorder. 'But there's clearly truth in it.'

'It's not susceptible to post-Enlightenment analysis,' the man opposite him says. 'It doesn't fulfil David Hume's criteria of judging miracles.'

'This is oral history, handed down,' the other man replies. 'It's poetry. Does that make it less true?'

There is another long pause. Then someone breaks the silence again.

'This was so shocking. God was so immense to them. They learnt these stories from memory. They hadn't got a written word. It was memorized and yet there's so much detail here.'

'The scandal of this is that the creator of the universe breaks into the utterly ordinary and everyday,' says the man next to me. 'That's scandalous, outrageous, extraordinary.'

'A son who would reign forever. It hardly makes any sense.'

'I struggle with the particularity of it – that almost focusing on it as a purely historical event makes it harder to connect with me than if it was something that is happening now. There's something miraculous about every conception and there's something divine about every baby. There's a risk of focusing on a purely historical approach to it.'

'There may be too much detail but it grounds what's being said. That works for me,' says another.

The candles continue to flicker, offering a warm, shimmering glow within the darkened room.

'We don't know if different bits were added, do we? It was a while later that Luke wrote this part. He wanted to root it in time and place.'

'But God is with us here now. That's why we are each hearing different aspects of it now.'

'I find it's very Trinitarian,' observes one man. 'The Most High, the Jewish way of saying the Father. Then there's the Son and his conception. And the Holy Spirit coming upon you. It's all very symbolic.'

'Perhaps we all have encounters with God and they're little nectar drops that we can't explain but leave us with something,' says a female voice. 'Not tangible like a baby but something that is of God. I don't think we should examine it so much. We should experience it. We should live it. If we have that encounter, we have seen God in some way.'

'That's lovely. The ultimate experience of the Other.'

The room falls silent. After a while, Kathleen Freeman reads the gospel passage again. There is a further silence for five minutes, then the bell rings.

I ask what image they have in their heads?

'It's not an image in my head. It's in my body,' a female voice responds.

There's another period of silence before further thoughts flow.

'I see a very simple room and then a vision.'

'A young woman is getting caught up in something beyond herself.'

'Frozen in time. Timeless.'

'I see it rather as a message of God for me now. God telling me something now.'

'It feels like it was the only way God could enter into the creative order in a new way.'

'It's like one of those ancient footprints we discover, made thousands of years ago. But this one is set in stone. It can't be washed away by time.'

'I feel I'm in the middle of experiencing it. I feel overwhelmed.'

I am particularly interested in these last responses. Those people did not describe the image they carried in their heads. Instead, they talked about feelings and meanings. Their responses seemed to generate from the heart, not the head.

'I think God's favour to Mary was an act of grace. There's no way we can win his favour,' comes a voice.

'Never be surprised what's just around the corner, is what I hear,' says another.

'Maybe this was all a dream. She was good at listening to her dreams.'

'I trained as a midwife,' comes a gentle female voice. 'I think we are often given the opportunity for pregnancy, for giving birth, for new ideas, but we often miss those opportunities because we don't listen. We don't listen deeply enough. Isn't that the message here?'

There's another long period of silence before a final prayer and then the lights are switched on. I thank everyone for allowing me to be with them.

As I leave, Kathleen Freeman hands me a small piece of paper entitled 'Listening, with Mary'. She says it comes from a prayer website called 'Sacred Space' created by Irish Jesuits. I read the words: 'Mary offers us a profound image of receptive silence. She is a woman wrapped in silence. She receives the word fully, because she is all space for it. She ponders the word and brings forth fruit.'

A few days later, Stephen, one of the people who took part in the Christian Meditation session, gets in touch with me by email:

> Our evening meditation and reflections on the Annunciation have stayed with me and I have continued to ponder. I've found myself staying with two of the questions you posed at the end. 'Did it happen?' and 'Is it a metaphor?' For me they are closely linked, and linked through something from which I increasingly find spiritual challenge and refreshment. This is an approach to the Scriptures which is founded on an understanding that they embody essentially non-historic but timeless truths of the human situation, and need constantly to be rescued from the concretisation of a largely historical theological approach. This is for me where I struggle with all too much of the Church's stance and an often unthinking presentation around the life of Christ, where apparent facts (said Gradgrind!) are proffered as the main reason for trying to live a faithful life. The stories of the virgin birth, of the incarnation, and indeed of the resurrection, have been, it feels to me, set down as 'facts', indeed, as often no more than facts, as templates for us to try and copy, and are thereby necessarily and inevitably rooted in specific time and place (subsequently one might add providing scope for endless tribal arguments as to who 'owns' which bit of the special and uniquely sanctified ground as justification for endless fighting). Many of the great religions share common symbols which, perhaps, if we acknowledged a little more, might make easier the finding of much needed shared ground and mutual respect with other faiths rather than our all too often monopolistic and 'uniqueness' starting point. There are, for instance, stories, I gather, of the birth of Buddha similar to that of the Annunciation, and the Greek myths (which certainly would have been familiar to the early Church non-Judaic writers and compilers) abound, of course, with stories of divine conceptions of Gods and heroes. This has moved me in recent years to a reading of Scripture which is deeply enriched by looking for, seeing the story, the 'myths' behind the events of the Bible, because I can identify through the experience of my own 'myth' or purpose, as intended by my Creator. Myth here is intended in the richest and life-affirming sense rather than as in 'just a myth'.
>
> So my somewhat drawn out and tortuous answer now to your questions would be, 'No, it didn't happen,' in the factual manner in which the Church is inclined to present it, and 'Yes, it is happening all the time if we can but have eyes to see and ears to hear.' And 'No, it's not a metaphor,' because that simply stands as an image to help us connect with something else conceptually in our reach. But it is a symbol, as in Joseph Campbell and C. G. Jung's understandings, as something which points us to a reality, a dimension of being which is beyond our understanding, which the divine must by definition be, (and thereby provides me at least with all my irritation as to the historical theology approach, with some hope of relating to our Saviour as God incarnated).
>
> I only hope this makes some sense and that it may spark a few more thoughts in your intriguing researches.'

It is 20 December and a special Christmas service takes place in the early evening at St Paul's church. Every seat is taken. The service card shows a drawing of the angel Gabriel. I am asked by the Rector to deliver Luke's story of the Annunciation from the lectern. Amusingly, he says, 'You're rather familiar with it.' Immediately afterwards, the congregation sings the beautiful Basque folk carol, 'The angel Gabriel from heaven came'. The words, by Sabine Baring-Gould, seem especially poignant tonight:

> The angel Gabriel from heaven came,
> His wings as drifted snow, his eyes as flame.
> 'All hail,' said he, 'thou lowly maiden, Mary,
> Most highly favoured lady.'
> Gloria!
>
> 'For known a blessed Mother thou shalt be.
> All generations laud and honour thee.
> Thy Son shall be Emmanuel, by seers foretold,
> Most highly favoured lady.'
> Gloria!
>
> Then gentle Mary meekly bowed her head.
> 'To me be as it pleaseth God,' she said.
> 'My soul shall laud and magnify his holy name.'
> Most highly favoured lady.'
> Gloria!
>
> Of her, Emmanuel, the Christ, was born,
> in Bethlehem, all on a Christmas morn,
> and Christian folk throughout the world will ever say,
> 'Most highly favoured lady.'
> Gloria!

Afterwards, the congregation hears a poem written by the former Rector of St Lawrence with St Swithun, David Scott, who now lives in retirement in Cumbria. Inspired by a woodcut he'd seen, it was published earlier in the year by Bloodaxe as part of his *Beyond the Drift* collection of poems. It is called 'A David Jones Annunciation':

> In such an ordinary room
> the angel came skidding to rest:
> she on a bench of prayer
> he to get news off his chest.
>
> Arrivals can happen like that
> on the day you least expect,
> when the washing's on the line
> and you've no idea what's next.
>
> He was such a gentle angel
> with a lily in his hand
> and his eyes so meekly angled
> you have to understand

The King is in search of a kingdom;
the time to be born is soon,
and God wants you to house him
in the byre of your womb.

She sat as still as the chair
staring at the cool, tiled floor
and the silence was deeper there,
than she'd ever heard before.

Neither knew how to break it.
Neither was wanting to press.
It was probably only a minute
but it felt like an hour to say 'yes'.

'Yes' was the shape of the farmhouse.
'Yes' was the trunk of the trees.
'Yes' was the gate of the hinges.
'Yes' brought the world to its knees.

The following morning is the Fourth Sunday of Advent and I am back in St Paul's for the Family Communion service. At the start, the youngest children come to the front to hear a story. The session is led by Tim Bissett, a member of the congregation and Director of the Christmas Appeal at St Martin-in-the-Fields. Previously, he was the chief executive of the Church Urban Fund. Twenty children gather in front of the altar, and sit on the floor.

'How many more sleeps are there before Christmas?' he asks. They work out together that there are four left. 'I think there'll be a few surprises for you on Christmas morning when you wake up,' he says. They all nod.

He has a kindly manner and is dressed in an informal, relaxed style with a baggy pullover and jeans.

'What's a surprise?' he asks them.

'Something you don't know about,' one of the children responds.

'Yes, exactly,' says Tim. 'When people get a surprise, what do they say?'

'Wow,' says one of the children.

He gets them all to shout 'Wow!' He then asks the whole congregation to shout out 'Wow!'

'Today's story is full of surprises,' he begins. 'An angel was sent from God.' He pushes his hands up and the children shout out,

'Wow!'

'He was sent to Nazareth – a nothing place, like going to Basingstoke.

'Wow!'

'The angel said to Mary, "You're beautiful. You will become pregnant and have a baby and you will call him Jesus",' he tells them.

'Wow!' they respond, chuckling.

'Mary wasn't expecting that, was she? She was going to have a baby and she was being told what to name him. What a surprise,' he says. On cue, the children immediately respond,

'Wow!'

He tells them to listen carefully. He says the angel then tells Mary that the baby is going to be great and be 'the Son of the Most High and his kingdom will have no end.' They look a little confused. 'This is one important baby, eh?' he says. 'But Mary isn't even married. The angel tells her not to be worried because the Holy Spirit will look after her. Now that sounds really surprising. That deserves a really big "Wow!" '

The children shout out the word. They are transfixed and fully attentive. It is a clever but simple way of telling the story to a very young audience.

'Mary said, "Ok, that's good. Yes, I see it all now. I'm ready to serve".'

'Wow!' the children respond again.

Tim asks them all to close their eyes and pray to God.

'We thank God for Mary and for her example to us. For that was the biggest surprise ever. Amen.'

Before the children head off for their various activities in the parish rooms, a little girl is asked to light the fourth and final pink candle on the Advent wreath. As she holds the taper, the priest tells the children the fourth candle represents 'the joy of the Virgin Mary. Today we especially remember Mary, how kind and good she was, her humility and courage when chosen to be the mother of Jesus.'

On this Fourth Sunday of Advent, the last before Christmas Day, the gospel reading is Luke's passage on the Annunciation. Stephen Adam, a Licensed Lay Minister who lives in the city, gives the sermon. As he stands to address the congregation, I am struck by how, for St Paul's, this is the day to celebrate the story of the Annunciation rather than earlier in the year on the feast day of 25 March. I include an extract from his sermon that he bases on the Annunciation:

144. Rembrandt *The Annunciation*, 1635. © Besançon, musée des Beaux-Arts et d'Archéologie. Photo: Pierre Guenat

In his book, *The Christmas Stories*, Trevor Dennis – a master storyteller – draws attention to a remarkable ink drawing of the scene where Rembrandt shows Mary literally fainting with shock and sliding off her chair, with Gabriel having to catch her to stop her falling on the floor. Maybe that's a more earthy realism than some of the technicolour Renaissance images that adorn our Christmas cards? Surely one of the most beautiful verses in the Psalms is Psalm 17:8:

Guard me as the apple of your eye,
Hide me in the shadow of your wings

Rembrandt catches this perfectly in the drawing...he depicts one of Gabriel's wings arching over Mary's head, curling around her like a comforting arm.

As we reflect upon the Annunciation, this encounter between the extraordinary and the ordinary, and the transformation that results from it, so it seems to me that this is very much a metaphor for what we are engaged in week by week when our worship is at its best and most genuine and heartfelt. It's through worship and liturgy that we are formed as disciples and equipped to witness the Good News of Christ. In our worship we come in all our ordinariness, with all our frailties and brokenness, and we encounter something extraordinary in the presence of God. This is most explicit in the Eucharist, which we will share shortly. The ordinary elements of broken bread and wine outpoured are recast as something extraordinary, and in the process we are remade – literally re-membered – and thereby empowered purely through God's grace. May we too experience our own Annunciations – those moments of contemplation, that sense of being in the presence of something holy and beyond ourselves – through our worship in this Christmas season and beyond. Amen.

––––––––––

The New Testament Church of God (NTCG) in Southampton is a thriving Evangelical Pentecostal church. Originally, the red brick building was used by Baptists but, fifty years ago, the style of worship changed to accommodate the needs of a growing local West Indian Christian community.

It is one of around 150 NTCG churches in the United Kingdom today, serving more than 30,000 Pentecostal worshippers. The Church is recognized as one of the UK's largest black majority Church organisations and is one of the fastest growing in the country. 'We are a welcoming international church that is enthusiastic about seeing growth and progress', states the NCTG's Facebook page. Indeed, according to *The Times* newspaper, for every Church of England church that has closed over the past six years, three independent Pentecostal churches have opened as inward migration changes the face of faith in Britain.

Indeed, Pentecostalism is one of the fastest growing denominations in the world with around five hundred million followers, based largely in West Africa, the Caribbean, North and South America and parts of Asia. The NTCG in the UK is part of a global movement called the Church of God International, which is present in more than 170 countries. It has over seven million members, and its headquarters are based in Cleveland, Tennessee. It was founded in 1886 and is based on justification by faith and the infallible authority of the Bible. Its first members are said to have felt an outpouring of the Holy Spirit that led them to speak in tongues and practise divine healing.

The New Testament Church of God was established in England in the early 1950s when West Indians began to arrive in the Midlands. Its services today are informal and highly charged with exuberant singing and overt spiritualism. Flags from different nations and the various Caribbean islands hang from the Southampton church's walls, promoting the international character of the congregation – Caribbean, as well as Nigerian, Kenyan, South African and Zimbabwean.

As I enter the building, a large overhead projector screen proclaims, 'Welcome to be blessed in the house of the Lord'. A poster on a wall states the Church of God's Declaration of Faith, listing fourteen statements of belief. These include: 'In the verbal inspiration of the Bible'; 'In one God eternally existing in three persons'; 'That Jesus Christ is the only begotten Son of the Father, conceived of the Holy Ghost and born of the Virgin Mary.' Other declarations proclaim, 'That all have sinned and come short of the glory of God, and that repentance is commanded of God for all and necessary for the forgiveness of sins'; 'Divine healing is provided for all in the Atonement'; and belief 'In the bodily resurrection, eternal life for the righteous, and eternal punishment for the wicked.'

This is the first time I have attended a service alongside a black majority evangelical congregation. The reason I have come here on this cold, wintry Sunday morning, is because the Minister, Bishop Wilfred Willins, is going to preach on Luke's story of the Annunciation.

The service is due to start at 11.15 a.m., but it begins twenty minutes late and people continue to arrive a good hour after the billed time. At first, I count thirty people scattered amongst the pews, but the congregation builds to more than seventy by the end of the service. All but three are black. Most are women, dressed in their Sunday best, some wearing lovely hats. They shout 'Hallelujah' and 'Praise the Lord' frequently. Proceedings are slightly chaotic but clearly enjoyable. A young woman called Kadian leads the gospel singing including 'Go Tell It on The Mountain', 'The Virgin Mary had a Baby Boy', and 'He Never Failed Me Yet'. Many of the congregation dance in the aisles as they sing. Tambourines, vigorous clapping and the sound of a loud electric guitar add to the vibrancy.

After singing 'Welcome, Welcome, Blessed Holy Ghost', everybody moves around the church welcoming and greeting each other. One woman is in tears. Another grabs me tightly and says, 'The Lord loves you deeply.'

A woman called Yvonne heads to the podium and says, 'Today is a good day because the Lord made today' before she reads Luke 1:26-38.

Again, people call out 'Amen' and 'Praise the Lord'.

One woman near me shouts, 'She knew to say yes, oh yes, how Mary knew that.'

After the reading, Bishop Wilfred takes to the stage. He wears a cream-coloured suit and a pink shirt and tie. In one hand he holds a microphone. In the other he holds a small black book entitled, *The Master's Healing Presence Bible*.

'The Bible tells us of the Virgin Birth in Isaiah 7:14,' he begins, 'The pronounced One was to be the seed of the woman – Genesis 3:15. The angel Gabriel told Mary of the coming of the virgin's birth – Luke 1:26-38. I see humanity's willing acceptance of God's action in Mary, a freely given acceptance of the task of being the mother of God. His name Emmanuel, being interpreted as God with us, and we see Jesus the Son of a personal God, the Son of a living God. Christ treated all men the same. He led people away from traditional religion. He captured the attention of the multitude. He was the perfect embodiment of his Father.'

'Oh yes he was,' a woman calls out.

Another shouts, 'Free acceptance. Freely given acceptance.'

'The Virgin Birth is a miracle you accept by faith,' Bishop Wilfred continues. 'The Bible says if we believe it, that settles it. Mary had to accept this miracle by faith. She had difficulty understanding it. Remember she replied, "How can this be, seeing that I know not a man?" – Luke 1:34. So we must all remember, "nothing is impossible with God" – Luke 1:37.'

A member of the congregation calls out, 'That's right, that's right, nothing is impossible for God.'

Bishop Wilfred's approach is to make a bold statement that he backs up with direct reference to a Bible verse. I notice that no one in the pews is holding or reading a Bible as they listen. When he finishes speaking, a quote appears on the large screen: 'Isaiah cried, Isaiah cried, Behold a virgin shall bear a son. Its name shall be called the Almighty God.'

Some children appear from a back room, dressed as angels, shepherds and kings. Young Mary and Joseph sit on two chairs in front of the lectern facing the congregation.

A girl wearing a white dress and with gold tinsel in her hair, holds the microphone. Angel Gabriel has arrived.

After this short simple Nativity play has been performed, we sing some more, and then move to the community room for a free Christmas lunch of Caribbean style chicken, pork and curry.

I speak with Bishop Wilfred in his tiny, sparse office. We immediately hit it off when I mention the Kensington Oval cricket ground in Barbados and the island's local hero, Sir Gary Sobers. 'Wow, I'm impressed,' he chuckles. He is remarkably young looking for his age with not a trace of grey or white in his hair. He has a kind face and speaks quietly and very slowly. Aged seventy, he was born and brought up on the west coast of Barbados.

'We have our baptisms in the sea there,' he tells me. 'Why not? That's where the water is. Services here are much less flamboyant than back in Barbados. There's more sunshine there so they're often held outside.'

His grandparents brought him up after his parents separated when he was a young child. His grandfather was a preacher and had a big influence on young Wilfred. He attended an evangelical wing within Anglicanism before moving on to the evangelical Church of Christ. He came to England in 1963 'to improve himself', worked in an engineering firm, and lived in Stafford where he joined an Elim Pentecostal church that inspired him with its liveliness. He felt a calling to ministry but always kept a secular job during the week. He moved to London where he was a security controller of government buildings in Whitehall for many years. He joined the New Testament Church of God and for twenty-five years he served as a minister with five London churches under his wing. Now retired, he travels to Southampton on Fridays to fill the role of minister for the weekend. His wife, Merle, to whom he has been married for fifty years, acts as the Ladies' President. They have been connected to the Southampton NTCG for the past nine years.

I begin by asking what the annunciation story means for him.

'To me, I see it as God laying aside his divine robes and wrapping himself in the rags of human nature, identifying himself with our humanity to pay the price of our redemption,' he responds.

I comment that I find his statement intriguing. Why did he use a clothing analogy?

'God is holy,' he replies. 'He covers himself in light. Darkness looks for a hiding place. He lays that aside to identify himself with us so that we can touch him with our infirmities because he became human and, therefore, he equated himself with our humanity and now we can touch him because he understands our hurts, our feelings and our disappointments. He gives us healing with his stripes – Isaiah 53. "With His stripes we are healed." We are healed mentally, physically and in every sense of the word.'

Does he believe that the annunciation story actually happened?

'I see it as real because to accept the Virgin Birth, you have to accept the Bible. I believe the Bible is right. Therefore, I accept the Virgin Birth. With God all things can happen. It's a miracle.'

Is it literal truth because it appears in Luke's Gospel?

'Not only because it is laid down by Luke,' he replies, 'but other writers have also spoken about it, not only in the New Testament but also go back to Isaiah, "A virgin shall conceive in her womb and bear a son and he will be called Emmanuel, God-is-with-us." And Moses, when he left Egypt with the people, they were complaining about the journey and the food. He said the day will come when God will raise a prophet like unto me, speaking of the coming of the prophet, the Messiah. I see it as fact because I believe in the word of God. I accept by faith because Mary accepted by faith.'

What does he feel about the statement that the Annunciation is the most important event in human history?

'Correct,' he responds immediately. 'I would agree with that one hundred per cent because, until then, we were lost. God became man to redeem man from sin. There can be no forgiveness without the shedding of blood. Sin must be punished. Christ became our sin bearer. He was punished on the Cross. He was the perfect lamb. Before him is BC. After him is AD. And the conception is the moment.'

Did God, through the angel Gabriel, command Mary to have the baby or did she have free will?

'We are free moral agents,' he says. 'I suppose she could have said no, but when the anointing of God is on your life, it is difficult to say no. "You are highly favoured. You shall conceive". The "shall" is a positive. She accepted by faith. I see her as a descendant of David from that royal line even though she was poor. She knew the history. Then she accepted and knew the Messiah was coming. She knew. She must have read the Torah time and time again. She went up to Jerusalem to worship on different occasions. She knew He was coming. How He was coming, she didn't know until Gabriel came and told her you are the one. "Let it be done according to your word". She was a willing and submissive vessel, accepting by faith.'

What does Mary mean to him?

'To me personally, she is just the mother of Christ. She is not one I should worship. She needed a saviour.'

Does he ever pray to her?

'No,' he says firmly. 'She needed a saviour. She's an ordinary human being but also the mother of Christ.'

Some would find that combination difficult to understand, I say.

'The Catholic Church would but Christ is the only mediator between God and Man. She is the mother of God but not a mediator.'

Is she a bridge or a barrier to closer relationships across the different Christian denominations?

'Neither,' he says. 'She's an ordinary person who was favoured by God. That's it. Yes, she is blessed but is not someone to worship. That's it. Oh dear, dear, dear,' he sighs. 'If I saw a statue of Mary, I would block it out of my mind. I don't see Christ either. I don't see Him. I've had dreams, good dreams. When I first received the baptism of the Holy Spirit, I had a vision of a man coming to me but I cannot say that I remember what he looks like. The whole Christian faith is an act of faith. You must believe God is God, the rewarder. I've never seen God. I've never seen Christ so to speak. But I see His work when I look on the trees and feel the wind.'

So how does he visualize Gabriel coming before Mary?

'I imagine this celestial figure…I see a human form light.'

I show him the Lemoyne painting of *The Annunciation*. What does he see?

He looks at the composition in silence.

Does he like it?

'I don't dislike it. I just see it as a picture because in my mind we're not supposed to…' he pauses before continuing, 'Exodus 20:4, "Thou shall not make unto thee any graven images or any likeness of anything that is in heaven above or that is in the earth beneath." A Jewish family would never have this in the house because they believe in the true God in heaven. And we are forbidden from having any images at all.'

I move from a Pentecostal minister to a Presbyterian one. The Reverend Dr Bert Tosh is an acclaimed scholar of Irish Presbyterian history and until 2013 was the senior producer for religion and ethics at BBC Northern Ireland, responsible for all religious output in what is the United Kingdom's most sectarian and divided religious community.

Patrick Loughrey, the Warden of Goldsmith's College at the University of London and a former Controller of BBC Northern Ireland, told me: 'Serious scholarship and spontaneous good humour are characteristics seldom associated with contemporary Ulster clergymen. Dr Tosh defies stereotype. He is entertaining, compassionate and has taken academic research far beyond the quiet uplands of the academy. Bert served congregations on both sides of the Irish border. His BBC career was a creative extension of his deeply committed Christian ministry. His work is not about pious preaching but rather a relentless search for truth. Successfully providing ambitious religious affairs programmes for people of all backgrounds during Ulster's darkest days is a remarkable achievement. It is even more notable when it is sustained over three decades and when that output has remained consistently popular in Northern Ireland and on BBC Radio 4.'

Aged sixty-nine, Bert Tosh describes himself today as 'a working theologian'. Originally a Chemistry graduate, he studied Divinity and was ordained in 1973 as a Presbyterian minister. He served congregations in Belfast, Londonderry and Donegal. His Ph.D. at Queen's University, Belfast focused on Irish Presbyterian worship and he has received awards for his scholarship on the history of the Presbyterian Church in Ireland. I worked alongside him at the BBC for twenty years. He is a big, burly bear of a man with a white beard, glasses and a deep voice, which he uses brilliantly to convey a rich array of memorable humorous anecdotes.

He has always emphasized the importance of religious literacy and of understanding the beliefs, practices and heritage of all denominations. He wrote to me recently: 'There has been in much Protestant Evangelicalism an emphasis on Redemption to the detriment of the Incarnation. To put it rather crudely, the only reason God became man was to save us. I have come to the position now of regarding each as complementary to the other and of equal importance. That has made me reflect rather more on the Annunciation and what it means than before.'

I connect with him by phone during the busy pre-Christmas period and ask what the annunciation story means for him?

'I suppose at a certain level it moves me emotionally. I wouldn't claim to know a great deal about the art of it but one thing that strikes me is that when I look at the art of the Annunciation, just how many different scenarios of it there are. It's a lovely story. I know that may sound trite. It was the first step in the incarnation of God as a human being and, therefore, it has huge significance. Now if you said, how do you interpret the story? do you believe it's literally true? I've probably moved on from asking questions about literal truth now. The story is true. What actually happened to my mind is of secondary importance but it is true because here is this God who describes himself in Isaiah as "the high and lofty one" who also dwells with the humble. This is God taking this first step to becoming, as the Creed says, "for us and for our salvation, he became man" or, if you prefer, a human being.'

Does he see a key theme in the story?

'I suppose I've often pondered on Mary. Probably a young teenage girl, she must have been terrified seeing an angel and then being told she was going to have a baby, and then being told it will be God. She seems quite calm,' he chuckles. 'The fourteen-year-old girls I know would run screaming from the room but there's a great calmness about her.

'I suppose that in a sense it has led in certain types of Catholicism to the picture of the meek woman who does what she is told,' he continues. 'But I can't see just that because she said, "Let it be done" that she should be seen as meek. She must have been quite strong actually to cope with it all. Yes, my key theme would be this is God drawing near.

'It no longer greatly worries me about literal truth. I doubt very seriously whether there was a single Adam and a single Eve and an apple and a snake. All I know is that story is true because it's true of every human being that ever existed. Now this is in a slightly different category. I've no qualms whatsoever about saying, "and became Man". I've no difficulty about the divinity of Jesus. All the explanations of the Greek philosophers who lived in the first four centuries are of interest to me intellectually but they don't get one terribly excited at the gut level. I think something happened. Mary became pregnant. I've no doubt about that. Whether she saw an angel or what or whether it appeared in a dream or she dreamt it or whatever…I mean the Old Testament has lots of childbearing stories – Hannah, Sarah – you can see parallels in the Old Testament.

'Now if we get on to the Virgin Birth for thirty seconds,' he says without any prompting, 'Emil Brunner, the Swiss theologian, said that if there was a virgin birth, it was a secondary miracle compared to the primary miracle of the birth of the Son of God. I would be agnostic about the Virgin Birth. But the fact I'm agnostic doesn't make me say if there wasn't a virgin birth, then Jesus wasn't God. That doesn't follow for me. My more fundamentalist friends would say I'm being horribly inconsistent and that may be true, but I believe Jesus is divine and human. How it happened is, to my mind, of secondary importance. The fact is it happened.'

What does he make of the statement that it is the most important event in human history?

'Did Cormac Murphy O'Connor say that?' he asks. 'It doesn't matter who but I think it's very difficult to say that. If you forced me into a corner and said, give me a hierarchy, I'd say the Resurrection. I can see how you can turn that round and say if there hadn't been an Annunciation, there'd be no Incarnation and no Resurrection. Interestingly, the Protestant theology in which I grew up and most evangelicals today would put Redemption much higher. The only reason God was incarnated was to redeem us. I think it's very dangerous to say what God can and cannot do and what God should and shouldn't do. One preacher here regularly used to talk about the crib and the cross and that you can't have one without the other. In a sense that Catholic bishop or whoever it was is right but to say it's the most important event in history…but maybe the moment of creation? Look, I wouldn't go that far but the Annunciation is very, very important. The theme I'd always want to emphasize is God drawing near and Mary's acceptance, and in her response, that sense of calling.

'I have preached about Mary,' he goes on. 'She played a very small part in my own theological development because of the fear that if you talked too much about her, you'd get landed into all sorts of positions you shouldn't be in. She is blessed. That is what the angel said to her. I wouldn't see her as a co-mediatrix or anything like that but I recognize her importance in God's plan and in the importance of the Incarnation. She stands as one brave woman who put up with a heck of a lot. She is a heroic figure. A misunderstood figure. Catholics praying to Mary not to God would be not an unusual notion still for many Protestants. Very conservative Evangelicals think the Catholic Church is misleading people about how to get to heaven. I think Mary is a factor but not a major factor. It's very difficult to generalize. It depends where you are. There was a *Songs of Praise* that took place here some time ago and there was a hymn with some reference to Mary and some of the Prods wouldn't go. Whether that would still happen now, I don't know.'

Is it necessary to believe in the Annunciation in order to be a Christian?

'No, but you have to believe that Jesus Christ is divine,' he replies. 'I don't think you necessarily have to believe how it happened according to Luke. Yes, to believe in the Incarnation and the Resurrection is vital but the Annunciation is not essential. It's secondary but not of no importance.'

Does the annunciation story divide the religious community in Northern Ireland or bring them together?

'I don't think it does either,' he says. 'I mean, let's remember most Protestant Evangelicals or fundamentalists would believe the annunciation story to be literally true. Of course they would. I think where the division comes is what you make of Mary beyond that – the Immaculate Conception, her perpetual virginity, the exemplar for all celibates. I've always had this notion that Mary has been adopted in certain Catholic minds to give God a feminine face. Now I think that's nonsense but, let's face it, God is thought of as a masculine, whatever that means, and I think Mary represented, understandably, the other side of the coin.'

He tells me he's looking at Lemoyne's painting on his computer screen via the National Gallery website. What does he think of it? I ask.

'A painting typical of its time,' he responds. 'A superior looking angel and Mary definitely not looking like a fourteen-year-old girl. I like the painting but it wouldn't be my first choice. I prefer the Rembrandt drawing, the Fra Angelico fresco where they are both looking at each other, and the Japanese artist, Sadao Watanabe. His Annunciations are so different, they really make you think about it. There's such great humanity in his work.'

There will be more on Watanabe a little later.

———

Elizabeth Stuart's office is festooned with Christmas cards. The University of Winchester's carol services are over for another year and the vast majority of the students have left the campus to return home for the festive period. As First Deputy Vice-Chancellor, it has been a challenging but fulfilling term, managing change and building the impact and reputation of the city's leading centre for higher education.

She sits by her small office table, under which her faithful friend, Arthur, a Jack Russell terrier, lies fast asleep. She wears a woolly jumper and a pair of distinctive black, round glasses that suit her face. She is ready for a well-earned Christmas break and is looking forward to staying with her sister in Brighton. Before she leaves, she has one last appointment...to talk with me about the Annunciation!

Liz Stuart joined the University in 1998 as Professor of Christian Theology and Director of the Centre for the Study of Sexuality and Religion. She is an internationally renowned scholar who has published widely on the theologies of sexuality and gender and is a leading proponent of Queer Theology. In the 1980s and 90s, she became a well-known activist for LGBT rights.

She has an interesting faith background too. Her mother was Catholic, her father Anglican and she was brought up a Roman Catholic in Gravesend in Kent. She attended two convent schools before going to the local grammar.

'From a very early age, I felt a calling to priesthood, from about the age of six,' she tells me. 'It made no sense because there were no women ministers anywhere. But it never went away and I channelled it into the study of theology.'

When the Church of England decided to ordain women deacons, she says she paused and thought about it but 'the sexuality thing and the debate around it was at its height then, and I thought there would be no integrity in me doing that. You would have had to have hidden the fact you were gay. I was in a relationship for twenty years. When that ended, I became aware of the Liberal Catholic tradition which had no issues with women priests or gays or anything, so I was ordained in that.'

In 2006, she became Archbishop of the Province of Great Britain and Ireland in the Liberal Catholic Church International. The denomination is not in full communion with the Roman Catholic Church. It promotes a high level of intellectual liberty in the interpretation of the creeds and supports freedom of conscience. It teaches the doctrine of the Holy Trinity and believes that the Holy Bible, the creeds and the Traditions of the Church are fundamental and true. This small group says that all Christian worship is valid so long as it is earnest and true. Its priests are described as 'ungendered', and when they celebrate Mass, they turn away from the congregation to face eastwards, in the old, pre-Vatican II, Catholic way.

I open by asking what the annunciation story means for her? There is a long pause before she speaks. It is as if she wants to choose the exact word, pick the right phrase.

'I think for me, primarily, it signals a new creation. It's the creation of a new humanity that is at one with God. A creation out of nothing in the sense that a child is born male but of no male matter, as the theologian, Graham Ward, has put it, as a result of a cooperation between the Virgin Mary and the divine. It's a new creation story that means things change. They change in the person of Christ and everything is changed as a result of that encounter.'

Does she believe it as fact or see it as a metaphor?

'I believe it,' she says. 'I absolutely believe it. I believe it on a theological level. It's too simplistic to say I believe it as a mere fact, but I believe it. What you see in the Gospels is early Christians trying to work out when it was that Jesus became divine. In Mark's Gospel, whoever wrote that thought it was at Jesus's baptism. In Matthew and Luke, the Spirit overshadows Mary and it's at the conception. In John, it's pushed back to eternity. So I would say something like it happened and that is what the author of the Gospel of Luke is trying to express – that in the person of Christ, a new creation came into being.'

When she says, 'I believe it', does she believe in the message or the event or both?

'I believe that Mary was a virgin,' she replies. 'I believe that she had a choice in whether to take part in this great story of salvation and this new beginning. The whole point is that it is a unique event. But it's a much richer and deeper thing than something that's just factual. That's what I'm trying to convey. It has a much deeper meaning than a historical event.'

What does she feel is the key meaning of the story?

'I think there are so many resonances in it. We are witnessing a new dawn. Everything is different. I think what we see in the example of Mary is the appropriate response to that, the freedom of it. There's absolute freedom to participate or cooperate in this or not. In the story, she is presented with a being whose sole purpose is to do the will of God. That's what angels do. She chooses to become like that being. It's interesting that at the moment she says yes, Gabriel disappears. He's done his job and she's become like him. She's become a being who's done the will of God. She becomes, in a sense too, the first priest. She's able to say in a way that nobody else is able to say, "This is my body and this is my blood". She's the mediator of the Christ in that very profound way. She becomes a model for priesthood in that very moment. And I think there are some very interesting things going on in terms of gender.'

Could you explain? I ask.

'Well, "the power of the most high will overshadow you" is a reference to the manifestation of God as the Shekinah – the presence of God as something that overshadows, which in Hebrew is represented in female form. So that female form overshadows the Virgin Mary and she conceives a child. So there's no male involvement at all. What we have is a male child born of no male matter. For me, that plays around with our notion of gender.'

So she believes that the Annunciation is not just a unique event in terms of a virgin birth.

'Part of this new era, part of this new creation that is brought in with Christ is one in which gender becomes quite slippery,' she says. 'And that's later expressed in the classic baptismal formula that Paul quotes: "In Christ, there is no male and female." What's happening here is a playing around with gender that makes gender non-ultimate as a theological category.'

So, is it true to say that the annunciation story acts as a sort of foundation stone to Queer Theology?

'Absolutely,' she replies. 'Queer Theology owes a lot to a secular philosopher called Judith Butler, who in her 1990 book, *Gender Trouble*, suggests that gender is not something stable or natural. It's conveyed to us in scripts and we're only aware we're following scripts when someone performs those scripts poorly. Grayson Perry would be a good example of that,' she chuckles. 'You could say in the story of the Annunciation, you have the story of the conception followed by the story of the birth, which, whilst recognized as classic script, also plays around with that script, demonstrating that our concepts of gender are just too flakey to build whole theologies upon. That's what Queer Theology is about. So gender just won't bear the weight of theological ultimacy. So you just can't discriminate against people on the basis of gender categories, whether that's male or female or gay or straight. They're just not of theological concern.'

I tell her about Bishop Philip Egan's comment that the Annunciation is 'the most important event in human history'.

'I agree,' she responds. 'I think as a Christian I believe Christ's coming into the world is the most important event in human history. I think it represents a fissure in human history after which nothing was the same.'

What does Mary mean to her?

'As I've got older, she's meant more and more to me. A favourite image of Our Lady, as I still call her, is the one outside Salisbury Cathedral – *The Walking Madonna* – because she looks powerful and determined and she's walking away from the church. I love that as an image. I was brought up on very saccharine images of Our Lady but, as time has gone on, I've come to see her primarily as priest.'

Does she venerate her?

'Yes, I will pray various devotions to her every day.'

Does she see her as a co-mediatrix?

'I wouldn't put it in those terms but I suppose I see her certainly as an expression of the female side of divinity. But more I see her as priest, disciple and mother of God. I have a number of statues of her at home. I went through a period in my life when I thought she wasn't helpful to women and I think the way she is often represented isn't helpful but I've come to the view of her as priest, having written a paper on Mary as priest and looking at various images of her throughout history. She's important to me.'

Is she a bridge or a barrier to Christian unity?

'It depends on the denomination,' she responds. 'The veneration of Our Lady is shared by a number of denominations. She can be a bridge between Roman Catholics and the Orthodox Church and at least some parts of the Anglican Communion. But there's still considerable suspicion amongst some denominations. It's very hard to convey the feeling that you do have if you venerate her and not to fall in to talking as though you are worshipping her. As a child, I thought she and the saints were your friends. They were there for you. I still feel that way.'

What about Mary's perpetual virginity?

She gives one of her signature pauses before responding.

'I do on a theological level. It doesn't matter to me whether it was true on a historical level or not but on a theological level I think the idea that she was the mediator of this new creation out of nothing, as the first creation, was important. The virginity is an expression of that to Luke.'

But why is it important that she remained a virgin all her life?

'She probably wasn't. It doesn't matter to me on a factual level but I've no problem affirming it on a theological level.'

Doesn't that make Mary less human? I suggest.

'My response to that is, why does having sex or children make her more human than someone who doesn't? In the world we're currently in where, thank God, everyone can get married, I think there's a danger that the commitment to living a celibate life or a single life will be completely marginalized and may disappear and I think that would be a shame. What Mary represents, and that whole strand of Christians committing themselves to be celibate represents, is a very important statement that ultimately all our desires, whoever we are, have only one end in God. All or desires – to eat, to drink, to have sex or whatever – the true end is in God. And we need images of people who have forgone the fulfilment of other desires to remind us of that.'

Liz Stuart says that it is right that the Roman Catholic Church asks questions about compulsory celibacy, but the idea that a voluntary commitment to celibacy could die out would, in her words, 'be a very great shame'.

How does she see her own celibacy?

'I experienced it very strongly as a calling,' she replies. 'I'd been in a relationship for twenty years that ended and after that I just knew. It's hard to convey. I just knew I was being called to celibacy for the rest of my life. "You are now meant to be celibate" was the calling. I knew it was a true calling because it made me a better person, a warmer person, a less selfish person.'

It must be tough and quite lonely, I observe.

'That's the point,' she says. 'I get very annoyed with people who write and talk about a difference between being alone and being lonely. Of course there's a difference but there are times when being alone, you are going to be lonely. To be human, whether you're in a relationship or not, there's times when you are going to be lonely and that's the point of choosing that kind of life – to power through that kind of loneliness to God, to experience it and, in that experience, to throw yourself onto God. It can be sacrificial if you find yourself falling in love with somebody and can't do anything about it. But it's more positive than sacrificial.'

Does she feel any parallel with Mary?

'I suppose in the sense that being presented with a possibility of choosing a pathway that would inevitably bring misunderstandings, difficulties, sadness and so on, but for the sake of something joyous and to be able to participate in a different way in the outworking of the gospel, I suppose yes.'

For the LGBT Christian community, does the Annunciation provide a story of hope and special comfort?

'I think so', she responds. 'I think the interesting thing about all this, certainly in the 1970s, 80s and for most of the 90s, it was very difficult to be a LGBT Christian. Churches were just awful and yet people persisted. There were some pretty awful statements put out during that period and some churches did not show themselves in a good light in the midst of the AIDS crisis. Some did but many didn't. But I was moved by how many gay people persisted in their faith and remained in the Church. That's something to do with stories like the Annunciation that reveal that the Church is queer. There is something queer about the gospel. That the heart of Christianity is doing something strange with gender and that is radically inclusive.

'The inclusive message of the gospel and the annunciation story can never be drowned out by the exclusive interpretation of it, and that's extraordinary,' she says. 'The Church is under a mandate because of stories like the Annunciation, the Church is absolutely called to offer a different model of gender to the world. And yes, you can absolutely root that in the Annunciation.'

When I ask whether one has to believe in the annunciation story to be a Christian, there is a very long pause before she responds.

'I think you have to believe in what the story is theologically about to be a Christian. It would be an odd Christian who didn't believe that Christ's birth and coming into the world marked something new. I don't believe Christians have to believe things in the same way. I would have no problem with someone not believing in the literal story or whatever. Actually, my experience is that an amazing number of people believe in angels and I don't know why Christians don't make more of this story. I've met so, so many people outside of the Churches who have a very powerful belief in angels.'

As our conversation draws to a close, we return to the theme of her calling. She tells me she was in the Liberal Catholic Church for sixteen years but recently has felt a new calling.

'I felt a different kind of call,' she tells me. 'It's slightly sensitive but I'm now exploring the possibility of being ordained in the Church of England. I don't know if you know the line in the psalm, "You have set my foot in a large room". Well, I feel a call to that large room.'

She describes being at a crossroads before she began to go through the discernment process. 'No one is more surprised than me,' she says. 'There was something of that kind of calling and having to decide whether to say yes or no to it and wanting to run away and pretend it was not happening.'

She retired from active ministry in the Liberal Catholic Church because the calling persisted so strongly.

'I saw the full riches of the Anglican Communion plus the sexuality question has got to the point that there's nothing more to be said. You just have to let the Holy Spirit do his work now and I think the Holy Spirit has spoken pretty loudly in the world. The Church just has to hear it.'

As I prepare to leave, I show her the Lemoyne painting. There's another long period of reflection before she breaks her silence.

'Her eyes are interesting. They're focused on the paper that's fallen off her reading desk. The angel has spoken. I like elements of it. I like the fact she's been studying, the scholarly dimension, but she doesn't look strong enough for me. She's too meek and mild.'

She walks me to the wall near her office window where a painting hangs.

'This is a painting I call *Annunciation* that I commissioned from the artist, Jill Coughman, at a feminist theology conference in Plymouth in 1999.' [Coughman herself originally entitled it, *Mary Receiving the Call*, saying it was a modern take on how, today, Mary would receive the message].

'I love the idea you pick up the phone and on the other end there might be an angel,' Liz Stuart chuckles. 'I like the thoughtfulness, the concern, the sense of fear. Look, she's hugging herself. But I also like the shape of the phone, which is taken up in the shape of the figure. In her response, she becomes a kind of angelic figure who chooses to do the will of God. She has to struggle but decides to say yes and becomes angelic, a messenger herself. We can all identify with picking up the phone and getting the kind of news that means you want to hug yourself in fear really. I just love it.'

145. Jill Coughman *Mary Receiving the Call*, 1999. © Jill Coughman

CHAPTER 37

AN INVITATION

It is Christmas Eve afternoon and St Paul's is full again, this time for the annual children's Nativity service. Adults make last minute adjustments to angel wings, tiaras, tinsel halos and shepherds clothing. Parents and grandparents wait expectantly, cameras poised.

There are ten minutes to go. Nine-year-old Eleanor Smith will play the coveted part of Mary and eleven-year-old Elizabeth Blunt is to be the angel Gabriel. Edmund Bissett will portray a rather cheeky looking Joseph. Bill Lucas, the Director of the production, shouts frantically, 'It's mayhem. Come on shepherds, focus please. Where have the Kings gone to?'

There is time for one last rehearsal of the opening scene. Bill Lucas takes the two young actors through their parts.

'What do you think's happening here?' he asks them.

'I'm telling her she's having a son, God's son,' Elizabeth says.

'I'm re-assuring her not to be worried. There's no need for a massive panic.'

'Will she be panicking?' he asks.

'She might be a bit,' she says, 'because she's just got engaged to somebody and then God says, "You're going to have my son." So it's quite a big thing.'

He tells her to shout 'Mary!' as loudly as she possibly can when she first appears. Then he asks Eleanor Smith, who plays Mary, how she should be feeling?

'Can she trust this thing?' she responds. 'It would be quite scary. She's never seen an angel before. She may not believe it because you can't have two dads. It would be really strange. Nobody has actually met God so it will be strange for an angel just to appear in your house and say, "You're going to have a baby." They had quite a few superstitions then. She may have thought the angel came because of a sin or something. She'd be all tense but then she starts to relax a bit. She probably doesn't believe it at first. It's a bit like a postman coming down and saying, "you're going to have a baby." Why would you say yes? I suppose because you want to feel honoured and involved.'

'What kind of person is Mary?' Bill Lucas asks her.

'She doesn't like to lie,' Eleanor responds. 'She's quite a holy person. She's quiet but when she has to, she can raise her voice quite loud.'

We turn towards Elizabeth Blunt who is playing the angel.

'Who is Gabriel?' Bill Lucas asks.

'He's the leader of the angels,' she replies. 'He's quite close to God. He's come from heaven as a messenger. God has told him what to say.'

'Is Gabriel a boy or a girl?' I ask.

'He's a boy,' she says, 'but it doesn't matter. There wasn't anyone else so my dad signed me up. I try to comfort Mary but it can't be done straight away.'

The production begins. Everyone sings 'Once in Royal David's City' before sitting down. Bill Lucas, now playing the part of The Storyteller, explains what is about to happen: 'One night Mary couldn't sleep. Perhaps it was Joseph's snoring in the house next door that kept her awake,' he proclaims.

The young boy playing Joseph, wearing a gown and a towel around his head, snores very loudly. Suddenly, the angel Gabriel appears from behind a pillar and calls out, 'Mary!' The angel has cardboard wings attached to her back and is wearing a full-length gold dress. Mary, wearing a long, light-blue headscarf and sitting on a chair in front of the altar, replies, 'Who's there? What do you want? The door's locked so you can't get in.'

'Mary!' the angel shouts out again.

'Who is it?' Mary asks. 'Joseph, is it you?'

Joseph is lying on the floor to the right of the altar. His snores echo around the church.

'How can he still be asleep?' Mary sighs.

The angel walks slowly towards her. 'An angel,' Mary proclaims as she gets down from the chair and kneels.

'Mary, you have been chosen. Listen to me!' says angel Gabriel. 'You are to have a child, a baby boy, God's own son. He will bring perfect love into the world. Do you understand?' She recites the words perfectly but is clearly nervous.

'A baby? God's son?' Mary asks. 'What are you talking about? What about Joseph?'

She looks across to Joseph who remains lying on the floor. 'We have no money. How will we buy food for a son? I don't know how to be a mother. This is all too much. Please, can I wake up now?'

146. The Annunciation encounter at the Nativity service, St Paul's Church, Winchester

Angel Gabriel replies, 'You are awake Mary. This is all real. You don't need to worry. God will give you strength. Lift up your voice, Mary! Do not be afraid. The Lord is near.'

There are many words to remember and at one point Gabriel needs a little prompt from her mother. The Storyteller walks towards the altar and stands just to the side of the angel Gabriel, Mary and Joseph.

'Now slowly the angel disappeared again, and Mary was left scratching her head,' he tells the audience. 'How can she trust a God who does strange things like this? What will she say to Joseph? But she has no time to think, my friends, because the story is moving on. The donkey is ready. And so are the musicians.'

A loud braying noise comes from the back of the church. Mary and Joseph head down the aisle as the congregation sings 'Little Donkey'. The play follows its traditional course as Mary and Joseph make their way to Bethlehem. There is a lovely moment at the end when all the angels, shepherds and kings gather around Mary and Joseph in the stable. Mary holds a real baby, born just nine days ago. Thankfully, he is as good as gold. One of the kings wanders off looking bored. Many of the angels wave to the audience and adoring mummies and daddies blow back kisses. For many families, this is a highlight of Christmas.

When the play is over, and all the photographs have been taken, I sit down with an exhausted Bill Lucas. His full-time job is Director of the Centre for Real-World Learning and Professor of Learning at the University of Winchester. He has written more than forty books on learning and creativity and, as a former teacher, he is ideally placed to answer how best to pitch the annunciation story to a young audience. I begin our conversation by asking how important is it for him that a Nativity play starts with the Annunciation scene?

'It's very important,' he replies. 'You can take all sorts of decisions about whether you have it in or not but, for me, this is a service. So I'm wanting to go right back to that moment of deep understanding when a mere mortal is faced with something quite impossible, quite unbelievable, quite extraordinary. For me, it's a really interesting acknowledgement of the role Mary plays and the fact that this isn't a virgin birth but a virgin conception. That's critically important to the overall story.'

I observe that in his version, Joseph is next to Mary, albeit fast asleep.

'Although I say it's a service, it has huge elements of pantomime,' he says. 'He's got to be there somehow, I think. They're not married so there's another agenda here. Even though Mary doesn't talk about the social opprobrium that might follow, we leave that space in for the adult minds to think about. So we have him there symbolically.'

How much can a child understand the overall story? I wonder.

'It's one of the most difficult things for children and adults,' he replies. 'I think in some ways, as children don't understand the mechanics, and this is a children's story, that's not very unusual at all. Think dragons, fables, the miraculous. It's actually very easy for them to take it in at a basic plot level. I think it's almost impossible for them to take in what's really going on here. Nevertheless, I'm stunned every year by the thoughtful diligence that whoever is playing the angel Gabriel and Mary manage to speak their lines. It's such a tricky concept. They're a sort of conduit, by saying their lines very simply and without any trace of irony.'

I notice he leaves out the word 'virgin'.

'Yes, I do,' he says. 'It makes no sense at all to them. It introduces something that means nothing. I don't think I need to for the audience that comes to the service. That's an interesting question. I may be wrong.'

I say I also notice he leaves out Mary's acceptance. Is that intentional?

'It's just to move it on. There's a sort of inevitable selection. If you think liturgically, there are some hymns that just have to be in. We need to move the story on. Overall, it's about thirty-five minutes and that's about the limit.'

I tell him that, as a child, I always thought that Gabriel simply told Mary she was having a child and she had no opportunity to say no. And it's the same here.

'You're asking good questions but they're too subtle to ask about our particular story,' he replies.

What does he think the youngest children understand about the Annunciation sequence?

'Gosh!' he answers. 'I think they know mummies have babies. They know, if they have younger siblings, that Mummy tells them she's going to have a baby. Almost immediately, they know it's Mummy and Daddy's baby. There's a tiny question mark in a young child's mind about what's going on here.'

Do they see the encounter between Gabriel and Mary as fact?

'With regard to the psychological development of a child, they can't distinguish between fact and metaphor early on. They just can't,' he says. 'For the littlest ones, the question wouldn't make any sense. It's not conceptually possible. By five, six, seven, depending on the child, you begin to realize there are other meanings. When you're given a token, it can mean something else. When you hear a story, it can have another meaning too. So I'd distinguish between those who are maybe three, four and just five and those who are five, six and seven. I wouldn't want to be precise. Jean Piaget [the renowned French clinical psychologist known for his pioneering work in child development] had a go at this and we now think he got it precisely wrong in his four stages of child development. Anyone in their middle primary years would start to understand the subtlety of all this.'

So, in his view, the vast majority, if not all, of the younger children taking part this afternoon, would see it as true.

'Oh yes. Absolutely. I think they do,' he responds.

I tell him how one Bishop describes the Annunciation as 'the most important event in human history'.

'I would absolutely agree. If your question begs a narrative, then existentially, if there's a concept of *before*, there must have been in the imagined mind of God, a *pre*, even greater moment, in which you sketch out that this is the hinge point on which all the Gospels hang and all the Old Testament prophecies will make sense. Conceptually, I think, there's a bigger miracle, which is the idea of God. The idea of God is almost the bigger idea. The idea of God so loving and shaping the world that all this is going to happen. But I do think the Annunciation is the hinge point.'

As 'Shepherd Bill', he has been directing the Nativity service here for the last twelve years. When he sees the Annunciation scene in action, what does he think?

'Every time I think different things. I always think, in amongst the muddle and trying to stay calm, different things. Each and every year, it raises different thoughts, different questions, different feelings. That's the beauty of it.'

––––––

The rector of my local church, has written a special message to his parishioners: 'The weeks before Christmas have become a very busy and often stressful time for people. The temptation to spend more than we can afford is all around us, and resisting this can be hard. Our faith challenges us to look beyond ourselves to the poor and homeless. The season of Advent is a wonderful opportunity to be reminded of what's most important – God's love for everyone.'

Peter Seal's favourite word of the year is resonance. He urges us to follow his example and ask ourselves each day, 'Does this activity have resonance in our lives? Does it touch us deep down? Does it connect with those things we believe most strongly and hold most dear?'

In his monthly address in the Parish Magazine he writes: 'What I'm discovering anew is the challenge of asking, "How does the Christian faith resonate with people's lives today?" This seems to me to be the crucial question – and the answers are varied and multi-layered. We live in an age where easy answers just don't work, but it's important to go on asking the big questions.'

It seems the ideal time to ask in what way the annunciation story resonates for him. I head to the Rectory on Cheriton Road. His study is extremely ordered – there's a neat desktop and his books are filed on various shelves. There are two photographs on the back wall. One shows him shaking hands with Pope John Paul II, taken when he was staying at the English College in Rome. The other is of his ordination in Wareham in Dorset in 1984, with his father and father-in-law, both Anglican priests, beside him.

He says he felt a first calling at thirteen, when his father had a parish in a rough area of Litchfield in Staffordshire.

'Some yobs smashed some red votive candles in the church and I told them to get out. I was enraged. It stayed with me for years. Looking back, I realize then that I held it all very dear,' he tells me.

At nineteen, he went to Exeter University to study Psychology and Sociology but 'in a dramatic moment' switched on his second day to Theology and, after graduating in 1980, went for selection to the priesthood. He trained at Lincoln Theological College and the English College in Rome.

Does he see a parallel between his experience and the annunciation story in that he heard a calling and said yes to the invitation?

'That's expressed perfectly,' he replies. 'She was free. I was free. I spent a long time saying no but my yes was pulled out of me.'

What does the story mean for him?

'It's our way of understanding God becoming human,' he says. 'It's the response of this slip of a girl – a teenage pregnancy but not – to God's invitation to her to do something she would never have dreamed of, couldn't believe, probably at lots of levels didn't want, but something in her said, "I'll do that." For me, it's the beginning of the Incarnation.'

Does he see it as the very moment of the Incarnation?

'What I find fascinating is that Jesus was present before the foundation of the world, so this was God's moment to choose that place and time. Quite why that time we'll probably never know. It does feel that it's profoundly different before and after and it does feel a historic time frame.'

Does he believe that Gabriel commanded Mary to have the baby or did she have free will?

'It feels like an invitation but one you probably wouldn't refuse,' he replies. 'It's possibly a bit like vocation to the priesthood. It is an invitation but you probably know you'd be unwise to decline or you wouldn't be fulfilled/happy if you decline. I think it's got to remain invitation and free will. I never talk about God having a plan. I prefer the word "purpose". It's not all mapped out. God has a dream for you, me and everyone else and we can take all sorts of variants and decisions to make that happen.'

Does he see the story as fact or metaphor?

'I see it, perhaps uncharacteristically, as fact. I think at this moment in time the woman Mary bore a human being that was completely divine and completely human. I think she had an overwhelming awareness from God that she understood and interpreted. Whether, literally, she saw an angel is less important to me.'

What does he think about those who say the story is a metaphor?

'Metaphor, myths, are real,' he responds. 'The story is talking about a deep reality. It doesn't mean it's not true. It's true. It's real.'

What does true mean for him?

'Certainly the message is true. At the most basic, it makes sense. You hear the story over the years again and again and you test it out. Does it make sense? Does it resonate? Does it connect deeply? For me, it's incredibly real. The possibility. The excitement. The dread.'

And was this a unique event?

'Whatever else, Jesus, the man, was unique. He was God on earth. Those who talk about becoming like Jesus, I say no! It's not our agenda. It's about you becoming Mark; me becoming like Peter. We're not God.'

Does he support the notion of the Virgin Birth?

'To be accurate, it's the virgin conception, not the Virgin Birth' he corrects me. 'I think I would. As I understand it, she became pregnant and then she had a normal gestation and gave birth naturally. But her perpetual virginity is not important to me. When they married, who knows? Mary and Joseph probably had normal marital relations. It doesn't trouble me at all.'

Peter Seal moved to Winchester in 1987 as chaplain at King Alfred's College before it became the University of Winchester. He has been the rector of the parish of St Matthew with St Paul in the city since 2000. He is almost sixty but has a boyish face and an air of innocence about him.

I ask what he thinks of the statement that the Annunciation is 'the most important event in human history'.

'That makes sense,' he says. 'It was the defining moment when our salvation unfolded in its fullest way. They all belong together, from conception through to resurrection, but, yes, that's the start.'

If there is one word that sums up the annunciation story for him, what would it be?

'Response,' he says confidently.

What does Mary mean to him? Does he venerate her?

'I regularly pray the Hail Mary,' he responds. 'In that prayer, we're not praying to Mary. We're asking Mary to pray for us. That I find very powerful. I think she's an exemplar, very close to the Godhead because of her place in salvation history. Mother Teresa wrote a lovely piece about Mary having a special affection for priests. I always found that rather powerful and supportive. I do believe the prayers of Mary are very strong.'

He sees Mary as a kind of protector, I suggest.

'I like that. I like that very much,' he says.

As a body, does he think Anglicanism has got Mary wrong?

'I have a sadness that a lot of people, being careful here, are missing out. There is a wealth of riches in an appropriate devotion of and to Mary. She's incredibly important. Understandably, some people say Mary is used as an intermediary. She is prayed to when you can only pray to Jesus, the one mediator.'

So, when he says the Hail Mary, is he praying to Mary?

'No,' he replies. 'I'm asking Mary to pray for me. I'm invoking the prayers of Mary, full of grace. At tough times. In the night. When you're really agonizing. She's very powerful.'

Is she a bridge or a barrier to greater unity between Roman Catholics and Anglicans?

'Potentially, she's a bridge but now she may well be a barrier,' he replies.

Recently, Peter Seal has been holding a series of get-togethers in the parish, aimed at those with no apparent belief, under the banner of 'Puzzling Questions'.

What would he say if I came along and told him I couldn't understand or believe the annunciation story?

'Don't worry,' he replies. 'Most of faith is a gift. I'd want to expose with them what it is they can believe. I often want to say, what is it you don't believe? You then often find much more common ground than you ever imagined. I remember someone describing the Creed as an agenda. It's much more than that for me. It's invaluable as a concise setting out of the Christian doctrine and belief. But different people will give different weight to different bits and I want to say, "Don't worry".'

What would he say if I said, I couldn't believe in the Resurrection?

'I suppose I usually find wondering whether someone is a Christian or not is pretty unhelpful,' he replies. 'The sort of definition of Christian and non-Christian, I never use it. Some may say that's a bit woolly. "Come on Peter, get defined, there must be boundaries." For me, it's a freedom, an inclusive outreach that is much more likely to lead people to a journey of further discovery rather than, "you must do this, you must believe that". I want to say within the Church, the Resurrection is a key bit of teaching. I believe it. Read John 2:20 and put yourself in Mary's place. Every time I read it, I'm completely arrested by it. I think it's completely real. But then there are so many conversations to be had about the nature of the resurrection body. He was radically different. Simple resuscitation? Forget it. He was dead, completely finished. The Resurrection is crucially important.'

Has his view of the annunciation story changed during his life?

'For me, the hugely deepening experience was being in Rome for five months,' he replies. 'That privilege to live alongside around eighty Roman Catholic seminarians. I got an understanding of what it was to be serious about faith, partly because of the celibacy they were having to embrace and I remember vivid experiences of praying in the Martyrs Chapel at the English College and being deeply touched. The whole area of the saints was opened up to me, including Mary. I hadn't thought about it much before if I'm honest but I started to think about the breadth and the depth. I think part of our calling here in England is to...', his voice tails off for a second or two, '...well, it's the breadth and the depth. I was at a service the other day. I didn't sense depth at all. I thought this has lost its way. We need to give people credit for serious thought and intelligent engagement. The Church needs to say we can drill down together. I'm still discovering every day. I think it's that element of response that has grown for me,' he continues. 'Here is this person hearing this invitation and saying yes. That has deepened in me.'

I suggest that it sounds as though his faith is rather grounded in Roman Catholicism.

'I have good friends from those days in Rome,' he says. 'There's a most wonderful, charming man, who's now a Catholic bishop in England, who took me out for a supper on my last day in Rome and we had a wonderful dinner and at the end he said, "I'm just checking, you don't think you're making a mistake?" But I've never thought I was. I'm happy in my Anglicanism but I was deeply and massively enriched there.'

I look behind me at the photograph of him with Pope John Paul II. He looks as if he is in awe. Can he see a day when Roman Catholicism and Anglicanism will come together as one?

'I don't see it,' he says. 'We've travelled enormously in terms of understanding and self-respect and we're actually in a better place than when I was first ordained thirty years ago when we really thought there would be one Church. Church membership is a complex psychological thing and there are different trends and personalities attracted to different styles of worship and I think we should say "Hooray!" to that. Every tradition has got its extraordinary riches and we should rejoice in that. There's something highly desirable in telling good stories about each other but also appropriate humility.'

I show him the Lemoyne painting.

'I see a dancing angel, a touch almost of frivolity, not unsexual, his low-cut dress, showing a leg. She is meek and composed. Appropriately confident, not fearful. I quite like it. I like the movement of the angel and the slight lightheartedness and especially her looking at ease, not fearful.'

———

At the Christmas Day morning service, I sit, by chance, next to Peter Seal's wife, Julia, and their son, Philip. Their daughter Katie is not there. Peter tells the congregation that she has recently joined the Sisters of St Andrew at Ameugny in France, near to the Taizé community. For five years, she has been exploring what God is calling her to do in a long journey of discernment. After much prayer, he says, she has concluded that she needs to see if God is calling her to live in a religious community as a Sister. The Order of the Sisters of St Andrew is founded on the life and teaching of St Ignatius of Loyola, more commonly known as the Jesuits. During this initial stage of discernment, she is called a postulant and can leave at any time. She is now known as Sister Katie. She has no mobile phone and her parents speak to her on the landline once a fortnight. Whilst supporting their beloved daughter, they struggle with the limited level of contact and this is clearly a tough time for them.

After the service, I talk with Katie's brother Phil, an English graduate who recently completed his doctorate at Balliol College at the University of Oxford. His thesis was on theological poetics, focusing on the poetry and prose writings of the mystic, Thomas Merton. Now he teaches English at a secondary school in Oxford. We talk about my Annunciation journey. 'Is there still time for me to write a poem for you?' he asks. 'Of course, I reply.'

A few days later, he sends me his poem, entitled 'Annunciations':

She is cornered: the night
Stalks strangely around her like
A predatory God. She will
Weep as the creature
Leaves its arrogant gift.

She is shocked: rude lights
Trespass the regular dreams
Of her teenage sleep. She will
Groan as the unsought
Burden settles and swells.

She is drawn: her eyes
Engage the angel's
Alien glow. She will
Ponder her awkward task
As the half-life stirs.

She is held: the surprising
Guardian offers his hand
To quell her fright. She will
Choose to accept the risks
Of blood and flesh.

She sings her yes: Gabriel
Greets the news with
Wide delight. Mary
Proclaims her Lord
And wants her child.

I write back, thanking him for his creative gift. I ask Philip Seal if he is familiar with Thomas Merton's 1957 poem, 'The Annunciation'. 'Not one of his very best,' he says.

Merton, of course, was one of the best known and most influential religious writers of the twentieth century. Born in 1915, he converted to Roman Catholicism at Columbia University and later, in 1941, became a Trappist monk, entering the Abbey of Gethsemane belonging to the Order of Cistercians of the Strict Observance. He died in 1968 aged 53 of an accidental electrocution whilst on a trip to Bangkok for a conference on East-West monastic dialogue. So enthralling are Merton's prolific and deeply spiritual reflections and commentaries that I decide his poem has to be part of my poetry compendium. Here is 'The Annunciation':

Ashes of paper, ashes of a world
Wandering, when fire is done:
We argue with the drops of rain!

Until One comes Who walks unseen
Even in elements we have destroyed.
Deeper than any nerve
He enters flesh and bone.
Planting His truth, He puts our substance on.
Air, earth, and rain
Rework the frame that fire has ruined.
What was dead is waiting for His Flame.
Sparks of His Spirit spend their seeds, and his
To grow like irises, born before summertime.
These blue things bud in Israel.

The girl prays by the bare wall
Between the lamp and the chair.
(Framed with an angel in our galleries
She has a richer painted room, sometimes a crown.
Yet seven pillars of obscurity
Build her to Wisdom's house, and Ark, and Tower.
She is the Secret of another Testament
She owns their manna in her jar.)

Fifteen years old —
The flowers printed on her dress
Cease moving in the middle of her prayer
When God, Who sends the messenger,
Meets His messenger in her Heart.
Her answer, between breath and breath,
Wrings from her innocence our sacrament!
In her white body God becomes our Bread.

It is her tenderness
Heats the world like David on his bed.
Times that were too soon criminal
And never wanted to be normal
Evade the beast that has pursued
You, me and Adam out of Eden's wood.
Suddenly we find ourselves assembled
Cured and recollected under several green trees.

Her prudence wrestled with the Dove
To hide us in His cloud of steel and silver:
These are the mysteries of her Son.
And here my heart, a purchased outlaw,
Prays in her possession
Until her Jesus makes my heart
Smile like a flower in her blameless hand.

CHAPTER 38

MY FAMILY

Most of the people I have encountered on this journey are 'believers'. They come from a Christian background and interpret Luke's story of the Annunciation from a position of faith. Each has his or her interpretation of the message and an opinion on whether or not it actually happened. But it is important to remember that a large percentage of the British population has no Christian faith. Many do not believe in the Annunciation, nor do they believe in the Incarnation or the Resurrection.

Whilst hearing such views is not the purpose of this book, I feel it is essential to capture some of the reasons why atheists, agnostics and non-believers dismiss the story.

I turn to my own family. It is the first time I have spoken to each of them at length about their thoughts on religion and, in particular, the Annunciation. My wife, Hilary, and my five adult children were all baptized in the Christian faith. Today, none of them believes in Jesus Christ, nor do they attend church. What do they make of Luke's story? What do they make of the proposition that it is the most important event in human history? And, lastly, what do they make of the Lemoyne painting? All will have views that I know I should hear.

147. Christmastime and the Byford family comes together

Hilary Byford was born Hilary Bleiker in Gibraltar in 1958. She describes her father, Paul, as an atheist and her mother, Cicely, as a 'traditional Church of England believer who went to church on a Sunday.'

I wonder if that difference between her parents confused her during childhood.

'I think it did,' she says. 'When one parent doesn't follow the other, then naturally you question that belief.'

She explains how, as a young child, she accepted what she was told regarding Jesus. 'It was just part of what you did, a bit like believing in Santa Claus, and there was a comfort in that.'

She played both an angel and Mary in her school Nativity plays. 'I remember my main worry was, would I drop the baby?' As a teenager, she went to church regularly on a Sunday, 'because my mother went and it was a part of my life for a while.' She stopped going when she turned sixteen.

'As you get older, you experience more of life and it becomes more important to know what you think and why you think it,' she tells me. 'I think human beings, as part of an evolutionary process, have developed a conscience, and understand that they need rules in order to carry on the species without falling into complete anarchy. I think religion is a human construct that is there to provide a framework of moral behaviour, to mollify the fact that death exists by giving a promise of life after death, and to try to explain the human race and where we sit in the universe. It's a way of answering those big questions that are essentially unanswerable. Why is the universe here? Why are we here? Man has always asked these questions. Aristotle and Plato for example – great philosophers who lived way before Jesus – were outstanding thinkers who questioned why we're here and where we stand in the universe. We still look back and study their words, looking for the answer, gaining meaning and understanding from them. The ancient Egyptians came up with their own belief system that was filled with different gods who influenced every aspect of life from the weather to human behaviour, and perpetuated the idea of life after death. Then the scientists had a go. Darwin attempted to explain how and why we are here in his theory of evolution. But he couldn't explain what happened before life on earth. I think religion is a manifestation of people trying to explain what life's all about, trying to make sense of it all. Why does the sun come up each morning? Why are we all here? Why do we have to die? What happens after we die? And all that.

'Jesus was possibly one of those great philosophers who understood that humans need morality and a set of rules,' she continues. 'His teachings were rather lucid, hold all kinds of truths about human behaviour and give guidance about how to lead a good life. I don't think the whole story is a complete myth. I think it's quite possible Jesus was a charismatic leader who claimed he was the Almighty, the Son of God. Strong leaders who stand the test of time crop up once in a while and are never forgotten. I definitely don't think he was Son of God. It is clear that he made a big impact on those around him, and the gospel writings are a way of making sure he wasn't forgotten. I don't believe he rose from the dead at all. I don't believe things that are not possible.

'Now we have science and technology to help us try to understand why we are here but then, more than 2,000 years ago, everything must have seemed so miraculous. Perhaps it's logical to think there must be a bigger being who created the universe and who will one day make himself known to us. It's understandable that people want to believe that.'

Hilary Bleiker studied English at the University of Leeds and graduated in 1980. We had met there two years previously and married two months after her graduation ceremony. She was twenty-one. I was twenty-two. Thirty-five years later, this is probably the most in-depth conversation we have ever had about religion and belief. We move on to discuss specifically the Annunciation.

'I don't believe it at all,' she says dismissively. 'It never happened. I believe it's an attempt to give retrospective significance to the mother of Jesus. It's trying to assign a religious context to the creation of Jesus. When the gospels were written, it was important to make the story as spectacular as possible. The writers would have thought, how can we make people sit up and listen to this story? It's embellishment.'

There is a striking confidence and certainty in her voice. As a non-believer, I wonder what she makes of the statement that the Annunciation is the most important event in human history.

'If you believe it happened, it would be, but, for me, it means nothing. I am incredulous that people believe it.'

What does she make of Mary's virgin conception?

'Ridiculous,' she replies. 'Of course it is. It can't happen.'

But that's the whole point, I suggest. That's what a miracle is.

'I understand that. But surely the people who wrote the New Testament, were thinking, how do we make this really special? To claim the conception happened when she was a virgin would immediately make Mary and Jesus stand out...both were special even before he was born. Of course, it's quite possible that Mary always contended she was a virgin but actually had been fooling around with Joseph. It's possible that although there was no full penetration, she still got pregnant. A lack of medical understanding might have led them to presume the conception was a miracle. There are explanations for most things.'

So, she wholly rejects the notion of an angel coming to Mary and announcing a virgin conception, I ask.

'That could be explained by the fact that she had a dream,' she responds. 'Perhaps as a way of trying to make sense of the pregnancy, someone seized on that idea. It's difficult because we have to judge things from a modern-day perspective. It could be their experience was totally different. I wouldn't be so arrogant though as to offer the explanation. Who am I to say my version is the correct one. No one knows. Certainly not me. It is certainly explainable from a scientific view. It is also possible that the gospel authors wanted to attribute retrospectively the godliness of Jesus or it could even be a combination of the two.'

So for her, I repeat, her perspective is that the Annunciation is mere fiction?

'Yes, absolutely,' she replies firmly. 'I would say I am a humanist. If someone comes up with a viable explanation and concrete proof then obviously, I would listen. But I just think I'm pragmatic by nature and I'm not prepared to say I believe in something just because others do. However, I am open to the idea that there may be a higher power – whether that resides in the laws of nature or the laws of physics – I don't know. And the problem is, neither does anyone else.'

She stares at me, wanting to see my reaction to her response. I remain impassive and continue to listen.

'I haven't mentioned psychological development,' she continues. 'I do think there are certain people who strive to find spirituality for a variety of reasons – genetics, personality, and later in life, upbringing and life experience. I think some people are born to be more open to religion. Not everybody has that. Those people want to believe in something outside themselves and will look until they find it. Then there are others who feel they don't need to do that to be fulfilled. They feel quite complete in themselves and their place in the world. I can understand that religion has much to offer – the wonderful architecture, literature and art that it has inspired, the sense of community it offers and the comfort it can provide. But it's not for me.'

What does she feel about those who say the Annunciation definitely happened just as Luke's account states?

'You've got people saying, "yes, I'm a Christian" but also claiming they don't believe in the Annunciation. They cherry pick those bits they want to believe in which, as a non-Christian, I think is a bit strange. Yet it's a good thing to question. I think those people who do believe it all without questioning are gullible. But if that's what makes their life complete and makes them feel better, then who am I to criticize? It does mystify me though.'

I show her the print of the Lemoyne picture. She has also seen close up the original painting at the National Gallery.

'The whole tone of the painting is rather sickly. It's very sentimental. Look at those cherubim. The problem is if you don't believe it, then it's just a story. It's so romanticized. Mary doesn't look traumatized. She looks almost grateful. She's so subservient, replicating the traditional role of women, which I don't like. It's almost referring back to mythology. People striving to understand. It's a human being's desire to have answers. This painting has that tone to it.'

She continues to gaze at the picture.

'The composition and colours are beautiful and the light is very well depicted. I'd glance at it but I certainly wouldn't linger.'

What about those believers who say the Annunciation is a metaphor – the story never actually happened but it carries an important message and explanation?

'I don't get that unless, of course, the whole thing is a metaphor, or it's allegorical. In which case, Jesus is a fictional character based on someone who existed,' she replies. 'Perhaps the Bible is like John Bunyan's *The Pilgrims Progress*, where all the characters and the situations they find themselves in are fictional but the story refers to another, deeper truth and serves as moral guidance to those who read it. An allegory. I could be open to that. It would take a huge leap of the imagination but I could get that. I don't think you can say that one part of the overall story is metaphor and another part is fact. Either all the events in the Bible happened or the story is a metaphor – a metaphor on how to live life well so the human race doesn't annihilate itself.'

Does she think she'll always hold such views?

'Yes, unless something new happens. The one question I would love to be answered is how the universe was created. If scientists get to that, I think they will either prove the existence of God, whatever that is, or destroy it.'

———

Christmas is the one time each year when all our five adult children are with us in the family home. This time, I want to take the chance to sit down with each one to discuss the Annunciation. All were baptized as babies in the Roman Catholic Church. All made their First Holy Communion at St Peter's church in Winchester, aged seven. All were educated in a local Church of England primary school and the same state comprehensive school and sixth form college in the city. All are university educated. They were encouraged to go to Mass every Sunday but were allowed to make up their own minds whether or not to attend when they were fifteen or sixteen. Today, none of them would describe themselves as Christian. Engaging with each of them about their thoughts on the annunciation story will provide me with a rare and valuable opportunity to try and understand why they hold those views.

My eldest son, Sam, is twenty-nine years old and lives in Tokyo, Japan. He studied English at Manchester University and is now the Asia Editor of a US based technology website called 'The Verge'. As a child, he was a voracious reader. He devoured books. One of his favourites was his *Children's Bible*.

'The annunciation story didn't feel unusual,' he recalls. 'The whole Bible is full of angels and booming voices from heaven.'

Did he believe the story as child? I ask.

'I didn't ever believe it. I have no memory of ever believing any Bible story,' he replies. 'To some degree, I believed it was based on some fact but I never thought it was literal truth. I didn't have much opinion on it. It never occurred to me that believing it was the particular point of the story. It seems to me that anyone who believes in every word of the Bible only believes it because of tradition. It necessarily implies that everyone born in countries that don't know the Bible are wrong, which is absolutely ridiculous. They're kind of fairy stories that people are brought up to believe in the same way North American Indians have their stories and Hindus have theirs and Muslims have theirs. For those saying they believe theirs is the absolute truth when the only reason they believe the stories is the way they were brought up and the traditions of their countries, I think, is ridiculous. But that does not mean that the stories don't have value. That's why religions continue to this day. But believing in the actual veracity of the story misses the whole point of it.

'I now have solid opinions and beliefs that I didn't have as a child,' he continues. 'I doubt I could articulate what I'm saying now when I was eight years old but I never ever believed it. I remember believing in Santa Claus as a child but I never believed in the Annunciation and the whole Nativity story.'

Does he hold to the view that a man called Jesus was conceived 2,000 years ago?

'Yes, historians are agreed on that,' he says. 'But I don't see any evidence he was divine other than the Bible, which I would say is shaky evidence. I studied linguistics at university. I know how much can get lost in translation. The language of the Bible isn't even spoken today. I don't think it's fair to see it as a historical document. It's a religious text and that doesn't have to be fact. If you have this figure who you want to centre a religion around, it makes sense to establish him as an Otherworldly character from the off, and an angel implanting a virgin is a good way of starting off from a story perspective. It's plausible.'

So he thinks the annunciation story is a metaphor?

'Of course,' he replies. 'It's pure story telling. It's a fairy story in the sense of a story about the supernatural. The metaphor itself is for religious scholars to work out. It's an evocative setting, an evocative happening. I don't know if Luke, who wrote this particular story, believed it. You could say it's a metaphor about calling or you could say it's just a story about calling. That's just semantics.'

Is it because you don't have facts that you don't think you can trust the story to be true? I suggest.

'That's rather an evasive way to frame it,' he responds. 'You need something to go on to even have the reason to trust in the story in the first place. I would put to you that the reason why Christians in the UK would trust it is because it was passed down to them. Very few people come to the decision, "I'm now going to start believing in it" as an adult. Yes, there are born-again Christians who may do that at a time in their lives when they're searching for something. Level-headed adults don't normally say, "I've read this book and I believe that everything in it happened." That's not how they think in the twenty-first century.

'I understand that it's about faith but it's important to know where the faith comes from. You can't just have faith for no reason. Don't get me wrong, I'm far from the atheist who preaches science and reason and logic and Richard Dawkin and all that. I think that's an obnoxious attitude. But at the same time, you can't say it's about truth with no basis for the faith. I don't think you would apply the same criteria to any other document from that age in terms of taking it at its word because the standards of record were not anywhere near that. We have the Bible and the Gospels because that's what we have to go on. There are other writings from that time that you, yourself, wouldn't believe in. I suppose that's when a leap of faith comes in. But you need a reason to believe it. Either a reason of culture or because it was passed down.'

I note that I passed it down to him and yet he has decided to say no.

'It was clear to me from an early age that Mum wasn't really religious,' he responds. 'I think when I was brought up, it was a different time to you. The country has become secular really fast. Maybe if you'd brought me up with a religious wife and living in America I would have believed it. Mum never said she didn't believe it but it was clear she didn't really care about it like you did and do.'

Did he feel that he was being indoctrinated as a child?

'I did have a sense that my Sunday mornings were being taken up for something I considered a waste of time. But I wouldn't say that was instructive in my belief or lack of belief.'

When he was seven, eight and nine, did he think going to church was a waste of time?

'I don't begrudge it. I think religion is interesting, a deep topic, and there's no harm in knowing about it. But, increasingly, it's not for me and people like me. Technically, I'm an atheist but I think that word has been hijacked by people I'd rather not be associated with. If you want to break down a definition, it's that no one really knows. No one knows. You, yourself, have a faith. If the angel Gabriel appeared to me now, I'd probably believe in God. Neither of us is a hundred per cent sure. That's the point. Everyone is agnostic to a point. I'm probably better described as agnostic. There's no reason for me to believe in a God.'

What does he think about those who believe that the Annunciation happened as stated in Luke's story, and that the virgin conception resulted in a child who was both divine and human?

'I think a lot of people are searching for something. For a lot of people, it's what's passed down and is the path of least resistance. It's what they grew up with. Clearly, it's not a sign of intelligence nor that they're wrong. It's what some people have in the world. Some believe. Some don't.'

Has his experience of living in Japan for the past seven years in any way shaped his thinking?

'I think Japan, of all countries, handles the question of religion the best. It takes the best of religion in terms of architecture, the traditions, and it renders them in the modern climate in a way that is very benign. There's no downside to it nor is there fundamentalism and the preaching of extremism. Young people are quite in touch with the traditions of Japan. They would go to a shrine to worship a god without the hint of belief in the god. It's a nice way to keep in touch with the traditions of the country. It's the norm. It's probably the most atheist country in the world but the vast majority of people would describe themselves as Buddhist. They're respectful of the tradition and the architecture. In the same way, I believe a guy called Jesus existed. There's enough historical evidence to persuade me of that and he must have had a mother.'

What does he think of the statement that the Annunciation is the most important event in human history?

'If you believe in Jesus as God then yes but that sounds a bit grandiose to me. As a non-Christian, that seems to be overstating it even if you believe it. I don't see how that event has such resonance. If you extend that logic, Muhammad Ali's birth is more important than the Rumble in the Jungle. It's a strange way of thinking. As a non-Christian, it seems to me that people believe Jesus came down from heaven to take the bullet for humanity. The Crucifixion and the Resurrection are far more evocative, strong and symbolic than the fact of his existence in the first place. Obviously, it's the start of the story but it seems to me to call the Annunciation the pivotal moment is to be missing the forest from the trees. At the end of it, you have a baby but the baby didn't do all those things.'

He looks at Lemoyne's painting.

'I don't dislike it but I wouldn't hang it on my wall. I don't think the idea of any organized religion would have any appeal to me. All the inter-denominational squabbling shows the absurdity of it all. That has nothing to do with personal faith and is missing the point. If you want to believe in God fine, but for me to align myself with an organized religion would have to be a transformative event, and that hasn't happened yet.'

———

My eldest daughter, Molly, is twenty-seven when we talk about the Annunciation. A Cardiff University graduate in English and Communication Studies, she is now a TV producer and director. She tells me that when she was five she can remember being an angel in a school Nativity production, performing in an old people's home. Then, the following year, she was Gabriel's assistant. But one of her earliest childhood memories is watching me act out the annunciation story using little woollen figures of an angel and Mary when she was three or four. I ask her for her thoughts.

'It's a story someone came up with thousands of years ago – a nice story that's been passed down and believed over generations. I don't believe the actual event ever happened. I suppose there could possibly have been a woman who had sex out of wedlock and this story developed to make the birth of Jesus seem extra special. But I think it's just a story. It's like Father Christmas. The story of Jesus is a make-believe story that makes people feel good about themselves and gives them a reason for their existence.'

What does she think of the notion that an angel actually appeared before a fourteen-year-old girl called Mary in Nazareth?

'It's ridiculous,' she intervenes. 'I don't believe in angels. I don't believe in spirits.'

What about the virgin conception?

'It's ridiculous too. I just don't believe a girl can get pregnant without having sex.'

But that's the whole point, I tell her. This was a one-off miracle.

'I don't believe in miracles,' she says. 'It's nothing but fantasy. It would be lovely if it were true. It's a lovely story. But I can't believe it.'

She tells me she doesn't believe in the Crucifixion or the Resurrection either.

'I don't believe there was a man called Jesus.'

But that's an historical fact, I say.

'Let me clarify,' she says. 'I don't believe there was a man called Jesus who did all the things the Bible says he did. It's physically impossible to turn water into wine, to feed 5,000 people with a bit of fish and some loaves. I don't believe there was someone with such super powers and I certainly don't believe the angel Gabriel story. The story was passed on by word of mouth for years so I think it's like Chinese whispers. I think the truth is that the story has been twisted to gain people's interest. If you believe in miracles then you can believe anything can happen. It's a hype mechanism.

'I remember being next to my elder brother, Sam, at church and I really wanted to be an altar boy,' she continues. 'There was a boy on the altar who used to ring the bell and he had the best job. And another held the incense, swinging it back and forth, and another held a big pole with a cross on it. I really, really wanted to be one of them too. I liked the way they dressed and the power. I liked the theatre, the spectacle, the costumes. As a child, it was fascinating. But I never believed any of it. I never ever believed the bread wafer turned into Jesus's body.'

What does she say to the Bishop who told me the Annunciation is the most important event in human history?

'He's got an incredible imagination and I'm very jealous he can believe that. What an amazing thing to believe. But what an absurd thing to believe. I can't understand why my brain can't believe it but it just can't. I'd love to believe it. But I'd love to believe in Father Christmas too. I need very, very strong facts. I think those who believe just accept it. They don't have any evidence in front of them and they don't question. There's no video footage because it didn't exist then, of course. They just have to believe in the words. It's like reading someone's diary and believing everything that's in there happened. It could be a load of make believe but they take it at face value. Why should I believe something someone wrote over 2,000 years ago when there is no hard evidence to back it up? An angel flew down. There was a light, and a voice told a woman something miraculous. I can't believe that. Why would I believe that?'

Does she think the annunciation story is a lie, a fabrication, an exaggeration or what?

'Perhaps a woman called Mary did become pregnant and they've come up with the best story in the world so she wouldn't be shunned. I think it's just a story. I've watched a lot of films about cults. There may have been a man named Jesus, who made people believe he had superpowers, which were then written into a story that became so spectacular that everyone believed it. But I just don't believe all that. I don't believe Mary existed as mother of God. I think religion attempts to explain why we are here and to give us hope that there's life after death. I believe that like any other animal on the planet, I'm here to continue a race – it's all about creation. There's no other reason for me being here. And I don't need to believe that there's life after death.

'I'm open to things if people can prove them to me,' she continues. 'I don't say religion isn't true. I don't believe in God now but I'm open to people trying to persuade me. There's still that one per cent. I'd like to believe. It does give you a purpose. It answers the questions most people can't answer. Wouldn't it be great if miracles could exist.'

She offers me a cheeky smile before offering a further thought.

'I've grown up in a family of five children with a religious dad, and we went to church every single Sunday to the age of fourteen or fifteen. As a child your mind is very easily influenced and you believe what your parents say to you. Yet I think it's quite telling that now, not one of us believes in God. Maybe Mum's influence was stronger than yours. But I think it's very strange that none of those influences and experiences in our earlier lives could determine our minds and make us have even a glimmer that maybe it's true.

'When you are young, you believe in a lot of things that are fantasy – the tooth fairy, Father Christmas, the Borrowers existing in your bath tub. And you would tell us the birth story of Jesus was true. Then, there was always that moment when we found out that those stories weren't true. Perhaps we just applied the same logic to the Bible stories – that they weren't true either. I guess that's part of childhood and growing up. We just believed in so many things and they were all really great to believe in and it was quite upsetting when we didn't believe them any longer.

'Maybe it was when Mum finally told me. When we were young she came to church and said she believed it all but it must have been that one day she told me she didn't believe. We know it's your thing Dad. You're the religious one and you quite like that. It's always you that's away with the fairies. You always have these big ideas about everything and you're like a child. You like to accept things and you'd rather believe something is true than question it and maybe change your mind. You just believe it whereas Mum is like me. She needs facts whereas you have one of those child-like minds.'

She has never been so candid with me before. I tell her I welcome her honesty. I show her the Lemoyne painting.

'I don't like it,' she says immediately. 'He looks way too authoritative and powerful and she looks so vulnerable and can't do anything about him. He's higher than her, stronger than her, and he's got his arm raised. There's something about his pose. And she looks weak and vulnerable and under his spell. Yes, it looks like he's casting a spell on a child. She doesn't look in control. It's so spooky. She's in the dark, looking all pathetic and inferior. And he's in the light, this great character. And yet it's supposed to be saying something lovely that thousands of people believe in.'

What would make her believe that the annunciation story is true?

'Video footage,' she chuckles. 'I don't think I'll ever believe it.'

––––––––––

Flora, a Bournemouth University graduate in Multi-Media Journalism, reads the words of the annunciation story again in the books that I have laid out on a table for her. It is the first time in years that my twenty-three-year-old daughter has thought about this.

There are three different children's Bibles and three books about the Christmas story, which I bought when they were children. One tiny book called *Christmas* by Jan Pienkowski has a wonderfully evocative illustration, featuring his trademark black silhouette figures, showing the angel arriving as Mary hangs out the washing. I ask her for her memories of the annunciation story.

'I remember Gabriel came to Mary to give her a message that she would have a baby called Jesus. I remember it mainly from primary school assemblies and Nativity plays,' Flora recalls.

What does the annunciation story mean for her today?

'Nothing really. I suppose the story means Christmas to me because I always associate it with the start of a Nativity play.'

Does she believe the story?

'No,' she replies firmly. 'Personally, I think the Bible teaches you morals and gives guidance for life. I agree with a lot of it but I don't think the events in it happened. I believe Jesus was a human being, a son of Mary, and he was a good man. But I don't believe he was the Son of God. He was just a man who did good deeds and was blessed.'

Does the story of the angel Gabriel and Mary have any message for her? I ask.

'If anything, it's about going with the unexpected and it teaches that the unexpected can sometimes be a blessing rather than an unhappy surprise.'

As a child, did she believe the story to be true?

'I was never certain about it,' she replies. 'I never thought the Nativity story actually happened. I think it's a nice comforter, to give people hope and tell them what they want to hear. But around sixteen years old, I started to talk about it with friends. I studied Religious Education GCSE at school until I was sixteen. I thought deeply about it and then realized, I don't believe in God. I don't think the things in the New Testament actually happened. It's all a metaphor about the human condition, a higher power and how to live your life.'

So, what of the statement that the Annunciation is the most important event in human history?

'If I was a Christian, I'd think otherwise. I'd say Christmas and Easter rather than just the announcement of the conception. Surely the sacrifice of Jesus is more important. That happened after all his teachings and, therefore, means more.'

I can see her studying a picture of Mary in one of the books. I ask what Mary means to her.

'She's quite vulnerable. She didn't choose it. I think she may have slept with someone else. I don't think badly of Mary. To bring up the Son of God would be a big task but she doesn't have an impact on me at all.'

I show her Lemoyne's painting.

'It's an amazing painting but it leaves me with no lasting religious feelings. It doesn't make me feel anything beyond the fact that I think it's a lovely painting. I'm an atheist but I don't like that word. They preach not to preach. I call myself a quiet atheist.'

—

My younger son Harry is twenty-one, a guitarist in a band, and studying Philosophy and Linguistics at the University of Leeds. I ask him his opinion of the annunciation story.

'Obviously the story is a metaphor,' he says. 'Anyone who doesn't think it's a metaphor is deluded. It's literally not something that could happen.'

But that is the whole point of the story, I say. It is a unique, one-off event.

'My view is that God's omnipotence doesn't come from the fact that he can bend the rules of physics and the laws of nature. The point is he is the laws of nature and his omnipotence doesn't come from the fact he can change things. He is everything that could happen. You can't pick and choose. He defines everything that is possible.'

But this was a one-off miraculous virginal conception – Jesus, divine and human.

'That's like Eastern mythology – Vishnu and the avatar – God coming down to earth in a physical form.'

What does he think of the notions of a virginal conception and the Incarnation?

'I don't respect the idea of the divine and human combined. It's misguided. It's mistaken. I've changed my mind in the last year. I used to say I don't believe in God. I categorically insisted God does not exist. But now I think I know what I mean by the word God. I understand what you believe in but you are assigning a quality to it that doesn't have to exist. For instance, consciousness – why does God have to be capable of decisions? Why does it have to be a who?

'You think you perceive the world through your senses, yeah? What you can sense through the physical realm. Anything beyond that is spiritual. But I would say the spiritual realm is an extension, an expansion. There's more in existence than we can sense. Like bats with extra perception, the use of infrared…it's an extension of physicality. I would say people mistake God for being something completely external instead of seeing it as something that embraces the entire spectrum. God is not a conscious being. It's literally everything and it's the rules that make everything work.'

He talks about Taoism, an ancient Chinese tradition of philosophy and belief that is as old as Christianity. He explains to me that Taoism is about The Tao, the ultimate creative principle of the universe to which all things are unified and connected. This seems to chime, in part, with Harry's description of what God is.

He continues, 'Before, I would have said God doesn't exist. Now, I'd say a religious person and I do believe in the same thing but the religious person assigns qualities to God that I do not believe, like consciousness. It's not a conscious force that can affect individuals or make decisions. It's the energy.

'All religions are striving for the same thing – a truth. But I'd say the aim should be to have something you no longer doubt. I'm not a fundamental sceptic but I think faith is the dangerous thing. Faith is essentially the abandonment and ignoring of evidence in order to preserve a belief that you already hold. Faith is a force that enables dogma.

'My God, that I believe in,' he continues, 'I'm able to change my opinion on, depending on the evidence that is presented to me so that everything I get wrong is my mistake, not God's. However, you, Dad, believe in something that comes up with some strict rules and if evidence provides something that may not be right, you would still follow your faith and reject the evidence in order to preserve your Christian belief. To have faith is to belittle scientific evidence.'

Isn't faith about a trust and commitment to what you believe is truth? I suggest.

'So, if you were presented with evidence that the Bible stories didn't happen, would you change your mind?' he asks. 'There's an equal stack of evidence that Jesus wasn't God. Why would you take the side you have chosen? Regardless of the fact you were taught it, you're old enough to decide for yourself so why did you decide it's true?'

I respond that believers commit to the veracity of a story. They trust it because they have a spiritual feeling that it is right.

'Everybody has that spiritual feeling or force,' he says, 'but assigning it to a deity that consciously rules over you is incongruous. Should you not assign that to the wholesomeness of nature and science? If you were not taught about God and had never heard about God or Jesus, you'd have never thought about God.'

So why would Luke 'make up' a story that a woman who had never had sex had a baby who would be God as well as human?

'Who am I to say that?' he says. 'I don't know the exact intentions of Luke. That's the classic comforting argument. You don't know the intellectual capacity of Luke. You don't know his intentions – whether he was writing this as a genuine story or just doing it as a comfort to his patron or whatever. Logically and reasonably, the story is metaphorical.'

'I remember hearing about the story first in my First Holy Communion class. Gabriel came to Mary and said, "You're pregnant with the Son of God".'

Lily, my youngest daughter aged nineteen, is recalling her first memory of the annunciation story. She is currently studying Psychology at the University of Leeds. Does she believe in the miracle of Mary's virginal conception?

'No,' she says. 'I believe there was a woman called Mary. She had a husband called Joseph. And they had a son called Jesus. I believe Jesus was conceived by Mary with Joseph or with someone else.'

So, does she think the virgin conception is a made-up story?

'I never believed the Mary-Gabriel story. I always thought of it as fictional. I was shown it in book form and I always thought it was like a fairy story.'

But was he conceived at the Annunciation as Son of God, divine and human?

'I think there was someone called Jesus but I don't believe he performed all the miracles they say in the Bible. He was probably just a very charismatic guy who had good morals.'

Does she believe in any God?

'No. We don't need a reason to be here,' she responds. 'People want a reason so they know how to live their life. I'd rather live it as I think I should. People use religion as a comfort or because their family believe. Some use it for guidance and some find it when something bad or sad happens and they find comfort in prayer. I've never thought of looking to someone else. I think people can get the answers they need themselves. If you're praying, you can get the answer in your head and work it out yourself.

'I want to know more about it,' she continues. 'I went to an evangelical church once with a friend and it's like one big family. But I think, I just don't need that. I've got a great family already. I hope you don't feel disappointed by the way I think. I'm open to it but I don't think I'm capable of being religious. It's really hard to explain.'

I show her the *Children's Bible* I used to read to her as a child. I ask her to read the Annunciation passage again.

'I don't feel any particular connection to it. It's like any other story.'

Would she like to believe it?

'If I'd like to believe it, I would but I don't have any motive to do so. A lot of my friends are religious at different levels. I think Christianity has changed a lot though. I think they all know I'm quite set in my ways.'

Why does she think the annunciation story is there in Luke's Gospel with the narrative about Jesus?

'To show the power of God,' she replies. 'To show he's omnipotent.'

She holds the Lemoyne picture in her hands and looks perturbed.

'She looks really sad. He's pointing up to God. We don't know if he's said anything yet. He's just arrived. It's a good painting, especially the light representing God.'

Mary was probably twelve to fourteen at the time of the Annunciation, I tell her.

'What?' she exclaims. 'That just makes me question it even more. Everyone has their opinion on things. I understand that. Metaphors are subjective. The interpretation of the Bible is subjective. Everyone sees religion in a different way. Don't expect to come to a final conclusion, Dad, about what the painting and the story mean. Everyone sees different things…in the painting and in the story. I'm sure we are all saying different things to you. Who's to say one's right and one's not.'

I keep thinking about the statement made by my eldest son, Sam. 'The reason why most Christians believe in it is because it's what's passed down and is the path of least resistance…I guess it's about faith but it's important to know where that faith comes from.'

148. The author's parents, Lawry and Muriel Byford

I decide to head to Yorkshire to see my parents. I have never had a serious conversation with them about religion before and have never asked what each of them believes. And yet they are the two people, more than anyone, who passed down their 'faith' and, without question, as a child, influenced my own thinking. What do they make of the annunciation story?

Lawrence (Lawry) and Muriel Byford live on a pleasant modern housing estate in a smart village called Pannal, just south of Harrogate. He is about to celebrate his ninetieth birthday and she is nearly eighty-four. He has been retired for nearly thirty years after a hugely successful career in the Police Service. She has been a loyal and steadfast housewife and homemaker. They have been married for more than sixty years and have three grown up children and eight grandchildren.

Lawry was born in 1925 in the pit town of Normanton in the West Riding of Yorkshire and was baptized a Roman Catholic. He was an altar boy at his local church, St John the Baptist, and the two earliest photographs I have of my father are of him dressed in a cassock and shawl, one standing by the altar at St John's and the other as an altar boy at the head of a Pentecost Day procession in the town, alongside his father, George. He has gone to Mass every Sunday without fail – religiously you may say. Although religion and the Christian faith play a central role in his life, he has always been rather private about it.

We go for a drive in his beloved Yorkshire Dales and stop off for a coffee and an English cooked breakfast at his favourite Tea Room, Wilding's in Pateley Bridge. I decide this is the best place to talk to him about the Annunciation.

He is dressed smartly in a collar and tie and woollen jacket. Physically he may be frailer than before but his mind remains as sharp as ever. As ever, he loves to talk and to reminisce.

What does he think of the annunciation story?

'When I was a boy, I used to hear the church bell ring out at noon every day at St John's, opposite our school, and we'd stand up automatically and the teacher would say, "The angel of the Lord declared unto Mary…". I used to think, I know we do it every day, but I don't really understand it – you don't at that age, eight or nine. It was more a discipline.'

He looks at the Lemoyne picture and ponders.

'It's a way of explaining to people who might not have the intellect to understand it. It's like a parable. It was there for people working on farms or whatever with no education whatsoever…and the reasons the bells went on the hour in Normanton was people then didn't have the…you just told them.'

'My history and knowledge is confined to narrow barriers,' he continues. 'What gets me, what I really believe in are things like Good Friday and the night before (Maundy Thursday). That's absolutely incredible in my mind.'

So, he thinks the Last Supper, the crucifixion definitely happened, I ask.

'Yes, and the resurrection too – Mary Magdalene outside the tomb, "Where's he gone?" she cries. It's the realism that's there. Oh yes, definitely.'

But he sounds as though he is not sure of the veracity of the annunciation story.

'Mm,' he ponders. 'I don't dispute that it happened but…' he pauses, 'the story's there in order to explain to ordinary people, well, it's like the parables. It's like what the Monsignor said at Mass on Sunday, "What's the best short stories you've ever read?" he asked us, and he then said the best short stories he'd ever read were in the Bible.'

Does he believe there was a virgin conception?

'It doesn't bother me,' he responds, staring at me. 'I never even think on those lines. No, no, no.'

So if the baby Jesus had been conceived in a natural way, it wouldn't bother him.

'Absolutely not,' he says.

Extraordinary as it may seem, I have never spoken with him in such a way before. Although the Christian faith has been such a pivotal part of family life, I have never asked him before about what he actually believes in. As Sam rightly put it, it's just been passed down from generation to generation. So whether the Annunciation happened or not, is he more interested in Jesus's later life than that moment of his conception?

'It never enters my mind,' he answers. 'What I greatly benefited from was being on the altar as a boy of eight and that's always had an influence on me. When we get to the deeply theological aspects of any religion, I don't want to go down that way. It's like reading *Robinson Crusoe* and asking was the sun shining on a particular day or were there coconuts on the trees? I mean it's the theme of the story that matters. Truly Mark, I've always believed someone has steered me on my way during my life, how the whole pattern of my life has come about. You're just sustained by something…'

His voice drops off. He takes a sip of his tea and continues eating his meal. Does he think there's an after-life? I wonder.

'Definitely,' he replies.

'For your spirit or your body?' I wonder.

'I don't know,' he says. 'I was very close to my father, and when he was dying after three or four years of being ill, Fr Keegan came to see him from St Austin's in Wakefield – he eventually became the Bishop's Secretary. I'll never forget it, when my father was close to death, Fr Keegan said, "I think we might say a prayer." I put my hand out and he knocked it out of the way and he put his hand on Fr Keegan's and there was such solace there.'

I realize as he speaks how he has such a simple faith – non-questioning, accepting, passed down. I wonder, when he says the Creed every week at Mass at his local Roman Catholic church, does he believe in every word?

'If I was going to be absolutely truthful,' he says, 'I never give it the thought you think I ought to be giving it. If I did, and I came to the conclusion, oh, I should leave that bit out and I'm not going to say those words, well, no, I never even think of it. It doesn't bother me. You're painting a picture I don't recognize.'

He meanders again with another anecdote unconnected with the Annunciation. I remark that he seems to be saying that the theme of the passage is to accept what God wishes.

'I'm not as meticulous as that. It's a wonderful painting is that,' he says pointing to the Lemoyne picture, 'but beyond that, is it possible the Virgin Mary conceived in accordance with Luke's story? I've no idea. All I know is she produced Jesus Christ and he turned out to be who he was and was created in what we've had in all our Christian beliefs over the centuries.'

He gazes further at the painting for a while in silence.

'Basically, something like that happened,' he says as he points to the picture, 'and it helps those who are not as intellectually privileged as we are to understand the story.'

I tell him about how different people have offered different interpretations of the story's substance and meaning whilst I have been on the journey. Some see it as fact whilst others see it as metaphorical. Some reject it altogether.

'That's the wonderful thing about the mind of individuals. It's not a general thing. It's how you're inspired, individually. Each to his own. If you can finish up with a satisfaction…let me put it this way in harsh terms. Am I better off than I might have been if I had been a non-Christian. Answer: yes. Has being a Christian been a great influence on my life? Answer: yes, but don't ask me how. I just know it has. It has been a good influence on me. When you are looking back on your life, are there incidents that point to, "there's something going on here," – definitely, and I'm thankful for that. I have difficulty saying long prayers but I often say, "Thank you God for everything you have done for me." You can say the Our Father, the Hail Mary, but that's better than any prayer, just saying thank you.

'You know they talk about divine intervention, well, I'm a great believer in it on the odd occasions it's happened to me. If there is such a thing as guardian angels, I've had a good one,' he says. 'I still think there must have been some divine intervention for all the things to have happened to me as they have.'

As I listen to him, I reflect a while. Here is a man who came from nothing, a poor working class background in a mining town south of Leeds and rose to the top as Chief Inspector of Constabulary of the Police Service in England and Wales. A Law graduate, a barrister, a knight of the realm. And yet he talks with such child-like simplicity. Is it indoctrination? Or is it a faith characterized by mature simplicity? For him, there is no desire to be touched by the 'progressive' Enlightenment tradition. There's a calmness of approach, a trusting acceptance, an assured character to his faith. Perhaps his is a maturity of thinking simply that goes beyond complexity.

As we finish off our tea and bacon and eggs, he says he rarely prays to Mary and accepts he was born a Roman Catholic and did not choose to be one. So, does it matter to him whether you are a Catholic or what, so long as you believe the Christian Gospels?

'Oh, yes it does,' he says. 'If you really push me to the quick, and I look at the Reformation and I look at Anglicans as our neighbourly relations, the sooner they come back under one flock under the Pope, the better. But let me give you a thought. I'll never forget this. When I worked in Turkey, I had Ishmael, who was the chief of police seconded to me and was my bodyguard. He was a lovely man. He said, "I must go to the mosque on Friday." I said, "I'll come with you." So I went off to the mosque in Ankara with him. I took my shoes off and whatever. I enjoyed it. Then on the Sunday, we went to Istanbul and I said, "I must go to the French church there for Mass." "I'll come with you," he said. I can see his face now, standing before a statue of St Anthony with the votive candles all lit, with his hat by his chest and I said, jokingly, "Ishmael, you're a hypocrite." He said, "Who is he?" and I said, "St Anthony, the saint of miracles." He said, "I knew it. Let me tell you something. You and I want water from the well. You have a bucket. I have a bucket. We both draw the water. We just use different buckets".'

He laughs at the recollection. 'I've never forgotten it. Can you think of a better example than that?'

———

Muriel Byford sits in her comfy 'Granny chair' where, every day, she completes the crossword in the *Daily Telegraph* and tackles her books of puzzles. Today is her eighty-fourth birthday. The lounge, like the rest of her house, is spotless. Everything is neat and tidy, clean and in its right place. Behind her on a window ledge is a twelve-inch wooden statue, carved by a dear friend now dead. It is a semi-abstract figure in ash and its shape and form make it clear it is of the Virgin Mary.

It is the only indication in the room of religion. The bookshelves behind her are full of biographies, dictionaries, novels and history books. There is no crucifix on any of the walls. No Catholic statues of the Sacred Heart. Faith and belief is a private affair here, not something to show off or to evangelize.

She was born Muriel Massey and was brought up in Altofts, near Normanton in Yorkshire, where her beloved father was a railwayman.

'When I was little, I used to go to Sunday school at a Methodist chapel in Altofts on Sunday afternoons, where we learnt Methodist hymns,' she tells me. 'My mother and father were Church of England and went regularly to Normanton Parish Church. He sang in the choir.'

As a teenager, she joined them and sat alongside her school friends. When she was married, she went to the more local Altofts church which was 'very high but it was convenient. Then when we had children, I went with your Dad to the Catholic church sometimes but I never took Communion because it wasn't allowed. When we moved to Halifax [in 1962], you were about to join St Malachy's Primary School. They were short of three teachers. I said I was willing to help out in any way and soon an application came in the post. As your brother and you were about to prepare for First Holy Communion classes, I thought it would be confusing for you to wonder why I didn't go. It would raise questions that would be difficult to answer. So I decided to become a Catholic. I called myself a "convenience Catholic". I still feel the same, a Catholic by convenience.

'I remember saying to the priest who received me into the Catholic Church,' she continues. 'He said, "Is there anything that gives you concern?" I said I can't honestly believe in the Assumption. It's just ridiculous that a person, having died, can go up bodily. Spiritually, I have no complaints but bodily where did she get off? Is she floating around? I mean it's ridiculous.' He said, "Muriel, I have my own private worries about that too." That made me feel better. Cradle Catholics are indoctrinated at every turn, who are in turn indoctrinated by their own parents and by school teachers, who are told what to teach. So they don't think for themselves. It makes it difficult for them. They may think, I don't believe that, but don't know why.'

We digress a little while to talk about her wedding day at St John's in 1950. Because she was not a Catholic at the time, she was not allowed music or flowers inside the church during the marriage service. 'It was never explained to me why. My dad and I walked up the aisle in complete silence. It felt annoying and made me feel second best. I feel resentful but that's how things were.'

She takes a sup from her cup of tea and looks straight ahead before continuing.

'With me, if I didn't go to church with your Dad, I probably wouldn't go at all. But I do have a relationship with God every day. I have a word with him but I absolutely believe one hundred and one per cent that God isn't just in a Catholic church or any building. He's everywhere. If I need him, I ask him. If I want to tell him something, I tell him. If it wasn't for your Dad, I'd probably go to the local church of England church here in Pannal.'

What is her first memory of the annunciation story?

'At Christmas, at Sunday school, as part of the Nativity plays. It was the opening chapter although not a lot was made of it. It wasn't a big deal.'

Did she think then the story of the angel Gabriel and Mary was true?

'I don't think it was as positive as that,' she says. 'It was just accepted that was how the story began but I don't think it was emphasized ever as the opening of Christianity. It was just the start of the Christmas story.'

What does she think now?

'It's all just part of the Christmas story. I've never sat down and really thought about it. I'm trying to think now about how I think about it. I can imagine that if the story of the virgin birth is true, then Mary probably either experienced that or thought she did. But I don't think I have any views on it that would impress anyone.'

Does she believe in the virgin conception?

'If it's a one-off in history and God said so, I'm prepared to accept it but that's the problem with all religions. There isn't one of them that can prove anything of them being right. Belief and faith aren't the same thing. I don't necessarily have faith in that particular event being true but I'm prepared to believe that perhaps Mary thought so. I think that there's another thing that rings true. That she went running off to tell Elizabeth because she knew Elizabeth was also expecting quite unexpectedly and she said, "Guess what's happened to me?" That gives it a smack of authenticity to me. That she believed it whether that was right or not. So you accept it as the start of the Christmas story. You just accept it.'

When she recites the Creed, does she believe all the words specifically relating to the Annunciation?

'Well, we just say so, don't we? We believe but we don't know. I think the significance of it to the Church is that it is the fulfilment of the prophecies of the Old Testament and that would authenticate the claims that Jesus was the Son of God. They'd been waiting hundreds and hundreds of years.'

I tell her some think the theme of the story is about acceptance, unexpectedness, duty or calling. Others see it as surrender. What is it for her?

'I won't say for me but I can see the purpose of the story of the Annunciation and the virgin birth as being part of the authenticity of Jesus being the Son of God and the Messiah.'

Does she believe it?

'I'm prepared to believe it,' she replies. 'If Jesus is the Son of God, I'm prepared to believe his conception happened in such a way, that that is how it happened.'

What does Mary mean to her? I wonder. What status does she have for her?

'Definitely not the Catholic side,' she says, 'but more influential than the Anglican view...a) in the way she brought up Jesus and b) she was there as his mother throughout his life. I think she did believe he was the Son of God.'

Does she ever pray to Mary?

'Yes, on Sundays,' she says. 'She's his mother and she's in heaven with him. We hope she is. She may just put a word in. But I never ask her for specific things. I respect her but I'm essentially not a Catholic. As a mother, I recognize the influence she would have had on her son.'

How would she describe herself in terms of religion?

'I am a believer in a supreme power. I think there is something other than the physical earth, the physical universe. I've no idea if it's scientific but it's bigger than anything we can understand. There's something that's influential. It's not somebody you can ask a favour of. It's a supreme force, an influential force.'

She takes another sup of tea and ponders a while.

'I do think the crucifixion and all that happened. Whether it was a fulfilment of something, I'd have to dig deeper and think more about all that but I believe in an influential force, not lauding it over or whatever, but some sort of force and power that is influential on what happens in time. That's my opinion, as certain as I can be. I can't see anything to argue against Jesus coming along and I think his influence is for nothing but good. If we lived by his teachings, the social requirements of being a Christian, the world would be a better place. Not necessarily all of us believing in Jesus but believing in what he said and then practising that.'

I pass the Lemoyne picture to her.

'I see what appears to be a rather feminine angel, androgynous, being sent with the cherubim by God from heaven. Mary is submissive and saying, "Who me? Surely not! You've got the wrong person," as he's saying the message to her. I don't dislike it but I'm not so keen on Mary. She wasn't a little, sweet innocent...she was a young girl...I also think there was a family of children after this. It might have been a virgin conception but she had more children after. Jesus had brothers and sisters. I'm absolutely convinced of that.'

As she gazes at the composition, I ask her whether she thinks it is the most important event in human history.

'If the story is true, then that could be true,' she responds. 'If your beliefs are true, then it's absolutely right.'

As she gets up to put the kettle on, I notice behind her, in a large bookcase, a tattered Ladybird book called *Baby Jesus*. I remember my mother reading it to me at bedtime when I was a small child living in Halifax in West Yorkshire. Tucked up in bed, listening to the comforting words of my mum, kneeling by my side. I open the book for the first time in more than fifty years. The memories come flooding back as I recognize instantly two classic Ladybird illustrations showing Mary with her water carrier in Nazareth and her then being confronted by an angel. I read the accompanying words:

> Mary was kind and good. She lived in Nazareth. The house had a flat roof. There were stone steps at the side of the house. Mary could climb the steps on to the roof.
>
> If Mary looked down from the roof, she would see the children playing. Mary loved children.
>
> One day, Mary was busy in her home. She sang as she worked. Then Mary sat down to rest.
>
> As she sat still, the room became very bright. Mary looked up and saw an angel.
>
> The angel said: 'God is sending a Baby Son to you. You shall call His name Jesus.'
>
> When the angel had gone, Mary was very happy. She was so glad God was sending her Baby Jesus.

149. Annunciation illustration from *Baby Jesus*, Ladybird book, 1961. © Ladybird Books Ltd 1961

CHAPTER 39

A GRAND JOURNEY

In late 1723, four years before he began work on *The Annunciation* at his studio in central Paris, François Lemoyne travelled to Italy with his patron, François Berger, and a certain Monsieur Croisil. During a seven month sojourn, involving research and painting, Lemoyne visited Bologna, Venice, Rome and Naples. There, he studied many great works by leading Renaissance artists. He noted the movement and thickness of their brushstrokes, the layering of paint, the innovative use of light and shade, the composition, perspective and symbolism deployed in each picture, and the rich variety of pigments and palettes. In particular, he studied the breathtaking techniques deployed by Titian and Tintoretto in Venice and Michelangelo at the Sistine Chapel in Rome. He returned in August 1724 informed, invigorated and inspired.

Reading about Lemoyne's 'grand journey' has given me the idea to start my own Annunciation quest. I dream of visiting some of the great centres of European art, to stand before a wide range of original Annunciation masterworks in the galleries and churches where they are displayed: stained glass, stone carvings, mosaics, sculptures and paintings from groundbreaking periods in the history of sacred art. My destinations will include Chartres, Amsterdam, Madrid, Barcelona, Venice, Florence and Rome. I wonder if such close encounters will help to inform my understanding of the story and its meaning.

Travelling south through northern France, fifty miles west of Paris, past the old towns of Evreux and Dreux, the startling edifice comes into view. Still many miles away, it looks like a mother spaceship, its tall steeples soaring above the flat cornfields like two lunar rockets waiting to take off. As we come closer, the distinctive outline of Chartres Cathedral gradually reveals some of the intricate details of its façade.

A Christian church was first established in Chartres around the fourth century and an altar, dedicated to the Blessed Virgin Mary, has been in place since the early sixth century. A royal decree in the eighth century named the structure St Mary's of Chartres. The growing devotion to Mary at Chartres was strengthened greatly in 876 when Charlemagne's grandson, Charles the Bald, gave the *Sancta Camisia* relic to the city, probably as a gift for the consecration ceremony of the new Carolingian cathedral.

The precious treasure was an oblong-shaped piece of silk, that was claimed to be part of a veil worn by Mary at the time of the Annunciation and when she gave birth to Jesus. The cloth, which had been gifted previously to Charlemagne by the Byzantine Empress, Irene of Constantinople, soon attracted thousands of pilgrims every month and Chartres became a major Marian pilgrimage shrine.

The building of a new Cathedral structure, the fifth on the site, started in 1134. But lightning caused a fire that destroyed most of the edifice in 1194 with only the crypt and part of the west front surviving. It was thought that the *Sancta Camisia* was lost in the fire but after four days, a group of priests revealed that they had locked themselves behind thick iron trap doors below the Treasury in order to protect it. The country's Cardinal claimed that the relic's survival was a miraculous sign from Mary herself.

Today, Chartres still attracts millions of visitors from around the world, some on religious pilgrimages, but most as tourists, admiring the craftsmanship of the intricately carved stonework, and the breathtaking beauty of its stained glass. One of the best preserved medieval ecclesiastical buildings in Western Europe, it has been designated a UNESCO World Heritage site.

I am sitting inside the Cathedral at the west end of the nave next to Malcolm Miller, an ecclesiastical historian of Chartres and a tour guide here for the past fifty-seven years. Now in his eighties, he first started his Cathedral tours in early 1958 and today he has already completed four academic talks and one public tour. 'Mary is omnipresent here, anywhere and everywhere that you look,' he tells me.

Miller read French at Durham in the 1950s and came to Chartres as part of his studies. That is when his intense love affair with the city and its Cathedral began. He tells me proudly that he has been awarded two of France's highest civilian honours – a knighthood in the National Order of Merit and another in the Order of Arts and Letters. Dressed in a linen suit and brown brogues, his manner is learned but brusque. It is mid-afternoon and not surprisingly he says he is feeling very tired.

We look up towards the sparkling Rose window and the three lancets below. Fortunately, bright sunlight streams through the panels giving the colours a magnificent radiance. These are the oldest windows in the Cathedral, dating back to the 1150s, and they survived the great fire of 1194. The art of stained glass was less than a century old when they were created at the St Denis atelier, where the distinctive blue colours were achieved with cobalt oxide. We focus on the central lancet, which tells the story of the Incarnation cycle. The first panel in the bottom left corner, shows an Annunciation scene.

150. The central lancet window on the west façade
at Chartres Cathedral featuring a stunning
Annunciation panel, 1150s, Chartres Cathedral.
© Fr Lawrence Lew O.P.

'We're looking at the oldest part of the Cathedral above ground and we have to remember these windows are not just there for their beauty,' Malcolm Miller whispers. 'They're didactic, teaching those who couldn't read or write about the Bible through pictures. We are looking at one of the best examples of twelfth-century stained glass, anywhere in the world'

The four-foot square panel of the Annunciation shows a green winged angel Gabriel, dressed in white and blue, arriving from the left, holding a staff and raising two fingers in salutation as he points towards Mary's ear. The haloed Mary has risen from her seat whilst holding a book. Looking perturbed, she has turned around to hear the voice, and her right hand is raised to her chest.

As we gaze at the panel through high-powered binoculars, I ask Malcolm Miller what the annunciation story means for him spiritually.

'That's an awkward question,' he answers, shuffling in his seat. 'I find myself being an agnostic Christian, dealing with these subjects doesn't make sense, like say the creation story. I'm aware people in my groups have so many different beliefs or non-beliefs. I never tell them my beliefs. I convey the history and the wonder of the beauty here. But I'd say, in the end, it's all rooted in Old Testament stories. My intelligence gets the better of me sometimes,' he says before closing his eyes.

In the evening I wander around the Cathedral precinct and see a spectacular son et lumiere show of extraordinary ambition that transforms the outside of the Cathedral into a blaze of colour and intricate animation. Early the following morning, greeted by a clear blue sky and warming sun, I head to the front of the Royal Portal to meet my second guide.

Wearing an ankle-length blue dress, her hair in a neat bob, Jill Geoffrion is taking photographs of a stone carving on the western façade using a telephoto lens. An expert in Labyrinth prayer, she guides organized groups here to walk the medieval labyrinth, which is situated at the west end of the nave. She also leads special prayer tours around the Cathedral, in her own words, 'to creatively inspire and encourage people to seek God and serve others.'

Today, I am accompanying her on a three-hour walk around the Cathedral focused specifically on the Annunciation. There are more than two hundred images of Mary around the building and Jill has designed a special tour to stop at ten different locations, inside and outside the building, where a different Annunciation scene is represented.

Born and brought up in Minnesota in the United States, Jill Geoffrion first came to Chartres in 1979 whilst studying Art History in Paris. The visit had an immediate and profound impact on her – 'an overwhelming experience of God's love,' – and since then she has made more than forty pilgrimages to the Cathedral. Married with two adult sons, she was raised in the Presbyterian Church in the US but, as a child, only went to church occasionally, at Christmas and Easter. She then went to boarding school where she underwent a 'charismatic conversion,' she tells me.

'I felt there was something incomplete. God wasn't sharing himself fully with me,' she recalls. After a year, she discovered Jesus and her life changed forever. 'I felt I was discovered at fourteen. I wasn't a very happy teenager. It was at the end of a church service on a Friday night. I went out in the woods and there was a big wind blowing and it felt like it was blowing into me. I felt totally different.'

Was it like an Annunciation moment for her? I wonder.

'It was,' she responds. 'The wind coming into me. I've never really thought of it before as a kind of annunciation but I can absolutely see it now. It was. There was an integration moment – the wind outside and the wind inside me. I've never had such an intense experience before or since.'

What did she do? I ask.

'At that moment, there was no resistance. I'd already said my yes. It was a total yes. It was beyond a yes. I didn't feel alone anymore. I've never felt alone again.'

From fourteen to twenty-six, she read her Bible, studied religion, felt a calling and recognized a need to go to a seminary. She served as an assistant Pastor in the American Baptist Church and studied for a Ph.D. in Women's Studies and Christian Spiritualities.

'It was vital to me that I was in a non-hierarchical environment,' she says. 'I've realized that's my calling. Praying, guiding, showing, reflecting and that's what I'm going to be doing with you right now.'

She lives in Chartres from October to Easter, sometimes with her husband but more often alone. During the rest of the year, she tries to visit Myanmar (Burma), other Christian seminaries in east Asia, and places as far afield as Congo and Ukraine. She spent only two months back home in the US last year but that doesn't bother her. 'I just want to make a meaningful connection with God, whenever, wherever,' she says.

We begin our tour outside standing by the Royal Portal at the Cathedral's western façade, where we admire two different sets of stone sculptures of the angel Gabriel and Mary, carved in 1154. 'Keep looking at the eye movement between them or the lack of it. That's important,' she says. Next to the statues of the two figures on the right tympanum is a depiction of the Visitation and then one of Mary lying down in bed as she gives birth to baby Jesus. She passes me one of her photos – a close up of this particular Annunciation carving, together with a meditation she has written. She asks me to read it:

'The Messenger'
Who gets to converse with an angel?
For that matter, who wants to speak to an angel – before it happens?

The low voice sent me scurrying inside myself;
trying to figure out what was happening.
What else would someone do
when overwhelmed with surprise?

I didn't take the angel seriously
when I was told not to be afraid.
First of all, unknown situations have a way of creating hesitation.
Also, being told that I would become pregnant was far from comforting.

What would you do if a messenger of God
turned your world upside down?

We move on and enter the Cathedral. Like Malcolm Miller, she wants to focus on the magnificent central lancet at the west end of the nave and, specifically, the stained-glass panel of the Annunciation. She passes me a second of her meditative pieces.

'Oh No!'
You've got to be kidding!
Get away from me!
What in the world is happening?
I wonder what this is all about!?

So many things can go through one's mind in a split second.

How do we react when God shows up?
We don't really expect it.
And we're not sure if it's a good or bad thing when it first happens.

How can we prepare ourselves
so that we won't run away
before we hear what God wants to communicate?

As we walk slowly up the nave, she points out more thirteenth-century, stained-glass representations of the Annunciation before we turn left through the north transept and move outside to view the north porch. It is time to reach for the binoculars again as we view the faces of Mary and Gabriel in an early thirteenth-century stone carving. It is also time to read another of Jill Geoffrion's meditations.

'Yes,'
I was made to say, 'Yes!'
I was raised to say, 'Yes.'
I like to say, 'Yes!'

But I wonder,
'What am I getting myself into?'
I know enough to know I have no idea.
But it's my nature to embrace 'Yes.'

Did you expect any other response?

Look who is saying, 'No!'

We sit quietly and reflect on the beauty of the stone sculptures. After a while, she passes me another of her Annunciation prayers to read.

'In Just Nine Months'
Nine months from now...
I will know that nothing is
impossible with God.

Nine months from now...
the truth of your words will
come to fruition.

Nine months from now...
I will have a son to care for.

Nine months from now...
the course of history will
begin to change.

Nine months from now...
I will not recognize my life as
I have known it.

In just nine months...

151. Statue of the Annunciation at the North Porch, Chartres Cathedral. © Jill K H Geoffrion, www.jillgeoffrion.com

152. Jean Soulas, stone carving of the Annunciation, sixteenth century, Chartres Cathedral

153. *Sancta Camisa*, Chartres Cathedral. © Fr. Lawrence Lew O.P.

Next, we move back inside the Cathedral to visit the Sacristy. Jill Geoffrion and a verger go to a safe and bring out two objects that are not usually on public view: two precious seventeenth-century gold chalices and a lovely detailed reliquary, each with an engraved depiction of the annunciation encounter. Then we move to the early sixteenth-century Choir Screen to see Jean Soulas's elaborate limestone carving of Mary kneeling below a canopy as the angel arrives

Finally, we sit in semi-darkness in the north-eastern part of the ambulatory, where the *Sancta Camisia* silk cloth is displayed inside a glass reliquary. Three women kneel in front of the cloth, praying. One of them is heavily pregnant. Someone has left four red roses and a small bouquet of flowers on the floor in front of the display cabinet. An assistant insists to passing visitors that no photographs are taken in the area. Jill whispers to me that when the cloth was tested late in the twentieth century, it was found to contain traces of pollen from first-century Palestine

I stare at the plain, off-white piece of silk cloth hanging inside the glass case and wonder. Could this really be the very veil or part of the tunic that Mary wore when she heard an angelic voice 2,000 years ago?

I look at Jill as she gazes ahead. Her eyes are filled with tears. I ask if she feels she is fulfilling the calling she first felt forty-two years ago when she experienced that sudden gust of wind.

'I truly don't feel worthy of that moment,' she says. 'It is so much bigger than any service I could ever do.'

Her soft voice becomes emotional. Even though we are in semi-darkness, I can see a tear trickling down her cheek.

'I love the image of water,' she whispers. 'If there's one image for God, I'd say it's a deep body of water. A raindrop becomes part of a lake. It's such an honour to be a raindrop in the lake.'

What does the Annunciation mean for her spiritually? I ask.

'I love the story,' she tells me. 'Whatever we expect from God, we have no idea. We just have to be open. We have to be in vision. Get up every morning and say yes.'

Does she see it as fact or metaphor?

'Yes, yes,' she replies with a smile.

So, she sees it as both? I ask.

'Yes, absolutely. But how can we know? We can't. But I believe it happened. To be honest, I've never really thought about that specific question before. I need to…how could we possibly know? But we can all imagine that story in a million different ways. What matters is a person was faced with accepting something that was so far beyond what was possible and she opened herself to that. A key element for me is that she pondered. The angel went on and on and on. But that was totally irrelevant to her. She said, "How could it be if I'm a virgin?" That's really interesting to me. Sometimes our responses are so silly. She had to do what she did to work it out for herself. I find that humorous. Don't hide whatever is important to you. The fact she was a virgin probably wasn't that big for God but it was huge for her. So there had to be that huge interaction.'

Is the notion of a virgin conception important to her?

'It doesn't seem like the crucial part of the story to me,' she replies. 'Do I believe in that or not? Yes, why not? But why would I focus on that? There's a much bigger story here of God's love for the world. Her story really isn't the story. It's God's story and she's part of the story. In the end, the story is about God's great love for the world. God is the main character here. If God really touches our lives, the story then is much bigger.'

Is there one word or phrase that best sums up the annunciation story for her? I wonder.

'Surprise. Seeking understanding. Maybe acceptance.' She pauses for a while. 'Courage, honesty, integrity, difficulty.'

Does she venerate Mary?

'Well, I did this morning. But no, not normally,' she replies. 'For me, when I was a child, she was just the mother of Jesus. Then I came to Chartres and sat in front of the veil and I saw the deep devotion to her all around me. Interestingly, I pray my family prayers here as a daughter, sister, mother, as part of a family. I like the idea that a Catholic prays to Mary in order to be introduced to her Son. And as a Protestant, that we pray to Jesus in order for him to introduce us to his mother.' She chuckles. 'And now, I've got a whole new perspective, having been with you today.'

I take the print of the Lemoyne painting from my bag and pass it to her. What does she see?

'Can I say what I feel?' she asks. 'This is a really, really repulsive image to me. I see Mary with pale skin. Her hands are in a very unnatural position, pointing to her neck. She's almost choking herself. Rather than a firm yes, she's holding back. I see that her inner red garment takes me to the harlot rather than to the Virgin, which makes me very angry. And why is there all that stuff on the floor? My heart wants her and the angel to connect but they're not even looking at each other. And those cherubs look like dead children. No, to me, this is a really distressing image. It's the stylisation that's hard, especially there in the face of Mary. I don't know anyone who looks like that, especially at a moment of spiritual awareness. My experience is that, usually, they look really upset at that moment. But she looks so disconnected and that upsets me. My experience as a spiritual leader is that at a God moment, people don't go inside themselves. It's a moment that's really distressing. That would feel so much more real for me.'

We sit in silence together for another fifteen minutes in front of the *Sancta Camisia*. Thinking. Reflecting.

––––––

There are so many depictions of the Annunciation throughout Paris, from all ages and in all materials. The problem is where to start?

I spend a wonderful two days trawling both banks of the Seine viewing some of the city's most acclaimed Annunciation representations. My first stop is a stained-glass panel in the ambulatory at the far end of Notre Dame Cathedral. Next, I seek out a number of Annunciation pieces on display at the fabulous National Museum of the Middle Ages, formerly called the Cluny. Amongst the inventory of more 24,000 medieval works of tapestries, fabrics, stained glass, sculptures, paintings and jewellery, there is a wool and silk tapestry of the Annunciation, made in Paris in 1499 for Bayeux Cathedral; a sixteenth-century polychrome and wood altarpiece; a two piece, late fifteenth-century vernon limestone sculpture from Normandy; and a beautiful thirteenth-century Limoges enamel.

The following morning I head to Room Four of the Musée d'Orsay to view Jean-François Millet's *The Angelus*, painted in 1859. The famous picture depicts two peasant workers in the fields at Barbizon, forty miles south of Paris, laying down their tools at six o'clock in the evening to recite the Angelus. The church bell inside the distant steeple at Chailly-en-Bière strikes the hour. In shadow of the diffused light, the man and woman have stopped digging potatoes and their pitchfork, basket, sacks and wheelbarrow are strewn around them on the empty plain.

154. Jean-François Millet *The Angelus*, 1859, Musée d'Orsay, Paris. Photo © Musée d'Orsay, Dist. RMN-Grand Palais/Patrice Schmidt

The idea for *The Angelus* came to Millet because he remembered that his grandmother, hearing the church bell ringing while they were working in the fields, always made them stop work to say the Angelus prayer. So it was a childhood memory that lies behind the wonderful painting, not Millet's desire to glorify some great religious feeling. The artist was not a church attendee. However, for the past 150 years, the picture has been an iconic symbol of prayerful meditation, which, for so many, radiates a deep religious contemplation.

As I continue to gaze at the picture, two things strike me powerfully. How many farm workers in secular France today will have even heard of the Angelus prayer, let alone the

Annunciation? And what of those two figures, the man holding his hat as he looks down to the ground whilst the woman clasps her hands together? The composition is similar to many of the Annunciation paintings of Gabriel and Mary I have seen over the past few months. Maybe, inadvertently, Millet captured a highly original and distinctive take on the biblical encounter.

Returning to Ile de la Cité, I view a wonderful stained-glass panel in Sainte-Chapelle, the Palatine chapel built as a High Gothic double church in 1248 in the oldest part of the city's medieval royal castle. Recently re-opened after years of restoration, the upper chapel, which was used by the monarch and his guests of honour, is a truly breathtaking site. The interior is bathed in a profusion of radiant colours as the light shimmers through the fifteen windows. In the bottom left hand corner of one of them is an exquisite panel featuring the encounter between the angel Gabriel and Mary.

155. Rogier van de Weyden *The Annunciation*, 1435-40, The Louvre, Paris. Photo © Musée du Louvre, Dist. RMN-Grand Palais/Angèle Dequier

At the Louvre, my final Parisian destination, I focus on one painting, *The Annunciation*, created by the Flemish master, Rogier van der Weyden, between 1435 and 1440. It is thought he painted the work in Brussels, probably for a Piedmontese banker living in Flanders at the time or for a member of his family back in Italy. Originally forming the central panel of a triptych, it is painted in the contemporary style for the period with a richly-dressed angel Gabriel, wearing a magnificent brocade cape, greeting Mary, who is reading a book in front of her elaborate bed. A ewer and basin on her side-table, along with a jar of lilies, emphasize her purity. The extinguished candle nearby symbolizes that the waiting is over for the coming light.

Four hundred years ago, the Rubenhuis museum in Antwerp, Belgium, was Peter Paul Rubens's flourishing studio and home, where he lived with his wife and children for the last thirty years of his life. Rubens was a prolific Flemish baroque painter who became

Flanders's leading artist of the early seventeenth century. His extravagant works are acclaimed for their emphasis on movement, colour and sensuality. He became particularly well known for his fleshy, curvaceous female bodies, often described as 'Rubenesque'.

Rubens was born in Westphalia in 1577 and was baptized a Calvinist. When he was ten, the family settled in Antwerp, which was then in the Spanish Netherlands. Rubens had a humanist education but later became a devout Catholic. Influenced by the great Italian Classical and Renaissance artists, he travelled to Italy in 1600 and stayed for eight years, inspired particularly by the magnificent works of Titian and Tintoretto in Venice, and Raphael and Michelangelo in Rome. Returning to Antwerp, Rubens developed a highly distinctive, flamboyant baroque style, full of dynamism, sensuous colouring and exuberance that combined Flemish realism with the Classical and Renaissance character of the Italian masterpieces. The design of his splendid house and garden in Antwerp was clearly influenced by his visit to Italy and has the appearance of a beautiful, grand palazzo.

His main studio now acts as a large gallery in the museum, displaying a number of his great works. It was here that Rubens and his assistants originally produced more than two thousand paintings. High on the right wall hangs his epic picture, *Annunciation*, that is more than three metres long. He drew the original composition as a preliminary model in

156. Peter Paul Rubens *The Annunciation*, 1628, Rubenhuis, Antwerp. © Rubens House, Antwerp
Photo: Michel Wuyts and Louis De Peuter

1610 and then immediately painted the right side of the canvas, including the figure of Mary, but, inexplicably, left the picture incomplete for seventeen years. In 1628, he finished it. The painting shows Mary caught in surprise as three cherubs hold a cloak over her. As the twisting angel Gabriel arrives from the left, a dove flies towards Mary, and a dramatic shaft of light shines down on her, illuminating the whole scene. The guide describes *Annunciation* as a vivid example of Rubens's later style: large scale, vertiginous, a harmonious composition, with lush brushwork, bright colours and whirling, dynamic poses.

The more I look at it, the more I see strong similarities with Lemoyne's *The Annunciation*, painted a hundred years later. The size of the work; the rounded arch at the top of the painting; the way the angel Gabriel points his finger upwards; his androgynous look; the colour of his outer garment; the way his thigh is exposed; the radiant light shining down from the top centre, illuminating the whole composition; the cherubs above

Mary; her bare exposed foot; the white linen in the straw basket. Yet there are also clear differences. Lemoyne's two main figures are on opposite sides to Rubens's picture; he has no flowers in a vase; no dove; in Rubens's depiction the two main figures look at each other, in Lemoyne's they do not; Rubens includes a cat licking its paw. But the similarities more than outweigh the differences. Did Lemoyne see this painting when visiting Antwerp, I wonder, or was he familiar with a copy? Did Rubens's work influence his own representation a century later? Interestingly, an earlier Rubens work, *Adam and Eve*, painted before he left for Italy, is hung directly below his Annunciation picture.

I leave the Rubenhuis museum and head for the Cathedral of Our Lady in the heart of the old city. It took 169 years for the present brick and white stone building to be completed and it is the largest Gothic structure in the Low Countries. The multi-tiered north tower is over a hundred and twenty metres high. For more than a thousand years, Antwerp's Catholics have honoured and revered Mary as 'Our Lady', the patroness of both the city and the Cathedral.

157. Maerten de Vos *St Luke painting the Virgin Mary*, 1602 Cathedral of Our Lady, Antwerp. © KMSKA – Lukas-Art in Flanders vzw. Photo: Hugo Maertens

Inside, there is a striking 1602 painting by the leading Flemish artist, Maerten de Vos, called *St Luke painting the Virgin Mary*. As I gaze at the canvas, I try to work out the possibility of this legendary story having any substance or credibility. Mary was possibly thirteen or fourteen at the time of Jesus's conception. Luke is thought to have written his Gospel account some eighty years after Jesus's birth. It is not beyond the realm of possibility that Mary could have met him in old age and recounted what had happened at the time of her pregnancy. Then later, Luke may have used the testimony to describe her encounter with the angel Gabriel. It is a highly unlikely proposition – Mary would have been in her early nineties – but not impossible. Most biblical scholars dismiss the idea of any meeting between Luke and Mary as the source of his Gospel narrative of the Annunciation. But I have heard many ordinary, faithful people on my journey tell me they believe Luke heard the detail directly from the Virgin's mouth, so to speak. They simply have belief that this is true and do not seem to need certainty based on clear historical evidence. I remember one woman in Chichester saying to me, 'Why would you want to question that? I never have and I'm glad I haven't.'

To the side of the de Vos painting is the Mary Chapel, where a lustrous sixteenth-century wooden statue of *Our Lady of Antwerp* stands on a globe above the altar. Holding her baby son in her left hand and a gold sceptre in her right, she wears a lavishly jewelled crown on her head and is dressed in gleaming white and gold robes. Here, Mary is depicted as the 'Queen of Heaven'. The candelabras in front of the altar host scores of tall, thin votive candles, whose flickering light give a particularly high Catholic atmosphere to the space. A guide states that many Belgians come to the Mary Chapel to pray to 'Our Lady in her capacity as ruler of heaven, in the hope of acquiring her blessing and favour.'

One British tourist visiting the Cathedral tells me she finds it 'kitsch, tasteless, even abhorrent. I can't explain why but it engenders a physical reaction,' she says. 'It's so artificial and manufactured. This cult of Mary was never intended in the Scriptures. I find it almost commercializing her, trivializing her, elevating her to a status that, for me, is repulsive.'

She says she doesn't believe in Christianity but I ask her why she has such a visceral reaction.

'I don't know. It cheapens religion and her. I can't explain it.'

A couple of minutes later, a middle-aged woman dressed all in black enters the Mary Chapel and lights a candle. She kneels before the statue and, closing her eyes, begins to pray. Half an hour on, she is still there.

During that time, I have seen some of Rubens's most famous paintings, which are displayed in the Cathedral including *The Descent from the Cross* and *The Resurrection of Christ*. In the Choir, the magnificently carved nineteenth-century, neo-Gothic oak choir stalls include a lovely rendition of the Annunciation. Designed by François Durlet, it forms part of a thirty-six-episode series that depicts the life of Mary in high relief. Mary turns away from her prie-dieu with her arms crossed over her chest. Angel Gabriel leans over with a raised finger, indicating he is giving her the message, as the dove descends on a beautifully carved beam of light.

The Rijksmuseum in Amsterdam showcases the most complete collection of Dutch Masters in the world. Altogether, more than 8,000 pieces are displayed, including treasures such as Rembrandt's *The Night Watch* and Vermeer's *The Milkmaid*. So it is somewhat ironic that my intention is to find two Annunciation sculptures, one by a German and the other by an Italian.

The first thing that catches my eye is a fifteenth-century Brabant sculpture. Made from oak with traces of polychromy, the small statue shows Joachim and Anna embracing at the Golden Gate in Jerusalem on hearing that Anna is finally pregnant. The statue, made around 1470, originally formed part of an altarpiece dedicated to the Virgin Mary. It is beautifully carved and shows such tenderness and love at a very intimate and joyous moment.

158. Tilman Riemenschneider *The Annunciation*, 1486, The Rijksmuseum, Amsterdam. © The Rijksmuseum, Amsterdam

After a while, I find what I have come looking for: *The Annunciation* by Tilman Riemenschneider, one of the most important German sculptors of the late Middle Ages. It is a small, two piece alabaster sculpture that was created in Würzburg in 1486. Gabriel's drapery billows as he arrives on the scene. His lips are parted and his right arm is raised in a greeting. His long, curly golden hair falls over his shoulders. Mary's left hand rests on the book she has been reading at her prie-dieu. She looks away from the angel, somewhat perturbed as she is clearly taken by surprise.

Next, I find two stunning figures carved in walnut by Francesco di Valdanbrino, a Tuscan sculptor who created them in Siena in 1423. The statues were made to flank the high altar of the church of San Francesco in Pienza in Tuscany. The long, thin statue of Gabriel wears a white and red robe with a golden sash and red shoes. He looks very Italian. Unusually, Mary is clothed in a full red dress. She appears to be raising her right hand in trepidation as she holds a book firmly in her left hand. She is dressed as a high society Tuscan woman.

It does seem incredible that there is no Dutch painting of the Annunciation anywhere in the Rijksmuseum. Moreover, there appears to be no Dutch masterpiece of the encounter in any church throughout the Dutch capital. Before the Reformation, churches and cathedrals in Amsterdam were filled with religious paintings, statues and reliquaries, made by some of the most skilled artists and craftsmen in Europe. Perhaps their absence today demonstrates the strength of anti-Marian feelings during the hard-line Protestant Reformation in the Netherlands. During this time, any image that could be considered idolatrous was destroyed.

159. Francesco di Valdanbrino *The Annunciation*, 1423, The Rijksmuseum, Amsterdam. © The Rijksmuseum, Amsterdam

As I prepare to leave Amsterdam, I call in on a small Catholic church on a suburban road near to the Beatrix Park in the south of the city. Its name is the Chapel of the Lady of All Nations. As I enter the plain building at eleven o'clock in the morning, I see around thirty people reciting the First Joyful Mystery of the Rosary that focuses on the Annunciation and Mary's humility. Most are middle-aged women. The majority is Dutch but there is a small group of women from Quezon City in the Philippines and a woman next to me is from the United States. The priest wears full vestments and three nuns sit at the back. I take a place on a bench at the side of the chapel. The priest looks across at me sternly. He makes a hand sign, which I don't understand, but he doesn't seem happy to see me and appears to be asking me to leave. The Blessed Sacrament is placed in a monstrance on the altar. Nearby is a large painting of Mary as *The Lady of All Nations*. It's festooned with yellow, mustard and orange coloured flowers.

The Lady of All Nations – the Blessed Virgin Mary – reportedly appeared and spoke to a middle-aged woman in Amsterdam over a period of fourteen years from 1945 to 1959. The name of the woman was Ida Peerdeman. The 'visions' have become known as the 'Amsterdam Apparitions' and they began on 25 March 1945. In that year, the feast day coincided with Palm Sunday. World War II was drawing to an end in Europe. The Netherlands was suffering from severe food shortages during the 'Hungry Winter' of 1944/5 and Amsterdam was still under German occupation. Thirty-nine-year-old Ida Peerdeman was with her sisters, huddled by a stove in her home when, she claimed, she saw a light in the corner of the adjoining room and was drawn to it. 'Out of the light came the Lady,' she said. On the guidance of a local priest, she wrote down all that 'the Lady' said, as the apparitions continued over the next fourteen years.

She claimed that the figure told her she was Mary but that she should be addressed as the 'Lady of All Nations'. The 'messages' included the prediction of the occurrence of Vatican II some years before it was called and a warning that the Church in the late twentieth century would face grave dangers, particularly 'a resurgence of the modernist heresy'. The Lady of All Nations also called for the 'final Marian dogma' to be endorsed such that she would be seen as 'Co-Redemptrix, Mediatrix and Advocate' and she promised she would then give 'peace, true peace to the world'. She wanted this to sit alongside the four established dogmas declared by the Roman Catholic Church: that she had an Immaculate Conception at birth and a bodily Assumption to Heaven at death, that she is the Mother of God, and a perpetual virgin.

Apparently, Mary requested of Ira Peerdeman that an image be made of her and described in detail how it should look. She wanted to be depicted standing on a globe with the loincloth of her Son wrapped around her as she is penetrated by an intense light. A wooden cross should stand directly behind her. The German artist, Heinrich Repke, under the direction of Ira Peerdeman, created the painting in 1951. That same year 'the Lady' communicated a special prayer to be said before the Cross:

> Lord Jesus Christ, Son of the Father, send now your Spirit over the earth.
> Let the Holy Spirit live in the heart of all nations.
> That they may be preserved from degeneration, disaster and war.
> May the Lady of All Nations, who was once Mary, be our Advocate.
> Amen.

The phrase 'who was once Mary' proved to be highly controversial within the higher echelons of the Roman Catholic Church. In 1956, the local bishop declared that there was no evidence that the apparitions were of a supernatural nature. In 1972 and 1974, the Congregation for the Doctrine of the Faith at the Vatican wrote, 'the supernatural nature is not determined' and called on the faithful to discontinue its propaganda with regard to the alleged apparitions. That remains the official position of the Vatican today. However, in the 1970s, the Foundation of the Lady of All Nations built the chapel on the Diepenbrockstraat in the south of the city and displayed Repke's painting to the side of the altar. Ira Peerdeman died in 1996. That same year, the local Bishop of Haarlem authorized public devotion to 'Our Lady of All Nations' and in 2002, the current Bishop, Joseph Maria Punt, declared that the apparitions accorded to Ide Peerdeman to be 'of a supernatural origin'.

Some commentators have suggested that the spread of the cult of 'Our Lady of All Nations' is to do with hardline, traditional, conservative Catholics in the Netherlands and beyond, standing against a growing liberalisation in the Church, particularly since the 1960s. One thing for sure: an alleged apparition on the feast of the Annunciation back in 1945 started an extraordinary chain of events here in Amsterdam.

———

The Prado in Madrid claims to have 'the greatest collection of religious art in the world'. For me, the most striking image is El Greco's *La Anunciación* created between 1596 and 1600. It is an extraordinary picture and, even after an hour standing before it, I keep discovering more and more. It is a towering image, the canvas measuring 315 cm x 174 cm. There is so much energy, movement and drama. Nobody else paints with such vivid expressionism, originality, intensity and fervour.

Born in 1541 in Crete, which was then under Venetian rule, Domenicos Theotocopoulos, nicknamed 'the Greek', moved to Venice and Rome to pursue his craft before settling in Toledo in 1577, where he became one of the most important artists of the late sixteenth century. In 1596, at the height of his powers, El Greco was commissioned

to paint the High Altar of the Colegio de la Encarnación in Madrid, an Augustinian seminary. *La Anunciación* formed the bottom, central section of the altarpiece.

In the centre of the picture, a dove comes spiralling down in a whirlwind of golden light towards Mary. Above the dove, a flamboyant ensemble of angels hangs in the clouds playing musical instruments. Below this group and the dove is a tall, thin Gabriel, wearing a bold, green tunic and clasping his hands together over his chest. His majestic wings are wide open. Mary, next to her prayer stand, looks towards him trustingly. On the ground lies her sewing gear. There is also a burning bush, which, by tradition, never goes out, symbolizing the divine presence and Mary as the receptacle of that divine presence.

The two central figures seem to float in a supernatural space. A semi-abstract group of angelic voices hovers behind Mary and Gabriel. Between her and the angel is the burning bush that appears to be lit by flickering white candle flames.

160. El Greco *La Anunciación*, 1596-1600, The Prado, Madrid. © Museo Nacional del Prado

I take the high-speed train from Madrid to Barcelona and less than four hours later, I am standing in front of one of the most extraordinary church buildings in the world: Antonio Gaudi's 'La Sagrada Familia' (Church of the Holy Family). If El Greco is a force of originality, Gaudi is in a different league. Gaudi spearheaded the 'modernisme' or Catalan Art Nouveau movement and this architectural gem is his most famous work. Indeed, La Sagrada Familia has become the emblematic symbol of Barcelona, famous around the world.

Born in 1852, Antonio Gaudi studied at the Barcelona School of Architecture. He was a profoundly Christian man, known for his piety, who attended Mass daily, and who was particularly devoted to the Virgin Mary. He began work on this spectacular building in 1882, aged thirty, and devoted the last part of his life wholly to the project from 1914 to his untimely death in 1926. Some ninety years later, it is still work-in-progress with gigantic cranes and high visibility clothed workmen moving all around the site. It has a likely completion date of around 2045.

You have to see this building close up to understand it. You need to walk around its vast internal spaces and pause for many minutes to take it all in. Words like spectacular, awesome, sublime, grandiose, unconventional, fairytale, do not do it justice. For me, the design of La Sagrada Familia walks a tightrope between absolute genius and an out-of-control imagination but, in the end, it is the most unique and memorable sacred building I have ever seen. Cardinal George Pell recently described it thus: 'This place speaks of God to the people of today (and tomorrow) more eloquently than any church I know.'

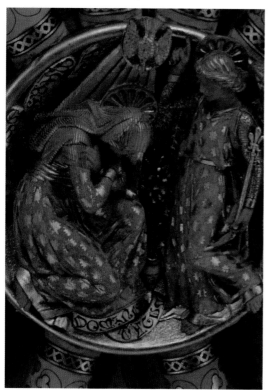

161. Joan Flotats designed roof boss in the Crypt, 1882, La Sagrada Familia, Barcelona

The crypt was the first part of the building to be completed in 1882 and the central keystone roof boss features a striking multi-coloured work by Joan Flotats depicting the Annunciation.

The Nativity façade on the church's northern side was the first part of the external structure to be completed in 1936. The design focuses on the theme of Christ's birth and childhood, and has three doorways relating to Faith, Hope and Charity. In front of the central doorway is a stone column with a serpent wound round from top to bottom with the apple of sin in its mouth. Above the column is a nativity scene and then directly above that are the stone figures of Mary and Gabriel at the Annunciation, designed by Jaume Busquets to Gaudi's original plans. Mary kneels down with her hands together and leans over in a humble pose – almost a willing surrender – as Gabriel places his right arm over her head.

162. Left: The author looks towards the Nativity façade at La Sagrada Familia, Barcelona. Right: Jaume Busquets designed Annunciation scene on the Nativity façade, La Sagrada Familia, Barcelona

As dusk falls and parakeets swoop over the neatly lit Nativity façade, an old woman passes me a card. It is entitled 'Prayer to the Holy Family':

Jesus, Mary and Joseph,
in whom we contemplate
the splendour of true love,
we confidently turn to you.

Holy Family of Nazareth,
make our families like yours,
places of communion,
and cenacles of prayer,
true schools of the Gospel and
little domestic churches.

Jesus, Mary and Joseph,
hear and answer our prayer.

Climbing to a height of 3,000 feet, the cable car docks at the Monastir de Montserrat. The views of Catalonia from the steep, jagged rocks along this serrated mountain ridge are spectacular. As the sun breaks through the light cloud cover, the Santa Maria monastery at Montserrat appears to glisten against the steep sedimentary rock face.

It is thought that the Benedictine monastery, thirty-five miles inland from Barcelona, was established here in the ninth century and today it is Catalonia's holiest shrine, attracting more than three million tourists and pilgrims every year. The reason is the legendary story of the Virgin of Montserrat, the patron saint of Catalonia. Around the year 880, a small group of nomad shepherd children were working in the area when they saw an intense light descending from the sky above the mountains. They claimed they could hear angels singing from inside a cave. They recounted what had taken place to their parents, who came to the place to find out what may have happened. They, too, witnessed the intense light and thought it was a sign from God. They brought the local priests to the location, and when they were inside the cave they discovered a statue of the Virgin Mary.

Tradition claims that St Luke made the statue in Jerusalem, and St Peter brought it to Montserrat around AD 50. Centuries later, the statue is said to have been hidden from the invading Moors in a 'holy cave' called the Santa Cora. Although the Virgin of Montserrat statue has been carbon dated to the twelfth century, that has not stopped worshippers from coming to see her and today she stands in the sanctuary of the monastery's domed Basilica on a richly enamelled altar. Queues form all day as pilgrims stand in front of La Moreneta (the dark maiden), one of a number of black or dark-chocolate coloured Madonna statues venerated across Europe. People are fascinated by the colour of these statues. One theory is that it has resulted from years of exposure to votive candle smoke. Another is that it is simply ageing varnish.

As I enter the Basilica, the bell strikes one o'clock and the Montserrat *escolania* (choir) of fifty boys start to sing the renowned Virolai hymn. I notice a small depository by the entrance where many dedications have been left…small toys, children's shoes, a wedding dress, a baby girl's white lace dress and scores of baby photographs. There are even red lipstick marks on the walls. La Moreneta is an important shrine for newly married couples and many Catalonian brides come here to pray for a happy and blessed marriage or for Mary to enable them to conceive a child or undergo successful childbirth. Of course, the small irony of these pilgrims praying to the Virgin Mary, who may never have experienced sexual intercourse, seems to go unnoticed.

163. *La Moreneta*, Santa Maria de Montserrat Abbey, Catalonia, Spain. Photo © Saleha Ullah

I follow three women up the stairs to face the gilded Romanesque statue, styled as the Virgin in Majesty. Ensconced within a glass frame with the baby Jesus on her lap, the crowned Mary's right hand holds an orb, which can be touched by the pilgrim through a small hole. One woman leaves a note; the second kisses the orb; and the third kneels on the floor, making the sign of the cross.

'What do you hope for?' I ask her as we leave the sanctuary.

'Children, children,' she replies. 'The Virgin Mary will help me. I know.'

I walk along a precipitous meandering path that leads to the Holy Grotto at Santa Cora, a mile away in the distance. The fourteen Stations of the Cross are used as staging posts along the way. At the cliff edge, there is a sheer drop of more than two thousand feet to the valley below, providing spectacular but rather scary views. Inside the small chapel at the Holy Grotto, hundreds of candles flicker in the dark. A small statue of Mary and the Christ Child stands on a ledge in the cave. To the side, there is another depository with baby clothes, children's dresses and baby shoes left in small boxes. On the walls, decorated with red lipstick marks, are photographs of young babies, and wedding dresses hang in plastic covers. A sign on the door indicates: 'Brought here as a thanksgiving offering to St Mary of Montserrat because of an ask which got favour or benefit.'

One card in the box states: 'Marina. 3/7: 11.30h Gracias!' Another is a handwritten note, 'Santa Maria de la Anunciación, madre de Dios, te amo, muchas gracias por mi bebe. Cristina' (Holy Mary of the Annunciation, mother of God, I love you, many thanks for my baby). A photograph of a proud and happy Cristina cradling her newborn child is attached.

CHAPTER 40

THREE ITALIAN CITIES

Venice is chock-a-block with images of the Annunciation if you know where to look.

No official records confirm the precise date of the founding of this unique place but tradition holds that at 12.00 noon on 25 March, AD 421, the city came into being. Small, scattered Veneti communities had lived on the lagoon islands for years, working as fishermen and salt harvesters. But it was on the 25 March that the first church was dedicated on the tiny islet of Rialto and, ever since, Venetians have celebrated the date as both 'natale di Venezia' – the birth of the city – and the feast day of the Annunciation.

When I arrive on 20 March at the eleventh-century church of San Giacomo, preparations are well underway to celebrate the city's birthday in the nearby marketplace. Inside the church, Marco Vecellio's *Annunciazione* painting is prominently displayed as a further reminder of the feast day's special importance.

A few yards east of the church of San Giacomo is the famous Rialto Bridge, half way down the Grand Canal and the site of the first crossing point of the city's main waterway. After a number of wooden structures collapsed, this stone bridge was designed in 1588 and completed in 1591. A beloved landmark on the Grand Canal, the southern archivolt features the key figures of the annunciation story on its façade. Gabriel is sited on the left side of the arch, his right hand pointing upwards, and Mary is on the right, holding her hand to her breast. The dove flies between them at the centrepoint of the archway. Every day, thousands of passengers on the vaporettos, water taxis and gondolas that pass under the Rialto Bridge would be reminded of the significance of the annunciation story to Venice… if only they know where to look.

164. Rialto Bridge, 1588-91, Venice.

By the time the Rialto Bridge was built, Venice had become one of the great mercantile and cultural centres of the world, a treasure trove of majestic churches and magnificent palazzi, and a place that inspired many of Europe's greatest Renaissance artists to produce their finest work.

As I head down the Grand Canal to St Mark's Piazza, the Campanile comes into view. Ninety metres high, the freestanding bell tower once acted as the city's lighthouse. Atop

537

the iconic structure stands the glistening, golden statue of the angel Gabriel, looking out onto the basino di San Marco and the island of San Giorgio Maggiore beyond. At the nearby St Mark's Basilica, thirteenth-century statues of Gabriel and Mary sit inside two *aediculos* on the corner of the main façade. Inside the Basilica, there is a wonderful tenth-century annunciation mosaic on the west side of the north transept and another glittering fifteenth-century depiction in the Chapel of Madonna del Mascoli.

165. Angel Gabriel on top of the Campanile, St Mark's Square, Venice

Close to St Marco's Piazza, there is an extraordinary marble altarpiece with beautifully sculptured figures by Heinrich Meyring of the angel Gabriel and Mary on either side of the main altar in the church of Santa Maria del Giglio (St Mary with the Lily.) In the Accademia Gallery there are annunciation masterpieces by Veneziano,

166. Heinrich Meyring Annunciation statues, seventeenth century, Santa Maria del Giglio, Venice

Bellini, Veronese and Parisati; and in the fine Gothic church of Madonna dell'Orto in the northern Cannaregio district, Palma il Giovane's *Annunciation* takes pride of place.

But, for me, the two most striking Venetian paintings of the Annunciation are sited inside the beautiful, early sixteenth-century Scuola Grande di San Rocco. The entrance to the ground floor hall displays a brilliant Tintoretto, painted between 1583 and 1587. With dramatic use of light and shade, it depicts a white-robed angel Gabriel flying through a hole in Mary's home. Mary, dressed in red with a dove hovering above her, looks utterly startled. Her home is one of stark contrasts: in part, very basic, with a dilapidated column of bricks centre stage, a frayed chair by her side and Joseph's carpentry tools stacked haphazardly by the side of the house. The inclusion of a group of twelve cherubim hovering above the angel Gabriel, the magnificent Venetian ceiling and the royal bed with its red silk drapes, offsets this apparent realism. Tintoretto seemingly wants to emphasize that Mary is a woman of two parts…the poor, pious girl from Nazareth and the Queen of Heaven.

As I walk up the wide, marble staircase towards the upper Great Hall, there's another magnificent Annunciation, this one painted by Titian in 1535. Titian uses a grand Renaissance setting, with a balustrade, colonnades and a chequer-board red and white marble floor. Angel Gabriel arrives carrying a lily stem, and the dazzling shafts of light on which the dove descends illuminate Mary's soft, pale face as she kneels at her prie-dieu with her arms crossed in a gesture of acceptance. A partridge by her feet symbolizes

167. Jacopo Tintoretto *The Annunciation*, 1583-87, Scuola Grandi di San Rocco, Venice. © Scuola Grandi di San Rocco

voluptuousness and fecundity. Apparently classical writers believed the female bird had extraordinary procreative powers, claiming it could conceive from the air or from the sound of a male voice – a highly appropriate bird for an artist to include to underpin the notion of a virginal conception. Next to the red-clawed partridge is a pome fruit from a quince, a reminder of Eve's contrasting disobedience in the Garden of Eden. By Mary's feet is a wicker basket with a white cloth tucked inside. Perhaps this symbol is a prediction of the shroud that will cover Mary's son at his future death.

168. Titian *The Annunciation*, 1535, Scuola Grandi di San Rocco, Venice. © Scuola Grandi di San Rocco

It is thrilling to think that François Lemoyne probably visited this very building and admired these same paintings 290 years ago.

My final destination in Venice is the San Salvatore church, a stunning example of early sixteenth-century High Renaissance architecture. Here, I find another Annunciation by Titian, painted in 1560–1565, thirty years after his earlier work in the San Rocco and ten years before his death. It is a grand picture, some twelve feet high, in which the angel Gabriel forms part of a cloud filled with angels as heavenly light pours down from an opening in the sky, symbolizing the transfer from the immaterial to the material. Mary lifts her headscarf exposing her right ear, to indicate her acceptance of the message of the Incarnation.

Fifteen representations of the Annunciation within a square mile in one of the world's most beautiful and unique cities. Even for me, that is quite enough for one day!

————

After a two hour high speed train journey, crossing through the north Italian regions of Veneto and Emilia-Romagna and the rolling Tuscan hills, I arrive in Florence, the 'cradle of the Renaissance' and home to some of the greatest art collections in the world. If Venice celebrates its birthday on the feast of the Annunciation, Florence recognizes 25 March as its second New Year's Day. For up until 1750, the feast of the Annunciation was still recognized in Florence as the beginning of the calendar year and, even to this day, celebrations take place on 25 March to mark the 'Cappodano Fiorentino', the Florentine New Year.

For hundreds of years, the people of Florence gathered in Piazza Santissima Annunziata to welcome the arrival of spring and mark both the feast day of the Annunciation and the coming of a new year. They entered the church of Santissima Annunziata and stood in front of a thirteenth-century Annunciation fresco in the chapel of the Holy Effigy and gave thanks. Legend has it that the artist Bartolomeo was commissioned to paint this Annunciation in 1252 and fell asleep after completing all but the face of the Virgin Mary. When he woke up, he discovered that an angel had finished the fresco for him, resulting in a beautiful Madonna. The painting soon became a place of veneration for pilgrims, who left a variety of votive offerings.

Today, every 25 March, a historical procession, the Corteo Storico, weaves its way from the Palagio di Parte Guelfa to the Piazza Santissima Annunziata to mark the Festa dell' Annunciazione with traditional Florentine costumes, medieval music and flag waving. In the square, market stalls offer traditional dishes including Brigidini biscuits and a special concert is held to honour this 'second New Year' tradition. Moreover, Florentine brides traditionally visit the fifteenth-century canopied tabernacle of the Annunciation just inside the entrance to the Basilica and leave their wedding bouquets there in the hope of a blessed and happy marriage. During my visit, I count fifteen bouquets and buttonholes left inside the church. Florence has always seen itself as a city under the special protection of the Virgin Mary and the lily is the symbol of the city.

Inside the church of Santissima Annunziata is a fresco, St Luke painting the Virgin, created by Giorgio Vasari in 1565. Luke sits in front of his easel looking at Mary and her young son, who are raised above the ground by five putti. An ox, the symbol of Luke, lies down next to him. As Luke prepares to add further colour to the canvas, Mary points out to Jesus his very own image in the picture. The work references the legend told during the late Middle Ages and Renaissance that Luke knew Mary personally.

169. Giorgio Vasari *St Luke painting the Virgin*, 1565, Church of Santissima Annunziata, Florence. © Darren Milligan

I arrive three days before the feast of the Annunciation and spend the next forty-eight hours soaking up the art and history that links Florence so closely with Luke's story. The climax will be seeing for the first time Fra Angelico's fresco – probably the most famous and acclaimed Annunciation image ever created.

After arriving at the Stazione Santa Maria Novella, I walk a few yards to the fourteenth-century Dominican church of the same name. There, I admire two Annunciation works by Santi di Toto and Petro di Minato. The next stop is the church of San Lorenzo to view Lippi's *Annunciation* of 1450. A few hundred yards south and I arrive in the Piazza San Giovanni, looking towards the Duomo. The huge dome dominates the Florentine skyline and its red tiles and white, green and red marble façade make this building a stunning sight. The Cathedral is dedicated to the Virgin Mary as Santa Maria del Fiore – St Mary of the Flower – the flower being Christ.

Opposite the Duomo is the twelfth-century Battistero or Baptistry, built on a large octagonal plan with the eight sides symbolizing the eighth day and the time of Christ being beyond earthly measured seven-day cycles. I have come especially to view the north doorway, one of three entrances to the Baptistry. Designed by twenty-two-year-old Lorenzo Ghiberti, following a special competition, and constructed between 1402 and 1425, the huge bronze door is made up of twenty-eight individual squares, each two-foot panel depicting an aspect of the life of Christ.

The third panel from the bottom on the left shows a dramatic yet graceful Annunciation scene. The bronze relief shows the striking figure of God the Father sending the dove of the Holy Spirit to fly above the angel Gabriel towards a tense, slender Mary, who leans back almost in retreat as she stands under a portico. It is a superb rendition and an extraordinary artistic achievement by goldsmith Ghiberti, who spent more than twenty years meticulously designing and constructing the doors. Inside, the magnificent ceiling includes an Annunciation scene as part of a dazzling series of thirteenth-century mosaics illustrating Old and New Testament stories.

I walk a few hundred yards towards the Arno River and arrive at the Uffizi Gallery, containing the world's finest collection of Renaissance art. I have earmarked three works in particular that I want to see.

170. Lorenzo Ghiberti Annunciation panel, 1402-25, The Baptistry, Florence

171. Simone Martini and Lippo Memmi *The Annunciation with St Margaret and St Ansanus*, 1333, Uffizi Gallery, Florence. © Gallerie degli Uffizi

Simone Martini's rendition of the Annunciation in 1333, using tempera on wood, is one of the masterpieces of fourteenth-century Sienese Gothic art. Created with the assistance of his brother-in-law, Lippo Memmi, Martini's large altarpiece was painted for the Saint Ansanus altar in Siena Cathedral. It shows a prostrate angel with beautiful wings and flowing mantle, having just touched the ground. He holds an olive branch as a sign of peace. A bouquet of lilies stands nearby in a gold vase. Mary looks visibly shocked as she recoils. She pulls her blue mantle close to her neck, as if for protection. The book she has been reading is half closed. The dove above them is encircled by a group of angels. The background includes pointed Gothic arches and is filled with rich gold leaf, giving the picture an aura of sanctification.

I move on to the Leonardo Room where a large, bustling crowd is gathered around one particular painting. It is difficult to see anything as tour guides, jostling for space, gather their groups around the picture. Many people hold their mobile phones high in the air, trying to take a photograph of the painting over other people's heads. I step back and sit down a few yards away. It is rather amusing to watch these visitors as they stand in front of Leonardo da Vinci's masterpiece, *The Annunciation*. Eventually, after waiting for half an hour, I find myself in front of the painting with just two other people.

Leonardo's *Annunciazione* was painted in 1472 when he was just twenty and still working in the studio of his master, Andrea del Verrocchio. Using oil and tempera on wood, it is thought to be a possible collaboration between them both. It was originally attributed to another painter, Domenico Ghirlandaio, but the consensus today among art experts is that this is one of Leonardo's earliest works. It was originally located in the Chiostro San Bartolomeo in Monteoliveto near Florence.

The setting is a Florentine villa with rolling Tuscan hills in the background – a classic Renaissance setting. The composition shows the angel Gabriel kneeling in reverence and

172. Leonardo da Vinci *The Annunciation*, 1472, Uffizi Gallery, Florence. © Gallerie degli Uffizi

holding a lily. Mary sits at a lectern in an almost full frontal pose. The interior of her bedroom can be glimpsed on her left. Art historians believe the elongated shape of the lectern and the formation of the Virgin's hand probably mean that the work was supposed to be viewed from further below the frame and to the right of the picture.

As I stand in front of the picture, studying the detail of Mary's beautifully lit face, more crowds enter the room and gather around it. I am gently pushed aside as people lean forward to hear their guide's commentary. I watch again from a distance as around fifty people cluster round the picture, many of them taking 'selfies' of themselves in front of the painting.

I move on to Sandro Botticelli's Annunciazione di Cestello, painted in 1489-90. Formerly in the Cestello church of the Cistercians in Borgo Pinti in Florence, the altarpiece is a brilliant depiction of the pivotal moment when Gabriel confronts Mary. There is a wonderful sense of drama as both figures hold out their hands but do not

173. Sandro Botticelli *Cestello Annunciation*, 1489, Uffizi Gallery, Florence. © Gallerie degli Uffizi

touch, referencing the way Mary conceived Jesus. The dynamic movement of the two central characters contrasts with the precise, static lines of the red floor tiles and the sense of perspective that takes the viewer out of the back window to the Tree of Life and the river beyond, emphasizing a sense of eternity. Below, carved on the frame in Latin, are the words from verse 35 of Luke's story: 'The Holy Ghost shall come upon thee and the power of the Highest shall overshadow thee.'

Whilst I gaze at the picture, I am reminded of my recent conversation with Professor Tim Gorringe who has a copy of this painting in his bedroom. He described the wonderful sense of dance between the divine and the human in which the divine approaches but does not overwhelm. That seems to me to be a brilliant exposition of what Botticelli is trying to express.

I leave the Uffizi Gallery and head down the via del Corso to the church of Santa Maria de Ricci to hear a rather strange story concerning the Annunciation. The church was founded in 1508 in reparation for an outrage committed by Antonio Rinaldeschi against an Annunciation painted on the side of the nearby church of Santa Maria deli Alberighi.

Rinaldeschi had spent the night of 21 July 1501 in the nearby Osteria del Fico, drinking and gambling. He is said to have handed over his cloak after losing at cards. Angered by his losses, he noticed the Annunciation image and picked up some horse dung in the road and threw it against the figure of the Virgin Mary. A passerby witnessed his actions and subsequently he was arrested and charged with sacrilege. Later, he was hanged from a window of the Bargello. The story goes that the dung, which had hit the face of Mary, subsequently transformed into the shape of a rose on the Virgin's cheek. The Ricci family built the Santa Maria de Ricci in response to the sacrilege, and the fresco was chiselled off the wall of the old, demolished church of Santa Maria deli Alberighi. Now it sits above the Ricci church's main altar and is known as the Madonna de Ricci. Nearby, a panel details the story of Antonio Rinaldeschi's crime, featured in nine scenes.

My next stop is Santa Croce, the largest Franciscan church in Italy. Inside is Donatello's superb sandstone sculpture of the Annunciation, created in 1435. The partly gilded figures of the angel Gabriel and Mary form a classic styled relief set within a tabernacle. Donatello created extraordinary, life-like folds of drapery from the local grey sandstone. The humble angel kneels before Mary as she stands listening to his words. Her body turns away but she looks down towards him with grace and humility. The sculpture is particularly striking for its sense of calmness and serenity.

My last destination in Florence is the site of probably the most famous and acclaimed Annunciation image of all time: Fra Angelico's fresco in the Convent of San Marco.

174. Donatello *The Annunciation*, 1435, Basilica di Santa Croce, Florence

Built between 1437 and 1452 in the northern part of the city, the former Dominican monastery is graced with a series of his wonderful frescos, which were painted along the dormitory corridors and inside each individual cell in order to inspire prayer, devotion and contemplation amongst the monastic community. The frescos are characterized by their simplicity and spirituality.

Fra Angelico was born as Guido di Pietro in 1395 and, as a Dominican friar became known as Fra Giovanni da Fiesole. He moved from Fiesole to San Marco as the monastery was being renovated and he became known as 'Il Beato Angelico' (the Blessed Angelic One) for the outstanding artwork that he created in the monks' cells and on the dormitory landings.

I walk up the staircase to the dormitories on the upper floor of the convent, and see for the first time Fra Angelico's famous *Annunciazione*, created in 1440. Through his brilliant use of perspective and harmonious colour, the viewer is given the impression that he/she is looking through an imaginary window onto a real space. Angel Gabriel has arrived, his multi coloured wings on full display. He is aglow with colour in shades of ochre and gold, whereas Mary, who sits on a stool, facing a fenced-in garden, wears more muted, dark robes. Spring flowers on the ground are in bloom and the trees sport thick green foliage. The protagonists meet under a loggia whose archways and vaulted ceiling are similar to the architecture of the San Marco convent. Behind Mary is a small window, similar to those in each of the monks' cells. It is clear Fra Angelico wanted to place the encounter in the very surroundings in which he and his fellow brothers lived. Siting the large Annunciazione fresco at the top of the stairs encouraged the monks to pause and meditate on the great mystery before each returned to his cell.

175. Fra Angelico *The Annunciation*, 1440, Convent of San Marco, Florence. © and by kind permission of Gabinetto Fotografico, Gallerie degli Uffizi

I stand alone in silence for ten minutes. This is the image that has been referenced by so many people I have spoken to. I almost have to pinch myself to remind myself that I am actually here. To my immense surprise, there is no one else here. Both life-size figures of Gabriel and Mary have their arms folded in mutual acceptance, emphasizing how both are submissive to a greater will. As they cast eyes on each other, there's a sense of stillness and serenity, quiet elegance and modesty. The harmonious colours offer a sense of calm and, at the bottom of the painting, there is a Latin inscription with the words: 'Hail, O Mother of Piety and noble domicile of the Holy Trinity.'

Along the first floor landings are two rows of more than forty small cells where each monk lived, slept and prayed. On each cell wall is a Fra Angelico fresco representing an episode in the life of Christ and placed as a model for meditation. In cell three on the east corridor, there is another annunciation scene where, again, the two slender, haloed figures cross their arms in acceptance. Angel Gabriel looks down on a thin looking Mary, who kneels in submission, a model of humility and obedience. Radiant light shines between them. The palette of colours is simple and subdued with a lovely pale pink sinopia used for the drapery. There is very little symbolism used because Fra Angelico recognized his fellow brothers already knew the story well. Here in cell three, the fresco includes an additional figure of Peter of Verona, one of the first Dominican martyrs, who looks on as an apparent witness to the annunciation encounter.

I stand in the cell for more than thirty minutes, looking at the detail of the fresco. A guide arrives eventually and tells me this is a highly unusual afternoon – normally the convent is packed full. It is a real privilege to see the two annunciation frescos in such solitude, just as the monks would have done.

A busy and highly memorable annunciation-themed stay in Florence draws to a close.

176. Fra Angelico *The Annunciation*, 1440, Cell 3, Convent of San Marco, Florence. © and by kind permission of Gabinetto Fotografico, Gallerie degli Uffizi

I arrive in Rome in readiness to celebrate the feast of the Annunciation with Pope Francis in St Peter's Square. Before it takes place, I take the opportunity to see five iconic Annunciation images, which are displayed in different parts of the city. The first is probably the most important depiction of the Annunciation that I will see on my whole pilgrimage because it's thought to be the oldest known image of the encounter between the angel Gabriel and Mary anywhere in the world.

I am on the via Salaria in northern Rome, at the Catacomb of Priscilla. The catacombs are underground cemeteries constructed outside the old city walls, where the early Christian dead were buried. The Roman authorities had serious concerns about dead spirits and poor hygiene, so they buried the bodies away from the city. During the Christian persecutions of the third and early fourth centuries, the various catacombs dotted around Rome received the remains of numerous martyrs and a number of Popes. The catacombs enabled Christians to come together discreetly to express their faith in relative safety.

Priscilla was a member of the Acilius Giabrio senatorial family and is thought to have granted the use of her land north of the city for Christian burial purposes. The catacombs were dug out within an *arenarium* (sandstone quarry) from the late second century to the early fifth century, to form a series of underground burial chambers. There were three levels, creating a maze of more than eight miles of underground passageways cut into the rock. The tombs and funeral chapels accommodated 40,000 graves. Rich and poor were buried in different parts of the complex, the rich in special decorated chambers, the poor in *loculi* (carved out wall compartments.)

By the fifth century, the Barbarians had ransacked all the tombs as they searched for gold and other treasures. The catacombs were sealed off until the seventh century when Christians opened the graves looking for relics of martyrs. They were pretty much forgotten until the sixteenth century when they were re-discovered and recognized at last for producing some of the earliest and most important depictions of Christian art.

Today, the Benedictine Sisters of Priscilla live above the tunnels in the House of the Catacombs and are entrusted with the care of the underground cemetery network. Every day they offer specially guided tours of parts of the complex. As I prepare to join one of the tour groups alongside twelve other people, I feel a strong sense of anticipation.

Sandro Luclam, a historian and Christian archaeologist, is our guide. As we descend a few steps and begin our journey along the dark, narrow passageways, he tells us the temperature at thirty-five metres underground will be around 13 ºC. (55 ºF.) The tunnels are low and just about wide enough for one person. A distinctive musty, sweet smell hangs in the air like thick perfume. The overall effect is claustrophobic and I am keen to keep up with the rest of the group. I don't want to get lost down here. As we meander through the never-ending web of tunnels, I imagine what it must have been like to pass through here 1,700 years ago with only oil lamps for guidance. Today, there are dim electric lights along the dark passageways although there are still parts where Sandro has to use a torch.

He explains to the group how, from the beginning of the third century, tombs and niches were hollowed out of the stone so that bodies could be stored on top of each other. The corpses were laid inside the tight compartments, wrapped in shrouds, sometimes sprinkled with scented oils, before the entrances were plastered over. Some martyrs were buried in a *cubiculum* (small chamber) or in an *arcosolium* (arched recess.) The walls and ceilings of these areas are covered with stunning frescos and stucco pieces, often depicting religious subjects.

At one point, we stand by a niche with a terracotta coloured fresco that is thought to be the oldest known image of the Virgin Mary, dating back to the middle of the second century. The Virgin holds her young child on her knee with a male adult figure by her side. 'Oh my God, I can't believe what I'm seeing,' says an American tourist directly in front of me.

After forty-five minutes of visiting the *Velatio*, the *Cryptoportico*, and the Greek Chapel with its second-century frescos of Old and New Testament scenes, we return to the surface via the labyrinth of tight passageways and retire to the Convent's waiting room.

I tell Sandro I enjoyed the visit but feel frustrated, as I had hoped to see the Annunciation fresco. He explains that it is not on a tour route and is in an area not normally accessible to the general public. I tell him about my 'special project' and the various encounters I have had over the past year. Luckily, he shows great interest and agrees to take me down to the Annunciation cubicle if there is time after he has finished his public tours. I wait around anxiously hoping he will fulfil his promise.

At the end of the afternoon, after a two hour wait, he returns and once more leads my wife and me through the dark passageways of Level One. Without him as the guide, we would be completely lost so we stay as close to him as we can. At times, we are walking in complete darkness save for his torchlight. He directs the light forward so that the person at the end of the line can see very little. It is enough to make us feel insignificant, vulnerable and not a little afraid. It is easy to let one's imagination get carried away when surrounded by tombs in an underground city of dark tunnels. Eventually, after meandering through narrow passageways, climbing down steps and crouching under arches, we come to a small room with a depiction of the Good Shepherd and then, in a niche on the wall, Sandro points out a representation of the resurrection of Lazarus. We walk a few more feet and enter cubicle P, which is in a dead end.

'We are here in the cubicle dell' Annunciazione,' Sandro declares as he shines a bright light on the ceiling of the small room. There above us is what is claimed to be the earliest known image of the Annunciation. It is a fresco painted by an unknown artist towards the end of the third century, probably around AD 280. I look up in awe and see a triple circle of festoons, consisting of small globes and red dots. Within these three rings, we see a woman wearing a stola according to the

177. Annunciation fresco, third century, Catacomb of Priscilla, Rome

Roman fashion of the time. Her hair is coiffed and, as Sandro describes, she is unveiled 'so she is uncovered like a virgin.' This is Mary, who is seated on a high back chair, apparently listening to a figure standing in front of her. He is wearing a tunic and pallium and is raising his right hand as if he is speaking to her. This is the angel Gabriel. The fresco is in excellent condition, the colours clearly visible.

'Normally, we do not allow photographs but please, just one for you,' Sandro says. I take a photograph of the fresco and he agrees to allow us one more of my wife, Hilary, and myself, both standing below it for posterity.

178. The author and his wife, Hilary, in the Catacomb of Priscilla, Rome

I gaze at the image. More than 1,700 years old. Created at the very beginning of Western Christianity. What an amazing experience and a great privilege.

The next stop is the Basilica of Santa Maria Maggiore, the largest and oldest shrine to the Virgin Mary in Rome. One legendary story in the Middle Ages suggested the original building was erected by Pope Liberius on the site on the Esquiline Hill in the early fourth century after he had seen a vision of the Virgin Mary at the height of summer in August. She told him to build her a church on the spot where snow would lie the next day. The story goes that snow duly fell on the site within twenty-four hours. Of course, there is no historical foundation to the story. It is thought that Pope Sixtus III built the church in the middle of the fifth century soon after Mary was declared 'Theotokos' – the God-bearer – at the Council of Ephesus in 431. The Basilica's central nave is filled with wonderful fifth-century mosaics that celebrate the Council's doctrinal declarations.

179. Annunciation mosaic, 432-440, Basilica of Santa Maria Maggiore, Rome. © Fr Lawrence Lew O.P.

The mosaics on the triumphal arch tell the story of Jesus, starting with the Annunciation on the left-sided spandrel. Thirteen different artists worked on the magnificent spectacle between AD 432 and 440. The Annunciation scene shows Mary accompanied by a retinue of white-robed angels. She sits on a large chair wearing golden robes and a girdle set with pearls, and she has a diadem in her hair. She looks like a Byzantine princess. She holds in her hand the red thread ready to be woven as told in the apocryphal Gospel of James. Mary looks straight ahead as she is about to hear the angel Gabriel's voice, with a dove hovering above her head. This is thought to be the first time that a dove, representing the Holy Spirit, is shown in an Annunciation scene. On the left, an *aedicule* with a closed gate symbolizes her virginity.

As I wander around the magnificent building, a special Mass begins, celebrating the twentieth anniversary of *Evangelium Vitae*, the encyclical of Pope John Paul II, which proclaimed the value, dignity and sanctity of each human life and its inviolability. Every pew is packed full.

In the second part of the service, entitled 'Affidare a Maria Il mistero della vita,' (Entrusting Mary with the mystery of life) Luke's story of the Annunciation (1:26-38) is read out. Many women walk towards the nearby Ave Regina Pacis (Hail Queen of Peace) statue of Mary clutching rosary beads and prayer cards. Some leave flowers as they kneel in adoration.

I leave the Basilica and head next to the Pantheon, which stands on the Piazza della Rotunda. One of ancient Rome's most spectacular buildings, it was originally built by Emperor Hadrian in AD 118–25 as a 'Temple of all Gods'. With its awe-inspiring dome a perfect hemisphere, it stands as a monument to the architectural brilliance of ancient

Rome. It was converted to the church of Santa Maria and the Martyrs in the seventh century and over the centuries Christian altars replaced the statues of the ancient gods that originally stood in the niches. In the Chapel of the Annunciation, there is a beautiful fifteenth-century fresco by Melozzo da Forli of the annunciation encounter.

The Basilica of Santa Maria in Trastevere is the oldest church in Rome dedicated to the Virgin Mary. According to tradition, an oil spring burst out here in 38 BC. It was considered to be a sign of the coming of Christ so the church was built on that exact spot in the third century. The medieval façade features a mosaic frieze from the twelfth century that depicts the Virgin Mary breastfeeding her child, surrounded by ten holy virgins bearing lighted oil lamps as signs of their virginity. Inside, there are wonderful mosaics in the apse covering the arch and half dome, including one of the Annunciation created in 1291 by Pietro Cavillini.

180. Melozzo da Fori *The Annunciation*, fifteenth century, The Pantheon, Rome. © Martyn Steel

Nestled between mosaics of the birth of Mary and the Nativity, the annunciation scene shows the angel Gabriel arriving with his black, white and red wings fully displayed. Mary sits on a classically designed throne with her right hand holding up her blue mantle for protection. She looks towards Gabriel while above her, God the Father sends down the dove in anticipation of the conception. The gold background shimmers in the light.

181. Pietro Cavillini Annunciation mosaic, 1291 Santa Maria in Trastevere, Rome © Fr Lawrence Lew O.P.

I leave the Basilica and walk along the bank of the River Tiber for twenty minutes before heading up the Via della Conciliazione to see the magnificent dome of St Peter's and the Piazza San Pietro straight ahead. I enter the Vatican Museum where I see an exquisite eighth-century Syriac silk fragment depicting the Annunciation. In the Contemporary Art Collection there is an extraordinarily detailed ceramic of the Annunciation by Angelo Biancini made in 1963. L'Annuncio by Salvador Dali is a 1960 preliminary study for his large surrealist painting *The Ecumenical Council* which was created by the Spanish artist to mark Pope John XXIII's announcement of the forthcoming Second Vatican Council.

Inside St Peter's, the largest church in the world and the Mother church for Catholics around the globe, I look down the spectacular nave towards Bernini's amazing baldachin of gilded bronze that canopies the Papal altar and, above it, Michelangelo's domineering dome. Before this extraordinary Renaissance and baroque church was built, the earliest structure on the site was erected under Emperor Constantine in the fourth century, over the grave of St Peter, after the Emperor had backed Christianity as an official Roman religion.

The Vatican Grottos, situated underneath the Papal altar, house Pope Paul VI's grave – a simple travertine slab. He was the Pope when I made my First Holy Communion in the 1960s and he served as the Pontiff from 1963 to 1978. He promulgated an apostolic exhortation in 1974 entitled *Marialis Cultus* emphasizing the importance of devotion to Mary developing 'in harmonious subordination to the worship of Christ'. As well as being the 'Mother of the Church', Pope Paul VI described her as 'truly our sister' and 'worthy of imitation because she was the first and most perfect of God's disciples.'

I head back upstairs to the tomb of the former Pope, John Paul II, in a side chapel on the right-hand side of the Basilica. The altar has the words 'Sanctus Joannes Paulus PP. II' (Pope and Pontiff) engraved in red on the white marble. More than thirty people kneel in front of the altar. Some hold pictures of the former pontiff. Others hold rosary beads. The person next to me is crying. On his death in April 2005, John Paul's body was buried in the Vatican Grottos below St Peter's. But in an extraordinary move six years later, following his beatification, the tomb was opened up and the wood coffin containing his body was extracted and taken to the altar of the Chapel of St Sebastian on the main floor of the Basilica, just up from Michelangelo's *Pieta*, so that more people could pay homage. Less than a year ago, he was canonized as a saint by Pope Francis and is now known as St John Paul the Great. It seems fitting that this hugely popular Pope should be buried so close to the most famous statue of Mary, for he revered her intensely.

I sit in a pew in front of the altar and read some of John Paul's most relevant declarations about Mary. He called her, 'the Mother of Mercy, who obtained mercy in a particular and exceptional way as no other person has. From Mary, we learn to surrender to God's will in all things. From Mary, we learn to trust even when all hope seems gone. Through Mary we come to her Son more easily. Mary is the sure path to our meeting with Christ.'

Devotion to the Mother of the Lord, when it is genuine, John Paul proclaimed, is always an impetus to a life guarded by the spirit and values of the gospel. 'Mary belongs indissolubly to the mystery of Christ and she belongs to the mystery of the Church from the beginning, from the day of the Church's birth.'

In his Evangelical Letter on the Virgin Mary, published on the feast of the Annunciation in 1987, he wrote: 'Every day Mary is in constant contact with the ineffable mystery of God made man, a mystery that surpasses everything revealed in the Old Covenant. From the moment of the Annunciation, the mind of the Virgin Mary has been initiated into the radical "newness" of God's self-revelation and has been made aware of the mystery.

She is the first of those "little ones" of whom Jesus will say one day, "Father…you have hidden these things from the wise and understanding, and revealed them to babes".'

In 1995, he described the Blessed Virgin Mary as the perfect realisation of the Church's holiness and its model: 'Mary is asked to assent to a truth never expressed before. She accepts it with a simple yet daring heart. With the question, "How can this be?" she expresses her faith in the divine power to make virginity compatible with her exceptional and unique motherhood. Mary exerts a decisive influence with her faith on the fulfilment of the mystery of the Incarnation, the beginning and the synthesis of Jesus's entire redeeming mission.'

The following year, in 1996, Pope John Paul II emphasized the virginal conception as a biological fact:

> The Church has constantly held that Mary's virginity is a truth of faith. In the episode of the Annunciation, the Evangelist Luke calls Mary a 'virgin', referring both to her intention to preserve her virginity, as well as to the divine plan, which reconciles this intention with her miraculous motherhood. The affirmation of the virginal conception, due to the action of the Holy Spirit, excludes every hypothesis of natural partheno-genesis and rejects the attempts to explain Luke's account as the development of a Jewish theme or as the derivation of a pagan mythological legend. The structure of the Lucan text resists any reductive interpretation. Its coherence does not validly support any mutilation of the terms or expressions which affirm the virginal conception brought about by the Holy Spirit.

John Paul ended: 'Mary's virginity is intimately linked to her divine motherhood and perfect holiness.'

I leave the Basilica and step onto the Piazza Retta, in front of the main façade of St Peter's. I look across the Square to a large Marian mosaic, high on the wall of one of the Vatican buildings. It is called *Mater Ecclesiae* and was commissioned by Pope John Paul II after the attempt on his life in St Peter's Square in 1981. The Pope was convinced that the Virgin Mary had protected him on that day and immediately expressed the desire that an image of the Madonna, symbolizing her as Mother of the Church, be placed facing the Square. Below the image of the crowned Virgin Mary holding her baby Son are the words, 'Totus Tuus' (totally thine).

I sit down and look across St Peter's Square. The last time I was here, Pope Benedict was waving to the massed crowds from a window in the Vatican apartments. Pope Benedict, both as Pontiff and in his previous role as Prefect of the Congregation for the Doctrine of the Faith when he was Cardinal Joseph Ratzinger, also had much to say on Mary and the Annunciation. He wrote that Mary was, 'the confluence of the streams of Israel. In prayer, she bore the misery and grandeur of its history and so enabled it to become fertile soil for the living God…Mary's maternity means that she willingly places her own substance, body and soul, into the seed so new life can grow.'

As Pope, he described Mary as the image of the Church in attentive hearing of the word of God, which took flesh in her. Mary symbolizes openness to God and others; an active listening which interiorizes and assimilates, one in which the word becomes a way of life. He stated there are two moments when God intervenes directly in the material world – the Virgin Birth and the resurrection from the tomb. 'These two moments are a scandal to the modern spirit…these two moments are the cornerstones of faith. If God does not have power over matter, then he simply is not God. But he does have this power, and through the conception and resurrection of Jesus Christ, he has ushered in a new creation. So as the Creator, he is also our Redeemer.'

As I sit in St Peter's Square, enjoying the lovely warm sunshine and the magnificent view, I wonder what Pope Francis will say at tomorrow's weekly Papal Audience on the feast of the Annunciation. What will he want to convey about the event in Nazareth and its meaning for the faithful today? I have done my homework, looking back at his previous homilies and addresses and consult my notes. In the past, he has described Mary's 'exceptional pilgrimage of faith as representing a constant point of reference for the Church. Mary let herself be guided by the Holy Spirit on a journey of faith towards a destiny of service and fruitfulness.'

He has said, 'Whenever we look at Mary, we come to believe again in the revolutionary nature of love and tenderness.' He has also declared, 'In her, we see that humility and tenderness are not virtues of the weak but of the strong.'

Exactly one year ago, on last year's feast of the Annunciation, he emphasized that salvation is a gift from the love that we ought to receive with humility and obedience, just as Mary did: 'In order to receive this salvation, we need a humble heart, a meek heart, an obedient heart like that of Mary. Salvation cannot be bought or sold – it's a gift. It's given to us. It's free. We cannot be saved through ourselves. Salvation is a totally free gift.'

I head to the nearby Piazza Pio XII, where I enter a large building overlooking St Peter's Square and walk up to the first floor to the Congregazione per il Culto Divino e la Disciplina dei Sacramenti (Congregation for Divine Worship and the Discipline of the Sacraments).

Thirty-three years ago, Arthur Roche, a Roman Catholic priest in Leeds, was charged with the task of organizing Pope John Paul II's visit to York as part of the Holy Father's visit to Britain. I was the BBC Television producer for the same event, also based in Leeds, and Arthur and I got to know each other well. Both of us were starting out on our respective careers. He went on to become Bishop of Leeds and today he is Archbishop Arthur Roche, Secretary of the Congregation for Divine Worship and Discipline of the Sacraments, based at the Vatican, and a member of the Pontifical Council for Culture.

Arthur Roche is at the heart of the Roman Curia, where he handles affairs relating to liturgical practices or, in Vatican language, 'the regulation and promotion of the sacred liturgy, primarily of the sacraments.' He helps to draw up and revise liturgical texts and review particular calendars and texts for the Mass and Divine Office. I am particularly interested in meeting again in order to discuss the spiritual meaning of the annunciation story and the current status of the feast of the Annunciation, which will be celebrated tomorrow.

When I arrive, he is dressed in grand formal regalia. He has just met a delegation of Japanese bishops to discuss liturgical developments in Japan. He goes off to change into more informal black clothing and clerical collar and then guides me into his modest meeting room, which looks out onto St Peter's Square. He is keen to take me out onto his balcony where he enjoys one of the most magnificent office views anywhere in the world, with the monumental dome of the Basilica and the beautifully curved Bernini colonnades dominating the vista.

'It was a big shock for me to be moved here,' he tells me, 'partly because I wasn't expecting it and I was getting to that age when you don't want to be moving too much in life. But, of course, I came and I've never looked back really.'

The sixty-five-year-old is a stockily built man with thinning grey hair, rimless glasses and a ruddy complexion. He was brought up in Batley Carr, West Yorkshire, and his northern accent is still detectable.

Does he miss being the bishop of his home patch in West Yorkshire? I wonder.

'Yes, but I don't think about it,' he replies. 'I've learnt through my priestly life that I've been asked to do things I wasn't well suited for but I've always found I've enjoyed doing them and found surprise in them. When you've had such happiness in a post, it's a mistake to look back when you move on because you can't live two realities simultaneously. It's a very strong Christian principle. The sacrament of the present moment of God is in reality, not in make believe or notion concepts. It's very privileged work here at the centre, working alongside the Pope. What we do is to make sure the reform of the Second Vatican Council is carried out and one of our major responsibilities is in overseeing the translation of the liturgical texts.'

What does the annunciation story mean for him?

'Of course, it's the most important event in history really – of God becoming Man,' he says. 'It's not only a point of reference bringing together so many theological and scriptural aspects. It also creates a difference in existence from that moment on. We suddenly see God, who created the prototype man in Adam, is actually reversing what happened at the dawn of creation. When I think of the Annunciation, I always think of Genesis because Adam and Eve were not only creatures like you and I, but they were the source of what we now are. Their position is very important in the human tree of genealogy. What they did is very important because they introduced a corruptible element through original sin to our existence. What was the choice of Adam and Eve? It was for sin. For self-preference. What we find in the Annunciation is that Mary makes God the preferential option. "Let it be according to your word." She's reversing actually what our first parents did. They enjoyed the paradise they were in. What she was doing was reversing their blunder by listening to God, understanding what she heard, accepting what she understood, and saying so. That's the reversal of what we hear of in Genesis.'

How important is it for him that she had the right to say no?

'It's clear from Scripture that God is conscious of one thing he cannot touch within human beings and that is their freedom to choose,' he replies. 'A gift he gives to them and which he cannot take back. He cannot take away your uniqueness to exercise freedom. He was wanting from his creature the most spontaneous, immediate response to the love that she received from him, back from the creative. Love is never a matter of coercion. It's got to be a choice and it's a massive choice. God gave man and woman freedom to choose. For Adam and Eve, it wasn't God that they chose.'

What if she had said no?

'It would have made an absolute nonsense…' He pauses for a short while. 'But that didn't happen, so…'

Does he see the story as wholly fact?

'Yes,' he responds. 'If it wasn't fact, it wouldn't be human and if it's not human…I think the Annunciation, the Incarnation, is all about God becoming human. That's the way I look on it. If it didn't happen, the question wasn't put, she hadn't listened, she hadn't responded, she hadn't said yes, then it would have taken away everything that is visibly human and with which we would recognize as being an honest response.'

Does it trouble him that the annunciation encounter only appears in Luke and not in the three other Gospels?

'No,' he replies firmly. 'They all have a thread running through but they are all written for different audiences and written by people who had different experiences. Luke's is the Gospel of compassion effectively, of a response to human affairs. He has the representation of being a doctor and doctors have to be very observant to give their diagnosis. The detail he brings is second to none. To me, it's not an issue. It's not that faith simply accepts it blindly. We have submitted our Scripture to very strict scientific measurement. That assists faith but it doesn't substitute faith.'

If the Annunciation is so significant, then why is the status of the feast so low today?

'It's a Solemnity,' he responds. 'So it's the highest grade of feast within the Catholic Church.'

But it isn't a holy day of obligation, is it?

'No, but not all Solemnities are. Has it lost the "reverence"?' he asks rhetorically. 'What happened at the moment of the Annunciation was one of the most humble happenings in Scripture and in history. But it happened within the midst of human reality. In a sense, it does rather occur to me the humbleness of what happened is reflected in the way we celebrate it. I wouldn't make a big thing of that but it was a very humble thing.'

Surely the status of the feast has been lessened today?

'The Church is very careful not to take away the effects of the resurrection and the feast of Easter,' he responds, 'and the Annunciation falls within Lent.' He looks into the distance and pauses for some time before continuing. 'Of course, the big challenge for some Christians too is the fact that the Incarnation talks of that little reality of a single cell being a human being. There are massive dogmatic things from this.'

I keep pursuing my point. I note that we bow our heads when we say the words in the Nicene Creed, 'by the power of the Holy Spirit he became incarnate from the Virgin Mary and was made man.' Surely, therefore, those are the most important words in the Profession of Faith?

'But it's also to acknowledge the humility of the act,' he responds. 'The divine condescension. Liturgical acts reflect…' he pauses again for a while, 'The most important gesture is that we stand for the gospel and the creed. Yes, it was the historical beginning of the most profound mystery of the depth of God's love for the human race.'

He strokes his chin and looks away for a moment.

'We don't commemorate conceptions,' he continues. 'We celebrate birthdays. In the Catholic tradition, the birthday is the day when a child is brought into the light – *dare alla luce* – to be given light from the darkness of the womb, which is also symbolic of the Resurrection.'

Would the Fourth Sunday of Advent be a better place in the liturgical year to focus on the Annunciation?

'The Sunday is always more important than a feast day,' he says. 'The fact that the Church puts the gospel story of the Annunciation also onto that Sunday is a massive statement in itself.'

He passes me the recently published Homiletic Directory, put together by his Congregation for Divine Worship and the Discipline of the Sacraments. It offers a guide to Catholic priests on constructing relevant and authoritative sermons throughout the liturgical year with the desire that, 'the homily can actually be an intense and happy experience of the Spirit, a consoling encounter with God's word, a constant source of renewal and growth.'

For the Fourth Sunday of Advent, it states, 'all the readings – from the prophets, from the Apostles, from the Gospels – cluster around the mystery announced to Mary by the angel Gabriel. The events have a special place in the devotional life of many Catholics.' The guidance indicates how the Annunciation is at the heart of the Hail Mary prayer; the First Joyful Mystery of the Rosary; the Angelus; and has inspired some of the greatest art in the history of the Christian faith. 'The homilist should build upon this firm foundation of Christian devotion and lead his people into a deeper penetration of these wondrous episodes.'

So, what is the key message of the annunciation story for him?

'I think, what I would say, the lesson for me in all of this is about attentiveness to the word of God. It seems to me she was so attuned to the word of God that she was able to say, "I accept and I will do this." She had the freedom to say no but she was brave.'

Was there a key moment in his own attentiveness that led him to say yes to his own calling?

'I don't think I'd made my First Holy Communion at that time so I must have been around six or seven,' he begins. 'Every morning when my mother and I came to St Joseph's primary school, we'd come through the back door of the church on the way to school to see the priest celebrating Mass. I remember knowing that this was massive. I just knew God was the most significant thing ever. It was massive. That's what I knew. Of course, I've had moments of doubt and trepidation but that time was an impressive one for me. I'm going to tell you something very personal that confirmed that experience for me in later life. I remember wanting to be a priest at nine and the thing that confirms to me what God wanted me to be was that at roughly the same time in the polio plague of the 1950s, I was felled with polio and I was the only boy to walk out of the hospital seven months later. I was the only lad to walk out of Pinderfields hospital in Wakefield under his own steam. And that was through my mother's very simple intercession to Martin de Porres before he became a saint. The realisation of that was massively significant to me. The strength of that feeling has rarely left me.'

I show him the print of the Lemoyne painting. What does he see?

'She's very serene, isn't she?' he observes. 'It's almost like she's collapsing. Yes, a fainting. It's sort of a human being knowing her smallness. Accepting this greatness but her human response is not just simply fear but being very deeply moved by it. She was very daring, wasn't she? I do like the angel. Very formidable. I like the way he's looking at her because he just knows. He's not pointing to the weakness she may be feeling at the time. He's pointing to the greatness of God. Yes, I like it. It's a very fine painting.'

As I gather my belongings, he offers a final thought: 'I think Mary is the touchstone for Christian orthodoxy. What you think about her will affect massively what you think of Christ. If she's not in the right place in your thinking, Christ won't be either. She gave up everything to give us Christ.'

It is 25 March, the feast day of the Annunciation, and I am in St Peter's Square attending the weekly General Audience with His Holiness, Pope Francis. It's pouring with rain and the piazza is a sea of multicoloured umbrellas and waterproofs. Thousands have come despite the inclement weather and all the allocated pens in the Square are full. Large screens relay events on the altar in front of St Peter's main façade. The Pope, dressed in white, sits on a large chair and there is a gigantic painting of the Madonna and Child to his side. Cardinals and bishops surround him. The curved roof above the altar keeps the Pope dry but every few minutes assistants sweep away the water that collects on the floor. Despite the torrential rain, the crowd cheers and applauds every time Pope Francis waves or makes a gesture. He says:

> With the Annunciation the Lord illuminates and strengthens Mary's faith as he will also do for her spouse Joseph, so that Jesus will be born into a human family. This is very beautiful: it shows us how deeply the mystery of the Incarnation, as God desired, encompasses not only conception in the mother's womb, but also acceptance in a

real family. Today I would like to contemplate with you the beauty of this bond, the beauty of God's condescension.

On 25 March, the Solemnity of the Annunciation, in many countries the Day of Life is celebrated. That is why, twenty years ago, St John Paul II on this day signed the encyclical, *Evangelium Vitae*. In order to commemorate this anniversary, there are many followers of the Pro-Life movement present in the Square today. In *Evangelium Vitae*, the family occupies a central place, as it is the womb of human life. A human couple was blessed from the beginning to form a community of love and life, entrusted with the mission to generate life. Christian spouses, celebrating the sacrament of marriage make themselves open to honour this blessing, with the grace of Christ, for their whole lives. The Church, for her part, is solemnly committed to care for the family that is born, as a gift of God for her life, in good times and in bad. The bond between the Church and the family is sacred and inviolable. The Church, as a mother, never abandons the family, even when it is downhearted, wounded and humiliated in so many ways. Neither when it falls into sin, nor moves away from the Church; she will always do everything to try to care for and heal it, to call it to conversion and to reconcile it to God.

He continues, speaking into a microphone, as the rain teems down, 'Jesus, Mary and Joseph, in you we contemplate the splendour of true love; to you we turn with trust. Holy Family of Nazareth, grant that our families may be places of communion and prayer, authentic schools of the gospel and small domestic churches.'

To be honest, I am a little disappointed by his address. One cannot describe it as intellectually stretching, particularly thought provoking or groundbreaking. After giving a papal blessing to the gathering, the Holy Father gets into his open 'Popemobile' and is driven around the Square, waving and blowing kisses to the adoring congregation. For each section of the crowd, there is the opportunity for a two-second close up view as he drives past. The crowds nearby go crazy, standing on chairs, waving and holding up rosary beads, crucifixes and family photographs. One couple from Chicago holds up a sign, 'Pope Francis: The People's Pontiff. We love you!' After twenty minutes, he has disappeared back into the Vatican offices and the large crowd has dispersed.

182. Pope Francis greets the crowds in St Peter's Square on the feast day of the Annunciation, Rome. © Reuters

I return inside St Peter's Basilica to reflect and dry out. In the domed apse at the far end, a Mass is being held to mark the twentieth anniversary of *Evangelium Vitae*. As people queue to receive Holy Communion, I gaze up at the baroque Bernini sculpture that dominates the space and admire its flamboyant extravagance. It is an explosion of bronze and marble with an oval alabaster window featuring a stained-glass image of a dove, in its centre. As one guide puts it: 'Natural light flooding through the glass makes it glow with spectacular effect, at the same time imparting a burnished sheen on the surrounding bronze structure.' My weeklong visit to Italy is over. My 'Grand Tour' of Western Europe is coming to an end.

Some months later, Pope Francis offered further thoughts on the Annunciation: 'When people do not want to say yes to God, they usually do not say no. They just hide like Adam and Eve did after they sinned…Even after the sin of Adam and Eve,' the Pope explains, 'God continually reached out to holy men and women – from Abraham to Moses to the prophets – asking them to cooperate in his plan of salvation. The Gospel speaks to us of the end of that *yes* chain and the beginning of another with Mary's willingness to carry God's Son. With this *yes*, God not only watches how humanity is proceeding; he not only walks with his people but he becomes one of us and takes on our flesh. Jesus himself is God's *yes*. The feast of the Annunciation is a perfect occasion to think about one's life and whether or not we always say yes or often hide, with our heads down, like Adam and Eve, not exactly saying no, but pretending not to know what God is asking.'

CHAPTER 41

JUDAISM AND ISLAM

Can the annunciation story connect the three monotheistic religions – Judaism, Christianity and Islam? Is there anything in the story that can promote interfaith dialogue? Or is the Incarnation – the result of Mary's encounter with the angel Gabriel – the very root of the division amongst these three faiths? I plan to pose these questions to three eminent people: Rabbi Julia Neuberger, Professor Mona Siddique and Dr Tim Winter, also known as Shaykh Abdul Hakim Murad.

Christians view Mary as a young Jewish girl who lived in the hamlet of Nazareth in Palestine Galilee. She came from the family line of David and was betrothed to Joseph. She was faithful to Judaism, listened to the Hebrew Scriptures, learned the messages of the Torah, kept the Sabbath and visited the synagogue. There is an undeniable Jewish backcloth to the encounter between her and the angel Gabriel.

Pope Francis said, 'Inside every Christian is a Jew.' Speaking to Spain's *La Vanguard* newspaper he said, 'I believe that inter-religious dialogue must investigate the Jewish roots of Christianity and the Christian flowering of Judaism. I understand it is a challenge, a hot potato, but it is possible to love as brothers. Every day, I pray the Psalms of David. My prayer is Jewish, then I have the Eucharist, which is Christian.'

It is a balmy Friday afternoon in the centre of London and I am outside the West London Synagogue near Marble Arch. This is the United Kingdom's flagship Reform Synagogue, which describes itself as 'a lively community of progressive Jews' and 'a welcoming intergenerational and inclusive centre of Jewish life, proud of its diverse forms of worship, progressive values, quest for learning and commitment to *Tikkun Olam*.'

Rabbi Baroness Julia Neuberger, the Senior Rabbi, arrives in the reception area and within seconds we are climbing the stairs heading to her office. Immediately, I am taken aback by her extraordinary intensity and drive. Before we reach her office, she has fired many questions at me and grumbled that she cannot understand why I would want to talk to her about the Annunciation when it has 'no relevance or resonance'. She turns around as she arrives at her office and tells me that rabbis are 'teachers not preachers'.

By coincidence, last night she was interviewed at a public event in Winchester, which I attended. There, in a lighthearted moment, she told her audience in the Guildhall that Jews are, 'bad at faith. Never ask a Jew what they believe. They behave as if they believe, rather than that they do. We're no good on faith. We are a fuzzy lot.'

She then continued in a more serious vein: 'Questions of practice rather than belief are what brings people in. It's linked to belief but primarily it's family and tradition. Belief comes second. Action is more important to Jews than belief. Belonging and community are more important than belief.'

Educated at Newnham College, Cambridge, she studied Assyriology and Hebrew Language before going on to the Leo Baeck College in London. One of the first female rabbis in Britain, she served in the South London Liberal Synagogue for twelve years and for a year was also a Professor of Divinity at Harvard. Then she became Chief Executive of the health charity, the King's Fund, from 1997 to 2004 before her appointment as a Peer in the House of Lords, where she has developed a strong reputation as a social campaigner and reformer. She has been the Senior Rabbi at the West London Synagogue since 2011 and welcomes the increasing 'feminisation of rabbis'. Married with two adult children, she is well known in Britain as a feisty social and religious commentator.

She opens our conversation by referring to the Hebrew Scriptures: 'The idea of an angel coming to announce a miraculous birth has considerable resonance because it occurs in the Hebrew Bible all over the place but the idea that this is the annunciation as opposed to, if you like, a literary construct to enable the story of an impossible birth to come into being, just seems to me extraordinary.

'We have in the Hebrew Bible, and therefore Christianity has too, various extraordinary births.' she continues. 'The most famous, I suppose, was Sarah. Of course, there were three angels in the story. [Genesis 18]. The word "angel" in Hebrew is *malak* and means messenger, and these three messengers turn up at Abraham's tent. Sarah, who's supposedly around ninety, is listening at the opening of the tent. They say she is going to give birth and Sarah roars with laughter. And that's the pun as to why Isaac is called *yitshāq* – he will laugh. The whole thing is a joke – it's all a play on words. The Hebrew Bible is full of internal interpretation and that's significant.'

She goes on to tell me that the Hebrew accounts of Hannah conceiving Samuel and of Samson's birth are also 'stories'. I suggest that the fact there are so many angels and miraculous births in the Hebrew Scriptures shows there is a resonance. She stops me in my tracks.

'In my view, that's where Christianity got it from,' she interrupts abruptly. 'They're stories. It's a way of explaining. It's a literary device and why wouldn't that go on into the Christian New Testament? It's the same tradition.'

So, does she have more respect for the Christian who sees the annunciation story as a metaphor rather than as fact?

'Yes, yes,' she responds. 'It's a way of explaining...' her voice tails off before continuing, 'and then we get into the complication of the Virgin Birth. The Hebrew word isn't virgin. There's a whole lot of stuff here that...well, that's what I mean about internal explanation. The stories get created and they are ways of explaining things or explaining what we'd describe as a faith tradition, where people can't quite get a grip of it. That occurs in both the Hebrew Bible and the New Testament. I wouldn't see why that should be any different. I mean these are not necessarily different in kind. In that sense, the story of the Annunciation is completely familiar to us but it's significance, we just think, well so what?'

Is it more than 'so what?' I suggest. Isn't this the very moment that starts to separate Judaism from Christianity?

'No, no,' she responds shaking her head frantically. 'Plenty of early Christians wouldn't have seen the Incarnation would they or wouldn't have even thought of it then. If you believe the scholars such as Geza Vermes who wrote *Jesus the Jew*, Jesus is a bit like a liberal rabbi. He's a teacher within the Jewish tradition but of a very radical kind. The idea that he was in some way God incarnate is later. Vermes looks at the expression "Son of Man" which is an expression in the Hebrew Bible as well. It's only when it's "Son of God" that...' she pauses again before continuing, 'but even Son of God could be just...you know everybody is the son or daughter of God. So the idea of the divinity of Jesus is clearly what divides us.

'But even more than that, what really divides us is the idea that anyone should die for my sins. What the hell is that about? I don't get it and we wouldn't get it. All that seems to be doing for us is taking the language and tradition of either the scapegoat idea or the idea that somehow sin can be moved from someone and the idea you can be somehow redeemed by this, and we think what is all that about? We don't understand it. But I don't think of a dividing line. It's not a line. It's a historical development.'

So the idea, I suggest, of Jesus being both divine and human...She interrupts again, saying firmly, 'I don't get it. I don't get it.'

I understand that the central belief of Judaism is the absolute unity and singularity of God. I recognize that Judaism forbids the worship of a person as idolatry. I realize that practising Jews regard Jesus as a human being: he cannot be God or Son of God in Jewish theology. Therefore, I suggest, that very moment when Jesus, divine and human, is conceived must be the key moment of division.

'No, I don't think it's that simple,' she retorts. 'I don't think the early Church had an absolute instant moment when they thought this is divinity in human form. Nor do I think the early ideas about the Messiah – the Messianic ideas which predate Christianity but then are developed within Christianity – remember there were forms of messianic Judaism at the same time as the rise of Christianity – I don't think there's a hard moment. That's not how it goes.

'I don't think religions are, "This is the truth and it happens right now." I just don't think that's how people are,' she says. 'They borrow all the time and they accumulate bits and pieces. It's about development.'

Does she see the annunciation story as a bridge or a barrier to interfaith dialogue between Judaism and Christianity?

'It's neither,' she replies. 'We just discuss it together. It wouldn't be a problem discussing it.'

I tell her I was interested in how she described Mary last night as 'carrying the flame for the feminine' and said that Roman Catholicism has some commendation in how it approaches Mary and her role.

'The Madonna figure in Christianity is the one strong feminine role model, almost an intermediary to God in Catholicism, which of course we don't have,' she responds. 'Interestingly, Kabbalistic Judaism, medieval mystical Judaism, developed something that is not wholly different – the Shekinah – the feminine presence of God. Clearly the need for and development of some sort of female presence in religious thought may well be medieval. After all, Mariolatry is medieval.'

So, I start to ask, when she looks from the outside in at Mary being promoted as...

'It gives women a role,' she intervenes before I can finish the question. 'It promotes the role of women.'

Does it intrigue her that something so central to Christianity is given such a comparatively low status in the liturgical calendar of the Church?

'It doesn't bother me,' she replies.

But does it intrigue her?

'Not particularly,' she says.

I move on to the 'Hand in Hand' charity she supports, which run integrated schools in Israel for Jewish, Arab Muslim and Arab Christian pupils side by side. She tells me they are a deliberate attempt 'to foster respect in different faiths and to experience a different faith without owning it.'

How would she want the annunciation story in Luke's Gospel to be communicated and explained to Jewish children in the schools?

'That it's hugely significant in terms of how Christians perceive the Incarnation but also that there's a history of this kind of miraculous birth that goes into your tradition too,' she replies. 'There's a tradition that explains miraculous births in this way.'

With some trepidation, I show her a print of Lemoyne's Annunciation painting.

'This is the sort of thing that absolutely I'd walk straight past,' she says immediately. 'It's my idea of hell, this kind of picture. I don't like the sentimentality of this period. It's too sweet. I'm quite interested in the drawing…the mannerist shapes…there's a very deliberate design which allows you to see almost a snaking, serpenty shape. Mannerists were very interested in how you shaped the canvas. It was a very deliberate way of describing so that people knew how to look at the canvas.'

I comment how in the picture, Mary doesn't look like a twelve-year-old Jewish girl.

'They never do in classic European painting. They are painted to look like the image of innocent beauty of the period. She wouldn't have worn clothes like that. But it doesn't bother me at all. It's Mary seen as an early eighteenth-century interpretation of Christian tradition. I do think it's a really horrible painting. It's pretty bad. It's very stylized.'

She continues to study the picture. 'We don't do much depiction of the human form,' she says. 'Remember, historically, Judaism didn't allow the depiction of the human form. The Orthodox bit of my family wouldn't have had the depiction of the human form in the house.'

Do religious paintings of Hebrew Scripture scenes resonate in her faith?

'No. I'm interested in art. My mother was a huge art collector. But images have no centrality in Judaism. In mainstream Judaism, you don't use the human form.'

As our conversation draws to a close, she comments on how Christians like answers and Jews like questions.

'The fundamental question here is why did they want to develop a doctrine of the Incarnation?' she says. 'Why was it necessary to make God human when the tradition from where many of the early Christians came from was that God was very different from human. That's the really interesting question. What was it about the early Church and the development of the stories of the early Church that made them want to develop this? Actually, the Annunciation bit is not so strange. It's the Incarnation bit that's strange. That would be so foreign to anyone who grew up Jewish. Is it that they wanted to make the relationship with God more intimate and more comprehensible? Is it about their own feelings of Jesus as a leader? That he was so remarkable that they had to make him in part divine? I don't know. One of the things we do know is that the period of the creation of early Christianity is also the period of huge religious ferment. Was this just one idea sweeping around at the time?'

We leave her office and head to the main sanctuary of the synagogue to sit and listen to the girls and boys rehearsing for their Bar Mitzvah the following day. It is 5.30 on a Friday afternoon and, in half an hour, she will lead the Erev Shabbat service, then the Kiddush ceremony straight afterwards, followed by a meal and light refreshments with the congregation. It's all go in the whirlwind life of Rabbi Julia Neuberger.

––––––––––

The imposing neo-Gothic Assembly Hall high up on the Mound in Edinburgh, is the annual meeting place of the General Assembly of the Church of Scotland. Perhaps surprisingly, I am here to meet one of Britain's leading Muslim academics. Professor

Mona Siddiqui is Professor of Islamic and Inter-Religious Studies at the University of Edinburgh and the School of Divinity is based in the Assembly Hall complex.

Born in Karachi, Pakistan, she moved to England with her family in 1968 when she was five. After spending her childhood in Huddersfield, she studied Arabic and French at the University of Leeds, took a Master's in Middle Eastern Studies at the University of Manchester, and then completed her Ph.D. there in Classical Islamic Law. Today, she is an academic specialist in Islamic Studies and Christian-Muslim relations and writes and broadcasts regularly as a respected and authoritative commentator. Diminutive with long black hair and rimless glasses, she jokes with me on arrival that she has been described as 'that Anglican Muslim'.

In her book, *Christians, Muslims & Jesus*, published in 2013, Mona Siddiqui explores Jesus's nature and role through the writings of key Muslim and Christian thinkers. It may be surprising to some readers to discover that Mary is mentioned more in the Qur'an than in the New Testament, with seventy verses referring to her and thirty-four specifically mentioning her name. In the Qur'an, she is known by her Syriac name, Maryam. One of the Qur'an's suras or chapters – 19 – is dedicated to Maryam and part of it, verses 16-34, describes the annunciation story and the subsequent birth of her son:

> Maryam withdrew from her family to an eastern place. She took a curtain to screen herself from them. And we sent Our Spirit to appear before her in the form of a perfected man. She cried, 'I seek the Lord of Mercy's protection against you. Go away if you have any fear God.' He said, 'I am only your Lord's messenger come to announce to you the gift of a pure son.' She said, 'How can I have a son when no man has touched me and I am not unchaste?' He said, 'This is what your Lord said: "It is easy for Me – we shall make him a sign to all people, a mercy from Us",' And so it was ordained and she conceived him. She withdrew to a distant place. And when the pains of childbirth drove her to [cling to] the trunk of the palm tree, she exclaimed, 'If only I had been dead and forgotten long before all this,' But a voice cried to her from below, 'Do not grieve, for your Lord has provided a stream at your feet and if you shake the trunk of the palm tree towards you, so it will drop juicy fresh dates upon you. So, eat and drink and be joyful. And when you see a human being, say 'I have vowed a fast to the Lord of Mercy to abstain from conversation and I will not speak to anyone today.'
>
> Then she went back to her people carrying the child and they said, 'O Mary, you have done something terrible; your father was not a bad man, your mother was not unchaste.' Then she pointed towards him. They said, 'How can we speak to someone who is still an infant?' But he said, 'I am God's servant. He has given me the Book and has made me a prophet. He has made me blessed wherever I may be and commanded me to pray and give alms as long as I live, to cherish my mother. He did not make me domineering or graceless. Peace was on me the day I was born and will be on the day I die and the day I am raised to life again.' Such was Jesus, son of Maryam.

There's another important reference earlier in the Qur'an in sura 3 verses 42-7:

> The angels said to Maryam: 'Maryam, God has chosen you and made you pure. He has truly chosen you above all women. Maryam be devout to your Lord, prostrate yourself in worship, bow down with those who pray…'
>
> The angels said, 'Maryam, God gives you glad tidings of a Word from Him whose name will be Messiah, Jesus, son of Maryam, who will be held in honour in this world and the next, who will be one of those brought to God. He will speak to people in his

infancy and in his adulthood. He will be one of the righteous.' She said, 'My Lord, how can I have a son when no man has touched me?' [The angel] said, 'This is how God creates what He will: when He ordained something,
He only says 'Be' and it is.

The Qur'an is the holy book of Islam, inspired by God, and is seen by Muslims as eternal and uncreated. It bears a revelation of universal wisdom that is complete, unalterable and final. Muslims believe that all sections of the Qur'an were communicated to Muhammad by the angel Gabriel over a period of twenty-three years at Mecca and Medina in Arabia. Angel Gabriel acted as the intermediary in all these revelations by God to Muhammad. Although scholars have highlighted how the Prophet Muhammad drew extensively from Jewish and Christian sources, both canonical and apocryphal, Muslims believe it gives the true facts about Jesus and his status.

There are some obvious and rather striking similarities between the Qur'an passages and Luke's story. In both, a messenger arrives to inform Mary about the pregnancy; she is a virgin; she is alone at the time and there was no natural father at the conception.

However, there are also some differences. In the Qur'an the messenger is not named specifically but is presumed to be the angel Gabriel (the illustrious messenger, cast as the angel of revelation, who appears when a new prophet is summoned to call his people to order). Also, Mary hears the announcement in an unspecified place, and is presumed to have left Jerusalem where, implicitly, she had been dedicated to some kind of service in the Temple. Later, she is said to feel birth pains, a description that emphasizes her humanity. But more than these differences, there is a fundamental discrepancy in the two versions that gets to the very heart of the difference between Christian and Islamic belief.

The crucial difference focuses on whether Jesus is God's prophet or God incarnate. The Incarnation – Jesus as divine and human – is a pivot of Christianity and is at the very heart of Luke's story. In the Qur'an, Jesus is seen as a prophet or messenger, sent as a spirit of God and as a precursor to Mohammad. He is special but not divine. He is the Messiah but only a prophet. In the Qur'an, a divine communication tells the reader of Jesus's conception as a human being. The revelation gets to the very heart of the tension between the two religions about Jesus's status and about self-revelation and transcendence. Here God is not revealed in Jesus. Jesus is his servant.

The Incarnation and the Trinity have always been major points of difference between Christianity and Islam (as well as Christianity and Judaism). In Islam, Mary, described as the daughter of Imran, is revered for her femininity, her righteousness and her pious devotion. She is seen as an example of virtue, obedience and purity. The Qur'an calls her a woman of faith, carrying the mercy of God. In the New Testament, the angel Gabriel greets her with 'Hail, O favoured one.' In the Qur'an, she is told, 'Allah has chosen you and purified you and chosen you above women of all peoples.' The crucial point, however, is that the Islamic faith does not recognize Mary as the mother of God.

I am keen to hear how Professor Siddiqui views the annunciation story and find out if she believes it exposes the central division between the two religions.

We meet in a bustling, noisy cafe in the Assembly Rooms building with a magnificent view towards Princes Street and Edinburgh's New Town beyond. I begin by asking what the annunciation story in the Qur'an means for her.

'I suppose it's a way of putting Jesus into the story,' she replies. 'Jesus being one of the primary messengers rather than just a prophet. But the Annunciation is not really part of the Islamic narrative, at least for most of us. Where you have Muslims and Christians living in the same area, then there can be a coming together around Mary.'

Most Christians have no idea, I suggest to her, that Mary is mentioned in the Qur'an more than in the Bible and that there's an annunciation story involving Mary and the conception of Jesus.

'I think that's partly because Jesus doesn't feature in the Qur'an in the same way that he is essential to Christianity. Everything about Jesus from an Islamic perspective doesn't fit into a Christian narrative,' she says. 'Muslims can accept that God can enable Mary's virgin birth but they don't talk about it because they don't think it's important in terms of Jesus's own relevance in terms of devotion, which is not central to Islam.'

How would she describe the place of Mary in Islam?

'She's the only woman mentioned by name in the Qur'an,' she responds. 'She's the only woman who has got a chapter with her name – quite a long sura. The most interesting thing is that it's the sura most often read by women in times of trouble. Women are encouraged to read it when they're praying for something and are vulnerable, often about family matters. Partly, it's because of Mary's own story in the Qur'an – she'd been kind of given away and was in seclusion when the angel appeared and is panic stricken. How on earth am I going to conceive? How do I go back to my community? What about my dignity and respect, and the shame? There's a lot that's evoked in that story. It's the holiness of Mary and her vulnerability that are so relevant. She's a good woman where there are many women who are temptresses or problematic. Mary is not problematic in that sense. She's embodies chastity and virtue and giving herself unto God. But there's an ambivalence to her too.'

What message would a woman hope to get from reading this story in the Qur'an? I ask.

'Blessings,' she says. 'Just blessings. You can read the same story a hundred times, even two hundred times. You can read it once a day or several times a day. You're reading something that's been signalled out as specifically relevant at a particular time in your life, a time of change. All the chapters are of equal worth but this one, at this time, may be more relevant.'

She tells me that she started reading sura 19, and the annunciation passage in particular, when she was pregnant with her first child. She was encouraged by her mother to read it at least once a day throughout her pregnancy. However, she says it did not really work for her.

'I read it just like any other chapter of the Qur'an. Maybe it was because I wasn't part of an Islamic tradition, where all the women around me were saying read this now. I read it every day but I failed to connect with it. But there are so many layers to the story. She is the holiest woman in the Qur'an, the most virtuous. At the same time, her story is eclipsed by Jesus's story. She has this presence but her presence fades because now a new messenger has arrived.

'There's a tension in the story between Muslims and Christians,' she continues. 'How can Muslims deny the ultimate status of Jesus as God's son when they accept the Virgin Birth, the miracle of it, accept the Immaculate Conception of Mary, but then they deny that he's God's son? There's so many ways of reading that story. There's no Marian cult in Islam, no devotion to her in that sense as a saint.'

So Christians and Muslims, I suggest, can agree on the following: Mary has a special purity; there was an annunciation moment involving an angel or messenger; there was a virgin birth through the spirit of God in some form.

'Tick, tick, tick,' she responds.

So the fundamental point at which they would divide is in that moment of the conception. Christians believe the baby is the Son of God, both divine and human, whereas in Islam he is regarded as a messenger?

'Sure,' she says, 'and it gets more complicated. There's a general Islamic tradition that Satan pricks everyone at birth and original sin is in them, except for Mary and Jesus who are not pricked at birth. There's an Islamic tradition that they remained kind of almost sinless.'

That would appear to bring Muslims closer to Catholics and their doctrine of the Immaculate Conception. And yet the status of Mary within Catholicism – as mother of God and as someone to venerate – is alien to Islam. Most Christians would have no clue about all this. Even though Christians say Jesus is the Son of God and Muslims say he is a special messenger, there are clear connections between both faiths.

'I agree,' she says. 'It's very powerful.'

The irony, if that's the right word, I suggest, is that Mary may have more significance and status in parts of Islam than in a low evangelical Protestant church.

'Absolutely and that's maybe in part that the Jesus God-like has been so pushed forward that the human aspects have been somewhat erased. She's human and he's human. She's central to the story but also let's remember there are huge differences between Christianity and Islam in how they understand God and the Trinity for example. There's a huge gulf between Catholics and Muslims in how they see Mary. She is not Theotokos. But there are different ways of looking at this whole idea. You can say Jesus is God but in my classes I then say, would you say God is Jesus? They look at you and some say "no, you couldn't say that". So we then think about what that means and we start to talk about how Mary comes into this. I want to keep Mary as significant for them but at the same time emphasize there is a sense she's done her bit, she was great, but now we have this new person. In Islam, no one talks about Mary. She's there. Once you've talked about her chastity, then what?'

Amid the noise and clatter of the cafe, Mona Siddiqui then makes a particularly interesting observation. 'Mary cannot be the idea of the embodiment of femininity in Islam because she denies herself,' she continues. 'She's given birth and then withdraws back to devotion. But in Islam, a woman is someone who lives, who has a husband, has children, she has a family, a home life, a full life and she is also part of a community. So the idea of abstinence from all that and giving yourself up to God at the expense of a lived life, a full life, is not what Islam is about for women.'

I explain to her that many of the people I have spoken to view the annunciation story as historic fact whereas others see it as a metaphor.

'It's just all words, isn't it?' she says. 'In the end it is all words. When I say I believe in the Virgin Birth, am I really thinking that through? What does that mean in my thought process today? Does it affect my feeling about life? It doesn't because I don't see Mary as an exemplar for a modern Islamic woman and what female life today is all about. I don't see her as a negative but the things that are still important – chastity, humility, devotion, self-respect, a sense of shame in the classical sense of shame – those are universal rights. You don't have to have scriptural women to say we must be like them because we can't be like them. We can use those principles and values to say how can I be today? All these great women, they don't mean anything in my life today in a sense that they're historical figures. Some of it can be read metaphorically, some of it can be read historically, but do I take from them? No, I take those principles from today's universal principles of what constitutes a good life.'

What, for her, are the universal principles within the annunciation story that chime in any religion or society?

'You can't prove any of this and maybe none of it happened but some of it [the story] sticks with you,' she says. 'It's not that I can defend it. It's part of a whole system of other beliefs that fit into that system. For me, God can do anything and could do anything. The biological arguments that, genetically, it could not happen are silly arguments to me. There's so much in religion that can't be proved. People believe because it fits into a larger ethos of how they view life. So it is with the Mary story.'

She observes how Catholicism emphasizes Mary's right to say no whereas Islam views God as omnipotent so Mary was not given a choice. It's just a different way of talking about God, she comments. Interestingly, she says just as the Christian story of the Annunciation marks a beginning – the Incarnation – in Islam the annunciation story is an ending because it finishes the telling of Jesus's arrival as a human being and as one of God's messengers.

What keeps her believing, she tells me, is a faith in God. When you strip away everything else, she says, there is a higher being that she feels connected with. She recognizes she is a Muslim by tradition and birth but there is something in Christianity that resonates with her too and is at the heart of her interfaith relations work. 'I don't feel a connection with Buddhism, Hinduism, Judaism but in Christianity there is some resonance,' she says.

She notes that many Christians express vulnerability and a sense of doubt when they talk about their faith whereas in Islam, there is certainty. However, she recognizes that Muslims are likely to have diverse views too and has come to appreciate that it is healthy to question one's beliefs from time to time. 'When Muslims and Christians worship, they may think of God in different ways,' she says, 'but I don't think it's a different God.' In the end, we are all judged by our actions. She talks of the need for a 'resurrection of Mary' as a bridge that can bring Muslims and Christians together to talk and understand each other in an atmosphere of mutual tolerance and respect.

I show her Lemoyne's painting of the Annunciation. What does she see?

'For me, it's such a Christian image – very soft, very heavenly. They're beautiful colours. There are too many figures for me as a Muslim in a sense of trying to convey the divine. Mary is completely meek and submissive. The irony is that she must have been really strong. She submitted to God, yes, but she was proud in some ways of what she did. You don't get that at all in this image. This is about somebody completely surrendering herself. Of course, you'd never have a picture like this in Islamic tradition.'

Would such a picture be seen as offensive, inappropriate or irrelevant? How would she like it to be?

'I don't know because I don't think in figures,' she replies. 'It doesn't speak to me. But I know what to expect here. I know this is a version of a Christian story with a Christian interpretation.'

So, what image does she see when she thinks of the annunciation story in sura 19?

'I see Mary in darkness. It's all very ethereal. I then see light – that's very important. I do see a figure. I see her in a blue garment. Yes, that's because that's the only image I have seen of her. If there was no Christian art, how would we all see her?'

———

Dr Tim Winter is one of Britain's leading Islamic academics and is based at the Faculty of Divinity at the University of Cambridge. The Shaykh Zayed Lecturer in Islamic Studies, he is an award-winning intellectual on Islamic Thought and Muslim-Christian relations. He is also Dean of the Cambridge Muslim College, which trains imams for British mosques. A Sunni Muslim who was brought up in a Christian household, Tim Winter is also known as Shaykh Abdal Hakim Murad.

We meet in his small, neat study in the Faculty of Divinity. Studious, pale skinned with thinning light hair and a beard, he talks quietly and slowly. Educated at Westminster School, he took a double first in Arabic at Cambridge before further studies in Cairo. Today, aged fifty-four, he has been described in *The Independent* newspaper recently as one of Britain's most influential Muslims.

'The Qur'an is a text with secrets and enigmas,' he tells me, 'and one of the most important, significant interfaces between Islam and the religion that immediately preceded it, is the way in which it, in a very distinctive but also in a very purposive way, describes the origins of the religion that, as it were, is Islam's nearest rival. So we see that there is nothing in the Qur'an about the birth of the prophet Muhammad for instance or about the birth of most of the significant figures of the biblical narrative. But we find this extraordinary effulgence of information and theological pointers and recasting of narratives when it comes to the origins of Christianity. The reason for that, probably, is to do with Islam's sense of itself as finally balanced between, on the one hand, a new religion, and on the other, a new religion that claims its legitimacy in terms of an ongoing narrative. In other words, it is Abrahamic, it is Christic, it is Mosaic, it is Adamic – it is not some completely unfamiliar message from the Arabian beyond. It's deliberately situating itself as a central part, as a culmination of the Judeo-Christian Abrahamic story. The way it constructs the annunciation, the nativity and the first moments of Christ's life is the way in which it demonstrates its legitimate pertinence or belonging to the rival story of the Byzantines in whom the Arabs had lived in the shadow for a long time.'

That is a very dense answer. I hope I will be able to keep the conversation going. I ask next what the Qur'an's annunciation story means for him.

'Essentially, it's a theological term but one that has its own distinct integrity and charm,' he says. 'The passages do not present themselves as polemic but as lyrical and loving evocations of a beautiful event. So the Virgin Mary is continued in Islam but is a peg on which the Qur'an hangs its own very distinctive Christology and hence its own justification.'

He, too, stresses how in the Qur'an, Mary is not the mother or bearer of God but is a distinctive archetype of faithful prayerfulness and patience in adversity. She is a starting point for Muslims on womanhood – an example of virtue, obedience, purity and moral excellence.

We move on to discuss the factual differences between the two narratives in the Qur'an and Luke's Gospel account.

'Gabriel is recast slightly in the Qur'an as the angel of revelation,' he says. 'The city from where Mary leaves is interpreted by the commentators as Jerusalem. It's one of those pregnant Qur'an narratives where a lot seems to be presumed such that commentators later have to scrabble around for information. When her time comes, she goes out to the desert to an unspecified eastern place. She then gives birth under a palm tree. There are no wise men; there is no star in the sky; there are no shepherds. She's wholly alone. The strong cultural implication is that it is a terrible and probably terminal situation for her to be in as an unmarried woman committing the capital crime of unchastity.'

He tells me that when Muslim women endure birth pains, they sometimes recite Marian prayers because it is the only time such birth pains are mentioned in the Qur'an.

In the Qur'an, does the announcement by Gabriel happen in Mary's home?

'It's not clear,' he replies. 'Either in her home or in a booth or a cell where she was secluded for worship in the Temple. A big question for contemporary scholarship is where does this very distinctive story of the annunciation and the nativity come from? Where is the palm tree? If we look back at the very ancient preserved Gospels and the apocryphal gospels, we find a wide range of different memories and stories, some of which are quite ancient. One possible source that has been proposed by some commentators is what's called the gospel of Nicodemus and another is the infant gospel of James, which does seem to include some of the Quranic features. Now that doesn't mean that academics can suddenly jump up and down in excitement and say there's a linear influence. In that world, one was looking at oral traditions, shared narratives, different religious groups taking stories, principles and themes that were of use to them from a shared cultural compost of narratives and ideas. No one would be able to put their hand on their heart and say the Qur'an is directly influenced by these texts. The Qur'an is inhabiting a huge world.'

I tell him I had read that in the Qur'an, 'virginity' means detached rather than intact.

'The word "virgin" doesn't appear in the Qur'an in this connection,' he responds. 'Instead, what you get is when she's having the annunciation and the angel is speaking to her, saying she's going to have a child, there's her response, "How can I have a child when no man has touched me?" That's normally interpreted by commentators as indicating she's a virgin but some would say maybe she was married and had relations before. The virginity trip is much less significant for Islam than it is for Christianity. Sexuality is identified there as a negative consequence of the Fall. Because we became mortal, we had to replicate ourselves so sexuality becomes necessary so that the species can survive but it's a regrettable reminder of sin, whereas in the Jewish and Islamic tradition, there isn't that connection between sexuality and sin. It's a positive thing, almost sacred. In Islam, her virginity doesn't become significant in terms of the qualities that are attributed to Jesus subsequently. The idea that God's word can only come through a pure, untouched vessel doesn't make much sense to Muslim imagination.'

He has described Mary as of 'slight relevance' within Islam. What does he mean?

'Well, she's not present in the liturgy whereas in the Christian liturgy, she's often very central. Generally in Muslim piety, although you have a whole chapter named after her in the Qur'an text, she doesn't play a role in the economy of salvation at all. She's simply presented really as a kind of female saint – a strong and independent figure – rather than the meek and mild figure in Christianity. Modern Muslims will say Mary is there but there are other ideal types as well. She's a useful point of contact with the religious other – particularly the Christian other.'

So, does he see her as a bridge or a barrier to interfaith dialogue?

'She invites Christians and Muslims to dialogue,' he replies. 'Catholics consider her to be the tender and pure heart of everything they think to be intrinsically theirs, and when they discover there's one other major world religion that has claims over her, they become intrigued. So it can be a prompt to dialogue and a point of contact. But when you get into the serious discussions, she can become quite divisive. The denial of the Trinity, the Incarnation, Original Sin – the key Christian doctrines – they are put down by the Qur'anic retelling of the story. So she's an invitation to further dialogue but often one runs up to the most serious issues that divide Muslims and Christians. She's a lightning rod. For example, to discuss Mary with the College of Cardinals in Rome is tricky for Muslims.'

I am interested to learn how a shy Christian teenager from Cambridge converted to Islam. Was there a sudden annunciation moment for him?

'I was brought up a Christian in a benign but not doctrinally precise Anglican kind of way,' he says. 'In terms of my own journey, there were two major episodes. One was at the age of sixteen when I'd never really considered monotheism as the true interpretation of reality. My parents sent me off on an exchange to learn French with a very vigorous and large French Jewish family in Corsica, who turned out to be enthusiastic nudists. I remember considering the incredible beauty of the daughters of the house aged fourteen to seventeen sitting on the beach eating peaches in the Mediterranean sun. At some point I felt, this is not nothing. The world is not a random concatenation of dead matter. There is something luminous here that has, at its most reasonable explanation, the idea that it is analogous to personal life that has given it this form, this beauty, this moral significance. I sometimes say, "I was converted by a French nudist teenager." That really was the moment I thought this is really important – the rhetoric of beauty.

'Over the next couple of years, I tried to make sense of ancestral Christianity. I spoke to a school chaplain who put on the blackboard reasons for belief and reasons for disbelief. The latter list was longer than the former. He thought the historic doctrines were early medieval elaborations rather than the teachings of Jesus. I shopped around for alternatives. It was the 1970s. A lot of people were on the hippy trail to Afghanistan, India and further east but I had no particular desire to be exotic. It struck me that if you are monotheist and that's in your bones, it's really difficult, it's a wrench, to transfer yourself to Tibet or to an ashram where there's not really an overlap. Judaism seemed to solve the problems but also seemed to be the spiritual path of a particular people. They didn't aspire to convert the world. And then Islam was kind of last on my list. It wasn't on anyone's horizon in the 1970s before Khomeini [Ayatollah Khomeini returning to Iran to lead the Iranian Revolution in 1979]. I started to take an interest in Islamic art and attended evening classes in that and finally put two and two together and that this was the Christology that made sense to me. I could have monotheism and the person of Jesus was also there. I wasn't exotic. I was middle England. I wasn't on the hippy trail. I thought this is only going to be valid for me if it enables me to discover more authentically what I have already concluded and is integral to myself. So it wasn't really a conversion, more a kind of articulating something.'

He describes how he went into Islam through a dry and bookish route comparing various philosophies and theologies.

'I didn't meet any Muslims beforehand. I didn't travel to any Muslim centres. So no, not really a road to Damascus experience, apart from the girl on the beach.'

He offers a rare smile. Of course, mosques never display images and religious

183. Ottoman miniature image of the Qur'an annunciation story from the manuscript, Kisadül-Enbiya, held at the Süleymaniye Library in Istanbul. © Süleymaniye Yazma Eser Library of the Turkish Writers Association, Hamidiye 980

imagery plays no part in Islam. However, he searches through his library in his office and finally finds a rare Ottoman depiction of the annunciation story with Mary standing below a tree as the angel delivers his message. She wears a long red dress and has hair flowing almost down to her thighs. She puts her hands to her ears as she hears the angel's voice.

I show him the Lemoyne painting.

'I see an early eighteenth-century European take. It's not my own even though I love baroque art. I like it but I'm not sure it conveys the original, white-hot puritan experience of God that you get in the Gospels or the Qur'anic narratives. It's too baroque. It's too elaborate, too adorned. Be focused on the word, that's my preference.

'I want my image to be somebody whose face would be transformed rather than the nice girl from a corner of western Europe three hundred years ago,' he continues. 'Somebody luminous, sanctified. Something more like an icon, that's not trying to give you a photograph but more the archetype – an eternal, platonic form. I think a lot of people nowadays are alienated from religion by being forced to see everything through a lens of a different time and place. The churches that do well are those that don't tend to meet in churches but meet in coffee houses or even in church halls. I love traditional English churches but the environment, the iconography, the pews, the dust, don't speak to young people. But take them to a simple, modern space and they lighten up. I don't know what the Church of England is going to do about that.'

CHAPTER 42

TO THE HOLY LAND

———

Jerusalem: the Golden City, the Eternal City, the Holy City. No other place means so much to so many of the faithful. It is unique in that it puts the three Abrahamic religions – Judaism, Christianity and Islam – into a historical melting pot. Each religion assigns special significance to Jerusalem and has claimed individual buildings and areas as sacred. However, the city is not neatly subdivided into equal parts, each one claimed by one faith group. All is jumbled together and occasionally overlaps. And that presents a unique challenge.

It is the holiest city in Judaism, the spiritual home of the Jewish people. In particular, the site of the First and Second Temples, the last remnant of which forms the Western Wall by Temple Mount, is a place of deep reverence for the Jewish people and is their most sacred place. Jewish tradition holds that the Holy of the Holies, which once housed the Ark of the Covenant, was sited in this area.

Christianity also regards Jerusalem as the holiest city. It is the place where Jesus was presented as a child at the Temple, and where the Last Supper was held. But most importantly, it is the place of the crucifixion at Golgotha and of his resurrection nearby. Today, the Church of the Holy Sepulchre encloses the sites of both these events.

Muslims, too, consider it a sacred city, which, they believe, was visited by the prophet Muhammad on a miraculous nocturnal journey before he ascended to heaven. It is the site of the Dome of the Rock on Haram al-Sharif and of the al-Aqsa mosque, the third holiest site for Muslims after Mecca and Medina.

Tensions are high in the week I visit Jerusalem and security services are very much in evidence everywhere I look. On the streets, there is a volatile atmosphere that is almost palpable. A fortnight ago, a Hamas militant killed two people after driving a van into a group of pedestrians, close to a tram stop. Just a few days ago, there was a deadly attack on a synagogue in West Jerusalem in which two Palestinians killed four rabbis before being shot dead. The perpetrators were armed with a pistol and meat cleavers. A policeman died later of his wounds. People in all areas of the city are worried, tense and despondent.

This follows weeks of rising unrest and violence, partly fuelled by tension over the disputed site of the Temple Mount/Haram al-Sharif. Many Palestinians believe that Israel is preparing to allow Jews to pray in the compound of the al-Aqsa mosque, but the Israeli government denies this emphatically. The prospect of a peace settlement in the region seems light-years away and Jerusalem is at the heart of the conflict. Israelis and Palestinians both claim the holy city as their capital, which is under Israeli control. The two sides are further apart than ever.

I have come to Jerusalem on my way to Nazareth because, in Christian tradition, the story of the Annunciation has roots in this ancient city. For this is the place where Mary's parents, Joachim and Anna, are said to have lived and where they apparently embraced at the Golden Gate on the Temple Mount's eastern wall upon hearing of Anna's miraculous conception. According to one tradition, it is also the birthplace of the Virgin Mary. The legendary account, proclaimed in the apocryphal Gospel of James, stands in some conflict, of course, to Luke's canonical annunciation narrative, which places Mary's home in Nazareth in Galilee, ninety miles north of here. The apocryphal Gospel of James also claims that Mary was presented at the Temple in Jerusalem as a three year old, less than half a mile from her home. To accept both of Luke and James's versions, you would have to believe that Mary was born and brought up in Jerusalem, stayed in the Temple as a child and then left for Nazareth as a teenager with her parents, to live alongside Joseph.

Having viewed the Golden Gate that has been walled up since the sixteenth century, I head into Old Jerusalem via Lion's Gate and make my way along the narrow al-Mujahideen Road to the Greek Orthodox and Roman Catholic churches of St Anne, both named after the mother of the Virgin Mary, and situated in the Muslim quarter of the city.

Above the door of the tiny Greek church, the words 'Birth Place of the Virgin Mary' are carved into the stone. The walls of the ground level room are crammed full of icons. Below, down a set of steep stairs, is a cave-like space that, according to Orthodox tradition, was the home of Joachim and Anna and the birthplace of Mary. A simple wooden relief panel featuring the three of them marks the place with the words: 'The House of the Righteous Ancestors of God, the Parents of the Virgin Mary, Joachim and Anna.'

But this is not the only building that claims to be the birthplace and childhood home of the Virgin Mary. Fifty yards up the road is the Roman Catholic church of St Anne. The present church was built on the site of the remains of the original Byzantine Basilica, which was erected in the seventh century. The Crusaders were firm in their belief that their new church was built over the grotto of Mary's birthplace and childhood home. This attractive Romanesque church was completed in 1138 and is the best-preserved Crusader church in Jerusalem. During the Muslim rule of Palestine, the church became an Islamic law school but then fell into disrepair and in 1856 was handed over to the French government. It has been looked after since 1878 by the Missionaries of Africa, commonly called the White Fathers, who, the sign in the courtyard indicates, 'came to Jerusalem to work for unity.'

The interior of the church of St Anne is simple and largely unadorned. On the south aisle, a flight of steps leads down to the crypt. This houses the grotto that Western Christian tradition claims was the home of Joachim and Anna, and the birthplace of Mary. A sign proclaims boldly: 'Welcome for Prayers. NO EXPLANATIONS IN THE BASILICA!'

Inside the tiny stone space, there is a simple altar together with a statue of a crowned Virgin Mary. A Russian icon, depicting her birth, is displayed on a wall showing Anna lying on a bed covered in a red blanket after having given birth. Below her bed, two maids hold the baby girl next to a basin filled with water. At the side, Joachim looks on proudly. A visitors' book, placed on a lectern nearby, is full of messages left by people from all over the world:

'Mary, please grant my children a good career.'

'Blessed Mary, thank you for protecting us during our pilgrimage. Let us not be afraid, just like you.'

'I pray to you for a child for my daughter.'

'I want some health from my asthma illness.'

'Mary, we pray to you for all unborn children.'

'We thank you dear Mary for bringing Jesus into the world.'

'My mother, I love you, pray for me.'

'Please Mary, wash my whole family of all their sins. Pray for getting higher marks for my son, and for prosperity for my family, and for getting a job for my son.'

'We pray for the end of abortion and the lasting union of marriage.'

'Wherever I will be, I will follow you Mary.'

I return upstairs to meet Fr Peter Smith, a seventy-one-year-old White Father, who has lived here for three years with the twenty other members of the St Anne community. For forty-four years, he was a missionary in Tanzania. There, a third of the East African country is Christian, a third is Muslim and a third practises one of the country's numerous indigenous religions or has no faith.

We sit at the back of the church in front of a large stone statue that shows Anna teaching her young daughter Mary. Fr Peter is dressed in the gandoura (long white cassock) of the White Fathers with a rosary and cross around his neck and bright sports trainers on his feet. I count more than fifty lit candles in front of the statue.

'This is one of the traditional birthplaces of Mary but it probably has the strongest and soundest tradition going back to the Protoevangelium of St James and it is also associated with the proximity to the Temple,' he tells me. 'Granted, all of these sources that we have are two to three hundred years after Mary's birth, but in the East all of them claim that Mary was born in Jerusalem. So it would have been a strong claim but we're not building our faith on that. It's a tradition built up around the idea that this was the home of Joachim and Anna. What historical value you want to place on that tradition is up to you. How sound it is historically is not for me to judge.'

What about the Greek Orthodox claim that its church sits on the site of Mary's birthplace?

'It's the same set of tunnels,' he replies. 'There are also the alternative claims that she was born in Sepphoris or Nazareth but this, here, is the soundest tradition. If you read the Qur'an, it too presumes she lived in Jerusalem. That's why this church survived under Salah ad-Din [the first Sultan of Egypt and Syria who took control of Jerusalem in 1187].'

Does he feel that Mary is a bridge or a barrier to interfaith dialogue between Christians and Muslims?

'It depends how critical you want to be,' he says. 'You can make anyone a bridge in any relationship. Anyone who calls Jesus, Son of God – and remember, that's not mentioned in the Bible – well that would be anathema to a Muslim, blasphemy.'

What does the annunciation story in Luke's Gospel mean to him?

'For me spiritually, I always had a great devotion to Our Lady throughout my time in Africa. I contrast Luke's account with the Qur'an. In the Qur'an, she's asked to bear a child and there's no real dialogue. For God, it's easy – "Be and it is". But in Luke's Gospel, and I know it's a small difference but a really important one, there's a dialogue. God entered into dialogue. He didn't just impose it. It's a dialogue almost of equals. In the Qur'an, it's more of a command, God taking the initiative. But in Luke's Gospel, in contrast, he wants to engage, to request. That's so important. It's that wonderful interaction between God and mankind in the dialogue between the angel and Mary. I love that.'

Does he see the Lucan account as fact or as metaphor?

'Absolute fact for myself,' he replies immediately. 'I'm not trying to prove it to anybody but I see it as historical fact. No question about it, on the basis of faith, of which Luke's Gospel is a contributory factor. If you have that faith, you don't need explanations. If you don't have faith, no explanation is possible. Everybody has to find his or her own way. But faith is a gift from God. Reason is involved, yes, but faith is a gift. There may be reason, science saying it couldn't happen, but then you're on a philosophical level of what God can and cannot do. For me, being brought up a Catholic, never having to question it, what limit are you going to put on God?'

When he was a White Father in Africa, how did he explain the annunciation story?

'By the time I got there, we had a pretty well established church. Acceptance of Mary and her role was not a problem. Of course, Muslims in Tanzania would reject that she was the mother of God. They'd have great respect for her but would always reject that.'

Does he agree with Bishop Philip Egan's phrase that the Annunciation is 'the most important event in human history'?

'Well…' he pauses, 'I know what he's trying to say. The hierarchy of truths: Creation, Incarnation, Crucifixion, Resurrection. We do like to slice things up, don't we?' he smiles. 'It's part of a whole surely rather than trying to split them up? Don't isolate one event from the others. God's will is the over-riding, most important thing.'

Did he ever have an annunciation moment?

'I was in a Catholic school in a Catholic atmosphere. Twenty-one boys and twenty-one girls were in the class. I was an altar boy. There was an attraction to the White Fathers for me when the [White Father's] priest came to visit us. I was ten. Yes, that was a decisive moment.'

I show him the Lemoyne painting. He pauses for a long while as he studies it.

'I personally find it very helpful for my own meditation,' he says. 'I prefer an angel to a beam of light. But I want to see a more feisty Mary myself.'

As I leave Fr Peter, a large group of Baptist singers from Louisiana in the southern United States arrives to sing in the church, which is renowned for its outstanding acoustics. Only a handful of them go down to the crypt to see Mary's alleged birthplace. The vast majority stays upstairs in the body of the church. 'I don't want to look at that,' one lady tells me. 'Why would I want to go there?'

A few minutes later and I am in a busy West Jerusalem cafe, meeting Professor Ora Limor from the Department of History, Philosophy and Judaic Studies at the Open University of Israel. Educated at the Hebrew University in Jerusalem, she takes a special research interest in Jewish-Christian polemics and cultural encounters in the Middle Ages. Her published papers include 'Mary and the Jews: Story, Controversy and Testimony' and 'Mary in Jerusalem: An Imaginary Map'.

'By tradition, Mary was born here in Jerusalem, living among Jews, raising her son as a Jewish boy, and dying among Jews,' she says. 'She never changed her religion. After her son's death, she was living in Jerusalem for another twenty-four years, according to tradition. But no Christian knows for sure. In the New Testament Gospels and in St Paul's Letters, Mary is not really involved. Her name appears only a few times. They tell us nothing of Mary's childhood and youth. Nobody really knows.'

Given Mary's great importance in Christian ritual, she states, it is surprising how little the Gospels refer to her. Any details of her background before and at the time of the Annunciation come from tradition, mainly through the apocryphal Protoevangelium of James. Although the work was never recognized by the Church as authoritative and was criticized for lacking any historical foundation, it greatly informed the Christians' view of Mary as a good, faithful Jewess and helped to fill out the details of her biography. Moreover, the legendary content soon spread rapidly across the Christian world.

'From the third century onwards, she becomes much more important a figure and finds a place in the doctrine of the Church,' she tells me. 'In 431 at the Council of Ephesus, she becomes known as the bearer of God – Theotokos – and then places of pilgrimage appear gradually over the fifth and sixth centuries here in Jerusalem and across the Holy Land for remembering her.'

She tells me how in her recent work 'Mary in Jerusalem: An Imaginary Map', part of a series of papers that form the book *Visual Constructs of Jerusalem*, published in 2014, she explains how the collection of Marian sacred sites in Jerusalem developed from the sixth century to include a new church of St Mary, built by Justinian in 543, and the church of St Anne, honouring her mother and Mary's birthplace.

'She soon became the enemy of the Jews because they didn't believe she gave birth as a virgin without a man,' Ora Limor tells me. 'They thought it was awful to think that God will find a place in the womb of a woman near to her organs, so close to the dirt of all that.'

This condemnation of Mary by Jews continued from the first century right through to the medieval period. Professor Limor makes reference to *Nizzahon Vetus*, a work written in Germany around 1300, at the time when the cult of the Virgin Mary and the intense devotion to her reached its peak across Europe:

> Consequently, how could this man be God, for he entered a woman with a stomach full of faeces who frequently sat him down in the privy during the nine months, and when he was born he came out dirty and filthy, wrapped in placenta and defiled by the blood of childbirth and impure issue. The Torah, on the other hand, warns against approaching a menstruate woman, a woman who has had an impure issue, and one who has just given birth, as it is written, 'And shall continue in blood of purification three and thirty days; she shall touch no hallowed thing until the day of her purification be fulfilled' (Leviticus 12:4). Hence he was not worthy of association with anything sacred.

Why did Jews focus their wrath on Mary in those early years of the Christian Church?

'Because she became such a big figure in Christianity, and her figure became so important in attracting believers,' she says. 'In Judaism, there is one God, thought to be a strong male-like character, a very masculine God. They could see she was being seen like the Pagan gods of femininity. From Jews, stories and beliefs started to spread that it cannot be. This story makes no sense for God to go into the womb of all places. They then took the stories to uglier places – of course, the baby was born without a proper father because she was a prostitute and then even further, that she was raped. They said the baby was illegitimate. These weren't official stories that had come from rabbis. The legends came from who knows where originally, but they continued until modern times, and were often told secretly. The Jews never said Jesus never existed or Mary never existed. There was a woman called Mary and she gave birth without a husband but not because of God – her son was a *mamzer*, a bastard. He was illegitimate.'

Does she think Jews here still proclaim that view?

'Secular Jews, of course not. Orthodox Jews and Reform Jews, of course not. But students in religious academies when they want to amuse themselves...I don't know what they say to each other. Although the big enemy is Islam, there is still a feeling in Jewish psychological thinking against Christianity as a reaction to anti-Semitism, which they feel is still there all the time.'

In that context, does she feel Mary is a bridge or a barrier to stronger interfaith dialogue between Jews and Christians?

'She's irrelevant today, I would say' she responds. 'I am absolutely secular but I feel when Jews and Christians talk with each other on polemics, she's not relevant. And, of course, the idea of a human God remains the fundamental barrier.'

She looks away for a short while, pausing to reflect. 'I think Mary replaced all the mythological goddesses and she came in their place. The barrier is the way Christianity then shaped her as the intercessory between God and humanity, standing at the gate of heaven, pleading for the spirits who were waiting to know whether they were going to heaven or hell and she would plead for their mercy. That idea is the barrier, as well as the idea that she is mother of God and mother of the Church.'

———

Of course, the main reference point for the location of the annunciation story is Luke's Gospel account. This has canonical authority for all denominations of the Christian Church and firmly places the location of the Annunciation in Nazareth, ninety miles north of Jerusalem in Galilee.

According to the Synoptic Gospels (Matthew, Mark and Luke), Nazareth was the home of Mary, and later was the childhood home of Jesus, who became known as Jesus of Nazareth. Indeed, early Christians were sometimes described as Nazarenes. Two thousand years ago, Nazareth (*Nazeret* in Hebrew, *an-Nasira* in Arabic) was an all-Jewish hamlet of a few hundred people. Today it is Israel's largest Arab city with a population of around 75,000. My annunciation journey would not be complete without a visit. So I head there, to my destination.

Known as the 'Cradle of Christianity' and described by Jerome in the fourth century as 'the Flower of Galilee', the old city of Nazareth lies on the rise between the Sea of Galilee and the Jezreel valley. It has been a place of Christian pilgrimage since the fourth century. A story is told that a Spanish pilgrim, Lady Egeria, visited Nazareth in 383 and recorded that she saw, 'a big, splendid cave in which Mary had lived and an altar being placed there.' A Byzantine basilica replaced the first shrine in the fifth century before the Persians arrived in 637 after invading Palestine. The Crusaders made it their Galilee chapel in 1099 and rebuilt the basilica but were then driven out a century later by Saladin, who returned Nazareth to Muslim control. From the mid-1200s, Christian clergy were banned from Nazareth and it fell into serious decline. By the end of the seventeenth century, Christian churches and shrines were being re-established in the town and the Franciscans acquired the site of the main basilica.

Today the vast majority of Nazareth's population is Arab. Seventy per cent is Muslim. Thirty per cent is Arab Christian, comprising Greek Orthodox, Melkite Greek Catholics and Roman Catholics. Before 1948, Nazareth was a city with a large Christian majority. Many of today's residents are part of the internally displaced Palestinian refugee families who came to Nazareth from nearby towns more than sixty years ago after the Arab-Israeli war of 1948, when the city became a part of the newly formed country of Israel. Today it is known as the Arab capital of Israel. Until recently, its Mayor was a non-practising Greek Orthodox resident called Ramez Jaraisi but since the last mayoral election in 2013, Ali Salam, a Muslim, has been in office. The majority of the population is poor and unemployment is comparatively high. Tourism is an important revenue source.

Up on the hill, above the old city, is Nazareth Illit (Upper Nazareth), a predominantly Jewish district of 40,000 people, established in the 1950s. Nazareth Illit has parks, wide roads, good modern housing and excellent public services. Around 20 per cent of its inhabitants are Arabs but there are no Arab schools nor any mosques there. It was declared a separate city in 1974. Its controversial right-wing Mayor, Shimon Gapso, recently described Nazareth Illit provocatively as a 'Jewish city now and forever. If that makes me a racist, then I'm the proud offshoot of a glorious dynasty of "racists".' Later, he commented that Nazareth Illit 'was founded to make the Galilee Jewish and must preserve this role.' Of the old city of Nazareth located below, he described it as 'a hostile city to Israel, a nest of terrorism in the heart of Galilee…waiting for an opportunity to stab Israel in the back.'

As well as visiting the various religious shrines in the old city, I am also interested in the present state of affairs in Nazareth and whether it still reflects the long history of conflict and dispute amongst Jews, Christians and Muslims across the region. With its unique status as a world renowned centre for Christian pilgrimage, with a majority Muslim population living in the largest Arab city in the State of Israel, can the city of Nazareth guide a way forward for interfaith relations and dialogue?

On arrival, I meet up with Jonathan Cook, an award-winning British writer and freelance journalist, who lives and works in Nazareth. He is the only foreign correspondent based in the city and has written three books on the Israeli-Palestinian conflict.

How would he describe Nazareth today?

'It's a city like all Palestinian communities inside Israel that's under an occupation but not the occupation we'd know in the Occupied Territories. I once described it as 'an occupation of the soul' because there is no Israeli identity here beyond some kind of formal one. Israel has this concept of Israeli citizenship but it's not really interested in it. It's interested in nationality and there are two main nationalities here, Jew and Arab. The bit that gives you most of your important rights is not your citizenship but your nationality. The only nationality that really counts is the Jewish nationality because it's a Jewish State and they even want to re-define it as the nation State of the Jewish people. So, if you're an Israeli Palestinian, or a Palestinian citizen of Israel, or an Israeli Arab, however you want to describe it, you are stripped of any meaningful sense of belonging to the State. It is an alien entity because it chooses to be in that relationship with you.'

Forty-eight-year-old Jonathan Cook says he prefers to describe himself as an activist journalist rather than a campaigning one. He graduated from Southampton University with a degree in Philosophy and Politics and then gained his Master's in Middle Eastern Studies at the School of Oriental and African Studies in London. He has written regularly for *The Guardian*, *The Observer* and *Le Monde*. In 2011, he won the Martha Gellhorn Special Prize for Journalism, the judges praising his work on Palestine and Israel, 'especially his de-coding of official propaganda and his overriding analysis of events often obfuscated in the mainstream that makes him one of the reliable truth-tellers in the Middle East.' He has lived in Nazareth for more than a decade and is raising his young family in a city he likes to describe as the capital of the Palestinian minority in Israel.

Slim, balding and wearing metal-rimmed spectacles, he is clearly passionate, almost fanatical, about the story he finds in Nazareth and says his mission is to communicate truthfully his own interpretation of what's happening here. He says there are striking and disturbing similarities between the experiences of the Palestinians inside Israel and those inside the Occupied Territories of the West Bank and Gaza. 'Nazareth is not supposed to have survived past 1948 as an Arab city. All the cities became Judaized except Nazareth and it is an accident that it survives. It's an anomaly.'

He describes how the surrender of Nazareth to the Jews was formalized in a written agreement during the 1948 war, whereby the town's leaders agreed to cease hostilities in return for promises from the Israeli commanders that no harm would come to the Arab civilians of the town. David Ben-Gurion, the incumbent leader of the Jewish community and Israel's first Prime Minister, feared that expelling Christian Arabs from Nazareth would provoke an outcry throughout the Christian world. That's why, at the end of the Arab-Israeli war, Nazareth saw a large influx of Arab refugees from the towns and villages around Galilee, who saw the city as a safe haven.

'The traditional story is that Ben-Gurion decided at the last minute not to attack Nazareth and expel the people,' he says. 'That's why Nazareth Illit was then built with the intention to swallow up Nazareth and turn it into a ghetto. Take Nazareth's land and box it in. But it never happened because of the Christian institutions here. Nazareth had all these resources that couldn't really be taken away from it – because they were Christian institutions, not because of anything to do with the Palestinians. So we have our three hospitals, a whole middle class of health professionals, ten or so private schools, founded by various religious orders. Unless you want to take on the international Christian community, you can't get rid of those things. That's why we have some of the best schools in the country here.'

Provocatively, he describes the political system in Nazareth as 'almost apartheid'. There have been reports of occasional skirmishes in recent years and when the Pope visited the city in 2000, some Muslims protested and demanded that a mosque be built close to the Islamic Shrine of Shahab e-Din, close to the Roman Catholic Basilica. However, despite assurances, it was never built. I suggest that perhaps the situation cannot be all that bad as he chooses to raise his family here. Jonathan Cook concedes it is not like the West Bank or Gaza and that the different religious communities here live in relative calm and harmony compared to Jerusalem.

'There's a sense of mutual dependency between the Christians and Muslims here,' he says. 'There's a cautious tolerance amongst the groups. People understand they need each other.'

As our conversation draws to a close, I ask again how he would describe Nazareth today?

'The problem is there's a situation for the Palestinians where the State is openly hostile to you and where you are excluded and marginalized. You can see some people drive great cars here. There are some very wealthy people in Nazareth who are doing very well but they have no communal success. As a community, as a collective, they are opposed at every level. There's no way to be successful here as a collectivity. The State's view of the Palestinians here is as temporary guest workers. You're here on licence, so long as you don't cause any problems – like having too many babies or bringing people in from the Occupied Territories or being ideologically hostile to the State. This is the atmosphere here,' he continues. 'It's a "Judaizing" context. Your possibilities are highly limited here. People are struggling over very limited resources and in a context where everything is hostile to them. That makes it easy to manipulate them. Israel always has a strategy of divide and rule. It's a very complicated picture.'

It has been fascinating to hear one man's view on present day Nazareth. The hour has passed and it is time for him to return to his nearby home. He describes the situation as 'a complicated picture'. That seems to be a fair assessment. Despite the inequality in standards of living and job opportunities, the city functions and its residents live in relative peace compared to many other areas in the Holy Land.

But what has all this got to do with the Annunciation and my visit tomorrow to the city's various religious shrines? Context is the answer. Over the past 2,000 years different religious groups in Nazareth have proffered completely different interpretations of the Lucan story and its significance, and at times have resorted to armed conflict and violence in the name of religion. So it is with the political situation in Nazareth today. There is a hidden tension here, a delicate balance that, for now, tolerates the serious differences in status and opportunity between the Jewish community up on the hill in Nazareth Illit, and the Christian Arabs and Muslims living in different parts of Nazareth.

The following morning heralds a lovely day with brilliant sunshine, a cloudless blue sky and temperatures rising to 90 °F. My first port of call is the church of St Gabriel, the Greek Orthodox Church of the Annunciation, built in 1750 above an older Crusader chapel. According to Greek Orthodox tradition, the Annunciation took place here while Mary was fetching water from a spring. The church is located directly above the source of the spring. A sea of brightly coloured frescos covers the inside walls and ceiling of the church. There are no other visitors inside save for a rather grumpy attendant who demands a donation and hands me a small candle. A barrel-vaulted crypt, covered with majolica tiles, leads me to the sound of trickling water. In the dark light, a priest, wearing a black cassock and scuff cap, kneels in front of the spring chanting prayers and filling up discarded water bottles. He washes his hands and face and then bows again in prayer.

The spring water flows southwards underground to a place 150 yards away where a dry fountain, called Mary's Well, is sited. The Eastern Orthodox Church believes this could be the place where Mary and the other women came to collect the daily water supply and do the washing. According to the apocryphal Gospel of James, there were two encounters between the angel Gabriel and Mary, the first at the well and the second at her home:

184. 'The site of the Annunciation', Church of St Gabriel, Greek Orthodox Church of the Annunciation, Nazareth

> And she took the jug and went out to fill it with water. Suddenly, a voice said to her, 'Rejoice, blessed one. The Lord is with you. You are blessed amongst women.' And Mary looked around to the right and to the left to see where this voice came from. And trembling, she went into her house. Setting down the jug, she took the purple thread and sat down on the chair and spun it. Suddenly, an angel stood before her saying, 'Do not be afraid Mary, you have found grace before the Lord of all. You will conceive from his Word.' Upon hearing this, however, Mary was distraught, saying to herself, 'If I conceive from the Lord God who lives, will I also conceive as all women conceive?' And the Angel of the Lord said, 'Not like that, Mary. For the power of God will come over you. Thus, the holy one who is born will be called Son of the Most High. And you will call his name Jesus for he will save his people from their sins.' And Mary said, 'See, I am the servant of the Lord before him. Let it happen to me according to your word.'

I continue walking south through the old city, calling in on the Abo Salem coffee house where old men play cards and backgammon, before passing through a maze of narrow alleyways to find the Arab souk with chickens, fish, trinkets and clothes for sale. I am struck by how few tourists there are. The place seems almost empty.

Within a few minutes, I arrive at the Roman Catholic Basilica of the Annunciation, the largest church in the Middle East. Western Christians believe that the Basilica stands on the site of Mary's home where the Annunciation took place. The plot is thought to have been a place of worship since the end of the first century when it was referred to as 'The House of Mary'. Conceived by the Italian architect, Giovanni Muzio, the present Basilica was built in the 1960s over the ruins of the fifth-century Byzantine church and was consecrated in 1969. The Franciscans took a big risk in commissioning the design, which is bold, modern and highly original. From the outside, a soaring lantern-topped conical dome dominates the striking concrete structure. A large relief sculpture of the angel Gabriel and Mary on the west front's façade greets visitors at the main entrance.

In the courtyard there are numerous depictions of Mary from countries around the world – Paraguay, Chile, Georgia, Sri Lanka, Vietnam, Thailand, Korea, Poland, China, Singapore, Ukraine…the list goes on. Some are paintings, others are sculptures or mosaics but all reflect the artistic style of the country that has donated them.

185. 'The site of the Annunciation', Roman Catholic Basilica of the Annunciation, Nazareth

The mighty Basilica is built on two levels. The upper floor serves as the parish church and is the place where daily Masses are held in Latin and Arabic. In the dimly lit lower level, the focus is on pilgrimage and next to the main altar in the centre of the space is the most venerated area in the Basilica, the grotto of the Annunciation.

Behind an iron grille and underneath a bronze canopy stands a small altar in front of the opening to a tiny cave. On the front are the words: '*Verbum Caro Hic Factum Est*' (Here the Word became flesh). Behind the altar, the small grotto, carved out of soft rock, is eighteen feet long and five feet high. A small flight of stone steps is visible at the back. Two thousand years ago, this was probably the cellar of the house. It is here that tens of thousands of pilgrims come to venerate Mary and to remember the moment of the Annunciation.

186. The grotto inside the Basilica, Nazareth. © Dennis Jarvis

Visitors form a line on the main floor of the upper church and descend via a spiral staircase towards the cave. A large party of Brazilians has just arrived as part of their pilgrimage to the Holy Land. In front of the locked entrance to the grotto, each person stops for a while and reflects. Many genuflect. Some go down on both knees and make the sign of the Cross. Two women leave their rosary beads. One or two others cry and find it difficult to leave. Three people want to take a 'selfie'. After a short while, they are asked to move on as there are people waiting patiently behind them in the queue. The next party is a group of Russian Orthodox women from Moscow all wearing headscarves. They stay only for five minutes, take photographs, and then leave. One woman tells me they cannot stay long because they are leaving for Cana and then on to Tiberias and Capernaum. There is a short gap before the next tour party arrives. Out come the mobile phones and cameras again and then it is off to the next destination.

At a quiet moment early in the afternoon, I read Luke's story of the Annunciation in front of the cave entrance. I am alone. As I look at the altar, I reflect on all that I have heard over the past few months. The range of views about the message of the annunciation story; the debated historicity of the narrative; the claim by Bishop Philip Egan that it is 'the most important event in the history of the world'. I take out of my bag the large print of Lemoyne's 1727 Annunciation painting and study the image carefully. Then I look at the space in front of me that holds so much resonance. I see a simple altar covered with a white cloth with a gold monstrance in the middle and two lit candles on either side. A red coloured altar lamp hangs above and there's a white-washed wall behind, together with some exposed mortar and stonework. I have come a long way. It is a hugely emotional moment.

I leave the Basilica and head for the nearby St Joseph's church. Walking through an open courtyard, I stop to look at a striking two-piece bronze sculpture of the Annunciation by Guglielmo Schiavina, dedicated to 'Jesus's mother from Janua Dei Trading, Namibia, for conciliation and harmony'. St Joseph's was built in 1914 on the site of an earlier twelfth-century church. From the seventh century onwards, it has traditionally been claimed that the site was the location for Joseph's carpentry workshop. Three stained-glass windows in the crypt detail important aspects of Joseph's life: the angel Gabriel telling him

187. Guglielmo Schiavina *The Annunciation*, 1990, Nazareth

in a dream not to leave Mary; the wedding ceremony of Joseph and Mary; and Mary and Jesus comforting Joseph in his final hours.

In the narrow streets of the old city, I visit the small Nazareth Synagogue church, now used by Melkite Greek Catholic Arabs. It is the location where Jesus is said to have preached as a young adult to his fellow Jews and to have read from the scroll of Isaiah: 'The Spirit of the Lord is on me because he has anointed me to proclaim good news to the poor.' Pilgrims have been visiting this site since the twelfth century.

The next stop is the White Mosque (Al-Abiad), which was built at the end of the eighteenth century and is an important historical and cultural place for the Muslim population of Nazareth. Hundreds regularly attend the Friday sermon here. It is the oldest mosque in the city with a distinctive pencil-shaped minaret, cream coloured walls and a white dome. A sign at the entrance states it is called the White Mosque as a symbol of optimism, purity and unity of all communities in Nazareth and as a place to promote peace and fraternity – a highly appropriate sentiment in these tense, troubled times.

I return to the Basilica area where, on the main street, aptly known as Annunciation Road (El Basharra), stands the Mary of Nazareth International Centre. Built directly opposite the Basilica's main entrance, this is an extraordinarily lavish new complex that was opened on 25 March 2011, the feast day of the Annunciation. The French *Chemin Neuf* (New Way) Roman Catholic community runs it as a non-profit venue to attract pilgrims and tourists visiting the city and to promote ecumenical understanding among Christian denominations and other religions. The large building, housed on three floors, includes an exposed archaeological excavation of the ruins of a first-century dwelling; a large public auditorium; a chapel for silent prayer; sophisticated interactive exhibits; and four rooms providing wide screen films about Mary and her life to promote greater awareness of her importance.

I take the guided tour that lasts almost two hours. It starts in a highly impressive theatrical space, where, to my surprise, there are no other visitors. 'Mary, take us with you on the path of light,' the opening commentary proclaims. I sit down in the large, dark room with lighting that is designed to create the appearance of a large cave. I am told we will be following in the footsteps of Mary and that she will be our guide through the Scriptures.

An opening film about Mary's early life and her encounter at the Annunciation follows much of the story from the Protoevangelium of James. I am astonished at its high production values and cinematic style, its use of sophisticated multi-screen elements and impressive graphics.

'On becoming a woman,' the commentary says, 'Mary goes to the man whom God had chosen for her – from the Royal line of David, Joseph of Nazareth. Joseph accepted Mary's desire to remain a virgin and lead a consecrated life.'

The dramatic sequence of the Annunciation follows the shape and words of Luke's narrative. We are told that the angel arrives at the 'climax' of human history and that God chose Mary among all women for his eternal plan.

'It's here in Nazareth that the Lord would like to enter in time and change the course of human history. But he chose to make the world's salvation hang upon her *yes*.'

When she accepts the angel's message with her fiat, bells ring out and the commentary speaks of 'Mary being overshadowed by the real presence of God as she becomes the ark of a new and everlasting covenant between God and humankind.' It continues, 'Imagine Mary's overwhelming joy as she carried in her womb the hope of her people who had waited for so many centuries. Dance and rejoice, O daughter of Zion. Shout O Israel. Rejoice with joy. The King of Israel is in your womb, daughter of Jerusalem.'

I move on to the next auditorium and watch two further films. The first is called 'Mary was a Jew' and emphasizes how Mary was a Jewish woman who lived here in the Second Temple period. It opens with comments from Dr Deborah Weissman, a specialist in Jewish education and the Jewish President of the International Jewish-Christian Council:

> She was probably the most important Jewish woman in history because, according to the narrative, she is the mother of Jesus,' she says. 'Jesus was born and died a Jew but his followers were the founders of what is today the world's largest religious group. A very important development in human history and I would go as far as to say, for some of us Jews, we are grateful that Christians have carried the God of Israel all over the world, which we couldn't do because Judaism is the religion of a particular people. We do not ascribe divinity to Jesus nor do we ascribe the messianism. For us, Jesus was not the Messiah nor the Saviour and certainly not the Son of God except in so far as all of us are sons and daughters of God. But we do believe, well many of us believe, that Jesus was a very great spiritual teacher, a very great leader. Jesus gave us a remarkable example of how to live a godly life. So I don't need to think he was God in order to say he showed us how to live a godly life and I wish more people in the world would follow his example.

As soon as the thirty-six minute film ends, the next one begins. Entitled 'Muslims talk about Mary', its opening commentary explains how, in the seventh century, Islam emerged out of a revelation from God that was made direct to the prophet Muhammad over a period of twenty-two years. These revelations were passed on by word of mouth to his companions and formed the Qur'an. For the believers of Islam, this sacred book is the actual word of God. The entire religion is founded on this text from heaven, the film says. It goes on to emphasize that Muslims do not pray to Mary, only to Allah. Jesus is a prophet, a spirit of God but he is not God, nor the Son of God. But it also stresses that, according to Hadith, Mary and Jesus, uniquely, were never tainted by sin, never touched by the devil.

Abdelhak Eddouk, a Muslim chaplain based in Paris, comments in the film: 'For Muslims, God exists. He is a unique God – the creator who gave life to all creatures. The Qur'an is the divine word, the revelation. It is also the book that is used by Muslims for their prayers.'

Mohammad Obeid, the Legal Islamic Judge of Nazareth, follows him: 'The one who is sent by God, Muhammad, peace and blessings be upon him, taught us as Muslims to respect the prophets and the Qur'an taught us by giving us the best possible example in respect of Mary, the daughter of Imran, because she is the noble one, the virgin, the pure one, the one who is irreproachable in the eyes of Islam. On the contrary, she is a woman who dedicated herself to God Almighty in adoration, fasting, faith and prayer. This is how Mary is perceived and how we think of her as one of the best women throughout history.'

At the end of the tour, I meet with Sister Beatrice Bourrat, a member of the *Chemin Neuf* community, who comes from Lyon in France. She describes herself as a missionary and has been a member of *Chemin Neuf* for the past thirty years working in Rome, London and Brazil. For the past year, she has helped to run the International Centre here in Nazareth. Diminutive, grey haired and bespectacled, she wears a white top, long light brown skirt and brown neck scarf, together with a large wooden cross around her neck.

She takes me to the roof terrace gardens where there is an outstanding panoramic view of the city, dominated by the huge dome of the Basilica. A small garden has been filled with various plants and species including dates, figs, olives, pomegranates, grapes, barley and wheat, that would have grown in biblical times. Sister Beatrice describes how the idea for the Centre began twenty years ago when a French man 'met Jesus Christ through Mary and was converted.'

Olivier Bonnassies came to Nazareth and founded the *Association Marie de Nazareth* with the vision of setting up a centre for evangelisation and ecumenism in the city. He wanted the museum to be a cutting-edge, multi-media experience. Twenty-five thousand donors, mainly French and including a variety of businesses, backed the project at a cost of between £12 and £14 million. The mission was 'to evangelize by introducing the general public to the awe-inspiring mystery of Mary as Mother of God and to the overall beauty, truth and depth of the Catholic faith.' Similar centres are planned for the Shrine of Our Lady of Guadalupe in Mexico, where twenty million pilgrims visit every year, and the Shrine of Our Lady of Aparecida in Brazil, which attracts eleven million pilgrims annually.

I tell her the International Centre here in Nazareth is impressive but I haven't seen many visitors.

'Very often I say to God, why did you build this place? What is happening to this Centre?' she responds. 'Tell us the truth and help us to go further as we still continue to find the vocation of this place. As you'll understand, there are many challenges here in the Holy Land, in Israel. I think God has a plan and He knows the way He wants to use this place. It's becoming more and more a place to speak and to pray for peace and to build bridges. Try to imagine we are a little bridge to that minaret over there.'

She points to the White Mosque in the old city and then to the larger al-Salam Peace Mosque further away in the distance.

'Yes, there are very few people at the moment,' she continues. 'It's not well known yet. It's a very big construction and one day will become well known but at the moment it's a little start.'

It is such a shame that so many people visit the Basilica but don't walk across the road and come here, I comment.

'It's a shame, yes,' she replies softly.

She tells me that 40,000 people have visited the Centre since it opened three years ago; 5,000 came in the first year, 10,000 in the second and 20,000 in the third. So it is growing but not by enough. Seven hundred thousand people visit Nazareth every year. 'Fifty thousand would be nice,' she says. 'It would be good because we could then balance the expenses for the maintenance and the productions.'

Although the building was erected and fitted out by the Mary of Nazareth Association, *Chemin Neuf* meets its running costs. I am surprised by how good it is, I tell her, but also by how few people come here. How disappointed does she feel about the current performance?

'When I see all the people visiting Nazareth and I see so many groups, I want to say, "Please, come and visit us!" but you can't. It's up to the groups and their itinerary. The guide has to decide. The bus driver has to decide. The pilgrims don't spend much time here.'

I tell her someone told me yesterday that the average time spent by a pilgrim in Nazareth is under an hour. Many people spend more time having a meal and a drink than visiting the shrines. 'Yes, I know,' she replies sadly.

How would she describe the current situation in Nazareth?

'Nazareth is a place of peace,' she replies. 'God manifests his love of peace here. Mary is a woman of peace. We want to honour Mary here but also honour other faiths. It is a town of peace. There is something special that makes it peaceful. The contacts up on the hill are good. We experience peace in this place but it's not the whole of Nazareth. The relationship between Muslims and Christians, I feel, are good in Nazareth. People refer to here. Muslims and Christians collaborate here in a place of peace. I do feel the Franciscans at the Basilica are protecting this place.'

As we look out over the city, the sun starts to set, creating a wonderful, rich orange sky, I ask her to tell me more about her life.

'I was born in Lyon. I was raised with a deep faith. But at fifteen to nineteen, I really felt it was very complicated to be a Christian. It seemed the opposite to the right fashion in France and God was very far. I almost lost my faith. I was rarely going to church. But still I always had something in my heart that said you have to fight for peace, you have to fight for love and to put your feet where you will be serving love. I wanted something authentic. I went to a simple, spontaneous prayer group with my sister in Lyon at the beginning of the *Chemin Neuf* community. I was very touched by it.'

You had a boyfriend? I ask.

'Yes, I was enjoying my life, having a real night life. That very evening I said there was a font of life here like finding a well. There is water down there and I just have to drop my bucket with a rope and bring up the water, which tastes so very good. I touched the heart of life. It was like a heartbeat. I was looking for life as well as love. I thought this will give me life.'

What did she say to her boyfriend?

'It took me six years to go further in reaching the well,' she laughs. 'I went to the prayer group. I bought a Bible. I started to go to church. I still had many boyfriends,' she laughs again, 'but my life had no meaning. I couldn't satisfy myself in anything. I was looking for something deeper. As part of my studies, I spent five months in the United States, living with a family but in reality often in solitude and I learnt of a fulfilment in prayer. I was touched by *Chemin Neuf* in Lyon whilst finishing my studies. I said for one year, I won't have boyfriends. I will have a year for God. I felt happy in a consecration for celibacy. I thought this was my life. I was very happy. I felt a conviction, an inner voice that comes and touches you inside. A pure feeling. Between twenty-five and twenty-eight I was hearing the call to celibacy and from twenty-seven, I was totally celibate. But it's not easy.'

Did she regret having had relationships in the past at that point?

'I really felt my whole life was a preparation for that moment,' she says. 'My personality is such that when I have an experience, I do it fully, passionately. I felt God was always close to me and had never abandoned me. Sometimes there is no one to take you out of this arid place. But there was a seed waiting to be planted and I knew I could trust that seed.'

Does she find it harder physically or mentally to commit to a celibate life?

'It depends on the period you are going through,' she replies. 'To understand celibacy, you really need to understand it's a point of intimacy with Jesus that fulfils your heart. It's a step of deepening your personal prayer.'

Surely, it is easier to be celibate when you've never experienced sexual relations before.

'Probably,' she smiles.

I respect the sacrifice, I tell her, but it is a very big ask.

'What I realize is that our personal relationships with Jesus are very, very personal and I feel my way of life was prepared with all those challenges.'

Has she ever lapsed? I wonder.

'No, no,' she says.

If she had been told when she was eighteen that she would become a nun, what would she have felt?

'I would have felt ashamed because it was so different,' she replies. 'I would have said God has to do a lot of work. There is a long way to go. But I wouldn't have rejected it. When I was five years old, I was in school, I remember, and there was a Sister with a black veil. She was so kind. I used to think I'd like to be like her. But then I would forget it. The word "nun" sounds austere but what I am discovering here is that you are not living your life in celibacy only with other nuns. There are married couples here, single people, a mixture. In *Chemin Neuf*, we commit ourselves to a consecrated life of celibacy to serve the coming of the Kingdom of God, by loving people, trusting people, building bridges, faith, hope and charity.'

Does she ever regret that she did not marry and have children?

'When you pass from a part of your life when you have relationships with men and you go to another step of your life where you choose not to have, it isn't a very easy process,' she says. 'It means you are leaving to put the roots of your life in different ground. They didn't used to be in this type of ground and it takes time to adapt. You have to respect the new ground. I never regretted it. But I have to choose again and again and again.'

Does she have doubts about the sacrifice she has made?

'I think doubts are part of my faith,' she responds. 'When doubt comes, I feel there is something deeper. I then look for reaching this place of stability lower down in this deep place.'

She places her right hand against her chest. I wonder, was the moment at the prayer group in Lyon like an annunciation moment for her?

'Yes, I think so,' she says. 'I had a preparation for that moment even though some aspects of my life were pointing in the opposite direction. I could express it as like the visit of an angel. For Mary, it was one single, concentrated moment. Her words were clear. For me, it has been little signs along the way. Little words along the way. It was the starting moment of an annunciation.'

What does the Lucan Gospel story of the Annunciation mean for her spiritually?

'I feel more and more touched by what happened in Nazareth and what is happening now in the revelation of God's love,' she responds. 'Sometimes I am struggling with Mary and saying, "Are you really someone like me? Are you really fully human? Born without sin, the Immaculate Conception. Are you really fully human?" And the answer is how I went to pray at the statue of Mary of Nazareth inside the Basilica this morning and I gave my hand and she said to me, "Yes, I am." The story of the Annunciation tells me about the value of the human being to God. Mary is an extraordinary person, totally pure and without evil. This is one of my main struggles in life – how not to cooperate with evil. I think, yes, God gave us Mary and Mary is without evil. She's perfect and yet she's also a very humble person. The story is also about trust – total trust and humility in the sense of accepting something very great in life in a very simple way.'

Does she think the annunciation story happened or does she see it as a metaphor?

'I believe it,' she smiles. 'To me, it is the biggest revelation of God's love. How do we say? The major revelation of God's love. Of course it happened. We cannot deny that the distance between God and one little human being was abolished at the Annunciation with the coming of the Holy Spirit. If the Holy Spirit touches the woman, it means the distance between God and humanity is abolished. Yes, this happened and the world's history from that moment goes forward. At that very moment. So yes, I agree with the statement but it happened in a hidden way. Nobody knew about the event except Mary.'

I take the print of Lemoyne's painting out of my bag and pass it to her.

'I notice the position of Mary looking down,' she observes. 'For me, this means the whole preparation. Mary is saying to herself in humility, "This is now getting accomplished." What I don't like about it is the baroque painting style but I do like the positioning of the angel. There's something light about him, hovering. He doesn't come and impose himself. He comes and says this is what I come to tell you. I offer you this message. I don't impose it. I like that.'

As we come to the end of our meeting and darkness starts to take its hold over Nazareth, she tells me that she'd prayed earlier today for our conversation to be 'authentic'. She offers a lovely, gentle smile.

'I think God sent me here to Nazareth because he needed me to understand that ordinary everyday life is blessed,' she says. 'Jesus was living thirty years here in an everyday, ordinary life. I had a hard time believing that ordinary life could be a blessed call and that it could be helpful for the coming of the Kingdom. For me it was all about to act, to be a missionary. But now when I work here, when I clean the floors, I feel my life is blessed and this gives me a lot of hope for the world. The Annunciation shows us that all the ordinary lives of the people of the world are blessed.'

———

The next morning I return to the Basilica. A pilgrimage from England is due to arrive. Before the coach appears, I wander round the various souvenir shops clustered around the precincts of the Basilica, looking to see what is on offer. They all sell the same things: small olive wood statues of Mary holding baby Jesus; cheap models of Mary and Joseph with baby Jesus in a crib in the classic Nativity scene; olive wood and plastic statues of Our Lady, her hands spread out in that famous humble pose. Jewish menorah candelabra and Islamic lanterns also fill the shelves. Israeli and Palestinian flags of all sizes are on offer too. Bookmarks, postcards and posters of Pope Francis sell particularly well, I am told. But there is not one annunciation scene anywhere. No angel Gabriel. No sculptural encounter between Mary and the angel of any kind in any of the shops. Not even a postcard. 'We have never been asked for that,' one shop owner tells me. Another says they used to stock a small wooden sculpture of the angel Gabriel and Mary with a dove in between but nobody would buy them.

'Why not?' I ask.

'I don't know,' he says. 'They want to see the baby. How do you say? The mother becoming a mother is too difficult. Many, I feel, do not understand the Annunciation.'

But that's why they are here, I say.

'I know, I know. It is strange, very strange,' he replies, shaking his head.

How much resonance, I wonder, does the story of the Annunciation have for people visiting the shrines? I go to a nearby cafe and ask a group of Spanish tourists that very question. The answers are varied. One tells me it is the beginning of the greatest story ever told. Another is amused that there is more than one location in the city that marks the place where it happened. One young woman says Nazareth is the highlight of her trip to the Holy Land. 'We are not going to Jerusalem and Bethlehem now. We have changed our plans. It is too dangerous there. So this is more important now. Nazareth is now more special but that is good, yes, because it is the very start of Jesus.'

I ask two guides who have just arrived with their coach tours why the pilgrimages and tourist trips do not visit the newly opened Mary of Nazareth International Centre.

'Time,' both of them reply simultaneously.

'We are only in Nazareth for one hour,' one of them tells me. 'The tourists only visit the Basilica and maybe the souvenir shops. They do not even go to the well or to the St Gabriel church. We have one day in Galilee and there is no time.'

The other, an experienced guide of twenty years standing, says she visited the Centre a few weeks ago.

'It's very good. Very professional and interesting. Very helpful. But the tour is very long. It takes more than an hour to watch the films. It is a good education about Mary but there is not enough time.'

They both observe that there has been a serious drop in the number of pilgrims coming to Nazareth this year.

'It's affecting the whole of the Holy Land,' one says. 'People are scared to come here. The Americans are cancelling trips every day. Now, the events in Jerusalem have made it much worse. What are we to do? Look at Nazareth. It is peaceful and a lovely place to visit. But people won't come. It is a tragedy.'

By midday, the Diocese of Westminster's annual pilgrimage to the Holy Land has arrived in Nazareth. This year 120 people are taking part. It is particularly special this time because the Archbishop of Westminster, Cardinal Vincent Nichols, is leading the group. Yesterday, on the opening day of their weeklong pilgrimage, they took a boat trip on the Sea of Galilee. Today, after stopping in Nazareth to celebrate Mass and enjoy a plentiful lunch, they are moving on to Mount Tabor, the traditional site of the Transfiguration, and then ending at Cana, the place where, according to John's Gospel, Jesus performed his first miracle, changing water into wine at a wedding reception.

The party makes its way to the upper church for Mass. The gospel reading, aptly, is Luke's story of the Annunciation. In the homily, given by Fr John Farrell OP, the Incarnation is described as 'the awesome mystery, more awesome than creation itself.' At twelve o'clock, the bells of the Basilica ring. The pilgrims make their way down to the grotto where they kneel whilst Cardinal Vincent recites the Creed. Then they have a quiet moment to reflect as they peer through the iron grille towards the small altar before heading outside.

Cardinal Vincent, dressed in a richly decorated gold and blue chasuble and scarlet zucchetto (or skullcap) goes inside the cave and kneels before the altar, praying in silence. He stays there for ten minutes seemingly in deep contemplation. Although he has visited Nazareth six times before, he has never been inside the grotto itself.

When he gets up, he heads to the sacristy to change before joining me on a seat I have placed in front of the grotto. We are all alone. I ask him how it felt to be inside the grotto for the first time.

'It was overwhelming, actually,' he replies. 'So immensely precious to be at the place where it all began. To think that this is the place chosen by God where his plan of salvation would begin. Of all the possible ways that God could show his love for this world – and we have to start with the view that this is God's created world and, therefore, is profoundly good but today is in a mess – of all the places he could choose, he chose here in such a humble and obscure way of literally planting a seed of new life and choosing a humble dwelling now surrounded by all this majesty. In there, I think I just got a profound sense of the bare simplicity of God's choice, which is so utterly confusing to us because we want to think of God as majestic, all powerful, eternal and infinite and able to do all things. But God's choice was to do it in this way and it never ceases to baffle me.'

I remind him of our previous meeting in Archbishop's House in Westminster, when he compared the photograph of the imminent execution of Steven Sotloff by Jihadi John with the composition of the annunciation scene in François Lemoyne's painting. Has being in the grotto made him think differently about Luke's annunciation story?

188. Cardinal Vincent Nichols prays inside the grotto, Basilica of the Annunciation, Nazareth

'Well, I think our earlier conversation was one which reflects our everyday experience of being torn between our desires and hopes and instincts for goodness and the realities of brutality and corruption. The brutality and corruption that we were talking about was on a very grand scale. It was the corruption of some of the most noble ideals and brutality of the most horrendous and blatant sort. That conversation was caught in the midst of the dilemma between good and evil. But here, I'm just overwhelmed by the sense of the immense, delicate, deferential goodness of God. It is just overwhelming.'

He is clearly emotional and wipes away a tear.

'What we see outside day by day in the streets is so mixed up in a maelstrom of good and bad,' he continues. 'But right here, God picks such an utterly simple way. Speaking here is what I'd want to reflect on and ponder and offer. Here everything about the potential for goodness in human nature, in our world, is affirmed, and it is affirmed by the gracious, all powerful God, but he affirms it in a way that deeply respects the freedom he has given us and deeply respects the fabric of humanity through which we live our bodies and our spirits and our relationships. He respects all of those things and builds from the tiniest seed into what is a promise of future glory for creation and for every single human being if we are open enough to receive it.'

I wonder what he was praying for when inside the grotto.

'There were two things really,' he says. 'One was probably a bit selfish because it was about myself. Just how, day by day, step by step, I might be more simply, whatever God wants me to be, an instrument in a sense. My experience, as you get older, is that it gets more difficult. Life becomes more complicated. I begin to understand, I think more deeply, the discrepancies and dilemmas that are deep inside. It's quite difficult to find that pure simplicity of heart that we are asked to try and allow the Lord to create within us. So there was that. And then there were also prayers for the peace of this land, especially in the context of the recent face of violence and that face of the opposite pathway to solutions. Right here, this is the pathway of peace and literal disarmament and simplicity. What we have seen most recently is the work of those who believe that what they hold to be good will be provoked into existence by frightful violence. They announce a different kingdom, a different way of the world, one that I abhor, that I would want to shun, and I think every person of good instinct would say is corrupt, violent and wrong. So I prayed about this simple seed of goodness that God has given in creation and gives again at the Annunciation in an even more concentrated form eventually in the form of a single man who we see absorbing into himself all the anger, corruption and sinfulness in the world and offering it back to the Father so it can be transformed in his Resurrection. And that begins right here and, therefore, that formed my second prayer.'

Did he believe that the Annunciation happened right there in the grotto?

'I don't see why not,' he replies. He points to the words engraved on the altar in the cave: 'Here the Word was made flesh.'

'To me, this place is overwhelming,' he says. 'The sense of the reality of what happened is palpable. You can almost touch it. Now whether it was here or a hundred yards down the road doesn't really matter. This is Nazareth. This is the place by tradition. This is the spot and that's good enough for me.'

I show him the photograph of Steven Sotloff, then one of Lemoyne's *The Annunciation*. I tell him that since we met, two more executions by Jihadi John have taken place.

'And yes, in recent days those deaths in the synagogue in Jerusalem as well. That is wrong. That is evil. Evil is in the world. It takes possession of men's hearts. It's in every heart. It's never that far away.' He points to Jihadi John. 'These executions are particular graphic annunciations of the power and presence of evil in our world.'

He takes hold of the Lemoyne picture and holds it in the air.

'But this is antithesis. This is the light. In a wonderful way the painting as it opens up to the light of heaven reflects the very architecture of this place around us. There's a kind of circle of heavenly light which is above us at this very moment.'

He points upwards to the oculus from where light streams down to the lower church.

'One subtle difference between these two images is that the knife is held more or less towards us and it's held as a warning. But here the arm of the angel and his finger is asking us to raise our minds and hearts in hope and joy and not tremble in fear at the threat of the blackness of this figure and the evil he intends. So that would be the contrast that you see in this place. From this tiny little cave, the whole of the architecture of the church raises our minds and hearts in exact configuration with the summons of the angel in Lemoyne's painting.'

As he finishes speaking, the sound of an organ fills the whole of the Basilica of the Annunciation. We look at each other. The Cardinal raises his eyebrows, nods his head and smiles. As he gets up to go, he takes out his mobile phone and walks towards the grotto to take a photo. He checks the image and again nods his head and smiles.

'One of the greatest moments of my life,' he says.

CHAPTER 43

MEMORABLE IMAGES FROM AROUND THE WORLD

Looking at images of Mary from around the world in the courtyard of the Basilica reminds me that most of the art of the Annunciation I have seen over the past two years has been western European in character.

The earliest image of the Annunciation in the Catacomb of Priscilla in Rome has her clothed in the Roman fashion of the third century. Most of the great medieval and Renaissance paintings have her dressed in western European styled robes, with western European features and porcelain skin, and the angel Gabriel is nearly always presented in classical Renaissance style.

But of course, the annunciation story has spread all over the world and there are distinctive artistic interpretations of the encounter on every continent. Here are some examples from the late twentieth and early twenty-first centuries that have made an impact on me.

Amy Bright Unfried is an American sculptor based in Jackson Hole, Wyoming. Brought up in Massachusetts, she studied Economics with Art History at Wellesley and Yale University before setting out on a successful professional career in economics and finance, primarily as an investment banker.

She describes herself as a mother of three grown up children, and a cradle Episcopalian who, in mid-life, felt a calling to be a sculptor. 'I felt I had to do it,' she says about embarking on a second career.

After travelling with her husband to Rome where she visited the Vatican Museums, and then going on a trip to Spain and seeing images of the Annunciation everywhere she looked, she decided to create her own distinct interpretation of the encounter. She says she wanted to tell the story in a new way.

Over a period of six months, in 2008, she created a stunning bronze in which 'angel Gabriel, like a flame, brings the Spirit to the kneeling Mary, combining abstract and realism in a single piece.'

The sculpture is twenty-two inches high and seventeen inches wide. From the original model a limited edition of nine bronze casts have been made. She says she likes to work in bronze for its endurance, beauty and extraordinary tensile strength.

'I'm very happy with the piece. It's one of the best pieces I've done,' she tells me. 'I wanted to find a fresh and original approach. Most of the time, they're on the same level. I wanted to create a swooping line from several angles with the angel above.'

She noted that most annunciation works create 'a gap of tension' between the two figures but in her version she has joined them together in a delicate balancing act.

'Technically, I couldn't have the Spirit floating. There's as little contact as possible so they touch at the fingertips,' she tells me. 'The part of the Spirit that's most clear is

189. Amy Bright Unfried *Annunciation*, 2008. © Amy Bright Unfried

the hand, then there's a head and then there's a flame. Mary gestures and is submissive to the Spirit but I didn't want her head to be down. She has eye contact but has a gesture of humility.'

The movement of the angel is dramatic and the different shades of patina create a sense of billowing flames. Mary's long hair is braided but her dress style is unspecific. 'I didn't want a particular period of history,' she emphasizes. The use of bronze makes this piece stand out from its western European counterparts.

The title of the piece is *Annunciation*, but she also gave it a subtitle: 'Inspiration'.

'It's an alternative view. If they're not into Bible stories, then they may be able to relate to it more as a story about inspiration,' she says.

When I ask what the Annunciation means for her, she replies, 'It's part of my history.'

Does she see it as fact or metaphor?

'I recently read a book by John Shelby Spong called *Born of a Woman* about the life of Jesus. I'm now inclined not to take the story literally but as a way of showing the greatness of Jesus and how special he was.'

The sculpture is a fantastic, highly distinctive piece, with an extraordinary sense of movement.

The late Andy Warhol famously once said, 'I'm afraid that if you look at a thing long enough, it loses all meaning.' Well this Annunciation journey seems to be having the opposite effect on me.

The leading pop artist of his generation, Warhol was born Andrew Warhola in 1928, the son of Slovak immigrants, who lived in the fervently Catholic Ruska Dolina district of Pittsburgh, Pennsylvania. He was brought up in a strong religious household, filled with the rituals and icons of the Ruthenian Byzantine Catholic Church.

He began his career as a successful commercial illustrator and went on to become one of the most prominent, prolific and influential artists of the twentieth century, known for his striking paintings, his brilliantly coloured silk screen prints, and his obsession with consumerism, excess and the cult of celebrity, which he believed were at the heart of modern day American life. His pop art images of contemporary culture became icons of their time.

Warhol lived with his devout mother, Julia, for the first forty years of his life and they are said to have prayed together at home regularly. Warhol attended Mass frequently at his local church in Manhattan right up to his death in 1987, aged fifty-eight. He always kept a crucifix and his well-worn prayer book by his bed. In April 1980, he attended Pope John Paul II's weekly audience in St Peter's Square and had the chance to shake hands and talk for a while with the Pope.

Andy Warhol was complex, enigmatic and full of contradictions. At his memorial service at St Patrick's Cathedral in New York City in April 1987, art historian and close friend, John Richardson, delivered a telling eulogy:

> Besides celebrating Andy Warhol as the quintessential artist of his time and place – the artist who held the most revealing mirror up to his generation – I'd like to recall a side of his character that he hid from all but his closest friends: his spiritual side. Those of you who knew him in circumstances that were the antithesis of spiritual may be surprised that such a side existed. But exist it did, and it's the key to the artist's psyche…
>
> The knowledge of this secret piety inevitably changes our perception of an artist who fooled the world into believing that his only obsessions were money, fame, glamour and that he was cool to the point of callousness. Never take Andy at face value. The callous observer was in fact a recording angel.

Each member of the congregation was given a prayer card with an image of Our Lady of Korsun on one side and a prayer on the other, including the words: 'Sweet Heart of Mary, be my salvation! Mary of Perpetual help, pray for us.'

In the final three years before his death, Warhol created a number of paintings, drawings and screen prints under the series title *Details of Renaissance Paintings,* all influenced by his admiration for the great Renaissance artists. In 1984, he created a portfolio of four differently coloured screen prints entitled, *Leonardo da Vinci, The Annunciation 1472.*

190. Andy Warhol *Leonardo da Vinci The Annunciation 1472,* 1984. © 2017 The Andy Warhol Foundation for the Visual Arts, Inc/Artist Rights Society (ARS) New York and DACS London

Warhol's image focuses on the central part of Leonardo's fifteenth-century painting *The Annunciation,* displayed in the Uffizi Gallery in Florence. Warhol has replaced the soft colours of the original picture with his trademark bright, garish pop art palette. He cropped the image, in order to concentrate solely on the hands of the angel Gabriel and Mary. On the left, we see Gabriel's index and middle fingers pointing towards Mary's hand, which rests on a lectern next to her book. In the background we see the cypress trees and mountain scene that feature in the original Leonardo painting.

Warhol believed there was no distinction between fine art and the commercial art used in books, magazines and on advertising boards. He once said sarcastically, 'An artist is somebody who produces things that people don't need to have.' However, his Annunciation work, which I first saw in a gallery in Georgetown, Washington DC, is a powerful example of how he references a previously well-known image and creates a new and highly original interpretation. By cropping the original image so severely, he brilliantly manages to capture the essence of the annunciation story – communication, conversation, and acceptance.

He produced four limited editions of his Annunciation screen print design, each using different colour combinations. The pencil signed prints, 32″ x 44″ in dimension, now sell for more than $20,000 apiece.

The contemporary American painter Alfonse Borysewicz's vocation, he says, is 'to find new ways to express an ancient faith.' He combines the visual language of abstraction with collage and figurative elements to craft contemporary religious paintings.

When we talk, his latest work is due to be exhibited in the Dadian Gallery at the prestigious Henry Luce III Centre for the Arts and Religion in Washington DC.

'In his hands, ordinary nests, honeycombs and pregnant mothers are transformed into poetic images of wonder,' writes the exhibition curator, Kiki McGrath. Borysewicz uses traditional and found materials on his canvases – oil paint, gold leaf, honeycombs, sheet music, plastic and cardboard. 'What authenticates my work is that undertow of mystery – the painting itself,' he says. 'The paintings are rooted in the gift of creation and hold the tension between the already and not yet.' The exhibition is called *Beginning Comes Last*, and features a new work of the same title that is rooted in the annunciation story.

Alfonse Borysewicz was born in 1957 and raised in Detroit. By his early twenties, he had completed four years of seminary training during which he was encouraged to travel to Jerusalem and Rome. Soon after, he opted out with a year of training still to complete. The trip, he says, made him realize, 'they'd closed down my future.' He studied theology before going to the Museum School of Fine Arts in Boston and then receiving a Guggenheim Fellowship in painting. For the past thirty years, he has lived in Brooklyn, New York. One American arts magazine recently described him as 'America's greatest living Catholic painter'. However, the reality is that he has fallen out of favour with many New York galleries because his work is now so focused on religious art.

He has created at least five different Annunciation works in recent years, of which *Beginning Comes Last* is his latest. It is a semi-abstract piece using oil and wax on linen, together with gold leaf. He has worked on it, on and off, for the past eight years. It is quite a small piece, 24″ x 21″ in size, and features Mary without a face and the outline of a foetus that appears lit from within.

What is it about the annunciation story that motivates him to paint so many versions? I wonder.

'I'm obsessed with the beginning of the story,' he replies. 'Yes, I think Christmas is a part of the story but I think the Annunciation is way more important.'

He explains how his paintings 'spin off' twelfth and thirteenth-century icons: 'I'm intrigued how they have the Christ child visible under the garment. The promise of what's to come. It's an Annunciation because the child is not yet quite visible. I'm hiding the image of the child but its silhouette is there. I love icon paintings but I'm also sometimes something of an iconoclast. Part of me wants to censor these Marian images because I do so many of them, but they seem to come back.'

The title of the work, *Beginnings Comes Last*, came to him when he was teaching a New Testament class. He heard a philosophy student describe the approach of learning about contemporary philosophers such as Martin Heidegger, as like a crab walking backwards.

'We start from the Resurrection and we work our way back,' he tells me. 'It's a wonderful mystery and that title stuck with me from Heidegger. I think of the story [of Jesus] backwards. The beginning comes last. It is of the

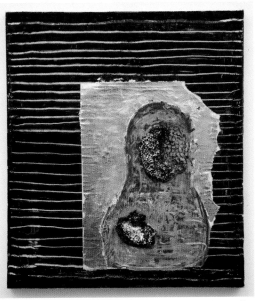

191. Alfonse Borysewicz *Beginning Comes Last*, 2016. © Alfonse Borysewicz

Annunciation. The image announces what happened first though we come at it much later in the life story of Christ – the womb being the first primal interiority of the Incarnation. By reflecting on what preceded us, we go forward – what is promised comes into better focus when we realize what initially happened. Of the Annunciation, as Pope Benedict wrote in his first encyclical, *Deus Caritas Est*: "a love story, between God and man/woman, was born".'

Borysewicz's semi-abstract image of Mary is magnetic, both mysterious and still. My eyes head straight to the golden light under her dress. For me, it is a very powerful image of the moment of the Incarnation.

'This work started with Mary with a sunflower image and then lots of other different images but the child figure kept appearing,' he recalls. 'I took a real honeycomb and collaged it into the painting. The lines of colour at the back are the revelation of Gabriel in a minimum abstract way.'

'My wife is Japanese,' he continues, 'and in Japan when you look at magazines you go the other way. Sometimes, I feel so many folk over-romanticize the beginning. We come to know a person and then, as much as we can, we walk backwards to know even more about them – well, that's what I do.'

He describes his approach to art as 'complex simplicity'. What does he mean?

'I think real genius is when you have to work through to where things become much more complex and then you arrive back at simplicity,' he says. He quotes Matisse as a fine example. 'I start simply, then keep re-working them and re-working them, and that's the complexity, and then I arrive back at this very simple silhouette image in the end.'

He says his art is there to express his own interiority.

'My interiority is very much shaped by my faith, perhaps faith itself. My art is a vocation. In one sense it's all intuitive but there's a cathedral within me that directs my hand and my heart.'

I ask what Luke's story of the Annunciation means for him?

'A seed was planted of love,' he responds. 'A cosmic wave and we are still at the beginning of it. The Church is still very young. It's a love story and that's the beginning of it.'

Does he see it as fact or metaphor?

'I probably see it as both,' he replies. 'I'm ok holding the line between an obsession with certainty and the mystery of it all. I think it happened but the logistics of it all, I don't know. I don't really care. I just feel it in my own Christian life.'

I tell him Bishop Philip Egan's quote of it being 'the most important event in human history'.

'I would agree. It's a cosmic change in our relationship with God and our neighbour. It's like the earth found a heart and it started to beat. The kingdom of God is happening right now. Life is not a dress rehearsal. This is it. Right now.'

———

Fifty-two-year-old Paulo Medina lives in Chihuahua, Mexico. He was born the fourth of five children to devout Roman Catholic parents who lived in the nearby agricultural centre of Delicias in the Conchos River Valley. As a child, he loved to paint and had hopes of becoming either a professional artist or an architect. But a car accident that killed his father and badly injured his elder brother changed his life.

'That time was a dramatic moment. I was born again and felt a real calling at that moment,' he tells me when we link up in vision via the Internet.

He studied English in California, then commercial art, before entering a seminary. A Bishop told him that his desire to be both an artist and a priest were not contradictory. Today, Fr Paulo is a successful artist and a clergyman of twenty-five years standing. He paints both figuratively and in abstract and his works sell for several thousand dollars. Although not exclusively a religious painter, it is his biblically influenced works that have been most acclaimed.

'Artistic experience, as a spectator, and then, more directly, as an artist, has meant the possibility of transcending and reaching certain spaces that are intangible, but lived daily,' he has said about his work. 'As a creator, to be in front of a blank canvas or a digital image to be manipulated, is to be faced with a challenge: that of translating to the language of forms, textures and colours something that has not yet been conceptualized, but that exists somewhere and that I desire to capture, expressing it through those materials and tools at my disposal. Thereby, it becomes a kind of game, in which time disappears and one enters into communion with the aesthetic experience with its infinity of moments, which go from pain to ecstasy. Self-taught experimentation in the field of art has been, for me, one of the great pleasures of life.'

During 2006, in Chihuahua, he created a large, striking abstract work in acrylic entitled *Annunciation*.

'Sometimes I paint an abstract that, while I'm doing it, I don't know its meaning,' he tells me. 'Later, reading or praying or what else, I have a gaze about what the painting means. I remember I'd created a painting about the Assumption and wanted to continue exploring something sacred around the Virgin Mary.'

Paulo Medina and I are talking on Skype so I can see that he has short black hair and wears thick black-rimmed spectacles. He is dressed casually in a blue jumper with an open neck shirt and T-shirt underneath. I notice that the walls of the room are filled with paintings, icons and crucifixes. He speaks good English with a heavy Mexican accent.

'I remember *Annunciation* was a difficult painting. In the beginning, I was trying to get close to a portrait of Mary but it was not coming. So I freed myself to paint what was then in my head. I turned it upside down. If you turn the painting around [180 degrees] you'll see there is a kind of outline portrait of her but I renounced that and turned it around. I then followed my intuition. I felt the colours and the texture. The work helped me to meditate and transcend. But anyone can interpret it as they want. I like that.'

I tell him that when I first saw the painting, I noticed immediately the small red cross in the middle and wondered if he was trying to show what was to come.

'That's a very good interpretation,' he responds enthusiastically. 'You discovered that and now it helps me to understand the painting. The cross

192. Paulo Medina *Annunciation*, 2006.
© Paulo Medina

you see, for me, is now an element that I won't forget.'

I comment how, for me, the abstract image depicts the very moment of the conception – if you like, the 'explosion' of the Incarnation.

'Exactly!' he says. 'That's what I feel about this painting.'

The moment the world turns upside down, I say.

He laughs and agrees enthusiastically.

'It's what is happening inside the womb at that time, and that and the colours made me give it the title. Often I don't give my pictures a title. But here, I thought, yes. It's both the biological moment and the spiritual, theological moment.'

What does Luke's annunciation story mean for him?

'The beginning of Christianity. The beginning of everything. Without that moment, there is no Incarnation.'

I tell him about Philip Egan's description of it as 'the most important event in human history'.

'I agree. I agree. Without conception and Incarnation, there is no crucifixion and no death.'

Does he think Luke's narrative of Mary encountering the angel is a description of what actually happened?

'I don't know how it happened,' he responds. 'It's a description but historically we don't know the detail. I believe there was an angel there – Gabriel as a messenger of some kind. A light or whatever.'

I tell him that I have seen many paintings of Mary and the angel Gabriel entitled *The Annunciation*, but perhaps his abstract work is, in a sense, the most accurate picture of them all.

'As a priest, it's not my way to sell paintings to make a living. It's not my life to create publicity,' he tells me. 'My paintings take their own way but sometimes I am very surprised how they come back to me many years later. I painted this Annunciation and then it was sold. If you hadn't contacted me, it would not be in my mind. But now it is. I like the way the painting has opened my own mind again to the Annunciation. That's because there is something in there. It's like something that has come unexpectedly. The painting has made its way to you. I'm surprised but now the painting has made its way to me again and has even more meaning for me, having spoken with you. When something like this happens, it confirms what I am doing.'

In the late 1940s, the Society of African Missions set up a unique project in south-western Nigeria. This involved an Irish Roman Catholic missionary, Fr Kevin Carroll, establishing the Oye-Ekiti workshop project in rural Yorubaland. The goal was to encourage local Yoruba artists to create work that would be a hybrid of their traditional craftsmanship and the Christian message. The result would be images with a greater local relevance and resonance than the western European styled images previously used by the missionaries.

Fr Carroll, a fluent Yoruba speaker, spent more than thirty-five years in the area and was convinced the project would produce work that would have greater appeal to the Yoruba speaking community. This fusion of Yoruban art and the Christian message, a highly controversial idea at the time, was first called 'adaptation' and later became known as 'inculturalisation'.

Yoruba artists traditionally focus on woodcarving, weaving, embroidery, beading and pottery. The main activity in the Oye workshop concentrated on wood carving using the local Opin style of the Ekiti region. Leading carvers such as George Bandele Areogun from Osi-Ilorin and Lamidi Olonade Fakeye joined the project. The result was a new style rooted in the traditions of the local Ifa religion but which focused on images from the Christian story. The workshop lasted seven years between 1947 and 1954 before it closed due to lack of funding. It received a mixed reception amongst Roman Catholic leaders and missionaries in Nigeria, some praising the move whilst others vehemently criticizing the initiative as a form of 'paganism'.

193. George Bandele *The Virgin Mary*, 1950, SMA African Art Museum, Tenafly, New Jersey © SMA African Art Museum, Tenafly, New Jersey

However, Carroll continued to work with the wood carvers after the project closed until his death in 1993. Indeed, by the end of the century, both George Bandele and Lamidi Fakeye had become internationally recognized for their craftsmanship.

In 1950, Bandele created a wood carving of the Virgin Mary, depicting her as a young Yoruban girl with African features and platted hair. He copied the Western tradition by putting her in a blue dress and white headscarf, but her clothing was of a Yoruban style. Mary opens her hands wide as she hears the message. She crushes a snake with her bare feet, symbolizing her status as the new Eve.

In 1964, fifty-six-year-old Bandele was commissioned by Fr Carroll to carve four large static wooden door panels for the African Art Museum of the Society of African Missions in Tenafly, New Jersey.

The top frieze of one of the four panels depicts an annunciation scene. Rather than holding a lily, the angel Gabriel extends a kola branch from a tree indigenous to Yorubaland, whilst Mary is shown as a young Yoruban girl dressed in traditional clothing with two chickens at her feet, engaged in the daily routine of pounding yams in a mortar.

At the turn of the millennium, Dr Nicholas Bridger, a teacher in World History and Art History at a secondary school in California, began investigating the history and impact of the Oye-Ekiti workshop initiative. In 2012 he published a book, *Africanizing Christian Art: Kevin Carroll & Yoruba Christian Art in Nigeria,* and curated an associated exhibition at the African Art Museum of the Society of African Missions Fathers, based at Tenafly in New Jersey. He spent almost a decade carrying out archival and field research in Nigeria, Ireland and the Vatican. 'In a way, it was a pilgrimage like yours,' the seventy-three-year-old tells me on the phone from his home in San Jose.

In 2007, two years before Lamidi's death, Nick Bridger commissioned Lamidi to carve an annunciation scene, to present to his wife, a devout Catholic. It was to be one of Lamidi's final Yoruba Christian art images and is now displayed in Nick Bridger's Californian home. Although Lamidi had converted to Islam as a teenager, he developed his outstanding carving skills creating Christian images in the Oye-Ekiti workshops. 'He didn't realise the Annunciation was in the Qu'ran as well,' he tells me. 'I just love it. Mary's not spinning the veil like in all those Renaissance paintings. She's pounding yam which is what they all eat in Nigeria. I thought it was such a great adaptation.' As we end our conversation, he emphasizes to me how there was a rapid expansion

194. Lamidi Olonade Fakeye *The Annunciation*, 2007,
© Dr Nicholas Bridger

of Christianity in Africa during the twentieth century from 9 million in 1900 to more than 500 million at the end of the century. 'The Oye-Ekiti workshop played its part in heralding this huge demographic shift,' he says.

Three annunciation images, not set in Nazareth, nor in the palatial surroundings of a Tuscan house or a Flanders castle, but in a simple, rural hamlet in Yorubaland in West Africa.

In the early 1970s in a higher part of west Africa, Mafa Christians living in northern Cameroon wanted to see pictures of the gospel stories incorporating their own culture. The Vie de Jesus Mafa project began with the support of French Catholic missionaries, led by François Vidil. As the villagers acted out Bible stories, photographs were taken and then an unnamed French artist painted the scenes, creating seventy-three pictures that showed stories from John the Baptist's birth through to the resurrection of Jesus.

Around a hundred thousand people form the Mafa ethnic group in Cameroon, a community primarily of corn farmers, scattered over the central part of the northern

Mandaras region. The Vie de Jesus Mafa initiative portrayed Jesus as a local Mafa and the paintings were used as a resource to help the people understand the New Testament in a way that directly connected with their own community.

As local church leaders, theologians and French missionaries used the paintings to evangelize the message of the gospel stories, the response from the minority Mafa Christian people was highly favourable as the images resonated with their own everyday experiences.

The knowledge of the initiative soon spread around Cameroon and other parts of west Africa, across the continent and beyond. In the past forty years, more than six million copies of the paintings have been distributed to more than eighty countries worldwide.

195. Vie de Jesus Mafa Project *The Annunciation*, 1970s, Cameroon

The third in the series is called *The Annunciation* and shows a black Mary cooking outside her simple mud and thatch home. It is daylight and there is no one else around. Food bowls lie on the ground as the meal cooks over the fire. The rest of the hamlet with its distinctive sare conical roofs can be seen in the background, and beyond the plateau are the Mokolo mountains. An angel, who looks like a local adult male, has arrived, dressed in a fawn cloth. Mary looks startled as she puts down her stirring stick to hear his message.

Once again, the Annunciation and Nazareth have been transferred to a west African setting, and in this painting, there is no sign of a luxurious blue mantle, a lily branch or a prie-dieu.

———

Thirty-one-year-old Evans Yegon was born and brought up in the rural Rift Valley county of Bomet in Kenya. His family background was farming but his father worked in Nairobi so the family moved there when he was twelve. He always wanted to be an artist. At school, he remembers sketching all the time. He studied Fine Art at the Buruburu Institute of Fine Art and has been a professional artist for the last seven years. Known by the pseudonym Yegonizer, he describes his style as 'vibrantism' and his work has been exhibited in the Nairobi National Museum.

In 2013, he painted a vivid picture of the Annunciation in oil. It shows Mary falling backwards as the winged angel arrives in blazing light. Jonathan Chapman, the head of the BBC bureau in Nairobi, sent me a copy of the image when he heard about my project.

'I wanted to show Mary blushing,' Yegonizer tells me from his Nairobi home as we link up via the Internet. 'Angel Gabriel has come and said something funny as well as saying the words used in Luke. I think there were more words said than those used in the Gospel story. There was some humour. I tried to make it homely. The earthenware jars and the curtain opening up the partition to the room. I like vibrant colours. I like to exaggerate the colours.'

196. Evans Yegon (Yegonizer) *The Annunciation* 2013 © Evans Yegon

I can see the Annunciation painting displayed on the wall behind him. I observe that he doesn't use Kenyan faces in his religious work.

'In the Bible, there was only one black man,' he laughs. He says he wanted to depict Mary authentically as a Palestinian woman rather than as a Kenyan or a European. 'If I paint you, I'd use a lot of yellow but for Mary or Jesus, I use a lot of red and white.'

Forty per cent of his work is religious art but it does not sell. He makes his living painting other subjects at his studio in the GoDown Arts Centre in the city. His prices range from 400 to 1,000 dollars. But he says he is determined to paint the life of Jesus in a series of pictures from the Annunciation to the Resurrection, 'as a way of spreading the gospel and keeping the message of Jesus out there.'

He turns around to look at his painting.

'People don't like to buy things of religious subjects because it is a big statement about Jesus and who they are,' he says. 'People like neutral subjects. It's a secular world and people want to be neutral. They don't want to hang something that's explicit about their religion. That's a shame. People are more secular, more westernized. Everything is getting eroded. It's very sad. But I'm hoping my religious canvases will last for a long time. I know one day someone will have a connection with this Annunciation and want to exhibit it.'

Yegonizer wears a loose-fitting, striped open-neck shirt and has short hair and brilliant white teeth. He has a happy disposition and smiles regularly.

A Presbyterian, he says he goes to church every Sunday and prays every day. Last year, he married his childhood sweetheart, Anne, whom he met at Sunday school. They grew up together but it was only a few months ago that he managed to save up enough money for their wedding.

Would it help sell more of his religious art if he used Kenyan faces? I ask.

'I'm not sure really,' he responds. 'There was a painting of Jesus chasing the people out of the Temple and they were all Kenyan faces but that painting is still at the college. It never sold. I don't think it would make any difference.'

Does he see the annunciation story as fact or metaphor?

'I definitely believe it actually happened,' he replies. 'I believe the story. I'm sure of it.'

Does he think you have to believe the detail of the annunciation story to be a Christian?

'I think you have to,' he says. 'Jesus is the Son of God. He didn't come from a man.'

What about the statement that the Annunciation is the most important event in human history?

'I agree to that,' he says. 'It's where Jesus starts his life but it has to be with the Crucifixion and the Resurrection too. They all have to be together. The Annunciation and the Resurrection.'

As I bid him farewell, he offers a final thought.

'I may not be able to buy land or cars but I'm happy. I feel satisfaction with my religious paintings and helping to spread the gospel.'

In 2002, I travelled to Jakarta, the Indonesian capital, on business. Although the country has the world's largest Muslim population, 20 per cent of Indonesians – fifty million people – are Christian. In the capital, only 11 per cent of the population is Christian, two thirds being Protestant and one third Catholic.

I have only just remembered that I had an annunciation 'experience' after I visited Jakarta Cathedral – Gereja Santa Perawan Maria Diangkat Ke Surga – the Cathedral Church of Our Lady of the Assumption. Built in 1901 in a neo-Gothic style, close to Merdeka Square, it is dwarfed by the nearby Istiqlal Mosque, the largest in south-east Asia. As I left the Cathedral, I noticed a local man selling handicrafts and spontaneously

197. Wood carving of 'an annunciation scene', 2002, Jakarta, Indonesia

decided to buy a carving that caught my eye. When I returned to the hotel and studied it closer, I noticed the word 'annunciation' written on the back in black ink.

I don't know if it is an authentic Indonesian carving of the biblical encounter but it looks as though it might be. The angel on the left wears a feathered headdress and confronts the woman who is kneeling and raising her right hand. She wears similar headgear, and a long skirt and looks rather regal. The figures are positioned unusually close together. Flowers surround them on a raised circular relief.

For the past fifteen years, it has been displayed on a wall in my home. But until now, I had completely forgotten that it is entitled *annunciation*.

My eldest son lives in Tokyo and while I was visiting him one summer, I became aware of the work of Sadao Watanabe.

Watanabe was born in Tokyo in 1913 and died in 1996. He was an internationally recognized print maker whose work was devoted to Christian stories from the Bible. What made him unique was the way he blended Christian themes with the Japanese Folk Art tradition, setting them within a familiar Japanese environment. By the end of his life he was Japan's foremost Christian artist, although that did not mean he was well known in his own country.

Buddhism and Shinto are the primary religions in Japan. Portuguese missionaries landed on Kyushu Island in southern Japan in 1543 and although they had some initial success in spreading Christianity, the followers became heavily persecuted and for a time the religion was banned. Today, fewer than one per cent of the population belongs to a Christian denomination.

Watanabe was influenced by his schoolteacher, became a devout Christian and was baptized in 1930, aged seventeen. As a youngster, he suffered from tuberculosis and vowed that if he recovered, he would study the Bible and spread the Christian message through art. An exceptionally shy man, he became an apprentice in a factory in Okinawa where he learnt *katazume*, the traditional technique of stencil dying used on kimonos. He then learnt *kappazuri*, the technique of stencil painting, from his artistic mentor, Serizawa Keisuke.

He applied this learning to his art, which focused on stencil prints of biblical scenes made in the 'mingei' Japanese folk art tradition – the handcrafted art of ordinary people described as 'the beauty in crafts of everyday life'. Watanabe was concerned that the biblical paintings and pictures that he saw in Japan all had a western European flavour. 'My task is to stand within the artistic tradition of Japan,' he said. 'Theology will not take deep root in Japanese soil if it is merely an import.' He dedicated his life to Christian stencil work and he was creating designs right up until his death, aged eighty-two. 'I owe my life to Christ and the gospel,' he once said. 'My way of expressing my gratitude is to witness my faith through the medium of biblical scenes.' Every one of the stencil prints that he created was unique because the colours were hand painted using natural pigments that were bound on the paper using soya bean milk.

I am on the thirty-fifth floor of the Maraunouchi Building in central Tokyo close to the main Tokyo Railway Station, looking out to the Imperial Gardens and the sprawling city beyond. Junko Watanabe (unrelated) and Mrs Fujie Mase unroll three large screen prints and hold them up for me to view. All three are entitled *The Annunciation* and were created by Sadao Watanabe. The earliest, made in 1966, is one of a limited edition of fifty prints. The second, created in 1972, is Watanabe's most popular Annunciation. The third is from 1974. Throughout his prolific career, Watanabe created many versions of the Annunciation. There are others from 1965, 1990 and 1992.

198. Junko Watanabe and Fujie Mase hold up Sadao Watanabe's *The Annunciation*, 1966. By kind permission of Mrs Fujie Mase (art dealer), Tokyo

Mrs Mase is a Tokyo art dealer and collector and was a close friend of Sadao Watanabe. On his death in 1996, Watanabe's widow, Harue, gave all his remaining screen prints to Mrs Mase to sell. She has more than sixty prints, which are priced at around 2,000 dollars each. Most buyers are Japanese but she tells me Americans also like to purchase them.

Mrs Mase is a very small, elegant woman with short, well-coiffured hair. Today, she is wearing a white silk shirt and sharp black trousers. She speaks very little English and much of our stilted conversation takes place through her friend, Junko. She hands me a catalogue of Watanabe's complete works as she gingerly unfolds the last of the three prints made on thin, wrinkled paper called *momi-gami*. She takes away the protective tracing paper and holds up the print with Ms Watanabe on the other side. 'We must be very careful,' she says. 'Fragile, fragile.'

The first two Annunciation prints she retains on behalf of a private collector. The third is still to be sold. A special exhibition of Watanabe's prints is being held next year in a Tokyo gallery and she hopes it will find a buyer. Watanabe was more popular in the 1980s and 90s, she says, but since his death, he is less well known.

His work is held in the Library of the National Museum of Modern Art in Tokyo. It has also been displayed in the Vatican, the British Museum, Museum of Modern Art (MoMA) in New York, and even at The White House when President Lyndon B. Johnson was in office in the 1960s. However, Sadao Watanabe preferred his prints to be displayed in ordinary places.

'I would like to see them hanging where ordinary people gather because Jesus brought the gospel to the people,' he once said.

'He didn't have many reference books, nor a camera,' Mrs Mase says. 'He read the Bible intensely every day and drew from that understanding. He read it honestly. For him, it was so honest, so personal.'

As we gaze in admiration at the 1966 print of *The Annunciation*, 27" x 22" in dimension, I ask her what she sees. She explains that she looks at it as a beautiful piece of art, not religion. 'I am not Christian. The people who buy it come because it is great art much more than because of the Christian dimension,' she says.

––––––––––

At the very start of my journey, I had a conversation with Dr Ralph Townsend, the headmaster of Winchester College, during which he showed me *Trilogy of Masterworks,* a book from his native Australia that highlights three works by Australian artist Tom Thompson. He told me that he had secured one of these three paintings, entitled *Annunciation, with distant town,* for Sydney Grammar School.

The picture was painted in the late 1980s. Some twenty years earlier, in the late 1960s to early 1970s, Tom Thompson worked on another painting featured in the book called simply *Annunciation*. Both pictures depict the encounter between the angel Gabriel and Mary and are set in the Southern Tablelands of south-eastern Australia.

Tom Thompson was born in 1923 in Narrabri in New South Wales. As a child, he loved art. Between 1950 and 1951, he came to London and worked as a night watchman and general hand at the National Gallery. He enjoyed studying the paintings on display and would spend many an hour alone sketching and drawing. On his return to Australia, he set himself up as a painter and art teacher, working at the National Art School. Then he established his own studio in the small town of Braidwood in the Southern Tableland region, 120 miles south of Sydney.

At the time I make contact with him to talk about his two Annunciation works, he has just reached ninety years of age and lives in the beachside suburb of Narrabeen, north of Sydney. He tells me his creation, *Annunciation*, was influenced by the great masters such as Leonardo, Raphael and Rubens but he wanted to set his painting in the bush area of the Southern Tablelands, where sheep, cattle and forestry are at the heart of the local economy. Thompson was living in the country town of Braidwood, a small community of around a thousand people, at the time. So a classic Italian porch becomes a veranda and the overall setting is a dilapidated Federation style house set in the Australian countryside.

199. Tom Thompson *Annunciation*, late 1960s to early 1970. © Manly Art Gallery & Museum

He worked on the painting, using egg tempera and acrylic on a composition board, between 1966 and 1973. Today, the painting is part of the Manly Art Gallery and Museum's collection. In the foreground, two red-eyed doves perch on an ornamental frame, which has a sign tied onto it declaring, 'HAIL: THE LORD IS WITH THEE: BLESSED ART THOU AMONG WOMEN.' A yellow cloth tied to the sign matches the colour of the scarf worn by the crouching messenger. We see a clothes-horse on the left side of the veranda with blankets hanging from it. In the foreground is a tall gum tree and the town of Braidwood is visible in the background. A bright light shines between the messenger and Mary as she sits on a bench.

'My father was a Presbyterian parson. His father was too,' Tom Thompson tells me on the phone from his New South Wales home. 'In childhood I went along with it all. But I then was questioning a lot of the biblical references. I came to my own opinion.'

He says the reason he painted the picture was that he was motivated to question the way the conception of Jesus was written by Luke.

'Was it an angel?' he asked himself. 'There's no living form to an angel. It's an inspiration that comes into the mind. It's a fairy story. Things don't happen that way. Jesus was born as one of us. I think it was written like that to exalt his magnificence. If this is going to be an adventure for us, then Jesus could be born in Australia. It could happen here.'

He says the Annunciation is all about a new life coming into an old world and tells me that fertility is represented on the right side of the painting whereas on the left is simply geometry.

'I'm making it happen in my way, even though the original story is told in a different way,' he says.

A decade later and Tom Thompson created a second annunciation painting, *Annunciation, with distant town,* an acrylic painted on a coachwood panel. This is the painting that Ralph Townsend acquired for the Sydney Grammar School collection. Tom Thompson tells me that the space between the messenger and Mary became his highest priority.

200. Tom Thompson *Annunciation, with distant town,* 1980s. © Sydney Grammar School

'She's looking at something new. Mary doesn't see the angel,' he says. 'She's looking above him. She's looking at the bright light in front of her. We see this vision of an angel but she doesn't see it. The reality is something very different. I wanted to hint at that.'

Why did he do the second painting? I wonder.

'It's just another version. That's all.'

The angel crouches in front of Mary on the wooden floor of the veranda. Mary stops reading her book and straightens her back as she hears the voice. Braidwood can be seen in the background, behind the house, with the coastal Budawang mountain range beyond. Joseph's carpentry lies underneath the wooden floor of the veranda and a shovel and a pickaxe lean against a metal drum. The brickwork is partly painted white.

I ask him whether he sees the annunciation story as fact or metaphor?

'I reasoned my way that it shouldn't be a fairy story but that's what it is – a fairy story. It's an intentional fairy story to get across the message, to aggrandize it. Remember, the story was written a long time after Jesus was alive.'

What does the annunciation story mean for him today?

'It can't better the story of your birth or my birth,' he replies. 'Jesus could have been the son of a carpenter who then had an awakening. It's a story. That's all it is.'

I had sent him a print of the Lemoyne painting in the post. What does he think of it?

'It's a most charming illustration, especially in its way of presenting the emotional figuration of the Virgin Mary and the angel,' he responds. 'The design is novel in its creation and compositional excitement. But it's a rather romantic version of the subject.'

CHAPTER 44

THE DEPTH OF THE IMPACT

My journey is nearing its end. I return to the National Gallery for one last encounter. Sir Nicholas Penny, the Director of the National Gallery, is about to stand down after seven years in the post. Undoubtedly, his most famous acquisitions have been two Venetian Renaissance masterpieces by Titian. *Diana and Actaeon* was bought in 2009 at a cost of £50 million and, three years later, *Diana and Callisto* was purchased for a similar amount. Both pictures are shared with the National Galleries of Scotland. Although it did not generate anything like the same headlines, the loan of Lemoyne's *The Annunciation* from Winchester College in 2011, has made a significant contribution to the National Gallery's eighteenth-century collection of French paintings. In his final month in office, the man who sanctioned this loan has agreed to meet me.

A renowned scholar, curator and art historian, sixty-five-year-old Nick Penny was knighted a month ago for his outstanding service to the arts. A record six and a half million visitors came to the National Gallery last year, a staggering 50 per cent increase in a decade, half of whom are from overseas. Almost 500,000 schoolchildren now visit each year. The fact that entry is free has much to do with that explosion in numbers. The Gallery, with its collection of more than two and a half thousand works, has maintained its reputation under Nick Penny as one of the world's pre-eminent collections of European paintings.

We walk through the gallery towards Room 33 in silence.

Nobody else is around. He unlocks various doors as we make our way alone through the large display rooms on the first floor. Sadly, Dr Penny's tenure is ending with a bitter staff dispute unresolved. Today is the fiftieth day of strike action by gallery assistants in a campaign against privatizing their jobs. Two thirds of the rooms are closed to the public today including Room 33.

Recently, the room re-opened after a year of building work, which has seen both improved natural roof lighting and new spotlight designs. The strike, whilst sad and unwelcome, offers us the chance to have the room all to ourselves with no distractions. Dressed in a collar and tie but no jacket, he is a tall, gangly figure with grey-black hair and a serious, scholarly disposition. He recalls first seeing the painting five years ago when it was in storage in Battersea.

'It's always difficult to appreciate the merit of a painting in a warehouse,' he tells me. 'They're sometimes propped up on an easel, often they're not. The lighting is horrible and the circumstances are very, very different to the Gallery. So I always think, if a picture strikes me as being very good in those circumstances, it's a very good sign. I wasn't at all sure what I'd see. Immediately, I thought the painting was in pretty good condition and probably in its original frame. That interested me.

He continues, 'There is this concern that the picture originally was intended to have an arch top, which, I think, compositionally, would have been rather more beautiful than a rectangle. There are so many curving elements in the composition. It seems to me all that would have been enhanced by the curved top. I'm struck right now by the shadow that's created by the rectangular frame. Probably if we had more daylight than spotlight it would…', he pauses and looks up to the ceiling, wondering aloud if a skylight would improve matters, 'however, it looks pretty good here. It looks a lot better than it did in the warehouse, although I could tell then that it was a fine picture.'

He takes a few steps back, puts his hand on his chin and nods in approval.

'Humphrey Wine [Curator of French Seventeenth- and Eighteenth-Century Paintings at the National Gallery] was very keen that we should bring the picture to the Gallery. I think he'd seen it before and knew about it, so we were very well disposed towards it. Of course I, as Director, made a decision but I would have found it difficult to turn this down had the curator made a persuasive case for it. On the other hand, were the curator against it, say if it took too many other important paintings off the wall, then I'd have had to think about it.'

He walks slowly towards the canvas again as his eyes dart around. He doesn't look at me but only at the picture as he continues to speak.

'It's a very, very important painting. It adds a new dimension to our presentation of French paintings of this period because, as you see, there isn't a single religious painting in the room. I would have thought that was a very good thing because there are plenty of very good religious paintings in France during this period. It's a period we associate with *fête galante* and the whole rise of new genres of secular paintings but there are still altarpieces being executed there by leading artists like Boucher. And we didn't have a Lemoyne either. That was another important consideration. I don't know if a collection like this has to have a Lemoyne. There are other artists we have to have. I was keen to have a Lemoyne but, actually, I was much keener that we should have a great French religious painting of this period and what could be more appropriate than one that was commissioned.'

I suggest it must have been quite controversial to bring such an altarpiece to Winchester College in the 1720s.

'It would be exceedingly interesting to know the circumstances,' he responds. 'My suspicion would be that it was a Wykehamist taking a slightly unofficial initiative because that would account for the kind of miscalculation with regard to its reception – people think what could they want more than this marvellous gift – and, importantly, it may account for the relative absence of any papers. It's very unlikely…' He pauses a while before continuing his thoughts. 'It's got to have been commissioned. This is not a picture done on spec. And because of its proportions, someone had already got a space ready to put it in. There may well have been some miscalculations when you take into account the arched top. That does rather concern me. People don't paint altarpieces on spec. What can happen sometimes is someone makes a commission for a particular church or chapel or oratory and it falls through in some way. They don't inherit the castle or they don't pay you for it.'

Suddenly, he becomes rather animated and turns to me with his eyes shining.

'Yes, yes, that is a possible circumstance. That this is a commission that went wrong and then Lemoyne had the painting hanging on his hands and then someone took it off.'

I tell him there is a copy of the painting in reverse displayed in a chapel at St Sulpice in Paris and that Languet de Gergy, the parish priest at St Sulpice, commissioned Lemoyne to decorate the cupola of the Chapel of the Virgin Mary with a fresco of the Assumption several years after *L'Annunciation* was completed.

The more I have thought about it, the more I have wondered, did something happen in 1727 at St Sulpice or at another place where the painting may have been originally destined? Did the person who commissioned the painting have second thoughts? Was there a dispute over payment? Was there an argument about something else? After all, Lemoyne was notoriously difficult to deal with. Why does no paperwork exist recording its original commission, either in Winchester or amongst Lemoyne's own papers? The only record Winchester College has is a single line entry about its actual purchase. Why was there a gap of two years between the date of the completion of the painting and its arrival at Winchester College? Why does it have a rounded arch at the top yet has been placed in a rectangular gilt wood frame? It was such a rarity for any early eighteenth-century French altarpiece to come to Britain at that time. The leading Lemoyne expert, Jean-Luc Bordeaux, told me he thought Dr Burton had commissioned Lemoyne but I have a niggling feeling that suggests otherwise. Could the original have been destined for the Church of St Sulpice in Paris, where the copy is now displayed?

'To my mind, that would make a lot of sense,' Sir Nicholas Penny responds. 'Commissions do happen, then there's a confusion about the commission or a change of mind on the part of the patron or they run out of money. Artists have things hanging around. Travellers come and admire the studio. They think of buying a small picture and then suddenly think, 'Well, that's a wonderful painting and I can give it to my college,' without much thought about where he'll put it or maybe how they would treat it. That, to me, would be a very plausible scenario. If you have gone to the trouble of commissioning Lemoyne to do this, which I think would have been sufficiently exceptional for some biographer to have picked up, if you'd done that, you'd take a great deal of care to find out how well it would be received by the college and how well it would fit in. If none of those things were done, and the absence of evidence perhaps suggests they were not done, then that could be explained by being an impromptu and amazing purchase. How very interesting.'

He looks closely at Mary's face.

'I think the important thing here is the response of the Virgin – "Let it be done according to thy word." To me, that is what this painting illustrates. Once you accept that – and her previous surprise is indicated by the disarray of her cloak and perhaps by the disarray of the work in her basket, and the fact she seems to have sunk to her knees, that suggests the previous disturbance has happened – then this is her acceptance. The angel is a permanent feature in the whole of this. He can't say, "I've done my greeting bit so now I can wind down." The angel is a continuing signal of the divine will. The angel could be lifting off and saying, "The light of the Lord will fall upon you," which, indeed, it is doing. I don't think it's a conflation of the arrival and her acceptance. I think the angel may vanish in a moment. I think that's one of the really clever aspects of this painting. The painting, of course, is an interior picture – a French baroque response to the inside and the outside. Here, the solution is to show that it's an interior. There's a brick wall with some plaster falling off. The soft bricky colour relates really nicely to the robe of the Virgin. And on the left, although it's not very apparent, there is this rather ragged drapery falling down. It's a curtain for sure and, therefore, a standard prop. It's a colour similar to the clouds but it is a clear mark of an interior. Actually, you also get the paradox in this painting of the Virgin coming from a very good family, descended from the lineage of David, with the posh prie-dieu and, in contrast, the exposed brick and the ragged curtain.'

He looks even closer.

'I'm a bit concerned actually, myself, if there was something underneath the hovering left hand of the angel. You see those shapes there. I'm not sure what they are.'

He takes five steps back and looks up, admiringly.

'The light is bursting out so it's hard to imagine anything about the top half of this painting other than it's the outside. It makes it more of an apparition. Yes, I think a really successful aspect of the whole painting is the degree to which the angel is made of less material substance than Mary. He is further away but it's not just that. It's the way the wings align with the clouds. Look how the colour of the tunic is similar to the clouds.'

I have been studying this painting for more than two years but it is wonderful to stand next to Sir Nicholas Penny and listen to his observations. He has seen, literally, hundreds of Annunciations during his professional career.

What strikes him most about this one in particular?

'Oh, I think the hands of the Virgin and her profile,' he replies. 'You feel that's the focus of this painting. Her gesture is rather unusual with her left hand coming forward and pressing her breast. It's a sort of gesture of acceptance and modesty. Certainly, that's what I spend most time looking at.'

He walks up close to the canvas again and says he is now looking at the Virgin's hair.

'It's quite dark, quite silky, a very beautiful character. And look at the light passing through the basket. That's an exquisite touch.'

Does he like it?

'Very, very much. It's beautiful. I don't know if it's amazingly popular. I'd be surprised if most visitors spend a lot of time looking at it. But those who do…well, I think…' His voice drops off. 'That to me is not an essential criterion.'

I tell him that when I have been in the room, most people walk straight past it. Indeed, Room 33 can sometimes feel a little like an anteroom. A place to pass through after the arriving hordes have admired the magnificent seventeenth-century Italian paintings in Room 32 including Caravaggio's *The Supper at Emmaus* and then headed to Room 34 (British Art 1750–1850) to admire paintings such as Turner's *The Fighting Temeraire*, Constable's *The Hay Wain* and Stubbs's *Whistlejacket*.

Sir Nicholas Penny walks up to the information card to the left of the frame.

'This label looks very good,' he says. 'I'm often quite critical of my colleagues' labels but I think this one is very good. He's used the maximum number of words, so if you add anything, you'd have to take something away. But what I wouldn't say is the archangel Gabriel announces to the Virgin that she will give birth to Jesus. I would say something to the effect, "The Virgin humbly accepts the news from the angel." I'd focus on the acceptance rather than the command. I'd have to drop the reference to Luke and possibly the archangel but I think I'd do that because that's what the painting is about.

'If you look at all the Annunciation pictures in the National Gallery,' he continues, 'you can say an artist has done it this way and another artist has done it that way. But then, if you sought them out not by date, or by school, or by place or origin, but by purpose, you'd probably find the altarpieces would emphasize the most important aspect of the Annunciation theologically – Mary's complete acceptance.'

As Sir Nicholas gazes at the canvas, he talks to himself. It is as if I am no longer in the room.

'Poussin's treatment is so unusual – very learned, but it could have got you into trouble if it had been displayed in a church.'

He stands on tiptoes to peer above the angel. 'How interesting,' he says. 'There's no dove but I just wonder if there wasn't something white hovering up there at the top of the lunette.'

I tell him there is a dove in the copy in St Sulpice and also a lily stem placed in the basket. I wonder if this original work had been toned down for Winchester College.

'My bet would be the other way round,' he says. 'The artist thought the real essentials of the picture did not require those accessories. How fascinating.'

What does he think about those who say the picture brings out a sense of interiority?

'I never use the word interiority,' he replies. 'What does it mean? I wish it was hung a little higher. If it was in a chapel, remember, you'd have to step up to the sanctuary and then step up to the altar.'

I watch from a distance, as the Director appears to take one last look at the painting. He says it is time for him to return to his office. As we walk back to the Gallery's main entrance, I ask what the message of the annunciation story is for him?

'You can put yourself in the position of someone...' His voice hesitates. 'We've all had that experience...that you might suddenly have to receive an unexpected message from somewhere.'

Would he agree with Bishop Philip Egan that it is the most important event in human history?

'Oh, yes...well, I wouldn't go that far,' he corrects himself, 'but I can see, from his point of view, from his perspective.'

Where does securing the loan of the picture sit within his achievements as Director of the National Gallery? Does he see it as a moment of significance?

'Yes, I do,' he responds. 'It hasn't been much noticed. But it reminds you what you do is not for popular acclaim or popular attention. We're not just buying or borrowing pictures for today's public. We're thinking in longer terms. You don't measure a painting necessarily only by how many it affects but also by the depth of the impact it may make on a few people.'

He looks at me, and then smiles. As we say our farewells, he hints that the National Gallery and Winchester College are about to come to an agreement to extend the loan, a decision he would be delighted with.

Four days later, in Sir Nicholas Penny's final week in office, Winchester College and the National Gallery announce that the painting will stay at the National Gallery for a further five years. *The Annunciation* by François Lemoyne will be displayed as part of one of the world's greatest art collections until at least 2021.

The circumstances surrounding its original commission remain a mystery, a bit like the painting's subject matter.

During the past three years, I have searched anywhere and everywhere to find the image of Lemoyne's *The Annunciation* in religious and history of art books. I uncovered only two examples. One, a coloured plate engraving in the 1770 edition of Reverend John Fleetwood's celebrated book, *The Life of Our Lord and Saviour Jesus Christ*. The other, rather bizarrely, in a tiny pamphlet called *Making God Visible: The Birth of Jesus in Art and Words*, published in 2013 by All Saints Press based in St Louis, Missouri. There is no postcard of the picture in the National Gallery shop. The image does not feature in any guide or art book in the National Gallery Library or in the National Art Library at the V&A. Whether or not it will gain prominence in future, remains to be seen. Certainly, the Winchester College Society has made a start, featuring the painting on its Christmas card.

As I close the chapter on François Lemoyne and the commission of *The Annunciation* a mystery still lingers. On 4 June 1737, did he really commit suicide at his studio in Paris or was his death something more sinister? Lemoyne had plenty of enemies as well as rivals at that time. Also, it is clear that his health had deteriorated rapidly during that year: he was depressed, suffered from painful headaches and felt ostracized and undervalued. His mental health was fragile and he was becoming increasingly paranoid. Indeed, at one point, he believed that Parisian policemen were following him. His friends recognized he was in urgent need of medical care. The night before his death, Berger arranged to take him for a trip to the countryside the following morning. According to Lemoyne's biographer, Caylus, Berger was intending to have him locked up for his own safety.

That morning, as usual, Lemoyne taught his pupils at his studio, but by the time Berger arrived, he had locked himself in his bedchamber, apparently suspicious that he was about to be taken away. He stabbed himself nine times with his sword, three times in the throat and six times in the chest. When Berger tried to force open the door, Lemoyne crawled to release the lock, staggered backwards and fell to the floor in a pool of blood. An autopsy was carried out soon after his death and suicide was the verdict.

But can a man really stab himself nine times with a sword, three times in the throat and six times in the chest? Would he have the strength and the fortitude? It seems incredible to me. I have a niggling doubt, this time about the cause of death.

By chance, I discovered that two members of the congregation at my local church are pathologists. Dennis Wright was appointed more than forty years ago as Professor of Pathology at the newly formed Medical School at the University of Southampton. Now retired, he remains Emeritus Professor of Pathology there. His wife, Dr Elizabeth Benjamin, is a senior clinical lecturer and consultant gynaecological pathologist at University College London (UCL). I send them all the papers I have relating to the autopsy following Lemoyne's death including the police and medical reports, together with Dr Hannah Williams's detailed paper, 'The Mysterious Suicide of François Lemoyne', published in the *Oxford Art Journal* in June 2015. Of course, they have no access to the corpse or the precise detail on how the autopsy was carried out by Dr de Vilars. But do they think the likely cause of death was suicide or was it more likely to be murder? A few days later, I receive an email from them both, supporting the original verdict:

> The circumstances described of Berger's arrival at Lemoyne's home and the opening of the bedchamber door indicate that the cause of death was suicide not murder. The nature of the wounds also supports this conclusion. Lemoyne as an artist had a fair knowledge of human anatomy. This was demonstrated by the stab wounds that he made, aiming first at the carotid artery, then when this failed, at the heart. In murder cases, stabbings are usually much more random, often involving the hands and arms of the victim as he attempts to fend off the attack.
>
> The wounds to the neck, aimed at the carotid artery, were presumably the first attempt. They failed because he was using a pointed weapon rather than a blade. The fourth wound penetrated the stomach 'through and through'. Had he not died of his later wounds this might have caused peritonitis, which at that time would probably have led to his death.
>
> The four stabs around the left breast penetrated the full depth of the chest, emerging at the back, testimony to the sharpness of the weapon. All four stabs penetrated the left lung and two also penetrated the left ventricle of the heart. The wounds to the lung would probably cause some collapse of the organ, but, on its own, this would probably not be fatal. The two stabbings that penetrated the left ventricle

of the heart would have caused death. The autopsy report recorded a 'massive effusion of blood'. This would be due to the blood being pumped out of the wounds in the left ventricle, which the autopsy report records as the cause of death.

The sword is described as an olinde, with a guard and grip of gilt steel. On cross section, the blade is triangular. While the tip of the blade is very sharp, the edges of the blade get blunter towards the hilt. When stabbing himself, Lemoyne presumably held the blunt upper blade in both hands. The sword was too long to have been held by the hilt.

To a person of sound mind it is difficult to imagine committing suicide with multiple stab wounds to the neck and chest. However, Lemoyne does not appear to have been of sound mind. The evidence given of his behaviour in the time leading to his suicide suggests that he was suffering from paranoid psychosis. At a time when suicide was a criminal offence, death by the sword may have been regarded as a more honourable method of achieving this end.

In a journey full of mystery and unresolved questions, at least this email seems to offer one definitive answer: the original verdict of suicide as the cause of Lemoyne's death was correct.

CHAPTER 45

A LIBERATING ROLE MODEL FOR WOMEN

The University of Winchester prides itself on being a leading centre in Britain for the study of feminist theology. So it is fitting that the latest art exhibition at the Link Gallery on the University's West Downs campus is entitled *Feminist Images of Mary/Miriam*. As I head to the opening night launch, I am intrigued to find out if there are any works specifically focused on the annunciation story. I am not to be disappointed.

The catalogue describes the exhibition as celebrating feminist reflections on Mary/Miriam by women artists and theologians from across Europe:

> Artists are from the Feminist Theology and Art Forum and the exhibition wishes to achieve, through the imagination of the artists, another way of viewing the full embodiment of women through the historical/religious subject of Mary/Miriam. Each artist has explored Mary's/Miriam's narrative through various feminist theological texts in connection to their artwork. The visual art presented here is an exploration hoping to expand the view of Mary/Miriam as liberating role model for women and re-visioning the narrative as feminist liberative praxis.

There is much talk at the reception about feminist thinking and body theologies and the recent re-examination of Mary, who has been embedded within our culture as the representation of the perfect woman in Christianity.

As I wander around the display, three paintings, in particular, grab my attention: *Overshadowed*, by the West Country artist Jill Coughman; *The Annunciation*, by a German painter, Annette Esser; and *The Annunciation – bondage*, by another German-born artist, Jana-Faye Jakumeit. All three works are heavily influenced by the portrayal of Mary in Luke's story of the Annunciation.

Jill Coughman tries to portray and celebrate women as active, strong independent individuals. 'The myth of the Virgin Mary, possibly one of the foremost religious icons in the western world, is a powerful one,' she comments. 'Her birth, her death, her age is never mentioned. For me as a painter, this allows me enormous freedom. I have been indoctrinated with images of the Virgin Mary and the rebel in me wants to see and portray another side of her.'

Overshadowed was created in her Plymouth studio earlier in the year and is based on the moment at which Mary has the visitation from the angel Gabriel.

'My drive as an artist is to paint positive images of women who are moving,' she tells me later. 'I grew up seeing very passive images of women. I'm constantly driven to paint women not as objects.

'I was trying to think, if this is going to happen today, who would Mary be; what would she be doing?' she continues. 'I spent quite a long time exploring Mary doing everyday tasks – washing up, hoovering – and trying to incorporate this sense of a shadow. I wanted to portray the visitation to her as very subtle and non-gender specific. I

201. Jill Coughman *Overshadowed*, 2016. © Jill Coughman

question myths and stories constantly. It came about because I couldn't make the composition work with her indoors, so I took her outdoors and I thought about what symbolism I could use to add more fibre to the story. I chose the flowers because of their symbolic meaning. I decided to have her picking flowers with this sense of something behind her. The shadow of an angel or a person standing with their arms out just behind her.'

The flowers, she says, allowed her to introduce an added layer of meaning to an ostensibly ordinary scene. The irises represent forthcoming good news and the forget-me-nots indicate that a partner cannot give you what you want. 'I'm always looking for ways that add sex to the meaning of the story I'm trying to convey,' she laughs.

In the catalogue, she states 'the non-gender-specific shadow is meant to be a subtle reference to the occasion which hopefully becomes more evident as the viewer looks at the image for longer.'

How critical was it for the shadow to be non-gender? I ask.

'That's my questioning of the annunciation story that we're being told and have been brought up on,' she says. 'I question everything and why do we believe one version of the story. I'm always looking if there's another explanation of the story or if there's another angle to the story.'

What does the annunciation story mean for her?

'I read Marina Warner's *Alone of All Her Sex* and I love her questioning. What's it mean to me?' she asks rhetorically before pausing. 'I think I'll have to pass on it,' she says hesitatingly.

Does she believe it to be fact or metaphor or something else?

'I don't believe it as fact,' she replies. 'I really believe miracles can happen. Amazing, fantastic things can happen but stories change as they're told, written down or painted, one year after another. And although there might have been a thing that did happen miraculously all that time ago,' she sighs heavily, 'it's very unlikely it happened as it is written in the Bible. And there are so many versions of miraculous happenings, depending on the faith you have. So, do I believe it happened as it said in the Bible? No.'

What does Mary mean to her?

'That's a really interesting question,' she replies. 'Symbolically, she's really complex. I believe...mm...mm...I can't say it really. I'm so afraid of being misunderstood. I feel she's had an awful lot of power taken away from her by...' She hesitates again. 'No, I can't talk about it. Symbolically, she's very important because she's been painted so many times. As an artist, I'd say she's been really central as a role model in our western culture. But I'm an artist, not a theologian. If you were going to ask a theologian to paint a picture and then ask them to explain all the research, the symbolism, their marking, their favourite shape of brush, they wouldn't have a clue. I'm very interested in theology and mythology but my language is one of image and pattern and colour, and that's how I communicate – through painting. I can't do it easily with words.'

I move on next to view Annette Esser's painting, *The Annunciation*. Born in Cologne in 1957, she studied theology and then completed a doctorate in feminist spirituality. Recently, as well as being a feminist theologian and the founder of the Scivias Institute of Art and Theology, she has taken up painting. She completed the picture earlier in the year after being hospitalized for a while.

As I look at her work, I am intrigued by her words in the exhibition catalogue:

> My image of Mary derives from my Catholic upbringing, yet not simply in a positive but also in a critical way. Mary was the Divine Mother of God and my relation to her was not at ease but rather very distant, as was the relation to my mother.
>
> While studying theology, rather God and Jesus were in the centre of my attention, at least at first. Only gradually did I discover more of the Biblical Mary and the fact that Mary was only a young woman or a girl of 14 or 15 when she got pregnant. It was then through feminist theology and having discovered my own sexuality that I also started to look more critically at the connection of being a mother and a virgin at once as an image that puts every other woman into a secondary position.
>
> Then I thought about my own experience. Actually, the moment when the nurse told me that I was positively tested for being pregnant. The moment she stared at me and waited for my reaction as she knew that this was not planned parenthood. And when for me, her question about the father of the child was of less interest than my sudden vision of this new life becoming real as a child in my body.

202. Annette Esser *The Annunciation*, 2016. ©
Annette Esser

I become conscious there is a tall, middle-aged woman standing close by as I view the painting. I continue to read:

> Thinking of painting Mary after years of feminist criticism and with the insight of depth psychology, I imagined Mary as a simple young woman in today's cloth…in my own imagination, I thought that the angel should be closer to Mary. Rather than being another figure outside of her, the angel presented a message inside herself that she became aware of in this very moment and that she treasured and pondered in

her heart. Mary's eyes are half-open. She is reflecting inside but she also perceives the reality outside of herself. The wings that depict Mary and the angel as one are, in fact, what I found to be the real experience. It is about the message and the messenger being one. It's the experience of when all is shining and glowing and radiating, when insight becomes outside, and when the whole body and the whole perspective is widened. And when what we see is still just a young woman, thinking and reflecting about some things that have just happened to her.

The woman is still there. I decide to act on my instinct.

'Hello, are you Annette Esser?' I enquire.

'Yah,' she replies in a strong German accent.

I ask her about her painting.

'I was thinking last year about the Fra Angelico image in San Marco and it inspired me a lot,' she begins. 'I was nineteen when I first saw it and I was touched by the colours. What touched me was that Mary and the angel were so far away from each other. Mary is meek and humble but the angel is so far away. So, my basic idea was how can they get closer? I suddenly had this image of Mary and the angel as one. The message and the messenger as one and what is happening in her is like one experience.'

She speaks with intense passion.

'It is an experiential experience because when I think of the moment that I was told I was pregnant, that was like a widening experience, the sudden realisation of this new life to come.' As she points to the wings, she continues, 'Something is widening like the horizontal things here. For me, these wings are showing what is going on inwardly. The message is of this new life to come and this new perspective. Something is coming to you but is not yet realized. The wings are the widening perspective but she is looking inwardly at this realisation of what's coming.

'And then the question of the father of this child is not as important as the perspective of this child as new life being born because you don't think about the father of this child. That's at least my own experience. That's not the really important question at this moment of conception. I suddenly thought of this child and I was stunned. It was a very intense moment. It's this very positive realisation of what is happening in you as a young woman.'

I am about to ask her a question but she carries on, oblivious. Her energy, though, is infectious.

'My god-daughter was just turning fourteen and she was wearing these red clothes at her confirmation. I took a picture of her and said, "You are my model now because Mary was a similar young woman when she found out." It was a good age to imagine Mary when she had her first realisation.'

She tells me this is only her fourth painting and is on offer for £1,700. She says she wanted to use beaten gold and a reddish burned umber. The sky above Mary's head is light blue with a little pink, apparently giving a hint to Mary as aurora. Heaven to the left is dark blue, showing the rising moon and on the right is the rising star – both celestial bodies being symbols of the Virgin Mary. In contrast to the dark blue sky, Mary stands on the earthly grass beneath her bare feet.

'I chose to do it in a very traditional way. I'd prefer it to be hung in a church or a chapel. Right now, I'm not in the mood for selling it but I hope it will go to the right place. It's a spiritual image.'

So when I look at this painting, I suggest, am I looking at her experience and Mary's experience at the same time?

'Yah,' she replies. 'When you look deeply at your own experience, you find a more general experience. Through the individual, you get through to objectivity. You just have to be honest about your own experience.'

She says she believes that Mary in this very special moment of conception/realisation was being transformed into an angel. So the messenger, the message and the one who received the message all became one. Showing Mary with angelic wings in the moment of the Annunciation is her attempt to reconcile the Catholic and Protestant traditions about Mary and angels.

When she was told she was pregnant at forty years of age, how did she feel at that very moment, especially as the pregnancy was unplanned?

'It was a *fascinosum et tremendum* experience,' she says. 'Fascination but also being scared. A "how did I do this?" moment. It's both. And this is what the angelic message is. It's big and new and going beyond yourself. It's a moment of innocence and humility. It's a very spiritual moment.'

She says it was unthinkable to have had an abortion. 'I'm a Catholic woman. I was a Ph.D. student in New York and I had to totally re-plan my life and go back to Europe.'

What is the key message of Luke's story of the Annunciation? I ask.

'It's not simply a historical story. Remember, it was written by him later. There's so much symbolism in it.'

Does she see it as fact or metaphor?

'When we talk about the story and all the signs, we also talk about something real. I think Mary knew her son, Jesus, was very special. Maybe she also believed him to be the Messiah. But we can't look into this.'

———

Whilst the opening night's invited guests move around the two floors of the Link Gallery, holding canapés and glasses of wine, I remain firmly ensconced in the same place on the ground floor. For next to Annette Esser's painting hangs another work that is so striking that it stops me in my tracks. A young woman, presumably the Virgin Mary, is naked and bound, kneeling on the floor. It is called *The Annunciation – bondage* and is inspired by the practices of BDSM (Bondage & Discipline, Dominance and Submission, Sadism and Masochism). A German-born artist called Jana-Faye Jakumeit, in collaboration with an urban drip painter named RKP, created it.

Jana-Faye Jakumeit is a Ph.D. student at the University of Winchester whose thesis explores, in the words of the exhibition catalogue, 'whether the lived experiences of BDSM practitioners are merely an expression of the eternal return of patriarchal oppression, or whether they offer a way of resistance to the totality of power and dualism. Jana-Faye's interest is to expand our understanding of sex, sexuality and the erotic by exploring sacred eroticism and spiritual experiences derived from pain.'

Striking, with short, angular blonde hair, Jana-Faye Jakumeit stands next to me and describes the work displayed directly in front of us. It is a mixed media work on canvas. Jana-Faye painted the central, tied down figure in non-white hues while the long vertical drips in the background, were created by RKP who mixed most of the highly-textured acrylic and oil paint in order to produce the distinctive green, gold and blue palette.

'One of the theological debates around the Annunciation is, did Mary consent and, if she did consent, did she have the capacity and capability to consent? Jana-Faye tells me. 'Are you as a human being able to consent to something so unconceivable, so unimaginable as bearing the Son of God and everything that happens in the story? Did she really have the freedom in will and the will power to deny this request? We are not aiming to provide resolution to that debate. We want to express the dilemma.

'Bondage and Discipline, Dominance and Submission, Sadism and Masochism – that's something where people deliberately seek these dilemmas,' Jana-Faye continues. 'They surrender their powers and their autonomy, as consenting adults, to someone they trust and who has their well-being at heart, but there's something really interesting and curious about people deliberately surrendering their autonomy and their power. What we find in Mary, in a feminist tradition, is we often see women as victims of patriarchy, the internalized patriarchy women have been socially constructed to be at the mercy of their body and bodily functions and women's

203. Jana-Faye Jakumeit *The Annunciation – bondage*, 2016.
© Jana-Faye Jakumeit

embodiment. They seem to be at a great disadvantage. In this painting, when we look at women, we also know that women are very valuable contributing members of society. There is a great strength in women or we wouldn't have made it this far and we wouldn't be here today. So we wanted to look at the strength in this apparent weakness.'

So even though she is tied up and surrendering, I comment, she is doing so willingly, in the same way as someone would in BDSM?

'That's the parallel that we are trying to draw,' Jana-Faye replies. 'Whether she willingly surrendered or not to giving herself to a cause completely. She surrendered willingly in that she raised her son and buried her son. She embodies the will to love. There's a level of dedication, devotion and consent there. She took on this challenge that she was being tested with.'

So what you are saying here, I suggest, is that in the same way that someone engaging in BDSM is submissive and trusts the other person, Mary is submissive and trusts the angel?

'Well, the angel is probably more representative of God but ultimately there's a trust in oneself,' Jana-Faye responds. 'A trust in oneself to be capable of doing this and being able to deal with it.'

Is the annunciation story fact or metaphor?

'No, there's very little value in a literal reading of any Scripture. That's where religion becomes a very dangerous tool that ends in violence because my literal reading then becomes the only truth and I don't think that's very resourceful. What you are doing in theology most of the time is actually finding all the different truths and appreciating there's a multitude of opportunity to interpret things and there is not one truth.'

When I ask what is the central message of the annunciation story, there is a long pause before the reply.

'I would say there is a strength in what we seem to see as a weakness. We see someone who is completely devoted, someone who has no other chance than doing what they're asked to do because they're tied down or that someone willingly surrenders into disempowerment. Anyone who is disempowered, we are failing to see that in the disempowerment they find power and strength. That's the central message for me.'

———————

Of course, the gospel story of the encounter between the angel Gabriel and Mary has been one of the most popular religious subjects in art throughout the ages. But I am about to meet one man who thinks poetry can be even more powerful than paintings in communicating the mystery of that angelic meeting and its meaning. Malcolm Guite is a Cambridge based poet, singer-songwriter, Anglican priest and academic, whose interest lies in the interface between theology and the arts.

I meet up with him in Winchester at the end of a day when he has been leading a five hour spiritual reflection session called 'Parable and Paradox – a poetic journey into the teachings of Jesus'. We head to a nearby patisserie for a coffee, croissant and conversation.

He looks slightly dishevelled, wearing an open-neck shirt, pullover, jacket and thick wool herringbone styled overcoat. His most distinctive feature is his long flowing grey hair and thick grey-white beard. The fifty-nine-year-old also wears a blue-grey fedora styled hat and walks with a stick. As we walk along the street chatting, he quotes verses of poetry regularly in a gravelly voice and is clearly passionate about words and language.

As we sit down on a low red sofa in the patisserie, he seems uninhibited by all the people at tables around him as immediately he starts to recite rather loudly his own sonnet entitled 'Annunciation', written in 2012 and published in his *Sounding the Seasons* collection:

We see so little, stayed on surfaces,
We calculate the outsides of all things,
Preoccupied with our own purposes
We miss the shimmer of the angels' wings,
They coruscate around us in their joy
A swirl of wheels and eyes and wings unfurled,
They guard the good we purpose to destroy,
A hidden blaze of glory in God's world.
But on this day a young girl stopped to see
With open eyes and heart. She heard the voice;
The promise of His glory yet to be,
As time stood still for her to make a choice;
Gabriel knelt and not a feather stirred,
The Word himself was waiting on her word.

There's something magical when a poet reads his or her own words. His rich, husky voice and precise intonation bring the sonnet alive as I sit with closed eyes and listen. At the end, I ask what inspired it?

'I've always loved that sense of the space between them,' he tells me. 'I was very struck that the feast often happens in the season of Lent with this sense of openness and glory.

That opening line, "We see so little, stayed on surfaces" and that particular word "stayed" was inspired by George Herbert and his poem, 'The Elixir' and those lines:

> A man who looks on glass,
> On it may stay his eye
> Or if he pleaseth, through it pass
> And then the heav'n espy

'The idea I suddenly saw in that poem is we're already in the midst of heaven, it's just we've got these little surfaces around us that stop us from seeing it and we can either let them remain opaque or allow them to become windows. In a sense, the angels never leave heaven. They are heaven and they're there and they bring heaven in and this girl sees it. And I love this idea, very characteristic of the New Testament, that it is so often the lowly, the least, the lost, who actually get the revelation. I love the idea the true thing in itself comes dancing in front of Mary and she sees it.'

His sonnet was written for 25 March as part of a collection of poetry that reflects the liturgical year. He calls the Annunciation the mysterious moment of awareness, assent and transformation in which eternity touches time.

'This is one of a number of poems I've written about Mary. I'm an Anglican priest but I've always been drawn to Mary, not by suddenly being in an Anglo-Catholic Church or something – my father was a Methodist and my mother was a Presbyterian – but I had a long ramble around Ireland when I was in my teens, and not a Christian at that time, and I found the devotion to Mary there very moving and the statues very moving. I was given a rosary by a friend and I wanted to do this thing but I didn't really believe it, so I said the Rosary in Latin on the basis that it would be more like a mantra. But for whatever reason, my sense of Mary and her grace is now very deep in me. She is the type of the soul. Her opening yes to God, which allows everything to happen – the Incarnation – is ours. It's what makes ours possible.'

He scurries through his bag, taking out papers and personal possessions in order to find a book. 'Here's another poem I wrote,' he says. 'It's just called "Mary" although, originally, when it was first published, I called it "Theotokos".' He reads aloud again:

> You bore for me the One who came to bless
> And bear for all and make the broken whole.
> You heard His call and in your open 'yes'
> You spoke aloud for every living soul.
> Oh gracious Lady, child of your own child,
> Whose mother-love still calls the child in me,
> Call me again, for I am lost, and wild
> Waves surround me now. On this dark sea
> Shine as a star and call me to the shore.
> Open the door that all my sins would close
> And hold me in your garden. Let me share
> The prayer that folds the petals of the Rose.
> Enfold me too in Love's last mystery
> And bring me to the One you bore for me.

'I'd be hard pressed in my purely Anglican-priest, theological mode to justify half of that,' he says, 'but you can't tell your muse what to say and that's just how I feel about things. With Mary's Annunciation, we're all involved in it in some way. It involves all of us.

At that moment, the Creator is coming into the creation. She's the point of the whole creation into which the utterly transcendent maker of all things is coming to be a creature in his own creation. So, in that sense, she is representative of all of us. She's actually speaking on our behalf. And I love the idea of her being the new Eve.'

I ask him whether he feels poetry can get to the heart of the annunciation story more than a painting can?

'My annunciation poem has the word "see" in it. I wrote, "We see so little stayed on surfaces" and then, "But on this day a young girl stopped to see with open eyes and heart." I'm acknowledging that the seeing is important but I actually think that sometimes it takes poetry, and the imagination through poetry, to help us to do that thing that George Herbert says, which is to see through rather than looking at.'

A poetic icon, I say.

'Yes, it is. Exactly like an icon,' he responds.

So, seeing through words, you can see more than in a painting, I observe.

'Yeah, yeah,' he replies enthusiastically. 'There's a lovely word, "ekphrastic", which means writing about painting. An ekphrastic poem tries to open out for the reader what it's like to look at a painting. If you read a really good ekphrastic poem, you can go back to the painting and see more. It's very difficult because if a picture paints a thousand words, what's the poem then? But it's genuinely the case that you can enable a poem to see more. You can license them to look deeper and allow them to realize there's more to see.'

Does he see the annunciation story as fact or metaphor or what?

'I see it as both,' he replies. 'I don't choose between fact and metaphor. Just because something is an absolutely fabulous metaphor doesn't mean it didn't happen. I see the Annunciation as the meeting of fact and metaphor, history and myth. I just think it's authentic. I see this gospel moment as eternally resonant. I see the whole narrative of Mary noticing the angel, her own openness and willingness to say yes, and then her bearing the child, is her pointing to glory. That's exactly what we, as Christians, are called to do and what the Church is meant to do – to bear him out to the world. The fact that that is a model of what we are meant to do both individually and as a Church doesn't mean it didn't happen. It happened the way it did precisely to be the pattern for us.'

I tell him about Bishop Philip Egan's statement that the Annunciation is the most important event in human history.

'The difficulty with saying that is you're picking and choosing events from a single event. The most important event in human history is the Incarnation, and the life, death, resurrection and ascension of God in humanity. That's one event. I don't think chopping it up is the right thing. It is all one shape, one event.'

What does the annunciation story mean for him? I ask.

'For me personally, it really is the turning point of the cosmos and the beginning of the story,' he responds. 'What it means in the end is as John Donne wrote in his Annunciation poem, "Immensity cloistered in thy dear womb". It means that the inaccessible, the unknowable, the infinite, has become accessible, knowable and finite. I'm very surprised there hasn't been a devotion in the long history of Christianity to Christ in the womb. There's a fabulous sermon by the Anglican preacher, Lancelot Andrewes, the late sixteenth and early seventeenth-century preacher who's a hero of mine, where he talks about Christ taking our nature at the very sill of our being and he talks about the foetus being even more helpless than a baby who's inarticulate. We carry some of that dependency and inarticulation through our lives and Christ takes that on too.'

Malcolm Guite was born in Nigeria. His father was a Methodist lay preacher. In his teens he lost his faith but then, in what he describes as his own annunciation moment, he returned to being a practising Christian when he heard a Franciscan friar speak. He tells me how he spoke about pregnancy and childbirth and how a babe is utterly dependent on a parent for survival and how the umbilical cord is key to being fed and being nourished. In the same way, he said, that dependency can be correlated to our own dependency on God. The theme rather reminds me of Rowan Williams's Annunciation sermon at the very start of my journey.

'Everything that we would want to say about our dependence on God is like the little infant connected to the umbilical cord,' he explains. 'And God says that's how I'm coming to you. One of the radical interpretations of the Incarnation is that it's God saying, "I'll be dependent as you are." Literally, he's dependent on the umbilical cord of Mary.'

The more I listen to him, the more his coarse, croaky voice reminds me of the actor, John Hurt.

'I was at Cambridge, in the Michaelmas term of my third year, at Fisher House and basically this guy was talking about the Mass and the understanding of the Eucharist in terms of incarnation. He started with this thing about how the babe in a womb is completely dependent. It was resonant for me because only a month earlier I'd had an epiphany, which was the awareness of the utter presence and glory of God and my own utter dependence, smallness and fragility. I felt a radiant presence. I was house sitting for someone in Ealing and I was reading the Psalms as background to English literature. I then went along to this thing and Eric Doyle, one of the Franciscans, said how the child attached to the umbilical cord can hardly move from its environment and its mother. All it can do is cry out and be dependent. I knew where this was going. This is how we are with God. But he said it's how God comes to us and makes his appeal to us. He just comes to us in love. At that point, the penny dropped and I said I'm a Christian. It was the first time in my life it felt right to be a human being…and that it was alright to be me.'

It was an annunciation moment for him, I suggest.

'Yes, it was a life-changing moment, without question.'

Does he think the status of the Annunciation has been lost?

'Well, if it's true, which I think it is, there's a sense it's never lost,' he says. 'It is what it is. If a few priests in one corner of the cosmos forget to remember it, it doesn't mean it's lost. But if you mean has it been lost in our ritual and cultural memory, it has been lost. It has been lost in the Church year. I do think there's huge value in remembering it in March. We have a peculiar difficulty in our country to do with history and the Reformation. They were so anxious as it were in a sense when they cleared out a lot of the unnecessary human accretions to get back to the pristine gospel, so anxious not to throw the divine baby out with the bath water, that they kind of threw out his mother instead. It was really ironic and paradoxical because the Annunciation is totally and utterly a biblical episode. In so far as you say *sola scriptura* – I need to have the Bible as my guide – you don't have the Immaculate Conception nor the Assumption, but you do have the Annunciation. Mary is there at the beginning, at the Cross, and at the end. She is, literally, the container of the whole of grace in the womb and she's also in some sense the vessel of the story. She's there at the beginning and the end and at various points between. She's absolutely essential from the scriptural point of view.

'So how do we recover that?' he asks rhetorically. 'I think we have to get over our inhibitions and recognize that Mary does not involve, in any way, diminishing the uniqueness of Christ's atoning out. Calling her theotokos – the God-bearer – is not to take away what God does for us in the uniqueness of Christ. Indeed, it's to enhance it. Mary is the one who most consistently points to Jesus. There's no danger of losing Jesus when you look at Mary. I think it's really important in the divisions of the Church that the Protestants remember Mary. It would do us good psychologically…having Mary and revering her at the Annunciation is not spikiness and prissiness and being obsessed with liturgical niceties. You don't have to buy in to all the ecclesiastical pap to buy into Mary as gracious and central. The problem is, to be honest, that of the people who want to proclaim Mary, some who do want to have also bought into all the ecclesiastical pap and a huge amount of historical baggage that we just need to let go of.'

Our time is almost up. He must get the next train and head back to Girton College, Cambridge. There's just time for one last question. Is there one word that, for him, sums up the annunciation story?

'Grace,' he replies immediately. 'It's God's grace in coming to us and her extraordinary grace in accepting. The most astonishing moment is when the angel says to Mary, "Hail Mary, full of grace". What the angel is actually bringing to the world is grace in Jesus Christ and yet he who is coming to earth in his very grace also recognizes grace in his recipient. She represents us and that there's grace in nature. Grace is the key word.'

With that he puts on his hat, rubs his right hand through his thick beard, gathers his things, takes hold of his stick and bids me farewell. Little does he know that he was my final interviewee.

CHAPTER 46

END REFLECTIONS

I am sitting in the newly re-opened Lady Chapel at the eastern end of Winchester Cathedral, which has been closed for the past four years. Originally built in the thirteenth century, the east bay of the Chapel was re-modelled around 1500, possibly as a thank-offering by Elizabeth of York, the wife of King Henry VII, for their son, Prince Arthur, who was baptized here in 1486.

The Virgin Mary's image is everywhere around me: on a golden Annunciation altarpiece straight ahead; on an Annunciation wall painting above a wooden door to my left; on a stained-glass window of the Annunciation just above that door on the north wall. As well as these images, there's a roof boss above me, on the west bay, showing a crowned Mary at her Assumption, flanked by six angels. By the side of the altar, there's a yarra wood Pieta sculpture of Mary holding the body of her son, crafted by Peter Eugene Ball in 1990, and paid for by the local Roman Catholic community.

204. C.E. Kempe *The Annunciation*, 1905, Winchester Cathedral. © Dr
John Crook, Winchester

I keep looking at those three Annunciation images. The reredos was designed by C. E. Kempe and commissioned in 1905 by the friends and admirers of the Hampshire writer, Charlotte Yonge, to commemorate her death four years earlier. The richly decorated relief has a classic composition with Gabriel on the left, Mary on the right at her prie-dieu, and the hovering dove in the middle above a vase of lilies. The Annunciation wall painting above the north door is part of a series depicting the legendary miracles of Mary. The panel is a modern, exact copy of the sixteenth-century grisaille wall painting, which lies underneath but is too fragile to be exposed. It was scraped and whitewashed at the Reformation although much of the white paint has now fallen off.

The Annunciation stained-glass image above it is made up of two panels, that form part of a 1900 window depicting the birth of Jesus, again designed by Charles Eamer Kempe.

As I sit alone in silence in one of the early sixteenth-century Tudor stalls – the only pre-Reformation stalls to have survived in a Lady Chapel in England – I start to reflect on my whole Annunciation project.

Although the point of this journey has been to open my mind to a wide range of insights and opinions from others, I have never forgotten what the Mother Prioress, Sister Mary, told me when I left the Carmelite of the Annunciation, many months ago: 'You're writing the book and, therefore, at the end, you've got to take from all the things you'll hear what you feel resonates with you. And you've got to be honest in the way you're writing it. Not that you don't have to take anybody's ideas…but you've got to always be yourself. That's what wholeness is. But it's good to hear what all these people say to you and to take their advice. Then you've to take it all in, drink it all in, and be honest and, at the end, write about what you believe. We've all got to be whole. Whatever you do, you've got to be genuine, it's no good trying to please everyone or be someone else. We've got to be the person whom God made us and be whole.'

Bishop Anba Angaelos from the Coptic Church took the point one step further when I met him at the Ecumenical Society of the Blessed Virgin Mary conference in Cambridge: 'Be open to listening but you can't just keep listening. You have to make a decision. There are always choices to make and the journey has to come to its destination at some point. You need to know what you believe – your anchor point – and then be exposed to other people's views and respect them. Don't ever expect it will make logical sense. It has to be a decision of the unknown and from the heart. It's not limited or confined to logic. But you have to get to a point on your journey when you have to make a decision.'

That point has finally arrived.

———

At the start of this journey, I was fifty-five years old. Little did I realize then that it would take me three years to complete.

I have always thought of myself as a practising Christian, inspired by a love of God and the words of Jesus. However, I have never been a strident evangelist, nor particularly pious. I am a person constantly questioning my faith and beliefs; a person who wants to live as Christ teaches us but often fails. I was baptized a Roman Catholic like my father, and his father – the grandfather I never met. My mother was brought up in the Church of England but converted to Catholicism in her early thirties, when I was five – a decision she describes as 'a move of convenience'.

I made my First Holy Communion a week after my seventh birthday; I was confirmed at ten; I served regularly as an altar boy at my local Roman Catholic Church until the age of twelve. I stopped going to Confession soon after I first experienced it. As a teenager, a curious mixture of duty, obligation, ritual and parental expectation blended together with hope, desire, nourishment, obedience and guilt determined my weekly attendance at Mass. But all of it was underlined by an ongoing belief in God and the teachings of Jesus.

I remember in my early years at grammar school in Lincoln, I would have to absent myself from the Scripture class each week and go to the library because of my Roman Catholic faith. I have since discovered it was the same for other Catholic pupils from different year groups, who experienced the same fate. Apparently, the local priest, Fr John Weaver, had requested our removal. Often, I would sit in the library next to a younger pupil, a member of the Plymouth Brethren, who had also been granted a special dispensation. At the time, the exclusion felt baffling and troublesome, and left the indelible impression that my faith was somehow a little odd and different.

Throughout my adult life, I would say my religious belief has remained pretty strong and steadfast and, even when challenged, has never seriously wavered. I have never given up the ritual of attending a Sunday service, nor of saying prayers to God every day. But I admit, until this journey, I have never really questioned what exactly I believe.

When I got married, aged twenty-two, my wife was an occasional churchgoer, who had a wavering faith based on tradition and hope. As time passed, she questioned the basis of any religious belief and now describes herself as a non-believer. Our five children were baptized in the Roman Catholic Church and attended Mass up to their early teenage years. Now they are adults, as the reader has discovered, none of them attend church and all regard themselves as atheists, agnostics or non-believers. Over the years, my wife encouraged lively family discussions about religion. She and our children occasionally expressed frustration that I was not prepared to question either my Church teachings or my faith but would accept them at face value and without challenge.

Fifteen years ago, my religious stability changed somewhat when I stopped going to Mass at St Peter's, my local Roman Catholic Church. The weekly homilies no longer resonated for me and, seemingly, ceased to have much relevance to my life. I realized that I was going to Mass in order to receive Communion but I was not inspired nor particularly engaged. Moreover, the Roman Catholic Church as an institution was increasingly troubling me. I admired so many aspects of it – the tradition, the certainty of belief that it instilled and much of its teaching. I liked many of the members of my local congregation. But I thought its specific stances on opposition to the ordination of women, enforced celibacy for its priesthood, the continuing rejection of artificial contraception, the ban on divorcees taking Holy Communion and its description of homosexuality as a moral disorder contrary to natural law were all either wrong or misguided. I felt like a silent hypocrite indirectly colluding with it all.

Moreover, the child abuse and corruption scandals that recently had rocked the Roman Catholic Church bewildered me. In particular, I thought the Church authorities in England had handled the child abuse issue poorly, without sufficient curiosity, conviction or compassion for the victims. I then discovered, to my horror, that Fr Michael O'Kelly, a former priest at St Peter's in the 1980s when I was a member of the congregation, had been jailed for nine months after being caught in 2001 with 18,000 indecent photographs and computer images of children, that were described in court as 'disturbing, degrading and disgusting'.

Of course, I recognise the Church of England has also been guilty of dreadful acts of mismanagement in its own handling of child abuse scandals. For example, in June 2017, an independent review concluded senior figures in the Church of England 'colluded' with a former bishop who abused young men. Peter Ball, the predatory former Bishop of Lewes and Gloucester was jailed for thirty-two months in October 2015 after admitting a string of sex offences between the 1970s and 1990s. Dame Moira Gibb's review highlighted a serious failure of the Church of England to respond appropriately to the gross misconduct over a period of many years. There was stinging criticism of the actions of the former Archbishop of Canterbury, George Carey.

Reluctantly, back in 2003, I decided to leave the flock at St Peter's RC church for a while and, during a period of reflection and re-examination started to attend a Parish Communion service at St Paul's, my nearest Church of England church. Immediately, I was deeply moved by the warmth of the welcome I received. I was impressed with the rector, Peter Seal, who worked hard to make his sermons thought provoking, inclusive and intelligent. A retired bishop, living in the parish, occasionally led the service. John Dennis was wonderfully wise, open, funny and compassionate. In addition, I liked the fact that the licensed reader then was a woman. I noticed immediately that everyone seemed to know each other and the warmth of the greeting was extraordinary. St Paul's was known for having 'soft edges', welcoming anyone and everyone, and encouraging people to ask questions. The parish was rooted in community and offered a variety of worship to all ages. It seemed to balance rather well a relaxed approach with a sense of the sacred. The published *Parish Theology* stated: 'We know how hard it can be to have faith, but the quest for meaning is at the heart of our humanity. We know that certainty is rarely possible and can be the enemy of faith.' This was a new concept for me but an attractive one.

Fourteen years on, I continue to attend the Parish Communion service at St Paul's every Sunday morning and I have become a member of the PCC (Parochial Church Council) and the Deanery Synod. However, understandably, my Roman Catholicism has not left me completely. I still use my battered *Weekday Missal* and my 1993 edition *Morning and Evening Prayer Book*. I like to call myself an ecumenical Christian, a catholic with a small 'c' by tradition, a respecter of all faiths and of those people with none. I note how in both Anglican and Roman Catholic services, we all say similarly: 'We believe in one holy catholic and apostolic Church' when reciting the Nicene Creed. I was conceived in September 1957 by an Anglican mother and a Roman Catholic father. That mixture is what has shaped me today. A Christian first and foremost, baptized a Roman Catholic but who practises now within an Anglican tradition. I pray every day for Christian unity. I am attracted to the goal of unity rather than uniformity – respectful of a range of views and interpretations held honestly within a Christian framework.

I still call in occasionally at St Peter's in the day to sit alone in silence. I still go to Mass when I am on holiday in continental Europe. I have also been to a special Roman Catholic Mass held in the Lady Chapel at Winchester Cathedral, which around fifty local Catholics attend on a Saturday morning, once a quarter. I often attend the Festal Services and Evensong at Winchester Cathedral to hear the beautiful singing in such magnificent surroundings. I find Winchester Cathedral to be one of the most awe-inspiring and spiritual buildings in the world. The silence and contemplation afforded by the Epiphany Chapel. The glory and wonder of that spectacular sight looking down the nave. The long history and sense of continuity of the Christian faith when sitting in the Quire and North Transept. I recognize that the Church of England has both strengths and considerable weaknesses, just like the Roman Catholic Church. This Annunciation journey has made me wish even more for both denominations to come closer together. They would both be stronger for it, in my view. But I suspect any significant movement will not happen in my lifetime.

I remember in September 2010 being in the Quire at Westminster Abbey for a special service of Evening Prayer in the presence of Pope Benedict and the incumbent Archbishop of Canterbury, Rowan Williams. It was the first time a Pope had visited the Abbey, the country's coronation church since 1066. For 600 years, it was a Benedictine abbey with close ties to Rome. Then came the Reformation and King Henry VIII's split from Papal authority.

As the two men walked past me, making their way slowly towards the Sanctuary and the High Altar, I remember feeling intense joy and satisfaction. It felt right – the Pope and the Archbishop of Canterbury side by side. For me, in that brief but special hour, it fulfilled a hope and a dream that the Roman Catholic Church and the Church of England could be as one. As Pope Benedict spoke I felt a warm glow: 'This noble edifice evokes England's long history, so deeply marked by the preaching of the gospel and the Christian culture to which it gave birth,' he said. 'I come here today as a pilgrim from Rome, to pray before the tomb of Saint Edward the Confessor and to join you in imploring the gift of Christian unity.'

At that point, I thought about my mother and how my own Christian life up to then had been shaped by both denominations. Dame Mary Tanner, the President of the World Council of Churches, read from St Paul's Letter to the Philippians. John Christie, the Moderator of the General Assembly of the Church of Scotland read the Gospel. Leah Wagstaff, Secretary of the Church of England Youth Council, spoke the following prayer: 'Let us praise God for the shared vision and witness of all Churches within the British Isles proclaiming afresh to every generation the Good News of God's love revealed in Jesus Christ: for their cooperation in this mission and ministry, and for their welcome and openness to all.'

Leaders from the Methodist and United Reformed Churches were also there alongside leaders from the Orthodox Church, the Baptist Union, the Lutheran Church and the Salvation Army.

The Pope and the Archbishop venerated the St Augustine Gospels, said to have been brought from Rome by St Augustine in 597 on his first mission to evangelize Britain, and the oldest illustrated Latin Gospel book still in existence. As they offered prayers at the tomb of Edward the Confessor, the Choir sang *Ubi caritas et amor, Deus ibi est* (Where charity and love are, there is God).

I remember turning to Mark Thompson, then the Director General of the BBC and a devout Roman Catholic, and saying, 'This feels right, Mark. This feels good.'

I had worked for the BBC as a journalist and editor for more than thirty years. Nine months after that service in Westminster Abbey, I left the Corporation. I'd started my career as a researcher and ended it as Deputy Director General and Head of BBC Journalism. In that role, I was responsible for all the BBC's news and current affairs output throughout the United Kingdom and around the world, across its radio, television and interactive services. At the heart of my trade was a curiosity about the world, an ability to listen, and to explain complex issues in an impartial, objective manner. I was trained not to express a view but to promote accuracy and fairness, to seek a wide range of voices and opinions in order to inform audiences and to help them to make up their own minds.

After I left the BBC in 2011, for the first time in years, I had the space and time for serious reflection on my beliefs. I found myself using those journalistic skills once again but in a way that I had not expected when in November 2013, quite by chance, I came across François Lemoyne's painting of the Annunciation at the National Gallery in London. The immediate and profound impact it made on me that day sparked the sudden urge to learn more about the picture's history and, most importantly, to understand more about the meaning of its subject matter.

Luke's story of the Annunciation: thirteen verses; fewer than three hundred words; less than ninety seconds to read.

Over the past three years, I have experienced more than a hundred encounters about that specific text with leading clerics, world-renowned biblical scholars, theologians, artists and art historians and I have heard more than a hundred different interpretations and commentaries. Each response was distinctive, shaped by the faith (or, sometimes, lack of it), histories, education and background of each individual. The discussions focused on belief and non-belief, certainty and doubt, spiritual imagination and interpretation, and the way in which life's experiences can shape a faith. Each time, I asked a set of probing questions and listened carefully and respectfully to the answers. I let the responses speak for themselves. The intimate conversations proved to be highly personal, profound, revealing and, at times, heart rending. When Bishop Philip Egan described the Annunciation as 'the most important event in human history', I decided to ask each interviewee if they thought he was right.

The Annunciation, alongside the Crucifixion, is the most popular Christian image in the history of art. I travelled around England to see many different examples, and I headed to France, the Low Countries, Spain and Italy to stand in front of many of the greatest ever artistic depictions of the story created over the past 2,000 years, including paintings, sculpture, tapestries and ceramics.

I headed to the Holy Land, wandered the streets of Nazareth, and experienced an unforgettable encounter with Cardinal Vincent Nichols as we sat in front of the very place that the Annunciation is believed by many to have taken place.

Now, having absorbed all those experiences, I must decide. What do I believe about the annunciation story? What are my feelings about the story's veracity and its meaning? What phrases from my conversations have proved most memorable and made the most significant impression? What, in particular, has resonated with me? Have I, in any way, changed my mind?

For more than fifty years, before setting out on this journey, I had understood the story of the Annunciation to be literally true in the way that Luke described. I believed that Mary was a virgin, betrothed to Joseph. I thought of her as a young woman, aged between eighteen and twenty. I pictured her wearing blue and white clothing, and presumed the unexpected event happened in her home in Nazareth. I always understood that she was told she was having a baby and assumed that she had no choice in the matter – that Gabriel was giving her an order. I believed the conception of Jesus, Son of God, divine and human, happened there and then. To be honest though, I had never given it much thought. It was simply a given. It is what I was told as a child, and I had never really considered it since. As St Paul wrote in his second Letter to Timothy, I took all the New Testament's words to be true:

> You must keep to what you have been taught and know to be true; remember who your teachers were, and how, ever since you were a child, you have known the holy Scriptures – from these, you can learn the wisdom that leads to salvation through faith in Christ Jesus. All scripture is inspired by God and can profitably be used for teaching, for refuting error, for guiding people's lives and teaching them to be holy. (2 Timothy 3:14-17)

Incredible as it may seem, I had never before considered the historicity of the Annunciation, interrogated its message, assessed its impact on women or determined its relevance for today. That is until I saw the Lemoyne painting three years ago. That moment in Room 33 was the catalyst for me to dig deep; to search; to question; to listen; to think. I began by reflecting on the key meaning of the annunciation story and asking, what is its contemporary message?

'It's the DNA of our faith...it's the story that has everything.' Those words from Professor David Ford in Cambridge strike me as being especially resonant. 'It's a God-sized event,' he told me, 'Luke is stretching our categories, our imaginations, stretching our hearts and minds in order to be open to something amazing, unique, unprecedented and yet deeply resonant with the Old Testament.' Later that same day, a frail Owen Chadwick described the Annunciation to me as, 'the most beautiful story in Scripture and the most important one.'

Sitting in the sacristy in St Paul's Cathedral, Canon Philippa Boardman's comment hit home, 'Mary made room for Christ in her womb. We need to make room for Christ to dwell in us.' Theologian Paula Gooder also struck a chord with her statement, 'It's about the joy that comes when you're able to accept the gift that God wants to give you, however unexpected it is.' I also remember the Anglican priest, Rose Hudson-Wilkin, speaking with passion about how 'the Annunciation draws me to a God who uses the powerless. It's God turning upside down society's way of looking at things. It's about God emptying himself.'

The Church historian, Diarmaid MacCulloch, had a good turn of phrase when he told me in his office in Oxford, 'It makes the Incarnation work metaphorically when opposites – divinity and humanity – shouldn't work together, can't be together. The Annunciation is the hinge on which they work.'

Canon Mark Oakley had a particularly exquisite expression, 'It's about awakening us out of sinful existence to a sense of numinous, the depths, whatever metaphors we want to fall into. Awakening us out of our daily lives to another voice. Awakening the soul to a resonance that is beyond the human – the mirror of God, the transcended – and we all know when it happens.'

In Nazareth, Sister Beatrice told me, 'the story is about trust – total trust and humility in the sense of accepting something very great in life in a very simple way.'

When I asked people to describe the Annunciation in a word or a single phrase, many of the responses stayed with me. Mike Chapman's 'surrender to win'; Vanessa Herrick's 'God's yes to humanity and our yes to God'; Tim Bissett's 'the biggest surprise ever'; and Sam Wells's 'the full revelation of earth to heaven and heaven to earth.'

At the very start of my journey, Brian Rees struck a chord, 'The Annunciation remains awesome in its wonder and power to transform us...it's the moment in time that changed time.' Tina Beattie called it 'the shock of the new – the moment creation finds its meaning.' Tim Gorringe summed it up in one word, 'gift', whilst Lucy Winkett said it means simply 'yes'.

I believe the story's message is essentially about calling and acceptance. It is about hearing the call of God at any moment, and having the chance to reject that call even though God has the power to determine the outcome. The important thing is to be open and ready to respond. For none of us must be afraid to listen to God's call.

For Richard Chartres, the Annunciation is about, 'being alert to the movement of God and being ready to be found.' Mark Wakelin, standing with me in front of the Lemoyne painting, called it, 'the mighty weight of God's promises hanging on the thread of human obedience.' Judith Maltby explained it as 'God's total immersion into human history. Without the Incarnation, I can't see the point of Christianity.' Ben Quash put it another way, 'The Annunciation is the point when the threshold is crossed and from then on redemption is possible.' I love how the Bishop of Salisbury, Nick Holtam, called it, 'the start of the journey' whilst the American artist, Alfonse Borysewicz described it as, 'the end of the journey'. Indeed, my old priest, David Forde, combined the two with his own phrase, 'It's the beginning of our journey back to God.'

I used to think that Jesus Christ was conceived at the Annunciation. Now I understand that it was Jesus who was conceived at that moment, whereas Christ had existed beforehand and exists now and after. That's a difficult concept for anyone to grasp. As the Orthodox priest, Kallistos Ware, put it to me, 'a new beginning but no new person – that's the uniqueness of Christ.'

Cardinal Vincent Nichols memorably called the Annunciation, 'an invitation to remember transcendence. The starting point, the foundation, an annunciation of our transcendence and of both our capacity and calling to understand and share in the life of God.'

The Bishop of Winchester, Tim Dakin, told me, 'The Annunciation is not just a personal encounter. This is God re-engaging with the history of the people [of Israel] that he might, in his mercy, engage with the wider history of the world. The fact that Jesus is going to be the Messiah is a statement about the future of the world. An extraordinary adjustment to reality at that very moment.'

Each of these statements really resonates with me. The more I listened to people, the more I realized that, for many of them, the story rests on the anchor point that Mary had the right to say no to the angel Gabriel. Although I had always presumed that the angel was commanding Mary rather than pleading with her, I now view the matter differently.

John Hall at Westminster Abbey called it, 'the decisive moment. Mary's response is the cosmic yes and the opportunity to say yes to God comes every moment, every day.' Nick Holtam at Salisbury emphasized for me that, 'an incredibly important part of the story is the acceptance. The willingness to go with it. She's the archetypal person there, like each of us, and has the chance or not to respond to God. Our acceptance is down to you and me.'

Jane Hedges at Norwich agreed, 'Mary had a choice. She could have said no. For me, that's fundamentally part of my spirituality. God has a will and a purpose for us but, with that, we have free will – bringing our will into line with God's will and that's what Mary did.' Indeed, Mary's right to choose is fundamental to how Vivienne Faull at York interprets the Annunciation as a story of 'empowerment, emancipation, independence.' Kallistos Ware emphasized how the Annunciation, 'was an invitation, not a compulsory order. God waited for her in full freedom.'

Yet Cardinal Cormac Murphy-O'Connor and others used the word 'surrender'. 'I'm here to do the will of God. We're involved in the mystery of salvation and we somehow have to surrender to it,' he said. The Ugandan born artist, Gloria Ssali, spoke of it being, 'an absolute abandonment to God.' The former Archbishop of Canterbury, George Carey, put it another way, 'the Annunciation is all about the surrendering to the will of God. The submissiveness is all about the freedom to choose. I think it is a very positive thing – the acceptance, the willingness to go the extra mile. Being true to oneself like Mary was.'

I believe the nuns at the Carmelite of the Annunciation got it right. Sister Thérèse described it as 'an act of faith, it's not just a story, we're all in there somewhere.' Sister Mary of Carmel said, 'the fundamental part of the story is asking her if she would say yes'; and Sister Ann Dodd memorably called it, 'a journey into the unknown'. The Annunciation is about listening without knowing the unknown. For we know that we don't know. Faith is deeper than rationality.

Lucy Winkett had an interesting perspective when she said, 'For me, the encounter with the divine presence is the irresistible invitation, which is a paradox. You are free to say no but you can't resist it.' James Atwell put it a different way, 'What you get in Mary and the Annunciation is a sense of God being powerless to make the world come to him. What he's got to do is to draw it to him of its own free will and Mary is the world saying yes to God. The lurch is prefigured in Mary and maybe the confirmation of creation is prefigured in Mary. It shows us transparently the way God works.'

In nearly all my encounters, I asked people if they saw Luke's annunciation story as fact, metaphor, myth, or something else? Perhaps, on reflection, that was the wrong phraseology. It may have been better simply to ask, is it true?

Most academic theologians and scholars appeared to be deeply sceptical about the historicity of the annunciation story. It is clear that belief in the event actually happening as Luke described cannot be rooted in certainty or hard evidence.

When I visited Norwich Cathedral, Jeremy Haselock put it this way, 'Every word of Luke's Gospel is profoundly and deeply true but it is not necessarily historical fact. The Fathers and theologians understood that in the Middle Ages. They could see how these themes were taken from the Old Testament and developed in the New Testament, and they saw it all as a wonderful narrative to enshrine, frame, the essential truth of the Incarnation.' He went on to say, 'It can't be proven to be historical fact but it is profoundly true.'

Sir Mark Tully took up this theme. 'I don't see it as fact but that doesn't mean I see it as a lie. Let's go back to the many ideas of truths. In many ways, whether it's fact or not doesn't really matter to me. That question is not relevant for the way I feel about it.'

Some of my interviewees were persuaded that it is historical fact.

'It's vitally important for me that it's fact because of the blending of divinity and humanity, the joining of heaven and earth,' Sue Wallace from Winchester Cathedral told me. 'It's saying something about transformative grace and I just feel in my guts it's more than a metaphor,' Judith Maltby commented. Not surprisingly, both the Roman Catholic Cardinals, the Carmelite nuns and many clerics took that view too, more in faith and hope than in absolute certainty, of course. They believe and trust that the encounter between the angel Gabriel and Mary actually happened.

I used to believe that the detail of the story was factually correct. However, after thinking about it deeply, I have changed my mind. Now I am more persuaded that the story was written by Luke as an addition to his Gospel to try to explain the uniqueness of Jesus. Mark never mentioned the event in Nazareth. Matthew deployed the parallel idea of Joseph hearing from the angel Gabriel in a dream. Indeed, later in his Gospel, Matthew suggests Joseph, Mary and Jesus only settled in Nazareth after returning from Egypt, where they had fled to escape from King Herod's wrath. John never referenced the angel Gabriel visiting Mary in his Gospel but proclaimed, 'The Word was made flesh and dwelt amongst us.' The angel Gabriel-Mary encounter is Luke's Sondergut (i.e., material unique to Luke's Gospel).

Now, I see his annunciation story more as metaphorical. I would love it to have happened as Luke wrote it. However, I agree with Rose Hudson-Wilkin that, 'the meaning of the story is more important than the actual story.' As Lucy Winkett put it, 'I think it could have happened but a metaphor is more true for me than fact. It's beyond a fact. I get to the truth behind it. So I think it's profoundly true.'

I remember the words of Jyoti Sahi to me, 'It's a Christian myth and myths are often more important than empirical facts.' Mark Oakley echoed his sentiments, 'The Annunciation is mythology. It's not about what happened. It's about what happens.' The Hampshire textile artist, Alice Kettle, said, 'I don't see it as fact. I see it as something deeply spiritual in a kind of celestial way. I'm not sure what it is. It's an archetypal myth that's humanizing – a transcendence.' The musician, Martin Neary, spoke to me on the same lines, 'The comprehension of the Annunciation is beyond me. But that doesn't mean I don't believe it. In a way, it doesn't matter that I can't comprehend it.' The Head of the Barbican, Nick Kenyon, commented, 'I see the story as meaningful myth. It embodies a great truth. The actual factual accuracy is not the main point about it. The central message is of accepting something from the outside over which you have no control. The possibility of a shock that can happen tomorrow. Who knows?' James Atwell, the retired Dean of Winchester Cathedral memorably told me, 'I'm on the frontier between fact and metaphor.'

Some may see that last response as a fudge but I think it is a good answer. I would like the Annunciation to have happened as Luke describes; I haven't a clue if it did, particularly in the way Luke sets out, but I somehow doubt it. However, it is the meaning of the story that is most important.

The American Franciscan priest, Richard Rohr, from the Centre for Action and Contemplation in New Mexico, wrote: 'All religious language is metaphor by necessity. It's always pointing towards the mystery that you don't know until you have experienced it. Without it, the metaphor largely remains empty.'

He stresses how we should look for meaning, not answers: 'Whether a myth is historical truth is not even important. We want and need them to be true. Such myths proceed from the deep and collective unconscious of humanity. Our myths are stories and images that are not always true in particular but entirely true in general. They're usually not historic fact but invariably they are spiritual genius. They hold life and death, the explainable and the unexplainable, together as one. They hold together the paradoxes that the rational mind cannot process by itself. Myths, as do good poems, make unclear and confused emotions brilliantly clear, even life changing. Myths are true because they work!'

Mariann Burke, in her book, *Re-Imagining Mary*, describes the Annunciation as 'a poetic truth – a myth rooted in intuitive thinking rather than rational thinking. The Annunciation and the Resurrection are myths. Jesus and his life is logos. Myths express truths closer to life's meaning than facts and resonate in the soul.'

I agree that the power of the annunciation story lies more in its symbolic truth, not its literal truth. However, I believe that the crucifixion and resurrection actually happened. I think that is central to the Christian faith. It seems to me that to interpret the crucifixion and the resurrection as purely metaphorical is to reject the central tenet of Christianity – that Jesus, the Christ figure, was both divine and human and did rise from the dead.

As St Paul said in his First Letter to the Corinthians: 'If Christ raised from the dead is what has been preached, how can some of you be saying that there is no resurrection of the dead? If there is no resurrection of the dead, Christ himself cannot have been raised, and if Christ has not been raised, then our preaching is useless and your believing it is useless; indeed we are shown up as witnesses who have committed perjury before God, because we swore in evidence before God that he had raised Christ to life.' (1 Cor. 15:12-15a)

George Carey, the former Archbishop of Canterbury, concurred when he commented, 'Personally, I can say with certainty, I accept the Resurrection. With the Virgin Birth, I'm not so sure but I accept it because it's the most satisfying version to make sense of the story.'

Philip Morgan told me his guidance to himself is to 'believe more and more in less and less. Believe more and more in the Resurrection and less and less in the rest of the gospel story as accurate, historic information.' Everybody who had anything to do with the production of the Gospels was convinced that the Resurrection had taken place, he observed, and they were working back from the Resurrection within the oral tradition. In that context, he was more persuaded that the annunciation story was a metaphor than historic fact.

Alfonse Borysewicz, the American artist, also started with the Resurrection and worked backwards. However, he told me he sees the annunciation story as both fact and metaphor. 'I'm ok holding the line between an obsession with certainty and the mystery of it all. I think it happened but the logistics of it all, I don't know. I don't really care. I just feel it in my own Christian life.'

For now, I think I am somewhere between both these last two perspectives. That is my view for now, but, of course, it could well change in future. As Steve Chalke commented, 'The Annunciation is like a goldmine that I can never finish mining. Even if I got to 150, I'd still be finding truths about it I'd never seen before. For me, the centrality of the story is about God's intention with ordinary people to bring about extraordinary things.'

Although I may have serious doubts now about the annunciation story's factual veracity, I no longer worry about that. Belief is not about striving for literal truth. It is about a trust and commitment to the annunciation story's key message and meaning. I like the late Gerald Priestland's turn of phrase in *Priestland's Progress*, his own pilgrimage described as 'one man's search for Christianity now', when broadcast in 1981 on BBC Radio: 'Christianity is not a way of unreasonable certainty. It is a far more interesting way of reasonable uncertainty.' He highlighted that the four gospel writers were telling 'the truth' as they saw it in terms natural to them at the time.

I believe in the Resurrection and I think of myself as a Christian. But do I have to believe in the Annunciation to be a Christian? I certainly don't think a Christian has to believe in the literal truth of an angel visiting Mary or even of a virgin conception. For me, the critical belief must be in the Incarnation. That Jesus was born, and was both divine and human. That God at that moment was both transcendent and immanent. I believe there has to be something supernatural to make sense of it all. However, the specific circumstances in which the Incarnation happened is no longer a pivotal factor in my belief.

I can see the theological convenience of the virgin conception – a one-off, miraculous event that creates the divine and the human in Jesus. But I no longer believe it to be crucial. I don't agree with Robin White's assertion that, 'the virgin conception is extremely important because it expresses the divine fatherhood of God.' I don't know how Jesus was created. The details thereof do not inform my faith.

I have also realized on this journey that I prefer the description of Jesus as Jesus Christ to that of Son of God. I think of Jesus as God in human form but I now shy away somewhat from some of the gender specific Trinitarian language of God the Father and God the Son. For me, God is the maker of heaven and earth, of all that is, seen and unseen. God is the living creation, past, present and future. As the first Letter of John says: 'God is love; and those who live in love live in God, and God lives in them' (1 John 4:16). I believe that the power of the Most High covers me and you with its shadow and that nothing is impossible to God. Rather than the language of 'God in three persons', I favour more 'one God in three dimensions': God the Almighty – the Creator; God the Christ – as Jesus the teacher and redeemer; God the Holy Spirit – the live communicator and active God in all of us.

I love John Taylor's description of the Holy Spirit as 'the Go-Between' and how in the annunciation story the Holy Spirit makes each of the two characters really see each other.

And it is through that spiritual force, that breath, that *rūach*, that I hope is the way God and I can communicate and can always be together.

I found Kenneth Cracknell's view on Luke's passage particularly thought provoking. That the Annunciation offers us, 'a midrash on something that doesn't actually happen but ought to have happened and deepens our understanding of what did happen. He [Luke] wants to say this is the inner meaning and the inner meaning is much more certain than history.' I like the notion of midrash.

Although I found John Shelby Sponge's language a little harsh and unequivocal, at the same time, it was enlightening: 'The idea of the virgin birth is nonsense. What it is really about is a proclamation of a living faith. The virgin birth allegory says that human life alone could not have produced the God presence that was found in Jesus of Nazareth. It's mythology but also profound faith. It forces us to see faith in dimensions larger than literal truth.'

One day, I was flicking through *The Complete Bible Handbook* by John Bowker – a former Dean of Trinity College, Cambridge, published in 1998. In a section on how accurate the Gospels were in recording what actually happened, he highlighted six approaches: source criticism, form criticism, redaction criticism, reader criticism, structuralist criticism and rhetorical criticism – before concluding:

> There is no final meaning of the text, only ways of discerning new and important layers of meaning but meanings that are nonetheless controlled by the text itself. The Bible does not depend on the extent to which it is a good or bad history book. Truth about God and about human beings can be found just as much in fiction as in fact, in a poem as in prose, in a novel as in a scientific paper, perhaps more so.

I also read an interesting book called *The Myth of God Incarnate*, published in 1977, which contains a set of provocative essays by nine theologians and was edited by John Hick, the then Professor of Theology at Birmingham University. The book argues that in the interests of truth, we should consider 'Jesus was "a man approved by God" for a special role within the divine purpose and that the later perception of him as God incarnate, the Second Person of the Holy Trinity living a human life, is a mythological or poetic way of expressing his significance for us.' It suggests 'the traditional doctrine of the Incarnation has long been something of a shibboleth, exempt from reasoned scrutiny and treated with unquestioning literalness.' Jesus is discussed as a human who offers 'the perception of God'. One theologian, Frances Young, describes it as seeing God in Jesus and that 'he is as-if-God for me'. This rejection of the notion of Jesus as both divine and human proved highly controversial at the time of the publication.

But as I believe Jesus to be uniquely divine and human, the promised one born to Mary, then I accept that Mary is the mother of God. She is the theotokos – the God-bearer. However, after fifty years of seeing her as 'Our Lady' and a person to venerate, I am now more cautious about her status. She was described to me as 'the pivotal point' and in one sense she is. But I accept now that the Roman Catholic Church has put her on such a pedestal, presenting her as the perpetual virgin who intercedes for us, and elevating her as the perfect one, that she can appear to have lost her humanity.

In his Mariological Apostolic Exhortation, *Marialis Cultus*, published in 1974, Pope Paul VI wrote: '[Mary] with her generous "fiat" (cf. Lk. 1:38) became through the working of the Spirit the Mother of God, but also the true Mother of the living, and, by receiving into her womb the one Mediator (cf. 1 Tim. 2:5), became the true Ark of the Covenant and true Temple of God.'

I want to regard her in much more human terms – as an ordinary woman who was called on unexpectedly to do something utterly extraordinary. When one thinks of Mary as a young Galilean girl, probably twelve to fourteen years of age, the shock of her trust and acceptance is even greater.

I remember Cardinal Cormac Murphy-O'Connor and I had a fascinating and frank conversation about Mary over a lunch. Describing her as 'the first disciple', he urged me to read the Anglican-Roman Catholic International Commission's statement on her entitled, *Mary: Grace and Hope in Christ*. I studied the text in detail, together with accompanying commentaries, essays and a study guide. Known as the Seattle Statement, it was published in 2005 as the agreed position of the ecumenical Commission on Christian faith and devotion relating to the Blessed Virgin Mary. ARCIC sought to agree what could be held in common within a common heritage for both Anglicans and Roman Catholics as it attempted to portray Mary 'within a pattern of grace and hope in Christ.'

ARCIC concluded that any interpretation of Mary must not obscure the unique mediation of Christ. It is Christ who is the sole mediator between God and humankind and any consideration of Mary must be linked with the doctrines of Christ and the Church. The Commission recognised Mary as Theotokos - the mother of God incarnate - and, in that context, the members agreed that Mary was prepared by grace to be the mother of the Redeemer, by whom she, herself, was received and redeemed with glory. ARCIC recognised Mary as a model of holiness, faith and obedience for all Christians and as a prophetic figure of the Church, concluding it was impossible to be faithful to Scripture without giving due attention to the person of Mary. Following a re-reception of the place of Mary in the faith and life of the Church, the Commission agreed that Christ's redeeming work 'reached 'back in Mary to the depth of her being and to her earliest beginnings.' It concluded that the 'teaching about Mary in the two definitions of the Immaculate Conception and the Assumption, understood within the biblical pattern of the economy of hope and grace, can be said to be consonant with the teachings of the Scriptures and the ancient common traditions.' Such agreement, ARCIC hoped, would place the question about authority which arise from the two definitions of 1854 and 1950 in a new ecumenical context.

In a Preface to the Agreed Statement, the Co-Chairs of ARCIC wrote:

> Mary, the Mother of Our Lord Jesus Christ, stands before us as an exemplar of faithful obedience, and her 'Be it to me according to your word" is the grace-filled response each of us is called to make to God, both personally and communally as the Church, the body of Christ. It is as figure of the Church, her arms uplifted in prayer and praise, her hands open in receptivity and availability to the outpouring of the Holy Spirit, that we are as one with Mary as she magnifies the Lord.

On this journey, I have come to realize more deeply how the positioning of Mary in the annunciation story can be divisive, particularly for women. I understand now that for some women, she can be a symbol of suppression, of obedience to patriarchy, of surrender to male dominance and how the promotion of her purity and virginity has damaged many a woman's psyche.

The Bible Society theologian, Paula Gooder, told me, 'Personally, I think [Mary's description in the Annunciation] has done enormous damage and particularly for those of us who ourselves are mothers. Mary is held up as an ideal none of us can achieve – to be a virgin and a mother.'

Feminist theologian, Lisa Isherwood conveyed the criticism much more starkly when she said, 'Mary has been an appalling message for women – you can be a virgin or a whore – and most women are neither.'

I appreciate how, in the annunciation story, Mary's motherhood promotes Jesus's humanity whilst her virginity promotes his divine status. I understand how the early Christian writers saw her obedience as a direct contrast to Eve's disobedience in the Genesis story in the Old Testament. However, for me, the idea of the preservation of Mary's virginity whilst giving birth (*virginitas in partu*) seems to be unnecessary and the notion of her perpetual virginity (*virginitas post partum*) to be without biblical foundation – neither element is referenced anywhere in any of the four canonical Gospels.

I believe that Mary had more children after Jesus. This is clearly referenced in Scripture and I cannot see the harm in believing that. Was her first pregnancy the result of a virginal conception? Possibly. Was she a perpetual virgin? I don't want to think so.

Whether or not Mary is 'the most influential leader in history after Jesus, a role model for us all,' as Nicky Gumbel described her to me, seems highly debatable but I like his phrase that 'her act is the greatest and most decisive act of faith in history.'

Ah yes, that gets us on to the claim from Bishop Philip Egan, that the Annunciation 'is the most important event in human history'. I can see how he gets there. You cannot have the Resurrection without the Crucifixion and for a Jesus that is both divine and human, there has to have been an Incarnation. According to Luke, that happened at the Annunciation. Everything starts with that moment; hence the claim that it is the most important event in human history. However, I am reluctant to earmark that one event above the others. I believe the Incarnation and the Resurrection are the two most important events in human history and the annunciation encounter is a pivotal moment in the sequence of events. I was struck by Mary Frances McKenna's words at the Ecumenical Society of the Blessed Virgin Mary conference in Cambridge, 'I think it's imperative the Annunciation is reconnected with the Incarnation because, in many ways, the meaning of each is so very different. There's no Mother without the Son and there's no Son without the Mother.'

I think it is such a pity that 25 March occurring within Lent reduces the importance of the feast of the Annunciation. Inevitably the solemnity of Lent dilutes the celebration or eclipses its significance completely. However, I feel strongly that the mystery of the Incarnation at that moment of conception needs to be marked more fully and distinctively within the liturgical year. Perhaps the Roman Catholic Church and the Anglican Communion could take a leaf out of the Orthodox Church and promote 25 March as one of the greatest feast days for celebration and contemplation, only superseded by Easter.

I believe that the Annunciation has far greater status and theological significance than the birth of Mary (8 September), the Solemnity of her as the Mother of God (so soon after Christmas on 1 January) and especially the Immaculate Conception (8 December) and the Assumption (15 August), both of which I struggle with. If Bishop Philip Egan is right that it is 'the most important event in human history' or if Cardinal Vincent Nichols's description of it as 'the most important word of consent ever uttered in human history' is correct, then surely all Christians should celebrate the feast of the Annunciation, and therein the moment of the Incarnation, more wholeheartedly. However, I doubt that anything will change in the near future.

Three years on from wandering the streets of Winchester on the feast day of the Annunciation, I did the same again on Saturday 25 March 2017. My pilgrimage was over, the manuscript pretty much completed. When I woke up, I checked my email box. Richard Rohr did not mention the Annunciation at all in his daily meditation piece for that day, sent to thousands of subscribers around the world, including me, via the Internet. Again, there were no services at the main Baptist church in Winchester or at the United Reformed church on Jewry Street. The Hope church in the centre of the city was again all locked up – the same as three years ago. My own church, St Paul's, was closed too. Even the Tractarian church of the Holy Trinity had no service.

There was a single Mass at 9 a.m. at the Roman Catholic church of St Peter's. Only nineteen people attended, all of them over fifty years old. The priest, Fr Tom McGrath, wore a white chasuble with a blue cross motif. In a distinct Irish brogue, he gave a very brief sermon that lasted less than ninety seconds.

'Mary had a lot of questions about what God was asking her to take on,' he said, 'and this is what she was prepared to do. Her response was, "Here I am Lord, I come to do your will." So all of us gathered here this morning – we want to make a similar response. God has called us to follow in his wake. All of us have many uncertainties about our future and maybe we don't understand many things as clearly as we should. But we do know we have been called and we want, generously, to make our response, our commitment to the way that we have been called.'

At Winchester Cathedral, there was no festal service, not even an Evensong with the choir. A Holy Communion Service according to the Book of Common Prayer was held at midday. It was taken by Canon Brian Rees, the priest who had conducted the Annunciation service there three years before. He welcomed the eight people who gathered in the small Epiphany Chapel, all of them well over sixty years of age.

'Nine months today is Christmas Day,' he told us. 'A long journey for Mary and for us in some ways too. The Annunciation is very important to many of us because it teaches us that God calls, not because of our greatness or intellect but in humility and gentleness, to give, whoever we are and whatever we are, the best of everything to God. Do take time to study the Annunciation. It is full of import.'

As he spoke, the glorious sunshine outside lit up the Burne-Jones Annunciation stained-glass window directly above me. At the end of the service, Brian Rees greeted me warmly and asked how the book was going? I told him it was almost finished. He said to a woman standing next to us, 'Now here's a man who has really felt a calling, an annunciation, this past three years.' I told her what the book is about. 'The Annunciation – it's completely lost today', she sighed as we walked along the north aisle of the nave. 'I don't know what can be done.'

The greatest artistic challenge with the Incarnation, along with the Resurrection, is that it cannot be visualized. That is why so much religious art features the angel Gabriel and Mary at the Annunciation. Luke's story gives us a visual handle on how to reflect the great mystery. Over the past three years I have seen so many artistic expressions of the Annunciation – at least one hundred and fifty of them close up. That image of Mary from my First Holy Communion book, *My Lord and My God*, will stay with me throughout my life. So, too, of course, will François Lemoyne's *The Annunciation*. No other painting has made such a dramatic impact on me, uniquely causing an abandonment of everyday life in pursuit of its story. Even so, I don't like it particularly. It is too romanticized and baroque for my taste. But I will never forget it. When I visit the National Gallery in future, I will always call in on Room 33 and say hello.

There were six other works of art, in particular, that made the biggest impression on me during the journey. Alfonse Borysewicz's *Beginning Comes Last*; Chris Gollon's *Annunciation*; Caroline Hall's *Annunciation 9*; Henry Moore's *Mother and Child : Hood*; the Joseph Pyrz statue *Annunciation 2*; and Henry Ossawa Tanner's *The Annunciation*.

Each in their own way fulfilled what Karl Biesenbach, the Chief Curator at Large at MoMA in New York said to *Time* magazine in June 2015: 'Art can change the way we look at the world. It can reveal a certain beauty or truth, and it definitely is a disruption, a disturbance or a moment of epiphany where we pause and our view of everything else changes.'

The unmediated experience of looking at each one of them made a connection, raised questions and challenged my opinion of the annunciation story.

As well as those stunning artistic images, it is Sir John Tavener's extraordinary piece of music, *Annunciation* that has spoken to me in an equally powerful way. Every time I listen to it, I am captivated. I often think of Tavener's words about his own musical search, whilst in discussion with Joan Bakewell in her BBC Radio 3 series, *Belief*: 'Music should be metaphysics. If it is not that, if it doesn't express love, if it doesn't express some kind of metaphysics, then for me, it's not doing anything at all...you have to find your own voice, you have to find the primordial voice. And one spends one's whole life looking for this primordial voice.'

By the end of his life, Tavener had distanced himself from the organized Church and spoke of the way he was inspired musically by 'virgin nature', which he saw in a sense as God's art. 'This is what the narrowness of Christianity doesn't comprehend,' he commented. 'It's not just the revelation of Jesus of Nazareth. Everywhere you look is God, if you look for it in the right places. Your wonder is nature. You're in his nature.'

In poetry, I will especially remember forever the stunning words and beautiful phraseology that both St John of the Cross and Denise Levertov deploy in their Annunciation inspired poems.

———

One thing I have learned during the past three years may seem simple and rather obvious: the more you look, the more you see; the more you listen, the more you hear. I realize that Christians respond to the story of the Annunciation as to a painting or a piece of music – imparting layers of interpretation that reflect their own life experience, beliefs and hopes. Hearing so many different interpretations does not weaken the important meaning of the story, its poetic truth. If anything, such diversity strengthens its resonance through listening, absorbing, questioning and reflecting.

Doubting its historicity does not mean failure or rejection of the story. Belief in the Annunciation is not rooted in certainty. Faith is not rooted in rational evidence. Trust, hope and commitment are at the heart of faith.

For fifty years, I had seen doubt as a kind of weakness: a route to undermining the whole foundation of my faith. Now I see it the other way around. Questioning, weighing up, doubting, is healthy and essential.

As Cardinal Basil Hume once said, 'It's only when I begin to doubt that I really make an honest act of faith.' Sister Julienne in the BBC television drama series, *Call the Midwife*, got it right when she remarked, 'Certainty is fleeting. That is why we must have faith.'

We can never prove the existence of God and, for me, the importance lies in a belief in the mystery of the Annunciation, not its literal truth. I see Luke's Gospel as a record and guide, not a direct communication from God. Whether the Annunciation actually happened as Luke describes, I doubt.

As my journey draws to a close, I remind myself of the words of Sister Thérèse at the Carmelite of the Annunciation, 'You're dealing with something vast here, way beyond our human understanding.'

The Bishop of Salisbury, Nick Holtam, advised me, 'You need to look in and you need to look out.' I have tried to do that over the past three years and this unique journey has been stimulating, profound and illuminating – an opportunity to listen to each contributor and to listen within.

But it has also made me recognize how, for so many people in Britain today, the Annunciation, Christianity and religion as a whole are irrelevant and meaningless. We live in a world where, apparently 96 per cent of UK citizens do not read the Bible and an extraordinary 45 per cent of children have never heard a Bible story other than the Nativity. So why did I not use my BBC training in accuracy, fairness and balance to ensure at least half of my dialogues were with atheists, agnostics or non-believers, who would dismiss the story completely?

The point of this journey has been to understand the meaning of the annunciation story and its contemporary message for a wide range of believers and for those who have been influenced directly by the annunciation story to produce an artistic work. It would not have taken the exploration very far to hear a consistent response that the Annunciation had no meaning whatsoever and that it is 'all rubbish'.

I approached the eminent scientist Professor Steve Jones because his pioneering genetic research highlights, scientifically, that a human virgin conception is impossible. I spoke to my own family because their relative lack of belief has resulted in me questioning and challenging my own faith. Grayson Perry may be a non-believer but he created a stunning tapestry, *The Annunciation of the Virgin Deal*, influenced in part by the annunciation story and I wanted to understand the inspiration behind it.

For atheists, the idea of God is at best irrelevant, at worst delusional, made up by humans to meet a human need. Faith, they say, is a desire for fulfilment, 'a brilliant invention' as Dr Jonathan Miller once described it.

I could have highlighted non-believing philosophers such as Marx, Freud and Ayer. How, for example, A. J. Ayer's idea of logical positivism, proclaimed in his 1936 thesis, *Language, Truth and Logic*, rejects any statement that cannot be verified by sense experience, thereby rendering such statements meaningless. A search for God may be emotionally understandable but not intellectually coherent. Freddie Ayer always said he just did not get religion and he certainly would have dismissed the Annunciation.

The late essayist and religious critic, Christopher Hitchens, claimed religion poisons everything. In his international best seller, *God Is Not Great*, published in 2007, he wrote:

> There still remain four irreducible objections to religious faith: that it wholly misrepresents the origins of man and the cosmos, that because of this original error it manages to combine the maximum of servility with the maximum of solipsism, that it is both the result and the cause of dangerous sexual repression, and that it is ultimately

grounded on wish-thinking…thus the mildest criticism of religion is also the most radical and the most devastating one. Religion is man-made.

If he was still alive, he would most likely have said the Annunciation was simply a made-up story with no credibility or substance.

I could have approached the well-known atheist, ethologist and evolutionary biologist Richard Dawkins to hear him tell me in no uncertain terms how the notion of religious faith was delusional but where would that have taken me in understanding the specific message of the Annunciation? For him, Darwinism is the only explanation for the existence of all life. 'I care about evidence as the reason for knowing what is true,' he once said.

But as Gerald Priestland wisely observed in 1984, no proof of God has ever been totally convincing or there would be no atheists. Nor has there been any total disproof or there would be no believers.

I am open to the possibility that God does not exist. I accept I have no proof. But faith is not about proof; it is not based on logic, rationality or science. I trust that God exists. I experience God every day. I accept God every hour. I connect with God, I hope, every moment. I try to feel God deep within me. I want to be challenged by my faith but I stand as a believer in Jesus Christ of my own free will. It is not a blind faith.

I am not ruled by dogma but I feel an omnipresence of God. It feels right to me. I am happy to be a member of the great universal Church of Christianity. A Church of tradition; a listening Church; a believing Church; a questioning Church.

I recognize that many people are agnostics or non-believers. Some may wish they could believe in the Annunciation and the Christian gospel teaching of Incarnation, Resurrection and Redemption but are unable to make such a leap of faith. They may believe in a supreme or supernatural force, even accepting a God-like notion but cannot accept Jesus as Christ, divine and human. Although some agnostics do not believe the Annunciation to be a historical event, they may still view it as a metaphorical truth expressed in story form.

I remember listening to Sir Mark Tully on BBC Radio 4 one early morning present a powerful and rather personal edition of *Something Understood* called 'The Myth of Christmas'. How should we interpret the traditional Christian stories, he asked, as we prepare for an increasingly secular holiday? Many of those who crowd into churches for midnight Mass or other services at Christmas, he said, will find it difficult to believe the gospel stories literally or to accept the traditional view of Jesus as God come down on earth. But they might well be moved by the liturgy, the carols, their memories of Christmases past, the sense that this is the one day when the world does stop. It may be that they wish they could find some meaning in the Christmas story. For them, the Virgin Birth could well be one of the stumbling blocks, which stand in the way of a credible Christmas. The intention of the programme was to discover that it is possible to find meaning in Christmas without believing the stories actually happened.

Sir Mark highlighted the power of mythical interpretation and explored the idea that regarding the story as myth can give meaning to Christmas without belief in the traditional Christology. He emphasized the validity of the Christmas myth across time and tradition and its reflection in other religions, for example, the birth story of the Hindu God Krishna. He was born divine. His mother was a virgin. As a baby he escaped miraculously from a tyrannical ruler who wanted to kill him.

A myth is not an untruth or a lie, Sir Mark said. There's truth, untruth and myth or mythical truth. He quoted the theologian, Karen Armstrong, in her book, *The Case for*

God, that, 'a myth was never intended as an accurate account of a historical event. A myth could tell us something profoundly true about our humanity. It showed us how to live more richly and intensely.'

Maybe the right question is not, is it true? Rather to ask, am I being true to the Annunciation's message? Am I alert to hearing the calling? Am I attentive to it? Am I alert to God's question and direction for me?

This journey has shown me how, by examining one important but small text of the New Testament, a whole range of interpretations and perspectives can be offered, even from Christian believers. So diverse have been the insights that I am aware they may potentially undermine the previous certainty and conviction of some readers. Indeed, it might lead some to wonder what would happen if each story in the New Testament was exposed to the same level of scrutiny and debate. Could that potentially undermine its reliability as a book of record? If so, what would be the consequences? Would the very notion of faith be put in question?

In fact, I have found the opposite to be true. Not only has the experience illuminated my understanding of my faith. It has strengthened it. I have come to realize that the message of each story in the Bible is far more important than the detail. The New Testament, of course, is the work of a range of writers. It was not literally written by God but was inspired by God. It is not infallible.

The late American writer, Madeleine L'Engle wrote in her 1997 book, *Bright Evening Star: Mysteries of the Incarnation*: 'Don't try to explain the Incarnation to me! It is further from being explainable than the furthest star in the furthest galaxy. It is love, God's limitless love enfleshing that love into the form of a human being, Jesus the Christ, fully human and fully divine.'

Chloë Reddaway, standing in front of François Lemoyne's painting at the National Gallery, told me, 'It's not just about understanding the story. It's about understanding the significance of the story – the meaning of the meaning.' I think that's exactly right.

Humphrey Wine, the former Curator of Seventeenth- and Eighteenth-Century French Painting there, was instrumental in bringing the Lemoyne picture to the National Gallery. Ironically, the words he used to describe the composition of the Lemoyne painting are a good summary of my own faith journey, 'The dynamic is like a spinning top. At the moment a spinning top is placed on the floor, it's in constant movement but it stays in the same place.'

My youngest daughter, Lily, although a non-believer, spoke some wise words to me, 'Don't expect to come to a final conclusion Dad about what the painting and the story mean. Everyone sees different things in the painting and in the story. I'm sure we all are saying different things to you. Who's to say one's right and one's not?'

Having heard so many views from such a variety of people, I just wish words such as 'right', 'wrong', 'confirm', 'reject', 'definitely' and 'certain' were used sparingly, if at all. George Carey memorably told me, 'I can't see why we can't live together as one family with our differences. In our family of twenty-three, when we get together, children and grandchildren and all, we disagree over many different things but we're still together because we love one another.'

Naïve, possibly. A child-like dream, maybe. But I say amen to that sentiment. Indeed, I feel some empathy with the perennial tradition that recognizes most religions in the world have a recurring theme of a divine reality, whether it be Judaism, Christianity, Islam, Hinduism or whatever. No religious tradition, I feel, holds the whole truth exclusively to itself. Of course, any religious person is influenced by birth, family background, social and cultural context and life experience. Different religious followers are all searching for wholeness and meaning.

I worry about the increasingly secular world and the diminishing place of God in people's lives. Recently, in his retirement, Pope Benedict made a profound observation about secular modernity: 'A society where God is absent destroys itself. This is what we have seen in the great totalitarian experiments of the last century.' Moreover, this sentiment also comes at a time when we live our lives increasingly in a world of post-truth politics, fake news and conspiracy theories. The search for 'truth' is emerging as one of the big philosophical ideas and political battlegrounds of the early twenty-first century. Fact, opinion, fiction and deceit all mix together on the Internet to create imagined truth. 'What is truth?' Pilate rightly asked (John 18:38). For me, the mystery of the Annunciation may not be rooted in fact but it is not untrue. It holds a profound and truthful message.

Rowan Williams has written recently in his wonderful, concise book, *Being Disciples*, about a loss of confidence in reason in our contemporary world: 'By that I don't mean a loss of confidence in rational procedures so much as a loss of patience with argument, real mutual persuasion; a loss of the ideas that by mutual persuasion and careful argument we might have our minds enlarged to receive more of the truth.'

My Annunciation journey has been liberating as well as insightful and has certainly enlarged my mind. I feel more passionate about my own faith, more confident and yet more humble, more steadfast and also more hopeful. I have had a wonderful opportunity to listen, to learn and to open myself up to fresh perspectives.

My own reflections, inevitably, whilst firmly held today, will be fluid. They are my views for now, but, of course, they could change in future. As Steve Chalke said to me, 'The Annunciation is like a goldmine that I can never finish mining. Even if I got to 150, I would still be finding truths about it I'd never seen before. For me, the centrality of the story is about God's intention with ordinary people to bring about extraordinary things.'

I recognize that a willingness to change is key to the continuity of my Christian faith. Change is a strength, not a weakness, as new ideas and fresh insights shape my future thinking.

The way ahead now will be to carry forward the Annunciation's message. To look out and listen for the calling; to read the Scriptures regularly; to discern and look deep within myself; to continue to discover; to say yes to God's love, kindness and compassion; to promote in any small way I can a world of integrity, fairness and justice; and always to be guided by Jesus's teachings. How the calling may manifest itself precisely in the months and years ahead is, as yet, unknown. But I am alert and ready. Open to the glimmer of God and God's love.

Pope Francis has spoken about the way in which people look for an escape from the call, and find ways of avoiding it, whilst God is looking, waiting for the response: 'Jesus himself is God's yes. The feast of the Annunciation is a perfect occasion to think about one's life and whether or not we always say yes or often hide with our heads down, like Adam and Eve, not exactly saying no but pretending not to know what God is asking.'

Richard Rohr, the Franciscan priest, summed it up powerfully in one of his eloquent daily meditations, entitled 'Love, Our First and Final Home':

> Human history is one giant wave of unearned grace, and you are now another wave crashing on the sands of time, edged forward by the many waves behind you. You are a fully adopted son or daughter in God's one eternal family. To accept such an objective truth is the only sense in which you need to be a Christian or believer. It's

the best and deepest understanding of how the Risen Christ spreads his forgiving heart through history. It is not a role or office we are passing on – that is not the meaning of 'apostolic succession'. We are passing on the very love of God from age to age.

When I sat quietly in the Slipper Chapel at Walsingham, I picked up a little book called *Message of Walsingham* by R. W. Connelly. He writes: 'The pilgrim is a seeker. He is searching for God, a deeper understanding of God's goodness and a closer personal relationship with him. He is always seeking; he will never find his final answer in this world. The true pilgrim is always in transit; he never really arrives.'

Three years on, in what is described increasingly as a post-modern, post-Christian world, I say, 'Let it be according to thy word', as I remain a pilgrim on a journey.

––––––––

It is May 2017, the manuscript is complete and I am checking through the final draft of the book. As I look through the final chapter, an unexpected message arrives by email. It comes from the new Dean of Winchester, The Very Reverend Catherine Ogle. The announcement of her appointment was made back in September 2016 and she is now settling into her new role. As the former Dean of Birmingham, she has succeeded James Atwell to become the first woman Dean in the history of Winchester Cathedral. She wonders if I can come and see her at her office by the Cathedral. I have met her briefly a couple of times since her arrival in the city. 'I'm seven weeks in now and I'm writing in the hope that we might meet up?' she asks.

A few days later, after we exchange pleasantries and I enquire about how she is settling in, she lands a most unexpected question. Having spoken with the Bishop of Winchester and members of Chapter, she announces that the Bishop and herself would like me to become an Honorary Lay Canon at the Cathedral and a member of the Cathedral Chapter. 'Pause and have a think about it,' she says. 'Don't rush.' I respond by saying that I am shocked and that their invitation is totally unexpected. 'The Lord works in mysterious ways,' I say.

Three weeks later, we meet again and I tell her I am both flattered and delighted to accept. I felt both humbled and thrilled to say yes. On 24th May, I receive the formal invitation from the Bishop and I am informed that the licensing and installation will take place at Choral Evensong on 16th July 2017.

At the service, Winchester Cathedral's Choir is on stunning form. Immediately after the formal proceedings are over, including me being led by the Dean's right hand to my assigned stall, the Choir deliver a soaring rendition of the Magnificat, set to John Ireland's music. As I stand and look across at the surpliced boys and men, the words from their mouths soar all around the exquisite fourteenth-century oak choir stalls :

> My soul doth magnify the Lord:
> > and my spirit hath rejoiced in God my Saviour.
> For he hath regarded:
> > the lowliness of his hand-maiden.
> For behold, from henceforth:
> > all generations shall call me blessed.
> For he that is mighty hath magnified me:
> > and holy is his name.

205. The Bishop of Winchester and the Dean of Winchester with the author at his licensing and installation as a Lay Canon and member of Chapter, July 2017, Winchester Cathedral